Psychology and the Challenges of Life

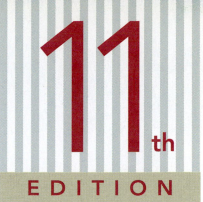

Adjustment and Growth

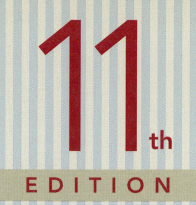

11th

E D I T I O N

Psychology and the Challenges of Life

Adjustment and Growth

Jeffrey S. Nevid
St. John's University

Spencer A. Rathus
New York University

WILEY

John Wiley & Sons, Inc.

Vice President & Executive Publisher	Jay O'Callaghan
Executive Editor	Christopher Johnson
Associate Editor	Eileen McKeever
Production Manager	Dorothy Sinclair
Senior Production Editor	Valerie A. Vargas
Marketing Manager	Danielle Torio
Creative Director	Harry Nolan
Senior Designer	Madelyn Lesure
Production Management Services	Ingrao Associates
Editorial Assistant	Mariah Maguire-Fong
Media Editor	Lynn Pearlman
Cover Photo Credit	Main Image: Martin Barraud/Getty Images, Inc. Thumbnails (left to right): Tetra Images/SuperStock; Photographer's Choice/SuperStock; MediaMagnet/StockBroker/SuperStock

This book was set in Times Ten Roman 10/12 by Prepare and printed and bound by Courier-Kendalville. The cover was printed by Courier-Kendalville.

To order books or for customer service, please call 1-800-CALL WILEY (225-5945).

ISBN-13 978-0-470-38362-9

Printed in the United States of America

10 9 8 7 6 5 4 3

Preface

Welcome to the new edition of *Psychology and the Challenges of Life*. With this 11th edition, we continue to reflect on the many ways in which psychology relates to the lives we live and the important roles that psychology can play in helping us adjust to the challenges we face in our daily lives. Throughout this text, we explore the many applications of psychological concepts and principles in meeting life challenges such as managing our time, developing our self-identity, building and maintaining friendships and intimate relationships, adopting healthier behaviors and lifestyles, coping with stress, and dealing with emotional problems and psychological disorders. In these uncertain times, we feel it is also appropriate to examine how we can face challenges that arise from broader threats we face as a nation, especially threats posed by natural disasters and acts of terrorism.

Our students today are part of the most wired, plugged in generation in human history. They are a Googling, I'ming, Facebooking, texting, and iPoding generation. Millenials—people born between 1980 and 2002—have never known a time without the Internet, the World Wide Web, and cell phones. The use of avatars, or altere-gos in cyberscape, is creating a whole new type of psychological identity. At the time that today's college-age students were born, a web was something that only spiders spun, and mobile phones were so bulky, cumbersome, and expensive that only a few business executives and military personnel used them.

This edition raises questions about the impact of modern technology on our psychological adjustment. But even as we reflect on these changes and the challenges they pose, we maintain our focus on core issues in the psychology of adjustment and personal growth.

With these goals in mind, we approached the writing of this edition with several clear objectives that have defined this text through many editions:

- To communicate the scientific bases of psychology through coverage of research methods, review of classic studies in psychology that inform our understanding of underlying issues, and comprehensive coverage of research reported in the scientific literature during the past few years;
- To apply psychological principles to help readers meet the challenges they face in daily life, to resolve problems, and to reach their unique potentials;
- To reflect the importance of human diversity in our lives today;
- To provide a comprehensive pedagogical package that stimulates learning and strengthens memory;
- To motivate students through the abundant use of humor and personal anecdotes; and
- To present abstract, complex concepts in energetic, accessible prose that speaks directly to students, not down to them.

What's New In This Edition

Online Self-Assessments

With this edition, we expand our use of instructional technology to make it easier for students to evaluate their attitudes and behaviors in the light of the psychological concepts described in the text. This textbook has long been recognized for its inclusion of many self-assessment questionnaires that allow students to go beyond merely reading about psychological concepts to applying these concepts to themselves and their life experiences. In this edition, students can administer these self-assessment questionnaires by either completing the printed versions in the textbook or accessing them online at the text companion website. The online versions are electronically scored and interpreted. We believe that providing online access to these materials will make them more convenient and accessible to your students.

Emphasis on Positive Psychology

Positive psychology is a growing movement within psychology that focuses on human virtues and assets rather than human weaknesses and deficits. Positive psychology studies many positive aspects of the human experiences, such as love, happiness, friendship, optimism, helping behavior, and the building of self-esteem. In this edition, we integrate positive psychology content throughout the text and highlight this material through the use of convenient icon (*Positive Psychology*). We introduced a new *Psychology and Modern Life* feature in Chapter 1 that focuses on emerging research in positive psychology that addresses the question, "What Makes People Happy?" We also provide a tabbing guide to positive psychology material in the text to make it more convenient for you and your students to locate these particular topics.

Linked Videos

Our students today are a part of a plugged-in generation that wants immediate access to video materials. In this edition, we include a new online feature that provides links to related videos that both enrich and expand the student's understanding of textual material. These videos will be embedded within *WileyPLUS*.

Comprehensive Updating

Research developments that inform our understanding of processes of adjustment and growth continue to unfold at a dizzying pace. We endeavor to continue to bring the latest research findings and scientific developments to our readers in a way that makes them interesting and accessible. At the same time, we weave into the narrative thread many of the classic studies in the field. We also strive to present technical and complex material in a succinct and readable form that is accessible to students of different levels of preparation.

Pedagogical Features

The Modular Format, a Learning Style Suited to Today's Busy Students

We believe that a textbook should be more than a compendium of knowledge and information; it should be a tool for learning. We try to never lose sight of the fact that we are teachers, whether we are standing in front of a class or sitting at a computer screen and writing a textbook. As teachers, we face the challenge of assisting students in acquiring and retaining knowledge to help them succeed in today's learning environment.

We teachers are challenged as never before. Our students are changing, and we must develop new ways of meeting the challenges we face in the classroom and in preparing textbooks for students today. In our classrooms we find increasing numbers of returning students, nontraditional students, and students struggling to balance family, work, and academic responsibilities.

To help students balance their many responsibilities, we have organized the text in a modular format that breaks down lengthy chapters into smaller, individualized study units. The modular approach helps students organize their study time by presenting information in more manageable units of instruction. Each module is a self-contained study unit that begins with a set of survey questions and ends with a review section in which students can test their knowledge of key concepts before moving ahead. With the modular format, students can nibble on individual modules rather than try to digest a whole chapter at a time.

Psychology in Daily Life

The capstone module in each chapter has been relabeled to reflect the central role that psychology can play in our daily lives. The *Psychology in Daily Life* feature module helps students see how psychological knowledge discussed in the chapter can be applied to modern life. We believe that the psychology of adjustment course should help students appreciate the applications of psychology to our daily lives.
Here is a listing of these modules:

Chapter 1:   Becoming a Successful Student
Chapter 2:   Understanding Yourself
Chapter 3:   Managing Stress
Chapter 4:   Becoming an Active Health Consumer
Chapter 5:   Finding Healthful Alternatives to Harmful Substances
Chapter 6:   Enhancing Self-Esteem
Chapter 7:   Becoming an Assertive Person (Winning Respect and Influencing People)
Chapter 8:   Helping a Friend in Crisis
Chapter 9:   Coping with Emotional Responses to Stress—Anxiety, Anger, Depression
Chapter 10:   Coping with the Costs of Gender Polarization
Chapter 11:   Coping with Loneliness
Chapter 12:   Making Relationships Work
Chapter 13:   Preventing HIV/AIDS and Other Sexually Transmitted Diseases
Chapter 14:   Successful Aging
Chapter 15:   Finding a Career That Fits

A Closer Look

These boxed features provide profiles of fascinating individuals from the history of psychology and from several of our contemporaries. We discuss the challenges faced by such important figures as Sigmund Freud, B. F. Skinner, Erik Erikson, Carl Rogers, Stanley Milgram, and Aaron Beck. We also highlight important issues of diversity in personal accounts by our colleagues Beverly Greene, Raphael Javier, and the late Jayne Thomas.

Your Personal Journal: Reflect Reflect Reflect

Journaling is an increasingly important tool for helping students relate course material to their own lives. There are many forms of journaling, including the traditional form of keeping a journal of daily experiences. We incorporate journaling in the form of writing assignments that direct students to reflect on how the text material relates to their personal beliefs and experiences. By encouraging students to focus on the personal relevance of text material, journaling fosters deeper processing that leads to more effective learning. Journaling and other forms of elaborative rehearsal in this text help strengthen new learning by encouraging students to actively work with the concepts presented in the text.

The journaling writing assignment is presented in the form of a feature at the end of each chapter called *Your Personal Journal: Reflect Reflect Reflect*. We encourage students to write answers to a set of personally meaningful questions relating to material discussed in the chapter. Here is a brief sampling of these questions:

- How would you describe your own personality traits in terms of the Big Five personality traits? What are your most prominent traits? Would others who know you agree or disagree with your appraisal? (Ch. 2)
- Have you experienced any of the types of psychological conflicts described in the text? Which type of conflict was it? How did you resolve the conflict? (Or didn't you?) (Ch. 3)
- The text discusses different stages of career development. In what "stage" of career development are you? Explain. (Ch. 15)

Journaling is among the many active learning features of this text. Throughout this text, we encourage active learning through personal writing, completing self-questionnaires, thinking critically about key issues, and applying material discussed in the chapters to one's personal experiences.

Adjustment and Modern Life

We continue to emphasize the important roles of psychology in helping us meeting the many challenges of contemporary life today. However, we have changed the label we use for these features from *Adjustment in the New Millennium* to *Adjustment and Modern Life*. It seems like only yesterday we were celebrating the arrival of the new millennium (and wary of the risk of the Y2K). Yet the new millennium is not so new anymore as it has celebrated its tenth birthday. *Adjustment and Modern Life* features cutting-edge research in the field, contemporary issues, and challenges of adjustment we face in life today. Here is a small sampling:

- What Makes People Happy? (Ch. 1)
- Multitasking: In a Word, When Studying, Don't (Ch. 1)
- Binge Drinking on Campus (Ch. 5)
- Your Self in Cyberspace: Which Self is It? (Ch. 6)
- Why Are More Women Depressed? (Ch. 8)
- Cell Phone Nation: Social Blessing or Curse? (Ch. 11)
- Emotional Intelligence: The Emotional Pathway to Success (Ch. 12)
- Challenges of a Changing Workplace (Ch. 15)

Integrated Coverage of Human Diversity

We cannot hope to understand human behavior without reference to the richness of human diversity. People differ not only as individuals, but also in terms of culture, gender, age, sexual orientation, and other factors.

This edition continues its exploration and celebration of the richness and diversity of American society today. We are a nation of many peoples of different heritages, nationalities, and ethnic groups. The United States itself is a nation of hundreds of different ethnic and religious groups. This diversity extends to the global village of nearly 200 nations and to those nations' own distinctive subcultures.

Material on diversity is integrated directly in the chapters themselves rather than segregated off in boxed features. Separating the material on diversity may give the mistaken impression that diversity is not part of mainstream psychology. We believe that diversity is part and parcel of modern psychology and should be integrated within the general discussion in the text.

We want students to consider how issues of diversity relating to culture, ethnicity, values, and lifestyle shape our adjustment to the world around us. By focusing on issues of diversity, students come to better understand not only how people differ but also how they are alike in many respects.

Student-Oriented Features

▪ ▪

As a tool for learning, we incorporate many student-centric, active learning features we believe will be of interest to students and help them succeed in the course.

Think About It

We encourage students to go beyond review and recitation by posing thought-provoking questions in the *Think About It* section in each module review. Here are some examples:

- Why is it incorrect to say biology is destiny?
- How might acculturation be something of a mixed blessing to immigrant groups? Explain.
- How is self-esteem developed? What advice would you give new parents about helping their children acquire self-esteem?
- If you were to advise college officials on ways of reducing prejudice and fostering tolerance on your campus, what steps would you suggest?
- How do cognitive therapists conceptualize the role of cognitions (thoughts and beliefs) in the development of emotional disorders?

Try This Out

This active learning feature encourages students to apply psychological concepts they learn about in the text to their own lives. Examples include the following:

- Testing Your Texting Skills
- Tips for Managing Your Time
- Taking It Off and Keeping It Off—Weight, That Is
- Examining Your Self-Concept
- Countering Persuasive Sales Tactics
- To Sleep, Perchance to Dream
- Get That Date!

"Did You Know That" Chapter Openers

We begin each chapter with a set of "*Did You Know That...*" questions. The questions stimulate interest in the chapter material and encourage students to read further. These questions help debunk common misconceptions, raise student awareness about important psychological and social issues, and draw their attention to recent research findings. Page numbers are provided so that students can quickly find the relevant information in the body of the chapter. Here is a sampling of these chapter openers:

Did You Know That...

- Cramming for a test is not more likely to earn you a good grade than spacing your study sessions?
- Exposure to racism can take a toll on a person's mental health and self-concept?
- Meditation can be good for your blood pressure?
- People who are high in conscientiousness not only tend to get their work in on time, but they also tend to live longer and happier lives?
- People who have blacked out from drinking may never wake up if they fail to receive prompt medical attention?
- When directed to do so by an experimenter, most participants in a landmark but controversial study administered to another person what they told were painful electric shocks?

- When it comes to measures of general intelligence, one gender doesn't appear to be any smarter than the other?
- Taller people tend to earn higher incomes than shorter people?
- Many people seeking romantic partners go from "texting" to "webcam" dates before actually meeting the person?
- When people are sexually aroused, their earlobes swell?
- The next best thing to a Fountain of Youth is your neighborhood gym?
- Women who wear perfume to interviews may be less likely to get the job, at least when they are interviewed by men?

Self-Assessment Exercises

Self-assessment exercises stimulate interest and deeper processing by engaging students in the process of applying psychological concepts to themselves. Students can evaluate where they stand in relation to many of the concepts discussed in the text. For example, they can examine whether they fit the Type A behavior and evaluate the level of stress in their lives in relation to college norms. As we described, this edition provides students with the opportunity to complete these questionnaires directly in the text, or if they prefer, filling them out online. The online version provides electronic scoring. The text version provides answer keys at the end of each chapter to make it convenient for students to evaluate their responses. Each chapter contains at least one self-assessment exercise. Here is a sampling of the self-assessment exercises:

- Dare You Say What You Think? The Social Desirability Scale (Ch. 1)
- Will You Be a Hit or a Miss? The Expectancy for Success Scale (Ch. 2)
- How Much Are You Stressed? (Ch. 3)
- Are You Type A or Type B? (Ch. 3)
- Are You Heart Smart? (Ch. 4)
- Are You Getting Your Z's? (Ch. 5)
- Why Do You Smoke? (Ch. 5)
- How Satisfied Are You with Your Body? (Ch. 6)
- Examining Your Self-Concept (Ch. 6)
- Are You Making Yourself Miserable? The Irrational-Beliefs Questionnaire (Ch. 9)
- Are You a "Chesty" Male or a "Fluffy" Female? The ANDRO Scale (Ch. 10)
- Do You Endorse a Traditional or a Liberal Marital Role? (Ch. 12)
- The AIDS Awareness Inventory (Ch. 13)
- What Are Your Attitudes Toward Aging? (Ch. 14)
- How Do You Feel about Your Work? The Job Satisfaction Index (Ch. 15)

Most students who take the psychology of adjustment course are first- or second-year college students. For many of them psychology of adjustment is their introductory course in psychology. To help them succeed in the course, we include the following pedagogical aids to foster more effective learning.

Study Aids
. . . .

The SQ4R Study Method

Originally developed by educational psychologist Francis Robinson, the SQ3R study method is based on five key steps: (1) survey, (2) question, (3) read, (4) recite, and (5) review. Many textbook authors use variations of the SQ3R method and for good reason: It enhances learning by encouraging students to adopt a more active role in the learning process. This text makes full use of the SQ3R study method and adds an important additional "R"—*reflect*.

The chapter introduction and survey questions at the start of each module introduce the student to the material they will be reading. We then encourage reflection, recitation, and review to help students master and retain the information they read.

1. Survey and Question. Each chapter opens with a numbered listing of the modules in the chapter. This helps students survey the material to be covered and how it is organized in the chapter. Each module begins with a set of survey questions that highlight important learning objectives in the module. These survey questions also serve as advance organizers for studying that students can use to test themselves on their knowledge of text material.

2. Read. The writing style in this text was carefully developed to be clear, as well as accessible and engaging. We seek to grab and hold the reader's interest, for we recognize that explicit learning required in college courses requires focused attention. One of the ways we engage readers is by addressing them directly and encouraging them to evaluate how the material in the text relates to their personal experiences.

3. Reflect. Students learn more effectively when they reflect on what they are learning. Psychologists who study learning and memory refer to reflection as elaborative rehearsal. One way of reflecting on subject matter is to relate it to things one already knows about, whether it be related material or events or experiences in our own lives. Reflection makes material meaningful and easier to remember. It also makes it more likely that students will be able to apply the information to their own lives.

We have incorporated the *Reflect* features of the text within the journaling feature we discussed earlier (*i.e., Your Personal Journal: Reflect Reflect Reflect*). Instructors may wish to assign these writing exercises for extra credit in the course.

4. Recite and Review. The module review section is structured in a fill-in-the-blanks style. This interactive approach challenges students to recite and review their knowledge of key concepts, rather than merely recognize the correct answer in a multiple-choice format. Recitation and review is further emphasized in the Recite Recite Recite summaries at the end of each chapter. Here, students recite their answers to the survey questions and then compare their own answers with the sample answers given in the text.

Running Glossary

Key terms are defined in the margins, at the points where they occur in the text. Many students do not make use of a glossary at the back of a book. Moreover, ready access to glossary items permits students to maintain their concentration on the flow of material in the chapter. Students need not flip back and forth between different sections of the book to decode the vocabulary. Key terms are boldfaced the first time they appear in the chapter, in order to signal students that definitions are available.

The Ancillaries

The eleventh edition of *Psychology and the Challenges of Life* is accompanied by an array of ancillaries that are intended to optimize learning and teaching.

Instructor's Supplements

The Instructor's Manual, Test Bank, Computerized Test Bank, and PowerPoint files will all be available on one convenient Instructor's Resource CD-ROM, as well as online at www.wiley.com/college/nevid.

Student's Supplements

The Self-Scoring Study Guide and Student Activities Manual is a great student resource. This guide contains chapter outlines, learning objectives, key term exercises, tear-out activities and questionnaires, chronological chapter reviews, and sample testing. *The Psychology and the Challenges of Life* student web site features exciting study aids such as online quizzing, critical thinking essays, chapter summaries, and vocabulary flash cards. Visit the web site at www.wiley.com/college/nevid.

Acknowledgments

. . . .

Although this is an eleventh edition of a well-established college text, we continue to approach our work with the same enthusiasm and vigor we brought to our first edition more than 30 years ago. We are invigorated in our efforts by our continued collaboration with the many talented people of John Wiley and Sons, Inc., who are dedicated to the highest level of professionalism in college publishing. We are especially indebted to our editor, Chris Johnson, our assistant editor Eileen McKeever, our production editor Valerie Vargas, and Suzanne Ingrao of Ingrao Associates for their contributions throughout the production process.

We are most highly indebted to our many professional colleagues over the years who have participated in the growth and development of *Psychology and the Challenges of Life*. First we would like to thank our professional colleagues who participated in the review of the manuscript for this text through our many editions:

Martha Kuehn, Central Lakes College; Jane Thompson, Clayton College; Fred Heilizer, DePaul University; Paul Bartoli, East Stroudsburg University; Ann Chapman, Eastern Kentucky University; Greg Thomas, Garden City Community College; Sharon Thomas, Miami-Dade Community College; Judith Rohr, Tennessee Technical University; Jim Calhoun, University of Georgia; and Diane Lodder, Wake Technical Community College. Bernardo Carducci, Shyness Research Institute Indiana University Southeast; Dorothy (Dot) McDonald, Sandhills Community College; Robert Osman, Onondaga Community College; Scott Potter, Marion Technical College; Richard W. Rogers, Daytona Beach Community College; Robert Schultz, Fulton-Montgomery Community College; Harold D. Andrews, Miami-Dade Community College-Wolfson Campus; Bob Arndt, Delta College; Bela Baker, University of Wisconsin-Green nevid_FM-i-xxix-hr2 11/16/06 10:23 AM Page xiv Bay; Helene Blakewell, Stephen F. Austin University; Jacinth Baubitz, Northwood Institute; Nancy Bowers, Pikes Peak Community College; Edward N. Brady, Belleville Area College; Kyle Ann Campos, Des Moines Area Community College; Desmond Cartwright, University of Colorado; David Chance, Central State College; Steven Coccia, Orange County Community College; Norma Crews, DeKalb Community College; Jean De Vany, Auburn University; Richard Dienstbier, University of Nebraska; Steve Donahue, Grand Canyon College; William Dugmore, Central Washington University; Thomas Eckle, Modesto Junior College; Richard M. Ehlenz, Rochester Community College; Ron Evans, Washburn University; Jennie Fauchier, Metro Technical Community College; Eugene Fichter, Northern Virginia Community College; Ronnie Fisher, Miami-Dade Community College; Sharon Fisher, El Paso Community College; Lynn Godat, Portland Community College; Peter Gram, Pensacola Community College; Lawrence Grebstein, University of Rhode Island; Myree Hayes, East Carolina University; Barbara J. Hermann, Gainesville College; Glady Hiner, Rose State College; Joseph Horvat, Weber State College; Richard Hudiburg, University of North Alabama; Gordon M. Kimbrell, University of South Carolina; Guadalupe King, Milwaukee Area Technical College; Clint Layne, Western Kentucky University; Gary Lesniak, Portland Community College; Arnold Le-Unes, Texas A&M University; Phyllis McGraw, Portland State University; Joseph McNair, Miami-Dade Community College North Campus; Louis A. Martone, Miami-Dade Community College; Frederick Medway, University of South Carolina; Roland

Miller, Sam Houston State University; Norma Mittenthal, Hillsborough Community College; Patrick Murphy, Spokane Community College; Tony Obradovich, DeVry Institute of Technology; Ginger T. Osborne, Rancho Santiago College; Arne Parma, Massachusetts Bay Community College; Carola Pedreschi, Miami-Dade Community College; Kathy Petrowsky, Southwestern Oklahoma State University; Robert Petty, University of Santa Clara; A. R. Peyrnan, Mississippi State University; Gary Piggrem, DeVry Institute of Technology; Chris Potter, Harrisburg Area Community College; Jay Pozner, Jackson Community College; Sara N. Andrews, Troy University; Kimberly D. Brown, Ball State University; John McNeeley, Daytona State College; Thomas L. Flagg, Eastern Michigan University; Richard G. Cavasina, California University of Pennsylvania, and Patricia Ann Perdue, Marshall University.

Finally, we invite your comments and suggestions. You may contact us at the following e-mail address: **jnevid@hotmail.com**

Jeff Nevid
Spencer Rathus

Contents in Brief

Contents

2 Personality 38

3 Stress: What It Is and How to Manage It 82

4 Psychological Factors and Health 118

5 Developing Healthier Behaviors 152

8 Psychological Disorders 256

14 Adolescent and Adult Development: Going Through Changes 454

15 The Challenge of the Workplace 492

Psychology and the Challenges of Life

Adjustment and Growth

CHAPTER

1

Psychology and the Challenges of Life

OUTLINE

Did you know that...

▌ **Module 1.1: Psychology and Adjustment**

▌ **Module 1.2: Human Diversity and Adjustment**

▌ **Module 1.3: Critical Thinking and Adjustment**

▌ **Module 1.4: How Psychologists Study Adjustment**

▌ **Module 1.5: Psychology in Daily Life: Becoming a Successful Student**

CHAPTER REVIEW *RECITE! RECITE! RECITE!*

YOUR PERSONAL JOURNAL *REFLECT REFLECT REFLECT*

Did you know that...

- Multitasking while studying can damage your grades? (p. 6)

- Genetics influences many psychological traits and even our preferences for different types of occupations? (p. 8)

- White, Euro-Americans are now a minority in the nation's most populous state? (p. 12)

- Women were once not permitted to attend college in the United States? (p. 13)

- You could survey a million voters and still not predict the outcome of a presidential election accurately? (p. 23)

- You are more likely to eventually get a divorce if you live together with your future spouse before getting married? (p. 27)

- Cramming for a test is not more likely to earn you a good grade than spacing your study sessions? (p. 33)

Oleg Prikhodko/iStockphoto

Beth, 22, a fourth-year chemistry major, has been accepted into medical school in Boston. She wants to do cancer research, but this goal means another seven or eight years at the grindstone. Kevin, her fiancé, has landed a solid engineering position in Silicon Valley, California. He wants Beth to come with him, take a year to start a family, and then go to medical school in California. But Beth hasn't applied to medical school in California, and there's no sure bet that she would "get in" there. If she surrenders her educational opportunity now, another one might not come along. Should she demand that Kevin accompany her to Boston, even though he hasn't been offered work there? Would he go? What if he gives up his golden opportunity and their relationship falters because of resentment? Also, she wonders how long she can safely put off childbearing. Though she thinks of herself as "a kid," her biological clock is ticking and she won't be finishing her medical training—assuming she goes to medical school—until she's past 30. And what if having children even then threatens to prevent her from getting established in her career? Beth has just been accepted into medical school—shouldn't she be happy?

John, 21, is a business student who is all business. Every day he reads the *Wall Street Journal* and the business pages of the *New York Times*. He is dedicated to his books and invests most of his energy in trying to construct a solid academic record so that he will get his career off on the right foot. He represents the first generation in his African American family to attend college, and he is determined to do college right. But sometimes he wonders why he bothers; he thinks of himself as one of those people who "just can't take tests." He begins to shake two days before a test. His thoughts become jumbled when the papers are distributed. He finds himself wondering if his professors will attribute poor grades to his ethnicity. By the time the papers are on his desk, his hand is shaking so badly that he can hardly write his name. His grades suffer.

Maria, 19, is a first-year college student. She has seen the TV talk shows and has gone to the R-rated films. She has read the books and the magazine articles about the new sexual openness, but her traditional Mexican American upbringing has given her a strong sense of right and wrong. Yet she perceives herself as well acculturated to the dominant, but more liberal, contemporary American culture. Despite the social and sexual pressures she finds in the dominant culture and her desire to fit in, she would prefer to wait for Mr. Right. At the very least, she is not going to allow social pressure to prevent her from carefully sorting out her values and her feelings. The young man she has been seeing, Mark, has been patient—from his point of view. But lately he's been pressuring Maria, too. He has told Maria they have more than a fly-by-night relationship and that other women are more willing to "express their sexual needs" with him. Maria's girlfriends say they understand her feelings. Yet they tell her they fear that Mark will eventually turn elsewhere. Quite frankly, Maria is concerned about more than virginity; she also thinks about sexually transmitted infections such as genital herpes and AIDS. After all, Mark is 22 years old and she doesn't know every place he's been. True, they can take precautions, but what is completely safe? In any event, Maria does not want to be pressured.

Lisa, 20, a hard-working college junior, is popular with faculty, dutiful with relatives. She works out regularly and is proud of her figure. But Lisa also has a secret. When she is sipping her coffee in the morning, she hopes that she won't go off the deep end again, but most of the time she does. She usually starts by eating a doughnut slowly; then she eats another, picking up speed; then she voraciously downs the remaining four in the box. Then she eats two or three bagels with cream cheese. If there is any leftover pizza from the evening before, that goes down, too. She feels disgusted with herself, but she hunts through her apartment for food. Down go the potato chips, down go the cookies. Fifteen minutes later she feels as though she will burst and cannot take in anymore. Half nauseated, she finds her way to the bathroom and makes herself throw up the contents of her binge eating. Tomorrow, she tells herself, will be different. But deep inside she suspects that she will buy more doughnuts and more cookies, and that tomorrow might be much the same. She worries that she may be bulimic and in need of professional help.

David, 32, is not sleeping well. He wakes before dawn and cannot get back to sleep. His appetite is off, his energy level is low, he has started smoking again. He has a couple of drinks at lunch and muses that it's lucky that any more alcohol makes him sick to his stomach—otherwise, he'd probably be drinking too much, too. Then he thinks, "So what difference would it make?" Sometimes he is sexually frustrated; at other times he wonders whether he has any sex drive left. Although he's awake, each day it's getting harder to drag himself out of bed in the morning. This week he missed one day of work and was late twice. His supervisor has suggested in a nonthreatening way that he "do something about it. " David knows that her next warning will not be unthreatening. It's been going downhill since Sue walked out. Suicide has even crossed David's mind. He wonders if he's going crazy.

Beth, John, Maria, Lisa, David—each of them is experiencing a challenge to adjustment and growth.

We face many challenges in life. For example, Beth is experiencing role conflict. She wants to attend medical school but also wants to maintain the relationship with Kevin and start a family. Although she might become a physician, she would probably retain the primary responsibility for childrearing. Even women who have become officers of their companies typically manage the household and childcare responsibilities. Kevin is not a chauvinist, however. As it turns out, he accompanies Beth to Boston and looks for work there.

John's challenge is test anxiety, plain but not-so-simple. Years of anxiety and fluctuating grades have led to a vicious cycle: He becomes so anxious that he often finds himself paying more attention to his bodily sensations and his troubled thoughts than to the test items themselves. His distraction then leads to poor grades and heightens his anxiety. His concerns have prevented him from performing up to his full potential. Fortunately, there is a notice on a bulletin board that his college counseling center is offering a program to help students with test anxiety.

Maria's challenges also involve conflict—conflict with Mark and conflict within herself. She decides not to be pressured into a sexual relationship, and it happens that Mark turns elsewhere. It hurts, but Maria is confident that other men who are more sensitive to her values will understand and appreciate her.

Lisa faces the challenge of dealing with *bulimia nervosa,* an eating disorder discussed in Chapter 5. The causes of eating disorders are complex and not fully understood, but they appear to be related to social pressures young women in our society face in adhering to unrealistic standards of thinness. Lisa does seek treatment, but only after her dentist informs her that the enamel on her teeth has begun to decay due to repetitive vomiting. Treatment is helpful in reducing episodes of binge eating and vomiting, but she continues to experience occasional lapses. "I'm on the right track," she says, "but I've still got a way to go."

David faces the challenges posed by another type of psychological disorder, depression. Feelings of depression are normal following a loss, such as the end of a relationship, but David's feelings have lingered. His friends tell him that he should get out and do things, but David is so down that he hasn't the motivation. After much prompting, David consults a psychologist who, ironically, also pushes him to get out and do things—pleasant events of the sort described in Chapter 9. The psychologist also shows David that part of his problem is that he thinks of himself as a loser who is just destined to fail in all his endeavors.

Beth, John, Maria, Lisa, and David all need to make adjustments to cope with the challenges in their lives. The challenges of life touch us all at one time or another. That is what this book is about: adjusting to challenges as we get on with the business of living—growing, learning, building relationships, making sense of our value systems, establishing careers, making ends meet, and striving to feel good about ourselves. This book portrays our quest for self-development and brings psychological knowledge to bear on problems that may block self-development. Some of these problems, such as anxiety, depression, or obesity, are personal in nature. Some involve intimate relationships and sexuality. Others involve the larger social context—the workplace, prejudice and discrimination, community disasters, pollution, and urban life.

Adjustment to College Life
Whether you are at a residential college or a commuter college, whether you are beginning college fresh out of high school or are a returning student, whether you are attending full time or part time, college life involves many changes that require adjustment. Many of the challenges of college life are academic and social, but some, like athletics, fighting commuter traffic, or climbing flights of steps, can have a strong physical component.

Tom Stewart/©Corbis

Most challenges offer us the opportunity not merely to adjust, but also to grow. We can grow in many ways, such as expanding our interests, our knowledge and skills, our self-awareness, and our ways of coping with the challenges we face. In this book you will learn how you can apply psychological knowledge to help you meet the challenges you face in life as well as to grow in directions that help you enrich your life and relate more effectively to others. You will also learn about the professional helpers and when and how to seek their intervention. This knowledge is important because life in the new millennium has in many ways become more challenging than ever.

In this chapter we first define the science of psychology and see that it is well suited to gathering information about, and suggesting applications for, our own adjustment and growth. We explore the richness of human diversity—facets of ourselves that contribute to our uniqueness and enable us to experience a sense of cultural pride. We discuss critical thinking, a scientific approach to life that enables us to analyze the claims and arguments of others to determine what is true and what is false. Then we examine the scientific procedures that psychologists use in gathering knowledge. Finally, we explore what psychologists have learned about student success—how we can study effectively, how we can make use of time spent in class, how we can ace tests, and how we can manage time to fit in academic responsibilities and leisure activities.

Psychology and Adjustment

- ▪ What is psychology?
- ▪ What is adjustment?
- ▪ What is the difference between adjustment and personal growth?
- ▪ Is biology destiny?
- ▪ What is the difference between the clinical approach and the healthy-personality approach to the psychology of adjustment?

▪ **Psychology** The science that studies behavior and mental processes.

The science of **psychology** is ideally suited to helping people meet the challenges of contemporary life. Psychology is the scientific discipline that studies behavior and mental processes. Psychologists traditionally attempt to understand or explain behavior in terms of the workings of the nervous system, the interaction of genetic and environmental influences ("nature" and "nurture"), the ways in which we sense and mentally represent the world, the roles of learning and motivation, and the nature of personality and social interaction.

Many psychologists are concerned with applying psychological knowledge in helping people adjust better to their work and social environments, overcome emotional

Adjustment and Modern Life

Multitasking: In A Word, When Studying, Don't

Are you a multitasker? Do you listen to your iPod or personal music player while studying? Do you talk on your cell phone while washing the dishes, watching TV, or shopping? Do you make lists on your PDA or scribble notes to yourself about your weekend plans while attending lectures? If you do, you're certainly not alone. People today say they are multitasking more than ever before.

As an example, most people (54%) reported in a recent poll that they read their e-mail while talking on the phone (Shellenbarger, 2003b). With the proliferation of ever more electronic gadgets, we have become accustomed to having one eye on one thing and another eye (or ear) on another. We are living increasingly multitasking lives, but how well do we handle the demands of performing two simultaneous tasks?

The word *multitasking* is derived from the field of computer science, where it was introduced to describe the ability of computer systems to allow users to perform two or more tasks at a time, such as surfing the web and using a word processor. But human beings are

Passengers, we're starting our descent into... woops, the pilot's on his cell phone and missed a turn... we'll update you when we know where we are exactly.

www.betsystreeter.com

not computer systems. Do we have the capacity to perform two tasks efficiently? The answer is *no* and *yes*. Let us explain.

Multitasking is certainly a timesaver, but scientific studies show that it is difficult for people to perform two things well at the same time (Oberauer & Kliegl, 2004; Rubinstein, Meyer, & Evans, 2001).

The problem is one of divided attention. As the Roman sage Publilius Syrus put it some 2,000 years ago, "to do two things at once, is to do neither." Since our attentional resources are limited, the resources we deploy to one task, such as watching TV, subtract from those we can direct to another task, such as talking with someone on the phone ("Multitasking," 2005; Shellenbarger, 2003a). The result, far too often, is that we do neither task well. Divided attention is not simply a problem of inefficiency; it can also lead to dangerous consequences, as when we divide our attention between driving and using a cell phone at the same time.

The risks of divided attention while driving extends beyond cell phone use (Conkle & West, 2008). Fussing with a child in the back seat, putting on makeup, fussing with children in the back seat, selecting songs to play on an iPod, eating or drinking, and texting (especially texting!) can be dangerously distracting.

problems, and develop healthier behaviors. But what, then, is adjustment? **Adjustment** is coping behavior that permits us to meet the demands we face in the environment. Sometimes the demands are physical. When we are cold, we can adjust by dressing warmly, turning up the thermostat, or exercising. Holding down a job to make ends meet, drinking to quench our thirst, meeting the daily needs of our children—these, too, are forms of adjustment needed to meet the kinds of demands we face in our lives.

▌ **Adjustment** Processes by which people respond to environmental pressures and cope with stress.

Sometimes the demands of adjustment have more of a psychological basis, as in psychological demands involved in living on our own when we leave for college or set up our own household. Coping with a major exam, a job interview, or the death of a loved one also poses adjustment challenges. There are many ways we might adjust to these kinds of demands, such as by making efforts to form new friendships when we move away from home, developing effective study skills, rehearsing what we'll say in a job interview, or seeking help from others in coping with a significant loss.

Sometimes we rely on ineffective coping strategies. We might pretend that problems do not exist. We might put a term paper out of our minds for weeks (or months). We might convince ourselves that we're sure to get that job because other people will naturally recognize our superior skills and talents. We might deal with emotional problems by dulling our feelings through the use of alcohol or other drugs. Or we might drift into a state of despair by telling ourselves that our problems are just so immense that there's no point to trying to cope with them. More constructively, we can see the pressures and problems we face for what they are. Then we can make decisions and formulate plans that will allow us to cope with them the best we can.

About one in eight female drivers responding to a recent insurance company survey reported applying makeup while driving, while about one in five male and female drivers reported texting messages (Alexander, 2007).

The problem of overloading our mental resources is especially keen when it comes to tasks that engage the same parts of the brain, such as listening to the TV while engaging in a conversation. If you engage in both of these tasks simultaneously, your conversant is likely to say to you, "Are you listening to me?" Recently, several winners of the prestigious MacArthur "genius" grants who were interviewed by a *New York Times* reporter said that they leave their cell phones and iPods off or tucked away while traveling so as to have downtime available just for thinking (Wallis & Steptoe, 2006).

On the other hand, we can multitask efficiently when one of the tasks is a well-practiced mechanical skill, such as washing dishes or vacuuming. In fact, paying too close attention to routine mechanical tasks like these may actually be counterproductive. In a recent study, investigators found that expert soccer players were more successful in dribbling a ball through a slalom course when they were distracted than when they focused their attention entirely on the side of the foot that had last made contact with the ball (Beilock et al., 2002). However, when using their nondominant foot, they performed better when they paid full attention to the position of their

Digital Vision/Getty Images, Inc

feet. Novice soccer players performed better with either their dominant or nondominant foot by paying close attention to the position of their feet when contacting the ball. This research example calls to mind what Vladimir Horowitz, one of the premier pianists of the twentieth century, had to say about concert pianists. Horowitz said that the worst thing that can befall concert pianists during a performance is to think about what their fingers are doing.

Think of other examples in which paying very close attention to performing mechanical tasks can be counterproductive, such as focusing on your fingers while typing (assuming you are a skilled typist). But the fact remains that for the kinds of challenging mental tasks needed to succeed in college, such as decoding the principles of calculus or theories of learning, studying for an exam, or learning a new skill, you need to concentrate fully on the task at hand. In other words, you can't expect to study as effectively if you divide your attention between your textbook and the music playing through your iPod or a TV show in the background. Use your iPod while jogging along an often-traveled course or while zoning out in your home, but not while decoding the basic principles of calculus or learning theory. As cognitive researcher David Meyer of the University of Michigan puts it, "If you can avoid it, don't multitask" ("The Thief of Time," 2005).

1.1.1 Touchpoints in Our Study of Adjustment

To get our bearings, let us address three core issues that underlie our study of adjustment.

Adjustment and Personal Growth: Two Aspects of the Psychology of Adjustment

Literally speaking, to adjust is to change so as better to conform to, or meet, the demands of one's environment. Adjustment is essentially reactive. It's like a tennis game: The environment serves up the balls, and we return them as best we can. When we adjust, we respond to pressures that require us to adapt. But the psychology of adjustment goes beyond adjusting to environmental demands. It also addresses issues of personal growth. Whereas adjustment is reactive, personal growth is proactive. Our study of the psychology of adjustment is based on the premise that people are not merely reactors to their environments. People are also actors. Things not only happen to us; we also make things happen. Not only does the environment affect us, but we also affect the environment. In fact, we create novel environments to suit our needs. We must extend the psychology of adjustment to accommodate the creative and active components of the human experience—the ability to grow or develop as a person. Not only do we react to stress, but we also act upon our environment in meeting our needs and pursuing our goals.

To achieve psychological fulfillment, we need to act, not merely react. We need to fill our lives with meaning and expand ourselves in directions that may not even be known today. Personal growth is more of a journey than a final destination, a process of development in which we continually examine who we are, where we are going, and what we want our lives to become.

Nature Versus Nurture: Is Biology Destiny?

▐ **Genes** The basic unit of heredity, consisting of a segment of deoxyribonucleic acid (DNA).

▐ **Chromosomes** Strands of DNA that consists of genes. People normally have 23 pairs of chromosomes.

Psychologists are concerned about the degree to which our traits and behavior patterns reflect our *nature*, or genetic factors, and our *nurture*, or environmental influences. Physical traits such as height, skin color, and eye color are biologically transmitted from generation to generation by **genes**. We have lungs rather than gills and arms rather than wings because of the genetic code embedded in our genes. Genes are segments of DNA (deoxyribonucleic acid), the stuff of which our **chromosomes** are composed. Genes give rise to our biological structures and physical traits, but how do they influence our psychological or behavioral traits? The answer is complex.

An increasing body of knowledge points to an important role for genetics in many psychological traits, including intelligence, shyness, aggressiveness, leadership potential, thrill seeking, aptitudes in music and art, and even preferences for different types of occupations (Bouchard, 2004; Ellis & Bonin, 2003; Plomin & Crabbe, 2000; Schwartz et al., 2003). Genetic factors are also involved in our propensity to marry (Johnson et al., 2004). Where genetic influences are involved in shaping personality or behavior, at work is a combination of genes interacting with environmental influences in complex ways. In other words, there is no one-to-one connection between any individual gene and any psychological trait.(Uhl & Grow, 2004).

Genetic influences also contribute to most of the adjustment problems we face in coping with stressful demands, such as emotional problems involving anxiety and depression, as well as more severe psychological disorders such as schizophrenia and bipolar disorder (formerly known as manic-depression), and even criminal or antisocial behavior (Baum et al., 2007; Gabbard, 2005; Gur et al., 2007; Koenen et al., 2008; Marx, 2007; Menzies et al., 2007). Genes also play a contributing role in the development of obesity and addiction to substances such as alcohol and nicotine (Hampton, 2006; Unger et al., 2007; Volkow, 2007).

"I'm the gene that causes alcoholism. I figured I'd cut out the middle man."

As we see in the *Adjustment and Modern Life* feature on page 10, researchers believe that people may even inherit a tendency toward a certain level of happiness. Despite the ups and downs of experience, people tend to drift back to their usual levels of cheerfulness or grumpiness.

Although genetic factors play a role in psychological adjustment and effective behavior, biology is not destiny. Genes create a *predisposition* or *likelihood*, not a *certainty*, that certain traits, behaviors, abilities, or problem behaviors will develop. We need to understand that life experiences and the choices we make in dealing with challenging situations also play important roles. For example, you may have inherited a genetic predisposition that puts you at increased risk of developing problems with alcohol or other drugs. But whether or not you develop these problems depends on many environmental and psychological factors, such as your exposure to drug-abusing peers, development of skills for coping with stress without using or abusing drugs, attitudes and expectancies concerning drug use, and parental modeling of alcohol use or misuse.

In sum, genes alone do not dictate who we become or what we do with our lives. Most psychologists believe that psychological traits are determined by a complex interplay or combination of nature (genetics) and nurture (environmental and learning influences), not simply by one or the other (Horwitz, Luong, & Charles, 2008; Plomin and McGuffin, 2003). By marshaling our personal resources, we can live up to our potential, whatever deck of genes we may have been dealt in life. This text focuses on the skills involved in marshaling these resources, such as acquiring more effective coping skills, developing more adaptive behaviors, and replacing maladaptive attitudes and beliefs with more adaptive alternatives.

The Clinical Approach versus the Healthy-Personality Approach

Most psychology-of-adjustment textbooks are written according to one of two major approaches—a clinical approach or a healthy-personality approach. The clinical approach focuses primarily on ways in which psychology can help people overcome personal problems and cope with stress.

The healthy-personality approach focuses primarily on healthful patterns of personal growth and development, including social and vocational development. The book you are holding in your hands was written with awareness of both approaches to the psychology of adjustment. We examine both effective and ineffective ways of coping with stress. But there is equal emphasis on optimizing our potential through preventive and self-actualizing behavior. We aim to be comprehensive and balanced in our approach, to provide ample theory, research, and applications for coping and for optimal development.

Psychologists focus mainly on individual people and are committed to the dignity of the individual. Yet psychologists also recognize that we cannot understand individuals without an awareness of the richness of human diversity. People differ from one another in many ways—in ethnicity, cultural background, gender, lifestyle and so on. When it comes to studying the psychology of adjustment, we need to consider the role of diversity in how we cope with the challenges we face and develop our unique potentials.

The healthy-personality approach is part of a growing movement in psychology called **positive psychology**. Founded by psychologist Martin Seligman of the University of Pennsylvania, positive psychology emphasizes the study of positive aspects of behavior, such as love, optimism, hope, helping behavior, and human happiness, rather than negative aspects such as psychological disorders, drug abuse, and antisocial behavior (Seligman, 2003; Seligman et al., 2005; Snyder & Lopez, 2007; Vallea, Huebner, & Suldo, 2006). Throughout this text we focus on these and other positive aspects of human experience, including successful aging, self-esteem, and self-actualization.

Creatas/SuperStock

■ **Positive Psychology** A developing movement in the field of psychology that emphasizes the positive aspects of our behavior, such as our assets and virtues, rather than our weaknesses and deficits.

Adjustment and Modern Life

Positive Psychology

What Makes People Happy?

The study of human happiness has emerged front and center in positive psychology, the movement in contemporary psychology that focuses on human assets and virtues. Today, psychologists are seeking to understand factors that contribute to happiness and ways of helping people increase their level of happiness and psychological well being.

One thing we've learned is that despite the popular belief, money does not breed happiness. People may think they'd be a lot happier if they were wealthier, but evidence does not bear out the belief that greater wealth translates into greater happiness (Kahneman et al., 2006). It turns out that above a certain moderate income level, about $50,000 in today's dollars, increasing wealth fails to add any substantial gains in happiness. As Harvard University psychologist and leading authority on personal happiness Daniel Gilbert puts it, "Once you get basic human needs met, a lot more money doesn't make a lot more happiness" (cited in Futrelle, 2006). Notice in Figure 1.1 that happiness levels off at higher income levels. Even the extremely wealthy, such as members of the Forbes 400 richest people in the United States, are only a tiny bit happier than the general public (Easterbrook, 2005). We have also learned that while winning a lottery jackpot has a temporary effect on happiness, any boost in happiness tends to fade within about a year or so (Corliss, 2003).

So if wealth isn't the answer to the eternal question of what makes people happy, what does? Happiness researchers believe they have some clues that are worth noting. Evidence to date points to several factors: heredity, having friends (a big plus), and religious faith (Paul, 2005; Wallis, 2005). Investigators suspect that people may have a genetically determined "set point" for happiness, a kind of personal thermostat that keeps their happiness and contentment around a certain level despite the ups and downs of life (Lykken & Csikszentmihalyi, 2001; Wallis, 2005). Concerning religious faith, we can't say whether happiness is connected to belonging to a religious community, or the sense

of meaning and purpose associated with religious belief, or a combination of factors. Having friends is a prescription for happiness that underscores the importance of connecting to people in meaningful and rewarding ways. In that sense, we might think of happiness as a kind of social contagion that can spread through networks of people who have close ties with one another (Fowler & Christakis, 2008; Roy-Byrne, 2009).

Even if happiness is influenced by genetic factors, feelings of happiness often change over time (Fujita & Diener, 2005; Lucas, 2007). Positive psychology offers some prescriptives that people can use to increase their levels of personal happiness. The founding figure in positive psychology, Martin Seligman (2003), believes that boosting happiness involves three fundamental challenges: (1) engaging in pleasurable activities, (2) becoming absorbed and engaged in activities in daily life, and (3) finding meaning or personal fulfillment through life activities. He also offers a number of specific techniques that people can use to boost their levels of happiness, including the following (adapted from Seligman, 2003; Seligman et al., 2005):

▮ *Gratitude visit.* With your eyes closed, think of someone who has had a major positive impact on your life but whom you've never really thanked. During the next week, write a letter of thanks to the person, but don't mail the letter. Instead, arrange a visit to the person and when you arrive, read the testimonial letter and discuss what he or she has meant to you.

▮ *Three blessings.* Each night before going to bed, think of three things that went well during the day. Write them down in a journal and take a moment to reflect upon them.

▮ *One door closes, another opens.* Reflect on the times in your life when a door has closed because of death or loss. But go further by linking this thought to a later experience in which a door opened for you. Come to appreciate the ebbs and flows of life experiences.

▮ *Savorings.* Plan a perfect day, but make sure to share the experience with another person.

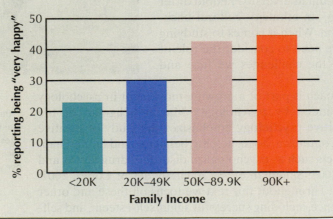

Figure 1.1

Happiness and Family Income

Notice how happiness begins to level off in relation to family income above a moderate income level of $50,000.

Source: Kahneman et al., 2006

Review It

(1) Psychology involves the scientific study of behavior and _____ processes.

(2) _____ is coping behavior that allows us to meet the demands the environment imposes on us.

(3) Personal growth involves _____ upon the environment to fulfill our needs, not merely reacting to it.

(4) By creating a predisposition, genes increase the _____ that we will develop certain traits, behaviors, abilities, or psychological disorders.

(5) Paying too close attention to performing _____ tasks can sometimes be counterproductive.

(6) The _____ _____ to the study of adjustment is concerned primarily with how people can use psychology to cope better with stress and overcome personal problems.

Think About It

Why is it incorrect to say biology is destiny?

MODULE 1.2

Human Diversity and Adjustment

- ▪ What is human diversity?
- ▪ Why is it important to study human diversity?
- ▪ What is an ethnic group?
- ▪ What forms of prejudice have women experienced in our society?

1.2.1 Ethnic Diversity

The nation and the world at large contain more kinds of people and more ways of doing and viewing things than most of us might imagine. One kind of diversity involves people's **ethnic groups**. But just what is an "ethnic group"?

An ethnic group is a subgroup within the general population that has a common cultural heritage, as distinguished by factors such as customs, race, language, and common history. One reason for studying ethnic diversity in the United States is that the experiences of various ethnic groups highlight the impact of social, political, and economic factors on human behavior and development. As we will see, factors such as discrimination and prejudice affect traditionally identified minority groups more than others. Some health concerns also affect some groups more than others. Another reason for studying ethnic diversity is to examine the dramatically changing ethnic composition of our society (as discussed in the *Adjustment and Modern Life* feature in this module). Studying human diversity also enables students to appreciate the rich cultural heritages and historical problems of the many ethnic groups in our society.

Yet another reason concerns psychological intervention and consultation. Psychologists are called upon to help people of all

▌ **Ethnic groups** Groups of people who can be distinguished by characteristics such as their cultural heritage, common history, race, and language. Not all ethnic groups differ according to all these features. For example, French Catholics and Protestants can be said to belong to different ethnic groups, but both groups are predominantly white, speak French, and share much of their cultural heritage and history.

PhotoDisc Red/Getty Images, Inc

Human Diversity

We as a society are becoming increasing ethnically diverse. How is your personal identity influenced by our cultural or ethnic heritage?

ethnic groups solve personal problems. Without knowledge of the history and cultural heritage of those groups, psychologists could not hope to understand the aspirations and problems of individuals from those groups.

How can psychologists understand African Americans or Latino and Latina Americans, for example, without being sensitive to the prejudice these ethnic groups have historically suffered? Moreover, should psychologists from the European American majority attempt to practice psychotherapy with people from ethnic minority groups? If so, what kinds of special education or training might they need to do so? What is meant by "culturally sensitive" forms of psychotherapy? We address these issues in Chapter 9.

Adjustment and Modern Life

Who We Are Today, Who We Will Be Tomorrow

We live in an ethnically diverse society that is becoming increasingly more diverse from year to year. Today, roughly one-third of the U. S. population comprises people from traditionally recognized ethnic minority groups (Hispanic, African American, Asian/Pacific Islander, and Native American) (see Figure 1.2) ("U.S. Minority Population," 2007). The traditional meaning of the word *minority* has been turned on its head, as white Americans of European ancestry (European Americans) now constitute a minority of the population in many U.S. cities and in the nation's most populous state (California). Canada, too, is also becoming increasingly ethnically diverse, though not quite at the same rate as the United States. The percentage of nonwhites in the Canadian population increased from 9% in the early 1990s to about 13% by the early years of the new millennium (Statistics Canada, 2003). Presently, Hispanics and African Americans comprise the largest minority groups in the United

States, with each accounting for about 13% of the population. Asian/Pacific Islanders account for about 4% of the U.S. population, whereas Native Americans constitute nearly 1%.

Ethnic diversity among American college students mirrors the general population, with about 30% reporting either Hispanic, black, or Asian ethnicity (U.S. Census Bureau, 2005). The two fastest-growing U.S. population groups are Hispanic Americans (whom we refer to as Latino and Latina Americans in this book) and Asian Americans. Notice how the makeup of the U.S. population is expected to change by the year 2050 (Figure 1.3).

By the middle of the century, it is projected that whites will constitute only a slim majority of the population. Not only is American society becoming increasingly diverse, but many people today reject traditional distinctions in defining their racial or ethnic identities. Increasing numbers of people in the United States and Canada have biracial backgrounds, including such prominent individuals as President Barack Obama, golfer Tiger Woods, baseball player Derek Jeter, and singer Mariah Carey.

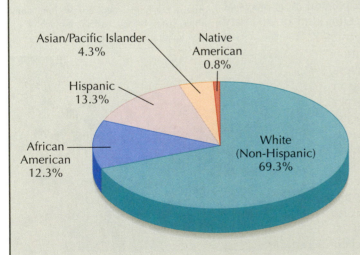

Figure 1.2
Ethnic/Racial Breakdown of U.S. Population

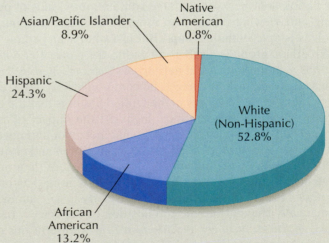

Figure 1.3
Ethnic/Racial Breakdown of U.S. Population in 2050 (projected)

1.2.2 Gender

Gender is the state of being male or being female, but it is a psychosocial concept, not a biological one. The term *sex* refers to the biological division between male and female, as when we describe the sexual organs (not gender organs) that distinguish the reproductive anatomy of men and women. A person's gender, however, is not simply a matter of her or his anatomy or chromosomal sex. Gender is wrapped up with a complex web of cultural expectations and social roles about how we are expected to act as women or men.

Just as there have been historical prejudices against members of ethnic minority groups, so, too, have there been prejudices against women. The careers of women have traditionally been channeled into domestic chores, regardless of their talents, wishes, or abilities. Not until relatively modern times were women in Western cultures provided opportunities to pursue higher educational opportunities. Even today, women in many parts of the world are prevented from pursuing educational and training opportunities afforded to men.

Women in colonial times in the United States were not permitted to attend college. In fact, college doors were not opened to women until 1833, when Oberlin College became the first school of higher education to welcome women. Women did not have an easy go of it in the early days of psychology. The earliest female pioneer in psychology, Christine Ladd-Franklin (1847–1930), was denied her doctoral degree—not because she lacked credits or failed to complete her thesis but because she was a woman, and women were not expected to pursue advanced degrees. The proverbial tide has now turned. Today, about two-thirds of the undergraduate degrees and about three-quarters of the doctorates in psychology are granted to women (Cynkar, 2007; see Figure 1.4). Today it is the norm for women to be in the workforce. However, as we will see in Chapter 15, women in general continue to be paid less than men in comparable positions.

▮ **Gender** The state of being female or being male. (In this book, the word *sex* refers to sexual behavior and is also used in phrases such as *sex hormones*.)

1.2.3 Other Meanings of Diversity

Human diversity touches on many differences among people, such as age, physical ability, ethnicity or racial identification, religious differences, and sexual orientation.

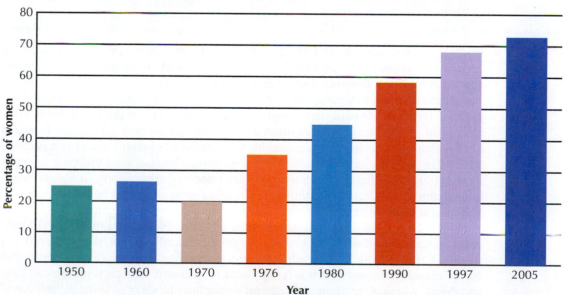

Figure 1.4
Percentage of Female Ph.D. Recipients in Psychology
Women now represent nearly three-fourths of new doctorate recipients in psychology, as compared to only one-fifth in 1970.
Source: Cynkar, 2007

Older people, people with disabilities, and gay males and lesbians have all suffered from various forms of discrimination.

Our focus on human diversity throughout the text will help us to better understand and fully appreciate the true extent of human behavior and mental processes. This broader view of psychology—and the world—is enriching for its own sake and heightens the accuracy and scope of our presentation.

Let us now consider how a scientific approach can help you cope with the challenges of life. This approach is characterized by critical thinking.

MODULE REVIEW

Review It

(7) Psychologists recognize that we need to consider the richness of human _____ in our efforts to develop a better understanding of individual behavior.

(8) Subgroups within the general population who have a common cultural heritage are called _____ groups.

(9) _____ is a psychosocial concept that distinguishes masculinity from femininity. Today, about two-thirds of the undergraduate degrees in psychology are awarded to (men or women).

Think About It

How can we gain a better appreciation of adjustment and personal growth by taking into account factors relating to human diversity?

MODULE 1.3

Critical Thinking and Adjustment

▪ What is critical thinking?

▪ What are some of the major features of critical thinking?

▪ How does critical thinking "protect" us from the claims of astrology and other pseudosciences?

▮ **Critical thinking** An approach to thinking characterized by skepticism and thoughtful analysis of statements and arguments—for example, probing the premises of arguments and the definitions of terms.

Psychology is a science, and the psychology of adjustment provides a scientific approach to coping with the challenges of life. One of the hallmarks of the scientific approach is **critical thinking**. But what is critical thinking?

Critical thinking has many meanings. On one level, it means taking nothing for granted. It means not believing things just because they are on the World Wide Web, or in print, or because they were uttered by authority figures or celebrities. It means not necessarily believing that it is healthful to express all of your feelings just because a friend in "therapy" urges you to do so. On another level, critical thinking refers to thoughtfully analyzing the statements and arguments of other people. It means examining definitions of terms, examining the premises or assumptions behind arguments, and then scrutinizing the logic with which arguments are developed.

Why is critical thinking essential to your adjustment? Critical thinking will help you determine whether the arguments of a political candidate are to be believed and trusted. Critical thinking will help you decide whether that clever quiz you found online actually measures what it is supposed to measure. Critical thinking can help you decide whether the arguments against eating fatty foods or in favor of "safer sex" apply to you. Critical thinking will help you decide whether a new diet craze has the potential to help you or hurt you. Critical thinking will help you examine the evidence as to whether the latest machine for giving you "abs" of steel is better than the last 10 machines that were supposed to give you abs of steel. Critical thinking will even help you figure out whether your friends' stories make sense.

1.3.1 Features of Critical Thinking

Let us consider some of the major features of critical thinking that can help you in your college years and beyond:

1 *Maintain a healthy skepticism.* Keep an open mind. Politicians and advertisers try to persuade you. Even research reported in the media or in textbooks may adopt a certain slant. Extend this principle to yourself. Are some of your own attitudes and beliefs superficial or unfounded? Accept nothing as true until you have examined the evidence.

2 *Examine the definitions of terms.* Some statements are true when a term is defined in one way but not when it is defined in another way. Consider the label on a container of "low-fat" ice cream: "97% Fat Free!" One day at the super-market we were impressed with an ice cream package's claims that the product was 97% fat free. Yet when we read the label closely, we found that a 4-ounce serving had 160 calories, 27 of which were contributed by fat. Fat, then, accounted for 27/160ths, or about 17%, of the ice cream's calorie content. But fat accounted for only 3% of the ice cream's weight—most of which was calorie-free water weight. The packagers of the ice cream knew that labeling the ice cream as "97% fat free" would make it sound more healthful than "Only 17% of calories from fat." Read carefully. Think critically.

3 *Examine the assumptions or premises of arguments.* Consider the statement that one cannot learn about human beings by conducting research on nonhuman animals. One premise in the statement seems to be that human beings are not animals. We are, of course. (Would you rather be a plant?)

4 *Be cautious in drawing conclusions from "evidence."* Self-help books tend to be filled with anecdotes about people who followed the methods in the books and improved their lives. "Psychics" point to predictions that prove to be accurate. Think critically: Do the self-help books report results with everyone who tried the method for losing weight or for achieving psychological well-being, or do they just report successes? Do so-called psychics report their failures or only their successes? Be especially skeptical when you hear "I know someone who …" Ask yourself whether this one person's reported experience—even if true—is satisfactory as evidence. When examining research findings, consider who paid for the research. Research evidence on the effectiveness of particular drugs may be less persuasive if the studies were underwritten by pharmaceutical companies selling the drugs rather than undertaken by independent researchers.

5 *Consider alternative interpretations of research evidence, especially of evidence that seems to show cause and effect.* What about this research question: "Does alcohol cause aggression?" Later in the chapter we see that evidence shows a clear connection, or "correlation," between alcohol and aggression. That is, many people who commit violent crimes have been drinking alcohol. But does the evidence show that this connection is causal? Could other factors, such as gender, age, willingness to take risks, or social expectations, account for both the drinking and the aggressive behavior?

6 *Don't oversimplify.* People's adjustment to the challenges of life can involve complex interactions of genetic influences, situational factors, and personal choice. Consider the question as to whether psychotherapy helps people with adjustment problems. A broad answer to this question—a simple yes or no—might be over-simplifying. It may be more worthwhile to ask, "What type of psychotherapy, prac-ticed by whom, is most helpful for what kind of client and what kind of problem?"

7 *Don't overgeneralize.* Consider again the statement that one cannot learn about human beings by conducting research on animals. Is the truth of the matter an all-or-nothing issue? Can we obtain certain kinds of information about people from research with animals? What kinds of things are you likely to be able to learn only through research with people?

8 *Apply critical thinking to all areas of life.* A skeptical attitude and a demand for evidence are useful not only in college but in all areas of life. Be skeptical when you are bombarded by TV commercials, when political causes try to sweep you up, when you see the latest cover stories about UFO sightings in supermarket tabloids. How many times have you heard the claim, "Studies have shown that …"? Perhaps such claims sound convincing, but ask yourself: Who ran the studies? Were the researchers neutral scientists, or were they biased toward obtaining certain results?

These principles of critical thinking guide psychologists' thinking as they observe behavior, engage in research, or advise clients as to how to improve the quality of their lives. They will also help you adjust to the challenges in your own life. Now let us turn to applying critical thinking skills to two areas that are very much in the public eye: astrology and self-help books. In the *Adjustment and Modern Life* feature on page 19, we focus on another area in which people need to exercise their critical thinking skills: surfing the Internet.

Evaluating Food Claims
Think before you buy. Is a low-fat ice cream that advertises itself as 97% fat free really healthy for you? What does this food claim really mean?

Sean Locke/iStockphoto

1.3.2 Thinking Critically about Astrology and Other Pseudosciences

Should you be concerned about your horoscope? Do "psychics" really help police find criminals and evidence? When you are troubled, should you examine the situation critically and solve your problems by yourself? If you believe you might profit from another person's advice, should you consult an astrologer, a psychic, or a mental health professional like a psychologist?

Psychologists are trained to be critical thinkers. They are skeptical. They insist on seeing the evidence before they will accept people's claims and arguments as to what is true and what is false. The same procedures can be applied to **pseudosciences** (false sciences) such as astrology. Pseudoscience beckons us from the tabloids at supermarket checkout counters. Each week, there are 10 new encounters with extraterrestrials. There are 10 new "absolutely proven effective" ways to take off weight and 10 new ways to beat stress and depression. There are 10 new ways to tell if your partner has been cheating and, of course, 10 new predictions by astrologers and psychics.

Let's focus on one example of pseudoscience—astrology. But first read this personality report. We wrote it about you:

> *You have your strengths and your weaknesses, but much of the time you do not give yourself enough credit for your strengths. You are one of those people who has the inner potential for change, but you need to pay more attention to your own feelings so that you can determine the right direction for yourself.*
>
> *You have many times found yourself to be in conflict as your inner impulses have run up against the limits of social rules and moral codes. Most of the time you manage to resolve conflict in a way that makes sense to you, but now and then you have doubts and wonder whether you have done the right thing. You would often like to be doing two or more things at the same time, and you occasionally resent the fact that you cannot.*
>
> *There is an inner you known to you alone, and you often present a face to the world that does not quite reflect your genuine thoughts and feelings. And now and then you look at the things you have done, and the path that you have taken, and you have some doubt as to whether it is all worth it.*

That's you, isn't it? It probably sounds familiar enough. The tendency to believe a generalized (but phony) personality report is called the **Barnum effect**, after nineteenth-century circus magnate P. T. Barnum, who once declared that a good circus had a "little something for everybody." The Barnum effect—the tendency for gen-

❚ **Pseudoscience** A method or system that claims to have a scientific basis but does not, such as astrology. A false or sham science.

❚ **Barnum effect** The tendency of people to accept overgeneralized descriptions of personality as accurate appraisals of their own personalities.

eral personality reports to have a "little something for everybody"—also allows fortune-tellers to make a living. That is, most of us have enough in common that a fortune-teller's "revelations" about us may ring true.

Most of us have personality traits in common. But what do tea leaves, bird droppings, palms (of your hands, not on the tropical sands), and the stars have in common? Let us see.

P.T. Barnum also once declared, "There's a sucker born every minute." The tendency to believe generalized personality reports has made people vulnerable to fakers and phonies throughout history. It enriches the pocketbooks of people who offer to "read their personalities" and predict their futures based on the movements of the stars and planets through astrology. Even in an age in which science has proved itself capable of making significant contributions to people's daily lives and health, many people today check their horoscopes rather than seek scientific information when they have to make a decision!

Astrology is based on the notion that the positions of the sun, the moon, and the stars affect human temperament and human affairs. For example, people born under the sign of Jupiter are believed to be full of playful good humor (jovial). People born under the sign of Saturn are thought to be gloomy and morose (saturnine). And people born under the sign of Mars are believed to be warlike (martial). One supposedly can also foretell the future by studying the positions of these bodies.

Astrologers maintain that the positions of the heavenly bodies at the time of our birth determine our personality and destiny. They prepare forecasts called horoscopes that are based on our birthdates and indicate what it is safe for us to do. If you get involved with someone who asks for your "sign" (for example, Aquarius or Taurus), he or she is inquiring about your birthdate in astrological terms. Astrologers claim that your sign, which reflects the month during which you were born, indicates whom you will be compatible with. You may have been wondering whether you should date someone of another religion. If you start to follow astrology, you may also be wondering whether it is safe for a Sagittarius to date a Pisces or a Gemini.

Apply principles of critical thinking to the claims of astrologers. For example, does the fact that there may be a long-standing tradition in astrology affect its scientific credibility? Are the tides of the seas comparable to human personality and destiny?

Psychology is a science. Science demands that beliefs about the behavior of cosmic rays, chemical compounds, cells, people—or the meaning of bird droppings or the movements of the stars—must be supported by evidence. Persuasive arguments and reference to authority figures are not scientific evidence. Astrologers and other pseudoscientists have made specific forecasts of events, and their accuracy—or lack of it—provides a means of evaluating astrology. Astrological predictions are no more likely to come true than predictions based on chance (Munro & Munro, 2000). Nor is there any scientific basis for beliefs that one's personality is related to one's birth sign (Hartmann, Reuter, & Nyborg, 2006). But does the lack of scientific support for astrology matter? Will followers of astrology be persuaded by facts? Maybe not. Many people seem to need some magic in their lives, even if the "magic" provided by psychics amounts to a heap of garbage. Sad to say, even in our age of scientific enlightenment, many people are more comfortable with stories and leaps of faith than they are with objective evidence and statistical probabilities.

Paul Brian/iStockphoto

What's Your Sign?
Can you really learn about an individual's personality or future prospects by consulting astrological signs? How can we distinguish between true science and pseudosciences like astrology?

1.3.3 Thinking Critically about Self-Help Books: Are There Any Quick Fixes?

Chicken Soup for the Soul; The Road Less Traveled; The 7 Habits of Highly Effective People; The Seven Spiritual Laws of Success; Don't Say Yes When You Want to Say No; Our Bodies Ourselves; The 8-Week Cholesterol Cure; Treating Type A Behavior and Your Heart; Feeling Good—The New Mood Therapy. . . . These are just a few of the self-help books that have flooded the marketplace in recent years. Every day, shy people, anxious people, heavy people, stressed people, and confused people scan bookstores and supermarket checkout racks in hope of finding the one book that will provide the answer. How can they evaluate the merits of these books? Some offer useful insights and advice. But others are just plain wrong. How can we separate the helpful wheat from the useless and sometimes harmful chaff?

Unfortunately, there are no easy answers. Many of us believe the things we see in print, and anecdotes about how chubby John lost 60 pounds in 60 days and shy Joni blossomed into a social butterfly in a month have a powerful allure. Especially when we are needy.

Be on guard. A price we pay for freedom of speech is that nearly anything can wind up in print. Authors can make extravagant claims with little fear of punishment. They can lie about the effectiveness of a new fad diet as easily as they can lie about being kidnapped by a UFO.

To help separate the meaningful wheat from the nonsensical chaff, try some critical thinking:

1 *First, don't judge the book by its cover or its title.* Good books as well as bad books can have catchy titles and interesting covers. Dozens, perhaps hundreds, of books are competing for your attention. It is little wonder, then, that publishers try to do something sensational with the covers.

2 *Avoid books that make extravagant claims.* If it sounds too good to be true, it probably is. No method helps everyone who tries it. Very few methods work overnight. People want the instant cure. The book that promises to make you fit in 10 days will outsell the book that says it will take 10 weeks. Responsible psychologists and health professionals do not make lavish claims.

3 *Check authors' educational credentials.* Be suspicious if the author's title is just "Dr." and is placed before the name. The degree could be a phony doctorate bought through the mail. It could be issued by a religious cult rather than a university or professional school. It is better if the "doctor" has an M.D., Ph.D., Psy.D., or Ed.D. after her or his name rather than "Dr." in front of it.

4 *Check authors' affiliations.* There are no guarantees, but authors who are affiliated with colleges and universities may be more credible than those who are not.

5 *Consider authors' complaints about the conservatism of professional groups to be a warning.* Do the authors boast that they are ahead of their time? Do they berate professional health organizations as pigheaded or narrow-minded? If so, be suspicious. Most psychologists and other scientists are open-minded. They just ask to see evidence before they jump on the bandwagon. Enthusiasm is no substitute for research and evidence.

6 *Check the evidence reported in the book.* Poor-quality self-help books tend to make extensive use of anecdotes—unsupported stories about the fantastic results achieved with a few individuals. Responsible psychologists and other health professionals check the effectiveness of techniques with carefully constructed samples of people. They carefully measure the outcomes and qualify their statements about their results, such as by saying "it appears that" and "subjects tended to improve. "

7 *Check the reference citations for the evidence.* Legitimate psychological research is reported in the journals you will find in the reference section of this book. These journals report only research methods and outcomes that meet scientific standards. If there are no reference citations, or if the list of references seems suspicious, you should be suspicious, too.

8 *Ask your instructor for advice.* Ask for advice on what to do, whom to talk to, what to read.

9 *Read textbooks and professional books, like this book, rather than self-help books.* Search the college bookstore for texts in fields that interest you. Try the suggested readings in textbooks.

10 *Stop by and chat with your psychology professor.* Talk to someone in your college or university health center.

In sum, there are few, if any, quick fixes to psychological and health problems. Do your homework. Become a critical consumer of self-help books.

Let us now look more deeply into a scientific approach to adjustment. We shall discuss the scientific method in general and then consider the ways in which psychologists gather evidence to support—or, sometimes, to disprove—their views.

Adjustment and Modern Life

Thinking Critically When Surfing Online

The Internet offers a host of services, from e-mail to shopping to news and information. It's no surprise that an increasing number of people are using online resources. As they click from site to site, they are exposed to a vast repository of information about psychology, self-help, relationships, health, and so on. Like self-help books, much of this information is helpful, but much of it is incomplete, misleading, difficult for the average person to understand, or just plain wrong (Benotsch, Kalichman, & Weinhardt, 2004). The beauty of the Web is that anyone can post information that others can access. Yet this freedom carries with it the risk that the information posted may be inaccurate.

Critical thinkers don't suspend their skeptical attitude when they go online. They check out the credentials of the source by asking questions such as these: Who is posting the material? Is the source a well-respected medical or scientific institution? Or is it an individual or group of individuals with no apparent scientific credentials and perhaps with an axe to grind with the scientific establishment? The most trustworthy online information comes from well-known scientific sources, such as leading scientific journals, government agencies like the National Institutes of Health, and major professional organizations like the American Psychological Association and the Association for Psychological Science. Articles in scientific journals undergo a process of peer review in which independent scientists first carefully scrutinize them before they are accepted for publication.

Critical thinkers should also be wary of product claims for health-related products. People sell virtually anything over the Internet these days. Don't assume that product claims are scientifically valid. Treat them as a form of electronic advertising, basically an Internet version of a television commercial. In other words, take them with the proverbial grain of salt and keep a tight grip on your wallet. Also, examine offers of money-back guarantees carefully. Read the fine print. These "guarantees" may not promise that the product will work as advertised. Rather, they might guarantee that you'll get your money back if the product fails, but often there are strings attached. As the expression goes, "Let the buyer beware." Sad to say, many of us never question the information that comes to us on the printed page or on our computer screens. Yet critical thinkers evaluate assertions and claims for themselves.

Though we should think critically about information posted on the Web, we should also recognize that the Internet can be an effective vehicle for distributing information that may not be accessible through other sources, such as information young people can use to prevent sexually transmitted diseases (Keller & Brown, 2002). Investigators have also found that women with breast cancer benefit psychologically from seeking health-related information on the Internet (Fogel, 2003).

Source: Nevid, J. S. *Psychology: Concepts and Applications.* (2nd ed.) Copyright © 2007 by Houghton Mifflin Company. Used with permission.

MODULE REVIEW

Review It

(10) The adoption of a skeptical, questioning attitude toward the claims or arguments of others is called _____ _____.

(11) One aspect of critical thinking is the careful examination of the _____ of terms.

(12) The term *pseudoscience* refers to a (true or false?) science.

(13) Though we should carefully evaluate information we obtain on the Internet, evidence from a recent study showed that women with breast cancer benefited _____ from seeking health-related information online.

Think About It

Do you accept the claims made for products or services advertised on TV or in newspapers or magazines at face value? How can you apply the principles of critical thinking to weigh the validity of these claims?

MODULE 1.4

How Psychologists Study Adjustment

■ What is the scientific method?

■ What is the case study method?

■ What is the survey method?

■ How do psychologists use samples to represent populations?

■ What is the naturalistic observation method?

■ What is the correlational method?

■ What is the experimental method?

■ **Scientific method** A method for obtaining scientific evidence in which a hypothesis is formed and tested.

Are women better than men at spelling? Are city dwellers less friendly toward strangers than small-town residents? Do laws against discrimination reduce prejudice? Does alcohol cause aggression? Is exercise good for your blood pressure? What are the effects of day care and divorce on children? Many of us have expressed opinions on questions such as these at one time or another, and psychological and medical theories also suggest a number of possible answers. But psychology is a science, and scientific statements about behavior must be supported by evidence. Strong arguments, reference to authority figures, celebrity endorsements, and even tightly knit theories don't qualify as scientific evidence. Scientific evidence is obtained by means of the **scientific method**.

1.4.1 The Scientific Method: Putting Ideas to the Test

The scientific method is an organized way that scientists use to test ideas and expand and refine their knowledge based on careful observation and experimentation. It is not a recipe that psychologists and other scientists follow, but rather a set of general principles that guides their research. Psychologists usually begin by formulating a research question. Research questions can have many sources. Our daily experiences, psychological theory, even folklore and intuition all help generate questions for research. But whatever the source of the question, psychologists do not substitute speculation or theorizing for gathering evidence.

A research question may be studied as a question or reworded as a **hypothesis** (see Figure 1.5). A hypothesis is a specific prediction about behavior or mental processes that is tested through research. One hypothesis about day care might be that preschoolers who are placed in day care will acquire greater social skills in relating to peers than will preschoolers who are cared for in the home. A hypothesis about exposure to TV violence might be that elementary school children who watch more violent TV shows tend to behave more aggressively toward their peers.

Psychologists next examine the research question or test the hypothesis through carefully conducted methods of research. For example, they might introduce children who are in day care, and children who are not, to a new child and observe how children in each group interact with the new acquaintance. Psychologists draw conclusions about their research questions or the accuracy of their hypotheses on the basis of their observations or findings. When evidence accumulates that fails to bear out hypotheses, psychologists may rethink their hypotheses or modify the theories from which they are drawn.

As psychologists draw conclusions from research evidence, they are guided by principles of critical thinking. For example, they do not confuse correlation with causation. **Correlation** is a statistical association or relationship between variables. Causation means that one variable directly causes or influences another. For example, psychologists may find a significant correlation in children between the amounts

Testing the Hypothesis
The scientific method is a systematic way of testing predictions, or hypotheses, in the light of evidence. For example, an investigator might test the hypothesis that dating couples who share similar attitudes and interests are more likely to stay together than those with dissimilar attitudes and interests. Sharing the same choice of clothing may have no bearing on the outcome of the relationship, however.

■ **Hypothesis** A prediction about behavior that is tested through research.

■ **Correlation** A statistical association or relationship between two variables, expressed in the form of a correlation coefficient.

of time spent watching violent TV shows and the level of aggressiveness shown in the schoolyard or the classroom. It may be tempting to conclude from this kind of evidence that TV violence causes aggressive behavior. But a **selection factor** may be at work—because the children studied choose (select) for themselves what they will watch. Perhaps more aggressive children are more likely than less aggressive children to tune in to violent TV shows. As we shall see, psychologists use experimental methods to tease out cause-and-effect relationships.

To better understand the effects of the selection factor, consider a study on the relationship between exercise and health. Imagine that we were to compare a group of people who exercised regularly with a group of people who did not. We might find that the exercisers were physically healthier than the couch potatoes. But could we conclude that exercise is a causal factor in good health? Perhaps not. The selection factor—the fact that one group chose to exercise and the other did not—could also explain the results. Perhaps healthy people are more likely to choose to exercise.

Some psychologists include publication of research reports in professional journals as a crucial part of the scientific method. Researchers are obligated to provide enough details of their work that others will be able to repeat or **replicate** it to see whether the findings hold up over time and with different subjects. Publication of research also permits the scientific community at large to evaluate the methods and conclusions of other scientists.

Psychologists may attempt to replicate a study in detail to corroborate the findings, especially when the findings are significant for people's welfare. Sometimes psychologists replicate research methods with different kinds of subjects to determine, for example, whether findings with women can be generalized to men, whether findings with European Americans can be generalized to ethnic minority groups, or whether findings with people who have sought psychotherapy can be generalized to people at large.

1.4.2 How Psychologists Do Research

• •

Let us now consider the research methods used by psychologists: the case study method, the survey method, the naturalistic observation method, the correlational method, and the experimental method. But first let us draw your attention to the historic underrepresentation of women and minorities in research.

Including Women and Members of Diverse Ethnic Groups in Research

There is a historic bias in favor of conducting research with men, especially in the field of health. For example, most of the large-sample research on relationships between lifestyle and health has been conducted with men. Investigators today, however, as well as the funding agencies that support research in the health sciences, recognize the importance of including traditionally underrepresented groups in research studies, including women and ethnic minorities.

One area in which more research is needed is the impact of work on women's lives. For example, how does working outside the home affect the division of labor within the home? Numerous studies have found that women are more likely than men to put in a "double shift." Women, that is, tend to put in a full day of work along with an equally long "shift" of shopping, mopping, and otherwise caring for their families. We should also note that findings from research studies based on male participants may not generalize to women in general, nor might findings based on European American women generalize to women of color. When women in general, or women of color and of lower socioeconomic status in particular, are not included in research studies, or when their responses are not sorted out from those of European American women, or more affluent women, issues of interest to them tend to get lost.

▮ **Selection factor** A source of bias that may occur in research findings when subjects are allowed to determine for themselves whether they will receive a treatment condition in a scientific study. Do you think, for example, that there are problems in studying the effects of a diet or of smoking cigarettes when we allow study participants to choose whether they will try the diet or smoke cigarettes? Why or why not?

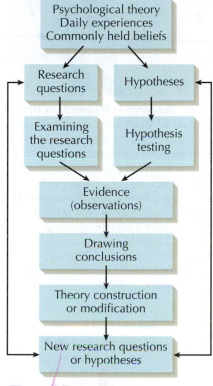

Figure 1.5
The Scientific Method
The scientific method is a systematic way of organizing and expanding scientific knowledge. Daily experiences, common beliefs, and scientific observations all contribute to the development of theories. Psychological theories explain observations and lead to hypotheses about behavior and mental processes. Observations can confirm the theory or lead to its refinement or abandonment.

▮ **Replicate** Repeat, reproduce, copy. What are some reasons that psychologists replicate the research conducted by other psychologists?

More Research Is Needed on the Impact of Work on Women's Lives

The great majority of American women—including women with infants—work outside the home. And who do you think continues to bear the main responsibility for homemaking and childrearing—the father or the mother? (Excellent guess.) Women, therefore, tend to have double shifts, one at home and one on the job. How does such overload affect their adjustment?

▌ **Case study method** A method of research based on a carefully drawn biography obtained through interviews, questionnaires, or psychological tests.

▌ **Social desirability bias** The tendency for people to respond in socially desirable ways.

▌ **Surveys** Means of information gathering by which large numbers of individuals are interviewed or asked to complete questionnaires in order to learn about their attitudes or behaviors.

▌ **Generalize** To extend from the particular to the general; to apply observations based on a sample to a population.

Research samples have also tended to underrepresent minority ethnic groups in the population. For example, personality tests completed by European Americans and by African Americans may need to be interpreted in diverse ways if accurate conclusions are to be drawn. The well-known Kinsey studies on sexual behavior (Kinsey et al., 1948, 1953) did not adequately represent African Americans, poor people, older people, and numerous other groups. The results of the National Health and Social Life Survey (NHSLS), reported later in the chapter, do reflect the behavior of diverse groups.

The Case Study Method

We begin our discussion of major research methods with the **case study method** because our own ideas about human nature tend to be based on our informal studies or observations of individuals and small groups. Most of us gather our information haphazardly. Often, we see what we want to see. Unscientific accounts of people's behavior are referred to as anecdotes. Through the use of the case study method, psychologists draw carefully constructed portraits of the lives of individuals in order to better understand their behavior. Sigmund Freud, whose work is discussed in Chapter 2, developed his theory of personality largely on the basis of intensive case studies of patients he had treated.

Freud studied his patients in great depth, seeking factors that seemed to contribute to notable patterns of behavior. He followed some patients for many years, meeting with them several times a week.

Of course, there are bound to be gaps in memory when people are questioned. People may also distort their pasts because of a **social desirability bias**—a tendency to present oneself in a socially desirable light. Interviewers may also have certain expectations and may subtly encourage subjects to fill in gaps in ways that are consistent with their theoretical perspectives. All in all, case studies may provide useful or revealing information, but they lack the rigorous controls found in experimental methods.

The Survey Method

Psychologists conduct **surveys** to learn about attitudes and behaviors that cannot be directly observed in the natural setting or studied experimentally. When conducting surveys, psychologists typically administer questionnaires or interviews to large numbers of individuals. Surveys have been conducted on many topics relating to adjustment, including dietary habits, exercise patterns, marital satisfaction, and even intimate sexual behavior.

Samples and Populations: Hitting the Target Population

Consider a piece of "history" that never happened: In 1936 the Republican candidate Alf Landon defeated the incumbent president, Franklin D. Roosevelt. Or at least Landon did so in a poll conducted by a popular magazine of the day, the *Literary Digest*. In the actual election, Roosevelt routed Landon in a landslide of 11 million votes. How, then, could the *Digest* predict a Landon victory? How was so great a discrepancy possible?

The *Digest*, you see, had phoned the voters it surveyed. Today, telephone sampling is a widely practiced and reasonably legitimate technique. But the *Digest* poll was taken during the Great Depression, when Americans who had telephones were much wealthier than those who did not. Americans at higher income levels are also more likely to vote Republican. No surprise, then, that the overwhelming majority of those sampled said that they would vote for Landon.

Psychologists use samples to represent populations. If samples accurately represent the population they are intended to reflect, we can **generalize** the results obtained from research samples back to the populations from which they were drawn.

In surveys such as that conducted by the *Literary Digest* and in other research methods, the individuals, or subjects, who are studied are referred to as a **sample**. A sample is a segment of a population. Psychologists and other scientists need to ensure that the subjects they observe represent their target population, such as Americans, not subgroups such as Southern California Yuppies or European American members of the middle class.

▌ **Sample** Part of a population selected for research.

Random Sampling

One way to achieve a representative sample is by means of *random sampling*. In a random sample, each member of a **population** has an equal chance of being selected to participate. Researchers may stratify their sample by first identifying subgroups in the population and then randomly sampling members of these subgroups in relation to the proportion of the subgroups in the population. For instance, 12% of the American population is African American; a stratified sample would thus be 12% African American. As a practical matter, a large, randomly selected sample will show reasonably accurate stratification. A **random sample** of 1,500 people will represent the general American population reasonably well. A haphazardly drawn sample of a million people, however, might not.

▌ **Population** A complete group of organisms or events.

▌ **Random sample** A sample drawn such that every member of a population has an equal chance of being selected.

Volunteer Bias

Popular magazines often conduct reader surveys to ascertain attitudes about relationships, sexuality, family issues, and so on. Although many thousands of readers complete these questionnaires and send them in, do they represent the general American population? Probably not. These studies and similar ones may be influenced by **volunteer bias**. The concept behind volunteer bias is that people who offer to participate in research studies, or who participate in surveys, differ in important ways from people who do not. In the case of research into sexual behavior, volunteers may represent subgroups of the population—or of readers of the magazines in question—who are willing to disclose intimate information. Volunteers may also be more interested in research than nonvolunteers and may also have more spare time. How might such volunteers differ from the population at large? How might such differences slant or bias the research outcomes?

▌ **Volunteer bias** A source of bias or error in research that reflects the prospect that people who offer to participate in research studies differ systematically from people who do not.

Surveying Intimate Behavior: The NHSLS Survey

Is it possible for scientists to describe the sex lives of people in the United States? There are many difficulties in gathering data, such as the refusal of many individuals to participate in research. Moreover, we must specify which people we are talking about. Are we talking, for example, about the behavior of women or men, younger people or older people, European Americans or African Americans?

A large nationwide survey of sexual practices, called the National Health and Social Life Survey (NHSLS), sampled 3,432 people (Laumann et al., 1994). Of this number, 3,159 were English-speaking adults aged 18 to 59. The other 273 respondents were drawn from African American and Latino and Latina American households. While the sample probably represents the overall U.S. population aged 18 to 59 quite well, it may include too few Asian Americans, Native Americans, and Jewish Americans to offer much information about these groups.

The NHSLS research team identified sets of households in various locales—addresses, not names. They sent a letter to each household describing the purpose and methods of the study. An interviewer visited each household one week later. The people targeted were assured that the purposes of the study were important and that their identities would be kept confidential. Incentives of up to $100 were offered to obtain a high completion rate of close to 80%.

The NHSLS considered the factors of gender, age, level of education, religion, and race/ethnicity in the numbers of sex partners people have (Laumann et al., 1994) (see

Table 1.1). Males in the survey report having higher numbers of sex partners than females do. For example, one male in three (33%) reports having 11 or more sex partners since the age of 18. This compares with fewer than 1 woman in 10 (9%). Most people in the United States, however, appear to limit their numbers of sex partners to a handful or fewer.

Note that the number of sex partners appears to rise with age into the forties. Why? As people get older, have they had more opportunity to accumulate life experiences, including sexual experiences? But reports of the numbers of partners fall off among people in their fifties; the reason is likely to be that people in this age group entered adulthood when sexual attitudes were more conservative.

Level of education is also connected with sexual behavior. Generally speaking, it would appear that education is a liberating influence. People with some college, or who have completed college, are likely to report having more sex partners than those who attended only grade school or high school. By contrast, having a conservative religious

Table 1.1 ▮ Number of Sex Partners Since Age 18 Based on NHSLS[a] Study						
	Number of Sex Partners (%)					
Factors	0	1	2–4	5–10	11–20	21 +
Gender						
Male	3	20	21	23	16	17
Female	3	32	36	20	6	3
Age						
18–24	8	32	34	15	8	3
25–29	2	25	31	22	10	9
30–34	3	21	29	25	11	10
35–39	2	19	30	25	14	11
40–44	1	22	28	24	14	12
45–49	2	26	24	25	10	14
50–54	2	34	28	18	9	9
55–59	1	40	28	15	8	7
Education						
Less than high school	4	27	36	19	9	6
High school graduate	3	30	29	20	10	7
Some college	2	24	29	23	12	9
College graduate	2	24	26	24	11	13
Advanced degree	4	25	26	23	10	13
Religion						
None	3	16	29	20	16	16
Liberal, moderate Protestant	2	23	31	23	12	8
Conservative Protestant	3	30	30	20	10	7
Catholic	4	27	29	23	8	9
Race/Ethnicity						
European American	3	26	29	22	11	9
African American	2	18	34	24	11	11
Latino and Latina American	3	36	27	17	8	9
Asian American[b]	6	46	25	14	6	3
Native American[b]	5	28	35	23	5	5

Note: Adapted from *The Social Organization of Sexuality: Sexual Practices in the United States* (Table 5.1C, p. 179), by E. O. Laumann, J. H. Gagnon, R. T. Michael, & S. Michaels, 1994, Chicago: University of Chicago Press.

[a]*National Health and Social Life Survey,* conducted by a research team centered at the University of Chicago.

[b]These sample sizes are quite small.

affiliation appears to be a restraining factor. Liberal Protestants (for example, Methodists, Lutherans, Presbyterians, Episcopalians, and members of the United Churches of Christ) and people who say they have no religion report higher numbers of sex partners than do Roman Catholics and conservative Protestants (for example, Baptists, Pentecostals, and members of the Churches of Christ and Assemblies of God).

Ethnicity is also connected with sexual behavior. The research findings in Table 1.1 suggest that European Americans and African Americans have the highest numbers of sex partners. Since Latino and Latina Americans are mostly Catholic, perhaps Catholicism provides a restraint on their sexual behavior. Asian Americans would appear to be the most sexually restrained ethnic group. However, the sample sizes of Asian Americans and Native Americans are too small to command much confidence in the results.

The Naturalistic Observation Method

You use **naturalistic observation** every day of your life. That is, you observe people in their natural habitats. So do scientists. But scientists use more systematic or formal methods when observing people than occurs in casual observation. For example, they may observe peer relationships of children in a schoolyard in order to better understand how children relate to one another. They may note how children form play groups and how they include or exclude other children. Psychologists may also observe differences in the eating behaviors of normal-weight and overweight patrons at fast-food restaurants. They may observe what people order, how long it takes them to consume their meals, and how many bites they take. Do the overweight eat more rapidly? Chew less frequently? Leave less food on their plates? This kind of information may help determine whether the eating habits of people of different weight classes differ.

▮ **Naturalistic observation** A scientific method in which organisms are observed in their natural environments.

Dare You Say What You Think? The Social Desirability Scale	*Self-Assessment*

Do you say what you think, or do you tend to misrepresent your beliefs to earn the approval of others? Do you answer questions honestly, or do you say what you think other people want to hear? Telling others what we think they want to hear is making the socially desirable response. Falling prey to social desirability may cause us to distort our beliefs and experiences in interviews or on psychological tests. The bias toward responding in socially desirable directions is also a source of error in the case study, survey, and testing methods. You can complete the following Social Desirability Scale devised by Crowne and Marlowe to gain insight into whether you have a tendency to produce socially desirable responses.

Directions: Read each item and decide whether it is true (T) or false (F) for you. Try to work rapidly and answer each question by circling the T or the F. Then turn to the scoring key at the end of the chapter to interpret your answers.

T F   1. Before voting I thoroughly investigate the qualifications of all the candidates.
T F   2. I never hesitate to go out of my way to help someone in trouble.
T F   3. It is sometimes hard for me to go on with my work if I am not encouraged.
T F   4. I have never intensely disliked anyone.
T F   5. On occasions I have had doubts about my ability to succeed in life.
T F   6. I sometimes feel resentful when I don't get my way.
T F   7. I am always careful about my manner of dress.
T F   8. My table manners at home are as good as when I eat out in a restaurant.
T F   9. If I could get into a movie without paying and be sure I was not seen, I would probably do it.
T F 10. On a few occasions, I have given up something because I thought too little of my ability.
T F 11. I like to gossip at times.
T F 12. There have been times when I felt like rebelling against people in authority even though I knew they were right.
T F 13. No matter who I'm talking to, I'm always a good listener.
T F 14. I can remember "playing sick" to get out of something.
T F 15. There have been occasions when I have taken advantage of someone.

T F   16. I'm always willing to admit it when I make a mistake.
T F   17. I always try to practice what I preach.
T F   18. I don't find it particularly difficult to get along with loudmouthed, obnoxious people.
T F   19. I sometimes try to get even rather than forgive and forget.
T F   20. When I don't know something I don't mind at all admitting it.
T F   21. I am always courteous, even to people who are disagreeable.
T F   22. At times I have really insisted on having things my own way.
T F   23. There have been occasions when I felt like smashing things.
T F   24. I would never think of letting someone else be punished for my wrongdoings.
T F   25. I never resent being asked to return a favor.
T F   26. I have never been irked when people expressed ideas very different from my own.
T F   27. I never make a long trip without checking the safety of my car.
T F   28. There have been times when I was quite jealous of the good fortune of others.
T F   29. I have almost never felt the urge to tell someone off.
T F   30. I am sometimes irritated by people who ask favors of me.
T F   31. I have never felt that I was punished without cause.
T F   32. I sometimes think when people have a misfortune they only got what they deserved.
T F   33. I have never deliberately said something that hurt someone's feelings.

Source: Crowne, D. P., & Marlowe, D. A. (1960). A new scale of social desirability independent of pathology, *Journal of Consulting Psychology, 24*, 351. Copyright 1960 by the American Psychological Association. Reprinted by permission.

For an interactive version of this self-assessment exercise, go to www.wileyplus.com

In naturalistic observation, psychologists and other scientists observe behavior in the field, or "where it happens." They try to avoid interfering with the behaviors they are observing by using **unobtrusive measures**. The naturalistic observation method provides descriptive information about behavior, but it cannot determine the underlying causes of behavior.

▌ **Unobtrusive measures** Research measures that do not interfere with the subject's behavior.

The Correlational Method: Seeing What Goes Up and What Comes Down

Are people with higher intelligence more likely to do well in school? Are people with a stronger need for achievement likely to climb higher up the corporate ladder? What is the relationship between stress and health? These kinds of questions are often addressed through correlational research.

In using the **correlational method**, psychologists investigate whether one observed behavior or measured trait is related to, or correlated with, another. Consider the variables of intelligence and academic performance. The variables of intelligence and academic performance are assigned numbers such as intelligence test scores and academic averages. Then the numbers or scores are mathematically related and expressed as a **correlation coefficient**. A correlation coefficient is a number that varies between −1.00 and +1.00. The closer to positive or negative 1.00, the stronger the magnitude of the relationship between the two variables.

When one variable increases as the other increases, the relationship between the two variables is expressed as a **positive correlation** (the sign of the correlation coefficient is positive). For example, investigators find a positive relationship between intelligence and measures of academic achievement, such as grades in school (e.g., Ridgell & Lounsbury, 2004).

Generally speaking, the higher people score on intelligence tests, the better their academic performance is likely to be. The scores attained on intelligence tests are positively correlated with overall academic achievement (see Figure 1.6).

There is a **negative correlation** between stress and various indices of health. As the amount of stress affecting us increases, the functioning of our immune system

▌ **Correlational method** A scientific method that studies the relationships between variables.

▌ **Correlation coefficient** A number between −1.00 and +1.00 that expresses the strength and direction (positive or negative) of the relationship between two variables.

▌ **Positive correlation** A relationship between variables in which one variable increases as the other also increases.

▌ **Negative correlation** A relationship between two variables in which one variable increases as the other decreases.

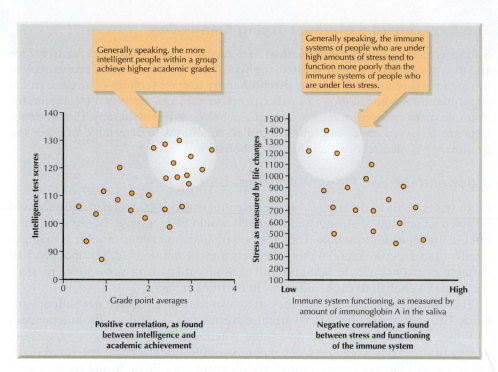

Figure 1.6
Positive and Negative Correlations
With a positive correlation between variables, as between intelligence and achievement, as one variable increases, the other tends to increase. By and large, the higher people score on intelligence tests, the better their academic performance is likely to be, as shown in the diagram to the left. (Each dot is located to represent an individual's intelligence test score and grade point average.) Similarly, there is a positive correlation between engaging in exercise and physical health, as we see in Chapter 5. On the other hand, there is a negative correlation between stress and health. As the amount of stress increases, the functioning of our immune system tends to decrease. Although correlational research may point to a possible causal effect, it does not demonstrate cause-and-effect relationships.

decreases (see Chapter 4). Under high levels of stress, many people show poorer health. A negative correlation is expressed by a correlation coefficient with a negative sign (for example: –.60).

Correlational research may suggest causal patterns but does not demonstrate cause-and-effect relationships. For instance, it may seem logical to assume that high intelligence makes it possible for children to profit from education. Research has also shown, however, that education contributes to higher scores on intelligence tests. Children placed in richly stimulating Head Start programs at an early age do better later on intelligence tests than other children who did not have this experience. It is also conceivable that intelligence and academic achievement have no causal relationship but that both are explained by a third variable, such as genetic factors or exposure to a stimulating home environment. The relationship between intelligence and academic performance may not be as simple as you might have thought. What of the link between stress and health? Does stress impair health, or is it possible that people in poorer health encounter higher levels of stress? Although correlational research may not pinpoint cause and effect, it may suggest possible causal factors that can be followed up through experimental methods.

Consider another example based on research on cohabitation ("living together"). A kind of folklore has developed concerning the advantages of premarital cohabitation or of trial marriage with one's future spouse. Many people believe that a trial period allows them to test their feelings and find out if they can adjust to another's quirks before they make a permanent commitment. It is thus ironic that studies show that cohabiting couples who later marry are more likely to divorce than are couples who did not cohabit before marriage (Cohan & Kleinbaum, 2002; Holman, 2000).

Do not jump to the conclusion that living together before marriage causes, or even heightens, the risk of divorce. We cite this research to highlight the fact that correlational research does not demonstrate cause and effect. Both variables—the high divorce rate and the choice to live together before marriage—might reflect another factor: liberal attitudes. That is, liberal attitudes could contribute to cohabitation and to divorce. Similarly, even though body height and weight are correlated, people do not grow taller because they weigh more.

The Experimental Method: Trying Things Out

▮ Experimental method A scientific method that seeks to confirm or discover cause-and-effect relationships by introducing independent variables and observing their effects on dependent variables.

Scientists use the **experimental method** to determine cause-and-effect relationships and to answer questions such as whether physical activity lowers blood pressure, alcohol incites aggressive behavior, or psychotherapy relieves feelings of anxiety. In the experimental method, a group of participants, or subjects, receives a treatment, for example, an exercise regimen, a dosage of alcohol, or a trial of therapy. Then the subjects are observed under carefully controlled conditions to determine whether the treatment has an effect on their health or behavior.

Independent and Dependent Variables

▮ Independent variable A condition in a scientific study that is manipulated so that its effects may be observed.

▮ Dependent variables A measure of an assumed effect of an independent variable.

In an experiment to determine whether alcohol causes aggression, subjects would be given an amount of alcohol and its effects would be measured. In this case, alcohol is an **independent variable**. The presence of an independent variable is manipulated by the experimenters so that its effects may be determined. The independent variable of alcohol may be administered at different levels, or doses, from none or very little to enough to cause intoxication or drunkenness.

The measured results, or outcomes, in an experiment are called **dependent variables**. The presence of dependent variables presumably depends on the independent variables. In an experiment to determine whether alcohol influences aggression, aggressive behavior would be a dependent variable. Other dependent variables of interest might include sexual arousal, visual-motor coordination, and performance on intellectual tasks such as defining words or doing numerical computations.

Experimental and Control Groups

▮ Treatment In experiments, a condition received by participants so that its effects may be observed.

▮ Random assignment A procedure for randomly assigning subjects to experimental or control groups.

▮ Experimental group A group of subjects who receive a treatment in an experiment.

▮ Control group A group of subjects in an experiment whose members do not obtain the treatment, while other conditions are held constant. Therefore, one may conclude that group differences following treatment result from the treatment.

Scientists determine the effects of an independent variable by comparing the behavior of experimental and control groups. Individuals in an experimental group receive the experimental manipulation, which is also called a **treatment**. Members of a control group do not. Every effort is made to ensure that all other conditions are held constant for both groups. This method enhances the researchers' ability to draw conclusions about cause and effect. In well-designed studies, subjects are assigned randomly to treatment or control groups. By using **random assignment**, experimenters have confidence that differences between treatment and control groups are due to the effects of the experimental manipulation, or independent variable, rather than differences in the types of subjects comprising these groups.

In a study on the effects of alcohol on aggression, members of the **experimental group** would ingest alcohol and members of the **control group** would not. In a complex experiment, different experimental groups might ingest different dosages of alcohol and be exposed to different types of social provocations.

Blinds and Double Blinds

▮ Placebo A bogus treatment that has the appearance of being genuine.

One early study on the effects of alcohol on aggression reported that men at parties where beer and liquor were served acted more aggressively than men at parties where only soft drinks were served (Boyatzis, 1974). But subjects in the experimental group knew they had drunk alcohol, and those in the control group knew they had not. Aggression that appeared to result from alcohol might not have reflected drinking per se. Instead, it might have reflected the subjects' expectations about the effects of alcohol. People tend to act in stereotypical ways when they believe they have been drinking alcohol. For instance, men tend to become less anxious in social situations, more aggressive, and more sexually aroused.

A **placebo**, or "sugar pill," often results in the kind of behavior that people expect. Physicians sometimes give placebos to demanding, but healthy, people, many of whom then report that they feel better. When subjects in psychological experiments are given placebos—such as tonic water—but think they have drunk alcohol, we can conclude that changes in their behavior stem from their beliefs about alcohol, not from the alcohol itself.

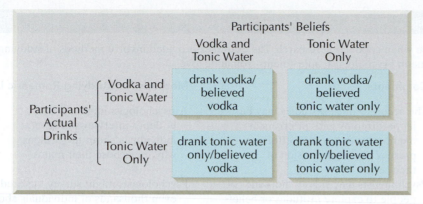

Figure 1.7
The Experimental Conditions in the Lang Study
The taste of vodka cannot be discerned when vodka is mixed with tonic water. For this reason, it was possible for subjects in the Lang study on the effects of alcohol to be kept "blind" as to whether they had actually drunk alcohol. Studies use blinds to control for the effects of subjects' expectations.

Well-designed experiments control for the effects of expectations by creating conditions under which subjects are unaware of, or *blind* to, the treatment. Yet researchers may also have expectations that bias their judgments. They may, in effect, be "rooting for" a certain treatment. Hence, it is often useful if the experimenters themselves are kept in the dark about which subjects received which treatments. Studies in which neither the subjects nor the experimenters know which subjects received the active drug and which received the placebo are called **double-blind studies**.

A U. S. watchdog agency, the Food and Drug Administration (FDA), requires double-blind drug studies before it allows the marketing of new drugs. The drug and the placebo look and taste alike. Experimenters assign the drug or placebo to subjects at random. Neither the subjects nor the observers know who is taking the drug and who is taking the placebo. After the final measurements have been made, a neutral panel (a group of people who have no personal stake in the outcome of the study) judges whether the effects of the drug differed from those of the placebo.

We turn back to a classic double-blind study on the effects of alcohol to illustrate. Alan Lang and his colleagues (1975) first pretested a highball of vodka and tonic water to determine that it could not be discerned by taste from tonic water alone. They then recruited college men who described themselves as social drinkers to participate in the study. Some of the men drank vodka and tonic water; others drank tonic water only. Of the men who drank vodka and tonic water, half were misled into believing they had drunk tonic water only (Figure 1.7). Of those who drank tonic water only, half were misled into believing their drink contained vodka. Thus, half the subjects were blind to their treatment. Experimenters who measured the men's aggressive responses were also blind concerning which subjects had drunk vodka. The research team found that men who believed they had drunk vodka responded more aggressively to a provocation than men who believed they had drunk tonic water only. The actual content of the drink didn't account for the results. That is, men who had actually drunk alcohol acted no more aggressively than men who had drunk tonic water only.

Double-blind controlled studies are not perfect, however. We've learned that prescribing physicians as well as their patients are able to guess at greater than chance levels of accuracy whether an active drug or a placebo is used (Kirsch et al., 2002; Kirsch, Scoboria, & Moore, 2002). Health care providers and their patients often discern whether an active drug is used based on telltale side effects. Even though double-blind designs sometimes resemble Venetian blinds with the slats slightly open, they remain an important means for determining the effectiveness of new medications (Leber, 2000; A.C. Leon, 2000).

Before moving ahead, you may want to review the different types of research methods psychologists use, as outlined in Table 1.2.

▌ **Double-blind studies** Experiments in which neither the subjects nor the researchers know who has been given the active treatment or drug and who has not.

Table 1.2 ▮ How Psychologists Do Research

Here we consider the methods psychologists use when conducting research. The examples provided involve methods of studying research questions concerning an important issue in psychological adjustment—romantic love.

What Researchers Do	Comments	Methods for Studying Romantic Love
In the *case study method*, the researcher interviews an individual (or small group of individuals) or examines historical records of the lives of particular individuals.	The accuracy of case studies may be jeopardized by gaps or errors in memory or by people's efforts to present a false impression of themselves.	A psychologist might conduct in-depth interviews of several individuals about the reasons why they chose their mates.
In the *survey method*, the researcher may use questionnaires, interviews, or public records to obtain information about a group of people.	Psychologists may survey thousands of people to explore attitudes or beliefs about such topics as abortion, premarital sex, or leisure pursuits.	Psychologists might survey hundreds or even thousands of individuals about the characteristics of people with whom they have had committed relationships or have married.
In the *naturalistic observation method*, the researcher observes behavior in the field— that is, where it occurs naturally.	Psychologists attempt not to interfere with the behaviors they are observing.	Psychologists might observe from a distance how lovers walk together and how they look at each other.
In the *correlational method*, the researcher uses statistical (mathematical) methods to reveal and describe positive and negative relationships (correlations) between variables.	This method may suggest but does not demonstrate the presence of cause and effect. The degree to which variables are statistically associated with each other is expressed in the form of a *correlation coefficient* that may vary from +1 to -1.	Psychologists might study relationships between feelings of love, self-esteem, and sexual satisfaction.
In the *experimental method*, the psychologist manipulates one or more independent variables (makes changes in the participants' environments) and observes their effects on one or more dependent (measured) variables. Experiments are conducted to establish cause-and-effect relationships between independent and dependent variables.	Participants in experimental groups receive an experimental treatment, but participants in control groups do not. All other conditions are held constant in order to draw conclusions about a causal link between the independent variable (treatment vs. control conditions) and the dependent variable (observed effect). Random assignment helps ensure that groups do not differ on important subject characteristics that might affect the outcome.	Psychologists might expose dating partners to an experimental treatment in which they share an arousing experience, such as watching an emotionally powerful movie, and then measure the treatment's effects on their feelings of attraction or love for each other. (Control participants would be exposed to a neutral movie.)

Adjustment and Modern Life

Do U Txt?

The popularity of text messaging took almost everyone by surprise. Text messaging was introduced as a piece of enterprise software to help workers maintain instant communication with managers and other workers, but its use has exploded in recent years, especially among adolescents and young adults. Texting has become the preferred method of communication for millions of Americans—more popular than telephone calls, e-mail, and even speaking (Steinhauer & Holson, 2008). To put the explosive growth of this new medium of communication in context, the number of text messages Americans sent increased more than 10-fold in just a three-year period, from 7.2 billion in June 2005 to some 75 billion in June 2008.

Texting is the process of sending an SMS (Short Message Service) message from a mobile phone to another mobile user.

With the current limit of 160 characters per message, users have developed a system of shortening words by using abbreviations. A simple example is the expression, "How r u?," meaning "How are you?" Other abbreviations used in both texting and instant messaging may not be so intuitive (see *Try This Out*).

Texting is basically a new form of brief communication, not simply an alternative to calling or conversing. As one college student whose text messages outnumber the phone calls he makes by 10 to 1 said, "It's not that I don't like to talk on the phone. . . Sometimes I just want to see what's going on, as opposed to having a conversation. So it is easier to send a text" (cited in Steinhauer & Holson, 2008, p. A17).

Educators have raised concerns about whether the use of abbreviated forms of communication might lead to poorer writing skills among American youths. Some linguists argue that the casual use of language in both texting and IM'ing is an assault on formal written English, which can lead to a breakdown in basic skills in using the language properly (Lee, 2002). Texting can also be dangerously distracting when driving and even walking across town. As with cell phone use, the human brain cannot devote the resources needed to perform two different complex tasks, like driving and texting, at the same time. A number of states have banned texting while driving, and many more states will surely follow.

D U txt? Has it affected your study habits? Some students claim that use of texting shorthand helps them keep better notes in class. But some heavy users of IM and texting may simply forget or neglect to use the proper form of the language in their formal writing, such as when turning in course assignments. Like many new technologies, texting can be a friend or a foe when it comes to effective study habits. If you find yourself inserting texting or IM abbreviations in formal writing where they don't belong, take the time to review your work before submitting it. Inappropriate usage or just plain sloppiness can be easily corrected.

Let us note that some linguists downplay the risks posed by texting. For example, linguist Carolyn Adger, director of the Language in Society Division of the Center for Applied Linguistics in Washington, notes that "Language and languages change.... Innovating with language isn't dangerous.... Besides, text messaging is making it easier for people to communicate (cited in "R ur txt msgs," 2003).

Texting and other new forms of communication, such as e-mail and IM, provide a new means of converting thoughts into words. Perhaps that's one reason why teenagers today are writing more than any other generation since letter writing began to wane in popularity generations ago (Helderman, 2003). The question of whether abbreviated communication poses a threat

...and there's the hands— It looks like—well, it looks like he's texting.

beep

Streeter

©Betsy Streeter

to formal writing is perhaps better framed in terms of suitability. Rather than discouraging this alternate mode of communication, perhaps we need to teach children that not all forms of expression are suitable in all situations. They can be taught that while abbreviations may be acceptable in e-mail, texting, or IM communications, they may be inappropriate when used in formal classroom writing, course examinations, or when drafting a letter or an official document (Fresco, 2005; O'Connor, 2005).

TRY THIS OUT   TESTING YOUR TEXTING SKILLS

Test your skills by filling in the answers in the blanks in the right column. The answers are shown on page 32.

Texting Expression	What it Means	Texting Expression	What it Means
AYEC		RUCMNG	
BCNU		TLK2UL8R	
BTW		WAN2	
FYEO		WTG	
IHNI		XLNT	
IMHO		:)	
L8R		: -)	
LOL		:-X	
NMP		:'-(	
NP		:(	
OTOH		>:-@!	
PCM		%-(	
PXT		:-D	
ROTFL			

Texting Expression	What it Means	Texting Expression	What it Means
AYEC	At your earliest convenience	RUCMNG	Are you coming?
BCNU	Be seeing you	TLK2UL8R	Talk to you later
BTW	By the way	WAN2	Want to?
FYEO	For your eyes only	WTG	Way to go
IHNI	I have no idea	XLNT	Excellent
IMHO	In my humble opinion	:)	Smile
L8R	Later	: -)	Happy
LOL	Laughing out loud	:-X	Kiss on the lips
NMP	Not my problem	:'-(	Cry
NP	No problem	:(	Frown
OTOH	On the other hand	>:-@!	Angry and swearing
PCM	Please call me	%-(	Confused and unhappy
PXT	Please explain that	:-D	Laughter
ROTFL	Rolling on the floor laughing		

Sources: The Joy of Text (www.bbc.co.uk), texting.com, Macmillan English Dictionary, www.webopedia.com

MODULE REVIEW

Review It

(14) The _____ _____ is a framework for testing ideas and acquiring knowledge through careful observation and experimentation.

(15) The _____ _____ method involves the development of a carefully drawn portrait of an individual.

(16) The method of research that involves the administration of questionnaires or interviews to large numbers of individuals is called the _____ method.

(17) A subset or segment of a population used in research is referred to as a _____.

(18) Investigators use the technique of random _____ to draw representative samples from the population of interest.

(19) Psychologists may employ _____ measures to help ensure that their observational methods do not interfere with the behavior of the people they observe.

(20) Psychologists use the correlational method to examine _____ between variables, though they recognize that the variables may not be causally connected.

(21) The experimental method studies cause-and-effect relationships by means of manipulation of one or more (independent or dependent?) variables in order to observe their effects on one or more (independent or dependent?) variables.

Think About It

People who exercise are generally healthier than people who do not. Does this relationship between exercise and health show that exercise is a causal factor in good health? Why or why not?

Psychology in Daily Life

Becoming a Successful Student—In This and Your Other Courses

Succeeding in meeting the academic challenges of college requires skills in both managing time and studying effectively. The *Psychology in Daily Life* modules in this book are found at the end of each chapter and apply psychology to the challenges that are likely to occur in your own life. The first of these is intended to help you do well in this and your other college courses.

Your second author had little idea of what to expect when he went to college. New faces, a new locale, responsibility for doing his own laundry, new courses. It all added up to an overwhelming assortment of changes.

Perhaps the most stunning change of all was his newfound freedom. It was completely up to him to plan ahead to get his coursework completed but somehow to manage to leave time for socializing and his addiction to the game of bridge.

Another big surprise was that it was not enough for him just to enroll in a course and plant himself in a seat. To see what we mean, visualize a simple experiment. Imagine that you put some water into a bathtub and then sit in the tub. Wait a few moments, then look around. Unless strange things are happening, you'll notice that the water is still there, even though you may have displaced it a bit. You are not a sponge, and you will not simply soak up the water. You have to take active measures to get it inside—perhaps a straw and patience would help.

1.5.1 Taking an Active Approach to Learning (We Don't Really "Soak Up" Knowledge)

The problems of soaking up knowledge from this and other textbooks are not entirely dissimilar. You won't accomplish much by sitting on it, except, perhaps, looking an inch taller. But psychological theory and research have taught us that an active approach to learning results in better grades than a passive approach. It is more efficient to look ahead and seek the answers to specific questions than to just flip through the pages. It is also helpful not to try to do it all in one sitting, as in cramming before tests, especially when a few bathtubsful of academic material are floating around you.

Plan Ahead

You can take an active approach to studying by first evaluating the amount of material you need to learn during the semester and the rate at which you learn. Establish a study plan to ensure that you have sufficient time to learn the material required in your texts and assigned readings. You may need to reevaluate your study schedule from time to time and be willing to review your original estimates.

Most of us learn better through spaced, or distributed, learning rather than through massed learning. Consequently, it makes sense to space out your studying fairly evenly throughout the semester, rather than cramming just before exams.

Here are some additional study tips that might be helpful:

- Know when the tests are scheduled and what material will be covered on each test.
- Ask your instructor which material is most important for you to learn.
- Review your lecture notes, use additional study materials such as study guides, and review the text material.
- Create a schedule that allows you enough time to master each of the assigned chapters and any additional readings before each exam.
- Prioritize your study tasks and establish a schedule for accomplishing them.
- As you read, generate possible test questions and quiz yourself.
- Review key terms, using flash cards or index cards to help you master these glossary terms.
- Identify key concepts by stopping after each section of text and asking yourself, "What key concepts was the author trying to get across? What were the main points the author was addressing?"
- Use practice tests in the textbook or ancillary study guides as dress rehearsals for "the real thing." Instructors sometimes draw exam questions from the practice tests, so answering these questions may give you an edge when it comes to taking exams.
- Break down practice tests into two parts by separating out odd and even questions. Answer the odd questions first. If you answer them perfectly, go on to the even questions. If not, review the material in the chapter again and then answer the even questions. Then compare your scores for the two parts. Chances are that the additional review will help boost your performance on the second set of questions.
- Keep a record of your performance on the practice tests so you can gauge how well you are progressing through the course of the semester.

Study Different Subjects Each Day

We have to admit that too much psychology may not be such a good thing. That is, we generally respond better to novel stimulation and variety. You may find it helpful to alternate your study efforts. Rather than studying psychology all day Monday and literature all day Tuesday, study some psychology and some literature each study day.

Become an Active Note Taker

By taking notes, you become an active learner. Rather than just passively absorbing lecture material (or perhaps spacing out), you become actively engaged in reviewing and organizing this material. None of us possess an encyclopedic memory for everything we hear or see. Taking careful notes helps you recall important lecture information that you might otherwise forget or perhaps never learned in the first place.

Expand Your Attention Span

Establish a schedule that gradually increases your study time by adding a few minutes each day. Most of us find it takes a period of time before we are fully in the groove. Also, you may find that your attention wanders when you've been studying for a length of time.

Take frequent breaks to minimize these lapses of attention. Get up and stretch your muscles. Take a brief walk or just take in the view from your window. When you return to studying, you're likely to be better able to focus your attention.

Eliminate Distractions

Select a study place that is free from distractions, especially noise and other people's chatter. Find a quiet study place that allows you to focus your attention, such as the library or study lounge. If you study at home, place a "Do Not Disturb" sign on your door. Control your phone calls by turning off your cell phone or by setting the answering machine for your landline to a silent (nonring) mode. Keep the TV and radio off. Avoid bringing magazines and other types of distractions to your study space.

Practice Self-Reward

Pat yourself on the back for meeting your study goals. You may also want to link specific rewards to meeting your study goals. For example, you may wish to reward yourself each weekend with a desirable activity if (and only if) you accomplish your weekly study goals.

Stick With It—College Pays Off

Sure, there may be times when you feel like cashing it in. But pursuing a college degree (or two) and sticking with it pays off, and in more ways than one. According to government statistics, people with college degrees earn more on the average than those without degrees (see Figure 1.8). Those with higher degrees tend to earn more than those with lower degrees. But the value of a college education is not measured merely in dollars. A college education can increase your knowledge and skills, broaden your perspectives, and help you become a more critical thinker and better informed citizen, parent, and worker. You may also make abiding, even lifetime, friendships with people you meet at college.

1.5.2 The SQ3R Study Method: Survey, Question, Read, Recite, and Review

The SQ3R study method is a widely used study technique developed by educational psychologist Francis Robinson (1970). It is designed to help students develop more effective study habits. SQ3R is an acronym that stands for five key steps to developing effective study skills: survey, question, read, recite, and review.

Survey

Preview each chapter by leafing through the pages to get a sense of the topics that are covered and the way the chapter is organized. Each chapter, including those in this text, is organized in terms of major and minor sections or parts. This text in particular is organized in terms of major sections called modules and subsections within modules. A module is a self-contained unit of instruction that focuses on a major topic within the chapter. Becoming familiar with the format and structure of your textbooks helps prepare you for the content you will need to learn.

Question

This text begins each module with a set of survey questions that are answered in the body of the text. These questions highlight key issues and points that are addressed in the module. Use these questions as a guide to your reading. Test yourself to see if you can answer each of the questions as you read the corresponding material in the module. You may also find it helpful to generate additional questions for yourself. The development of good questioning skills helps you become a more active learner and can help expand your comprehension of the text material.

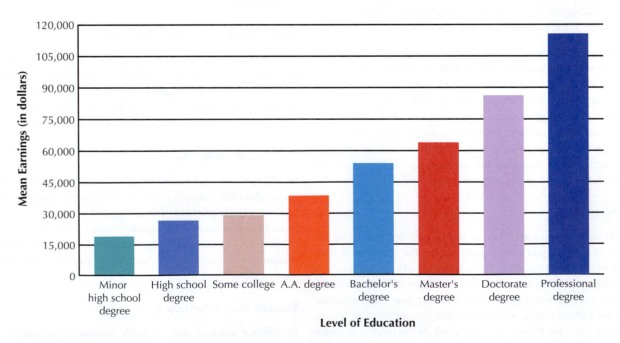

Figure 1.8
College—It Pays Off
Yes, college pays off, but not just in future earnings potential.
Source: U. S. Bureau of the Census, 2005. Note that earnings are based on 2003 dollars.

Read

Try to answer the survey questions as you read the chapter material. Also, pick out the key terms and key concepts and make sure you understand them before moving ahead.

Recite

Recite your answers to each survey question aloud. Hearing yourself speak these answers helps strengthen your retention and mastery of the material. To further reinforce your learning, practice writing down your answers in a notebook.

Review

Use the *Module Review* sections at the end of each module to review your knowledge of the material. First, complete the fill-in-the-blank questions found in the *Review It* section. Then answer the *Think About It* questions posed in the review. These critical thinking questions help stimulate your thinking and challenge you to carefully evaluate and examine issues that are discussed in the text. Many college texts today contain critical thinking questions.

This text also contains sample answers to survey questions, which you will find in the *Recite-Recite-Recite* chapter reviews at the end of each chapter. Compare your answers with the sample answers provided and review the relevant sections of the text if your answer doesn't quite measure up. In the *Your Personal Journal* section at the end of the chapter, you'll find opportunities to reflect on how the concepts introduced in the chapter relate to your personal experiences. Reflection encourages deeper processing of material, which can translate into better performance in class.

Review the text material on a regular study schedule, such as once weekly. Review your answers to the survey questions and test yourself on your knowledge of key terms and concepts. Reread the subject matter if you stumble.

All in all, taking a more active approach to studying may help you improve your grades and gain more pleasure from the learning process.

1.5.3 Coping with Test Anxiety

Like John, whom we introduced at the beginning of the chapter, many college students face the challenge of coping with test anxiety. Test anxiety can lead us to tense up during examinations and make it difficult to focus our attention and perform to the best of our ability. Test anxiety is often linked to exaggerated, catastrophic thoughts, such as those shown in Table 1.3. If you experience test anxiety that interferes with your test performance, it may be worthwhile to examine your thoughts and take steps to replace irrational, catastrophizing thoughts with the kinds of rational alternatives shown in Table 1.3. Here are some steps you can use to restructure your thinking:

1. Identify irrational catastrophizing thoughts.
2. Construct incompatible rational alternatives.
3. Substitute rational alternative thoughts.
4. Reward yourself for making these changes.

Prepare yourself for test situations by rehearsing rational alternatives you can use if you need them. Attend to your thoughts during the examination. If you begin thinking irrational thoughts, substitute rational alternatives. Reward yourself for making a mental switch by saying to yourself, "Way to go. I'm not going to let my thoughts make things worse for me. I can decide what I say to myself."

You may also find it helpful to practice relaxation techniques, such as those described in Chapter 3, to help you relax before examinations. Also, like John, you might benefit from checking out whether your college offers help in coping with test anxiety.

Table 1.3 ▌ Rational Alternatives to Irrational Thoughts	
Irrational, Catastrophizing Thoughts	**Rational Alternatives**
"I'm never going to be able to do this. It's impossible."	"Nonsense. You studied this stuff. Just take it a step at a time."
"If I flunk, my life is ruined."	"Don't exaggerate. It would be unfortunate, but it's not the end of the world. Take deep breaths and focus on the test."
"Everyone else is so much smarter than me."	"Stop putting yourself down. They are probably struggling just as hard as you are."
"Everyone's leaving. They must know all the answers."	"Working fast is no guarantee of good work. Take the time you need to finish."
"My mind is a blank. I just can't remember a thing!"	"Okay, settle down. Take a deep breath and then refocus. If you still don't know the answer, skip this one and come back to it later."
"I'll never be able to finish this in time."	"Just take it one question at a time. Do your best and don't get bent out of shape."

CHAPTER REVIEW

RECITE! RECITE! RECITE! RECITE! RECITE! RECITE! RECITE!

Study Tip: Reciting the answers to these study questions will help you become a more effective learner. First try answering the questions by yourself, either reciting them out loud or writing them in a notebook or on the computer. Then compare your answers with the sample answers provided below.

1. **What is psychology?**
Psychology is the science of behavior and mental processes.

2. **What is adjustment?**
Adjustment is behavior that permits us to meet the challenges of life. Adjustment is also referred to as coping or coping behavior.

3. **What is the difference between adjustment and personal growth?**
Adjustment is reactive—coping with the challenges of life. Personal growth is proactive. It involves conscious, active self-development.

4. **Is biology destiny?**
No. Genes (nature) may determine the ranges for the expression of traits, but environmental conditions and our chosen behavior patterns minimize the influence of genetic risk factors and maximize our genetic potential.

5. **What is the difference between the clinical approach and the healthy-personality approach to the psychology of adjustment?**
The clinical approach focuses on ways in which problems can be corrected, whereas the healthy-personality approach focuses on optimizing our development along personal, social, physical, and vocational lines.

6. **What is human diversity?**
Human diversity refers to many sources of differences among people, including ethnic or racial differences, gender differences, and differences in disability status and sexual orientation.

7. **Why is it important to study human diversity?**
Awareness of the richness of human diversity enhances our understanding of the individual and enables students to appreciate the cultural heritages and historical problems of various ethnic groups. Knowledge of diversity helps psychologists understand the aspirations and problems of individuals from various groups so that they can successfully intervene to help group members.

8. **What is an ethnic group?**
An ethnic group comprises people who share factors such as cultural heritage, history, race, and language in common. Minority ethnic groups have frequently experienced prejudice and discrimination by members of the dominant culture.

9. **What forms of prejudice have women experienced in our society?**
There have been historical prejudices against women. The careers of women have been traditionally channeled into domestic chores, regardless of women's wishes as individuals. Much of the scientific research into gender roles and gender differences assumes that male behavior represents the norm.

10. **What is critical thinking?**
Critical thinking is the adoption of a skeptical questioning attitude and evaluation of arguments or claims in the light of evidence. Critical thinking is a hallmark feature of psychology and other sciences.

11. **What are some of the major features of critical thinking?**
Critical thinking involves examining the definitions of terms, examining the premises or assumptions behind arguments, and scrutinizing the logic with which arguments are developed. Critical thinkers are cautious in drawing conclusions from evidence. They do not oversimplify or overgeneralize.

12. **How does critical thinking "protect" us from the claims of astrology and other pseudosciences?**
Critical thinking guides us to examine the evidence for and against astrology and other pseudosciences.

13. **What is the scientific method?**
The scientific method is an organized way of expanding and refining knowledge. Psychologists reach conclusions about their research questions or the accuracy of their hypotheses on the basis of their research observations or findings.

14. **What is the case study method?**
The case study method involves the crafting of carefully constructed portraits of individuals to help shed light on their behavior.

15. **What is the survey method?**
The survey method involves the administration of questionnaires or interviews to large numbers of individuals to learn more about their attitudes and behavior patterns.

16. **How do psychologists use samples to represent populations?**
The subjects who are studied are referred to as a sample. A sample is a segment of a population. Women's groups and health professionals argue that there is a historical bias in favor of conducting research with men. Research samples have also tended to underrepresent minority ethnic groups in the population. Researchers use random and stratified samples to represent populations. In a random sample, each member of a population has an equal chance of being selected to participate. In a stratified sample, identified subgroups in the population are represented proportionately.

17. **What is the naturalistic observation method?**
The naturalistic observation method involves careful and unobtrusive observation of behavior where it happens—in the "field."

18. **What is the correlational method?**
The correlational method reveals relationships between variables but does not determine cause and effect. In a positive correlation, two variables increase together; in a negative correlation, one variable increases while the other decreases.

19. **What is the experimental method?**
Experiments are used to discover cause and effect—that is, the effects of independent variables on dependent variables. Experimental groups receive a specific treatment, whereas control groups do not. Blinds and double blinds may be used to control for the effects of the expectations of the subjects and the researchers. Results can be generalized only to populations that have been adequately represented in the research samples.

YOUR PERSONAL JOURNAL

REFLECT   REFLECT   REFLECT   REFLECT   REFLECT   REFLECT   REFLECT

Study Tip: Reflecting on how the concepts in the chapter relate to your own experiences encourages deeper processing, which makes the material more personally meaningful and fosters more effective learning. Use additional pages if needed to complete your answers.

1. Recall the discussion of study tips on pages 33–35. What study tips described in the text can you incorporate into your study efforts? Based on your reading, is it better to space your study sessions or cram just before exams? How will this knowledge affect your study practices?

    _____

    _____

    _____

    _____

2. This chapter discussed the role of sociocultural factors in psychological adjustment. What impact has your own ethnic or cultural background had on your daily life? On your adjustment to the stresses you face?

    _____

    _____

    _____

    _____

ANSWERS TO MODULE REVIEWS

Module 1.1

1. mental
2. Adjustment
3. acting
4. likelihood
5. mechanical
6. clinical approach

Module 1.2

7. diversity
8. ethnic
9. Gender/women

Module 1.3

10. critical thinking

11. definitions
12. pseudoscience/false
13. psychologically

Module 1.4

14. scientific method
15. case study
16. survey
17. sample
18. sampling
19. unobtrusive
20. relationships
21. independent/dependent

17. T_____
18. T_____
19. F_____
20. T_____
21. T_____
22. F_____
23. F_____
24. T_____
25. T_____

26. T_____
27. T_____
28. F_____
29. T_____
30. F_____
31. T_____
32. F_____
33. T_____

SCORING KEY FOR THE SOCIAL DESIRABILITY SCALE

Place a checkmark on the appropriate line of the scoring key each time your answer agrees with the one listed in the scoring key. Add the checkmarks to compute your total score.

1. T_____
2. T_____
3. F_____
4. T_____
5. F_____
6. F_____
7. T_____
8. T_____

9. F_____
10. F_____
11. F_____
12. F_____
13. T_____
14. F_____
15. F_____
16. T_____

INTERPRETING YOUR SCORE

LOW SCORERS (0–8). About one respondent in six earns a score between 0 and 8. Such respondents answered in a socially *undesirable* direction much of the time. It may be that they are more willing than most people to respond to tests truthfully, even when their answers might meet with social disapproval.

AVERAGE SCORERS (9–19). About two respondents in three earn a score between 9 and 19. They tend to show an average degree of concern for the social desirability of their responses, and it may be that their general behavior represents an average degree of conformity to social rules and conventions.

HIGH SCORERS (20–33). About one respondent in six earns a score between 20 and 33. These respondents may be highly concerned about social approval and respond to test items in such a way as to avoid the disapproval of people who may read their responses. Their general behavior may show high conformity to social rules and conventions.

iStockphoto

- According to Sigmund Freud, fingernail-biting and smoking are leftover signs of conflicts experienced during early childhood? (p. 44)

- John Watson, the father of behaviorism, believed he could turn any healthy and well-formed infant into a doctor, lawyer, successful businessperson, or a beggar or a thief if he were able to raise the child in any way he chose? (p. 50)

- The humanistic psychologist Carl Rogers believed that children should be prized for themselves regardless of their behavior? (p. 62)

- Driving behavior is linked to a major underlying personality factor? (p. 66)

- People who are higher in conscientiousness tend not only to get their work in on time but also tend to live longer and happier lives? (p. 66)

- Acculturation may be something of a double-edged sword when it comes to immigrant groups adjusting to life in the United States? (p. 72)

- Some personality tests rest on the belief that people project aspects of their personalities into their responses to ambiguous stimuli? (p. 75)

There is an ancient tale about three blind men who encounter an elephant. Each touches a different part of the elephant, but each is stubborn and claims that he alone has grasped the true nature of the beast. One grabs the elephant by the leg and describes it as firm, strong, and upright, like a pillar. To this, the blind man who touched the ear of the elephant objects. From his perspective, the animal is broad and rough, like a rug. The third man has become familiar with the trunk. He is astounded at the gross inaccuracy of the others. Clearly the elephant is long and narrow, he declares, like a hollow pipe.

Each of this trio came to know the elephant from a different perspective. Each was bound by his own point of view. Each was blind to the beliefs of his fellows and to the real nature of the beast—not just because of his physical limitations, but also because his initial encounter led him to think of the elephant in only a certain way.

In a similar way, our conceptions about people, and about ourselves, may be bound up with our own perspectives. Different ways of encountering people lead us to view people's personalities from different perspectives. A commonly held view equates personality with liveliness, as in "She's got personality." But psychological theorists look deeper. Some characterize personality as consisting of the person's most striking traits, as in people with a "shy personality" or a "happy-go-lucky personality." Still other theorists focus on how personality is shaped by learning or by underlying biological influences. Those schooled in the Freudian tradition look at personality as consisting of underlying mental structures that are continually jockeying with each other outside the range of our ordinary awareness. And to the humanistic theorists, personality is not something people possess but rather the ways in which they express personal choices that give meaning and personal direction to their lives. Then, too, sociocultural theorists remind us that we need to take into account the influences of culture, race, and ethnicity. In all, we have different views of the elephant in our study—the human personality. None of these views may offer a complete portrait, but each may contribute something unique to our understanding. Before we examine these different theoretical views, let us define our subject matter.

39

▌**Personality** The distinctive patterns of behavior, thoughts, and feelings that characterize a person's adjustment to the demands of life.

Psychologists define **personality** as the reasonably stable patterns of emotions, motives, and behavior that distinguish one person from another. We shall see what each has to say about human nature and what each suggests about our abilities to cope with the challenges of life and how we develop as individuals.

MODULE 2.1

Psychodynamic Theories

- Why is Freud's theory of personality deemed a psychodynamic model?
- What is the structure of personality in Freud's view?
- What is Freud's theory of psychosexual development?
- What are the views of some other psychodynamic theorists on personality?
- How do psychodynamic theorists view the healthy personality?

▌**Psychodynamic theories** Theories based on Freud's view that clashes between different elements or forces within the personality shape behavior, thoughts, and emotions.

There are several **psychodynamic theories** of personality, each of which owes its origin to the thinking of Sigmund Freud. These theories have a number of features in common. Each teaches that personality is characterized by a dynamic struggle between different elements within the personality. At any given moment our behavior, thoughts, and emotions represent the outcome of these inner contests. Let us set the stage for our review of the psychodynamic perspective by considering Freud's theory of personality.

2.1.1 Sigmund Freud's Theory of Personality

Sigmund Freud was trained as a physician specializing in neurological problems. Early in his practice he treated patients who, despite an absence of any medical disorder, suffered from unexplained physical symptoms, such as loss of feeling in a hand or paralysis of the legs. He observed how these odd symptoms could sometimes disappear, at least for a time, when patients were hypnotized or when, fully conscious, they recalled and expressed strong emotions. He became convinced that these symptoms were psychological in nature, but that their causes must be buried in the recesses of the mind beyond the reach of ordinary conscious awareness. Based on his clinical work, he began to construct the first psychological theory of personality, setting himself the task of exploring the interior of the human mind.

The Geography of the Mind

▌**Preconscious** In psychodynamic theory, the part of the mind whose contents are not in awareness but are capable of being brought into awareness by focusing of attention.

▌**Unconscious** In psychodynamic theory, the part of the mind whose contents are not available to ordinary awareness.

▌**Repression** In psychodynamic theory, a defense mechanism that protects the self from anxiety by keeping unacceptable wishes, impulses, and ideas out of awareness.

We can think of Freud's concept of the mind as a human iceberg. Only the tip of an iceberg rises above the surface of the water; the great mass of it is hidden in the depths (see Figure 2.1). Freud came to believe that people, similarly, are aware of only a small portion of the ideas and impulses that dwell within their minds. He argued that a much greater portion of the mind—our deepest images, thoughts, fears, and urges—remains beneath the surface of conscious awareness, where little light illumines it. Freud labeled the region of the mind that pokes through into the light of awareness the conscious. He called the regions below the surface the **preconscious** and the **unconscious**. The preconscious mind contains elements of experience that are out of awareness but can be made conscious simply by focusing on them. The unconscious is shrouded in mystery. It contains biologically based instincts, such as sexual and aggressive instincts, that give rise to unacceptable urges or impulses that are kept out of awareness through **repression**, the automatic ejection of anxiety-evoking material from awareness. Freud believed that repression

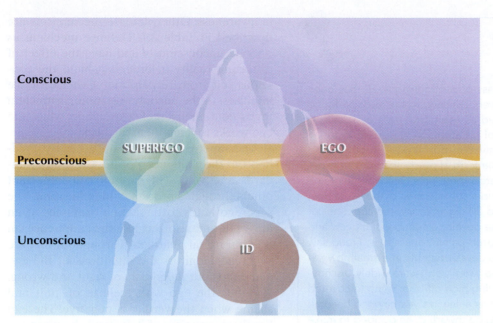

Figure 2.1
"The Human Iceberg"
Using an iceberg metaphor to represent the psychoanalytic view of personality, we see that only the tip of the mind rises above the surface into conscious awareness. Material in the preconscious can become conscious if we direct our attention to it, but unconscious material tends to remain shrouded in mystery.

also works on troubling or painful memories, keeping this material safely away from consciousness. Repression may also protect us from perceiving morally unacceptable impulses.

The unconscious mind does not easily give up its contents. To explore the unconscious, Freud engaged in a form of mental detective work called **psychoanalysis**. For this reason, his theory of personality is also referred to as psychoanalytic theory. In psychoanalysis, people are prodded to talk about anything that pops into their mind while they lie comfortably on a couch. They may gain self-insight by pursuing some of the thoughts that pop into awareness. But they also are motivated to avoid awareness of underlying sexual or aggressive wishes or thoughts that might elicit anxiety if consciously expressed. So patients may show **resistance** to exploring unacceptable wishes or thoughts, perhaps even cancelling therapy sessions when these subjects are touched upon.

▮ **Psychoanalysis** In this usage, Freud's method of exploring human personality.

▮ **Resistance** A blocking of thoughts whose awareness could cause anxiety.

Structure of Personality

Freud proposed that the human personality is composed of three mental or **psychic structures**: the id, the ego, and the superego. These structures represent the clashing forces within the personality. Psychic structures cannot be seen or measured directly, but their presence is suggested by behavior, expressed thoughts, and emotions.

The **id** is present at birth. In Freud's view, it contains instinctual drives, such as sex and aggression, and operates entirely in the unconscious. Freud described the id as "a chaos, a cauldron of seething excitations" (1933/1964, p. 73). The id follows what Freud termed the **pleasure principle**. It demands instant gratification of instincts without consideration of law, social custom, or the needs of others.

The **ego** begins to develop during the first year of life, largely because not all of a child's demands for gratification can be met immediately. The ego stands for reason and good sense, for rational ways of coping with frustration. It curbs the appetites of the id and makes plans that fit social conventions. Thus, a person can find gratification and yet avoid social disapproval. The id informs you that you are hungry, but the ego decides to microwave enchiladas.

The ego is guided by the **reality principle**. It takes into account what is practical along with what is urged by the id. The ego also provides the person's conscious sense of self. Although most of the ego is conscious, some of its business is carried out unconsciously. For instance, the ego also acts as a censor that screens the impulses of the id. When the ego senses that improper impulses are rising into awareness, it may use psychological defenses, such as repression, to prevent them from surfacing

▮ **Psychic structures** In psychodynamic theory, a hypothesized mental structure that helps explain different aspects of behavior.

▮ **Id** The psychic structure, present at birth, that represents physiological drives and is fully unconscious (a Latin word meaning "it.")

▮ **Pleasure principle** The guiding principle of the id, directing pursuit of instant gratification of instinctual demands without regard to social requirements or the needs of others.

▮ **Ego** The second psychic structure to develop, characterized by self-awareness, planning, and the delay of gratification (a Latin word meaning "I.")

▮ **Reality principle** The guiding principle of the ego, directing pursuit of satisfaction of instinctual demands within the constraints of social living.

A CLOSER LOOK

Sigmund Freud

Sigmund Freud (1856–1939) was a mass of contradictions. He has been lauded as the greatest thinker of the twentieth century, the most profound of psychologists. He has been criticized as overrated, even a "false and faithless prophet." He focused much of his attention in prudish Victorian Vienna on the importance of sexual motivation, but he was himself a model of sexual restraint. He invented a popular form of psychotherapy but experienced lifelong psychologically related problems such as migraine headaches, bowel problems, fainting under stress, hatred of the telephone, and an addiction to cigars. He smoked 20 cigars a day and could not or would not break the habit even after he developed cancer of the jaw and needed to undergo more than two dozen painful operations. Freud saw himself as an outsider. He was born to Jewish parents in a small town in the Austro-Hungarian Empire, at a time when Jews were widely discriminated against and prevented from holding high office or rising to coveted academic appointments. Knowing that as a Jew his yearnings to become a distinguished academic scholar would be thwarted, he decided to make his living in clinical practice. Although he considered himself Jewish, he proclaimed himself to be an atheist. He spent nearly all of his adult life in Vienna, fleeing to England to escape the Nazi threat only a year before his death. He left a rich legacy that continues to inspire spirited debate and to challenge our understanding of ourselves.

▌ **Defense mechanism** In psychodynamic theory, an unconscious function of the ego that protects the self from anxiety-evoking material entering conscious awareness.

▌ **Superego** The third psychic structure, which functions as a moral guardian and sets forth high standards for behavior.

▌ **Identification** In psychodynamic theory, the incorporation within the personality of another person's moral standards, values, or behaviors.

▌ **Eros** In psychodynamic theory, the basic instinct to preserve and perpetuate life.

▌ **Libido** (1) In psychoanalytic theory, the energy of eros; the sexual instinct. (2) Generally, sexual interest or drive.

▌ **Erogenous zones** Areas of the body that are sensitive to sexual sensations.

▌ **Psychosexual development** In psychodynamic theory, the process by which libidinal energy is expressed through different erogenous zones during different stages of development.

▌ **Oral stage** The first stage of psychosexual development, during which gratification is hypothesized to be attained primarily through oral activities.

in awareness. Other defense mechanisms are described in Table 2.1. **Defense mechanisms** operate unconsciously and have the effect of distorting reality in order to shield the conscious self from recognition of unacceptable impulses. In the unconscious mind, instinctual urges continually seek expression while the ego works to keep them in check.

The **superego** develops during early childhood, as the child incorporates the moral standards and values of parents and important others through a process of **identification**. The superego holds forth shining examples of an ideal self and also acts like the conscience, an internal moral guardian. Throughout life, the superego monitors the intentions of the ego and hands out judgments of right and wrong. It floods the ego with feelings of guilt and shame when the verdict is negative. The ego hasn't an easy time of it. It stands between the id and the superego, striving to satisfy the demands of the id and the moral sense of the superego. From the Freudian perspective, a healthy personality has found ways to gratify most of the id's demands without seriously offending the superego. Most of the id's remaining demands are contained or repressed. If the ego is not a good problem solver or if the superego is too stern, the ego will have a hard time of it, and psychological problems, such as troubling fears, obsessive concerns, or depression, may result.

Stages of Psychosexual Development

Freud aroused controversy in his day by arguing for the importance of sexual motivation in personality development, even among children. Freud believed that sexual motives are closely linked to children's basic ways of relating to the world, such as sucking on their mother's breasts and moving their bowels.

Freud believed that we possess a basic instinct, which he termed **eros**, that has as its aim the preservation and perpetuation of life. Eros is fueled by psychological, or psychic, energy, which Freud labeled **libido**. Libidinal energy is the energy of the sexual instinct. As a child develops, libidinal energy becomes expressed through erotic or sexual feeling in different parts of the body, which he termed **erogenous zones**. To Freud, psychological development involves the transfer of libidinal energy from one erogenous zone to another, so in fact development is psychosexual in nature. He hypothesized five periods of **psychosexual development**: *oral, anal, phallic, latency,* and *genital*.

During the first year of life a child experiences much of its world through the mouth. If it fits, into the mouth it goes. This is the **oral stage**. Freud argued that oral activities such as sucking and biting give the child sexual gratification as well as nourishment.

Freud believed that children encounter conflict during each stage of psychosexual development. During the oral stage, conflict centers on the nature and extent of oral gratification. Early weaning (cessation of breast feeding) could lead to frustration. Excessive gratification, on the other hand, could lead an infant to expect that it will routinely be given anything it wants. Insufficient or excessive gratification in any stage could lead to **fixation** in that stage and to the development of traits that

Table 2.1 ▮ Defense Mechanisms, According to Psychodynamic Theory

Defense Mechanism	What It Is	Examples
Repression	The ejection of anxiety-evoking ideas from awareness	<ul><li>A student forgets that a difficult term paper is due.</li><li>A client in psychoanalysis forgets an appointment when anxiety-evoking material is about to be brought up.</li></ul>
Regression	The return, under stress, to a form of behavior characteristic of an earlier stage of development	<ul><li>An adolescent cries when forbidden to use the family car.</li><li>An adult becomes dependent again on his parents following the breakup of his marriage.</li></ul>
Rationalization	The use of self-deceiving justifications for unacceptable behavior	<ul><li>A student blames her cheating on her teacher for leaving the room during a test.</li><li>A man explains his cheating on his income tax by saying, "Everyone does it."</li></ul>
Displacement	The transfer of ideas and impulses from threatening or unsuitable objects to less threatening objects	<ul><li>A worker picks a fight with her spouse after being criticized sharply by her supervisor.</li></ul>
Projection	The thrusting of one's own unacceptable impulses onto others so that others are assumed to harbor them	<ul><li>A hostile person perceives the world as being a dangerous place.</li><li>A sexually frustrated person interprets innocent gestures of others as sexual advances.</li></ul>
Reaction formation	Assumption of behavior in opposition to one's genuine impulses in order to keep impulses repressed	<ul><li>A person who is angry with a relative behaves in a "sickly sweet" manner toward that relative.</li><li>A sadistic individual becomes a physician.</li></ul>
Denial	Refusal to accept the true nature of a threat	<ul><li>A person believes that he will not contract cancer or heart disease although he smokes heavily.</li><li>"It can't happen to me."</li></ul>
Sublimation	The channeling of primitive sexual or aggressive impulses into positive, constructive efforts	<ul><li>A person paints nudes for the sake of "beauty" and "art."</li><li>A hostile person becomes a tennis star.</li></ul>

Dan Dalton/Digital Vision/Getty Images, Inc.

A Sign of Fixation in the Oral Stage?

Is the food delicious? Is the person starved? Or does fixation in the oral stage of development have something to do with the momentary inhalation of this treat?

❚ **Fixation** In psychodynamic theory, a form of arrested development, marked by the appearance of traits associated with an earlier stage of psychosexual development.

❚ **Anal stage** The second stage of psychosexual development, when gratification is attained through anal activities.

❚ **Phallic stage** The third stage of psychosexual development, characterized by a shift of libido to the phallic region. (From the Greek *phallos*, referring to an image of the penis. However, Freud used the term phallic to refer both to boys and girls.)

❚ **Oedipus complex** A conflict of the phallic stage in which the boy wishes to possess his mother sexually and perceives his father as a rival in love.

❚ **Electra complex** A conflict of the phallic stage in which the girl longs for her father and resents her mother.

❚ **Displaced** Transferred.

❚ **Latency** A phase of psychosexual development characterized by repression of sexual impulses.

❚ **Genital stage** The mature stage of psychosexual development, characterized by preferred expression of libido through intercourse within the context of marriage.

are characteristic of that stage. Oral traits include dependency, gullibility, and excessive optimism or pessimism (depending on the child's experiences with gratification).

Freud theorized that adults with an oral fixation could experience exaggerated desires for "oral activities," such as smoking, overeating, alcohol abuse, and nail biting. Like the infant whose very survival depends on the mercy of its caretakers, adults with oral fixations may be disposed toward clinging, dependent relationships.

During the **anal stage**, sexual gratification is attained through contraction and relaxation of the muscles that control elimination of waste products from the body. Elimination, which was controlled reflexively during most of the first year of life, comes under voluntary muscular control, even if such control is not reliable at first. The anal stage is said to begin in the second year of life.

During the anal stage, children learn to delay the gratification that comes from eliminating as soon as they feel the urge. The general issue of self-control may become a source of conflict between parent and child. Anal fixations may stem from this conflict and lead to two sets of traits in adulthood. So-called *anal-retentive traits* involve excessive self-control. They include perfectionism, a strong need for order, and exaggerated neatness and cleanliness. *Anal-expulsive traits*, on the other hand, "let it all hang out." They include carelessness, messiness, even sadism.

Children enter the **phallic stage** during the third year of life. During this stage, the major erogenous zone is the phallic region (the penis in boys and the clitoris in girls). Parent–child conflict is likely to develop over masturbation, to which parents may respond with threats or punishment. During the phallic stage, children may develop strong sexual attachments to the parent of the other gender and begin to view the parent of the same gender as a rival for the other parent's affections. Thus, boys may want to marry Mommy and girls may want to marry Daddy.

Children have difficulty dealing with feelings of lust and jealousy. Home life would be tense indeed if they were consciously aware of them. These feelings, therefore, remain unconscious, but their influence is felt through fantasies about marriage with the parent of the other gender and hostility toward the parent of the same gender. In boys, this conflict is labeled the **Oedipus complex**, after the legendary Greek king who unwittingly killed his father and married his mother. Similar feelings in girls give rise to the **Electra complex**, the female counterpart to the Oedipus complex in males. According to Greek legend, Electra was the daughter of King Agamemnon. She longed for him after his death and sought revenge against his slayers—her mother and her mother's lover.

The Oedipus and Electra complexes are resolved by about age 5 or 6. Children then repress their hostilities toward the parent of the same gender and begin to identify with her or him. Identification leads them to incorporate the social and gender roles of that parent and to internalize his or her values. Sexual feelings toward the parent of the other gender are repressed for a number of years. When the feelings emerge again during adolescence, they are **displaced**, or transferred, to socially appropriate members of the other gender.

Freud believed that by the age of 5 or 6, the pressures of the Oedipus and Electra complexes cause children to repress all their sexual urges. In so doing, they enter a period of **latency** during which their sexual feelings remain unconscious. During the latency phase, it is not uncommon for children to prefer playmates of their own gender.

Finally, Freud held that children enter the final stage of psychosexual development, the **genital stage**, at around puberty. Adolescent males again experience sexual urges toward their mother, and adolescent females experience such urges toward their father. However, the incest taboo causes them to repress these impulses and displace them onto other adults or adolescents of the other gender. Boys might seek girls "just like the girl that married dear old Dad." Girls might be attracted to boys who resemble their fathers.

To Freud, psychosexual maturation involves finding a marital partner of the opposite sex with whom one can achieve sexual gratification through intercourse in the context of marriage. In Freud's view, other forms of sexual gratification, such as oral or anal stimulation, masturbation, and sexual activity with people of the same sex represent immature forms of sexual conduct.

2.1.2 Other Psychodynamic Theorists

Several personality theorists are among Freud's intellectual heirs. Their theories, like his, include dynamic movement of psychological forces, conflict, and defense mechanisms. In other respects, their theories differ considerably.

Carl Jung

Carl Jung (1875–1961) was a Swiss psychiatrist who had been a member of Freud's inner circle. He fell into disfavor with Freud when he developed his own psychodynamic theory—**analytical psychology**. In contrast to Freud (for whom, he said, "the brain is viewed as an appendage of the genital organs"), Jung downplayed the importance of the sexual instinct. He saw it as just one of several important instincts. He also placed greater emphasis than did Freud on the present than on infantile or childhood experiences. Jung posited the existence of the "Self," the unifying force in the personality that gives direction and purpose to human behavior. According to Jung, heredity dictates that the Self will persistently strive to achieve wholeness or fullness. Jung believed that a deeper understanding of human behavior needs to take into account conscious processes such as self-awareness and pursuit of life goals, or self-direction, as well as unconscious impulses (Boynton, 2004).

Jung, like Freud, was intrigued by unconscious processes. He believed that we have not only a personal unconscious that contains repressed memories and impulses but also an inherited **collective unconscious**. The collective unconscious contains primitive images, or **archetypes**, that reflect the history of our species. Examples of archetypes are the all-powerful God, the young hero, the fertile and nurturing mother, the wise old man, the hostile brother—even fairy godmothers, wicked witches, and themes of rebirth or resurrection. Archetypes themselves remain unconscious, but Jung declared that they influence our thoughts and emotions and cause us to respond to cultural themes in stories and films, such as those images of good and evil represented in popular films like the *Star Wars* series.

Alfred Adler

Alfred Adler (1870–1937), another follower of Freud, also felt that Freud had placed too much emphasis on sexual impulses. Adler believed that people are basically motivated by an **inferiority complex**. In some people, feelings of inferiority may be based on physical problems and the need to compensate for them. Adler believed, however, that all of us encounter some feelings of inferiority because of our small size as children and that these feelings give rise to a **drive for superiority**. For instance, the English poet Lord Byron, who had a crippled leg, became a champion swimmer. As a child Adler was crippled by rickets and suffered from pneumonia, and it may be that his theory developed in part from his own childhood striving to overcome repeated bouts of illness.

Adler believed that self-awareness plays a major role in the formation of personality. He spoke of a **creative self**, a self-aware aspect of personality that strives to overcome obstacles and develop the individual's potential. Because each person's potential is unique, Adler's views have been termed **individual psychology**. Adler also emphasized the importance of birth order in shaping personality. He believed that parents tend to set high expectations for their first-born children, leading them to become high achievers and to seek power or leadership positions. Second-born children may be more competitive and want to overtake the first-born, setting the stage for rivalry.

Keith Hamshere/The Kobal Collection, Ltd.

The Power of Archetypes
Archetypes are primitive images or symbols that Carl Jung believed are embedded within a collective unconscious that humans share in common. Adventure stories such as *The Lord of the Rings* and *Star Wars* tap into archetypal figures, such as the young hero, the wise old man, and the dark evildoer.

▌ **Analytical psychology** Jung's psychodynamic theory, which emphasizes the collective unconscious and archetypes.

▌ **Collective unconscious** Jung's hypothesized store of vague memories of our ancestral past.

▌ **Archetypes** Basic, primitive images or concepts hypothesized by Jung to reside in the collective unconscious.

▌ **Inferiority complex** Feelings of inferiority hypothesized by Adler to serve as a central motivating force in the personality.

▌ **Drive for superiority** Adler's term for the desire to compensate for feelings of inferiority.

▌ **Creative self** Adler's term for the self-aware part of the personality that directs goal-seeking efforts.

▌ **Individual psychology** The term describing Adler's personality theory that emphasizes the uniqueness of the individual.

Karen Horney

Karen Horney (1885–1952) was drummed out of the New York Psychoanalytic Institute because she took issue with the way psychoanalytic theory portrayed women. Early in the twentieth century, psychoanalytic theory taught that a woman's place was in the home. Women who sought to compete with men in the business world were assumed to be suffering from unconscious penis envy. Psychoanalytic theory taught that little girls feel inferior to boys when they learn that boys have a penis and they do not. Horney accepted the general principle of penis envy, but she believed that we must understand the development of young women within a social context as well. She argued that it was not penis envy that made women feel inferior, but rather envy of the social power and authority that men hold in modern society (Stewart & McDermott, 2004).

Trained in psychoanalysis, Horney agreed with Freud that childhood experiences are important factors in the development of adult personality. Unlike Freud, she asserted that unconscious sexual and aggressive impulses are less important than interpersonal relationships in children's development. She also believed that genuine and consistent love can alleviate the effects of even the most traumatic childhood.

Horney believed that people relate to others in three basic ways. They may move *toward others* by seeking to establish supportive, loving relationships. Or they might move *away from others* by emphasizing their independence and self-sufficiency. Or they might move *against others* by seeking to control or dominate others. To Horney, a person with a healthy personality is able to balance these three ways of relating to people. But problems can arise when people get stuck in one particular style of relating to others. They may move too much in the direction of meeting others' needs, leading them to become overly compliant and self-sacrificing out of fear of losing approval. Or perhaps they move too far away from others, becoming isolated and emotionally detached. Or perhaps they can relate to people only in ways that allow them to dominate, exploit, or control them.

❙ **Psychosocial development** Erikson's theory of personality and development, which emphasizes social relationships and eight stages of personal growth.

❙ **Identity crisis** Erikson's term for a period of serious soul-searching about one's beliefs, values, and direction in life.

A CLOSER LOOK

Erik Erikson—"Who Am I, Really?"

His natural father deserted his mother just before his birth, and Erik Erikson was raised by his mother and his stepfather, a physician named Theodor Homburger. They did not want the boy to feel different, so he was not told about his father until many years later. Though both his mother and his stepfather were Jewish, Erikson resembled his father, a Dane with blond hair and blue eyes. In his stepfather's synagogue, he was considered a Gentile. To his classmates, he was a Jew. He began to feel different from other children and alienated from his family. He fantasized that he was the offspring of special parents who had abandoned him. The question "Who am I?" permeated his adolescent quest for identity. As he matured, Erikson faced another identity issue: "What am I to do in life?" His stepfather encouraged him to attend medical school, but Erikson sought his own path. As a youth he studied art and traveled through Europe, leading the Bohemian life of an artist. This was a period of soul-searching that Erikson came to label an **identity crisis.**

As a result of his own search for identity, he became oriented toward his life's work—psychotherapy. He left his wanderings and plunged into psychoanalytic training under the supervision of Sigmund Freud's daughter, Anna Freud.

Despite Erikson's grueling search for identity, he appears to have denied his own children information about their family. He and his wife institutionalized their fourth child, Neil, who was born with Down syndrome. But his biographer (Friedman, 1999) writes that the Eriksons told their older children that Neil had died after birth. Perhaps Erikson's upbeat view of life did not prepare him to handle such harsh reality, so he pushed it away (Edmundson, 1999).

Erik H. Erikson

Erik Erikson (1902–1994), like Sigmund Freud, is known for devising a comprehensive theory of personality development. But whereas Freud focused on stages of psychosexual development, Erikson proposed stages of **psychosocial development** (see Table 2.2). For Erikson, each stage presents a psychosocial challenge that can have one of two outcomes. For example, the first stage of psychosocial development is labeled the stage of *trust versus mistrust* because of its two possible outcomes: (1) A warm, loving relationship with the mother (and others) during infancy might lead to a sense of basic trust in people and the world. (2) A cold, ungratifying relationship might generate a pervasive sense of mistrust. Erikson believed that most people would wind up with some blend of trust and mistrust—hopefully more trust than mistrust. A sense of mistrust could interfere with the formation of relationships unless it was recognized and challenged. Erikson extended Freud's five developmental stages to eight to include the evolving concerns of adulthood. For Erikson, the goal of adolescence is

Table 2.2 ▮ Erikson's Stages of Psychosocial Development		
Time Period	**Life Crisis**	**The Developmental Task**
Infancy (0–1)	Trust versus mistrust	Coming to trust the mother and the environment— to associate surroundings with feelings of inner goodness
Early childhood (1–3)	Autonomy versus shame and doubt	Developing the wish to make choices and the self-control to exercise choice
Preschool years (4–5)	Initiative versus guilt	Adding planning and initiative to choice, becoming active and on the move
Elementary school years (6–12)	Industry versus inferiority	Becoming eagerly absorbed in the development of useful skills and performance of productive tasks
Adolescence	Ego identity versus role diffusion	Connecting skills and social roles to formation of career objectives; developing a sense of who one is and what one stands for
Young adulthood	Intimacy versus isolation	Committing the self to another; engaging in sexual love
Middle adulthood	Generativity versus stagnation	Needing to be needed; guiding and encouraging the younger generation; being creative
Late adulthood	Integrity versus despair	Accepting the time and place of one's life cycle; achieving wisdom and dignity

the attainment of **ego identity**, not genital sexuality. The focus is on who we see ourselves as being and what we stand for, not on sexual interests.

We explore Erikson's views on adolescent and adult development further in Chapter 14. Erikson, like Horney, believed that Freud had placed undue emphasis on sexual instincts. He asserted that social relationships are more crucial determinants of personality than sexual urges. To Erikson, the nature of the mother–infant relationship is more important than the details of the feeding process or the sexual feelings that might be stirred by contact with the mother. Erikson also argued that to a large extent we are the conscious architects of our own personalities. His view grants more powers to the ego than Freud did. In Erikson's theory, it is possible for us to make real choices. In Freud's theory, we may think that we are making choices but may actually be merely rationalizing the compromises forced upon us by internal conflicts.

▮ **Ego identity** Erikson's term for the sense of who we are and what we stand for.

2.1.2 The Healthy Personality

Each theory of personality is connected with a perspective on what makes up the healthy personality. Psychodynamic theories were developed by working with troubled individuals, so the theoretical emphasis has been on the development of psychological disorders, not a healthy personality. Nevertheless, the thinking of the major theorists can be combined to form a picture of psychological health.

Positive Psychology

The Abilities to Love and to Work

Freud is noted to have equated psychological health with the abilities *lieben und arbeiten*—that is, "to love and to work." Healthy people can care deeply for others. They can engage in sexual love within an intimate relationship and lead a productive work life. To accomplish these ends, sexual impulses must be allowed expression in a relationship with an adult of the opposite gender, and other impulses must be channeled into socially productive directions.

Ego Strength

The ego of the healthy individual has the strength to control the instincts of the id and to withstand the condemnation of the superego. The presence of acceptable outlets for the expression of some primitive impulses decreases the pressures within the id and, at the same time, lessens the burdens of the ego in repressing the remaining impulses. Being reared by reasonably tolerant parents might prevent the superego from becoming overly harsh and condemnatory.

A Creative Self

Both Jung and Adler spoke of a "Self"—a unifying force that provides direction to behavior and helps develop a person's potential. The notion of a guiding self provides bridges between psychodynamic theories, social-cognitive theory (which, as we will see, speaks of self-regulatory processes), and humanistic theory (which, as we also will see, speaks of a self as the core of our experience in the world).

Compensation for Feelings of Inferiority

None of us can be "good at everything." According to Adler, we attempt to compensate for feelings of inferiority by excelling in one or more of the arenas of human interaction. So Adler views choosing productive arenas in which to contend—finding out what we are good at and developing our talents—as healthful behavior.

Erikson's Positive Outcomes

A positive outcome within each of Erik Erikson's psychosocial stages also contributes to the healthy personality. It is healthful to develop a basic sense of trust during infancy, to develop a sense of industry during the grammar school years, to develop a sense of who we are and what we stand for during adolescence, to develop intimate relationships during young adulthood, to be productive during middle adulthood, and so on.

2.1.3 Evaluation of Psychodynamic Approaches

Psychodynamic thinking has had a rich and pervasive influence on our culture. Terms like *defense mechanisms, ego, id, superego,* and *fixations* have entered our popular vocabulary, though not always with the same meanings as Freud intended. Works of art and literature have been strongly influenced by Freudian themes or undertones. Psychodynamic theorists focused our attention on our inner experiences—on our dreams, our hidden motives, and the forces or influences within our personalities.

They also brought to light a fuller appreciation of the importance of childhood experiences in shaping the adult personality. To some observers, Freud and his followers allow us to peer into the inner recesses of the human mind. But many critics, including some of Freud's own followers, believe that he placed too much emphasis on the importance of sexuality and underemphasized social relationships. Critics also claim that the psychodynamic perspective remains mired in fanciful theorizing rather than resting on scientific foundations. Other critics state that unconscious processes, such as repression, fall outside the range of scientific tests because they cannot be directly observed. Yet, even today, a number of researchers believe that it is possible to develop scientific approaches to test many of Freud's concepts (e.g., Cramer, 2000; Westen & Gabbard, 2002). For example, researchers can examine how the mind links ideas to each other automatically, without conscious thought or reflection (Westen, 2002). As we shall see in Chapter 9, Freud himself made use of this concept, called *free association*, in developing a model of psychotherapy. All in all, the psychodynamic perspective remains a major model of personality that continues to both fascinate and challenge us.

MODULE REVIEW

Review It

(1) Psychodynamic theories believe that personality is shaped by _____ between unconscious forces within the mind.

(2) Freud posited that a psychic structure called the _____ is present at birth and operates according to the pleasure principle.

(3) The ego operates according to the _____ principle.

(4) The _____ is the moral sense and develops by internalizing the standards of parents and others.

(5) The stages of psychosexual development include the oral, anal, _____, latency, and genital stages.

(6) _____ in a stage may lead to the development of traits associated with the stage.

(7) In the Oedipus and Electra complexes, children long to possess the parent of the (same or other?) gender and become jealous of, or resentful toward, the parent of the same gender.

(8) Jung believed that in addition to a personal unconscious, people also have a _____ unconscious.

(9) Adler believed that people are motivated by an _____ complex.

(10) Whereas Freud proposed psychosexual stages of development, Erikson posited _____ stages of development.

Think About It

A man who is passed over for promotion at work takes his anger out on his wife. Explain this behavior in terms of Freud's concept of defense mechanisms.

MODULE 2.2

Learning Theories

- How do behaviorists conceptualize personality?
- What is classical conditioning?
- What is operant conditioning?
- What are the different types of reinforcers?
- Are negative reinforcement and punishment the same thing?
- How does social-cognitive theory differ from the behaviorist view?
- How do learning theorists view the healthy personality?

Psychodynamic theorists look at personality and behavior in terms of the outcomes of conflicts between internal mental structures. Learning theories take us in a different direction. Rather than focusing on the structure of personality, they focus on our capacity to learn and adapt to the environments we face. In this section we consider two leading examples of learning theories and how they relate to adjustment: traditional learning theory, or behaviorism, and a contemporary learning theory model called social-cognitive theory.

2.2.1 Behaviorism

Behaviorism An early school of psychology based on the belief that psychology should limit itself to the study of observable behavior.

Behaviorism was an early movement in psychology predicated on the belief that psychology would not develop as a science unless it limited itself to the study of observable behavior. The behaviorists rejected the study of the mind as unscientific because the contents or processes of the "mind" could not be directly observed. They also believed that our behavior is determined by our learning experiences in the environment. At Johns Hopkins University in 1924, psychologist John B. Watson announced the battle cry of the behaviorist movement:

> *Give me a dozen healthy infants, well-formed, and my own specified world to bring them up in and I'll guarantee to take any one at random and train him to become any type of specialist I might suggest—doctor, lawyer, merchant-chief and, yes, even beggar-man and thief, regardless of his talents, penchants, tendencies, abilities, vocations, and the race of his ancestors.*
>
> (Watson, 1924, p. 82)

No one, of course, took up Watson's challenge, so we'll never know what would have happened to these children. We suspect that few psychologists today subscribe to the view that the environment completely determines behavior, as Watson implies. For example, we now know that genetics plays an important role in shaping personality. But his proclamation underscores the behaviorist view that personality is malleable, or "plastic"—that situational variables or environmental influences, not internal, personal factors like intrapsychic forces, traits, or even conscious choice, are the key shapers of human wants and behaviors. In contrast to the psychodynamic theorists of his day, Watson argued that unseen, undetectable mental structures must be rejected in favor of that which can be seen and measured.

To the behaviorist, personality is nothing more than the sum total of an individual's response repertoire. A response repertoire is the range of a person's behaviors, which are developed on the basis of environmental influences, such as rewards and punishments. Personality is what a person *does,* not what a person is. Behaviorism discounts concepts of personal freedom, choice, and self-direction as mere illusions or myths. If we fully understood all the environmental influences that impinge upon us—all the rewards and punishments that shape our behavior—we would see that our behavior is just as determined as the movements of billiard balls on a pool table. Even our thinking that we have free will is determined by the environment. To examine how environmental influences affect behavior, behaviorists investigated two types of learning processes: classical and operant conditioning.

Classical Conditioning: Learning by Association

Classical conditioning A simple form of learning in which one stimulus comes to bring forth the response usually brought forth by a second stimulus as a result of being paired repeatedly with the second stimulus.

Classical conditioning is a form of learning by association. It was discovered by accident by a Russian physiologist, Ivan Pavlov (1849–1936). Pavlov, who was awarded the Nobel Prize for his work on digestive processes, was studying the biological pathways of dogs' salivation glands. However, the animals themselves botched his results by what, at first, looked like random salivation. Upon investigation, Pavlov noticed that the dogs were actually salivating in response to his assistants' entering the lab or the inadvertent clanking of metal on metal. So Pavlov initiated a series of experiments to demonstrate that the dogs salivated in response to stimuli that had been associated with being fed.

If you place meat on a dog's tongue, it will salivate. Salivation in response to food is a reflex—a simple form of unlearned behavior. We, too, have many reflexes, such

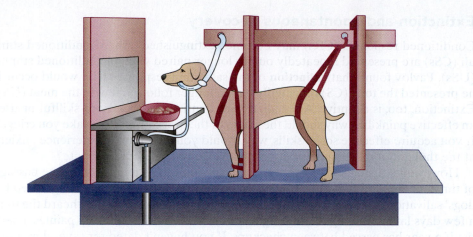

Figure 2.2
Pavlov's Demonstration of Conditioned Reflexes in Laboratory Dogs
From behind the one-way mirror, a laboratory assistant sounds a tone and then drops meat powder on the dog's tongue. After several repetitions, the dog salivates to the tone alone. Saliva is collected by means of a tube. The amount of saliva is a measure of the strength of the dog's learned responses.

as the knee jerk in response to a tap below the knee and the eyeblink in response to a puff of air.

A change in the environment, such as placing meat on a dog's tongue or tapping below the knee, is called a stimulus. A reflex is one kind of response to a stimulus. Reflexes are unlearned, but they can also be associated with, or conditioned to, different stimuli.

In his research on digestion in dogs, Pavlov (1927) strapped an experimental animal into a harness (see Figure 2.2). He placed meat powder on the dog's tongue, and the dog salivated. He repeated the process several times, with one difference. Each time, he preceded the meat with the sound of a tone. After several pairings of the tone and meat powder, Pavlov sounded the tone but did not present the meat. What did the dog do? It salivated anyway. The dog had learned to salivate in response to the tone because it had been repeatedly paired with the meat.

In this experiment, meat is an **unconditioned stimulus** (abbreviated US or UCS), and salivation in response to meat is an **unconditioned response** (abbreviated UR or UCR). *Unconditioned* means "unlearned." At first the tone is a neutral stimulus in the sense that it does not evoke the designated response (salivation). But through repeated pairing with the US (meat), the tone becomes a learned or **conditioned stimulus** (CS), which is capable of evoking, or eliciting, the salivation response. Salivation to the tone is a learned or **conditioned response** (CR).

> ■ **Unconditioned stimulus** A stimulus that elicits a response from an organism without learning.
>
> ■ **Unconditioned response** An unlearned response; a response to an unconditioned stimulus.
>
> ■ **Conditioned stimulus** A previously neutral stimulus that elicits a conditioned response because it has been paired repeatedly with a stimulus that already brought forth that response.
>
> ■ **Conditioned response** A response to a conditioned stimulus.

Conditioning of Fears

Can you identify classical conditioning in your own life? Perhaps you automatically cringe or grimace in the waiting room when you hear the dentist's drill. The sound of the drill may have become a conditioned stimulus (CS) for conditioned responses (CRs) of muscle tension and fear. John Watson and his future wife Rosalie Rayner (1920) demonstrated how fears could be conditioned. They presented an 11-month-old lad, "Little Albert," with a laboratory rat and then clanged steel bars behind his head. At first the boy reached out to play with the animal. After several pairings of animal and clanging, however, the boy cried when he saw the rat and attempted to avoid it.

Adjustment often requires responding appropriately to conditioned stimuli—stimuli that have been associated or linked to other stimuli that naturally elicit a particular response. After all, if we did not learn to fear touching a hot stove after one or two pairings of seeing the reddened burner and experiencing pain, we would suffer many needless burns. If we did not develop an aversion to food that nauseates us, we might become poisoned.

But adjustment can also require coping with excessive or irrational conditioned fears. If the sound, or the thought, of the drill is enough to keep you away from the dentist's office, you may wish to consider one of the fear-reduction techniques we discuss in Chapter 9.

Extinction and Spontaneous Recovery

∎ **Extinction** In classical conditioning, repeated presentation of the conditioned stimulus in the absence of the unconditioned stimulus, leading to suspension of the conditioned response.

Conditioned responses (CRs) may become "extinguished" when conditioned stimuli (CSs) are presented repeatedly but no longer paired with unconditioned stimuli (USs). Pavlov found that **extinction** of the salivation response (CR) would occur if he presented the tone (CS) repeatedly but no longer followed it with the meat (US). Extinction, too, is adaptive. After all, if your dentist becomes more skillful or uses an effective painkiller, why should the sound of the drill continue to make you cringe? If you acquire effective social skills, why should you continue to experience anxiety at the thought of meeting new people or asking someone out on a date?

∎ **Spontaneous recovery** In classical conditioning, the eliciting of an extinguished conditioned response by a conditioned stimulus after some time has elapsed.

However, extinguished responses may return simply as a function of the passage of time; that is, they may show **spontaneous recovery**. After Pavlov extinguished his dogs' salivation in response to a tone, they would again salivate if they heard the tone a few days later. You might cringe again in the office of the (recently painless) dentist if a year has passed between checkups. If you haven't dated for several months, you might experience anxiety at the thought of asking someone out. Is spontaneous recovery adaptive? It seems so; as time passes, situations may change again.

Operant Conditioning: Learning by Consequences

In classical conditioning we learn to connect stimuli, so a simple, usually passive response evoked by one is then evoked by the other. In the case of Little Albert, clanging noises were associated with a rat, so the rat came to elicit the fear response brought forth by the noise. Let us now turn our attention to **operant conditioning**, a form of "learning by consequences."

∎ **Operant conditioning** A form of learning in which the frequency of behavior is increased by means of reinforcement or rewards.

Operant conditioning helps to explain the acquisition and maintenance of more complex, voluntary behaviors. Through the process of operant conditioning, organisms learn to perform behaviors that produce certain rewarding effects on the environment. These behaviors are called operant responses (or simply *operants*) because they operate on the environment to produce rewarding consequences.

Operant behaviors can foster adjustment, as when we learn to say "please" and "thank you" because doing so brings social approval. Yet operants can also be maladaptive. For example, through classical conditioning we may have learned to experience the involuntary response of fear whenever we enter a dentist's office or see a hypodermic syringe. Through operant conditioning, we may learn to avoid dental visits or necessary injections because such behaviors are rewarded by relief from anxiety. However, such avoidance may be counterproductive to our health and overall adjustment. Perhaps the lesson here is that learning processes can have both healthful and unhealthful consequences.

The scientist who coined the term *operant conditioning* and who studied its properties was the Harvard psychologist B. F. Skinner. Skinner (1938) showed that hungry pigeons will learn to peck buttons when pecking is followed by food pellets dropping into their cages. The pecking is an operant response that produces the effect of releasing the food pellets. It may take the pigeons a while to happen upon the first response (button-pecking) that is followed by food, but after the pecking–food association has occurred a few times, pecking becomes fast and furious until the birds have eaten their fill. Similarly, hungry rats will learn to press levers to attain food or to get a burst of electrical stimulation in the reward pathways in the brain that produce feelings of pleasure.

Classical conditioning explains how such involuntary responses as salivation, eyeblinks, or fears are learned. Operant conditioning helps explain how more complex, voluntary responses, including everything from a pigeon pecking at a target to a young person learning a tennis serve, are acquired.

∎ **Reinforcement** A stimulus that increases the frequency of the behavior it follows.

In operant conditioning, organisms acquire responses or develop skills that lead to **reinforcement**. A reinforcement is a change in the environment (that is, a stimulus) that increases the frequency of the behavior that precedes it. A reward, by contrast, is defined as a pleasant stimulus that increases the frequency of behavior. Skinner preferred the concept of reinforcement to that of reward because it is fully defined in terms of observable behaviors and environmental contingencies.

The definition of reinforcement does not rely on "mentalistic" assumptions about what another person or lower organism finds pleasant or unpleasant. However, many psychologists use the terms *reinforcement* and *reward* interchangeably.

Types of Reinforcers

Positive reinforcers increase the frequency of particular behaviors when they *occur* following the behaviors. Money, food, sexual pleasure, and social approval are common examples of positive reinforcers. **Negative reinforcers** also increase the frequency of behaviors, but they do so when they are *removed* following the particular behaviors. Pain, anxiety, and social disapproval can function as negative reinforcers.

That is, we learn behaviors that lead to their removal or elimination. For example, we learn to open an umbrella when rain starts beating down on our head or to turn on a fan or air conditioner in stiflingly hot weather. In both cases, the learned behaviors are operants that lead to the removal of unpleasant stimuli (negative reinforcers).

Adjustment requires learning responses or skills that enable us to attain positive reinforcers and to avoid or remove negative reinforcers. In the examples given, adjustment means acquiring skills that allow us to attain money, food, and social approval, and to avoid or remove pain, anxiety, and social disapproval. When we do not have the capacity, the opportunity, or the freedom to learn these skills, our ability to adjust is impaired.

We can also distinguish between *primary* and *secondary* reinforcers. **Primary reinforcers** have their value because of the biological makeup of the organism. We seek primary reinforcers such as food, liquid, affectionate physical contact with other people, sexual excitement and release, and freedom from pain because of our biological makeup. **Secondary reinforcers** (also called *conditioned reinforcers*) acquire their reinforcing value through association with established reinforcers. We learn to value money because it can be exchanged for primary reinforcers such as food and heat (or air conditioning). Or we may learn to seek social approval—another secondary reinforcer—because approval may lead to affectionate embraces or the meeting of various physical needs.

The Role of Reinforcement

Nancy Louie/iStockphoto

The behaviorist B. F. Skinner believed that reinforcers, whether positive or negative, increase the frequency of the behaviors they follow. Children learn to raise their hands in class and develop other desirable habits in the classroom because these behaviors are reinforced by teachers in the form of attention or praise. What were the reinforcing influences in your life? What effects have they had on your behavior?

▌ **Positive reinforcer** A reinforcer that increases the frequency of behavior when it is presented—for example, food and approval.

▌ **Negative reinforcer** A reinforcer that increases the frequency of behavior when it is removed—for example, pain, anxiety, and social disapproval.

▌ **Primary reinforcer** An unlearned reinforcer, such as food, water, warmth, or pain.

▌ **Secondary reinforcer** A stimulus that gains reinforcement value as a result of association with established reinforcers. Money and social approval are secondary reinforcers.

▌ **Punishment** An unpleasant stimulus that suppresses behavior.

Punishment

Punishments are unpleasant consequences or painful or aversive stimuli that suppress or decrease the frequency of the behavior they follow. A **punishment** is not the same thing as a negative reinforcer. A negative reinforcer is an event whose removal increases the frequency of the preceding behavior. If a room is uncomfortably hot, turning on the air conditioner is an operant response that is negatively reinforced by relief from the heat.

Punishment can rapidly suppress undesirable behavior. For this reason it may be warranted in emergencies, such as when a child tries to run out into the street. But many theorists suggest that punishment is usually undesirable, especially in rearing children. For example, punishment does not in and of itself teach an alternative, acceptable form of behavior.

Basketball-Shooting Raccoon

JP Laffont/Sygma/©Corbis

In an early example of operant conditioning, psychologists used rewards, or positive reinforcers, to train a raccoon to shoot a basketball. We're not really sure about its 3-point shot ability, however.

A CLOSER LOOK

B. F. (Burrhus Frederic) Skinner

During his first TV appearance, Skinner was asked, "Would you, if you had to choose, burn your children or your books?" He said he would choose to burn his children, since his contribution to the future lay more in his writings than in his genes. B. F. Skinner (1904–1990) delighted in controversy, and his response earned him many TV appearances. Skinner was born into a middle-class Pennsylvania family. As a youth he was always building things—scooters, sleds, wagons, rafts, slides, and merry-go-rounds. Later he would build the so-called Skinner box, as a way of studying operant behavior. He earned an undergraduate degree in English and turned to psychology only after failing to make his mark as a writer in New York's Greenwich Village.

A great popularizer of his own views, Skinner used reinforcement to teach pigeons to play basketball and the piano—sort of. On a visit to his daughter's grammar school class, it occurred to him that similar techniques might work with children. Thus he developed *programmed learning*. In programmed learning, the learner proceeds at his or her own pace to master a set of learning tasks, receiving reinforcement for completing each step in the series. Although he had earlier failed at writing, he gathered a cultish following when he published *Walden II*, a novel that depicts a utopian society in which principles of reinforcement are applied to help people lead happier and more productive lives.

Skinner and his followers have applied his principles not only to programmed learning but also to behavior modification programs for helping people with disorders ranging from substance abuse to phobias to sexual dysfunctions. He died eight days after receiving an unprecedented Lifetime Contribution to Psychology award from the American Psychological Association.

Punishment also tends to suppress undesirable behavior only under circumstances in which delivery is guaranteed. It does not take children long to learn that they can "get away with murder" with one parent, or one teacher, but not with another. Moreover, punishment may be imitated as a way of solving problems or of coping with stress. Children learn by observing other people. Even if they do not immediately imitate behavior, they may do so as adults when they are under stress, with their own children as targets. Table 2.3 compares reinforcement and punishment.

Psychologists encourage parents to use positive reinforcement to reward children for desirable behavior rather than punish them for misbehavior. Ironically, some children can gain the reward of adult attention only by misbehaving. In such cases, punishment may function as a positive reinforcer—that is, children may learn to misbehave in order to gain the attention (expressed through punishment) of the people they care about.

Operant conditioning is not just a laboratory procedure. It is used every day in the real world. Consider the socialization of children. Parents and peers influence children to acquire behavior patterns that are appropriate to their gender through dispensing rewards and punishments. Parents usually praise children for sharing and punish them for being too aggressive. Peers take part in socialization by playing with children who are generous and nonaggressive and, often, by avoiding those who are not.

Table 2.3 ▌ Comparing Reinforcement and Punishment

	What Happens	When It Occurs	Example	Consequence on Behavior
Positive reinforcement	A positive event or stimulus is introduced.	After a response	Your instructor smiles at you (a positive stimulus) when you answer a question correctly.	The response (answering questions in class) becomes more likely to occur.
Negative reinforcement	An aversive stimulus is removed.	After a response	Taking an aspirin makes a headache (an aversive stimulus) stop.	Taking an aspirin becomes more likely when you have a headache.
Punishment (application of aversive stimulus)	An aversive stimulus is applied.	After a response	A parent scolds a child for slamming a door.	The child becomes less likely to slam doors.
Punishment (use of unpleasant consequences)	Unpleasant consequences are applied, such as monetary penalties or "timeout."	After a response	You get a parking ticket for failing to feed the meter.	You become less likely to let a parking meter expire in the future.

2.2.2 Social-Cognitive Theory

In contrast to the traditional behaviorism of Watson and Skinner, **social-cognitive theory** proposes a broader view of learning. It was primarily developed by theorists Albert Bandura (1999, 2004), Julian Rotter (Rotter, 1990), and Walter Mischel (Mischel & Shoda, 1999; Mischel, 2004). Social-cognitive theorists focus on cognitive processes, such as expectations we hold about the anticipated outcomes of events, and on learning by observing the behavior of others in social situations. Social-cognitive theorists differ from behaviorists in that they see people as influencing their environment just as their environment influences them. Bandura, for example, uses the term **reciprocal determinism** to describe this mutual pattern of influence of the environment, behaviors, and cognitions (see Figure 2.3).

To social-cognitive theorists, people are not simply at the mercy of the environment. Instead, they are self-aware, purposeful learners. They seek to learn about their environment and to alter it in order to make reinforcers available. Social-cognitive theorists believe that classical and operant conditioning are important forms of learning; but so, too, they argue, is learning through observation.

Observational learning (also termed **modeling**) refers to acquiring knowledge by observing others. For operant conditioning to occur, an organism (1) must engage in a response and (2) that response must be reinforced. But observational learning occurs even when the learner does not perform the observed behavior. Therefore, direct reinforcement is not required either. Observing others extends to reading about them or seeing what they do and what happens to them in books and films, on TV and radio. For example, a large body of psychological research supports the view that exposure to violence on television or other media contributes to aggressive behavior in children and adolescents (Bushman & Anderson, 2001; Huesmann et al., 2003; Uhlmann & Swanson, 2004).

Social-cognitive theorists believe that behavior reflects both **person variables,** which are factors that lie within the person, and **situational variables,** which are factors such as rewards and punishments that lie in the environment. One goal of psychological theories is the prediction of behavior. Social-cognitive theorists believe we cannot predict behavior from knowledge of situational variables alone. Whether a person will behave in a certain way depends not only on situational variables but also on the person's expectancies about the outcomes of that behavior and the perceived or subjective values of those outcomes—that is, the importance individuals place on particular outcomes. We spoke about the role of rewards and punishments in our discussion of behaviorism. Here we consider several types of person variables: competencies, encoding strategies, expectancies, and self-regulatory systems and plans (Mischel, 2004; Mischel & Shoda, 1995) (see Figure 2.4).

Competencies: What Can You Do?

Competencies include knowledge and skills that are needed to adjust in our social environment. Our ability to use information to make plans depends on our competencies. Knowledge of the physical world and of cultural codes of conduct are important competencies. So are academic skills such as reading and writing, athletic skills such as swimming and tossing a football, social skills such as knowing how to ask someone out on a date, and many others.

Individual differences in competencies reflect genetic variation, learning opportunities, and other environmental factors. People do not perform well on given tasks unless they have the competencies needed to do so.

Encoding Strategies: How Do You See It?

Different people **encode** the same stimuli in different ways. Their encoding strategies are an important factor in their behavior. One person might encode a tennis game as a chance to bat the ball back and forth and have some fun; another person

---

▪ **Social-cognitive theory** A cognitively oriented theory in which observational learning, values, and expectations play major roles in determining behavior. Formerly termed *social-learning theory*.

▪ **Reciprocal determinism** Bandura's term for the social-cognitive view that people influence their environment just as their environment influences them.

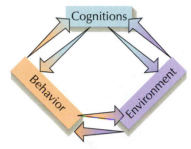

Figure 2.3
Bandura's Model of Reciprocal Determinism
Bandura believes that cognitions, behaviors, and environmental factors mutually interact with each other in determining behavior.
Source: Adapted from Bandura, 1986

▪ **Observational learning/Modeling** Learning by observing the behavior of others.

▪ **Person variables** Factors within the person, such as expectancies and competencies, that influence behavior.

▪ **Situational variables** Factors in the environment, such as rewards and punishments, that influence behavior.

▪ **Competencies** Knowledge and skills that enable us to adapt to the demands we face in our social environment.

▪ **Encode** To symbolize, transform, or represent events or information.

Figure 2.4
Person and Situational Variables in Social-Cognitive Theory
According to social-cognitive theory, person and situational variables interact to influence behavior.

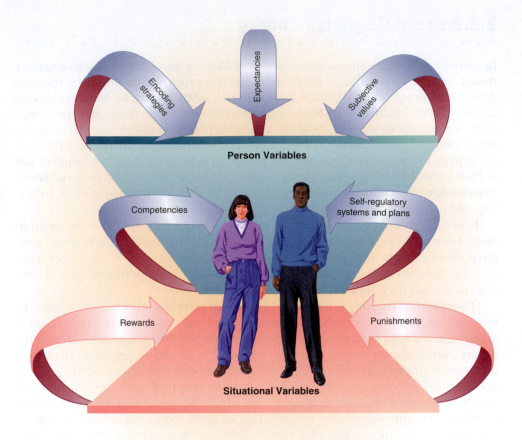

might encode the game as a demand to perfect his or her serve. One person might encode a date that doesn't work out as a sign of her or his inadequacy; another person might encode it as evidence that not all people are "made for each other."

We may make ourselves miserable by encoding events in self-defeating ways. A linebacker may encode an average day on the field as a failure because he didn't make any sacks. We may suffer feelings of hopelessness if we encode a failing grade on an exam as a sign of general stupidity or incompetence rather than an isolated failure.

Expectancies: What Will Happen?

Expectancies are personal predictions about the outcomes of events. **Self-efficacy expectations** are beliefs that we can accomplish certain things, such as speaking before a group, doing a backflip into a swimming pool, or solving math problems. We are more likely to attempt behaviors that we believe we can succeed in accomplishing.

Outcome expectancies are expectations about the outcomes of behaviors. If you expect that studying for an exam will improve your chances of getting a good grade, you are more likely to study than if you felt it would be pointless.

Competencies influence expectancies. Expectancies, in turn, influence motivation to perform. People with positive self-efficacy expectations tend to have higher self-esteem (Sanna & Meier, 2000) and are more likely to attempt difficult tasks than people who do not believe that they can master those tasks. People with higher levels of self-efficacy are also less likely to relapse after quitting smoking or completing substance abuse treatment and are more likely to follow a regular exercise or physical activity program (Ilgen, McKellar, & Tiet, 2005; Motl et al.,

∎ **Expectancies** Personal predictions about the outcomes of events.

∎ **Self-efficacy expectations** Beliefs about one's ability to perform specific tasks successfully.

2002; Shiffman et al., 2000). People who are high in self-efficacy are also better able to pick up the pieces of their lives after experiencing calamitous events, such as natural disasters and terrorist attacks (Benight & Bandura, 2004). On the other hand, a lack of self-efficacy is associated with depression and hopelessness (Bandura et al., 1999) and with lower levels of physical activity in adolescents (Motl et al., 2002). One way that psychotherapy helps people is by changing their self-efficacy expectations from "I can't" to "I can." As a result, people are motivated to try new things.

Is there a downside to self-efficacy? Perhaps. Self-efficacy is generally an asset in performance situations, such as in the classroom, on the playing field, or in the corporate office (Bandura & Locke, 2003). But too high a level of self-efficacy may lead to overconfidence, which in turn can handicap performance (Vancouver et al., 2002).

Self-Regulatory Systems and Plans: Getting from Here to There

We tend to regulate our own behavior, even in the absence of observers and external constraints. We set our own goals and standards. We make plans to achieve them. We congratulate or criticize ourselves, depending on whether we achieve them (Bandura, 1999).

Self-regulation allows us to influence, even control, our environments. We can select the situations to which we expose ourselves and the arenas in which we will compete. Depending on our expectancies, we may choose to enter the academic or athletic worlds. We may choose marriage or the single life. And when we cannot readily select our environment, we can to some degree organize our behavior within the environment to cope more effectively. For example, if we are undergoing an uncomfortable medical procedure, we may try to reduce the stress by focusing on something else—an inner fantasy or an environmental feature such as the cracks in the tiles on the ceiling. This is one of the techniques used in prepared, or "natural," childbirth.

2.2.3 The Healthy Personality

Positive Psychology

Behaviorists do not usually speak in terms of a healthy personality, since a personality cannot be observed or measured directly. We must sidestep this question—slightly. Rather than using the words *health* and *healthy*, which have a medical flavor, learning theorists prefer to speak in terms of adaptive behaviors or behaviors that permit the learner to obtain reinforcement.

Ideally, we should learn to anticipate positive events with pleasure and potentially harmful events with fear. In this way, we will be motivated to approach desirable stimuli and to avoid noxious stimuli. Fears should be sufficient to warn of real danger but not so extreme that they inhibit necessary exploration of the self and the environment. Similarly, "healthy" people have acquired skills (operant responses) that enable them to meet their needs and avert punishments.

Social-cognitive theorists view the healthy personality in terms of opportunities for observational learning and in terms of person variables:

- *Learning by observing others.* Since much human learning occurs by observation, we need to be exposed to a variety of models and to make the most of these learning opportunities.

- *Learning competencies.* Getting along and getting ahead require knowledge and skills—competencies. Competencies are acquired by conditioning and observational learning. We require accurate, efficient models and the opportunities to practice and enhance skills.

- *Accurate encoding of events.* We need to encode events accurately and productively. One failure should not be magnified as a sign of total incompetence. A social provocation may be better encoded as a problem to be solved than as an injury that must be avenged.

© Davis Barber/PhotoEdit

"Yes, I Can"
Self-efficacy expectations, or beliefs in our ability to accomplish what we set out to do, influence our willingness to attempt difficult or challenging tasks. If your self-confidence is lagging, what can you do to change the "I cant's" to the "I can's"?

Self-Assessment

Will You Be a Hit or a Miss? The Expectancy for Success Scale

Life is filled with opportunities and obstacles. What happens when you are faced with a difficult challenge? Do you rise to meet it, or do you back off? Social-cognitive theorists note that our self-efficacy expectancies influence our behavior. When we believe that we are capable of succeeding through our own efforts, we marshal our resources and apply ourselves.

The following scale, created by Fibel and Hale (1978), can give you insight as to whether you believe that your own efforts are likely to meet with success. You can compare your own expectancies for success with those of other undergraduates taking psychology courses by turning to the scoring key at the end of the chapter.

Directions: Indicate the degree to which each item applies to you by circling the appropriate number, according to this key:

1 = highly improbable
2 = improbable
3 = equally improbable and probable, not sure
4 = probable
5 = highly probable

In the Future I Expect That I Will:

T F	1.	Find that people don't seem to understand what I'm trying to say		1 2 3 4 5
T F	2.	Be discouraged about my ability to gain the respect of others		1 2 3 4 5
T F	3.	Be a good parent		1 2 3 4 5
T F	4.	Be unable to accomplish my goals		1 2 3 4 5
T F	5.	Have a stressful marital relationship		1 2 3 4 5
T F	6.	Deal poorly with emergency situations		1 2 3 4 5
T F	7.	Find my efforts to change situations I don't like are ineffective		1 2 3 4 5
T F	8.	Not be very good at learning new skills		1 2 3 4 5
T F	9.	Carry through my responsibilities successfully		1 2 3 4 5
T F	10.	Discover that the good in life outweighs the bad		1 2 3 4 5
T F	11.	Handle unexpected problems successfully		1 2 3 4 5
T F	12.	Get the promotions I deserve		1 2 3 4 5
T F	13.	Succeed in the projects I undertake		1 2 3 4 5
T F	14.	Not make any significant contributions to society		1 2 3 4 5
T F	15.	Discover that my life is not getting much better		1 2 3 4 5
T F	16.	Be listened to when I speak		1 2 3 4 5
T F	17.	Discover that my plans don't work out too well		1 2 3 4 5
T F	18.	Find that no matter how hard I try, things just don't turn out the way I would like		1 2 3 4 5
T F	19.	Handle myself well in whatever situation I'm in		1 2 3 4 5
T F	20.	Be able to solve my own problems		1 2 3 4 5
T F	21.	Succeed at most things I try		1 2 3 4 5
T F	22.	Be successful in my endeavors in the long run		1 2 3 4 5
T F	23.	Be very successful working out my personal life		1 2 3 4 5
T F	24.	Experience many failures in my life		1 2 3 4 5
T F	25.	Make a good first impression on people I meet for the first time		1 2 3 4 5
T F	26.	Attain the career goals I have set for myself		1 2 3 4 5
T F	27.	Have difficulty dealing with my superiors		1 2 3 4 5
T F	28.	Have problems working with others		1 2 3 4 5
T F	29.	Be a good judge of what it takes to get ahead		1 2 3 4 5
T F	30.	Achieve recognition in my profession		1 2 3 4 5

Source: Reprinted with permission from Fibel & Hale, 1978, p. 931.
For an interactive version of this self-assessment exercise, go to www.wileyplus.com

- *Accurate expectations and positive self-efficacy expectations.* Accurate expectancies enhance the probability that our efforts will pay off. Positive self-efficacy expectations increase our motivation to take on challenges and our persistence in meeting them.
- *Efficient self-regulatory systems.* Methodical, efficient self-regulatory systems facilitate our performances. For example, thoughts such as "One step at a time" and "Don't get bent out of shape" help us to cope with difficulties and pace ourselves.

2.2.4 Evaluation of Learning Theories

Learning theory perspectives on personality have arguably had a larger influence on modern psychology than any other set of theories. They have focused our attention on the role of the environment in shaping our learning experiences and determining our behavior. On a personal level, to better understand your present behavior as a student or a worker, we need to learn more about your individual history of rewards and punishments. To the traditional behaviorist, your personality is nothing more than the sum total of your learned behaviors. Many contemporary learning theorists, however, take a broader view of the learning process. These theorists, generally called social-cognitive theorists, expand the traditional view of learning to include cognitive factors such as expectancies and observational learning. Social-cognitive theorists view people as active seekers and interpreters of information in the environment, not merely as reactors to environmental forces acting on them. But like psychodynamic theory, learning theory models of personality have also been subject to criticism.

To some critics, learning models fail to account for the roles of unconscious influences in determining behavior. Others have voiced concern that learning models fail to give sufficient attention to the influence of heredity, or that they give insufficient attention to the development of personality traits or styles, or that they lack the ability to provide a meaningful account of self-awareness.

Now let us turn our attention to humanistic theory, which, like social-cognitive theory, emphasizes cognitive processes and conscious experience.

MODULE REVIEW

Review It

(11) Classical conditioning is a simple form of learning in which an originally _____ stimulus comes to elicit the response usually brought forth by another stimulus by being paired repeatedly with that stimulus.

(12) A response to an _____ stimulus is called an unconditioned response.

(13) _____ reinforcers increase the probability of responses when they occur following the responses.

(14) Negative reinforcers (strengthen or weaken?) responses when they are withdrawn following the responses.

(15) _____ reinforcers such as food have their value because of the biological makeup of the organism.

(16) _____ reinforcers, such as money, acquire their value through association with established reinforcers.

(17) A _____ is an aversive stimulus that suppresses the frequency of behavior.

(18) Social-cognitive theorists believe that we must consider both person variables and _____ variables to predict behavior.

Think About It

How do behaviorism and social-cognitive theory differ in their views of human nature and personal freedom?

MODULE 2.3

Humanistic Theory

- What is the humanistic perspective on personality?
- How do humanistic theories differ from psychodynamic and behaviorist theories?
- What is your self?
- What is self theory?
- How do humanistic theorists view the healthy personality?

∎ **Humanism** The view that people are capable of free choice, self-fulfillment, and ethical behavior.

∎ **Existentialism** The view that people are completely free to choose their courses of action and are ultimately responsible for their actions.

You are unique, and if that is not fulfilled, then something has been lost.
—Choreographer Martha Graham

Humanistic psychologists focus our attention on the meaning of life—or, rather, the meaning with which we imbue our lives. The term **humanism** has a long history and many meanings. It became a third force in American psychology in the 1950s and 1960s, partly in response to the predominant model of determinism espoused by psychodynamic and behavioral theorists. To the humanistic theorists, humans are not puppets on a string controlled by the invisible puppet masters of internal mental structures or environmental influences. Humanism was also a philosophical reaction to the "rat race" spawned by industrialization and automation. Humanists felt that work on assembly lines produced "alienation" from inner sources of meaning. Two of the leading humanistic theorists were the psychologists Abraham Maslow and Carl Rogers.

Humanistic psychologists drew upon the school of European philosophy called **existentialism**. Although there are perhaps as many forms of existentialism as there are existentialists, the central view of this philosophy is that we humans are fundamentally free, even "painfully" free in making decisions about what we do with our lives. We are free to choose how we lead our lives, and we cannot escape from the responsibility that comes with the ability to choose. We may make choices that imbue our lives with meaning and a sense of purpose. Or we may choose to live *inauthentically* by allowing others to determine who we are and what we should do.

Freud argued that defense mechanisms prevent us from seeing the world as it is. Therefore, the concept of free choice is meaningless. Behaviorists view freedom as merely an illusion. We may think of ourselves as free because we may not see the strings, the rewards and punishments, that actually control our behavior. To humanistic and existentialist thinkers, free choice is the veritable essence of what it means to be human.

Bettmann/©Corbis

Bettmann/©Corbis

What Do These Two People Share in Common?
The humanistic psychologist Abraham Maslow considered these two people, Albert Einstein and Eleanor Roosevelt, to be self-actualizers. But you needn't be a celebrated historical figure to become a self-actualizer. Any one of us can become self-actualizing by striving to fulfill our own unique potentials as individuals.

2.3.1 Abraham Maslow and the Challenge of Self-Actualization

Humanists see Freud as preoccupied with the "basement" of the human condition. Freud wrote that people are basically motivated to gratify biological drives and that their perceptions are distorted by their psychological needs. The humanistic psychologist Abraham Maslow argued that people also have a conscious need for **self-actualization**—to become all that they can be—and that people can see the world as it is.

∎ **Self-actualization** In humanistic theory, an innate tendency to strive to realize one's potential. Self-initiated striving to become all one is capable of being.

Because people are unique, they must follow unique paths to self-actualization. People are not at the mercy of unconscious, primitive impulses. Rather, one of the main threats to individual personality development is control by other people. We must each be free to get in touch with and actualize our selves. But self-actualization requires taking risks. Many people prefer to adhere to the "tried and true," even though what is true for one person may be untrue for another. People who adhere to the "tried and true" may find their lives degenerating into monotony and predictability.

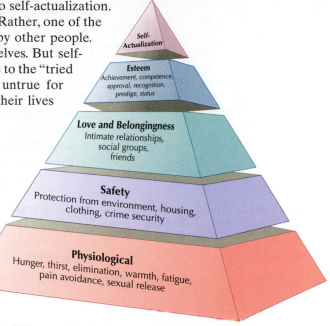

The Hierarchy of Needs: What Do You Do When You're No Longer Hungry?

Maslow believed that there was an order, or **hierarchy of needs**, that ranged from basic biological needs, such as hunger and thirst, to self-actualization (see Figure 2.5).

Freud saw all motivation as stemming from the id, and he argued that our beliefs that we possess conscious and noble intentions are either self-deceiving or sublimated expressions of basic sexual drives. By contrast, Maslow saw all levels of needs as real and legitimate in their own right. Maslow believed that once we had met our lower-level needs, we would strive to fulfill higher-order needs for personal growth. We would not snooze away the hours until lower-order needs stirred us once more to act. In fact, some of us—as in the stereotype of the struggling artist—will sacrifice basic comforts to devote ourselves to higher-level needs.

Maslow's hierarchy of needs includes the following:

1 *Biological needs.* Water, food, elimination, warmth, rest, avoidance of pain, sexual release, and so forth.

2 *Safety needs.* Protection from the physical and social environment by means of clothing, housing, and security from crime and financial hardship.

3 *Love and belongingness needs.* Love and acceptance through intimate relationships, social groups, and friends. Maslow believed that in a well-fed and well-housed society, a principal source of maladjustment lies in the frustration of needs at this level.

4 *Esteem needs.* Achievement, competence, approval, recognition, prestige, status.

5 *Self-actualization.* Personal growth, the development of our unique potentials. At the highest level are also needs for cognitive understanding (as found in novelty, understanding, exploration, and knowledge) and aesthetic experience (as found in order, music, poetry, and art).

How far have your personal growth and development proceeded up through the hierarchy of needs? At what levels have you adequately met your needs? What levels are you attacking now?

Let us learn more about the nature of the self by examining Carl Rogers's self theory. Rogers offers insights into the ways in which the self develops—or fails to develop—in the real social world.

Figure 2.5
Maslow's Hierarchy of Needs
Maslow believed that we progress toward higher psychological needs once our basic survival needs have been met. Where do you fit into this picture?

■ **Hierarchy of needs** Maslow's progression from basic, physiological needs to social needs to aesthetic and cognitive needs.

PhotoDisc Green/Getty Images, Inc

To Become All You are Capable of Being
The psychologist Abraham Maslow emphasized the importance of self-actualization as a higher human need. Self-actualization is not an end-state, but a journey of self-discovery in which you strive to achieve whatever your unique potential happens to be. What is your pathway toward self-actualization?

2.3.2 Carl Rogers's Self Theory

The humanistic psychologist Carl Rogers (1902–1987) wrote that people shape themselves—their selves—through free choice and action.

Rogers defined the **self** as the center of experience. Your self is your ongoing sense of who and what you are, your sense of how and why you react to the environment and how you choose to act on the environment. Your choices are made on the basis of your values, and your values are also part of your self. Rogers's self theory focuses on the nature of the self and the conditions that allow the self to develop freely. Two of his major concerns are the self-concept and self-esteem.

Our self-concepts consist of our impressions and beliefs about ourselves. Rogers believed that we all have unique ways of looking at ourselves and the world—that is, unique **frames of reference**. We may each use a different set of dimensions in defining ourselves, and we may judge ourselves according to different sets of values. To one person, achievement–failure may be the most important dimension in self-evaluation. To another person, the most important dimension may be decency–indecency. A third person may not even think in terms of a dimension of decency–indecency.

Self-Esteem and Positive Regard

Rogers assumed that we all develop a need for self-regard, or self-esteem, as we develop and become aware of ourselves. At first, self-esteem reflects the esteem in which others hold us. Parents help children develop self-esteem when they show them **unconditional positive regard**—that is, when they accept them as having intrinsic merit regardless of their behavior at the moment. But when parents show children **conditional positive regard**—that is, when they accept them only when they behave in a desired manner—children may develop **conditions of worth**. That is, they may come to think that they have merit or worth only when they behave as their parents wish them to behave. They come to think of themselves as unworthy for failing to meet parental standards ("You're a bad boy").

Because each individual is thought to have a unique potential, children who develop conditions of worth must be somewhat disappointed in themselves. We cannot fully live up to the wishes of others and remain true to ourselves. This does not mean that the expression of the self inevitably leads to conflict. Rogers was optimistic about human nature. He believed that we hurt others or act in antisocial ways only when we are frustrated in our efforts to develop our own potential. But when parents and others are loving and tolerant of our differences, we, too, are loving—even if some of our preferences, abilities, and values differ from those of our parents.

Children in some families, however, learn that having their own ideas or feelings meets with social disapproval. They may come to see themselves as bad or undeserving and label their feelings as selfish, wrong, or evil. If they wish to retain a consistent self-concept and self-esteem, they may have to deny many of their feelings or disown aspects of themselves. In this way the self-concept becomes distorted—a reflection of how others want them to be, not what they truly are. They may become like strangers to themselves. According to Rogers, anxiety often stems from recognition of feelings and desires that are inconsistent with a distorted self-concept. Since anxiety is unpleasant, people may deny the existence of their genuine feelings and desires whenever anxiety surfaces.

According to Rogers, the path to self-actualization requires getting in touch with our genuine feelings,

---

■ **Self** To Rogers, the center of our conscious experience that organizes how we relate to the world as a distinct individual.

■ **Frames of reference** One's unique patterning of perceptions and attitudes, according to which one evaluates events.

■ **Unconditional positive regard** Acceptance of others as having intrinsic merit regardless of their behavior at the moment. Consistent expression of esteem for the value of another person.

■ **Conditional positive regard** Judgment of another person's value on the basis of the acceptability of that person's behaviors.

■ **Conditions of worth** Standards by which the value of a person is judged.

IT Stock

Unconditional Positive Regard
Rogers highlighted the importance of unconditional positive regard in the development of self-esteem.

accepting them, and acting on them. This is the goal of Rogers's method of psychotherapy, *client-centered therapy*.

Rogers also believed that we have mental images of what we are capable of becoming. These are termed **self-ideals**. We are motivated to reduce the discrepancy between our self-concepts and our self-ideals.

According to humanistic-existential theory, self-esteem is central to our sense of well-being. Self-esteem helps us develop our potential as unique individuals. It may originate in childhood and reflect the esteem others have for us.

▎ **Self-ideals** One's concepts of what one is capable of being.

2.3.3 The Healthy Personality

Positive Psychology

Humanistic-existential theorists put the "self" front and center in their concept of the healthy personality. People who are well adjusted are true to themselves—they know themselves and make authentic choices that are consistent with their individual needs, values, and goals. People with healthy personalities show the following qualities:

- *Experiencing life in the here and now.* They do not dwell excessively on the past or wish their days away as they strive toward future happiness.
- *Being open to new experience.* They do not turn away from ideas and ways of life that might challenge their own perceptions of the world and values.
- *Expressing their true feelings and beliefs.* They assert themselves in interpersonal relationships and are honest about their feelings. They believe in their own inner goodness and are not afraid of their urges and impulses.
- *Seeking meaningful activities.* They strive to live up to their self-ideals, to enact fulfilling roles.
- *Being capable of making major changes in their lives.* They can find more convenient ways to interpret experiences, strive toward new goals, and act with freedom.
- *Becoming their own persons.* They have developed their own values and their own ways of construing events. As a consequence, they take risks and can anticipate and control events.

2.3.4 Evaluation of Humanistic Theory

The greatest value of the humanistic approach—the recognition of the importance of conscious, subjective experience—may also be its greatest weakness. By its nature, conscious experience is private and subjective. It cannot be detected by scientific observation and measurement. Your "consciousness" is available to an audience of one—you. To strict behaviorists, the study of internal mental experience lies beyond the purview of scientific study. How can we accurately perceive the conscious experience of others—to clearly see the world through another person's eyes? But to humanistic psychologists, limiting the scope of study to that which can be directly measured or observed misses what is truly unique about the human experience—that "show" between our ears that gives rise to our sense of self-awareness. Humanistic theorists counter that even though we cannot put consciousness under a microscope, we can move toward a better understanding of consciousness by having people report their thoughts and feelings in ways that help us to understand what they are experiencing. To trait theorists, whose work we encounter next, humanistic theories, like learning theories, fail to account for the role of personality traits in explaining the continuity or consistency in behavior over time and from situation to situation.

MODULE REVIEW

Review It

(19) The humanistic view argues that people (are or are not?) capable of free choice and self-fulfillment.

(20) Maslow argued that people have growth-oriented needs for _____.

(21) The need for self-actualization is the highest in Maslow's _____ of needs.

(22) Rogers's theory begins with the assumption of the existence of the _____.

(23) According to Rogers, we see the world through unique frames of _____.

(24) The self is most likely to achieve optimal development when the individual experiences (conditional or unconditional?) positive regard.

Think About It

How does the humanistic view of personality differ from the psychodynamic and behavioral views?

MODULE 2.4

Trait Theories

▪ What are traits?

▪ How do contemporary trait models conceptualize the underlying dimensions of personality?

▪ How do trait theorists view the healthy personality?

© Jeff Isaac Greenberg/Photo Researchers, Inc.

Unique
According to humanistic psychologists like Carl Rogers, each of us is unique and views the world from a unique frame of reference. Rogers also believed that people are basically prosocial and would develop their unique talents and abilities if they received unconditional positive regard in childhood.

In most of us by the age of thirty, the character has set like plaster, and will never soften again.

—*Psychologist William James*

The notion of **traits** is very familiar. If we asked you to describe yourself, you would probably do so in terms of traits such as bright, sophisticated, and witty. (That is you, isn't it?) We also describe other people in terms of traits.

Traits are reasonably stable elements of personality that are inferred from behavior. If you describe a friend as "shy," it may be because you have observed social anxiety or withdrawal in that person's encounters with others. Traits are assumed to account for consistent behavior in diverse situations. You probably expect your "shy" friend to be retiring in most social confrontations—"all across the board," as the saying goes. The concept of traits is also found in other approaches to personality. Freud linked the development of certain traits to children's experiences in each stage of psychosexual development.

2.4.1 Hans Eysenck

Psychologist Hans J. Eysenck (2000) was born in Berlin but moved to England in 1934 to escape the Nazi threat. Ironically, he was not allowed to enter the British military to fight the Nazis during World War II because he was still a German citizen (Farley, 2000).

Eysenck developed the first British training program for clinical psychologists and focused much of his research on the relationships between two general personality

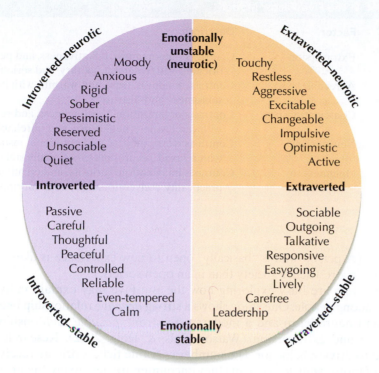

Figure 2.6
Eysenck's Personality Types
Here we see how various personality traits can be used to create four basic personality types in Eysenck's model, as represented in the four quadrants.

■ **Trait** A relatively stable aspect of personality that is inferred from behavior and assumed to give rise to consistent behavior.

■ **Neuroticism** Eysenck's term for emotional instability.

■ **Introversion** A trait characterized by preference for solitary activities and tendencies to inhibit impulses.

■ **Extraversion** A trait characterized by tendencies to be socially outgoing and to express feelings and impulses freely.

traits: introversion–extraversion and emotional stability–instability (Eysenck & Eysenck, 1985). (Emotional instability is also known as **neuroticism**.) Carl Jung was first to distinguish between introverts and extraverts. Eysenck added the dimension of emotional stability–instability to **introversion–extraversion**. He catalogued various personality traits according to where they are situated along these dimensions or factors (see Figure 2.6). For instance, an anxious person would be introverted and neurotic—that is, solitary and reserved as well as emotionally unstable.

2.4.2 The Five-Factor Model

Today the leading contemporary trait model of personality, the *five-factor model*, represents the five major traits or personality factors found most consistently in personality research (Costa & McCrae, 2006; McCrae et al., 2004). These five traits include two found in Eysenck's model—extraversion and neuroticism—along with the traits of conscientiousness, agreeableness, and openness to experience (see Table 2.4).

These five factors of personality are found consistently in personality research conducted in many parts of the world, including Western countries such as the United States, Canada, and the United Kingdom, as well as Israel, China, Korea, and Japan (Egger et al., 2003; McCrae et al., 2004; Paunonen, 2003). A study of more than 5,000 German, British, Spanish, Czech, and Turkish people suggests that the factors have a substantial genetic contribution (McCrae et al., 2000). The researchers interpret the results to suggest that our personalities tend to mature rather than be shaped by environmental conditions, although the expression of personality traits is certainly affected

Table 2.4 ❙ The Five-Factor Model		
Number	Factor	Description
I	Extraversion	Contrasts outgoingness, talkativeness, and people-oriented with reserved, solitary, and serious-minded
II	Agreeableness	Contrasts kindness, trust, and warmth with hostility, selfishness, and distrust
III	Conscientiousness	Contrasts organization, thoroughness, and reliability with carelessness, negligence, and unreliability
IV	Neuroticism	Contrasts worry, anxiety, and emotional instability with relaxed, secure, and emotionally stable
V	Openness to experience	Contrasts imagination, curiosity, and creativity with practicality, conventionality, and conformity

by culture. (A person who is "basically" open to new experience is likely to behave less openly in a restrictive society than in an open society.)

Investigators are busy exploring how the Big Five may explain individual differences among people. One study shows a strong *negative* relationship between self-esteem and neuroticism and a moderate to strong *positive* relationship between self-esteem and extraversion (Watson, Suls, & Haig, 2002). Research has even extended to driving behavior. The number of traffic tickets drivers receive and the number of motor vehicle accidents they encounter are negatively (inversely) linked to the Big Five factor of agreeableness (Cellar, Nelson, & Yorke, 2000). As we have long suspected, it's safer to share the freeway with agreeable people.

People who are higher in conscientiousness tend to live longer, perhaps because they tend to be safer drivers, to take better care of their health, to adopt healthier diets, and to limit their use of alcohol (Bogg & Roberts, 2004; Kern & Friedman, 2008). On the other hand, people who tend to be flexible and nonjudgmental—who are likely to put up with your every whim, like puppy dogs—tend to score low on conscientiousness (they don't examine you too closely) and high on agreeableness (Bernardin, Cooke, & Villanova, 2000).

As for college students, the trait of conscientiousness predicts higher grades as well as motivation to set performance goals and pursue them vigorously (Chamorro-Premuzic & Furnham, 2003; Judge & Ilies, 2002). On the other hand, neuroticism is associated with lower final exam grades. If you are somewhat lacking in conscientiousness, don't despair. Conscientiousness typically increases during young adulthood and middle age, perhaps because this is the time in life when people generally take on more career and family responsibilities (Caspi, Roberts, & Shiner, 2005).

Researchers are also studying how the five factors are connected with ways in which people interact with their friends, lovers, and families. In one study with college students, investigators found links between higher levels of neuroticism and lower levels of reported satisfaction with intimate relationships (White, Hendrick, & Hendrick, 2004). Conversely, agreeableness and extraversion were associated with greater relationship satisfaction. We should not be surprised that personality traits and relationship factors are closely intertwined.

Not all researchers accept the Big Five model. Some believe that reducing human personality to a mere five dimensions fails to capture the fullness and richness of human personality or to account for differences in how individuals behave in specific environmental contexts.

Paulus Rusyanto/iStockphoto

Conscientiousness
Conscientiousness is one of the five personality traits in the five-factor model of personality. The other four are extraversion–introversion, agreeableness, neuroticism (emotional instability–emotional stability), and openness to experience.

2.4.3 The Healthy Personality

Trait theory is mainly descriptive, and it is generally assumed that heredity has a great deal to do with the development of specific personality traits. Genetic factors may create dispositions for certain traits, but how those traits are expressed is influenced to a large extent by our learning experiences, development of skills, and abilities to choose our own course of action. But it seems responsible to seek a fit between our underlying traits and the jobs and activities that may suit us best. For example, an imaginative, intelligent, and talented individual may fare better as a creative artist than as an accountant.

Positive Psychology

▌ **Neurotransmitters** Chemicals in the nervous system that carry messages from one nerve cell, or neuron, to another.

Adjustment and Modern Life

Are Our Traits Imprinted in Our Genes?

Scientists recognize that many personality traits are influenced by genetic factors. But whether genetic propensities or dispositions for particular traits become expressed depends on the interactions of genes and environmental influences, such as our unique learning experiences (Yang et al., 2009).

An increasing body of evidence points to an important role for genetics in shaping personality (Bouchard, 2004). Evidence points to a genetic contribution to many behavioral and personality characteristics, including shyness, neuroticism, aggressiveness, extraversion, agreeableness, emotional stability, problem drinking, smoking, and novelty-seeking (e.g., Harro et al., 2009; Malouff, Rooke, & Schutte, 2008; Price & Jaffee, 2008; Stambor, 2006b).

Genes influence personality by way of creating a *predisposition* or likelihood—not a certainty—of certain personality traits and behavioral patterns emerging. For example, people may have certain genes that increase their likelihood of becoming shy, extraverted, or emotionally unstable. But whether these traits actually emerge depends on the interaction of genetic influences with life experiences or environmental factors.

Scientists have begun exploring the role of specific genes in shaping personality (e.g., Lahti et al., 2006; Zuckerman, 2006). Consider the findings from a group of Israeli researchers (Benjamin, Ebstein, & Belmaker, 2002). They found that people with higher levels of the novelty-seeking trait often possessed a particular form of a gene that helps regulate the body's production of the chemical *dopamine*, a type of **neurotransmitter**, or chemical messenger, that ferries nerve impulses from one nerve cell to another. People with high levels of the novelty-seeking trait are often described by others as impulsive, exploratory, fickle, excitable, and quick-tempered. They tend to be adventurous risk-takers who like to do things just for the thrill of it. We know that dopamine plays an important role in regulating exploratory behavior in other animals, so it is not surprising that it may be involved in explaining inquisitive, exploratory behavior in humans. In the brain, dopamine activates reward circuits,

producing feelings of pleasure. One intriguing possibility that needs to be studied further is whether people who possess the form of the gene linked to novelty-seeking have an irregularity in how their brain utilizes dopamine.

Scientists today have moved beyond the old nature–nurture debate. It is no longer a question of whether genes or environment influence our personalities. Rather, the question is how genes interact with environment in leading to expression of behavioral traits such as shyness, dominance, extraversion, and anxiety (Diamond, 2009; Rutter, 2008). Research along these lines is still in its infancy. But just as heredity may shape personality, early life experiences may affect how our brains develop, which in turn may influence our personalities.

Mel Yates/Getty Images, Inc

Changing the Unchangeable: Is Biology Destiny?

What can we do to adjust to counterproductive traits, such as neuroticism and shyness? Such traits tend to be enduring and seem to be at least partly biologically based. Is it healthful to be self-accepting and say, "That's me—that's my personality," and then settle for what one's "traits" will allow? Or is it more healthful to try to change self-defeating behavior patterns, such as social withdrawal and tenseness?

Rather than thinking in terms of changing embedded traits, it may be more productive to think about changing, or modifying, behaviors. Rather than attempting to change an abstract trait such as social withdrawal, one can work on modifying socially withdrawn behavior. Rather than eliminating neuroticism (emotional instability), we can learn to tone down our bodily arousal and develop skills that enable us to better handle the stressors we face. If people acquire consistent new behavior patterns, aren't they, in effect, changing their traits, whether or not the traits are biologically based? Even when a trait seems to be "deeply embedded," it may sometimes only mean that we need to work somewhat harder to change our behavior or develop better coping skills.

This is a perfect time to consider a learning theory perspective. According to learning theorists, if we practice a behavior often enough (if we work at it) and are rewarded or reinforced for our efforts, new adaptive behavior patterns can become habits. Habitual behavior patterns can be ingrained in a way that makes them somewhat akin to traits.

2.4.4 Evaluation of Trait Theories

Trait theories have a natural appeal. We tend to explain people's behaviors in terms of the traits they possess. If John regularly fails to get his work in on time, we might say that he is lazy (has a trait of laziness). But critics contend that trait theories lead to circular arguments that merely label behavior rather than explain it. That is, they may restate what is observed rather than truly explain what is observed. Saying that John fails to get his work in on time because he is lazy is a circular explanation; we have used his behavior to determine the trait he possesses and then used the trait to explain his behavior. Another major criticism of trait theory is that it fails to account for situational variability in behavior. Critics claim that behavior varies more from situation to situation than trait theory would suggest. But even though people's behaviors may vary with the demands they face in particular situations, people do display some enduring patterns of behavior over time that are consistent with certain personality traits, including the Big Five.

In recent years, a developing consensus appears to be emerging around the concept of *interactionism*—the belief that behavior reflects an interaction between trait dispositions and situational or environmental factors (Pincus et al., 2009; Tett & Burnett, 2003; Webster, 2009; Wu & Clark, 2003). People clearly respond differently in different situations. For example, you may be outgoing and assertive with your friends but deferential and laid-back with your professors or employers. Yet people don't completely reinvent themselves from situation to situation. They tend to have fairly typical ways of relating to others that cut across various situations (Fleeson, 2004). Even Walter Mischel, a leading figure in social-cognitive theory, recognizes that people vary in their underlying characteristics, with some being more sociable, open-minded, punctual and so on than others (Mischel, 2004). Trait theorists help us conceptualize these consistent patterns in terms of underlying traits. Interactionism helps us move beyond the trait-versus-situation debate toward a synthesis that recognizes an important role for both traits and situational factors.

Review It

(25) _____ are enduring personality characteristic that account for behavioral consistency.

(26) Eysenck described the underlying dimensions of personality in terms of two basic traits: introversion–extraversion and _____.

(27) Five-factor theory suggests that there are five basic personality factors: introversion–extraversion, emotional stability, conscientiousness, _____, and openness to experience.

Think About It

Do you tend to explain other people's behavior in terms of their traits? How about your own behavior?

MODULE 2.5

The Sociocultural Perspective

■ Why is sociocultural theory important to the understanding of personality?

■ What is meant by individualism and collectivism?

■ How does acculturation affect the adjustment of immigrant groups?

■ How do sociocultural theorists view the healthy personality?

In multicultural societies such as those of the United States and Canada, personality cannot be understood without reference to **sociocultural theory**—the view that our sense of ourselves and our adjustment to society is influenced by social and cultural factors such as ethnicity, gender, culture, discrimination, and socioeconomic status. According to a *New York Times* poll, 91% of people in the United States agree that "being an American is a big part" of who they are (Powers, 2000). In addition, 79% say that their religion has played a big role or some role in making them who they are, and 54% report that their race has played a big role or some role. Moreover, trends in birth rates and immigration are making the population an even richer mix. Different cultural groups in the United States have different attitudes, beliefs, norms, self-definitions, and values.

Consider Hannah—a Korean American teenager. She strives to become a great violinist, yet she talks back to her parents and insists on choosing her own friends, clothing, and so on. She is strongly influenced by her peers and completely at home wearing blue jeans and eating French fries. She is also a daughter in an Asian American immigrant group that tends to view education as the key to success in American culture. Belonging to this ethnic group has certainly contributed to her ambition. But being a Korean American has not prevented her from becoming an outspoken American teenager, when children back in Korea—especially girls—generally follow the wishes of their parents. Her outspoken behavior strikes her traditional mother as brazen and inappropriate.

As Hannah's experience illustrates, we cannot fully understand the challenge of adjusting to the demands of our environment without understanding the cultural beliefs and socioeconomic conditions that affect the individual. Here we focus on the relationships between sociocultural factors and the concept of the self, as well as on the challenges facing immigrant groups as they struggle to adjust to life in a new country.

▌ **Sociocultural theory** The view that focuses on the roles of ethnicity, gender, culture, and socioeconomic status in personality, behavior, and adjustment.

2.5.1 Individualism versus Collectivism

❙ **Individualists** People who define themselves in terms of their own personal traits and give priority to their own goals.

❙ **Collectivists** People who define themselves in terms of relationships to other people and groups and who give priority to group goals.

Hannah sees herself as an individual and an artist to a greater extent than as a family member and a Korean girl. Cross-cultural research reveals that people in the United States and many northern European nations tend to be individualistic in their sense of self. **Individualists** emphasize individual achievement, value self-sufficiency, define themselves in terms of their personal identities, and give priority to their personal goals and aspirations (Dwairy, 2002; Triandis & Suh, 2002). When asked to complete the statement "I am...," they are likely to respond in terms of their personality traits ("I am outgoing," "I am artistic") or occupational identities ("I am a nurse," "I am a systems analyst").

In contrast, most of the world's population—some 80% according to some estimates—live in collectivistic cultures, mainly in Africa, Asia, and Central and South America (Dwairy, 2002). **Collectivists** tend to define themselves in terms of the groups to which they belong and to give priority to the group's goals (Choi et al., 2003; Triandis & Suh, 2002). They connect their identity with their social roles and obligations, such as being a good son or good daughter and a good worker (Sedikides, Gaertner, & Toguchi, 2003) (see Figure 2.7). They emphasize communal values, such as respect for one's elders and authorities, conformity, cooperation, and avoiding conflicts with others (Nisbett, 2003). When asked to complete the statement "I am...," they are more likely to respond in terms of their families, gender, or nation ("I am a father," "I am a Buddhist," "I am Japanese").

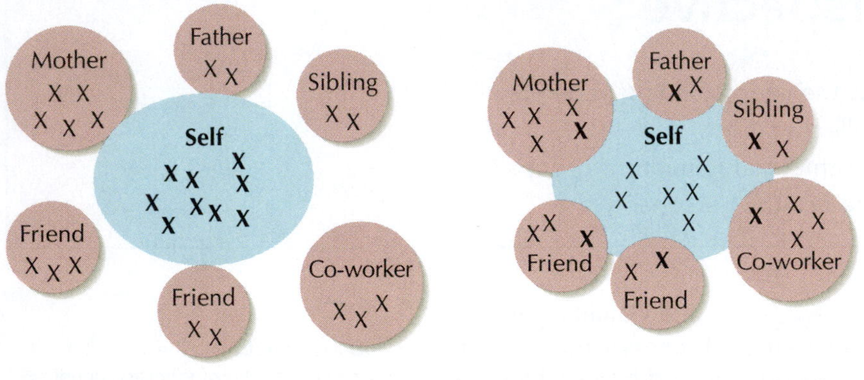

The seeds of individualism and collectivism are found in the culture in which a person grows up. The capitalist system fosters individualism. It assumes that individuals are entitled to amass personal fortunes and that the process of doing so creates jobs and wealth for large numbers of people. By contrast, Eastern cultures exalt people who resist personal temptations in order to do their duty and promote the welfare of the group.

Though important differences exist between individualistic and collectivistic cultures, we should point out that the human mind has the ability to think both individualistically and collectivistically depending on the particular circumstances (Oyserman, Coon, & Kemmelmeier, 2002). In other words, people from collectivistic cultures can strive to succeed on an individual level, whereas people from individualistic cultures can hold deeply embedded beliefs regarding their social responsibilities and obligations to others. Yet let us touch upon an example that puts these cultural differences into context. Acting honorably in fulfilling social obligations extends even to turning in cash someone has dropped on a sidewalk (Onishi, 2004). In collectivistic Japan a few years ago, Tokyo residents turned in some $23 million in cash to lost-and-found centers they found lying on the sidewalks. In one case, a 24-year-old woman, Hitomi Sasaki, found $250 on the sidewalk outside the restaurant where she worked. She promptly turned it in. How many residents of Chicago, New York, Seattle, Houston, or other U.S. cities and towns would follow Ms. Sasaki's lead if they discovered cash lying in the street? How about you? Would you return the cash?

Cultural factors also shape concepts of social identity, including what it means to be an American. Investigators posed the following question to groups of Chinese American and European American students in the San Francisco Bay area: "What does it mean to be an American?" (Tsai et al., 2002). As you can see in Figure 2.8, Chinese American students more often referenced customs and traditions, whereas European American students often mentioned ethnic diversity. The groups did not differ significantly in emphasizing political ideology.

A. Independent View of Self   B. Interdependent View of Self

Figure 2.7
The Self in Relation to Others from the Individualist and Collectivist Perspectives
To an individualist, the self is separate from other people (Part A). To a collectivist, the self is complete only in terms of relationships to other people (Part B).
Source: Based on Markus & Kitayama, 1991

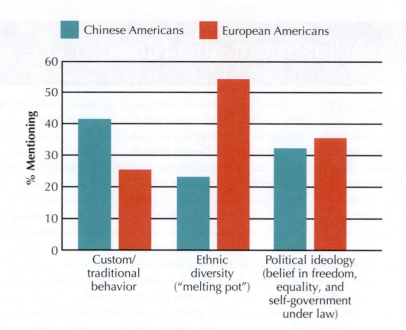

Figure 2.8
Cultural Differences in What It Means to Be an American
What does it mean to be an American? In this student sample, Chinese Americans more often mentioned the importance of customs and traditions, whereas European American students more often emphasized the importance of ethnic diversity as a foundation of American society.
Source: Adapted from Tsai et al. (2002)

2.5.2 Sociocultural Factors and the Self

Differences along the collectivist–individualistic dimension may serve as a buffering influence in bolstering self-esteem. Evidence shows that African Americans and other ethnic minorities in the United States, such as Hispanic Americans and Asian Americans, show more of a collectivist orientation than do white Americans of European background. In other words, ethnic minorities endorse more of a "we-orientation" than the "me-orientation" that is prominent among European Americans (Gaines et al., 1997; Oyserman, Gant, & Ager, 1995). Consequently, self-esteem among ethnic minorities may be more closely tied to fulfilling one's roles as parent, brother, and elder than to achieving individual success. African Americans draw upon a traditional African cultural heritage that places a strong emphasis on social connectedness and responsibility to others within the same group or tribe (Boykin & Ellison, 1995).

Perhaps this buffering influence of cultural heritage explains the findings that African American girls are likely to be happier with their appearance than European American girls are. Sixty-five percent of African American elementary school girls said that they were happy with the way they were, compared with 55% of European American girls. By high school, 58% of African American girls remained happy with the way they were, compared with a surprisingly low 22% of European Americans. It appears that the parents of African American girls teach them that there is nothing wrong with them if they do not match the unrealistic ideals of the dominant culture. The world mistreats them because of prejudice, not because of who they are as individuals (Williams, 1992). The European American girls are more likely to blame themselves for not attaining the ideal, however unreachable it may be.

2.5.3 The Healthy Personality

Positive Psychology

From a sociocultural framework, the development of a healthy personality involves coming to understand who we are in the collective sense. It also involves balancing the social and individual parts of the self. We need to understand something of our cultural background, our family history, and the continuity that exists in families from generation to generation. But in so doing, we also need to consider how to function within a Western individualistic society in which one's own interests, ambitions, and achievements are incorporated within the mainstream values of the larger society.

Adjustment and Modern Life

Acculturation: A Double-Edged Sword?

Should Hindu women who emigrate to the United States surrender the sari in favor of California casuals? Should Russian immigrants speak to their children only in English? Should African American children be acquainted with the music and art of Africa or those of Europe? These activities are examples of **acculturation**, the process by which immigrants become acclimated to the customs and behavior patterns of their new host culture.

Some immigrants become completely acculturated or acclimated, adopting the language, style of dress, and customs of the host country. Others maintain almost complete separation. They retain the language and customs of their country of origin and never acclimate to those of the new country. Still others adopt a bicultural identity—preserving their traditional customs, preferences for types of music, food, and dress, as well as adopting new customs and language proficiencies of the host culture. They blend the customs and values of both cultures and can switch "mental gears." That is, they may blend into the mainstream culture in the workplace but raise their children to speak the language and adopt values and customs of their traditional culture. Relationships between acculturation and psychological adjustment are complex. Acculturation turns out to be something of a double-edged sword. Let us take a closer look at the research evidence, which has focused mainly on Latinos.

It seems that more acculturated groups may acquire some of the unhealthy patterns of the host culture. Some investigators find more acculturated Latinos to be at higher risk of developing psychological disorders than their less acculturated counterparts (Ortega et al., 2000). Acculturation is also associated with an increased risk of smoking among Latino adolescents (Unger et al., 2000). The erosion of traditional cultural values may help explain findings of higher rates of sexual intercourse among more acculturated Hispanic teens and higher rates of drug dependence among Hispanic women born in the United States than among those who immigrated ("Studies Focus," 2007; Turner, Lloyd, & Taylor, 2006). We also have recent evidence showing poorer mental health among Mexican Americans who were born in the United State as compared to Mexican nationals and Mexican immigrants (Escobar & Vega, 2000).

On the other hand, investigators also find less acculturated Mexican Americans who are poorly proficient in English to have more signs of depression (Salgado de Snyder, Cervantes, & Padilla, 1990). Minimal acculturation is a frequent marker for lower socioeconomic status, and financial hardship is a major source of stress linked to depression. The pressure of an English-speaking culture may well be the predominant source of stress relating to acculturation of Latinos. Not surprisingly, the stress associated with acculturative pressures is linked to poorer psychological adjustment (Crockett et al., 2007; Schwartz, Zamboanga, & Jarvis, 2007).

If anything, research underscores the value of a bicultural pattern. Evidence shows the highest levels of self-esteem are found among bicultural immigrant groups (Phinney, Cantu, & Kurtz, 1997; Phinney & Devich-Navarro, 1997). If "Americanization" has damaging effects on the adjustment of immigrant groups, it appears that maintaining ethnic identity and retaining cultural traditions might provide a protective or buffering effect.

To round out this discussion, consider the results of studies of Asian American adolescents which show that those who maintain their ethnic identity are generally better adjusted psychologically and have higher self-esteem than their peers (Huang, 1994). Ethnic identity is a critical component of adjustment for adolescents of color (French et al., 2006) and appears to be a stronger predictor of self-esteem among African Americans and Hispanic Americans than among European Americans (Gray-Little & Hafdahl, 2000; Umaña-Taylor, 2004). For ethnic minorities, the ability to identify strongly with their ethnic heritage may help them maintain self-esteem in the face of continuing racism and prejudice.

Elena Ray/iStockphoto

How Does Acculturation Affect Adjustment?
This Latina American is highly acculturated to life in the United States. Some immigrants are completely assimilated by the dominant culture of their host nation and abandon the traditions and customs—even the language—of their country of origin. Others retain the traditions and language of their country of origin and never become accustomed to the culture and language of the new host country. Still others become bicultural: Truly bicultural people are "at home" both with the language and traditions of their country of origin and with the language and culture of their host country. Other things being equal, bicultural individuals appear to be the best adjusted.

Balancing Competing Cultural Demands

In Western nations, adjustment may mean having an individualistic perspective—for example, experiencing and trying to actualize personal ambitions, being self-assertive, and so on. In other parts of the world, adjustment may mean viewing oneself and society from a collectivist point of view. Yet some of us, like Hannah, need to function within very different societies in the school or work environment we face in our daily lives and the family environment we face at home. We may come to experience clashes of cultures that may revolve around such issues as when (or if) young people go off on their own before marriage, whether to pursue one's own ambitions in terms of career or vocation or to fulfill one's family obligations, and whether to adopt the social customs of the mainstream culture or remain true to one's cultural traditions. In some cases, a frank discussion about these competing demands within the family may yield a resolution. In other cases, seeking help from a counselor or mental health professional may lead to alternative solutions.

Coping Effectively with Discrimination

Most of us belong to groups that have experienced—or are currently experiencing—discrimination. People experience discrimination on the basis of their ethnic background, their gender, their sexual orientation, their age, and so on. People with healthy personalities try not to allow discrimination to affect their self-esteem. If you have experienced discrimination, it is not you as an individual who is at fault. The problem lies within those who judge you on the basis of your sociocultural background rather than your individual traits and abilities. You will find advice for coping with prejudice and discrimination in Chapter 6.

Becoming Acculturated Without Losing Your Cultural Identity

Maintaining strong ethnic identification is linked to better psychological health among immigrant and ethnic minority groups (Phinney, 2000; Rieckmann, Wadsworth, & Deyhle, 2004). Ethnic identity can be expressed in many ways, from retaining traditional values, languages, and other trappings of one's ethnic background to experiencing pride in one's heritage. In other words, you can develop a bicultural identification by making efforts to adapt to the dominant culture while also maintaining your own ethnic identity.

2.5.4 Evaluation of the Sociocultural Perspective

The sociocultural perspective embraces a broader view of personality than those associated with traditional psychological models. Sociocultural theorists have focused much needed attention on factors such as ethnicity, gender, culture, discrimination, and socioeconomic status in shaping our personalities. We exist in a social community, not merely within our own skin. On the other hand, the sociocultural perspective must itself be broadened to include in the mix of personality our unique individual experiences, our genetic heritage, and our subjective experiences of ourselves.

MODULE REVIEW

Review It

(28) _____ define themselves in terms of their personal identities and give priority to their personal goals.

(29) _____ define themselves in terms of the groups to which they belong and give priority to group goals.

(30) Immigrants who identify with the bicultural pattern of assimilation typically have the (highest or lowest?) self-esteem.

(31) Ethnic identity appears to be a (weaker or stronger?) predictor of self-esteem among African Americans and Hispanic Americans than among European Americans.

Think About It

How might acculturation be something of a mixed blessing to immigrant groups? Explain.

MODULE 2.6

Assessing Personality

▪ ▪

▮ How is personality assessed?

▮ What are objective personality tests?

▮ What are projective personality tests?

Psychologists are interested in measuring personality for a number of reasons. Some use information from personality tests to help people make important academic and vocational decisions, such as whether a person is well suited for a certain type of work or college major. Others may use personality tests to help them better understand their clients or to shed light on their clients' psychological or interpersonal problems.

Personality tests are not the only ways of assessing personality. We can also learn a good deal about people by carefully observing them or by administering structured interviews that ask them a set of specific questions about themselves. Behavior-rating scales are also used to assess behavior in settings such as classrooms or mental hospitals. With behavior-rating scales, trained observers usually check off each occurrence of a specific behavior within a certain time frame—say, 15 minutes. Behavior-rating scales are growing in popularity, especially for use with children (Kamphaus, Petoskey, & Rowe, 2000). However, more formal tests of personality, such as objective and projective tests, are used more frequently, and we will focus on them in this module.

2.6.1 Objective Personality Tests

▪ ▪

Objective tests present respondents with a standard group of test items in the form of a questionnaire. Respondents are limited to a specific range of answers so that they can be scored objectively. One test might ask respondents to indicate whether items are true or false for them. (We have included self-assessments of this sort in several chapters of this book.) Another might ask respondents to select the preferred activity from groups of three. A leading objective personality test, the Minnesota Multiphasic Personality Inventory, has a true–false format that can be objectively scored, thereby yielding highly reliable results.

The Minnesota Multiphasic Personality Inventory

The Minnesota Multiphasic Personality Inventory (MMPI), now in a revised edition called the MMPI-2, contains 567 true–false items. The MMPI is designed to be used by clinical and counseling psychologists to help confirm diagnostic impressions or to

Table 2.5 ▮ Minnesota Multiphasic Personality Inventory (MMPI-2) Scales		
Scale	**Abbreviation**	**Possible Interpretations**
Validity Scales		
Lie	L	Lies or is highly conventional
Frequency	F	Exaggerates complaints or answers items haphazardly; may have bizarre ideas or disturbed behavior or wants to make it appear that way
Correction	K	Denies problems
Clinical Scales		
Hypochondriasis	Hs	Has bodily concerns and complaints
Depression	D	Is depressed; has feelings of guilt and helplessness
Hysteria	Hy	Reacts to stress by developing physical symptoms; lacks insight
Psychopathic deviate	Pd	Is immoral, in conflict with the law; has stormy relationships
Masculinity/Femininity	Mf	High scores suggest interests and behavior considered stereotypical of the other gender
Paranoia	Pa	Is suspicious and resentful, highly cynical about human nature
Psychasthenia	Pt	Is anxious, worried, high-strung
Schizophrenia	Sc	Is confused, disorganized, disoriented; has bizarre ideas
Hypomania	Ma	Is energetic, restless, active, easily bored
Social introversion	Si	Is introverted, timid, shy; lacks self-confidence

reveal aspects of the individual's underlying personality or areas of concern. The MMPI was developed on the basis of an empirical approach in which items were included in the scale when they tended to be answered differently by people diagnosed with psychological problems—such as depression, hypochondriasis, and schizophrenia—than by groups of normal individuals.

The MMPI-2 also contains scales designed to reveal problematic concerns, such as anxiety, depression, health-related concerns, and family problems. By examining an individual's scores on the individual scales that make up the MMPI in relation to the norms for each scale, the examiner can assess where an individual places on the particular traits that the scale is believed to measure or identify areas of concern that may warrant therapeutic attention. The MMPI is presently the most widely used self-report personality inventory in the world (Camara, Nathan, & Puente, 2000). A large number of research studies support both the reliability of the test (its consistency of measurement) and its validity (ability to measure what it purports to measure) (Graham, 2000; Kubiszyn et al., 2000).

The MMPI also contains a number of validity scales, including those shown in Table 2.5. They are used to measure response sets, or biases, that may color how people respond to the test items. For example, they may give answers they deem to be socially acceptable. But even these validity scales may not be able to detect all sources of bias. The clinical scales of the MMPI assess the problems shown in Table 2.5, as well as stereotypical masculine or feminine interests and social introversion.

2.6.2 Projective Personality Tests

Projective personality tests are derived from the belief in psychodynamic theory that people tend to project or impose their unconscious needs, impulses, or motives onto their responses to unstructured or vague stimuli. In projective personality tests there are no clear, specified answers. People are shown ambiguous stimuli such as inkblots or ambiguous drawings and asked to say what they look like or to tell stories about them. Or they may be given a series of incomplete sentences and asked to give short responses that complete each of the sentences. For projective tests, there is no one correct response. The meanings people attribute to ambiguous stimuli, or the responses they give when filling in the blanks of incomplete sentences, are assumed

Figure 2.9

Lambert/Getty Images, Inc.

A Rorschach Inkblot
The Rorschach is the most widely used projective personality test. What does this inkblot look like to you? What could it be?

to reflect their own psychological needs, drives, and motives. Hence, it is assumed that people project something of their own personalities into their responses. Unlike objective tests, the scoring on projective tests depends more on the subjective impressions and level of skill of the examiner.

The Rorschach Inkblot Test

The Rorschach test, named after its developer, the Swiss psychiatrist Hermann Rorschach, asks people to look at a set of inkblots one by one and to say what each of them looks like or could be. A response that reflects the shape of the blot is considered a sign of adequate "reality testing"—that is, accurate perception of the world around one. A response that richly integrates several features of the blot is considered a sign of high intellectual functioning.

Although there is no single "correct" response to the Rorschach inkblot shown in Figure 2.9, some responses are not in keeping with the features of the blots. Figure 2.9 could be a bat or a flying insect, the pointed face of an animal, the face of a jack-o'-lantern, or many other things. But responses like "diseased lungs" or "a metal leaf in flames" are not suggested by the features of the blot and may indicate personality problems.

But is the Rorschach a valid test? Supporters of the test believe it may provide insight into a person's psychological traits, internal conflicts, general intelligence, and other variables. Yet critics argue that the Rorschach has failed to meet general tests of scientific utility and validity (Garb et al., 2002; Hamel, Shafer, & Erdberg, 2003; Hunsley & Bailey, 2001). On the other hand, proponents provide evidence that supports the use of at least certain Rorschach scores or responses in making specific predictions (Garb et al., 2005; Meyer et al., 2001; Perry, 2003). For example, evidence suggests that Rorschach responses can be used to predict success in psychotherapy (Meyer, 2000), to detect some forms of disturbed thinking (Lilienfeld, Fowler, & Lohr, 2003), and to distinguish between different types of psychological disorders (Kubisyzn et al., 2000). Still, the validity of the Rorschach remains a subject of continued and sometimes strident debate.

Figure 2.10

A Card Similar to Those on the Thematic Apperception Test
Can you make up a story about this card? Who are the people? What are they thinking and feeling?

The Thematic Apperception Test

The Thematic Apperception Test (TAT) was developed in the 1930s by Henry Murray and Christiana Morgan. It consists of drawings, like the one shown in Figure 2.10, that are open to a variety of interpretations. Individuals are given the cards one at a time and asked to make up stories about them, to say what was happening at the particular time, what led up to these events, and what will happen in the future.

The TAT is widely used in research on motivation and personality. The notion is that we are likely to project our own needs into our responses to ambiguous situations, even if we are unaware of them or reluctant to talk about them. The TAT is also widely used to assess attitudes toward other people, especially parents, lovers, and spouses.

Like the Rorschach, the TAT has had it share of critics. One frequent criticism is that the responses people give may have more to do with the stimulus properties of the test materials rather than projections of one's underlying personality (Murstein & Mathes, 1996). Again, proponents take the view that, in skilled hands, projective tests can yield information about personality and clinical problems that cannot be obtained from self-report tests or interviews (Stricker & Gold, 1999). In Chapter 15 we will see how you can take advantage of personality tests to help you assess what kinds of careers will "fit" your personality.

Review It

(32) A test that offers a limited set of response options is called an (objective or projective?) test.

(33) People with high scores on the MMPI ___ scale may be trying to present themselves as disturbed.

(34) With _____ tests there are no are no clear, specified answers.

(35) The MMPI is an example of an objective test, whereas the _____ and TAT are examples of projective tests.

Think About It

Can a psychological test be reliable (consistent over time) but not valid? Explain your answer.

Psychology in Daily Life   MODULE 2.7

Understanding Yourself

Despite their diversity, each theory of personality and behavior touches on meaningful aspects of human nature. Rather than worry about which is the one true theory, why not consider how each might contribute to your self-understanding? Let us put together a list of some of the basic ideas set forth by these theories.

Each of the ideas in the following list might not apply equally to everyone, but such a list might reflect something of what you see in yourself and in other people. Let's try it out by first classifying each of the following principles according to the theoretical framework it represents. Place a checkmark next to each of these principles using the following code (the answer key is shown at the end of the chapter):

    P = Psychodynamic
    T = Trait theory
    B = Behaviorism
    SC = Social-cognitive theory
    H = Humanistic
    S = Sociocultural

1. ____ The behavior patterns that comprise our personalities were shaped by the experiences we had in the environment.

2. ____ Our cognitive processes can be distorted so that we may see what we want to see and hear what we want to hear.

3. ____ Some of your traits, such as your intelligence, outgoingness, emotional stability, social dominance, and interest in arts and crafts may be in part genetically determined.

4. ____ It is useful to consider seeking jobs and social activities that are compatible with your psychological traits.

5. ____ We are influenced by hidden drives and motives of which we may not be aware.

6. ____ Our expectancies about forthcoming events may lead us to feel pleasure or fear.

7. ____ Our behavior is shaped by our history of rewards and punishments.

8. ____ We model much of our behavior after that of people we observe, especially those we admire.

9. ____ We need to reach into ourselves to know what is meaningful and important to us.

10. ____ Our behavior and personalities are affected by our cultural backgrounds.

11. ____ How we balance our basic needs with the demands of society has an important bearing on our adjustment and well-being.

12. ____ Each of us has something unique to offer, although it may not always seem very important to other people.

13. ____ When we close ourselves off to new experiences, we are less likely to find things that are of value to us and to develop as individuals.

14. ____ Sometimes we act in ways that are contrary to our real needs, wants, and desires.

15. ____ We may encounter conflict when the demands or values of the larger society conflict with those of our families or cultural traditions.

Each of the major approaches to understanding personality views the "elephant" from a different perspective, but each sheds light on aspects of human nature. Which teachings from these models of personality can you draw upon to understand yourself? To understand others? To understand what you are capable of becoming?

Before we end, let us draw upon one of the major theoretical perspectives on personality—the humanistic perspective—to take a good, hard look at ourselves. Let us consider whether our journey through life is leading us toward self-actualization—toward realizing our own unique potentials.

2.7.1 Do You Strive to Be All That You Can Be?

Are you a self-actualizer? Do you strive to be all that you can be? Psychologist Abraham Maslow attributed the following eight characteristics to the self-actualizing individual. How many of them describe you? Why not check them and undertake some self-evaluation?

1 *Do you fully experience life in the present—the here and now?* (Self-actualizers do not focus excessively on the lost past or wish their lives away as they strive toward distant goals.)

2 *Do you make growth choices rather than fear choices?* (Self-actualizers take reasonable risks to develop their unique potentials. They do not bask in the dull life of the status quo. They do not "settle.")

3 *Do you seek to acquire self-knowledge?* (Self-actualizers look inward; they search for values, talents, and meaningfulness. The questionnaires in this book offer a decent jumping-off point for getting to know yourself. It might also be enlightening to take an "interest inventory"—a test frequently used to help make career decisions—at your college testing and counseling center.)

4 *Do you strive toward honesty in interpersonal relationships?* (Self-actualizers strip away the social façades and games that stand in the way of self-disclosure and the formation of intimate relationships.)

5 *Do you behave self-assertively and express your own ideas and feelings, even at the risk of occasional social disapproval?* (Self-actualizers do not bottle up their feelings for the sake of avoiding social disapproval.)

6 *Do you strive toward new goals? Do you strive to be the best that you can be in a chosen life role?* (Self-actualizers do not live by the memory of past accomplishments. Nor do they present second-rate efforts.)

7 *Do you seek meaningful and rewarding life activities? Do you experience moments of actualization that humanistic psychologists refer to as peak experiences?* (Peak experiences are brief moments of rapture filled with personal meaning. Examples might include completing a work of art, falling in love, redesigning a machine tool, suddenly solving a complex problem in math or physics, or having a baby. Again, we differ as individuals, and one person's peak experience might bore another person silly.)

8 *Do you remain open to new experiences?* (Self-actualizers do not hold themselves back for fear that novel experiences might shake their views of the world or of right and wrong. Self-actualizers are willing to revise their expectations, values, and opinions.)

CHAPTER REVIEW

RECITE! RECITE! RECITE! RECITE! RECITE! RECITE! RECITE!

Study Tip: Reciting the answers to these study questions will help you become a more effective learner. First try answering the questions by yourself, either reciting them out loud or writing them in a notebook or on the computer. Then compare your answers with the sample answers provided below.

1. Why is Freud's theory of personality deemed a psychodynamic model?

Freud's theory is termed psychodynamic because it assumes that we are driven largely by unconscious motives and forces within our personalities. People experience conflict as basic instincts of hunger, sex, and aggression come up against social pressures to follow rules and moral codes. At first this conflict is external, but as we develop, it is internalized.

2. What is the structure of personality in Freud's view?

The personality consists of three mental states: the id, the ego, and the superego. The unconscious id represents psychological drives and seeks instant gratification. The ego, or the sense of self or "I," develops through experience and takes into account what is practical and possible in gratifying the impulses of the id. Defense mechanisms such as repression protect the ego from anxiety by repressing unacceptable ideas or distorting reality. The superego is the moral conscience and develops through the process of identification with important figures in one's life.

3. What is Freud's theory of psychosexual development?

People undergo psychosexual development as psychosexual energy, or libido, is transferred from one erogenous zone to another during childhood. There are five stages of development: oral, anal, phallic, latency, and genital. Fixation in a stage leads to development of traits associated with the stage.

4. What views on personality are attributed to some other psychodynamic theorists?

Carl Jung's theory, analytical psychology, focuses on a collective unconscious and archetypes, both of which reflect the history of our species. Alfred Adler's theory, individual psychology, focuses on the inferiority complex and the compensating drive for superiority. Karen Horney's theory focuses on parent–child relationships and the possible development of feelings of anxiety and hostility. Erik Erikson's theory of psychosocial development highlights the importance of early social relationships rather than the gratification of childhood sexual impulses. Erikson extended Freud's five developmental stages to eight, including stages that occur in adulthood.

5. How do psychodynamic theorists view the healthy personality?

Psychodynamic theorists equate the healthy personality with the abilities to love and work, ego strength, a creative Self (Jung and Adler), compensation for feelings of inferiority (Adler), and positive outcomes to various psychosocial challenges (Horney and Erikson).

6. **What are traits?**

Traits are elements of personality that are inferred from behavior and account for consistency in behavior. Heredity is believed to play a large role in the development of traits.

7. **How do contemporary trait models conceptualize the underlying dimensions of personality?**

Hans Eysenck described personality in terms of two broad personality dimensions: introversion–extraversion and emotional stability–instability (neuroticism). The major contemporary model, the five-factor model, posits five key factors of personality: extraversion, agreeableness, conscientiousness, emotional stability, and openness to experience.

8. **How do trait theorists view the healthy personality?**

Trait theorists to some degree equate the healthy personality with having the fortune of inheriting traits that promote adjustment. The focus of trait theory is description of traits people possess, not the origins or modification of traits. To behaviorists, personality is the sum total of an individual's response repertoire, which is developed on the basis of experience. Behaviorists believe we should focus on observable behavior rather than hypothesized unconscious forces and that we should emphasize the situational determinants of behavior. They also consider the sense of personal freedom or ability to exercise free will to be an illusion.

9. **How do behaviorists conceptualize personality?**

To behaviorists, personality is the sum total of an individual's response repertoire, which is developed on the basis of experience. Behaviorists believe we should focus on observable behavior rather than hypothesized unconscious forces and that we should emphasize the situational determinants of behavior. They also consider the sense of personal freedom or ability to exercise free will to be an illusion.

10. **What is classical conditioning?**

Classical conditioning is a simple form of associative learning in which a previously neutral stimulus (the conditioned stimulus, or CS) comes to elicit the response evoked by a second stimulus (the unconditioned stimulus, or US) as a result of repeatedly being paired with the second stimulus.

11. **What is operant conditioning?**

Operant conditioning is a form of learning in which organisms learn to engage in behavior that is reinforced. Reinforced responses occur with greater frequency.

12. **What are the different types of reinforcers?**

These include positive, negative, primary, and secondary reinforcers. A positive reinforcer increases the probability that a response will occur when it occurs following the response. A negative reinforcer increases the probability that a response will occur when it is removed following the response. Primary reinforcers, such as food or sexual pleasure, attain their value because of the organism's biological makeup. Secondary reinforcers, such as money and social approval, attain their value through association with primary reinforcers.

13. **Are negative reinforcement and punishment the same thing?**

They are not the same thing. Punishments are aversive stimuli, such as pain, that suppress behavior; punishments decrease the probability that the targeted behavior will occur. Negative reinforcers are also unpleasant stimuli, but they serve to increase the rate of response of behaviors that lead to their removal.

14. **How does social-cognitive theory differ from the behaviorist view?**

Social-cognitive theory focuses on cognitive and social influences on behavior, such as expectancies and learning by observing others in social environments. To predict behavior, social-cognitive theorists believe we need to consider both situational variables (rewards and punishments) and person variables, such as competencies, expectancies, and self-regulatory processes.

15. **How do learning theorists view the healthy personality?**

Learning theorists prefer to speak of adaptive behaviors rather than a healthy personality. Nevertheless, they would probably concur that the following will contribute to a "healthy personality": having opportunities for observational learning, acquiring competencies, encoding events accurately, having accurate expectations, having positive self-efficacy expectations, and regulating behavior productively to achieve goals.

16. **What is the humanistic perspective on personality?**

Humanistic theorists argue that our personalities are shaped by what we make of our lives. To the humanists, we are all capable of free choice, self-fulfillment, and ethical behavior. Humanistic psychologists draw upon the philosophy of existentialism, the belief that humans are free to determine their lives and cannot escape responsibility for the choices and the meaning or lack of meaning with which they imbue their lives.

17. **How do humanistic psychologists differ from psychodynamic and behaviorist theorists?**

Both psychodynamic and behaviorism believe that our behavior is determined either by internal forces within the personality, as Freud believed, or by external forces in the environment as the behaviorists maintained. But humanistic psychologists believe that people can exercise personal choice and strive for self-actualization.

18. **What is your self? What is self theory?**

According to Rogers, the self is an organized and consistent way in which a person perceives his or her "I" in relation to others. Self theory begins by assuming the existence of the self and each person's unique frame of reference. The self attempts to actualize (develop its unique potential) and does so best when the person receives unconditional positive regard. Conditions of worth may lead to a distorted self-concept, to disavowal of parts of the self, and to anxiety.

19. **How do humanistic-existential theorists view the healthy personality?**

Humanistic-existential theorists view the healthy personality as experiencing life here and now, being open to new experience, expressing one's genuine feelings and ideas, trusting one's feelings, engaging in meaningful activities, making adaptive changes, and being one's own person.

20. Why is sociocultural theory important to the understanding of personality?
One cannot fully understand the personality of an individual without understanding the cultural beliefs and socioeconomic conditions that have affected that individual. Sociocultural theory encourages us to consider the roles of ethnicity, gender, culture, and socioeconomic status in the development of personality and behavior.

21. What is meant by individualism and collectivism?
Individualists define themselves in terms of their personal identities and give priority to their personal goals. Collectivists define themselves in terms of the groups to which they belong and give priority to the group's goals. Many Western societies are individualistic and foster individualism in personality. Many Eastern societies are collectivist and foster collectivism in personality.

22. How does acculturation affect the adjustment of immigrant groups?
Relationships are complex, with negative outcomes associated with both high and low levels of acculturation. Healthier adjustment may be related to maintaining ethnic identity while balancing the demands of living in the host country.

23. How do sociocultural theorists view the healthy personality?
Sociocultural theorists view the healthy personality as functioning adaptively within one's cultural setting, balancing competing cultural demands, coping with discrimination, and becoming adequately acculturated in a new society while, at the same time, retaining important traditional values and customs.

24. How is personality assessed?
Various methods are used, including observation and interviewing techniques, behavior-rating scales, and objective and projective tests of personality.

25. What are objective tests?
Objective tests, such as the MMPI, present sets of items or questions that allow for only a limited range of responses so that they can be objectively scored. The examiner compares the individual's scores to relevant norms in order to determine how an individual places on particular psychological traits or to identify areas of concern.

26. What are projective tests?
Projective tests, such as the Rorschach and the TAT, present ambiguous test materials that are answered in ways that may reveal underlying aspects of the individual's personality.

YOUR PERSONAL JOURNAL

REFLECT   REFLECT   REFLECT   REFLECT   REFLECT   REFLECT   REFLECT

Study Tip: Reflecting upon how the concepts in the chapter relate to your own experiences encourages deeper processing, which makes the material more personally meaningful and fosters more effective learning. Use additional pages if needed to complete your answers.

1. Think of a friend who is single. If you were trying to fix him or her up on a date and you were asked what kind of "personality" he or she had, what would you answer? What models(s) of personality described in the chapter relate most closely to your description?

_____

_____

_____

_____

2. How would you describe your own personality traits in terms of the Big Five personality traits? What are your most prominent traits? Would others who know you agree or disagree with your appraisal?

_____

_____

_____

_____

ANSWERS TO MODULE REVIEWS

Module 2.1

1. conflicts
2. id
3. reality
4. superego
5. phallic
6. Fixation
7. other
8. collective
9. inferiority
10. psychosocial

Module 2.2

11. neutral
12. unconditioned
13. Positive
14. strengthen
15. Primary
16. Secondary
17. punishment
18. situational

Module 2.3

19. are

20. self-actualization
21. hierarchy
22. self
23. reference
24. unconditional

Module 2.4

25. Traits
26. emotional stability
27. agreeableness

Module 2.5

28. Individualists
29. Collectivists
30. highest
31. stronger

Module 2.6

32. objective
33. F
34. projective
35. Rorschach

SCORING KEY FOR THE EXPECTANCY FOR SUCCESS SCALE

In order to calculate your total score for the expectancy for success scale, first reverse the scores for the following items: 1, 2, 4, 6, 7, 8, 14, 15, 17, 18, 24, 27, and 28. That is, change a 1 to a 5; a 2 to a 4; leave a 3 alone; change a 4 to a 2; and a 5 to a 1. Then add the scores. The range of total scores can vary from 30 to 150. The higher your score, the greater your expectancy for success in the future—and, according to social-learning theory, the more motivated you will be to apply yourself in facing difficult challenges. Fibel and Hale administered their test to undergraduates taking psychology courses and found that women's scores ranged from 65 to 143 and men's from 81 to 138. The average score for each gender was 112.

ANSWER KEY FOR PSYCHOLOGY IN DAILY LIFE QUIZ

1. B
2. C
3. T
4. T
5. P
6. SC
7. B
8. SC
9. H
10. S
11. P
12. H
13. H
14. P
15. S

▌ According to a recent national survey by the American Psychological Association, about one in three Americans say they are facing extreme levels of stress in their lives? (p. 84)

▌ Stress is the most common reason that college students seek help from college counseling centers? (p. 84)

▌ Exposure to racism can take a toll on a person's mental health and self-concept? (p. 88)

▌ Hot temperatures make us hot under the collar—that is, they prompt aggression? (p. 101)

▌ Meditation can be good for your blood pressure? (p. 112)

▌ To relax muscles, it may help to tense them first? (p. 113)

Pascal Gensest/iStockphoto

Perhaps too much of a good thing can make you ill. You might think that marrying Mr. or Ms. Right, finding a prestigious job, and moving to a better neighborhood all in the same year would propel you into a state of bliss. It might. But the impact of all these events, one on top of the other, could also lead to headaches, high blood pressure, and asthma. As pleasant as they may be, they all involve major life changes, and change is a source of **stress**. But just what is stress? In physics, stress is defined as a pressure or force exerted on a body. Tons of rock pressing on the earth, one car smashing into another, a rubber band stretching—all are types of physical stress. Psychological forces, or stresses, also press, push, or pull. We may feel "crushed" by the weight of a big decision, "smashed" by adversity, or "stretched" to the point of snapping. We may encounter high levels of stress in our daily lives in the form of demands involved in juggling school, work, and family responsibilities; caring for infirm relatives; or coping with financial adversity or health problems. In psychology, stress is any demand made on an organism to adapt, cope, or adjust.

Some stress is healthful and necessary to keep us alert and occupied. But intense or prolonged stress can overtax our physical and mental resources, making us more vulnerable to stress-related disorders that range from digestive ailments to allergic conditions to heart disease and depression (Kemeny, 2003). Although some of us can cope better with stress than others, we all have our limits. Over time, stress can dampen our moods, impair our ability to experience pleasure, and harm the body. Though occasional stress may not be harmful, persistent high levels of daily stress can weaken the immune system, the body system responsible for protecting us from disease-causing organisms (Fan et al., 2009). Consequently, exposure to chronic stress can make us more vulnerable to various types of diseases, as we shall see in Chapter 4.

In this chapter, we focus on stress from three vantage points: the sources of stress, the psychological factors that help buffer or moderate stress, and the ways in which psychologists and other health professionals help people manage stress more effectively.

▌ **Stress** (1) An event that exerts physical or psychological force or pressure on a person. (2) The demand made on an organism to adjust.

83

MODULE 3.1

Sources of Stress

∎ What are the major sources of stress?

∎ How is it that too much of a good thing can make you ill?

∎ How do irrational beliefs create or compound stress?

∎ What kinds of disasters are there? How do they affect us?

∎ How do environmental factors such as noise, temperature, pollution, and crowding affect our adjustment?

Nearly half of adult Americans (47% according to a recent survey) are concerned with the amount of stress in their lives ("Americans Engage," 2006). And it is no wonder, as there are many sources of stress. In this module we consider several major sources of stress: daily hassles; life changes; pain and discomfort; conflict; irrational beliefs; Type A behavior; and environmental factors such as disasters, noise, and crowding. If you are like most college students, you probably experience at least some of these sources. It's no surprise, then, that stress is the number-one reason that college students seek help at college counseling centers (see Table 3.1) (Gallagher, 1996).

Table 3.1 ∎ Students' Reasons for Seeking Counseling

Reason	Percent Reporting Reason
Stress, anxiety, nervousness	51
Romantic relationships	47
Low self-esteem, self-confidence	42
Depression	41
Family relationships	37
Academic problems, grades	29
Transition to the career world	25
Loneliness	25
Financial problems	24

Many Americans also say that the level of stress in their lives is on the rise. The American Psychological Association recently conducted a nationwide survey, which showed that nearly half of Americans say that stress has increased during the past five years and one-third say they face extreme levels of stress in their lives (American Psychological Association, 2006, 2007a). Stress is also taking its toll. Nearly half (43%) of those surveyed in the APA poll reported negative psychological and physical health problems resulting from stress (see Figure 3.1).

Figure 3.1

Psychological and Physical Symptoms Resulting from Stress

Americans report many symptoms of stress, especially such psychological symptoms as irritability, anger, nervousness, and lack of motivation, as well as such physical symptoms as fatigue, headaches, and upset stomach.

Source: Stress in America Survey, American Psychological Association, 2007b. Reprinted with permission.

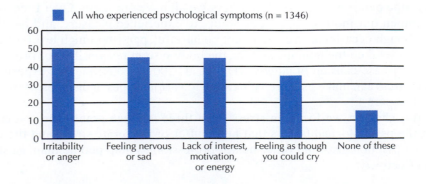

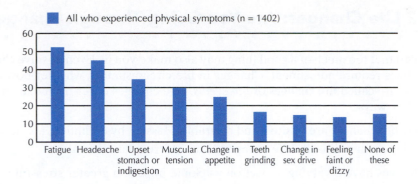

All who experienced physical symptoms (n = 1402)

(bar chart with y-axis from 0 to 60 and categories: Fatigue, Headeache, Upset stomach or indigestion, Muscular tension, Change in appetite, Teeth grinding, Change in sex drive, Feeling faint or dizzy, None of these)

3.1.1 Daily Hassles: The Stress of Everyday Life

Which straw will break the camel's back? The last straw, according to the saying. Similarly, stresses can pile up until we can no longer cope with them. Some of these stresses are daily hassles. **Daily hassles** are regularly occurring conditions and experiences that can threaten or harm our well-being (see Figure 3.2). Others are life changes. Lazarus and his colleagues (1985) analyzed a scale that measures daily hassles and their opposites—termed **uplifts**—and found that hassles could be grouped as follows:

1 *Household hassles:* preparing meals, shopping, and home maintenance.
2 *Health hassles:* physical illness, concern about medical treatment, and side effects of medication.
3 *Time-pressure hassles:* having too many things to do, too many responsibilities, and not enough time.
4 *Inner-concern hassles:* being lonely and fearful of confrontation.
5 *Environmental hassles:* crime, neighborhood deterioration, and traffic noise.
6 *Financial responsibility hassles:* concern about owing money such as mortgage payments and loan installments.
7 *Work hassles:* job dissatisfaction, not liking one's duties at work, and problems with co-workers.
8 *Future security hassles:* concerns about job security, taxes, property investments, stock market swings, and retirement. These hassles are linked to psychological variables such as nervousness, worrying, inability to get started, feelings of sadness, and feelings of loneliness.

▌**Daily hassles** Routine sources of annoyance or aggravation that have a negative impact on health.

▌**Uplifts** Lazarus's term for regularly occurring enjoyable experiences.

Maartje van Caspel/iStockphoto

Daily Hassles

Traffic jams... running late... juggling work and school demands... worrying about paying bills These are just some examples of the common stressful occurrences of daily life. What are the hassles you regularly face? What can you do about them to reduce your stress burden?

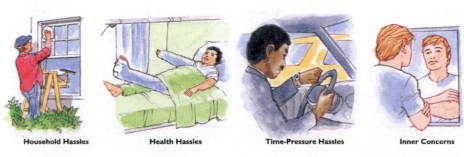

Household Hassles   Health Hassles   Time-Pressure Hassles   Inner Concerns

Environmental Hassles   Financial Responsibility Hassles   Work Hassles   Future Security Hassles

Figure 3.2
Daily Hassles
Daily hassles are recurring sources of aggravation. Which of the hassles shown here are regular parts of your life?

3.1.2 Life Changes: Are You Going Through Changes?

▌ **Life changes** Major changes in life circumstances, such as getting married, starting (or losing) a job, or losing a loved one.

Not All Stress Is Bad
Positive life changes, such as the birth of a child or a promotion at work, can be sources of stress. They increase the demands placed on us to adjust. Though positive life changes may make life more meaningful and fulfilling, even good stress can affect our health when it strains our ability to cope and adds to our general stress burden.

We noted that too much of a good thing may also make you ill. Even positive changes in our lives require adjustment. Changes in life circumstances, whether positive or negative, are called **life changes** or *life events*. Life changes differ from daily hassles in two key ways:

1 Many life changes are positive and desirable. Hassles, by definition, are negative.

2 Hassles occur regularly. Life changes occur at irregular intervals.

Life changes have a varying impact on us. Some impose a greater stressful burden than others. As you can see in Figure 3.3, negative changes such as divorce or death typically impose a greater stressful burden than positive changes, such as marriage or going on vacation.

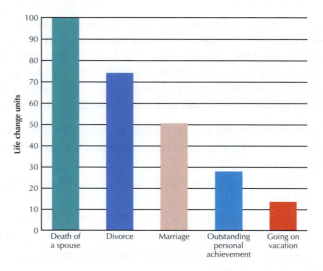

Figure 3.3
Life Changes and Stress
Both positive and negative life changes can be stressful. This graph shows the stressful burden assigned to various life changes. As you can see, even going on vacation incurs some stress, though certainly not of the same magnitude as divorce or the death of a spouse.

How Much Are You Stressed?

Self-Assessment

How stressful is your life? The College Life Stress Inventory provides a measure of stress associated with life changes or events that college students may encounter. Circle each of the events that you have experienced during the past 12 months. Then sum the stress ratings for each of the circled responses to yield a total stress score. The scoring key located at the end of the chapter can help you interpret your score.

EVENT	STRESS RATING
1. Being raped	100
2. Finding out that you are HIV-positive	100
3. Being accused of rape	98
4. Death of a close friend	97
5. Death of a close family member	96
6. Contracting a sexually transmitted disease (other than AIDS)	94
7. Concerns about being pregnant	91
8. Finals week	90

9. Concerns about your partner being pregnant	90
10. Oversleeping for an exam	89
11. Flunking a class	89
12. Having a boyfriend or girlfriend cheat on you	85
13. Ending a steady dating relationship	85
14. Serious illness in a close friend or family member	85
15. Financial difficulties	84
16. Writing a major term paper	83
17. Being caught cheating on a test	83
18. Drunk driving	82
19. Sense of overload in school or work	82
20. Two exams in one day	80
21. Cheating on your boyfriend or girlfriend	77
22. Getting married	76
23. Negative consequences of drinking or drug use	75
24. Depression or crisis in your best friend	73
25. Difficulties with parents	73
26. Talking in front of a class	72
27. Lack of sleep	69
28. Change in housing situation (hassles, moves)	69
29. Competing or performing in public	69
30. Getting in a physical fight	66
31. Difficulties with a roommate	66
32. Job changes (applying, new job, work hassles)	65
33. Declaring a major or concerns about future plans	65
34. A class you hate	62
35. Drinking or use of drugs	61
36. Confrontations with professors	60
37. Starting a new semester	58
38. Going on a first date	57
39. Registration	55
40. Maintaining a steady dating relationship	55
41. Commuting to campus or work, or both	54
42. Peer pressures	53
43. Being away from home for the first time	53
44. Getting sick	52
45. Concerns about your appearance	52
46. Getting straight A's	51
47. A difficult class that you love	48
48. Making new friends; getting along with friends	47
49. Fraternity or sorority rush	47
50. Falling asleep in class	40
51. Attending an athletic event (e.g., football game)	20

Source: M. J. Renner & R. S. Mackin (1998). A life stress instrument for classroom use. *Teaching of Psychology, 25,* 46–48. Reprinted with permission.

For an interactive version of this self-assessment exercise, go to www.wileyplus.com

The Challenges of Acculturative Stress

The feelings of tension and anxiety that accompany efforts to adapt to or adopt the orientation and values of the dominant culture are termed **acculturative stress**. Research has shown that for African Americans, acculturative stress is embedded within a history of racist treatment and is associated with feelings of anxiety and tension and physical health problems, such as hypertension. Exposure to racism and discrimination is linked to many adverse effects, including diminished self-esteem,

▮ **Acculturative stress** The feelings of tension and anxiety that accompany efforts to adapt to or adopt the orientation and values of the dominant culture.

feelings of alienation and role confusion (confusion over who one is and what one stands for), and poorer psychological and physical health (e.g., King, 2005; Mays, Cochran, & Barnes, 2007). Because of such links, investigators suggest that African American parents should help their children become more aware of the value of their own culture to help buffer the effects of racism and acculturative stress (Thompson, Anderson, & Bakeman, 2000). Developing a strong ethnic identity and taking pride in one's own culture can bolster a person's ability to cope with the stressful effects of racism and prejudice (Greene et al., 2006). A recent study of ninth-graders showed that stronger ethnic identity also predicted greater academic success among students from Mexican and Chinese backgrounds (Fuligni, Witkow, & Garcia, 2005).

3.1.3 Ethnic Identity as a Buffer Against Stress

Don Terry was experiencing acculturative stress. Don Terry's mother is European American; his father is African American. When he was a child, he said to his mother, "You're white and Dad's black, so what does that make me?" (Terry, 2000). Half European American, half African American, he had a foot in two cultures and felt compelled to be at home in each. But it's not easy. African American students whose values are at variance with those of the dominant culture often feel pressured to change. They feel compelled to acculturate, to become bicultural—capable of getting by among African Americans and European Americans—in an often-hostile environment. "Oh, I see," she said. "Well, you're half-black and you're half-white, so you're the best of both worlds."

However, life experiences taught Don that in the United States it is difficult, if not impossible, to be "half" European American and "half" African American. Consider some of his experiences at college and how he "chose" to be African American. Don chose to attend Oberlin College because of its reputation for enlightened race relations. But when he began his freshman year, he found a very different picture. When he walked into the dining room, he found African American students sitting together at one group of tables and European American students at others. African American fans usually sat with other African American fans at football and basketball games, while European American fans sat with European Americans.

One night, Don was visiting a European American girl and her European American roommate in their dorm. They were just chatting, with the door open. Another African American student was there, flirting with the roommate. Don was about to leave when a European American girl who was passing by stuck in her head. Looking disgusted, she said "What's this? A soul-brother session?" Don was stunned. Why was race a part of it? He and his friend were just chatting with a couple of girls and getting nowhere. The girl Don was visiting looked embarrassed. He didn't know if she was embarrassed about her neighbor sticking her nose in or because her neighbor had "caught" a couple of African American males in her room.

Don was fed up. He embraced blackness as a shield and a cause. He enrolled in courses in Black Studies. The courses were crucial to his academic and personal development. They helped him forge an identity. They also helped him to understand—for the first time—his African American father's anger toward the discriminatory dominant culture.

Don got in touch with his disappointment and his rage that race was so important, even at his "progressive" college. He was angry that he could not be himself—a complex individual named Don Terry, with a European American mother and an African American father. Instead, he saw that he would always be lumped in the racial category of being black and treated like a caricature, not a person. "Disgusted by the world's refusal to see me as mixed and individual," writes Don Terry (2000), "I chose 'blackness.'" And part of that identity comprised racist feelings of his own.

Like Don Terry, African Americans hear themselves called derogatory names. They hear people telling insulting jokes about them. They are still barred from many social and occupational opportunities. They are taunted. They are sometimes the butt of physical aggression. Their parents often warn them that if they are stopped by the police, they are to keep their hands low and in clear sight and are to avoid sounding threatening; otherwise, they may be shot.

It is no secret that African Americans encounter racism in their interactions with European Americans and other people, even in "progressive" places like Oberlin College. Some European Americans consider them to be a criminal class. African American college students, most of whom attend predominantly European American colleges and universities, also encounter racism. In addition to worrying about grades, dating, finances, health, and all the other hassles experienced by college students, they are also hassled by students who think that they do not belong at "their" college or university. Even "open-minded" European American students often assume that the African American students were admitted on the basis of affirmative action or other racial programs rather than on the basis of their own individual merits.

©Lawrence Migdale/Getty Images, Inc

Ethnic Self-Identity
Pride in one's cultural heritage and ethnic identity may help buffer the stressful effects of racism and prejudice.

3.1.4 Coping with Acculturative Stress

C. Patricia Thompson and her colleagues (2000) note that many African American college students have poorly defined personal identities and are subject to being buffeted about by acculturative stress. Some African American students attempt to cope by becoming as Eurocentric as possible. Others undergo a process that may begin with idealization of the dominant culture in the United States but ends with a solid African American identity. Some event—perhaps personal exposure to prejudice, realization of the horror of historic atrocities such as lynchings, or the race-related misfortunes of a friend or family member—causes them to reject Eurocentric culture and undergo a search for an African American identity. They immerse themselves in African American culture and withdraw from unnecessary contacts with European Americans. Don Terry writes that at this stage he chose "blackness" and took coursework in "black nationalism." Rejection of the dominant culture helps foster feelings of hostility toward European Americans. The forging of links with other African Americans and the adopting of pride in African American culture eventually work to lessen feelings of hostility and resentment so that individuals like Don Terry become calmer, more secure, and less hostile. Individuals who emerge with an African American viewpoint but who can cope with and even befriend European Americans appear to experience the least acculturative stress (Thompson et al., 2000). That, perhaps, is where Don Terry, a reporter for the *New York Times*, is today.

3.1.5 Pain and Discomfort: Your Body's Warning Signal

For many people, pain is a major adjustment problem. Headaches, backaches, toothaches—these are only a few of the types of pain that most of us encounter from time to time. According to a national Gallup survey of 2,002 adults in the United States (Arthritis Foundation, 2000), 89% experienced pain at least once a month. More than half (55%) of people age 65 and over say they experience pain daily; sad to say, these people are most likely to attribute pain to getting older (88%), for example, being more likely to develop arthritis. By contrast, people aged 18 to 34 are more likely to attribute pain to tension or stress (73%), to overwork (64%), or to their lifestyle (51%). When we assume that there is nothing we can do about pain, we are less likely to try. Yet 43% of Americans say that pain curtails their activities, and 50% say that pain puts them in a bad mood. There are also a number of gender differences in the experiencing of and response to pain, as shown in Table 3.2.

Table 3.2 ∎ Results of Pain Survey of American Adults		
Percent who report...	Women	Men
Experiencing daily pain	46	37
Feeling they have a great deal of control over their pain	39	48
Feeling that tension and stress are their leading causes of pain	72	56
Going to see the doctor about pain only when other people urge them to do it	27	38
Balancing the demands of work and family life to be the key cause of their pain	35	24
Frequent headaches	17	8
Frequent backaches	24	19
Arthritis	20	15
Sore feet	25	17

Source of data: Arthritis Foundation, 2000.

Pain means something is wrong in the body. Yet pain is also adaptive, if unpleasant, because it motivates us to do something about it. For some of us, however, chronic pain—pain that lasts once injuries or illnesses have cleared—saps our vitality and interferes with the pleasures of everyday life.

We can sense pain throughout most of the body, but it is usually sharpest where nerve endings are densely packed, as in the fingers and face. Pain can also be felt deep within the body, as in abdominal pain and back pain. Even though headaches may seem to originate deep inside the head, there are no nerve endings for pain in the brain. Brain surgery can be done with a local anesthetic that prevents the patient from feeling the drilling of a small hole through the skull. Can it be that the lack of nerve endings in the brain is evolution's way of saying that, normally speaking, when someone has a reason to experience pain deep inside the brain, it might be too late to do anything about it?

Pain usually originates at the point of contact, as with a stubbed toe. The pain message is relayed from the point of contact to the spinal cord and from there to the brain, making us aware of the location and intensity of the damage. In response to pain signals, the brain releases chemicals, including **prostaglandins**, which heighten circulation to the injured area, causing the redness and swelling that we call inflammation. Inflammation serves the biological function of attracting infection-fighting blood cells to the affected area to protect it against invading germs. **Analgesic** drugs such as aspirin and ibuprofen work by inhibiting the production of prostaglandins.

A leading expert of pain, Ronald Melzack (1999), points to various factors in our physiology and psychology that determine our reaction to pain. For example, our emotional response affects the degree of pain, and so do the ways in which we respond to stress. For example, if the pain derives from an object we fear, perhaps a knife or needle, we may experience more pain. If we perceive that there is nothing we can do to change the situation, perception of pain may increase. If we have self-confidence and a history of successful response to stress, the perception of pain may diminish.

Endorphins

In response to pain, the brain also triggers release of **endorphins**, which are a class of neurotransmitters, or chemical messengers, involved in transmitting signals within the nervous system. The word *endorphin* is the contraction of *endogenous morphine*. *Endogenous* means "developing from within." Endorphins are similar to the narcotic morphine in their functions, and we produce them naturally in our own bodies. Endorphins block pain by "locking into" receptors in the nervous system for chemicals that transmit pain messages to the brain. Once the endorphin "key" is in the "lock," the chemicals that carry pain signals are prevented from transmitting their messages.

∎ **Prostaglandins** Substances derived from fatty acids that are involved in body responses such as inflammation and menstrual cramping.

∎ **Analgesic** A drug that helps relieve pain.

∎ **Endorphins** Neurotransmitters that are composed of chains of amino acids and are functionally similar to morphine.

Coping with Pain

Coping with that age-old enemy—pain—has traditionally been a medical issue. The primary treatment has been chemical, as in the use of painkilling drugs. However, psychological factors play a major role in how people cope with pain. For example, the availability of social support, of people showing concern and lending a helping hand, can help blunt the psychological effects of enduring pain. Here we focus on some other psychological factors involved in helping people manage pain more effectively.

Obtaining Accurate Information
Many pain sufferers try not to think about why things hurt, but remaining in the dark about the source of their pain may prevent them from obtaining the medical treatment they need to diagnose and treat the underlying problem. Physicians, for their part, often neglect the human aspects of relating to their patients. That is, they focus on diagnosing and treating the causes of pain, but they often fail to discuss with patients the meaning of the pain and what the patient can expect. Obtaining accurate medical information can reduce stress by helping people maintain a sense of control over their situation. They feel they are doing something about their medical condition, rather than simply trying to ignore it.

Using Distraction and Fantasy
Experimental studies show that that people report lower levels of pain if they focus their attention away from their pain (Coderre, Mogil, & Bushnell, 2003). Distraction can take many forms, from exercising to becoming immersed in a good book or movie. Imagine that you've injured your leg and you're waiting to see the doctor in an emergency room. You can distract yourself by focusing on details of your environment. You can count ceiling tiles or the hairs on the back of a finger. You can describe (or criticize!) the clothes of medical personnel or passersby.

Using Hypnosis
In 1842, London physician W. S. Ward amputated a man's leg after using a rather strange anesthetic: **hypnosis**. According to reports, the man experienced no discomfort. Several years later, operations were being performed routinely under hypnosis at his infirmary. Today, hypnosis is often used to reduce chronic pain and as an anesthetic in dentistry, childbirth, and even in some forms of surgery (e.g., Coderre et al., 2003; Keefe, Abernethy, & Campbell, 2005).

Scholars continue to debate not only how hypnosis works but even what it is. One prominent view is that hypnosis is a *trance state*, or altered state of awareness, in which the person becomes highly suggestible, or responsive to suggestions. Other psychologists reject the view that hypnosis involves any special state of awareness or "trance." Their view is that hypnosis is best understood in terms of the social dynamics between the hypnotist and the subject—that by adopting the role of a good hypnotic subject, people obligingly follow along with the hypnotist's directions.

Although investigators continue to debate the nature of hypnosis, the practice is widely used to help people cope better with nagging pain. The hypnotist may instruct the pain patient that he or she feels nothing or that the pain is distant and slight. Hypnosis can also aid in the use of distraction and fantasy. For example, the hypnotist can instruct the person to imagine that he or she is relaxing on a warm, exotic shore. Although hypnosis may have therapeutic benefits in treating pain, it should be used only as an adjunct to treatment, not as a substitute for conventional treatments.

Practicing Relaxation Training and Biofeedback Training
When we are in pain, we often tense up. Tensing muscles is uncomfortable in itself, arouses the sympathetic nervous system, and focuses our attention on the pain. Relaxation counteracts these self-defeating behavior patterns. Some psychological methods of relaxation focus on relaxing muscle groups (see *Psychology in Daily Life*). Some involve breathing exercises, and others use relaxing imagery: The imagery distracts the person and deepens feelings of relaxation. **Biofeedback training (BFT)** is also used to help people relax targeted muscle groups that are often tensed during periods of pain. BFT has been used effectively in treating many forms of pain, including headache and lower back and jaw pain (Gatchel, 2001; Nestoriuc, Rief, & Martin, 2008).

▮ **Hypnosis** An altered state of consciousness associated with a heightened susceptibility to suggestions.

▮ **Biofeedback training (BFT)** A means of training people to gain some degree of control over internal bodily responses through the use of physiological monitoring equipment that provides feedback (information) about changes in these responses.

Tuning in Your Body

Through biofeedback training, people learn to alter certain physical responses in their bodies, such as states of muscle tension. Reducing muscle tension in the forehead may help lessen pain associated with tension headaches.

Cindy Charles/PhotoEdit

Taking Control of Your Thoughts   Taking control of your thoughts is an important coping skill for dealing with persistent pain (Nuland, 2003). Pain patients who hold pessimistic thoughts, such as believing that their pain will never end, tend to cope more poorly with pain than those who maintain more hopeful, optimistic attitudes. More generally, maintaining a sense of control—seeing ourselves as taking an active role in managing pain rather than becoming a helpless victim—can increase our ability to cope with pain.

Closing the "Gate" on Pain   Simple remedies like applying an ice pack or rubbing the injured area frequently help relieve pain. Why? One possible answer lies in the *gate theory of pain* originated by Melzack (1999). From this perspective, a gating mechanism in the spinal cord opens and closes, letting pain messages get through to the brain or shutting them out. Note that the "gate" is not an actual physical structure in the spinal cord, but a representation of a pattern of the nervous system activity that results in controlling the flow of pain signals through the spinal cord to the brain. Using an ice pack, or even rubbing the injured area, transmits stimulation to the spinal cord that can compete with pain signals (Coderre et al., 2003). Consequently, pain signals may be prevented from reaching the brain. Think of it as a switchboard being flooded with calls. The flooding prevents many of the calls (the pain signals) from getting through.

If you feel pain in a toe, for example, try squeezing all your toes. When you feel pain in your calf, rub your thighs. People around you may wonder what you're doing, but you're entitled to try to "flood the switchboard" so that some pain messages don't get through. But for sudden or persistent pain, don't simply treat the symptoms—see a physician. Pain is a sign that something is wrong in the body that requires medical attention.

Acupuncture   For thousands of years, Chinese doctors have been inserting thin needles into particular points in the body and rotating them in order to relieve pain. This practice, called **acupuncture**, has been used to treat a wide range of disorders in addition to pain, from asthma to drug addiction. Though evidence of its effectiveness is mixed, the strongest evidence supporting the benefits of acupuncture involves treatment of pain, such as chronic headaches, and nausea (Vickers et al., 2004). However, recent evidence suggests that the benefits of acupuncture can be explained by a placebo effect, rather than by the insertion and manipulation of needles (Brinkhaus et al., 2006; Haake et al., 2007; Linde et al., 2005).

∎ **Acupuncture** A traditional Chinese healing practice consisting of inserting and rotating thin needles in various parts of the body in the belief that it releases the body's natural healing energy.

3.1.6 Frustration: When the Wall Is Too High

You may wish to be a point guard for the varsity basketball team but lose the ball every time you dribble. You may have been denied a job or an educational opportunity because of your ethnic background or favoritism. These situations give rise to **frustration**, the emotional state that occurs when a person's attempts to attain a goal are thwarted or blocked (see Figure 3.4, part A). Frustration is another source of stress. Many sources of frustration are obvious. Adolescents are used to being told they are too young to wear makeup, drive, go out, engage in sexual activity, spend money, drink, or work. Age is the barrier that requires them to delay gratification. We may frustrate ourselves as adults if our goals are set too high or if our self-demands are irrational. If we try to earn other people's approval at all costs, or insist on performing perfectly in all of our undertakings, we doom ourselves to failure and frustration.

∎ **Frustration** The thwarting of a desire to obtain a goal.

The Frustrations of Commuting

One of the common frustrations of contemporary life is commuting. Distance, time, and driving conditions are some of the barriers that lie between us and our work or school. How many of us fight the freeways or crowd ourselves into train cars or buses for an hour or more before the workday begins? For most people, the stresses of commuting are mild but persistent. Still, lengthy commutes on crowded highways are linked to increases in heart rate, blood pressure, chest pain, and other signs of stress. Noise, humidity, and air pollution all contribute to the frustration involved in driving to work. If you commute by car, try to pick times and roads that provide lower volumes of traffic. It may be worth your while to take a longer, more scenic route that has less stop-and-go traffic.

Psychological Barriers

Anxiety and fear may serve as emotional barriers that prevent us from acting effectively to meet our goals. A high school senior who wishes to attend an out-of-state college may be frustrated by the fear of leaving home. A young adult may not ask an attractive person out on a date because of fear of rejection. A woman may be frustrated in her desire to move up the corporate ladder, fearing that co-workers, friends, and family will view her assertiveness as compromising her femininity.

Tolerance for Frustration

Getting ahead is often a gradual process that requires us to live with some frustration and delay gratification. Yet our **tolerance for frustration** may fluctuate. Stress heaped upon stress can lower our tolerance. We may laugh off a flat tire on a good day. But if it is raining, the flat may seem like the last straw. People who have encountered frustration but learned that it is possible to surmount barriers or find substitute goals are more tolerant of frustration than those who have never experienced it or have experienced it in excess.

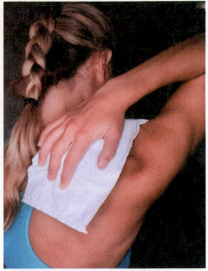

Corbis/SuperStock

Blocking Pain
Applying an ice pack or rubbing an injured area may temporarily help relieve pain by blocking pain messages from reaching the brain. But pain is a signal that something is wrong and requires medical attention.

▌ **Tolerance for frustration** The ability to delay gratification, to maintain self-control when a goal is thwarted.

3.1.7 Conflict: "Darned If You Do, Darned If You Don't"

Should you eat dessert or try to stick to your diet? Should you live on campus, which is more convenient, or should you rent an apartment, where you may have more independence? Choices like these can place us in conflict. In psychology, conflict is the feeling of being pulled in two or more directions by opposing motives. **Conflict** is frustrating and stressful. Psychologists often classify conflicts into four types: approach–approach, avoidance–avoidance, approach–avoidance, and multiple approach–avoidance.

Approach–approach conflict (Figure 3.4, part B) is the least stressful type. Here, each of two goals is desirable, and both are within reach. You may not be able to decide between pizza or tacos, Tom or Dick, or a trip to Nassau or Hawaii. Such conflicts are usually resolved by making a decision. People who experience this type of conflict may vacillate until they make a decision.

Avoidance–avoidance conflict (Figure 3.4, part C) is more stressful because you are motivated to avoid each of two negative goals. However, avoiding one of them requires approaching the other. You may be fearful of visiting the dentist but also afraid that your teeth will decay if you do not make an appointment and go. You may not want to contribute to the Association for the Advancement of Lost Causes, but you fear that your friends will consider you cheap or uncommitted if you do not. Each goal in an avoidance–avoidance conflict is negative. When an avoidance–avoidance conflict is highly stressful and no resolution is in sight, some people withdraw from the conflict by focusing on other matters or doing nothing. Highly conflicted people have been known to refuse to get up in the morning and start the day.

▌ **Conflict** A condition characterized by opposing motives, in which gratification of one motive prevents gratification of the other.

▌ **Approach–approach conflict** Conflict involving two positive but mutually exclusive goals.

▌ **Avoidance–avoidance conflict** Conflict involving two negative goals, with avoidance of one requiring approach of the other.

Figure 3.4

Models for Frustration and Conflict

Part A is a model for frustration in which a person (P) has a motive (M) to reach a goal (G) but is thwarted by a barrier (B). Part B shows an approach–approach conflict, in which the person cannot simultaneously approach two positive goals. Part C shows an avoidance–avoidance conflict in which avoiding one negative goal requires approaching another. Part D shows an approach–avoidance conflict in which the same goal has positive and negative features. Part E shows a multiple—in this case, double— approach–avoidance conflict in which more than one goal has positive and negative features.

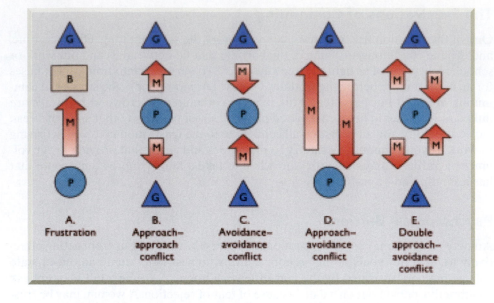

▌**Approach–avoidance conflict** Conflict involving a goal with positive and negative features.

▌**Multiple approach–avoidance conflict** Conflict involving two or more goals, each of which has positive and negative aspects.

When the same goal produces both approach and avoidance motives, we have an **approach–avoidance conflict** (Figure 3.4, part D). People and things have their pluses and minuses, their good points and their bad points. A cheesecake may be delicious, but oh, the calories! Goals that produce mixed motives may seem attractive from a distance but undesirable from up close. Many couples repeatedly break up and then reunite. When they are apart and lonely, they may recall each other fondly and swear that they could make the relationship work if they got together again. But after they spend time together again, they may find themselves thinking, "How could I ever have believed that this so-and-so would change?"

The most complex form of conflict is the **multiple approach–avoidance conflict**, in which each of several alternative courses of action has pluses and minuses. An example with two goals is shown in Figure 3.4, part E. This sort of conflict might arise on the eve of an examination, when you are faced with the choice of studying or, say, going to a film. Each alternative has both positive and negative aspects: "Studying's a bore, but I won't have to worry about flunking. I'd love to see the movie, but I'd just be worrying about how I'll do tomorrow."

All forms of conflict entail motives that aim in opposite directions. When one motive is much stronger than the other, such as when you feel starved and are only slightly concerned about your weight, it will probably not be too stressful to act in accordance with the powerful motive—in this case, to eat.

When each conflicting motive is powerful, however, you may experience high levels of stress and confusion about the proper course of action. At such times you are faced with the need to make a decision. Yet decision making can also be stressful, especially when there is no clear correct choice.

3.1.8 Irrational Beliefs: Ten Doorways to Distress

Psychologist Albert Ellis (1913-2007) believed that our beliefs about events, as well as the events themselves, can be stressors that challenge our ability to adjust (Ellis & Dryden, 1996). Consider a case in which a person is fired from a job and is anxious and depressed about it. It may seem logical that losing the job is responsible for the misery, but Ellis points out how the individual's beliefs about the loss compound his or her misery.

Let us examine this situation according to Ellis's A → B → C approach. Losing the job is an activating event (A). The eventual outcome, or consequence (C), is misery.

Between the activating event (A) and the consequence (C), however, lie beliefs (B), such as these: "This job was the most important thing in my life," "What a no-good failure I am," "My family will starve," "I'll never find a job as good," "There's nothing I can do about it." Beliefs such as these compound misery, foster helplessness, and divert us from planning and deciding what to do next. The belief that "There's nothing I can do about it" fosters helplessness. The belief that "I am a no-good failure" internalizes the blame and may be an exaggeration. The belief that "My family will starve" may also be an exaggeration. We can diagram the situation like this:

$$\text{Activating events} \rightarrow \text{Beliefs} \rightarrow \text{Consequences}$$
$$\text{or}$$
$$A \rightarrow B \rightarrow C$$

Anxieties about the future and depression over a loss are normal and to be expected. However, the beliefs of the person who lost the job tend to catastrophize the extent of the loss and contribute to anxiety and depression. By heightening the individual's emotional reaction to the loss and fostering feelings of helplessness, these beliefs also impair coping ability. They lower the person's self-efficacy expectations.

Ellis proposes that many of us adopt irrational beliefs that become our personal doorways to unhappiness. He argues that we make ourselves miserable by adopting the kinds of irrational beliefs listed in Table 3.3. When we hold to these kinds of beliefs, we inevitably find that either we or the world at large comes up short, which leaves us feeling upset, angry, or depressed.

Ellis finds it understandable that we would want the approval of others but irrational to believe that we cannot survive without it. It would be nice to be competent in everything we do, but it's unreasonable to expect it. Sure, it would be nice to be able to serve and volley like a tennis pro, but most of us don't have the time or natural ability to perfect our game. Demanding perfection prevents us from going out on the court on weekends and batting the ball back and forth just for fun. Belief number 5 is a prescription for perpetual emotional upheaval. Belief numbers 7 and 9 lead to feelings of helplessness and demoralization. Sure, Ellis might say, childhood experiences can explain the origins of irrational beliefs, but it is our own cognitive appraisal—here and now—that causes us to be miserable.

Research findings support the connections between irrational beliefs (e.g., excessive dependence on social approval and perfectionism) and feelings of anxiety and depression (Blatt et al., 1995). Perfectionists are also more likely than other people to commit suicide when they are depressed (Pilkonis, 1996).

Table 3.3 ▮ Ellis's Irrational Beliefs

Irrational Belief 1: You must have the sincere love and approval of almost everyone who is important to you almost all of the time.

Irrational Belief 2: You must succeed in virtually everything you attempt in order to feel that you are a competent person.

Irrational Belief 3: Things must go the way you want them to go or life is just awful.

Irrational Belief 4: Other people must treat everyone fairly and justly, and you can't stand it when they don't.

Irrational Belief 5: When there is danger or fear in your world, you must be preoccupied with it and be continually upset by it.

Irrational Belief 6: People and things should turn out better than they do. It's awful and horrible when you don't find quick solutions to life's hassles.

Irrational Belief 7: Your emotional misery stems from external pressures that you have little or no ability to control. Unless these external pressures change, you must remain miserable.

Irrational Belief 8: It is easier to evade life's responsibilities and problems than to face them and undertake new challenges.

Irrational Belief 9: Your past has a determining influence on your feelings and behavior today.

Irrational Belief 10: You can achieve happiness by inertia and inaction.

©Tom McCarthy//PhotoEdit

I Must Make This Sale or Else!
Do you believe you must succeed in virtually everything you set out to accomplish in order to feel good about yourself? Or can you take disappointments in stride without feeling like a total failure? Which, if any, of Ellis's irrational beliefs describe your own views?

▌ **Type A behavior pattern** A pattern of stress-producing behavior, characterized by aggressiveness, perfectionism, unwillingness to relinquish control, and a sense of time urgency.

Ulli Seer/Stone/Getty Images, Inc

Are You Type A?
Do you feel rushed or pressured all the time? Are you quicker to lose patience than most people? Are you intense, even at play? Do you find it difficult to take things easy? How much of the stress in your life is self-imposed?

Like other cognitive-behavioral psychologists who examine how our thoughts and behavior influence each other, Albert Ellis shows us how we can be our own worst enemies when stressors strike. For example, do any of these experiences sound familiar?

1 You have difficulty with the first item on a test and become convinced that you will flunk?

2 You want to express your genuine feelings but think that you might upset another person by doing so?

3 You haven't been able to get to sleep for 15 minutes and assume that you will lie awake the whole night and feel "wrecked" in the morning?

4 You're not sure what decision to make, so you try to put your conflicts out of your mind by going out, playing cards, or watching TV?

5 You decide not to play tennis or go jogging because your form isn't perfect and you're in less than perfect condition?

If you have had such experiences, it may be because you harbor irrational beliefs of the sort identified by Albert Ellis—beliefs that make you overly concerned about the approval of others (experience 2) or that are perfectionistic (experience 5). They may lead you to think that you can relieve yourself of life's problems by pretending that they do not exist (experience 4) or that a minor setback must lead to greater problems (experiences 1 and 3). The unjustified assumption that an event is or will become awful is called catastrophizing. That is, you turn a setback into a catastrophe.

How, then, do we change irrational or catastrophizing thoughts? Cognitive-behavioral psychologists present a challengingly simple answer: We change these thoughts by changing them. However, change can require some work. Before we can change our thoughts, we must first become aware of them. Cognitive-behavioral psychologists (e.g., Marks & Dar, 2000) outline a multistep procedure for controlling the irrational or catastrophizing thoughts that often accompany feelings of anxiety, conflict, or tension.

First, develop awareness of the thoughts that seem to be making you miserable by careful self-examination. Study the examples of irrational beliefs in Table 3.3 and ask yourself whether any of them rings true of you. Also, when you encounter anxiety or frustration, pay close attention to your thoughts.

Next, evaluate the accuracy of the thoughts. Are they guiding you toward a solution, or are they compounding your problems? Do they reflect reality, or do they blow things out of proportion? Do they misplace the blame for failure or shortcomings? And so on.

Then, prepare thoughts that are incompatible with the irrational or catastrophizing thoughts and practice saying them firmly to yourself. (If nobody is nearby, why not say them firmly aloud?)

Finally, reward yourself with a mental pat on the back for making effective changes in your beliefs and thought patterns.

Controlling catastrophizing thoughts reduces the impact of a stressor, whether it is pain, anxiety, or feelings of frustration. It gives you a chance to develop a plan for effective action. When effective action is not possible, controlling our thoughts increases our capacity to tolerate discomfort. So does relaxing, which we discuss in *Psychology in Daily Life.*

The Type A Behavior Pattern: Burning Out from Within?

Some people create stress for themselves through the **Type A behavior pattern**. Type A people are highly driven, competitive, impatient, and aggressive. They feel rushed and under pressure all the time and keep one eye firmly glued to the clock. They are not only prompt for appointments but often early. They eat, walk, and talk rapidly and become restless when others work slowly. They attempt to dominate group discussions.

Type A people find it difficult to give up control or share power. They are often reluctant to delegate authority in the workplace, and as a result they increase their own workloads.

Type A people find it difficult just to go out on the tennis court and bat the ball back and forth. They watch their form, perfect their strokes, and demand continual self-improvement. They hold to the irrational belief that they must be perfectly competent and achieving in everything they undertake.

Type B people, in contrast, relax more readily and focus more on the quality of life. They are less ambitious and less impatient, and they pace themselves. They are able to stop and smell the roses rather than just rushing by them on the way to a meeting.

Are you a Type A person? The accompanying self-assessment should afford you some insight into this question.

Reducing Type A Behavior
Even jackrabbits slow down at times. If you are Type A, what steps can you take to slow down the pace of your daily life?

3.1.9 Environmental Stressors: It Can Be Dangerous Out There

We may face many stressors in the environment, from the routine stressors of blaring traffic noise on city streets to traumatic stressors, such as natural and technological disasters and acts of terrorism.

Are You Type A or Type B?

Self-Assessment

Complete this self-assessment by placing a checkmark under Yes if the behavior pattern described is typical of you and under No if it is not. Try to work rapidly and leave no items blank. Then read the section on Type A behavior and turn to the scoring key at the end of the chapter.

Do You:	Yes	No
1. Strongly accent key words in your everyday speech?	___	___
2. Eat and walk quickly?	___	___
3. Believe that children should be taught to be competitive?	___	___
4. Feel restless when watching a slow worker?	___	___
5. Hurry other people to get on with what they're trying to say?	___	___
6. Find it highly aggravating to be stuck in traffic or waiting for a seat at a restaurant?	___	___
7. Continue to think about your own problems and business even when listening to someone else?	___	___
8. Try to eat and shave or drive and jot down notes at the same time?	___	___
9. Catch up on your work while on vacations?	___	___
10. Feel guilty when you spend time just relaxing?	___	___
11. Find that you're so wrapped up in your work that you no longer notice office decorations or the scenery when you commute?	___	___
12. Find yourself concerned with getting more things rather than developing your creativity and social concerns?	___	___
13. Try to schedule more and more activities into less time?	___	___
14. Always appear for appointments on time?	___	___
15. Clench or pound your fists or use other gestures to emphasize your views?	___	___
16. Credit your accomplishments to your ability to work rapidly?	___	___
17. Feel that things must be done now and quickly?	___	___
18. Constantly try to find more efficient ways to get things done?	___	___
19. Insist on winning at games rather than just having fun?	___	___
20. Interrupt others often?	___	___
21. Feel irritated when others are late?	___	___
22. Leave the table immediately after eating?	___	___
23. Feel rushed?	___	___
24. Feel dissatisfied with your current level of performance?	___	___

For an interactive version of this self-assessment exercise, go to www.wileyplus.com

Disasters: Of Fire and of Ice

Some say the world will end in fire,
Some say in ice.

—ROBERT FROST

Earthquakes, hurricanes, blizzards, tornadoes, windstorms, ice storms, monsoons, floods, mudslides, avalanches, and volcanic eruptions—these are a sampling of the natural disasters to which we are prey. The devastation wreaked upon New Orleans and other Gulf states by Hurricane Katrina in 2005 is a testament to the raw destructive power of nature.

Natural disasters are hazardous in themselves and also cause life changes to pile atop one another by disrupting community life. Services that had been taken for granted, such as electricity and water, may be lost. Businesses and homes may be destroyed, so that people must rebuild or relocate. Natural disasters reveal the thinness of the veneer of technology on which civilization depends. It is understandable that many survivors report stress-related problems such as anxiety and depression for months after the fact.

Perhaps it is also understandable that the suicide rate rises after natural disasters like hurricanes, floods, and earthquakes. Ètienne Krug and his colleagues (1998) at the Centers for Disease Control and Prevention speculate that well-intentioned government disaster loans contribute to the suicide rate by placing victims under the stress of repaying the loans.

We owe our dominance over the natural environment to technological progress. Yet technology can also fail or backfire and cause disaster, such as in the case of airplane accidents, major fires, bridge collapses, leakage of poisonous gases or toxic chemicals, and blackouts. These are but a sampling of the technological disasters that befall us. When they do, we feel as though we have lost control of things and suffer traumatic forms of stress.

Survivors of natural and technological disasters may suffer psychological and physical effects of stress for years afterwards. The stress of piecing together one's life or grieving for lost loved ones may be compounded by the additional burdens of filing claims and even by pursuing lawsuits against those identified as responsible for adverse consequences of human origin.

©AP/Wide World Photos

Traumatic Stress
Traumatic events, such as the shootings at Virginia Tech, can have profound effects on our psychological and physical adjustment. Stress-related problems may linger for years in the form of posttraumatic stress disorder (PTSD).

Terrorism: When Our Sense of Security in Our Own Land Is Threatened

On September 11, 2001, everything changed. Americans, who had always felt secure and protected from acts of terrorism within the borders of their own country, now experienced the sense of vulnerability and fear that had unfortunately become a staple of daily life in many other parts of the world. Though we endeavored to return to a sense of normality, many of us are still reeling from the events of 9/11. Many of us lost friends and loved ones or are still feeling the emotional consequences of that awful day. Survivors of traumatic events like 9/11 or of devastating hurricanes or floods may suffer from lingering emotional effects, such as posttraumatic stress disorder (PTSD), which we discuss in Chapter 8. But the effects of traumatic events like 9/11 affect most all of us in one way or another. As you can see from Table 3.4, a clear majority of

Table 3.4 ▮ Stress-Related Symptoms Reported by Americans in the Week Following the Terrorist Attacks of September 11, 2001			
	Depression	Lack of Focus (Difficulty Concentrating)	Insomnia
Men	62	44	26
Women	79	53	40
Genders combined	71	49	33

Source: Pew Research Center. (2002, September, 20). *American psyche reeling from terror attacks.* www.people-press.org/terroist01rpt.htm.

Adjustment and Modern Life

Warning Signs of Trauma-Related Stress

People normally experience psychological distress in the face of trauma. If anything, it would be abnormal to remain blasé at a time of crisis or disaster. But stress reactions that linger beyond a month and affect an individual's ability to function in meeting the tasks of everyday life may be a cause for concern.

The American Psychological Association lists the following symptoms as warning signs of traumatic stress reactions. If you or a loved have experienced these symptoms for more than a month, it would be worthwhile to seek professional mental health assistance. Assistance is available through your college health services (for registered students) or through networks of trained professionals. For more information or a referral, you may contact your local American Red Cross chapter or the American Psychological Association at 202-336-5800.

1. Having recurring thoughts or nightmares about the event.
2. Having trouble sleeping or changes in appetite.
3. Experiencing anxiety and fear, especially when exposed to events or situations reminiscent of the trauma.
4. Being on edge, being easily startled, or becoming overly alert.
5. Feeling depressed, sad; having low energy.
6. Experiencing memory problems, including difficulty in remembering aspects of the trauma.
7. Feeling "scattered" and unable to focus on work or daily activities.
8. Having difficulty making decisions.
9. Feeling irritable, easily agitated, or angry and resentful.
10. Feeling emotionally "numb," withdrawn, disconnected, or different from others.
11. Spontaneously crying; feeling a sense of despair and hopelessness.
12. Feeling extremely protective of, or fearful for, the safety of loved ones.
13. Not being able to face certain aspects of the trauma; avoiding activities, places, or even people that remind you of the event.

Source: American Psychological Association, *Warning Signs of Trauma Related Stress.* http://www.apa.org/practice/ptsd.html. Copyright 2002 by American Psychological Association. Reprinted by permission.

Americans reported feeling depressed in the immediate aftermath of 9/11, and a sizable proportion had difficulty concentrating or suffered from insomnia.

How to Talk to Your Children About Terrorist Attacks

Terrorism, once a problem limited to foreign countries, has become a reality within our own borders. The 2001 terrorist attacks did not spare the children of the nation. Children saw these terrible events unfolding on their television screens and heard the adults in their lives discussing the tragic events. Yet many adults don't know how to talk to children about this disaster and the risk of future ones, and many don't know how to recognize that their children are feeling distress.

FEMA for Kids, the part of the FEMA (Federal Emergency Management Agency) website devoted to children, offers advice on how parents can discuss terrorism with their children. The site also includes general guidelines about dealing with the impact of disaster on children and gives schools the opportunity to submit artwork children have done in an effort to share their feelings. The web address for the site is www.fema.gov/kids.

Children affected by disasters may suddenly act younger than they are or may appear stoic—not crying or expressing concern. According to Holly Harrington, the FEMA for Kids manager, "Parents can help their children by talking to them, keeping them close, and even spoiling them for a little while. We also advise that children not be overexposed to the news coverage of the terrorist events."

Talking to children about terrorism can be especially problematic because it is difficult to provide them with safety guidelines to protect themselves from terrorism. According to psychologists, questions about terrorism are teaching opportunities. Adults should answer questions about terrorism by providing understandable information and realistic reassurance. And children don't need to be overwhelmed with information, so less is better than more in terms of details.

Children may exhibit many kinds of behaviors after a disaster. Some of the more common patterns include the following:

1 Change from being quiet, obedient, and caring to being loud, noisy, and aggressive, or from being outgoing to being shy and afraid.
2 Develop nighttime fears or have nightmares or bad dreams.
3 Be afraid the event will recur.
4 Become easily upset, crying and whining.
5 Lose trust in adults. After all, adults were not able to control the disaster.
6 Revert to younger behavior such as bed-wetting and thumb-sucking.
7 Not want parents out of their sight and refuse to go to school or child care.
8 Have symptoms of physical illness, such as headaches, vomiting, or fever.
9 Worry about where they and their family will live.

What to Say, What to Do

The federal government offers a number of suggestions for parents to help their children cope with the emotional consequences of a terrorist attack:[1]

1 Talk with the children about how they are feeling and listen without judgment.
2 Let the children take time to figure things out. Don't rush them.
3 Help them learn to use words that express their feelings, such as *happy, sad, angry,* or *mad.*
4 Assure children that you will be there to take care of them. Reassure them often.
5 Stay together as a family as much as possible.
6 Let them have some control, such as choosing what outfit to wear or what meal to have for dinner.
7 Encourage the children to share with their parents any pictures they have drawn or things they have written.
8 Help children regain their faith in the future by helping them develop plans for activities that will take place later—next week, next month.
9 Allow the children to grieve losses.

3.1.10 Noise: Of Muzak, Rock 'n Roll, and Low-Flying Aircraft

Psychologists help people adjust by applying knowledge of sensation and perception to design environments that produce positive emotional responses and contribute to human performance. They may thus suggest soundproofing certain environments or using pleasant background sounds such as music or recordings of water in natural environments (rain, the beach, brooks, and so on). Noise can be aversive, however, especially loud noise. How do you react when chalk is scraped on the blackboard or when a low-flying airplane screeches overhead?

The decibel (dB) is used to express the loudness of noise (see Figure 3.5). The hearing threshold is defined as 0 dB. Your school library is probably about 30 to 40 dB. A freeway is about 70 dB.

High noise levels are stressful and can lead to health problems ranging from hypertension to neurological and intestinal disorders. Levels of 85 dB or higher can

---

[1] Adapted from Federal Emergency Management Agency (FEMA) web posting, September 2001.
FEMA Offers Advice on How to Talk to Children About Terrorist Attacks.

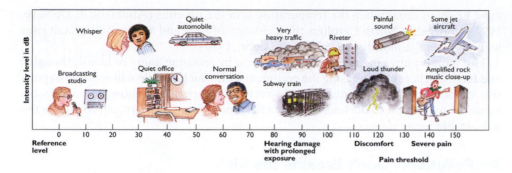

Figure 3.5
Decibel Levels of Various Sounds
Loud noise is an environmental stressor that can raise the blood pressure and interfere with learning and performance.

trigger the body's natural stress response, leading to elevated blood pressure and causing indigestion. At about 125 dB and beyond, noise becomes physically painful. Noise at 150 dB can rupture your eardrums. But you can suffer permanent damage to your hearing before pain sets in, as from prolonged exposure to noise at 85 dB or higher or exposure to brief bursts of noise of 120 dB or louder.

Just how loud is 120 dB? Rock concerts frequently fall in this range, subjecting both musicians and concertgoers to the risk of hearing impairment. Many young people who blast music through headphones attached to their iPod or MP3 players are exposing themselves to similarly dangerous volumes, day after day. They (you?) may not realize the damage they are doing to their ears until many years afterward, when long-term hearing loss develops.

High noise levels such as those imposed by traffic or low-flying airplanes also impair daily functioning. They can lead to forgetfulness, perceptual errors, and even the tendency to drop things. Preschool children who are exposed to loud noise in their day-care setting are less advanced in their prereading skills (Maxwell & Evans, 2000).

Couples may enjoy high noise levels at a dance club, but grating noises of 80 dB seem to decrease feelings of attraction. They cause people to stand farther apart. Loud noise also reduces helping behavior. People are less likely to help pick up a dropped package when the background noise of a construction crew is at 92 dB than when it's at 72 dB (Staples, 1996). They're even less willing to make change for a dollar to help a passerby.

What can you do to safeguard your hearing? Here are some suggestions:

- When you can't avoid excessive noise, as at worksites, wear hearing protectors or soft foam or silicone-type earplugs.
- Use your fingers (carefully!) as earplugs in an emergency.
- Turn down the volume on your stereo, especially when using earphones.
- Do not attend ear-splitting concerts.
- Sound-protect your home with heavy curtains, acoustical ceiling and wall tiles, double-paned windows, and thick carpeting. Caulk windows and doors that let in sounds.

Temperature: "Getting Hot Under the Collar"

"Summertime," goes the song from *Porgy and Bess*, "and the livin' is easy. Fish are jumpin', and..." —and if you live in Minneapolis, the rate of property crime is high. Ellen Cohn and James Rotton (2000) studied property crime rates in that northern city over a two-year period and discovered that warm weather encourages outdoor activity, including going from house to house to steal. Outdoor activity is more difficult during Minneapolis's bitter winters, which helps explain why people's property is safer then.

Rising temperatures may also make some people hot under the collar. Higher temperatures are linked to increased levels of aggressive behavior (Bell, 2005; Bushman, Wang, & Anderson, 2005). One consequence of the temperature–aggression effect: The frequency of honking at traffic lights in Phoenix tends to increase as the temperature rises (Kenrick & MacFarlane, 1986). In Houston, murders and rapes are most likely to occur when the temperature is in the nineties (Anderson & DeNeve, 1992). In Raleigh, North Carolina, the incidence of rape and aggravated assault rises with the average monthly temperature (Cohn, 1990).

Hot temperatures incite aggressive behavior by arousing angry or hostile thoughts and feelings, thereby increasing the readiness with which people will respond aggressively when provoked or frustrated. At very hot temperatures, however, aggressive behavior may begin to decline, as people become primarily motivated to escape the unbearable heat.

Air Pollution: "Don't Breathe the Air"

Psychologists and other health scientists investigate the effects of pollution and noxious odors on our health and adjustment. For example, the lead in auto fumes is known to impair children's intellectual functioning in the same way that eating lead paint does. High levels of air pollution are linked to higher mortality rates in cities (Samet et al., 2000). Unpleasant-smelling pollutants, like other forms of aversive stimulation, decrease feelings of attraction and heighten aggression (Baron & Byrne, 2000).

Crowding and Other Stresses of City Life

Big-city dwellers are more likely to experience stimulus overload and to fear crime than suburbanites and rural folk (Herzog & Chernick, 2000). Overwhelming crowd stimulation, bright lights, shop windows, and so on cause them to narrow their perceptions to a particular face, destination, or job. The pace of life increases, even how quickly we walk through city streets. All major population groups in the United States—African Americans, Asian Americans, European Americans, and Latino and Latina Americans—find high-density living conditions to be uncomfortable, even aversive (Evans, Wells, et al., 2000).

Yet not all cities are the same. Cross-cultural research reveals that cities in Europe and Japan function at a faster pace than cities in less-developed countries, as measured by the pace of walking the streets, the time taken to complete a simple task, and the accuracy of public clocks (Levine & Norenzayan, 1999). They may get more done, but people in "faster" cities are also more likely to smoke and to die from coronary disease (Levine & Norenzayan, 1999). Farming, anyone?

Personal Space

One adverse effect of crowding is the invasion of one's personal space. Personal space is an invisible boundary, a sort of bubble surrounding you. You are likely to become anxious and perhaps angry when others invade your space. This may happen when someone sits down across from or next to you in an otherwise empty cafeteria or stands too close to you in an elevator.

Personal space appears to serve both protective and communicative functions. People usually sit and stand closer to people who are similar to themselves in race, age, or socioeconomic status. Dating couples come closer together as the attraction between them increases.

Some interesting cross-cultural research has been done on personal space. For example, North Americans and northern Europeans apparently maintain a greater distance between themselves and others than southern Europeans, Asians, and Middle Easterners do (Baron & Byrne, 2000).

People in some cultures apparently learn to cope with high density and also share their ways of coping with others. Asians in crowded cities such as Tokyo and Hong Kong interact more harmoniously than North Americans and Britons, who dwell in less dense cities. The Japanese are used to being packed sardinelike into subway cars by white-gloved pushers employed by the transit system. Imagine the rebellion that would occur if such treatment were attempted in American subways! It has been suggested that Asians are accustomed to adapting to their environment, whereas Westerners are more prone to trying to change it.

Review It

(1) Daily _____ are regularly occurring annoyances or events that threaten our well-being.

(2) Life _____, even pleasant ones, are stressful because they require adjustment.

(3) Members of immigrant groups may encounter _____ stress when they attempt to adjust to the values and behavior patterns of the host culture.

(4) Chemical messengers in the body that help block pain signals are called _____.

(5) The emotional state of _____ occurs when a person's attempts to accomplish a goal are thwarted.

(6) The feeling of being pulled in two or more directions by opposing motives is called a _____.

(7) The psychologist Albert Ellis believes that our _____ about events can be sources of stress.

(8) _____ behavior is characterized by a sense of time urgency, competitiveness, and aggressiveness.

(9) Disasters (increase or decrease?) our sense of control over our lives.

(10) High levels of heat tend to (increase or decrease?) aggressiveness.

Think About It

How do our cognitions—our attitudes and beliefs—affect the impact that external stressors have on us?

Psychological Moderators of Stress

■ How do our self-efficacy expectations affect our adjustment?

■ What characteristics are connected with psychological hardiness?

■ Is there any evidence that "a merry heart doeth good like a medicine"?

■ How do predictability and control help us adjust?

■ Is there evidence that social support helps people adjust?

Some people are more resilient in the face of stress than others. Though we all have our limits, there is no one-to-one relationship between the amount of stress we experience and outcomes such as physical disorders or psychological distress. Biological factors account for some of the variability in our responses. For example, some people apparently inherit predispositions toward certain physical and psychological disorders. But psychological factors also play a role. Psychological factors can influence, or moderate, the impact of sources of stress.

This module focuses on some key moderators of stress: self-efficacy expectations, psychological hardiness, a sense of humor, predictability and control, and social support.

3.2.1 Self-Efficacy Expectations: "The Little Engine That Could"

Self-efficacy expectations Beliefs to the effect that one can perform a task successfully or manage a stressor.

Our confidence in our abilities, or **self-efficacy expectations**, is linked to our ability to withstand stress (Montpetit & Bergeman, 2007). People who have confidence in their abilities to meet the challenges they face are less likely to be disturbed by adverse events. People with higher levels of self-efficacy are generally better able than their more self-doubting counterparts to master challenges such as losing weight and not relapsing after quitting smoking; they are also more likely to adhere to a regimen of physical activity (Motl et al., 2002; Shiffman et al., 2000). A study of Native Americans found that alcohol abuse was correlated with self-efficacy expectations (M. J. Taylor, 2000). That is, individuals who believed that they were powerless were more likely to abuse alcohol, perhaps as a way of lessening the stresses in their lives. In the face of calamitous or traumatic events, people with higher levels of self-efficacy show better rates of recovery, perhaps because they take a more direct role in mending their lives (Benight & Bandura, 2004).

3.2.2 Psychological Hardiness—Are You Tough Enough?

Psychological hardiness A cluster of traits that buffer stress and are characterized by commitment, challenge, and control.

Locus of control The place (locus) to which an individual attributes control over the receiving of reinforcers—either inside or outside the self.

Psychological hardiness also helps people resist stress. Our understanding of this phenomenon is derived largely from the pioneering work of Suzanne Kobasa and her colleagues (1994). They studied business executives who seemed able to resist illness despite stress. The psychologically hardy executives in Kobasa's research showed three key characteristics:

1 *Commitment.* They were strongly committed to their work and pursuit of their life goals.
2 *Challenge.* They felt challenged by new experiences and opportunities. They believed that change, rather than stability, is normal in life, not a threat to their security.
3 *Control.* They were high in perceived control over their lives. They felt and behaved as though they were influential, rather than helpless, in facing the various rewards and punishments of life. Psychologically hardy people tend to have what Rotter (1990) terms an internal **locus of control**.

Hardy people tend to interpret stress as a fact of life that makes life more interesting. For example, they see a conference with a supervisor as an opportunity to persuade the supervisor rather than as a risk to their position. Other researchers find that psychologically hardy people tend to report fewer physical symptoms, have better immune system responses, cope better with stress, and encounter less depression than their less hardy peers (Dolbier et al., 2001; Ouellette & DiPlacido, 2001; Pengilly & Dowd, 2000). More hardy undergraduates also tend to achieve higher grades, perhaps because they view their academic success as a challenge (Sheard & Golby, 2007).

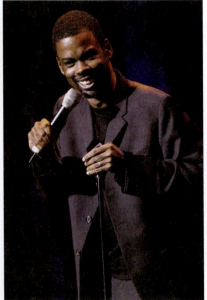

Karl Walter/Getty Images, Inc

Humor Can Be Good Medicine
Humor can help lighten the burdens of life, including the stressful burdens we face in everyday life. Feeling stressed out? Here is a prescription you might find entertaining—why not take in a comedy tonight?

3.2.3 Sense of Humor: "A Merry Heart Doeth Good Like a Medicine"

The idea that humor lightens the burdens of life and helps people cope with stress has been with us for millennia. Consider the biblical maxim, "A merry heart doeth good like a medicine" (Proverbs 17:22). A dose of humor not only makes us laugh but also helps get our minds off the sources of stress in our lives, at least for a time. Though scientific findings on the potential benefits of humor are inconclusive, you may find that humor can help you cope with the stressful burdens you face in your daily life. Why not try a dose of something amusing tonight, a comedy perhaps?

3.2.4 Predictability and Control: "If I Know What's Coming, I Can Better Prepare for It"

Blend Images/Getty Images, Inc

Psychological Hardiness
Psychologically hardy individuals are more resilient to the effects of stress. They are committed to their work and other activities, are open to new challenges, and feel in control of their lives.

The ability to predict a stressor apparently moderates its impact. Predictability allows us to brace ourselves for the inevitable and, in many cases, plan ways of coping with it. A sense of control is one of the keys to psychological hardiness (Folkman & Moskowitz, 2000b; Tennen & Affleck, 2000). Examples from everyday life, including shopping in crowded stores (Machleit, Eroglu, & Mantel, 2000), suggest that a sense of control over the situation—of being able to choose—also helps us cope with the stress of being packed in. When we are at a concert, disco, or sports event, we may encounter higher density than we do in a frustrating ticket line. But we may be having a wonderful time. Why? Because we have chosen to be at the concert and are focusing on our good time (unless a tall or noisy person is sitting in front of us). We feel that we are in control. We tend to moderate the effects of high density in subway cars and other vehicles by ignoring our fellow passengers and daydreaming, reading newspapers and books, or finding humor in the situation. Some people catch a snooze and wake up just before their stop.

The accompanying self-assessment will afford you insight as to whether you believe that you are in charge of your own life.

Control—even the illusion of being in control—allows us to feel that we are not at the mercy of the fates (Folkman & Moskowitz, 2000b; Tennen & Affleck, 2000). There is also a relationship between the desire to assume control over one's situation and the usefulness of information about impending stressors (Lazarus & Folkman, 1984). Predictability is of greater benefit to people who wish to exercise control over their situations. People who want information about medical procedures and what they will experience cope better with pain when they undergo those procedures (Ludwick-Rosenthal & Neufeld, 1993).

The Locus of Control Scale | *Self-Assessment*

Psychologically hardy people tend to have an internal locus of control. They believe that they are in control of their own lives. In contrast, people with an external locus of control tend to see their fate as being out of their hands.

Are you "internal" or "external"? To learn more about your perception of your locus of control, respond to this self-assessment, which was developed by Stephen Nowicki and Bonnie Strickland (1973). Place a checkmark in either the Yes or the No column for each question. When you are finished, turn to the answer key at the end of the chapter.

	YES	NO
1. Do you believe that most problems will solve themselves if you just don't fool with them?	___	___
2. Do you believe that you can stop yourself from catching a cold?	___	___
3. Are some people just born lucky?	___	___
4. Most of the time, do you feel that getting good grades meant a great deal to you?	___	___
5. Are you often blamed for things that just aren't your fault?	___	___
6. Do you believe that if somebody studies hard enough he or she can pass any subject?	___	___
7. Do you feel that most of the time it doesn't pay to try hard because things never turn out right anyway?	___	___
8. Do you feel that if things start out well in the morning, it's going to be a good day no matter what you do?	___	___
9. Do you feel that most of the time parents listen to what their children have to say?	___	___
10. Do you believe that wishing can make good things happen?	___	___
11. When you get punished, does it usually seem it's for no good reason at all?	___	___
12. Most of the time, do you find it hard to change a friend's opinion?	___	___
13. Do you think cheering more than luck helps a team win?	___	___
14. Did you feel that it was nearly impossible to change your parents' minds about anything?	___	___

15. Do you believe that parents should allow children to make most of their own decisions? ___ ___
16. Do you feel that when you do something wrong there's very little you can do to make it right? ___ ___
17. Do you believe that most people are just born good at sports? ___ ___
18. Are most other people your age stronger than you are? ___ ___
19. Do you feel that one of the best ways to handle most problems is just not to think about them? ___ ___
20. Do you feel that you have a lot of choice in deciding who your friends are? ___ ___
21. If you find a four-leaf clover, do you believe that it might bring you good luck? ___ ___
22. Did you often feel that whether or not you did your homework had much to do with what kind of grades you got? ___ ___
23. Do you feel that when a person your age is angry with you, there's little you can do to stop him or her? ___ ___
24. Have you ever had a good luck charm? ___ ___
25. Do you believe that whether or not people like you depends on how you act? ___ ___
26. Did your parents usually help you if you asked them to? ___ ___
27. Have you ever felt that when people were angry with you, it was usually for no reason at all? ___ ___
28. Most of the time, do you feel that you can change what might happen tomorrow by what you did today? ___ ___
29. Do you believe that when bad things are going to happen, they are just going to happen no matter what you try to do to stop them? ___ ___
30. Do you think that people can get their own way if they just keep trying? ___ ___
31. Most of the time, do you find it useless to try to get your own way at home? ___ ___
32. Do you feel that when good things happen, they happen because of hard work? ___ ___
33. Do you feel that when somebody your age wants to be your enemy, there's little you can do to change matters? ___ ___
34. Do you feel that it's easy to get friends to do what you want them to do? ___ ___
35. Do you usually feel that you have little to say about what you get to eat at home? ___ ___
36. Do you feel that when someone doesn't like you, there's little you can do about it? ___ ___
37. Did you usually feel it was almost useless to try in school, because most other children were just plain smarter than you were? ___ ___
38. Are you the kind of person who believes that planning ahead makes things turn out better? ___ ___
39. Most of the time, do you feel that you have little to say about what your family decides to do? ___ ___
40. Do you think it's better to be smart than to be lucky? ___ ___

For an interactive version of this self-assessment exercise, go to www.wileyplus.com

Positive Psychology

3.2.5 Optimism: Is the Glass Half Full or Half Empty?

Are you the type of person who sees the proverbial glass as half full or as half empty? People with more optimistic attitudes—who see the glass as half full—tend to be more resilient than others to the effects of stress, including stress associated with physical disorders. For example, investigators link optimism to lower levels of emotional distress among heart disease and cancer patients and to lower levels of reported pain and emotional distress among cancer patients (Bjerklie, 2005; Carver et al., 2005; Shnek et al., 2001; Trunzo & Pinto, 2003). Optimism in pregnant women even predicts better birth outcomes, as measured, for instance, by higher infant birth weights (Lobel et al., 2000). Optimism in coronary artery bypass surgery patients is also associated with fewer serious postoperative complications (Scheier et al., 1999). On the other hand, people with more pessimistic attitudes tend to report greater emotional distress in the form of depression and social anxieties (Hardin & Leong, 2005).

We have also learned that more optimistic people tend to live longer and to have more satisfying and happy romantic relationships (Assad, Donnellan, & Conger, 2007; Giltay et al., 2006). Optimism is certainly an adaptive attitude, but let us caution that people with overly optimistic attitudes may be less well prepared than people with more balanced attitudes in handling setbacks in life (Sweeny, Carroll, & Shepperd, 2006).

Health researchers recognize that linkages between optimistic attitudes and better health outcomes are based on correlational relationships. So we should be careful about inferring causal links. Nonetheless, it makes sense that facing the stressors in our lives with an optimistic attitude may help us persevere and muster the resources we need to meet these challenges. The accompanying self-assessment will help you evaluate whether you are someone who sees the proverbial glass as half full or half empty.

3.2.6 Social Support: On Being in It Together

People are social beings, so it is not surprising that social support acts as a kind of buffer against the effects of stress (Taylor et al., 2007; Wills & Filer Fegan, 2001). Sources of social support include the following:

1 *Emotional concern*, such as by listening to people's problems and expressing feelings of sympathy, caring, understanding, and reassurance.

2 *Instrumental aid*, such as material support and services that facilitate adaptive behavior. For example, after a disaster the government may arrange for low-interest loans so that survivors can rebuild. Relief organizations may provide food, medicines, and temporary living quarters.

Assessing Your "LOT" in Life: The Life Orientation Test

Self-Assessment

Do you consider yourself to be an optimist or a pessimist? Do you expect good things to happen, or do you find the cloud around the silver lining? The Life Orientation Test may provide you with insight into your general outlook on life.

Directions: Indicate whether or not each of the items represents your feelings by writing a number in the black space according to the following code. Then turn to the scoring key at the end of the chapter.

> 4 = strongly agree
> 3 = agree
> 2 = neutral
> 1 = disagree
> 0 = strongly disagree

_____ 1. In uncertain times, I usually expect the best.
_____ 2. It's easy for me to relax.
_____ 3. If something can go wrong for me, it will.
_____ 4. I always look on the bright side of things.
_____ 5. I'm always optimistic about my future.
_____ 6. I enjoy my friends a lot.
_____ 7. It's important for me to keep busy.
_____ 8. I hardly ever expect things to go my way.
_____ 9. Things never work out the way I want them to.
_____ 10. I don't get upset too easily.
_____ 11. I'm a believer in the idea that "every cloud has a silver lining."
_____ 12. I rarely count on good things happening to me.

Source: Michael F. Scheier & Charles S. Carver (1985), Optimism, coping, and health: Assessment and implications of generalized outcome expectancies. *Health Psychology, 4,* 219–247. Reprinted with permission.

For an interactive version of this self-assessment exercise, go to www.wileyplus.com

Ghislain & Marie David DeLossy/Getty Images, Inc

Reaching Out
Social support is an important buffer against the effects of stress, such as the stress we face due to significant illness or the loss of loved ones.

3 *Information,* such as guidance and advice that enhances people's ability to cope.

4 *Appraisal,* such as feedback from others about how one is doing. This kind of support involves helping people interpret, or "make sense of," what has happened to them.

5 *Socializing,* such as through simple conversation, recreation, even going shopping with another person. Socializing has beneficial effects, even when it is not oriented specifically toward solving problems.

Research validates the value of social support. Introverts, people who lack social skills, and people who live by themselves appear more prone to developing infectious diseases such as colds under stress (Cohen & Williamson, 1991; Gilbert, 1997). Evidence also teaches that social support helps immigrants cope with the stresses of acculturation (Hovey, 2000).

MODULE REVIEW

Review It

(11) People with (higher or lower?) self-efficacy expectations tend to cope better with stress.

(12) Kobasa found that psychologically hardy executives are high in _____, challenge, and control.

(13) Being able to predict and control the onset of a stressor (increases or decreases?) its impact on us.

(14) Linkages between optimism and better health outcomes are (correlational or experimental?) in nature.

(15) The material support we receive that helps us adjust to stressors is called _____ aid.

Think About It

How do factors like high self-efficacy expectations, control, and humor help us adjust to stress?

Psychology in Daily Life
MODULE 3.3

Managing Stress

Stress management does not seek to eliminate stress from your life. After all, stress is a part of life, and at least some amount of stress is needed to help us remain active, alert, and motivated. Stress management is a set of techniques designed to help us manage the stress we experience more effectively—to prevent stress from becoming a source of distress. Some people have good coping resources for handling stress. But others rely on defensive means of coping with stress.

What do you do when the pressures of work or school begin to get to you? What do you do when you feel that your instructor or your supervisor doesn't appreciate your performance? When your

steady date finds someone else? When you're uptight before a test, or irritated because you're stuck in traffic? Do you choose defensive coping or active coping? Let us contrast these two different ways of coping, defensive coping and active coping.

3.3.1 Defensive Coping: Copping Out, Not Coping

Many techniques for coping with stress are defensive. Defensive coping reduces the immediate impact of the stressor, but at a cost. Costs include socially inappropriate behavior (as in alcoholism, aggression, or regression), avoidance of problems (as in withdrawal), or self-deception (as in rationalization or denial).

Image Source/Getty Images, Inc

Defensive Coping

Methods of defensive coping with stress—such as drinking, withdrawal, or use of defense mechanisms—can reduce the immediate impact of the stressor, but with some cost. Costs include socially inappropriate behavior (as in substance use or aggression), avoidance of problems (as in withdrawal), or self-deception (as in the use of some defense mechanisms). Active coping recognizes stressors for what they are and aims to manipulate the environment (in socially acceptable ways) to remove the stressors or to change our responses to cushion their impact.

Defensive coping grants us time to marshal our resources but does not deal with the source of stress or enhance the effectiveness of our responses to stress. In the long run, defensive methods can be harmful if we do not use the chance they provide to find better ways of coping. Note the following examples of defensive coping:

Withdrawal When you face a stressful situation you feel unable to control, you may want to withdraw from the situation. Withdrawal can be emotional, as in loss of interest, or physical, as in moving or changing one's lifestyle. Rape survivors often move to a new location in order to avoid painful memories and future threats. Temporary withdrawal can be helpful by providing the chance to find better methods of coping. But withdrawal from social involvement prevents people from getting on with their lives and finding other sources of support. In one case, a young man who had always dreamed of becoming a firefighter withdrew from the training academy after only three days because he found it too stressful. He later regretted his decision and fortunately was able to become reinstated. Given a second chance, he successfully completed the program and fulfilled his lifelong ambition.

Denial People who rely on denial when facing the stress of coping with a serious illness refuse to acknowledge the seriousness of their health situation. They may minimize the seriousness of their condition ("Oh, it's no big deal"), misattribute their symptoms to benign causes ("It's probably just my arthritis acting up"), or assume that symptoms will pass if left alone. But people who dismiss chest pains or suspicious lumps as "no big deal" may not avail themselves of the medical assistance they may require. Denial may minimize the effects of stress in the short run, but the eventual consequences of leaving a serious medical condition untreated can be tragic.

Sigmund Freud considered denial a type of defense mechanism that operates unconsciously to protect us from anxiety that might stem from recognition of unacceptable ideas and impulses (see Table 2.2). According to psychodynamic theory, everyone uses defense mechanisms, at least to some degree. However, defense mechanisms can become problems in adjustment when people begin to rely on them to cope with stress or when they lead people to forgo seeking necessary medical treatment or making desirable life changes.

Substance Use Another common, but also ineffective, means of handling stressful situations is the use of alcohol or other drugs. The use of psychoactive substances may blunt awareness of sources of stress but fails to resolve the underlying problem. Moreover, drinking regularly or using other drugs to cope with stress can lead to a drug dependence, which only compounds the problems the person is facing.

Aggression Some people lose their tempers when they feel stressed and become verbally or physically abusive to other people. Violence is often used to cope with social provocations and, sometimes, as a response to frustration. But lashing out at others verbally or physically is a source of stress in itself, can damage relationships, and can have serious consequences, even lethal results in the case of physical assault. Physical violence is not only illegal but dangerous. Aggressive behavior also heightens interpersonal conflict by creating motives for retaliation.

3.3.2 Active Coping: Dealing Directly with Stress

We can see that some ways of handling stress can make matters much worse. Now let us consider healthier ways of managing stress. Direct or active coping methods for managing stress aim to manipulate the environment (in socially acceptable ways) to remove stressors or to change our response patterns to buffer their harmfulness. Through active coping, we willingly face stressors for what they are. Sometimes stressors cannot be eliminated or modified. Active coping then involves rational evaluation of our capacities to manage them as best we can and planning efficient ways to cushion their impact.

Here are some strategies for active coping with the stressors of everyday life.

Keep Stress at Manageable Levels Think about your daily life. Do things run smoothly from day to day? Do you have enough time to "stop and smell the roses"? Or do you find yourself running frantically from place to place just to keep up with the many demands on your time? Does it seem that no matter how hard you try, there is still much more that needs to be done? If the demands on your time keep piling up, you may be facing more stress than you can handle. Here are some ways to turn down the level of stress in your life:

1. *Don't bite off more than you can chew.* Don't take on more tasks than you can reasonably accomplish given the other demands on your time. Don't sacrifice family or personal needs so as to cram more work-related activities into your busy schedule.

2. *Reduce daily hassles.* What can you do to reduce daily hassles? Might you be able to change your schedule to avoid the morning traffic jam? Can you carpool? Being stuck in traffic may be more tolerable if you are not the one behind the wheel and can use the time to catch up on your reading. What other daily hassles can you minimize or eliminate?

3. *Develop time-management skills.* Does it seem like there's never enough time to accomplish all that you need to do? Wouldn't it be nice to stop time in its tracks or lengthen the day by a couple of hours? Well, short of making the world stand still, there is a lot you can do to make time work for you rather than against you (see Table 3.5).

Table 3.5 ▌ Tips for Managing Your Time

Here are some suggestions you may find helpful to organize your time more efficiently:

- *Use a monthly calendar.* Fill in appointments and important events (like upcoming exams, doctor's visits, family get-togethers, etc.). Make sure there's a time for everything and everything is in its time.
- *Prioritize tasks.* Use to-do lists and organize tasks by priority. Start each day with a list of things you feel you need to do. Then prioritize them, using a 3-point code. Assign a #1 to things you must absolutely get done today. Assign a #2 to things you'd like to get done today but don't absolutely need to get done. Then give a #3 to things you'd like to get done today if time allows. Also, break down larger tasks into smaller, manageable doses. Take that term paper that's been staring you in the face. Don't try to finish it off in just one or two marathon sittings. Break it down into smaller pieces and then tackle the pieces one by one.
- *Lessen the duration of stressors.* Try to manage stress by taking it in manageable doses. Take things more slowly. Take more frequent breaks. If possible, stretch deadlines when stressful burdens become too taxing. Reduce the impact of studying for exams by starting to study earlier than you normally would. You can then afford some study breaks. Perhaps, too, you can stretch some deadlines to ease your stress burden. We're not suggesting that you compromise your work ethic but rather that you spread out your workload into less stressful doses. Your final products may even be better in quality.

Become More Aware of Your Body's Response to Stress

Don't ignore the signs of stress. Become aware of how your body reacts to stress. Does your back hurt more than usual? Is that nagging headache becoming a daily occurrence? Are you biting your nails? Are you exhausted at the end of the day? These physical and psychological symptoms may signal that you've reached or exceeded your stress threshold. Also, prepare your body for coping with stress. Follow a nutritionally balanced diet. Get enough sleep. Have regular medical checkups. Avoid tobacco and other harmful substances. Keep active and fit.

Know What to Expect

Stressors are more manageable when you know what to expect. Knowing that a final exam is coming in three or four weeks puts you on notice that you need to adjust your study routine to prepare for it. In the case of unexpected stressors, like blackouts, you may be able to prepare in general by having flashlights and candles in the house. Or at least you can brace yourself for their impact. Knowing what to expect gives you time to develop coping strategies. People with accurate knowledge of medical procedures tend to cope with them more effectively than people who remain in the dark. When you face a particular stressor, learn what you can about it. If you don't understand something, ask one of your professors or school counselors to help you.

Reach Out and Be Touched by Someone

Social support buffers the effects of stress. Early important studies with medical students and dental students, two highly stressed groups, show that students who had more friends had better immune system functioning than those with fewer friends (Jemmott et al., 1983; Kiecolt-Glaser et al., 1984). Lonely students have poorer immune functioning than students with more social support. Hospitalized people who receive strong emotional support have speedier recoveries than people with weak

emotional support networks. Receiving social support is only one side of the proverbial coin. Giving support to others can also help buffer the impact of stress and can be personally fulfilling.

How can you broaden your own social support network? The Social Support Inventory (see Table 3.6) offers suggestions for getting the kinds of social support that people rely upon, especially in times of stress. Let us offer another suggestion. There are probably numerous clubs and organizations on your campus or in your community that can provide opportunities to make new friends. Check it out with your office of student life or college counseling services.

Work It Out by Working Out

Exercise not only builds up your physical resources but also directly combats stress. Many people work off the tensions of the day with a vigorous game of racquetball, a run around the park, or a dozen laps in the pool. How does exercise help us cope with stress? One answer may lie in the fact that exercise promotes fitness. It strengthens bodily systems, such as the cardiovascular system, that are affected by stress.

Another possibility involves endorphins, the morphinelike hormones that block pain and induce feelings of well-being. Vigorous exercise raises the levels of endorphins in the bloodstream. Exercise also reduces key responses to stress, muscle tension, and anxiety, at least for a few hours. Perhaps, then, exercise restores a more relaxed state of mind and body.

You need not push your body to extremes to benefit from the stress-reducing effects of exercise. Even mild levels of exercise—a gentle swim, a brisk walk in the park—can relieve stress. Regardless of the reasons that exercise relieves stress, exercise has a remarkable effect on our moods. It calms us down and improves our psychological outlook. Choose a physical activity that you enjoy. Pushing yourself to do something you detest will only increase the stress you experience.

Table 3.6 ▮ Social Support: What It Is, How to Get It

Type of Support	What It Is	How to Get It
Emotional concern	Having others available who will listen to your problems and express understanding, sympathy, caring, and reassurance	Develop friendships and maintain relationships with present friends and family members. Make contact with trusted advisors in your community, such as your local priest, minister, or rabbi. Get involved in social organizations or community activities that provide opportunities to expand your social network.
Instrumental aid	Having material assistance and services needed to support adaptive behavior in times of stress.	Know about the resources in your community that assist people in times of need. Become acquainted with government support programs and the work of voluntary support agencies.
Feedback	Having feedback from others that tells us how we're doing when we're under stress	Develop a give-and-take relationship with several people whose opinions you trust.
Socializing	Having opportunities to socialize with others in our free time	Invite friends and family members to get together with you on a regular basis, perhaps organized around enjoyable activities like playing cards, going to dinner or shows, or going bowling.

Change Stressful Thoughts to Stress-Busting Thoughts

What are you telling yourself about the events that distress you? Are you sizing things up correctly, or are you blowing them out of proportion? Do you react to disappointing experiences by feeling disillusioned and hopeless? Do you press yourself to accomplish everything you set out to do? Do you refuse to compromise? Do you feel miserable when you fall short of your expectations? If these thought patterns ring true, you may wish to replace black-and-white thoughts with rational alternatives. Allow for shades of gray. Don't focus only on the negative parts of your experiences.

One category of stressful thoughts are thoughts that blow stressors out of proportion. Table 3.7 gives examples of some common stressful thoughts and some alternative thoughts that help keep things in perspective.

Table 3.7 ▮ Thoughts That Blow Stressors Out of Proportion and Rational Alternatives That Help Keep Things in Perspective

Thoughts That Blow Stressors Out of Proportion	Rational Alternative Thoughts That Help Keep Things in Perspective
"Oh my God, it's going to be a mess! I'm losing all control!"	"This is annoying and upsetting, but I haven't lost all control yet, and I don't have to."
"This is awful. It'll never end."	"It's bad, but it doesn't have to get the best of me. And upsetting things do come to an end, even if it's sort of hard to believe right now."
"I just can't stand it when Mom (Dad/my roommate/my date) gives me that look."	"Life is more pleasant when everyone is happy with me, but I have to be myself, and that means that other people are going to disagree with me from time to time."
"There's no way I can get up there and perform/give that speech! I'll look like an idiot."	"So I'm not perfect; that doesn't mean I'm going to look like an idiot. And so what if someone thinks I look bad? It doesn't mean I am bad. And if I am bad, so what? I can live with that, too. I don't have to be perfect every time. So stop being such a worrywart and get up and have some fun."
"My heart's beating a mile a minute! It's going to leap out of my chest! How much of this can I take?"	"Take it easy! Hearts don't jump out of chests. Just slow down a minute—stop and think. I'll find a way out. And if I don't for the time being, I'll survive. Some day I'll look back on this and laugh at how upset I got myself."
"What can I do? I'm helpless! It's just going to get worse and worse."	"Take it easy. Just stop and think for a minute. Just because there's no obvious solution doesn't mean that I won't be able to do anything about it. There's no point to getting so upset. Why don't I just take it from minute to minute for the time being. If I can't think of anything to do, I can always talk to other people about it."

Express Your Feelings When something is bothering you, don't keep it inside. Talk it over with someone you trust. Or write down your feelings in a personal journal. Evidence shows that expressing one's feelings is especially helpful in coping with stressful or traumatic events (de Moor et al., 2003; Pennebaker, 2004; Sloan & Marx, 2004). Keeping disturbing thoughts and feelings to yourself may place additional stress on your autonomic nervous system. Persistent high levels of stress can impair your immune system and make you more vulnerable to stress-related disorders. Talking or writing about stressful experiences has positive effects on the immune system. You can also consult a health professional to help talk things out.

The positive effects of expressing your feelings in writing extend to positive as well as negative experiences. Researchers at Southern Methodist University instructed undergraduate students to write about either intensely positive experiences or about neutral (control) topics for 20 minutes each day for three days (Burton & King, 2004). Students who wrote about positive experiences reported better moods and had fewer medical visits to the campus health center in the several months following the study.

Try a Little Humor: It's Good Medicine Humor can help buffer the effects of stress. By making us laugh, humor can get our minds off our troubles, at least for a time. A regular dose of humor may make stress more bearable.

Do Something Each Day That You Enjoy Stress is more manageable when you do something each day that brings you joy. Perhaps you would enjoy some leisure reading each day. Perhaps you would prefer to watch or participate in a sports event. Or maybe you would rather work on the car or surf the Web.

Change "I Can'ts" into "I Can's" A strong sense of self-efficacy enhances our ability to withstand stress. People with higher self-efficacy expectations also bounce back more easily from failure. Life's challenges seem less stressful to them.

If you believe you can accomplish what you set out to do, you are likely to marshal your resources and apply yourself until you reach your goal. If you doubt yourself, you may give up when you encounter the first setback. Start with small, achievable goals that will help boost your confidence and encourage you to move forward. Treat disappointments as opportunities to learn from your mistakes, not as signs of failure.

Practice Meditation Meditation induces a relaxed state accompanied by lower levels of bodily arousal. Many different forms of meditation exist; in most of them, the practitioner narrows attention by repeating a word, thought, or phrase or by maintaining a steady focus on a particular object, such as a burning candle or the design on a vase.

One of the most widely practiced forms is transcendental meditation (TM), an Indian meditation practice distinguished by the repetition of mantras—relaxing, sonorous sounds like *ieng* and *om*. Another form of meditation long practiced by Buddhist monks is mindfulness meditation. Practitioners focus entirely on their thoughts and physical sensations on a moment-to-moment basis (Grossman, 2008; Ludwig & Kabat-Zinn, 2008). The principle underlying mindfulness meditation is to concentrate attention completely on each moment in time, without analyzing, judging, or evaluating these unfolding experiences. The

Dalai Lama, the Buddhist spiritual leader, described mindfulness as "a state of alertness in which the mind does not get caught up in thoughts or sensations, but lets them come and go, much like watching a river flow by" (quoted in Gyatso, 2003, p. A29).

Both TM and mindfulness meditation produce a relaxation response that is characterized by a reduction in heart rate and respiration and a drop in blood pressure. Physicians and psychologists are actively exploring the use of these and other forms of meditation to promote physical and mental health. Evidence shows that meditation can have positive effects in relieving chronic pain, reducing high blood pressure, countering stress, and improving emotional well-being (Anderson, Liu, & Kryscio, 2008; Barnes, Treiber, & Johnson, 2004; Zautra et al., 2008). Meditators also produce more frequent alpha waves—brain waves associated with feelings of relaxation. Meditation also increases nighttime concentrations of the hormone melatonin, which induces sleepiness (Buscemi et al., 2006; Wright et al., 2006).

The following instructions will help you to try meditation as a means of lowering the arousal connected with stress:

1. Begin by meditating once or twice a day for 10 to 20 minutes.
2. In meditation, what you *don't* do is more important than what you *do* do. Adopt a passive, "what happens, happens" attitude.
3. Create a quiet, nondisruptive environment. For example, don't face a light directly.
4. Do not eat for an hour beforehand; avoid caffeine for at least two hours.
5. Assume a comfortable position. Change it as needed. It's okay to scratch or yawn.
6. As a device to aid concentrating, you could focus on your breathing or seat yourself before a calming object such as a plant or burning incense. Try "perceiving" (rather than mentally saying) the word *one* on every outbreath. This means thinking the word but "less actively" than usual (good luck). Others suggest thinking or perceiving the word *in* as you are inhaling and *out*, or *ah-h-h*, as you are exhaling.
7. If you are using a mantra (like the syllable *om*, pronounced *ommm*), you can prepare for meditation and say the mantra out loud several times. Enjoy it. Then say it more and more softly. Close your eyes and think only the mantra. Allow yourself to perceive, rather than actively think, the mantra. Again, adopt a passive attitude. Continue to perceive the mantra. It may grow louder or softer, disappear for a while, and then return.
8. If disruptive thoughts enter your mind as you are meditating, you can allow them to "pass through." Don't get wrapped up in trying to squelch them, or you may raise your level of arousal.
9. Allow yourself to drift. (You won't go too far.) What happens, happens.
10. Above all, take what you get. You cannot force the relaxing effects of meditation. You can only set the stage for it and allow it to happen.

Relax Yourself! There are many relaxation techniques. Health professionals at your college or university counseling center can introduce you to them.

One method, called *progressive muscle relaxation*, was developed by the physiologist Edmund Jacobson. Jacobson noticed that people

Jutta Klee/Stone/Getty Images, Inc

Meditation
Psychologists have studied meditation as a way of focusing one's consciousness to allow the stresses of the world to fade away. Many people endeavor to practice spiritual forms of meditation, but psychologists tend to focus on observable effects such as changes in muscle tension and blood pressure.

tend to tense their muscles when they are under stress, although they may not be aware of it. Since muscle contractions are associated with emotional tension, Jacobson reasoned that relaxing muscles can reduce states of tension. Many of the people he worked with, however, didn't have a clue as to how to relax their muscles.

Jacobson taught people first to tense, then to relax specific muscle groups in the body. The method is "progressive" in that people progress from one group of muscles to another, literally from head to toe. You can get a feel for this technique by practicing on a particular muscle group, say the muscles in your right hand. First, make a tight fist in your right hand, but not so tight that you risk injuring your hand. Just tight enough to feel the tension. After tensing for a few seconds, let go of tensions completely. Study the difference between the states of tension and relaxation. Notice how the muscles in your hand seem to unwind and let go of the tension. As you gain experience with the technique, you may find that you can relax your muscles by "just letting them go" without first having to tense them.

You can practice progressive relaxation by using the following instructions. Why not tape them or have a friend read them aloud?

First, create a conducive setting. Settle down on a reclining chair, a couch, or a bed with a pillow. Pick a time and place where you're not likely to be interrupted. Be sure that the room is warm and comfortable. Dim the lights. Loosen tight clothing.

Use the following instructions. Tighten each muscle group about two-thirds as hard as you could if you were using maximum strength. If you feel that a muscle may go into spasm, you are tensing too hard. When you let go of your tensions, do so completely.

The instructions can be memorized (slight variations from the text will do no harm), taped, or read aloud by a friend. An advantage to having someone read them is that you can signal the person to speed up or slow down by lifting a finger or two.

After you have practiced alternate tensing and relaxing for a couple of weeks, you can switch to relaxing muscles only.

Relaxation of Arms (time: 4–5 minutes) Settle back as comfortably as you can. Let yourself relax to the best of your ability.... Now, as you relax like that, clench your right fist, just clench your fist tighter and tighter, and study the tension as you do so. Keep it clenched and feel the tension in your right fist, hand, forearm... and now relax. Let the fingers of your right hand become loose, and observe the contrast in your feelings.... Now, let yourself go and try to become more relaxed all over.... Once more, clench your right fist really tight... hold it, and notice the tension again.... Now let go, relax; your fingers straighten out, and you notice the difference once more.... Now repeat that with your left fist. Clench your left fist while the rest of your body relaxes; clench that fist tighter and feel the tension... and now relax. Again enjoy the contrast.... Repeat that once more, clench the left fist, tight and tense.... Now do the opposite of tension—relax and feel the difference. Continue relaxing like that for a while.... Clench both fists tighter and together, both fists tense, forearms tense, study the sensations... and relax; straighten out your fingers and feel that relaxation. Continue relaxing your hands and forearms more and more.... Now bend your elbows and tense your biceps, tense them harder and study the tension feelings... all right, straighten out your arms, let them relax and feel that difference again. Let the relaxation develop.... Once more, tense your biceps; hold the tension and observe it carefully.... Straighten the arms and relax; relax to the best of your ability.... Each time, pay close attention to your feelings when you tense up and when you relax. Now straighten your arms, straighten them so that you feel the most tension in the triceps muscles along the back of your arms; stretch your arms and feel that tension.... And now relax. Get your arms back into a comfortable position. Let the relaxation proceed on its own. The arms should feel comfortably heavy as you allow them to relax.... Straighten the arms once more so that you feel the tension in the triceps muscles; straighten them. Feel that tension... and relax. Now let's concentrate on pure relaxation in the arms without any tension. Get your arms comfortable and let them relax further and further. Continue relaxing your arms even further. Even when your arms seem fully relaxed, try to go that extra bit further; try to achieve deeper and deeper levels of relaxation.

Relaxation of Facial Area with Neck, Shoulders, and Upper Back (time: 4–5 minutes) Let all your muscles go loose and heavy. Just settle back quietly and comfortably. Wrinkle up your forehead now; wrinkle it tighter... And now stop wrinkling your forehead, relax and smooth it out. Picture the entire forehead and scalp becoming smoother as the relaxation increases.... Now frown and crease your brows and study the tension.... Let go of the tension again. Smooth out the forehead once more.... Now close your eyes tighter and tighter... feel the tension... and relax your eyes. Keep your eyes closed, gently, comfortably, and notice the relaxation.... Now clench your jaws, bite your teeth together; study the tension throughout the jaws.... Relax your jaws now. Let your lips part slightly.... Appreciate the relaxation.... Now press your tongue hard against the roof of your mouth. Look for the tension.... All right, let your tongue return to a comfortable and relaxed position.... Now purse your lips, press your lips together tighter and tighter.... Relax the lips. Note the contrast between tension and relaxation. Feel the relaxation all over your face, all over your forehead and scalp, eyes, jaws, lips, tongue, and throat. The relaxation progresses further and further.... Now attend to your neck muscles. Press your head back as far as it can go and feel the tension in the neck; roll it to the right and feel the tension shift; now roll it to the left. Straighten your head and bring it forward, press your chin against your chest. Let your head return to a comfortable position, and study the relaxation. Let the relaxation develop.... Shrug your shoulders, right up. Hold the tension.... Drop your shoulders and feel the relaxation. Neck and shoulders relaxed.... Shrug your shoulders again and move them around. Bring your shoulders up and forward and back. Feel the tension in your shoulders and in your upper back.... Drop your shoulders once more and relax. Let the relaxation spread deep into the shoulders, right into your back muscles; relax your neck and throat, and your jaws and other facial areas as the pure relaxation takes over and grows deeper... deeper... ever deeper.

Relaxation of Chest, Stomach, and Lower Back (time: 4–5 minutes)

Relax your entire body to the best of your ability. Feel that comfortable heaviness that accompanies relaxation. Breathe easily and freely in and out. Notice how the relaxation increases as you exhale... as you breathe out just feel that relaxation..... Now breathe right in and fill your lungs; inhale deeply and hold your breath. Study the tension.... Now exhale, let the walls of your chest grow loose and push the air out automatically. Continue relaxing and breathe freely and gently. Feel the relaxation and enjoy it.... With the rest of your body as relaxed as possible, fill your lungs again. Breathe in deeply and hold it again.... That's fine, breathe out and appreciate the relief. Just breathe normally. Continue relaxing your chest and let the relaxation spread to your back, shoulders, neck, and arms. Merely let go... and enjoy the relaxation. Now let's pay attention to your abdominal muscles, your stomach area. Tighten your stomach muscles, make your abdomen hard. Notice the tension.... And relax. Let the muscles loosen and notice the contrast.... Once more, press and tighten your stomach muscles. Hold the tension and study it.... And relax. Notice the general well-being that comes with relaxing your stomach.... Now draw your stomach in, pull the muscles right in and feel the tension this way.... Now relax again. Let your stomach out. Continue breathing normally and easily and feel the gentle massaging action all over your chest and stomach.... Now pull your stomach in again and hold the tension.... Now push out and tense like that; hold the tension... once more pull in and feel the tension... now relax your stomach fully. Let the tension dissolve as the relaxation grows deeper. Each time you breathe out, notice the rhythmic relaxation both in your lungs and in your stomach. Notice thereby how your chest and your stomach relax more and more.... Try and let go of contractions anywhere in your body.... Now direct your attention to your lower back. Arch up your back, make your lower back quite hollow, and feel the tension along your spine... and settle down comfortably again, relaxing the lower back.... Just arch your back up and feel the tensions as you do so. Try to keep the rest of your body as relaxed as possible. Try to localize the tension throughout your lower back area.... Relax once more, relaxing further and further. Relax your lower back, relax your upper back, spread the relaxation to your stomach, chest, shoulders, arms, and facial area. These parts relax further and further and further and ever deeper.

Relaxation of Hips, Thighs, and Calves Followed by Complete Body Relaxation (time: 4–5 minutes)

Let go of all tensions and relax... Now flex your buttocks and thighs. Flex your thighs by pressing down your heels.... Relax and note the difference.... Straighten your knees and flex your thigh muscles again. Hold the tension.... Relax your hips and thighs. Allow the relaxation to proceed on its own.... Press your feet and toes downward, away from your face, so that your calf muscles become tense. Study that tension.... Relax your feet and calves.... This time, bend your feet toward your face so that you feel tension along your shins. Bring your toes right up.... Relax again. Keep relaxing for a while.... Now let yourself relax further all over. Relax your feet, ankles, calves and shins, knees, thighs, buttocks, and hips. Feel the heaviness of your lower body as you relax still further.... Now spread the relaxation to your stomach, waist, lower back. Let go more and more. Feel the relaxation all over. Let it proceed to your upper back, chest, shoulders, and arms and right to the tips of your fingers. Keep relaxing more and more deeply. Make sure that no tension has crept into your throat; relax your neck and your jaws and all your facial muscles. Keep relaxing your whole body like that for a while. Let yourself relax.

Now you can become twice as relaxed as you are merely by taking in a really deep breath and slowly exhaling. With your eyes closed so that you become less aware of objects and movements around you and thus prevent any surface tensions from developing, breathe in deeply and feel yourself becoming heavier. Take a long, deep breath and let it out very slowly.... Feel how heavy and relaxed you have become. In a state of perfect relaxation you should feel unwilling to move a single muscle in your body. Think about the effort that would be required to raise your right arm. As you think about raising your right arm, see if you can notice any tensions that might have crept into your shoulder and your arm.... Now you decide not to lift the arm but to continue relaxing. Observe the relief and the disappearance of the tension.... Just carry on relaxing like that. When you wish to get up, count backwards from four to one. You should then feel fine and refreshed, wide awake and calm.

Breathe (Deeply, Through Your Diaphragm)

Has anyone ever told you to take a few deep breaths when you were feeling stressed or anxious? When we are tense, our breathing becomes shallow. We may hyperventilate, or breathe more rapidly than usual. When we breathe, we exchange oxygen for carbon dioxide. But when we hyperventilate, we breathe off too much carbon dioxide, which can cause feelings of dizziness or lightheadedness. Breathing slowly and deeply from the diaphragm tones down the body's response to stress and restores a correct balance between oxygen and carbon dioxide in our bloodstream.

Diaphragmatic breathing can be learned by practicing some simple skills:

1. *Breathe through the nose only.*
2. *Take the same amount of time to inhale and exhale.*
3. *Make inhaling and exhaling continuous and leisurely.* You can count silently to yourself (*one-thousand-one, one-thousand-two, one-thousand-three,* etc.) as you breathe in and out. Or you may use a particularly resonant-sounding word, like *relax,* on each outbreath (elongate the *x*-sound as you breathe out).
4. *Lie on your back in bed.* Place your hands lightly on your stomach. Breathe deeply and slowly in such a way that your stomach rises as you inhale and lowers as you exhale. You can also prac-

tice the technique while sitting upright in a comfortable chair. Place your right hand lightly on your stomach (or your left hand if you are left-handed). Place your other hand on your upper chest. Breathe in such a way that you can see your stomach move outward each time you inhale and move inward each time you exhale. By monitoring your chest movements, you can determine that you are not breathing through your throat, which is what happens when your breathing becomes shallow. If the hand positioned on your upper chest remains still while your hand monitoring your abdomen moves outward and inward with each inbreath and outbreath, you are breathing diaphragmatically.

As you become more familiar with diaphragmatic breathing, you may be able to breathe diaphragmatically by simply focusing your attention on taking deep, slow breaths, without any need to monitor the movements of your abdomen and chest with your hands. Many people find it helpful to continue using their relaxation word (such as *relax* on each outbreath) as a cue to help restore a relaxation effect.

When you are tense, anxious, or in pain, diaphragmatic breathing may help distract you from your discomfort. Monitoring your breaths can also help block out disturbing thoughts.

To sum up, stress is an inescapable part of life. Some stress is beneficial. It keeps us alert and motivated. Yet too much stress can overtax our ability to cope and put us at risk of stress-related health problems.

Handling stress means averting unnecessary stressors, keeping stress at manageable levels, and toning down the body's reaction to stress. Stress may be a fact of life, but it is a fact we can learn to live with. In the next chapter, we explore how stress and other psychological factors affect our physical health.

CHAPTER REVIEW

RECITE! RECITE! RECITE! RECITE! RECITE! RECITE! RECITE!

Study Tip: Reciting the answers to these study questions will help you become a more effective learner. First try answering the questions by yourself, either reciting them out loud or writing them in a notebook or on the computer. Then compare your answers with the sample answers provided below.

1. **What are the major sources of stress?**
   These include daily hassles; life events; acculturative stress; pain; frustration; conflict; Type A behavior; natural and technological disasters; terrorism; and environmental factors such as noise, extremes of temperature, pollution, and overcrowding.

2. **How do irrational beliefs create or compound stress?**
   Albert Ellis shows that negative activating events (A) can have more aversive consequences (C) when irrational beliefs (B), such as tendencies to catastrophize negative events, compound their effects. Two common irrational beliefs are excessive needs for social approval and perfectionism. Both set the stage for disappointment and increased stress.

3. **What kinds of disasters are there? How do they affect us?**
   There are natural and technical disasters. Not only do such disasters do physical and personal damage when they strike, but they also damage our support systems and our sense of control over our situations and our lives. The effects of disasters may linger for years after the physical damage is done. Terrorism is a source of stress that can shake our sense of living securely in our own homes and communities.

4. **How do environmental factors such as noise, temperature, pollution, and crowding affect our adjustment?**
   High noise levels are stressful and can impair learning and memory, as well as lead to health problems such as hearing loss, hypertension, and neurological and intestinal disorders. Loud noise also dampens helping behavior and heightens aggressiveness. Extremes of temperature tax the body, are a source of stress, and impair performance. High temperatures are also connected with aggression. The lead in auto fumes may impair learning and memory. Overcrowded living conditions are experienced as aversive and lead to feelings of intrusion into one's personal space. A sense of control or choice—as in choosing to attend a concert or athletic contest—helps us cope with the stress of high density.

5. **How do our self-efficacy expectations affect our adjustment?**
   When we feel capable of accomplishing tasks and meeting challenges, we are more likely to persist in difficult tasks and to endure discomfort.

6. **What characteristics are connected with psychological hardiness?**
   Suzanne Kobasa found that psychological hardiness among business executives is characterized by high levels of commitment, challenge, and control.

7. **Is there truth to the statement that "A merry heart doeth good like a medicine"?**
   We can't say, because evidence is not conclusive about the potential health benefits of humor or laughter. But we can say that humor does make us feel good, and there is something to be said for feeling good.

8. **How do predictability and control help us adjust?**
   Predictability allows us to brace ourselves for stress. Control permits us to plan and execute ways of coping with stress.

9. **Is there evidence that social support helps people adjust?**
   Social support may help bolster resistance to infectious diseases such as colds. It may also help people cope with the stress of cancer and other health problems. The kinds of social support include expression of emotional concern, instrumental aid, information, appraisal, and simple socializing.

YOUR PERSONAL JOURNAL

REFLECT   REFLECT   REFLECT   REFLECT   REFLECT   REFLECT   REFLECT

Study Tip: Reflecting on how the concepts in the chapter relate to your own experiences encourages deeper processing, which makes the material more personally meaningful and fosters more effective learning. Use additional pages if needed to complete your answers.

1. Hassles are an important source of stress in our lives. Describe some daily hassles you regularly encounter. How many are connected with your role as a student? What can you do about them?

   _____

   _____

   _____

   _____

2. Have you experienced any of the types of psychological conflicts described in the text? Which type of conflict was it? How did you resolve the conflict? (Or didn't you?)

   _____

   _____

   _____

   _____

ANSWERS TO MODULE REVIEWS

Module 3.1

1. hassles
2. changes
3. acculturative
4. endorphins
5. frustration
6. conflict
7. beliefs
8. Type A
9. decrease
10. increase

Module 3.2

11. higher
12. commitment
13. decreases
14. correlational
15. instrumental

SCORING KEY FOR COLLEGE LIFE STRESS INVENTORY SELF-ASSESSMENT

The developers of the College Life Stress Inventory administered their inventory to a sample of 257 students in Introductory Psychology. Though we can't say that their student sample was representative of undergraduate students in general, the scores they report provide a context for interpreting your own stress level. The average or mean score of the students was 1,247. About two of three students scored in the range of 806 to 1,688. Scores outside that range could be considered to reflect either low or high stress levels, respectively.

ANSWER KEY FOR "ARE YOU TYPE A OR TYPE B" SELF-ASSESSMENT

"Yes" answers suggest the Type A behavior pattern, which is marked by a sense of time urgency and constant struggle. In appraising your type, you need not be overly concerned with the precise number of "yes" answers; we have no normative data for you. But as Freidman and Rosenman (1974, p. 85) note, you should have little trouble spotting yourself as "hard core" or "moderately afflicted"—that is, if you are honest with yourself.

ANSWER KEY FOR THE "LOCUS OF CONTROL SCALE"

Place a checkmark in the blank space in the following scoring key each time your answer agrees with the answer in the key. The number of checkmarks is your total score.

Scoring Key

1. Yes	11. Yes	21. Yes	31. Yes
2. No	12. Yes	22. No	32. No
3. Yes	13. No	23. Yes	33. Yes
4. No	14. Yes	24. Yes	34. No
5. Yes	15. No	25. No	35. Yes
6. No	16. Yes	26. No	36. Yes
7. Yes	17. Yes	27. Yes	37. Yes
8. Yes	18. Yes	28. No	38. No
9. No	19. Yes	29. Yes	39. Yes
10. Yes	20. No	30. No	40. No

Interpreting Your Score

LOW SCORERS (0–8). About one respondent in three earns a score of from 0 to 8. Such respondents tend to have an internal locus of control. They see themselves as responsible for the reinforcements they attain (and fail to attain) in life.

AVERAGE SCORERS (9–16). Most respondents earn from 9 to 16 points. Average scorers may see themselves as partially in control of their lives. Perhaps they see themselves as in control at work, but not in their social lives—or vice versa.

HIGH SCORERS (17–40). About 15% of respondents attain scores of 17 or above. High scorers largely tend to see life as a game of chance, and success as a matter of luck or the generosity of others.

SCORING KEY FOR LIFE ORIENTATION TEST

In order to arrive at your total score for the test, first reverse your score on items 3, 8, 9, and 12. That is,

a. 4 is changed to 0
b. 3 is changed to 1
c. 2 remains the same
d. 1 is changed to 3
e. 0 is changed to 4

Now add the numbers of items 1, 3, 4, 5, 8, 9, 11, and 12. (Items 2, 6, 7, and 10 are "fillers"; that is, your responses are not scored as part of the test.) Your total score can vary from 0 to 32. Scheier and Carver (1985) provide the following norms for the test, based on administration to 357 undergraduate men and 267 undergraduate women. The average (mean) score for men was 21.03 (standard deviation = 4.56), and the mean score for women was 21.41 (standard deviation = 5.22). All in all, approximately two-thirds of undergraduates (men and women combined) obtained scores between 16 and 26. Scores above 26 may be considered quite optimistic, and scores below 16, quite pessimistic. Scores between 16 and 26 are within a broad average range, and higher scores within this range are relatively more optimistic.

Dragan Trifunovic/ iStockphoto

Some of us are our own best friends. We mind what we eat, we exercise regularly, and we monitor the sources of stress in our lives so that we can regulate their impact. Some of us are our own worst enemies. We share contaminated needles or engage in reckless sexual behavior despite knowledge that HIV/AIDS can be transmitted in these ways. We eat foods high in cholesterol and fats despite knowledge that we heighten the risks of coronary heart disease and cancer. And, of course, we continue to smoke even though we know full well that we are not invulnerable. As we shall see in this chapter, scientists have learned that psychological factors, such as stress and behavior patterns, play major roles in determining our vulnerability to potentially life-threatening diseases, such as heart disease, cancer, and diabetes, as well as the length and quality of our lives. In the following chapter, we examine the health benefits of developing healthier eating, fitness, and sleep habits. In this chapter, we consider ways in which our behavior patterns either help safeguard our health or put our health in jeopardy. We also explore the psychology of adjustment to physical illness, such as how people cope when faced with a serious illness.

MODULE 4.1

Physical, Emotional, and Cognitive Effects of Stress

▪ What is health psychology?
▪ What is the general adaptation syndrome?
▪ What are the emotional and cognitive effects of stress?
▪ How does the immune system work and how does stress affect it?

▌ **Health psychology** The field of psychology that studies the relationships between psychological factors (e.g., attitudes, beliefs, situational influences, and overt behavior patterns) and the prevention and treatment of physical illness.

Health psychology is the subfield of psychology that studies relationships between psychological factors and the prevention and treatment of physical health problems. Health psychologists study the ways in which:

- Psychological factors such as stress, behavior patterns, and attitudes lead to or aggravate physical health problems.
- People can cope with stress.
- Stress and pathogens (disease-causing organisms such as bacteria and viruses) interact to influence the immune system.
- People decide whether to seek health care.
- Psychological forms of intervention such as health education (for example, concerning nutrition, smoking, and exercise) and behavior modification programs can contribute to physical health.

One of health psychology's major areas of research is the effects of stress on physical health. Exposure to high levels of stress taxes our coping resources and puts us at risk of developing physical disorders ranging from headaches to heart disease. In this module we take a closer look at how stress affects the body.

4.1.1 The Body's Response to Stress

▌ **General adaptation syndrome (GAS)** Selye's term for a hypothesized three-stage response to stress.

Stress is more than a psychological event; it is more than "knowing" it is there; it is more than "feeling" pushed and pulled. Stress also has clear effects on the body. Famed stress researcher Hans Selye outlined the sequence of changes that occur in the body in response to stress, which he called the **general adaptation syndrome (GAS)**, or *stress response*. The body under persistent stress is apparently much like a clock with an alarm system that does not shut off until its energy has been depleted.

The General Adaptation Syndrome

Selye (1976), who was playfully called "Dr. Stress," observed that the body's response to different stressors shows certain similarities, whether the stressor is a bacterial invasion, perceived danger, or a major life change. For this reason, he labeled this response the *general adaptation syndrome (GAS)*. The GAS is a cluster of bodily changes that occur in three stages: an *alarm stage*, a *resistance stage*, and an *exhaustion stage*.

▌ **Alarm stage** The first stage of the GAS, which is "triggered" by the impact of a stressor and characterized by activity of the sympathetic branch of the autonomic nervous system.

▌ **Fight-or-flight reaction** Cannon's term for an innate adaptive response to the perception of danger.

▌ **Endocrine system** A body system involved in regulating many bodily processes and consisting of ductless glands that empty their secretions, called hormones, directly into the bloodstream.

▌ **Autonomic nervous system (ANS)** The part of the nervous system that regulates glands and involuntary activities such as heartbeat, respiration, digestion, and dilation of the pupils of the eyes.

▌ **Sympathetic nervous system** The division of the ANS that is most active during activities and emotional responses—such as anxiety and fear—that spend the body's reserves of energy.

▌ **Parasympathetic nervous system** The division of the ANS that is most active during processes that restore the body's reserves of energy, such as digestion.

The Alarm Stage   The **alarm stage** (also called the *alarm reaction*) is the body's initial response to a stressor. This reaction mobilizes or arouses the body in preparation to defend itself against a stressor. Early in the twentieth century, physiologist Walter B. Cannon (1929) termed this alarm response the **fight-or-flight reaction**. The alarm reaction is triggered by various types of stressors. It prepares the body to fight or flee from a threatening stressor or source of danger (Wargo, 2007).

The alarm reaction involves a number of body changes that are initiated by the brain and are further regulated by the **endocrine system** and the **autonomic nervous system (ANS)**. The autonomic nervous system is the part of the nervous system that automatically (*autonomic* means "automatic") controls involuntary bodily processes such as heartbeat and respiration. It consists of parts or divisions, the **sympathetic nervous system** and the **parasympathetic nervous system**. These systems have largely opposite effects. The sympathetic nervous system accelerates bodily processes, such as heart rate and breathing, and leads to the release of energy from stored reserves during times when the body needs additional oxygen and fuel to work harder or to defend itself against threats. The sympathetic nervous system takes control during the alarm reaction. The parasympathetic nervous system tones down states of bodily arousal and controls bodily processes that replenish resources, such as digestion. Let us now consider the roles of the endocrine and autonomic nervous systems in the stress response. First, however, you may wish to examine Figures 4.1 and 4.2 to learn more about the glands of the endocrine system and autonomic nervous system.

Stress has a domino effect on a set of endocrine glands that are labeled the *hypothalamus-pituitary-adrenal* (HPA) axis (Ellis, Jackson, & Boyce, 2006; Marin et al., 2007; Miller, Chen, & Zhou, 2007). Here's how it works:

1 A small structure in the brain called the **hypothalamus** secretes corticotropin-releasing hormone (CRH).

2 CRH causes the pituitary gland to secrete *adrenocorticotropic hormone* (ACTH).

3 ACTH then causes the *adrenal cortex*, the outer layer of the adrenal glands, to secrete **corticosteroids**, or *steroidal hormones*.

Corticosteroids help the body resist stress by making nutrients, which are stored in the body, available for use in meeting the demands for energy required to cope with stressful events (Ditzen et al., 2008; Het & Wolf, 2007; Kumsta et al., 2007). Although these hormones initially help the body cope with stress, continued secretion can be harmful to the cardiovascular system, which is one rea-

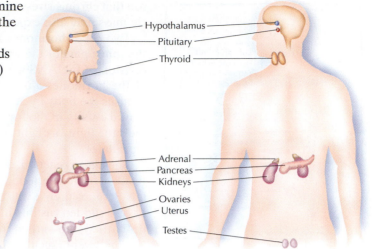

Figure 4.1

Glands of the Endocrine System
The endocrine system consists of a network of glands located throughout the body that secrete hormones directly into the bloodstream. The endocrine system plays important roles in reproduction, growth, metabolism, and the body's response to stress.

▮ **Hypothalamus** A small, pea-sized structure in the brain involved in regulating many bodily processes, including hunger, sleep, emotions, and body temperature.

▮ **Corticosteroids** Hormones produced by the adrenal cortex that increase resistance to stress in ways such as fighting inflammation and causing the liver to release stores of sugar. Also called *steroidal hormones*.

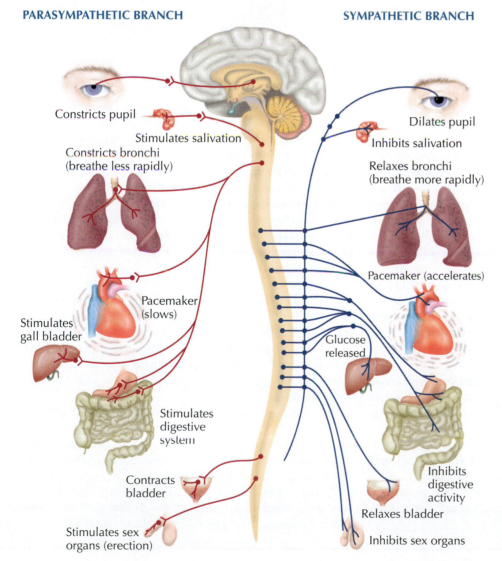

Figure 4.2

The Autonomic Nervous System
The autonomic nervous system (ANS) helps regulate automatic bodily responses, such as heart rate, respiration, and digestion. The parasympathetic branch, or division, of the ANS is generally dominant during activities that replenish the body's store of energy, such as digestion and rest. The sympathetic branch, or division, is most active during activities in which the body needs to expend energy, such as fighting or fleeing from a threatening stressor, and when we experience strong emotions such as fear and anger.

son that chronic stress can impair one's health. People who use steroids to build muscle mass may also experience cardiovascular problems.

Two other hormones that play a major role in the alarm stage are secreted by the inner part of the adrenal glands, called the *adrenal medulla*. The sympathetic division of the ANS activates the adrenal medulla, causing it to release a mixture of the hormones *adrenaline* and *noradrenaline*. This mixture of stress hormones arouses the body by accelerating the heart rate and stimulating the liver to release stored energy in the form of glucose (sugar). This process provides the energy that fuels the fight-or-flight reaction, which prepares the body to either fight or flee from a predator.

The alarm reaction, or fight-or-flight mechanism, is like an internal alarm system. It stems from a period in human prehistory when many stressors were life-threatening. Perhaps then it was triggered by the sight of a predator at the edge of a thicket or by a sudden rustling in the undergrowth. Today it may be aroused when you need to "battle" stop-and-go traffic or when you are confronted with an upsetting or challenging event, such as taking an examination. Once the threat is removed, the parasympathetic nervous system takes control and the body returns to a lower state of arousal. Many of the bodily changes that occur in the alarm reaction are outlined in Table 4.1.

Adjustment and Modern Life

"Fight or Flight" or "Tend and Befriend"? Understanding Gender Differences in Response to Stress

Nearly a century ago, Harvard University physiologist Walter Cannon labeled the body's response to stress the "fight-or-flight" reaction. He believed that the body was prewired to become mobilized or aroused in preparation for combat when faced with a predator or a competitor or, if the predator was threatening enough, that "discretion"—that is, a "strategic retreat"—would sometimes be the "better part of valor." The fight-or-flight reaction includes a cascading sequence of bodily changes involving the autonomic nervous and endocrine systems, under control of structures in the brain.

Emerging research examines stress-related responses through the lens of gender. UCLA psychologist Shelley Taylor and her colleagues (2000) argue that at least half of us are more likely to tend to the kids or "interface" with family and friends in the face of stress than to fight or flee. Which half of us would that be? The female half.

Taylor explains that her interest in the fight-or-flight reaction was prompted by an offhand remark of a student who had noticed that nearly all of the rats in studies of the effects of stress on animals were male. Taylor did an overview of the research on stress with humans and noted that prior to 1995, when federal agencies began requiring more equal representation of women if they were to fund research, only 17% of the subjects were female.

Quite a gender gap—and one that had allowed researchers to ignore the question of whether females responded to stress in the same way as males.

Taylor and her colleagues then dug more deeply into the literature and found that "men and women do have some reliably different responses to stress" (Taylor et al., 2000). She called the characteristic response to stress in women the "tend-and-befriend" response. It involves nurturing and seeking the support of others rather than fighting or fleeing. Taylor and her colleagues reviewed studies showing that when women faced a threat, a disaster, or even an especially bad day at the office, they often responded by caring for their children and seeking contact and support from others, particularly other women. After a bad day at the office, men are more likely to withdraw from the family or start arguments. This response may be prewired in female humans and in females of other mammalian species.

From the perspective of evolutionary theory, we might suggest that the tend-and-befriend response became imprinted in our genes because it promoted the survival of females who are tending to their offspring. (Females who choose to fight may die or at least be separated from their offspring—no evolutionary brass ring here.) Gender differences in behavior are frequently connected with gender differences in **hormones** and other biological factors.

This one is no different. Taylor and her colleagues point to the effects of the pituitary hormone *oxytocin*. This hormone stimulates labor and causes the breasts to eject milk when women nurse. It is also connected with nurturing behaviors such as affiliating with and cuddling one's young in many mammals (Taylor et al., 2000). The literature also shows that when oxytocin is released during stress, it tends to have a calming effect on both rats and humans, making them less afraid and more social.

Table 4.1 ▮ Components of the Alarm Reaction

Corticosteroids are secreted.
Adrenaline is secreted.
Noradrenaline is secreted.
Respiration rate increases.
Heart rate increases.
Blood pressure increases.
Muscles tense.
Blood shifts from internal organs to the skeletal musculature.
Digestion is inhibited.
Sugar is released from the liver.
Blood clotting increases.

The Resistance Stage If the alarm reaction mobilizes the body and the stressor is not removed, we enter the adaptation or **resistance stage** of the GAS. Levels of endocrine and sympathetic nervous system activity are lower than in the alarm reaction but still higher than normal. In this stage the body attempts to restore lost energy and repair bodily damage.

▮ **Hypertension** High blood pressure.

▮ **Hormones** Substances secreted by endocrine glands that regulate various body functions. (From the Greek *horman*, meaning "to stimulate" or "to excite.")

▮ **Resistance stage** The second stage of the GAS, characterized by prolonged sympathetic activity in an effort to restore lost energy and repair damage. Also called the *adaptation stage*.

But wait a minute! Men also release oxytocin when they are under stress. So why the gender difference? The answer may lie in the presence of other hormones, the sex hormones estrogen and testosterone. Females have more estrogen than males do, and estrogen appears to enhance the effects of oxytocin.

Males, on the other hand, have more testosterone than females, and testosterone may mitigate the effects of oxytocin by prompting feelings of self-confidence (which may be exaggerated) and fostering aggression (A. Sullivan, 2000). It is thus possible that males are more aggressive than females under stress because of biological differences in the hormone balance in their bodies, while females are more affiliative and nurturant. It makes evolutionary sense, at least. In order to perpetuate the human species and even make it tougher as the generations progress, it takes only a few tough men (does this sound like a commercial for the Marines?) to impregnate a large number of women. But men, even tough ones, may not outlive women. "Men are more likely than women to respond to stressful experiences by developing certain stress-related disorders, including **hypertension**, aggressive behavior, or abuse of alcohol or hard drugs," Taylor added in a UCLA press release (S.E. Taylor, 2000):

"Because the tend-and-befriend regulatory system may, in some ways, protect women against stress, this biobehavioral pattern may provide insights into why women live an average of seven and a half years longer than men."

Not all psychologists agree with an evolutionary or biological explanation. Psychologist Alice Eagly (2000) allows that gender differences in response to stress may be rooted in hormones but suggests we consider an alternative: Differences may reflect learning and cultural conditioning. "I think we have a certain amount of evidence that women are in some sense more affiliative, but what that's due to becomes the question. Is it biologically hard-wired? Or is it because women have more family responsibility and preparation for that in their development?

That is the big question for psychologists." A very big question, indeed.

Ghisiain & Marie David de Lossy/Image Bank/Getty Images, Inc.

"Fight-or-Flight" or "Tend-and-Befriend"?
Walter Cannon labeled the body's prewired response to stress the "fight-or-flight" reaction. However, new research by psychologist Shelley Taylor and her colleagues suggests that women may be "prewired" to take care of others ("tend") or affiliate with others ("befriend") when they encounter stressful events.

▍ **Exhaustion stage** The third stage of the GAS, characterized by weakened resistance and possible deterioration.

The Exhaustion Stage   If the stressor is still not dealt with adequately, we may enter the **exhaustion stage** of the GAS. Individual capacities for resisting stress vary, but the body will eventually become exhausted when stress continues indefinitely. The muscles become fatigued. The body is depleted of the resources required for combating stress. With exhaustion, the parasympathetic nervous system comes to dominate. As a result, our heartbeat, respiration rate, and bodily arousal may slow down. It might sound as if we would profit from the respite, but remember that we are still under stress—possibly an external threat. Continued stress in the exhaustion stage may lead to what Selye calls *diseases of adaptation*. These medical disorders can range from allergies to hives to even coronary heart disease (CHD)—and, ultimately, death.

Though people differ in their ability to sustain stress, high levels of persistent or unrelieved stress eventually overtax the body's resources to the point where the person becomes more susceptible to stress-related disorders (Cohen, Janicki-Deverts, & Miller, 2007; Kemeny, 2003). Later in the chapter we explore a number of these stress-related illnesses.

Emotional Effects of Stress

Emotions color our lives. We are green with envy, red with anger, blue with sorrow. Poets paint a thoughtful mood as a brown study. Positive emotions such as love and desire can fill our days with pleasure, but negative emotions, such as those induced by stress, can fill us with dread and make each day an intolerable chore. Let us consider three important emotional responses to stress: anxiety, anger, and depression.

Anxiety   Anxiety tends to occur in response to threats posed by such stressors as physical danger, loss, and failure. Anxiety is a stressor in its own right (it places demands on us) as well as an emotional response to stress.

▍ **Trait anxiety** Anxiety as a personality variable, or persistent trait.

▍ **State anxiety** A temporary condition of anxiety that may be attributed to a specific situation.

Psychologists frequently distinguish between **trait anxiety** and **state anxiety**. Trait anxiety is a personality variable. People with trait anxiety have persistent feelings of dread and foreboding—cognitions that something terrible is about to happen. They are chronically worried and concerned. State anxiety is a temporary condition of arousal that is triggered by a specific situation, such as the eve of a final exam, a big date, a job interview, or a visit to the dentist.

On a biological level, sympathetic nervous system arousal in response to stress is associated with physical symptoms such as rapid heartbeat and breathing, sweating, and muscle tension. These physical responses are often accompanied by strong emotions such as terror, fright, anxiety, rage, or anger. (Think back to a time when you experienced fear or anger. Was your heart beating rapidly? Did you break out in a sweat—perhaps a cold sweat?) Because sympathetic nervous activation predominates when you are under stress, digestion is inhibited. Thus, fear may be accompanied by indigestion.

Anger   Anger usually occurs in response to stressors such as frustration and social provocation. Hostility differs from anger in that it is an enduring trait. Anger usually involves cognitions (thoughts and beliefs) to the effect that the world should not thwart our efforts to meet our needs (in the case of frustration) or that another person has no right to treat us in a certain way (in the case of a social provocation). Like anxiety, it is accompanied by strong bodily responses, such as rapid heartbeat and breathing.

Depression   Depression usually occurs in response to stressors such as the loss of a friend, lover, or relative; to failure; to inactivity or lack of stimulation; or to prolonged stress. Why does depression sometimes stem from inactivity and lack of stimulation? People have needs for stimulation, and some "stress" is desirable and healthful.

Why does depression stem from prolonged exposure to stress? On a biological level, depression is characterized by parasympathetic dominance, and parasympathetic activity is characteristic of the exhaustion stage of the GAS.

Emotions and Behavior Emotions motivate certain kinds of behavior. Negative emotions such as anxiety, anger, and depression can motivate us to behave in maladaptive ways. For example, anxiety tends to motivate escape behavior; anger, aggressive behavior; and depression, withdrawal.

It is helpful for us to perceive negative emotional responses as signs that something is wrong, to learn what we can about the sources of stress, and then to plan behavior that will enable us to remove or buffer stressors. But when our emotions "run too high," they can disrupt our cognitive processes and interfere with adaptive behavior.

Cognitive Effects of Stress

Under stress, we may have difficulty thinking clearly or remaining focused on the tasks at hand. The high levels of bodily arousal that characterize the alarm reaction can impair memory functioning and problem-solving ability. During examinations—a source of stress that can trigger the alarm reaction—you may have experienced such high levels of negative arousal (anxiety) that you are unable to recall material you were sure you had banked in memory. Afterward, you might think, "I just drew a blank." Also, in a state of high arousal, we may become so focused on our body responses or expectations of failure or doom that we cannot keep our thoughts on the problems at hand.

4.1.2 Effects of Stress on the Immune System

Given the complexity of the human body and the fast pace of scientific change, we often feel that we are dependent on trained professionals to cope with illness. Yet we actually do most of this coping by ourselves, by means of the body's **immune system**. The immune system is the body's line of defense against disease and defective cells (Jiang & Chess, 2006; Kay, 2006). The immune system dispatches billions of specialized white blood cells that engulf and kill **pathogens** such as bacteria, fungi, and viruses, as well as worn-out and cancerous body cells. The technical term for white blood cells is **leukocytes**. Leukocytes conduct microscopic warfare. They engage in search-and-destroy missions in which they "recognize" and eradicate foreign agents and unhealthy cells. These white blood cells are the microscopic warriors in our bodies that continually carry out search-and-destroy missions against foreign agents that may have entered the body. Leukocytes recognize foreign agents (viruses and bacteria, for example) to enhance the effectiveness of future combat. The surfaces of the foreign agents are termed **antigens** (*anti*body *gen*erators) because the body reacts to their presence by generating specialized proteins, or **antibodies**, that fit into these foreign bodies like a key fitting a lock, inactivating them and marking them for destruction by killer white blood cells (Greenwood, 2006; Kay, 2006). The immune system "remembers" how to battle these foreign invaders by maintaining antibodies in the bloodstream.

Inflammation is another function of the immune system. When injury occurs, blood vessels in the area first contract (to stem bleeding) and then dilate. Dilation increases the flow of blood to the damaged area, causing the redness and warmth that characterize inflammation. The increased blood supply also floods the region with white blood cells to combat invading microscopic life-forms such as bacteria, which otherwise might use the local damage as a port of entry into the body. Psychologists, biologists, and medical researchers have combined their efforts in a field of study that addresses the relationships among psychological factors, the nervous system, the endocrine system, the immune system, and disease: **psychoneuroimmunology** (Ader,

▌ **Immune system** The system of the body that recognizes and destroys foreign agents (antigens) that invade the body.

▌ **Pathogens** Microscopic organisms (e.g., bacteria or virus) that can cause disease.

▌ **Leukocytes** White blood cells. (Derived from the Greek words *leukos*, meaning "white," and *kytos*, literally meaning "a hollow," but used to refer to cells.)

▌ **Antigens** Substances that stimulate the body to mount an immune system response. (The contraction for *anti*body *gen*erator.)

▌ **Antibodies** Substances formed by white blood cells that recognize and destroy antigens.

▌ **Inflammation** Increased blood flow to an injured area of the body, resulting in redness, warmth, and increased supply of white blood cells.

▌ **Psychoneuroimmunology** The field that studies the relationships between psychological factors (e.g., attitudes and overt behavior patterns) and the functioning of the immune system.

Corbis/SuperStock

Stress and the Common Cold
Chronic stress can leave us more vulnerable to disease, including the common cold.

Felten, & Cohen, 2001). One of its major concerns, as we see next, is the effect of stress on the immune system.

Though occasional stress may not harm us, chronic or persistent stress can weaken the immune system, making us more vulnerable to many forms of disease (Fan et al., 2009; Gorman, 2007). Chronic stress affects our physical health in many ways. For example, it is linked to impaired wound healing and to lower production of the body's own natural killer cells—immune system cells that eradicate pathogens from the body (Dougall & Baum, 2001 Robles, Glaser, & Kiecolt-Glaser, 2005).

Chronic stress also increases the body's production of *corticosteroids*—steroidal hormones produced by the adrenal glands. Over time, these hormones suppress (dampen) the functioning of the immune system (Fan et al., 2009). Suppression has negligible effects when steroids are secreted intermittently—every so often. However, persistent secretion of these steroids reduces the body's production of antibodies. As a consequence, we become more vulnerable to various illnesses, including the common cold. The immune system is also weakened by the regular use of synthetic steroids, which are a class of drugs that have legitimate medical uses but are often abused by some athletes seeking to build up muscle mass.

Stress hormones may even affect the health of our relationships. A recent study measured stress hormones in newlyweds; those whose bodies pumped out more of these hormones during the fitrst year of marriage were more likely to get divorced within 10 years than were others with a lower stress response (Kiecolt-Glaser et al., 2003). Social support may moderate the damaging effects of persistent stress on the body. An early study of dental school students showed that those who had many friends had better immune system functioning during times of stress than did those with fewer friends (Jemmott et al., 1983). The lesson here is that we may be better able to maintain our health through times of stress if we have a strong social network to draw on. In later research, investigators showed that people with a wider social network were more resistant to the common cold after they were intentionally exposed to a cold virus than were others with a narrower range of social contacts (Cohen et al., 1997).

Life Changes and Physical Health

Another way of examining links between stress and illness is by comparing health outcomes in relation to the number of life changes (or life events) people experience. You'll recall from Chapter 3 that life changes are stressful because they impose burdens on people that require adjustment. Evidence shows that people who experience more life changes during a given period of time are more likely to encounter both psychological and physical health problems (Dohrenwend, 2006). However, we need to be cautious when interpreting these linkages. For one thing, the relationships between life events and physical health problems are generally small in magnitude. For another, researchers are not convinced that the causal connections are all that clear.

Let us consider a number of limitations in the research on the connections among daily hassles, life changes, and health problems:

1 *Correlational evidence.* Links between life changes and illness are based on correlational rather than experimental research. It may seem logical that the hassles and life changes caused the disorders, but these variables were not manipulated experimentally. Other explanations of the data are possible. One possible explanation is that people who are predisposed to medical or psycho-

logical problems encounter more hassles and experience more significant life changes. For example, medical disorders may contribute to sexual problems, arguments with spouses or in-laws, changes in living conditions and personal habits, and changes in sleeping habits.

2 *Positive versus negative life changes.* Other aspects of the research on the relationship between life changes and illness have also been challenged. For instance, we may need to distinguish the effects of hassles and negative life changes from positive changes. In other words, positive changes may be stressful, but they are less of a hassle than negative changes.

3 *Personality differences.* We may also need to account for personality differences. For example, people with different kinds of personalities may respond to life stresses in different ways. People who are easygoing or psychologically hardy are less likely to become ill under the impact of stress.

4 *Cognitive appraisal.* The stress impact of an event reflects the meaning of the event to the individual (Folkman & Moskowitz, 2000a). Pregnancy, for example, can be a positive or negative life change, depending on whether one wants and is prepared to have a child. We evaluate stressful events in terms of their perceived danger, our values and goals, our beliefs in our coping ability, our social support, and so on. The same event will be less taxing to someone with greater coping ability and support than to someone who lacks these advantages.

We can see that the relationships between life changes and physical health are complex. Nonetheless, since hassles and life changes require adjustment, it seems wise to be aware of them and how they may affect us.

We may be better able to protect our health during times of stress simply by writing about the sources of stress in our lives. Evidence shows that writing about stressful events can improve both physical and psychological health and even improve immune system functioning (Frattaroli , 2006; Langens & Schuler, 2007; Low, Stanton, & Danoff-Burg, 2006; Pennebaker, 2004). Though additional research is needed on the therapeutic value of this form of personal writing, there may be benefits to the time-honored custom of keeping a diary of your daily experiences, stresses and all. Even if writing about the stresses in your life doesn't improve your physical health, it may help relieve the psychological effects of daily stress.

Photodisc Red/Getty Images, Inc.

"Gotta Have Friends"
Evidence supports the view that having a wide range of social contacts helps us maintain our health during times of stress.

© Biology Media/Photo Researchers, Inc.

Microscopic Warfare
The immune system helps us to combat disease. It produces white blood cells (leukocytes), such as the one shown here, that routinely engulf and kill pathogens like bacteria and viruses.

MODULE REVIEW

Review It

(1) _____ _____ studies the relationships between psychological factors and the prevention and treatment of physical illness.

(2) The general adaptation syndrome has three stages: alarm, _____, and exhaustion.

(3) Cannon called the alarm reaction the _____ _____ _____ reaction.

(4) Women may show a _____ _____ _____ response to stress rather than fight-or-flight.

(5) Under stress, pituitary ACTH causes the adrenal cortex to release _____ that help the body respond to stress.

(6) Two hormones that play a role in the alarm reaction are secreted by the adrenal medulla: adrenaline and _____.

(7) The emotion of _____ tends to occur in response to threats.

(8) Trait anxiety is a personality variable, whereas _____ _____ is triggered by a specific threat.

(9) Anxiety involves predominantly (sympathetic or parasympathetic?) arousal.

(10) Strong arousal (aids or impairs?) problem-solving ability.

(11) The immune system produces (red or white?) blood cells, called _____, that routinely engulf and kill pathogens.

(12) Some leukocytes produce _____, or specialized proteins that bind to their antigens and mark them for destruction.

(13) Evidence shows that stress can weaken the _____ system.

(14) Life _____ are correlated with physical health problems, but the causal linkages remain unclear.

Think About It

In what ways does prolonged stress impair our ability to adjust?

MODULE 4.2

Factors in Health and Illness

▪ ▪

▪ What is the multifactorial approach to health?

▪ How are factors of ethnicity, gender, and socioeconomic status related to physical health?

▪ **Multifactorial model** The view that health and illness are a function of multiple factors involving biological, psychological, and cultural domains—and their interactions.

Why do some people become ill while others maintain their health and vitality? Why do some people develop cancer? Why do some have heart attacks? Why do some of us seem to come down with everything that is going around, while others ride out the roughest winters with nary a sniffle? A leading contemporary model in health psychology, the **multifactorial model**, recognizes that there is no single, simple answer to these questions. The likelihood of contracting an illness—be it the flu or cancer—can reflect the interaction of many factors, including genetic factors and lifestyle factors. Biological factors such as pathogens, inoculations, injuries, age, gender, and a family history of disease may strike us as playing obvious roles in determining the risk of illness.

Genetics, in particular, tempts some people to assume there is little they can do about their health. However, as Jane Brody (1996b), a leading health writer for the *New York Times,* put it, "a bad family medical history" does not portend doom but should be recognized as an opportunity to "keep those nasty genes from expressing themselves." For example, genetic factors are involved in breast cancer (T. Walsh et al., 2006). However, rates of breast cancer among women who have recently immigrated to the United States from rural Asia are similar to those in their countries of origin and nearly 80% lower than the rates among third-generation Asian American women, whose rates are similar to those of European American women (Hoover, 2000). From such evidence we come to see that factors related to one's lifestyle (diet, smoking, exercise, etc.) are intimately connected with the risk of developing serious illnesses, such as cancer, heart disease, and diabetes (Mitka, 2003; Mokdad et al., 2003). The good news is that practicing healthier behaviors can save lives—even yours (see Table 4.2).

As shown in Figure 4.3, psychological (behavior and personality) factors, sociocultural factors, environmental factors, and stressors all play roles in health and illness. Many health problems are affected by psychological factors, such as attitudes,

Table 4.2 ▌ Healthier Behaviors Save Lives

- Elimination of tobacco use could prevent 440,000 deaths each year from cancer, heart and lung diseases, and stroke.
- Improved diet and exercise could prevent 300,000 deaths from conditions such as heart disease, stroke, diabetes, and cancer.
- Control of underage and excess drinking of alcohol could prevent 100,000 deaths from motor vehicle accidents, falls, drownings, and other alcohol-related injuries.
- Immunizations for infectious diseases could prevent up to 100,000 deaths.
- Safer sex or sexual abstinence could prevent 20,000 deaths from sexually transmitted infections (STIs).

Sources: National Center for Health Statistics, U.S. Department of Health and Human Services, Centers for Disease Control and Prevention

Biological Factors
Family history of illness
Exposure to infectious organisms
  (e.g., bacteria and viruses)
Functioning of the immune system
Inoculations
Medication history
Congenital disabilities, birth complications
Physiological conditions (e.g., hypertension,
  serum cholesterol level)
Reactivity of the cardiovascular system to stress
  (e.g., "hot reactor")
Pain and discomfort
Age
Gender
Ethnicity (e.g., genetic vulnerability to
  Tay-Sachs disease or sickle-cell anemia)

Environmental Factors
Vehicular safety
Architectural features (e.g., crowding,
  injury-resistant design, nontoxic
  construction materials, aesthetic
  design, air quality, noise insulation)
Aesthetics of residential, workplace,
  and communal architecture and
  landscape architecture
Water quality
Solid waste treatment and sanitation
Pollution
Radiation
Global warming
Ozone depletion
Natural disasters (earthquakes, blizzards,
  floods, hurricanes, drought, extremes
  of temperature, tornadoes)

Behavior
Diet (intake of calories, fats, fiber, vitamins, etc.)
Consumption of alcohol
Cigarette smoking
Level of physical activity
Sleep patterns
Safety practices (e.g., using seat belts; careful driving; practice
  of sexual abstinence, monogamy, or "safer sex"; adequate
  prenatal care)
Having (or not having) regular medical and dental checkups
Compliance with medical and dental advice
Interpersonal/social skills

Sociocultural Factors
Socioeconomic status
Family circumstances (social class, family size, family conflict, family disorganization)
Access to health care (e.g., adequacy of available health care, availability of health
  insurance, availability of transportation to health care facilities)
Prejudice and discrimination
Health-related cultural and religious beliefs and practices
Health promotion in the workplace or community
Health-related legislation

Personality
Seeking (or avoiding) information about
  health risks and stressors
Self-efficacy expectations
Psychological hardiness
Psychological conflict (approach–approach,
  avoidance–avoidance, approach–avoidance)
Optimism or pessimism
Attributional style (how one explains one's
  failures and health problems to oneself)
Health locus of control (belief that one is or
  is not in charge of one's own health)
Introversion/extraversion
Chronic hostility
Tendencies to express or hold in feelings of
  anger and frustration
Depression/anxiety
Hostility/suspiciousness

Stressors
Daily hassles (e.g., preparing meals, illness, time pressure,
  loneliness, crime, financial insecurity, problems with co-workers,
  day care)
Major life changes such as divorce, death of a spouse,
  taking out a mortgage, losing a job
Frustration
Pain and discomfort
Availability and use of social support vs. peer rejection or isolation
Climate in the workplace (e.g., job overload, sexual harassment)

Figure 4.3
The Multifactorial Model of Health and Illness
The multifactorial model holds that a wide range of factors, including those listed here, determine our health and susceptibility to illness. Which of these factors are beyond your ability to control? Which are you capable of controlling?

Figure 4.4
Numbers of Deaths in United States Due to Behavioral Causes
Source: Schroeder, 2007

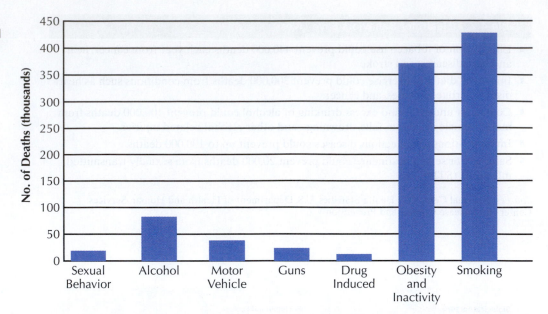

emotions, and behavior. And, as shown in Figure 4.4, nearly 1 million deaths could be prevented each year in the United States if people adopted healthier behaviors (Schroeder, 2007). Stopping smoking, eating right, exercising, and controlling alcohol use would prevent nearly 80% of these deaths. Psychological states such as anxiety and depression can also impair the functioning of the immune system, rendering us more vulnerable to physical disorders. Identifying and treating these emotional problems not only would improve one's mental health but also might reduce the risks of physical illness.

In this module, we consider sociocultural factors associated with physical health and illness. We then examine the role of psychological factors in some leading health problems, including headaches, heart disease, and cancer. In each case we consider the interplay of biological, psychological, social, technological, and environmental factors in their development. We also explore ways in which psychologists can make important contributions to the treatment of physical health disorders.

Other measures for preventing needless deaths include improved worker training and safety to prevent accidents in the workplace, wider screening for breast and cervical cancer, and control of high blood pressure and elevated blood cholesterol levels.

Human Diversity and Health: A Land of Many Nations

From the perspective of health and health care, we are many nations and not just one. Many factors influence whether people engage in healthful behaviors or whether they have access to advances in medical treatment. These factors include ethnicity, gender, level of education, and socioeconomic status.

Ethnicity and Health Although life expectancy has been steadily rising for all ethnic/racial groups in the United States, the life expectancy of African Americans still lags behind that of European Americans by about seven years on the average. An important contributor to these differences is socioeconomic status (SES): African Americans are disproportionately represented among the lower income levels in our society and people on the lower rungs of the socioeconomic ladder typically have lower life expectancies and poorer qualities of life (Siegler, Bosworth, & Poon, 2003). Other factors may also contribute, including differences in diet, exercise patterns, and access to health care, as well as genetic factors.

The United States and Canada have the resources to provide the most advanced health care in the world. But not all of us have access to these advantages. Because of lower SES and lack of affordable health insurance, African Americans tend to have less access to quality health care than do European Americans (Etchason et al., 2001; Lurie, 2005; Vaccarino et al., 2005).

African Americans also tend to receive different levels of treatment by medical practitioners. African Americans are less likely to receive hip and knee replacements, kidney transplants, and even mammograms and flu shots (Epstein & Ayanian, 2001; Freeman & Payne, 2000). Why these discrepancies? Various explanations have been offered, including cultural differences, patient preferences, lack of information about health care, and racism.

Disproportionately high numbers of African Americans and Latino and Latina Americans in the United States are living with HIV/AIDS. Nearly half of the men and three-quarters of the women with AIDS are African American or Latino and Latina American, even though these groups make up only about one-quarter of the population. Death rates due to AIDS are higher among African Americans and Latino and Latina Americans than among European Americans, in large part because European Americans have greater access to high-quality health care.

African Americans are more likely than European Americans to have heart attacks and strokes and to die from them. Figure 4.5 compares the death rates from heart disease of African American women and women from other ethnic backgrounds in the United States. Early diagnosis and treatment might help decrease the racial gap. However, African Americans with heart disease are less likely than European Americans to obtain aggressive and potential life-saving treatments such as cardiac catheterization and coronary artery bypass surgery, even when they would benefit equally from them (e.g., Chen et al., 2001; Freeman & Payne, 2000; Vaccarino et al., 2005). Moreover, when European Americans and African Americans show up in the emergency room with heart attacks or other severe cardiac problems, physicians are more likely to misdiagnose the conditions among the African Americans (Pope, Kouri, & Hudson, 2000). Do emergency room physicians pay less attention to the health concerns of African Americans?

African Americans with high blood pressure also have the highest risk of dying from heart disease due to hypertension of any U.S. population group (Wright et al., 2005). One in three African Americans have the disorder. African Americans have higher rates of obesity and diabetes than the general population, and both of these factors are linked to an increased risk of high blood pressure (Brown, 2006; Ferdinand, 2006). Possible genetic differences in sodium (salt) sensitivities may be involved. Yet another factor, exposure to racism and prejudice on a regular basis, is linked to poorer physical and psychological health among ethnic minorities (King, 2005; Mays, Cochran, & Barnes, 2007). On the other hand, having a strong sense of ethnic identity and pride in one's cultural heritage can strengthen one's ability to cope with racism and prejudice (Greene et al., 2006).

In addition, African Americans have higher rates of cancer than persons of any other racial or ethnic group in our society (National Center for Chronic Disease Prevention and Health Promotion, 2005). They also have higher death rates from cancer than any other American group except Native Americans (Freeman & Payne, 2000). As an illustration, see Figure 4.6, which shows rates of lung cancer cases among several major racial/ethnic groups in our society. What might account for racial/ethnic differences in rates of cancer and deaths due to cancer?

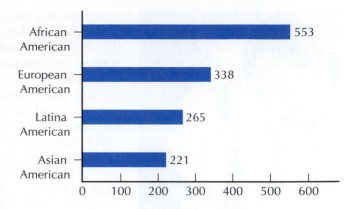

Figure 4.5
Deaths per 100,000 Women Aged 35 and Above from Heart Disease
African American women have experienced a higher annual death rate from heart attacks (553 per 100,000) than women from any other ethnic group in the United States.

Figure 4.6
Rates of Lung Cancer Among Major Racial/Ethnic Groups
The rates of lung cancer are higher among men than women. They also differ for different racial and ethnic groups, as shown in this figure. Black men have higher rates of lung cancer than men from other groups. Asian/Pacific Islander men and Hispanic men have the lowest rates. Among women, white women have the highest rate of lung cancer. Asian/Pacific Islander women and Hispanic women have the lowest rates, which shouldn't be surprising given the fact that they also have the lowest smoking rates.
Source: National Cancer Institute.

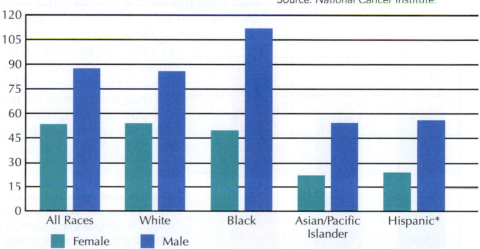

Rates are per 100,000 persons and are age adjusted to the 2000 U.S. standard population; rates cover approximately 92% of the U.S. population.
*The ethnic category Hispanic may include different race categories (white, black, Asian/Pacific Islander).

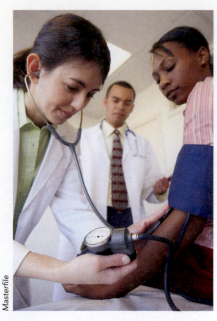

Masterfile

Ethnicity and Hypertension
African Americans are more likely than European Americans to have high blood pressure. Since you cannot directly sense your level of blood pressure, you need to be checked regularly for it. (You can also do self-testing with a kit you can purchase in nearly any pharmacy.) African Americans may be genetically more vulnerable than European Americans to hypertension, but psychological factors found among many African Americans, such as stress, diet (especially a diet high in salt), and smoking, also contribute to high blood pressure (in anyone).

African Americans are disproportionately represented among the lower-income groups in our society. People from poorer communities have higher cancer death rates than those from more affluent areas, in part because people from poorer areas tend to have more risk factors (physical inactivity, smoking) and in part because they often lack access to early detection (screening) programs and treatment services. Once they develop cancer, African Americans are more likely than European Americans to die from it. The higher cancer death rates for African Americans are more likely connected with their lower socioeconomic status and relative lack of access to health care than to biological differences in the cancer itself (Bach et al., 2003).

The case of breast cancer is somewhat different. Overall, African American women are less likely than European American women to develop breast cancer. However, when they do, they often do so at an earlier age, tend to be diagnosed with it somewhat later, and are more likely to die from it (National Cancer Institute, 2000; see Figure 4.7). The later diagnosis may be a result of less access to health care, but genetic factors may also be involved.

Let us also consider cultural differences in dietary factors. A study that followed more than 40,000 women for five years found that women who ate diets high in fruits and vegetables and low in saturated fats tended to live longer (Kant et al., 2000). It has also been shown that death rates from cancer are higher in such nations as the Netherlands, Denmark, England, Canada, and—yes—the United States, where average daily fat intake is high (Cohen, 1987). Death rates from cancer are much lower in such nations as Thailand, the Philippines, and Japan, where average daily fat intake is much lower. Thailand, the Philippines, and Japan are Asian nations, but do not assume that the difference is racial! The diets of Japanese Americans are similar in fat content to those of other Americans—and so are their rates of death from cancer.

There are health care "underusers" among American ethnic/racial groups. For example, Latino and Latina Americans visit physicians less often than African Americans and European Americans do because of lack of health insurance, difficulty speaking English, misgivings about medical technology, and—for illegal aliens—concerns about deportation.

Gender and Health One prominent risk factor for coronary heart disease (CHD) is male gender. Men are more likely than women to develop CHD until about age 65, when the rates begin to even out. The estrogen circulating in a woman's body may have a protective effect on her heart and blood vessels. CHD in women is uncommon until menopause but then rises sharply with increasing age as estrogen production falls off sharply (Mendelsohn & Karas, 2005). But gender may also play a role in how cardiac incidents are treated. When women and men show up in the emergency room with symptoms of heart attacks and other serious cardiac problems, the conditions are more likely to be misdiagnosed in women (Pope et al., 2000).

The gender of the physician can also make a difference. According to a study of more than 90,000 women, women whose internists or family practitioners are women are more likely to have screening for cancer (mammograms and Pap smears) than women whose internists or family practitioners are men (Lurie et al., 1993). It is unclear from this study, however, whether female physicians are more likely than their male counterparts to encourage women to seek preventive care,

Figure 4.7
Ethnic/Racial Difference in Death Rates[*] for Breast Cancer
Here we see the racial disparities in death rates from breast cancer. Health researchers recognize that we need to overcome barriers to screening if the benefits of early detection are to be achieved for all population groups.
[*]Per 100,000 population, age-adjusted.
Source: Mortality Rates for Four Major Cancers, by Sex and Race/Ethnicity—United States, 1990–1998. Morbidity and Mortality Weekly Report, Vol. 51, 2002, 49–53.

(Bar graph: y-axis 0 to 30. Overall ≈ 22.5, Whites ≈ 22, Blacks ≈ 29.5)

or whether women who choose female physicians are also more likely to seek preventive care. Other research shows that female physicians are more likely than male physicians to conduct breast examinations properly (J.A. Hall et al., 1990).

On the average, women live about five years longer than men (life expectancies are 75.2 years for men versus 80.4 years for women). Although the gender gap in longevity has been narrowing, men typically don't live as long as women in part because they are more likely to die from acts of violence, accidents, cirrhosis of the liver (related to alcoholism), and suicide. Yet another factor may be lack of attention to their health. Surveys of physicians and of the general population find that women are generally more willing than men to seek health care (Courtenay, 2000). Men often let symptoms go until a problem that could have been prevented or readily treated becomes serious or life-threatening. "Health is a macho thing," notes one physician (cited in Kolata, 2000b). "Men don't like to be out of control. So they deny their symptomology."

We've underscored the importance of taking socioeconomic status into account when considering ethnic or racial differences in health and longevity. There is an element of truth to the notion that the rich get healthier and the poor get sicker. More affluent people typically have better access to quality health care and are generally better educated than poorer people. Better-educated people tend to smoke less, exercise more, and take better care of their health than less well educated people. So the relationship between SES and poorer health may be at least partly explained by education. The challenge to health providers and educators is to disseminate knowledge about healthier behaviors more broadly within society (not only through the college classroom), as well as to assist the economically disadvantaged members of society to gain better access to quality health care and develop healthier lifestyles.

MODULE REVIEW

Review It

(15) The belief that our health depends on an interaction of factors, including genetic and lifestyle factors, is called the _____ _____.

(16) African Americans tend to have (more or less?) access to health care than European Americans do.

(17) African Americans are (more or less?) likely than European Americans to have heart attacks and contract most forms of cancer.

(18) Men's life expectancies are five years (longer or shorter?) than women's.

Think About It

Why is it incorrect to say that our health is just a matter of luck or genes?

MODULE 4.3

Psychological Factors in Physical Health Problems

▮ How has psychology contributed to understanding and treating headaches?

▮ How has psychology contributed to understanding and treating menstrual problems?

▮ How has psychology contributed to understanding and treating coronary heart disease?

▮ How has psychology contributed to understanding and treating cancer?

We might think that problems of the mind and body, of mental illness and physical illness, represent two completely separate domains. But the workings of the mind and the body are actually much more closely intertwined than they may appear at first blush. In Chapter 8 we will explore the role of biological factors in patterns of abnormal behavior called *mental disorders* or *mental illnesses*. But psychological factors play a role in a great many physical disorders. In this module, we examine the role of psychological factors in the two leading killer diseases in our society—heart disease and cancer. But first we will focus on the psychological dimensions of two common physical problems—headaches and premenstrual syndrome. While the physical health problems we review in this module are medical disorders, psychological factors play important roles in understanding and treating them.

4.3.1 Headaches: Pounding Away

Headaches are among the most common stress-related physical ailments. Nearly 20% of people in the United States suffer from severe headaches. Two of the most common types of headaches are muscle-tension and migraine headaches.

Muscle-Tension Headache

The single most frequent kind of headache is the muscle-tension headache. During the first two stages of the GAS, we are likely to contract muscles in the shoulders, neck, forehead, and scalp. Persistent stress can lead to constant contraction of these muscles, causing muscle-tension headaches. Psychological factors, such as the tendency to catastrophize negative events—that is, blow them out of proportion—can also bring on a tension headache. Catastrophizing is a psychological event, but it has effects on the body, such as leading us to tense muscles in the neck, shoulders, and forehead. Tension headaches usually come on gradually. They are most often characterized by dull, steady pain on both sides of the head and feelings of tightness or viselike pressure throughout the head.

Migraine Headache

Stress plays a role in a type of headache that affects 1 in 10 Americans, some 28 million people—**migraine headache** (Mulvihill, 2000). Migraines are intense, throbbing headaches that often affect one side of the head (Durham, 2004). They may last hours or even days. Sensory and motor disturbances often precede the pain; a warning "aura" may include vision problems and perception of unusual odors. The migraines themselves are often accompanied by sensitivity to light, loss of appetite, nausea, vomiting, sensory and motor disturbances such as loss of balance, and changes in mood. Imaging techniques suggest that when something triggers a migraine, neurons at the back of the brain fire in waves that ripple across the top of the head, then down to the brainstem, the site of many pain centers in the brain. The underlying causal mechanisms of migraine are complex and not well understood. They appear to be related to changes in blood flow in the brain, which in turn may be affected by imbalances in the neurotransmitter **serotonin**.

Neurotransmitters are chemical messengers in the nervous system. Triggers for migraine headaches include many factors, such as stress, hormonal fluctuations, changes in barometric pressure, exposure to glaring lights, pollen, use of certain drugs, ingestion of certain chemicals such as monosodium glutamate (MSG) (used to enhance flavor), and even chocolate and ripened cheese (Mulvihill, 2000).

Behavioral responses to headaches may play a role in coping. For example, investigators in one study found that women who experienced regular migraines, as opposed to those who did not, tended to be more self-critical, more likely to catastrophize stress and pain, and less likely to seek social support when under stress (Hassinger, Semenchuk, & O'Brien, 1999). Although this evidence is correlational,

▌ **Migraine headache** A throbbing headache caused by wavelike firing of neurons on the brain, which creates ripples of neural activity that reach pain centers in the brainstem.

▌ **Serotonin** A neurotransmitter, imbalances of which have been linked to mood disorders, anxiety, insomnia, and changes in appetite.

▌ **Neurotransmitters** The chemical messengers in the nervous system that carry nerve signals from one nerve cell to another.

it suggests that we may unwittingly propel ourselves into a vicious cycle. Migraine or other types of recurrent headaches are significant stressors that can lead us to catastrophize our situation, to heap blame or criticism on ourselves, or to withdraw from social interactions or fail to make use of available social support. In so doing, we may further compound our pain and emotional distress.

Headache Treatment

Aspirin, acetaminophen, ibuprofen, and many prescription drugs are used to fight headache pain. Some inhibit the production of hormones called **prostaglandins**, which help initiate transmission of pain messages to the brain. Newer prescription drugs can help prevent many migraines, such as drugs that help regulate serotonin levels in the brain (Lohman, 2001; Silberstein et al., 2000). Behavioral methods, such as relaxation training and biofeedback training, can also help (Gatchel, 2001; Holroyd, 2002). People who are sensitive to MSG or red wine can request meals without MSG and switch to white wine. People can also gain better control over migraines by identifying triggers for attacks, such as chocolate or fluorescent lights, and avoiding them as much as possible.

■ **Prostaglandins** Hormones that initiate pain messages and also cause muscle fibers in the uterine wall to contract, as during labor.

4.3.2 Menstrual Problems

Menstruation is a perfectly natural biological process. Nevertheless, 50% to 75% of women experience some discomfort prior to or during menstruation (Sommerfeld, 2002). Table 4.3 contains a list of commonly reported symptoms of menstrual problems. One of the most common forms of menstrual discomfort is **premenstrual syndrome (PMS)**.

Premenstrual Syndrome (PMS)

Premenstrual syndrome (PMS) refers to the biological and psychological symptoms that may affect women during the four- to six-day interval that precedes menstruation. For many women, premenstrual symptoms persist during menstruation.

Most cases of PMS involve mild to moderate discomfort. An estimated 5% to 8% of women suffer from severe premenstrual syndrome (Yonkers, O'Brien, & Eriksson, 2008). About 2 or 3% of women report symptoms severe enough to markedly impair their social, academic, or occupational functioning (Mortola, 1998). But PMS does produce significant discomfort, and it should not be taken lightly—or as a matter of course—by the medical community.

The causes of PMS are not fully understood. The prevailing view is that negative attitudes toward menstruation—for example, believing that menstruating women are unclean—can worsen menstrual problems but that PMS primarily has a biological

Dragan Trifunovic/iStockphoto

Migraine!
Migraine headaches tend to come on suddenly and are usually identified by severe throbbing pain on one side of the head. There is no doubt that migraines are connected with tension, but they may also be triggered by strong light, barometric pressure, pollen, certain drugs, MSG, chocolate (oh no!), aged cheese, beer, champagne, red wine, and—as millions of women know—the hormonal changes connected with menstruation. Newer medicines have some effectiveness against migraines, and people can learn to avoid some of the triggers. Women are advised to be assertive with their physicians: If one approach to treating migraines doesn't work, try another—and, if necessary, find a physician who will help you do just that.

Table 4.3 ▮ Symptoms of Menstrual Distress	
Physical Symptoms	**Psychological Symptoms**
Swelling of the breasts	Depressed mood, sudden tearfulness
Tenderness in the breasts	Loss of interest in usual social or recreational activities
Bloating	Anxiety, tension (feeling "on edge" or "keyed up")
Weight gain	Anger
Food cravings	Irritability
Abdominal discomfort	Changes in body image
Cramping	Concern over skipping routine activities, school, or work
Lack of energy	A sense of loss of control
Sleep disturbance, fatigue	A sense of loss of ability to cope
Migraine headache	
Pains in muscles and joints	
Aggravation of chronic disorders such as asthma and allergies	

■ **Premenstrual syndrome (PMS)** A cluster of physical and psychological symptoms that afflict some women prior to menstruation.

▮ **Gamma-aminobutyric acid (GABA)** A neurotransmitter that appears to help calm anxiety reactions.

basis. Investigators suspect that female reproductive hormones (estrogen and progesterone) play an important role. PMS also appears to be linked with imbalances in the brain of neurotransmitters such as serotonin. Chemical imbalances involving serotonin are also linked to changes in appetite. Women with PMS do show greater premenstrual increases in appetite than other women. Another neurotransmitter, **gamma-aminobutyric acid (GABA)**, also appears to be involved in PMS, as we know that medications that affect the levels of GABA may help relieve symptoms of PMS. Premenstrual syndrome appears to be caused by a complex interaction between female sexual hormones and neurotransmitters (Bäckström et al., 2008).

Women today have many options available for treating premenstrual symptoms. These include exercise, dietary control (for example, eating several small meals a day rather than two or three large meals; limiting salt and sugar; vitamin supplements), hormone treatments (usually progesterone), and medications that affect concentrations of GABA or serotonin in the nervous system. The accompanying *Try This Out* feature offers additional suggestions that may be helpful to women coping with menstrual discomfort.

TRY THIS OUT — COPING WITH MENSTRUAL DISCOMFORT

Women with persistent or severe menstrual distress may find the following suggestions helpful:

1. *First of all, don't blame yourself!* Again, this is where psychological as opposed to medical advice comes in handy. Menstrual problems were once erroneously attributed to women's "hysterical" nature. This is nonsense. Menstrual problems appear, in large part, to reflect oversensitivity to cyclical changes in hormone levels throughout the body and fluctuations in the levels of chemical messengers (neurotransmitters) in the brain. Even though researchers have not yet fully identified all the causal elements and patterns, there is no basis in fact to claim that women who have menstrual problems are "hysterical."

2. *Keep track of your menstrual symptoms to help you (and your doctor) identify patterns.*

3. *Develop strategies for dealing with days when you experience the greatest distress—strategies that will help enhance your pleasure and minimize the stress affecting you on those days.* Psychologists have found that it is useful to engage in activities that distract people from pain. Why not try things that will distract you from your menstrual discomfort? See a film or get into that novel you've been meaning to read.

4. *Ask yourself whether you harbor any self-defeating attitudes toward menstruation that might be compounding distress.* Do close relatives or friends see menstruation as an illness, a time of "pollution," a "dirty thing"? Have you adopted any of these attitudes—if not verbally, then in ways that affect your behavior, as by restricting your social activities during your period?

5. *See a doctor about your concerns, especially if you have severe or persistent symptoms.* Severe menstrual symptoms are often caused by health problems such as endometriosis and pelvic inflammatory disease (PID). Check it out.

6. *Develop nutritious eating habits—and continue them throughout the entire cycle (that means always).* Consider limiting intake of alcohol, caffeine, fats, salt, and sweets, especially during the days preceding menstruation.

7. *If you feel bloated, eat smaller meals (or nutritious snacks) throughout the day rather than a couple of highly filling meals.*

8. *Some women find that vigorous exercise—jogging, swimming, bicycling, fast walking, dancing, skating, even jumping rope—helps relieve premenstrual and menstrual discomfort.* Try it out. But don't engage in exercise only prior to and during your period! Irregular bursts of strenuous activity may be an additional source of stress. Consider weaving exercise into your regular lifestyle.

9. *Check with your doctor about vitamin and mineral supplements (such as calcium and magnesium).* Vitamin B_6 appears to help some women.

10. *Ibuprofen (brand names: Medipren, Advil, Motrin, etc.) and other medicines available over the counter may be helpful for cramping.* Various prescription drugs such as tranquilizers (e.g., alprazolam) and serotonin reuptake inhibitors may also be of help. Ask your doctor for a recommendation. Note that in these cases, you are not taking a drug to quell anxiety or to treat depression. You are taking a drug to treat imbalances in neurotransmitters that may lead to premenstrual distress as well as give rise to anxiety or depression.

11. *Remind yourself that menstrual problems are time limited.* Don't worry about getting through life or a career. Just get through the next couple of days.

4.3.3 Coronary Heart Disease: Taking Stress to Heart

Coronary heart disease (CHD) is the leading cause of death in the United States, accounting for some 900,000 deaths annually (Ferdinand, 2006). Most of these deaths result from heart attacks, but the underlying problem most often involves narrowing of arteries (*arteriosclerosis*) from the buildup of fatty deposits (*plaque*) along artery walls (Stoney, 2003). Blood clots are more likely to lodge in arteries clogged by these fatty deposits. If a clot should lodge in an artery that provides blood to the heart, the supply of blood to the heart can become choked off, causing a heart attack or *myocardial infarction* (MI). Heart tissue literally dies during a heart attack. Whether a person survives depends on the extent of the damage to heart tissue as well as the delicate electrical system that regulates the heart rhythm.

We've learned a great deal about the factors that increase a person's chances of suffering from CHD. Here we focus on the major identified risk factors (Lee, 2007; Mendelsohn & Karas, 2005; Mukamal et al., 2003). We will see that behavioral factors such as eating patterns, smoking, and exercise have a great deal to do with the risk of CHD.

1 *Age and family history.* Two factors over which you have no control (age and family history) play a key role in determining risk. Older adults and people with a family history of CHD stand a higher risk of developing CHD.

2 *Physiological conditions.* Obesity, high blood cholesterol levels, and hypertension are important risk factors for CHD (Jones et al., 2002; Manson & Bassuk, 2003). These factors are controllable to a certain extent. We can make changes in our diet and exercise patterns to lose excess weight or prevent obesity from developing. We can control high blood cholesterol and blood pressure through diet and exercise, and, if need be, through use of medication. Unfortunately, evidence shows that many people fail to control these factors. For example, investigators found that only about one-quarter of adults with high blood pressure (*hypertension*) were taking medications to control their blood pressure (Hyman & Pavlik, 2001). Clearly, more needs to be done to help people reduce the risk factors they can control.

3 *Lifestyle factors.* How we lead our lives plays an important role in determining our risk of developing CHD. Unhealthy patterns include heavy drinking, smoking, inactivity, overeating, and eating food that is high in cholesterol, like saturated fats (Hajjar & Kotchen, 2003). Smoking alone doubles the risk of heart attacks and is linked to more than one in five deaths from CHD. On the other hand, moderate use of alcohol seems to be good for the heart. Evidence links moderate drinking (one to two drinks per day) to a lower risk of heart attacks and strokes and to lower death rates overall (e.g., Carmichael, 2003; Mukamal et al., 2003). Investigators suspect that moderate use of alcohol boosts levels of high-density lipoproteins (HDL), the "good" cholesterol that helps sweep away artery-blocking fat deposits (Goldberg et al., 2001a; Wood, Vinson, & Sher, 2001).

4 *Type A behavior.* Although early research pointed to a connection between Type A personality pattern and increased risk of CHD, later investigations cast doubt on this relationship (Geipert, 2007). Yet there is one element of the Type A behavior pattern that is more consistently related to higher risks of heart disease and other serious health problems: hostility (Boyle, Jackson, & Suarez, 2007; Olson et al., 2006; Smith, 2006).

   Hostility is a trait that describes people who tend to have "short fuses" and are prone to get angry easily and often. They also hold cynical and mistrustful attitudes toward others. Investigators find that chronic hostility and proneness to anger are the components of the Type A behavior pattern most strongly linked to the development of CHD (Eckhardt, Norlander, & Deffenbacher, 2004; Haas et al., 2005). Whether the other features of the Type A behavior pattern, such as the hurried pace of life, directly contribute to health problems remains open to further study.

Flirt/Superstock

Anger
People who anger easily and often are at greater risk of developing coronary heart disease. Is anger a problem for you? What can you do to manage anger more effectively?

5 *Negative emotions.* How might hostility translate into heart disease? One strong possibility focuses on the role of anger. Hostile people get angry often and stay angry for extended periods of time. Evidence shows that anger is closely associated with the risk of coronary heart disease (Contrada & Guyll, 2001; DiGiuseppe & Tafrate, 2007; Pressman & Cohen, 2005). To put the effects of anger in context, researchers statistically controlled for influences of high blood pressure and cholesterol levels, smoking, and obesity and found that people who easily become angered were about three times as likely as calmer people to experience heart attacks (J. E. Williams et al., 2000).

The underlying mechanisms explaining the links between anger and hostility and cardiovascular problems remains to be determined. But investigators suspect that the stress hormones adrenaline (also called epinephrine) and noradrenaline (also called norepinephrine) play key roles (Sanders, 2007). These hormones are released in response to stress. They speed up the heart rate and raise blood pressure, which places increased burdens on the cardiovascular system. Over time, chronic or recurring stress may eventually weaken the cardiovascular system, setting the stage for heart attacks, especially in vulnerable people. An overproduction of stress hormones may also affect the stickiness of the clotting factors in the blood, which in turn may heighten the risk of potentially dangerous blood clots forming that can cause heart attacks or strokes. People who are chronically hostile and angry have higher levels of blood cholesterol and blood pressure, which are two major risk factors for CHD and early death (Iribarren et al., 2000; Suinn, 2001).

Most of the research linking negative emotions to heart disease has focused on hostility and anger. Recently, however, researchers have begun looking at

Figure 4.8
The Job-Strain Model
This model highlights the psychological demands of various occupations and the amount of personal (decision) control they allow. Occupations characterized by both high demands and low control place workers at greater risk of heart-related problems.

the role of other strong negative emotions, such as anxiety and depression. What they find is that these negative emotions are linked to higher risks of cardiovascular problems as well as other health problems (e.g., Goldston & Baillie, 2007; Underwood, 2004).

A new personality type has entered the discussion of the role of negative emotions in coronary heart disease—the *Type D personality.* The *D* stands for "distressed." People with a Type D personality are typically unhappy, insecure, anxious, and irritable. However, they tend to keep their negative feelings bottled up out of fear of saying anything that could lead people to disapprove of them. Some early evidence shows an increased risk of coronary heart disease, and deaths from heart disease, among people with the Type D personality (Pedersen et al., 2004). We should caution, however, that more research is needed to determine whether these connections will stand up to further scientific scrutiny.

6 *Job strain.* Overtime work, assembly-line labor, and exposure to conflicting demands can all contribute to CHD. High-strain work, which makes heavy demands on workers but gives them little personal control, puts workers at the highest risk (Aboa-Éboulé et al., 2007; Krantz et al., 1988; see Figure 4.8). Figure 4.9 shows the increased risks associated with risk factors such as high cholesterol, smoking, hypertension, and inactivity.

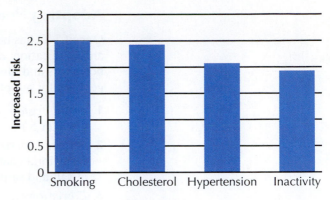

Figure 4.9
Risk Factors for Coronary Heart Disease
Here we see the added risk of the major risk factors of smoking, cholesterol, hypertension, and inactivity. For example, smokers are 2.5 times more likely to develop CHD than are nonsmokers.

Self-Assessment

Are You Heart Smart?

Test your heart disease IQ by answering the following questions. Then check your answers against those at the end of the chapter.

YES	NO	
___	___	1. A heart attack occurs when the heart stops beating.
___	___	2. You can have a heart murmur without actually having heart disease.
___	___	3. Cardiovascular disease does not begin until people reach their forties.
___	___	4. People can generally tell if their blood pressure is elevated.
___	___	5. Overweight people are not any more likely to have hypertension than people of normal weight.
___	___	6. People with cardiovascular disease should avoid physical exercise.
___	___	7. The pumping of the heart is controlled by the heart muscle.
___	___	8. Whites are about as likely to die from coronary heart disease (CHD) as African Americans.
___	___	9. Your risk of having a heart attack is in the cards—either you have a family history or you don't.
___	___	10. All forms of cholesterol are harmful to the heart.

For an interactive version of this self-assessment exercise, go to www.wileyplus.com

Adopting Healthier Habits to Reduce the Risk of CHD

Once CHD has been diagnosed, a number of medical treatments, including surgery and medication, are available. Importantly, we can all take steps in changing our behaviors and lifestyles to help prevent CHD from developing. Here are some suggestions for adopting a heart-healthy lifestyle:

1 *Avoid or stop smoking, control weight, and follow a healthful diet.* (See Chapter 5.)

2 *Reduce hypertension.* Medication is available for reducing hypertension, but behavioral changes can help, such as following a healthy diet that limits intake of salt and saturated fats, not smoking, and adopting a regular exercise routine.

3 *Lower low-density lipoprotein (LDL) serum cholesterol.* Again, drugs are available to reduce levels of the harmful form of blood cholesterol, LDL cholesterol.

   Yet other behavioral measures may also help, including exercising and cutting down on foods that are high in cholesterol and saturated fats. Lowering LDL is helpful at any time of life, even during older adulthood. However, even young adults should think about their LDL levels, since elevated LDL in young adulthood can establish a pattern that places one at risk for cardiovascular disease later in life.

4 *Modify Type A behavior*, especially hostility (see the accompanying *Try This Out* feature).

5 *Exercise.* You don't need to become a triathlete to reduce your risk of CHD. Investigators find that even moderate exercise, such as brisk walking, reduces the risk of developing CHD if it is incorporated as a part of your lifestyle (Blumenthal et al., 2005; Borjesson & Dahlof, 2005; Meyers, 2007).

TRY THIS OUT — MODIFYING TYPE A BEHAVIOR

Type A behavior is identified by characteristics such as a sense of time urgency and hostility. Cardiologist Meyer Friedman, one of the originators of the Type A concept, and Diane Ulmer reported in 1984 on some of the results of the San Francisco Recurrent Coronary Prevention Project (RCPP). The RCPP was designed to help Type A heart attack victims modify their behavior in an effort to avert future attacks. After three years, subjects who learned to reduce Type A behavior patterns had only one-third as many recurrent heart attacks as a control group.

Two of the RCPP guidelines addressed participants' sense of time urgency and their hostility.

Alleviating Your Sense of Time Urgency

Stop driving yourself—get out and walk! Too often we jump out of bed to an abrasive alarm, hop into a shower, fight commuter crowds, and arrive at class or work with no time to spare. Then we become involved in our hectic day. For Type A people, the day begins urgently and never lets up. The first step in coping with a sense of time urgency is confronting and replacing the beliefs that support it. Friedman and Ulmer (1984) note that Type A individuals tend to harbor the following beliefs:

- "My sense of time urgency has helped me gain social and economic success" (p. 179). The idea that impatience and irritation contribute to success, according to Friedman and Ulmer, is absurd.
- "I can't do anything about it" (p. 182). Of course, the belief that we cannot change ourselves is also one of Ellis's doorways to distress (see Chapter 3). Even in late adulthood, note Friedman and Ulmer, old habits can be discarded and new habits can be acquired.

   Here are some suggestions for combating the sense of time urgency (adapted from Friedman & Ulmer, 1984):

1. *Spend more time socializing with friends and family.*
2. *Take a few minutes each day to think about your earlier life experiences.* Examine old photographs of friends and family.

3. *Cultivate enjoyable leisure activities.* Read for pleasure, but avoid books on business and climbing the corporate ladder.
4. *Immerse yourself in cultural activities.* Visit museums and galleries. Cultivate your aesthetic sense.
5. *Lighten up on yourself.* Don't impose impossible schedules on yourself. Don't attempt to do too many things at once.
6. *Enjoy mealtimes.* Make meals an occasion for conversation, not for wolfing down your food.
7. *Slow down.* Take a daily walk around the neighborhood, but leave the cell phone at home.

Psychologist Richard Suinn (1982, 1995) also suggests the following:

1. *Get a nice-sounding alarm clock!*
2. *Move about slowly when you awake.* Stretch.
3. *Drive more slowly.* Note that the posted speed limit is the maximum allowed by law, not the minimum.
4. *Don't wolf lunch.* Get out; make it an occasion.
5. *Don't tumble words out.* Speak more slowly. Interrupt less frequently.
6. *Get up earlier to sit and relax, watch the morning news with a cup of tea, or meditate.* This may mean going to bed earlier.
7. *Leave home earlier and take a more scenic route to work or school.* Avoid rush-hour jams.
8. *Don't carpool with last-minute rushers.* Drive with a group that leaves earlier or use public transportation.
9. *Have a snack or relax at school or work before the "day" begins.*
10. *Don't do two things at once.* Avoid scheduling too many classes or appointments back to back.
11. *Use breaks to read, exercise, or meditate.* Limit intake of stimulants like caffeine. Try decaffeinated coffee.
12. *Space chores.* Why have the car repaired, work, shop, and drive a friend to the airport all in one day?
13. *If rushed, allow unessential work to go to the next day.* Friedman and Ulmer add, "Make no attempt to get everything finished by 5:00 P.M. if you must pressure yourself to do so" (Suinn, 1984, p. 200).
14. *Set aside some time for yourself:* for music, a hot bath, exercise, relaxation. (If your life will not permit this, get a new life.)

Controlling Hostility

Hostility, like time urgency, is supported by a number of irrational beliefs. Again, we need to begin by recognizing our irrational beliefs and replacing them. Beliefs that support hostility include the following:

- "I need a certain amount of hostility to get ahead in the world" (Friedman & Ulmer, 1984, p. 222). Becoming readily irritated, aggravated, and angered does not contribute to getting ahead.
- "I can't do anything about my hostility" (p. 222). Need we comment?
- "Other people tend to be ignorant and inept" (p. 223). Yes, some of them are, but the world is what it is. As Ellis notes, we expose ourselves to aggravation by demanding that other people be what they are not.
- "I don't believe I can ever feel at ease with doubt and uncertainty" (p. 225). There are ambiguities in life; certain things remain unpredictable. Becoming irritated and aggravated doesn't make things less uncertain.
- "Giving and receiving love is a sign of weakness" (p. 228). This belief is rugged individualism carried to the extreme. It can isolate us from social support.

Friedman and Ulmer offer suggestions beyond replacing irrational beliefs:

1. Don't get into discussions on topics about which you know that you and the other party hold divergent and heated opinions.
2. When other people do things that fall short of your expectations, consider situational factors that may explain their behavior, such as their level of education or cultural background. Don't assume that they intended to upset you.
3. Look for the beauty and joy in things.
4. Stop cursing so much.
5. Express appreciation for the help and encouragement of others.
6. Play to lose, at least some of the time. (Ouch?)
7. Say "Good morning" in a cheerful manner.
8. Look at your face in the mirror throughout the day. Search for signs of aggravation and ask yourself if you need to look like that.

Purestock

Taking it Easy
Research suggests that even if you are Type A, you can learn to stop and smell the daisies (or yuccas or eucalyptus or whatever). Spend more time (relaxing, not competing!) with friends. Go to the movies. Read books, but not those on getting ahead in corporate America!

■ **Carcinogenic** Relating to an agent that gives rise to cancerous changes.

Overall, there is much we can do to reduce our risks of CHD and suffering a heart attack. Even people with established heart disease can lower their risk of heart attack by making lifestyle adjustments such as stopping smoking, exercising regularly, and following a healthier diet. But as noted, in far too many cases, modifiable risk factors remain uncontrolled. Psychologists and other health professionals need to find more effective ways of helping people make heart-healthy changes in their behavior. (For suggestions for integrating regular physical exercise into your lifestyle, see Chapter 5.)

4.3.4 Cancer: Swerving off Course

Each year more than 1.4 million Americans receive the dreaded diagnosis of cancer, and more than a half a million die from it. Cancer is a disease characterized by the development of abnormal, or mutant, cells that may take root anywhere in the body: in the blood, bones, digestive tract, lungs, genital organs, and so on. If their spread is not controlled early, the cancerous cells may *metastasize*—that is, spread by establishing colonies elsewhere in the body. Although the immune system destroys cancerous cells, a developing cancer may overwhelm the ability of the body to combat it. Table 4.4 shows the relative lifetime risks of being diagnosed with different types of cancer.

Risk Factors

There are many causes of cancer, including heredity, exposure to cancer-causing chemicals, and even viruses (Lynch et al., 2004; T. Walsh et al., 2006). As with many other disorders, people can inherit a disposition toward developing certain types of cancer, such as breast cancer, prostate cancer, or colorectal cancer (cancer of the colon or rectum) (Piño et al., 2005; Wideroff et al., 2005). **Carcinogenic** genes may remove the brakes from cell division, allowing cells to multiply wildly. Or they may allow mutations to accumulate unchecked. Yet people often fail to recognize the important roles of unhealthy behaviors in the development of cancer. Health experts recognize that many, perhaps even most, cancer deaths in the U.S. could be prevented

Table 4.4 ■ Lifetime Risk of Being Diagnosed with Cancer by Major Sites		
Site	**Men**	**Women**
All sites combined	1 in 2	1 in 3
Prostate	1 in 6	***
Breast	1 in 909	1 in 7
Lung and bronchus	1 in 13	1 in 18
Colon/rectum	1 in 17	1 in 18
Melanoma	1 in 53	1 in 78
Urinary bladder	1 in 28	1 in 88
Non-Hodgkin's lymphomas	1 in 46	1 in 56
Leukemia	1 in 68	1 in 96
Kidney and renal pelvis	1 in 68	1 in 114
Cervix	***	1 in 125
Ovary	***	1 in 58
Pancreas	1 in 80	1 in 80
Oral cavity and pharynx	1 in 71	1 in 147

Note: Ratios reported above are rounded from percentages. These risks are based on the general population. Your individual risks may vary in relation to your personal risk factors, including family history and lifestyle.

Source: Fay, M. P. *Estimating Age-Conditional Probability of Developing Cancer Using a Piecewise Mid-Age Jointpoint Model to the Rates.* Statistical Research and Applications Branch, NCI, Technical Report # 2003-03, 2004.

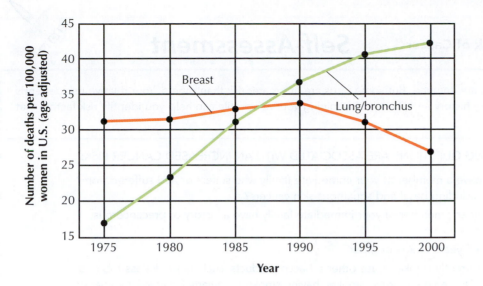

Figure 4.10
Rates of Death Due to Lung Cancer and Breast Cancer in Women
By the 1990s, lung cancer had surpassed breast cancer as the leading cancer killer of U. S. women.
Source: National Cancer Institute, 2005a

▌ **DNA** Acronym for deoxyribonucleic acid, which makes up genes and chromosomes and carries genetic information from generation to generation.

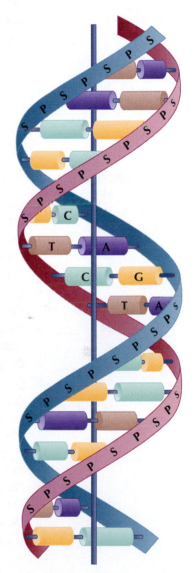

if people made certain healthy changes in their lifestyles, especially avoiding smoking, adopting a healthy diet and maintaining a healthy body weight, avoiding excess sun exposure, and exercising regularly (Lobb et al., 2004).

Nearly 9 in 10 deaths due to lung cancer are directly caused by smoking. But did you know that many other types of cancer, including bladder cancer and colorectal (colon and rectal) cancer, are also linked to smoking? You may be surprised to learn that lung cancer has surpassed breast cancer as the leading cancer killer of women (see Figure 4.10). Lung cancer is also the leading cause of cancer deaths among men.

The accompanying self-assessment feature helps you assess your relative risk of developing cancer.

Stress and Cancer One area of active research is the exploration of links between stress and cancer. A number of researchers have also turned their attention to the effects of stress on **DNA** and the implications for development of cancer. Twisted strands of DNA (the acronym for deoxyribonucleic acid) make up our genes (see Figure 4.11).

The links between stress and cancer in humans continue to be actively investigated. Presently, we cannot yet reach any firm conclusions on what role, if any, stress plays in the development of cancer (Delahanty & Baum, 2001; Dougall & Baum, 2001). In the meantime, it would be prudent to play it safe by taking reasonable steps to modulate the level of stress we experience. We should also become better aware of the early warning signs of cancer so that we might be able to identify cancer in its earliest and most treatable stages.

Psychological Treatment of Cancer Patients

People with cancer must cope not only with the physical effects of the illness itself. They also need to cope with many other challenges, including feelings of anxiety and depression, troubling side effects of treatment, changes in body image after the removal of a breast or testicle, and family problems. Health professionals recognize that cancer patients may benefit from psychological interventions, such as group support programs that provide support, encouragement, and assistance in developing coping skills and resources. Evidence shows that psychological interventions focusing on developing skills for coping with cancer and managing stress can help improve the psychological adjustment and well-being of cancer patients (Helgeson, 2005; Tyre, 2004). Recent evidence based on a study of women with breast cancer also suggests that these kinds of psychological interventions can increase the survival rate (Andersen et al., 2008).

Figure 4.11
Twisting Strands of DNA
Segments of DNA form a double helix made up of genes that determine physical traits such as height and eye color. Genes are also involved in determining psychological traits and susceptibility to various kinds of illness.

Assessing Your Personal Risk of Cancer

Self-Assessment

Cancer can strike anyone; none of us are immune. But some of us are at greater risk than others. Your relative risk depends on many factors, especially your family history and lifestyle. Examining your risk profile can help you identify risk factors that you can change.

"YES" ANSWERS TO THE FOLLOWING QUESTIONS ARE ASSOCIATED WITH AN INCREASED CANCER RISK:

_____ 1. Do you have a member of your immediate family who suffers or had suffered from cancer, excluding basal and squamous skin cancers?

_____ 2. Do you or any member of your immediate family have a history of precancerous growths?

_____ 3. Are you 45 years of age or older?

_____ 4. Do you currently smoke or use other tobacco products, such as smokeless tobacco or snuff? Or are you a former smoker, having smoked regularly for at least a year or more?

_____ 5. Are you overweight?

_____ 6. Do you have two or more drinks of alcohol daily?

_____ 7. Have you had a history of severe sunburns, even back in childhood? Do you enjoy sunbathing and fail to adequately protect your skin with sunscreen lotion?

"YES" ANSWERS TO THE FOLLOWING QUESTIONS ARE ASSOCIATED WITH A LOWER CANCER RISK:

_____ 1. Do you watch your fat intake, making sure not to consume more than of 30% of your total caloric intake in the form of dietary fat?

_____ 2. Do you eat a diet rich in fruits, vegetables, and dietary fiber?

_____ 3. Do you generally avoid foods that are smoke-, nitrite- or salt-cured?

_____ 4. Do you limit your alcohol intake to fewer than two drinks per day?

_____ 5. Do you use sunscreen protection (SPF value of 15 or higher) when you go out in the direct sun for longer than a few minutes?

_____ 6. Do you protect your skin from overexposure to the sun by wearing protective clothing?

_____ 7. Do you avoid use of all tobacco products?

_____ 8. Do you exercise regularly and take generally good care of your health?

_____ 9. Do you get regular health checkups and follow recommended cancer screening guidelines given your age and family history, such as Pap smears, prostate cancer screening tests, clinical breast exams and mammograms, and digital rectal exams?

_____ 10. If you are a woman, do you regularly examine your breasts for lumps? If you are a man, do you regularly examine your testicles for lumps?

_____ 11. Do you limit your exposure to environmental hazards such as asbestos, radiation, and toxic chemicals?

_____ 12. Do you avoid tanning salons and home sunlamps?

_____ 13. Is your diet rich in sources of essential vitamins and minerals?

No particular score translates into a precise risk estimate. The more "Yes" answers to the first set of questions and the fewer "Yes" answers to the second set, the greater your overall cancer risk. Examine these risk factors carefully. Ask yourself which risk factors you can change to help improve your chances of remaining healthy and cancer-free.

Source: Adapted from Nevid & Rathus (2007).

For an interactive version of this self-assessment exercise, go to www.wileyplus.com

Psychological treatments are also used to combat the nausea that often accompanies chemotherapy. Patients undergoing chemotherapy who receive training in relaxation skills and guided imagery techniques to help distract them from their discomfort may be better able to tolerate chemotherapy than those not receiving this training (Redd & Jacobsen, 2001). Children and adolescents find that playing video games also reduces the discomfort of chemotherapy. They focus on battling computer-generated enemies rather than the side effects of drugs.

Prevention of, and Coping with, Cancer

Although cancer is indeed frightening, and for good cause, we are not helpless in the face of this disease. We can take a number of steps, including the following, to reduce our risks of developing cancer and to detect cancer at its earliest and most treatable stages:

- *Avoid smoking and heavy use of alcohol.*
- *Modify diet by reducing intake of saturated fats and increasing intake of fruits and vegetables.* Plant foods contain many naturally occurring chemicals that may have cancer-preventive effects (American Cancer Society, 2005b). (Yes, Grandma was right about veggies.)
- *Exercise regularly.* Evidence continues to mount suggesting that regular exercise can help reduce the risk of some forms of cancer, such as breast cancer and colorectal cancer (National Cancer Institute, 2005b; Willett, 2005).
- *Have regular medical checkups so that cancer will be detected early.*
- *Minimize exposure to excess stress and learn to more effectively manage stress you can't avoid.*
- *If you are living with cancer, maintain hope and a fighting spirit and take an active role in managing your health care.*

We conclude this section with good news for readers of this book: Better-educated people—that means you—are more likely to alter unhealthy behavior patterns and to reap the benefits of change. College may not only help you prepare for a better job—it may save your life.

In this chapter we have examined relationships between psychological factors and health. In the following chapter we focus on issues in health that involve nutrition, fitness, sleep, and drugs.

MODULE REVIEW

Review It

(19) The most common kind of headache is the _____ _____ headache.

(20) The _____ headache has a sudden onset and is identified by throbbing pain on one side of the head.

(21) Pain or discomfort in the days preceding menstruation is called _____ syndrome.

(22) Premenstrual syndrome appears to be linked with imbalances in neurotransmitters such as _____.

(23) Risk factors for coronary heart disease include family history, obesity, hypertension, high levels of serum cholesterol, heavy drinking, smoking, hostility, and _____ strain.

Think About It

Based on your reading of the text, how would you dispute an assertion that psychology has little to offer in the prevention or treatment of killer diseases, such as heart disease and cancer?

Psychology in Daily Life

Becoming an Active Health Care Consumer

Health care is more complicated today than ever before. The tradition of the family doctor as an independent practitioner is giving way to an increasingly complex mix of medicine and big business. We live in an age of managed care—a system that has one hand on the stethoscope and the other on the pocketbook. With the bewildering array of health care plans available today, it is no surprise that many of us find it difficult to make informed health care choices. One of the major challenges of modern life is learning to become an active health care consumer. Taking an active role in managing your health will help ensure that you get the quality of care you need and deserve.

But what does it mean to be an active health care consumer? It means taking an active role in managing your health care by educating yourself about your health care options, choosing your health care providers wisely, and weighing treatment alternatives carefully.

On the other hand, what does it mean to be a passive health care consumer? Passive consumers wait until they get sick to seek health care or learn about health care options. They may carry an insurance card but know little about the range of health services covered by their plan. Passive health care consumers typically do not get the best possible health care. They indirectly participate in the escalation of health care costs because they do not use services, such as regular physical examinations, that might prevent the development of serious and costly medical conditions or reduce their severity.

Passive health care consumers may think of the health care system as too complicated to understand. Their attitudes and beliefs undercut their motivation to manage their own health care: "I prefer to just leave medical matters in the hands of my doctor," "I do not really care what it costs, my insurance will cover it anyway," and "I basically believe that all health care providers are competent and have my best interests at heart."

By contrast, people who take an active role in managing their health care ask questions—plenty of them—of their health care providers to help ensure they get the best-quality care and understand the treatment alternatives available. They believe that they, not their health care providers or their insurance carriers, are ultimately responsible for managing their own health care. They take steps to protect themselves from mismanaged care.

What about you? Are you an active or a passive health care consumer? You can gain insight into the matter by completing the following self-assessment. Then ask yourself what changes you can make in your attitudes and behavior to get the most out of your health care.

4.4.1 Talking to Your Doctor: Being Seen and Being Heard

Hearing "the doctor will see you now" is not merely an invitation to be seen. It is also an invitation to be heard. People who take an active role in managing their health care let their doctors know what is ailing them and gather as much information as they need to make informed decisions regarding treatment. Many people feel that their doctors don't give them the time they need to discuss their complaints or concerns. Although your doctor's time is valuable (as is yours), you have the right to be heard and to ask your doctor to fully explain your medical condition and treatment recommendations in language you can understand. When talking to your doctor . . .

1. Describe your symptoms and complaints as clearly and as fully as possible. Don't hold back, cover up, or distort your symptoms. After all, your health is at stake. But don't embellish your symptoms or repeat yourself. If your doctor interrupts you, say something like, "Doctor, if I may just finish. I'd like you to have the full picture . . ." If your doctor seems more interested in ushering you through the door than hearing you out, think about finding another doctor.

2. Don't accept a treatment recommendation that you don't want. If your doctor's rationale for the treatment plan leaves you shaking your head, get another opinion. Don't be pressured into accepting a treatment plan that doesn't seem right to you.

3. Insist on explanations in plain language. Many patients complain that the doctor does not explain things clearly. You can't make informed choices regarding treatment choices if you don't understand them.

©Jose Luis Pelaez, Inc./CORBIS

Talking to Your Doctor
Be seen and be heard when talking to your doctor. You are responsible for your own health care. Be certain that you take the time to communicate your health issues to your doctor, and make certain that her or his interpretations and suggestions are spoken in plain English. If you don't understand an explanation, say so. Ask the doctor to rephrase it in a way that you can understand. If you have a bad feeling about the doctor, or the diagnosis or the suggested course of treatment, get a second opinion. If you can't get to see a doctor, get a lawyer. If you can't afford a lawyer, ask the information operator for "legal services."

4. Don't be swayed by a doctor who claims your problems are "all in your head." Doctors may not take complaints seriously when there are no findings on physical examination or laboratory tests, especially if symptoms seem vague, like feelings of fatigue. If your doctor is stumped, you may need to consult another doctor.

4.4.2 Preventing Mismanaged Care

Successful managed care is a dual responsibility. Managed care organizations should provide quality medical care and disclose service limitations and any incentives for limiting patient care. But consumers are responsible for leading a healthy lifestyle, consuming medical resources wisely, and exercising personal initiative to help make managed care work. Consumers who take an active role in managing their health care—including managing their managed care plans—can take several steps to protect themselves against mismanaged care

1. *Look under the hood and "kick the tires" before joining an HMO or other health plan* (see Table 4.5).
2. *Discuss coverage for hospital stays.* If you're planning major surgery, find out in advance what costs your managed care company will cover and how long a period of hospitalization you'll be permitted. Discuss whether your coverage is reasonable for your type of surgery with your physician.
3. *Insist on your right to see a specialist.* If you feel that your condition calls for a specialist, and one is not available to you as a member of the managed care plan, demand one. If you must go outside your plan to obtain a specialist's services, have the specialist cite his or her medical findings that justify the need for these services. Use this document to appeal the denial of coverage.
4. *Learn what to do in case of emergencies.* If you are faced with a medical emergency, your first concern is to get proper care, not to haggle over costs with your managed care company. But before an emergency arises, you should take the time to learn about the provisions in your plan for obtaining emergency care. Most plans require that you first contact a participating doctor, who will then direct you to an emergency room covered by the

Photodisc Red/Getty Images, Inc

Managing Your Health Care
Taking an active role in managing your health care involves "looking under the hood" and "kicking the tires" of health plans or HMOs before enrolling. What steps can you take to ensure that you receive quality medical care?

plan. However, many HMOs refuse to pay for emergency services if they later decide that the patient's condition did not require them. It may not matter even if the plan's own doctors advise the patient to go to the nearest emergency room. The hospital may then seek payment from the patient.

5. *If you are refused coverage.* If you are refused coverage for medical services not covered by your plan, file an appeal. (The appeals process is typically explained in the plan's handbook.) Document the need for services. Include supporting documents from physicians who referred you or provided the services. If the managed care company still refuses to pay, file an appeal. If an appeal doesn't succeed, your employer's benefits manager may be able to intercede on your behalf. You may also file a formal complaint with your state department of insurance, which establishes a paper trail supporting your case. As a last resort, you may wish to consult a lawyer.

Table 4.5 ▌ Looking Under an HMO's Hood

Besides asking about location and cost, here is a checklist of some points to consider when shopping for a managed care plan:

- What percentage of the plan's network doctors are board certified and what percentage leave each year?
- Has the plan been audited by the National Committee for Quality Assurance or other organization, and if so, can you inspect the report?
- What's in the sample benefits contract?
- How many complaints filed with the state insurance department against the plan have been upheld?
- Must primary care physicians receive permission from the HMO before making referrals to specialists? And for women, does that rule include gynecologists?
- How easy is it to file an appeal when medical treatment is denied?
- What portion of the plan's premium dollars is spent on medical care?
- What financial incentives do doctors receive for holding down the cost of medical care?
- What type of preventive care, like immunizations, does the plan offer?
- What kind of preauthorization is needed for hospitalization?
- Is a prescription drug you regularly take on the plan's list of medications approved for payment?

Are You an Active or a Passive Health Care Consumer?

Self-Assessment

Do you take active charge of your health care, or do you sit back and wait for things to happen? Are you doing what is best for you? Check by circling the statement that best represents your beliefs and attitudes concerning your health care. Then interpret your answers by checking the key at the end of the chapter

I avoid thinking about my health care until a health care need arises.	Or	I make an effort to think about my health care needs and plan ahead to meet these needs.
I don't know how to locate a personal physician and other health care providers in my area.	Or	I have established a relationship with a primary health care provider and other health care providers, such as a dentist, an eye care specialist, and (if I'm a woman) a gynecologist.
I'm not aware of the major hospitals, clinics, and other medical facilities in my area or, if I am aware of them, I don't know what services they provide.	Or	I not only know where the major health care facilities in my area are located, I know what services they offer and how to get there in case of emergency.
I don't keep a listing of phone numbers handy for hospitals and doctors I could call in case of medical need.	Or	I keep handy a listing of phone numbers and know whom I would call in the case of a medical emergency or other medical needs.
I usually skip regular medical examinations, either because I don't have the time or don't know how to go about arranging for a physical.	Or	I have regular medical exams and have established a relationship with a primary health care provider who knows my health record.
I lack the means of paying for health care and have not made arrangements in case I need medical services.	Or	I maintain health care coverage.
To be honest, I tend to ignore symptoms for as long as possible in the hope that they will disappear.	Or	I pay attention to any changes in my body and bring any symptoms or complaints to the attention of my primary health care provider.
I sometimes use emergency services, such as ambulances, police, and emergency units, when they are not necessary.	Or	I always work through my primary health care provider when I am in need of health care.
I frankly wouldn't know where I would go if I needed emergency care.	Or	I know how to handle a medical emergency—whom I would call and where I would go to get emergency care.
I sometimes or often fail to keep medical appointments or arrive late for them.	Or	I keep appointments and arrive on time.
I sometimes or often fail to call to cancel appointments ahead of time.	Or	I always call to cancel appointments if necessary.
I sometimes hold back information from my health care provider or believe that doctors should just know what's bothering me without my having to tell them.	Or	I readily offer information to my health care provider and describe my symptoms as clearly as possible.
I sometimes or often give incomplete information on medical histories due to embarrassment, forgetfulness, or inattention.	Or	I give complete information and do not withhold, embellish, or distort information concerning my health.
I sometimes or often fail to pay attention to the instructions I receive from my doctor.	Or	I listen carefully to instructions, take notes, and ask for explanations of my medical condition.
I generally don't ask my physician to explain medical terms I don't understand.	Or	I always ask my doctor to explain any terms I don't understand.
I generally accept everything my doctor tells me without questioning.	Or	I assertively ask questions when I don't understand or agree with the treatment plan.
I sometimes or often fail to follow instructions that I have agreed to follow, such as not filling prescriptions or not taking medications according to schedule.	Or	I carefully follow instructions that I agreed upon; if I'm not sure of the directions to follow, I call my doctor (or pharmacist) and ask for clarification

I sometimes or often fail to keep follow-up appointments or neglect to call to update my health care provider on my condition.

Or

I reliably keep follow-up appointments and make update calls when indicated.

I simply stop following a treatment that has troubling effects or no effects and don't bother to inform my health care provider.

Or

If a treatment doesn't appear to be working or produces negative effects, I call my health care provider for a consultation before making any changes in the treatment plan.

I don't examine medical bills carefully, especially those that are paid by my insurance company.

Or

I carefully examine bills for any errors or duplication of services charged and bring any discrepancies to the attention of my health care provider.

I don't question any charges for medical services, even if I think they are excessive or inappropriate.

Or

I question my health care provider about any charges that appear excessive or inappropriate.

I generally neglect filling out insurance claim forms for as long as possible.

Or

I promptly complete insurance forms and drop them in the mail as soon as possible.

I generally don't keep records of my medical treatments and insurance claims.

Or

I keep full and complete records of my medical visits and copies of insurance claim statements.

For an interactive version of this self-assessment exercise, go to www.wileyplus.com

CHAPTER REVIEW

RECITE! RECITE! RECITE! RECITE! RECITE! RECITE! RECITE!

Study Tip: Reciting the answers to these study questions will help you become a more effective learner. First try answering the questions by yourself, either reciting them out loud or writing them in a notebook or on the computer. Then compare your answers with the sample answers provided below.

1. What is health psychology?

Health psychology studies the relationships between psychological factors (e.g., behavior, emotions, stress, beliefs, and attitudes) and the prevention and treatment of physical health problems.

2. What is the general adaptation syndrome?

The GAS is a cluster of bodily changes triggered by stressors. The GAS consists of three stages: alarm, resistance, and exhaustion. The bodily responses involve the endocrine system (hormones) and the autonomic nervous system. Corticosteroids help resist stress by fighting inflammation and allergic reactions. Adrenaline arouses the body by activating the sympathetic division of the autonomic nervous system, which is highly active during the alarm and resistance stages of the GAS. Sympathetic activity is characterized by rapid heartbeat and respiration rate, release of stores of sugar, muscle tension, and other responses that deplete the body's supply of energy. The parasympathetic division of the ANS predominates during the exhaustion stage of the GAS.

3. What are the emotional and cognitive effects of stress?

Anxiety tends to occur in response to threatening stressors. Anger usually occurs in response to stressors such as frustra-tion and social provocation. Depression occurs in response to losses, failure, and prolonged stress. High levels of stress are connected with high levels of arousal, which, in turn, evoke maladaptive cognitions and behavior patterns and impair problem-solving ability.

4. How does the immune system work, and how does stress affect it?

Leukocytes (white blood cells) engulf and kill pathogens, worn-out body cells, and cancerous cells. The immune system also "remembers" how to battle antigens by marshaling antibodies in the bloodstream. The immune system also facilitates inflammation, which increases the number of white blood cells that are transported to a damaged area. Prolonged or intense stress depresses the functioning of the immune system, in part because it stimulates release of corticosteroids. These steroids counter inflammation and interfere with the formation of antibodies.

5. What is the multifactorial approach to health?

This view recognizes that many factors, including biological, psychological, sociocultural, and environmental factors, affect our health.

6. How are factors of ethnicity, gender, and socioeconomic status related to physical health?

African Americans live about seven years less than European Americans, largely because of sociocultural and economic factors that are connected with less access to health care and greater likelihood of eating high-fat diets, smoking, and living in unhealthful neighborhoods. Women are less likely than men to have heart attacks in early and middle adulthood due to the protective effects of estrogen. Women outlive men by five years on the average. One reason is that women are more likely than men to consult health professionals about health problems.

7. How has psychology contributed to understanding and treating headaches?

Psychologists have studied how stress contributes to muscle-tension and migraine headaches. Psychologists help people alleviate these kinds of headaches by using psychological techniques, such as biofeedback training, to counter states of bodily tension associated with stress or change patterns of blood flow in the body.

8. How has psychology contributed to understanding and treating menstrual problems?

Psychologists have participated in research that is exploring the connections among menstrual discomfort, psychological factors (e.g., anxiety, depression, irritability, attitudes toward menstruation), physical symptoms (e.g., bloating, cramping), and changes in the available levels of hormones and neurotransmitters. PMS afflicts many women for a few days prior to menstruation. In most cases, the symptoms are mild to moderate, but they are severe in some women. Psychologists have helped devise strategies women can use to adjust to menstrual and premenstrual discomfort, including not blaming themselves, engaging in pleasant activities, maintaining a healthy diet, exercising, and actively seeking medical assistance when needed.

9. How has psychology contributed to understanding and treating coronary heart disease?

Psychologists have participated in research showing that the risk factors for coronary heart disease include family history; physiological conditions such as hypertension and high levels of serum cholesterol; behavior patterns such as heavy drinking, smoking, and eating fatty foods; work overload; chronic tension and fatigue; and physical inactivity. They help people achieve healthier cardiovascular systems by stopping smoking, controlling weight, reducing hypertension, lowering LDL levels, changing Type A behavior, reducing hostility, and exercising.

10. How has psychology contributed to understanding and treating cancer?

Psychologists have participated in research showing that the risk factors for cancer include family history, smoking, drinking alcohol, eating animal fats, sunbathing, and possibly stress. Making healthy changes in behavior can help reduce the risk of cancer, such as by avoiding smoking, having regular medical checkups, controlling alcohol use, adopting a healthy diet, and avoiding sunbathing. Psychologists help cancer patients and their families cope with the disease and maintain a "fighting spirit."

YOUR PERSONAL JOURNAL

REFLECT   REFLECT   REFLECT   REFLECT   REFLECT   REFLECT   REFLECT

Study Tip: Reflecting on how the concepts in the chapter relate to your own experiences encourages deeper processing, which makes the material more personally meaningful and fosters more effective learning. Use additional pages if needed to complete your answers.

1. Have you or has someone in your immediate family been affected by a life-threatening disease, such as coronary heart disease or cancer? Based on your reading, what steps can you take to reduce your risks of developing these diseases? (We mean steps you can take now, not in the distant future, when it may already be too late to avert serious illness.)

_____

_____

_____

2. Based on your reading of the text, do you consider yourself to be an active health care consumer? If so, how so? If not, what steps can you take to become more actively involved in managing your health care?

_____

_____

_____

_____

ANSWERS TO MODULE REVIEWS

Module 4.1

1. Health psychology
2. resistance
3. fight-or-flight
4. tend-and-befriend
5. corticosteroids
6. noradrenaline
7. fear
8. state anxiety
9. sympathetic
10. impairs
11. white/leukocytes
12. antibodies
13. immune
14. changes

Module 4.2

15. multifactorial model
16. less
17. more
18. shorter

Module 4.3

19. muscle-tension
20. migraine
21. premenstrual
22. serotonin
23. job

ANSWERS TO HEART SMART QUIZ

1. *False.* The heart continues to beat during a heart attack, but a severe heart attack can lead to a disruption in the electrical system that controls the heart rhythm or to complete heart failure.

2. *True.* Some people with healthy hearts suffer from heart murmurs (abnormal heart sounds). A physician can determine whether heart murmurs are a sign of heart disease.

3. *False.* Cardiovascular disease may even begin in childhood.

4. *False.* Most people with hypertension (high blood pressure) have no telltale symptoms. The only way to determine whether you have high blood pressure is to have it tested by a health professional.

5. *False.* Overweight people have a higher risk of developing hypertension, a major risk factor for CHD.

6. *False.* Exercise is good for the heart, even for people with cardiovascular disease. Exercise helps strengthen the heart. But people with established heart disease need to consult with their health providers to determine the type of exercise program that is appropriate and safe for them.

7. *False.* The electrical (nervous) system of the body controls the pumping of the heart.

8. *False.* African Americans are more likely to suffer from CHD and to die from the disease.

9. *False.* Though heredity plays a part in determining your risk, modifiable lifestyle factors, such as diet, avoidance of tobacco, and regular exercise, also play important roles.

10. *False.* The form of cholesterol called low-density lipoproteins (LDL) is harmful to the heart since it leads to the buildup of fatty deposits along artery walls that can set the stage for a heart attack. Yet another type of cholesterol, called high-density lipoproteins (HDL), is actually healthful because it sweeps away fatty deposits, or plaque.

SCORING KEY FOR "ARE YOU AN ACTIVE OR A PASSIVE HEALTH CARE CONSUMER?"

Statements in the left-hand column reflect a passive approach to managing your health care. Statements in the right-hand column represent an active approach. The more statements you circled in the right column, the more active a role you are taking in managing your health care. For any statements in the left column you circled, consider how you can change your behavior to become an active rather than a passive health care consumer.

- Dieting has become a customary way of eating for women in the United States? (p. 161)

- Exercise can help relieve feelings of depression? (p. 172)

- About one in three adults in the United States regularly go to bed after midnight? (No wonder so many of us feel tired much of the time.) (p. 174)

- Alcohol remains the BDOC (big drug on campus)? (p. 180)

- People who have blacked out from drinking may never wake up if they fail to receive prompt medical attention? (p. 182)

- More people in the United States die each year from smoking-related illnesses than from motor vehicle accidents, alcohol and drug abuse, suicide, homicide, and AIDS combined? (p. 186)

- Coca-Cola once "added life" by using the stimulant cocaine as an ingredient? (p. 188)

Tom & Dee Ann McCarthy/ Corbis Images

Mark Twain quipped that it was easy to give up smoking—he had done it a dozen times. Your authors have both quit smoking cigarettes to reduce the chances of coronary heart disease and the threat of cancer of the lungs, pancreas, bladder, larynx, and esophagus. We gave it up a dozen times—between us. But we've both been tobacco-free for more than 25 years. In recent years, knowledge of the benefits of exercise and the hazards of various substances has been amassed. Health-food stores have opened in every shopping mall. The fitness craze is upon us. Large numbers of us have taken to exercise and modified our diets in an effort to enhance our physical well-being and attractiveness. Some of us have even kept to our regimens.

In this chapter, we examine a number of ways in which our behavior affects our health, including nutrition, fitness, sleep, and use and abuse of psychoactive substances. We begin our discussion with nutritional patterns, and we see that there are ways in which we can do ourselves much more good than harm.

MODULE 5.1

Nutrition: The Stuff of Life

- What are the essential ingredients of a healthful diet?
- Is obesity a matter of lack of willpower?
- What are the major kinds of eating disorders?
- What is known about the origins of eating disorders?

We are what we eat—literally. Our bodies convert what we consume into bones, muscles, nerves, and other bodily tissues. What we consume also plays an important role in our health. As we shall see, health scientists have established strong links between healthy nutrition and avoidance of serious chronic diseases, such as cardiovascular disease and some forms of cancer. As many as one in three deaths due to cancer, and many other deaths due to heart disease, diabetes, or stroke, are linked to poor nutrition, especially consumption of a high-fat, high-calorie diet. But many of us don't watch what we eat. For some busy college students, out of sight is out of mind. They skip meals, especially breakfast. Many students eat on the run—catch as catch can. Others are slaves to the colorful trays of food that line the glass cases at the cafeteria. Their food cards allow them to take at least one of everything, and they do so with a vengeance. Still others chomp through bags of potato chips and jars of peanuts while they are studying. Others heed the call when someone suggests going out for pizza—even if they are not hungry.

Nutritional matters are on the back burner for many college students. But adopting healthy nutritional habits is not just a problem for college students. We Americans eat far too much junk food that is laden with fat—foods such as high-fat meats, french fries, potato chips, and cheese. We may also fool ourselves into thinking we are eating healthy when we order fish or chicken—but then eat these foods deeply fried or baked in butter or sauces.

"The time has come, the walrus said, to talk of many things"—so begins a poem in *Alice in Wonderland*. Unfortunately, many of us live in a wonderland when it comes to nutrition. The time has come to talk—and think—about nutrition, now. "Nutrition?" Let us then talk about nutrition. Let us not be preachy about what you should or should not eat. Rather, let us talk about providing you with information to help you make the best-informed choices about your diet.

5.1.1 Nutrients: Ingredients in a Healthful Diet

The word **nutrition** (from the Latin root *nutria*, meaning "to feed") is the process by which organisms consume and utilize foods. Foods provide **nutrients**. Nutrients furnish energy and the building blocks of muscle, bone, and other tissues. Essential nutrients include protein, carbohydrates, fats, vitamins, and minerals.

Proteins

Proteins are **amino acids** that build muscles, blood, bones, fingernails, and hair. Proteins also serve as enzymes, hormones, and antibodies. We must obtain several proteins from food. We manufacture others for ourselves. The most popular sources of protein are meat, poultry, eggs, fish, and dairy products such as milk and cheese. Legumes (beans, lentils, and peas) and grains are also fine sources of protein. Americans tend to eat more protein than they need. Protein deficiencies are rare in well-fed societies like the United States and Canada. Any excess protein we consume is converted into fat.

Carbohydrates

Carbohydrates are the major sources of energy in our diet. There are two major types of *carbs:* simple and complex. *Complex carbohydrates* include starches and dietary fiber. They provide a steady source of energy, as well as vitamins and minerals. In contrast, simple carbohydrates, which comprise various types of sugars, offer little more than a spurt of energy. Many nutritionists recommend that starches account for 50% to 60% of our daily calorie intake. Foods rich in complex carbohydrates include whole grains and cereals; citrus fruits; crucifers, such as broccoli, cabbage, and cauliflower; leafy green vegetables; legumes; pasta (also high in protein, low in fats); root vegetables like potatoes and yams; and yellow fruits and vegetables, like carrots and squash. Many starches are also rich in **dietary fiber**, which aids digestion and may have other health benefits, such as helping to protect us from heart disease (Pereira et al., 2004). Many health experts recommend that we consume 20 to 35 grams of dietary fiber a day (some recommend 25 grams minimum). Yet only half of Americans consume more than 10 grams of fiber a day.

▮ **Nutrition** The process by which plants and animals consume and utilize foods.

▮ **Nutrients** Essential food elements that provide energy and the building blocks of muscle, bone, and other tissues: protein, carbohydrates, fats, vitamins, and minerals.

▮ **Proteins** Organic molecules that comprise the basic building blocks of body tissues.

▮ **Amino acids** Organic compounds from which the body manufactures proteins.

▮ **Carbohydrates** Organic compounds forming the structural parts of plants that are important sources of nutrition for animals and humans.

▮ **Dietary fiber** Complex carbohydrates that form the structural parts of plants, such as cellulose and pectin, that cannot be broken down by human digestive enzymes.

Table 5.1 ▌ Recommended Daily Totals of Dietary Fat at Specified Calorie Levels

Calories per Day in the Diet	Amount of Fat (the Grams) That Provides 30% of Calories
1,500	33 to 58
2,000	44 to 78
2,500	56 to 97
3,000	67 to 117

Source: U.S. Department of Agriculture, Dietary Guidelines for Americans 2005.
Note: Each gram of fat comprises 9 calories.

In recent years, many people have adopted "high-protein, low-carb" diets to control body weight. Leading health organizations, including the American Heart Association, take issue with these diets (such as the popular Atkins diet) (American Heart Association, 2005). They point to the lack of nutritional balance and emphasis on high-fat sources of protein (meat, eggs, and cheese) that can contribute to heart disease. Although these diets may promote quick weight loss, much of the loss may be in the form of water weight (bodily fluids) as the result of cutting carbohydrates. We lack any conclusive evidence that these diets are safe and effective in the long term.

Fats

Fats provide stamina, insulate us from extremes of temperature, nourish the skin, and store vitamins A, D, E, and K. However, most Americans, especially fast-food addicts, consume more fat in their diets than they need. Saturated fat, which comes from animal sources such as meat and dairy products, greatly increases levels of unhealthy blood cholesterol. Monounsaturated and polyunsaturated fats (check the food labels), such as that found in certain vegetable oils like olive oil and canola oil, are healthier forms of dietary fat.

Health officials recommend that adults limit their total fat intake to 20% to 35% of their daily calorie consumption. Saturated fat should account for no more than 10% of daily calories. Table 5.1 shows the recommended limits for total daily fat intake; Table 5.2 decodes some high-fat food choices that are definitely *not* heart-healthy.

▌ **Fats** Organic compounds that form the basis of fatty tissue of animals, including humans (body fat), and are also found in some plant materials.

Table 5.2 ▌ Find That Fat! (16 Heart Attacks on a Plate)

If you are selecting a meal from a restaurant menu, beware of dishes described with the following delightful, mostly foreign terms. They are superhigh in fat—sort of a heart attack on a plate.

- **Alfredo** *in a cream sauce*
- **au gratin** *in cheese sauce*
- **au fromage** *with cheese*
- **au lait** *with milk*
- **à la mode** *with ice cream*
- **escalloped** *with cream sauce*
- **hollandaise** *with cream sauce*
- **bisque** *cream soup*
- **basted** *with extra fat*
- **buttered** *with extra fat*
- **casserole** *extra fat*
- **creamed** *extra fat*
- **crispy** *fried*
- **pan-fried** *fried with extra fat*
- **sautéed** *fried with extra fat*
- **hash** *with extra fat*

When you find these terms on the menu, you can ask for the dish to be prepared in a more healthful way. Instead of cooking in butter, you could ask that a dish be prepared with the least amount of olive oil possible. You can also request that fried dishes be grilled, poached, or baked instead.

Table 5.3 ❚ Vitamins: Myths vs. Facts	
Myth	**Fact**
Popping a vitamin pill can correct a poor diet.	Vitamin pills will not compensate for a poor diet. A multivitamin pill can ensure that you receive essential vitamins but will not provide the other nutrients you need for your health.
The more vitamins you take, the better.	Excess doses of some vitamins can be harmful. Regularly taking just five times the recommended allowances (RDAs) of vitamin D can lead to serious liver damage, for example. High doses of niacin (vitamin B_3) can also cause liver damage. Check with your health care provider before taking supplements of any vitamins or other nutrients
Vitamin supplements will help boost athletic performance.	Vitamins will not improve your game or increase your performance in sports.
Taking "stress vitamins" will help me to cope better with my emotional problems.	So-called stress vitamins help the body counter the effects of physical stress, such as changes in temperature. There is no evidence that vitamins help people cope with emotional stress.
"Natural" vitamins are better than synthetic vitamins.	There is no evidence that your body can tell the difference between natural and synthetic vitamins.

❚ **Vitamins** Organic substances needed by the body in small amounts to maintain essential bodily processes.

❚ **Free radicals** Metabolic waste that may damage cell membranes and genetic material.

❚ **Osteoporosis** A bone disorder primarily affecting older people in which the bones become porous, brittle, and more prone to fracture.

Vincent Ricardel/Photonica/Getty Images, Inc.

Nutrition
Many people today adopt poor diets because they eat on the run or don't pay close attention to what they are eating. Young adults, emerging from adolescence, also have a way of considering themselves to be invulnerable to the effects of a poor diet. Or they tell themselves that they will eat more carefully later in life. How is your own diet? After reading the text, do you think you need to make any changes in what you eat?

Vitamins and Minerals

Vitamins are essential organic compounds that need to be eaten regularly. Vitamin A is found in orange produce, such as carrots and sweet potatoes, and deep green vegetables. It is also abundant in liver, but "organ meats" like liver are extremely high in cholesterol (find more healthful sources). Vitamins A and D are found in fortified dairy products. B vitamins are abundant in legumes, vegetables, nuts, and whole-grain products. Fruits and vegetables are rich in vitamin C. Vitamins like A, C, and E are *antioxidants*; that is, they deactivate substances in some foods, called **free radicals**, that might otherwise contribute to the development of cancer. (Don't let those radicals go free.)

We also need minerals such as calcium (for conducting nerve impulses and making bones and teeth), iron, potassium, and sodium. Calcium and vitamin D help maintain good bone health and reduce the risks in later life of **osteoporosis**—a bone disease characterized by brittleness of the bones that leads them to become more susceptible to fractures (NIH Consensus Development Panel, 2001). Readers are advised to consult with physicians, pharmacists, and dieticians about their daily requirements of vitamins and minerals. Overdoses can be harmful. Don't assume that more is better and mindlessly pop megavitamin pills.

Applying the critical thinking skills discussed in Chapter 1 can help us make healthier food choices. We are bombarded daily with health-related claims we see in television commercials or read in product advertisements or product packaging. Just take a casual walk through any supermarket or health-food store and begin counting the many health claims on product boxes.

Critical thinkers maintain a healthy skepticism toward advertising and product information. They carefully consider the source of any claim and demand evidence that supports its validity. For example, they recognize that saying a product "may boost the immune system" is not the same thing as saying "does boost the immune system." Even claims that a food or supplement "boosts the immune system" or "protects against heart attacks" may simply stem from a copywriter's imagination, not hard scientific evidence. One aspect of thinking critically is separating myth from fact, as described in Table 5.3.

Relationships between nutritional patterns and health have grown clearer in recent years. For example, many cases of heart disease and cancer can be linked to poor diet (see Chapter 4). Food preservatives, high intake of animal fat, and vitamin deficiencies pose particular risks. High levels of cholesterol heighten the risks of cardiovascular disorders. On the other hand, vitamins, calcium, and fruits and vegetables appear to reduce the risk of cancer. Following a diet that is low in saturated and trans-fats and rich in fruit, vegetables, fish, and whole grains can also reduce the risk of heart attacks by as much as 80% (Haskell & Eisenberg, 2002; Rimm & Stampfer, 2005).

In an affluent society like ours, relatively few people suffer from nutritional deficiencies. By contrast, the major nutritional imbalance we face is stacked in the other direction—overconsumption. The intake of excessive quantities of calories—food energy—leads to what might well be our number-one nutrition-related problem—obesity.

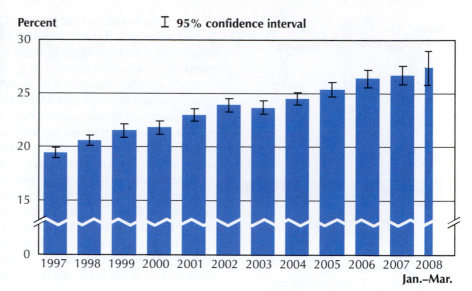

Figure 5.1
America's Expanding Waisline
The prevalence of obesity among U.S. adults has increased sharply in recent years.
Source: Early Release of Selected Estimates Based on Data from the January–March 2008 National Health Interview Survey, Centers for Disease Control, http://www.cdc.gov/nchs/data/nhis/earlyrelease/200809_06.pdf

5.1.2 Obesity—Are We Losing the Battle of the Bulge?

Consider some facts about obesity:

- Nearly two out of three adult Americans are overweight and about one in four are classified as obese (Howard et al., 2006; McNeil, 2005; Powell, Calvin, & Calvin, 2007) (see Figure 5.1).

- Overweight and obesity are rising rapidly. The prevalence of obesity among U.S. adults jumped 41% in the period of 1997 to 2008, up from 19.4% to 27.4% (CDC, 2008). The proportion of young Americans who are overweight has doubled over the past 25 years (Dietz, 2004; Hedley et al., 2004).

- If present trends continue, say health experts, obesity will cut the life expectancy of today's children by as much as two to five years as compared to their parents' generation (Olshansky et al., 2005; Preston, 2003).

- Americans eat more than a total of 800 billion calories of food each day (200 billion calories more than they need to maintain their weights). The extra calories could feed a nation of 80 million people, or the entire nation of Germany.

American culture idealizes slender heroes and heroines. For those who "more than measure up" to TV and film idols, food may have replaced sex as the central source of guilt. Why is obesity such a concern? The reason is clear: Obesity is a major health risk. Evidence shows that obesity is strongly related to a range of serious and potentially life-threatening medical problems, including cardiovascular disease, stroke, diabetes, gallbladder disease, gout, respiratory problems, arthritis, and even some forms of cancer (e.g., Hossain, Kawar, & El Nahas, 2007; Lyssenko et al., 2008; Reeves et al., 2007). All told, obesity accounts for more than 100,000 excess deaths in the United States every year and reduces the life expectancy of the average person by 6 to 7 years (Fontaine et al., 2003; Flegal et al., 2007).

Why are the collective midsections of Americans expanding? The answers, experts say, are clear: too many calories consumed coupled with too little vigorous activity. Many of us have become "cyberslugs" and "couch potatoes," eating too much fattening food while sitting around too much and exercising too little. According to the federal government, Americans today consume about 12% more calories daily, on the average, than they did just 20 years ago (Martin, 2007). There is some good news we can report: Even though rates of obesity in American adults remain high, they have begun to level off in recent years (Ogden et al., 2006).

Max Blain/iStockphoto

Cutting Fat?
Can you think of ways to cut back on your consumption of dietary fat?

Inactivity is another fat booster. Did you know that living in the suburbs is linked to increased risk of obesity? The reason, health researchers believe, is an overreliance on the automobile and the corresponding reduction in walking and physical activity as compared to city-dwellers (Warner, 2004).

Body weight is basically a balancing act between calories consumed and calories expended through physical activity and maintenance of bodily processes (see Figure 5.2). When calorie intake exceeds calorie expenditure, we gain body weight. To lose weight, we need to reduce the number of calories consumed or increase the calories we expend. Maintaining a stable weight involves balancing calories consumed with calories used.

What about you? Are you overweight? Obese? Health authorities gauge overweight and obesity by a measure called the **body mass index (BMI)**. The BMI is a measure of weight that takes height into account (see Figure 5.3). According to the National Institutes of Health, people with a BMI of 25 to 29 are overweight. Those with a BMI of 30 or higher are classified as obese.

Let us now consider the underlying causes of obesity. Obesity is a complex medical condition involving both biological and psychosocial factors.

Biological Factors

Biological factors contributing to obesity include heredity, adipose tissue (body fat), and body metabolism (the rate at which the body converts **calories** to energy). Scientists today recognize that heredity plays a central role in obesity (Couzin, 2006, 2007; Silventoinen et al., 2007; Unger et al., 2007).

The efforts of obese people to maintain a slender profile may also be sabotaged by microscopic units of life within their own bodies: **fat cells**. No, fat cells are not obese cells. They are adipose tissue, or cells that store fat. As time passes after a meal,

Figure 5.2
Weight: A Balancing Act
Our body weight is determined by the balance between our calories (food energy) consumed and calories used in the course of the day.
Source: Physical Activity and Weight Control, National Institutes of Diabetes and Digestive and Kidney Diseases (NIDDK), http://win.niddk.nih.gov/publications/physical.htm

■ **Body mass index (BMI)** A widely used index of weight that takes into account a person's height.

■ **Calories** Food energy; scientifically, units expressing the ability to raise temperature or give off body heat.

■ **Fat cells** Cells that contain fat; adipose tissue.

Figure 5.3
Body Mass Index (BMI)
The BMI is a measure of weight that takes height into account. To calculate your own BMI, first find your height and then move your finger across the table to find your weight. The number in the top row shows your BMI. Health authorities classify people with BMIs of 25 to 29 as overweight and those with BMIs of 30 or higher as obese.

BMI

Height (inches)	19	20	21	22	23	24	25	26	27	28	29	30	31	32	33	34
58	91	96	100	105	110	115	119	124	129	134	138	143	148	153	158	162
59	94	99	104	109	114	119	124	128	133	138	143	148	153	158	163	168
60	97	102	107	112	118	123	128	133	138	143	148	153	158	163	168	174
61	100	106	111	116	122	127	132	137	143	148	153	158	164	169	174	180
62	104	109	115	120	126	131	136	142	147	153	158	164	169	175	180	186
63	107	113	118	124	130	135	141	146	152	158	163	169	175	180	186	191
64	110	116	122	128	134	140	145	151	157	163	169	174	180	186	192	197
65	114	120	126	132	138	144	150	156	162	168	174	180	186	192	198	204
66	118	124	130	136	142	148	155	161	167	173	179	186	192	198	204	210
67	121	127	134	140	146	153	159	166	172	178	185	191	198	204	211	217
68	125	131	138	144	151	158	164	171	177	184	190	197	203	210	216	223
69	128	135	142	149	155	162	169	176	182	189	196	203	209	216	223	230
70	132	139	146	153	160	167	174	181	188	195	202	209	216	222	229	236
71	136	143	150	157	165	172	179	186	193	200	208	215	222	229	236	243
71	140	147	154	162	169	177	184	191	199	206	213	221	228	235	242	250
73	144	151	159	166	174	182	189	197	204	212	219	227	235	242	250	257
74	148	155	163	171	179	186	194	202	210	218	225	233	241	249	256	264
75	152	160	168	176	184	192	200	208	216	224	232	240	248	256	264	272
76	156	164	172	180	189	197	205	213	221	230	238	246	254	263	271	279

Body weight (pounds)

blood sugar levels drop. Fat is then drawn from fat cells to provide further nourishment. A small structure in the brain, the hypothalamus, detects fat depletion and triggers the hunger drive (Woods et al., 2000). Obese people have more fat cells than people of normal weight, billions more (Underwood & Adler, 2004). People with more fatty tissue (fat cells) than others feel food-deprived earlier, even though they may be equal in weight. This might occur because more fat-depletion signals are being sent to the brain. Unfortunately, when we lose weight, we do not lose fat cells (they sort of "shrivel up"). Thus, many people who have lost weight complain that they are always hungry when they try to maintain normal weight levels.

Fatty tissue also metabolizes ("burns") food more slowly than does muscle. For this reason, a person with a high fat-to-muscle ratio metabolizes food more slowly than a person of the same weight with a lower fat-to-muscle ratio. That is, two people who are identical in weight may metabolize food at different rates, depending on the distribution of muscle and fat in their bodies. Obese people therefore are doubly handicapped in their efforts to lose weight—not only by their extra weight but also by the fact that much of their body is composed of adipose tissue. Ironically, the very act of dieting can make it progressively more difficult to lose additional weight. This is because people on diets and those who have lost substantial amounts of weight burn fewer calories. That is, their metabolic rates slow down (Major et al., 2007).

Our bodies are designed to preserve stored reserves of energy—body fat (Underwood & Adler, 2004). This fat-sparing mechanism may have been adaptive to ancestral humans who had to endure times of famine, but it has become a liability to us today when we attempt to lose weight and keep it off. The pounds seem to come off more and more reluctantly. That's not to say we shouldn't try to lose excess weight. But we should understand what we're up against.

Psychosocial Factors

Environmental and psychosocial factors also play key roles in obesity (Hill et al., 2003). Adults and children in the United States are exposed to thousands of food-related environmental cues, such as commercials for fast-food restaurants that emphasize high-fat menu selections. These types of environmental cues can trigger hunger even when our bodies are satiated. Efforts to maintain a healthy weight may also be impeded by negative emotions like depression and anxiety, which can serve as cues leading to excess eating or even binges.

Restaurants today are using larger dinner plates and piling on the food, pizzerias are using larger pans, and fast-food restaurants are offering "big gulp" soft drinks that pack an incredible 800 calories into a 64-ounce cup! The increased availability of fast-food restaurants combined with increased portion sizes ("Did anyone say supersize it?") may also be contributing to increased rates of obesity. And consider this: The character Ronald McDonald is now the second most widely recognized figure, after Santa Claus, among children (Parloff, 2003). Portion size is yet another factor. Recent experimental studies indicate that people generally eat larger amounts of food when it is served in larger portion sizes (Geier, Rozin, & Doros, 2006; Martin, 2007). As one of the researchers explained, "If it's there, people are going to eat it, and they aren't necessarily going to notice it" (cited in Martin, 2007, p. 9).

Might obesity be catching? No, this is not a trick question. Evidence shows that obesity tends to be shared among people in social networks involving friends, neighbors, spouses, and family members (Christakis & Fowler, 2007). The people in our social networks may influence how much we eat and what we eat and affect our judgments about the acceptability of obesity. Investigators suspect that social networks may be an even stronger determinant of obesity than genes (Barabási, 2007).

What's the bottom line on maintaining a healthy weight? Health experts recognize that quickie diets and weight-loss pills are not the answer to long-term weight management (Mann et al., 2007). The answer, they say, is making healthy eating and exercise habits part of one's regular lifestyle (Lamberg, 2006; Powell et al., 2007; Wadden et al., 2005). Psychologists offer a number of helpful suggestions for developing healthier eating behaviors, such as those found in the accompanying *Try This Out* feature.

Francisco Cruz/SuperStock

All in the Family?
Although genetics plays a key role in obesity, psychosocial factors such as leading a sedentary lifestyle and consuming a high-fat diet and large meal portions certainly contribute to the problem.

TRY THIS OUT ▌ TAKING IT OFF AND KEEPING IT OFF—WEIGHT, THAT IS

Managing your weight does not require drastic and dangerous fad diets, such as fasting, eliminating carbohydrates, or downing gobs of grapefruit or rice. Rather, effective weight management involves examining your eating habits and making healthy changes in behavior to help you manage your weight more effectively. The methods include setting reasonable goals, improving nutritional knowledge, decreasing calorie intake, exercise, behavior modification, and tracking your progress (Manson et al., 2004; Underwood & Adler, 2004).

Setting Calorie Goals

For example, select a reasonable goal for your post-diet weight. You can use the BMI information in Figure 5.3, but your ideal weight also depends on how much muscle you have (muscle weighs more than fat). Your physician may be able to make a judgment about how much fat you have by using (painless!) skinfold calipers.

Gradual weight loss is usually more effective than crash dieting. Assume that you'll lose 1 to 2 pounds per week, and focus on the long-term outlook. Eating fewer calories is the key factor to weight loss, so we need some nutritional knowledge. One pound of body weight roughly equals 3,500 calories. As a rule of thumb, if you eat 3,500 more calories than your body requires in order to maintain its proper weight, you will gain a pound or so. If you eat 3,500 fewer calories than you burn, you will lose a pound or so. How many calories do you burn in a day? Your calorie expenditure is a function of your activity level and, yes, of your weight. Gender and age figure in somewhat but not as much.

Table 5.4 ▌ Calories Expended in One Hour According to Activity and Body Weight

Activity	Body Weight (In Pounds)				
	100	125	150	175	200
Sleeping	40	50	60	70	80
Sitting quietly	60	75	90	105	120
Standing quietly	70	88	105	123	140
Eating	80	100	120	140	160
Driving, housework	95	119	143	166	190
Walking slowly	133	167	200	233	267
Walking rapidly	200	250	300	350	400
Swimming	320	400	480	560	640
Running	400	500	600	700	800

The guidelines in Table 5.4 will help you arrive at an estimate. Let's follow Paul, a rather sedentary office worker, through his day. He weighs 150 pounds. First, he records eight hours of sleep a night. As we see in Table 5.5, that's 8 times 60, or 480 calories. He spends about six hours a day at the desk, for another 900 calories. He eats for about an hour (120 calories) and drives for an hour (143 calories). He admits to himself that he spends about five hours a day in quiet sitting,

Table 5.5 ▌ Approximate Number of Calories Burned by Paul* on a Typical Weekday

Activity	Hours/Day			Calories/Hour Subtotal
Sleeping	8	×	60	= 480
Desk work	6	×	150	= 900
Driving	1	×	143	= 143
Eating	1	×	120	= 120
Sitting quietly	5	×	105	= 525
Hobbies	2	×	150	= 300
Walking rapidly	1	×	300	= 300
Totals	24			2,768

*Based on a body weight of 150 pounds.

watching television or reading (525 calories). He has begun an exercise program of walking rapidly for an hour a day—that's 300 calories. Another couple of hours of desk work at home—working on his stamp collection and other hobbies (300 calories)—accounts for the remainder of the day. In this typical weekday, Paul burns up about 2,768 calories. If you weigh less than Paul, your calorie expenditure will probably be less than his, unless you are more active.

The information in Table 5.4 can help you estimate the number of calories you burn each day. To lose weight, you need to take in fewer calories, burn more calories through vigorous physical activity, or do both.

To lower calorie intake, consult a calorie book and a physician. The book will provide calorie information to help you track your calorie intake. The physician will tell you how much you can safely reduce your calorie intake in light of your general health condition. Establish specific weight-loss plans, including daily calorie intake goals. If the daily goal sounds forbidding—such as eating 500 calories a day fewer than you do now—you can gradually approach it. For example, reduce daily intake, say, by 100 calories for a few days or a week, then 200 calories, and so on.

Before cutting down, you may wish to determine your calorie-intake baseline. Track the calories you consume throughout the day by jotting down the following:

▪ What you have eaten or drunk (everything that passes your lips)
▪ Estimated number of calories (use the calorie book)
▪ Time of day, location, and activity

Your record may suggest foods that you need to cut down on or eliminate; places you should avoid; activities associated with unwanted snacking (such as talking on the telephone or watching TV); and times of day, such as midafternoon or late evening, when you are particularly vulnerable to snacking. You can plan small, low-calorie snacks (or distracting activities) for these times so that you won't feel deprived and then go on a binge.

Once you have established your baseline, maintain a daily record of calories consumed throughout the weight-loss program. You may weigh yourself regularly (we suggest once a week), but use calories, not weight, as your guiding principle.

By meeting your calorie reduction goals, your weight will eventually follow suit.

Changing the *ABCs* to Control Your Eating Behavior
The behavioral techniques outlined in Table 5.6 are designed to help you gain better control over the *A*s (the antecedent cues or stimuli that trigger the behavior), the *B*s (the problem behaviors themselves), and the *C*s (the consequences of the problem behaviors). Use those that seem to apply to you and use your ingenuity to develop your own strategies.

5.1.3 Eating Disorders

Did you know that dieting is now the normative pattern for young women in the United States today? Young women today have come of age in an American culture that is obsessed with thinness, especially thinness in women. Eating disorders are not normal; in many cases they arise from distorted eating behaviors that are grounded in excessive dieting or the pursuit of unrealistic standards of thinness. The major types of eating disorders are **anorexia nervosa** and **bulimia nervosa**.

By and large, eating disorders develop in women during adolescence and young adulthood when social pressures to conform to an unrealistically thin ideal are at their peak (McKnight Investigators, 2003; Nolen-Hoeksema et al., 2007). Recent estimates peg the prevalence of anorexia nervosa in women at slightly less than 1% of women and the prevalence of bulimia among adult women at 1% to 2% (Hudson et al., 2006; Wilson, Grilo, & Vitousek, 2007). Women with eating disorders outnumber men with them by at least 6 to 1 (Goode, 2000). The incidences of anorexia nervosa and bulimia nervosa have increased markedly in recent years. Not only are eating disorders disturbing and dangerous in themselves, but they also frequently set the stage for clinical depression (Stice et al., 2000b).

▪ **Anorexia nervosa** An eating disorder characterized by maintenance of an abnormally low body weight, intense fear of weight gain, a distorted body image, and, in females, lack of menstruation.

▪ **Bulimia nervosa** An eating disorder characterized by recurrent episodes of binge eating followed by purging and by persistent overconcern with body shape and weight.

Table 5.6 ▮ Changing the *ABCs* of Eating Behavior		
Changing the *As* of Overeating—The Stimuli That Trigger Problem Behavior		
	Strategy	**Examples of Use of the Strategy**
 "Limit your exposure to cues that trigger overeating"	**Controlling external stimuli**	▪ Avoid settings that trigger overeating. (Eat at The Celery Stalk, not The Chocolate Gourmet.) ▪ Don't leave tempting treats around the house. ▪ Serve food on smaller plates. Use a lunch plate rather than a dinner plate. ▪ Don't leave seconds on the table. ▪ Serve preplanned portions. Do not leave open casseroles on the table. Immediately freeze leftovers. Don't keep them warm on the stove. ▪ Avoid the kitchen as much as possible. ▪ Disconnect eating from other stimuli, such as watching television, talking on the telephone, or reading. ▪ Establish food-free zones in your home. Imagine there is a barrier at the entrance to your bedroom that prevents the passage of food.
 "Learn to cope with upsetting feelings in more constructive ways than overeating."	**Controlling internal stimuli**	▪ Don't bury disturbing feelings in a box of cookies or a carton of Mocha Delight ice cream. ▪ Relabel feelings of hunger as signals that you're burning calories. Practice saying to yourself, "It's okay to feel hungry. It doesn't mean I'm going to die or pass out. Each minute I delay eating, more calories are burned." ▪ Practice relaxation or meditation when feeling tense rather than turning to food.
Changing the *Bs* of Overeating		
	Strategy	**Examples of Use of the Strategy**
 "Put your fork down after every bite to allow your brain to catch up to your stomach"	**Slow Down the Pace of Eating**	▪ Put down utensils between bites. ▪ Take smaller bites. ▪ Chew thoroughly. ▪ Savor each bite. Don't wolf each bite down to make room for the next. ▪ Take a break during the meal. Put down your utensils and converse with your family or guests for a few minutes. (Give your rising blood sugar level a chance to signal your brain.) ▪ When you resume eating, ask yourself whether you need to finish every bite. Leave something over to be thrown away or enjoyed later.
 "Prepare a shopping list before grocery shopping."	**Modify shopping behavior**	▪ Shop from a list. Don't browse through the supermarket. ▪ Shop quickly. Don't make shopping the high point of your day. ▪ Treat the supermarket like enemy territory. Avoid the aisles containing junk food and snacks. If you must walk down these aisles, put on mental blinders and look straight ahead. ▪ Never shop when hungry. Shop after meals, not before.

"Substitute a nonfood activity for a food activity."

Competing responses	▪ Substitute nonfood activities for food-related activities. When tempted to overeat, leave the house, take a bath, walk the dog, call a friend, or walk around the block.
	▪ Substitute low-calorie foods for high-calorie foods. Keep lettuce, celery, or carrots in the middle of the refrigerator so they are available when you want a snack.
	▪ Fill spare time with nonfood-related activities: Volunteer at the local hospital, play golf or tennis, join exercise groups, read in the library (rather than the kitchen), take long walks.

"Set a kitchen timer to delay snacking."

| Chain breaking | ▪ Stretch the overeating chain. Before allowing yourself to snack, wait 10 minutes. Next time wait 15 minutes, and so on. |
| | ▪ Break the eating chain at its weakest link. It's easier to interrupt the eating chain by taking a route home that bypasses the bakery than to exercise self-control when you're placing your order. |

Changing the Cs of Overeating

| Reward yourself for meeting your calorie-reduction goals. | One pound of body weight is equivalent to 3,500 calories. To lose 1 pound per week, you need to cut 3,500 calories per week, or 500 calories per day, from your typical calorie intake level, assuming your weight has been stable. |
| | Reward yourself for meeting weekly calorie goals. Reward yourself with gifts you would not otherwise purchase for yourself, such as a cashmere sweater or tickets to a show. Repeat the reward program from week to week. If you deviate from your dietary program, don't lose heart. Get back on track next week. |

Source: Adapted form Nevid, Rathus, & Greene (2003), p. 360. Used with permission of Prentice Hall, Inc.

Anorexia Nervosa

There is a saying that you can never be too rich or too thin. We can't say whether you could ever be too rich (though we'd like to try it for a while), but, as in the case of Karen, we *can* certainly say that you can be too thin.

Karen was the 22-year-old daughter of a renowned English professor. She had begun her college career full of promise at the age of 17. But two years ago, after "social problems" occurred, she had returned to live at home and taken progressively lighter courseloads at a local college. Karen had never been overweight, but about a year ago her mother noticed that she seemed to be gradually "turning into a skeleton."

Karen spent hours every day shopping at the supermarket, butcher, and bakeries as well as in conjuring up gourmet treats for her parents and younger siblings. Arguments over her lifestyle and eating habits had divided the family into two camps. The camp led by her father called for patience. That headed by her mother demanded confrontation. Her mother feared that Karen's father would "protect her right into her grave" and wanted Karen placed in residential treatment "for her own good." The parents finally compromised on an outpatient evaluation.

At an even 5 feet, Karen looked like a prepubescent 11-year-old. Her nose and cheekbones protruded crisply, like those of an elegant young fashion model. Her lips were full, but the redness of the lipstick was unnatural, as if too much paint had been dabbed on a corpse for the funeral. Karen weighed only 78 pounds, but she had dressed in a stylish silk blouse, scarf, and baggy pants so that not one inch

Landov

Starved to Death

Brazilian fashion model Ana Carolina Reston was just 21 when she died from medical complications due to anorexia. Unfortunately, the problem of anorexia and other eating disorders among fashion models is widespread, as it is in other situations in which pressure is imposed to attain unrealistic standards of thinness.

of her body was revealed. More striking than her mouth was the redness of her rouged cheeks. It was unclear whether she had used too much makeup or whether minimal makeup had caused the stark contrast between the parts of her face that were covered and those that were not. Karen vehemently denied that she had a problem. Her figure was "just about where I want it to be," and she engaged in aerobic exercise daily. A deal was struck in which outpatient treatment would be tried as long as Karen lost no more weight and showed steady gains back to at least 90 pounds. Treatment included a day hospital with group therapy and two meals a day. But word came back that Karen was artfully toying with her food—cutting it up, sort of licking it, and moving it about her plate—rather than eating it. After three weeks, Karen had lost another pound. At that point her parents were able to persuade her to enter a residential treatment program where her eating could be carefully monitored. (From the author's files)

Karen was diagnosed with anorexia nervosa, which is a potentially life-threatening psychological disorder characterized by refusal to maintain a healthful body weight, intense fear of being overweight, a distorted body image, and, in women, lack of menstruation (Striegel-Moore & Bulik, 2007).

Women with anorexia may lose 25% or more of their body weight in a year. Sadly, they may become so emaciated that they succumb, as in the recent case of a Brazilian model named Ana Carolina Reston, who died at age 21 from medical complications due to anorexia. At the time of her death, the 5'7" young woman weighed but 88 pounds.

In the typical anorexic pattern, a girl notices some weight gain after menarche and decides that it must come off. However, dieting—and, often, exercise—continue at a fever pitch. They persist even after the girl reaches an average weight and even after family members and others have told her that she is losing too much. Girls with anorexia almost always adamantly deny that they are wasting away. They may point to their extreme exercise program as proof of their fitness. But their body images are distorted. Others may perceive them as "skin and bones." But the women themselves frequently sit before the mirror and see themselves as still having unsightly pockets of fat.

Many people with anorexia become obsessed with food. They engross themselves in cookbooks, take on the family shopping chores, and prepare elaborate dinners—for others.

Bulimia Nervosa

The case of Nicole is a vivid account of a young woman who was diagnosed with bulimia nervosa:

Nicole awakens in her cold dark room and already wishes it was time to go back to bed. She dreads the thought of going through this day, which will be like so many others in her recent past. She asks herself the question every morning, "Will I be able to make it through the day without being totally obsessed by thoughts of food, or will I blow it again and spend the day [binge eating]"? She tells herself that today she will begin a new life, today she will start to live like a normal human being. However, she is not at all convinced that the choice is hers. It turns out that this day Nicole begins by eating eggs and toast. Then she binges on cookies; doughnuts; bagels smothered with butter, cream cheese, and jelly; granola; candy bars; and bowls of cereal and milk—all within 45 minutes. When she cannot take in any more food, she turns her attention to purging. She goes to the bathroom, ties back her hair, turns on the shower to mask any noise she will make, drinks a glass of water, and makes herself vomit. Afterward she vows, "Starting tomorrow, I'm going to change." But she knows that tomorrow she will probably do the same thing. (Adapted from Boskind-White & White, 1983, p. 29)

Bubbles Photolibrary/Alamy Limited

On a Binge

The psychological disorder bulimia nervosa is characterized by recurrent cycles of binge eating and dramatic measures to purge the food, such as self-induced vomiting. Binge eating often follows strict dieting, and people with the problem—nearly all young women—tend to be perfectionistic about their body shape and weight.

Nicole's problem, bulimia nervosa, is characterized by recurrent cycles of binge eating followed by dramatic measures to purge the food. Binge eating frequently follows food deprivation—for example, severe dieting. Purging includes self-induced vomiting, fasting or strict dieting, use of laxatives, and/or vigorous exercise. Like young women with anorexia, those with bulimia tend to hold perfectionistic views about body shape and weight and express unhappiness with their own body shape. But unlike women with anorexia, those with bulimia generally maintain a relatively normal weight level.

Causes of Eating Disorders

The underlying causes of eating disorders are complex and involve multiple factors, including body dissatisfaction (not liking your body), which is closely linked to social pressure to adhere to an unrealistically thin body ideal (Forbush, Heatherton, & Keel, 2007; Grabe, Ward, & Hyde, 2008; Striegel-Moore & Bulik, 2007). Some psychodynamic theorists suggest that anorexia represents a female's effort to revert to **prepubescence**. In this view, anorexia allows her to avoid growing up, separate from her family, and assume adult responsibilities. Because of the loss of fat tissue, her breasts and hips flatten. In her fantasies, perhaps, a woman with anorexia remains a child, sexually undifferentiated.

Adolescent girls may use refusal to eat as a weapon against their parents. Evidence points to disturbed relationships within the family in many cases. For example, parents of adolescents with eating disorders were relatively more likely to be unhappy with their family's functioning, to have problems with eating and dieting themselves, to think that their daughters should lose weight, and to consider their daughters to be unattractive (Baker, Whisman, & Brownell, 2000). Some researchers speculate that adolescents may develop eating disorders as a way of coping with feelings of loneliness and alienation they experience in the home. Could binge eating symbolize the effort to gain parental nurturance? Does purging symbolically rid one of negative feelings toward the family?

Social-cognitive theorists suggest that young women with anorexia set unreasonable demands on themselves in the pursuit of perfection, including what in their minds is the "perfect body" (Cockell et al., 2002; Halmi et al., 2000). Yet "perfection" is an impossible goal, even for fashion models who are themselves prone to develop eating disorders because of pressures to match an idealized image.

Investigators find that many young women with eating disorders have issues of control as well as perfectionism. These women may feel that eating is the only part of their lives over which they can exercise control (Shafran & Mansell, 2001). Consider the sociocultural aspects of eating disorders: The quintessential U.S. role model, Miss America, has been slimming down over the years. Since the beginning of the pageant in 1922, the winner of the contest has gained 2% in height but lost 12 pounds in weight. In the 1920s, her weight as compared to her height was in what is today considered the "normal" range, according to the World Health Organization (WHO)—that is, a body mass index in the 20–25 range. The WHO considers people with a BMI lower than 18.5 to be undernourished, and many recent Miss Americas have had a BMI of about 17 (Rubinstein & Caballero, 2000). Miss America has become another undernourished role model.

As the cultural ideal grows slimmer, women with average or heavier-than-average figures feel more pressure to slim down (Winzelberg et al., 2000). Investigators find that even in children as young as eight, disproportionately more girls than boys are dissatisfied with their bodies (Ricciardelli & McCabe, 2001). Recent evidence shows that young girls exposed to images of Barbie dolls afterwards felt worse about their bodies and had a greater desire for a thinner body shape than did girls who were exposed to more realistically proportioned dolls (Dittmar, Halliwell, & Ive, 2006).

Gender differences in weight perceptions also occur among college students; a greater percentage of college females believe they are either slightly or very overweight than do college males (American College Health Association, 2005) (see Table 5.7). To punctuate the point about unrealistic pressures placed on young women, about one in seven college women said they would be embarrassed to even buy a chocolate bar in a store (Rozin, Bauer, & Catanese, 2003).

Let's not lose sight of the fact that some men develop eating disorders (Greenberg & Schoen, 2008). Men with eating disorders are often involved in sports or occupations that require them to maintain a certain weight, such as dancing, wrestling, and modeling (Goode, 2000). (Women ballet dancers are also at special risk of developing eating disorders.) Men are more likely than women to control their weight through

▍ **Prepubescence** The years just prior to puberty.

©Jill Greenberg Studio

To Be Barbie
The Barbie doll has long represented the buxom but thin (impossibly thin!) feminine form. Were women's bodies to be proportioned like those of the Barbie doll, they would look something like the woman depicted on the right. Achieving these proportions, however, would require the average young woman shown on the left to grow nearly a foot in height, slim her waistline by 5 inches, and add 4 inches to her bustline. Do you think the idealized image of the Barbie doll has influenced the self-image and eating habits of young women in our society? Why or why not?

Table 5.7 ∎ Students' Reported Descriptions of Weight

Descriptor	Total		Female		Male	
	n	%	n	%	n	%
Very underweight	142	0.7	67	0.6	69	1.2
Slightly underweight	1,935	10.2	976	8.0	851	14.6
About the right weight	10,038	52.9	6,407	52.7	3,118	53.4
Slighly overweight	6,188	32.6	4,201	34.6	1,649	28.2
Very overweight	687	3.6	502	4.1	152	2.6

Note: Refers to question: "How do you describe your weight?" Because of missing data by sex, the response categories do not always equal the total.

Source: American College Health Association, 2005. Reprinted by permission of the American College Health Association.

intense exercise. Men, like women, are under social pressure to conform to an ideal body image—one that builds their upper bodies and trims their abdomens. Gay males tend to be more concerned about their body shape than heterosexual males and are therefore more vulnerable to eating disorders (Strong et al., 2000).

It's important to note that eating disorders predominantly affect young women from Western cultures who are repeatedly exposed to images promoting the ultrathin ideal, especially in the United States. But even in our own society, eating disorders appear to be much less common among African American women and other minority women, for whom body image is not tied as closely to body weight as it is among European American women (A. Roberts et al., 2006; Wonderlich et al., 2007). Finally, body dissatisfaction is not limited to women; it also occurs among men, especially when it becomes linked to attaining idealized standards of leanness and muscularity (Hobza et al., 2007; Ricciardelli et al., 2007; Tiggemann, Martins, & Kirkbride, 2007).

Biological factors, such as genetic influences and brain mechanisms that control feelings of hunger and satiety, play important roles in eating disorders (Bulik et al., 2006; Klump & Culbert, 2007). For example, irregularities in how the brain utilizes the neurotransmitter serotonin are implicated in bulimic binges, since antidepressant drugs that increase availability of the chemical often help curb eating binges in bulimic women (Walsh et al., 2004). The connection with serotonin is not surprising because the neurotransmitter functions like a behavioral seat belt in constraining impulsive behaviors—and bingeing certainly qualifies as an impulsive act (Crockett et al., 2008). Also, negative emotions such as depression and anxiety can trigger binge eating (Reas & Grilo, 2007).

Although eating disorders are difficult to treat and relapses are common, promising results have been reported in using such treatment approaches as cognitive behavioral therapy and antidepressant drugs (Schmidt et al., 2007; Walsh et al., 2004; Wilson et al., 2007).

MODULE REVIEW

Review It

(1) _____ are amino acids that build muscles, blood, bones, fingernails, and hair.

(2) _____ provide the body with energy.

(3) _____ provide stamina, insulate us from extremes of temperature, nourish the skin, and store vitamins.

(4) (Fat or Muscle?) metabolizes (burns) food more rapidly.

(5) Anorexia nervosa is characterized by intense fear of being overweight, a distorted _____ image, and, in females, lack of menstruation.

(6) Bulimia nervosa is defined as recurrent cycles of _____ _____ followed by purging food.

Think About It

Why are females more likely than males to develop eating disorders?

Fitness: Run (at Least Walk) for Your Life

■ What are the two major types of exercise?
■ What are the physical benefits of exercise?
■ What are the psychological benefits of exercise?

Fitness is not just a matter of strength or of whether you can run a mile in eight minutes or less. Fitness is the ability to engage in moderate to vigorous levels of physical activity without undue fatigue. The bad news is that 75% of adults in the United States do not engage in enough physical activity to maintain even moderate fitness (CDC, 2001). Fewer than 50% engage in regular physical activity (see Figure 5.4). Inactivity among teenage girls in particular has reached the point that many hardly move at all! If you cannot walk from the parking lot to the classroom or the office, or climb several floors of stairs, without shortness of breath or fatigue, consider yourself unfit.

Does fitness matter? After all, few of us intend to run marathons or to compete in the Olympics. Nonetheless, fitness does matter for us all, as it is associated with lower risk of cardiovascular disease (heart and artery disease) (Wessel et al., 2004). The good news is that you may not be destined to remain unfit. Nor do you need to endure pain to reap the benefits of exercise.

The U.S. Centers for Disease Control and Prevention (CDC, 2001) suggest that half an hour of moderate activity—such as brisk walking, swimming, or even raking leaves—five times per week may reap health benefits for most people. You can even divide up your exercise into three 10-minute sessions (Stenson, 2003; see Table 5.8).

Corbis Stock Market

Running for Life
Many thousands of Americans engage in long-distance running to keep fit. But you needn't become a marathon runner to reap the health benefits of exercise. Many kinds of regular physical activity can improve fitness and health.

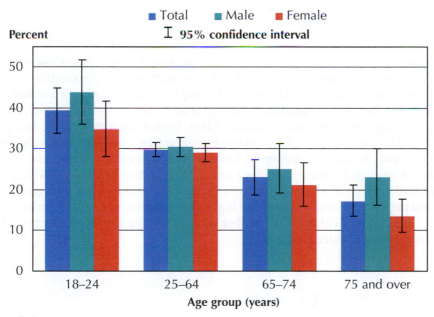

Figure 5.4
Let's Get Moving, America
We see here that less than 50% of adults at all age levels engage in regular physical activity during their leisure (nonwork) hours. Moreover, the percentage of adults who engage in regular leisure-time physical activity decreases with age.
Source: Early Release of Selected Estimates Based on Data. From the January–March 2008 National Health Interview Survey, Centers for Disease Control, http://www.cdc.gov/nchs/data/nhis/earlyrelease/200809_07.pdf.

Table 5.8 ■ Health Facts About Physical Activity

- Adults 18 and older need 30 minutes of physical activity five or more days a week to be healthy; children and teens need 60 minutes of activity a day for their health.
- Significant health benefits can be obtained by including a moderate amount of physical activity (e.g., 30 minutes of brisk walking or raking leaves, 15 minutes of running, 45 minutes of playing volleyball). Additional health benefits can be gained through greater amounts of physical activity.
- Engaging in 30 to 60 minutes of physical activity, broken into smaller segments of 10 or 15 minutes throughout the day, has significant health benefits.
- Moderate daily physical activity can substantially reduce the risk of developing or dying from cardiovascular disease, type 2 diabetes, and certain cancers, such as colon cancer. Daily physical activity helps to lower blood pressure and cholesterol, helps prevent or retard osteoporosis, and helps reduce obesity, symptoms of anxiety and depression, and symptoms of arthritis.
- Physically inactive people are twice as likely to develop coronary heart disease as regularly active people. The health risk posed by physical inactivity is almost as high as that posed by such risk factors as cigarette smoking, high blood pressure, and high cholesterol.

Source: Adapted from "Physical Activity Fact Sheet," The President's Council on Physical Fitness and Sports, Department of Human Services, as updated March 2005. Reprinted from Nevid & Rathus, 2007, by permission of Thomson Custom Publishing.

Thus, the great majority of readers can improve their fitness by making exercise a regular part of their lifestyles. You should consult with a physician before starting any vigorous exercise program, especially if you have special health conditions, such as high blood pressure or asthma. Your physician can prescribe an exercise program that would be healthful for you.

In this section we discuss types of exercise, the physiological effects of exercise, the health benefits (and hazards!) of exercise, and the psychological effects of exercise. Before we do so, review Table 5.8, which lists some important health facts about physical activity compiled by the President's Council on Physical Fitness and Sports.

5.2.1 Types of Exercise

Aerobic exercise Exercise that requires sustained increase in oxygen consumption, such as jogging, swimming, or riding a bicycle.

Anaerobic exercise Exercise that does not require sustained increase in oxygen consumption, such as weightlifting.

The two major types of exercise are **aerobic exercise** and **anaerobic exercise**. Aerobic exercise requires a sustained increase in the body's consumption of oxygen and promotes cardiovascular fitness. Examples of aerobic exercise include running and jogging, running in place, walking (at more than a leisurely pace), aerobic dancing, jump rope, swimming, bicycle riding, basketball, racquetball, and cross-country skiing (see Figure 5.5). Anaerobic exercises, by contrast, involve short bursts of muscle activity. Examples include weight training, calisthenics (which allow rest periods between exercises), and sports such as baseball, in which there are sporadic bursts of strenuous activity. Anaerobic exercise can strengthen muscles and improve flexibility. Figure 5.5 highlights the pros and cons of various kinds of exercise. Table 5.4 shows the number of calories you can expect to burn from various kinds of physical activities.

5.2.2 Effects of Exercise

Fitness (1) The ability to perform physically demanding tasks without undue fatigue. (2) Cardiovascular fitness refers to the ability of the heart and lungs to function under stress.

The major physiological benefit of aerobic exercise is **fitness**. Fitness is not a matter of how strong you are or whether you can run an eight-minute mile. Rather, it involves your body's ability to withstand moderate levels of stress and pressure without undue fatigue, such as when climbing stairs or carrying packages. Various aspects of fitness include muscle strength and endurance, muscle suppleness or flexibility, and cardiorespiratory (or aerobic) fitness.

Figure 5.5 Types of Physical Activities

Indoor Activities			
Activity	**Pros**	**Cons**	**Tips**
Working out with exercise equipment (e.g., ski machine, treadmill, stationary bike, step aerobics, weight training, rowing machine, stair climber, etc.)	Weight training can strengthen muscles and build bones; aerobics equipment like treadmills, stair climbers, skiers, and rowers can give you a good aerobics workout to build cardiovascular endurance, take off pounds, and strengthen and tone selected muscle groups (e.g., the rowing machine is great for the biceps, quads, upper back, abs, and legs). Most equipment these days has electronic gauges that give you feedback on intensity, calories expended, and time spent exercising.	Equipment can be expensive if you purchase it for home use, especially motorized treadmills. Club memberships, too, tend to be expensive and may not guarantee access to the equipment when you want to use it, especially during peak hours. Many people are initially attracted to exercise equipment (some in the misguided belief that the equipment will do the work for them) but quickly lose interest when they find the routines too demanding or monotonous. Using such equipment may result in injuries if you push yourself too hard too fast.	Don't overdo it. Build up intensity and duration slowly. Allow your body to adjust to the increased demand. Alternate between machines to increase variety and combat boredom. Also, combat boredom and help the time pass more quickly by watching TV, reading (if possible), or listening to music on your personal stereo. Most important: Get checked out first by a health professional.
Working out with an exercise video 	This is great for aerobics training without the expense and effort of going to an exercise studio or health club; there is only a one-time expense for the video.	You may get bored with same routine and may lose motivation if someone isn't there exhorting you on.	Start with an exercise program at a local club or studio to learn proper technique and style. Ask the instructor for recommended videos that fit your needs and style. Have several exercise videos available and alternate among them to prevent boredom. Invite a friend over and exercise together.
Swimming laps 	Swimming improves cardiovascular endurance; it's great for shedding pounds and toning muscles; as a low-impact activity, it poses little risk of injury; it's relaxing and soothing to the mind as well.	Pools may be crowded or inconvenient. Use of pools may require expensive membership fees.	Start slowly and build up gradually. Don't push yourself to extremes. Increase the number of laps and lap speed gradually. Find a pool with swim hours that fit your particular schedule.
Aerobics classes 	Classes are a good way to build up cardiovascular endurance and drop excess pounds. If you're the type of person who needs a push every now and then, having an instructor exhorting you on may help you to get the most out of yourself. Instructors also help you with technique and can tailor the routine to your ability and level of endurance.	Classes can be expensive. They may not be offered at convenient times or locations. Some people may be intimidated or self-conscious about exercising in front of others. Depending on the instructors, some classes may be too demanding. The repetitive routines may become boring or mind-numbing.	Choose an instructor who is right for you, someone who takes the time to get to know your personal capabilities and needs. Start with a beginner's class and gradually work your way up to more challenging classes. Go with a friend. It's more likely that you'll stick with it if you feel that someone else is depending on you.

Figure 5.5 Continued

Outdoor Activities

Activity	Pros	Cons	Tips
Competitive sports (e.g., baseball, basketball, handball, racquetball, tennis, golf, etc.) 	Sports that require more continuous exertion, such as basketball and tennis, can improve cardiovascular fitness. Even sports requiring less frequent bursts of physical activity, like baseball or softball, can burn calories and help you meet your goal of 30 minutes daily of moderate physical activity. Golfing can be a good workout, but only if you leave the golf cart in the clubhouse and carry your own golf bag.	Competition can bring out the best in people, but also the worst. It may also diminish self-esteem if you connect your self-worth with winning and wind up on the losing end. Team sports may be difficult to coordinate with people's busy schedules. Accessibility to courts or ball fields may be limited. Games may be washed out due to the weather.	Choose a sport you enjoy and in which you have a modicum of skill. Play for enjoyment, not to trounce your opponent. Remember, it is only a game.
Brisk walking 	Depending on the pace, it can be a source of cardiovascular endurance (at 5+ mph) or general fitness (3–4 mph); requires no special equipment other than good walking shoes; you can enjoy the scenery, which may be especially appealing on long nature walks.	There is not too much on the downside, which is perhaps why walking has become America's most popular fitness activity, practiced by more than 70 million people. Yet there are some potential disadvantages. Walking may be unpleasant or difficult in inclement weather. It may become boring if you walk the same route every time. Injuries can occur if you fail to warm up correctly, use improper shoes, take a misstep because of an uneven surface, or push your body too hard too fast.	Wear a comfortable, well-fitting athletic shoe that is specially designed for walking. Remember to start any workout, including brisk walking, with some warm-up exercises, including stretching. This will help cut down on the chances of injuries such as sprains and strains. Afterwards, cool down by walking at a slower pace for about five to seven minutes and then finish off with some stretching. Start with a slower pace and for a limited period of time, say about 10 or 15 minutes. Then gradually increase your speed to about 3–4 miles an hour for about a 30-minute period (Poppy, 1995).
Running 	Running is excellent aerobic exercise for cardiovascular fitness and weight reduction. It requires minimal equipment, though good running shoes are a must.	Injuries to feet and ankles are common due to the high impact of running, especially on hard surfaces. Excessive running can overtax body resources, impairing immunological functioning.	Get your doctor's approval before beginning any vigorous exercise routine. Stretching exercises are a must when warming up and cooling down. Run in pairs or groups for safety's sake, especially at night. Like other exercises, take it slow at first and build up speed and endurance gradually. Seek medical attention for any persistent pain or soreness.

Figure 5.5 Continued

Outdoor Activities

Activity	Pros	Cons	Tips
Cycling 	You can set the pace for moderate or vigorous activity; cycling improves cardiovascular fitness at higher speeds; it has less impact on feet and ankles than running, reducing the risk of injury. Love that passing scenery!	There is a potential risk of injuries from falls; it requires the purchase of a quality bicycle for safety's sake and accessories including (a must!) a Snell-certified helmet; it may be dangerous on slippery surfaces and city streets; it's not suitable for inclement weather.	Never bicycle without a safety helmet; like other demanding exercises, work up pace and distance gradually and consult your doctor first; alternate between level and hilly terrain; have your bicycle checked regularly for malfunctions; avoid cycling on congested city streets.
In-line skating 	This was the fitness boom of the 1990s, with the numbers of in-line skaters surpassing those of cyclists in some city parks. Depending on the pace, this sport can be a source of moderate or vigorous exercise, with less impact on feet than running or fast walking.	There is a high risk of injuries to wrists, knees, and ankles from falls; it's especially dangerous if you are weaving around other in-line skaters or cyclists; there is the expense of initial outlays for in-line skates and safety accessories.	Learn proper technique before setting out, and check first with your doctor concerning any physical restrictions; use proper safety equipment, which includes a safety helmet, wrist and knee pads, and a quality pair of in-line skates that provide good ankle support. Avoid highly congested areas and never skate in vehicular traffic.
Cross-country skiing 	This is excellent aerobic exercise that spares the feet of the pounding associated with running. Enjoy the beauty of nature in all its winter wonder. It's less expensive than downhill skiing and may be free in public areas or parks.	Skiing is limited to winter and available only in colder climates; it requires the purchase of skis, boots, and ski clothing; there is the risk of injury to the lower extremities from falls or severe twists of the ankles or knees; there is also the risk of cold-weather injuries.	Get your doctor's approval before beginning any vigorous exercise routine. Learn proper technique from an expert before setting out. Dress warmly in removable layers; waterproof outer clothing is a must. Work up gradually.

Muscle strength is promoted by contracting muscles and then returning gradually to the starting position. Weight training and calisthenics such as push-ups and chin-ups facilitate muscle development by offering resistance. Flexibility is enhanced by slow, sustained stretching exercises. Flexibility is desirable in its own right and also because it helps prevent injuries from other types of exercises. This is why many people stretch before running. Stretching exercises can be incorporated into the warm-up and cool-down phases of an aerobic exercise program.

Cardiorespiratory fitness, or "condition," means that the body can use greater amounts of oxygen during vigorous activity and pump more blood with each heartbeat.

Since the conditioned athlete pumps more blood with each beat, he or she usually has a slower pulse rate—fewer heartbeats per minute. But during aerobic exercise, the person may double or triple his or her resting heart rate for minutes at a time. Exercise raises the metabolic rate and burns more calories than sedentary activity.

Exercise and Physical Health

▮ **High-density lipoproteins (HDL)** The so-called good cholesterol because it sweeps away cholesterol deposits from artery walls for elimination from the body, thereby lowering the risk of cardiovascular disease.

Even couch potatoes can reduce their risk of cardiovascular disease by becoming more physically active. Regular vigorous exercise has many healthy effects on the heart and circulatory system, including reducing hypertension, lowering the risk of heart attacks and strokes, and boosting levels of good cholesterol, the **high-density lipoproteins (HDL)** that sweep away fatty deposits from the artery wall (Borjesson & Dahlof, 2005; Manson et al., 2002; Stampfer et al., 2000). But even moderate exercise such as brisk walking can reduce the risks of developing heart disease (I.M. Lee et al., 2001; Manson et al., 2002). Exercise helps maintain muscle tone and reduces the risks of obesity and osteoporosis (NIH Consensus Development Panel, 2001). We shouldn't be surprised that investigators find that people who exercise regularly tend to live longer (Gregg et al., 2003).

Regular exercise helps people lose weight and, more importantly, keep it off. Exercise promotes weight loss in ways other than burning calories. The body often compensates for lessened food intake by slowing the metabolic rate, but regular aerobic exercise elevates the metabolic rate of dieters throughout the day. Health researchers find that dieting plus exercise is more effective than dieting alone for shedding pounds and keeping them off (Jeffery, Epstein, et al., 2000; Jeffery, Hennrikus, et al., 2000).

Exercise and Mental Health

Aerobic exercise helps normalize levels of neurotransmitters implicated in negative emotional states such as depression. Exercise can be enjoyable in its own right and can provide a break from the strains of everyday life, which are yet other ways in which it counters depression. Evidence from controlled studies shows that exercise can help alleviate depression in combination with other treatments (Babyak et al., 2000). All in all, regular exercise, especially vigorous aerobic exercise, can help sustain our mental as well as physical health.

5.2.3 Making Physical Activity a Part of Your Lifestyle

Note that we use the term *physical activity* rather than *exercise*. Regular exercise is an excellent way of getting in shape, but you don't need to pound the treadmill at your local health club to meet the recommended guidelines for daily physical activity (see Table 5.9). Many daily activities fit the bill, including the following:

- Climbing stairs rather then taking the elevator
- Raking leaves
- Taking a brisk walk in the neighborhood or on your way home from work
- Riding a stationary bicycle or working out while watching TV
- Pushing a hand lawnmower (not the power kind)
- Playing singles tennis or swimming laps
- Performing strenuous odd jobs around the house

Most people should aim for 30 minutes a day of moderate physical activity. The good news is that you needn't accumulate all those minutes at one time or from only one activity. You can combine short bouts of different activities throughout the day. You'll gain even more healthful benefits if you combine regular physical activity with a structured exercise program. But before beginning an exercise program, you should note the following:

1 *Unless you have engaged in sustained and vigorous exercise recently, seek the advice of a medical expert.* If you smoke, have a family history of cardiovascular disorders, are overweight, or are over 40, get a stress test.

2 *Consider joining a beginner's exercise class.* Group leaders are not usually experts in physiology, but at least they "know the steps." You'll also be among other beginners and derive the benefits of social support.

3 *Get the proper equipment to facilitate performance and help avert injury.*

Table 5.9 ▍ Recommended Guidelines for Physical Activity

Engage in regular physical activity and reduce sedentary activities to promote health, psychological well-being, and a healthy body weight.

- To reduce the risk of chronic diseases in adulthood: Engage in at least 30 minutes of moderate-intensity physical activity, above usual activity, at work or home on most days of the week.
- For most people, greater health benefits can be obtained by engaging in physical activity of more vigorous intensity or longer duration.
- To help manage body weight and prevent gradual, unhealthy body weight gain in adulthood: Engage in approximately 60 minutes of moderate- to vigorous-intensity activity on most days of the week while not exceeding caloric intake requirements.
- To sustain weight loss in adulthood: Participate in at least 60 to 90 minutes of daily moderate-intensity physical activity while not exceeding caloric intake requirements. Some people may need to consult with a health care provider before participating in this level of activity.

Achieve physical fitness by including cardiovascular conditioning, stretching exercises for flexibility, and resistance exercises or calisthenics for muscle strength and endurance.

Source: 2005 Dietary Guidelines for Americans, Key Recommendations for the General Population, USDA, January 12, 2005.

Note: These guidelines apply to the general population. People with special health needs should consult their health care providers.

4 *Read up on the activity you are considering.*

5 *Select activities you can integrate within your lifestyle.* Enjoy yourself, and your strength and endurance will progress on their own. If you do not enjoy what you're doing, you're not likely to stick to it.

6 *Keep a diary or log and note your progress.* If running, note the paths or streets you follow, the distance you run, the weather conditions, and any remarkable details that come to mind. Check your notes now and then to remind yourself to try more enjoyable runs.

7 *If you feel severe pain, don't try to exercise "through" it.* Passing feelings of soreness are to be expected for beginners (and some old-timers now and then). But sharp pain or persistent soreness is abnormal and a sign that something is wrong.

Check Your Physical Activity and Heart Disease IQ

Self-Assessment

Test how much you know about how physical activity affects your heart. Mark each question true or false. See how you did by checking the scoring key at the end of the chapter.

T F   1. Regular physical activity can reduce your chances of getting heart disease.
T F   2. Most people get enough physical activity from their normal daily routine.
T F   3. You don't have to train like a marathon runner to become more physically fit.
T F   4. Exercise programs do not require a lot of time to be very effective.
T F   5. People who need to lose some weight are the only ones who will benefit from regular physical activity.
T F   6. All exercises give you the same benefits.
T F   7. The older you are, the less active you need to be.
T F   8. It doesn't take a lot of money or expensive equipment to become physically fit.
T F   9. There are many risks and injuries that can occur with exercise.
T F 10. You should always consult a doctor before starting a physical activity program.
T F 11. People who have had a heart attack should not start any physical activity program.
T F 12. To help stay physically active, include a variety of activities.

For an interactive version of this self-assessment exercise, go to www.wileyplus.com

MODULE REVIEW

Review It

(7) According to the CDC, _____ % of adults in the United States do not engage in enough physical activity to maintain even moderate fitness.

(8) According to the President's Council on Physical Fitness and Sports, adults need _____ minutes of physical activity on five or more days a week to maintain good health.

(9) _____ exercise requires a sustained increase in the consumption of oxygen.

(10) _____ exercise involves short bursts of muscle activity, as in weight training and sports like baseball.

(11) Regular exercise (raises or lowers?) the metabolic rate.

Think About It

Why does exercise lessen the risk of heart attacks and strokes?

MODULE 5.3

Sleep: A Time for Renewal

▮ Why do we sleep?

▮ What are the causes of insomnia?

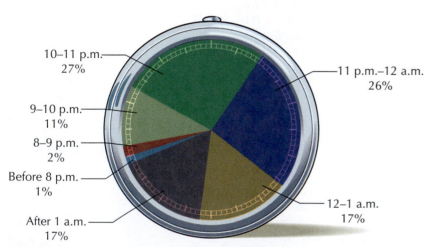

10–11 p.m.
27%

9–10 p.m.
11%

8–9 p.m.
2%

Before 8 p.m.
1%

After 1 a.m.
17%

11 p.m.–12 a.m.
26%

12–1 a.m.
17%

Figure 5.6
When Do You Go to Bed?
Many Americans are going to bed too late to get the seven to nine hours of sleep they need.
Source: Adapted from Sleepless in America, a survey conducted by the AC Nielsen Company, April 2005, retrieved from http://us.acnielsen.com/news/20050404.shmtl.
Note: Percentages are rounded off.

Here's a surprise (Not): Americans are not getting enough sleep. Most people need between seven and nine hours of sleep to feel fully rested and able to function at their best. But more than six in ten Americans get fewer than the recommended number of hours of sleep and about one in ten adults (about 8%) sleep less than six hours a night (CDC, 2008; Winerman, 2004). One in four adults say that their lack of sleep interferes with their ability to function during the day (National Sleep Foundation, 2005). Even more ominous, more than one in five people polled in this same survey said they had fallen asleep at the wheel during the past year.

What about college students? How much do they sleep on an average night? Surveys of college students show that they average between 6 to 6.9 hours sleep a night, which is less than the recommended level and may help explain why many feel groggy or drowsy while attending lectures or walking about campus during the day (Markel, 2003). Only about 15% of American high school students get the recommended 8.5 hours of sleep they need (Kantrowitz & Springen, 2003; Song, 2006).

One reason we've become a nation of sleepyheads is that many of us are going to bed too late. We are increasingly living in a 24/7 world where it is possible to order pizzas at two in the morning or watch 24-hour news channels that never take a break. The results of a recent survey showed that about one in three adults in the U.S. (34 percent) say they regularly go to bed after midnight (see Figure 5.6). No surprise that

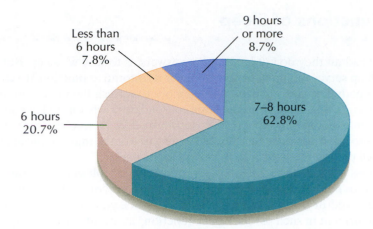

Figure 5.7
How Long Do We Sleep?
About six in ten Americans get the recommended seven to nine hours of sleep a night, but nearly one in three report sleeping six hours or less a night.
Source: CDC, 2008.

many of us are not getting the 7 to 9 hours of sleep we need (see Figure 5.7). Are you a member of this midnighter club?

We know we need an adequate amount of sleep to function at our best. But why do we need sleep? What functions does it serve?

Are You Getting Your Zs?	# Self-Assessment

Many, if not most, college students complain that they do not get enough sleep. How about you? This questionnaire will help you determine whether you are getting your Zs. If you answer several of these items in the affirmative, chances are that you are having trouble sleeping or suffering from insomnia. If that's the case, the suggestions in the accompanying *Try This Out* feature may be helpful. If the problem continues, it makes sense to consult your health provider.

Directions: Read the following items and check whether each one is mostly true or mostly false for you. Try to work rapidly and answer every item.

TRUE FALSE

_____ _____ I have trouble staying awake when I do things in the evening.
_____ _____ I used to get more sleep than I do now.
_____ _____ I find myself hitting the snooze bar over and over again to grab a few more minutes of sleep.
_____ _____ I often have to fight to get out of bed in the morning.
_____ _____ Warm rooms can put me right to sleep.
_____ _____ I find myself nodding off during classes or at work.
_____ _____ I will suddenly realize that I haven't heard what someone is saying to me.
_____ _____ Sometimes it is almost impossible to keep my eyes open while I am driving.
_____ _____ I often fall asleep after I have had a drink or two.
_____ _____ I am one of those people who often falls asleep when "my head hits the pillow."
_____ _____ I have "bags," or dark circles, under my eyes.
_____ _____ I have to set the alarm clock loud in order to get up at the right time.
_____ _____ There are not enough hours in the day.
_____ _____ During the day I am often grumpy and worn out.
_____ _____ My eyes will sort of glaze over while I am working on something.
_____ _____ I need coffee or tea to get going in the morning.
_____ _____ I will be thinking about something, like solving a problem, and all of a sudden everything will go out of my mind.
_____ _____ I have trouble staying awake after eating a heavy meal.
_____ _____ I try to catch up on lost sleep over the weekend, but I never quite do so.

For an interactive version of this self-assessment exercise, go to www.wileyplus.com

Dynamic Graphics/IT Stock Free/Alamy Limited

What's Wrong with This Picture?
People who suffer from insomnia often have poor sleep habits, such as using their bed for many other daily activities, such as eating, reading, working, and talking on the phone. Let your bed be a place for winding down, not gearing up.

❚ **Insomnia** A disorder characterized by persistent difficulty falling asleep or remaining asleep.

5.3.1 Functions of Sleep

Researchers admit they do not have all the answers as to why we sleep. But they suspect that sleep serves multiple functions. One is a restorative function; it helps rejuvenate a tired body. But sleep may be needed more to refresh the mind than the rest of the body (Song, 2006). Sleep helps the brain consolidate newly formed memories of life experiences into more lasting ones (Hu, Stylos-Allan, & Walker, 2006; Rasch et al., 2007). Sleep may also serve a survival function by keeping us from roaming about at night when we might fall prey to predators lurking about in the dark.

If you miss a few hours of sleep or experience a sleepless night, you will probably be able to muddle through the next day, although you may feel groggy. But if you are deprived of normal sleep for several nights, you are likely to suffer substantial impairment in such psychological functions as attention, learning, and memory. The National Sleep Foundation (2000b) estimates that sleep deprivation is linked to about 100,000 vehicular crashes and 1,500 vehicular deaths each year. Sleepiness is becoming a way of life for many Americans (Minerd & Jasmer, 2006). People who suffer chronic sleep deprivation, such as those of shifting work schedules, stand an increased risk of serious health problems, including cardiovascular disease, as well as psychological disorders and problems with mental alertness and concentration (Hampton, 2008; Latta & Van Cauter, 2003).

People often need more sleep during times of stress, such as a change of job, an increase in workload, or an episode of depression. Sleep may help us recover from stress. Newborn babies tend to sleep about 16 hours a day, and teenagers seem to sleep around the clock. It is widely believed that older people need less sleep than younger adults do. However, sleep in older people is often interrupted by physical discomfort or the need to go to the bathroom. Older people often sleep more during the day to make up for sleep lost at night.

Many people have so much difficulty falling asleep, remaining asleep, or falling back to sleep after a middle-of-the night awakening that they cannot make up for lost sleep. They suffer from chronic insomnia, a significant health problem that affects many of us at one time or another, sometimes for years.

5.3.2 Insomnia: "When Sleep Eludes Us"

Perhaps all of us have occasional trouble falling asleep. But about one in ten adult Americans suffer from persistent or chronic **insomnia**, the most common form of sleep disorder (Smith & Perlis, 2006). Insomnia is a common and persistent complaint among many adolescents and young adults (Roberts, 2008).

People with chronic insomnia complain of difficulty falling asleep, remaining asleep, or returning to sleep after nighttime awakenings (Morphy et al., 2007). Insomnia has many causes, including pain or physical disorders, mental disorders such as anxiety and mood disorders, or substance abuse. Other factors that may contribute to insomnia are intrusions from children; environmental factors such as noise, light, and temperature; even a partner's snoring. Insomnia often comes and goes with many people, increasing during periods of stress. Table 5.10 shows some gender differences in reporting of factors that disturb sleep.

Table 5.10 ❚ Gender Differences in Factors Reported as Disrupting Sleep		
Factor	Percent of Women Reporting Factor	Percent of Men Reporting Factor
Stress: 22% of adults overall	26	20
Pain: 20% of adults overall	25	13
Children: 17% of adults overall	21	12

Table 5.10 ▌ (Continued)		
Factor	Percent of Women Reporting Factor	Percent of Men Reporting Factor
Partner's snoring: 16% of adults overall	22	7
Pauses in partner's breathing: 8% of adults overall	11	2

Source: Based on data reported by the National Sleep Foundation (2000b).

MODULE REVIEW

Review It

(12) Sleep (does or does not?) appear to serve a restorative function.

(13) Sleep may also serve a _____ function of protecting us from predators by keeping us from wandering about at night.

(14) Sleep_____ can impair attention, learning, and memory.

(15) Difficulty falling asleep or remaining asleep through the night is called _____.

Think About It

Account for why it's not a good idea to try to force yourself to sleep.

TRY THIS OUT   TO SLEEP, PERCHANCE TO DREAM

No question about it: The most common medical method for fighting insomnia in the United States is taking sleeping pills. Pills (sleep medication) may work—for a while. They generally work by reducing arousal, which makes your brain more receptive to sleep. Positive expectations of success (the so-called placebo effect) may also contribute to their effectiveness. But there are problems with sleeping pills. First, if you fall asleep more easily, you are likely to attribute your success to the pill, not to yourself. You thus may come to depend on taking pills. Second, you develop tolerance for many kinds of sleeping pills. With regular use, you need higher doses to achieve the same effects. Third, high doses of these chemicals can be dangerous, especially if mixed with alcohol. Fourth, sleeping pills do not enhance your skills at handling insomnia. Thus, when you stop taking them, insomnia is likely to return. And fifth, regular use of sleep medications can lead to physical or psychological dependence. If these drugs are used at all, they should be used only for a brief period of time, a few weeks at most, and only under a physician's care.

Psychological methods based on behavioral and cognitive techniques have emerged as the most effective treatment for insomnia, even more effective than sleep medications (e.g., Lamberg, 2008; McCurry et al., 2007; Perlis et al., 2008; Vincent, Lewycky, & Finnegan, 2008). Although sleep medication may produce faster results, behavioral treatment typically produces longer-lasting results (Pollack, 2004). After all, taking sleep medication doesn't help people learn more adaptive sleep habits. Cognitive-behavioral therapists use a combination of techniques to help people overcome insomnia, including the following:

1. *Relax yourself.* Take a hot bath at bedtime or try meditating. Releasing muscle tension can reduce the amount of time needed to fall asleep and the incidence of waking up during the night.

2. *Challenge exaggerated fears.* You need not be a sleep expert to realize that thinking that your next day will be ruined unless you get to sleep right now may increase, rather than decrease, bedtime tension. However, cognitive-behavioral psychologists note that smart and knowledgeable people often exaggerate the problems they believe will befall them if they do not get a good night's rest (Edinger et al., 2001). Table 5.11 shows some beliefs that increase bedtime tension and some alternatives.

3. *Don't ruminate in bed.* Worrying or ruminating about your daily concerns interferes with sleep, in part because it engenders increased bodily arousal (Thomsen et al., 2003). Don't plan or worry about the next day while lying in bed. When you lie down for sleep, you may organize your thoughts for the day for a few minutes, but then allow yourself to relax or engage in mental excursions or fantasy. If an important idea comes to you, jot it down on a

handy pad so that you won't lose it. If thoughts persist, however, get up and follow them elsewhere. Let your bed be a place for relaxation and sleep—not your second office. A bed—even a waterbed—is not a think tank.

4. *Establish a regular routine.* Sleeping late can make matters worse by altering your body's natural wake–sleep cycle. Set your alarm for the same time each morning and get up, regardless of how long you have slept. By rising at a regular time, you'll allow your body to fall into a regular sleep–wake pattern.

5. *Try a little fantasy.* Fantasies or daydreams are almost universal and may occur naturally as we fall asleep. You can allow yourself to "go with" fantasies that occur at bedtime or plan particular fantasies in nightly installments. You may be able to ease yourself to sleep by focusing on a sun-drenched beach with waves lapping on the shore or on a walk through a mountain meadow on a summer day. You can construct your own "mind trips" and paint in the details. With mind trips, you conserve fuel and avoid delays at airports.

Table 5.11 ▌ Beliefs That Increase Nightly Tension and Calming Alternatives

Beliefs That Increase Nightly Tension	Calming Alternatives
If I don't get to sleep, I'll feel wrecked tomorrow.	Not necessarily. If I'm tired, I can go to bed early tomorrow night.
It's unhealthy for me not to get more sleep.	Not necessarily. Some people do very well on only a few hours of sleep.
I'll wreck my sleeping schedule for the whole week if I don't get to sleep right away.	Not at all. If I'm tired, I'll just go to bed a bit earlier. I'll get up about the same time with no problem.
If I don't get to sleep, I won't be able to concentrate on that big test/conference tomorrow.	Possibly, but my fears may be exaggerated. I may just as well relax or get up and do something enjoyable for a while.

Above all: Accept the idea that it's not the end of the world if you don't get a full night's sleep this night. You will survive. (You really will, you know.) In fact, you'll do just fine.

MODULE 5.4

Substance Abuse and Dependence: When Drug Use Causes Harm

- What are substance abuse and substance dependence?
- What are the causes of substance abuse and dependence?
- What are the effects of alcohol?
- What are the effects of opioids?
- What are the effects of barbiturates?
- What are the effects of nicotine?
- What are the effects of amphetamines?
- What are the effects of cocaine?
- What are the effects of LSD and other hallucinogenic drugs?
- What are the effects of marijuana?

The world is a supermarket of drugs. The United States is flooded with drugs that distort perceptions and change mood—drugs that take you up, let you down, and move you across town. Some people use drugs because their friends do or because their parents tell them not to. Others get started with doctors' prescriptions, coffee, or their first aspirin tablet. Some are seeking pleasure; others, relief from pain; still others, inner truth.

For better or worse, drugs are part of life in the United States. The majority of high school seniors report using illicit drugs at some point in their lives. Marijuana is the most widely used illicit drug—whether by young people or adults ("Fewer Youths Using," 2004). About 6% of American adults are current users of marijuana. Though rates of illicit drug use remain high, especially among younger people, the proportion of teens using illicit drugs has continued a decade-long decline ("Getting High," 2008). Yet a new wrinkle in the war on drugs is the rising prevalence of illicit use of prescription drugs, such as tranquilizers and sleeping pills, on many high school and college campuses. Despite general declines in illicit drug use among U.S. teens, the abuse of prescription drugs, such as the painkillers Vicodin and OxyContin, is on the rise (Friedman, 2006). Yet the most popular drugs on campus remain the longtime favorites: alcohol and tobacco. Tobacco contains a mild but highly addictive stimulant—nicotine.

Among college students, 21% report smoking cigarettes and more than two-thirds (69%) report using alcohol during the past month (see Figure 5.8). About one in six (16.5%) report using marijuana. Overall, however, 40% of college students report having used marijuana at least once (American College Health Association, 2005). Yet for every person who experiments with marijuana for the first time, some 250 people light up their first cigarette (Stout, 2000).

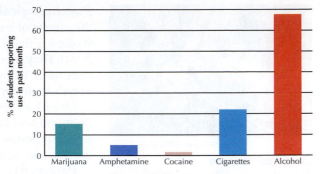

Figure 5.8

Drug Use on Campus
Alcohol and cigarettes remain the most popular psychoactive substances used on campus.
Source: American College Health Association, 2005.

5.4.1 Substance Abuse and Dependence: Crossing the Line

The American Psychiatric Association (2000) defines **substance abuse** as repeated use of a substance despite the fact that it is causing or compounding social, occupational, psychological, or physical problems. If you are missing school or work because you are drunk or "sleeping it off," you are abusing alcohol. The amount you drink is not as crucial as the fact that your pattern of use disrupts your life.

Substance dependence (more commonly called *addiction*) is more severe than abuse. Dependence has both behavioral and biological aspects. Behaviorally, dependence is often characterized by loss of control over use of the substance. Dependent people may organize their lives around getting and using a substance. Biological or physiological dependence is typified by tolerance, withdrawal symptoms, or both.

Tolerance is the body's habituation to a substance, so that with regular usage, higher doses are required to achieve similar effects. Addictive drugs have characteristic withdrawal symptoms when the level of usage suddenly drops off. The withdrawal syndrome (also called an *abstinence syndrome*) encountered by people who suffer from **alcoholism** may involve **delirium tremens** ("the DTs"). The DTs are characterized by heavy sweating, restlessness, **disorientation**, and terrifying hallucinations—often of creepy, crawling animals.

Causal Factors in Substance Abuse and Dependence

Substance abuse and dependence usually begin with experimental use in adolescence. Why do people experiment with drugs? The reasons are many: curiosity, conformity to peer pressure, parental modeling of drug use, rebelliousness, temporary escape from boredom or pressing personal problems or negative emotions, and the seeking of states of pleasure or personal enlightenment (Engels et al., 2006).

We should recognize that drug-use patterns established during adolescence foreshadow future substance abuse problems. For example, drinking in early adolescence is a risk factor for alcohol abuse in adulthood. Let us take a closer look at factors involved in substance abuse and dependence.

▮ **Substance abuse** Continued use of a substance despite knowledge that it is dangerous or that it is linked to social, occupational, psychological, or physical problems.

▮ **Substance dependence** Dependence is shown by signs such as persistent use despite efforts to cut down, marked tolerance, and withdrawal symptoms.

▮ **Tolerance** The body's habituation to a drug, so that with regular use, increasingly higher doses of the drug are needed to achieve similar effects.

▮ **Alcoholism** A term used to describe alcohol dependence, which is characterized by impaired control over the use of alcohol and development of a physiological dependence on the drug.

▮ **Delirium tremens** A condition characterized by sweating, restlessness, disorientation, and hallucinations.

▮ **Disorientation** Gross confusion. Loss of sense of time, place, and the identity of people.

Andrew Lichtenstein/The Image Works

Drugs on Campus
Though many different types of drugs are used by college students, alcohol remains the "big drug on campus."

Psychological Factors Social-cognitive theorists suggest that expectations about the effects of a substance are powerful predictors of its use. In one study, researchers studied a diary of stress, expectations about alcohol, and drinking (Armeli et al., 2000). They found that men who expected that alcohol would lessen feelings of stress were more likely to drink on stressful days. But men who expected that alcohol would impair their coping ability drank less on stressful days.

Use of a substance may be reinforced by peers or by the drug's positive effects on mood and its reduction of unpleasant sensations such as anxiety, fear, and tension. For people who are physiologically dependent, avoidance of withdrawal symptoms is also reinforcing.

Parents who use drugs may be modeling drug-using behavior for their children. In effect, they may be showing their children when and how to use them—for example, to drink alcohol to reduce tension or to "lubricate" social interactions.

Biological Views Evidence points to an important genetic contribution to many different forms of substance abuse and dependence, including alcoholism, opiate addiction, and even cigarette smoking (e.g., Gelernter et al., 2007; Hampton, 2006; Lynskey et al., 2007; Redgrave et al., 2007).

But what is the inherited component? Although the question remains under study, several clues have begun to emerge (Edenberg et al., 2005; Radel et al., 2005). Investigators suspect that people may inherit a tendency to reap greater pleasure from drugs such as alcohol as well as a reduced sensitivity to the negative effects of excessive alcohol use (e.g., upset stomach, dizziness, and headaches). In effect, people may inherit a tendency to be better able to "hold their liquor" and consequently incur greater risk of developing drinking problems than others. Other people whose bodies more readily "put the brakes" on excess drinking may be less likely to develop problems in moderating their drinking. The major classes of psychoactive drugs are depressants, stimulants, and hallucinogens. Let us consider the effects of drugs in these classes.

5.4.2 Depressants: Drugs that Slow You Down

▌ **Depressants** Drugs that decrease the rate of activity of the central nervous system.

▌ **Central nervous system (CNS)** The part of the body's nervous system that consists of the brain and spinal cord.

Depressants are not drugs that cause depression. Rather, they are drugs that depress or slow down the activity of the **central nervous system (CNS)**, the part of the nervous system that consists of the brain and spinal cord. In high doses, these drugs can slow down the CNS to such an extent that death may result from respiratory (breathing) arrest or cardiovascular collapse. Psychologically, these drugs have relaxing or sedating effects and may induce feelings of euphoria. Here we focus on the major types of depressants: alcohol, barbiturates, and opioids.

Alcohol—The "Swiss Army Knife" of Psychoactive Substances

One friend had been struck by Leslie's piercing green eyes. Another recounted how Leslie had loved to dance barefoot at parties. A roommate remembered how Leslie ate handfuls of chocolate chips straight from the bag and picked the marshmallows out of Lucky Charms cereal. She even remembered the time that Leslie baked a tuna casserole without removing the Saran Wrap. Leslie had been an art major and her professors described her work as promising (Winerip, 1998). Her overall GPA at the University of Virginia had been 3.67, and she had been in the middle of preparing her senior essay on a Polish-born sculptor. But she did not finish the essay or graduate. Instead, Leslie died from falling down a flight of stairs after binge drinking alcohol. While deaths from heroin or cocaine overdoses may get more publicity, hundreds of college students die from alcohol-related causes (overdoses, accidents, and the like) each year (Li et al., 2001). As many as 10 or so University of Virginia students alone wind up in a hospital emergency room each weekend due to alcohol-related causes.

So why do people choose to drink alcohol? Perhaps because no drug has meant so much to so many. Alcohol is our dinnertime relaxant, our bedtime sedative, our

Table 5.12 ▮ Alcohol on Campus: The Annual Toll	
600,000	physical assaults
500,000	injuries
70,000	sexual assaults
1,400	deaths due to overdose and accidents

Source: Hingson et al., 2002

Note: These figures represent the estimated annual numbers of alcohol-related physical assaults, injuries, sexual assaults, and deaths among U.S. college students ages 18 to 24.

cocktail-party social facilitator. We use alcohol to celebrate holy days, applaud our accomplishments, and express joyous wishes.

People use alcohol like a Swiss Army knife. It does it all. Alcohol is the all-purpose medicine you can buy without prescription. Some people use it as a form of self-medication to curb negative feelings such as anxiety, depression, or loneliness (Tomlinson et al., 2006). Yet we should recognize that most people use alcohol because of its positively reinforcing effects, such as for the pleasurable or relaxing effects it produces, or because it is linked to enjoyable social occasions.

But the army knife has a blade. It is also true that no drug has been so abused as alcohol. More than 10 times as many Americans suffer from alcoholism than use heroin or cocaine regularly. All in all, some 10 million to 20 million Americans suffer from *alcoholism*, or *alcohol dependence* as it is called by the psychiatric profession. Excessive drinking is linked to many negative social, economic, and health outcomes, including lower productivity, loss of employment, and downward movement in social status.

Alcohol-related accidents are also the leading cause of death among young Americans in the 17- to 24-year age range (Ham & Hope, 2003). Most of these deaths occur on the nation's roads. In any given year, some 1,400 U.S. college students lose their lives as the result of alcohol-related motor vehicle accidents (Sink, 2004; see Table 5.12). Moreover, alcohol use is implicated in many types of violent crimes, from domestic violence to homicide and rape (e.g., Fals-Stewart, 2003; Giancola & Corman, 2007).

Effects of Alcohol Alcohol has many effects on the mind and body, with the effects varying with dose and duration of use. Although alcohol is a depressant, low doses may actually be mildly stimulating. However, higher doses have a relaxing or sedating effect. Alcohol relaxes people and deadens minor aches and pains. It impairs cognitive functioning, slurs the speech, and reduces motor coordination. Overall, alcohol is involved in about half of all fatal automobile accidents in the United States.

Phototake/Alamy Limited

Alcohol Use as a Form of Self-Medication
Many people turn to alcohol or other drugs to cope with disturbing emotions, such as depression and anxiety. Relying on alcohol as a form of self-medication does nothing to help resolve underlying problems but may make matters worse by setting the stage for problem drinking.

Adjustment and Modern Life

Binge Drinking on Campus

Many college officials view binge drinking—not cocaine, ecstasy, or even marijuana—as the major drug problem on campus. Despite widespread marijuana use, alcohol remains the drug of choice among adolescents and college students. Binge drinking is becoming a social epidemic on college campuses and a serious cause for concern. People who engage in binge drinking—typically defined as having five or more drinks on a single occasion for a man or four or more drinks for a woman—show increased rates of aggressive behavior, poor grades, unprotected promiscuous sex (and sexually transmitted diseases), motor vehicle accidents, and

development of substance abuse or dependence (Birch, Stewart, & Brown, 2007; Brewer & Swahn, 2005; Keller et al., 2007).

Binge drinking is even ritualized in celebrations of reaching the legal drinking age of 21. In a a recent survey at the University of Missouri, about one in three college men and about one in four college women claimed to have consumed at least 21 drinks or more on their 21st birthdays (Rutledge, Park, & Sher, 2008). This level of drinking leads to severe alcohol intoxication and can result in significant health risks, including coma and even death.

We see in Table 5.13 the results of a recent large-scale nationwide survey of U.S. college students, which polled more than 19,000 students on 33 campuses (American College Health

Table 5.13 ∎ Number of Alcoholic Drinks Students Reported Consuming the Last Time They Partied						
	Total		Female		Male	
Number of Drinks	*n*	%	*n*	%	*n*	%
0	4,146	21.5	2,715	22.2	1,180	19.9
1–4	6,987	36.3	5,114	41.8	1,492	25.1
5–8	5,331	27.7	3,447	28.2	1,635	27.5
≥ 9	2,799	14.5	966	7.9	1,633	27.5

Source: American College Health Association, 2005. Reprinted by permission of The American College Health Association.

Note: Refers to Question 13: "The last time you partied/socialized, how many alcoholic drinks did you have?" Because of missing data by sex, the response categories do not always equal the total.

Association, 2005). These data show that more than one in four students (27.7%) reported drinking five or more drinks the last time they partied. Overall, nearly half of American college students engage in binge drinking.

Excessive or underage drinking has long been a problem in many fraternal organizations such as college fraternities and sororities (Park, Sher, & Krull, 2006). In response to these concerns, many Greek organizations encourage their members to drink responsibly, while some others have banned alcohol use entirely, including beer (Denizel-Lewis, 2005).

Consider some of the immediate dangers of heavy drinking. Binge drinking and other forms of excessive drinking, such as drinking games (e.g., beer chugging or downing a series of shots), can put drinkers at immediate risk of coma or even death from alcohol overdoses (Zernike, 2005).

Many of these needless deaths are caused by choking on one's own vomit. You see, drinking heavily can induce vomiting, but the drug's depressant effects may suppress the normal vomiting response. Consequently, vomit accumulates in the air passages, which can cause asphyxiation and death. Unfortunately, people who play drinking games may not stop until they're too drunk or sick to continue.

Image Source Black/SuperStock

Dangerous Games
Heavy drinking and drinking games can lead to dangerous, even fatal consequences. What should you do if a friend passes out as the result of drinking?

Alcohol overdosing is a serious medical condition that requires immediate medical attention. Don't just assume a friend will "sleep it off." Some friends never wake up.

What should you do if a friend blacks out from drinking? Is he (she) just sleeping it off? Should you just let the person "sleep it off"? Can you tell if the person has drunk too much? Should you turn the other way or call the authorities? What would you do? What would you say?

Here are some suggestions about what you can do in a situation in which you suspect someone may have overdosed. First, look for signs of alcohol overdose, such as the following:

- Failure to respond when talked to or shouted at
- Failure to respond to being pinched, shaken, or poked
- Inability to stand up on his or her own
- Failure to wake up
- Purplish color or clammy-feeling skin
- Rapid pulse rate or irregular heart rhythms, low blood pressure, or difficulty breathing

Do not leave a person who is unresponsive or unconscious alone. Treat the situation as a medical emergency that requires immediate attention. Don't simply assume that they'll "sleep it off." Stay with the person until you or someone else can obtain medical attention. Place the person on his or her side, or, if possible, have the person sit up with the head bowed. Do not give the person any food or drink. Do not induce vomiting. If the person is at all responsive, find out if he or she took other drugs or had taken any medication that might have interacted with the alcohol, or if the person has an underlying illness that could be contributing to the problem, such as diabetes or epilepsy. Reach (carefully) into the person's mouth and clear the airway if the person vomits; provide artificial respiration or CPR if necessary. Most important, call a physician or local emergency number immediately and ask for advice.

It may seem easier to walk away from the situation and let the person "sleep it off." You may think you have no right to interfere. You may have doubts about whether the person is truly in danger. But ask yourself: If you were in the place of the person who showed signs of overdosing on alcohol, wouldn't you want one of your friends to intervene to save your life?

Source: Adapted from Nevid (2006). Reprinted with permission of Houghton Mifflin Co.

Alcohol lowers inhibitions and impairs our ability to weigh the consequences of our behavior. Consequently, when we drink, we may say or do things we later regret, take excessive risks, or act impulsively without thinking (Donohue et al., 2007).

You may recall the slogan from an AIDS awareness public health campaign: "First you get drunk. Then you get stupid. Then you get AIDS." When people drink, they may be less able to foresee the consequences of their behavior and are less likely to summon up their moral beliefs.

Positive expectancies about the effects of alcohol are a major determinant of alcohol use, especially among young people (Morawska & Oei, 2005). People may use alcohol because they expect it will make them more popular or fun to be around. Alcohol may also induce feelings of elation and euphoria that may wash away self-doubts. It is also associated with a liberated social role in our culture. Drinkers may place the blame on alcohol ("It's the alcohol, not me"), even though they choose to drink.

Regardless of how or why one starts drinking, regular drinking can lead to physiological dependence. Once dependence develops, people maintain their alcohol intake to avoid withdrawal symptoms. Still, even when people with alcoholism have "dried out"—withdrawn from alcohol—many return to drinking. Perhaps they still seek to use alcohol as a way of coping with stress or escaping from it.

Alcoholism, Gender, and Ethnicity

Men are much more likely than women to develop alcoholism. A cultural explanation is that tighter social constraints on drinking are usually placed on women. A biological explanation is that alcohol hits women harder. If, for example, you have the impression that alcohol "goes to women's heads" more quickly than to men's, you are probably correct. Women seem to be more affected by alcohol because they break down less of it directly in the stomach. Thus, more alcohol reaches women's bloodstreams and brains relatively intact, which may put the brakes on excessive drinking. (Women have less of an enzyme that metabolizes alcohol in the stomach than men do.) Women mainly metabolize alcohol in the liver. For women, reports one health professional, "drinking alcohol has the same effect as injecting it intravenously" (Lieber, 1990). Strong stuff, indeed. Despite their greater responsiveness to small quantities of alcohol, women who drink heavily are apparently as likely as men to develop alcoholism.

Treating Alcoholism

Many treatment approaches are available to help people who suffer from alcoholism. The most widely used program is Alcoholics Anonymous (AA), a self-help program in which individuals provide mutual support in a context in which people progress through 12 designated steps toward sobriety. Yet AA has a strong spiritual focus that may not be suited to every individual. Evidence shows that a variety of approaches may be as effective as AA.

The National Institute on Alcohol Abuse and Alcoholism funded a large-scale study in which more than 1,700 problem drinkers were randomly assigned to AA's 12-step program, cognitive-behavioral therapy, or "motivational-enhancement therapy" (Ouimette, Finney, & Moos, 1997). The cognitive-behavioral treatment taught problem drinkers how to cope with temptations and how to refuse offers of drinks. Motivational enhancement was designed to enhance drinkers' desire to help themselves. The treatments worked equally well for most people, with some exceptions. For example, people with psychological problems fared somewhat better with cognitive-behavioral therapy. People who participate in AA typically do better when they make a commitment to abstinence, have a strong intention to avoid high-risk situations associated with alcohol use, and stick with the program longer (McKellar, Stewart, & Humphreys, 2003; Moos & Moos, 2004; Morgenstern et al., 2002).

Ironically, therapeutic drugs may be used to treat people with problems of substance abuse or dependence. In effect, one drug may be used to break a destructive pattern of use of another drug. For example, the nicotine patch provides a steady supply of nicotine to the body, which can help wean nicotine-dependent smokers from dependence on tobacco (Cepeda-Benito, Reynoso, & Erath, 2004; Strasser et al., 2005). Antidepressant drugs that increase the availability of serotonin in the brain (Prozac is one) help normalize serotonin activity and may help bring drug cravings for cocaine

Courtesy Sam Spady Foundation

Death By Alcohol
Tragically, alcohol overdoses claim the lives of 1,400 U.S. college students each year. One tragic example was 19-year old Samantha Spady of Colorado State University, who died after a night of heavy drinking with her friends.

©Bruce Ayres/Getty Images, Inc.

Does Alcohol Go More Quickly to Womens Heads Than to Men's?
In a word: yes. It was once thought that women were more susceptible because they weighed less. However, research now suggests that women are more sensitive to the effects of alcohol because they metabolize less of it in the stomach. There are also genetic differences in sensitivity to the effects of alcohol. For example, Asians are more likely than Europeans or European Americans to show a "flushing" response to alcohol.

or other drugs under control (Johnson et al., 2000; Kranzler, 2000). Deficiencies of the neurotransmitter serotonin may contribute to drug cravings (strong urges).

Another drug, naltrexone (brand name ReVia), blocks the high one normally gets from alcohol, which may help break the vicious cycle in which one drink creates a strong desire for another, leading to binge drinking in alcohol-dependent people (Anton, 2008; Myrick et al., 2008; O'Brien et al., 2008). But investigators recognize that drug therapies need to be combined with psychological approaches to help people with alcohol and other drug problems learn to live drug-free lives and to cope more effectively with their problems without turning to alcohol (e.g., Carroll & Onken, 2005).

Self-Assessment

How Do You Know If You Are "Hooked"?

Has drinking become a problem for you? How would you know if you were hooked? You may get some guidance on this important question by completing the following scale. The scale contains items adapted from the National Council on Alcoholism's self-test. Place a checkmark in the Yes or No column for each item. Then consult the scoring key at the end of the chapter for additional suggestions.

	YES	NO
1. Do you sometimes go on drinking binges?	___	___
2. Do you tend to keep away from your family or friends when you are drinking?	___	___
3. Do you become irritated when your family or friends talk about your drinking?	___	___
4. Do you feel guilty now and then about your drinking?	___	___
5. Do you often regret the things you have said or done when you have been drinking?	___	___
6. Do you find that you fail to keep the promises you make about controlling or cutting down on your drinking?	___	___
7. Do you eat irregularly or not at all when you are drinking?	___	___
8. Do you feel low after drinking?	___	___
9. Do you sometimes miss work or appointments because of drinking?	___	___
10. Do you use more and more to get drunk or high?	___	___

Source: Adapted from *Newsweek*, February 20, 1989, p. 52.
For an interactive version of this self-assessment exercise, go to www.wileyplus.com

Opioids

▮ **Opioids** A group of depressants derived from the opium poppy, or similar in chemical structure, that are used to relieve pain but that can also provide a euphoric rush.

▮ **Narcotic** A drug, such as heroin, with pain-relieving and sleep-inducing properties that has a strong addictive potential.

Opioids are a class of **narcotic** ("sleep-inducing") drugs that include natural opiates derived from the opium poppy, such as morphine and heroin, and chemically similar drugs that are synthesized to produce opiate-like effects, such as codeine and methadone. Like other depressants, opioids slow down the activity of the central nervous system. Opioids have legitimate medical uses, especially relief from pain. But they are also widely abused as street drugs. Illicit use of prescription painkillers, such as the opiate *OxyContin*, has emerged as a significant drug-abuse problem in the United States (Friedman, 2006).

Morphine was introduced in the United States in the 1860s, at about the time of the Civil War, and in Europe during the Franco-Prussian War (1870–1871). It was liberally used to deaden pain from wounds. Physiological dependence on morphine therefore became known as the "soldier's disease." *Heroin* was so named because it made people feel "heroic." It was also hailed as the "hero" that would cure physiological dependence on morphine. Yet heroin proved to be just as addictive as morphine.

Heroin can provide a strong and euphoric "rush." Users claim that it is so pleasurable it can eradicate any thought of food or sex. Regular users develop tolerance for heroin, leading them to take yet higher doses, which can cause potentially life-threatening overdoses.

Heroin is illegal. Because the penalties for possession or sale are high, it is also expensive. For this reason, many physiologically dependent people support their habit through dealing (selling heroin), prostitution, or selling stolen goods. Opiate addicts face extremely unpleasant withdrawal syndromes, which may begin with flulike symptoms and progress through tremors, cramps, chills alternating with sweating, rapid pulse, high blood pressure, insomnia, vomiting, and diarrhea. However, these syndromes are variable from one person to another and can be managed medically.

Methadone, a synthetic opiate, is used widely in treating heroin addiction because it prevents the highly unpleasant withdrawal symptoms that occur when heroin addicts stop using heroin. Methadone does not produce the druglike state or "rush" associated with heroin, so people maintained on methadone can hold jobs and get their lives back on track. However, methadone programs need to be strictly monitored, since overdoses can be lethal and the drug can become abused as a street drug (Belluck, 2003).

Methadone treatment is often combined with psychological counseling or other forms of drug rehabilitation. Eventually, people maintained on methadone may gradually be withdrawn from the drug. Methadone treatment programs have clearly helped saved the lives of many opiate addicts (Krantz & Mehler, 2004), but this treatment does not work in all cases; some individuals return to using heroin, while others are unable to tolerate the withdrawal symptoms when they stop using methadone (Dyer et al., 2001; Goode, 2001).

Barbiturates

Barbiturates are a class of sedating drugs that have calming and relaxant properties. Some common examples of barbiturates include *amobarbital, pentobarbital, phenobarbital,* and *secobarbital.* These drugs have some legitimate medical uses, including relief from pain and treatment of epilepsy. However, barbiturate use can quickly lead to physiological and psychological dependence. They are popular as street drugs not only because of their relaxing effects but also because they produce a state of mild euphoria. High doses of barbiturates result in drowsiness, motor impairment, slurred speech, irritability, and poor judgment. A physiologically dependent person who is withdrawn abruptly from barbiturates may experience severe convulsions that can lead to death. Thus, it is important that withdrawal be carefully monitored. Barbiturates have additive effects with other drugs, which makes them especially dangerous when mixed with alcohol and other depressants.

▮ **Barbiturates** Addictive depressants used to relieve anxiety or induce sleep.

5.4.3 Stimulants: Drugs that Speed You Up

We now turn to a class of drugs that have effects on the central nervous system opposite to those of depressants. **Stimulants** accelerate, or speed up, central nervous system activity, which heightens states of bodily arousal and mental alertness. But stimulants such as amphetamines and cocaine can also lead to a powerful "rush" or feelings of pleasure, which helps explain their powerful appeal and potential for abuse. We begin our discussion with nicotine—a mild stimulant that poses a grave threat to our health and well-being because of the means by which it is usually administered—smoking.

▮ **Stimulants** A drug that increases the rate of activity of the central nervous system.

Nicotine

Nicotine is a stimulant drug found in tobacco products, such as cigarettes, cigars, and chewing tobacco. It is a highly addictive drug (Nonnemaker & Homsi, 2007).

▮ **Nicotine** A mild but highly addictive stimulant drug found in tobacco.

Smoking is not just a bad habit; with repeated practice, it becomes a form of addiction in which smokers regulate their smoking to maintain fairly even levels of nicotine in their bloodstream. Addiction (chemical dependence) develops quickly, often within the first few weeks of smoking.

When dependence develops, smokers experience withdrawal symptoms if they abruptly stop smoking. These symptoms include nervousness, drowsiness, loss of energy, headaches, irregular bowel movements, lightheadedness, insomnia, dizziness, cramps, palpitations, tremors, and sweating. Nicotine-dependent smokers often resume smoking to control these withdrawal symptoms. Smokers may quit, then suffer withdrawal symptoms, and then resume smoking—a pattern that may occur repeatedly in the form of a vicious cycle.

As a stimulant, nicotine speeds up bodily processes such as heart rate and metabolic rate; curbs appetite; and increases concentration, alertness, and arousal. Some people smoke cigarettes in order to control their weight. Others tend to eat more when they stop smoking, which may lead them to return to smoking. Nicotine also produces mild feelings of pleasure (euphoria), and, paradoxically, it may induce feelings of mental calmness or relaxation. Consequently, smokers may come to depend on nicotine to lift them up and settle them down.

The Perils of Smoking   You know smoking is unhealthy—but just how dangerous is it? *Very* dangerous. So dangerous, in fact, that it is the leading preventable cause of death in the United States, causing nearly 450,000 deaths annually from smoking-related illnesses each year (American Lung Association, 2007). This is the equivalent of two jumbo jets colliding in midair each day with all passengers lost. Each year more Americans die from smoking-related diseases than from motor vehicle accidents, alcohol and drug abuse, suicide, homicide, and AIDS combined. Worldwide, smoking claims the lives of about 4 million people annually (Mokdad, Marks, & Stroup, 2004; Schneiderman, 2004). We do have some good news to report on the nonsmoking front. The percentage of American adults who smoke cigarettes has declined by more than half, from more than 42% in 1966 to slightly less than 20% today (Benincasa, 2008; Thorne et al., 2009).

Every cigarette smoked steals about seven minutes of a person's life. Nicotine is not the most dangerous constituent of cigarette smoking; that dishonor falls on such other ingredients as carbon monoxide and tars. The carbon monoxide in cigarette smoke impairs the blood's ability to carry oxygen, causing shortness of breath and compromising the cardiovascular system. The hydrocarbons ("tars") in cigarette and cigar smoke are believed to be responsible for causing lung cancer (American Lung Association, 2000). Nearly 9 out of 10 cases of lung cancer are due to smoking.

You may be aware that smoking causes lung cancer. But as the U.S. surgeon general pointed out in a recent report, smoking damages nearly *every* organ and system in the body. It is a major contributor to cardiovascular disease (heart and artery disease); emphysema and other chronic lung disorders; and many cancers, including cancer of the cervix, kidney, pancreas, and stomach ("Surgeon General Warns," 2004). Moreover, women smokers show reduced bone density, increasing the risk of fractures of the hip and other bones. Pregnant women who smoke have a higher risk of miscarriage, preterm births, low-birthweight babies, and stillborn babies.

Cigar smokers are less likely to inhale than cigarette smokers, so some cigar smokers had assumed (wrongly) that cigar smoking was relatively safe. Researchers from the American Cancer Society and the Centers for Disease Control and Prevention report that cigar smokers are five times as likely as nonsmokers to develop lung cancer, even when they do not inhale ("Cigars Increase," 2000). When they do inhale, cigar smokers run 11 times the risk of lung cancer as nonsmokers. Cigar smokers also run increased risks of cancers of the mouth, throat, and esophagus (Baker et al., 2000).

Passive smoking is also connected with respiratory illnesses, asthma, and other health problems. Prolonged exposure to household tobacco smoke during childhood is a risk factor for lung cancer. Because of the noxious effects of second-hand smoke, smoking has been banished from many public places such as airplanes, restaurants, and elevators.

Picture Contact/Alamy Limited

Smoking Kills
Smoking is the nation's leading preventable cause of death, accounting for more than one in five deaths among Americans. How can you avoid becoming yet another grim statistic?

▮ **Passive smoking** Inhaling smoke from other people's tobacco products; also called second-hand smoking.

Why, then, do people smoke? For many reasons—such as the desire to look sophisticated (although these days smokers are more likely to be judged foolish than sophisticated), to quell nervousness, to have something to do with their hands, and—of course—to regulate their intake of nicotine.

| Why Do You Smoke? | Self-Assessment |

These are some statements made by people to describe what they get out of smoking cigarettes. If you smoke, indicate how often you feel the way described in the statement by circling the appropriate number. Then check the scoring key at the end of the chapter to interpret your responses.

IMPORTANT: Answer every question

1 = never
2 = seldom
3 = occasionally
4 = frequently
5 = always

A.	I smoke cigarettes in order to keep myself from slowing down.	1 2 3 4 5
B.	Handling a cigarette is part of the enjoyment of smoking it.	1 2 3 4 5
C.	Smoking cigarettes is pleasant and relaxing.	1 2 3 4 5
D.	I light up a cigarette when I feel angry about something.	1 2 3 4 5
E.	When I have run out of cigarettes, I find it almost unbearable until I get them.	1 2 3 4 5
F.	I smoke cigarettes automatically without even being aware of it.	1 2 3 4 5
G.	I smoke cigarettes to stimulate myself, to perk myself up.	1 2 3 4 5
H.	Part of the enjoyment of smoking a cigarette comes from the steps I take to light up.	1 2 3 4 5
I.	I find cigarettes pleasurable.	1 2 3 4 5
J.	When I feel uncomfortable or upset about something, I light up a cigarette.	1 2 3 4 5
K.	I am very much aware of the fact when I am not smoking a cigarette.	1 2 3 4 5
L.	I light up a cigarette without realizing I still have one burning in the ashtray.	1 2 3 4 5
M.	I smoke cigarettes to give me a "lift."	1 2 3 4 5
N.	When I smoke a cigarette, part of the enjoyment is watching the smoke as I exhale it.	1 2 3 4 5
O.	I want a cigarette most when I am comfortable and relaxed.	1 2 3 4 5
P.	When I feel "blue" or want to take my mind off cares and worries, I smoke cigarettes.	1 2 3 4 5
Q.	I get a real gnawing hunger for a cigarette when I haven't smoked for a while.	1 2 3 4 5
R.	I've found a cigarette in my mouth and didn't remember putting it there.	1 2 3 4 5

For an interactive version of this self-assessment exercise, go to www.wileyplus.com

Amphetamines

Amphetamines are a group of stimulants that were first used by soldiers during World War II to help them remain alert through the night. Truck drivers have used them to stay awake all night, students have used them to stay up for all-night cram sessions, and dieters have used them to quell feelings of hunger. These drugs can be taken orally, smoked, snorted, or injected.

Called speed, uppers, bennies (for Benzedrine), and dexies (for Dexedrine), these drugs are often used for the euphoric "rush" they can produce, especially in high doses. Regular users may stay awake and "high" for days on end. Such highs must come to an end. People who have been on prolonged highs sometimes "crash," or fall into a deep sleep or depression. Due to tolerance, many of them take doses that would kill a laboratory animal.

■ **Amphetamines** A class of stimulant drugs, including methamphetamine, which can increase states of alertness and induce pleasurable feelings.

© AP/Wide World Photos

Ecstasy

Rather than inducing ecstasy, the drug can lead to unpleasant emotional reactions, impaired memory functioning, and even death when used in high doses.

■ **Ecstasy** An amphetamine-like drug that has mild euphoric and hallucinogenic effects.

© Jan Halaska/Photo Researchers, Inc.

Snorting Cocaine

A century ago, the stimulant cocaine was an ingredient in the soft drink Coca-Cola. Sigmund Freud used it (the drug, not Coca-Cola) to fight depression. However, cocaine also spurs sudden spikes in blood pressure, constricts the coronary arteries, and quickens the heart rate—events that now and then trigger respiratory and cardiovascular collapse, even in well-conditioned athletes. Overdoses cause restlessness and insomnia, tremors, headaches, nausea, convulsions, and mental symptoms such as hallucinations and delusions.

People can become psychologically dependent on amphetamines, especially when they are routinely used to cope with stress or depression. Tolerance develops rapidly. Recent evidence suggests that regular use of methamphetamine, a particularly powerful amphetamine, can also lead to physiological dependence or addiction (Jonkman, 2006). High doses of amphetamines may cause restlessness, insomnia, loss of appetite, and irritability. Amphetamine use can also induce a form of psychosis ("break with reality") characterized by hallucinations and delusions that mimic the symptoms of paranoid schizophrenia.

Methamphetamine is the most abused amphetamine, with more than 1.5 million Americans reporting using the drug regularly (Jefferson, 2005). Heavy use of methamphetamine—also known as meth, chalk, ice, crystal, and glass—is also linked to cognitive and emotional problems as well as to possible neurological damage. Brain-imaging studies show that methamphetamine use can damage the brain, causing problems with learning, memory, and other cognitive functions (Thompson et al., 2004; Toomey et al., 2003).

Amphetamine, like cocaine, another stimulant, releases bursts of dopamine in the brain, the neurotransmitter involved in producing feelings of pleasure (Jefferson, 2005; Leyton et al., 2002). Over time, heavy use of "meth" reduces the brain's production of dopamine (Volkow et al., 2001a). Consequently, long-term users come to increasingly rely on having methamphetamine in their bodies in order to experience any pleasure in life.

Another stimulant, *methylphenidate* (Ritalin), has a legitimate clinical use in the treatment of attention-deficit/hyperactivity disorder in children (Evans et al., 2001). However, Ritalin may also become a drug of abuse when used by adolescents or adults for its stimulating effects.

Ecstasy: The Latest "Rave"?

Marijuana has long held the dubious distinction of being the most widely used illicit drug in the United States. But a chemical cousin of amphetamine is well on its way to surpassing marijuana in popularity (Kuhn & Wilson, 2001). The drug established a foothold in late-night dance clubs, or *raves,* in American cities in the 1990s and early 2000s. It is called **ecstasy**, technically MDMA (3,4-methylenedioxymethamphetamine), though its long-term effects belie its appealing name. Ecstasy, a synthetic drug manufactured in the laboratory, produces mild euphoric and hallucinogenic effects (Lamers et al., 2006).

Many users, especially teens, believe it to be relatively safe, but health officials warn that the drug poses both serious physical and psychological risks. It raises blood pressure and heart rate—physiological reactions that can be dangerous to people with cardiovascular conditions. It can also lead to a tense or chattering jaw and in high doses can be deadly. Psychologically, it can produce unpleasant symptoms such as depression, anxiety, insomnia, and even psychotic features, such as extreme paranoia. Heavy use of the drug can lead to problems with learning, memory, and attention (Eisner, 2005; Lamers et al., 2006). If you think this cleverly named drug will leave you ecstatic, think again. The good news is that the number of new users has begun to decline; still, more than 10 million Americans report having used the drug at least once (SAMHSA, 2005).

Cocaine

Do you recall the commercials claiming that "Coke adds life"? Given its caffeine and sugar content, "Coke"—*Coca-Cola,* that is—should provide quite a lift. But Coca-Cola hasn't been "the real thing" since 1906, when the company discontinued the use of the stimulant cocaine in its formula. Cocaine is derived from coca leaves—the plant from which the soft drink took its name.

Cocaine is a powerful stimulant. It can produce feelings of euphoria, curb hunger, deaden pain, and bolster self-confidence. It may be brewed from coca leaves as a "tea," "snorted" in powder form, or injected in liquid form. Repeated snorting constricts blood vessels in the nose, drying the skin and sometimes exposing cartilage and perforating the nasal septum. These problems require cosmetic surgery. A hardened form of cocaine, called crack, is sold in small, ready-to-use smokeable doses that are affordable to many adolescents, leading many of them to quickly become regular users.

Cocaine is a highly addictive drug that gives rise to a withdrawal syndrome characterized by intense cravings for the drug, depressed mood, and failure to experience pleasure from the ordinary pleasant experiences of daily life. Users may also become psychologically dependent on the drug, using it compulsively to deal with life stress.

Cocaine is also a highly dangerous drug. It stimulates sudden rises in blood pressure, constricts the coronary arteries and thickens the blood (both of which decrease the oxygen supply to the heart), and quickens the heart rate. Overdoses may result in respiratory and cardiovascular collapse, leading in some cases to sudden death. Over time, use of cocaine damages brain circuits that regulate feelings of pleasure ("Cocaine Impairs," 2003). This may account for the fact that cocaine abusers often become depressed and unable to reap pleasure from ordinary life experiences when they stop using the drug.

Cocaine—also called snow and coke, like the slang term for the soft drink—has been used as a local anesthetic since the early 1800s. In 1884 it came to the attention of a young Viennese neurologist named Sigmund Freud, who used it to fight his own depression and published an article about it titled "Song of Praise." Freud's early ardor was tempered when he learned that cocaine is habit-forming and can cause hallucinations and delusions.

5.4.4 Hallucinogens: Drugs That Twist You Inside Out

Hallucinogens (also called *hallucinogenic drugs* or **psychedelics**) are drugs that induce sensory distortions and **hallucinations**. The most widely used hallucinogen is LSD ("acid"). We also discuss marijuana in this section, because it is often classified as a mild hallucinogen.

LSD and Other Hallucinogens

LSD ("acid") is the abbreviation for *lysergic acid diethylamide*, a synthetic hallucinogenic drug. More than a half million Americans report using LSD (NIDA Notes, 2004). Some users claim that it expands consciousness and opens up new worlds to them. Sometimes people believe they have achieved great insights while using LSD, but when it wears off they don't seem able to apply or even recall these discoveries. As a powerful hallucinogenic, LSD produces vivid and colorful hallucinations. Some LSD users experience **flashbacks**—distorted perceptions or hallucinations that mimic the LSD "trip" but occur days, weeks, or longer after usage.

Other hallucinogens include *mescaline* (derived from the peyote cactus) and *phencyclidine* (PCP). Regular use of hallucinogens may lead to tolerance and psychological dependence. But hallucinogens are not known to lead to physiological dependence. High doses may induce frightening hallucinations, impaired coordination, poor judgment, mood changes, and paranoid delusions.

Marijuana

Marijuana is derived from the *Cannabis sativa* plant, which grows wild in many parts of the world. Marijuana has complex effects. It can induce feelings of relaxation, elevate mood, and produce mild hallucinations. The active psychoactive substance in marijuana is *delta-9-tetrahydrocannabinol* (THC). THC is found in the branches and leaves of the plant, but it is highly concentrated in the sticky resin. **Hashish** ("hash") is derived from the resin and is more potent than marijuana.

Marijuana is the most widely used illicit drug in the United States, with about 6% of adults reporting current use, according to recent reports (NIDA Notes, 2004). In the nineteenth century, marijuana was used as much as aspirin is used today for headaches and minor aches and pains. It could be bought without a prescription in any drugstore.

Marijuana may have some legitimate medical uses, such as in reducing pressure within the eyes in patients with glaucoma or treating the nausea and vomiting that often follows the administration of chemotherapy in cancer patients. However, many experts believe that more studies are needed to fully evaluate the potential medical

▮ **Psychedelics** Drugs that cause hallucinations and delusions or heighten perceptions.

▮ **Hallucinations** Perceptions in the absence of sensation that are confused with reality.

▮ **LSD** The acronym for lysergic acid diethylamide, a hallucinogenic drug.

▮ **Flashbacks** Distorted perceptions or hallucinations that mimic the LSD experience but occur long after usage.

▮ **Hashish** A potent drug derived from the resin of the marijuana plant.

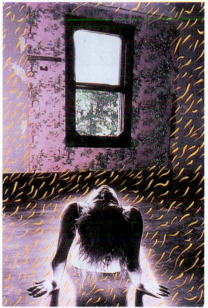

© A. Rousseau/The Image Works

Tripping the Life (Too) Fantastic
LSD is a powerful hallucinogenic drug that induces vivid and colorful hallucinations (perceptions in the absence of sensation). Some users of "acid" claim that it "expands consciousness" and opens new worlds to them, but they do not seem to be able to communicate or make use of their insights once the "trip" is over. High doses of hallucinogenics may cause frightening hallucinations, impaired coordination, poor judgment, mood changes, and paranoid delusions.

uses of the drug. Marijuana use elevates the heart rate and, in some people, the blood pressure. This higher demand on the heart and circulation poses a threat to people with hypertension and cardiovascular disorders.

Like alcohol, marijuana affects perceptual-motor coordination and so impairs driving ability. Heavy use can damage brain tissue and impair memory functioning and learning ability (Egerton et al., 2006; Lamers et al., 2006; Yücel et al., 2008). Although many users report positive mood changes, others experience disturbing feelings of anxiety and confusion and, occasionally, even psychotic reactions such as a heightened state of anxiety, confusion, and even paranoia. Heightened awareness of bodily sensations may lead some marijuana users to fear that their heart will "run away" with them. Some smokers find the disorientation that often occurs to be frightening or threatening. Smoking marijuana also introduces cancer-causing substances into the body.

People can become psychologically dependent on marijuana, but marijuana has not been classified as an addictive drug because it is not clearly connected to an identifiable withdrawal syndrome. Recent research, however, suggests that regular users of marijuana may indeed experience signs of physiological dependence, such as tolerance (need for increased amounts of the substance with repeated use) and some withdrawal symptoms upon abrupt cessation of use (Budney et al., 2007).

Marijuana affects areas of the brain involved in learning and memory, so long-term use may lead to problems in cognitive functioning (Solowij et al., 2002). Currently, evidence of cognitive impairment associated with long-term use of the drug is correlational, but we should caution that marijuana use conceivably does have damaging effects on the brain.

MODULE REVIEW

Review It

(16) Substance use becomes _____ when it causes or worsens social, occupational, psychological, or physical problems.

(17) Substance _____ is characterized by loss of control over the substance.

(18) _____ dependence is evidenced by tolerance or by a withdrawal syndrome when one discontinues use of the substance.

(19) Some people have _____ predispositions to physiological dependence on certain substances.

(20) Alcohol is an intoxicating depressant that (does or does not?) lead to physiological dependence.

(21) Women seem to be (more or less?) affected by alcohol than men.

(22) _____ are depressants that are used in medicine to relieve pain, but because of the euphoric rush they provide, they are bought "on the street."

(23) The synthetic opioid _____ is often used to treat heroin dependence.

(24) The stimulant _____ is found in products containing tobacco.

(25) Cocaine is a _____ that boosts alertness and self-confidence, but high doses can lead to restlessness, insomnia, and psychotic reactions.

(26) _____ produce euphoria in high doses, but high doses may also cause restlessness, insomnia, psychotic symptoms, and a "crash" upon withdrawal.

(27) _____ is widely used to treat attention-deficit/hyperactivity disorder in children.

(28) LSD may produce _____ long after it is used.

Think About It

Why do people experiment with various substances? What factors contribute to continued use of these substances, even in people who realize how these substances are damaging their lives?

| Psychology in Daily Life | MODULE 5.5 |

Finding Healthful Alternatives to Harmful Substances

Most of us use psychoactive drugs in one way or another. We may start our day with a cup of coffee or tea (which contains the mild stimulant *caffeine*) and end it with a "nightcap" (which contains alcohol). Or we may smoke or use illicit drugs. This discussion focuses on avoiding drugs that can cause harm, including tobacco and illicit drugs, and excessive or inappropriate use of alcohol.

Cognitive-behavioral psychologists note that an important step in changing patterns of substance abuse lies in raising our awareness of what we tell ourselves and other people about our behavior. For example, if you're going to quit smoking, why not tell your family and friends that you're quitting? By making a public commitment

to do so, you shore up your resolve. Also plan a target date for quitting, perhaps a date when you will be on vacation or away from the usual settings in which you smoke. You can use a nicotine substitute like a skin patch to help cut down before the target date and to prove to yourself that you can survive on fewer cigarettes (and, ultimately, on no cigarettes). You can plan specific things to tell yourself when you feel the urge to smoke: how you'll be stronger, free of fear of cancer, ready for the marathon, and so on. Once you have stopped, you can remind yourself repeatedly that the first few days are the hardest. After that, withdrawal symptoms weaken dramatically. And don't be afraid to pat yourself on the back by reminding yourself that you are accomplishing something that may literally be a lifesaver. For suggestions for changing the *ABC*s of substance-using behavior, see Table 5.14.

Table 5.14 ▌ Self-Control Strategies for Modifying the ABCs of Substance Abuse

Changing the *A*s (Antecedent Cues) of Substance Abuse

Learn to control the stimuli that trigger cravings for psychoactive substances by:

- Removing drinking and smoking paraphernalia from the home, including alcoholic beverages, beer mugs, carafes, ashtrays, matches, cigarette packs, lighters, and so on.
- Restricting the stimulus environment in which drinking or smoking is permitted. Limit use of the substance to a stimulus-deprived area of the home, such as the garage, bathroom, or basement. Remove all other stimuli that might be connected to using the substance, such as TV, reading materials, radio, or telephone. In this way, substance abuse becomes detached from many of the triggering stimuli.
- Avoiding socializing with people who have substance abuse problems and avoiding situations linked to use of the substance, such as bars, the street, bowling alleys, and so on.
- Socializing more with people who abstain from harmful substances.
- Frequenting substance-free environments, such as lectures or concerts, a gym, or museums, or by attending evening classes and eating in restaurants without liquor licenses.
- Managing the internal triggers for abuse, such as by practicing self-relaxation or meditation, not using substances to ease stress or states of tension, expressing angry feelings by writing them down, or seeking counseling for prolonged feelings of depression rather than turning to alcohol, pills, or cigarettes.

Changing the *B*s (Behaviors) of Substance Abuse

Learn to prevent and interrupt the behavior associated with substance abuse by:

- Breaking abusive habits by physically preventing them from occurring or making them more difficult, such as by not bringing alcohol home or cigarettes to the office.
- Using competing responses when tempted to engage in use of the substance. Handle substance-related situations armed with appropriate ammunition, such as mints, sugarless chewing gum, and so on. Other competing responses that interfere with use of a substance include taking a bath or shower, walking the dog, walking around the block, taking a drive, calling a friend, spending time in a substance-free environment, practicing meditation or relaxation, or exercising.
- Making abuse more difficult or labor-intensive, such as buying one can of beer at a time; storing matches, ashtrays, and cigarettes far apart; wrapping cigarettes in foil to make smoking more cumbersome; pausing for 10 minutes when struck by the urge to drink, smoke, or use another substance and asking oneself, "Do I really need *this* one?"

Changing the *C*s (Consequences) of Substance Abuse

Learn to control the consequences of using psychoactive substances by:

- Switching to brands of beer and cigarettes you don't like.
- Setting gradual substance-reduction schedules and rewarding yourself for sticking to them.
- Punishing yourself for failing to meet your substance-reduction goals. For example, you might assess yourself a monetary penalty for each slip and donate the cash to an unpalatable cause, such as a brother-in-law's birthday present.

Table 5.14 ▌ Continued

- Rehearsing motivating thoughts or self-statements you can write down on index cards to have available when temptations arise. For example:
  - Each day I don't smoke adds another day to my life.
  - Quitting smoking will help me breathe deeply again.
  - Foods will smell and taste better when I quit smoking.
  - My lungs will become clearer each and every day I don't smoke.
  - Smokers can carry a list of 20 to 25 such statements and read several of them at various times throughout the day. They can become parts of one's daily routine, a constant reminder of one's goals.

Source: Adapted from Nevid, Rathus, & Greene, 2006. Reprinted with permission of Prentice-Hall, Inc.

From time to time, all of us feel depressed, tense, or just plain bored. Many of us are intrigued by the possibility of exploring the still-dark reaches of our inner selves. Now and then we may feel inadequate to face the challenges of college life. Some of us see our futures as bleak and unrewarding, envisioning only a vast wilderness or desert before us.

We all have feelings like these occasionally. Do we turn to drugs to provide magical answers, or do we seek healthful alternatives—alternatives without drugs? If drugs seem the only answer, perhaps we should think again. Here are some drug-free alternatives to consider.

If you are...

- Feeling tense or anxious, try practicing self-relaxation or meditation, or exercising, or listening to relaxing music.
- Feeling bored, find a new activity or interest. Start an exercise program or get involved in athletics. Take up a hobby. Become involved in a political campaign or social cause.
- Feeling angry, write down your feelings or channel your anger into constructive pursuits.
- Feeling worthless, hopeless, or depressed, or putting yourself down, seek assistance from a friend or loved one. Focus on your abilities and accomplishments, not on your deficits. If that doesn't help, visit the college counseling center or health center. You may be suffering from a treatable case of depression.
- Wanting to probe the inner depths of your consciousness, try meditation or yoga. Or seek the advice of a counselor or minister, priest, or rabbi.
- Pressured into using drugs by friends, learn how to say no politely but firmly. If you need help saying no, read a self-help book on self-assertion or go to the college counseling center for advice. If necessary, get new friends. (A real friend will not push you into doing anything that makes you feel uncomfortable, including using drugs.)
- Seeking to heighten your sensations, try dancing, jogging, parachuting, snowboarding, in-line skating, or mountain climbing. There are many ways to get your adrenaline flowing without relying on chemical stimulants.

- Feeling stressed out to the point where you can't take it anymore, sit down to figure out the pressures acting upon you. List your priorities. What must be done right now? What can wait? If this approach fails, see your academic adviser or visit the college counseling center or health center. If you can afford the time, you may choose to take a day or two off. Sometimes the key is to establish more reasonable expectations of yourself. No drug will help you do that.
- Wanting to discover new insights into the human condition, take classes or workshops on philosophy and theology. Attend lectures by prominent thinkers. Read great works of literature. Ponder great works of art. Attend the symphony. Visit a museum. Let your mind connect with the great minds of the past and present.
- Searching for deeper personal meaning in life, become more involved in spiritual activity. Do volunteer work in hospitals or charitable organizations. Get involved in a cause you believe in. Or seek personal counseling to get in touch with your inner self. (There's an important person there. Get to know him or her.)

John Clines/IStockphoto

Motivating Yourself
Practicing motivating self-statements can help you develop healthier habits, such as by saying to yourself, "Each day I don't smoke adds another day to my life."

CHAPTER REVIEW

RECITE! RECITE! RECITE! RECITE! RECITE! RECITE! RECITE!

Study Tip: Reciting the answers to these study questions will help you become a more effective learner. First try answering the questions by yourself, either reciting them out loud or writing them in a notebook or on the computer. Then compare your answers with the sample answers provided below.

1. **What are the essential ingredients of a healthful diet?**
People need to consume a balanced diet that provides sufficient quantities of proteins, carbohydrates, fats, vitamins, and minerals. But we tend to eat too much protein and fats. Complex carbohydrates (starches) are better sources of nutrients than simple carbohydrates (sugars). Consumption of high levels of dietary cholesterol and saturated fat, along with obesity, heightens the risk of cardiovascular disorders.

2. **Is obesity a matter of lack of willpower?**
No. Obesity is a complex health problem that involves biological factors, such as heredity, amount of adipose tissue (body fat), and metabolic rate (the rate at which the individual converts calories to energy), as well as psychological factors, such as stress and the use of food to alleviate negative emotions.

3. **What are the major kinds of eating disorders?**
The major eating disorders are anorexia nervosa and bulimia nervosa. Anorexia is characterized by refusal to eat and maintenance of an unhealthy low body weight. Bulimia is characterized by cycles of binge eating and purging. Women are more likely than men to develop these disorders.

4. **What is known about the origins of eating disorders?**
Psychodynamic theorists propose that young women who are conflicted about their developing sexuality and womanhood may refuse to eat in order to maintain a childlike appearance. However, other theorists emphasize the role of cultural idealization of the slender female—and the pressure that such idealization places on young women—as the major contributor.

5. **What are the two major types of exercise?**
Aerobic exercise involves activities in which there is a sustained increase in the consumption of oxygen, such as working out on a treadmill or jogging. Anaerobic exercise, by contrast, involves short bursts of muscle activity, such as lifting weights. Both types of exercise have healthful benefits.

6. **What are the physical benefits of exercise?**
Regular exercise helps us maintain a healthy weight by directly burning calories and by building muscle mass (muscle tissue burns more calories than fats). Regular exercise also reduces the risks of cardiovascular disease and osteoporosis.

7. **What are the psychological benefits of exercise?**
Evidence indicates that exercise can help relieve depression, decrease anxiety and hostility, and boost self-esteem.

8. **Why do we sleep?**
Sleep apparently serves a restorative function, a memory-consolidation function, and a survival function.

9. **What are the causes of insomnia?**
Insomnia is connected with stress, physical and psychological disorders, and states of bodily tension. We can also set the stage for insomnia by worrying whether we will be able to get to sleep, or get enough sleep, to meet our daily responsibilities.

10. **What are substance abuse and substance dependence?**
Substance abuse is use of a substance that persists even though it impairs one's social or occupational functioning or general health. Substance dependence has behavioral and physiological aspects. It may be characterized by a lack of control over the use of a substance and by the development of tolerance, withdrawal symptoms, or both.

11. **What are the causes of substance abuse and dependence?**
People usually try drugs out of curiosity or because of peer pressure, but drug use comes to be reinforced directly by anxiety reduction or by feelings of euphoria or other desirable effects. Once people become physiologically dependent on a drug, they continue to use it to avert the development of unpleasant withdrawal symptoms. People may have genetic predispositions to become physiologically dependent on certain substances.

12. **What are the effects of alcohol?**
Alcohol is a depressant drug that induces states of relaxation by slowing the activity of the central nervous system. It can lead to physiological dependence and may cause death in overdoses. Alcohol lowers inhibitions, makes it difficult to weigh the consequences of our actions, and provides an excuse for failure or for undesirable behavior. A drink a day seems to be healthful, but most professionals do not recommend drinking because of concern that the individual may develop a drinking problem. Heavy drinking is connected with liver damage and other health problems.

13. **What are the effects of opioids?**
The opioids morphine and heroin are depressants that relieve pain, but they are also bought on the street because of the euphoric "rush" they provide. Opioid use can lead to physiological dependence.

14. **What are the effects of barbiturates?**
Barbiturates are sedating drugs that have legitimate medical uses, but they can lead rapidly to physiological and psychological dependence and can be abused as street drugs.

15. **What are the effects of nicotine?**
Nicotine is an addictive stimulant found in tobacco that can paradoxically help people relax. Cigarette smoking is a major contributor to heart disease, cancer, and other health problems.

16. **What are the effects of amphetamines?**
Stimulants are substances that act by increasing the activity of the central nervous system. Amphetamines are stimulants that produce feelings of euphoria when taken in high doses. But high doses may also cause restlessness, insomnia, psychotic symptoms, and a "crash" upon withdrawal. Amphetamines and a related stimulant, Ritalin, are commonly used to treat hyperactive children.

17. **What are the effects of cocaine?**
Psychologically speaking, the stimulant cocaine evokes feelings of euphoria and bolsters self-confidence. Physiologically, it causes sudden rises in blood pressure and constricts blood vessels. Overdoses can lead to restlessness, insomnia, psychotic reactions, and cardiorespiratory collapse.

18. **What are the effects of LSD and other hallucinogenic drugs?**
LSD is a hallucinogenic drug that produces vivid hallucinations. Some LSD users have flashbacks to earlier experiences.

19. **What are the effects of marijuana?**
Marijuana's active ingredients, including THC, often produce relaxation, heightened and distorted perceptions, feelings of empathy, and reports of new insights. Mild hallucinations may occur. Marijuana use elevates the heart rate, impairs perceptual-motor skills, and may damage the developing brain. The smoke also brings cancer-causing compounds into the body.

YOUR PERSONAL JOURNAL

REFLECT REFLECT REFLECT REFLECT REFLECT REFLECT REFLECT

Study Tip: Reflecting on how the concepts in the chapter relate to your own experiences encourages deeper processing, which makes the material more personally meaningful and fosters more effective learning. Use additional pages if needed to complete your answers.

1. What did you learn about the basic nutrients (protein, carbohydrates, fats, vitamins, minerals) in reading this chapter that you didn't know before? In what ways, if any, did reading this chapter raise your awareness about your own dietary patterns?

_____

_____

_____

_____

2. Based on your reading of the text, why is it important not to assume that someone who has passed out from drinking should be left to "sleep it off"? Did reading the text raise your awareness about the risks of alcohol overdose? Has it changed your own behavior or willingness to get involved if you were to encounter someone at risk of an alcohol overdose?

_____

_____

_____

_____

_____

ANSWERS TO MODULE REVIEWS

Module 5.1

1. Proteins
2. Carbohydrates
3. Fats
4. Muscle
5. body
6. binge eating

Module 5.2

7. 75
8. 30
9. Aerobic
10. Anaerobic
11. raises

Module 5.3

12. does
13. survival

14. deprivation
15. insomnia

Module 5.4

16. abuse
17. dependence
18. Psychological
19. genetic
20. does
21. more
22. Opioids
23. methadone
24. nicotine
25. stimulant
26. Amphetamines
27. Ritalin
28. flashbacks

SCORING KEY FOR THE "CHECK YOUR PHYSICAL ACTIVITY AND HEART DISEASE IQ" SELF-ASSESSMENT

1. *True.* Heart disease is almost twice as likely to develop in inactive people. Being physically inactive is a risk factor for heart disease, along with cigarette smoking, high blood pressure, high blood cholesterol, and being overweight. The more risk factors you have, the greater your chance for heart disease. Regular physical activity (even mild to moderate exercise) can reduce this risk.

2. *False.* Most Americans are very busy, but not very active. Every American adult should make a habit of getting 30 minutes of low to moderate levels of physical activity daily. This includes walking, gardening, and walking up stairs. If you are inactive now, begin by doing a few minutes of activity each day. If you only do some activity every once in a while, try to work something into your routine every day.

3. *True.* Low- to moderate-intensity activities, such as pleasure walking, stair climbing, yardwork, moderate to heavy housework, dancing, and home exercises can have both short- and long-term benefits. If you are inactive, the key is to get started. One great way is to take a walk for 10 to 15 minutes during your lunch break or take your dog for a walk every day. At least 30 minutes of physical activity every day can help improve your heart health and lower your risk of heart disease.

4. *True.* It takes only a few minutes a day to become more physically active. If you don't have 30 minutes in your schedule for an exercise break, try to find two 15-minute periods or even three 10-minute periods. Once you discover how much you enjoy these exercise breaks, they'll become a habit you can't live without.

5. *False.* People who engage in regular physical activity experience many positive benefits. Regular physical activity gives you more energy, reduces stress, helps you to relax, and helps you to sleep better. It helps to lower high blood pressure and improves blood cholesterol levels. Physical activity helps to tone your muscles, burns off calories to help you lose extra pounds or stay at your desirable weight, and helps control your appetite. It can also increase muscle strength, help your heart and lungs work more efficiently, and let you enjoy your life more fully.

6. *False.* Low-intensity activities—if performed daily—can have some long-term health benefits and can lower your risk of heart disease. Regular, brisk, and sustained exercise for at least 30 minutes, four or more times a week, such as brisk walking,

jogging, or swimming, is necessary to improve the efficiency of your heart and lungs and burn off extra calories. These kinds of activities are called aerobic—meaning the body uses oxygen to produce the energy needed for the activity. Other activities may give you other benefits such as increased flexibility or muscle strength, depending on the type of activity.

7. *False.* Although we tend to become less active with age, physical activity is still important. In fact, regular physical activity in older persons increases their capacity to do everyday activities. In general, middle-aged and older people benefit from regular physical activity just as young people do. What is important, no matter what your age, is tailoring the activity program to your own fitness level.

8. *True.* Many activities require little or no equipment. For example, brisk walking only requires a comfortable pair of walking shoes. Also, many communities offer free or inexpensive recreation facilities and physical activity classes. Check your shopping malls, as many of them are open early and late for people who do not wish to walk alone, in the dark, or in bad weather.

9. *False.* The most common risk in exercising is injury to the muscles and joints. Such injuries are usually caused by exercising too hard for too long, particularly if a person has been inactive for some time. To avoid injuries, try to build up your level of activity gradually, listen to your body for early warning pains, be aware of possible signs of heart problems (such as pain or pressure in the left or mid-chest area, left neck, shoulder, or arm during or just after exercising, or sudden lightheadedness, cold sweat, pallor, or fainting), and be prepared for special weather conditions.

10. *True.* You should ask your doctor before you start (or greatly increase) your physical activity if you have a medical condition such as high blood pressure, have pains or pressure in the chest and shoulder area, tend to feel dizzy or faint, get very breathless after mild exertion, are middle-aged or older and have not been physically active, or plan a fairly vigorous activity program. If none of these apply, start slow and get moving.

11. *False.* Regular physical activity can help reduce your risk of having another heart attack. People who include regular physical activity in their lives after a heart attack improve their chances of survival and can improve how they feel and look. If you have had a heart attack, consult your doctor to be sure you are following a safe and effective exercise program that will help prevent heart pain and further damage from overexertion.

12. *True.* Pick several different activities that you like doing because you will be more likely to stay with them. Plan short-term as well as long-term goals. Keep a record of your progress, and check it regularly to see the progress you have made. Get your family and friends to join in. They can help keep you going.

SCORING KEY FOR THE "HOW DO YOU KNOW IF YOU ARE "HOOKED"?" SELF-ASSESSMENT

"Yes" answers to *any* of these items may indicate a developing problem with alcohol. If you answered any of these items in the affirmative, you should seriously examine what drinking means to you. You may also wish to discuss these concerns with a helping professional who can assist you in evaluating whether you have a drinking problem or are at risk of developing one.

SCORING KEY FOR THE "WHY DO YOU SMOKE" SELF-ASSESSMENT

1. Enter the number you have circled for each question in the spaces below, putting the number you have circled to question A over line A, to question B over line B, and so on.
2. Add the three scores on each line to get your totals. For example, the sum of your scores over lines A, G, and M gives you your score on Stimulation–lines B, H, and N give the score on Handling, and so on.

				Totals
____ +	____ +	____	=	____
A	G	M		Stimulation
____ +	____ +	____	=	____
B	H	N		Handling
____ +	____ +	____	=	____
C	I	O		Pleasurable Relaxation
____ +	____ +	____	=	____
D	J	P		Crutch:Tension Reduction
____ +	____ +	____	=	____
E	K	Q		Craving: Psychological Addiction
____ +	____ +	____	=	____
F	L	R		Habit

Scores can vary from 3 to 15. Any score of 11 or above is high; any score of 7 or below is low.

What kind of smoker are you? What do you get out of smoking? What does it do for you? This test is designed to provide you with a score on each of six factors relating to smoking. Your smoking may be characterized by only one of these factors or by a combination of two or more factors. In any event, this test will help you identify what you use smoking for and what kind of satisfaction you think you get from smoking.

The six factors measured by this test describe different ways of experiencing or managing certain kinds of feelings.

Three of these feeling-states represent the positive feelings people get from smoking: a sense of increased energy or stimulation; the satisfaction of handling or manipulating things; and the enhancement of pleasurable feelings accompanying a state of well-being. The fourth relates to decreased-negative feeling states such as anxiety, anger, and shame. The fifth is a complex pattern of increasing and decreasing "craving" for a cigarette, representing the psychological addiction to smoking. The sixth is habit smoking, which takes place in an absence of feeling—purely automatic smoking.

A score of 11 or above on any factor indicates that this factor is an important source of satisfaction for you. The higher your score (15 is the highest), the more important a particular factor is in your smoking and the more useful the discussion of that factor can be in your efforts to quit.

Did you know that...

- "A rose by any other name" could smell just plain awful? (p. 201)

- Having higher self-esteem is linked to getting better grades in college? (p. 208)

- An identity crisis can be a good thing? (p. 208)

- A prospective employer may form a first impression of you even before you walk through the door? (p. 214)

- Waitresses who touch their patrons while making change receive bigger tips? (p. 215)

- Playing on the same team with people of other ethnicities can help break down prejudice? (p. 220)

- Men are more likely than women to interpret a woman's smile or friendliness toward a man as flirting? (p. 223)

- People from Eastern countries such as Japan and China are more likely to blame themselves for failures than are people from Western countries such as the United States and Canada? (p. 223)

iStockphoto

Y ou say you've had it tough getting from place to place? You complain that you've waited in lines at airports or that you've been stuck in freeway traffic? These are ordeals, to be sure, but according to Greek mythology, some ancient travelers had a harder time of it. They met up with a highwayman named Procrustes (pronounced pro-CRUSS-tease).

Procrustes had a quirk. He was interested not only in travelers' pocketbooks but also in their height. He had a concept—what cognitive psychologists refer to as a **schema**—of how tall people should be. When people did not fit his schema, they were in for it. You see, Procrustes also had a very famous bed—a "Procrustean bed." He made his victims lie in the bed. When they were too short for it, he stretched them to make them fit. When they were too long for it, he is said to have practiced surgery on their legs. Many unfortunate passersby failed to survive.

The myth of Procrustes may sound absurd, but it reflects a quirky truth about us as well. We all carry mental Procrustean beds around with us—our unique ways of perceiving the world. And we try to make things and people fit these concepts. Many of us carry around the Procrustean beds of gender-role stereotypes—an example of a **role schema**—and we try to fit men and women into them. For example, when a career woman oversteps the bounds of the male chauvinist's role schema, he metaphorically chops off her legs.

We carry many other kinds of schemas around with us, and they influence our adjustment and personal development. Our first impressions of others lead us to form **person schemas**, which we can think about as mental frameworks that color our future observations. For example, if we form an initial schema of someone as a "jerk," this impression tends to be anchored in our minds even if the person's later behavior no longer fits the part.

Schema A set of beliefs and feelings about something. Examples include stereotypes, prejudices, and generalizations.

Role schema A schema about how people in certain roles (e.g., boss, wife, teacher) are expected to behave.

197

Person schema A schema about how a particular individual is expected to behave.

Self-schemas The set of beliefs, feelings, and generalizations we have about ourselves.

Some schemas concern our ways of "reading" body language. We infer personality traits from behavior. Other schemas concern groups of people; they involve prejudices toward certain racial and ethnic groups. We will examine the origins of prejudice and make a number of suggestions as to what we can do to combat it. But we will begin with the cores of our psychological worlds—our selves. We will see that we carry inward-directed schemas, or **self-schemas**, that affect our feelings about ourselves and influence our behavior. Our selves include our physical selves, our social selves, and our personal selves. We will address key issues that relate to the self, such as the self-concept, the self-ideal, self-identity, and self-esteem. Finally, we will see that we have schemas that influence the ways in which we interpret the successes and shortcomings of other people and ourselves. These particular schemas are called attributions, and they have a major impact on our relationships with others.

As we progress, a theme will emerge: We do not perceive ourselves and other people directly. Instead, we process information about the self and others through our existing schemas. We perceive ourselves and others as through a glass—and sometimes darkly. And when other people do not quite fit our schemas, we have a way of perceptually stretching them or of chopping off their legs. Nor do we spare ourselves this cognitive pruning.

MODULE 6.1

The Self: The Core of Your Psychological Being

- What is the self?
- What are the parts of the self?
- What's in a name?
- What is the importance of our values?

Self The totality of our impressions, thoughts, and feelings, such that we have a conscious, continuous sense of being in the world.

Many psychologists write about the **self**. The psychodynamic theorists Carl Jung and Alfred Adler both spoke of a self that serves as a guiding principle of personality. Erik Erikson and Carl Rogers spoke of ways in which we are, to some degree, the conscious architects of ourselves. Your self is your ongoing sense of who and what you are, your sense of how and why you react to the environment, and, more importantly, how you choose to act on your environment. To Rogers, the sense of self is inborn—a "given." It is an essential part of the experience of being human in the world and the guiding principle behind personality structure and behavior.

Let us consider some parts of your self: your *physical self*, your *social self*, and your *personal self*.

6.1.1 Your Physical Self: My Body, Myself

Physical self One's psychological sense of one's physical being—for example, one's height, weight, hair color, race, and physical skills.

You see yourself when you look in the mirror, but that is only one part of yourself. The physical person—your **physical self**—plays an influential role in your self-concept. You may tower above others or always have to look up to them—literally. Because of your physical appearance, others may smile and seek your gaze, or they may pretend that you do not exist. Your health and conditioning are other aspects of your physical self. Your physical self may be up to athletic challenges or perhaps only down to observing others compete. Our self-concepts are also intertwined with our physical makeup. We think of ourselves as male or female based on the types of sexual organs we possess. We may also think better or worse of ourselves depending on the degree to which our bodies measure up to our expectations. Whereas some aspects of the physical self, such as hair length and weight, change as we grow, gender and race are permanent features of our physical identities.

For most of us, adjustment to traits such as height, gender, and race is closely linked to our self-acceptance and self-esteem. Other physical traits, such as weight, athletic condition, and hairstyle, can be modified. Our motivation, behavior, and the choices we make can be more influential than heredity in shaping these latter aspects of the self.

Large numbers of Americans, particularly American women, are dissatisfied with the appearance of their bodies. Many, if not most, women today would prefer to be thinner. And no wonder, given the ultrathin feminine figure that has been incorporated as an ideal within contemporary American society (see Chapter 5).

Despite the persistence of racial prejudices, a survey by the American Association of University Women (1992) found that African American girls are likely to be happier with their physical appearance than are European American girls. Why the difference?

It appears that the parents of African American girls teach them that there is nothing wrong with them if they do not match the American ideal; the world treats them negatively because of prejudice (Williams, 1992). European American girls are more likely to look inward and blame themselves for not attaining an unreachable physical ideal. Consequently, we should not be surprised by findings showing that eating disorders are less prevalent among African American women than European American women (Lamberg, 2003; Striegel-Moore et al., 2003). These disorders also occur less commonly among groups of women from other minority groups for which body image is not as closely tied to body weight as it is among non-Hispanic white women. That said, we should be aware of the risk that eating disorders among women of color may rise with increased identification with mainstream culture and with greater exposure to the ultrathin ideals of feminine beauty found in the larger society (Gilbert, 2003).

Before leaving this topic, let us note that racial differences in body satisfaction may also reflect more general differences in self-esteem, as investigators find that African Americans overall tend to have higher self-esteem than European Americans (Hafdahl & Gray-Little, 2002; Twenge & Crocker, 2002). Moreover, ethnic identity emerges as a stronger predictor of self-esteem among African Americans and Hispanic Americans than among European Americans (Gray-Little & Hafdahl, 2000; Umaña-Taylor, 2004).

PhotoDisc/SuperStock

The Physical Self
The physical person you carry around with you plays an enormously influential role in your self-concept. You may tower above others or have to look up to them—literally. Other people may smile at you because of your physical appearance, or they may act as if you do not exist. Our adjustment to our physical traits—height, gender, race, and so on—is connected with our self-acceptance and self-esteem.

Peter McBride/Getty Images, Inc.

Ethnic Identity
Investigators find that ethnic identity is more strongly linked to self-esteem among African Americans and Hispanic Americans than among European Americans. How important is your ethnic identity to your self-concept?

6.1.2 The Social Self: The Self You Show to Others

The **social self** refers to the social masks we wear, the social roles we play—suitor, student, worker, husband, wife, mother, father, citizen, leader, and follower. Psychologists distinguish between two general types of psychological identity or self-concept, a personal or individual identity and a social or group identity (Ellemers, Spears, & Doosje, 2002; Verkuyten & De Wolf, 2007). Our identity, thus, is composed of both who were are as individuals and the roles we assume as members of social groups.

▮ **Social self** The composite of the social roles one plays—suitor, student, worker, husband, wife, mother, father, citizen, leader, follower, and so on. Roles and masks help one adjust to the requirements of one's social situation.

Roles and masks are adaptive responses to the social world. In a job interview, you might choose to project enthusiasm, self-confidence, and commitment to hard work but not to express self-doubts or reservations about the company. You may have prepared a number of roles for different life situations.

We shouldn't think of social roles or masks as deceptions or lies. For example, we expect that by the time you got to college, you had integrated the student role into your behavioral repertoire. You know what is expected of you in the classroom—to sit attentively, raise your hand before asking a question, and so on. Is your behavior deceptive if you comport yourself in terms of such expected social roles? We think not. You may "be yourself" with close friends but act differently at work or school. For example, on a job interview you may accentuate your strengths and gloss over your weaknesses. You may perceive yourself to be something of a rebel, but it would be understandable if you were respectful when stopped by a highway patrol officer. This is not dishonesty; it is an effort to meet the requirements of the situation. If you did not understand what respect is, or did not have the social skills to act respectfully, you would not be able to enact a respectful role—even when it is required to do so.

When our entire lives are played behind masks, however, it may be difficult to discover our true inner selves. Partners tend to be reasonably genuine with one another in a mature intimate relationship. They drop the masks that protect and separate them. Without an expression of genuine feelings, life can be the perpetual exchange of one cardboard mask for another.

6.1.3 Your Personal Self—The Inner You

Personal self One's private, continuous sense of being oneself in the world.

Mark Twain's classic novel *The Prince and the Pauper* gives us insight into the **personal self**. In the novel, a young prince is sabotaged by enemies of the throne. He seeks to salvage the kingdom by exchanging places with Tom Canty, a pauper who happens to look just like him. It is a learning experience for both of them. The pauper is taught social graces and learns how the powerful are flattered and praised. The prince learns what it means to stand or fall on the basis of his own efforts, not his status as royalty.

Toward the end of the tale, there is a dispute. Which is the prince and which is Tom Canty? The lads are identical in appearance and behavior, and by now, even in experience. Does it matter? Both, perhaps, can lead the realm equally well. But court officials seek the one whose personal self—whose *inner identity*—is that of the prince. The tale ends happily. The prince retakes the throne, and Tom earns the permanent protection of the court.

Your personal self is visible to you and you alone. It is the day-to-day experience of being you, a changing display of sights, thoughts, and feelings to which you hold the only ticket of admission.

There are other aspects of our personal selves. For example, our name and values are important aspects of our self-identity. How we think of ourselves—our self-concept—is also a major determinant of our feelings of self-worth or self-esteem.

What's in a Name?

> Alice: *Must a name mean something?*
> Humpty-Dumpty: *Of course it must…. My name means the shape I am….*
>   *With a name like yours, you might be any shape, almost.*
>
> —*LEWIS CARROLL,*
> THROUGH THE LOOKING GLASS

What's in a name? Quite a bit, perhaps. As we explore in the nearby *Adjustment and Modern Life* feature, names may carry certain connotations about one's public identity or career choice. After all, "Puff Daddy" sounds more like a contemporary rap artist than Sean Combs. J. Lo sounds more dynamic than Jennifer (Lopez, that is). But, says University of Connecticut psychologist Antonius Cillessen, "There are other factors that are much more important.... Names are sort of in the category of athletic ability and physical attractiveness. Most of us think those are of primary importance in determining a child's acceptance or happiness, but in truth factors such as ability to show concern for others and social behavior are far more significant" (cited in Doner, 1998).

Names even have an influence on perceptions of physical attractiveness. In an early experiment, photographs of women who had been rated equal in attractiveness were assigned various names at random (Garwood et al., 1980). They were then rated by a new group of subjects with the assigned names in view. Women given names such as Jennifer, Kathy, and Christine were rated as significantly more attractive than women assigned names such as Gertrude, Ethel, and Harriet. There are two messages in this: First, names do not really serve as an index to beauty. But second, if your name is a constant source of irritation, there might be little harm in using a more socially appealing nickname.[1]

Our names and nicknames can also reflect our attitudes toward ourselves. Although we may have one legal given name, the variations or nicknames we select say something about our self-schemas. For example, are you a Bob, Bobby, or Robert? An Elizabeth, Betty, or Liz? Shakespeare wrote that a rose by any other name would smell as sweet, but perhaps a rose by the name of skunkweed would impress us as smelling just plain awful. Names have an influence on our social perceptions.

According to psychiatrist Eric Berne (1976), the names our parents give us, and the ways in which they refer to us, often reflect their expectations about what we are to become: Charles and Frederick were kings and emperors. A boy who is steadfastly called Charles or Frederick by his mother, and insists that his associates call him that, lives a different lifestyle from one who is commonly called Chuck or Fred, while Charlie and Freddie are likely to be horses of still another color.

Berne offers another example—the names of two individuals whose names may have had something to do with their chosen profession: H. Head and W. R. Brain. They were both neurologists.

Schoolchildren with unusual or odd names tend to be less popular than their schoolmates with more common monikers (Tierney, 2008). In the schoolyard, Michael and Maria find it easier to make friends than do Regis or Drimini. But investigators find no differences in personality between students with common names and those with names that are ambiguous with respect to gender (e.g., Ronnie and Leslie) or misleading (e.g., boys named Marion or Robin). But another study found that college women with masculine names (such as Dean or Randy)—who used them—were less anxious, more culturally sophisticated, and had greater leadership potential than women with masculine names who chose to use feminine nicknames (Ellington, Marsh, & Critelli, 1980). The women who used their masculine names showed no signs of maladjustment. A woman who uses a given masculine name may be asserting that she is not about to live up to the stereotype of taking a backseat to men.

LAN/Retna

Jennifer Lopez or J. Lo?
Jennifer Lopez announced that she wanted her moniker changed from Jennifer Lopez—already a star—to J. Lo (a more slam-dunk star?). Following his acquittal in a trial in which he was accused of carrying and firing a gun, her former boyfriend, Sean ("Puffy" or "Puff Daddy") Combs, said he wanted to get off to a new start under the name of P. Diddy. What's in a name? Does a rose by any other name smell as sweet? What do you think?

What Do You Value?

Our values involve the importance we place on objects and things. If we're hot, we may value air conditioning more than pizza. We may value love more than money, or money more than love. How many of us are in conflict because our values do not mesh fully with those of our friends, spouses, or employers?

Our values give rise to our personal goals and tend to place limits on the means we use to reach them. We may experience feelings of guilt if the means we use to achieve our goals are inconsistent with our values.

---

[1] Yes, we are being inconsistent. Remember Ralph Waldo Emerson's remark, "A foolish consistency is the hobgoblin of little minds."

Ethics Standards for behavior. A system of beliefs from which one derives standards for behavior.

We all have unique sets of values, but we probably get along best with people whose values resemble our own. Values are often derived from our parents and the religious teachings to which we were exposed. But we may also derive values and **ethics**, our standards of conduct or behavior, through reasoned analysis of standards of right and wrong. According to psychologist Lawrence Kohlberg (1981), the highest level of moral reasoning involves developing principled positions on issues that

Adjustment and Modern Life

Ms. Rose, by Any Other Name, Might Still Be a Florist

Guess what Dilip Doctor does for a living? (*Hint:* His receptionist answers the phone, "Doctor's office.")

"Back home in India, we had a different last name that began with a *Z* and in school I would always be called on last," Dr. Doctor, a Queens urologist, recalled. "One day I was complaining to my teacher, and he said because my father and mother were both physicians, why not call yourself Doctor? That was 40 years ago. And then I figured if they called me doctor, I might as well become one."

Then there are the cases of baseball's Cecil Fielder, news executive Bill Headline, the poet William Wordsworth, the pathologist (not gynecologist) Zoltan Ovary, the novelist Francine Prose, the poker champion Chris Moneymaker, the musicians Paul Horn and Mickey Bass, the British neurologist Lord Brain, and the entertainer Tommy Tune.

Think, too, of all those fictional characters and the real-life doctors and dentists named Payne, Blank the anesthesiologist, Kramp the swim coach, Blechman the gastroenterologist, Faircloth the fashion designer, Goodness the church spokesman, Slaughter the murderer, and the funeral director named Amigone. "I once had a doctor named Gore," recalls Anne Bernays, who, with her husband, Justin Kaplan, wrote *The Language of Names*.

Originally, professions were one way of establishing surnames (the most common American surname is Smith, of whom there are more than a million, far more than the number of blacksmiths). Then there are the names of people who succeeded in their professions despite their names: Dr. Kwak, Judge Lawless, or Orson Swindle, a member of the Federal Trade Commission. Long before Armand Hammer bought Arm & Hammer, the baking soda company, many people assumed he owned it.

"Some people think I'm a bird specialist, which I'm not," said Dr. Meredith Bird, a Rhode Island veterinarian, who added that she doubted that her name influenced her career choice. "I loved animals since I was a little kid. But I was forever grateful my mother didn't name me Robin."

Others believe names truly are destiny. "Names and 'life script,' researchers say, are not merely coincidental but, indeed, causative in considerable measure."

Professor Ralph Slovenko of Wayne State University Law School has written: "Dr. Robert E. Strange, director of the

Northern Virginia Mental Health Institute, tells people that he had no choice but to be a psychiatrist."

David J. Lawyer, who practices in Bellevue, Washington, says: "My routine answer on most days is I do not know why I became a lawyer. But I do know of people who have been inspired by their names. I was deposing an arborist, a tree doctor, and the guy said his name was Greenforest. I said, 'I get a lot of snickers about my name. You must, too.' He said, 'That's why I chose it.' And I did get a call from a fisherman once with a damaged boat full of fish. It was taking on water and he goes to a pay phone and all the attorneys in the yellow pages were ripped out, so he looks up lawyer in the white pages and finds me."

Mr. Lawyer said that two of his uncles are attorneys but that it's unlikely his three children will follow in his footsteps. "They all vow not to become lawyers," he said. Cleveland Kent Evans, a psychologist at Bellevue University in Nebraska, commented: "It is certainly possible that when someone's name corresponds with a word which is associated with a particular interest or profession in their culture, it might make them somewhat more likely to go into that profession.

But the people involved themselves wouldn't necessarily consciously know that or consciously want to admit it when it would happen."

Dr. Lewis P. Lipsitt, professor emeritus of psychology at Brown, agrees that the influence of a name is often subliminal:

"You wouldn't expect people to reply that they had a strong awareness of moving toward a profession or occupation or a preoccupation just because their name signified that they should," he said, "but I think there is a real process at work to gravitate people toward occupations and preoccupations suggested by their names. I was lecturing to my class one day, telling them to be careful because coincidences do happen. To illustrate, I said I could probably convince you people's names cause them to go into certain occupations. I mentioned Mrs. Record who keeps alumni records, Professor Fiddler in the music department, Dr. Fish of the Oceanographic Institute. By the time I got that deeply into it off the top of my head, I'm beginning to think there might be a causal relationship. And then a student said, and you, Dr. Lipsitt, you study sucking behavior in babies. And that had never occurred to me."

Source: Adapted from Roberts, 2005.

reflect our own moral standards. Clarifying our values is a crucial aspect of self-development. Without a sense of values, our behavior may seem meaningless, purposeless. During some periods of life, especially during adolescence, our values may be in flux. For most of us, this is an unsettling experience, and we are motivated to make our beliefs consistent and meaningful. But until we do, we may be subject to the whims and opinions of others—concerned about risking social disapproval because we have not yet established stable internalized standards for self-approval.

Values Clarification—What Is Important to You?   # Self-Assessment

Freedom, recognition, beauty, eternal salvation, a world without war—which is most important to you? Are people who put pleasure first likely to behave differently from people who rank salvation, wisdom, or personal achievement number one? Milton Rokeach devised a survey of values that allows us to rank our life goals according to their relative importance to us. How will you rank yours?

Directions: Eighteen values are listed below in alphabetical order. Select the value that is most important to you and write a 1 next to it in Column I. Then select your next most important value and place a 2 next to it in the same column. Proceed until you have ranked all 18 values. By turning to the key at the end of the chapter, you can compare your rankings to those of a national sample of American adults.

Now would you like to participate in a brief experiment? If so, imagine how someone very close to you, perhaps an old trusted friend or relative, would rank the 18 values. Place his or her rankings in Column II. Then think of someone with whom you have had a number of arguments, someone whose way of life seems at odds with your own. Try to put yourself in his or her place, and rank the values as he or she would in Column III. Now compare your own ranking to the rankings of your friend and your adversary. Are your own values ranked more similarly to those in Column II or in Column III? Do you and your good friend or close relative have rather similar values? Is it possible that you and the person represented in Column III do not get along, in part, because your values differ?

As a class exercise, compare your rankings to those of classmates or to the class average rankings. Do class members share similar values? Do they fall into groups with characteristic values? Does the behavior of different class members reflect differences in values?

VALUE	I	II	III
A COMFORTABLE LIFE a prosperous life	___	___	___
AN EXCITING LIFE a stimulating, active life	___	___	___
A SENSE OF ACCOMPLISHMENT lasting contribution	___	___	___
A WORLD AT PEACE free of war and conflict	___	___	___
A WORLD OF BEAUTY beauty of nature and the arts	___	___	___
EQUALITY brotherhood, equal opportunity for all	___	___	___
FAMILY SECURITY taking care of loved ones	___	___	___
FREEDOM independence, free choice	___	___	___
HAPPINESS contentedness	___	___	___
INNER HARMONY freedom from inner conflict	___	___	___
MATURE LOVE sexual and spiritual intimacy	___	___	___
NATIONAL SECURITY protection from attack	___	___	___
PLEASURE an enjoyable, leisurely life	___	___	___
SALVATION saved, eternal life	___	___	___
SELF-RESPECT self-esteem	___	___	___
SOCIAL RECOGNITION respect, admiration	___	___	___
TRUE FRIENDSHIP close companionship	___	___	___
WISDOM a mature understanding of life	___	___	___

For an interactive version of this self-assessment exercise, go to www.wileyplus.com

MODULE REVIEW

Review It

(1) A gender-role stereotype is an example of a (role schema? personal schema?).

(2) Your health and conditioning are two aspects of your _____ self.

(3) Researchers find that African American girls are (more likely or less likely?) to be happier with the way they are than European American girls.

(4) Gender and race are permanent features of the _____ self.

(5) The _____ self refers to the social masks we wear and the social roles we play.

(6) The aspects of self that are visible to you and you alone are called the _____ self.

(7) Names (do or do not?) influence perceptions of physical attractiveness.

(8) The term _____ applies to the importance we place on things.

Think About It

What aspects of your self are fixed or given? What aspects can be changed?

MODULE 6.2

Self-Concept, Self-Esteem, and Self-Identity

■ What is the self-concept?

■ What are the origins of self-esteem?

■ What is the ideal self?

■ What is self-identity?

■ What are identity statuses?

■ What are the connections between ethnicity and other sociocultural factors—such as gender—and identity

■ **Self-concept** One's perception of oneself, including one's traits and an evaluation of these traits. The self-concept includes one's self-esteem and one's ideal self.

@Felici a Martinez/Photo Edit

Who Are You?
How would you describe your self-concept? How high is your self-esteem? How would you describe the real you? Do you see the actual you as being close to, or far apart from, the ideal you?

Your **self-concept** is your impression or concept of yourself. It reflects the traits or qualities you ascribe to yourself, such as fairness, competence, sociability, and so on. Your self-concept has a major impact on your basic attitude toward yourself—your self-esteem. Self-esteem depends on many factors, including social approval, competence, and the discrepancy between the way you see yourself and what you think you ought to be—your *self-ideal* or ideal self.

The nearby *Try This Out* exercise provides an opportunity for you to evaluate your self-concept on a number of dimensions and to size up how closely your self-concept matches your concept of an ideal self. If your self-concept lags behind your ideal self, don't throw in the towel. The *Psychology in Daily Life* module at the end of the chapter offers some suggestions for bolstering your self-esteem.

The ability to invent different cyberidentities creates ethical, moral, and even legal challenges. Certainly it's no surprise that many people overstate their accomplishments and understate their age when they list themselves on computer dating services. Sexual predators create false personals as they prowl the Net looking for unsuspecting victims. The creation of cyberselves raises some provocative questions:

■ How much information should we reveal about ourselves when we go online?

■ Is it wrong or even immoral to assume another identity when interacting with others in a computer chat room?

■ What aspects of our Internet personas can we (should we) try to bring into our real selves?

TRY THIS OUT   EXAMINING YOUR SELF-CONCEPT

You can examine your self-concept as follows. First, rate yourself on each of the dimensions shown below. There is also room for you to add other dimensions that are important to you. Use the following code to check the number that corresponds to your concept of yourself along each dimension:

1 = extremely
2 = rather
3 = somewhat
4 = equally _____ and _____; not sure
5 = somewhat
6 = rather
7 = extremely

Fair	_ : _ : _ : _ : _ : _ : _	Unfair
	1 2 3 4 5 6 7	
Independent	_ : _ : _ : _ : _ : _ : _	Dependent
	1 2 3 4 5 6 7	
Religious	_ : _ : _ : _ : _ : _ : _	Nonreligious
	1 2 3 4 5 6 7	
Unselfish	_ : _ : _ : _ : _ : _ : _	Selfish
	1 2 3 4 5 6 7	
Self-confident	_ : _ : _ : _ : _ : _ : _	Lacking confidence
	1 2 3 4 5 6 7	
Competent	_ : _ : _ : _ : _ : _ : _	Incompetent
	1 2 3 4 5 6 7	
Important	_ : _ : _ : _ : _ : _ : _	Unimportant
	1 2 3 4 5 6 7	
Attractive	_ : _ : _ : _ : _ : _ : _	Unattractive
	1 2 3 4 5 6 7	
Educated	_ : _ : _ : _ : _ : _ : _	Uneducated
	1 2 3 4 5 6 7	
Sociable	_ : _ : _ : _ : _ : _ : _	Unsociable
	1 2 3 4 5 6 7	
Kind	_ : _ : _ : _ : _ : _ : _	Cruel
	1 2 3 4 5 6 7	
Wise	_ : _ : _ : _ : _ : _ : _	Foolish
	1 2 3 4 5 6 7	
Graceful	_ : _ : _ : _ : _ : _ : _	Awkward
	1 2 3 4 5 6 7	
Intelligent	_ : _ : _ : _ : _ : _ : _	Unintelligent
	1 2 3 4 5 6 7	
Artistic	_ : _ : _ : _ : _ : _ : _	Inartistic
	1 2 3 4 5 6 7	
Tall	_ : _ : _ : _ : _ : _ : _	Short
	1 2 3 4 5 6 7	
Obese	_ : _ : _ : _ : _ : _ : _	Skinny
	1 2 3 4 5 6 7	

Add other traits of importance to you:

_____ ___ : ___ : ___ : ___ : ___ : ___ : ___ _____   _____ ___ : ___ : ___ : ___ : ___ : ___ : ___ _____
          1   2   3   4   5   6   7   1   2   3   4   5   6   7

_____ ___ : ___ : ___ : ___ : ___ : ___ : ___ _____
          1   2   3   4   5   6   7

Now consider your self-ratings. Did you rate yourself toward the positive or negative end of these dimensions? People with higher self-esteem tend to rate themselves more positively than those with lower self-esteem. Some dimensions, such as "wise–foolish," may have more of a bearing on your self-esteem than other dimensions. The general pattern of your ratings should give you insight into your overall self-concept and how it affects your self-esteem.

Now, repeat the exercise with a marker of a different color. Or make an X instead of a checkmark. But this time indicate where you think you *ought* to be according to each dimension by marking the space above the corresponding number. Ignore your original ratings at this time. (Ratings for some dimensions might overlap, indicating a match between your self-concept and your ideal self.)

Now consider the *differences* between your ratings of your present self and ideal self on each dimension. Pay particular attention to dimensions you consider most important. The higher the *differences* between your actual self and your ideal self, the *lower* your self-esteem is likely to be. The *closer* your self-perceptions are to your ideal self, the *higher* your self-esteem is likely to be.

What aspects of your personality show the greatest discrepancies? Which, if any, of these characteristics would you like to change in yourself? Do you think it is possible to move closer to your desired self? How would you do it? What would you need to change about yourself and how you relate to others?

Adjustment and Modern Life

Your Self in Cyberspace: Which Self Is It?

Not very long ago, a person's public identity was represented by a name—first name, last name, perhaps a middle initial or two. Today, we need to carve out multiple identities or handles by which to identify ourselves in the world of cyberspace.

We have e-mail names and screen names and user names and the like—so many different names in fact that you may forget who you are when you navigate the Web. *(Now, what was my user name?)* The anonymity of the Internet affords us the opportunity to create alternate or false identities or personas. As psychologist John Suler (2002) notes, cyberspace gives us license to play with our identities, even experiment with many alternate selves:

One of the interesting things about the Internet is the opportunity it offers people to present themselves in a variety of different ways. You can alter your style of being just slightly or indulge in wild experiments with your identity by changing your age, history, personality, physical appearance, even your gender. The user name you choose, the details you do or don't indicate about yourself, the information presented on your personal web page, the persona or avatar you assume in an online community—all are important aspects of how people manage their identity in cyberspace.

The Internet can be a mixed blessing with respect to constructing our personal identities. On the positive end, the ability to create alternate cyberidentities can free us to express ourselves in ways that we might be reluctant to in real life. We can explore feelings, needs, and desires that we might otherwise keep hidden, even from ourselves. On the other hand, how do we reconcile the discrepant parts of ourselves that we reveal only in the relative safety of cyberspace? Moreover, is it right to mislead others? To claim to be something we're not? And what of our cyberbuddies? Are they misleading us? Does it matter?

Perhaps not, if we recognize that cyberspace is a place where fantasies intersect, not a place where people in real life interact with each other (and depend on each other). The advent of cyberidentities raises even more fundamental questions:

What is our true identity? Is it the social persona we show to others in our daily lives? Or is it the alternate identity or identities we enact online? Or is it perhaps some intermingling of the two? Might there be parts of our cyberselves that we can integrate into our daily selves? We raise these questions not to offer any final answers but simply to encourage readers to think about how they shape their identities when they enter the realm of cyberspace.

"On the Internet, nobody knows you're a dog."

6.2.1 Self-Esteem

As suggested by the nearby *Try This Out* feature, **self-esteem** may depend on the degree to which our impressions of ourselves square with our **ideal self** (or *self-ideal*)—the self we feel we ought to be. But what are the determinants of self-esteem? Self-esteem may begin with reflection of how others see us, beginning in childhood with parental love and approval. Children who are prized by their parents usually come to see themselves as being worthy of love. They are likely to learn to love and accept themselves.

In classic research, Coopersmith (1967) studied self-esteem among fifth- and sixth-grade boys and found that boys with higher self-esteem more often came from homes with strict but not cruel parents. Such parents were highly involved in their sons' activities. Parents of boys low in self-esteem were more permissive but tended to be harsh when they did use discipline. Children whose parents expect more of them accomplish more, and accomplishment is linked to self-esteem. The parents of boys with higher self-esteem were more demanding of their sons but also highly involved in their lives. Involvement communicates interest and concern—qualities associated with worthiness.

Though self-esteem tends to be relatively stable, it is not fixed or unchangeable. As seen in Figure 6.1, self-esteem among people in general tends to fall during adolescence and then begins stabilizing and rising gradually during adulthood before falling sharply in late adulthood (years 70+) (Robins & Trzesniewski, 2005; Robins et al., 2002). Self-esteem may also rise or fall depending on external events and one's

■ **Self-esteem** Self-approval. One's self-respect or favorable opinion of oneself.

■ **Ideal self** One's perception of what one ought to be and do. Also called the *self-ideal*.

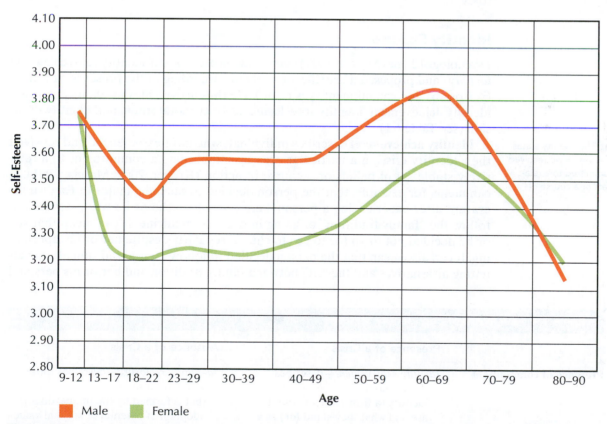

Figure 6.1

Self-Esteem Across the Lifespan

Here we see mean levels of self-esteem for males and females across the lifespan. Notice how self-esteem tends to fall during adolescence and then increases gradually until later adulthood, when it begins to decline sharply.

Source: Robins & Trzesniewski, 2005.

Erik Erikson
The theorist Erik Erikson examined how people come to terms with their personal identity—who they are, what they believe, and where they are headed in life.

■ **Identity crisis** A period of serious self-examination and self-questioning of one's values and direction in life.

■ **Identity achievement** The identity status that describes individuals who have resolved an identity crisis and committed to a relatively stable set of beliefs or a course of action.

emotional reaction to them (Nezlek & Plesko, 2001). For example, events such as poor test grades or a job loss are not only blows to the GPA and the wallet; they also tend to lower self-esteem (Martella & Maass, 2000). But it's not just events themselves that shape our self-esteem. As we will see in Chapter 9, cognitive theorists recognize that the judgments we impose on events determine the effects these events have on our emotional reactions. However self-esteem may be shaped, research underscores its importance. For example, investigators find self-esteem to be associated with better physical health and psychological well-being (DuBois & Flay, 2004), with higher GPAs in college (Di Paula & Campbell, 2002; S.E. Taylor et al., 2003), and with the ability to cope with the stress associated with the transition to college (Paul & Brier, 2001).

6.2.2 Self-Identity and Identity Crisis

We tend to think of the word *crisis* in negative terms. Yet the psychological theorist Erik Erikson, who coined the term **identity crisis**, believed that a crisis of self-identity is a normal part of development and can be a growth experience that leads to the formation of clear and consistent beliefs and direction in life or the life role. Moreover, Erikson believed that the fundamental challenge of adolescence is the creation of one's own adult self-identity. Your self-identity is your sense of who you are and what you stand for. Erikson believed that the key to identity achievement was the choice and commitment to an occupational or life role. But not everyone experiences an identity crisis. Nor does everyone develop a commitment to a life role, or roles.

Identity Statuses

Psychologist James Marcia (1991) studied the process of self-identity (also called *ego identity*) and proposed a classification scheme according to the presence of a crisis (yes or no) and commitment (yes or no). He thus arrived at four identity statuses: identity achievement, identity foreclosure, identity moratorium, and identity diffusion (see Table 6.1).

Identity achievement describes individuals who have experienced and resolved their identity crisis in a particular area by establishing a commitment to a relatively stable set of beliefs or a course of action (Kroger, 2000; Marcia, 1991). It can mean, for example, that the person decided to pursue a major in English literature after experiencing a personal crisis in which she or he was pressured to follow the "family tradition" of going into law or medicine. It can mean that she or he decided not to go (or to go) to church regularly despite her or his upbringing. It can also mean that the person decided to follow family tradition after evaluating alternatives and the "fit" between family tradition and her or his personal

Table 6.1 ■ Four Types of Ego Identity Statuses		
	Presence of a Crisis	**Absence of a Crisis**
Presence of commitment	*Identity achievement*—describes those who have achieved a sense of identity (a firm sense of who they are and what they stand for) as a result of going through a crisis	*Identity foreclosure*—describes those who have a sense of identity, but one that is formed by the unquestioning adoption of parental or societal values
Absence of commitment	*Identity moratorium*—describes those who are in the throes of an identity crisis, actively struggling to sort out values and achieve identity	*Identity diffusion*—describes those who do not have a sense of identity but are not presently concerned about it

beliefs and preferences. External forces such as family and social pressures can aid the achievement of identity but can also serve as barriers to identity formation, especially when they run counter to the values and likes of the individual (Danielsen, Lorem, & Kroger, 2000; Yoder, 2000). In terms of their personal traits, people who reach identity achievement tend to be emotionally stable and conscientious in their pursuits (Clancy & Dollinger, 1993).

Are You One of Your Favorite People?

Self-Assessment

Following are a series of statements that reflect your perceptions of your self-acceptance and self-worth. Read each statement and reflect honestly on how *true* or *false* it is for you according to the scale given below. Then check the scoring key at the end of the chapter.

1 = completely true
2 = mostly true
3 = half true, half false
4 = mostly false
5 = completely false

____ 1. I'd like it if I could find someone who would tell me how to solve my personal problems.

____ 2. I don't question my worth as a person, even if I think others do.

____ 3. When people say nice things about me, I find it difficult to believe they really mean it. I think maybe they're kidding me or just aren't being sincere.

____ 4. If there is any criticism or anyone says anything about me, I just can't take it.

____ 5. I don't say much at social affairs because I'm afraid that people will criticize me or laugh if I say the wrong thing.

____ 6. I realize that I'm not living very effectively, but I just don't believe I've got it in me to use my energies in better ways.

____ 7. I look on most of the feelings and impulses I have toward people as being quite natural and acceptable.

____ 8. Something inside me just won't let me be satisfied with any job I've done—if it turns out well, I get a very smug feeling that this is beneath me, I shouldn't be satisfied with this, this isn't a fair test.

____ 9. I feel different from other people. I'd like to have the feeling of security that comes from knowing I'm not too different from others.

____ 10. I'm afraid for people that I like to find out what I'm really like, for fear they'd be disappointed in me.

____ 11. I am frequently bothered by feelings of inferiority.

____ 12. Because of other people, I haven't been able to achieve as much as I should have.

____ 13. I am quite shy and self-conscious in social situations.

____ 14. In order to get along and be liked, I tend to be what people expect me to be rather than anything else.

____ 15. I seem to have a real inner strength in handling things. I'm on a pretty solid foundation and it makes me pretty sure of myself.

____ 16. I feel self-conscious when I'm with people who have a superior position to mine in business or at school.

____ 17. I think I'm neurotic or something.

____ 18. Very often, I don't try to be friendly with people because I think they won't like me.

____ 19. I feel that I'm a person of worth, on an equal plane with others.

____ 20. I can't avoid feeling guilty about the way I feel toward certain people in my life.

____ 21. I'm not afraid of meeting new people. I feel that I'm a worthwhile person and there's no reason why they should dislike me.

____ 22. I sort of only half-believe in myself.

____ 23. I'm very sensitive. People say things and I have a tendency to think they're criticizing me or insulting me in some way, and later when I think of it, they may not have meant anything like that at all.

____ 24. I think I have certain abilities and other people say so, too. I wonder if I'm not giving them an importance way beyond what they deserve.

____ 25. I feel confident that I can do something about the problems that may arise in the future.

____ 26. I guess I put on a show to impress people. I know I'm not the person I pretend to be.

____ 27. I do not worry or condemn myself if other people pass judgment against me.

_____ 28. I don't feel very normal, but I want to feel normal.

_____ 29. When I'm in a group, I usually don't say much for fear of saying the wrong thing.

_____ 30. I have a tendency to sidestep my problems.

_____ 31. Even when people do think well of me, I feel sort of guilty because I know I must be fooling them—that if I were really to be myself, they wouldn't think well of me.

_____ 32. I feel that I'm on the same level as other people and that helps to establish good relations with them.

_____ 33. I feel that people are apt to react differently to me than they would normally react to other people.

_____ 34. I live too much by other people's standards.

_____ 35. When I have to address a group, I get self-conscious and have difficulty saying things well.

_____ 36. If I didn't always have such hard luck, I'd accomplish much more than I have.

Source: Based on a measure originally developed by Emanuel M. Berger of the University of Minnesota, Minneapolis.
For an interactive version of this self-assessment exercise, go to www.wileyplus.com

∎ **Identity foreclosure** The identity status that describes individuals who have adopted a commitment to a set of beliefs or a course of action without undergoing an identity crisis.

∎ **Identity moratorium** The identity status that describes individuals who are in the throes of an identity crisis—an intense examination of alternatives.

Radius/SUPERSTOCK

Who Am I?
One of the major psychological challenges we face in life is carving out a sense of personal identity with respect to who we are, what we believe, and where we are headed in life.

Identity foreclosure refers to individuals who have commited themselves to a set of beliefs or a course of action without undergoing a personal identity crisis. Frequently, they have adopted the views of their parents or other role models without seriously questioning them (Kroger, 2000; Schwartz et al., 2000).

Most people follow the same religion as their parents, for example, but some do so after a period of personal questioning and others never particularly think about it. Identity foreclosure is most likely found in homogeneous societies or isolated subcultures in which "everybody's doing it" (Danielsen et al., 2000; Yoder, 2000). In terms of personal traits, people who foreclose their opportunity to develop their uniqueness may be closed to new experiences. As we see in the nearby (p. 212), psychologist Carl Rogers's father tried to insulate his children from the surrounding society to foreclose their options in developing personal ethical and religious beliefs. Rogers rebelled, however, and experienced a great deal of inner turmoil by doing so. Despite the tumult, he did not allow himself to be foreclosed, and he ultimately reached identity achievement.

Identity moratorium describes people who are in the throes of an identity crisis. It is a period of intense examination of alternatives. The alternatives might refer to career choices, whether to become sexually active (and with whom), whether to have a child, whether to attend church or change religions, or whether to join a political party. In the effort to arrive at stable commitments, people in this identity status carefully evaluate their values, attitudes, feelings, and the possibilities that are open to them.

Finally, **identity diffusion** describes people who have neither arrived at a commitment as to who they are and what they stand for nor experienced an identity crisis. They have not fashioned a stable set of beliefs or a coherent course of action. Nor are they attempting to do so. Such individuals may be given to acting on a whim and on the suggestions of others.

In early work by your first author and colleague Caroline Waterman (Waterman & Nevid, 1977), we surveyed 70 male and 70 female first- and second-year students at the University at Albany to determine whether they had developed a commitment to a set of personal beliefs concerning occupational choice, religious and political views, and sexual behavior (mainly the issue of premarital sex). We determined whether these beliefs had developed during a period of serious examination of the alternatives, or, as Erikson labeled it, an identity crisis. On the basis of their responses, students were assigned to one of the four identity statuses—identity achievement, identity foreclosure, identity moratorium, identity diffusion—in each area of life. We found that the development of a set of firm beliefs about sexual morality, not occupational choice, occupied center stage in the resolution of personal identity. College students can postpone occupational decisions, at least for a while, but sexual decision making is an issue that many college students face every

Table 6.2 ▮ Students in Each Identity Status in Various Areas of Commitment, According to the Waterman and Nevid Study				
	Occupational Choice	Religious Values	Political Beliefs	Sexual Values
Females				
Identity achievement	17%	23%	9%	39%
Identity moratorium	24	17	14	16
Identity foreclosure	20	20	13	39
Identity diffusion	39	40	64	7
Males				
Identity achievement	17	23	20	21
Identity moratorium	23	13	6	6
Identity foreclosure	21	36	10	64
Identity diffusion	39	29	64	9

week, or at least every weekend. Table 6.2 reveals that the lowest incidence of identity diffusion was in the area of sexual morality and the highest in political ideology. College students may be able to postpone commitments in the realms of careers, religion, and—especially—politics, but most adopt a philosophy about sexual permissiveness by the time they enter college or early in their college careers.

There were no gender differences in commitment to an occupational identity status, but the gender differences concerning sexual matters were revealing. Most men (64%) were foreclosers on sex, whereas women were equally split (39% and 39%) between identity achievement and foreclosure, with another 16% remaining in identity moratorium—that is, still seeking to make choices about sexual matters. Most men expressed the attitude, "There's nothing wrong with premarital sex. If we're getting it on together, fine." But the majority had never seriously examined their beliefs about sexual permissiveness. They had simply adopted the double standard that makes premarital sexual activity more acceptable for males ("Boys will be boys"). This does not imply that the women were puritanical. The majority of them also endorsed premarital sex but more often in the context of a meaningful relationship. To arrive at their views, the women had more frequently undergone an identity crisis in which they rejected more restrictive parental values. Adolescent females commonly feel caught between parental pressure to show restraint and peer pressure to "get with it." The development of their identity status concerning sexual matters involves a stage of crisis.

▮ **Identity diffusion** The identity status that describes individuals who have neither arrived at a commitment as to who they are and what they stand for nor experienced a crisis.

Human Diversity and Identity Formation

Don Terry (2000), the writer to whom we introduced you in Chapter 3, used to do anything he could to put off going to bed. One of his favorite delaying tactics was to engage his mother in a discussion about the important questions of the day, questions he and his friends had debated in the backyards of their neighborhood that afternoon— like who did God root for, the Cubs or the White Sox? (The correct answer was, and still is, the White Sox. Or so says the second author. The first author, fondly remembering summer days at Wrigley Field, still has a soft spot for the Cubs.) Then one night he remembers asking his mother something he had been wondering for a long time. "Mom," he asked, "What am I?"

"You're my darling Donny," she said.

"I know. But what else am I?"

"You're a precious little boy who someday will grow up to be a wonderful, handsome man."

"What I mean is, you're white and Dad's black, so what does that make me?"

"Oh, I see," she said. "Well, you're half-black and you're half-white, so you're the best of both worlds."

A CLOSER LOOK

Carl Rogers - A Case Study in Identity Achievement

Carl Rogers spent his early years in a wealthy Chicago suburb, where he attended school with the children of famed architect Frank Lloyd Wright. His family, with its six children, was religious and close-knit. His father viewed such activities as smoking, drinking, playing cards, and going to the movies as questionable. It was all right to be tolerant of them, but relationships with those who engaged in them were discouraged. When Rogers was 12, his family moved to a farm farther from the city to protect the children from what his father perceived to be unwholesome influences. Rogers (1902–1987) took refuge in books and developed an interest in science. His first college major was agriculture. During a student visit to China in 1922, he was exposed for the first time to people from different ethnic backgrounds. It was during this period that he wrote his parents proclaiming his independence from their conservative views. Shortly thereafter, he developed an ulcer and had to be hospitalized. It is unclear whether Rogers's rebellion against his father and the development of the ulcer were causally linked, but the coincidence seems quite noteworthy. Rogers then attended New York's Union Theological Seminary with the goal of becoming a minister. At the same time, he took courses in psychology and education across the street at Columbia University. After a couple of years of further exploration of his personal identity, he came to believe that—at least for him—psychology might be the better way of helping people get in touch with their own feelings and to develop as the unique individuals they were. So he transferred to Columbia. Perhaps in response to his parents' efforts to "protect" him from other ways of thinking, Rogers developed a form of therapy—client-centered therapy—intended to help people get in touch with their genuine feelings and pursue their own interests, regardless of whether doing so earned the approval of other people. Rogers had a positive view of human nature and did not believe that encouraging individuals to find and develop their unique selves would make them selfish. He thought that people were naturally prosocial—not antisocial—and that successful personal development would have the effect of allowing them to be even more generous and loving. Rogers believed that people's behavior took ugly turns only when their personal development was thwarted by the disapproval of other people.

Carl Rogers
In order for him to actualize his own self, Rogers had to overcome the influences of his rigid father and earn his father's disapproval. Rogers's personal experiences led him to believe that we must each be permitted to develop in our own ways.

Roger Ressmeyer/©Corbis

The next day, he told his friends that he was neither "black" nor "white." "I'm the best of both worlds," he announced proudly. "Man, you're crazy," one of the backyard boys said. "You're not even the best of your family. Your sister is. That girl is fine."

For much of his life, he has tried to believe his mother. Having grown up in a family of blacks and whites, he had long thought he saw race more clearly than most people. He appreciated being able to get close to both worlds, something few ever do. It was like having a secret knowledge.

And yet he has also known from an early age that things are more complicated than his mother made them out to be. Our country, from its beginnings, has been obsessed with race. Being European American or African American, or both, is part of one's identity. So is being male or female, Christian or Muslim or Jew.

Erik Erikson's views of the development of identity were intended to apply primarily to males. In Erikson's theory, the stage of identity development includes embracing a philosophy of life and commitment to a career. Erikson believed that the development of interpersonal relationships was more important to women's identity than occupational and ideological issues because women's identities were more intimately connected with their roles as wives and mothers. Men's identities did not depend on their roles as husbands and fathers. Erikson's theories were formed at a time when most women with young children were not employed outside the home. Today, most mothers are in the labor force, including most mothers with preschool children.

Reflective of the changes in career aspirations with which young women in the United States are raised today, women's identities are strongly connected with occupational issues. Thus, adolescent girls today voice almost as much concern about their occupational plans as boys do. But girls also express concern about how to balance the needs of a career and a family in their daily lives. Although most women will be full-time workers, they still usually bear the primary responsibility for rearing the children and maintaining the home.

Identity formation is often more complicated for adolescents from ethnic minority groups (Collins, 2000). These adolescents may be faced with two sets of cultural values: those of their ethnic group and those of the dominant culture (Phinney, 2000; Phinney & Devich-Navarro, 1997). When these values are in conflict, minority adolescents need to reconcile the differences and, frequently, decide where they stand. A Muslim American adolescent explains why she skipped the prom: "At the time of the prom, I was sad, but just about everyone I knew had sex that night, which I think was immoral. Now, I like saying that I didn't go. I didn't go there just because it was a cool thing to do" ("Muslim Women," 1993, p. B9).

Biracial adolescents whose parents are of different religions wrestle with yet another issue as to what constitutes their own dominant cultural heritage (Collins, 2000; Phinney, 2000). Parents from different ethnic groups may decide to build their lives together, but their values sometimes do not dwell contentedly side by side in the minds of their children.

MODULE REVIEW

Review It

(9) The concept or impression you hold about yourself is called your _____.

(10) _____ appears to begin with parental love and approval.

(11) Coopersmith found that middle school boys with high self-esteem tended to come from homes with (strict or permissive?) parents.

(12) High self-esteem (does or does not?) help college students cope with college life.

(13) Self-esteem is based on the difference between our self-descriptions and our _____ selves.

(14) Your _____ is your sense of who you are and what you stand for.

(15) The four types of identity status are identity achievement, identity _____, identity _____, and identity diffusion.

(16) Each identity status is characterized by the presence or absence of _____ and of crisis.

(17) People who adopt the views of others without seriously questioning them are said to be in the status of identity _____.

(18) In trying to form identity, adolescents from ethnic minority groups may need to evaluate two sets of cultural values—those of their ethnic group and those of the _____ culture.

Think About It

How is self-esteem developed? What advice would you give new parents about helping their children acquire self-esteem?

MODULE 6.3

Perception of Others

■ What is social perception?
■ Why are first impressions so important?
■ Why should we think about people's body language?

Thus far we have considered the ways in which we perceive ourselves. But let's turn the discussion around to **social perception**—how we perceive others in our social environment. We begin by seeing that first impressions prompt the development of schemas that resist change. Then we discuss our schemas concerning body language and prejudice.

■ **Social perception** The process by which we form understandings of others in our social environment, based on observations of how others act and information we receive.

6.3.1 The Importance of First Impressions

▮ **Primacy effect** The tendency to evaluate others in terms of first impressions.

Stockbyte/SuperStock

First Impressions
You never get a second chance to make a first impression. What factors influence first impressions? How can you make the most of the first impressions that others have of you?

▮ **Recency effect** The tendency to evaluate others in terms of the most recent impression.

First impressions tend to be lasting impressions. First impressions become lasting because of the **primacy effect**. That is, we tend to form a quick impression of a person's traits when we first encounter the person. We infer a person's traits from the person's behavior, style of dress, or general mannerisms. We then use these impressions as mental frameworks, or *person schemas*, when interpreting people's behaviors. So if Reggie acts in a way when we first meet him that we interpret as snobbish, we expect him to act snobbishly when we encounter him again. Even when his future behavior doesn't square with the schema we formed of him, we're likely to interpret his behavior as an exception to the rule—as justified by circumstances or external factors. We may eventually change our impression if enough counterinstances occur, but first impressions tend to be stubborn things.

How can we encourage people to pay more attention to more recent impressions? One way is to avoid making snap judgments when meeting people. We can suspend judgment until we get to know people better. We can also attend more closely to the person's recent behavior. We call the phenomenon in which the most recent impressions govern the formation of the person schema the **recency effect**.

Yes, first impressions tend to persist, but they are not engraved in stone. New information, or advice to focus on all the evidence, can modify them.

Managing First Impressions

Though first impressions may not be engraved in stone, they can affect how others perceive us. There are a number of ways in which you can manage first impressions to enhance the perceptions that others form of you:

- *First, be aware of the first impressions you make on others.* When you meet people for the first time, remember that they are forming person schemas about you. Once formed, these schemas resist change.
- *When you apply for a job, your "first impression" may reach your prospective employer before you walk through the door.* The first impression you make is conveyed by your résumé. Make it neat and present some of your more important accomplishments at the beginning.
- *Why not plan and rehearse your first few remarks for a date or a job interview?* Imagine the situation and, in the case of a job interview, things you are likely to be asked. If you have some relatively smooth statements prepared, along with a nice smile, you are more likely to be considered as socially competent, and competence is respected.
- *Smile.* You're more attractive and appear friendlier when you smile.
- *Be aware of your style of dress and physical mannerisms on job interviews, college interviews, first dates, or other important meetings.* Then again, people start forming impressions of you based on your dress, mannerisms, and other characteristics even before you first open your mouth to speak to them. So become more aware of what your body language and attire may be saying about you. Ask yourself: What type of dress is expected for this occasion? How can I make a positive first impression?
- *When you answer essay questions, attend to your penmanship.* It is the first thing your instructor notices when looking at your paper. If need be, print. Present relevant knowledge in the first sentence or paragraph of the answer, or restate the question by writing something like, "In this essay I will show how..."
- *In class, seek eye contact with your instructors.* Look interested. That way, if you do poorly on a couple of quizzes, your instructor may conceptualize you as a "basically good student who paid attention in class but made a couple of errors" rather than "a poor, uninterested student who is revealing his (her)

shortcomings." (Don't tell your instructor that this paragraph is in the book. Maybe he or she won't notice.) When speaking to your instructor, express interest in the subject material—no really, find something that interests you.

Now let's turn the tables. To avoid boxing someone into a corner of first impressions from which they may never escape, ask yourself the following:

- *Am I being fair to the other person?* If your date's parents are a bit cold toward you when you first meet them, maybe it's because they don't know you and are concerned about their son's or daughter's welfare. If you show them that you are treating their son or daughter decently, they may come around. Don't assume that they're basically prunefaces.

- *Does my first impression capture the "real person" or just one instance of the person's behavior?* Give other people a second chance, and you may find that they have something to offer. After all, would you want to be held accountable for everything you've ever said and done? Haven't you changed for the better as time has gone on? Haven't you become more sophisticated and knowledgeable? People are not always at their best. Don't carve person schemas in stone on the basis of one social exchange.

Body Language

Body language is an important contributor to forming person schemas. It provides important cues about a person's thoughts, attitudes, and feelings—assuming that we read the information correctly.

For example, the way people carry themselves provides cues as to how they feel and are likely to behave. When people are "uptight," their bodies are often rigid and straight-backed. Relaxed people often literally "hang loose." Various combinations of eye contact, posture, and distance between people provide cues as to their moods and their feelings toward their companions.

When people face us and lean toward us, we may assume that they like us or are interested in us. If we are privy to a conversation between a couple and observe that the woman is leaning toward the man but that he is sitting back and toying with his hair, we may rightly infer that he is not interested or not receptive to what she is saying. Touch also communicates. Women are more likely than men to touch other people when they are interacting with them (Stier & Hall, 1984). In an early touching experiment, Kleinke (1977) showed that appeals for help can be more effective when the distressed person engages in physical contact with the people being appealed to for aid. A woman received more dimes for phone calls when she touched the arm of the person she was asking for money. Similarly, waitresses who touch customers' arms are likely to receive higher tips. Touching often induces positive behavior. Like spoken language, body language varies from culture to culture. The same gesture may have a very different meaning in one culture than it does in another. For example, people in Bulgaria shake their heads up and down to signal no (Laroche, 2003). When using their fingers to display the number 8, people in China extend the thumb and the adjoining finger. In North America, the same gesture is interpreted as pointing a gun.

Looking someone in the eye may be received less favorably in some non-Western cultures than it is in Western cultures. Cultural differences also affect how far people stand from each other. People from some African cultures tend to stand far apart, even as much as 3 feet apart (Thiederman, 2002). But people in Middle Eastern cultures tend to get very close to each other, even less than 18 inches. The exact distance people stand from each other also depends on their social relationships. The closer or more intimate the relationship, the closer people tend to stand to each other. In these experiments, touching was nonintrusive. It was usually gentle and brief, and it occurred in familiar, public settings. However, when touching suggests greater intimacy than is desired, it can be seen as negative or as a form of sexual harassment.

We also learn things from eye contact. When other people "look us squarely in the eye," we may assume that they are being assertive or open with us. Avoidance of

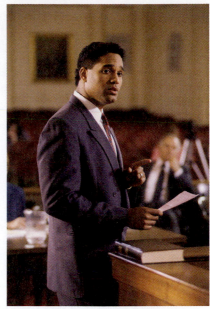

Ron Chapple/Getty Images, Inc.

Impression Management
Why do we dress up and put on our best behavior for job interviews? Why do attorneys get their clients haircuts and have them shave and dress well when they are on trial? First impressions are important. Initial impressions may persuade us to see people in certain ways and to have certain expectations of their behavior.

Bavaria/Getty Images, Inc

Body Talk
Body language is an important contributor to forming impressions of others. What does the body language of these people convey to you?

eye contact may suggest deception or depression. Gazing is interpreted as a sign of liking or friendliness. In one penetrating study, men and women were asked to gaze into each other's eyes for two minutes (Kellerman, Lewis, & Laird, 1989). After doing so, they reported having passionate feelings toward each other. (Watch out!)

Gazes are different, of course, from persistent "hard" stares. Hard stares may be interpreted as provocations or signs of anger. When the second author was in high school, adolescent males engaged in "staring contests" to assert their dominance. The adolescent who looked away first "lost."

In a series of field experiments, Ellsworth, Carlsmith, and Henson (1972) subjected drivers stopped at red lights to hard stares from riders of motor scooters. Recipients of the stares crossed the intersection more rapidly than other drivers did when the light changed. Greenbaum and Rosenfeld (1978) found that recipients of hard stares from a man seated near an intersection also drove off more rapidly after the light turned green.

Using Body Language to Foster Adjustment and Enhance Social Relationships

Consider some suggestions for using body language to improve your social relationships:

- *Be aware of what other people are telling you with their body language.* If they are looking away as you are telling them something, perhaps you are "turning them off." If they are leaning toward you, nodding, and meeting your gaze, they are probably agreeing with you. Make mental notes of their reactions to get a fix on their attitudes and feelings about you.

- *Pay attention to your own body language as a way of helping to make the desired impressions on other people.* Are you maintaining eye contact but nodding yes when you want to say no? If so, you can't be very happy with yourself. Would you like to be encouraging but wear a perpetual frown? If so, you may be pushing other people away without intending to.

- *Pay attention to your own body language as a way of learning about yourself— as a way of getting "in touch" with your own feelings.* If you are agreeing to something, but you are leaning away from the other person and your back is rigid, perhaps you would like to rethink your assent. Or perhaps you are staring when you think you might be gazing. Could it be that you are more upset by something than you had imagined?

MODULE REVIEW

Review It

(19) First impressions are important because of the _____ effect.

(20) The phenomenon in which the most recent impressions govern our impressions is called the _____ effect.

(21) When people feel "uptight," their bodies are often _____ and _____.

(22) When people lean (away from or toward?) us, we may assume that they are interested in us.

(23) Waitresses who touch customers' arms are likely to receive (higher or lower?) tips.

(24) When men and women gaze into each other's eyes for a while, they are likely to develop feelings of (antagonism or passion?).

Think About It

Why is body language important to understanding how we adjust to our social environment?

Prejudice and Discrimination

- ❚ What is prejudice?
- ❚ What is discrimination?
- ❚ What are stereotypes?
- ❚ What are the origins of prejudice and discrimination?

Too often we consider race as something only Blacks have, sex orientation as something only gays have, gender as something only women have. If we don't fall into any of these categories, then we don't have to worry.

—Henry Louis Gates, Jr.

I imagine one of the reasons people cling to their hates so stubbornly is because they sense, once hate is gone, they will be forced to deal with pain.

—James Baldwin

Some people have condemned billions of other people without ever meeting them, without ever learning their names. The reason is prejudice.

Prejudice is a preconceived attitude toward a group or person. It is formed without a critical evaluation of the facts or evidence and often without any direct knowledge of the group or person. Prejudice generally involves negative evaluations of others. (In some cases, we may form prejudices in favor of certain groups—such as our own ethnic or cultural group.) Prejudice is linked to expectations that the target group will perform poorly, in school or the workplace, or engage in undesirable behavior, such as criminal activity. Emotionally speaking, prejudice is associated with negative feelings such as dislike or hatred. Behaviorally, prejudice is expressed by avoidance of the targeted group (keeping a distance), by direct aggression toward them, or by discrimination against them.

Racism is a negative prejudice or bias held toward members of particular groups. Yet it is not the only form of prejudice. *Sexism* involves negative attitudes toward women, such as holding beliefs that women are incapable of assuming managerial or executive positions. In recent years, we have become more sensitive to another form of prejudice—ageism. "Ageists" assume that older people are less capable of performing on the job or that they are easily irritated or "crotchety." Many ageists assume that senior citizens cannot (or should not) engage in sexual activity (Rathus, Nevid, & Fichner-Rathus, 2008). None of these schemas are statements of fact. Yet senior citizens may also internalize these prejudices, leading them to foreclose on opportunities for productive work or intimate relations.

Prejudice is an attitude people hold toward particular groups or people. It sets the stage for **discrimination**, or overt negative behavior or actions toward members of a particular group or groups. Discrimination can take many forms, including denial of jobs, housing, voting rights, club memberships, and even seats in restaurants. Many groups in the United States have encountered discrimination—women, gay males and lesbians, older people, and ethnic groups such as African Americans, Asian Americans, Latino and Latina Americans, Irish Americans, Jewish Americans, and Native Americans.

Discrimination is also associated with **stereotypes**. A stereotype is a fixed, conventional belief about members of a particular group. For example, do you believe that women are emotional? That Jews are shrewd? That African Americans are superstitious? That Asians are inscrutable? That people with disabilities are unable to work? If you hold such views, you are endorsing stereotypes. How many of these stereotypes do you believe? Do you have evidence for them? If you identify with any of these

❚ **Prejudice** The belief that a person or group, on the basis of assumed racial, ethnic, sexual, or other features, will possess negative characteristics or perform inadequately.

❚ **Discrimination** The denial of privileges to a person or group on the basis of prejudice.

❚ **Stereotypes** Fixed, conventional ideas about a group that can lead us to process information about members of the group in a biased fashion.

groups, how does it make you feel to read these stereotypes about your own group? Do you believe more of the stereotypes about other groups than your own? If so, why?

Some stereotypes have an element of truth (e.g., the French tend to like wine) (McCrae & Terracciano, 2005). But despite these kernels of truth, stereotypes are overgeneralizations and fail to take into account individual differences (some French people do abstain from wine and other alcoholic beverages). Negative stereotypes can damage relationships among groups and be used to justify social inequalities. For example, stereotyped beliefs among the European colonial powers that Africans lacked the ability to govern themselves was long used as an excuse for maintaining colonial rule. Stereotyping obese people as lazy or undisciplined can lead us to pass them over for promotions or turn them down for demanding jobs.

6.4.1 Sources of Prejudice and Discrimination

Prejudice and discrimination bring out the worst aspects of human nature. The sources of prejudice and discrimination are many and complex, such as those described in Table 6.3. Let us consider these sources in more depth.

- *Dissimilarity.* We tend to like people who hold attitudes similar to our own. People of different religions and races often have different backgrounds, however, giving rise to dissimilar attitudes. Even when people of different races share important values, they may assume that they do not.
- *Social conflict.* There is also a lengthy history of social and economic conflict between people of different races and religions. For example, southern whites and African Americans have competed for jobs, giving rise to negative attitudes, even lynchings (Green, Glaser, & Rich, 1998).
- *Social learning.* Children acquire some attitudes from others, especially their parents. Parents who model prejudiced attitudes may transmit these ways of thinking to their children, especially if they reinforce their children for expressing prejudiced beliefs. ("Yeah, you're right, son. Those people aren't to be trusted"). The mass media can also perpetuate stereotypes. Even today, TV commercials often portray European Americans, especially men, as being more prominent and wielding more authority than African Americans (Coltraine & Messineo, 2000).
- *Information processing.* From a cognitive point of view, we can think of prejudice as a type of filter through which we perceive the social world. It is easier to attend to, and remember, instances of behavior that are consistent with our

Table 6.3 ❚ Sources of Prejudice	
Dissimilarity	People prefer to affiliate with people who have similar attitudes. People of different religions and races often have different backgrounds, which may give rise to dissimilar attitudes. People also tend to assume that people of different races have different attitudes, even when they do not.
Social conflict	Social and economic conflict give rise to feelings of prejudice. People of different races and religions often compete for jobs, giving rise to feelings of prejudice.
Social learning	Children acquire some of their attitudes by observing other people, especially their parents. Parents often reinforce their children for behaving in ways that express their attitudes, including prejudices.
Information processing	Prejudices serve as cognitive schemes or anchors, filters through which people perceive the social world. It is usually easier to remember instances of behavior that are consistent with prejudices than those that might force people to reconstruct their mental categories.
Social categorization	People tend to divide their social world into "us" and "them." People usually view people who belong to their own groups—the "ingroup"—more favorably than those who do not—the "outgroup" (Bettencourt et al., 2001).

prejudices (our mental filters or schemas) than it is to reconstruct our concepts (Kashima, 2000). If you believe that Jews are stingy, it is easier to recall a Jewish person's negotiation of a price than a charitable donation. If you believe that Californians are airheads, it may be easier to recall TV images of surfing than of scientific conferences at Caltech and Berkeley.

■ *Social categorization.* The cognitive perspective also focuses on people's tendencies to divide the social world into "us" and "them." People usually view those who belong to their own groups—the "ingroup"—more favorably than those who do not—the "outgroup" (Aboud, 2003; Dovidio et al., 2003). Moreover, we tend to assume that outgroup members are more alike, or homogeneous, in their attitudes and behavior than members of our own groups, whom we tend to view as "different as snowflakes" (Nelson, 2002). Our isolation from outgroup members makes it easier to maintain our stereotypes.

6.4.2 Combating Prejudice and Discrimination

Prejudice has existed throughout history, and we doubt that "miracle cures" are at hand to eradicate it fully. However, as we shall see, a number of measures have met with some success. In many cases, it is easier to deal with discrimination, the behavioral manifestation of prejudice. For example, laws now prohibit denial of access to jobs, housing, and other social necessities on the basis of race, religion, disability status, and related factors. Let us consider ways of combating prejudice.

Role Reversal: An Immunization Technique?

In a classic experiment by Weiner and Wright (1973), white third-graders were assigned at random to "Green" or "Orange" groups and identified with armbands. First, the "Green" people were labeled inferior and denied social privileges. After a few days, the pattern was reversed. Children in a second class did not receive the "Green–Orange treatment" and served as a control group.

Following this treatment, children from both classes were asked whether they wanted to go on a picnic with African American children from another school. It was found that 96% of the "Green–Orange" group expressed a desire to go on the picnic, as compared with 62% of the controls. The experience of prejudice and discrimination apparently led the "Green–Orange" children to think that it was wrong to discriminate on the basis of color. Perhaps being discriminated against made them more mindful of the sensitivities and feelings of members of outgroups. Unless we are encouraged to actively consider our attitudes toward others, we may automatically rely on previously conceived ideas, and these ideas are very often prejudiced.

Intergroup Contact

Intergroup contact can help break down stereotypes and reduce prejudice. But, as recognized by psychologist Gordon Allport (1954), intergroup contact alone is not enough. In fact, some forms of intergroup contact may actually increase negative attitudes by bringing differences between groups into sharper focus.

As Allport recognized, in order for intergroup contact to reduce prejudice and group tensions, four conditions need to be met (Brewer & Brown, 1998):

1 *Social and institutional support.* People in positions of authority or responsibility must support efforts to bring groups together rather than keeping them apart.

2 *Acquaintance potential.* Opportunities must exist for people of different groups to get acquainted with each other. In this way, people come to see that members of other religious and racial groups have varying values, abilities, interests, and personalities. Awareness of individual variation in turn can weaken stereotypical thinking (Hewstone & Hamberger, 2000; Sherman & Frost, 2000).

ColorBlindImages/Getty Images, Inc

Intergroup Contact
Intergroup contact can reduce feelings of prejudice, especially when people work together toward common goals. Intergroup contact also heightens awareness that individuals within an ethnic group vary, and this knowledge can lead us to abandon stereotypical thinking.

3 *Equal status.* Groups must occupy similar positions of status when they come together. When groups meet on an equal footing, it is more difficult to maintain prejudiced beliefs.

4 *Intergroup cooperation.* Working cooperatively with members of other groups to accomplish common goals can help reduce prejudice (Dixon, Durrheim, & Tredoux, 2007; Pettigrew & Tropp, 2006). Playing on the same team, working together on an educational project, or working on the yearbook are examples. Finally, let us add that prolonged contact is more effective than brief contact.

Seeking Compliance with the Law

On a personal level, it is appropriate to demand legal recourse if we have been discriminated against on the basis of race, religion, disability, or ethnicity. While "we cannot legislate morality," people can be compelled to modify illegal behavior.

Self-Examination

We may not be able to screen out all prejudiced and stereotyped thoughts, but we can make conscious decisions to challenge and correct them, and at the very least, not act upon them. As individuals, we can take steps to counter prejudiced thinking. But simply telling ourselves not to think in stereotypical terms may actually backfire by strengthening prejudiced thinking by virtue of bringing these beliefs more readily to mind. Nonetheless, evidence teaches that it is possible to change prejudiced attitudes (Livingston & Drwecki, 2007).

Social psychologists offer a number of suggestions to counter prejudiced thinking. Here are a handful of suggestions (e.g., Kunda & Spencer, 2003; Nelson, 2002; Turner, Hewstone, & Voci, 2007):

- Practice rejecting prejudiced and stereotypical thoughts when they occur.
- Picture positive examples of people from other groups.
- Participate in cooperative activities in which you interact with people of different backgrounds.
- Take part in diversity education programs, such as workshops or seminars on prejudice and intergroup conflict.

Raising Tolerant Children

Reducing prejudice may begin with helping our children develop more tolerant attitudes. We can do so by setting a good example of tolerance and promoting positive attitudes toward members of other groups.

We can begin setting a better example for our children by reducing our own prejudices. For example, we can reject prejudiced beliefs when they occur, rehearse positive images in our minds of members of others groups, and participate in intergroup activities and diversity education programs.

MODULE REVIEW

Review It

(25) _____ is an attitude toward a group that leads people to evaluate members of that group negatively.

(26) Denial of access to rights and privileges on the basis of group membership is termed _____.

(27) A _____ is a fixed, conventional idea about a group.

(28) Sources of prejudice include assumptions of attitudinal (similarity or dissimilarity?).

(29) Among the ways of combating prejudice and discrimination are role reversal, fostering intergroup contact, seeking compliance with the law, _____ of attitudes, and raising tolerant children.

(30) Helping children develop more _____ attitudes can help reduce the development of prejudice.

Think About It

If you were to advise college officials on ways of reducing prejudice and fostering tolerance on your campus, what steps would you suggest?

MODULE 6.5

Attribution Theory and Personal Adjustment

▪▪▪▪▪▪▪▪▪▪▪▪▪▪▪▪▪▪▪▪▪▪▪▪

- ▌ What is the attribution process?
- ▌ What are two major types of attributions?
- ▌ What are some types of attributional biases?

The pizza delivery man comes 30 minutes late. Do you assume that he's late because he's lazy or undisciplined? Or do you think he was late because he got stuck in traffic or had to wait for other pies to come out of the oven? Either case is an example of an **attribution**—a personal explanation of the causes of behavior. In this module we focus on the **attribution process**—the ways in which people draw conclusions about the factors that influence behavior. The attribution process is important to adjustment because our attributions lead us to perceive other people, and ourselves, as either purposeful actors or victims of circumstances.

Social psychologists describe two general types of attributions—dispositional attributions and situational attributions. In making **dispositional attributions**, we ascribe a person's behavior to internal factors, such as personality traits and free will. In making **situational attributions**, we attribute a person's actions to external factors such as social influence or socialization. Let's return to the pizza delivery guy. Which type of attribution are you using if you believe his lateness was due to laziness? Which are you using if you ascribe his behavior to getting stuck in traffic?

The Fundamental Attribution Error

In cultures that view the self as independent, people tend to attribute other people's behavior primarily to internal factors such as personality, attitudes, and personal choice (Kitayama et al., 2003). This bias in the attribution process is known as the **fundamental attribution error**. In such individualistic societies, people tend to focus on the behavior of others rather than on the circumstances surrounding their behavior. For example, if a teenager gets into trouble with the law, people in individualistic societies are more likely to blame the teenager than the social environment in which the teenager lives.

When it comes to explaining why the pizza arrived cold, you're likely to blame the pizza delivery guy, not the traffic conditions. When involved in difficult negotiations, the tendency is to attribute the toughness to the personalities of the negotiators on the other side rather than the nature of the process of negotiation. One reason for the fundamental attribution error is that we tend to infer traits from behavior. But in cultures that stress interdependence, such as Asian cultures, people are more likely

▌ **Attribution** A belief concerning why people behave in a certain way.

▌ **Attribution process** The process by which people draw inferences about the motives and traits of themselves and others.

▌ **Dispositional attribution** An assumption that a person's behavior is determined by internal causes, such as personal attitudes or goals.

▌ **Situational attribution** An assumption that a person's behavior is determined by external circumstances, such as the social pressure found in a situation.

▌ **Fundamental attribution error** The tendency to assume that others act on the basis of choice or will, even when there is evidence suggesting the importance of their situations.

Sean Locke/iStockphoto

Cold Pizza
How does the fundamental attribution error come into play in making attributions about why the pizza delivery guy arrives late?

▌ **Actor-observer effect** The tendency to attribute our own behavior to external, situational factors but to attribute the behavior of others to internal, dispositional factors such as choice or will.

▌ **Self-serving bias** The tendency to view one's successes as stemming from internal factors and one's failures as stemming from external factors.

to attribute other people's behavior to a person's social roles and obligations. For example, Japanese people might be more likely to attribute a businessperson's extreme competitiveness to the "culture of business" rather than to his or her personality.

The fundamental attribution error is linked to another bias in the attribution process: the *actor-observer effect*.

The Actor-Observer Effect

With apologies for overusing the same example, when we arrive late, why are we less likely to blame ourselves than we are to blame others who arrive late? The answer may be explained by the **actor-observer effect** (Pronin, Gilovich, & Ross, 2004). When we see people (including ourselves) doing things that we do not like, we tend to see the others as willful actors but to see ourselves as victims of circumstances. The tendency to attribute other people's behavior to dispositional factors and our own behavior to situational influences is called the actor-observer effect.

Consider an example. Parents and children often argue about the child's choice of friends or dates. In such situations, the parents tend to infer traits from behavior and to see the children as stubborn and resistant. The children also infer traits from behavior. Thus, they may see their parents as bossy and controlling. Parents and children alike attribute the others' behavior to internal causes. That is, both make dispositional attributions about other people's behavior.

How do the parents and children perceive themselves? The parents probably see themselves as being forced to take action by their children's foolishness. If the parents become insistent, it is in response to the children's stubbornness. The children probably see themselves as responding to social pressures to "fit in" and, perhaps, to sexual urges that may have come from within but seem like a source of outside pressure.

Both parents and children tend to see their own behavior as motivated by external forces. That is, they make situational attributions for their own behavior. The actor-observer effect extends to our perceptions of both ingroups (groups with which we identify) and outgroups (other groups). Consider conflicts between nations, for example. Both sides may engage in brutal acts of violence. Each side usually considers the other to be calculating, inflexible, and—not infrequently—sinister. Each side also typically views its own people as victims of circumstances and its own violent actions as justified or dictated by the situation. After all, we may consider the other side to be in the wrong, but can we expect them to agree with us?[2]

The Self-Serving Bias

Daniel told his buddy that he got an A in history but that his chemistry professor gave him a D. How might you explain the discrepancy in Daniel's explanation of his grades, the difference between what he "got" (an A) and what he was "given" (a D)?

Psychologists point to a common attributional bias, the **self-serving bias**, to explain this pattern of thinking (Roese & Olson, 2007). The self-serving bias is the tendency to ascribe our successes to factors within ourselves (internal or dispositional factors) but explain our failures to factors outside ourselves (external or situational influences) (Mezulis et al., 2004). For instance, when we have done well in a college course or impressed a date, we are likely to credit ourselves for our intelligence or charm. But when we fail, we are likely to blame external factors, such as bad luck, an unfair professor, or our date's bad mood. In this way, the self-serving bias serves to bolster our self-esteem.

---

[2] We are not suggesting that all nations are equally blameless (or blameworthy) for their brutality toward other nations. We are pointing out that there is a tendency for people of a nation to perceive themselves as being driven to undesirable behavior. Yet they are also likely to perceive other nations' negative behavior as willful.

There are exceptions to the self-serving bias. In accord with the bias, when we work in groups, we tend to take the credit for the group's success but to pin the blame for group failure on someone else. But the outcome is different when we are friends with other group members: Then we tend to share the credit for success or the blame for failure (Campbell et al., 2000). Another exception is that depressed people are more likely than other people to ascribe their failures to internal factors, even when external forces are mostly to blame.

Let us note a prevalent gender difference in attributions for friendly behavior. Men are more likely than women to interpret a woman's smile or friendliness toward a man as flirting (Buss, 2000). Such cues may be misread, of course, leading men to believe that women are more interested in them than they actually are.

Cultural Differences in Attributional Biases

Let's say two people take and fail the same exam. One person is a Chinese national; the other, a person from the United States or Canada. One says, "It was all my fault. I'll strive to do better the next time." The other says, "The test was unfair. I'd like another chance to prove what I know."

Can you guess which individual is likely to be the Chinese national and which the North American? Chances are that the first was Chinese and the other was the North American. The question is: Why?

The self-serving bias (SSB) is more widespread in Western cultures, such as the United States and Canada, than it is in East Asian cultures, such as Japan, China, and Taiwan (Chang & Asakawa, 2003; Mezulis et al., 2004). Consequently, the Chinese are more likely to attribute personal failure to lack of ability and successes to luck, which is the opposite of the pattern we typically find among North Americans. Recall our discussion of collectivist cultures from Chapter 2. Collectivist cultures are organized around the social connections and obligations among people (Oyserman, Coon, & Kemmelmeier, 2002). Taking credit for individual achievement is frowned upon. But expressing *proper humility* and self-criticism in the face of failure and affirming the need to work harder to improve oneself is deemed honorable (Nisbett, 2003). People in Western cultures tend to prize individual achievement and believe that they should be credited for their successes. But because they also value self-esteem, they rely on the self-serving bias to bolster their self-worth in the face of failure or disappointment.

Layne Murdoch/Getty Images, Inc.

"We're Number One!"
Ever notice how people tend to identify more with winning teams and to distance themselves from losing teams? They are more apt to say "We're number one!" when their favorite team wins but "They stink!" when the team loses. We tend to bask in reflected self-esteem when the team we support wins and protect our self-esteem by distancing ourselves from a losing team.

MODULE REVIEW

Review It

(31) The ways in which we infer the motives and traits of others based on observation of their behavior is called the_____ process.

(32) _____ attributions ascribe a person's behavior to internal factors, whereas _____ attributions attribute a person's actions to external factors such as social influence.

(33) The tendency to attribute other people's behavior primarily to internal factors such as personality, attitudes, and free will is known as the_____ _____ error.

(34) The tendency to attribute other people's behavior to dispositional factors and our own behavior to situational influences is known as the _____ effect.

(35) Chinese people are (less likely or more likely?) to attribute personal failure to lack of ability than are people in Western cultures.

Think About It

Explain why we tend to hold others accountable for their misdeeds but excuse ourselves for the bad things we do.

Psychology in Daily Life

MODULE 6.6

Enhancing Self-Esteem

No one can make you feel inferior without your consent.

— *Eleanor Roosevelt*

In this chapter we reviewed theory and research concerning the self—your physical self, your social self, and your personal self. Self-esteem is a major part of your personal self, and low self-esteem is a key source of psychological distress. Evidence from cross-cultural studies shows that humans the world over appear to have a need to feel good about themselves (DuBois & Flay, 2004; Sheldon, 2004).

High self-esteem is linked to many positive outcomes, including higher grade point averages, greater persistence in striving toward goals, and emotional stability or well-being (Di Paula & Campbell, 2002; Trzesniewski et al., 2006). Although self-esteem tends to be relatively stable throughout life (Trzesniewski, Donnellen, & Robins, 2003), we can give it a boost. In this module, we focus on ways of raising self-esteem.

6.6.1 Expand Your Competencies

The bookstores are stacked with self-improvement books—everything from becoming a better gardener to learning how to dress for success. What can you do to improve yourself? What skills can you strengthen or acquire? Whether you are 20 or 50, you can develop new skills and interests. The first author recalls asking his ski instructor how long he had been skiing. "Eighteen months," he said. "I started when I was 52." Then there are the things that interest you. Are you a movie buff? Why not read up on the history of cinema? Do you enjoy listening to piano? Why not take some lessons? Do you like dance but are a few pounds overweight? Check out the local studios and you'll find people of many body types in those leotards. The point is that you do not have to become perfect at the things that interest you. Through self development, you will enhance your self-esteem and give yourself more things to chat about with others at the same time.

6.6.2 Challenge the Tyranny of the "Oughts" and "Shoulds"

Our "oughts" and "shoulds" can create such perfectionistic standards that we are constantly falling short and experiencing frustration. One way of adjusting to perfectionistic self-demands is to challenge them and, when appropriate, to revise them. It may be harmful to abolish worthy and realistic goals, even if we do have trouble measuring up now and then. However, some of our goals or values may not stand up under our close scrutiny, and it is always healthful to be willing to consider them objectively.

Table 6.4 shows the kinds of thoughts that can be damaging to our self-esteem and alternatives that can enhance it. There is no mystery to making our thoughts more productive. Cognitive-behavioral psychologists suggest that we can work to directly change the thoughts with which we make ourselves miserable. We can read through the thoughts in the left-hand column of the table and consider whether we assault ourselves with them, or with thoughts like them. Then we can read over the suggested alternatives in the right-hand column. The suggested alternatives may fit you well, or they may not. If the suggested alternatives are not ideally suited to you, don't latch onto their shortcomings as reasons for tossing them onto the scrap heap. Instead, ask yourself what kinds of thoughts are more closely suited to your personality and your situation. Then work on using them to replace the thoughts that make you miserable. Again, read through the list.

When you come across thoughts that characterize you, consider the alternatives. Then, when you find yourself thinking those self-

Building Self-Esteem
Self-esteem is the hallmark of a healthy personality. People can boost their self-esteem by developing skills or competencies that help them achieve their goals, by striving toward realistic, attainable goals, and by coming to accept themselves when they fall short of perfection.

Table 6.4 ▌ Thoughts That Undermine Self-Esteem and Alternatives That Can Enhance Self-Esteem	
Irrational Thoughts That Undermine Self-Esteem	**Rational Thoughts That Lead in the Direction of Enhancing Self-Esteem**
There's nothing I can do to feel better about myself.	There are things I can do to feel better about myself, even if I can't think of them this minute. Take your time; don't give up the ship.
I have to be perfect at everything I do.	Nobody is perfect at everything. It's better to pick one or a few things that I'm pretty good at and develop them.
It's awful if _____ doesn't approve of me.	I'd prefer to have _____'s approval, but I can live without it. And maybe I'd have to do things that seem wrong to me to earn _____'s approval.
My body is a disaster.	My body isn't perfect, true, but is it really a "disaster" or am I judging myself according to unrealistic standards of perfection? And if there are shortcomings, what is to be gained by thinking of myself as a disaster? Let me think instead about what can be changed for the better and how I can do it—according to a reasonable schedule. Change can take time, and I need to work at things and give myself time to improve. When it comes to the things that can't be changed, I'll live with them; and since they got changed, there's no point in being down on myself because of them.
I have no idea what to do about my personal problems.	Okay, at this minute I don't know what to do about them. And if I can't come up with solutions, would it be a good idea for me to get some help? From whom? How should I go about it?
It really hurts when someone criticizes me.	Most people feel bad when they're criticized. If the criticism is justified, maybe it's something I can work on. If it's not, then it's the other. How will I go about it?
It really hurts when someone criticizes me.	Most people feel bad when they're criticized. If the criticism is justified, maybe it's something I can work on. If it's not, then it's the other person's problem, not mine.
I'm different from other people.	No two people are exactly alike, and that's a good thing. How can I develop and take full advantage of my differences?
If people knew the real me, they would despise me.	Nobody's perfect. We probably all have urges and ideas that we're better off to keep to ourselves. But is there something I should be changing? If so, how will I go about it?
I should try to be what other people want me to be.	No—if I try to be what other people want me to be, I'm foreclosing the opportunity to learn about my own capabilities and preferences. What can I do to figure out who *I* am? What can I do to develop the person that I am?
I'm just going to put my problems out of my mind.	It's not a bad idea to put problems on hold if they're not too painful and there are other things that have to get done right now. But is that the story with me now, or am I trying to pretend that they don't exist? If so, will they get worse, or will they go away by themselves? I have some thinking and decision making to do before I just push things out of my mind.
I should avoid striking up a conversation because I'll just be rejected.	Maybe I will be rejected, but my own opinion of myself can withstand possible rejection by others. You hit it off with some people and don't with others—that's reality. On the other hand, could I profit from developing some conversation skills? If so, how should I go about it?
I wish I could be like other people.	Danger! I'm myself; I'm not other people. Who am I? What are my real feelings about things? What can I do to arrive at my own decisions and maximize my own potential? I may never quarterback the football team, but perhaps I can write a good story. I may never be the world's hottest social magnet, but perhaps I can make myself more interesting by having experiences and interests that are worth talking about.
You can't blame me for being down on myself when you consider how hard my family was on me.	My family may have done things to hurt my self-esteem, but I'm a big girl/boy now and I'm responsible for my own feelings and my own behavior. It's time for me to maximize my own potential—not the things my family expected of me—and to get out into the world on my own.

defeating thoughts, challenge them and think the alternatives. Why not bookmark the page for easy reference for a while? (It couldn't hurt.)

We can also note that the second and third thoughts—those that indicate perfectionism and a powerful need for social approval—have been identified by psychologist Albert Ellis as the kinds of thoughts that are guaranteed to make us miserable and keep us miserable. We will refer to them repeatedly throughout this book. Get rid of them. They're not doing you any good.

6.6.3 Have a Crisis (Really? Perhaps the Answer Is Yes)

Your conception of your ideal self may not reflect the "you" that you'd like to become. Let's untwist that for you. You may be clinging to someone else's concept of what you ought to be, not your own. The truth is that it will never fit you; it will never feel right. Spend the time—and have the courage—to carefully evaluate the you that you'd really like to become, not someone else's version of you. Perhaps you foreclosed the opportunity to develop a real you by adopting other people's values and their goals for you.

A crisis can be good for you. (Really.) If you haven't yet experienced an identity crisis—carefully evaluated your values and your direction in life, thought deeply about who *you* are and what *you* stand for—perhaps the time to do so is now, or very soon. If you're studying for a big test or the like, why not "make an appointment" with yourself to sit down and begin to think things through the day after or on the weekend? You would make an appointment to see the doctor or an adviser, wouldn't you? Making an appointment with yourself to begin to come to grips with who you are and what it all means could be one of the most important "meetings" in your life.

6.6.4 Substitute Realistic, Attainable Goals for Unattainable Goals

It may be that we shall never be as artistic, as tall, or as graceful as we would like to be. We can work to enhance our drawing skills, but if it becomes clear that we shall not become Michelangelos, perhaps we can just enjoy our scribbles for what they are and also look to other fields for satisfaction. We cannot make ourselves taller (once we have included our elevator shoes or heels, that is), but we can take off five pounds and we can cut our time for running the mile by a few seconds. We can also learn to whip up a great chicken cacciatore.

Build Self-Efficacy Expectations

Our self-efficacy expectations, or confidence in our ability to accomplish tasks, are a major determinant of our willingness to undertake challenges and persist in meeting them. Our self-efficacy expectations define the degree to which we believe that our efforts will bring about a positive outcome. We can build self-efficacy expectations by selecting tasks that are consistent with our interests and abilities and then working at them. Many tests have been devised to help us focus on our interests and abilities. They are often available at your college testing and counseling center. But we can also build self-efficacy expectations by working at athletics and on hobbies.

Remember: Realistic self-assessment, realistic goals, and a reasonable schedule for improvement are the keys to building self-efficacy expectations. The chances are that you will not be able to run a four-minute mile, but after a few months of reasonably taxing workouts under the advice of a skilled trainer, you might be able to put a couple of 10-minute miles back to back. You might even enjoy them!

CHAPTER REVIEW

RECITE!   RECITE!   RECITE!   RECITE!   RECITE!   RECITE!   RECITE!

Study Tip: Reciting the answers to these study questions will help you become a more effective learner. First try answering the questions by yourself, either reciting them out loud or writing them in a notebook or on the computer. Then compare your answers with the sample answers provided below.

1. **What is the self?**
   The self is the core or center of your psychological being. It is an organized and consistent way of perceiving yourself as a unique being—an "I." The self also involves your perceptions of the ways in which you relate to the world.

2. **What are the parts of the self?**
   The self has physical, social, and personal aspects. Our social selves are the masks and social roles we don to meet the requirements of our situations. Our personal selves are our private inner identities.

3. **What's in a name?**
   Names are linked to expectations by parents and society at large. People with common names are usually rated more favorably, but people with unusual names often accomplish more. We have given names, but the names we choose to go by—often nicknames—can say much about how we view ourselves.

4. **What is the importance of our values?**
   Our values give rise to our personal goals and tend to place limits on the means we use to reach them. We are more subject to social influences when we do not have personal values or when our values are in flux.

5. **What is the self-concept?**
   Your self-concept is your impression or concept of yourself. It includes your perception of the traits (fairness, competence, sociability, and so on) you possess and the degree to which you deem these traits to be important in defining yourself.

6. **What are the origins of self-esteem?**
   Self-esteem begins to develop as the reflected appraisal of how we are regarded by important figures in our lives, especially parents. Children who are cherished by their parents, and receive their approval and support, usually come to see themselves as being worthy of love. Research suggests that

the children of strict parents are more likely than the children of permissive parents to develop high self-esteem. Although self-esteem can be a relatively stable element of personality, it can also vary depending on external events—such as test grades or other people's acceptance—and our emotional reaction to them.

7. What is the ideal self?

The ideal self is our concept of what we ought to be. The more your self-description is in keeping with your ideal self, the higher your self-esteem is likely to be.

8. What is self-identity?

Self-identity is your sense of who you are and what you stand for.

9. What are identity statuses?

Identity statuses are categories that describe an individual's level of self-identity. The psychologist James Marcia identified four identity statuses: identity achievement, identity foreclosure, identity moratorium, and identity diffusion. The status of identity achievement describes people who have resolved an identity crisis and are committed to a relatively stable set of beliefs or a course of action. Identity foreclosure describes people who have adopted a commitment to a set of beliefs or a course of action without undergoing an identity crisis. Identity moratorium describes people who are in the throes of an identity crisis; they are undergoing an intense examination of alternatives. Identity diffusion describes people who have neither arrived at a commitment as to who they are and what they stand for nor experienced a crisis.

10. What are the connections between ethnicity and other socio-cultural factors—such as gender—and identity?

People from ethnic minority groups often need to come to terms with conflicting values—those that characterize their particular ethnic background and those that characterize the dominant (European American, middle-class) culture in the United States. Erikson's views of identity development were intended to apply mainly to males because they focused on embracing a philosophy of life and commitment to a career at a time when most women remained in the home. Today, however, identity achievement in terms of a career is as important to women as it is to men in our society.

11. What is social perception?

Through the process of social perception, we come to form impressions of other people and develop attitudes about people and social issues.

12. Why are first impressions so important?

First impressions obtain their importance from the primacy effect. That is, we tend to infer traits from behavior. If people act considerately at first, they are conceptualized as considerate people, and their future behavior is interpreted according to that view of them.

13. Why should we think about people's body language?

People's body language provides important information about their thoughts and feelings, which can help us adjust in social situations. For example, when people lean toward us, they are usually showing interest in us.

14. What is prejudice?

Prejudice is a preconceived attitude toward a group that typically leads people to evaluate members of that group in negative terms.

15. What is discrimination?

Discrimination is negative behavior or actions that result from prejudice. It includes denial of access to jobs and housing.

16. What are stereotypes?

Stereotypes are fixed conventional ideas about groups of people, such as the stereotypes that Italian Americans are hot-tempered and Chinese Americans are deferential.

17. What are the origins of prejudice and discrimination?

Sources of prejudice include dissimilarity (or assumptions of dissimilarity), social conflict, social learning, the relative ease of processing information according to stereotypes, and social categorization ("us" versus "them").

18. What is the attribution process?

The attribution process involves the ways in which people infer their own and others' motives and traits.

19. What are two major types of attributions?

In dispositional attributions, we attribute people's behavior to internal factors such as their personality traits and personal decisions. In situational attributions, we attribute people's behavior to external circumstances or forces.

20. What are some types of attributional biases?

According to the actor-observer effect, we tend to attribute the behavior of others to internal, dispositional factors. However, we tend to attribute our own behavior to external, situational factors. The so-called fundamental attribution error is the tendency to attribute too much of other people's behavior to dispositional factors. The self-serving bias refers to the finding that we tend to attribute our successes to internal, stable factors and our failures to external, unstable factors.

YOUR PERSONAL JOURNAL

REFLECT   REFLECT   REFLECT   REFLECT   REFLECT   REFLECT   REFLECT

Study Tip: Reflecting on how the concepts in the chapter relate to your own experiences encourages deeper processing, which makes the material more personally meaningful and fosters more effective learning. Use additional pages if needed to complete your answers.

1. How has your social self—the self you show to others—been influenced by your family, your community, and your ethnic heritage? For example, what social roles are you expected to play in your life?

   _____

   _____

   _____

   _____

2. One aspect of your personal self, or the inner you, is your development of personal values. Based on your reading of the text, what values are most important to you?

   _____

   _____

   _____

   _____

   _____

ANSWERS TO MODULE REVIEWS

Module 6.1

1. role schema
2. physical
3. more likely
4. physical
5. social
6. personal
7. do
8. values

Module 6.2

9. self-concept
10. Self-esteem
11. strict
12. does
13. ideal
14. self-identity
15. foreclosure/moratorium
16. commitment
17. foreclosure
18. dominant

Module 6.3

19. primacy
20. recency
21. rigid/straight-backed
22. toward
23. higher
24. passion

Module 6.4

25. prejudice
26. discrimination
27. stereotype
28. dissimilarity
29. self-examination
30. tolerant

Module 6.5

31. attribution
32. Dispositional/situational
33. fundamental attribution
34. actor-observer
35. more likely

RESPONSES OF A NATIONAL SAMPLE TO THE VALUES CLARIFICATION SURVEY

The following table shows the average rankings assigned the values by a recently drawn national sample of adults. The sample ranked security, peace, and freedom at the top of the list. Beauty, pleasure, and social recognition were ranked near the bottom, and accomplishment and physical comfort were placed about halfway down the list. Apparently, we're an idealistic bunch who place hard work ahead of physical pleasure—or so it seems from the survey of values. There are a number of interesting response patterns. In one, peace and freedom were ranked second and third on the list, but it appears that peace and freedom were not perceived as being linked to national security, which was ranked eleventh. Friendship was also apparently considered more valuable than love.

Ranking of Values, According to a National Sample

Family security	1	True friendship	10
A world at peace	2	National security	11
Freedom	3	Equality	12
Self-respect	4	Inner harmony	13
Happiness	5	Mature love	14
Wisdom	6	An exciting life	15
A sense of accomplishment•	7	A world of beauty	16
A comfortable life	8	Pleasure	17
Salvation	9	Social recognition	18

SCORING KEY TO SELF-ACCEPTANCE SCALE

To score this key, first *reverse* the numbers you wrote in for the following items: 2, 7, 15, 19, 21, 25, 27, and 32. For each of these items,

a. change a 1 to a 5
b. change a 2 to a 4
c. do not change a 3
d. change a 4 to a 2
e. change a 5 to a 1

Then add the numbers assigned to each item and write your total score here: _____.

INTERPRETATION

Your total score can vary from 36 to 180.

LOW SCORERS (36–110): Scorers in this range are expressing little self-acceptance. The lower your score, the less your self-acceptance. Your low self-acceptance is apparently related to feeling that there is something wrong with you, to general lack of confidence, and to shyness or withdrawal when social opportunities arise. Although many factors are related to low self-acceptance, one of them may be poor social skills. If your lack of self-acceptance and your social interactions are sources of distress to you, you may profit from trying some personal problem solving or seeking professional counseling.

AVERAGE SCORERS (111–150): Most of us score in this range. Most of us tend to be more self-accepting in some areas than in others, to have more self-confidence in some areas than in others, to feel more comfortable with some people than with others. Our self-acceptance can be enhanced in some cases by challenging irrational goals and self-expectations. In other cases, we may profit from enhancing our vocational, personal, or interpersonal skills.

HIGH SCORERS (151–180): Scorers in this range are highly self-accepting and self-confident. Your consistent sense of worth tends to provide you with support as you meet new people and confront new challenges.

- When you are trying to persuade someone, it helps to present both sides of the argument? (p. 234)

- People are more likely to donate money to worthy causes when they are in a good mood? (p. 246)

- When told to do so by an experimenter, most participants in a landmark but controversial study administered to another person what they had been told were painful electric shocks? (pp. 238–239)

- Coloring your hair purple or wearing rings through your nose may be a way of conforming to a social norm? (p. 242)

- Another famous study showed that three out of four people would express a belief held by other members of a group even if it was obvious that the group's belief was just plain wrong? (p. 243)

- People will do things as members of a mob that they would never do on their own? (p. 244)

- Women in Atlanta were more likely than men to receive help, especially from men, when they dropped coins on the street than were women in Seattle or Columbus? (p. 247)

Keren Su/Stone/
Getty Images, Inc

Most of us would be reluctant to wear blue jeans to a funeral, to walk naked on city streets, or, for that matter, to wear clothes at a nudist colony. Other people and groups can exert enormous pressure on us to behave according to their wishes or according to group norms. Social psychologists refer to this sort of pressure as **social influence**. Social influence is the area of social psychology that studies the ways in which people alter the thoughts, feelings, and behavior of other people. The key thing about social influence for you—as a citizen and as a student of the psychology of adjustment—is recognizing social influence for what it is, being able to evaluate when it is appropriate, and, when necessary, being able to resist it.

Social influence The area of social psychology that studies the ways in which people influence the thoughts, feelings, and behavior of other people.

In this chapter, then, let us elaborate on the influences of other people as they affect our feelings and our behavior. In doing so, we will touch on some fascinating topics, such as the power of TV commercials to persuade us to buy and the possibility that most of us—if not all of us—can be pressured to do things that are repugnant to us.

But this chapter offers more than a "warning." We suggest a way in which you can prevent yourself from being pressured by other people: the adoption of assertive behavior. Assertive behavior allows you to express your genuine feelings and to say no to unreasonable requests. Assertive behavior not only helps you resist the demands of others. It also helps you to express positive feelings of appreciation, liking, and love.

Let us move on to our first topic in the psychology of social influence: persuasion. Then we will consider obedience to authority (which is not always a good thing), group behavior, conformity, and altruism and helping behavior (which may not occur as often as it should).

MODULE 7.1

Persuasion: Of Hard Pushing, Soft Pedaling, and You

▪ What are the two routes by which persuasive appeals can change attitudes?
▪ What factors foster persuasion?
▪ What is the foot-in-the-door technique?
▪ What is low-balling?
▪ What is the bait-and-switch technique?

Think about how often during the day someone tries to influence you. When you watch TV, you are bombarded with commercials trying to persuade you to buy the products advertised. Your teachers, your doctors, your religious leaders, politicians, your parents—even the authors of the books you read—try to influence you to think or act in a certain way. But can you really change people? The answer is decidedly yes. Marketers wouldn't spend millions in advertising fees if they didn't have evidence that their money was well spent. And as for your teachers, parents, and the like, you may not always agree with them, but chances are that they, too, succeed in persuading you to see things their way at least some of the time.

7.1.1 Factors of Persuasion

In this module we examine factors related to getting a message across: factors related to the content of the message itself, factors related to the messenger or source of the message, and factors related to the recipient of the message (see Figure 7.1). We also examine several commonly used sales techniques designed to elicit compliance from customers: the foot-in-the-door technique, low-balling, and bait-and-switch. We begin with a contemporary model of persuasion, the *elaboration likelihood model*, which proposes two different channels, or routes, by which persuasive appeals lead to attitude change.

A New Model of Persuasion: You Take the Low Road, I'll Take the High Road

▮ **Elaboration likelihood model** The view that persuasion occurs through two routes, a central route involving careful evaluation (elaboration) of the content of a persuasive message, and a peripheral route involving attention to associated cues that are peripheral to the content of the message.

The **elaboration likelihood model** of persuasion (ELM) focuses on two different routes by which persuasion works (Petty & Brinol, 2006; Petty, Wheeler, & Tormala, 2003). The first route, called the *central route*, involves careful consideration of the merits of the arguments and of the evidence at hand. The second route, called the *peripheral route*, involves persuasion by means of associating a persuasive message with cues that are peripheral to, or "to the side of," the content or meaning of the message.

Figure 7.1
Factors Involved in Getting Your Message Across
The effectiveness of persuasive appeals depends on characteristics of the source of the message, the message itself, and the recipient of the message.

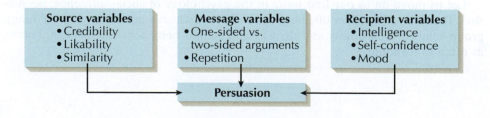

Source variables	Message variables	Recipient variables
• Credibility	• One-sided vs. two-sided arguments	• Intelligence
• Likability	• Repetition	• Self-confidence
• Similarity		• Mood

Persuasion

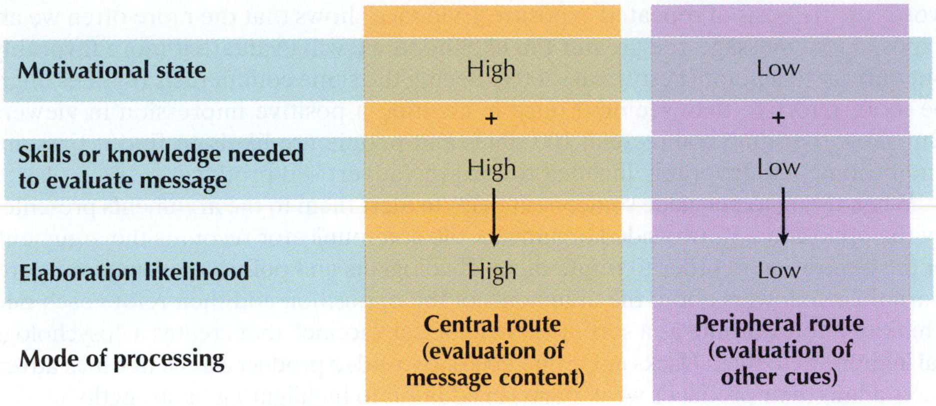

Motivational state	High	Low
	+	+
Skills or knowledge needed to evaluate message	High	Low
	↓	↓
Elaboration likelihood	High	Low
Mode of processing	Central route (evaluation of message content)	Peripheral route (evaluation of other cues)

Figure 7.2
The Elaboration Likelihood Model

The elaboration likelihood model holds that persuasion may occur through either a central or a peripheral route of cognitive processing. Under conditions in which elaboration likelihood is high, persuasion is more likely to occur through a central route whereby we carefully evaluate the content of the message itself. But when elaboration likelihood is low, as when we have little interest in the message or are too tired to pay close attention, persuasion may occur through a peripheral route involving the processing of cues that are unrelated to the content of the message.

For example, when you see a sports figure endorse a product, the marketer hopes that the appeal of the sports figure, a peripheral cue, will create a positive impression of the product. We may wind up purchasing a particular product because "such-and-such" endorses it, not because we've carefully researched the product to determine its value. Peripheral cues include such factors as the trustworthiness and attractiveness of the communicator. The elaboration likelihood model posits that people are more likely to carefully evaluate ("elaborate") a persuasive message when their motivational state is high (i.e., when the message is personally meaningful or important to them) and when they possess the skills or knowledge needed to evaluate the information (see Figure 7.2).

Advertisements may rely on either a central or peripheral route of persuasion. Some ads focus on the quality of the product (central route). But many others attempt to associate the product with appealing images (peripheral route). Ads for healthy cereals, which highlight their nutritional benefits, seek to persuade us through the central route. But ads that show football players heading for Disney World or choosing a brand of beer operate at the peripheral level of persuasion. We can think of the central route as the "high road" to persuasion, since it relies on more elaborate cognitive processing. The "low road," or peripheral route, relies on cues that are not directly related to the content of the message.

Let's apply the elaboration likelihood model to account for which road people are likely to use when evaluating a persuasive message. Consider a political debate. If viewers are well informed and interested in the issues, the likelihood is high that they will carefully evaluate the arguments each candidate makes. Thus, persuasion would occur through a central route (high elaboration). But if viewers are distracted or uninterested or lack the skills needed to weigh the merits of each candidate's arguments, elaboration likelihood will be low and the candidate with the winning smile may carry the day. That is, persuasion would occur through a peripheral route, in which the candidate's appearance, rather than the gravity of his or her views, would determine the outcome. Figure 7.2 shows the factors involved in determining the likelihood of elaboration—that is, whether attitude change is likely to occur through a central route or a peripheral route.

The Persuasive Message: Say What? Say How? Say How Often?

One factor involved in creating positive impressions is mere repetition. You might not be crazy about *zebulons* and *worbus* at first, but Robert Zajonc's (1968) classic research found that people began to react favorably toward these bogus foreign

© Reuters NewMedia Inc./Corbis Images

Would You Want This Man to Endorse Your Products?
Advertisers use a combination of central and peripheral cues to sell their products. What factors contribute to the persuasiveness of messages? To the persuasiveness of communicators? Why is Tiger Woods a sought-after commodity by advertisers?

▌ **Emotional appeals** A type of persuasive communication that influences behavior on the basis of feelings that are aroused instead of rational analysis of the issues.

words on the basis of repeated exposure. Evidence shows that the more often we are exposed to a message, the greater the likelihood we will evaluate it more favorably, but only up to a point (Petty et al., 2003). Seeing the same commercial 10 times might be more effective than seeing it once in creating a positive impression in viewers. But show the same commercial 100 times and people are likely to find it tiresome and become less favorably inclined toward the advertised product.

When trying to persuade someone, it helps to alert them to the arguments presented by the opposition. In two-sided arguments, the communicator recounts the arguments of the opposition in order to refute them. Theologians and politicians sometimes forewarn their followers about the arguments of the opposition and then refute each one. Think of a forewarning as a sort of "psychological vaccine" that creates a "psychological immunity" to them (Jacks & Devine, 2000). Two-sided product claims, in which advertisers admit their product's weak points in addition to highlighting its strengths, tend to be the most believable. For example, a motel chain advertised that it doesn't offer a swimming pool or room service but pointed out that the customer therefore saves money.

Emotional appeals, including fear appeals, often have strongly persuasive effects. In an illustrative study, women who were warned of the dire risk they would face if they failed to be screened for breast cancer were more likely to obtain mammograms than other women who were only informed of the benefits of mammography (Banks et al., 1995). But fear appeals need to be couched in terms of adverse outcomes that are more personally meaningful. In another study, health warnings about the risks of sun exposure were more effective in changing behavior when students were made aware of risks to their appearance (premature aging, wrinkling, and scarring of the skin) than when the warning dealt with the risk to their health (increased risk of skin cancer) (Jones & Leary, 1994). Why should fear of wrinkles motivate healthy behavior more than fear of cancer? The answer may be that personal appearance is more central to the student's present concerns. Fears about cancer may be relegated to the "do not open until age 50" mental bin. Audiences also tend to believe arguments that appear to run counter to the vested interests of the communicator. If the president of Ford or General Motors said that Toyotas and Hondas were superior, you can bet that we would prick up our ears. (Don't count on it.) But when an heir to the R. J. Reynolds tobacco fortune gave testimony to the U.S. Congress about the grievous health consequences of smoking, people listened.

The Persuasive Communicator: Whom Do You Trust?

Would you buy a used car from a person who had been convicted of larceny? Would you leaf through fashion magazines featuring homely models? Probably not. Persuasive communicators are characterized by such characteristics as credibility, likeability, trustworthiness, attractiveness, and similarity to their audiences. Because of the adoration of their fans, sports superstars such as Tiger Woods have also solidified their places as endorsers of products.

Health professionals enjoy high status in our society and are considered experts. It is not coincidental that toothpaste ads boast that their products have the approval of the American Dental Association.

We are reared not to judge books by their covers, but we are more likely to find attractive people persuasive. Corporations do not gamble millions on unappealing actors to hawk their products. Some advertisers seek out the perfect combination of attractiveness and plain, simple folksiness with which the audience can identify. Ivory Soap commercials sport "real folks" with comely features who are so freshly scrubbed that you might think you can smell Ivory Soap emanating from the TV set.

The Context of the Message: Get 'Em in a Good Mood

You are too shrewd to let someone persuade you by buttering you up, but perhaps someone you know would be influenced by a sip of wine, a bite of cheese, and a sincere compliment. Elements of the immediate environment, such as music, increase the likelihood of persuasion. Also, people tend to be more receptive to persuasive appeals when they are in a good mood (Park & Banaji, 2000). They are also more likely to give money to worthy causes when they are feeling good (Batson, Daniel, & Powell, 2003). Perhaps they tend to see things in a more positive light when they are feeling good. But prior warnings that a persuasive appeal is coming may stiffen resistance; people tend to be less persuaded when they receive a prior warning than when they are taken by surprise (Wood & Quinn, 2003).

The Persuaded Audience: Are You a Person Who Can't Say No?

Why do some people have sales resistance, whereas others enrich the lives of every telemarketer and door-to-door salesperson? For one thing, people with high self-esteem might be more likely to resist social pressure than people with low self-esteem. Moreover, people who are anxious when interacting with others may be more easily persuaded than people who are more self-assured.

In a classic study, Schwartz and Gottman (1976) identified thought patterns associated with social anxiety that make it more difficult for people to refuse requests. People who more readily comply with unreasonable requests are more apt to report thoughts like the following:

- "I was worried about what the other person would think of me if I refused."
- "It is better to help others than to be self-centered."
- "The other person might be hurt or insulted if I refused."

But people who refused unreasonable requests reported thoughts like these:

- "It doesn't matter what the other person thinks of me."
- "I am perfectly free to say no."
- "This request is unreasonable."

The lesson here is that the ability to assert ourselves in the face of unreasonable demands depends in large part on our inner dialogue—the thoughts we think or say to ourselves in these situations.

7.1.2 Sales Ploys: Saying No to Persuasive Sales Tactics

Have you ever paid more for a product than you intended when you walked into the store because a salesperson convinced you it was a good deal? Has a salesperson ever tried the old "bait-and-switch" ruse on you? Effective adjustment in our social world involves protecting your wallet or pocketbook by learning how to handle persuasive sales tactics.

The Foot-in-the-Door Technique

You might suppose that contributing money to door-to-door solicitors for charity will get you off the hook. Perhaps they'll take the cash and leave you alone for a while. Actually, the opposite is true. The next time they mount a campaign, they may call on you to go door to door on their behalf! Organizations compile lists of people they can rely on. They have learned that the "foot in the door" works. What is the **foot-in-the-door technique**? It's the technique that salespeople use when they get customers to accede to minor requests in order to prime them to agree to larger requests later on. Today telemarketers often call and ask people to answer "just a few" survey questions that will take "just a few minutes." But after the "survey" is taken, the sales pitch begins, and the telemarketer has gotten her or his foot in the door with you.

We can point to a number of reasons that people who accede to small requests become more amenable to larger ones, including their desire to be consistent (if you agreed once, you'll agree again) and their self-perception as the kind of people who

∎ **Foot-in-the-door technique** A method for inducing compliance in which a small request is followed by a larger request.

Purestock

Are You Being Low-Balled?
Have you ever been on the receiving end of a manipulative sales tactic, such as low-balling, bait-and-switch, or the foot-in-the-door technique? How well prepared are you to handle these social influence tactics?

▪ **Low-balling** A method in which extremely attractive terms are offered to induce a person to make a commitment. Once the commitment is made, the terms are revised.

▪ **Bait-and-switch** The sales tactic of baiting customers with low-priced but inferior merchandise and then switching them to a higher-priced item of more acceptable quality.

help in this way. Regardless of how the foot-in-the-door technique works, if you want to say no, it may be easier to do so (and stick to your guns) the first time a request is made. Later it may be more difficult, but forewarned is forearmed.

Low-Balling

Have you ever had a salesperson promise you a low price for merchandise, agreed to buy at that price, and then had the salesperson tell you that he or she had been in error or that the manager had not agreed to the price? Have you then canceled the order or stuck to your commitment? You might have been a victim of **low-balling**.

Low-balling is a sales method—also referred to as "throwing the low ball"—in which you are persuaded to purchase a product at an attractive price. But just before the deal is closed, it is abruptly yanked off the table and replaced by a less attractive offer. Let's say you agree to purchase a car for a certain amount, but the salesperson says he or she first needs to run it by the sales manager. The salesperson returns, mouthing something about the trade-in value of your old car coming in less than expected, and, well you could have the car, but it'll cost another $1,000. You've been low-balled. Committing yourself to accept the more favorable offer may make you more susceptible to agreeing to the subsequent, but less favorable, offer.

How might you protect yourself against low-balling? One possibility is to ask the salesperson whether he or she has the authority to make the deal and then to have him or her write out the terms and sign the offer. Unfortunately, the salesperson might later confess to misunderstanding what you meant by his or her having the "authority" to make the deal. Perhaps the best way to combat low-balling is to be willing to take your business elsewhere when the salesperson tries to back out of an arrangement.

Bait-and-Switch

Another frequently used sales technique designed to obtain compliance is the **bait-and-switch**. Here, a salesperson offers merchandise at an extremely low price. But when you examine the merchandise, it turns out to be missing some expected features or is of shoddy quality. Then comes the switch, as the salesperson offers a higher-quality, but more expensive, item in its place. The salesperson knows that, having expressed initial interest in the product, you may be more willing to buy the more expensive one. How prepared are you to handle these kinds of sales ploys? The nearby *Try This Out* will help you anticipate what you could say if you were faced with these manipulative sales ploys.

MODULE REVIEW

Review It

(1) According to the _____ _____ model, there are central and peripheral routes to persuasion.

(2) Messages that are delivered repeatedly tend to be (more or less?) effective than messages delivered once.

(3) Health professionals and celebrities (do or do not?) make effective salespeople in our society.

(4) According to the _____ _____ _____ _____ effect, people are more likely to agree to large requests after they have agreed to smaller ones.

(5) In the method of _____ _____, the customer is persuaded to make a commitment on favorable terms, and the salesperson then claims that he or she must revise the terms.

Think About It

Suppose you pursued a career in advertising. How would you use the information in this section to create a persuasive advertisement?

TRY THIS OUT — COUNTERING MANIPULATIVE SALES TACTICS

Let's say you are in the market for a new car. The salesperson shows you a model you like and after haggling for a while, you settle on a price that seems fair to you. The salesperson then says, "Let me get this approved by my manager and I'll be right back." What would you say to protect yourself against the types of influence tactics described in the text?

For each of the following examples, write your response in the column provided below. Then compare your answers with some sample responses you'll find at the end of the chapter.

Type of Tactic	What the Salesperson Says	What Do You Say Now?
Low-ball	"I'm sorry. He says we can't let it go for this amount. It has nothing to do with you, but he's getting more pressure from the boss. Maybe if we went back to him with another two or three hundred dollars, he'd accept it."	_____
Bait-and-switch	"My manager tells me that we're having difficulty placing orders for that model. Something to do with a strike in Osaka. We can definitely get the LX version, however. It's got some great features."	_____
Foot-in-the-door	"Okay, we can get you the car." After completing some of the paperwork, the salesperson slips in the following comment: "You know, you really should think about this factory-installed security system. You can never be too safe these days, you know."	_____

Source: Nevid (2007), p. 645. Reprinted with permission of Houghton Mifflin Company.

MODULE 7.2

Group Influences: Of Obedience, Conformity, and Mob Behavior

- Why are so many people willing to commit immoral acts when they are ordered to do so? (Why don't they refuse?)
- What is conformity?
- What factors enhance conformity?
- What is deindividuation and what factors foster it?

You may recall the famous quote from the sixteenth-century English poet John Donne, who wrote, "No man is an island, entire of itself." Today, we might paraphrase in gender-neutral language by saying that no one of us is an island, entire of itself. But Donne recognized that none us live in a social vacuum. We are social creatures and are influenced by the groups with which we interact in our daily lives. Here we examine several types of group influence—tendencies to obey the dictates of authority, tendencies to conform our behavior to social expectations, and tendencies to lose our individuality by becoming part of a mob.

Figure 7.3
The "Aggression Machine"
In the Milgram studies, pressing levers on the "aggression machine" constituted the operational definition of aggression.

7.2.1 Obedience to Authority: Does Might Make Right?

Throughout history, soldiers have followed orders—even when it comes to slaughtering innocent civilians. We may say we are horrified by such crimes and we cannot imagine why people engage in them. But how many of us would refuse orders issued by authority figures?

Victims of atrocities are often degraded by propaganda as being criminals or subhuman, which is used to justify maltreatment. Atrocities are also made possible through the compliance of people who are more concerned about the approval of their supervisors than about their own morality. Psychologists have long been concerned about understanding the nature of blind obedience. They have sought to answer the question: Why are so many people willing to commit crimes against humanity when they are ordered to do so? (Why don't they refuse?)

The Milgram Studies: Shocking Stuff at Yale

Psychologist Stanley Milgram also wondered how many of us would resist authority figures who made immoral requests. To find out, he ran a series of classic experiments at Yale University that still have many observers shaking their heads in disbelief. In an early phase of his work, Milgram (1963) placed ads in New Haven, Connecticut, newspapers asking for subjects for studies on learning and memory. He enlisted 40 men ranging in age from 20 to 50 from different "walks of life"—teachers, engineers, laborers, salespeople, men who had not completed elementary school, men with graduate degrees.

Let us suppose you had answered an ad. You would have shown up at the university for a fee of $7.50 (in 1960s dollars), for the sake of science or for your own curiosity. You might have been impressed. After all, Yale is a venerable institution that dominates the city. You would not have been less impressed by the elegant labs where you would have met a distinguished behavioral scientist dressed in a white laboratory coat and another newspaper recruit—like you. The scientist would have explained that the purpose of the experiment was to study the effects of punishment on learning. The experiment would require a "teacher" and a "learner." By chance, you would be appointed the teacher and the other recruit, the learner.

You, the scientist, and the learner would enter a laboratory room with a rather threatening chair with dangling straps. The scientist would secure the learner's cooperation and strap him in. The learner would express some concern, but this was, after all, for the sake of science. And this was Yale University, wasn't it? What could happen to a person at Yale?

You would follow the scientist to an adjacent room from which you would do your "teaching." This teaching promised to be effective. You would punish the "learner's" errors by pressing levers marked from 15 to 450 volts on a fearsome-looking console (see Figure 7.3). Labels described 28 of the 30 levers as running the gamut from "Slight Shock" to "Danger: Severe Shock." The last two levers resembled a film unfit for anyone under age 17: they were rated simply "XXX." Just in case you had no idea what electric shock felt like, the scientist gave you a sample 45-volt shock. It stung. You pitied the fellow who might receive more.

Your learner was expected to learn word pairs. Pairs of words would be read from a list. After hearing the list once, the learner would have to produce the word that was paired with the stimulus word. He would do so by pressing a switch that would signify his choice from a list of four alternatives. The switch would light one of four panels in your room (see Figure 7.4). If it was the correct panel, you would proceed to the next stimulus word. If not, you would deliver an electric shock. With each error, you would increase the voltage of the shock.

You would probably have some misgivings. Electrodes had been strapped to the learner's wrists (see Figure 7.5), and the scientist had applied electrode paste to "avoid blisters and burns." You were also told that the shocks would cause "no

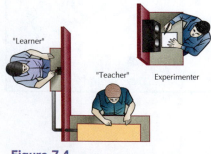

Figure 7.4
The Experimental Arrangement in the Milgram Studies
When the "learner" makes an error, the experimenter prods the "teacher" to deliver a painful electric shock.

permanent tissue damage," although they might be extremely painful. Still, the learner was going along, and, after all, this was Yale.

The learner answered some items correctly and then made some errors. With mild concern, you pressed the levers up through 45 volts. You had tolerated that much yourself. Then a few more mistakes were made. You pressed the 60-volt lever, then 75. The learner made another mistake. You paused and looked at the scientist. He was reassuring: "Although the shocks may be painful, there is no permanent tissue damage, so please go on." Further errors were made, and quickly you were up to a shock of 300 volts. But now the learner was pounding on the other side of the wall! Your chest tightened and you began to perspire. *Damn science and the $7.50!* you thought. You hesitated and the scientist said, "The experiment requires that you continue." After the delivery of the next stimulus word, there was no answer at all. What were you to do? "Wait for five to ten seconds," the scientist instructed, "and then treat no answer as a wrong answer." But after the next shock, there was again that pounding on the wall! Now your heart was racing and you were convinced that you were causing extreme pain and discomfort. Was it possible that no lasting damage was being done? Was the experiment that important, after all? What to do? You hesitated again. The scientist said, "It is absolutely essential that you continue." His voice was very convincing. "You have no other choice," he said, "you must go on." You could barely think straight, and for some unaccountable reason you felt laughter rising in your throat. Your finger shook above the lever. What were you to do?

On Truth at Yale To his own dismay, Milgram (1963, 1974) discovered what most people would do. Although some participants disobeyed commands to inflict painful and potentially dangerous shocks on learners, most of the people tested acceded to these commands (Packer, 2008). About two of three participants (65%) in an early phase of the study complied with the directives from the experimenter throughout the entire series of apparent shocks, inflicting what they were led to believe were 450-volt, XXX-rated shocks.

Were these newspaper recruits simply unfeeling? Not at all. Milgram was impressed by their signs of stress. They trembled, they stuttered, they bit their lips. They groaned, they sweated, they dug their fingernails into their flesh. There were fits of laughter, though laughter was inappropriate. One salesperson's laughter was so convulsive that he could not continue with the experiment.

What about women, who are supposedly less aggressive than men? Milgram conducted a later experiment with women and achieved results similar to those produced by the men. Milgram wondered if college students, heralded for independent thinking, would show more defiance. But a replication of the study with Yale undergraduates yielded similar results. All of this in a nation that values independence and the free will of the individual.

On Deception at Yale

You are probably skeptical enough to wonder whether the "teachers" in the Milgram study actually shocked the "learners" when they pressed the levers on the console. They didn't. The only real shock in this experiment was the 45-volt sample given to the teachers. Its purpose was to lend credibility to the procedure.

The learners in the experiment were actually confederates of the experimenter. They had not answered the newspaper ads but were in on the truth from the start. Teachers were the only real subjects. Teachers were led to believe that they were chosen at random for the teacher role, but the choosing was rigged so that newspaper recruits would always become teachers.

Milgram's research is now more than 40 years old, so we might ask whether people today would be as likely to commit bad deeds in situations where they are led to blindly follow authority. No experimenter has attempted a full replication of the Milgram studies because ethical guidelines now preclude the use of deception in studies that impose the kind of stress experienced by Milgram participants

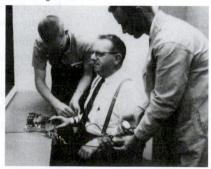

Figure 7.5
A "Learner" in the Milgram Studies on Obedience to Authority
This learner could be in for quite a shock.

(Burger, 2009; Elms, 2009). One recent study involving a partial replication of the Milgram procedure that stopped short of the highest level of shock (so as to avoid imposing undue stress on participants) showed similar rates of compliance to those in Milgram's original study (Burger, 2009). However, since some psychologists question the validity of the partial replication procedure (Elms, 2009; Miller, 2009; Twenge, 2009), the scientific jury is still out on whether people today are as likely as those in Milgram's time to obey such immoral commands.

The Big Question: Why? We have shown that most people obey the commands of others, even when pressed to perform immoral tasks. But we have not answered the most pressing question: Why? Why did Nazi soldiers in Germany during the Third Reich follow orders and commit atrocities? Why did "teachers" in the Milgram studies obey orders from the experimenter? We do not have all the answers, but we can offer a number of hypotheses (see Table 7.1):

1 *Propaganda.* Propaganda is used to dehumanize other groups. For example, Nazi propaganda held Jews and Gypsies to be subhumans—as infestations rather than people. Thus, slaughtering these people was likened to ridding the culture of vermin.

2 *Socialization.* Despite the expressed American ideal of independence, we are socialized to obey authority figures such as parents and teachers from early childhood on. Obedience to immoral demands may be the ugly sibling of socially desirable respect for authority figures.

3 *Lack of social comparison.* In Milgram's experimental settings, experimenters displayed command of the situation. Teachers (subjects), however, were on the experimenter's ground and very much on their own, so they did not have the opportunity to compare their ideas and feelings with those of other people in the same situation.

4 *Perception of legitimate authority.* One phase of Milgram's research took place within the hallowed halls of Yale University. Subjects might have been overpowered by the reputation and authority of the setting. An experimenter at Yale might have appeared to be a highly legitimate authority figure—as might a government official or a high-ranking officer in the military. Yet further research showed that the university setting contributed to compliance but was

Table 7.1 ❙ Factors That May Foster Blind Obedience	
Propaganda	People to be victimized are often degraded as being criminals or subhuman.
Socialization	People are socialized from early childhood to obey authority figures such as parents and teachers.
Lack of social comparison	Being on their own, subjects ("teachers") did not have the opportunity to compare their feelings with those of other people in the same situation.
Perception of legitimate authority	When Milgram's research took place at Yale University, subjects may have been influenced by the reputation and authority of the setting. An experimenter at Yale may have appeared to be a legitimate authority figure.
The foot-in-the-door technique	Once they had begun to deliver shocks to learners, subjects may have found it progressively more difficult to pull out of the situation.
Inaccessibility of values	People are more likely to act in accordance with their attitudes when their attitudes are readily available, or accessible. Most people believe that it is wrong to harm innocent people, but strong emotions interfere with clear thinking. As the subjects in the Milgram experiments became more upset, their attitudes may have become less accessible.
Buffers	Buffers may have decreased the effect of the learners' pain on the subjects (the "teachers"). For example, the learners were in another room.

not fully responsible for it. The percentage of individuals who complied with the experimenter's demands dropped from 65 to 48% when Milgram (1974) replicated the study in a dingy storefront in a nearby town.

At first glance, this finding might seem encouraging. But the main point of the Milgram studies is that most people are willing to engage in morally reprehensible acts at the behest of a legitimate-looking authority figure. Hitler and his henchmen were authority figures in Nazi Germany. Slobodan Milosevic was the authority figure in Serbia in the 1990s. "Science" and Yale University legitimized the authority of the experimenters in the Milgram studies. The problem of acquiescence to authority figures remains.

5 *The foot-in-the-door technique.* The foot-in-the-door technique might also have contributed to the obedience of the teachers. Once they had begun to deliver shocks to learners, they might have found it progressively more difficult to extricate themselves from the situation. Similarly, soldiers are first taught to obey orders unquestioningly in unimportant matters such as dress and drill. By the time they are ordered to risk their lives, they have been saluting smartly and following commands without question for a long time.

A CLOSER LOOK

Stanley Milgram: The Man Who Shocked the World

Stanley Milgram was born in the Bronx, New York, in 1933, the son of Jewish immigrants from Eastern Europe. Milgram excelled in school and achieved an IQ score of 158, the highest score among his high school classmates. He went on to attend Harvard University, where he studied with the famed personality theorist Gordon Allport and with a visiting professor, the social psychologist Solomon Asch. Asch's work on conformity (which is discussed later in the chapter) had a profound influence on the young Milgram, who devoted his dissertation study to national differences in conformity between people from Norway and France. But when Milgram graduated and embarked on an academic career in the early 1960s, he knew he needed to develop an important and distinctive research program to call his own. His decision to study obedience was rooted in his Jewish heritage and his determination to better understand the atrocities of the Holocaust. Milgram later wrote:

[My] laboratory paradigm…gave scientific expression to a more general concern about authority, a concern forced upon members of my generation, in particular upon Jews such as myself, by the atrocities of World War II…. The impact of the Holocaust on my own psyche energized my interest in obedience and shaped the particular form in which it was examined." (quoted in Blass, 2004, p. 62)

Milgram developed an experimental paradigm in which ordinary people were prodded by an experimenter to inflict on others what they were led to believe were painful electric shocks. The fundamental question Milgram would ask was, "Just how far would a person go under the experimenter's orders?" (Blass, 2004, p. 62).

Source: Adapted from *The Man Who Shocked the World* by Thomas Blass (Basic Books, 2004); reprinted from Nevid, 2007, p. 647, by permission of Houghton Mifflin Company.

6 *Inaccessibility of values.* People are more likely to act in accordance with their attitudes when they can easily bring them to mind (Kallgren, Reno, & Cialdini, 2000). Most people believe that it is wrong to harm innocent people. But powerful emotions disrupt clear thinking. As the teachers in the Milgram experiments became more aroused, their attitudes might thus have become less accessible to conscious awareness. As a result, it might have become progressively more difficult for them to behave according to their underlying attitudes.

7 *Buffers.* Several buffers decreased the effect of the learners' pain on the teachers. For example, the learners (who were actually confederates of the experimenter) were in another room. When they were in the same room with the teachers—that is, when the teachers had full view of their victims—the compliance rate dropped from 65% to 40%. Moreover, when the teacher held the learner's hand on the shock plate, the compliance rate dropped to 30%. In modern warfare, opposing military forces may be separated by great distances. They may be little more than a blip on a radar screen. It is one thing to press a button to launch a missile or aim a piece of artillery at a distant troop carrier or mountain ridge. It is quite another to hold a weapon to a victim's throat.

There are thus many possible explanations for obedience. Milgram's research has alerted us to a real danger—the tendency of many, if not most, people to obey the orders of an authority figure even when they run counter to moral values. It has happened before. It is happening now. What will you do to stop it?

7.2.2 Conformity: Do Many Make Right?

The police wouldn't cart you away to jail if you arrived at work in your pajamas (though the "fashion police" might). But someone would probably make a snickering comment and suggest you go home to change. Then again, you might be heralded as making a fashion statement and perhaps even start a new trend. Perhaps not; but in any event, we are expected to **conform** our behavior to **social norms**—the widely adopted standards of acceptable conduct that govern social behavior. Explicit social norms are often made into rules and laws such as those that require us to whisper in libraries and to slow down when driving past a school. There are also unwritten or implicit social norms, such as the manner of dress deemed appropriate in different social occasions and the expectation that we should face the front in an elevator. But what if other people on the elevator were facing the rear? Would you conform and turn in the same direction? Cornell University psychologist James Maas refers to a segment from the classic *Candid Camera* TV show that posed this social dilemma. A naive subject boards an elevator and faces the front. Then the next three people who board the elevator face the rear. The subject doesn't know that all three are actors who are in league with the producers of the show. By the time the third confederate boards the elevator, the naive subject has conformed and turned to face the rear (cited in Rakoff, 2000).

The tendency to make our behavior conform to social norms affects many aspects of our social behavior, from covering our mouths when we sneeze to not cutting in line to even choosing the "right" college ("You're going to State, just like your brother, isn't that right?"). You may fancy yourself a noncomformist by coloring your hair purple or wearing a nose-ring, but your behavior may fall in lockstep with your purple-haired nose-ringed peers.

The tendency to conform to social norms is often good. After all, we should be thankful when people cover their mouths when they sneeze. But group norms can also promote maladaptive behavior, as when people engage in risky behavior because "everyone is doing it." We don't necessarily conform under all circumstances. Sometimes we go against the crowd. But classic research by psychologist Solomon Asch in the early 1950s showed that we are more likely to conform than we might think.

Seven Line Judges Can't Be Wrong, Can They? The Asch Study

Do you believe your eyes and stick to your guns, even when others see things differently? Not if you were a subject in Asch's (1956) study. Imagine yourself in the following situation:

You enter a laboratory room with seven other subjects, supposedly taking part in an experiment on visual discrimination. At the front of the room stands a man holding cards with lines drawn on them.

The eight of you are seated in a series. You are given the seventh seat, a minor fact at the time. The man explains the task. There is a single line on the card on the left. Three lines are drawn on the card at the right One line is the same length as the line on the other card. You and the other subjects are to call out, one at a time, which of the three lines—1, 2, or 3—is the same length as the one on the card on the left. Simple.

The subjects to your right speak out in order: "3," "3," "3," "3," "3," "3." Now it's your turn. Line 3 in this first example is clearly the same length as the line on the first card, so you say "3." The fellow after you then chimes in: "3." That's all there is to it. Then another set of card is set up at the front of the room (see Figure 7.6). This time line 2 is clearly the same length as the line on the first card.

The six people on your right speak in turn: "1," "1..." Wait a second! "... 1," "1." You forget about dinner and study the lines briefly. No, line 1 is too short by a good half inch. But the next two participants say "1" and suddenly it's your

---

■ **Conform** To change one's attitudes or behaviors to adhere to social norms.

■ **Social norms** Explicit and implicit rules that reflect social expectations and influence the ways people behave in social situations.

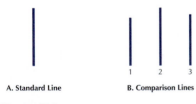

A. Standard Line   B. Comparison Lines

Figure 7.6
Stimuli Used in the Asch Study on Conformity
Which line on card B—1, 2, or 3—is the same length as the line on card A? Line 2, right? But would you be willing to say "2" if you were a member of a group and six other people had already answered "1"? Are you sure?

turn. Your hands have become sweaty, and there's a lump in your throat. You want to say "2," but is it right? There's really no time, and you've already paused noticeably. You say "1," and so— matter-of-factly—does the fellow who comes after you.

Now your attention is riveted on the task. Much of the time you agree with the other seven judges, but sometimes you don't. And for some reason beyond your understanding, they are in perfect agreement even when they are wrong—assuming you can believe your eyes. The experiment is becoming an uncomfortable experience, and you begin to doubt your judgment.

The discomfort in the Asch study was caused by the pressure to conform. Actually, the other seven recruits were confederates of the experimenter. They had pre-arranged a number of incorrect responses. The sole purpose of the study is to see whether you will conform to the erroneous group judgments.

How many people in Asch's study caved in? How many went along with the crowd rather than give what they thought to be the right answer? *Seventy-five percent*— three out of four agreed with the majority's wrong answer at least once. Asch himself was surprised by the results, for he didn't expect that so many people would bow under the pressure to conform and make an obviously incorrect response.

Why did they conform? Social psychologists suggest several explanations: (1) Participants may have assumed that the majority must be correct; (2) participants may have been more concerned with being liked by the group than caring whether their answers were correct; and (3) participants may have felt it was easier just to "go along" than to stand their ground and risk ridicule by others (Cialdini & Trost, 1998; Nowak, Vallacher, & Miller, 2003).

© Merrim/Photo Researchers, Inc.

Conformity
In the military, individuals are taught to conform until the group functions in machinelike fashion. What pressures to conform do you experience? Do you surrender to them? Why or why not?

Factors Influencing Conformity

Although we may all bend to conformity pressures in some situations, some of us are more likely to conform than others. Psychologists focus on both personal and situational factors to account for differences in conformity, including the following factors (Cialdini et al., 1999; Kallgren et al., 2000):

- Membership in a collectivist rather than an individualistic society
- Desire to be liked by other members of the group (but valuing being right over being liked decreases the tendency to conform)
- Low self-esteem
- Social shyness
- Lack of familiarity with the task

Other factors affecting conformity include group size and social support. The likelihood of conformity, even to incorrect group judgments, increases rapidly as group size grows to perhaps four or five members, then levels off with additional members. Yet finding just one other person who supports your minority opinion apparently is enough to encourage you to stick to your guns (Morris, Miller, & Spangenberg, 1977).

Getting Mobbed: Watch Out for the "Beast with Many Heads"

Mob actions such as race riots and lynchings sometimes seem to operate according to a psychology of their own, as we see next.

The Lynching of Arthur Stevens   In their classic volume *Social Learning and Imitation*, Neal Miller and John Dollard (1941) vividly described a lynching in the South. Arthur Stevens, an African American, was accused of murdering his lover, a European American woman, when she wanted to break up with him. Stevens was arrested and confessed to the crime. The sheriff feared violence and moved Stevens to a town 200 miles away during the night. But his location was uncovered. The next

© Paul Meredith/Getty Images, Inc

A Beast with Many Heads
Moblike behavior is irrational, like a "beast with many heads." Police know that it is best to break up mobs early, before outrage and deindividuation have spread among its members. Of course, there are constitutional issues involved, since people have the right to assembly. Put simply: The laws of the land often ask, "Where does your right to move your fist end—and my right to prevent my nose from being punched begin?"

day, a mob of a hundred persons stormed the jail and returned Stevens to the scene of the crime.

Outrage spread from person to person like a plague bacillus. Laborers, professionals, adolescents, and law enforcement officers alike were infected. Stevens was tortured and killed. His corpse was dragged through the streets. Then the mob went on a rampage in town, chasing and assaulting other African Americans. The riot ended only when troops were sent in to restore law and order.

Deindividuation   When people act as individuals, fear of consequences and self-evaluation tend to prevent them from engaging in antisocial behavior. But in a mob, they may experience deindividuation. **Deindividuation** is a state of reduced self-awareness and lowered concern for social evaluation. Many factors lead to this state (Cialdini & Goldstein, 2004; Nowak et al., 2003). These include anonymity (wearing a hood, for example, that conceals one's identity); **diffusion of responsibility** (the presence of others diffuses any sense of individual responsibility); arousal due to noise and crowding; and attending to, and conforming with, the social norms of the group rather than one's own core values. Under these circumstances, crowd members behave more aggressively than they would as individuals. But as individuals, we can resist deindividuation by cueing ourselves to stop and think whenever we begin to get swept up in the actions of a group. We can dissociate ourselves from such groups when they deviate from our personal values and thus be more likely to avoid behavior that we might later regret.

▮ **Deindividuation** The process by which group members discontinue self-evaluation and adopt group norms and attitudes.

▮ **Diffusion of responsibility** The dilution or loss of individual responsibility for behavior when members of a group act in unison.

MODULE REVIEW

Review It

(6) Milgram's research suggests that most people (do or do not?) comply with the demands of authority figures, even when the demands are immoral.

(7) When Milgram replicated his study with Yale students, he found that (fewer or about the same percentage of?) participants shocked the "learner."

(8) When he replicated the study with women, he found that (fewer or about the same percentage of?) participants shocked the "learner."

(9) The following factors contribute to obedience: socialization, lack of social _____, perception of experimenters as legitimate authority figures, and inaccessibility of values.

(10) Members of a (collectivist or individualistic?) society are more likely to conform to group norms.

(11) In Asch's studies of conformity, ____% of the subjects agreed with an incorrect majority judgment at least once.

(12) People who resist conforming to group norms tend to be (high or low?) in self-esteem.

(13) In *Social Learning and Imitation*, Miller and Dollard use the example of a _____ in their description of mob behavior.

(14) When people are members of mobs, they may experience _____, which is a state of reduced self-awareness and lowered concern for social evaluation.

(15) Factors that lead to deindividuation include anonymity, diffusion of _____, arousal, and group norms.

Think About It

Using the factors described in Table 7.1, account for why soldiers may be prompted to commit atrocities that go against their moral values.

Altruism and Helping Behavior: Preventing the Social Fabric from Tearing

Positive Psychology

- ▪ What is altruism?
- ▪ What factors foster helping behavior?
- ▪ Why do people sometimes ignore people who are in trouble?

We are all part of vast social networks—schools, industries, religious groups, communities, and society at large. Although we each have individual pursuits, in some ways our adjustment and personal development are intertwined. To some degree we depend on one another. What one person produces, another consumes. Goods are available in stores because other people have transported them, sometimes halfway around the world. A medical discovery in Boston saves a life in Taiwan. An assembly-line foul-up in Detroit places an accident victim in a hospital in Florida.

Altruism is a form of *prosocial* behavior, which is behavior that benefits the welfare of others (Warneken & Tomasello, 2006). Sharing, cooperation, comforting, and expressing empathy are other forms of prosocial behavior. Altruism is also characterized by helping behavior, whether it takes the form of pitching in to help a family in need, participating in a walk for a charitable cause, or donating blood or even bone marrow. Altruism sometimes takes the form of self-sacrificing behavior. Humans have been known to sacrifice themselves to ensure the survival of their children or of comrades in battle. Yet sometimes a victim's desperate cries for help go unheeded. Are people who simply stand by and do nothing while others die simply heartless?

▪ **Altruism** Unselfish concern for the welfare of others.

▪ **Bystander effect** The tendency for bystanders to fail to act to help a person in need.

Shannon Stapleton/Landov LLC

Altruism
There are many expressions of altruistic behavior, from helping a friend in need in heroic acts of self-sacrifice, such as those of the firefighters and police officers on 9/11 who raced up the stairs of the World Trade Center towers as they were burning to rescue people trapped above. But yet people stood by and did nothing when Kitty Genovese was viciously attacked. How could this have happened? Why did people fail to help?

7.3.1 The Bystander Effect: Some Watch While Others Die

How, one might ask, could the 1964 murder of 28-year-old Kitty Genovese have happened? It took place in New York City more than 40 years ago, but the shock it generated throughout the culture continues to resonate through the generations. Kitty screamed for help as her killer stalked her for more than half an hour and stabbed her in repeated attacks. A number of neighborhood residents (the exact number is unknown) heard the commotion and Kitty's cries for help. Yet nobody came to her aid. Only one person called the police—but only after the first attack had ended (Manning, Levine, & Collins, 2007). Why didn't people help?

The tendency to stand by and do nothing when others are in need is termed the **bystander effect**. Why did witnesses allow Kitty Genovese to die alone in the street? But as the heroic efforts of firefighters, police officers, and ordinary citizens who rushed into the burning towers on that terrible September day in 2001 illustrate so poignantly, people often do help others in need, even at the risk of their own lives. Consequently, we need to better understand the factors that underlie helping. Under what conditions do people tend to assist others in need? Under what conditions do they just pass by or do nothing?

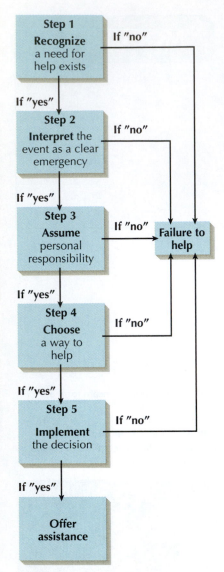

Figure 7.7
Decision-Making Model of Helping
Psychologists Bibb Latané and John Darley developed a five-step model of helping that posits that bystanders need to make a series of decisions before they will offer assistance to someone in need.

Bystander Intervention: Deciding to Help ... or Not?

Psychologists Bibb Latané and John Darley (1970) developed a decision-making model to explain why some bystanders help people in distress while others walk on by. The model proposes that for helping to occur, a bystander must make five independent decisions. But saying no at any one of these decision steps leads to a failure to help (see Figure 7.7).

1 *Bystanders must recognize that a need for help exists.* For a person to offer to help, the person must first recognize that a need for help exists. Does the other person need help, or can that person manage on his or her own?

2 *Bystanders must decide an emergency exists* (Baron & Byrne, 2000). Perhaps some people who heard Kitty Genovese's calls for help were not certain about what was happening. Perhaps they were confused about what they heard and whether it was a true emergency. Others admitted they did not want to get involved.

3 *Bystanders must assume the responsibility to act* (Staub, 2000; Suedfeld, 2000). It may seem logical that a group of people would be more likely to have come to the aid of Kitty Genovese than a lone person. After all, a group could more effectively have overpowered her attacker. Yet research by Darley and Latané (1968) suggests that a lone person may have been more likely to try to help her.

In their classic experiment, male subjects were performing meaningless tasks in cubicles when they heard a (convincing) recording of a person apparently having an epileptic seizure. When the men thought that four other persons were immediately available, only 31% tried to help the victim. When they thought that no one else was available, however, 85% of them tried to help. In other words, the presence of others may diffuse the sense of personal responsibility to get involved (Garcia et al., 2002). When people are in a group, they seem willing to let George (or Georgette) do it. When George isn't around, they may be more willing to help others in need. (Perhaps some who heard Kitty Genovese thought, "Why should I get involved? Other people can hear her, too.")

4 *Bystanders must choose a way to help* (Baron & Byrne, 2000). We hear of cases in which people impulsively jump into the water to save a drowning child and then drown themselves. Most of the time, however, people do not try to help unless they know what to do and feel they are capable of rendering help. Bystanders who are not sure that they can take charge of the situation may stay on the sidelines for fear of making a social blunder and being ridiculed. Or they may fear getting hurt themselves. (Perhaps some who heard Kitty Genovese thought, "If I try to help, I may get killed or make an idiot of myself.")

5 *Bystanders must implement the plan.* Choosing a way to help must be followed up by a decision to put the plan into action.

The Helper: Who Helps?

Many other factors affect helping behavior, including mood and empathy. For one thing, observers are more likely to help when they are in a good mood (Batson & Powell, 2003). Perhaps good moods impart a sense of personal power—the feeling that we can handle the situation. For another, people with a better-developed sense of empathy toward others are more likely to help people in need (Darley, 1993). Empathic people feel the distress of others, feel concern for them, and can imagine what it must be like to be in need. Women are more likely than men to be empathic and thus are more likely to help people in need (Trobst, Collins, & Embree, 1994).

The Victim: Who Is Helped?

People are more likely to help others they know (Staub, 2000; Suedfeld, 2000). Aren't we also more likely to give to charity when asked directly by a coworker or supervisor in the socially exposed situation of the office as compared with a letter received in the privacy of our own homes?

From the standpoint of evolutionary theory, altruism may be seen as part of our genetic nature, as it may have helped enable ancestral humans who carried our genetic code to survive a harsh and dangerous environment. Sacrificing one's interests for the sake of the group may have helped close relatives or other kinfolk who carried similar genes to survive. Thus, self-sacrifice may be an adaptive trait from a genetic or evolutionary point of view by virtue of helping to perpetuate a genetic code similar to our own. This view suggests that we are more likely to be altruistic with our relatives rather than with strangers, a view that is supported by research showing that people are more likely to help their kin than nonkin (Gaulin & McBurney, 2001). The Kitty Genoveses of the world may remain out of luck unless they are surrounded by kinfolk or friends.

People are also more likely to help people who are similar to themselves or with whom they identify (Penner et al., 2005). Similarity even extends to manner of dress, as evidence shows that people are more likely to help others who are dressed in a similar way than those in different attire (Cialdini & Trost, 1998).

Women are also more likely than men to be helped when their cars have broken down on the highway or they are hitchhiking. Is this gallantry, or are there sexual overtones to some of this "altruism"? There may be sexual overtones because attractive and unaccompanied women are most likely to be helped by men.

Although women are more likely than men to help people in need, it is traditional for men to help women, particularly in the South. Women were more likely than men to receive help, especially from men, when they dropped coins in Atlanta (a southern city) than in Seattle or Columbus (northern cities) (Latané & Dabbs, 1975). Why? The researchers suggest that traditional gender roles persist more strongly in the South.

People with more baby-faced features are also more likely to receive help than those with more mature features (Keating et al., 2003). Perhaps people with baby-faced features appear less able to fend for themselves.

Then there's the issue of race or ethnicity. Recent evidence suggests that blacks are less likely to receive help than whites under some conditions—when helping requires more time, when it involves more risk or effort, and when the person in need is farther away (Saucier, Miller, & Doucet, 2005). People may latch onto these reasons for not helping, rather than acknowledging to themselves or others that underlying racial prejudices play a role.

What will you do the next time you pass by someone who is obviously in need of aid? Will you help or will you stand by? Consider too that more than 40 million people worldwide are infected with HIV, with the great majority of cases occurring in developing countries in Africa and Asia (Ostermann et al., 2007). Many people infected with the virus will eventually die in agony unless wealthy nations like ours help them get the medicines they need. Are we going to help or will we just stand by?

©Howard Dratch/The Image Works

Would You Help This Stranded Motorist?
What factors determine whether people will assist someone in need? Would it make a difference if the stranded motorist were a woman? Why or why not?

MODULE REVIEW

Review It

(16) _____ is defined as selfless concern for the welfare of others.

(17) Altruism is characterized by _____ _____.

(18) The tendency to stand by and do nothing when others are in need is called the _____ effect.

(19) People are less likely to help others when they are among other people because of diffusion of _____.

(20) People are more likely to help people who are (similar or dissimilar?) to themselves.

Think About It

Why do many evolutionary psychologists believe that altruism is a natural aspect of human nature?

Psychology in Daily Life

MODULE 7.4

Becoming an Assertive Person (Winning Respect and Influencing People)

Positive Psychology

Short of living on a deserted island or in a cabin in the woods, we are all subject to social influences. The need to handle social pressures without losing our own individuality and stifling our needs and interests brings us to the issue of assertiveness. Assertive behavior involves many things—expressing your genuine feelings, standing up for your legitimate rights, and refusing unreasonable requests. It means withstanding undue social influences, disobeying *arbitrary* authority figures, and refusing to conform to *arbitrary* group standards. Since many of our feelings such as love and admiration are positive, assertive behavior also means expressing positive feelings ("That was great! You're wonderful!").

Assertive people also use the power of social influence to achieve desired ends. That is, they influence others to join them in worthwhile social and political activities. They may become involved in political campaigns, consumer groups, conservationist organizations, and other groups to advance their causes.

Alternatives to assertive behavior include submissive, or *unassertive*, behavior and *aggressive* behavior. When we are submissive, our self-esteem plummets.

Unexpressed feelings sometimes smolder as resentments and then catch fire as socially inappropriate outbursts. Aggressive behavior includes physical and verbal attacks, threats, and insults. Sometimes we get our way through aggression, but we also earn the condemnation of others. And, unless we are unfeeling, we condemn ourselves for bullying others.

Before reading further, you may wish to take the nearby self-assessment to gain insight into your level of assertiveness. Perhaps you can't become completely assertive overnight, but you can decide *now* that you have been unassertive long enough and plan to change. There may be times when you want to quit and revert to your unassertive ways.

Expressing your genuine beliefs may lead to some immediate social disapproval. Others may have a stake in your remaining a doormat, and the people we wind up confronting are sometimes those who are closest to us: parents, spouses, supervisors, and friends. If you choose to move ahead, you can use the following four methods to become more assertive: (1) self-monitoring, (2) challenging irrational beliefs, (3) modeling, and (4) behavior rehearsal.

Bob Handelman/Getty Images, Inc

Assertive Behavior
Psychologists distinguish between assertive behavior, unassertive (submissive) behavior, and aggressive behavior. Assertive behavior involves the expression of one's genuine feelings, standing up for one's legitimate rights, and refusing unreasonable requests. But it also has a more positive side: expressing feelings such as love and admiration.

The Rathus Assertiveness Schedule: Do You Speak Your Mind or Do You Hold Back?

Self-Assessment

What about you? Do you enrich the pockets of every telemarketer, or do you say no? Do you stick up for your rights, or do you allow others to walk all over you? Do you say what you feel or what you think other people want you to say? Do you initiate relationships with attractive people, or do you shy away from them?

One way to gain insight into how assertive you are is to take the Rathus Assertiveness Schedule. Once you have finished, turn to the end of the chapter to find out how to calculate your score. You'll find a table that allows you to compare your assertiveness to that of a sample of 1,400 students drawn from 35 college campuses across the United States. If you believe that you are not assertive enough, why not take the quick course in self-assertion offered here? You need not spend your life imitating a doormat.

Directions: Indicate how well each item describes you by using this code:

- 3 = very much like me
- 2 = rather like me
- 1 = slightly like me
- −1 = slightly unlike me
- −2 = rather unlike me
- −3 = very much unlike me

_____ 1. Most people seem to be more aggressive and assertive than I am.*

_____ 2. I have hesitated to make or accept dates because of "shyness."*

_____ 3. When the food served at a restaurant is not done to my satisfaction, I complain about it to the waiter or waitress.

_____ 4. I am careful to avoid hurting other people's feelings, even when I feel that I have been injured.*

_____ 5. If a salesperson has gone to considerable trouble to show me merchandise that is not quite suitable, I have a difficult time saying "No."*

_____ 6. When I am asked to do something, I insist upon knowing why.

_____ 7. There are times when I look for a good, vigorous argument.

_____ 8. I strive to get ahead as well as most people in my position.

_____ 9. To be honest, people often take advantage of me.*

_____ 10. I enjoy starting conversations with new acquaintances and strangers.

_____ 11. I often don't know what to say to people who are sexually attractive to me.*

_____ 12. I will hesitate to make phone calls to business establishments and institutions.*

_____ 13. I would rather apply for a job or for admission to a college by writing letters than by going through with personal interviews.*

_____ 14. I find it embarrassing to return merchandise.*

_____ 15. If a close and respected relative were annoying me, I would smother my feelings rather than express my annoyance.*

_____ 16. I have avoided asking questions for fear of sounding stupid.*

_____ 17. During an argument, I am sometimes afraid that I will get so upset that I will shake all over.*

_____ 18. If a famed and respected lecturer makes a comment which I think is incorrect, I will have the audience hear my point of view as well.

_____ 19. I avoid arguing over prices with clerks and salespeople.*

_____ 20. When I have done something important or worthwhile, I manage to let others know about it.

_____ 21. I am open and frank about my feelings.

_____ 22. If someone has been spreading false and bad stories about me, I see him or her as soon as possible and "have a talk" about it.

_____ 23. I often have a hard time saying "No."*

_____ 24. I tend to bottle up my emotions rather than make a scene.*

_____ 25. I complain about poor service in a restaurant and elsewhere.

_____ 26. When I am given a compliment, I sometimes just don't know what to say.*

_____ 27. If a couple near me in a theater or at a lecture were conversing rather loudly, I would ask them to be quiet or to take their conversation elsewhere.

_____ 28. Anyone attempting to push ahead of me in a line is in for a good battle.

_____ 29. I am quick to express an opinion.

_____ 30. There are times when I just can't say anything.*

Source: Reprinted from Rathus (1973), pp. 398–406.

For an interactive version of this self-assessment exercise, go to www.wileyplus.com

7.4.1 Self-Monitoring: Following Yourself Around the Block

Self-monitoring of social interactions can help you pinpoint problem areas and increase your motivation to behave more assertively. Keep a diary for a week or so. Jot down brief descriptions of any encounters that lead to negative feelings, such as anxiety, depression, or anger. For each encounter, record:

- The situation
- What you felt and said or did
- How others responded to your behavior
- How you felt about the behavior afterward

Here are some examples of self-monitoring. They involve an office worker (Kim), a teacher (Michael), and a medical student whose husband was a professor of art and archaeology (Leslie), all in their twenties:

Kim: Monday, April 6

9:00 A.M. I passed Artie in the hall. I ignored him. He didn't say anything. I felt disgusted with myself.

Noon. Pat and Kathy asked me to join them for lunch. I felt shaky inside and lied that I still had work to do. They said all right, but I think they were fed up with me. I felt miserable, very tight in my stomach.

7:30 P.M. Kathy called me and asked me to go clothes shopping with her. I was feeling down and I said I was busy. She said she was sorry. I don't believe she was sorry—I think she knows I was lying. I hate myself. I feel awful.

Kim's record reveals a pattern of fear of incompetence in social relationships and resultant avoidance of other people. Her avoidance may once have helped her to reduce the immediate impact of her social anxieties, but it has led to feelings of loneliness and depression. Now, because of Kim's immediate self-disgust, her defensive avoidance behavior doesn't even seem to help her in the short run.

Michael: Wednesday, December 17

8:30 A.M. The kids were noisy in homeroom. I got very angry and screamed my head off at them. They quieted down but sneaked looks at each other as if I were crazy. My face felt red and hot, and my stomach was in a knot. I wondered what I was doing.

4:00 P.M. I was driving home from school. Some guy cut me off. I followed him closely for two blocks, leaning on my horn but praying he wouldn't stop and get out of his car. He didn't. I felt shaky as hell and thought someday I'm going to get myself killed. I had to pull over and wait for the shakes to pass before I could go on driving.

8:00 P.M. I was writing lesson plans for tomorrow. Mom came into the room and started crying—Dad was out drinking again. I yelled that it was her problem. If she didn't want him to drink, she could confront him with it, not me, or divorce him. She cried harder and ran out. I felt pain in my chest. I felt drained and hopeless.

Michael's record showed that he was aggressive, not assertive. The record pinpoints the types of events and responses that had led to higher blood pressure and many painful bodily sensations. The record also helped him realize that he was living with many ongoing frustrations instead of making decisions—as to where he would live, for example—and behaving assertively.

Leslie: Tuesday, October 5

10:00 A.M. I was discussing specialization interests with classmates. I mentioned my interest in surgery. Paul smirked and said, "Shouldn't you go into something like pediatrics or family practice?" I said nothing, playing the game of ignoring him, but I felt sick and weak inside. I was wondering if I would survive a residency in surgery if my supervisors also thought that I should enter a less pressured or more "feminine" branch of medicine.

Thursday, October 7

7:30 P.M. I had studying to do but was washing the dinner dishes, as per usual. Tom was reading the paper. I wanted to scream that there was no reason I should be doing the dishes just because I was the woman. I'd worked harder that day than Tom, my career was just as important as his, and I had studying to do that evening. But I said nothing. I felt anxiety or anger—I don't know which. My face was hot and flushed. My heart rate was rapid. I was sweating.

Even though Leslie was competing successfully in medical school, men apparently did not view her accomplishments as being as important as their own. It may never have occurred to Tom that he could help her with the dishes or that they could rotate responsibility for household tasks. Leslie resolved that she must learn to speak out—to prevent male students from taunting her and to enlist Tom's cooperation around the house.

7.4.2 Confronting Irrational Beliefs: Do Your Own Beliefs Trigger Unassertive or Aggressive Behavior?

While you are monitoring your behavior, try to observe irrational beliefs that may lead to unassertive or aggressive behavior. These beliefs may be fleeting and so ingrained that you no longer pay any attention to them. But by ignoring them, you deny yourself the opportunity to evaluate them and to change them if they are irrational.

Kim feared social incompetence. Several irrational beliefs heightened her concerns. She believed, for example, that she must be perfectly competent in her social interactions or else avoid them.

She believed that it would be awful if she floundered at a social effort and another person showed disapproval of her, even for an instant. She also believed that she was "naturally shy," that heredity and her early environment must somehow have forged a fundamental shyness that she was powerless to change. She also told herself that she could gain greater happiness in life through inaction and "settling" for other-than-social pleasures like reading and television—that she could achieve contentment even if she never confronted her avoidance behavior. When shown Albert Ellis's list of 10 basic irrational beliefs (see Chapter 3), even Kim had to admit that she had unknowingly adopted nearly all of them.

Many of Michael's frustrations stemmed from a belief that life had singled him out for unfair treatment. How *dare* people abuse him? The *world* should change. With the world so unfair and unjust, why should he have to search out his *own* sources of frustration and cope with them? For example, Michael was attributing his own miseries to external pressures and hoping that if he ignored them, they would go away. With an alcoholic father and a weak mother, he told himself, how could *he* be expected to behave appropriately?

Shyness is another factor contributing to nonassertiveness. In the accompanying *Adjustment and Modern Life* feature, shyness expert Bernardo Carducci writes about the process of becoming successfully shy.

Women and Assertive Behavior: Problems Caused by Early Socialization Messages

Leslie failed to express her feelings because she harbored subtle beliefs to the effect that women should not be "pushy" and that they cause resentments when they compete in areas traditionally reserved for men. She kidded herself that she could "understand" and "accept" the fact that Tom had simply been reared in a home atmosphere in which women carried out the day-to-day household chores. She kidded herself that it was easier for her to remain silent on the issue instead of making a fuss and expecting Tom to modify lifelong attitudes.

Many women receive early socialization messages that underlie irrational beliefs in adult life. Among these messages are the following: "I need to rely on someone stronger than myself—a man," "Men should handle large amounts of money and make the big decisions," "It is awful to hurt the feelings of others," "A woman does not raise her voice," and "I should place the needs of my husband and children before my own." In the area of sexual behavior, women have frequently received these early socialization messages: that they need to be guided by men to achieve satisfaction; that only men should initiate sexual activity; that sexually assertive women are sluttish or castrating; and that women must use artificial means such as makeup and scented sprays to make themselves attractive. Beliefs such as these endorse the stereotypical feminine gender role and traits like dependence, passivity, and nurturance (at all costs). In short, they deny women *choice*.

Changing Irrational Beliefs

Do any of Kim's, Michael's, or Leslie's irrational beliefs also apply to you? Do they prevent you from behaving assertively? From making the effort to get out and meet people? From expressing your genuine feelings? From demanding your legitimate rights?

Do they sometimes prompt aggressive rather than assertive behavior? If so, you may decide to challenge your irrational beliefs. Ask yourself: Do they strike you as logical and well founded, or are they simply as habits of thought? Do they help you act assertively, or do they lead you to squelch your feelings or needs? What will

Adjustment and Modern Life

"Becoming Successfully Shy": Bernardo Carducci in His Own Words

As a researcher in the area of shyness for almost 25 years, I am frequently asked, "What can be done to cure shyness?" First of all, shyness is not a disease, a psychiatric disorder, a character flaw, or a personality defect that needs to be "cured." To deal effectively with their shyness, shy individuals need to increase their understanding of the nature of shyness. Since shyness involves excessive self-consciousness and self-preoccupation, along with difficulty meeting and talking to new individuals, the key to controlling shyness is to become more focused on others (Carducci, 2000a). One of the best ways I know to offset self-focused tendencies and difficulties associated with making connections with others is to become more involved in the lives of others by becoming a volunteer (Carducci, 2000b). Volunteering can serve to help shy people overcome many of the common difficulties created by being shy by offering the following benefits:

1. *Minimizing self-consciousness: You don't have to be perfect.* As a volunteer, the performance expectations on you are more relaxed—you don't have to be an expert, just someone who wants to help. Consequently, shy individuals can be less self-conscious and self-critical, and feel freer to be themselves and to devote more of their attention to the task at hand—helping others.

2. *Relieving social pressure: Expanding your comfort zone.* Volunteering allows shy individuals to experience new situations without the pressure to perform that they typically experience in social situations. The more places you can volunteer, the more comfortable you will feel in a variety of other social situations interacting with a variety of people.

3. *Having something to say: Built-in topics of conversation.* Since shy individuals typically have difficulty starting and maintaining conversations, they can use their volunteer experience to initiate conversations with other volunteers. Topics of conversation can be related to the motives for volunteering, services provided by the agency, news events related to the agency (e.g., more intact families coming to shelters), and any previous and additional experiences as a volunteer. Shy individuals can also use their volunteer experience as part of the basic steps needed to make successful conversation in social situations

(Carducci, 1999), including practicing such skills as personal introductions (e.g., "Hi, I'm Ronald; I'm a psychology major and volunteer at the animal shelter"), conversation starters (e.g., "I saw a cat do the funniest thing yesterday at the animal shelter"), and building ongoing topics of conversation (e.g., "Speaking of animals, I saw this wonderful documentary last week on pet therapy for the elderly").

4. *Expanding your social network: Fellow volunteers can become friends.* The people shy individuals meet through their volunteer activities can also become friends with whom they can socialize. Since they have already established a relationship with them through their volunteer efforts, the task of socializing with them becomes easier. For example, a shy individual can invite fellow volunteers for coffee or to attend an art opening, movie, or sporting event.

5. *Everybody benefits: A win–win solution.* In addition to the benefits gained by shy individuals through volunteerism, individuals who are the recipients of their services also benefit. So volunteerism is a win–win situation for everybody.

I propose a new solution to overcoming shyness—becoming "successfully shy" (Carducci, 2000b). Successfully shy individuals do not need to change who they are—remember, there is nothing wrong with being a shy person. Successfully shy individuals change the way they think and act. They think less about themselves and more about others and take actions that are more other-focused and less self-focused. They do not view shyness as a deficit. Instead, they view shyness as a characteristic feature of who they are and as an element of their personality they need to take into account, not something about themselves they despise. The key to being successfully shy is accepting one's shyness and responding proactively to control it, instead of letting shyness be in control.

Courtesy of Indiana University

As a shy adolescent and successfully shy adult, Bernardo J. Carducci, Ph.D., has been studying shyness for more than 25 years and is director of the Indiana University Southeast Shyness Research Institute and author of the book *Shyness: A Bold New Approach* (Carducci, 2000a).

If you think you, or someone you know, might want to deal directly with controlling your shyness, instead of letting your shyness control you, you can also find assistance in Dr. Carducci's 2005 book, *The Shyness Workbook: 30 Days to Dealing Effectively with Shyness,* which is published by Research Press.

happen if you try something new? What if your new behavior has a few rough edges at first? Will the roof cave in if someone disapproves of you? Will the consequences be as severe as you expect? Are exaggerated expectations of negative consequences holding you back?

7.4.3 Modeling: Creating the New—Well, Almost New—You

Much of our behavior is modeled after that of people we respect and admire, people who have seemed capable of coping with situations that posed some difficulty for us. Here and there we adopt a characteristic, a gesture, a phrase, a tone of voice, a leer, a sneer.

Therapists who help clients become more assertive use extensive modeling. They may provide examples of specific things to say. When we are interacting with other people, our ability to establish eye contact, our posture, and our distance from them also communicate strong messages. Direct eye contact, for example, suggests assertiveness and honesty. So therapists help clients shape nonverbal behaviors as well—whether to lean toward the other person, how to hold one's hands, how far away to stand, and so on. Then the client tries it. The therapist provides feedback—tells the client how well he or she did.

7.4.4 Behavior Rehearsal: Practice Makes Much Better

At first it is a good idea to try out new assertive behaviors in nonthreatening situations, such as before your mirror or with trusted friends. This is behavior rehearsal. It will accustom you to the sounds of assertive talk as they are born in your own throat. Therapists have clients rehearse assertive responses in individual or group sessions. They may use role playing, in which they act the part of a social antagonist or encourage you or other group members to take the roles of important people in your life. They alert you to posture, tone of voice, and the need to maintain eye contact.

Joan was a recently divorced secretary in her twenties. She returned home to live with her parents, and six months later her father died. Joan offered support as her mother, in her fifties, underwent several months of mourning. But Joan eventually realized that her mother had become excessively dependent on her. She no longer drove or went anywhere alone. Joan felt she must persuade her mother to regain some independence—for both their sakes. Joan explained her problem in an assertiveness-training group, a specialized form of group therapy that focuses on helping people develop assertiveness skills. The therapist and group members suggested things that Joan could say. A group member then role-played her mother while Joan rehearsed responses to her mother's requests.

Her goal was to urge independent behavior in such a way that her mother would eventually see that Joan was interested in her welfare. Joan showed that she understood her mother's feelings by first paraphrasing them. But she clung to her basic position through the broken-record technique in which she repeatedly held her ground, as in this sample dialogue:

MOTHER ROLE: Dear, would you take me over to the market?

JOAN: Sorry, Mom, it's been a long day. Why don't you drive yourself?

MOTHER ROLE: You know I haven't been able to get behind the wheel of that car since Dad passed away.

JOAN: I know it's been hard for you to get going again [paraphrase], but it's been a long day [broken record] and you've got to get started doing these things again sometime.

MOTHER ROLE: You know that if I could do this for myself, I would.

JOAN: I know that you believe that [paraphrase], but I'm not doing you a favor by driving you around all the time. You've got to get started sometime [broken record].

MOTHER ROLE: I don't think you understand how I feel. *[Cries.]*

JOAN: You can say that, but I think I really do understand how awful you feel but I'm thinking of your own welfare more than my own, and I'm not doing you a favor when I drive you everywhere [broken record].

MOTHER ROLE: But we need a few things.

JOAN: I'm not doing you any favor by continuing to drive you everywhere [broken record].

MOTHER ROLE: Does that mean you've decided not to help?

JOAN: It means that I'm *not* helping you by continuing to drive you everywhere. I'm thinking of your welfare as well as my own, and you have to start driving again sometime [broken record].

Joan's task was difficult, but she persisted. She and her mother reached a workable compromise in which Joan at first accompanied her mother while her mother drove. But after an agreed-upon amount of time, her mother began to drive by herself. We can use modeling on our own by carefully observing friends; business acquaintances; characters on television, in films, and in books—and noting how effective they are in their social behavior. If their gestures and words seem effective and believable in certain situations, we may try them out. Ask yourself whether the verbal and nonverbal communications of others would fit you if you trimmed them just a bit here and there. Sew bits and pieces of the behavior patterns of others together; then try them on for size. After a while you may find that they need a bit more altering. But if you wear them for a while once they have been shaped to fit you, you may come to feel as if you have worn them all your life.

CHAPTER REVIEW

RECITE! RECITE! RECITE! RECITE! RECITE! RECITE! RECITE!

Study Tip: Reciting the answers to these study questions will help you become a more effective learner. First try answering the questions by yourself, either reciting them out loud or writing them in a notebook or on the computer. Then compare your answers with the sample answers provided below.

1. What are the two routes by which persuasive appeals can change attitudes?

The central route involves the careful weighing of the content of messages. The peripheral route involves persuasion through cues that are peripheral to the content of the message.

2. What factors foster persuasion?

Emotional appeals are more effective with most people than are logical presentations. Repeated messages are usually more effective than messages presented once. People tend to be persuaded by celebrities, experts, and people who seem to be similar to themselves. People are more likely to be persuaded when they are in a good mood. People with low sales resistance tend to have low self-esteem and to worry about the impression they will make if they say no.

3. What is the foot-in-the-door technique?

With the foot-in-the-door technique, salespeople encourage customers to accede to minor requests to prime them to agree to larger requests later on.

4. What is low-balling?

Low-balling is a sales method in which the customer is persuaded to make a commitment on favorable terms, but the salesperson then says that he or she must revise the terms.

5. What is the bait-and-switch technique?

The customer is baited by an offer of merchandise at an extremely low price. But the merchandise appears to be of inferior quality or missing desirable features. The salesperson then pulls the switch by offering higher-quality but also more expensive merchandise.

6. Why are so many people willing to commit immoral acts when they are ordered to do so? (Why don't they refuse?)

Milgram found that the great majority of participants in his research would deliver a strong electric shock to an innocent party when instructed to do so by an experimenter. Possible reasons why people will commit atrocities include propaganda (degrading the victims), socialization, lack of social comparison, perception of the authority figure as being legitimate, inaccessibility of one's personal values, and lack of buffers.

7. What is conformity?

Conformity is changing one's behavior to adhere to social norms, such as facing forward in elevators or wearing what "people like us" are wearing.

8. What factors enhance conformity?

Factors that enhance the likelihood of conformity include belonging to a collectivist culture, the desire to be liked by others, low self-esteem, shyness, and lack of personal expertise in the situation.

9. What is deindividuation, and what factors foster it?

Deindividuation is a state of reduced self-awareness and lowered concern for social evaluation. Factors that foster deindividuation include anonymity, diffusion of responsibility, high levels of arousal, and focus on group norms rather than on one's own values. As members of crowds, many people engage in behavior they would find unacceptable if they were acting alone.

10. What is altruism?

Altruism is selfless concern for the welfare of others, which is characterized by helping others.

11. What factors foster helping behavior?

People are more likely to help others when they are in a good mood, are empathic, believe that an emergency exists, assume the responsibility to act, know what to do, and are acquainted with those in need.

12. Why do people sometimes ignore people who are in trouble?

When we are members of groups or crowds, we may ignore people in trouble because of diffusion of responsibility. We may be less likely to help when we feel that others are available to offer help, when we don't perceive a clear need for help, when we don't feel capable of helping, or when we fear being harmed ourselves.

YOUR PERSONAL JOURNAL

REFLECT   REFLECT   REFLECT   REFLECT   REFLECT   REFLECT   REFLECT

Study Tip: Reflecting on how the concepts in the chapter relate to your own experiences encourages deeper processing, which makes the material more personally meaningful and fosters more effective learning. Use additional pages if needed to complete your answers.

1. Put yourself in the position of one of Milgram's subjects. Would you have obeyed the experimenter's command to pull the shock lever? If not, why not? How confident are you that you could predict your response in this type of situation?

_____

_____

_____

_____

2. Had you been one of the people who heard Kitty Genovese's screams, would you have helped? Are you sure? What factors described in the text would probably increase your likelihood of helping someone in need? What factors might discourage your getting personally involved?

_____

_____

_____

_____

ANSWERS TO MODULE REVIEWS

Module 7.1

1. elaboration likelihood
2. more
3. do
4. foot-in-the-door
5. low-balling

Module 7.2

6. do
7. about the same percentage of
8. about the same percentage of
9. comparison

10. collectivist
11. 75
12. high
13. lynching
14. deindividuation
15. responsibility

Module 7.3

16. Altruism
17. helping behavior
18. bystander
19. responsibility
20. similar

SCORING KEY FOR THE RATHUS ASSERTIVENESS SCHEDULE (RAS)

Tabulate your score as follows: For those items followed by an asterisk (*), change the signs (plus to minus; minus to plus). For example, if the response to an asterisked item was 2, place a minus sign (–) before the two. If the response to an asterisked item was –3, change the minus sign to a plus sign (+) by adding a vertical stroke. Then add up the scores of the 30 items. Scores on the assertiveness schedule can vary from +90 to –90. The table will show you how your score compares to those of 764 college women and 637 college men from 35 campuses across the United States. For example, if you are a woman and your score was 26, it exceeded that of 80% of the women in the sample. A score of 15 for a male exceeds that of 55% of the men in the sample.

Percentiles for Scores on the RAS

Women's Scores	Percentile	Men's Scores
55	99	65
48	97	54
45	95	48
37	90	40
31	85	33
26	80	30
23	75	26
19	70	24
17	65	19
14	60	17
11	55	15
8	50	11
6	45	8
2	40	6
−1	35	3
−4	30	1
−8	25	−3
−13	20	−7
−17	15	−11
−24	10	−15
−34	5	−24
−39	3	−30
−48	1	−41

Source: Nevid and Rathus (1978).

SAMPLE RESPONSES TO "TRY THIS OUT"

1. *Low-ball technique.* You might say, "Sorry, that's my best offer. We agreed on a price and I expect you to stick to it."
2. *Bait-and-switch.* You might say, "If I wanted the LX version, I would have asked for it. If you're having problems getting the car I want, then it's your problem. Now, what are you going to do for me?"
3. *Foot-in-the-door technique.* You might say, "If you want to lower the price, we can talk about it. But the price I gave you is all I can afford to spend."

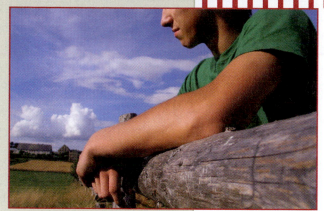

iStockphoto

This is the chapter in the text that students often turn to first. Perhaps they are curious about that odd fellow who mumbles to himself on the street. Or perhaps they have a friend or relative who has suffered from mental health problems such as depression or even schizophrenia and want to learn more about these conditions. Or perhaps they themselves are affected by psychological disorders or fear that they might be. If they are, they are certainly not alone. Psychological disorders, which the medical professional calls *mental disorders* or *mental illnesses*, are more common than people tend to think.

Chances are that you or someone close to you will suffer a diagnosable psychological disorder at one time or another. A major national study in the United States showed that psychological disorders affect about one in two adult Americans at some time in their lives (Kessler, Berglund, et al., 2005). All in all, psychological disorders are a major source of personal suffering and a major economic burden to society at large. When we take into account the people directly affected by psychological disorders and their families, as well as the economic costs of caring for people with mental health problems, then virtually every one of us is affected by these disorders.

Many effective treatments are available to help people suffering from psychological disorders, including psychotherapy and various types of psychiatric drugs. Despite these treatment alternatives, most people affected by psychological disorders do not receive adequate mental health care (Wang et al., 2005).

In this chapter we review the major types of psychological disorders. We discuss their symptoms or features and our current understanding about their causes. Learning about these disorders may raise your awareness about the kinds of psychological problems that you or people you know may encounter. But this chapter is not intended to make you a diagnostician. If you find that the discussion of these problems hits close to home, it would make sense to discuss your concerns with a qualified health professional.

MODULE 8.1

What Are Psychological Disorders?

❚ How do we define psychological disorders?

❚ How are psychological disorders grouped or classified?

❚ What are adjustment disorders?

As we noted in Chapter 1, psychology is the study of behavior and mental processes. Psychological disorders are behaviors or mental processes that are connected with various kinds of distress or impaired functioning. However, they are not expectable responses to specific events. For example, some psychological disorders are characterized by anxiety, but many people are anxious now and then without being considered disordered. It is appropriate to be anxious before an important date or on the eve of a midterm exam. When, then, are feelings like anxiety deemed to be abnormal or signs of a psychological disorder? For one thing, anxiety may suggest a disorder when it is not appropriate to the situation. It is inappropriate to be anxious when entering an elevator or looking out of a fourth-story window. The magnitude of the problem may also suggest disorder. Some anxiety is usual before a job interview. However, it is not usual to feel that your heart is pounding so intensely that it might leap out of your chest—and then avoiding the interview.

8.1.1 Criteria for Determining Abnormal Behavior

Mental health professionals apply a number of criteria in determining behavior they consider abnormal or disordered. These criteria include the following:

❚ **Hallucinations** Perceptions that occur in the absence of sensory stimulation and that are confused with reality.

❚ **Ideas of persecution** Erroneous beliefs that one is being victimized or persecuted.

1 *Unusualness.* Behaviors associated with psychological disorders may be unusual, but uncommon behavior or mental processes are not abnormal in themselves. Only one person holds the record for running or swimming the fastest mile. That person is different from you and me but is not abnormal. Only a few people qualify as geniuses in mathematics, but mathematical genius is not a sign of a psychological disorder.

Rarity or statistical deviance may not be sufficient for behavior or mental processes to be labeled abnormal, but it helps. Most people do not see or hear things that are not there, and "seeing things" and "hearing things" are considered abnormal. We must also consider the situation. Although many of us may feel "panicked" when we realize that a term paper or report is due the next day, most of us do not have full-fledged panic attacks, or episodes of sheer terror, that seem to come "out of the blue."

2 *Faulty perception or interpretation of reality.* Our society considers it normal to be inspired by religious beliefs but abnormal to believe that God is literally speaking to you. "Hearing voices" and "seeing things" are considered **hallucinations**. Similarly, **ideas of persecution**, such as believing that the Mafia or the FBI are "out to get you," are considered signs of disorder (unless, of course, they *are* out to get you).

3 *Significant personal distress.* Anxiety, fears, depression, and other psychological states are sources of personal distress, and personal distress beyond what would be expected in light of the person's life situation may be considered abnormal.

Scott Bohem/Getty Images, Inc.

Is This Behavior Abnormal?
One of the criteria professionals use to identify abnormal behavior is social deviance or acceptability. The style of dress and behavior of these men might not be considered deviant in the context of a football game but might be labeled abnormal in a work or school setting.

4 *Self-defeating behavior.* Behavior or mental processes that lead to personal misery rather than happiness and fulfillment may be suggestive of a psychological disorder. Chronic drinking or other forms of drug abuse that impair one's health and one's work and family life may therefore be deemed abnormal.

5 *Dangerousness.* Behavior or mental processes that are hazardous to the self or others may be suggestive of psychological disorders. People who threaten or attempt suicide may be considered abnormal, as may people who threaten or attack others. But, again, we need to take the situation into account. Criminal behavior may be dangerous to others (or to oneself) but not represent the product of a disordered mind. Controlled aggressive behavior in sports may be rewarded with lucrative contracts, not with a diagnosis of a psychological disorder.

6 *Social unacceptability in a given culture.* Mental health professionals take the cultural context into account in determining whether a particular behavior pattern is normal. Behavior that is acceptable in one culture may be considered abnormal in another. Among some North American Indian tribes, for example, it is understood that people may hear the voices of their departed loved ones speak out to them as they ascend to the afterlife. But such experiences may be considered signs of mental illness in contemporary American society.

8.1.2 Classifying Psychological Disorders

The most widely used classification scheme for psychological disorders (called mental disorders by the psychiatric profession) is the *Diagnostic and Statistical Manual* (DSM) of the American Psychiatric Association (2000). The current edition of the DSM is the DSM-IV-TR (Fourth Edition–Text Revision). The development of the next revision of the DSM, the DSM-V, is presently under way (Krueger & Markon, 2006).

The DSM uses a "multiaxial" system of assessment that provides information about a person's overall functioning, not just a diagnosis. The axes in the multiaxial system are shown in Table 8.1. People may receive either an Axis I (clinical syndromes) or Axis II (personality disorders and mental retardation) diagnosis, or a combination of the two.

Axis III, General Medical Conditions, lists physical disorders or problems that may affect people's functioning or their response to psychotherapy or drug treatment.

Table 8.1 ▍ The DSM Multiaxial Classification System

Axis	Type of information	Comments
Axis I	Clinical Syndromes	Includes psychological disorders that impair functioning and are stressful to the individual (a wide range of diagnostic classess, such as substance-related disorders, anxiety disorders, mood disorders, schizophrenia, somatoform disorders, and dissociative disorders).
Axis II	Personality Disorders (also used to code Mental Retardation)	Personality disorders are deeply ingrained, maladaptive ways of relating to others and behaviors that are stressful to the individual or to persons who relate to that individual.
Axis III	General Medical Conditions	Includes chronic and acute illnesses, injuries, allergies, and so on, that affect functioning and treatment.
Axis IV	Psychosocial and Environmental Problems	Identifies stressors that occurred during the past year that may have contributed to the development of a new mental disorder or the recurrence of a prior disorder, or that may have exacerbated an existing disorder.
Axis V	Global Assessment of Functioning	An overall judgment based on a 1-100 scale of the person's current level of functioning and the highest level of functioning in the past year according to psychological, social, and occupational criteria. For instance, a rating in the middle range of 51-60 would indicate a moderate level of symptoms (e.g., occasional panic attacks) or moderate difficulties in social, occupational, or school functioning (e.g., has few friends, has conflicts with co-workers).

Table 8.2 ❚ Psychosocial and Environmental Problems in the DSM System	
Problem categories	**Psychosocial and environmental problems**
Problems with primary support groups	Death of family members; health problems of family members; marital disruption in the form of separation, divorce, or estrangement; physical or sexual abuse in the family birth of a sibling
Problems related to the social environment	Death or loss of a friend; living alone or in social isolation; problems in adjusting to a new culture (acculturation problems); discrimination; problems in adjusting to the transitions of the life cycle, such as retirement
Educational problems	Academic problems; illiteracy; problems with classmates or teachers; impoverished or inadequate school environment
Occupational problems	Work-related problems, including problems with supervisors and co-workers, heavy workload, unemployment, adjustment to a new job, job dissatisfaction, sexual harassment, discrimination
Housing problems	Homelessness or inadequate housing; problems with landlords or neighbors; an unsafe neighborhood
Economic problems	Financial hardships or poverty; inadequate public support
Problems with access to health care	Lack of health insurance; inadequate health care services; problems with transportation to health care facilities
Problems related to the legal or criminal justice systems	Victimization by crime; involvement in a lawsuit or trial; arrest, imprisonment
Other psychosocial or environmental problems	Natural or technological disaster; war; lack of social services

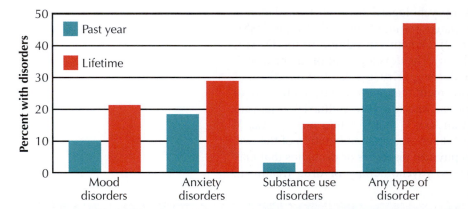

Figure 8.1
Prevalence of Psychological Disorders
These data, drawn from a national representative sample of U.S. adults age 15 to 49, show that nearly one in two have suffered from a diagnosable psychological disorder. About one in four have suffered from a psychological disorder during the past year.
Sources: Kessler, Berglund, et al., 2005; Kessler, Chiu, et al., 2005 based on data from National Comorbidity Survey Replication (NCS-R)

Axis IV, Psychosocial and Environmental Problems, includes difficulties that may affect the diagnosis, treatment, or outcome of a psychological disorder (see Table 8.2). Axis V, Global Assessment of Functioning, allows the clinician to rate the client's current level of functioning and her or his highest level of functioning prior to the onset of the psychological disorder. The purpose is to help determine the level of psychological functioning that may be likely to be restored through therapy.

Just how many people are affected by psychological disorders? We noted at the outset that about half of American adults suffer from a psychological disorder at some point in their lifetimes. About one in four adults suffer from a diagnosable psychological disorder in any given year (Kessler, Chiu, et al., 2005). In Figure 8.1 we see the prevalence rates of several major categories of psychological disorders.[1]

The conceptualization of abnormal behavior patterns as mental illnesses or disorders has received its share of criticism. Some professionals, such as psychiatrist Thomas Szasz (1970), believe that the categories described in the DSM are really "problems in living" rather than "illnesses" or "disorders." At least, they are not illnesses in the sense that heart disease, cancer, and the flu are bona fide illnesses. Szasz argues that labeling people with problems in living as "sick" is merely a way society uses to discredit behavior that deviates from accepted social norms by treating it as a sign of underlying illness. But many mental health professionals believe that critics like Szasz go too far in claiming that mental illness is merely a label used to stigmatize people who act in socially deviant ways.

Let us also note that conceptions of abnormal behavior vary from place to place (i.e., what is considered normal in one culture may be deemed abnormal in another).

---

[1] To be precise, the survey was not quite national, because the sample was limited to people residing in the 48 states in the U.S mainland.

Conceptions also vary from one period of time to another. For example, homosexuality was once viewed by the psychiatric profession as a diagnosable mental disorder. But in 1973, the American Psychiatric Association removed homosexuality from the DSM listing of diagnosable disorders (Drescher & Merlino, 2007). Homosexuality is now viewed by mental health professionals as a variation of human sexuality, not as a psychological or mental disorder.

Types of Psychological Disorders

Psychological disorders range from relatively mild disorders to more severe and chronic ones, such as schizophrenia and bipolar disorder. Among the mildest forms of psychological disorders is **adjustment disorder**. This disorder is a maladaptive reaction to an identified stressor and is characterized by academic, occupational, or social problems that exceed those normally caused by the stressor. The maladaptive response can be resolved if the person learns to cope with it or if the stressor is removed. If a love relationship ends and you cannot keep your mind on your coursework, you may fit the bill for an adjustment disorder. The diagnosis sounds more official than "not being able to get one's homework done," but it alludes to similar kinds of problems. If your uncle Pablo has been feeling down and pessimistic since his divorce from your aunt Sonya, he, too, may be diagnosed as having an adjustment disorder. If, since the breakup, your cousin Ricky has been cutting classes and spraying obscene words on the school walls, he may also have an adjustment disorder.

Considering an "adjustment disorder" to be a psychological or mental disorder highlights the problem of attempting to define where normal behavior leaves off and abnormal behavior begins. When something important goes wrong, it is normal to feel bad about it. If there is a business crisis, if we are victimized by violent crime, if there is an earthquake or a flood, anxiety and depression are understandable reactions. Under such circumstances, it might be abnormal not to react maladaptively—at least for a while. Leaving home for the first time to attend college is an identified stressor. Temporary feelings of loneliness and mild depression because of separation from one's family and friends, or anxiety about successfully completing academic assignments and making new friends, may be normal adjustments to such a stressor. But when a person's emotional complaints exceed the expected level, or when her or his ability to function is impaired, the diagnosis of adjustment disorder may be warranted. For example, if the student avoids social interactions at college or has difficulty getting out of bed or attending classes, the adjustment reaction may be excessive and warrant the diagnosis. But there are no precise boundaries between an expected reaction and an adjustment disorder.

© Esbin-Anderson/The Image Works

Not Being Able to Focus on Homework, or an Adjustment Disorder?
Adjustment disorders are mild as psychological disorders go, but they can be painful. They are defined as maladaptive reactions to identified stressors, such as the breakup of a romantic relationship. Being unable to focus on work because of the end of a relationship could qualify as an adjustment disorder. Considering such issues in adjustment to be psychological disorders highlights the problem of attempting to define where normal behavior leaves off and disordered behavior begins.

∎ **Adjustment disorder** A maladaptive reaction to one or more identified stressors that occurs shortly following exposure to the stressor(s) and causes impaired functioning or signs of distress beyond that which would normally be expected.

MODULE REVIEW

Review It

(1) Behavior is labeled abnormal when it is unusual, is socially unacceptable, involves faulty _____ of reality (as with hallucinations), and is dangerous, self-defeating, or distressing.

(2) The DSM incorporates a _____ system of assessment.

(3) Within this system, General Medical Conditions is coded on Axis _____.

(4) An _____ disorder is a maladaptive reaction to an identified stressor.

(5) Labeling an adjustment disorder as a psychological disorder highlights the problem of attempting to define precisely where normal behavior leaves off and _____ behavior begins.

Think About It

Where would you draw the line between a normal process of adjustment and an adjustment disorder?

MODULE 8.2

Anxiety Disorders

- ▪ What are the different types of anxiety disorders?
- ▪ What is known about the origins of anxiety disorders?

Anxiety is an emotional state that is accompanied by subjective, behavioral, and physical features. Subjective features include worrying, fear of the worst things happening, fear of losing control, nervousness, and inability to relax. Physical features reflect arousal of the sympathetic branch of the autonomic nervous system. They include trembling, sweating, a pounding or racing heart, elevated blood pressure (a flushed face), and faintness. The behavioral features of anxiety are dominated by avoidance of situations or cues associated with the source of the anxiety. For example, dental anxiety is associated with avoidance (or delay) of dental examinations and treatment. Anxiety experienced in specific situations or in response to particular objects (like insects or large animals) or situations is labeled fear. Excessive or inappropriate fear is classified as *phobia*.

Anxiety is an appropriate response to a real threat. It can be abnormal, however, when it is excessive or when it comes out of nowhere — that is, when events do not seem to warrant it. There are different types of anxiety disorders, but all of them are characterized by excessive or unwarranted anxiety.

8.2.1 Types of Anxiety Disorders

The classification of anxiety disorders includes phobias, panic disorder, generalized anxiety, obsessive-compulsive disorder, and traumatic stress disorders. Table 8.3 shows the rate or prevalence of these disorders and provides a description of their major symptoms and associated features.

Phobias

There are several types of phobias, including specific phobia, social phobia, and agoraphobia. **Specific phobia** is an excessive, irrational fear of a specific object or situation, such as snakes or heights. One specific phobia is fear of elevators. Some people will not enter elevators despite the hardships they incur as a result (such as walking up six flights of steps). Yes, the cable could break. The ventilation could fail. One could be stuck in midair waiting for repairs. These problems are uncommon, however, and it does not make sense to most people to walk up and down several flights of stairs to elude them. Similarly, some people with a specific phobia for hypodermic needles will not have injections, even to treat severe illness. Injections can be painful, but most people with a phobia for needles would gladly suffer an even more painful pinch if it would help them fight illness. Other specific phobias include **claustrophobia** (fear of tight or enclosed places); **acrophobia** (fear of heights); and fear of mice, snakes, and other creepy-crawlies. Fears of animals and imaginary creatures are common among children. Table 8.4 shows the typical ages of onset for various specific phobias.

Social phobia (also called *social anxiety disorder*) is a persistent fear of social interactions in which one might be scrutinized or judged negatively by others. Social phobia tends to develop early, by around age 15 on the average (Stein & Stein, 2008). People with social phobia live in constant fear of doing something that will be humiliating or embarrassing. Fear of public speaking is a common social phobia. Social phobia can severely affect daily functioning, leading people to avoid socializing with others or accepting jobs or promotions that would bring them into closer contact with others.

▪ **Specific phobia** Persistent fear of a specific object or situation.

▪ **Claustrophobia** Fear of tight, small places.

▪ **Acrophobia** Fear of high places.

▪ **Social phobia** An irrational, excessive fear of public scrutiny.

Table 8.3 ▮ Overview of Anxiety Disorders

Type of Disorder	Lifetime Prevalence in Population (approximate)	Description	Associated Features
Panic disorder	(a) Overall: 5.1% (b) With agoraphobia: 1.1% (c) Without agoraphobia: 4%	Repeated panic attacks (episodes of sheer terror accompanied by strong physiological symptoms, thoughts of imminent danger or impending doom, and an urge to escape)	Fears of recurring attacks may prompt avoidance of situations associated with the attacks or in which help might not be available; attacks begin unexpectedly but may become associated with certain cues or specific situations; may be accompanied by agoraphobia, or general avoidance of public situations
Generalized anxiety disorder	4%	Persistent anxiety that is not limited to particular situations	Excessive worrying; heightened states of bodily arousal, tenseness, being "on edge"
Specific phobia	9%	Excessive fears of particular objects or situations	Avoidance of phobic stimulus or situation; examples include acrophobia, claustrophobia, and fears of blood, small animals, or insects
Social phobia	5%	Excessive fear of social interactions	Characterized by an underlying fear of rejection, humiliation, or embarrassment in social situations
Agoraphobia (without panic disorder)	0.17%	Fear and avoidance of open, public places	May occur secondarily to loss of supportive others due to death, separation, or divorce
Obsessive-compulsive disorder	2% to 3%	Recurrent obsessions (recurrent, intrusive thoughts) and/or compulsions (repetitive behaviors the person feels compelled to perform)	Obsessions generate anxiety that may be at least partially relieved by performance of the compulsive rituals
Acute stress disorder	Unknown	Acute maladaptive reaction in the days or weeks following a traumatic event	Similar features as PTSD, but characterized more by dissociation or feelings of detachment from oneself or one's environment — being in a "daze"
Posttraumatic stress disorder	8%	Prolonged maladaptive reaction to a traumatic event	Reexperiencing the traumatic event, avoidance of cues or stimuli associated with the trauma; general or emotional numbing, hyperarousal, emotional distress, and impaired functioning

Sources: APA, 2000; Conway et al., 2006; Grant et al., 2005; Grant et al., 2006a, 2006b; Kessler, Berglund et al., 2005; Ozer & Weiss, 2004. Reprinted from Nevid, J.S., Rathus, S. A., & Greene, B. (2008). *Abnormal Psychology in a Changing World* (7th ed.). Upper Saddle River, NJ: Pearson Education. Reprinted with permission of Pearson Education.

Agoraphobia is fear of open or crowded places. The term *agoraphobia* is derived from the Greek words meaning "fear of the marketplace," or fear of being out in open, busy areas. Persons with agoraphobia fear being in places from which it might be difficult to escape or in which help might not be available if they experience

▮ **Agoraphobia** Fear of open, crowded places.

Table 8.4 ▮ Typical Age of Onset for Various Types of Specific Phobia

	Number of Cases	Mean Age of Onset
Animal phobia	50	7
Blood phobia	40	9
Injection phobia	59	8
Dental phobia	60	12
Social phobia	80	16
Claustrophobia	40	20
Agoraphobia	100	28

Martin Barraud/Getty Images, Inc.

Agoraphobia
Agoraphobia is excessive fear of venturing into open or crowded places, such as department stores, busy streets, or public conveyances. In some severe cases, the person with agoraphobia becomes essentially housebound out of fear of leaving the security of the home.

panicky symptoms (Berle et al., 2008; White et al., 2006). People who receive this diagnosis often refuse to venture out of their homes, especially by themselves. They find it difficult to hold a job or to maintain an ordinary social life.

The Case of Helen

Helen, a 59-year-old widow, became increasingly agoraphobic after the death of her husband three years earlier. By the time she came for treatment, she was essentially housebound, refusing to leave her home except under the strongest urging of her daughter, Mary, age 32, and only if Mary accompanied her. Her daughter and 36-year-old son, Pete, did her shopping for her and took care of her other needs as best they could. Yet the burden of caring for their mother, on top of their other responsibilities, was becoming too great for them to bear. They insisted that Helen begin treatment and Helen begrudgingly acceded to their demands.

Helen was accompanied to her evaluation session by Mary. Helen was a frail looking woman who entered the office clutching Mary's arm and insisted that Mary stay throughout the interview. Helen recounted that she had lost her husband and mother within three months of one another; her father had died 20 years earlier. Although she had never experienced a panic attack, she always considered herself an insecure, fearful person. Even so, she had been able to function in meeting the needs of her family until the deaths of her husband and mother left her feeling abandoned and alone. She had now become afraid of "just about everything" and was terrified of being out on her own, lest something bad would happen and she wouldn't be able to cope with it. Even at home, she was fearful that she might lose Mary and Pete. She needed constant reassurance from them that they too wouldn't abandon her. (From the authors' files. Reprinted from Nevid, Rathus, & Greene, 2006, with permission of Prentice Hall, Inc.)

Panic Disorder

It happened while I was sitting in the car at a traffic light. I felt my heart beating furiously fast, like it was just going to explode. It just happened, for no reason. I started breathing really fast but couldn't get enough air. It was like I was suffocating and the car was closing in around me. I felt like I was going to die right then and there. I was trembling and sweating heavily. I felt this incredible urge to escape, to just get out of the car and get away. I somehow managed to pull the car over to the side of the road but just sat there waiting for the feelings to pass. I told myself if I was going to die, then I was going to die. I didn't know whether I'd survive long enough to get help. Somehow—I can't say how—it just passed and I sat there a long time, wondering what had just happened to me. (From the authors' files.)

▌**Panic disorder** The recurrent experiencing of attacks of extreme anxiety in the absence of external stimuli that usually elicit anxiety.

In **panic disorder**, people experience abrupt attacks of acute, intense anxiety or sheer terror called *panic attacks*. At first these attacks occur spontaneously, as if arising "out of the blue." Over time they may become associated with cues in situations in which they have previously occurred, such as boarding an elevator or airplane. Panic attacks are accompanied by strong physical symptoms of anxiety, such as shortness of breath, heavy sweating, tremors, and pounding of the heart. It is not unusual for the victims to think they are having a heart attack. Saliva levels of cortisol (a stress hormone) are elevated during attacks (Bandelow et al., 2000). Many panic sufferers have difficulty breathing and may feel as though they are suffocating. They may experience nausea, numbness or tingling, flushes or chills, and fear of going crazy or losing control. Panic attacks usually last for minutes but may continue for hours. Afterward, the person usually feels drained.

Some people who have panic attacks stay home for fear of having an attack in public. They are diagnosed as having panic disorder with agoraphobia. About 5% of the general population suffers from panic disorder at some point in their lives.

Generalized Anxiety Disorder

The central feature of **generalized anxiety disorder** (GAD) is a general state of anxiety that becomes expressed in the form of persistent worrying. The anxiety cannot be attributed to a phobic object, situation, or activity. Rather, it seems to have a "free-floating" quality. Symptoms may include motor tension (shakiness, inability to relax, furrowed brow, fidgeting), autonomic overarousal (sweating, dry mouth, racing heart, lightheadedness, frequent urination, diarrhea), feelings of dread and foreboding, and excessive worrying and vigilance. People with GAD seem to worry about every little thing, not just one particular thing. GAD affects about 4% of the general population.

Generalized anxiety disorder A psychological disorder involving persistent feelings of worry accompanied by states of bodily tension and heightened arousal.

Obsessive-Compulsive Disorder

In obsessive-compulsive disorder (OCD), people have recurrent, troubling obsessions, compulsions, or both. The obsessions or compulsions cause personal distress or impaired functioning. An **obsession** is a recurrent, anxiety-provoking thought or image that seems irrational and beyond one's ability to control. Obsessions are so compelling and recurrent that they disrupt daily life. They may include doubts about whether one has locked the doors and shut the windows, or images such as one mother's repeated fantasy that her children had been run over on the way home from school. In another case, a woman became obsessed with the notion that she had contaminated her hands with Sani-Flush and that the contamination was spreading to everything she touched.

Obsession A recurring thought or image that seems beyond one's ability to control.

A **compulsion** is a seemingly irresistible urge to perform a specific act, often repeatedly, such as elaborate washing after using the bathroom. The impulse is recurrent and forceful, interfering with daily life. The woman who felt contaminated by Sani-Flush spent three to four hours at the sink each day and complained, "My hands look like lobster claws." Compulsions may temporarily reduce the anxiety connected with obsessions, but the obsessive thoughts typically return, leading to a vicious cycle of obsessive thoughts followed by compulsive behaviors, which are followed by more obsessive thoughts and compulsive behaviors, and so on. About 2% to 3% of American adults develop OCD at some point in their lives (American Psychiatric Association, 2000).

Compulsion An apparently irresistible urge to repeat an act or engage in ritualistic behavior such as hand washing.

The Case of Jack

Jack, a successful chemical engineer, was urged by his wife Mary, a pharmacist, to seek help for "his little behavioral quirks," which she had found increasingly annoying. Jack was a compulsive checker. When they left the apartment, he would insist on returning to check that the lights or gas jets were off, or that the refrigerator doors were shut. Sometimes he would apologize at the elevator and return to the apartment to carry out his rituals. Sometimes the compulsion to check struck him in the garage. He would return to the apartment, leaving Mary fuming. Going on vacation was especially difficult for Jack. The rituals occupied the better part of the morning of their departure. Even then, he remained plagued by doubts.

Mary had also tried to adjust to Jack's nightly routine of bolting out of bed to recheck the doors and windows. Her patience was running thin. Jack realized his behavior was impairing their relationship as well as causing himself distress. Yet he was reluctant to enter treatment. He gave lip service to wanting to be rid of his compulsive habits. However, he also feared that surrendering his compulsions would leave him defenseless against the anxieties they helped ease. (From the authors' files. Reprinted from Nevid, Rathus, & Greene, 2006, with permission of Prentice Hall, Inc.).

Posttraumatic Stress Disorder and Acute Stress Disorder

Exposure to trauma in the form of physical attacks, combat, medical emergencies, witnessing a death or near-death, accidents, and terrorist attacks can lead to the development of a maladaptive stress reaction called **posttraumatic stress disorder (PTSD)**. PTSD may not begin for many months or years after exposure to trauma, but it may last for years or even decades afterward.

Posttraumatic stress disorder (PTSD) A prolonged maladaptive reaction to a traumatic event that is characterized by intense fear, avoidance of stimuli associated with the event, and reliving of the event.

Robert Sullivan/Getty Images, Inc.

Traumatic Stress and PTSD

PTSD can result from many traumatic experiences, including combat, fires, stabbings, shootings, suicides, medical emergencies, accidents, explosions, and natural disasters like hurricanes and earthquakes. Though many people associate PTSD most strongly with combat trauma, the most commonly linked traumatic events are motor vehicle accidents.

PTSD is characterized by a variety of anxiety-related symptoms, such as rapid heart rate and feelings of anxiety and helplessness that are caused by a traumatic experience. PTSD frequently affects combat veterans, people whose homes and communities have been swept away by natural disasters or who have been subjected to toxic hazards, survivors of sexual assaults or childhood sexual abuse, and people directly exposed to the horrific events of September 11, 2001. Investigators estimated that some 425,000 New Yorkers, or about 7% of the city's population, developed PTSD related to the attacks within the first few months thereafter ("New Yorkers Battle Tensions," 2002).

A national study of more than 4,000 women found that about one woman in four who had been victimized by crime experienced PTSD (Resnick et al., 1993; see Figure 8.2). Violent crime, including rape, is more likely to lead to PTSD than are natural disasters like hurricanes and tornadoes (Gray & Acierno, 2002; Norris et al., 2003). Even so, the most commonly linked traumatic event is not combat or even crimes of violence, but rather motor vehicle accidents (Blanchard & Hickling, 2004). In PTSD, the traumatic event is revisited in the form of intrusive memories, recurrent dreams, and flashbacks—the sudden feeling that the event is recurring. People with PTSD typically try to avoid thoughts and activities connected to the traumatic event. They may also find it more difficult to enjoy life and may have sleep problems, irritable outbursts, difficulty concentrating, extreme vigilance, and an exaggerated "startle" response to sudden noise.

The Case of Margaret

Margaret was a 54-year-old woman who lived with her husband Travis in a small village in the hills to the east of the Hudson River. Two winters earlier, in the middle of the night, a fuel truck had skidded down one of the icy inclines that led into the village center. Two blocks away, Margaret was shaken from her bed by the explosion ("I thought the world was coming to an end. My husband said the Russians must've dropped the H-bomb.") when the truck slammed into the general store. The store and the apartments above were immediately engulfed in flames. The fire spread to the church next door. Margaret's first and most enduring visual impression was of shards of red and black that rose into the air in an eerie ballet. On their way down, they bathed the centuries-old tombstones in the church graveyard in hellish light. A dozen people died, mostly those who had lived above and in back of the general store. The old caretaker of the church and the truck driver were lost as well.

Margaret shared the village's loss, took in the temporarily homeless, and did her share of what had to be done. Months later, after the general store had been leveled to a memorial park and the church was on the way toward being restored, Margaret started to feel that life was becoming strange, that the world outside was becoming a little unreal. She began to withdraw from her friends and scenes of the night of the fire would fill her mind. At night she now and then dreamt the scene. Her physician prescribed a sleeping pill which she discontinued because "I couldn't wake up out of the dream." Her physician turned to Valium, an antianxiety drug, to help her get through the day. The pills helped for a while, but "I quit them because I needed more and more of the things and you can't take drugs forever, can you?"

Over the next year and a half, Margaret tried her best not to think about the disaster, but the intrusive recollections and the dreams came and went, apparently on their own. By the time Margaret [sought help], her sleep had been seriously distressed for nearly two months and the recollections were as vivid as ever. (From the authors' files. Reprinted from Nevid, Rathus, & Greene, 2006, with permission of Prentice Hall, Inc.)

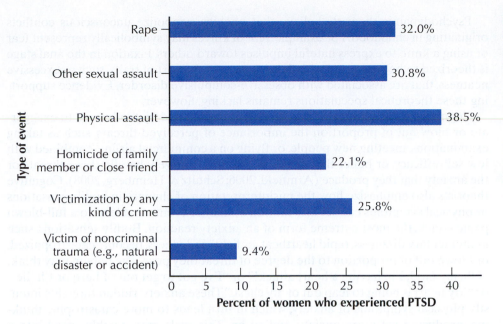

Figure 8.2
Posttraumatic Stress Disorder Among Female Victims of Crime and Among Other Women
The study by Resnick and colleagues showed that about one woman in four (25.8%) who was victimized by crime could be diagnosed with PTSD at some point following the trauma. By contrast, fewer than one woman in ten (9.4%) who was not victimized by crime experienced PTSD.
Source: Adapted from Resnick et al., 1994.

Not everyone exposed to trauma develops PTSD; fortunately, only a minority are affected to that degree. Vulnerability to PTSD depends on many factors, with the likelihood of occurrence increasing with the degree of exposure to the trauma and its perceived threat to one's life, childhood history of sexual abuse, lack of active coping responses for dealing with stress, feelings of shame, and lack of social support, among other factors (e.g., Ehlers et al., 2003). Overall, although roughly half of U.S. adults experience a traumatic event in their lifetimes, only about 8% eventually develop PTSD (Ozer & Weiss, 2004).

Acute stress disorder (ASD) is characterized by feelings of intense anxiety and feelings of helplessness during the first month following exposure to a traumatic event. By contrast, PTSD can occur months or years after the traumatic event and may persist for years or even decades. In many cases, however, ASD leads to the development of more persistent PTSD.

▮ **Acute stress disorder** A maladaptive reaction to a traumatic event occurring during the month following the event and characterized by feelings of intense anxiety and helplessness.

8.2.2 Causal Factors

As a prelude to our discussions of the causal factors of psychological disorders, let us note that psychological disorders are complex problems that defy simple explanations. Although important strides have been made in understanding these disorders, their origins remain to a great extent elusive. Here let us consider the most prominent theories of the origins of anxiety disorders, beginning with psychological viewpoints.

Psychological Views

Some phobias are learned on the basis of classical conditioning. For example, a person who is trapped in an elevator for hours may develop a fear of riding on elevators. In this case, previously neutral stimuli (cues associated with the elevator) become conditioned stimuli that evoke a conditioned response, or learned fear. Some phobias may be conditioned fears that were acquired in early childhood and are beyond memory. Other learning factors, such as observational learning, also play a role in the development of phobic behavior. If parents squirm, grimace, and shudder at the sight of mice, insects, or blood, children might assume that these stimuli are threatening and learn to imitate their parents' behavior. In any event, the avoidance of the phobic stimulus or feared object or situation becomes reinforced by the reduction of anxiety.

Psychodynamic theorists believe that phobias symbolize unconscious conflicts originating in childhood. For example, fear of knives may symbolically represent fear of using a knife to express hateful impulses toward others. Fixation in the anal stage is theorized to be connected with development of the sort of traits, such as excessive neatness, that are associated with obsessive-compulsive disorder. Evidence supporting these theoretical speculations remains lacking, however.

Cognitive theorists suggest that anxiety is maintained by tendencies to exaggerate or blow out of proportion the importance of perceived threats, such as taking examinations, meeting new people, or flying on a commercial airline, combined with low self-efficacy, or belief that one is unable to effectively handle these threats or the anxiety that they produce (Armfield, 2006; Schultz & Heimberg, 2008). Cognitive theorists also emphasize how the misinterpretation of changes in bodily sensations or physical symptoms can set into motion a chain of events that lead to a full-blown panic attack, the most extreme form of an anxiety reaction. Bodily sensations, such as momentary dizziness, rapid heartbeat, or lightheadedness, become catastrophized, or blown out of proportion to the degree of threat they pose. The person may think, "Oh, my God, I'm having a heart attack!" or "I've got to get out of here or I'll die," or "My heart is going to leap out of my chest." These anxiety-ridden thoughts intensify physical symptoms of anxiety, which in turn leads to more catastrophic thinking, producing yet more anxiety, and so on. This cycle may quickly spiral into a full-fledged panic attack.

Biological Views

Evidence underscores the important role that biological factors play in anxiety disorders. Genetic factors are implicated in many anxiety disorders, such as phobic disorders, panic disorder, generalized anxiety disorder, and obsessive-compulsive disorder (Coryell et al., 2006; Koenen et al., 2008; Leckman & Kim, 2006; Menzies et al., 2007; Smoller et al., 2008).

But if genetics does play a role in anxiety disorders, as investigators believe, how is that role expressed? Although scientists are still trying to understand the underlying mechanisms, let us offer some possible causal models. One model gaining favor is that genetic factors may increase the sensitivity of brain mechanisms responsible for responding to fearful stimuli (Hariri et al., 2002). Individuals possessing a particular form of a gene showed greater nervous system activity in response to fearful stimuli in parts of the brain that become activated in response to fearful or threatening stimuli.

Other investigators find that people with anxiety disorders such as OCD, PTSD, and social phobia have higher than expected levels of brain activity in the parts of the brain involved in states of worry and anxiety (Stein & Stein, 2008; Szeszko et al., 2004). For people with OCD, the brain may be repeatedly sending messages that something is terribly wrong and needs immediate attention, which may then lead to the kinds of nagging obsessive thoughts we tend to see in people with OCD. Whether genetic factors account for these patterns of overactivity remains to be determined.

We also know that genetic factors affect the manufacture and regulation of neurotransmitters and the numbers of types of receptor cells where these neurotransmitters dock. Genetic factors may account for faulty regulation of levels of the neurotransmitters *serotonin* and *norepinephrine* in the brain, leading to unusually high levels of anxiety in response to particular threats. Another possibility is that receptor sites in the brain may not be sensitive enough to the neurotransmitter **gamma-aminobutyric acid (GABA)**, which acts in the nervous system to calm down nervous system activity. The **benzodiazepines**, a class of drugs that reduce anxiety, appear to work by increasing the sensitivity of receptor sites to GABA.

This brings us to a more general comment. Though genetic factors may be involved in many psychological disorders, in no cases yet discovered do genes tell the whole story. Unlike some physical disorders, which are genetically transmitted,

▌ **Gamma-aminobutyric acid (GABA)** An inhibitory neurotransmitter that is implicated in anxiety reactions.

▌ **Benzodiazepines** A class of drugs that reduce anxiety.

psychological disorders are not explained by genes alone or by any one gene in particular. Where genetics does play a role, many genes are likely involved in creating a predisposition or propensity that makes it more likely that the disorder will develop under certain conditions. But genetic vulnerability is not genetic inevitability. Whether a person develops psychological disorders depends on a number of factors, not genes alone. Under favorable conditions, such as the availability of a warm and loving family, a relatively low level of stressful events, and the availability of coping resources, a disorder may never emerge despite a genetic tendency. Thus, genes and environment interact in a complex interplay of factors that give rise to abnormal behavior patterns (Haeffel et al., 2008; Levine & Schmelkin, 2006; Moffitt, Caspi, & Rutter, 2006).

MODULE REVIEW

Review It

(6) _____ phobia is an excessive fear of a specific object or situation.

(7) _____ disorder is characterized by sudden attacks in which people typically fear that they are about to die or lose control.

(8) In _____ _____ _____ disorder people are troubled by intrusive thoughts or impulses to repeat some activity.

(9) _____ _____ _____ disorder is caused by a traumatic experience and characterized by reexperiencing it in the form of intrusive memories, recurrent dreams, and flashbacks.

(10) _____ theory relates obsessive-compulsive traits to fixation in the oral stage of psychosexual development.

(11) Learning theorists see phobias as _____ fears.

(12) Genetic factors are implicated in creating a _____ to certain psychological disorders.

Think About It

Is anxiety normal? How are anxiety disorders abnormal? What might evolutionary psychologists say about the heritability of fears?

MODULE 8.3

Dissociative and Somatoform Disorders

▮ What are the major types of dissociative disorders?
▮ What is known about the origins of dissociative disorders?
▮ What are the major types of somatoform disorders?
▮ What is known about the origins of somatoform disorders?

In the **dissociative disorders** there is a separation of mental processes such as thoughts, emotions, identity, memory, or consciousness—the processes that make the person feel whole. These disorders are relatively uncommon, or even rare. In the case of **dissociative identity disorder** (formerly *multiple personality disorder*), many professionals even disagree about whether it is a distinct disorder or a form of elaborate role playing.

▮ **Dissociative disorders** A class of psychological disorders involving changes in consciousness or self-identity.

▮ **Dissociative identity disorder** A disorder in which a person appears to have two or more distinct identities or personalities, which may alternate in controlling the person.

I Somatoform disorder A class of psychological disorders in which people have physical complaints that cannot be explained medically or attribute their physical problems to grave causes despite assurances to the contrary.

People with a **somatoform disorder** may present with a physical problem such as paralysis, numbness, or mysterious pain that defies any medical explanation, or have a persistent belief that they have a serious disease despite a lack of medical evidence (Creed & Barsky, 2004; Rief & Sharpe, 2004). Dissociative and somatoform disorders are often grouped together because of the traditional psychodynamic view that they represent psychological defenses that shield the self from anxiety. Here we examine the major types of dissociative disorders and somatoform disorders and beliefs about their causes.

8.3.1 Types of Dissociative Disorders

The DSM lists four specific types of dissociative disorders: dissociative amnesia, dissociative fugue, dissociative identity disorder, and depersonalization disorder.

Dissociative Amnesia

I Dissociative amnesia A dissociative disorder marked by loss of personal memories or self-identity; skills and general knowledge are usually retained.

Dissociative amnesia is believed to be the most common form of dissociative disorder (Maldonado, Butler, & Spiegel, 1998). People with this disorder become suddenly unable to recall important personal information about themselves, such as past experiences or even their name. The loss of memory cannot be attributed to organic problems such as a blow to the head or alcoholic intoxication. It is thus a psychological disorder, not an organic one. In the most common example, the person cannot recall events for a number of hours after a stressful incident, as in warfare or in the case of an uninjured survivor of an accident. In generalized amnesia, people forget their entire lives. Amnesia may last hours or even years.

Dissociative Fugue

I Dissociative fugue A dissociative disorder in which one experiences amnesia and then flees to a new location.

In **dissociative fugue**, the person abruptly leaves his or her home or place of work and travels to another place, having lost all memory of his or her past life. While at the new location, the person either does not think about the past or reports a past filled with invented memories. The new personality is often more outgoing and less inhibited than the "real" identity. Following recovery, the events that occurred during the fugue are not recalled.

Susan Greenwood/Liason/Getty Images, Inc.

"Jane Doe"
Claiming to have no memory of who she was, the woman called "Jane Doe" was found wandering in a Florida park in a dazed state. She was eventually reunited with her family, who recognized her from a televised news report. "Jane" reportedly never regained her memory.

Dissociative Identity Disorder

In dissociative identity disorder (DID), two or more identities or personalities, each with distinct traits and memories, "occupy" the same person. Each identity may or may not be aware of the others (Dorahy, 2001; Huntjens et al., 2005). The alternate personalities of people with dissociative identity disorder can be very different from one another. Some investigators report that these alternates might even have different allergic reactions, different responses to medication, and even different eyeglass prescriptions (Birnbaum, Martin, & Thomann, 1996; Braun, 1988).

A few celebrated cases of this disorder have been portrayed in the popular media. One of them became the subject of the film *The Three Faces of Eve*. A timid housewife named Eve White harbored two other identities. One was Eve Black, a sexually aggressive, antisocial personality. The other was Jane, an emerging identity who was able to accept the existence of her primitive impulses and yet engage in socially appropriate behavior. Finally, the three faces merged into one—Jane. Ironically, later on, Jane (Chris Sizemore in real life) reportedly split into 22 identities. Another well-publicized (but recently disputed) case is that of Sybil, a woman with 16 identities who was portrayed by Sally Field in the film *Sybil*.

Some psychologists challenge the existence of DID as a distinct disorder. They don't deny that people with multiple personalities have disturbed behavior. But they ascribe their behavior to a form of attention-seeking role playing (Lilienfeld et al., 1999; Spanos, 1994). These theorists argue that people with DID may have constructed these alternate personalities as roles they play to act out confusing and conflicting emotions they experience. Over time, these roles may have become so deeply ingrained in their personalities that they seem to have become distinct personalities in their own right.

Depersonalization Disorder

Depersonalization disorder is characterized by persistent or recurrent feelings that one is detached from one's own body, as if one is observing one's thought processes from the outside or walking about in a fog. People with the disorder experience changes in attention and perception, making it difficult for them to focus clearly on events (Guralnik, Schmeidler, & Simeon, 2000). As a result, they may feel as though they are functioning on automatic pilot or as in a dream.

The case of Richie illustrates a transient episode of depersonalization:

> *We went to Orlando with the children after school let out. I had also been driving myself hard, and it was time to let go. We spent three days "doing" Disneyworld, and it got to the point where we were all wearing shirts with mice and ducks on them and singing Disney songs like "Yo ho, yo ho, a pirate's life for me." On the third day I began to feel unreal and ill at ease while we were watching these middle-American Ivory-soap teenagers singing and dancing in front of Cinderella's Castle. The day was finally cooling down, but I broke into a sweat. I became shaky and dizzy and sat down on the cement next to the 4-year-old's stroller without giving [my wife] an explanation. There were strollers and kids and [adults'] legs all around me, and for some strange reason I became fixated on the pieces of popcorn strewn on the ground. All of a sudden it was like the people around me were all silly mechanical creatures, like the dolls in the "It's a Small World" [exhibit] or the animals on the "Jungle Cruise." Things sort of seemed to slow down, the way they do when you've smoked marijuana, and there was this invisible wall of cotton between me and everyone else.*
>
> *Then the concert was over and my wife was like "What's the matter?" and did I want to stay for the Electrical Parade and the fireworks or was I sick? Now I was beginning to wonder if I was going crazy and I said I was sick, that my wife would have to take me by the hand and drive us back to the [motel]. Somehow we got back to the monorail and turned in the strollers. I waited in the herd [of people] at the station like a dead person, my eyes glazed over, looking out over kids with Mickey Mouse ears and Mickey Mouse balloons. The mechanical voice on the monorail almost did me in and I got really shaky. I refused to go back to the Magic Kingdom. I went with the family to Sea World, and on another day I dropped [my wife] and the kids off at the Magic Kingdom and picked them up that night. My wife thought I was goldbricking or something, and we had a helluva fight about it, but we had a life to get back to and my sanity had to come first. (From the authors' files.)*

▮ **Depersonalization disorder** A dissociative disorder in which one experiences persistent or recurrent feelings of detachment from one's own experiences or body.

© Werner H. Muller/Peter Arnold, Inc.

Depersonalization
People with depersonalization disorder feel as though they are detached from their bodies or observing their thoughts from outside. They or the world seem unreal. Stressful experiences can cause them to feel as though they are in a dream or functioning on "automatic pilot."

8.3.2 Causal Factors in Dissociative Disorders

The dissociative disorders are some of the odder psychological disorders. Before discussing psychological theories of the dissociative disorders, we should note that there is some skepticism about their existence. Some people diagnosed with dissociative amnesia or dissociative identity disorder may be faking their symptoms. Others may have adopted the role of a multiple personality—a role that may be inadvertently cued and reinforced by therapists and others. Playing a role doesn't mean that a person is purposefully trying to deceive others. We all adopt roles in our social lives, such as the roles of student, worker, and friend. In some people with dissociative identity disorder, the role of a multiple personality may have become so ingrained in their personalities through repeated practice that it becomes a seemingly natural part of themselves.

We don't know how many cases can be explained by either outright fabrication or role playing. But we do know that the case histories of people with DID show that the great majority suffered terrible sexual or physical abuse in childhood, typically beginning before age five and usually at the hands of a caretaker or relative (Burton & Lane, 2001). Many report both physical and sexual abuse. Children who go on to develop multiple personalities may have learned early in life to distance themselves from the abuse by psychologically escaping into these alternate selves. Dissociative symptoms may represent the only means of escape from an intolerable situation. Psychologists of different theoretical persuasions have also offered hypotheses about the origins of dissociative identity disorder and other dissociative disorders. According to psychodynamic theory, for example, people with dissociative disorders use massive repression to prevent them from recognizing improper impulses or remembering ugly events (Vaillant, 1994). In dissociative amnesia and fugue, the person simply forgets, or banishes from memory, a profoundly disturbing event or impulse. In dissociative identity disorder, the person expresses unacceptable impulses through alternate identities. In depersonalization, the person stands outside—removed from the turmoil within. According to learning theorists, people with dissociative disorders have learned to redirect their thinking away from troubling memories or disturbing impulses in order to avoid feelings of anxiety, guilt, and shame. Both psychodynamic and learning theories suggest that dissociative disorders help people keep disturbing memories or ideas out of mind.

Perhaps all of us are capable of dividing our awareness so that we become unaware, at least temporarily, of events that we usually focus more attention on. The dissociative disorders raise fascinating questions about the nature of human self-identity and memory. Perhaps it is no surprise that attention can be divided. Perhaps the surprising thing is that human consciousness normally integrates an often-chaotic set of experiences into a meaningful whole.

8.3.3 Types of Somatoform Disorders

Two major types of somatoform disorders are conversion disorder and hypochondriasis.

Conversion Disorder

▌ **Conversion disorder** A disorder in which anxiety or unconscious conflicts are "converted" into physical symptoms that often have the effect of helping the person cope with anxiety or conflict.

Conversion disorder is a rare disorder characterized by a major change in, or loss of, a physical function, such as blindness or paralysis or loss of feeling in a limb (Sar et al., 2004). However, there are no medical findings to explain the loss of functioning. Nor are the symptoms intentionally produced. That is, the person is not consciously faking. Conversion disorder is so named because it appears to involve the "conversion" of a source of stress or anxiety into a physical problem.

▌ **La belle indifférence** A French term descriptive of the lack of concern sometimes shown by people with conversion disorders toward their symptoms.

If you lost the ability to see at night, or if your legs became paralyzed, you would understandably show concern. But some people with conversion disorder show indifference to their symptoms, a remarkable feature referred to as **la belle indifférence**. During World War II, some bomber pilots developed night blindness. They could not carry out their nighttime missions, although no damage to the optic nerves was found. In rare cases, women with large families have been reported to become paralyzed in the legs, again with no medical findings. More recently, a Cambodian woman who had witnessed atrocities became blind as a result.

Hypochondriasis

A more common type of somatoform disorder is **hypochondriasis**. People with this disorder insist that their physical complaints are due to serious underlying illness, even though there is no medical justification to support their concerns (Abramowitz, Olatunji, & Deacon, 2008; Barsky & Ahem, 2004). They become preoccupied with thoughts that they are seriously ill, and they cannot be shaken from this fear despite medical reassurances. People with hypochondriasis do not "make up" their symptoms; rather, they experience nagging physical complaints that they attribute to dire causes. They may run from doctor to doctor, believing that their doctors may be misinformed or have missed something.

▮ **Hypochondriasis** A psychological disorder characterized by the persistent belief that one has a serious medical disorder despite lack of medical findings.

Are Somatoform Disorders the Special Province of Women?

The word *hysterical* derives from the Greek word *hystera*, meaning "uterus" or "womb." The use of *hysteria* stemmed from the ancient belief that it was a sort of female trouble that was caused by a wandering uterus. It was erroneously thought that the uterus could roam through the body—that it was not anchored in place! As the uterus meandered, it could cause pains and odd sensations almost anywhere. The Greeks also believed that pregnancy would anchor the uterus and thus would end hysterical complaints. Even in the earlier years of the twentieth century, it was suggested that strange sensations and medically unfounded complaints were largely the province of women. But evidence showed that hysterical complaints were not limited to women. During World War II, as noted earlier, a number of bomber pilots developed night blindness, which prevented them from carrying out dangerous missions and shielded them from guilt for killing any civilians who happened to be in the vicinity of bombing raids. The night blindness of the pilots shows that conversion disorders are not the special province of women—whether or not they were once labeled hysterical.

8.3.4 Causal Factors in Somatoform Disorders

The somatoform disorders have been richly mined by psychological theorists probing for causes of these puzzling disorders. But recognize that these theoretical accounts remain speculative, as empirical evidence that would help us better understand these puzzling but relatively uncommon problems remains sparse.

To psychodynamic theorists, beginning with Freud, hysterical symptoms symbolize underlying psychological conflict. A person who loses the use of an arm for no apparent medical reason may be harboring unconscious desires to use the arm to express an unacceptable impulse, such as harming others or harming oneself. The ego fashions a compromise solution—repressing the underlying aggressive impulse by creating a symptom (paralysis of the arm) that prevents the impulse from expression. If this view is correct, it may account for the fact that many (but certainly not all) people with conversion symptoms seem strangely apathetic to these symptoms, as though the symptoms were serving some underlying purpose.

From a learning theory perspective, conversion symptoms represent learned responses that are reinforced by avoidance of painful or anxiety-evoking situations. For example, people with conversion disorder may incur sympathy from others and be relieved of stressful burdens or responsibilities.

Evidence also points to a role for cognitive factors in somatoform disorders, such as distorted thinking patterns. For example, investigators find that people with hypochondriasis tend to "make mountains out of molehills" (Barsky et al., 2003; Cororve & Gleaves, 2001). Cognitive biases may underlie the tendency to exaggerate the importance of minor physical ailments that we find in people with hypochondriasis.

MODULE REVIEW

Review It

(13) _____ involves forgetting personal information.

(14) In _____ _____ _____, the person behaves as if multiple, distinct personalities occupy the body.

(15) In _____ _____, people feel as if they are detached from their bodies.

(16) Both psychodynamic and learning theories suggest that _____ disorders help people keep disturbing memories or ideas out of mind.

(17) Many people with dissociative disorders have a history of physical or sexual _____.

(18) In _____ _____, there is a major change in or loss of physical functioning with no organic basis.

(19) In _____, people persist in believing they have a serious disease despite medical reassurances.

Think About It

How would you explain dissociative and somatoform disorders as maladaptive ways of handling troubling memories or sources of anxiety?

MODULE 8.4

Mood Disorders

■ What are the different types of mood disorders?

■ Why are women more likely than men to become depressed?

■ What is known about the origins of mood disorders?

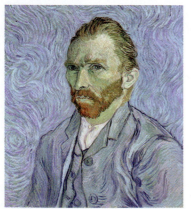

The Bridgeman Art Library International

Starry, Starry Night
In this self-portrait, the famed artist Vincent Van Gogh strikes a melancholy pose that reveals the deep sense of despair he endured. After suffering repeated bouts of deep depression, Van Gogh died of a self-inflicted gunshot wound at the age of 37.

■ **Mood disorders** A class of psychological disorders characterized by significant disturbances of mood.

Mood disorders are characterized by severe or persistent disturbances of mood. The disturbed mood may take the form of depression or elation. Most all of us experience fluctuations in our moods. We feel joyful when fortune shines on us or deflated when we fail or experience disappointments. If you have failed an important test, if you have lost money in a business venture, or if your closest friend becomes ill, it is understandable and fitting for you to be sad about it. It would be odd, in fact, if you were not affected by adversity. But in mood disorders, the disturbance of moods is either extreme, persistent, or out of keeping with the events the person has experienced.

8.4.1 Types of Mood Disorders

Here we consider two major types of mood disorders: major depression and bipolar disorder.

Major Depression

Major depression (also called *major depressive disorder* or MDD) has been described as the "common cold" of psychological problems, affecting some 16% of adults at some point in their lives (Duenweld, 2003; Kessler et al., 2003). Unfortunately, less than a third of people with major depression seek professional treatment (Pratt & Brody, 2008).

People with major depression may experience a downcast mood and lose interest or pleasure in activities they might otherwise enjoy. They may complain of feeling "down in the dumps" or have a sense of hopelessness about the future. They may have difficulty concentrating or summoning the energy to get going in the morning or even to get out of bed. They may experience changes in appetite (eating too much or too little) and sleep (sleeping either too much or too little or having difficulty getting back to sleep following early-morning awakenings). They may be tearful at times and even contemplate or attempt suicide. In extreme cases, they may experience **psychotic** behaviors, including hallucinations and delusions, such as believing that their body is rotting away.

Michael Ochs Archives/Getty Images, Inc.

Carrie Fisher
The actress Carrie Fisher, who portrayed Princess Leia in the original *Star Wars*, was diagnosed with bipolar disorder in her twenties.

Bipolar Disorder

People with **bipolar disorder**, formerly known as *manic-depression*, have mood swings from great elation to deep depression (Mansell & Pedley, 2008). The cycles seem to be unrelated to external events. In the elated, or **manic** phase, the person may show excessive excitement or silliness, such as by carrying jokes too far. The manic person may be argumentative. He or she may show poor judgment, destroying property, making huge contributions to charity they can ill afford, or giving away expensive possessions. People often find manic individuals abrasive and avoid them. They are often oversexed and too restless to sit still or sleep restfully. They often speak rapidly (showing "pressured speech") and jump from topic to topic (showing rapid **flight of ideas**). It can be hard to get a word in edgewise.

Depression is the other side of the proverbial coin. In the depressive phase, people with bipolar disorder have a downcast mood, often sleep more than usual, and feel lethargic. They may become socially withdrawn and irritable. Some people with bipolar disorder attempt suicide when the mood shifts from the elated phase toward depression (Jamison, 2000). They will do almost anything to escape the depths of depression that lie ahead. A leading authority on bipolar disorder is the psychologist Kay Redfield Jamison, who herself suffers from the disorder. Her bipolar disorder began in her teens, but like many patients, it wasn't diagnosed until many years later, when she was 28 (Ballie, 2002). In her memoir *An Unquiet Mind*, Jamison (1995) described how her early manic episodes were "absolutely intoxicating states" that led to "great personal pleasure, an incomparable flow of thoughts, and a ceaseless energy that allowed the translation of new ideas into papers and projects" (p. 5). But then

> ...as night inevitably goes after the day, my mood would crash, and my mind again would grind to a halt. I lost all interest in my schoolwork, friends, reading, wandering, or daydreaming. I had no idea of what was happening to me, and I would wake up in the morning with a profound sense of dread that I was going to somehow make it through another entire day. I would sit for hour after hour in the undergraduate library, unable to muster up enough energy to go to class. I would stare out the window, stare at my books, rearrange them, shuffle them around, leave them unopened, and think about dropping out of college.... I understood very little of what was going on, and I felt as though only dying would release me from the overwhelming sense of inadequacy and blackness that surrounded me. (Jamison, 1995)

Is There a Thin Line Between Genius and Madness?

You may have heard the expression, "There is a thin line between genius and madness."It may sound as if the "madness" in question should be schizophrenia because there are flights of fancy in that disorder as well as among geniuses. You may recall the Oscar-winning film *A Beautiful Mind*, in which actor Russell

Major depression A mood disorder in which the person may have a dampened mood, changes in appetite and sleep patterns, and lack of interest or pleasure.

Psychotic Relating to a break with reality, as manifest by delusional thinking or hallucinations.

Bipolar disorder A mood disorder in which mood alternates between two extreme poles (elation and depression).

Manic Related to episodes of highly elated mood and excessive excitement.

Flight of ideas Jumping rapidly from topic to topic, a characteristic train of thought during manic episodes.

Adjustment and Modern Life

Why Are More Women Depressed?

Women are about two times more likely to be diagnosed with depression than men—approximately 12% of men versus about 21% of women (Conway et al., 2006; Hyde, Mezulis, & Abramson, 2008). Gender differences in risks of depression begin to emerge in adolescence. But what explains this gender difference?

Although biological factors, such as hormonal influences relating to the menstrual cycle and childbirth, may contribute to the greater risk of depression in women, we also need to take into account the greater stressful burdens many women carry (Mazure & Keita, 2006; Plaisier et al., 2008). Women often face a disproportionate level of stress, such as holding a job and shouldering the bulk of housekeeping and childcare responsibilities. Women are also more likely to experience such stresses as physical and sexual abuse, poverty, single parenthood, and sexism. Women are also more likely than men to help other people who are under stress or to assume caregiving responsibilities for sick or disabled family members.

Gender difference in depression may also reflect different social expectations and social pressures. In our culture, for example, men are less likely than women to admit to depression or seek treatment for depression. "I'm the John Wayne generation," admitted one man, a physician. "'It's only a flesh wound'; that's how you deal with it. I thought depression was a weakness—there was something disgraceful about it. A real man would just get over it" (cited in Wartik, 2000).

Differences in coping styles between men and women may also play a role. The psychologist Janet Nolen-Hoeksema believes that men are more likely to cope with depression by distracting themselves from their feelings, whereas women are more likely to ruminate about their problems (Nolen-Hoeksema, 2006). Distraction may help take one's mind off one's problems, while rumination may only compound one's feelings of misery (Gilbert, 2004). Yet men are more likely to distract themselves by turning to alcohol. They thus may expose themselves and their families to another set of problems. Rumination is not limited to women; tendencies to ruminate or brood about one's problem are linked to depression in both men and women (Lo, Ho, & Hollon, 2008).

Let us also note that women do not have the privileges of men in our society, and social inequality creates many of the problems that lead people to seek therapy. Women—especially single mothers—have lower socioeconomic status than men, and depression and other psychological disorders are more common among poor people. Even capable, hard-working women may feel depressed when society limits their opportunities. A part of "therapy" for women, then, is to modify the overwhelming demands that are placed on women today. The pain may lie in the individual, but the cause often lies in society.

Dave Anthony/Taxi/Getty Images, Inc.

Why Are Women More Likely Than Men to Be Diagnosed with Depression?
There are so many possibilities. For one thing, women are more likely than men to admit to feelings of depression. Another factor could be the hormonal changes that accompany the menstrual cycle. Women who are in the work force—and that includes the great majority of women today—also tend to continue to bear the stress of having the main responsibility for homemaking and childrearing. And because of sexism, women are also treated in many cases like second-class citizens. Former APA president Bonnie Strickland has expressed surprise that even more women are not depressed, given the burdens that they bear.

▌**Schizophrenia** A severe and persistent psychological disorder characterized by a break with reality, disturbances in thinking, and disturbed behavior and emotional responses.

Crowe portrayed John Nash, a Nobel Prize–winning mathematician who was diagnosed with **schizophrenia**. However, the work for which he was to later receive the Nobel Prize occurred before he had deteriorated to the point that he was hospitalized.

Researchers have found links between creative genius and mood disorders of depression and bipolar disorder (McDermott, 2001; Nettle, 2001). Many artists seem to have peered into the depths of their own despair to find inspiration, but an alarming number of writers—including Virginia Woolf, Sylvia Plath, and Ernest Hemingway—have taken their own lives. You probably know what the artist Vincent van Gogh did to his ear during a depressive episode.

As noted by psychologist Kay Redfield Jamison (1997), artists are 18 times more likely to commit suicide than the general population. They are 8 to 10 times more likely to be depressed and 10 to 20 times as likely to have bipolar disorder. Many writers, painters, and composers were also at their most productive during manic periods, including the poet Alfred Lord Tennyson and the composer Robert Schumann. On the other hand, not every study has found a link between creativity and psychological disorders (Bailey, 2003). Perhaps we should reserve judgment on the nature of the relationship and what it might mean. But it is conceivable that some creative artists are able to channel their apparently boundless supplies of energy during manic episodes and the accompanying rapid stream of ideas toward the production of artistic works.

Anthony Potter Collection/Hulton Archive/Getty Images, Inc

Between Genius and Madness
The life experiences—and suicides—of many artists, including writer Ernest Hemingway, pictured here, were plagued by emotional highs and lows. Psychologist Kay Redfield Jamison has noted that creative artists are many times more likely than the general population to be diagnosed with depression or bipolar disorder and to commit suicide. Is there a thin line between creative genius and madness?

8.4.2 Causal Factors

What is known about the origins of mood disorders? Although the mood disorders are connected with processes within the individual, let us begin by noting that many kinds of stressful situations are also connected with depression (Cohen, Janicki-Deverts, & Miller, 2007). Many sources of stress are linked to increased risk of depression, including loss of loved ones, marital conflict, physical illness, low income, prolonged unemployment, and work-related pressure (Drieling, van Calker, & Hecht, 2006; Monroe et al., 2007). Clearly, the causes of mood disorders are complex and rest on the interplay of psychological and biological factors, together with life stress.

Psychological Factors

Sigmund Freud viewed depression as anger turned inward. People who are overly concerned about hurting other people's feelings or losing their approval may hold in feelings of anger rather than express them. Or they may have ambivalent (mixed) feelings toward deceased loved ones—both loving and hating them. But rather than directly confronting their angry feelings, they turn them inward against the internal representations of these individuals that they've incorporated within their own personalities after the loss (or threatened loss) of the other person. Anger is turned inward and is experienced as misery and self-hatred. From the psychodynamic perspective, bipolar disorder may be seen as alternating states in which the personality is dominated first by the superego and then by the ego. In the depressive phase of the disorder, the superego dominates, producing exaggerated ideas of wrongdoing and associated feelings of guilt and worthlessness. After a while the ego asserts supremacy, producing the elation and self-confidence often seen in the manic phase. Later, in response to the excessive display of ego, feelings of guilt return and plunge the person into depression once again.

Many learning theorists suggest that depressed people lack sufficient reinforcement in their lives to maintain their mood and behavior. Moreover, social-cognitive theorists point out that many people with depressive disorders have an external locus of control. That is, they do not believe they can control events so as to achieve reinforcements. Research conducted by learning theorists has also found links between depression and **learned helplessness**. In classic research, psychologist Martin Seligman and his colleagues (Overmier & Seligman, 1967; Seligman & Maier, 1967) exposed dogs to inescapable electric shock. The dogs learned they were helpless to escape the shock.

▮ **Learned helplessness** A model for the acquisition of depressive behavior, based on findings that organisms in aversive situations learn to show inactivity when their responses go unreinforced.

Do Your Own Thoughts Put You Down in the Dumps?

Self-Assessment

Cognitive theorists note that we can depress ourselves through negative thoughts. The following list contains negative thoughts that are linked to depression.

Directions: Using the code given below, indicate how frequently you have the following thoughts. There is no scoring key for this inventory. Try, however, to consider whether your negative thoughts are accurate and appropriate to your situation and how they may be affecting your moods.

1 = Never
2 = Seldom
3 = Often
4 = Very often

_____ 1. It seems such an effort to do anything.
_____ 2. I feel pessimistic about the future.
_____ 3. I have too many bad things in my life.
_____ 4. I have very little to look forward to.
_____ 5. I'm drained of energy, worn out.
_____ 6. I'm not as successful as other people.
_____ 7. Everything seems futile and pointless.
_____ 8. I just want to curl up and go to sleep.
_____ 9. There are things about me that I don't like.
_____ 10. It's too much effort even to move.
_____ 11. I'm absolutely exhausted.
_____ 12. The future seems just one string of problems.
_____ 13. My thoughts keep drifting away.
_____ 14. I get no satisfaction from the things I do.
_____ 15. I've made so many mistakes in the past.
_____ 16. I've got to really concentrate just to keep my eyes open.
_____ 17. Everything I do turns out badly.
_____ 18. My whole body has slowed down.
_____ 19. I regret some of the things I've done.
_____ 20. I can't make the effort to liven up myself.
_____ 21. I feel depressed with the way things are going.
_____ 22. I haven't any real friends anymore.
_____ 23. I do have a number of problems.
_____ 24. There's no one I can feel really close to.
_____ 25. I wish I were someone else.
_____ 26. I'm annoyed at myself for being bad at making decisions.
_____ 27. I don't make a good impression on other people.
_____ 28. The future looks hopeless.
_____ 29. I don't get the same satisfaction out of things these days.
_____ 30. I wish something would happen to make me feel better.

Source: Reprinted with permission of The Free Press, a division of Macmillan, Inc., from *The Psychological Treatment of Depression: A Guide to the Theory and Practice of Cognitive-Behavior Therapy* by J. Mark G. Williams. Copyright (1984) by J. Mark G. Williams.

Later, a barrier to a safe compartment was removed, offering the animals a way out. But when the dogs were shocked again, they made no effort to escape. Their helplessness apparently prevented them from attempting to escape. The lethargy and lack of motivation they displayed resembled that seen in people who are depressed. In humans, the failure to garner reinforcements for one's efforts—to continually try but fail—may also produce the lethargy and sense of helplessness that Seligman observed in dogs. In the face of continued lack of reinforcement for our efforts, we may begin to give up and resign ourselves to having a lack of control over potential reinforcements.

Cognitive theorists such as Aaron Beck and psychologist Albert Ellis believe that the ways we interpret negative life events leads to emotional disorders such as depression. For example, Beck (Beck et al., 1979; DeRubeis, Tang, & Beck, 2001) argues that people who are prone to depression tend to see the world through a kind of darkened mental filter that slants or biases how they interpret life experiences. Minor disappointments, such as getting a poor grade on a test, become blown out of proportion. They come to expect the worst and tend to focus only on the negative aspects of events. Beck calls these faulty thinking patterns "cognitive distortions" and believes that they pave the way for depression in the face of negative life events. Table 8.5 lists some examples of the cognitive distortions associated with depression.

The case of Christie illustrates a number of cognitive factors in depression:

Christie was a 33-year-old real estate sales agent who suffered from frequent episodes of depression. Whenever a deal fell through, she would blame herself, "If only I had worked harder...negotiated better...talked more persuasively...the deal would have been set." After several successive disappointments, each one followed by self-recriminations, she felt like quitting altogether. Her thinking became increasingly dominated by negative thoughts, which further depressed her mood and lowered her self-esteem: "I'm a loser.... I'll never succeed.... It's all my fault.... I'm no good and I'm never going to succeed at anything." Christie's thinking included cognitive errors such as the following: (1) mistaken responsibility (believing herself to be the sole cause of negative events); (2) name calling (thinking of herself as a "nothing"); (3) misfortune telling (predicting a dismal future on the basis of a present disappointment); and (4) negative focusing (judging her entire personality on the basis of her disappointments). In therapy, Christie was helped to think more realistically about events and not to jump to conclusions that she was automatically at fault whenever a deal fell through, or to judge her whole personality on the basis of disappointments or perceived flaws within herself. In place of this self-defeating style of thinking, she began to think more realistically when disappointments occurred, as in telling herself, "Okay, I'm disappointed. I'm frustrated. I feel lousy. So what? It doesn't mean I'll never succeed. Let me discover what went wrong and try to correct it the next time. I have to look ahead, not dwell on disappointments in the past." (From the authors' files. Reprinted from Nevid, Rathus, & Greene, 2006, with permission of Prentice Hall, Inc.)

Seligman's original conceptualization of learned helplessness underwent a significant revision in the form of the *reformulated helplessness theory* (Abramson, Seligman, & Teasdale, 1978). The revised theory held that perception of lack of control over reinforcement alone did not explain the persistence and severity of depression. It was also necessary to consider cognitive factors, especially people's attributions about the causes of events— that is, how they explain to themselves their failures and disappointments. Let us explain. When things go wrong, we may think of the causes of failure along three dimensions— as internal or external, stable or unstable, and global or specific. These personal styles of explanation, or **attributional styles**, can be illustrated using the example of having a date that does not work out. An internal attribution involves self-blame (as in "I really loused it up"). An external attribution places the blame elsewhere (as in "Some couples just don't take to each other" or "She was the wrong sign for me"). A stable attribution ("It's my personality") suggests a problem that cannot be changed. An unstable attribution ("It was because I had a head cold") suggests a temporary condition. A global attribution of failure ("I have no idea what

▮ **Attributional styles** Tendencies to attribute one's behavior to internal or external factors, stable or unstable factors, and global or specific factors.

Table 8.5 ▮ Cognitive Distortions Associated with Depression		
Type of Cognitive Distortion	**Description**	**Examples**
All or Nothing Thinking	Viewing events in black-or-white terms, as either all good or all bad	Do you view a relationship that ended as a total failure, or are you able to see some benefits in the relationship? Do you consider any less-than-perfect performance as a failure? Do you berate yourself for getting a less-than-perfect grade?
Misplaced Blame	Tendency to blame or criticize yourself for disappointments or setbacks while ignoring external circumstances	Do you automatically assume when things don't go as planned that it's your fault? Do others tell you that you are too hard on yourself or expect too much of yourself?
Misfortune Telling	Tendency to think that one disappointment will inevitably lead to another	If you get a rejection letter from a job you applied for, do you assume that all the other applications you sent will meet the same fate?
Negative Focusing	Focuses your attention only on the negative aspects of your experiences	Do you tend to harp on the negative side of events and overlook the positive? When you get a job evaluation, do you overlook the praise and focus only on the criticism?
Dismissing the Positives	Snatching defeat from the jaws of victory by trivializing or denying your accomplishments; minimizing your strengths or assets	When someone compliments you, do you find some way of dismissing it by saying something like, "It's no big deal," or "Anyone could have done it"? Do you give yourself short shrift when sizing up your abilities?
Jumping to Conclusions	Drawing a conclusion that is not supported by the facts at hand	Do you always expect the worst to happen? If you meet someone new, do you naturally assume that they couldn't possibly like you? If you feel a passing tightness in your chest, do you assume that it must be a sign of heart trouble?
Catastrophizing	Exaggerating the importance of negative events or personal flaws (making mountains out of molehills)	Do you react to a disappointing grade on a particular examination as though your whole life is ruined? Does your mind automatically run to the worst possible case?
Emotion-Based Reasoning	Reasoning based on your emotions rather than on a clear-headed evaluation of the availble evidence	Do you think that things are really hopeless because it feels that way? Do you believe that you must have done something really bad to feel so awful about yourself?
Shouldisms	Placing unrealistic demands on yourself that you "should" or "must" accomplish certain tasks or reach certain goals	Do you think that you *should* be able to ace this course or else you're just a loser? Do you feel that you *should* be further along in your life than you are now? Do you feel you *must* ace this course? (Not that it wouldn't be desirable to ace the course, but is it really the case that you *must*? Think about the consequences to your emotional well-being and self-esteem to continually impose *musts and shoulds* on yourself.)
Name Calling	Attaching negative labels to oneself or others as a way of explaining your own or someone else's behavior	Do you think that people fail to meet your needs because they are *selfish*? Do you label yourself *lazy* or *stupid* when you fall short of reaching your goals?
Mistaken Responsibility	Assuming that you are the cause of other people's problems	Do you automatically assume that your partner is depressed or upset because of something you said or did (or didn't say or do)?

Source: Nevid (2003). Reprinted with permission of Houghton Mifflin Co. Adapted from Burns, 1980.

to do when I'm with other people") suggests that the problem is quite large. A specific attribution ("I have problems making small talk at the beginning of a relationship") chops the problem down to a manageable size.

Research has shown that people who are depressed are more likely to attribute the causes of their failures to internal, stable, and global factors—factors that they are relatively powerless to change (Lewinsohn, Rohde, et al., 2000; Riso et al., 2003). Consistent with Beck's cognitive theory, evidence links negative, distorted thinking to depression (e.g., Beevers, Wells, & Miller, 2007; Riso et al., 2003). That said, psychologists continue to debate whether attributional styles or distorted thinking cause depression or merely reflect the effects of depression (Otto et al., 2007). As this debate continues to play out, we may find that causal linkages work both ways—in other words, negative or distorted thinking patterns affect our moods and our moods affect how we think.

Biological Factors

Evidence points to an important role for genetic factors in major depression and, most especially, in bipolar disorder (Baum et al., 2007; Holmans et al., 2007; López-León et al, 2008; Serretti & Mandelli, 2008). For example, identical twins, who share 100% genetic overlap, are more likely to have bipolar disorder in common than are fraternal twins, who share 50% of their genes in common.

Research into depression has identified irregularities in the brain's use of the neurotransmitter serotonin, a brain chemical involved in regulating states of pleasure and processing emotional stimuli (Oquendo et al., 2007; Sharp, 2006). People with clinical depression often respond to drugs that increase the availability of serotonin in the brain, such as the antidepressants Prozac, Zoloft, and Celexa.

Relationships between mood disorders and biological factors are complex and under intense study. Even if people are biologically predisposed toward depression, cognitive factors, exposure to stressful life situations, and availability of reinforcement play important contributing roles in determining whether this predisposition is expressed in the development of mood disorders (Kendler, Gardner, & Prescott, 2002; Leonardo & Hen, 2006). All things considered, mood disorders are complex problems reflecting the roles of many factors and their interactions (Belmaker & Agam, 2008; Haeffel et al., 2008).

MODULE REVIEW

Review It

(20) Two major types of mood disorder are major depression and _____ disorder.

(21) (Men or Women?) are more likely to suffer from major depression.

(22) In bipolar disorder there are mood swings between _____ and depression.

(23) People in a manic state may have grand, delusional schemes and show rapid _____ of ideas.

(24) Seligman and his colleagues have explored links between depression and learned _____.

(25) Depressed people are more likely than other people to make (internal or external?), stable, and global attributions for failures.

(26) There is greater concordance between (identical or fraternal?) twins in the development of bipolar disorder.

(27) Irregularities in the utilization of the neurotransmitter _____ are linked to the development of depression.

Think About It

When is depression considered a psychological disorder? How does bipolar disorder differ from the ordinary "ups and downs" of life?

MODULE 8.5

Schizophrenia

▪ ▪

■ What is schizophrenia?
■ What are the different types of schizophrenia?
■ What is known about the origins of schizophrenia?

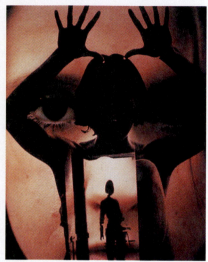
© Richard Frieman/Photo Researchers, Inc.

Paranoid Schizophrenia
People with paranoid schizophrenia often have delusions of grandeur and persecution. They may also have delusions of jealousy. They frequently have hallucinations, as in "hearing" people talk about them. They may believe that news stories refer to them in some sort of code. Despite these perceptual distortions, their cognitive functioning remains relatively intact when they are compared with people with disorganized schizophrenia or catatonic schizophrenia.

▮ **Hallucinations** Sensory experiences in the absence of external stimuli, such as "hearing voices" or seeing things that are not physically there.

▮ **Delusions** False but unshakable beliefs.

Jennifer was 19. Her husband David brought her into the emergency room because she had cut her wrists. When she was interviewed, her attention wandered. She seemed distracted by things in the air or something she might be hearing. It was as if she had an invisible earphone.

She explained that she had cut her wrists because the "hellsmen" had told her to. Then she seemed frightened. Later she said that the hellsmen had warned her not to reveal their existence. She had been afraid that they would punish her for talking about them.

David and Jennifer had been married for about one year. At first they had been together in a small apartment in town. But Jennifer did not want to be near other people and had convinced him to rent a bungalow in the country. There she would make fantastic drawings of goblins and monsters during the day. Now and then she would become agitated and act as if invisible things were giving her instructions.

"I'm bad," Jennifer would mutter, "I'm bad." She would begin to jumble her words. David would then try to convince her to go to the hospital, but she would refuse. Then the wrist-cutting would begin. David thought he had made the cottage safe by removing knives and blades. But Jennifer would always find something. Then Jennifer would be brought to the hospital, have stitches put in, be kept under observation and medicated with antipsychotic drugs. She would explain that she cut herself because the hellsmen had told her that she was bad and must die. After a few days she would deny hearing the hellsmen, and she would insist on leaving the hospital. Once she was stabilized, she would be released, but the pattern would continue. (From the authors' files.)

When the emergency room staff examined Jennifer's wrists and heard that she believed she had been following the orders of "hellsmen," they suspected she suffered from schizophrenia, a severe and persistent psychological disorder that touches every aspect of a person's life. It is characterized by disturbances in thought and language, perception and attention, motor activity, emotional states, and interpersonal functioning.

Schizophrenia is a chronic, lifelong disorder that corresponds most closely to popular concepts of "madness" or "insanity." It is characterized by a break with reality that may take the form of **hallucinations** (hearing or seeing things that are not there), **delusions** (fixed, false beliefs), and bizarre, irrational behavior. The onset of the disorder is typically during late adolescence or early adulthood, at the very time that people are starting to make their way in the world (Walker & Tessner, 2008).

Schizophrenia affects about 1% of the general population, or about 2.5 million people in the United States (Berenson, 2007; Perälä et al., 2007). Schizophrenia occurs somewhat more often in men than in women, and the disorder typically occurs earlier and in more severe forms in men (Tandon, Keshavan, & Nasralla, 2008).

People with schizophrenia have problems in memory, attention, and communication. Their thinking becomes unraveled. Unless we are allowing our thoughts to wander, our thinking is normally tightly knit. We start at a certain point, and thoughts that come to mind (our associations) tend to be logically connected. But people with schizophrenia often think illogically. Their speech may be jumbled. They may combine parts of words into new words or make meaningless rhymes. They may jump from topic to topic, conveying little useful information. They usually do not recognize that their thoughts and behavior are abnormal.

Many people with schizophrenia have delusions—for example, delusions of grandeur, persecution, or reference. In the case of delusions of grandeur, a person may believe that he is a famous historical figure such as Jesus or a person on a special mission. He may have grand, illogical plans for saving the world. Delusions tend to be unshakable even in the face of evidence that they are not true. People with delusions of persecution may believe that they are sought by the Mafia, CIA, FBI, or some other group. A woman with delusions of reference said that news stories contained coded information about her. A man with such delusions complained that neighbors had "bugged" his walls with "radios." Other people with schizophrenia have had delusions that they have committed unpardonable sins, that they were rotting away from disease, or that they or the world did not exist.

Jennifer apparently hallucinated the voices of "hellsmen." Other people who experience hallucinations may see colors or even obscene words spelled out in midair. Auditory hallucinations are the most common type, however. In individuals with schizophrenia, motor activity may become wild or become so slow that the person enters a state of **stupor**. They may make strange gestures and facial expressions. The person's emotional responses may be flat, or blunted, or inappropriate—as in giggling upon hearing bad news. People with schizophrenia have problems understanding other people's feelings, tend to withdraw from social contacts, and become wrapped up in their own thoughts and fantasies.

Stupor A condition in which the senses and thinking processes are dulled.

8.5.1 Types of Schizophrenia

There are three major types of schizophrenia: paranoid, disorganized, and catatonic.

Paranoid Type

People with **paranoid schizophrenia** exhibit systematized delusions and, frequently, related auditory hallucinations. They usually have delusions of grandeur and persecution, but they may also have delusions of jealousy, in which they believe that a spouse or lover has been unfaithful. They may show agitation, confusion, and fear, and may experience vivid hallucinations that are consistent with their delusions. People with paranoid schizophrenia often construct complex or systematized delusions involving themes of wrongdoing or persecution.

Paranoid schizophrenia A type of schizophrenia characterized primarily by delusions—commonly of persecution—and by vivid hallucinations.

Disorganized Type

Disorganized schizophrenia is characterized by incoherent speech, loosening of associations, disorganized behavior, fragmentary delusions or hallucinations, and flattened or highly inappropriate emotional responses. Extreme social impairment is common. People with this type of schizophrenia may also exhibit silliness and giddiness of mood, giggling, and nonsensical speech. They may neglect their appearance and personal hygiene and lose control of their bladder and bowels.

Disorganized schizophrenia A type of schizophrenia characterized by incoherent speech, disorganized or fragmentary delusions, and vivid hallucinations.

Catatonic Type

People with **catatonic schizophrenia** exhibit disturbed motor (movement) activity. They may slow down to a state of stupor and then suddenly change to an agitated phase. People with catatonic schizophrenia may maintain unusual, even difficult, postures for hours, even as their limbs grow swollen or stiff. A striking feature of this condition is **waxy flexibility**, in which the person maintains positions into which he or she has been manipulated by others. These individuals may also show **mutism**, but afterward they usually report that they heard what others were saying at the time.

Catatonic schizophrenia A type of schizophrenia characterized by striking impairment in motor activity.

Waxy flexibility A feature of catatonic schizophrenia in which persons maintain postures into which they are placed.

Mutism Failure to speak.

8.5.2 Causal Factors

The causes of schizophrenia remain elusive, but most researchers believe that schizophrenia is a brain disorder that arises from a combination of factors, including heredity, abnormal brain development, and stressful life experiences. Let us examine what we have learned and what remains to be discovered about this severe, disabling condition.

Genetic Factors

Genetics plays an important role in determining the risk of developing schizophrenia (e.g., Gur et al., 2007; Sands, 2008). The more closely related two people are by blood, the more likely they are to share the disorder in common. Scientists believe that multiple genes are at work, rather than any single gene (Braff, Schork, &. Gottesman, 2007; Walker & Tessner, 2008; Yeo, Gangestad, & Thoma, 2007). A number of research teams across the world are trying to track down the specific genes that increase susceptibility to schizophrenia (e.g., Gurling et al., 2006; Hamilton, 2008).

Although genetics clearly plays a key role in determining vulnerability to schizophrenia, it is not the only risk factor. If it were, we would expect a 100% **concordance rate** (percent of agreement) between identical twins, as opposed to the 40% to 50% rate we do find (Carpenter & Buchanan, 1994). Other (nongenetic) factors are clearly involved.

Some of these factors are biological in origin. Evidence of structural abnormalities in the brains of schizophrenia patients is large and growing, such as development of larger ventricles (hollow spaces) in the brain indicative of loss of brain tissue (gray matter) (e.g., Ettinger et al., 2007; Szeszko et al., 2005). We should recognize, however, that genetics may affect the development of brain structures, so perhaps genetic factors are intermingled with the development of brain abnormalities.

In sum, the accumulating evidence indicates that schizophrenia is a brain disorder. The parts of the brain most strongly implicated are those that enable us to organize our thoughts, develop and carry out planned actions, process emotional experiences, and maintain attention—the very functions that are often impaired in schizophrenia patients (e.g., Barch & Csernansky, 2007; Reichenberg & Harvey, 2007; Tregellas, 2009). These brain abnormalities may develop during prenatal development when the brain is forming or shortly after birth or during early childhood when it is still maturing.

Problems in the nervous system may involve brain chemistry as well as brain structures, and research along these lines has led to the dopamine theory of schizophrenia.

The Dopamine Theory of Schizophrenia

According to the dopamine theory of schizophrenia, people with schizophrenia overutilize the neurotransmitter dopamine (i.e., they use more of it than other people do) (Huttunen et al., 2008; McGowan et al., 2004). However, their brains do not appear to produce too much dopamine. Rather, their brains may have an excess number of dopamine receptors or their receptors may be overly sensitive to the chemical (Walker et al., 2004).

Overreactivity or overabundance of these receptors may explain some of the symptoms of schizophrenia, such as hallucinations and delusional thinking. This explanation is bolstered by evidence that antipsychotic drugs that help control these symptoms reduce dopamine activity in the brain by blocking receptors for dopamine. Though antipsychotic drugs may help quell the symptoms of schizophrenia, they are not a cure (Walker & Tessner, 2008).

How can we integrate the various factors that underlie schizophrenia? Although a complete model of how schizophrenia develops remains to be determined, most investigators today favor a multifactorial model. According to this model, genetic factors create a predisposition, or **diathesis**, toward schizophrenia (see Figure 8.3). Genetic vulnerability to the disorder—the diathesis—interacts with stress, such as complications during pregnancy and birth, life changes, and poor quality of parenting, in leading to the development of the disorder.

Concordance rate The rate of agreement or co-occurrence, as in the percentage of twins who share a particular disorder with their co-twins.

Diathesis A predisposition or vulnerability to a particular disorder.

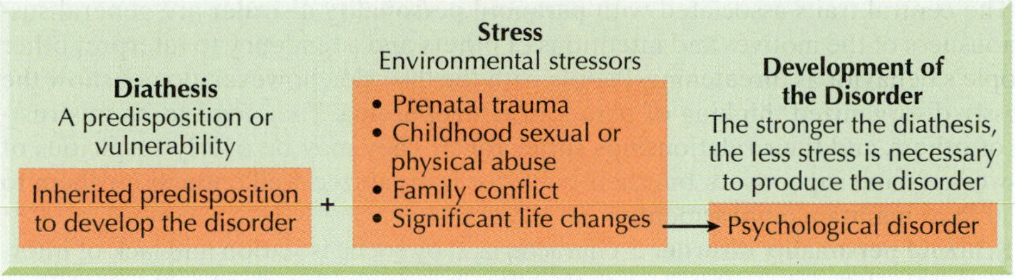

Figure 8.3 The Diathesis–Stress Model of Schizophrenia
According to the diathesis–stress model, an inherited predisposition, or diathesis, interacts with stress in giving rise to the development of schizophrenia.
Source: Adapted from Nevid, Rathus, & Greene, 2008.

MODULE REVIEW

Review It

(28) _____ is characterized by disturbances in thought and speech (as in the loosening of associations and in delusions), in attention and perception (as in hallucinations), in motor activity, in emotional states, and by withdrawal, among other features.

(29) _____ schizophrenia is characterized by impaired motor activity and waxy flexibility.

(30) Schizophrenia (does or does not?) tend to run in families.

(31) Evidence points to (larger or smaller?) empty spaces in the brains of many people with schizophrenia.

(32) The brains of people with schizophrenia may utilize more of the neurotransmitter _____ than do the brains of other people.

Think About It

What does it mean to say that schizophrenia is best understood from a multifactorial perspective?

MODULE 8.6

Personality Disorders

■ What are the different types of personality disorders?
■ What is known about the origins of personality disorders?

Personality disorders, like personality traits, are characterized by enduring patterns of behavior. Yet with personality disorders, these patterns are inflexible and maladaptive, causing difficulties in social, personal, or occupational functioning. These rigid patterns may also become a source of distress to the individual or to other people.

▌ **Personality disorders** Enduring patterns of maladaptive behaviors that are sources of distress to the individual or others.

8.6.1 Types of Personality Disorders

The DSM system lists 10 specific types of personality disorders that are organized in three general clusters according to their general behavioral features:

Cluster A: Odd or eccentric behavior. This cluster includes paranoid, schizoid, and schizotypal personality disorders.
Cluster B: Behavior that is overly dramatic, emotional, or erratic. This cluster consists of antisocial, borderline, histrionic, and narcissistic personality disorders.
Cluster C: Anxious or fearful. This cluster includes avoidant, dependent, and obsessive-compulsive personality disorders.

▌ **Paranoid personality disorder** A personality disorder characterized by persistent suspiciousness but not involving the disorganization of paranoid schizophrenia.

▌ **Schizoid personality disorder** A personality disorder characterized by social detachment or isolation.

▌ **Schizotypal personality disorder** A personality disorder characterized by oddities of thought and behavior but not involving bizarre behaviors associated with schizophrenia.

▌ **Borderline personality disorder** A personality disorder characterized by failure to develop a stable self-image, by a pattern of tumultuous moods and stormy relationships with others, and by difficulties controlling impulsive behaviors.

▌ **Histrionic personality disorder** A personality disorder characterized by overly dramatic and emotional behavior; by excessive needs to be the center of attention; and by constant demands for reassurance, praise, and approval.

Pam Francis/Getty Images, Inc.

Antisocial Personality
The serial killer Henry Lee Lucas, a drifter and violent career criminal, embodied many of the personality features of the antisocial personality. In 1998, then Texas governor George W. Bush commuted Lucas's death sentence to life imprisonment. Lucas died in his cell of heart failure in 2001. Though Lucas fits the stereotype of an antisocial personality, not all antisocial personalities run afoul of the law.

The central traits associated with **paranoid personality disorder** are general suspiciousness of the motives and intentions of others and a tendency to interpret other people's behavior as threatening. People with the disorder, however, do not show the grossly disorganized thinking of paranoid schizophrenia. They tend to be mistrustful of others, and their relationships suffer for it. They may be overly suspicious of co-workers and supervisors, but their behavior is organized well enough for them to be able to maintain employment.

Schizoid personality disorder is characterized by social isolation and lack of interest in social relationships. People with this disorder are characterized as "loners." They do not develop warm, tender feelings for others. They tend to have few friends, are unlikely to marry, and display flat or blunted emotions (i.e., they rarely if ever experience strong emotions such as anger, joy, or sadness).

Schizotypal personality disorder is characterized by difficulties forming close relationships with others; peculiarities of thought, perception, or behavior, such as excessive fantasy and suspiciousness; feelings of being unreal; or odd usage of words. People with schizotypal personality disorder may hold odd beliefs or exhibit peculiar behaviors (such as believing they can foretell the future), but their thoughts and behavior are not as disturbed as those of people with schizophrenia.

People with **borderline personality disorder** tend to have tumultuous moods, stormy relationships with others, and fail to develop a stable self-image and sense of direction in life (Gunderson, 2007; Trull et al., 2008). They are also prone to impulsive, acting-out behavior, such as cutting themselves (Ferraz et al., 2009).

Histrionic personality disorder characterizes people who are overly dramatic and emotional in their behavior and who make excessive demands to be the center of people's attention. They tend to have strong, unfulfilled needs for reassurance, praise, and approval.

People with **narcissistic personality disorder** have an inflated or grandiose self-image. They see themselves as having special talents or beauty and require constant admiration and praise, lest their self-esteem plummet.

People with **antisocial personality disorder** show a flagrant disregard for the interests, needs, and feelings of others as well as for usual social customs and rules. Their antisocial behavior may bring them into conflict with the law, yet they may show a superficial charm and have at least average intelligence. They may show little if any remorse over their misdeeds and a lack of anxiety about potential punishment for their behavior (Goldstein et al., 2006; Kiehl, 2006). Antisocial personality disorder is associated with a greater risk of engaging in criminal activity, but it's important to note that not all people with the disorder are criminals and not all criminals have antisocial personalities (Kosson, Lorenz, & Newman, 2006; Mahmut, Homewood, & Stevenson, 2008). The disorder occurs disproportionately more often among men—3% to 6% in men versus 1% in women (American Psychiatric Association, 2000; Cale & Lilienfeld, 2002).

People with **avoidant personality disorder** have such strong fears of rejection that they are often unwilling to enter relationships without strong assurances of acceptance. As a result, they may have few close relationships outside their immediate families. Unlike people with schizoid personality disorder, however, they have a strong interest in having relationships and are capable of developing feelings of warmth toward other people. People with **dependent personality disorder** are excessively dependent on others and have difficulties making independent decisions, such as deciding what clothes to buy, or whom to date, or where to live. In people with **obsessive-compulsive personality disorder**, there is an excessive need for orderliness and attention to detail, perfectionism, as well as overly rigid ways of relating to others. All in all, the personality traits associated with personality disorders are found in many individuals, but they are expressed to an excessive degree in people with these disorders.

8.6.2 Causal Factors

Many of the theoretical explanations of personality disorders are derived from the psychodynamic model. Traditional Freudian theory focuses on Oedipal problems as the source of many psychological disorders, including personality disorders. Faulty resolution of the Oedipus complex might lead to antisocial personality disorder, since the moral conscience, or superego, is believed to depend on proper resolution of the Oedipus complex.

Learning theorists suggest that childhood experiences can contribute to maladaptive ways of relating to others in adulthood—that is, can lead to personality disorders. Cognitive psychologists find that antisocial adolescents interpret social information in ways that bolster their misdeeds. For example, they tend to interpret other people's behavior as threatening, even when it is not (Dodge et al., 2002). Cognitive therapists work with antisocial adolescents to help them see social provocations as problems to be solved rather than as threats to their "manhood."

Let us also note that children raised in harsh, uncaring home environments may fail to develop a sense of empathy toward others and a concern for their welfare. They lack a moral compass that guides their actions. The lack of a moral compass may explain how they can act so callously toward others without a sense of guilt or remorse. Perhaps the genetics of antisocial personality disorder involves abnormalities in the prefrontal cortex of the brain, a part of the brain connected with emotional responses. Evidence indicates that men with antisocial personality disorder may have brain abnormalities that make it difficult for them to curb their impulses and aggressive behavior (e.g., Kiehl, 2006; Siegle, 2008).

▮ **Antisocial personality disorder** A personality disorder characterized by a pattern of antisocial and irresponsible behavior, a flagrant disregard for the interests and feelings of others, and lack of remorse for wrongdoing.

▮ **Avoidant personality disorder** A personality disorder in which the person is generally unwilling to enter relationships without assurance of acceptance because of extreme fears of rejection and criticism.

▮ **Dependent personality disorder** A personality disorder characterized by excessive dependence on others and difficulties making independent decisions.

▮ **Obsessive-compulsive personality disorder** A personality disorder described by excessive needs for attention to detail and demands for orderliness, as well as perfectionism and highly rigid ways of relating to others.

MODULE REVIEW

Review It

(33) _____ _____ are inflexible, maladaptive behavior patterns that impair personal or social functioning and are a source of distress to the individual or to others.

(34) The defining trait of paranoid personality disorder is undue _____.

(35) Social isolation is the major characteristic of the _____ personality.

(36) Persons with _____ personality disorder violate the rights of others, show little or no guilt for their misdeeds, and are undeterred by punishment.

(37) Research suggests that people with _____ personalities typically come from homes that lack parental warmth.

Think About It

What is the difference between saying that a person has a "bad personality" and saying that the person has a personality disorder?

Psychology in Daily Life

MODULE 8.7

Helping a Friend in Crisis

After motor vehicle accidents, what would you say is the next leading cause of death among college students today? Homicide? AIDS? Drugs? The answer is suicide (Rawe & Kingsbury, 2006). More than 1,000 college students annually, and approximately 30,000 Americans overall, commit suicide each year. Table 8.6 highlights some of the findings on the costs to the nation from suicide, based on a recent report from the U.S. Surgeon General.

8.7.1 Factors in Suicide

Most suicides are linked to mood disorders such as major depression and bipolar disorder and especially to deep feelings of hopelessness that may accompany these disorders (Bernal et al., 2007; Borges et al., 2008). Between 2% and 15% of depressed patients eventually commit suicide, generally at a point in their lives when they feel both utterly hopeless about their lives and helpless to change it for the better (Friedman & Leon, 2007). Other factors that may be involved in the complex web of factors that can lead to suicide include other psychological disorders, such as alcohol and substance abuse disorders, as well as persistent physical pain, severe chronic illness, and prolonged unemployment. Exposure to other people who committed suicide can increase the risk of suicide among adolescents. Copycat suicides contribute to a so-called cluster effect among adolescents.

Suicide attempts are more common after stressful events, especially events that entail loss of social support—as in the loss of a spouse, friend, or relative. People under stress who consider suicide may have difficulty resolving problems they face, especially problems or conflicts with others. They may see no other way of resolving their problems than taking their own lives.

Biological factors are also implicated in suicide. Like depression, suicide may involve irregularities in brain neurotransmitters and genetic factors, possibly involving genes that play a role in regulating neurotransmitter functioning (Joiner, Brown, & Wingate, 2005; Jokinen et al., 2008). Reduced availability in the brain of serotonin is linked to depression, so the linkage between suicide and serotonin is not surprising. But it may be that serotonin's influence on curbing impulsive behavior, including impulses to harm oneself, plays a more direct role.

© Mary Kate Denny/PhotoEdit

Suicide Prevention
Nearly 30,000 Americans commit suicide each year. Contrary to myth, the majority warn people of their intentions. They may even have had failed suicide attempts. Suicide expert Edwin Shneidman speaks of suicide as a result of "psychache" (1999)—unbearable psychological pain that the person decides must be brought to an end.

8.7.2 Who's at Higher Risk?

Some groups in our society are at greater suicide risk than others. Consider some facts about suicide:

- More teenagers and young adults die from suicide than from cancer, heart disease, AIDS, birth defects, stroke, pneumonia and influenza, and chronic lung disease combined.
- Suicide is more common among college students than among people of the same age who do not attend college. Each year about 10,000 college students attempt suicide. That said, suicide rates increase with age and are highest among older adults in the 65+ age range, especially older white males (Pearson & Brown, 2000).
- More women than men attempt suicide, but about four times as many men succeed in killing themselves (Cochran & Rabinowitz, 2003; Houry, 2004; Miller, Azrael, & Hemenway, 2004).

- Among people who attempt suicide, men prefer to use guns or hang themselves, while women prefer to use sleeping pills. Males tend to use quicker and more lethal means.
- European Americans and Native Americans have higher suicide rates than other ethnic or racial groups, such as African Americans and Hispanic Americans (Garlow, Purselle, & Heninger, 2005; Joe et al., 2006). Among young American Indians, the suicide rate is more than three times the national average group (Meyers, 2007). Feelings of hopelessness and alienation from mainstream society among many young Native Americans set the stage for alcohol and drug abuse and form the backdrop that gives rise to depression and suicide.
- The suicide rate among older people who are separated or divorced is double that of older people who are married (CDC, 2000c).

Table 8.6 | U.S. Surgeon General's Report on Suicide: Cost to the Nation

- Every 17 minutes, another life is lost to suicide. Every day, 86 Americans take their own lives and over 1,500 attempt suicide.
- Suicide is now the eighth leading cause of death in Americans.
- For every two victims of homicide in the United States, there are three deaths from suicide.
- There are now twice as many deaths due to suicide than due to HIV/AIDS.
- Between 1952 and 1995, the incidence of suicide among adolescents and young adults nearly tripled.
- In the month prior to their suicide, 75% of elderly persons had visited a physician.
- Over half of all suicides occur in adult men, ages 25 to 65.
- Many who make suicide attempts never seek professional care immediately after the attempt.
- Males are four times more likely to commit suicide than are females.
- More teenagers and young adults die from suicide than from cancer, heart disease, AIDS, birth defects, stroke, pneumonia and influenza, and chronic lung disease, combined.
- Suicide takes the lives of more than 30,000 Americans every year.

Source: Center for Mental Health Services, 2001; from Nevid, J. S., Rathus, S. A., & Greene, B. (2008). *Abnormal psychology in a changing world.* (7th ed.) Upper Saddle River, NJ: Prentice-Hall. Reprinted with permission of Pearson Education.

8.7.3 Myths about Suicide

You may have heard that individuals who threaten suicide are only seeking attention; those who are serious just "do it." Actually, it is not true that people who threaten suicide are only seeking attention. Most people who commit suicide give warnings about their intentions or consult a health provider (Luoma, Martin, & Pearson, 2002).

Recognize that many people who committed suicide had made prior unsuccessful attempts. In fact, a recent study showed that among adolescents who attempted suicide and were treated in hospital emergency rooms, rates of later completed suicide were more than 10 times higher in females and more than 20 times higher in males than were the rates in the general adolescent population (Olfson et al., 2005). Recognize, too, that contrary to widespread belief, discussing suicide with a person who is depressed does not prompt the person to attempt suicide. Extracting a promise not to commit suicide before calling or visiting a helping professional may actually prevent some suicides.

Some believe that only "insane" people would take their own lives. However, suicidal thinking is not necessarily a sign of an underlying disorder. Instead, people may consider suicide when they think they have run out of options.

Regardless of the myths about suicide, there are some things you can do if someone confides in you that he or she is contemplating suicide.

8.7.4 What Do You Say Now? What Do You Do Now?

Imagine that you are having a heart-to-heart talk with Jamie, one of your best friends. Things haven't been going well. Jamie's grandmother died a month ago, and they were very close. Jamie's coursework has been suffering, and things have also been going downhill with the person Jamie has been seeing. But you are not prepared when Jamie looks you in the eye and says, "I've been thinking about this for days, and I've decided that the only way out is to kill myself."

If someone tells you that he or she is considering suicide, you may become frightened and flustered or feel that an enormous burden has been placed on you. You are right: it has. In such a case, your objective should be to encourage the person to consult a health care provider, or to consult one yourself, as soon as possible. But if the person refuses to talk to anyone else and you feel that you can't break free for a consultation, there are a number of things you can do:

1. *Keep talking.* Encourage the person to talk to you or to some other trusted person (Los Angeles Unified School District, 2000). Draw the person out with questions like "What's happening?" "Where do you hurt?" "What do you want to happen?" Questions like these may encourage the person to express frustrated needs and provide some relief. They also give you time to think.

2. *Be a good listener.* Be supportive with people who express suicidal thoughts or feel depressed, hopeless, or worthless. They may believe their condition is hopeless and will never improve, but let them know that you are there for them and are willing to help them get help. Show that you understand how upset the person is. Do not say, "Don't be silly."

3. *Suggest that something other than suicide might solve the problem, even if it is not evident at the time.* Many suicidal people see only two solutions—either death or a magical resolution of their problems. Therapists try to "remove the mental blinders" from suicidal people.

4. *Emphasize as concretely as possible how the person's suicide would be devastating to you and to other people who care.*

5. *Ask how the person intends to commit suicide.* People with concrete plans and a weapon are at greater risk. Ask if you might hold on to the weapon for a while. Sometimes the answer is yes.

6. *Do not tell people threatening suicide that they're acting stupid or crazy.* Nor should you insist on contact with specific people, such as parents or a spouse. Conflict with these people may have led to the suicidal thinking in the first place.

7. *Suggest that the person go with you to obtain professional help now.* Call the local emergency room, suicide hotline, campus counseling center or infirmary, campus or local police station, or 911 for assistance. Explain that your friend is threatening suicide and you require immediate assistance. Offer to accompany the person to a helping professional or facility. If you cannot maintain contact with the suicidal person before the person can be brought to a helping professional, get professional assistance as soon as you separate.

You can also check out the following resources for assistance:

❚ The national suicide hotline: 1-800-SUICIDE (1-800-784-2433).

❚ American Association of Suicidology: Its website (www.suicidology. org) provides information on ways to prevent suicide. You will also find a list of crisis centers.

❚ American Foundation for Suicide Prevention: Its website (www.afsp.org) offers information about suicide and links to other suicide and mental health sites.

❚ American Psychological Association (APA): The APA website (www.apa.org) provides information about risk factors, warning signs, and prevention.

❚ National Institutes of Mental Health (NIMH): Its website (www.nimh.nih.gov) contains information on depression and other psychological disorders.

❚ Suicide Awareness—Voices of Education (SA/VE): SA/VE's website (www.save.org) offers educational and practical information on suicide and depression. It highlights ways in which family members and friends can help suicidal people. The Suicide Information & Education Centre (SIEC) website (www.siec.ca) also offers a specialized library on suicide.

CHAPTER REVIEW

RECITE! RECITE! RECITE! RECITE! RECITE! RECITE! RECITE!

Study Tip: Reciting the answers to these study questions will help you become a more effective learner. First try answering the questions by yourself, either reciting them out loud or writing them in a notebook or on the computer. Then compare your answers with the sample answers provided below.

1. How do we define psychological disorders?

Psychological disorders are characterized by such criteria as unusual behavior, socially unacceptable behavior, faulty perception of reality, personal distress, dangerous behavior, or self-defeating behavior.

2. How are psychological disorders grouped or classified?

The most widely used classification scheme is found in the *Diagnostic and Statistical Manual* (DSM) of the American Psychiatric Association.

3. What are adjustment disorders?

Adjustment disorders are maladaptive reactions to one or more identified stressors that occur shortly following exposure to the stressor(s) and cause impaired functioning or signs of distress beyond that which would be normally expected. Adjustment disorders are usually resolved when the stressor is removed or the person learns to cope with it.

4. What are the different types of anxiety disorders?

These disorders include irrational, excessive fears, or phobias; panic disorder, characterized by sudden attacks of panic in which people typically fear that they may be losing control, going crazy, or having a heart attack; generalized anxiety disorder, a generalized pattern of worrisome, anxious behavior and heightened bodily arousal; obsessive-compulsive disorder, in which people are troubled by intrusive thoughts and/or impulses to repeat some behavioral ritual; and posttraumatic stress disorder and acute stress disorder, which involve maladaptive reactions to a traumatic event.

5. What is known about the origins of anxiety disorders?

The psychodynamic perspective views anxiety disorders in terms of underlying psychological conflicts. Learning theorists view phobias as conditioned fears. Cognitive theorists focus on ways in which people interpret threats. Some people may also be genetically predisposed to acquire certain kinds of fears. Biochemical factors—which could be inherited—may create a predisposition toward anxiety disorders.

6. What are the major types of dissociative disorders?

Dissociative disorders are characterized by sudden, temporary changes in consciousness or self-identity. They include dissociative amnesia, in which personal memories are forgotten; dissociative fugue, which involves forgetting plus fleeing and adopting a new identity; dissociative identity disorder (multiple personality disorder), in which a person behaves as if more than one personality occupies his or her body; and depersonalization disorder, which is characterized by feelings that one is not real or that one is standing outside oneself.

7. What is known about the origins of dissociative disorders?

Many psychologists suggest that dissociative disorders help people keep disturbing memories or ideas out of mind. Childhood abuse or trauma figures prominently in the case histories of many people with dissociative disorders.

8. What are the major types of somatoform disorders?

In conversion disorder, a person loses a physical function or capability without any apparent medical cause. The person may show la belle indifférence (indifference to the symptom), which suggests that the symptom serves a psychological purpose. In hypochondriasis, people have exaggerated fears about the significance of their physical complaints and fail to be reassured when their doctors tell them their fears are groundless.

9. What is known about the origins of somatoform disorders?

These disorders remain puzzling but may represent ways of dealing with underlying psychological conflicts or ways of avoiding painful or anxiety-evoking situations. Distorted cognitions (thoughts) also play a role.

10. What are the different types of mood disorders?

Major depression is characterized by persistent feelings of sadness, loss of interest, feelings of worthlessness or guilt, inability to concentrate, and physical symptoms that may include disturbances in regulation of eating and sleeping. Even hallucinations and delusions may be present. Bipolar disorder is characterized by dramatic swings in mood between elation and depression. Manic episodes may involve pressured speech and rapid flight of ideas.

11. Why are women more likely than men to be depressed?

Part of the gender difference may reflect biological influences, but women typically also experience greater stress than men in our culture—including the stress that accompanies carrying a greater proportion of household and childcare responsibilities.

12. What is known about the origins of mood disorders?

Research emphasizes possible roles for learned helplessness, attributional styles, and underutilization of serotonin in depression. People who are depressed are more likely than other people to make internal, stable, and global attributions for failures. Genetic factors involving regulation of neurotransmitters may also be involved in mood disorders.

13. What is schizophrenia?

Schizophrenia is a most severe and persistent psychological disorder that is characterized by disturbances in thought and language, such as loosening of associations and delusions; in perception and attention, as found in hallucinations; in motor activity, as shown by a stupor or by excited behavior; in mood, as in flat (blunted) or inappropriate emotional responses; and in social interaction, as in social withdrawal.

14. What are the different types of schizophrenia?

The major types of schizophrenia are paranoid, disorganized, and catatonic. Paranoid schizophrenia is characterized largely by systematized delusions; disorganized schizophrenia, by incoherence; and catatonic schizophrenia, by motor impairment.

15. What is known about the origins of schizophrenia?

According to the multifactorial model, genetic vulnerability to schizophrenia may interact with other factors, such as stress, complications during pregnancy and childbirth, and quality of parenting, to cause the disorder to develop. According to the dopamine theory of schizophrenia, people with schizophrenia use more dopamine than other people do, perhaps because of an overabundance of dopamine receptors in the brain.

16. What are the different types of personality disorders?

The defining trait of paranoid personality disorder is suspiciousness. People with schizotypal personality disorders show oddities of thought, perception, and behavior. Social withdrawal is the major characteristic of schizoid personality disorder. People with antisocial personality disorders persistently violate the rights of others and are in conflict with the law. They show little or no guilt or shame over their misdeeds and are largely undeterred by punishment. People with avoidant personality disorder tend to avoid entering relationships for fear of rejection and criticism.

17. What is known about the origins of personality disorders?

Psychodynamic theory connected many personality disorders with hypothesized Oedipal problems. Genetic factors may be involved in some personality disorders. Antisocial personality disorder may develop from a combination of factors, including genetic vulnerability and harsh or neglectful parenting in childhood.

YOUR PERSONAL JOURNAL

REFLECT REFLECT REFLECT REFLECT REFLECT REFLECT REFLECT

Study Tip: Reflecting on how the concepts in the chapter relate to your own experiences encourages deeper processing, which makes the material more personally meaningful and fosters more effective learning. Use additional pages if needed to complete your answers.

1. Have you ever known anyone whose behavior appeared odd or bizarre? Do you believe the person suffered from a psychological or mental disorder? What criteria did you use to form such a judgment? How did the criteria you used square with those described in the text?

_____

_____

_____

2. In what ways do your beliefs affect your emotions? Can you think of an example in which you have engaged in ways of thinking that Beck would describe as cognitive distortions? For example, have you been merciless in your self-criticism when you fell short of your goals? Have you engaged in misfortune telling, dismissing the positives, or catastrophizing unfortunate events? Explain.

_____

_____

_____

ANSWERS TO MODULE REVIEWS

Module 8.1

1. perceptions
2. multiaxial
3. III
4. adjustment
5. abnormal

Module 8.2

6. Specific
7. Panic
8. obsessive-compulsive
9. Posttraumatic stress

10. Psychodynamic
11. conditioned
12. predisposition

Module 8.3

13. amnesia
14. dissociative identity disorder
15. depersonalization disorder
16. dissociative
17. abuse
18. conversion disorder
19. hypochondriasis

Module 8.4

20. bipolar
21. Women
22. elation
23. flight
24. helplessness
25. internal
26. identical
27. serotonin

Module 8.5

28. Schizophrenia
29. Catatonic

30. does
31. larger
32. dopamine

Module 8.6

33. Personality disorders
34. suspiciousness
35. schizoid
36. antisocial
37. antisocial

- A major form of psychotherapy encourages clients to just talk about whatever happens to be on their minds at the moment? (p. 295)

- Sigmund Freud believed that clients reenact childhood conflicts they had with their parents and other important figures in the relationship they form with their therapists? (p. 296)

Getty Images, Inc

- Lying around in a reclining chair and fantasizing can be an effective way of confronting your fears? (Really) (p. 293)

- Cognitive therapists believe that our emotional reactions to disappointments in life are determined by our beliefs about these events, not by the events themselves? (p. 308)

- You can use the Internet these days not only to download music and check your e-mail but also to consult an online therapist? (p. 313)

- About three of four people who undergo psychotherapy show significant positive changes within the first six months of treatment? (p. 315)

- People who are severely depressed may benefit from having jolts of electricity passed through their heads? (p. 322)

- The originator of a surgical technique intended to reduce violence learned that it was not always successful when one of his patients shot him? (p. 322)

Jasmine is a 19-year-old college sophomore. She has been crying almost without letup for several days. She feels that her life is falling apart. Her college dreams are in shambles. She feels she has brought shame on her family. Thoughts of suicide have crossed her mind. She can barely drag herself out of bed in the morning. She is avoiding her friends. She can pinpoint some sources of stress in her life: a couple of poor grades, an argument with a boyfriend, and friction with roommates. Still, her misery seemed to descend on her out of nowhere.

Jasmine is depressed—so depressed that her family and friends have finally prevailed on her to seek professional help. Depending on the therapist Jasmine sees, she may be doing the following:

1 Lying on a couch talking about anything that pops into her mind and exploring her dreams as a guide to her unconscious mind
2 Sitting face to face with a warm, gentle therapist who accepts Jasmine as she is and encourages her to do the same
3 Listening to a frank, straightforward therapist who explains how Jasmine's way of thinking is making her depressed and how by changing her thinking she can overcome her depression
4 Taking medication to alleviate her depression
5 Receiving a combination of these approaches

Had Jasmine broken her leg, her treatment by a qualified professional would have followed a fairly standard course. Yet treatment of psychological problems and disorders like depression may be approached from very different perspectives. In this

293

▌**Psychotherapy** A systematic interaction between a therapist and a client that brings psychological principles to bear on influencing the client's thoughts, feelings, or behavior to help that client overcome abnormal behavior or adjust to problems in living.

chapter we examine these different ways of helping, including the major approaches to psychotherapy and biological approaches to treatment. We begin with the question, "What is **psychotherapy**?"

Although there are many approaches to psychotherapy, they all have certain common characteristics. Let us begin with a definition: Psychotherapy is the systematic interaction between a therapist and a client that applies psychological principles to affect the client's thoughts, feelings, or behavior in order to help the client overcome psychological disorders, adjust to problems in living, or develop as an individual. Quite a mouthful? True, but note the essentials:

1 *Systematic interaction.* Psychotherapy is a systematic interaction between a client and a therapist. The therapist applies a theoretical viewpoint and an understanding of the client's cultural and social background in structuring the therapy process.

2 *Psychological principles.* Psychotherapy is based on psychological theory and research in areas such as personality, learning, motivation, emotion, and abnormal behavior.

3 *Thoughts, feelings, and behavior.* Psychotherapy influences clients' thoughts, feelings, and behavior. It can be aimed at any or all of these aspects of human psychology.

4 *Psychological disorders, adjustment problems, and personal growth.* Psychotherapy is often used with people who have psychological disorders. Other people seek help in adjusting to other types of problems such as shyness, weight problems, or loss of a spouse. Still other clients want to use psychotherapy in order to learn more about themselves and to reach their full potential as individuals, parents, or creative artists.

Bearing in mind the common ground of psychotherapy, let us now consider the distinct features of the major schools of therapy today.

MODULE 9.1

Psychodynamic Therapies: Digging Deep Within

▌ What is traditional Freudian psychoanalysis?

▌ How do modern psychodynamic approaches differ from traditional psychoanalysis?

▌**Psychoanalysis** Freud's method of psychotherapy.

Psychodynamic therapies are based on the thinking of Sigmund Freud, the founder of psychodynamic theory. Freud believed that people don't know themselves as well as they think they do, that all of us are driven by forces outside of our awareness. Freud assumed that the forces involve conflicts between three psychic structures or mental states—the id, ego, and superego (see Chapter 2). The origins of these conflicts trace back to childhood and revolve around difficulties reconciling primitive sexual and aggressive urges with the demands of social acceptability. Psychological problems arise when these long-hidden (repressed) sexual or aggressive impulses threaten to break through the ego's defenses and emerge into consciousness or when the superego floods us with excessive guilt. Freud's method of therapy, called **psychoanalysis**, was the first psychodynamic therapy. It seeks to help people develop insight (self-awareness) into the dynamic struggles occurring within the psyche between these mental states—conflicts that, in Freud's view, were at the root of psychological problems such as anxiety and depression. Once these conflicts are brought into consciousness and worked through during the course of therapy, clients will be free of psychological symptoms and can pursue more adaptive behaviors.

9.1.1 Traditional Psychoanalysis: "Where Id Was, There Shall Ego Be"

If you consulted a traditional Freudian psychoanalyst, you would probably be asked to lie on a couch in a slightly darkened room. You would sit behind the therapist, who would encourage you to talk about anything that comes to mind, no matter how trivial, no matter how personal. To avoid interfering with your self-exploration, the analyst might say little or nothing at all for session after session. A course of analysis is likely to last for years, even many years.

As developed by Freud, psychoanalysis aims to provide insight into the conflicts that are presumed to lie at the roots of a person's problems. Freud was fond of saying, "Where id was, there shall ego be." In part, he meant that psychoanalysis could shed the light of ego on the inner workings of the unconscious mind, the stage on which these unconscious conflicts are played out. He also sought to replace impulsive and defensive behavior with coping behavior. In this way, for example, a man with a phobia for knives might discover that he had been repressing the urge to harm someone who had taken advantage of him. The obvious symptom, the phobia for knives, was a defensive behavior because it helped the man keep a distance from objects he might use to express his destructive urges. On the surface, the man remained unaware of repressed destructive impulses he harbored within his unconscious mind. Through therapy, the man comes to recognize these impulses and to learn other ways of expressing his anger that would not incur social disapproval or harm himself or others. For example, he might find ways to confront the person verbally.

The unconscious does not lightly give up its secrets. Its contents are shrouded in mystery and cannot be accessed by ordinary attention or mental focusing. Freud thus developed several techniques to bring the light of awareness to bear on the dark recesses of the unconscious mind, including free association, analysis of transference, and dream analysis.

Free Association

Early in his career as a therapist, Freud found that hypnosis allowed his clients to focus on repressed conflicts and talk about them. The relaxed "trance state" provided by hypnosis seemed to allow clients to "break through" to topics of which they would otherwise be unaware. Freud also found, however, that many clients denied the accuracy of this material once they were out of the trance. Other clients found the disclosures to be emotionally painful. Freud therefore turned to free association, a more gradual method of breaking through the walls of defense that block a client's insight into unconscious processes.

In **free association**, the client is made comfortable—for example, lying on a couch—and asked to talk about any topic that comes to mind. No thought is to be censored—that is the basic rule. Psychoanalysts ask their clients to wander "freely" from topic to topic, but they do not believe that the process occurring within the client is fully free. Repressed impulses clamor for release, and eventually the client's verbal meanderings touch on these deeper concerns. The ego persists in trying to repress these unacceptable impulses and threatening conflicts. As a result, clients might show **resistance** to recalling and discussing threatening ideas. A client about to entertain such thoughts might claim, "My mind is blank." The client might accuse the analyst of being demanding or inconsiderate. He or she might "forget" the next appointment when threatening material is about to surface.

In subtle ways, perhaps, the analyst tips the balance in favor of verbalizing unconscious material. Now and then the analyst offers an **interpretation** of the client's remarks and resistance, showing how they may suggest deep-seated feelings and conflicts. A gradual process of self-discovery and self-insight ensues.

Traditional Psychoanalysis
In a traditional psychoanalysis, the client is made comfortable and asked to talk about any topic that comes to mind. No thought is to be censored. Psychoanalysts believe that repressed impulses seek release but that the ego tries to keep them repressed in order to avoid feelings of anxiety, guilt, or shame. The analyst attempts to tip the balance in favor of utterance.

▌ **Free association** In psychoanalysis, the uncensored uttering of all thoughts that come to mind.

▌ **Resistance** The tendency to block the free expression of impulses and primitive ideas—a reflection of the defense mechanism of repression.

▌ **Interpretation** An explanation of a client's utterance according to psychoanalytic theory.

■ **Transference** Responding to one person (such as a spouse or the psychoanalyst) in a way that is similar to the way one responded to another person (such as a parent) in childhood.

Transference

Freud believed that clients responded to him not only as individuals but also in ways that reflected their underlying attitudes and feelings toward other people in their lives. He labeled this process **transference**. For example, a young woman might respond to him as a father figure and *displace* her feelings toward her father onto Freud, perhaps seeking affection and wisdom. A young man could also see Freud as a father figure, but rather than wanting affection from him, he might view Freud as a rival, responding to him in terms of his own unresolved Oedipal rivalry with his own father.

Analyzing and working through the transference is a key aspect of psychoanalysis. This doesn't happen overnight but typically takes years to fully work through. Freud believed that clients reenact their childhood conflicts with their parents and other important figures in their lives during the course of therapy. Clients might thus transfer the feelings of anger, love, or jealousy they felt toward their own parents onto the analyst. Childhood conflicts often involve unresolved feelings of love, anger, or rejection. A client may interpret a suggestion by the therapist as a criticism and see it as a devastating blow, transferring feelings of self-hatred that he had repressed because his parents had rejected him in childhood. Transference can also distort clients' relationships with other people here and now, such as relationships with spouses or employers. The following therapeutic dialogue illustrates the way in which an analyst might interpret a client's inability to communicate his needs to his wife as an expression of transference. The purpose is to provide his client, Mr. Arianes, with insight into how his relationship with his wife has been colored by his childhood relationship with his mother:

ARIANES: I think you've got it there, Doc. We weren't communicating. I wouldn't tell [my wife] what was wrong or what I wanted from her. Maybe I expected her to understand me without saying anything.

THERAPIST: Like the expectations a child has of its mother.

ARIANES: Not my mother!

THERAPIST: Oh?

ARIANES: No, I always thought she had too many troubles of her own to pay attention to mine. I remember once I got hurt on my bike and came to her all bloodied up. When she saw me she got mad and yelled at me for making more trouble for her when she already had her hands full with my father.

THERAPIST: Do you remember how you felt then?

ARIANES: I can't remember, but I know that after that I never brought my troubles to her again.

THERAPIST: How old were you?

ARIANES: Nine. I know that because I got that bike for my ninth birthday. It was a little too big for me still, that's why I got hurt on it.

THERAPIST: Perhaps you carried this attitude into your marriage.

ARIANES: What attitude?

THERAPIST: The feeling that your wife, like your mother, would be unsympathetic to your difficulties. That there was no point in telling her about your experiences because she was too preoccupied or too busy to care.

ARIANES: But she's so different from my mother. I come first with her.

THERAPIST: On one level you know that. On another, deeper level there may well be the fear that people—or maybe only women, or maybe only women you're close to—are all the same, and you can't take a chance at being rejected again in your need.

ARIANES: Maybe you're right, Doc, but all that was so long ago, and I should be over that by now.

THERAPIST: That's not the way the mind works. If a shock, or a disappointment is strong enough it can permanently freeze our picture of ourselves and our expectations of the world. The rest of us grows up—that is, we let ourselves learn about life from experience and from what we see, hear, or read of the experiences of others, but that one area where we really got hurt stays unchanged. So what I mean when I say you might be carrying that attitude into your relationship with your wife is that when it comes to your hopes of being understood and catered to when you feel hurt or abused by life, you still feel very much like that nine-year-old boy who was rebuffed in his need and gave up hope that anyone would or could respond to him.

Source: Basch (1980), pp. 29–30.

Dream Analysis

Freud often asked clients to jot down their dreams upon waking so that they could discuss them in therapy. Freud considered dreams the "royal road to the unconscious." He believed that the content of dreams is determined by unconscious processes as well as by the events of the day. Unconscious impulses tend to be expressed in dreams as a form of **wish fulfillment**.

But unacceptable sexual and aggressive impulses are likely to be displaced onto objects and situations that reflect the client's era and culture. These objects become symbols of unconscious wishes. For example, long, narrow dream objects might be **phallic symbols**, but whether the symbol takes the form of a spear, rifle, stick shift, or spacecraft partially reflects the dreamer's cultural background.

In Freud's theory, the perceived content of a dream is called its overt or **manifest content**. Its presumed hidden or symbolic content is its **latent content**. If a man dreams he is flying, flying is the manifest content of the dream. Freud usually interpreted flying as symbolic of erection, so concerns about sexual potency might make up the latent content of the dream. Freud allowed that the same dream content might have different meanings for different people, so the analyst needs to explore what a particular dream might mean for each individual client (Lear, 2000).

9.1.2 Modern Psychodynamic Approaches

Some psychoanalysts adhere faithfully to Freud's techniques. They engage in protracted therapy that continues to rely heavily on free association, interpretation of dreams and the transference, and other traditional methods. In recent years, however, more modern forms of psychodynamic therapy have been devised. Modern psychodynamic therapy is briefer and less intense, making treatment available to clients who do not have the time or money for long-term therapy. Many modern psychodynamic therapists do not believe that prolonged therapy is needed or justifiable in terms of the ratio of cost to benefits. Some modern psychodynamic therapies continue to focus on revealing unconscious material and the gradual breaking down of psychological defenses. Nevertheless, they differ from traditional psychoanalysis in several ways. One difference is that the client and therapist usually sit face to face (the client does not lie on a couch). The therapist engages in a more direct dialogue with clients and takes a more directive stance. That is, therapists may suggest to clients helpful behavior and ways of looking at their problems instead of focusing on generating self-insight alone. Finally, there is usually more focus on the ego as the "executive" of personality and less emphasis on the id. For this reason, many modern psychodynamic therapists are considered **ego analysts**.

Many of Freud's followers, the "second generation" of psychoanalysts—from Carl Jung and Alfred Adler to Karen Horney and Erik Erikson—believed that Freud had placed too much emphasis on sexual and aggressive impulses and underestimated the role of the ego. Erikson, for instance, spoke to clients directly about their values and concerns, encouraging them to develop desired behavior patterns. Even Freud's daughter, the psychoanalyst Anna Freud (1895–1982), was more concerned with the ego than with unconscious forces and conflicts.

Wish fulfillment The satisfaction of an underlying wish, desire, or impulse in the form of a dream or mental fantasy.

Phallic symbols Signs that represent the penis.

Manifest content In psychodynamic theory, the reported content of dreams.

Latent content In psychodynamic theory, the symbolized or underlying content of dreams.

Ego analysts Psychodynamically oriented therapists who focus on the conscious, coping behavior of the ego instead of the hypothesized, unconscious functioning of the id.

David Buffington/Photodisc Green/Getty Images, Inc.

Modern Psychodynamic Psychotherapy

Unlike classical psychoanalysts, many contemporary psychodynamic therapists use a briefer, more direct form of therapy involving face-to-face interactions with clients. They tend to focus on a more direct exploration of the person's defenses and transference relationships than would traditional analysts.

MODULE REVIEW

Review It

(1) In psychoanalytic therapy as developed by Sigmund Freud, the therapist attempts to shed light on the _____ conflicts presumed to lie at the roots of the client's problems.

(2) Psychoanalysis focuses on helping clients develop _____ into their underlying conflicts.

(3) The techniques of traditional psychoanalysis include free association, analysis and working through of the _____, and dream analysis.

(4) Freud considered _____ to be the "royal road to the unconscious."

(5) Freud distinguished between two types of dream content: _____ content and _____ content.

Think About It

How do "modern" psychoanalytic approaches differ from Freud's traditional method? Why do they differ?

MODULE 9.2

Humanistic-Existential Therapies: Becoming Oneself

■ What is Carl Rogers's method of client-centered therapy?
■ What is Fritz Perls's method of Gestalt therapy?

■ **Client-centered therapy** Carl Rogers's method of psychotherapy, which emphasizes the creation of a warm, therapeutic atmosphere that frees clients to engage in self-exploration and self-expression.

■ **Gestalt therapy** Fritz Perls's form of psychotherapy, which attempts to integrate conflicting parts of the personality through directive methods designed to help clients perceive their whole selves.

Psychodynamic therapies focus on internal conflicts and unconscious processes. Humanistic-existential therapies focus on the quality of the client's subjective, conscious experience. Traditional psychoanalysis focuses on early childhood experiences. Humanistic-existential therapies usually focus on what clients are experiencing "here and now." Therapists in the humanistic-existential tradition were influenced by the teachings of *existentialism*, a modern philosophical movement that emphasized that we are free, indeed painfully free, to make our own choices and imbue our lives with a sense of meaning and purpose.

The humanistic-existential therapists did not dismiss the importance of the past. The past has a way of influencing current thoughts, feelings, and behavior. Carl Rogers, the originator of **client-centered therapy**, and Fritz Perls, the originator of **Gestalt therapy**, recognized that early incorporation of other people's values and expectations often leads clients to "disown" parts of their own personalities.

9.2.1 Client-Centered Therapy: Removing Roadblocks to Self-Actualization

Carl Rogers (1902–1987) developed a form of therapy, called *client-centered therapy*, that encourages individuals to rely on their own values and frames of references (Raskin, Rogers, & Witty, 2008). His method is intended to help people get in touch with their genuine feelings and pursue their own interests, regardless of other people's wishes.

Rogers believed that we are free to make choices and control our destinies, despite the burdens of the past. He also believed that we have natural tendencies toward health, growth, and fulfillment. Psychological problems arise from roadblocks placed in the path of self-actualization—that is, what Rogers believed was an inborn tendency to strive to realize one's potential. If, when we are young, other people only approve of us when we are doing what they want us to do, we may learn to disown the parts of ourselves to which they object. We may don social masks or façades to garner approval to such an extent that we become strangers to ourselves. We may learn to be seen but not heard—not even by ourselves. As a result, we may experience anxiety when our true feelings begin to surface.

Client-centered therapy aims to provide insight into the parts of us that we have disowned so that we can feel whole. It creates a warm, therapeutic atmosphere that encourages self-exploration and self-expression. The therapist's acceptance of the client is intended to foster self-acceptance and self-esteem. Self-acceptance frees the client to make choices that develop his or her unique potential.

Client-centered therapy is *nondirective*. The client takes the lead, stating and exploring problems. An effective client-centered therapist has several qualities:

1 **Unconditional positive regard**: unconditional respect for clients as human beings with unique values and worth, regardless of their particular behavior.

2 **Empathic understanding**: accurate recognition of the client's experiences and feelings. Therapists attempt to view the world through the client's frame of reference by setting aside their own values and listening closely.

3 **Genuineness**: modeling genuine or authentic feelings in the therapy session to encourage clients to do the same.

The following excerpt from a therapy session shows how Carl Rogers demonstrates empathic understanding and paraphrases or reflects back a client's (Jill's) feelings. His goal is to help her recognize feelings that she has partially disowned:

JILL: I'm having a lot of problems dealing with my daughter. She's 20 years old; she's in college; I'm having a lot of trouble letting her go.... And I have a lot of guilt feelings about her; I have a real need to hang on to her.

C.R.: A need to hang on so you can kind of make up for the things you feel guilty about. Is that part of it?

JILL: There's a lot of that.... Also, she's been a real friend to me, and filled my life.... And it's very hard... a lot of empty places now that she's not with me.

C.R.: The old vacuum, sort of, when she's not there.

JILL: Yes. Yes. I also would like to be the kind of mother that could be strong and say, you know, "Go and have a good life," and this is really hard for me, to do that.

C.R.: It's very hard to give up something that's been so precious in your life, but also something that I guess has caused you pain when you mentioned guilt.

JILL: Yeah. And I'm aware that I have some anger toward her that I don't always get what I want. I have needs that are not met. And, uh, I don't feel I have a right to those needs. You know... she's a daughter; she's not my mother. Though sometimes I feel as if I'd like her to mother me... it's very difficult for me to ask for that and have a right to it.

C.R.: So, it may be unreasonable, but still, when she doesn't meet your needs, it makes you mad.

JILL: Yeah I get very angry, very angry with her.

C.R.: (Pauses) You're also feeling a little tension at this point, I guess.

JILL: Yeah. Yeah. A lot of conflict.... (C.R.: M-hm.) A lot of pain.

C.R.: A lot of pain. Can you say anything more about what that's about?

Source: Farber et al. (1996), pp. 74–75.

Client-centered therapy is practiced widely in college and university counseling centers, not just to help students experiencing, say, anxieties or depression, but also

▍ **Unconditional positive regard** Nonjudgmental acceptance of the value of another person, regardless of the person's behavior at the particular point in time.

▍ **Empathic understanding** Ability to perceive a client's feelings from the client's frame of reference—a quality of the good client-centered therapist.

▍ **Genuineness** Recognition and open expression of the therapist's own feelings.

© Erich Hartmann/Magnum Photos, Inc.

Client-Centered Therapy
The client-centered therapist allows the client to provide the direction of therapy and exemplifies the therapeutic qualities of unconditional positive regard, empathic understanding, and genuineness. Thus, the therapist creates an atmosphere in which the client feels free to explore his or her genuine feelings.

to help them make important life decisions. Many college students have not yet made career choices or wonder whether they should become involved in intimate relationships or terminate unsatisfying relationships. Client-centered therapists do not tell clients what to do. Instead, they help clients arrive at their own decisions.

9.2.2 Gestalt Therapy: Piecing It Together

Gestalt therapy was originated by Fritz Perls (1893–1970). Perls was trained as a psychoanalyst but became dissatisfied with the lack of attention in traditional analysis on the client's subjective experiences in the present. Like client-centered therapy, Gestalt therapy assumes that people disown parts of themselves that might meet with social disapproval or rejection. It helps individuals integrate or blend the conflicting parts of their personalities. Perls borrowed the term **gestalt** from the *Gestalt* school of psychology, the early school of psychology that focused on how individuals come to perceive the world as composed of organized wholes or patterns rather than disconnected bits and pieces of sensory data. Perls used the term *gestalt* to signify his interest in giving the conflicting parts of the personality an integrated form or shape. He aimed to have his clients become aware of inner conflict, accept the reality of conflict rather than deny it or keep it repressed, and make productive choices despite misgivings and fears. People in conflict frequently find it difficult to make choices, and Perls sought to encourage (*compel* might be a better word) them to do so.

❚ **Gestalt** Derived from the German, meaning "organized form" or "pattern."

Although Perls's ideas about conflicting personality elements owe much to psychodynamic theory, his form of therapy, unlike psychoanalysis, focuses on the here and now. In Gestalt therapy, clients perform exercises to heighten their awareness of their current feelings and behavior, rather than exploring the past. Perls also believed, along with Rogers, that people are free to make choices and to direct their personal growth. But the charismatic and forceful Perls was unlike the gentle and accepting Rogers in temperament. Thus, unlike client-centered therapy, Gestalt therapy is highly directive. The therapist leads the client through planned experiences. There are a number of Gestalt exercises and games, including the following (Greenberg & Malcolm, 2002; Wagner-Moore, 2004):

- *The dialogue.* In this game, the client undertakes verbal confrontations between opposing wishes and ideas to heighten awareness of internal conflict. An example of these clashing personality elements is "top dog" and "underdog." One's top dog might conservatively suggest, "Don't take chances. Stick with what you have or you might lose it all." One's frustrated underdog might then rise up and assert, "You never try anything. How will you ever get out of this rut if you don't take on new challenges?" Heightened awareness of the elements of conflict can clear the path toward resolution, perhaps through a compromise of some kind.

- *I take responsibility.* Clients end statements about themselves by adding, "and I take responsibility for it."

- *The empty chair.* Clients are asked to imagine that someone with whom they have had a troubled relationship—perhaps a mother, father, spouse, or boss—is sitting in an empty chair next to them. They then are asked to express their feelings toward this person. In this way, they can work through "unfinished business" with this person and explore their innermost feelings and unmet needs without fear of criticism from the other person.

Body language also provides insight into conflicting feelings. Clients might be instructed to attend to the ways in which they furrow their eyebrows and tense their facial muscles when they touch upon certain concerns. In this way, they often find that their body language asserts feelings they have been denying in their spoken statements.

The following excerpt from a therapy session with a client named Max shows how Perls would make clients take responsibility for what they experience. One of his techniques is to show how clients are treating something they are doing (a "verb") like something that is just out there and beyond their control (a "noun"):

MAX: I feel the tenseness in my stomach and in my hands.
PERLS: The tenseness. Here we've got a noun. Now the tenseness is a noun.
         Now change the noun, the thing, into a verb.
MAX: I am tense. My hands are tense.
PERLS: Your hands are tense. They have nothing to do with you.
MAX: I am tense.
PERLS: You are tense. How are you tense? What are you doing?
MAX: I am tensing myself.
PERLS: That's it.

Source: Perls (1971), p. 115.

Once Max understands that he is tensing himself and takes responsibility for it, he can choose to stop tensing himself. The tenseness is no longer something out there that is victimizing him; it is something he is doing to himself.

Psychodynamic theory views dreams as the "royal road to the unconscious," but Perls saw the content of dreams as representing disowned parts of the personality. He would often ask clients to role-play elements of their dreams in order to get in touch with these parts of their personality.

MODULE REVIEW

Review It

(6) In contrast to psychoanalytic therapy, _____-existential therapies focus on clients' subjective, conscious experience.

(7) Client-centered therapy is a (directive or nondirective?) method that provides clients with an accepting atmosphere that enables them to overcome roadblocks to _____-actualization.

(8) The client-centered therapist shows (conditional or unconditional?) positive regard, empathetic understanding, and _____.

(9) Gestalt therapy provides (directive or nondirective?) methods that are designed to help clients accept responsibility and integrate conflicting parts of the personality.

Think About It

What do the humanistic-existential therapies of Rogers and Perls have in common? How do they differ?

MODULE 9.3

Behavior Therapy: Adjustment Is What You Do

■ What is behavior therapy?
■ What are some behavior therapy methods for reducing fears?
■ How do behavior therapists use aversive conditioning to help people break bad habits?
■ How do behavior therapists apply principles of operant conditioning?

Psychodynamic and humanistic-existential forms of therapy tend to focus on what people think and feel. Behavior therapists tend to focus on what people do. **Behavior therapy**—also called *behavior modification*—is a form of therapy that applies principles of learning to help people make desired behavioral changes.

■ **Behavior therapy** Systematic application of the principles of learning to the direct modification of a client's problem behaviors.

Adjustment and Modern Life

Finding Help

In most areas in the United States and Canada, there are pages upon pages of clinics and health professionals in the telephone directory. Many people have no idea whom to call for help. If you don't know where to go or whom to see, there are a number of steps you can take to ensure that you receive appropriate care:

1. *Seek recommendations from respected sources, such as your family physician, course instructor, clergyperson, or college health service.*

2. *Seek a referral from a local medical center or local community mental health center.* When making inquiries, ask about the services that are available or about opportunities for referral to qualified treatment providers in the area.

3. *Seek a consultation with your college counseling center or health services center.* Most colleges and universities offer psychological assistance to students, generally without charge.

4. *Contact professional organizations for recommendations.* Many local or national organizations maintain a referral list of qualified treatment providers in your area. If you would like to consult a psychologist, contact the American Psychological Association in Washington, DC (by telephone at 202-336-5650 or on the web at www.apa.org), and ask for local referrals in your area. Alternatively you can call your local or state psychology association in the United States or your provincial or territorial psychological association in Canada.

5. *Let your fingers do the walking—but be careful!* Look under "Psychologists," "Physicians," "Social Workers," or "Social and Human Services" in your local Yellow Pages. However, be wary of professionals who take out large ads and claim to be experts in treating many different kinds of problems.

6. *Make sure the treatment provider is a licensed member of a recognized mental health profession, such as psychology, medicine, counseling, or social work.* In many states, anyone can set up practice as a "therapist," even as a "psychotherapist." These titles may not be limited by law to licensed practitioners. Licensed professionals clearly display their licenses and other credentials in their offices, usually in plain view. If you have any questions about the licensure status of a treatment provider, contact the licensing board in your state, province, or territory.

7. *Inquire about the type of therapy being provided (e.g., psychoanalysis, family therapy, behavior therapy).* Ask the treatment provider to explain how his or her particular type of therapy is appropriate to treating the problems you are having.

8. *Inquire about the treatment provider's professional background.* Ask about the person's educational background, supervised experience, and credentials. An ethical practitioner will not hesitate to provide this information.

Behavior therapists draw upon the principles of classical and operant conditioning as well as observational learning (discussed in Chapter 2). They work with clients to help them overcome phobias, self-defeating behavior patterns such as overeating and smoking, and troubling emotional problems such as anxiety and depression. They also help clients acquire adaptive behavior patterns such as the social skills required to initiate and maintain social relationships or say no to insistent salespeople.

Like humanistic-existential therapists, behavior therapists remain very much in the present—the here and now. Although they understand that past is prelude to the present, they argue that we can only change behavior in the present. Behavior therapists, like other therapists, seek to develop warm, therapeutic relationships with clients, but they believe that the effectiveness of their techniques derives from specific, learning-based procedures rather than the therapeutic relationship. They insist that their methods be tested through controlled research and outcomes assessed in terms of measurable behavior. Behavior therapists use a variety of learning-based techniques, including those we survey in this section.

9.3.1 Fear-Reduction Methods

Many people seek the services of behavior therapists because of fears and phobias that interfere with their functioning. Behavior therapists use a variety of techniques to help people overcome these problems, including flooding, gradual exposure, systematic desensitization, counterconditioning, and modeling.

9. *Inquire whether the treatment provider has had experience treating other people with similar problems.* Ask about their results and how they were measured.

10. *Once the treatment provider has had the opportunity to conduct a formal evaluation of your problem, discuss the diagnosis and treatment plan before making any commitments to undertake treatment.*

11. *Ask about costs and insurance coverage.* Ask about what types of insurance are accepted by the provider and whether co-payments are required on your part. Ask whether the provider will adjust his or her fees on a sliding scale that takes your income and family situation into account. If you are eligible for Medicaid or Medicare, inquire whether the treatment provider accepts these types of coverage. College students may also be covered by their parents' health insurance plans or by student plans offered by their colleges. Find out if the treatment provider participates in any health maintenance organization to which you may belong.

12. *Find out about the treatment provider's policies regarding charges for missed or canceled sessions.*

13. *If medication is to be prescribed, find out how long a delay is expected before it starts working.* Also inquire about possible side effects, and about which side effects should prompt you to call with questions. Don't be afraid to seek a second opinion before undergoing any course of medication.

14. *If the treatment recommendations don't sound quite right to you, discuss your concerns openly.* An ethical professional will be willing to address your concerns rather than feeling insulted.

15. *If you still have any doubts, request a second opinion.* An ethical professional will support your efforts to seek a second opinion. Ask the treatment provider to recommend other professionals—or select your own.

16. *Be wary of online therapy services.* As we explore later in the chapter, the use of online counseling and therapy services is growing rapidly, even as psychologists and other mental health professionals raise the yellow flag of caution. Concerns arise because unqualified practitioners may be taking advantage of unwary consumers, as we lack a system for ensuring that online therapists have the appropriate credentials and licensure to practice. We also lack evidence that therapy can be effective when people interact with a therapist they never meet in person. Unless and until proper safeguards and clear evidence of treatment benefits are established, it's prudent to be wary of online therapy services.

Source: Nevid et al. (2007). Reprinted with permission of Houghton Mifflin.

Flooding

Flooding is based on the learning principle of *extinction* (see Chapter 2). In this method, a person is exposed for prolonged intervals to a fear-evoking but harmless stimulus until the fear is extinguished. For example, an individual with a fear of heights might try to remain for as long as possible in a height situation, or at least as long as it takes for the fear to dissipate. Because flooding engenders high levels of anxiety, the therapist or another helper may be present to assist the person during these encounters.

Gradual Exposure

Gradual exposure is similar to flooding in that it relies on exposure to fearful stimuli. But unlike flooding, the person is first exposed to minimally fearful stimuli and then gradually works upward in a hierarchy (ordered series) of progressively more fearful stimuli. Gradual exposure is used to treat many different types of fears, from fear of heights to fear of social interactions (e.g., Bradley et al., 2005; Choy, Fyer, & Lipsitz, 2006; Hofman, 2008; McEvoy, 2008). For example, a person with a fear of riding on elevators might begin by first standing outside an elevator, then standing in the elevator with the door open, then standing in the elevator with the door closed, then taking the elevator down one floor, then up one floor, then down two floors, and so on. The person must feel comfortable and free of anxiety at each step in the series before progressing to the next step. This procedure progresses until the person can comfortably take an elevator all the way up and all the way down.

© Rick Friedman/Stockphoto.com

Overcoming Fear of Flying
This woman has undergone systematic desensitization with other people who sought to overcome the fear of flying. For several sessions, she engaged in tasks such as viewing pictures of airports and airplanes and imagining herself entering and flying in an airplane. Now that she is in the final phases of her treatment program, she actually flies in an airplane with the support of group members and her therapist. Eventually, of course, she will fly by herself.

Systematic Desensitization

In systematic desensitization, exposure takes the form of imaginary encounters with fearful stimuli.

> *Adam has a phobia for receiving injections. His behavior therapist treats him as he reclines in a comfortable padded chair. In a state of deep muscle relaxation, Adam observes slides projected on a screen. A slide of a nurse holding a needle has just been shown three times, 30 seconds at a time. Each time, Adam has shown no anxiety. So now a slightly more discomforting slide is shown: one of the nurse aiming the needle toward someone's bare arm. After 15 seconds, our armchair adventurer notices twinges of discomfort and raises a finger as a signal (speaking might disturb his relaxation). The projector operator turns off the light, and Adam spends two minutes imagining his "safe scene"— lying on a beach beneath the tropical sun. Then the slide is shown again. This time Adam views it for 30 seconds before feeling anxiety.*

▌ **Systematic desensitization** Behavior therapy method for reducing fears by associating a hierarchy of images of fear-evoking stimuli with deep muscle relaxation.

▌ **Counterconditioned** Referring to counterconditioning, the therapeutic method by which a response that is incompatible with anxiety—such as relaxation—is made to appear under conditions that usually elicit anxiety.

▌ **Hierarchy** An arrangement of stimuli according to the amount of fear they evoke.

Adam is undergoing **systematic desensitization**, a method for reducing phobic responses. Systematic desensitization is a gradual process in which the client learns to handle increasingly disturbing stimuli while anxiety to each one is being **counterconditioned**. About 10 to 20 stimuli are arranged in a sequence, or **hierarchy**, according to their capacity to elicit anxiety. In imagination or by being shown photos, the client travels gradually up through this hierarchy, approaching the target behavior. In Adam's case, the target behavior was the ability to receive an injection without undue anxiety.

Systematic desensitization is based on the assumption that anxiety responses, like other behaviors, are learned and can be unlearned by means of counterconditioning or extinction. In counterconditioning, a response that is incompatible with anxiety is made to appear in situations that usually elicit anxiety. As a result, the bonds between fear-inducing cues and the fear response are weakened. Muscle relaxation is incompatible with anxiety. For this reason, Adam's therapist is teaching him to relax in the presence of (usually) anxiety-evoking slides of needles.

Remaining in the presence of phobic imagery, rather than running away from it, is also likely to enhance self-efficacy expectations—beliefs in one's ability to handle the situation without fear. As you'll recall from Chapter 2, self-efficacy expectations are beliefs we hold about our ability to perform particular tasks. If we believe we can cope with fearful or threatening stimuli, we're more likely to attempt to accomplish these tasks than if we doubted our ability.

Modeling

Modeling relies on observational learning. In this method clients observe, and then imitate, people who approach and cope with objects or situations the clients fear. Bandura, Blanchard, and Ritter (1969) found that modeling worked as well as systematic desensitization—and more rapidly—in reducing fear of snakes. Like systematic desensitization, modeling is likely to increase self-efficacy expectations in coping with feared stimuli.

▌ **Aversive conditioning** A behavior therapy technique in which stimuli associated with undesired responses become aversive by pairing noxious stimuli with them.

▌ **Rapid smoking** An aversive conditioning method for quitting smoking in which the smoker inhales every six seconds, thus rendering once-desirable cigarette smoke aversive.

9.3.2 Aversive Conditioning

Behavior therapists may use **aversive conditioning** to help people overcome self-defeating behavior patterns, such as smoking or problem drinking. In aversive conditioning, painful or aversive stimuli are paired with unwanted responses, such as smoking cigarettes in order to make the stimulus (cigarettes) less appealing. To help problem drinkers, tastes of different alcoholic beverages might be paired with drug-induced nausea and vomiting or with electric shock. With smokers, a **rapid smoking** procedure may be used in which the would-be quitter is instructed to inhale every six seconds. Rapid smoking induces nausea, which may help create a conditioned aversion to cigarette smoke. However, the effectiveness of aversive conditioning is uncertain, and effects may not transfer outside the treatment setting (Lancaster et al., 2000). However, aversive conditioning methods may be used as part of a broader treatment program.

9.3.3 Operant Conditioning Procedures

We usually prefer to be around people who smile at us rather than ignore us and to take courses in which we do well rather than fail. In other words, we repeat behavior that is reinforced. Behavior that is not reinforced is likely to become extinguished. Behavior therapists use these principles of operant conditioning with a range of problem behaviors. They train parents to apply reinforcement programs in the home that aim at increasing desirable behavior in children. They also work with hospital staff to implement behavior change programs designed to foster adaptive behavior in hospitalized mental patients.

The Token Economy

The **token economy** is a behavior change program in which institutionalized patients earn tokens, such as poker chips, when they perform appropriate behavior (Dickerson, Tenhula, & Green-Paden, 2005). The tokens can then be used to purchase desirable rewards, such as extra visits to the canteen or special privileges. The tokens are reinforcements for productive activities such as making beds, brushing teeth, and socializing.

▌**Token economy** A controlled environment in which people are reinforced for desired behaviors with tokens (such as poker chips) that may be exchanged for later privileges.

Social Skills Training

In social skills training, behavior therapists help people alleviate social anxiety and build social skills through a program in which participants rehearse social behaviors in a group setting and receive feedback and encouragement from the therapist and other group members. The behaviors of interest might be date-seeking skills, conversational skills, or conflict resolution skills. Group members can role-play important people—such as parents, spouses, or potential dates—in the lives of other members. Participants receive social reinforcement (praise) from the group leader and other group members for demonstrating effective social skills. Social skills training has also been used to help formerly hospitalized mental patients develop the social skills and job-related skills they need to function in community living situations. For example, patients learn job interviewing skills and skills needed to initiate and maintain a conversation.

Biofeedback Training

Through **biofeedback training (BFT)**, therapists help clients become more aware of, and gain control over, various bodily functions. Clients are hooked up to physiological recording devices that measure bodily functions such as heart rate or muscle tension (Gatchel, 2001). "Bleeps" or other electronic signals are used to indicate (and thereby reinforce) changes in the desired direction—for example, a slower heart rate. (Knowledge of results is a powerful reinforcer.) One device, the *electromyograph* (EMG), monitors muscle tension. It has been used to augment control of muscle tension in the forehead and other parts of the body, which can help relieve states of tension, anxiety, stress, and even headaches.

BFT also helps clients voluntarily regulate functions once thought to be beyond direct conscious control, such as heart rate and blood pressure. Hypertensive clients use a blood pressure cuff and electronic signals to gain some degree of control over

▌**Biofeedback training (BFT)** The systematic feeding back to an organism of information about a bodily function so that the organism can gain control of that function.

their blood pressure. The electroencephalograph (EEG) monitors brain waves and can be used to teach people how to produce brain wave patterns that are associated with states of relaxation. BFT has helped people overcome insomnia by learning to produce brain wave patterns associated with sleep (Murtagh & Greenwood, 1995). It has also been used successfully to reduce headache and low-back pain and in helping children with attention-deficit/hyperactivity disorder (ADHD) develop relaxation skills (Gatchel, 2001; Robbins, 2000).

MODULE REVIEW

Review It

(10) Behavior therapy is based on the systematic application of the principles of _____ to bring about desired behavioral changes.

(11) Behavior therapy methods for reducing fears include flooding, _____ exposure, systematic desensitization, and modeling.

(12) _____ conditioning associates undesired behavior with painful stimuli to decrease the frequency of the behavior.

(13) _____ conditioning methods reinforce desired responses and extinguish undesired responses.

Think About It

What are some of the learning principles on which behavior therapy is based?

MODULE 9.4

Cognitive Therapies: Adjustment Is What You Think (and Do)

▮ What is Aaron Beck's method of cognitive therapy?
▮ What is Albert Ellis's method of rational-emotive behavior therapy (REBT)?

There is nothing either good or bad, but thinking makes it so.
— SHAKESPEARE, *HAMLET*

A thing is important if anyone thinks it is important.
— WILLIAM JAMES

In the line from *Hamlet*, Shakespeare did not mean to suggest that injuries and misfortunes are painless or easy to manage. Rather, he meant that our appraisals of unfortunate events can heighten our discomfort and impair our coping ability. In so doing, Shakespeare was providing a kind of motto for cognitive therapists.

Cognitive therapists focus on helping people change the beliefs, attitudes, and automatic types of thinking that are believed to underlie psychological problems such as anxiety and depression (Beck & Weishaar, 2008; Dryden & Ellis, 2001). Cognitive therapists, like psychodynamic and humanistic-existential therapists, help clients develop self-insight, but they aim to increase insight into their thinking patterns in the present as well as their past experiences. Cognitive therapists also aim to help clients directly change distorted, faulty thinking into more constructive, adaptive thinking.

Most behavior therapists today directly incorporate cognitive methods into their treatment approach, practicing a broader form of behavior therapy called cognitive-behavioral therapy (CBT). Cognitive-behavioral therapy is based on an underlying assumption that cognitions (thoughts and beliefs) influence behavior and that changes in cognitions can lead to desirable behavioral changes. A strong body of evidence exists supporting the effectiveness of cognitive-behavioral therapy for treating a wide range of psychological disorders, from depression to anxiety disorders (Butler et al., 2006).

Let us now look at the approaches and methods of two leading cognitive therapists, Aaron Beck and Albert Ellis.

9.4.1 Cognitive Therapy: Correcting Errors in Thinking

Cognitive therapy was developed by the psychiatrist Aaron Beck (Beck, 2005; Beck & Weishaar, 2008). Beck encourages clients to become their own personal scientists to identify distorted ways of thinking and replace them with more adaptive thoughts and beliefs.

Beck questions people in a way that encourages them to see the irrationality of their thinking patterns. For example, he works with depressed people to help them see how they tend to minimize their accomplishments and jump to conclusions that the worst will always happen. Distorted thoughts can be fleeting and occur automatically, without conscious effort. This makes it difficult to detect them (Persons, Davidson, & Tompkins, 2001). Beck encourages clients to keep records of disturbing thoughts and the negative feelings they elicit. He then helps them challenge the validity of these thoughts and replace them with more rational alternatives.

Beck used cognitive and behavioral techniques on himself before he became a psychiatrist. One of the reasons he went into medicine was to confront his own fear of blood. He had a series of operations as a child, and from then on the sight of blood had made him feel faint. During his first year of medical school, he forced himself to watch operations. In his second year, he became a surgical assistant. By directly confronting fearful situations, he found that his fear gradually disappeared. Later, he dealt with a fear of tunnels by repeatedly pointing out to himself that his expectations of danger had no basis in reality.

As a psychiatrist, Beck first practiced psychoanalysis. However, he could not find scientific evidence for psychoanalytic beliefs. Psychoanalytic theory explained depression as anger turned inward. Beck's own clinical experiences led him to believe that it is more likely that depressed people experience cognitive distortions such as a "cognitive triad" of negative beliefs about themselves ("I'm no good"), the world at large ("This is an awful place"), and the future ("Nothing good will ever happen"). Beck's methods are active. He encourages clients to challenge beliefs that are not supported by evidence. Beck notes particular types of cognitive errors of the kinds described in Chapter 8 (see Table 8.5).

The concept of pinpointing and modifying errors may become clearer with the following excerpt from a case in which a 53-year-old engineer obtained cognitive therapy for severe depression. The engineer had left his job and become inactive. As reported by Beck and his colleagues, the first goal of treatment was to foster physical activity—even things like raking leaves and preparing dinner—because activity is incompatible with depression. Then:

[The engineer's] cognitive distortions were identified by comparing his assessment of each activity with that of his wife. Alternative ways of interpreting his experiences were then considered.

In comparing his wife's résumé of his past experiences, he became aware that he had (1) undervalued his past by failing to mention many previous accomplishments, (2) regarded himself as far more responsible for his "failures" than

▮ **Cognitive therapy** A form of therapy that focuses on how clients' cognitions (expectations, attitudes, beliefs, etc.) lead to distress and may be modified to relieve distress and promote adaptive behavior.

Clem Murray/Philadelphia Inquirer/MCT/NewsCom

Aaron Beck.

she did, and (3) concluded that he was worthless since he had not succeeded in attaining certain goals in the past. When the two accounts were contrasted, he could discern many of his cognitive distortions. In subsequent sessions, his wife continued to serve as an "objectifier."

In midtherapy, [he] compiled a list of new attitudes that he had acquired since initiating therapy. These included:

1. *"I am starting at a lower level of functioning at my job, but it will improve if I persist."*
2. *"I know that once I get going in the morning, everything will run all right for the rest of the day."*
3. *"I can't achieve everything at once."*
4. *"I have my periods of ups and downs, but in the long run I feel better."*
5. *"My expectations from my job and life should be scaled down to a realistic level."*
6. *"Giving in to avoidance [e.g., staying away from work and social interactions] never helps and only leads to further avoidance."*

He was instructed to reread this list daily for several weeks even though he already knew the content. (adapted from Rush, Khatami, & Beck, 1975)

The engineer gradually became less depressed and returned to work and an active social life. Along the way, he learned to combat inappropriate self-blame for problems, perfectionistic expectations, magnification of failures, and overgeneralization from past failures to future situations (i.e., failing in the past means that one will inevitably fail in the future).

9.4.2 Rational-Emotive Behavior Therapy: Overcoming "Musts" and "Shoulds"

The deepest principle of Human Nature is the craving to be appreciated.
—WILLIAM JAMES

▌**Rational-emotive behavior therapy (REBT)** Albert Ellis's form of therapy that encourages clients to challenge and correct irrational expectations and maladaptive behaviors.

The developer of **rational-emotive behavior therapy (REBT)**, psychologist Albert Ellis, who died at the age of 93 in 2007, pointed out that it is our beliefs about events, not the events themselves, that determine our emotional reactions (Dryden & Ellis, 2001; Ellis, 2001, 2008). We noted in Chapter 3 that many people harbor irrational beliefs that can give rise to problems or magnify their impact. Two examples of irrational beliefs are the belief that we *must* have the love and approval of everyone who is important to us and the belief that we *must* be competent in everything we undertake in order to feel a sense of self-worth.

Ellis, like Beck, began as a psychoanalyst. But he was put off by the essentially passive role of the analyst and by the slow process of therapy. Alternatively, Ellis's REBT methods are active and directive. He did not sit back like the traditional psychoanalyst and only occasionally offer an interpretation. Instead, he continually pointed out to clients when they express an irrational belief and showed them the emotional consequences of clinging to these beliefs and how they could be changed.

Ellis straddled behavioral and cognitive therapies. He originally dubbed his method of therapy rational-emotive therapy because his focus was on the cognitive–irrational beliefs and how to change them. However, he also understood the importance of making behavioral changes, both to strengthen cognitive changes and to develop more adaptive behaviors. In keeping with his broad philosophy, he later changed the name of rational-emotive therapy to rational-emotive behavior therapy or REBT. Beck's cognitive therapy also incorporates many behavioral principles, such as prescribing homework assignments in which clients are directed to try out new behaviors and gather evidence to test the validity of their beliefs. With Beck and Ellis, we see the convergence of behavioral and cognitive forms of therapy today that is generally classified under the umbrella term of cognitive-behavioral therapy (Butler et al., 2006).

Not only are behavioral and cognitive approaches to therapy converging, but many therapists today identify with an eclectic orientation. Eclectic therapists draw upon the principles and techniques of multiple approaches to therapy. A survey of 200 therapists found that about half use a combination of cognitive-behavioral and psychodynamic techniques in practice (Holloway, 2003b). In addition, another poll of clinical psychologists showed that the eclectic/integrative orientation narrowly surpassed the cognitive orientation as the most widely held theoretical orientation (Norcross, Karpiak, & Santoro, 2005) (see Figure 9.1). Interestingly, eclectic therapists tend to be older and more experienced than other therapists (Beitman, Goldfried, & Norcross, 1989). We might speculate that eclectic therapists have learned through experience the value of drawing upon different approaches in the practice of therapy.

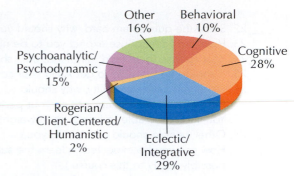

Figure 9.1
Therapeutic Orientations of Clinical Psychologists
As you can see from this graph, the leading therapeutic orientations among clinical psychologists are integrative/eclectic (29%) and cognitive (28%).
Source: Norcross, Karpiak, & Santoro (2005).

Are You Making Yourself Miserable? The Irrational-Beliefs Questionnaire

Self-Assessment

Do you make yourself miserable? Do your attitudes and beliefs set you up for distress? Do you expect other people to always put your needs first? Do you make such great demands of yourself that you must inevitably fall short? Do you think that you can be happier by sliding along than by applying yourself? Do you feel like dirt when other people disapprove of you? The following self-quiz may help you gain some insight into your belief patterns.

Directions: Following are a number of irrational beliefs that serve as examples of Ellis's set of basic irrational beliefs. Place a checkmark to the left of each one that might apply to you. (If you're in doubt, check it. Nobody's going to fault you for having more checkmarks than the person sitting next to you, and it'll give you something to think about!) This is not a formal test, so there are no norms. But recognizing irrational beliefs is the first step toward correcting them. It will enhance your self-knowledge and give you some things to work on.

_____ 1. Since your parents don't approve of your date, you must give him/her up.
_____ 2. Since your date doesn't approve of your parents, you must give them up.
_____ 3. It is awful if your teacher doesn't smile at you.
_____ 4. It's awful when your boss passes you in the hall without saying anything.
_____ 5. You're a horrible parent if your children are upset with you.
_____ 6. How can you refuse to buy the vacuum cleaner when the salesperson will be disappointed?
_____ 7. Unless you have time to jog 5 miles, there's no point in going out at all.
_____ 8. You must get A's on all your quizzes and tests; a B now and then is a disaster.
_____ 9. Your nose (mouth, eyes, chin, etc.) should be (prettier/more handsome) or else your face is a mess.
_____10. Since you are 15 pounds overweight, you are totally out of control and must be sickened by yourself.
_____11. Since you can't afford a Mercedes, how can you possibly enjoy your Honda?
_____12. Every sexual encounter should lead to a huge orgasm.
_____13. You can't just go out on the courts and bat the ball back and forth a few times; you have to perfect your serves, returns, and volleys.
_____14. You can't be happy with your life from day to day when people who are no more talented or hard-working make more money than you do.
_____15. The cheerleader/quarterback won't go out with you, so why go out at all?
_____16. Your boss is awful because a coworker got a promotion and you didn't.
_____17. White people are awful because they'd usually rather associate with white people.
_____18. African Americans are awful because they'd usually rather associate with African Americans.
_____19. Since there is the possibility of nuclear war, you must spend all your time worrying about it—and, of course, there's no point to studying.
_____20. How can you be expected to do your best on the job after you didn't get the raise?
_____21. Given all your personal problems, how can your teachers expect you to study?

_____22. Since the quizzes are hard, why should you study for them?

_____23. How can your spouse expect you to be nice to him/her when you've had an awful day on the job?

_____24. Your spouse (boyfriend, girlfriend, etc.) should know what's bugging you and should do something about it.

_____25. It should be possible to get A's in your courses by quick cramming before tests.

_____26. Since you have the ability, why should you have to work at it? (That is, your teacher/boss should appraise you on the basis of your talents, not on your performance.)

_____27. You should be able to lose a lot of weight by dieting for just a few days.

_____28. Other people should be nicer to you.

_____29. How can you be expected to learn the subject matter when your instructor is a bore? (_Note_: This belief couldn't possibly apply to this course.)

_____30. Your spouse (boyfriend, girlfriend, mother, father, etc.) is making you miserable, and unless he/she changes, there's nothing you can do about it.

_____31. Since you didn't get the promotion, how can you be happy?

_____32. How can you be expected to relax unless college gets easier?

_____33. Since college is difficult, there's a bigger payoff in dropping out than in applying yourself for all those years.

_____34. You come from a poor background, so how can you ever be a success?

_____35. Your father was rotten to you, so how can you ever trust a man?

_____36. Your mother was rotten to you, so how can you ever trust a woman?

_____37. You had a deprived childhood, so how can you ever be emotionally adjusted?

_____38. You were abused as a child, so you are destined to abuse your own children.

_____39. You come from "the street," so how can you be expected to clean up your act and stop cursing with every other word?

_____40. It's more fulfilling just to have fun than to worry about college or a job

_____41. You can be happier dating a bunch of people than by investing yourself in meaningful relationships.

MODULE REVIEW

Review It

(14) An underlying assumption of cognitive therapy is that changes in _____ (thoughts and beliefs) can lead to desirable behavioral and emotional changes.

(15) One of the reasons Beck became a physician was to overcome his fear of_____.

(16) Ellis's REBT confronts clients with the ways in which _____ beliefs contribute to problems such as anxiety and depression.

Think About It

How do cognitive therapists conceptualize the role of cognitions (thoughts and beliefs) in the development of emotional disorders?

MODULE 9.5

Group, Couple, and Family Therapy: When Therapy Goes Beyond the Individual

■ What are the advantages and disadvantages of group therapy?

■ What is couple therapy?

■ What is family therapy?

Some forms of therapy focus on more than one client at a time. In group therapy, a group of unrelated people are treated together. In family therapy, the client is the family, not any one individual in the family.

9.5.1 Group Therapy: We're in This Together

When a psychotherapist has several clients with similar problems—anxiety, depression, adjustment to divorce, lack of social skills—it often makes sense to treat them in a group rather than in individual sessions. The methods and characteristics of the group reflect the needs of the members and the theoretical orientation of the leader. In group psychoanalysis, clients might interpret one another's dreams. In a client-centered group, they might provide an accepting atmosphere for self-exploration. Members of behavior therapy groups might be jointly desensitized to anxiety-evoking stimuli or might practice social skills together.

Group therapy has the following advantages (Davison, 2000; Dugas et al., 2003; Haaga, 2000):

- *It is economical.* It is typically less costly than individual therapy, since therapists can work with several clients at the same time.
- *Compared with one-to-one therapy, group therapy provides more information and life experience for clients to draw upon.*
- *Appropriate behavior receives group support.* Clients usually appreciate an outpouring of peer approval.
- *When we run into troubles, it is easy to imagine that we are different from other people or inferior to them.* Affiliating with people with similar problems is reassuring.
- *Group members who show improvement provide hope for other members.*
- *Many individuals seek therapy because of problems in relating to other people.*

People who seek therapy for other reasons also may be socially inhibited. Members of groups have the opportunity to practice social skills in a relatively non-threatening atmosphere. In a group consisting of men and women of different ages, group members can role-play one another's employers, employees, spouses, parents, children, and friends. Members can role-play asking one another out on dates, saying no (or yes), and so on.

But group therapy is not for everyone. Some clients fare better with individual treatment. Many prefer not to disclose their problems to a group. They may be overly shy or want individual attention. It is the responsibility of the therapist to insist that group disclosures be kept confidential, to establish a supportive atmosphere, and to ensure that group members obtain the attention they need.

9.5.2 Couple Therapy: When the Group Is the Couple

Couple therapy helps couples improve their relationships by improving their communication and problem-solving skills and helping them manage conflicts more effectively (Christensen et al., 2004). Couple therapy—called *marital therapy* when the couple is a marital unit—helps correct power imbalances in the relationship so that partners can explore alternative ways of relating to each other that respect each other's needs. Ironically, in couples marred by domestic violence, the partner with less power in the relationship is usually the violent one. Violence sometimes appears to be a way of compensating for inability to share power in other aspects of the relationship (Rathus & Sanderson, 1999).

The leading contemporary approach to couple therapy is based on cognitive-behavioral principles (Rathus & Sanderson, 1999). It teaches couples communication skills (such as how to listen to one another and how to express feelings), ways of handling feelings like depression and anger, and ways of solving problems.

David Harry Stewart/Stone/Getty Images, Inc.

Group Therapy
Group therapy is not just more economical (less expensive) than individual therapy. Group members also gain from the experiences and emotional support of other group members.

∎ **Couple therapy** A form of therapy that focuses on helping distressed couples resolve their conflicts and improve their communication skills.

9.5.3 Family Therapy: When the Group Is the Family

Family therapy A form of therapy in which the family unit is treated as the client.

Family therapy is a form of group therapy in which one or more families constitute the group. Family therapy may be undertaken from various theoretical viewpoints. One is the *systems approach*, in which the family is conceptualized in terms of a system of interactions. The family therapist helps the family change the system by which the family functions in order to enhance the growth of individual family members and of the family unit as a whole.

Family members with low self-esteem often cannot tolerate different attitudes and behaviors in other family members. Faulty communication within the family also creates problems. In addition, it is not uncommon for the family to present an "identified patient"—that is, the family member who has the problem and is causing all the trouble. Yet family therapists usually assume that the identified patient is a scapegoat for other problems within and among family members. It is a sort of myth: Change the bad apple (identified patient) and the barrel (family) will be functional once more.

The family therapist—often a specialist in this field—attempts to teach the family to communicate more effectively and encourages growth and autonomy in each family member.

MODULE REVIEW

Review It

(17) Group therapy tends to be (more or less?) economical than individual therapy.

(18) _____ therapy seeks to correct power imbalances in relationships between two people.

(19) In the _____ approach to _____ therapy, family interactions are modified to enhance the growth of family members and the family unit as a whole.

Think About It

Under what circumstances would you recommend that someone go for group therapy rather than individual therapy?

MODULE 9.6

The Effectiveness of Psychotherapy

▌ Does psychotherapy work?

▌ What kinds of problems do researchers encounter when they conduct research on psychotherapy?

Does it work? We have seen that psychotherapy is practiced in different ways and in different modalities, such as individual and group therapies. But does psychotherapy work? And if so, for whom? Investigators employing a statistical averaging method called meta-analysis have strongly suggested that psychotherapy is, in fact, effective. That research is reviewed in this section. But before we report on the research dealing with the effectiveness of therapy, let us review some of the problems of this kind of research.

Adjustment and Modern Life

Positive Psychology

Internet Counseling: Psychological Help May Be Only a Few Mouse Clicks Away

You can do most anything on the Internet these days, from ordering concert tickets to downloading music or whole books. You can also receive counseling or therapy services from an online therapist. But as the numbers of online counseling services mushroom, many professionals voice concerns about the clinical, ethical, and legal issues regarding their use.

One problem is that while psychologists are licensed in particular states, Internet communications easily cross state and international borders. It remains unclear whether psychologists or other mental health professionals can legally provide online services to residents of other states in which they are not licensed. Psychologists and other helping professionals may face ethical problems and liability issues in offering services to clients they never meet in person. Many therapists also express concerns that interacting with a client by computer would prevent them from evaluating nonverbal cues and gestures that might signal deeper levels of distress than are verbally reported or typed on a keyboard (Rehm, 2008).

Yet another problem is that online therapists living at great distances from their clients may not be able to provide the more intensive services that clients need during times of emotional crisis. Professionals also express concern about the potential for unsuspecting clients to be victimized by unqualified practitioners, or "quacks." We presently lack a system for ensuring that online therapists are licensed and otherwise qualified practitioners.

Despite these drawbacks, evidence supporting the therapeutic benefits of online consultation and counseling services is mounting for treating problems such as anxiety disorders and insomnia, helping people quit smoking and learn stress management techniques, and even helping college students avoid the extreme drinking associated with 21st-birthday celebrations (Andersson et al., 2006; Carlbring et al., 2006; Comas-Diaz, 2006;

Neighbors et al., 2009; Orbach, Lindsay, & Grey, 2007; Walters, Wright, & Shegog, 2006).

There are also potential advantages of online treatment services. For one thing, easily accessible online consultation may encourage people who out of shyness or embarrassment have hesitated to seek professional help. Online consultation may also make people feel more comfortable about receiving help and may become a first step toward meeting a therapist in person. In addition, online therapy may provide people living in remote areas, where finding a therapist is difficult, or those lacking mobility, with services they might not otherwise receive (Morgan, Patrick, & Magaletta, 2008).

The bottom line about Internet counseling, says Russ Newman, executive director for professional practice of the American Psychological Association, is the need for monitoring and evaluating this emerging technology (cited in Lauerman, 2000). Psychologists are not writing off so-called e-therapy, but they remain cautious in endorsing its widespread use (Mora, Nevid, & Chaplin, 2008).

Source: Adapted from Nevid, Rathus, & Greene (2008).

IT Stock/Jupiter Images Corp

Internet Counseling
Online counseling services are sprouting up all over the web. Though psychologists don't discount the potential value of these types of services, they are concerned about the potential clinical, ethical, and legal issues that may arise regarding their use.

9.6.1 Problems in Comparing Different Forms of Psychotherapy

The ideal method for evaluating a treatment—such as a method of therapy—is the randomized controlled experiment. However, such experiments on therapy methods are difficult to arrange and control.

Consider psychoanalysis. In well-run experiments, people are assigned at random to treatment groups. A true experiment comparing psychoanalysis with behavior therapy would require randomly assigning people seeking therapy to one form of therapy or the other. But a person may have to remain in traditional psychoanalysis for years to attain beneficial results, whereas behavior therapy may have shorter-term objectives. Moreover, many people specifically seek psychoanalysis or behavior therapy per se, not psychotherapy in general. Would it be feasible or even ethical to assign them at random to particular forms of treatments?

In an ideal experiment, subjects and researchers are "blind" with regard to the treatment the subjects receive. Blind research designs allow researchers to control for subjects' expectations. In an ideal experiment on therapy, individuals would be blind regarding the type of therapy they are obtaining—or whether they are obtaining a placebo. However, it is difficult to mask the type of therapy clients are obtaining.

Even if we could conceal it from clients, could we hide it from therapists? Different therapies also differ in how they measure outcomes (Shadish et al., 2000). For example, behavior therapists define their goals in behavioral terms—such as a formerly phobic individual being able to obtain an injection or look out of a 20th-story window. But psychodynamic and client-centered therapists seek to foster insight and self-growth in their clients—qualities we cannot directly measure on the basis of observed behaviors. We must assess what clients say and do and make inferences about them.

9.6.2 Analyses of Therapy Effectiveness

Problems in directly testing one therapy against another have led investigators in the field to focus on the relative effects of therapies against control groups, typically waiting-list groups but sometimes psychological "placebo" groups that offer general forms of treatment but not specific therapeutic techniques. By examining the magnitude of difference between specific forms of therapy versus control groups, we can estimate how much benefit an average person is likely to receive from a particular form of therapy.

Meta-Analysis: Averaging the Results of Individual Studies

∎ **Meta-analysis** A method for statistically combining and averaging the results of individual research studies.

The most widely used statistical technique for determining the magnitude of difference between specific therapies and control groups is called **meta-analysis**. Many meta-analyses of psychotherapy effectiveness have been performed, with the evidence strongly supporting the effectiveness of psychotherapy (Butler et al., 2006; McLeod & Weisz, 2004; Wampold, 2007).

These meta-analyses show that various forms of psychotherapy produce larger effects than control conditions. In a classic study by Smith, Glass, and Miller (1980) of 400 controlled studies in which various types of therapy (psychodynamic, behavioral, humanistic, etc.) were compared against control groups, the average person receiving psychotherapy achieved better results than 80% of those placed in waiting-list control groups (see Figure 9.2).

Generally speaking, the more therapy the better; that is, people who have more psychotherapy tend to fare better than people who have less of it. About half of

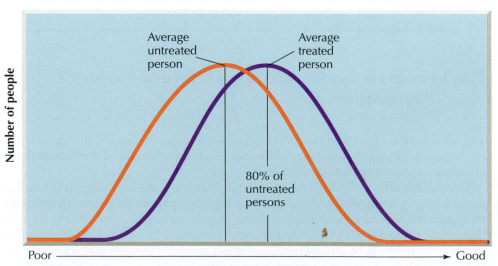

Figure 9.2
Results of Meta-Analysis of Psychotherapy Outcome Studies

patients receiving psychotherapy show clinically meaningful change within about three or four months of starting treatment. By about six months, this figure rises to about 75% (Anderson & Lambert, 2001). Meta-analyses also support the effectiveness of other forms of therapy, including marital, family, and group therapy (Butler et al., 2006; McDermut, Miller, & Brown, 2001; McLeod & Weisz, 2004; Shadish & Baldwin, 2005).

Does Therapy Help Because of the Specific Method or Because of Nonspecific Factors?

To what extent do the benefits of therapy stem from the nature of the therapeutic relationship rather than from the specific techniques used by therapists? Investigators have come to recognize that the general features of the therapeutic relationship that are common among different forms of therapy have beneficial effects quite apart from the specific techniques themselves (Norcross, 2002). These more general features of therapy, called **nonspecific factors**, include therapist warmth, concern, and attention and the instillation of hope or expectancies of positive outcomes. Evidence shows that the development of a strong **therapeutic alliance**, or close working relationship between the client and therapist, is an important ingredient in determining treatment outcomes (Baldwin, Wampold, & Imel, 2007; Elvins & Green, 2008; Vasquez, 2007). Still, investigators believe that specific techniques explain about twice the amount of therapeutic factors (Stevens, Hynan, & Allen, 2000).

Speaking of the effects of specific forms of therapy, we need to address the question of which therapy is most effective for which type of problem. We also need to know about the advantages of particular forms of therapy and about their limitations. This brings us to investigation of empirically supported treatments (ESTs).

❚ **Nonspecific factors** General factors in therapy that apply to different forms of therapy, such as the instillation of hope.

❚ **Therapeutic alliance** The close working relationship between a client and therapist.

Empirically Supported Treatments (ESTs)

How well do particular forms of therapy do in treating particular types of problems? In today's health care environment, there is increasing emphasis on accountability—that is, using treatments with demonstrated effectiveness (Weisz, Jensen-Doss, & Hawley, 2006). Psychologists, among other professional groups, have identified particular forms of therapy that were demonstrated to have therapeutic benefits in treating particular problems based on carefully controlled research ("APA Presidential Task Force on Evidence-Based Practice," 2006). Table 9.1 contains a partial listing of these treatments,

Table 9.1 ❚ Examples of Empirically Supported Treatments (ESTs)

Treatment	Conditions for Which Treatment Is Effective
Cognitive therapy	Depression
Behavior modification or behavior therapy	Depression
	Persons with developmental disabilities
	Headache
	Enuresis (bed-wetting)
	Agoraphobia and other specific phobias
	Obsessive-compulsive disorder
Cognitive-behavioral therapy	Panic disorder
	Generalized anxiety disorder
	Bulimia
	Smoking cessation
Interpersonal psychotherapy (a relatively brief form of psychodynamic therapy focused on interpersonal relationships)	Depression
Parent training programs	Children with oppositional behavior

Sources: Adapted from Chambless et al., 1998, Chambless & Ollendick, 2001; Deegear & Lawson, 2003.

which are called *empirically supported treatments*, or ESTs. Other treatments may be added to the list as evidence accumulates supporting their effectiveness.

Other therapies may be added to the list as additional evidence is gathered to support their effectiveness. The inclusion of a particular therapy does not mean the therapy is effective in all cases, nor does it mean that the therapy is necessarily sufficient in itself in treating the particular disorder. Some cases may be treated more effectively with a combination of different therapies, as in the form of eclectic therapy, or with a combination of psychotherapy and medication. The development of ESTs comes during a time when more attention is being given to the need for health care providers to demonstrate the effectiveness of their treatments. One of the task force members, psychologist William Sanderson, puts the issue this way: "Society wants proof that a treatment works—whether it be medication, surgery, or psychotherapy—before it is administered."

As we see in the following section, we must also consider the sociocultural features of clients in determining how to make therapy most effective. Failure to do so leaves many people who would profit from therapy on the wayside.

MODULE REVIEW

Review It

(20) The method of _____-analysis is used to evaluate results from a large number of outcome studies of the effectiveness of psychotherapy.

(21) Research shows that psychotherapy (is or is not?) effective in the treatment of adjustment problems.

(22) _____ supported treatments have demonstrated therapeutic benefits for particular problems or disorders.

Think About It

What problems do researchers face when they are attempting to directly compare different forms of therapy against one another?

MODULE 9.7

Psychotherapy and Human Diversity

■ How do issues of diversity come into play in therapy?

Let us not forget the question: For whom does psychotherapy work? This question is more important than ever before because the United States and Canada, they are a-changing. The numbers of African Americans, Asian Americans, and Latino and Latina Americans are growing rapidly, yet most forms of therapy were developed with European American clients.

People from ethnic minority groups are less likely than European Americans to seek therapy. Reasons for their lower participation rate include such factors as unawareness that therapy would help; lack of information about the availability of professional services or inability to pay for them (USDHHS, 2001); distrust of professionals, particularly European American professionals and (for women) male professionals; and language barriers. A recent report from the U.S. Surgeon General highlighted the ethnic and racial disparities in mental health services (see Table 9.2).

Table 9.2 ▌ Disparities in Mental Health Care: Major Findings from the Surgeon General's Report

- The percentage of African Americans receiving needed care for mental health problems is only half that of non-Hispanic whites. African Americans have less access to mental health care than whites, partly because a greater percentage of African Americans lack health insurance.
- Of all American ethnic groups, Hispanic Americans are the least likely to have health insurance. Moreover, the limited availability of Spanish-speaking mental health professionals means that many Hispanic Americans who speak little or no English lack the opportunity to receive care from linguistically similar treatment providers.
- Largely because of lingering stigma and shame associated with mental illness, Asian Americans/Pacific Islanders often fail to seek care until their problems are more advanced than is the case with other groups. Moreover, accessibility is limited by scarcity of treatment providers with appropriate language skills.
- American Indians/Alaska Natives have a suicide rate that is 50% higher than the national average, but little is known about how many people within these groups receive needed care. In addition, the rural, isolated locations in which many Native Americans live place a severe constraint on the availability of mental health services.

Sources: Adapted from Stenson, 2001a; USDHHS, 2001. Reprinted from Nevid et al., 2006.

A major factor explaining these disparities is a disproportionate number of minorities who either are uninsured or underinsured. Consequently, many of them are unable to afford mental health treatment and suffer from undiagnosed and untreated psychological problems, such as depression.

9.7.1 Psychotherapy and Ethnic Minority Groups

Therapists need to develop a better understanding of and sensitivity to differences in the cultural heritage, language, and values of their clients (Hansen et al., 2006; Sue, 2003; Wong et al., 2003). They also need to adapt their therapeutic approach to the cultural and social realities of clients from diverse backgrounds (Awad & Ladhani, 2007; Hwang, 2006). That is, they need to develop multicultural competence and adjust their approach to therapy to the cultural and social realities faced by clients from diverse backgrounds. Therapists also need to become aware of their own cultural biases in order to avoid stereotyping clients from other cultural groups (Stuart, 2004). Let us briefly touch upon some of these issues as they relate to psychotherapy with African Americans, Asian Americans, Latino and Latina Americans, and Native Americans.

African Americans

In addition to addressing the psychological problems of African American clients, therapists often need to help them cope with the effects of prejudice and discrimination. Psychologist Beverly Greene (1993) notes that some African Americans develop low self-esteem because they internalize negative stereotypes.

African Americans often are reluctant to seek psychological help because of cultural assumptions that people should manage their own problems and because of mistrust of the therapy process. They tend to assume that people are supposed to solve their own problems. Signs of emotional weakness such as tension, anxiety, and depression are stigmatized (Boyd-Franklin, 1995; Greene, 1993).

Many African Americans are also suspicious of their therapists—especially when the therapist is a European American. They may withhold personal information because of the society's history of racial discrimination (Boyd-Franklin, 1995; Greene, 1993).

Nancy Sheehan/PhotoEdit

Culturally Sensitive Therapy
Therapists need to be sensitive to cultural differences and how they affect the therapy process and be respectful of differences in cultural backgrounds of the clients they treat.

Asian Americans

Asian Americans tend to stigmatize people with psychological disorders. As a result, they may deny problems and refuse to seek help for them (Sue, 1991). Asian Americans, especially recent immigrants, also may not understand or believe in Western approaches to psychotherapy. For example, Western psychotherapy typically encourages people to express their feelings openly. This mode of behavior may conflict with the Asian tradition of restraint in public. Many Asians prefer to receive direct concrete advice than is typically the case in Western-style psychotherapy. However, more acculturated Asian Americans tend to make greater use of Western-style psychological services (Barry & Grilo, 2002).

Because of a cultural tendency to turn away from painful thoughts, many Asians experience and express psychological complaints as physical symptoms (Zane & Sue, 1991). Rather than thinking of themselves as being anxious, they may focus on physical features of anxiety such as a pounding heart and heavy sweating. Rather than thinking of themselves as depressed, they may focus on fatigue and low energy levels.

Latino and Latina Americans

Therapists need to be aware of potential conflicts between the traditional Latino and Latina American value of interdependency in the family and the typical European American belief in independence and self-reliance (De la Cancela & Guzman, 1991). Measures such as the following may help bridge the gaps between psychotherapists and Latino and Latina American clients:

■ Interacting with clients in the language requested by them or, if this is not possible, referring them to professionals who can do so.

■ Using methods that are consistent with the client's values and levels of acculturation, as suggested by fluency in English and level of education.

■ Developing therapy methods that incorporate clients' cultural values. Malgady, Rogler, and Costantino (1990), for example, use *cuento therapy* with Puerto Ricans. Cuento therapy uses Latino and Latina folktales (*cuentos*) with characters who serve as models for adaptive behavior. Culturally sensitive therapists also need to recognize the strongly held spiritual beliefs of many of their Latino clients.

Native Americans

Many psychological disorders experienced by Native Americans involve the disruption of their traditional culture caused by European colonization (LaFramboise,1994). Native Americans have also been denied full access to key institutions in Western culture. Loss of cultural identity and social disorganization have set the stage for problems such as alcoholism, substance abuse, and depression. Theresa LaFramboise (1994) argues that if psychologists are to help Native Americans cope with psychological disorders, they must do so in a way that is sensitive to their culture, customs, and values. Efforts to prevent such disorders should focus on strengthening Native American cultural identity, pride, and cohesion.

Some therapists use ceremonies that reflect clients' cultural or religious traditions (Csordas, Storck, & Strauss, 2008; Rabasca, 2000a,b). Purification and cleansing rites are therapeutic for many Native Americans. Such rites are commonly sought by Native Americans who believe that their problems are caused by failure to placate malevolent spirits or perform required rituals (Lefley, 1990).

9.7.2 Feminist Psychotherapy

Feminist psychotherapy is not a particular method of therapy. It is an approach to therapy rooted in feminist political theory and philosophy. Feminism challenges the validity of stereotypical gender-role stereotypes and the tradition of male dominance (Greene,1993).

Feminist therapy developed as a response to male dominance of health professions and institutions. It suggested that the mental health establishment often worked to maintain inequality between men and women by trying to help women "adjust" to traditional gender roles when they wished to challenge these roles in their own lives. Feminist therapists note that many women experience depression and other psychological problems as a result of being treated as second-class citizens, and they argue that society, rather than the individual woman, must change if these psychological problems are to be alleviated.

9.7.3 Therapy for Gay Males and Lesbians

Gay males and lesbians experience adjustment problems, just like everyone else does. But when they seek psychotherapy to help them with their problems, they may encounter therapists who are uncomfortable with their sexual orientation or may even try to change it. Some gays and lesbians even seek therapy to change their sexual orientations on their own. Psychotherapists need to ask whether it is ethical to try to change the sexual orientation of gay males and lesbians—even when they ask for such a change.

The American Psychiatric Association (2000) does not now consider a gay male or a lesbian sexual orientation to be a psychological disorder, though it did list homosexuality as a mental disorder until 1973. Many efforts have been made to "help" gay males and lesbians change their sexual orientation. Many critics argue that it is unprofessional to try to help people change their sexual orientations (Sleek, 1997). They note that the great majority of gay males and lesbians are satisfied with their sexual orientations and seek therapy only because of conflicts that arise from social pressure and prejudice. They believe that the purpose of therapy for gay males and lesbians should be to help relieve conflicts caused by prejudice so that they will find their lives more gratifying. In sum, psychotherapy is most effective when therapists attend to and respect people's sociocultural as well as individual differences. Therapists also need to recognize their ethical responsibilities if they are not comfortable with, or do not have the skills to work with, a particular client to refer that individual to another treatment provider.

A CLOSER LOOK

Beverly A. Greene: In Her Own Words

Our colleague, Beverly A. Greene, teaches at St. John's University and has contributed widely to the literature on diversity in psychotherapy. She is coeditor of the award-winning text *Women of Color: Integrating Ethnic and Gender Identities in Psychotherapy* and editor of *Ethnic and Cultural Diversity Among Lesbians and Gay Men*. Greene writes of herself as follows.

I am an African American woman, descended from African American and Native American peoples. I was raised in urban northeastern New Jersey in the shadows of New York City. Born and raised in Mississippi and Georgia from the late 1920s through the 1940s, my parents survived America's apartheid and its lynch mobs. My grandparents were the children and grandchildren of slaves and Cherokees in Georgia, the Carolinas, and Tennessee.

Memories of my childhood contain images garnered on visits South, where the signposts of racial segregation were visible and uncompromising, and stretch back North, where the signs were more subtle and insidious. Those early visits meant spending time with my century-old maternal great-grandmother. Her journey from a long-forgotten island in the British West Indies did not bring her to the liberating portals of Ellis Island with other American immigrants, but rather to the auction block just after the beginning of the Civil War. The doors of Ellis Island were never open to America's involuntary immigrants; they entered America through the back door.

With others in my generation, I emerged from this crucible of struggle and survival with a keen awareness of my membership in groups of proud but exploited peoples. My parents instructed us by word and example that we must never accept uncritically the outside world's images of us, nor define our potential with their distorted yardsticks. Similarly, we were warned not to be too quick to accept what the dominant culture had to say about other folks either. It was clear that the majority had a propensity to distort the identities of anyone who did not fit narrow definitions of who was acceptable to them. A clear appreciation for intellectual curiosity and achievement and a love for the written word were nurtured through the purchase of books of all types whenever possible. We were helped to understand that we would not always be treated fairly but that we always had the right to demand fair treatment. Because I lived in the midst of a society that constantly violated what it professed to be deeply held principles of Christian fairness and equality, my curiosity about human behavior grew. It seems in some ways to be a logical extension of being a member of groups forced to stand on the outside and observe the workings of those in power. Those skills developed long ago continue to serve me well.

Psychologist Beverly A. Greene Greene's early memories include visits with her century-old great-grandmother, whose journey from an island in the British West Indies brought her to the auction block, not to the liberating portals of Ellis Island.

Courtesy of Beverly A. Greene

MODULE REVIEW

Review It

(23) One common factor that leads many African Americans to be reluctant to seek therapy is cultural _____ of European American professionals.

(24) There may be conflict between the traditional Latino and Latina American value of _____ in the family and the typical European American belief in independence.

(25) _____ psychotherapists challenge the validity of stereotypical gender-role stereotypes and the traditional role of male dominance.

(26) Many critics argue that it is _____ to try to help gay males and lesbians change their sexual orientation because those who seek such therapy are usually responding to social pressure and prejudice.

Think About It

Is it correct to assume that psychotherapy is value-free? Why or why not?

MODULE 9.8

Biomedical Therapies

∎ What kinds of drug therapy are available for psychological disorders?

∎ What is electroconvulsive therapy (ECT)?

∎ What is psychosurgery? How is it used to treat psychological disorders?

∎ What do we know about the effectiveness of biomedical therapies?

The therapies we have discussed to this point in the chapter are psychological in nature—forms of psychotherapy. Psychotherapies apply psychological principles to treatment, and these principles are based on psychological theories of personality, learning, and motivation. But many people with psychological problems seek biomedical approaches rather than psychotherapy for help in overcoming their problems.

In this module we discuss three forms of biomedical treatment for psychological disorder. One form, drug therapy, is used widely. Another, electroconvulsive therapy (ECT), has much more limited use. The third, psychosurgery, is used rarely, if at all.

Let us note that biomedical therapies, including psychotherapeutic drugs and ECT, are administered by medical doctors, such as psychiatrists. Psychiatrists are physicians who specialize in the diagnosis and treatment of mental disorders. Yet the issue of prescription privileges for psychologists has emerged as a hotly contested issue between psychologists and psychiatrists as well as within the field of psychology itself (e.g, Bradshaw, 2008; Brehm, 2008). Many psychologists believe that, with proper training, they, too, should be permitted to prescribe psychotherapeutic drugs. In fact, some psychologists have been trained in specialized programs to administer psychotherapeutic drugs and are doing so safely and effectively. As of this writing, two states—New Mexico and Louisiana—have enacted legislation to permit specially trained psychologists to prescribe psychiatric medications. Whether prescription privileges will become more widely available to psychologists remains to be seen (Meyers, 2007).

9.8.1 Drug Therapy: In Search of the Magic Pill?

∎ **Psychotropic drugs** Drugs used to control symptoms associated with mental disorders such as anxiety disorders, mood disorders, and schizophrenia.

Psychotropic drugs (also called *psychotherapeutic drugs*) are prescription drugs that are widely used to help relieve disturbing emotional states, such as anxiety or depression, or to control symptoms of schizophrenia or other severe and persisting disorders, such as bipolar disorder. Let us examine the three major classes of psychotropic drugs used to treat psychological disorders: antianxiety drugs, antipsychotic drugs, and antidepressants.

Antianxiety Drugs

Most antianxiety drugs (also called *minor tranquilizers*) belong to the chemical class known as *benzodiazepines*. This class of drugs includes diazepam (Valium), chlordiazepoxide (Librium), oxazepam (Serax), and alprazolam (Xanax). As the name suggests, antianxiety drugs help quell symptoms of anxiety and induce feelings of calmness. In the body, they depress (slow) the activity of the central nervous system (CNS), slowing such bodily processes as heart rate and breathing rate as well as relieving feelings of nervous arousal. Many people come to tolerate antianxiety drugs very quickly. When tolerance occurs, dosages must be increased for the drug to remain effective. Sedation (feelings of being tired or drowsy) is the most common side effect of antianxiety drugs. Problems associated with withdrawal from these drugs include **rebound anxiety**. That is, people who regularly use these drugs may experience greater anxiety after discontinuing their use than they did before they started to use them. Antianxiety drugs can also lead to physical dependence, as evidenced by the development of withdrawal symptoms, such as tremors, sweating, insomnia, and rapid heartbeat, following abrupt cessation of use. Although these drugs are generally safe when used as prescribed, they can be dangerous, even lethal, when misused or used in combination with alcohol or other drugs.

Antipsychotic Drugs

People with psychotic disorders, such as schizophrenia, are often treated with **antipsychotic drugs** (also called *major tranquilizers* or *neuroleptics*). These drugs control the more flagrant symptoms of schizophrenia, such as delusions, hallucinations, and agitated or disturbed behavior (Essock et al., 2000; Lindenmayer & Khan, 2004). Many antipsychotic drugs, including the class of phenothiazines (for example, Thorazine and Mellaril) and a newer generation of so-called atypical antipsychotics, such as clozapine (Clozaril), risperidone (Risperdal), and olanzapine (Zyprexa), are thought to act by blocking dopamine receptors in the brain (Davis, Chen, & Glick, 2003; Lieberman et al., 2005). Research along these lines supports the theory that schizophrenia is connected with overactivity of the dopamine receptors in the brain.

Antidepressants

As the name implies, **antidepressants** are a group of drugs that help relieve depressive symptoms. Interestingly, some antidepressant drugs help treat a range of other disorders, including bulimia, generalized anxiety, panic disorder, posttraumatic stress disorder (PTSD), social anxiety, and obsessive-compulsive disorder (e.g., Katon, 2006; Katon et al., 2006; Schneier, 2006; Simpson et al., 2008; Walsh et al., 2004). They apparently work by altering chemical balances in brain systems that regulate such processes as emotional states and appetite. More specifically, antidepressants increase the availability of certain neurotransmitters in the brain, especially serotonin and norepinephrine, which are chemical messengers that carry signals in the brain. Three major classes of antidepressants are used today.

Monoamine oxidase (MAO) inhibitors, such as Nardil and Parnate, block the activity of an enzyme that breaks down noradrenaline and serotonin in the gap, or synapse, between neurons (nerve cells). Thus, more of these neurotransmitters become available in the synapse. **Tricyclic antidepressants** such as Tofranil and Elavil prevent the reuptake (reabsorption) of norepinephrine and serotonin by the transmitting neuron. **Selective serotonin reuptake inhibitors (SSRIs),** such as Prozac and Zoloft, also block the reuptake of serotonin by transmitting neurons but have actions that are more specific to serotonin (Sibille & Lewis, 2006). Although there is little difference in levels of effectiveness between the SSRIs and the older generation of tricyclic antidepressants, the SSRIs, like Prozac and Zoloft, are widely preferred because they are associated

©Paul S. Howell /Getty Images News and Sport Services

Drug Therapy?
What are the benefits of drug therapy? What are the limitations? Why would psychologists prefer to help individuals learn other methods of adjusting to anxiety that accompanies a big test, a first date, or a job interview?

■ **Rebound anxiety** Strong anxiety that can attend the suspension of usage of a tranquilizer.

■ **Antipsychotic drugs** Drugs that help relieve psychotic symptoms.

■ **Antidepressants** Drugs that help relieve depression.

■ **Monoamine oxidase (MAO) inhibitors** Antidepressant drugs that work by blocking the action of an enzyme that breaks down noradrenaline and serotonin.

■ **Tricyclic antidepressants** Antidepressant drugs that work by preventing the reuptake of noradrenaline and serotonin by transmitting neurons.

■ **Selective serotonin reuptake inhibitors (SSRIs)** Antidepressant drugs that work by blocking the reuptake of serotonin by transmitting neurons.

with less severe side effects and are less dangerous in overdose situations (Gartlehner et al., 2008; Qaseem et al., 2008; Serrano-Blanco et al., 2006).

Antidepressant drugs must usually build up to a therapeutic level over several weeks. They can also produce a range of side effects, such as dry mouth, headache, agitation, insomnia, lack of sexual drive, arousal, and delayed orgasm.

Lithium

The ancient Greeks and Romans were among the first to use the metal lithium as a psychoactive drug. They prescribed mineral water—which contains lithium—for people with bipolar disorder. They had no inkling as to why this treatment sometimes helped. A salt of the metal lithium (lithium carbonate), in tablet form, helps stabilize the moods of people with bipolar disorder (manic-depression) (Fountoulakis et al., 2008; Geddes et al., 2004). Although we still don't know precisely how lithium works, scientists believe it normalizes neurotransmitter functioning in the brain. People with bipolar disorder may have to use lithium indefinitely, just as a person with diabetes must use insulin to control the illness. Yet many people, at least 30% to 40% of those treated with the drug, either fail to respond to it or cannot tolerate it because of side effects.

The most common side effects are hand tremors, memory impairment, and excessive thirst and urination. The most common reason people discontinue lithium is because of problems with memory. As an alternative to lithium, some people with bipolar disorder achieve good results with anticonvulsive drugs commonly used in the treatment of epilepsy (Ceron-Litvoc et al., 2009; Weisler et al., 2008; Zhang et al., 2008). Divalproex (brand name Depakote) is one. (This just goes to show that a drug used for one purpose may also have other uses.)

Electroconvulsive Therapy

It sounds barbaric: An electric shock is passed through the brain in order to produce convulsions. Yet evidence shows that **electroconvulsive therapy (ECT)** can help relieve severe depression, even in many patients who have been unresponsive to antidepressants (Ebmeier, Donaghey, & Steele, 2006; Reifler, 2006). An estimated 100,000 Americans undergo ECT each year to help relieve severe depression.

People usually receive ECT in a series of 6 to 12 treatments spread over several weeks. Electrodes are attached to the temples, and an electrical current strong enough to produce a convulsion is induced. Patients are given a brief-acting general anesthetic to put them to sleep during the procedure, and a muscle relaxant is administered to prevent any jarring movements that might cause injury (Fink & Taylor, 2007).

ECT is controversial for many reasons; many professionals, for instance, are distressed by the thought of passing an electric shock through a patient's head and producing convulsions. Other concerns are possible side effects, including memory loss for events occurring around the time of treatment (Lisanby et al., 2000; Weiner, 2000). Yet another problem is the high rate of relapse following treatment (Prudic et al., 2004). All in all, many professionals view ECT as a treatment of last resort to be used only when other treatment options have been tried but failed.

Psychosurgery

We include **psychosurgery** as a footnote to our discussion of biomedical therapies, if only because it has become virtually extinct. The use of psychosurgery—surgical procedures used to alter deviant behavior—was pioneered by a Portuguese neurologist, Antonio Egas Moniz, and brought to the United States in the 1930s. Moniz's procedure, called a **prefrontal lobotomy**, involved severing the nerve pathways linking the prefrontal lobes of the brain to the thalamus. The theoretical rationale for the operation was vague and misguided, and Moniz's reports of success were exaggerated. Nevertheless, by 1950 prefrontal lobotomies had been performed on more than a thousand people in an effort to reduce violent and highly agitated behavior. Anecdotal evidence of the method's unreliable outcomes is found in an ironic footnote to history: One of Dr. Moniz's "failures" shot the doctor, leaving a bullet lodged in his spine and paralyzing his legs.

▌ **Electroconvulsive therapy (ECT)** Treatment of disorders like major depression by passing an electric current (which causes a convulsion) through the head.

▌ **Psychosurgery** Surgery intended to promote psychological changes or to relieve disordered behavior.

▌ **Prefrontal lobotomy** The severing or destruction of part of the frontal lobe of the brain.

Prefrontal lobotomy had a host of side effects, including hyperactivity and distractibility, impaired learning ability, overeating, apathy and withdrawal, epileptic-type seizures, reduced creativity, and, now and then, death. Prefrontal lobotomy is no longer practiced. Today, psychosurgery is limited to a treatment of last resort in some cases of severe obsessive-compulsive disorder, bipolar disorder, and major depression (Dubovsky, 2008; Shields et al., 2008; Steele et al., 2008). Even then, concerns are raised about the potential long-term complications of these procedures.

Evaluating Biomedical Therapies

There is little question that drug therapy has helped many people suffering from a range of psychological disorders, from panic disorder to depression to bulimia to schizophrenia. The introduction of antipsychotic drugs made it possible for hundreds of thousands of mental hospital residents to return to their homes and communities, where they could continue to receive supportive care.

Yet psychiatric drugs are no panaceas. Antipsychotics, for example, are only partially effective and can produce serious side effects, including metabolic disturbances and an apparently irreversible movement disorder called *tardive dyskinesia*, a physical disorder associated with involuntary lip-smacking and other uncontrollable movements. Antidepressant drugs can raise the risk of suicidal thoughts in children and adolescents (Bridge et al., 2007; Friedman & Leon, 2007). Some psychiatric drugs, such as Valium, can lead to psychological and physical dependence (addiction) when used regularly over time.

It is important to note that antidepressants bring complete symptom relief in only about a third or fewer of depressed patients and that their effects overall are only modestly stronger than those of placebos (inert drugs) (Lespérance et al., 2007; Menza, 2006; Nelson, 2006). Moreover, relapse rates following withdrawal of psychiatric drugs are high (Tang et al., 2007; Yager, 2006).

Consider, too, that many comparisons of cognitive therapy and drug therapy for depression suggest that cognitive therapy is as effective as, or more effective than, antidepressants (e.g., Beck, 2005; DeRubeis et al., 2005). Moreover, psychological treatment may reduce relapse rates because the learning that takes place during therapy carries past the end of treatment.

In sum, psychiatric drugs may provide patients with temporary relief from anxiety or depression but will not teach them new skills or ways of coping with their difficulties, other than relying on medication. Then again, some evidence suggests that the combination of cognitive therapy and psychiatric drugs may be superior in some cases to either treatment alone in treating problems relating to depression and anxiety (e.g., Domino et al., 2008; Feldman & Rivas-Vazquez, 2003; Harris, 2004). No one treatment approach is best in all circumstances. Some people respond well to psychotherapy, others to medication, and still others to a combination of treatments.

MODULE REVIEW

Review It

(27) Drugs used to quell psychotic symptoms are believed to work by blocking the action of the neurotransmitter _____.

(28) Antidepressants heighten the action of the neurotransmitter _____ .

(29) ECT is used mainly to treat severe cases of _____.

(30) The best-known, but no longer practiced, psychosurgery technique is _____ lobotomy.

Think About It

Compare the relative benefits of psychotherapy and drug therapy in treating mental health problems.

Coping with Emotional Responses to Stress—Anxiety, Anger, Depression

Modern life is filled with stresses and strains. This chapter is about taking charge of our lives rather than riding out the winds of our situations and our emotional responses. In this module, we describe some cognitive-behavioral strategies for reducing our fears, controlling our anger, and lifting our moods. You may not always succeed, but when faced with these situations, you will now have something to do about them. But if your emotional responses are strong and you are not managing well enough by yourself, talk to your professor, visit your college counseling center, or contact a private psychologist or other helping professional. Much of the time we can solve our problems on our own, but it is comforting to know that there are others who can, and would like to, help us.

9.9.1 Coping with Anxieties and Fears

Adjustment often requires that we approach and master the objects and situations that frighten us. Maintaining our health can require mastering fear of what the doctor may tell us. Getting ahead in school or in business can require speaking before groups, so some of us may need to cope with public speaking anxiety, the most common form of social anxiety.

You can reduce fears by gradually approaching, or confronting, feared objects or situations. Although your initial tendency might be to flee from a threatening (but physically harmless) situation, you may find yourself better able to cope with these situations by directly confronting them.

First, define the feared object or situation as the target, such as fear of riding on elevators, fear of heights, or fears of specific objects, such as large dogs.

Then list specific behaviors that make up a gradual approach of the target. A hierarchy of fear-evoking stimuli is called a fear-stimulus hierarchy. Strategies may include decreasing the distance between yourself and the target step by step—first approaching it with a friend, then approaching it alone, and gradually increasing the amount of time you remain in contact with the target. To be certain that the behaviors are listed in order of increasing difficulty, you can write down 10 to 20 steps on index cards. Then order and reorder the cards until you are satisfied that they are in a hierarchy. If there seems to be too great a jump between steps, one or two intermediary steps can be added.

Let's say you are troubled by fear of heights. Create a hierarchy (ordered list) of height situations in your community or neighborhood. Then begin using gradual exposure, starting with the least threatening height situation. Remain in the situation long enough for any fear to dissipate. Then repeat the experience another two or three times but before moving to the next step. If you stumble at a particular step, that's okay. Try again and again. If you still find it insurmountable, use a step halfway up in difficulty between the last accomplished step and the next-highest step. Talk calmly and rationally to yourself during each exposure experience and don't

catastrophize. Consider the case of Kathy, a college junior, as an example.

Kathy suffered from fear of driving, which made her dependent on her sister Marian and friends for commuting to work, shopping, and recreation. Driving 30 miles back and forth to work was identified as the target. She constructed this fear-stimulus hierarchy:

1. Sitting behind the wheel of her car with an understanding friend
2. Sitting alone behind the wheel of her car
3. Driving around the block with her friend
4. Driving around the block alone
5. Driving a few miles back and forth with her friend
6. Driving a few miles back and forth alone
7. Driving the route to work and back on a nonworkday with her friend
8. Driving the route to work and back on a nonworkday alone
9. Driving the route to work and back on a workday with her friend
10. Driving the route to work and back on a workday alone

Kathy repeated each step until she experienced no discomfort. As the procedure progressed, Kathy became aware of how her cognitive appraisal of driving had created and compounded her fears. Later she saw how cognitive reappraisal aided her coping efforts. At first she catastrophized: "What a baby I am! Marian is so understanding, and here I am ruining her day with my stupidity."

After discussing her self-defeating thoughts with a professional, Kathy learned to lighten up on herself for her imperfect performances. She recognized that self-efficacy develops gradually, and she rewarded herself for her steady progress. As time passed, she entertained thoughts like, "I don't like my fears, but I didn't get them on purpose and I'm working to overcome them. I am grateful to Marian, but I don't have to feel guilty about inconveniencing her. In the long run, this will make things easier for her, too. Now, this isn't so bad—I'm sitting behind the wheel without going bananas, so I'll give myself a pat on the back for that and stop condemning myself. I'm gradually gaining control of the situation. I'm taking charge and mastering it, bit by bit."

9.9.2 Managing Anger

Anger is a common emotional response to negative feelings such as frustration and to social provocations such as insults or threats. Anger is adaptive when it motivates us to surmount obstacles in our paths or to defend ourselves against aggressors. But anger is troublesome when it leads to excessive arousal or self-defeating aggression. Prolonged arousal is stressful and may lead to diseases of adaptation such as high blood pressure. Insulting, threatening, or attacking other people can cause us to get fired, be expelled from school, get into legal trouble, and get hurt or hurt people we care about.

From a cognitive perspective, we become angry because we say angering things to ourselves. It may seem that we become angry because we experience angering events—events in which we feel that other people treat us unfairly or take advantage of us. But two people may face the same angering situation, and one may remain cool as the proverbial cucumber while the other gets hot under the collar. The difference, cognitive theorists tell us, does not lie in the situation itself but in how each person responds to the situation.

We may become angry when we mutter to ourselves under our breath how unfair it is to be treated the way we are and how we just can't stand it. We may become angry when our thinking is dominated by "musts" and "shoulds" about how other people behave, such as people *must* treat us fairly and *should* put our needs first. It may be desirable to live in a world in which everyone is mutually respectful of one another's needs and feelings. But believing that the world must live up to these idealized expectations is a recipe for frustration and anger.

The thoughts that trigger anger may occur automatically, without any effort on our part to put them in our minds. Many automatic thoughts (see Table 9.3) are irrational and seem to just pop into our minds. We thus have to work to tune in to them. Then we need to work to replace them with rational, calming alternatives. In other words, we need to take an active role in managing our anger by identifying and correcting the kinds of thoughts that make us fume.

Evidence shows that people with anger management problems can benefit from anger management training (e.g., Del Vecchio & O'Leary, 2004; DiGiuseppe & Tafrate, 2003; Holloway, 2003a). Here, let us consider some of the cognitive-behavioral strategies that therapists use to help clients develop better anger management skills:

- *Monitor your reactions in angering situations.* Notice when you are becoming hot under the collar. Use this awareness as a cue to calm down and examine your thoughts. Take a moment to examine your thoughts and replace anger-inducing thoughts with calming, rational thoughts.

- *Stop and think.* Are you blowing things out of proportion? Are you jumping to a conclusion that the other person means you harm? What else might be going on? Are you taking things too personally?

- *Practice competing responses and competing thoughts.* Disrupt an anger response by taking a moment to visualize a peaceful scene in your mind's eye. Or take a walk around the block. Or just count to 10. If that doesn't help calm you down, do what the writer Mark Twain suggested and count to 100.

Table 9.3 ▌ Irrational Thoughts that Intensify Feelings of Anger and Rational Alternatives to These Thoughts

Activating Event	Irrational Thoughts	Rational Alternatives
Your mother asks,"Did you see a nice movie?"	"Why does she always ask me that?" "That's my business!"	"She probably just wants to know if I had a good time." "She's not really prying. She just wants to share my pleasure and make conversation."
You are caught in a traffic jam.	"Who the hell are they to hold me up?" (Road-rage alert!) "I'll never get there! It'll be a mess!"	"They're not doing it on purpose. They're probably just about as frustrated by it as I am." "So I'm late. It's not my fault and there's nothing I can do at the moment."
Your husband says, "The baby's crying pretty hard this time."	"Are you blaming me for it?" "So do something about it!"	"Don't jump to conclusions. He just made a statement of fact." "Stop and think. Why not ask Mr. Macho to handle it this time?"
Your roommate asks, "How's that paper of yours coming?"	"He's got nothing to do tonight," has he?" "Wouldn't he love it if I failed?"	"The paper is difficult, but that's not his fault." "I shouldn't assume I can read his mind. Maybe it's a sincere question. And if it's not, why should I let him get me upset?"
Your boss asks, "So how did that conference turn out?"	"I can handle conferences by myself!" "Always checking up on me!" "Dammit, I'm an adult!"	"Take it easy! Relax. Of course I can handle them. So why should I get bent out of shape?" "Maybe he's just interested, but checking up is a part of her job, after all is said and done." "Of course I am. So why should I get upset?"
Your fiancée asks, "Did you have a good time tonight?"	"She's always testing me!" "Didn't *she* have a good time tonight?"	"Stop and think! Maybe it's an innocent question—and if she is checking, maybe it's because she cares about my feelings." "Stop reaching and digging for reasons to be upset. She only asked if I had a good time. Deal with the question."

Table 9.4 ▌ Assertive Responses to Activating Events	
Activating Events	**Assertive Responses**
You are caught in a traffic jam	You admit to yourself, "This is annoying." But you also think, "But it is *not* a tragedy. I will control the situation rather than allow the situation to control me. *Relax.* Let those muscles in the shoulders go. When I arrive, I'll just take it step by step and make an honest effort. If things work out, fine. If they don't, getting bent out of shape about it won't make things better."
Your roommate asks, "How's that paper of yours coming?"	You say, "It's a pain! I absolutely hate it! I can't wait till it's over and done with. Don't tell me you have free time on your hands. I'd find that annoying."

- *Practice coping thoughts in place of angering self-statements.* Say to yourself, "There's no sense getting steamed about this. Just relax and figure out what I can say or do in this situation."

- *Practice self-relaxation.* When you feel angry, take a deep breath, tell yourself to relax, and exhale. Allow the bodily sensations of relaxation to "flow in" and replace feelings of anger.

- *Don't impose unrealistic expectations on others.* People will sometimes do hurtful or dumb things. People will not always meet your needs or meet them as quickly as you'd like. You can rail against the world or just accept people on their own terms. If a person acts unfairly, you can tell yourself the person is acting like a jerk, but that's no reason to get bent out of shape yourself.

- *Replace anger with empathy.* Empathy helps diffuse anger. Try to understand the situation from the other person's perspective. What do you think the other person is feeling that might explain the person's actions. Be assertive but show you understand what the other person is feeling, such as by saying, "I understand you are...; however, I would like for you to... now."

- *Depersonalize the situation.* Rather than curse out the other person under your breath, say to yourself, "He (she) must really have problems to be acting like this. But it's not my problem."

- *Keep your voice down.* Avoid shouting or cursing. You can keep your cool, even as others are losing their heads.

- *Act assertively, not aggressively.* When you act assertively, you express genuine feelings and stick up for your rights, but without putting the other person down. Assertive behavior does not include insulting, threatening, or attacking. However, it is assertive (not aggressive) to express strong disapproval of another person's behavior and to ask that person, respectfully, to change his or her behavior.

- *Express positive feelings.* Tell others how much you care about them. They will likely reciprocate in kind.

- *Give yourself a pat on the back for keeping your cool.* Reward yourself for handling a stressful situation without anger or aggression.

In Table 9.4 we review some of the situations noted earlier, but now we suggest assertive responses as a substitute for aggressive responses to activating events. And in Table 9.5 we present some new situations and compare potential assertive and aggressive responses.

By replacing irrational, enraging thoughts with rational alternatives, we can avoid uncalled-for feelings of anger and aggressive outbursts.

9.9.3 Lifting Your Mood (Getting Yourself Out of the Dumps)

Be not afraid of life. Believe that life is worth living and your belief will help create the fact.

—William James

Depression is characterized by inactivity, feelings of sadness, and cognitive distortions. If you suspect that your feelings may fit the picture of a major depressive episode or bipolar disorder, why not talk things over with your instructor or visit the college counseling or health center? But there are also things, such as the following, that you can do on your own to lift your mood and cope with milder feelings of depression:

- Engaging in pleasant events
- Thinking rationally
- Exercising

Increasing Pleasant Events

What we do is related to how we feel. Maintaining our moods on an even keel depends on keeping reinforcement levels flowing. But when we withdraw from pleasurable activities, we suffer a shortfall of reinforcement that can dampen our moods and motivation. You may be able to lift your mood by increasing your level of pleasant events.

1. Table 9.6 is a widely used checklist of pleasant activities. Check off those items that you find personally appealing.
2. Engage in at least three of these checkmarked pleasant events each day.
3. Record your activities in a diary. Add other activities and events that strike you as pleasant, even if they are unplanned.
4. Toward the end of each day, rate your response to each activity, using a scale like this one:
   - 3 = Wonderful
   - 2 = Very nice
   - 1 = Somewhat nice
   - 0 = No particular response
   - −1 = Somewhat disappointing
   - −2 = Rather disappointing
   - −3 = The pits
5. After a week or so, check the items in the diary that received positive ratings.
6. Repeat successful activities and experiment with new ones.

Table 9.5 ▌ A Comparison of Aggressive and Assertive Responses to Provocative Activating Events		
Provocation (Activating Event)	**Aggressive Response**	**Assertive Response**
Your supervisor says, "I would have handled that differently."	"Well, that's the way I did it. If you don't like it, fire me."	"What are you thinking?" If the supervisor becomes argumentative say, "I believe that I handled it properly because..." If you think that you were wrong, admit it straightforwardly. (It is assertive to express genuine recognition of incorrect behavior.)
A coworker says, "You are a fool."	"Drop dead."	"That's an ugly thing to say. It hurts my feelings, and if you have any hope of maintaining our relationship, I would recommend that you apologize."
A provocateur says, "So what're you gonna do about it?"	You shove or strike the provocateur.	You say, "Goodbye," and leave.
Your roommate has not cleaned the room.	"You're such a pig! Living with you is living in filth!"	"It's your turn to clean the room You agreed to clean it, and I expect you to stick to that. Please do it before dinner." (Reminding someone of an agreement and requesting compliance is assertive.)

Thinking Rationally

Public opinion is a weak tyrant compared with our own private opinion. What a man thinks of himself, that it is which determines... his fate.

—Henry David Thoreau, *Walden*

Depressed people tend to blame themselves for failures and problems, even when they are not at fault. They internalize blame and see their problems as stable (lasting) and global (pervasive)—as all but impossible to change. Depressed people also make cognitive errors such as catastrophizing their problems and minimizing their accomplishments.

Column 1 in Table 9.7 illustrates a number of irrational, depressing thoughts. How many of them have you had? Column 2 indicates the type of cognitive error being made (such as internalizing or catastrophizing), and column 3 shows examples of rational alternatives.

You can pinpoint irrational, depressing thoughts by identifying the kinds of thoughts you have when you feel low. Look for the fleeting thoughts that can trigger mood changes. It helps to jot them down. Then challenge their accuracy. Do you characterize difficult situations as impossible and hopeless? Do you expect too much from yourself and minimize your achievements? Do you internalize more than your fair share of blame?

You can use Table 9.7 to classify your cognitive errors of the type described in Table 8.5 in Chapter 8. Then construct rational alternatives to substitute for these distorted thoughts. Write these rational alternatives next to each distorted thought. Review them from time to time. When you are alone, you can read the distorted thought aloud. Then follow it by saying to yourself firmly, "No, that's irra-

tional!" Then read the rational alternative aloud twice, emphatically. After you have thought or read aloud the rational alternative, think, "That makes more sense! That's a more accurate view of things! I feel better now that I have things in perspective."

9.9.4 Exercise: Work it Out by Working Out

Exercise, as noted in Chapter 5, does not just foster physical health and conditioning. It can also enhance psychological well-being and help us cope with depression. Depression is characterized by inactivity and feelings of helplessness. Exercise, in a sense, is the opposite of inactivity. Research evidence bolsters the view that exercise can alleviate feelings of depression (Babyak et al., 2000; Colcombe

Galina Barskaya/iStockphoto

Playing with a Dog, Fighting Depression, or Some of Each?
Engaging in pleasant events is a way of combating depression. Because of individual differences, self-assessment techniques like the catalogue of pleasant events can help us focus on what might be of use to us.

Table 9.6 ▍ A Catalogue of Pleasant Events

1. Being in the country
2. Wearing expensive or formal clothes
3. Making contributions to religious, charitable, or political groups
4. Talking about sports
5. Meeting someone new
6. Going to a rock concert
7. Playing baseball, softball, football, or basketball
8. Planning trips or vacations
9. Buying things for yourself
10. Being at the beach
11. Doing artwork (painting, sculpture, drawing, moviemaking, etc.)
12. Rock climbing or mountaineering
13. Reading the Scriptures
14. Playing golf
15. Rearranging or redecorating your room or house
16. Going naked
17. Going to a sports event
18. Going to the races
19. Reading stories, novels, poems, plays, magazines, newspapers
20. Going to a bar, tavern, club
21. Going to lectures or talks
22. Creating or arranging songs or music
23. Boating
24. Restoring antiques, refinishing furniture
25. Watching television or listening to the radio
26. Camping
27. Working in politics
28. Working on machines (cars, bikes, radios, television sets)
29. Playing cards or board games
30. Doing puzzles or math games
31. Having lunch with friends or associates
32. Playing tennis
33. Driving long distances
34. Woodworking, carpentry
35. Writing stories, novels, poems, plays, articles
36. Being with animals
37. Riding in an airplane
38. Exploring (hiking away from known routes, spelunking, etc.)
39. Singing
40. Going to a party
41. Going to church functions
42. Playing a musical instrument
43. Snow skiing, ice skating
44. Wearing informal clothes, "dressing down"
45. Acting
46. Being in the city, downtown
47. Taking a long, hot bath
48. Playing pool or billiards
49. Bowling
50. Watching wild animals
51. Gardening, landscaping
52. Wearing new clothes
53. Dancing
54. Sitting or lying in the sun
55. Riding a motorcycle
56. Just sitting and thinking
57. Going to a fair, carnival, circus, zoo, amusement park
58. Talking about philosophy or religion
59. Gambling
60. Listening to sounds of nature
61. Dating, courting
62. Having friends come to visit
63. Going out to visit friends
64. Giving gifts
65. Getting massages or backrubs
66. Photography
67. Collecting stamps, coins, rocks, etc.
68. Seeing beautiful scenery
69. Eating good meals
70. Improving your health (having teeth fixed, changing diet, having a checkup, etc.)
71. Wrestling or boxing
72. Fishing
73. Going to a health club, sauna
74. Horseback riding
75. Protesting social, political, or environmental conditions
76. Going to the movies
77. Cooking meals
78. Washing your hair
79. Going to a restaurant
80. Using cologne, perfume
81. Getting up early in the morning
82. Writing a diary
83. Giving massages or backrubs
84. Meditating or doing yoga
85. Doing heavy outdoor work
86. Snowmobiling, dune buggying
87. Being in a body-awareness, encounter, or "rap" group
88. Swimming
89. Running, jogging
90. Walking barefoot
91. Playing frisbee or catch
92. Doing housework or laundry, cleaning things
93. Listening to music
94. Knitting, crocheting
95. Making love
96. Petting, necking
97. Going to a barber or beautician
98. Being with someone you love
99. Going to the library
100. Shopping
101. Preparing a new or special dish
102. Watching people
103. Bicycling
104. Writing letters, cards, or notes
105. Talking about politics or public affairs
106. Watching attractive women or men
107. Caring for houseplants
108. Having coffee, tea, or Coke, etc., with friends
109. Beachcombing
110. Going to auctions, garage sales, etc.
111. Water skiing, surfing, diving
112. Traveling
113. Attending the opera, ballet, or a play
114. Looking at the stars or the moon
115. Surfing the Net
116. Playing video games

Table 9.7 ∎ Irrational, Depressing Thoughts and Some Rational Alternatives		

Many of us create or compound feelings of depression because of cognitive errors such as those in this table. Have you had any of these irrational, depressing thoughts? Are you willing to challenge them?

Irrational Thought	Types of Distorted Thoughts	Rational Alternative
"There's nothing I can do."	Catastrophizing, Jumping to Conclusions	"I can't think of anything to do right now, but if I work at it, I may."
"I'm no good."	Misplaced Blame, Name Calling	"I did something I regret, but that doesn't make me evil or worthless as a person."
"This is absolutely awful."	Catastrophizing	"This is pretty bad, but it's not the end of the world."
"I just don't have the brains for college."	Name Calling, Jumping to Conclusions	"I guess I really need to go back over the basics in that course."
"I just can't believe I did something so disgusting!"	Catastrophizing	"That was a bad experience. Well, I won't be likely to try that again soon."
"I can't imaging ever feeling right."	Jumping to Conclusions	"This is painful, but if I try to work it through step by step, I'll probably eventually see my way out of it."
"It's all my fault."	Misplaced Blame, Mistaken Responsibility	"I'm not blameless, but I wasn't the only one involved. It may have been my idea, but he went into it with his eyes open."
"I can't do anything right."	Negative Focusing, All-or-Nothing Thinking	"I sure screwed this up, but I've done a lot of things well, and I'll do other things well."
"I hurt everybody who gets close to me."	Misplaced Blame, Mistaken Responsibility	"I'm not totally blameless, but I'm not responsible for the whole world. Others make their own decisions, and they have to live with the results, too."
"If people knew the real me, they would have it in for me."	Dismissing the Positives, Jumping to Conclusions, All-or-Nothing Thinking	"I'm not perfect, but nobody's perfect. I have positive as well as negative features, and I am entitled to self-interests."

& Kramer, 2003; O'Neil, 2003; Weuve et al., 2004). Why not use the exercise strategies described in Chapter 5 as a guide?

When we commit ourselves to monitoring and working on our negative feelings, we take direct charge of our emotional lives rather than condemning ourselves to passively riding out the winds of whatever emotion is driving us from moment to moment. If the strategies do not help you, why not talk things over with your professor or visit the college health or counseling center?

CHAPTER REVIEW

RECITE! RECITE! RECITE! RECITE! RECITE! RECITE! RECITE!

Study Tip: Reciting the answers to these study questions will help you become a more effective learner. First try answering the questions by yourself, either reciting them out loud or writing them in a notebook or on the computer. Then compare your answers with the sample answers provided below.

1. What is traditional Freudian psychoanalysis?
The goals of psychoanalysis are to provide self-insight into unconscious conflicts and replace defensive behavior with coping behavior. The major techniques used are free association, dream analysis, and interpretation of the transference. For example, a psychoanalyst might help clients gain insight into the ways in which they are transferring feelings toward their parents onto a spouse or even onto the analyst.

2. How do modern psychodynamic approaches differ from traditional psychoanalysis?
Modern approaches are briefer and more directive, and the therapist and client usually sit face to face.

3. What is Carl Rogers's method of client-centered therapy?
Client-centered therapy uses nondirective methods to help clients overcome obstacles to self-actualization. The therapist

shows unconditional positive regard, empathic understanding, and genuineness.

4. **What is Fritz Perls's method of Gestalt therapy?**
Perls's highly directive method aims to help people integrate conflicting parts of their personality. He aimed to make clients aware of conflict, accept its reality, and make choices despite fear.

5. **What is behavior therapy?**
Behavior therapy relies on learning principles (for example, conditioning and observational learning) to help clients develop adaptive behavior patterns and eliminate maladaptive ones.

6. **What are some behavior therapy methods for reducing fears?**
These include flooding, gradual exposure, systematic desensitization, and modeling. Flooding exposes a person to high levels of fear-evoking stimuli without aversive consequences until fear is extinguished. In gradual exposure, the person progresses through a series of exposure encounters with increasingly fearful stimuli. Systematic desensitization reduces fears by gradually exposing clients to a hierarchy of fear-evoking stimuli while they remain relaxed. Modeling encourages clients to imitate another person (the model) in approaching fear-evoking stimuli.

7. **How do behavior therapists use aversive conditioning to help people break bad habits?**
This is a behavior therapy method for discouraging undesirable behaviors by repeatedly pairing stimuli associated with self-defeating goals (for example, drinking alcohol, smoking cigarettes) with aversive stimuli so that the undesirable stimuli evoke an aversive response.

8. **How do behavior therapists apply principles of operant conditioning?**
These are behavior therapy methods that foster adaptive behavior through applying principles of reinforcement. Examples include token economies, social skills training, and biofeedback training.

9. **What is Aaron Beck's method of cognitive therapy?**
Aaron Beck notes that clients develop emotional problems such as depression because of cognitive errors that lead them to minimize accomplishments and catastrophize failures. He found that depressed people experience cognitive distortions such as the cognitive triad; that is, they expect the worst of themselves, the world at large, and the future. Beck teaches clients how to dispute cognitive errors.

10. **What is Albert Ellis's method of rational-emotive behavior therapy (REBT)?**
Albert Ellis originated rational-emotive behavior therapy, which holds that people's beliefs about events, not only the events themselves, shape people's responses to them. Ellis points out how irrational beliefs, such as the belief that we must have social approval, can worsen problems.

11. **What are the advantages and disadvantages of group therapy?**
Group therapy is more economical than individual therapy. Moreover, group members benefit from the social support and experiences of other members. However, some clients cannot disclose their problems in the group setting or risk group disapproval. They need individual attention.

12. **What is couple therapy?**
In couple therapy, a couple is treated together in the attempt to help them improve their communication skills and manage conflicts more effectively.

13. **What is family therapy?**
In family therapy, one or more families make up the group. Family therapy undertaken from the "systems approach" modifies family interactions to enhance the growth of individuals in the family and the family as a whole.

14. **Does psychotherapy work?**
Yes, statistical analyses using the technique of meta-analysis provide impressive evidence for the effectiveness of psychotherapy. Evidence from controlled research trials also supports the therapeutic benefits of particular forms of therapy (called empirically supported treatments) for particular disorders.

15. **What kinds of problems do researchers encounter when they conduct research on psychotherapy?**
Investigators face such problems as difficulties in randomly assigning participants to different methods of therapy; problems with measurement of outcome; and problems in sorting out the effects of nonspecific therapeutic factors, such as instillation of hope, from the specific effects of particular methods of therapy.

16. **How do issues of diversity come into play in therapy?**
Therapists need to be sensitive to cultural differences. For example, they should understand how people from ethnic minority groups that have been subject to oppression and prejudice may be mistrustful of European American therapists. Therapy methods and goals may also conflict with a client's own cultural values. Feminist therapy attempts to increase awareness of sociocultural issues that contribute to women's problems and challenges the tradition of male dominance. Many professionals believe that psychotherapy should not attempt to change a gay male or lesbian's sexual orientation but should help that person adjust to social and cultural pressures to be heterosexual.

17. **What kinds of drug therapy are available for psychological disorders?**
Antianxiety drugs help quell anxiety, but tolerance and dependence may develop over time. Antipsychotic drugs help many people with schizophrenia by blocking the action of dopamine receptors. Antidepressants often help people with severe depression, apparently by raising the levels of serotonin available to the brain. Lithium often helps stabilize mood swings in people with bipolar disorder.

18. **What is electroconvulsive therapy (ECT)?**

    In ECT an electrical current is passed through the temples, inducing a seizure and frequently relieving severe depression. ECT is controversial because of side effects such as memory loss and because of the highly invasive nature of the procedure.

19. **What is psychosurgery? How is it used to treat psychological disorders?**

    Psychosurgery is an even more controversial (and rarely, if ever, practiced) technique for controlling severely disturbed behavior through surgery on the brain.

20. **What do we know about the effectiveness of biomedical therapies?**

    There is controversy as to whether psychotherapy or drug therapy should be used with people with anxiety disorders or depres-

sion. Drugs do not teach people how to solve problems and build relationships. Having said that, antidepressants may be advisable when psychotherapy does not help people with depression. Furthermore, ECT appears to be helpful in some cases of severe depression in which neither psychotherapy nor drug therapy (antidepressants) is of help. Antipsychotic drugs can help control more flagrant symptoms of schizophrenia. Psychosurgery has been all but discontinued because of questions about its effectiveness and the occurrence of serious side effects.

YOUR PERSONAL JOURNAL

REFLECT   REFLECT   REFLECT   REFLECT   REFLECT   REFLECT   REFLECT

Study Tip: reflecting on how the concepts in the chapter relate to your own experiences encourages deeper processing, which makes the material more personally meaningful and fosters more effective learning. Use additional pages if needed to complete your answers.

1. Having read this chapter, would you be more or less willing to seek the help of a therapist if you experienced a psychological disorder? Which type of therapy do you think you would prefer? Why?

   _____

   _____

   _____

   _____

   _____

2. If you suffered from an anxiety disorder or mood disorder, would you consider using antianxiety or antidepressant drugs to treat it? Why or why not? Did reading the text alter your views in any ways?

   _____

   _____

   _____

   _____

   _____

ANSWERS TO MODULE REVIEWS

Module 9.1

1. unconscious
2. insight
3. transference
4. dreams
5. manifest/latent

Module 9.2

6. humanistic
7. nondirective/self
8. unconditional/genuineness
9. directive

Module 9.3

10. learning
11. gradual
12. Aversive
13. Operant

Module 9.4

14. cognitions
15. blood
16. irrational

Module 9.5

17. more
18. Couple
19. systems/family

Module 9.6

20. meta
21. is
22. Empirically

Module 9.7

23. mistrust
24. interdependency
25. Feminist
26. unethical

Module 9.8

27. dopamine
28. serotonin
29. depression
30. prefrontal

Did you know that...

- A student who successfully completed all requirements for a doctorate in psychology was denied the degree because she was a woman? (p. 333)

- When it comes to measures of general intelligence, one gender doesn't appear to be any smarter than the other? (p. 341)

- Women in our culture typically smile more often than men? (p. 343)

- For some forms of aggression, girls tend to be more aggressive than boys? (p. 343)

- Some people believe they are trapped in the body of the opposite sex by a mistake of nature? (p. 344)

- Women's bodies (as well as men's) produce the male sex hormone testosterone? (p. 349)

- In one preliterate society in New Guinea, it is expected that men will stay home and take care of the children while the women go off to hunt? (p. 350)

H. Armstrong Roberts/ Corbis Images

In the year 1882 a young woman had completed all her degree requirements for a Ph.D. (Doctor of Philosophy) degree from Johns Hopkins University, but the university refused to award her the degree. The reason? She was a woman, the earliest woman pioneer in psychology, Christine Ladd-Franklin (1847–1930). At the time that Ladd-Franklin studied psychology, the university, like many other universities in the United States, did not issue doctoral degrees to women. It was assumed that a woman's place was in the home or in occupations, such as teaching, which did not require doctoral-level training. But Ladd-Franklin was not to be deterred by the sexism of her time. She persevered and went on to a distinguished research career in psychology, finally receiving her Ph.D. degree some 44 years later, in 1926.

Times have changed and are changing still. Women now comprise the majority of psychology students at both the undergraduate and graduate levels. In fact, as noted in Chapter 1, women now account for about three-quarters of doctoral degree recipients in psychology.

And it's not just psychology. Other traditionally masculine-dominated professions, such as law and medicine, have seen increasing representation of women in their ranks. Women are also serving in combat, piloting aircraft, and commanding naval vessels. But as a leading feminist writer, Gloria Steinem, put it, we're only halfway there. Steinem was speaking here about the need to train our sons as well as our daughters to develop human qualities that were long misidentified as "feminine," such as empathy and compassion. But she might just as well have been speaking about the sexual inequalities that continue to exist today. Many occupational roles remain as gender-typed today as they were generations ago. For example, women continue to constitute the great majority of registered nurses and flight attendants.

Women still continue to bear a disproportionate share of household and childcare responsibilities, despite the fact that most women today also work outside the home. Or to put it another way, women today are expected not only to bring home the bacon but to fry it in the pan; to change the baby's diapers; and to transport the kids to play dates, doctor's visits, and, of course, the now-proverbial soccer games. What does it mean to be male in our society? To be female? How are men and women seen as different from each other? How different are they in fact? We discuss societal views of men and women and examine gender differences in the light of evidence. We also explore the origins of gender differences and the many costs of gender stereotyping to the individual and society.

MODULE 10.1

Gender Roles and Gender Stereotypes: What Does It Mean to Be Masculine or Feminine?

- ▌ What is a stereotype?
- ▌ What are our cultural beliefs about gender roles?
- ▌ What is gender polarization? What are perceived as the "natural" gender roles?
- ▌ What is psychological androgyny?
- ▌ How is psychological androgyny related to adjustment?

"Why Can't a Woman Be More Like a Man?" You may remember this song from the classic musical *My Fair Lady*. In the song, Professor Henry Higgins laments that women are emotional and fickle, whereas men are logical and dependable. We suspect that if Professor Higgins had been female, she might have wondered why a man can't be more like a woman. But just how do men and women differ apart from their obvious anatomical and reproductive differences? For example, do they differ in intelligence or other cognitive abilities? In personality and social behavior? And if differences exist, are they a matter of biology or culture? Before we consider what scientists have learned about gender differences, we should recognize that concepts of gender are embedded within a cultural framework.

Let us begin by recognizing that each society establishes a set of expectations, or **gender roles**, which designate the kinds of behaviors considered appropriate for men and women to perform. Gender roles prescribe how men and women should act, how they should dress, and even the kind of work they should do. The designation of certain jobs as "men's work" and others as "women's work" are examples of gender roles. According to traditional gender roles in Western society, men are expected to be breadwinners and women homemakers.

Layered over these gender roles are the *gender stereotypes* that people tend to hold about men and women. A *stereotype* is a fixed, conventional idea about the attributes, characteristics, or behaviors of members of a particular group or category, such as an ethnic or a racial group, a religious group, or, in the case here, a gender category (men or women). A gender stereotype is a generalized belief about what men and women are like. Stereotypes often give rise to prejudice and discrimination, as in the form of sexism and racism. For example, if we stereotype women as lacking managerial ability, we are likely to favor male candidates over female candidates for managerial positions.

Stereotyping can have more subtle effects. Members of stereotyped and stigmatized groups may be "on guard" for cues or signals associated with stereotypes like "girls can't do math" or "blacks don't do well on IQ tests" (Kaiser, Vick, &

▌ **Gender roles** A complex cluster of ways in which males and females are expected to behave.

Major, 2006; Steele & Ambady, 2006). This sense of being on guard when a stereotype is in the air may negatively affect how well people of stigmatized groups perform in competitive situations (Schmader, Johns, & Forbes, 2008). For example, drawing attention to gender stereotypes may undermine women's performance on math tests by diverting their attention to worrying about their performance (Good, Aronson, & Harder, 2008; Kiefer & Sekaquaptewa, 2007; Krendl et al., 2008; Muzzatti & Agnoli, 2007).

How are men and women viewed differently in our culture? In our culture, some of the more commonly held stereotypes of women are that they are nurturing, gentle, dependent, warm, emotional, kind, helpful, patient, and submissive. You can see that some stereotypes may depict positive attributes (kind, helpful), whereas others may carry a negative tone (submissive, dependent). The stereotypical male is seen as independent, competitive, tough, logical, self-reliant, dominant, and protective.

Cross-cultural studies confirm that gender-role stereotypes are widespread across different cultures (see Table 10.1). For example, in their survey of 30 countries, John Williams and Deborah Best (1994) found that men are more likely to be judged to be active, adventurous, aggressive, arrogant, and autocratic (and we have only gotten through the *A*s). Women are more likely to be seen as fearful, fickle, foolish, frivolous, and fussy (and these are only a handful of the *F*s).

When men and women in various cultures rate themselves, women tend to perceive themselves as more open to their emotions, whereas men tend to perceive themselves as more assertive (Costa, Terracciano, & McCrae, 2001). So self-perceptions also reflect the prevailing gender-role stereotypes.

Stereotypes also affect the opportunities open to men and women in Latino/Latina American communities, as can be seen in the nearby *Adjustment and Modern Life* feature.

Table 10.1 ▌ Gender-Role Stereotypes Around the World

Stereotypes of Males		Stereotypes of Females	
Active	Opinionated	Affectionate	Nervous
Adventurous	Pleasure-seeking	Appreciative	Patient
Aggressive	Precise	Cautious	Pleasant
Arrogant	Quick	Changeable	Prudish
Autocratic	Rational	Charming	Self-pitying
Capable	Realistic	Complaining	Sensitive
Coarse	Reckless	Complicated	Sentimental
Conceited	Resourceful	Confused	Sexy
Confident	Rigid	Dependent	Shy
Courageous	Robust	Dreamy	Softhearted
Cruel	Sharp-witted	Emotional	Sophisticated
Determined	Show-off	Excitable	Submissive
Disorderly	Steady	Fault-finding	Suggestible
Enterprising	Stern	Fearful	Superstitious
Hardheaded	Stingy	Fickle	Talkative
Individualistic	Stolid	Foolish	Timid
Inventive	Tough	Forgiving	Touchy
Loud	Unscrupulous	Frivolous	Unambitious
Obnoxious		Fussy	Understanding
		Gentle	Unstable
		Imaginative	Warm
		Kind	Weak
		Mild	Worrying
		Modest	

Source: Data from Williams & Best (1994), p. 193, Table 1.

Adjustment and Modern Life

Acculturation and Changing Gender Roles—Rafael Javier in His Own Words

Cultural differences influence gender stereotypes. Consider the machismo/marianismo stereotype within traditional Hispanic cultures. **Machismo** is a cultural stereotype that defines masculinity in terms of an idealized view of manliness. To be macho is to be strong, virile, and dominant. Each Latino and Latina culture puts its own particular cultural stamp on the meaning of machismo, however. In the Spanish-speaking cultures of the Caribbean and Central America, the macho code encourages men to restrain their feelings and maintain an emotional distance. In my travels in Argentina and some other Latin American countries, however, I have observed that men who are sensitive and emotionally expressive are not perceived as compromising their macho code. More research is needed into differences in cultural conceptions of machismo and other gender roles among various Latino/Latina groups.

In counterpoint to the macho ideal among Latino/Latina peoples is the cultural idealization of femininity embodied in the concept of **marianismo**. The marianismo stereotype, which derives its name from the Virgin Mary, refers to the ideal of the virtuous woman as one who "suffers in silence," submerging her needs and desires to those of her husband and children. With the marianismo stereotype, the image of a woman's role as a martyr is raised to the level of a cultural ideal. According to this cultural stereotype, a woman is expected to demonstrate her love for her husband by waiting patiently at home and having dinner prepared for him at any time of day or night he happens to come home, to have his slippers ready for him, and so on.

The feminine ideal is one of suffering in silence and being the provider of joy, even in the face of pain. Strongly influenced by the patriarchal Spanish tradition, the marianismo stereotype has historically been used to maintain women in a subordinate position in relation to men.

Acculturation—the process in immigrant groups of developing the customs of the host culture—has challenged this traditional machismo/marianismo division of marital roles among Latino/Latina American couples in the United States. In my own work in treating Latino/Latina American couples in therapy, I have seen that marriages are under increasing strain from the conflict between traditional and modern expectations about marital roles. Latina Americans have

Psychologist Rafael Javier.

Courtesy Rafael Javier

© Esbin-Anderson/The Image Works

A Latino/Latina American Couple
In many traditional Latino/Latina American cultures, we find a tradition of machismo among males and marianismo among females. But bear in mind that there are significant individual differences and that most cultures have some concept of a "macho" male, even though the word will differ. And, of course, most cultures around the world have traditionally viewed women as subordinate to men.

been entering the workforce in increasing numbers, usually in domestic or childcare positions, but they are still expected to assume responsibility for tending their own children, keeping the house, and serving their husbands' needs when they return home. In many cases, a reversal of traditional roles occurs in which the wife works and supports the family, while the husband remains at home because he is unable to find or maintain employment. It is often the Latino American husband who has the greater difficulty accepting a more flexible distribution of roles within the marriage and giving up a rigid set of expectations tied to traditional machismo/marianismo gender expectations. Although some couples manage to reshape their expectations and marital roles in the face of changing conditions, many relationships buckle under the strain and are terminated in divorce. While neither the machismo nor the marianismo stereotype is expected to disappear entirely, greater flexibility in gender-role expectations may be a product of continued acculturation.

▍ **Machismo** The Latino and Latina American cultural stereotype that defines masculinity in terms of strength, virility, dominance, and emotional restraint.

▍ **Marianismo** The Latino and Latina American cultural stereotype that defines the feminine ideal as subordinating her needs and desires to those of her husband and children and, when necessary, suffering in silence.

▍ **Acculturation** Process of adapting the customs of a host culture.

10.1.1 Adjustment and Psychological Androgyny: The More Traits the Merrier?

We commonly think about masculinity and femininity as opposite poles of one continuum. We may assume that the more masculine people are, the less feminine they are, and vice versa. So a man who shows "feminine" traits of nurturance, tenderness, and emotionality might be considered less masculine for it. Women who compete with men in the business world are seen not only as more masculine than other women but also as less feminine. But many psychologists look upon masculinity and femininity as independent dimensions. That is, people who score high on measures of masculine traits need not score low on feminine traits. People who show skill in the business world can also be warm and loving. People who possess both stereotypically masculine and feminine traits are said to show psychological androgyny. People who are low in both stereotypical masculine and feminine traits are "undifferentiated" according to masculinity and femininity (see Figure 10.1).

Undifferentiated people seem to encounter distress. Undifferentiated women, for example, are viewed less positively than more feminine or more masculine women, even by their friends (Baucom & Danker-Brown, 1983). And undifferentiated women tend to be less satisfied with their marriages (Baucom & Aiken, 1984). However, psychologically androgynous people, as we shall see, may be more resistant to stress.

Contributions of Psychological Androgyny to Well Being, Adjustment, and Personal Development

There is a good deal of evidence that androgynous people are relatively well adjusted. It appears that psychologically androgynous individuals can summon up both "masculine" and "feminine" traits to express their talents and desires and to meet the demands of different situations.

In terms of Erik Erikson's concepts of ego identity and intimacy, androgynous college students are more likely than feminine, masculine, and undifferentiated students to show a combination of "high identity" and "high intimacy" (Schiedel & Marcia, 1985). That is, they are more likely to show a firm sense of who they are and what they stand for (identity), and they have a greater capacity to form intimate, sharing relationships.

Psychologically androgynous individuals tend to be more creative than masculine or feminine-typed individuals (Norlander, Erixon, & Archer, 2000). Traits that are commonly identified with psychological androgyny include "masculine" independence under group pressures to conform and "feminine" nurturance in interactions with a kitten or a baby. They feel more comfortable performing a wider range of activities in different contexts, including (the "masculine") nailing of boards and (the "feminine") winding of yarn. In adolescence, they report greater interest in pursuing nontraditional occupational roles. They show greater self-esteem and greater ability to bounce back from failure. They are more likely to try to help others in need. Androgynous people are more willing to share leadership in mixed-gender groups;

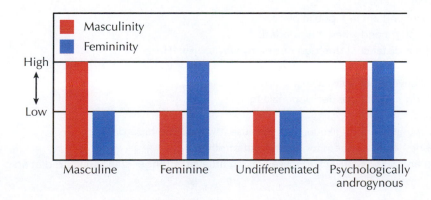

Figure 10.1
Psychological Androgyny
Many psychologists today believe that masculinity and femininity represent independent dimensions, so a person may possess high levels of both (psychological androgyny), high levels of either traditional masculinity or femininity, or low levels of both (undifferentiated).

masculine people attempt to dominate such groups, and feminine people tend to be satisfied with taking a backseat. Androgynous women rate stressful life events as less undesirable than do feminine women.

Traditionally defined feminine traits may contribute to marital happiness, whether they are found in women or men. In early research, Antill (1983) found not only that husbands' happiness was positively related to their wives' femininity but also that wives' happiness was positively related to their husbands' femininity. Wives of psychologically androgynous husbands are happier than women whose husbands adhere to a strict, stereotypical masculine gender role. Other investigators reported that androgynous men in a research sample were more tolerant of their wives' or lovers' faults and more likely to express loving feelings than were "macho" males (Coleman & Ganong, 1985). Women, like men, appreciate

---

Are You a "Chesty" Male or a "Fluffy" Female? The ANDRO Scale	**Self-Assessment**

What about you? Do you adhere to strict, traditional gender roles? Are you, in the words of psychologist Sandra Bem, a "chesty" male or a "fluffy" female? Or is psychological androgyny—the expression of both "masculine" and "feminine" traits—more your style?

Directions: To find out, indicate whether the following items are mostly true or mostly false for you by circling the T or the F. Use the tables at the end of the chapter to compare your score to those of a national sample of respondents. Then have some other people in your life take the test. How many chesty males and fluffy females do you know?

T F 1. I like to be with people who assume a protective attitude toward me.
T F 2. I try to control others rather than permit them to control me.
T F 3. Surfboard riding would be dangerous for me.
T F 4. If I have a problem I like to work it out alone.
T F 5. I seldom go out of my way to do something just to make others happy.
T F 6. Adventures where I am on my own are a little frightening to me.
T F 7. I feel confident when directing the activities of others.
T F 8. I will keep working on a problem after others have given up.
T F 9. I would not like to be married to a protective person.
T F 10. I usually try to share my problems with someone who can help me.
T F 11. I don't care if my clothes are unstylish, as long as I like them.
T F 12. When I see a new invention, I attempt to find out how it works.
T F 13. People like to tell me their troubles because they know I will do everything I can to help them.
T F 14. Sometimes I let people push me around so they can feel important.
T F 15. I am only very rarely in a position where I feel a need to actively argue for a point of view I hold.
T F 16. I dislike people who are always asking me for advice.
T F 17. I seek out positions of authority.
T F 18. I believe in giving friends lots of help and advice.
T F 19. I get little satisfaction from serving others.
T F 20. I make certain that I speak softly when I am in a public place.
T F 21. I am usually the first to offer a helping hand when it is needed.
T F 22. When I see someone I know from a distance, I don't go out of my way to say "Hello."
T F 23. I would prefer to care for a sick child myself rather than hire a nurse.
T F 24. I prefer not being dependent on anyone for assistance.
T F 25. When I am with someone else, I do most of the decision making.
T F 26. I don't mind being conspicuous.
T F 27. I would never pass up something that sounded like fun just because it was a little hazardous.
T F 28. I get a kick out of seeing someone I dislike appear foolish in front of others.
T F 29. When someone opposes me on an issue, I usually find myself taking an even stronger stand than I did at first.

T̶ F 30. When two persons are arguing, I often settle the argument for them.

T̶ F 31. I will not go out of my way to behave in an approved way.

T̶ F 32. I am quite independent of the people I know.

T̶ F 33. If I were in politics, I would probably be seen as one of the forceful leaders of my party.

T F̶ 34. I prefer a quiet, secure life to an adventurous one.

T̶ F 35. I prefer to face my problems by myself.

T F̶ 36. I try to get others to notice the way I dress.

T̶ F 37. When I see someone who looks confused, I usually ask if I can be of any assistance.

T̶ F 38. It is unrealistic for me to insist on becoming the best in my field of work all of the time.

T F̶ 39. The good opinion of one's friends is one of the chief rewards for living a good life.

T F̶ 40. If I get tired while playing a game, I generally stop playing.

T F̶ 41. When I see a baby, I often ask to hold him.

T F̶ 42. I am quite good at keeping others in line.

T F̶ 43. I think it would be best to marry someone who is more mature and less dependent than I.

T̶ F 44. I don't want to be away from my family too much.

T̶ F 45. Once in a while I enjoy acting as if I were tipsy.

T F̶ 46. I feel incapable of handling many situations.

T̶ F 47. I delight in feeling unattached.

T F̶ 48. I would make a poor judge because I dislike telling others what to do.

T̶ F 49. Seeing an old or helpless person makes me feel that I would like to take care of him.

T F̶ 50. I usually make decisions without consulting others.

T F̶ 51. It doesn't affect me one way or another to see a child being spanked.

T F̶ 52. My goal is to do at least a little bit more than anyone else has done before.

T̶ F 53. To love and to be loved is of greatest importance to me.

T F̶ 54. I avoid some hobbies and sports because of their dangerous nature.

T F̶ 55. One of the things which spurs me on to do my best is the realization that I will be praised for my work.

T F̶ 56. People's tears tend to irritate me more than to arouse my sympathy.

Source: Reprinted from Berzins, Welling, & Wetter (1977).

For an interactive version of this self-assessment exercise, go to www.wileyplus.com

spouses who are sympathetic, warm, tender, and love children. The ANDRO Scale in the nearby self-assessment will offer you insight into your own gender-role orientation.

Challenges to Androgyny

One challenge to androgyny is the belief that masculinity, not androgyny, accounts for greater self-esteem. Self-esteem is an important factor in our psychological well-being. Yet it may be that the relationship between psychological androgyny and self-esteem in both men and women is not based on the combination of masculine and feminine traits but rather on the presence of "masculine" traits per se (Ward, 2000; Williams & D'Alessandro, 1994). That is, traits such as independence and assertiveness contribute to high self-esteem in both genders.

Some feminist writers have criticized the view that psychological androgyny is a worthwhile goal—for a quite different reason. Feminists note that psychological androgyny is defined as the possession of both masculine and feminine personality traits. However, this very definition relies on the presumed authenticity of masculine and feminine gender-role stereotypes. Feminists argue that we need to move beyond traditional stereotypes and treat people as individuals, regardless of their gender. That said, many scholars believe that the concept of psychological androgyny holds value for describing people who combine traditionally defined "masculine" and "feminine" traits in their personalities (Arnett, 2004).

Review It

(1) _____ are fixed, conventional ideas about a group of people.

(2) Our expectations of how men and women should behave are called _____ _____ stereotypes.

(3) Psychological _____ describes people who possess both masculine-typed and feminine-typed traits.

(4) Research shows that psychologically androgynous people tend to have (higher or lower?) levels of creativity than people who are masculine-typed and feminine-typed.

(5) Critics connect the higher self-esteem of psychologically androgynous women with traditional (masculinity or femininity), not with androgyny per se.

Think About It

How have gender-role expectations changed in recent years? To what extent have they remained the same?

MODULE 10.2

Gender Differences: *Vive La Différence or Vive La Similarité?*

▊ What gender differences do researchers find in cognitive abilities?

▊ What gender differences do researchers find in social behavior?

The French have an expression, *Vive la différence*, which means "Long live the difference" (between men and women). Yet modern life has challenged our concepts of what it means to be a woman or a man. The anatomical differences between women and men are obvious and are connected with the biological aspects of reproduction. Biologists therefore have a relatively easy time of it describing and interpreting the gender differences they study. The task of psychology in examining gender differences in behavior and abilities is more complex and is wrapped up with social, cultural, and psychological factors, not just biological factors.

Let's put it another way: to reproduce, women and men have to be biologically different. Throughout history, it has also been assumed that women and men must be psychologically different in order to fulfill different roles in the family and society. But what are the psychological differences between women and men? Let us begin by asking the question: What are the gender differences in cognitive abilities?

10.2.1 Gender Differences in Cognitive Abilities

Here's a question that's bound to start an argument in mixed company: Who's smarter—men or women? It was long believed in Western society that males were more intelligent than females because of their greater knowledge of world affairs and their skill in science and industry. What was overlooked—largely by men—was that women were systematically excluded from full participation in world affairs, science, and industry. Scientific evidence does not square with the assessment of men as the brighter gender; in fact, tests of intelligence do not show any gender differences in overall intelligence or cognitive abilities (Halpern & LaMay, 2000). As former American Psychological Association president Diane Halpern put it, "There is no evidence that one sex is smarter than the other" (Halpern, 2004, p. 139).

Although males and females are similar in general intelligence, evidence does show some gender differences in specific cognitive skills. For example, girls are somewhat superior to boys in verbal fluency, or ease of use of spoken and written language (Spelke, 2005). Girls seem to acquire language somewhat faster than boys do. Also, in the United States far more boys than girls have reading problems, ranging from reading below grade level to severe disabilities (Rutter et al., 2004). On the other hand, males headed for college seem to catch up in verbal skills.

Boys have the edge in certain visual-spatial abilities of the sort used in math, science, and even map reading (Halpern et al., 2007; Johnson & Bouchard, 2007; see Figure 10.2). This advantage may help explain the tendency for men to excel in certain kinds of games and tasks, such as playing chess or solving geometry problems. One study compared the navigation strategies of 90 male and 104 female university students (Dabbs et al., 1998). In giving directions, men more often referred to miles and directional coordinates in terms of north, south, east, and west, whereas women were more likely to refer to landmarks and turns to the right or left ("Let's see, it's a left at the gas station and then the next right at the stop sign"). Men tend to have the advantage in spatial abilities, such as mentally rotating figures in space and finding figures embedded within larger designs (see Figure 10.2) (Levine et al., 2005; Quaiser-Pohl, Geiser, & Lehmann, 2006).

Studies in the United States and elsewhere find that males generally obtain higher scores on standardized math tests than females (Collaer & Hill, 2006; Halpern et al., 2007). That said, the math gap between the genders has been shrinking, so much

Commercial Eye/Iconica/Getty Images, Inc.

Who's Smarter—Men or Women?
When it comes to general intelligence, let's call it a tie. But some gender differences do exist with respect to more specific cognitive abilities.

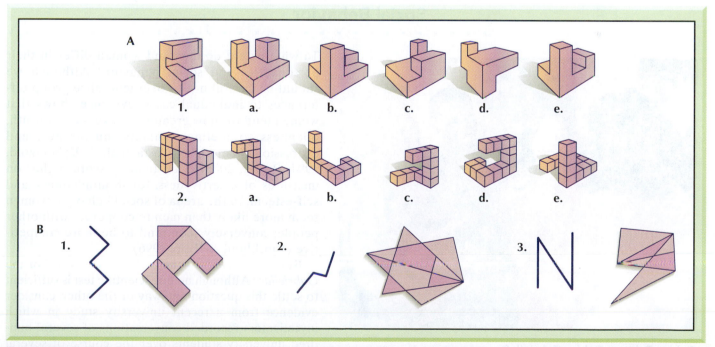

Figure 10.2
Spatial-Relations Skills
Males as a group tend to outperform females on the types of spatial-relations skills shown here, including matching three-dimensional figures that are rotated in space (A) and finding embedded figures or forms (B).

Math Is Me
The faulty conclusion that math ≠ me can discourage young women from pursuing advanced training in math and science.

Masterfile

so that average scores of boys and girls on standardized math tests today are actually quite close (Ripley, 2005). Among college students, men and women today show equal aptitude for mathematics (Spelke, 2005). Although gender differences in cognitive abilities exist, we should note the following qualifications:

1 _Gender differences are small._ Actually, differences within people of the same gender are much greater than differences across genders. Differences between men and women in cognitive abilities are overshadowed by the similarities (Hyde, 2005a; Spelke, 2005).

2 _Gender differences are group differences._ There is greater variation in these skills between individuals within the groups than between males and females. That is, there may be a greater difference in, say, verbal skills among women than between men and women. Millions of females outdistance the "average" male in math and spatial abilities. Men have produced their Shakespeares. Women have produced their Madame Curies. Men and women appear to be equally capable of learning science (Spelke, 2005). No woman or young girl should be discouraged from pursuing a career in math or science based on misguided notions that "girls don't do math (or science)."

3 _Some differences certainly reflect sociocultural influences._ In our culture, spatial and math abilities are stereotyped as masculine, so young men may receive greater encouragement to pursue these interests than young women. Yet training and experience matter. Recently, investigators found that the edge men show in certain spatial skills was reduced when women were given a mere 10 hours of training in playing visually challenging video games (Feng, Spence, & Pratt, 2007). Spatial skills are important in fields such as mathematics, engineering, and science, so offering specific training experiences in developing these skills may help redress the traditional imbalance between men and women in these fields.

10.2.2 Gender Differences in Personality and Social Behavior

Gabby Gabe or Gabby Gabriella?
According to the results of a recent study, there is no significant difference between men and women in the numbers of words they speak over the course of a day.

Kevin Dodge/©Corbis

To what extent do men and women differ in their personalities and social behavior? Although we should be careful not to overgeneralize group differences to individual cases, evidence shows that women tend to show greater extraversion, warmth, openness to feelings, anxiety, nurturance, and expression of emotions (Costa et al., 2002; Feingold, 1994; Ripley, 2005). Men tend to score higher on measures of assertiveness, tough-mindedness, and self-esteem. In the arena of social behavior, women seem more likely than men to cooperate with other people; conversely, men tend to be more competitive (Bjorklund & Kipp, 1996).

But who's gabbier—the _Gabes_ of the world or the _Gabriellas_? Although no one scientific test is sufficient to settle this question one way or the other, consider evidence from a recent university study in which investigators recorded conversations of several hundred university students over the course of several days through the use of tiny microphones (Mehl et al., 2007). The results showed a virtual tie in the number of words emitted per day by men and women, about

16,000 words in total. Taken together with other related research (see Leaper & Ayres, 2007), the stereotype that women are more talkative than men just doesn't square with scientific evidence.

Perhaps you've noticed differences in the relationships that men and women tend to have with their friends. Men's friendships with other men tend to be shallower and less supportive than women's friendships with other women. Research with 565 college students suggests that emotional restraint and fear of gay males (homophobia) partly explain men's relative lack of intimacy with other men (Bank & Hansford, 2000). Competitive striving with other men played a lesser role.

Women in our culture tend to smile more than men and typically are more expressive of their feelings and personal experiences (LaFrance, Hecht, & Paluck, 2003). In many societies, men aren't supposed to show their emotions openly, let alone cry. On the other hand, women are given more latitude to express emotions such as joy, love, fear, and sadness (Ripley, 2005). Yet men are typically given more latitude when it comes to expressing the emotion of anger. Men learn that anger is a "masculine" emotion and that acting out on anger through physical aggression may be perceived as "manly." "But for girls," says anger researcher Sandra Thomas of the University of Tennessee, Knoxville, "acting out in that way is not encouraged.... Women usually get the message that anger is unpleasant and unfeminine" (cited in Dittmann, 2003b). Still, women learn other ways of expressing anger, such as "writing off" people who offend them by intending never to speak to them again. Although cultural learning clearly plays a role in determining whether and how emotions are expressed, we should allow that the brains of men and women may be wired in different ways that have a bearing on both the felt experience of emotions and the expression of emotions (Canli et al., 2002).

Women tend to interact at closer distances than men do. They also typically seek to keep more space between themselves and strangers of the other gender than men do (Rüstemli, 1986). Men are made to feel more uncomfortable by strangers who sit across from them, whereas women are more likely to feel "invaded" by strangers who sit next to them. In libraries, men tend to pile books protectively in front of them. Women place books and coats in adjacent seats to discourage others from taking them.

■ **Relational aggression** Manipulating relationships as a means of inflicting harm on others.

Gender differences also exist in sexual behavior and aggressive behavior. Women are more likely to want to combine sex with a romantic relationship (Fisher, 2000). Men typically express more interest in casual sex and in having multiple sex partners. In most cultures, it is the males who march off to war and battle for glory (and sneaker ads in TV commercials). Researchers find that boys and men show more aggressive behavior than their female counterparts—at least in most cultures and under most circumstances (Archer, 2004; Baillargeon et al., 2007; Feder, Levant, & Dean, 2007). The issue is whether this gender difference is inborn or reflects sociocultural factors.

The caution about overgeneralizing also extends to the form of aggression. Studies of children consistently paint a picture of boys engaging in more physical or overt aggression. But girls more often engage in **relational aggression**, in which they use relationships as means of inflicting harm on others. For example, girls are more likely to express aggression by excluding others from friendship groups or by starting rumors.

But the question remains, are men more physically aggressive as the result of nature or nurture? We explore this question in the following module.

Peter Correz/Getty Images, Inc.

Relational Aggression
Although boys are generally more physically aggressive than girls, girls show more relational aggression, such as expressing aggression through spreading rumors or excluding others.

MODULE REVIEW

Review It

(6) Evidence shows that men and women are (similar or different?) in general intelligence.

(7) (Girls or Boys?) have the edge when it comes to verbal skills such as spoken and written language, but (girls or boys?) tend to be somewhat better at certain visual-spatial abilities.

(8) When giving directions, men tend to rely on directional coordinates whereas women more often utilize _____.

(9) (Women or Men?) tend to be more assertive and tough-minded.

(10) Girls tend to engage more often in _____ aggression.

Think About It

How do actual gender differences fail to fit the pattern of traditional gender-role stereotypes?

MODULE 10.3

Gender-Typing: On Becoming a Woman or a Man

▮ What are some biological views of gender-typing?
▮ What are some psychological views of gender-typing?

▮ **Gender-typing** The process or processes by which males and females develop psychological gender differences.

▮ **Gender identity** One's sense of being male or being female.

▮ **Sexual orientation** The directionality of our erotic or sexual attraction—toward members of the same sex, the opposite sex, or both sexes.

▮ **Gender identity disorder (GID)** A psychological disorder characterized by cross-gender identification.

In the preceding module, we saw that men and women differ in some respects in their cognitive abilities and social behaviors. But what is the origin of these differences?

The process by which men and women develop these differences is called **gender-typing**. In this module we explore several theoretical views on sources of gender-typing, beginning with the biological view that differences between men and women are part of the natural order of things. First, however, let us clarify some terms that often get confused. One such term is **gender identity**, which refers to one's psychological sense of being male or female. Your perception of yourself as either male or female is your gender identity.

Gender identity is not the same as **sexual orientation**. As we shall discuss further in the next chapter, sexual orientation is a statement about the direction of one's sexual attraction—that is, whether one is attracted to members of one's own sex, or the opposite sex, or both sexes. A gay male and a heterosexual male, for example, both have a male gender identity (they both think of themselves as men).

For most of us, our gender identity is consistent with our anatomic or biological sex. But people with **gender identity disorder (GID)** have a gender identity that is opposite to their anatomical (chromosomal) gender. Adults with GID are sometimes called *transsexuals* or *transgendered* individuals. They may undergo gender-reassignment surgery to undo what they perceive to be a mistake of nature.

People with a transgendered identity offer us a unique perspective on masculinity and femininity. Others respond to them as being members of one sex while all the time harboring the deep feeling that their exterior self does not reflect their true self. Here, a psychologist, Jayne Thomas, herself a transgendered individual, expressed what it was like for her to have a gender identity that was at variance with her anatomical sex:

All of my life, I harbored the strongest conviction that I was inappropriately assigned to the wrong gender—that of a man—when inside I knew myself to be a woman. Even so (and like so many other GIDs) I continued a life-long struggle with this deeply felt mistake; I was successful in school, became a national swimming champion, received my college degrees, married twice (fathering children in both marriages) and was respected as a competent and good man in the workplace. However, the persistently unrelenting wrongfulness of my life continued. Not until my fourth decade was I truly able to address my gender issue.

Jay Thomas, Ph.D. underwent gender reassignment and officially became Jayne Thomas, Ph.D. in November of 1985, and what has transpired in the ensuing years has been the most enlightening of glimpses into the plight of humankind. As teachers we are constantly being taught by those we purport to instruct. My students, knowing my background (I share who I am when it is appropriate to do so), find me accessible in ways that many professors are not. Granted, I am continually asked the titillating questions that one watching Geraldo might ask and we do have fun with the answers (several years ago I even appeared on a few of the Geraldo shows). My students, however, are able to take our discussions beyond the sensational and superficial, and we enter into meaningful dialogue regarding gender differences in society and the workplace, sexual harassment, power and control issues in relationships, and what it really means to be a man or a woman.

Dr. Thomas was chairperson of the Psychology Department at Southern California's Mission College. Sadly, she passed away in 2002. She is missed by her colleagues and by the general psychological community for her pioneering efforts to shed light on the experience of transgender identity. More of Dr. Thomas's views, both professional and personal, are found in *A Closer Look* on page 347.

10.3.1 Biological Influences on Gender-Typing: It's Nature's Way

Evolutionary psychology is a developing movement within psychology that seeks to apply the theory of evolution to explaining human social behavior, including the development of gender-typed behavior. According to evolutionary psychologists, gender differences were fashioned by the process of natural selection in response to problems in adaptation that were likely to have been encountered by ancestral humans (e.g., Buss, 2000). Ancestral humans who possessed physical and behavioral traits that enabled them to survive in a harsh and unforgiving environment were able to pass along their characteristics to their offspring, whereas others who were less fortunately endowed simply died off. Over time, these adaptive characteristics, which may have included certain gender-linked differences, were passed along the genetic highway all the way to us. This evolutionary process may be expressed through structural differences between males and females, as are found in the brain, and through differences in body chemistry, as are found in the endocrine system.

▌ **Evolutionary psychology** The subfield of psychology that applies principles of evolution to explaining human behavior.

Brain Organization

Evolutionary psychologists speculate that ancestral human societies were organized according to strict gender roles in which men were hunters and warriors and women were responsible for gathering edible plants and tending the children (Gaulin & McBurney, 2001; Kenrick, Li, & Butner, 2003; Maestripieri & Roney,

2006). They argue that the physical differences between men and women support this natural division of labor. For example, men's greater upper-body strength makes them better suited than women to roles as hunters and warriors. Their physical strength may have enabled them to spear fleeing game and overpower adversaries.

Contemporary researchers find evidence in brain-imaging studies that brains of men and women are organized somewhat differently (Riepe, 2000; Ritter, 2000). For example, the brains of boys and men appear to be more highly specialized for certain kinds of visual-spatial skills, such as map reading. But how do the brains become specialized? We know that sex hormones, especially the male sex hormone testosterone, and other chemical substances in the body influence the development and differentiation of the sex organs during prenatal development (Davis, Grattan, & McCarthy, 2000). Investigators suspect that hormonal influences of body chemicals during prenatal development also serve to "masculinize" or "feminize" the developing brain, creating behavioral predispositions consistent with gender-role behaviors (Collaer & Hines, 1995; Crews, 1994).

Gender identity (sense of maleness or femaleness) may also be influenced by biological factors, possibly involving sexual differentiation of the brain during prenatal development under the influence of the male sex hormone testosterone. Although prenatal influences may influence the sexual differentiation of the brain, gender identity does not appear to be stamped by nature at birth. For example, we have research evidence based on a sample of children born with ambiguous genitalia as the result of congenital defects who went on to develop gender identities consistent with the gender in which they were reared, regardless of their sex chromosomal pattern (XX for girls or XY for boys) (Slijper et al., 1998).

Women tend to have better-developed verbal skills than men and to be more nurturant and emotionally expressive—traits that might have a biological basis. Might it be that nature has equipped women with the attributes they need to be sensitive to the needs of infants, children, and others?

Riepe (2000) speculates that women's brains may be organized to keep landmark cues in mind, whereas men's brains might reflect a more geometric approach. We might speculate that the use of geometric cues may have been an advantage to ancestral hunters who may have lacked familiar landmarks when they ventured away from their home base. It is possible that gender differences in brain organization might explain, at least in part, why women excel in verbal skills, whereas men seem to have the upper hand in specialized spatial-relations tasks such as interpreting road maps and visualizing objects in space.

What can we reasonably conclude about the role of biology in gender-typed behavior? Although definitive conclusions may be lacking, many investigators today believe that both biological and environmental factors interact in determining the development of gender-specific behaviors (Bryant & Check, 2000). Biological influences may underlie certain behavioral predispositions or action tendencies, such as the tendencies for boys to show greater rough-and-tumble play and physically aggressive behavior than girls (Archer, 2004; Baillargeon et al., 2007; Feder et al., 2007). Yet biology is not destiny. We should recognize that gender-role behaviors are neither universal (people vary from one another) nor fixed. How children are raised also has an important bearing on their behavior, including their gender-role behavior (Bryant & Check, 2000). This brings us, then, to consider psychosocial influences on gender-typed behavior.

10.3.2 Psychosocial Influences on Gender-Typing

▪ **Identification** In psychodynamic theory, the process of incorporating within the personality elements of others. In social-cognitive theory, a broad, continuous process of learning by observation and imitation.

The two leading psychosocial perspectives on gender-typing today are social-cognitive theory and gender-schema theory. However, we begin with psychodynamic theory in part because of its historic interest and because it sets the framework for investigating the psychological dimensions of gender-typed behavior.

Psychodynamic Theory

Sigmund Freud explained how boys come to act "like boys" and girls "like girls" in terms of the process of **identification**. He believed that gender-typing occurs around the age of 5 or 6, as the child comes to resolve the Oedipus or Electra complex. The resolution of the complex occurs when boys identify with their fathers (i.e., develop masculine traits) and give up the wish to sexually possess their mothers. Girls resolve their complex by giving up the wish to have a penis and by then identifying with their mothers and their mother's role in life—to bear and rear children.

We lack evidence supporting Freud's views on the development of gender-typed behavior. Even the existence of the Oedipus complex has been questioned (see Kupfersmid, 1995), let alone its primary role in gender-typing. We have also learned that boys and girls begin to track differently in their behavior patterns and preferences for toys and activities at much earlier ages than we would expect from Freudian theory.

Even within their first year, boys are more explorative and independent. Girls are relatively quieter, more dependent, and more restrained. By 18 to 36 months, girls are more likely to prefer soft toys and dolls and to dance. Boys of this age are more likely to prefer blocks and toy cars, trucks, and airplanes. Many contemporary theorists depart from the traditional Freudian view on how gender-typed behavior develops. These theorists, as we shall see, emphasize the importance of cognitive factors.

Two major cognitive theories have emerged to explain gender-typed behavior: social-cognitive theory and gender-schema theory.

Social-Cognitive Theory

To social-cognitive theorists, gender-typing is a function of (1) the development in early childhood of mental concepts of gender-appropriate behavior and (2) learning experiences in which children are encouraged or rewarded for behaviors considered appropriate to their gender (Bandura & Bussey, 2004).

Children learn much of what is considered masculine or feminine by observational learning or modeling, as suggested by a classic experiment conducted by David Perry and Kay Bussey (1979). In this study, children learned how behaviors are gender-typed by observing the relative frequencies with which men and women performed them. The adult role models expressed arbitrary preferences for one item from each of 16 pairs of items—pairs such as oranges versus

A CLOSER LOOK

Jayne Thomas, Ph.D.—In Her Own Words

The "glass ceiling," male bashing, domestic violence, nagging, PMS, Viagra— these are but a few of the important issues examined in the human sexuality classes I instruct. As a participant-observer in my field, I see many of these topics aligning themselves as masculine/feminine or male/female.

Ironically, I can both see and not see such distinctions. Certainly women have bumped up against, smudged, and in some cases even polished this metaphorical limitation of women's advancement in the workplace (i.e., that glass ceiling). And most assuredly men have often found themselves "bashed" by angry women intent upon extracting a pound of flesh for centuries of felt unjust treatment.

As previously mentioned, these distinctions between masculine and feminine for me often become blurred; I must add that, having lived my life in both the roles of man and woman, I offer a rather unique perspective on masculinity and femininity.

Challenging Concepts of Masculinity and Femininity

Iconoclastically, I try to challenge both the masculine and feminine. "I know something none of you women know or will ever know in your lifetime," I can provocatively address the females in my audiences as Jayne. "I once lived as a man and have been treated as an equal. You never have nor will you experience such equality." Or, when a male student once came to my assistance in a classroom, fixing an errant video playback device and then strutting peacocklike back to his seat as only a satisfied male can, I teasingly commented to a nearby female student, "I used to be able to do that." Having once lived as a man and now as a woman, I can honestly state that I see profound differences in our social/psychological/biological being as man and woman. I have now experienced

Courtesy of Dr. Jayne Thomas

Psychologist Jayne Thomas Dr. Thomas was chair of the Psychology Department at Mission College in Southern California. Her specialty was the psychology of gender.

many of the ways in which women are treated as less than men. Jay worked as a consultant to a large banking firm in Los Angeles and continued in that capacity as a woman following her gender shift. Amazingly, the world presented itself in a different perspective. As Jay, technical presentations to management had generally been received in a positive manner and credit for my work fully acknowledged. Jayne now found management less accessible, credit for her efforts less forthcoming and, in general, found herself working harder to be well prepared for each meeting than she ever had as a male. As a man, her forceful and impassioned presentations were an asset; as a woman, they definitely seemed a liability. On one occasion, as Jayne, when I passionately asserted my position regarding what I felt to be an important issue, my emotion and disappointment in not getting my point across (my voice showed my frustration) was met with a nearby colleague (a man) reaching to touch my arm with words of reassurance, "There, there, take it easy, it will be all right." Believe me; that never happened to Jay. There was also an occasion when I had worked most diligently on a presentation to management only to find the company vice president more interested in the fragrance of my cologne than my technical agenda.

Certainly there are significant differences in the treatment of men and women, and yet I continue to be impressed with how similar we two genders really are. Although I have made this seemingly enormous change in lifestyle (and it is immense in so many ways), I continue as the same human being, perceiving the same world through these same sensory neurons. The difference—I now find myself a more comfortable and serene being than the paradoxical woman in a man's body, with anatomy and gender having attained congruence.

Adjusting the Shifting Gender Roles

Does the shifting of gender role create difficulties in the GID's life? Most assuredly it does. Family and intimate relationships rank highest among those issues most problematic for the transitioning individual to resolve. When one shifts gender role, the effects of such a change are global; as ripples in a pond, the transformation radiates outward, impacting all that have significantly touched the GID's life. My parents had never realized that their eldest son was dealing with such a lifelong problem. Have they accepted or do they fully understand the magnitude of my issue? I fear not.

After almost 15 years of my having lived as a female, my father continues to call me by my male name. I do not doubt my parents' or children's love for me, but so uninformed are we of the true significance of gender identity that a clear understanding seems light-years away. Often I see my clients losing jobs, closeness with family members, visitation rights with children and generally becoming relegated to the role of societal outcast. Someone once stated that "Everybody is born unique, but most of us die copies"—a great price my clients often pay for personal honesty and not living their lives as a version of how society deems they should.

Having lived as man and woman in the same lifetime, one personal truth seems clear. Rather than each gender attempting to change and convert the other to its own side, as I often see couples undertaking to accomplish (women need be more logical and men more sharing of their emotions), we might more productively come together in our relationships, building upon our gender uniqueness and strengths. Men and women have different perspectives, which can be used successfully to address life's issues.

apples and toy cows versus toy horses—while 8- and 9-year-old boys and girls watched them. The children were then asked to show their own preferences. Boys selected an average of 14 of 16 items that agreed with the "preferences" of the men. Girls selected an average of only 3 of 16 items that agreed with the choices of the men. In other words, boys and girls learned gender-typed preferences even though those preferences were completely arbitrary.

Social-cognitive theorists also recognize a role for identification, but not in the Freudian sense of the term. Social-cognitive theorists view identification as a continuous learning process in which children are influenced by rewards and punishments to imitate adults of the same gender—particularly the parent of the same gender.

Socialization also plays an important role. Parents—and other adults and even other children—model sex-appropriate behavior and encourage children to adopt behaviors deemed appropriate to their gender (Leaper, 2000).

Parents may reward children for gender-typed behavior or punish (or fail to reinforce) them for behavior they consider inappropriate. Girls, for example, are given dolls while they are still sleeping in their cribs. They are encouraged to use the dolls to rehearse caretaking behaviors in preparation for traditional feminine adult roles.

Concerning gender and aggression, a classic review paper by psychologists Eleanor Maccoby and Carol Jacklin (1974) noted how aggression is more actively discouraged in girls through punishment, withdrawal of affection, or being told that "girls don't act that way." If girls retaliate when they are insulted or attacked, they usually experience social disapproval. They therefore learn to feel anxious about the possibility of acting aggressively. Boys, on the other hand, are usually encouraged to strike back—to stand up for themselves.

Children are also exposed to the modeling of traditional gender-role expectations through depictions in popular media sources, such as TV, movies, and books and magazines. Despite changes in the past generation or two, the media continue to depict men and women in stereotypical roles (Bryant & Check, 2000). As one observer noted, "Women are often still depicted on television as half-clad and half-witted, and needing to be rescued by quick-thinking, fully clothed men" (Adelson, 1990, p. C18). Some argue that the media merely hold up a mirror to society, but we might point out that the continued stereotypical depiction of women serves to perpetuate and reinforce these stereotypes. Social-cognitive theory outlines ways in which social learning leads to the development of gender-typed behavior, through processes such as modeling, identification, and socialization. With gender-schema theory, we explore how children blend their developing self-concepts with cultural expectations.

Gender-Schema Theory

You have probably heard the expression "looking at the world through rose-colored glasses." According to Sandra Bem, the originator of **gender-schema theory**, people look at the social world through a set of gender schemas—"the lenses of

▌**Socialization** As applied to gender-typed behavior, the fostering of gender-typed behavior patterns by providing children with information and using rewards and punishments to encourage the adoption of these behavior patterns.

▌**Gender-schema theory** The view that one's knowledge of the gender schema in one's society (the distribution of behavior patterns that are considered appropriate for men and women) guides one's assumption of gender-typed preferences and behavior patterns.

gender." Gender schemas are mental representations, formed in childhood, of the qualities and behaviors associated with masculinity and femininity (S.L. Bem, 1993; Eddleston, Veiga, & Powell, 2006). Once we acquire these schemas, we begin to organize our behavior around them and come to reject behaviors—in ourselves and others—that deviate from them. Children's self-esteem soon becomes wrapped up in the ways in which they measure up to their gender schemas. For example, boys soon learn to hold a high opinion of themselves if they excel in sports and girls when they perceive themselves as beautiful or graceful. Once children understand the labels *boy* and *girl*, they have a basis for blending their self-concepts with the gender schema of their culture. No external pressure is required. Children who have developed a sense of being male or being female, which usually occurs by the age of 3, actively seek information about their gender schema. As in social-cognitive theory, children seek to learn through observation what is considered appropriate for them.

Polarized gender schemas serve as kinds of cognitive anchors within our culture. In an important early study, researchers showed 5- and 6-year-old boys and girls pictures of actors engaged in "gender-consistent" or "gender-inconsistent" activities (Martin & Halverson, 1983). The gender-consistent pictures showed boys playing with trains or sawing wood. Girls were shown cooking and cleaning. Gender-inconsistent pictures showed actors of the other gender engaged in these gender-typed activities. Each child was shown a randomized set of pictures that included only one picture of each activity. One week later, the children were asked who had engaged in the activity, a male or a female. Both boys and girls gave wrong answers more often when the picture they had seen showed gender-inconsistent activity. In other words, they distorted what they had seen to conform to the gender schema.

Somos/Veer/Getty Images, Inc.

Like Father, Like Son
Modeling is an important influence of the development of gender-typed behavior.

Are Men Naturally More Aggressive Than Women?

If men are more aggressive than women by nature, perhaps the male sex hormone testosterone is responsible. Although the bodies of men and women both produce this hormone, greater amounts are produced in men than in women. By virtually every gauge, men are more physically aggressive than women (Archer, 2004). Even on the playground, we find consistent gender differences showing more aggressive behavior, including more rough-and-tumble play, among boys (Kimura, 2002; Martin & Fabes, 2001). Moreover, physical aggressiveness is connected with higher levels of the male sex hormone testosterone in both men and women (Pope, Kouri, & Hudson, 2000; A. Sullivan, 2000). But we shouldn't think of testosterone as a kind of on–off switch for aggression. The role of testosterone in aggressive behavior is much more complex. Whatever the role of biological influences in gender-typed behavior turns out to be, we should recognize that biology is not destiny. Most leading authorities in the field recognize that biological and social environmental factors interact in the development of gender-typed behavior (e.g., Bryant & Check, 2000). Biology may create a disposition, or tendency, that increases the likelihood that stereotypical gender-role behaviors will emerge, such as greater rough-and-tumble play and aggressive behavior in boys and men. Boys' play also tends to be more competitive, in contrast to the cooperative, taking-turns style of play we typically see in girls (Cohen, 2001). But gender-typed behavior is not predestined or fixed by nature. Whether this tendency becomes expressed in behavior depends in large part on the culture and families in which children are reared (Bryant & Check, 2000).

We shouldn't lose sight of the role of cultural learning in explaining gender differences in aggression. Young boys in our culture are regularly exposed to action figures who pummel and kill their opponents. When boys mature, they are exposed to male heroes in movies and action television shows who are more likely to use fists and guns than reasoned arguments in dealing with conflict with others. Our culture also lionizes male aggressiveness on the gridiron and in the hockey rink and other sports venues. Is it surprising, then, that boys may inculcate aggressiveness as part and parcel of what it means to be a man?

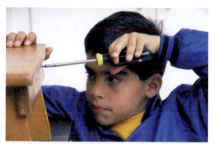

Tony Freeman/PhotoEdit

Gender-Typing
According to cognitive theories of gender-typing, once children become aware of their gender, they are motivated to behave in ways that they believe are consistent with their gender. Children actively seek information as to what types of behavior are deemed appropriate for people of their gender.

On a broader level, anthropologists lead us to recognize how gender roles represent cultural adaptations to the demands that societies face in their environments. For example, the famed anthropologist Margaret Mead (1935) wrote of one preliterate New Guinea culture she studied in which both men and women shared childcare responsibilities. In another New Guinea culture, traditional gender roles were reversed: The men stayed home and took care of the children, and the women went off to hunt. Mead's evidence leads us to recognize that the expectations we have about men and women may have more to do with the culture in which they are reared than with their biological differences.

Here's a case in point. The Sambians of New Guinea are a warlike people with rigidly defined gender roles. Boys are trained to be warriors, while women tend the children and stay close to home (Herdt, 1981). But among the !Kung people of Africa, women have more autonomy and play a more active role in tribal affairs (Drapers, 1975). How might such differences arise? Until recently, the Sambians had a history of fending off enemy attacks by neighboring tribes. They were only able to survive by training their sons to be warriors (Wender & Cohen, 1990). The rigid gender roles that characterized their society may have been a cultural adaptation that helped them survive the continued attacks by their enemies. The !Kung subsist by foraging for food in small groups. Men and women contribute in equal measure to gathering food, and both genders are permitted considerable autonomy and social influence. The more flexible gender roles in their society may reflect the equality between the genders in their respective contributions to the survival of the tribe.

Again, when it comes to examining the roles of biology and environment, of nature and nurture, in determining behavior, we can't offer any final answers. Scientists today believe that our study of gender differences in behavior is best approached by considering how biological and social factors interact (Berenbaum & Bailey, 2003).

In sum, brain organization and sex hormones may create dispositions toward gender-typed behavior and play roles in the development of gender-linked differences in verbal ability, math skills, and aggression. Social-cognitive theory outlines environmental factors that influence children to engage in gender-appropriate behavior. Gender-schema theory focuses on how children blend their self-identities with the gender schema of their culture. Table 10.2 summarizes the various perspectives on gender-typing.

Table 10.2 ▋ Influence on Gender-Typing

Biological Influences

Brain organization	The brain hemispheres are apparently more specialized in males than in females. As a result, women may exceed men in verbal skills that require some spatial organization, such as reading and spelling, while men may excel at more specialized spatial-relations tasks, such as visualizing objects in space.
Sex hormones	Prenatal sex hormones may "masculinize" or "feminize" the brain by creating predispositions that are consistent with gender-role stereotypes, such as the greater activity levels and physical aggressiveness of males.

Psychosocial Influences

Psychodynamic theory	Freud connected gender-typing with resolution of the Oedipus and Electra complexes. However, research shows that gender-typing occurs prior to the age at which these complexes would be resolved.
Social-cognitive theory	Social-cognitive theorists explain gender-typing in terms of observational learning, identification (as a broad form of imitation), and socialization.
Gender-schema theory	Children come to look at the social world through a set of gender schemas—"the lenses of gender." Our culture polarizes females and males by organizing social life around mutually exclusive gender roles. Children come to accept these roles without realizing it and attempt to construct identities that are consistent with the proper gender script or schema.

Review It

(11) In _____ psychology, gender differences are seen as products of _____ selection.

(12) Research in brain imaging suggests that the brain hemispheres are more specialized in (males or females?)

(13) Behaviors such as maze learning and aggression appear to be connected with exposure to the hormone _____.

(14) _____ _____ theorists note that children learn what is considered masculine or feminine by means of early social-learning experiences.

(15) According to _____ _____ theory, children develop a mental framework, or schema, of gender-appropriate behavior.

(16) Children's _____ then becomes wrapped up in how well they fit their developing gender schemas.

Think About It

What do you think were the major influences on your development of gender-typed behavior—biological, cultural background, learning experiences, or a combination? Explain.

Psychology in Daily Life

MODULE 10.4

Coping with the Costs of Gender Polarization

Gender polarization is the tendency to see men and women as opposites and to treat them accordingly. Gender polarization imposes significant costs on men and women in terms of education, careers, psychological well-being, and interpersonal relationships.

10.4.1 Costs in Terms of Education

Polarization has historically worked to the disadvantage of women. In past centuries, girls were considered unable to learn. Even the great eighteenth-century philosopher Jean-Jacques Rousseau, who was in the forefront of a movement toward a more open approach to education, believed that girls are basically irrational and naturally disposed to childrearing and homemaking—certainly not to commerce, science, and industry, pursuits for which education is required. Although the daughters of royal or sophisticated families have always managed to receive some tutoring, only in the twentieth century were girls fully integrated into the public schools. But even within these systems, boys seem to receive more encouragement and more direct instruction. Certain courses still seem to be considered part of the "male domain."

Intelligence tests show that boys and girls are about equal in overall learning ability (Halpern, 2004). Yet there remain some dif-

▌ **Gender polarization** The cultural tendency to see males and females as psychological and sexual opposites.

ferences in expectations, and these stereotypes limit the horizons of both genders. Nevertheless, girls are expected to excel in language arts and boys, in math and science.

Consider reading. Reading is a most basic educational skill, opening doorways to other academic subjects. Problems in reading generalize to nearly every area of academic life. It turns out that far more American boys than girls have had reading problems, either reading below grade level or the much more severe problem of dyslexia. Psychologists have offered many hypotheses as to why girls, as a group, read better than boys. Many of these hypotheses involve biological factors, such as different patterns of specialization of the hemispheres of the brain in boys and girls. But it may also be that cultural factors play a role in gender differences in reading.

Evidence for this view is found in the fact that gender differences in reading tend to disappear or to be reversed in other cultures (Matlin, 1999). Reading is stereotyped as a feminine activity in the United States and Canada, and girls surpass boys in reading skills in these countries. But boys score higher than girls on most tests of reading in Nigeria and England, where boys have traditionally been expected to outperform girls in academic pursuits, including reading.

Girls, however, tend to have less confidence in their ability at math and are more likely than their male counterparts to blame difficulties on their lack of ability than on the nature of the task (Ehrlinger & Dunning, 2003; Vermeer, Boekaerts, & Seegers, 2000). Recent evidence also shows that among male and female college students of the same level of math ability, men expressed greater confidence in using computers (Beyer et al., 2003). Lack of confidence and negative social expectations may dissuade girls from taking advanced courses in the so-called male domain. Math courses open doors for them in fields such as natural science, engineering, and economics. Several cultural factors explain why boys are more likely than girls to feel at home with math (AAUW, 1992; Tenenbaum & Leaper, 2003):

- Fathers are more likely than mothers to help children with math homework.
- Parents may believe their daughters are less interested in science and will find it more than difficult than their sons.
- Advanced math courses are more likely to be taught by men.
- Teachers often show higher expectations for boys in math courses.
- Math teachers spend more time working with boys than with girls.

All in all, many young women in our society learn a lesson in simple deduction based on a faulty premise (Nosek, Banaji, & Greenwald, 2003):

> (Faulty) Premise: Math is masculine
> If Me = Female
> Therefore Math ≠ Me

Given these experiences and expectations, we should not be surprised that by junior high, boys view themselves as more competent in math than girls do, even when they receive the same grades (AAUW, 1992). Boys are more likely to have positive feelings about math. Girls are more likely to have math anxiety. Even girls who excel in math and science are less likely than boys to choose courses or careers in these fields.

If women are to find their places in professions related to math, science, and engineering, we may need to provide more female role models in these professions. Role models will help shatter the stereotype that these are men's fields. We also need to encourage girls to take more courses in math and science.

10.4.2 Costs in Terms of Careers

Women are less likely than men to enter higher-paying careers in math, science, and engineering. Women account for perhaps one in six of the nation's scientists and engineers.

Although women are awarded more than half of the bachelor's degrees in the United States, they receive fewer than one-third of the degrees in science and engineering. Why? It is partly because math, science, and engineering are perceived as being inconsistent with the feminine gender role. Many little girls are dissuaded from thinking about professions such as engineering and architecture because they are given dolls rather than trucks and blocks as toys. Many boys are likewise deterred from entering childcare and nursing professions because others scorn them when they play with dolls.

There is also the issue of how women appraise their abilities in science. Evidence from a recent study showed that women underestimated their abilities in science as compared to men, even though they performed equally as well as men on a science quiz (Ehrlinger & Dunning, 2003). Underestimating their abilities may lead women to avoid pursuing careers in science.

There are also inequalities in the workplace. In nearly every occupation, women earn less on the average than men for the same work (Fairfield, 2009). Women physicians and college professors, for exam-

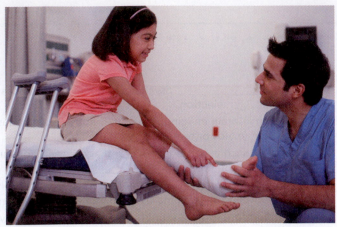

Blend Images/Superstock

An M.D.? Guess Again
Gender polarization has its costs in terms of education, careers, psychological well-being, and relationships. This man has the courage to follow his inner compass and do in life that which he wishes to do—nursing. How many other men with similar inclinations would fear that people would belittle them for entering a "women's profession"? On the other hand, women have been breaking down the doors in careers that have traditionally been considered part of the male domain—particularly in medicine, law, and the military.

ple, typically earn less than men in the same positions. Women are also less likely than men to be promoted into high-level managerial positions. Once women enter managerial positions, they often feel pressured to be "tougher" than men in order to seem just as tough. Moreover, the same kinds of behavior may be labeled positively for men but negatively for women. For example, a woman who is described as "all business" may be perceived negatively as unfeminine or cold, whereas a man is viewed positively as a skilled executive.

Women may also feel pressured to be careful about their appearance because coworkers pay more attention to what they wear, how they style their hair, and so forth. If they don't look crisp and tailored every day, others may think they are not in command. But if they dress up too much, they may be denounced as fashion plates rather than serious workers! Female managers who are deliberate and take time making decisions may be seen as "wishy-washy." What happens when female managers change their minds? They run the risk of being labeled fickle and indecisive rather than flexible.

Women who work also usually have the responsibility of being the major caretaker for children in the home. Research shows that when young couples do not have children, moves to another city are usually planned to benefit both partners' careers (Nasser, 2000). But once children arrive on the scene, such moves usually mean a promotion for the man but set the woman's career back.

Women are less likely than men to be promoted into responsible managerial positions. Many women are prevented from reaching the top echelons of management by glass ceilings. Women who have (or openly discuss plans to have) children are also often placed in "mommy tracks" in their organizations. They are not prevented from working, but they are channeled into less demanding (and less rewarding!) career paths. The organization makes less of an investment in them because of the assumption that mothers cannot make as much of an investment in the organization as child-free women can.

All in all, gender stereotyping discourages women from making their highest possible contributions to the workforce and to society. In case it is not self-evident, let us note that men also have a stake in reversing these pressures on women. Mistreatment of women by men hurts women who are loved and cared about by other men. Also, misery in the workplace does not stop at 5:00 P.M. It carries over into home life. Men have women in their home lives as wives, mothers, and daughters. So mistreatment on the job comes to affect the quality of home life. There is also the larger picture. If we, as a society, utilize the best talents of all of our people, we produce more, we invent more, and we increase our standard of living.

Men, too, have sought the freedom to break away from gender-role stereotypes. For example, they are now taking positions that were previously restricted to women, such as teaching in elementary school, nursing, and secretarial work.

10.4.3 Costs in Terms of Psychological Well-Being and Relationships

Educational frustrations and problems on the job are stressors that can make us anxious and depressed and interfere with our relationships with others. We have noted the ways in which gender stereotypes affect our educations and our careers. Gender polarization also interferes with our psychological well-being and our interpersonal relationships—in many ways (Baron & Byrne, 2000; Matlin, 1999; Rathus, Fichner-Rathus, & Nevid, 2005).

Compared to women who identify with more flexible gender roles, women who adopt traditional feminine gender roles:

- Appear to have lower self-esteem.
- Find stressful events more aversive than women who also show some masculine-typed traits.
- Are less capable of bouncing back from failure experiences than women who also show some masculine-typed traits.
- Are more likely to believe that women are to be seen and not heard. Therefore, they are unlikely to assert themselves by making their needs and wants known. As a consequence, they are likely to encounter frustration.
- Are more likely to conform to group pressure.

Compared to men who identify with more flexible gender roles, men who adopt traditional masculine gender roles:

- Are more likely to be upset if their wives earn more money than they do!
- Are less likely to feel comfortable performing the activities involved in caring for children, such as bathing them, dressing them, and feeding them.
- Are less likely to ask for help—including medical help—when they need it.
- Are less likely to be sympathetic and tender and to express feelings of love in their marital relationships.
- Are less likely to be tolerant of their wives' or lovers' faults.

Having read the last item above, the authors' spouses suggest that the authors leave this chapter now, before they get into even deeper trouble.

CHAPTER REVIEW

RECITE! RECITE! RECITE! RECITE! RECITE! RECITE! RECITE!

Study Tip: Reciting the answers to these study questions will help you become a more effective learner. First try answering the questions by yourself, either reciting them out loud or writing them in a notebook or on the computer. Then compare your answers with the sample answers provided below.

1. What is a stereotype?
A stereotype is a fixed conventional idea about a group that can give rise to prejudice and discrimination. A gender stereotype is a fixed, conventional idea about how men and women ought to behave.

2. What are some common gender stereotypes?
Women are typically perceived as nurturing, gentle, dependent, warm, emotional, kind, helpful, patient, and submissive. Men are typically stereotyped as independent, competitive, tough, logical, self-reliant, dominant, and protective.

3. What is psychological androgyny?
Throughout history it has been widely assumed that the more masculine a person is, the less feminine he or she is, and vice versa. However, many psychologists look upon masculinity and femininity as independent dimensions.

The construct of psychological androgyny characterizes people who possess both stereotypically masculine and feminine traits.

4. How is psychological androgyny related to adjustment?
Psychologically androgynous individuals can apparently summon up both "masculine" and "feminine" traits to express their talents and desires and to meet the demands of their situations. Psychologically androgynous people show high "identity" and "intimacy"—using the concepts of Erik Erikson. They show both independence and nurturance, depending on the situation. They have higher self-esteem and greater ability to bounce back from failure. Wives of psychologically androgynous husbands are happier than wives of husbands who adhere to a strictly stereotypical masculine gender role.

5. What gender differences do researchers find in cognitive abilities?

Boys have traditionally excelled in math and spatial-relations skills, whereas girls have had the edge in language skills. However, these differences are small and growing narrower.

6. What gender differences do researchers find in social behavior?

Females are typically more extraverted and nurturant than males. Males are typically more tough-minded and aggressive than females. Men tend to express more interest than women in casual sex and having multiple sex partners.

7. What are some biological views of gender-typing?

Biological views of gender-typing focus on the roles of evolution, genetics, and prenatal influences in predisposing men and women to gender-linked behavior patterns.

8. What are some psychological views of gender-typing?

According to psychodynamic theory, gender-typing stems from resolution of the conflicts of the phallic stage. However, children assume gender roles at much earlier ages than the theory would suggest. Social-cognitive theory explains gender-typing in terms of observational learning, identification, and socialization. Gender-schema theory proposes that children use the gender schema of their society to organize their self-perceptions and that they then evaluate themselves in relation to this schema.

YOUR PERSONAL JOURNAL

REFLECT   REFLECT   REFLECT   REFLECT   REFLECT   REFLECT   REFLECT

Study Tip: Reflecting on how the concepts in the chapter relate to your own experiences encourages deeper processing, which makes the material more personally meaningful and fosters more effective learning. Use additional pages if needed to complete your answers.

1. Do any of the gender differences discussed in the text square with, or counter, your own observations over the years? Explain.

2. Do you feel you have been hampered by gender-role expectations? Have traditional expectations of what it means to be a man or a woman influenced your occupational choices? Your relationships? Your interests?

ANSWERS TO MODULE REVIEWS

Module 10.1

1. Stereotypes
2. gender-role
3. androgyny
4. higher
5. masculinity

9. Men
10. relational

Module 10.3

11. evolutionary/natural
12. males
13. testosterone
14. Social-cognitive
15. gender-schema
16. self-esteem

Module 10.2

6. similar
7. Girls/boys
8. landmarks

SCORING KEY FOR THE ANDRO SCALE

People who score high on masculinity alone on this scale endorse traditionally masculine attitudes and behaviors, whereas people who score high on femininity alone hold traditionally feminine ways of relating to the world. Many psychologists now believe that you will experience life more fully and be better adjusted if you score relatively high on both masculinity and femininity. Scoring high on both suggests that you are psychologically androgynous and can summon up characteristics attributed to both genders, as needed. That is, you can be assertive but caring, logical but emotionally responsive, strong but gentle.

You can determine your own masculinity and femininity scores by seeing how many of your answers agree with those on the key in Table A.

Use B to compare your masculinity and femininity scores to those of 386 male and 723 female University of Kentucky students. Your percentile score (%) means that your own score equaled or exceeded that of the percentage of students shown.

Table A ▮ Key for Determining Total Masculinity and Femininity

	Masculinity						Femininity				
Item no.	Key	Score: 1 if same as key, 0 if not	Item no.	Key	Score: 1 if same as key, 0 if not	Item no.	Key	Score: 1 if same as key, 0 if not	Item no.	Key	Score: 1 if same as key, 0 if not
2.	T	1	30.	T		1.	T		32.	F	
3.	F		31.	T		5.	F		36.	T	
4.	T		33.	T		9.	F		37.	T	
6.	F		34.	F		13.	T		39.	T	
7.	T		35.	T		14.	T		41.	T	
8.	T		38.	F		16.	F		43.	T	
10.	F		40.	F		18.	T		44.	T	
11.	T		42.	T		19.	F		45.	T	
12.	T		46.	F		20.	T		49.	T	
15.	F		47.	T		21.	T		51.	F	
17.	T		48.	F		22.	F		53.	T	
25.	T		50.	T		23.	T		55.	T	
26.	T		52.	T		24.	F		56.	F	
27.	T		54.	F		28.	F				
29.	T										

Total Masculinity Score: (Maximum Score = 29) _23_   Total Femininity Score (Maximum Score = 27) _15_

To determine your masculinity and femininity scores on the ANDRO Scale, place a 1 in the appropriate blank space each time your answer agrees with the answer (T or F) shown on the key. Place a 0 in the space each time your answer disagrees with the answer shown on the key. Then add up the totals for each. *Source:* Data from Berzins et al., 1977.

Table B ▮ Percentile Rankings of Masculinity and Femininity Scores of College Students Sample

Raw score	Males (%)	Females (%)	Combined (%)	Raw score	Males (%)	Females (%)	Combined (%)
29	99	99	99	27	99	99	99
28	99	99	99	26	99	99	99
27	99	99	99	25	99	99	99
26	99	99	99	24	99	99	99
25	98	99	99	23	99	98	99
24	96	98	97	22	99	94	96
23	92	96	94	21	98	87	92
22	88	96	92	20	95	78	86
21	80	94	87	19	91	65	78
20	73	93	83	18	85	53	69
19	63	88	75	17	76	42	59
18	54	83	68	16	65	32	48
17	47	78	60	15	56	24	40
16	39	72	56	14	47	17	32
15	30	65	48	13	37	12	25
14	23	58	40	12	28	6	17
13	17	50	33	11	20	4	12
12	13	41	27	10	14	3	8
11	10	34	22	9	7	2	4
10	6	28	17	8	4	1	3
9	4	21	13	7	3	0	2
8	2	16	9	6	2	0	1
7	2	11	6	5	2	0	1
6	1	9	5	4	1	0	0
5	1	5	3	3	0	0	0
4	0	2	1	2	0	0	0
3	0	1	0	1	0	0	0
2	0	0	0	0	0	0	0
1	0	0	0				
0	0	0	0				

Source: Data from Berzins et al., 1977.

Interpersonal Attraction: Of Friendship and Love

OUTLINE

Did you know that...

- The major factor determining initial attraction is physical attractiveness? (p. 358)

- Taller people tend to earn higher incomes than shorter people? (p. 359)

- "Birds of a feather" most certainly do flock together when it comes to interpersonal attraction? (p. 364)

- People are even more likely to select mates who have first or last names similar to their own? (p. 364)

- Sexual orientation is not a matter of choice? (p. 367)

- Cell phones have been adopted at a faster rate than any other technology in human history? (p. 372)

- There are many different types of love, not just romantic love? (p. 373)

- Loneliness is not merely a psychological problem but is also associated with high blood pressure and poorer immune system functioning? (p. 379)

David Raymer/Corbis Images

What attracts you to other people? What leads you to like some people and dislike others? What turns you on and what turns you off? We're not speaking here just of sexual attraction. Psychologists use the term **attraction** more broadly to apply to feelings of liking we have toward others, not just toward romantic partners. The feeling of liking we hold toward friends is a form of attraction. But attraction involves more than feelings; it also involves having positive thoughts toward others and the inclination to act in positive ways toward them. By contrast, we can think of negative attraction as a force that draws us apart or repels us from others.

In nature, we can speak of attraction as a force that draws two objects or bodies toward each other, like the opposite poles of a magnet. Similarly, in the interpersonal world, we can think of attraction as the tendency to feel drawn toward other people as friends or lovers. In this chapter we examine the factors that contribute to attraction. We shall see how many of us adjust to fear of rejection by potential dating partners and to other difficulties.

Two forms of interpersonal attraction are friendship and love. But what is *love*? When the second author was a teenager, the answer was, "Five feet of heaven in a ponytail."[1] But this answer may be deficient in scientific merit. In this chapter, we also attempt to define the enigmatic concept of love.

Attraction and love also have a way of leading to the formation of intimate relationships, a subject we explore in Chapter 12. But not everyone develops friendships or love relationships. Some of us remain alone, and lonely. Loneliness is the subject of the final module in the chapter, *Psychology in Daily Life,* in which we discuss ways of overcoming loneliness.

Attraction A force that draws people together.

357

---

[1] The editor does not understand why the second author insists on notifying the world that he could have witnessed the signing of the Declaration of Independence.

MODULE 11.1

Attraction: The Force That Binds

- ▮ What factors contribute to attraction in our culture?
- ▮ What are some common stereotypes of attractive people?
- ▮ Do males and females find the same traits to be attractive in dating partners and mates?
- ▮ What is the matching hypothesis?
- ▮ What is sexual orientation?
- ▮ How do researchers explain sexual orientation?
- ▮ How do people in our society react to gay or bisexual people?
- ▮ Given the general societal reaction to gay males and lesbians, what challenges to adjustment are they likely to encounter?

Feelings of attraction can lead to liking and perhaps to love and to a more lasting relationship. In this section we see that attraction to another person is influenced by factors such as physical appearance and attitudes. We will see that most people are heterosexual; that is, they are sexually attracted to people of the opposite sex. However, some people have a gay male or lesbian sexual orientation; that is, they are erotically attracted to people of their own sex. But what factors contribute to feelings of attraction? In this module we explore the determinants of romantic attraction that stretch across sexual orientations, including physical attractiveness, attitude similarity, proximity, and reciprocity.

11.1.1 Physical Attractiveness: How Important Is Looking Good?

You might like to think that we are all so intelligent and sophisticated that we rank physical appearance low on the roster of qualities we seek in a date or mate—below sensitivity and warmth, for example. But evidence shows that physical appearance is the key factor determining romantic attraction (e.g., Li & Kenrick, 2006; Wilson et al., 2005). Without the spark of physical attraction, we may never have the opportunity to learn about each other's deeper qualities and so move the relationship along. What determines physical attractiveness? Are our standards subjective, or is there some agreement?

Some aspects of beauty appear to be cross-cultural (Langlois et al., 2000). For example, a study of people in England and Japan found that both British and Japanese men consider women with large eyes, high cheekbones, and narrow jaws to be most attractive (Perret, 1994). In his research, Perret created computer composites of the faces of 60 women and, as shown in part A of Figure 11.1, of the 15 women who were rated the most attractive. He then used computer enhancement to exaggerate the differences between the composite of the 60 and the composite of the 15 most attractive women. He arrived at the image shown in part B of Figure 11.1. Part B, which shows higher cheekbones and a narrower jaw than part A, was rated as the most attractive image. Similar results were found for the image of a Japanese woman. Works of art suggest that the ancient Greeks and Egyptians favored similar facial features.

In our society, it literally pays to be tall. Evidence links greater height to higher incomes in both men and women (although the effects are larger in men) (Dittmann, 2004; Judge & Cable, 2004). Why the height–income connection? The reason, say these investigators, is that taller workers are more likely to be selected for favored

XianPix Pictures Agency/NewsCom

"Looking Good"
Who is good-looking? To many people, stars like Angelina Jolie and Brad Pitt personify standards for beauty in contemporary American culture. How important is physical attractiveness in our selection of dates and mates?

sales and executive positions. Another possible reason: Height may contribute to self-esteem, which may translate into better performance on the job (Shea, 2007).

Tallness is a social asset in other ways, at least for men (Pawlowski & Koziel, 2002). Men tend to prefer women who are of average height, but women typically seek out taller men (Kurzban & Weeden, 2005; Swami & Furnham, 2008). Tall women, however, tend to be viewed less positively. College men typically prefer women who are about 4½ inches shorter than themselves (Gillis & Avis, 1980). Both men and women are perceived as more attractive when they are smiling (Reis et al., 1990). Thus there is good reason to, as the song goes, "put on a happy face" when you are meeting people or looking for a date.

Men and women in the United States tend to judge the hourglass figure in women as most attractive (Singh, 1994a, b). But there is a catch: Among women at least, curvaceousness is associated with female attractiveness, but only when a curvaceous figure is lean and does not have large hips (Forestell, Humphrey, & Stewart, 2004). The popular belief that men prefer women with large breasts may be somewhat exaggerated. Researchers in one study showed young men and women (ages 17 to 25 years) a continuum of male and female figures that differed only in the size of the bust for the female figures and of the pectorals for the male figures (Thompson & Tantleff, 1992). The participants were asked to indicate the ideal size for their own gender and the size they believed the average man and woman would prefer.

The results supported the "big is better" stereotype—for both men and women. Women's conception of ideal bust size was greater than their actual average size. Men favored women with still larger busts, but not nearly as large as the busts women *believed* that men prefer. Men believed that their male peers favored women with much larger busts than the peers actually said they preferred. Ample breast or chest sizes may be preferred by the other gender, but people seem to have an exaggerated idea of the sizes the other gender actually prefers.

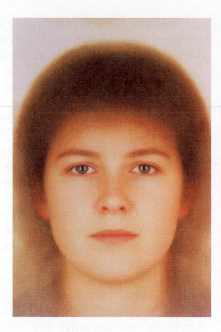

Figure 11.1

What Features Contribute to Facial Attractiveness?

In both England and Japan, features such as large eyes, high cheekbones, and narrow jaws contribute to perceptions of female attractiveness. Part A (left) shows a composite of the faces of 15 women rated as the most attractive of a group of 60. Part B (right) is a composite in which the features of these 15 women are exaggerated—that is, developed further in the direction that separates them from the average of the entire 60.

Photodisc./SUPERSTOCK

It Pays to Be Tall

Taller workers even tend to outearn their shorter counterparts. The question is: Why?

Even though people might prefer larger-than-average breasts, large-breasted women encounter negative stereotyping. People tend to perceive them as less intelligent, competent, moral, and modest than women with smaller breasts (Kleinke & Staneski, 1980).

Although preferences for facial features may transcend time and culture, preferences for body weight and shape may be more culturally determined. For example, plumpness is valued in some cultures. Grandmothers who worry that their granddaughters are starving themselves often come from cultures in which stoutness is acceptable or desirable. In contemporary Western society, there is pressure on both males and females to be slender, but greater pressure is placed disproportionately on women (Furnham, Petrides, & Constantinides, 2005; Wilson et al., 2005). Women generally favor men with a V-taper—broad shoulders and a narrow waist.

On the other hand, men and women typically perceive obese people in unfavorable terms such as lazy, unproductive, and unattractive (Polinko & Popovich, 2001). These negative perceptions can lead to discrimination, such as when obese people are rejected for jobs or passed over for promotion.

What about self-perceptions of our body weight in relation to what we expect the opposite sex to perceive as ideal? In an early but illuminating study, investigators found that college women generally saw themselves as heavier than the figure that men found most attractive (see "other attractive" in Figure 11.2) and heavier still than what they perceived as the ideal female figure (Fallon & Rozin, 1985). By contrast,

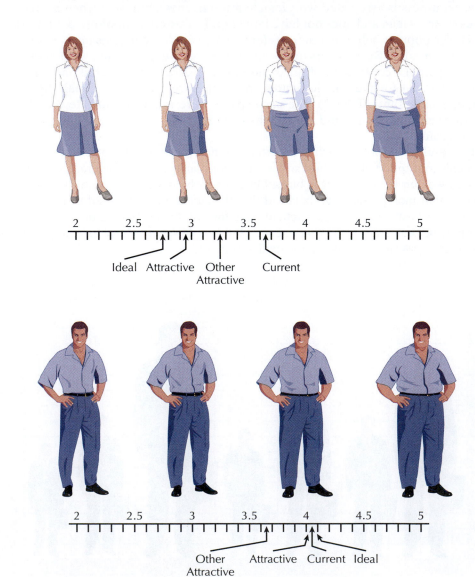

Figure 11.2

Can You Ever Be Too Thin?
The answer to this question is a resounding yes. Research suggests that most college women believe that they are heavier than they ought to be. However, men actually prefer women to be somewhat heavier than women imagine. Physical attractiveness aside, excessive thinness can be deadly, as in some cases of anorexia nervosa.

college men found their own physique to be similar to the ideal male build and to the one ("other attractive") that women reported was most appealing to them (see Figure 11.2) (Fallon & Rozin, 1985). Yet both men and women erred in their estimates of the other gender's preferences. Men actually preferred women to be heavier than women expected they would—about halfway between the girth of the average woman and what the woman thinks is most attractive. Women preferred men to be somewhat thinner than men had assumed.

Gender Differences in the Perception of Attractiveness

Do males and females find the same traits to be attractive in dating partners and mates? The answer, to be precise, is yes and no. That is, males and females tend to value similar qualities, but the emphases are not quite the same.

Studies on attraction and choice of mates find that women place relatively greater emphasis than men on such traits as vocational status, earning potential, expressiveness, kindness, consideration, dependability, and fondness for children. Men place greater emphasis on physical attractiveness of potential dates and mates than women do, as well as on cooking ability ("Why can't they switch on the microwave by themselves?") and frugality (Buss, 1994; Nevid, 1984; Shackelford, Schmitt, & Buss, 2005; Sprecher, Sullivan, & Hatfield, 1994).

In an important large-scale study, Susan Sprecher and her colleagues (1994) surveyed a national probability sample of 13,017 English- or Spanish-speaking people, age 19 or above, living in households in the United States. In one section of their questionnaire, they asked respondents how willing they would be to marry someone who was older, younger, of a different religion, not likely to hold a steady job, not good-looking, and so forth. Each item was followed by a 7-point scale in which 1 meant "not at all" and 7 meant "very willing." As shown in Table 11.1, women were more willing than men to marry someone who was not good-looking. On the other hand, women were less willing to marry someone not likely to hold a steady job.

Some behavioral and social scientists believe that evolutionary forces favor the survival of men and women with mating preferences such as these because they bestowed reproductive advantages on our early ancestors (Fisher, 2000). These preferences may reflect inherited factors that were passed down along the genetic highway all the way to us. Some physical features such as cleanliness, good complexion, clear eyes, good teeth and good hair, firm muscle tone, and a steady gait are found to be universally appealing to both genders (Fink & Penton-Voak, 2002; Rathus, Nevid, & Fichner-Rathus, 2005). Perhaps such traits have value as markers of better reproductive potential in prospective mates. Because of a woman's "biological clock," a woman's appeal may be strongly connected with her age and health, both of which are markers of reproductive capacity. The value of men as reproducers, however, is more intertwined with factors that contribute

Table 11.1 ▮ Gender Differences in Mate Preferences

How willing would you be to marry someone who...	Men	Women
▪ Was not "good-looking"?	3.41	4.42
▪ Was older than you by 5 or more years?	4.15	5.29
▪ Was younger than you by 5 or more years?	4.54	2.80
▪ Was not likely to hold a steady job?	2.73	1.62
▪ Would earn much less than you?	4.60	3.76
▪ Would earn much more than you?	5.19	5.93
▪ Had more education than you?	5.22	5.82
▪ Had less education than you?	4.67	4.08
▪ Had been married before?	3.35	3.44
▪ Already had children?	2.84	3.11
▪ Was of a different religion?	4.24	4.31
▪ Was of a different race?	3.08	2.84

to a stable environment for childrearing than age per se—factors such as social standing and reliability. Evolutionary theorists speculate that these qualities may have grown relatively more alluring to women over the millennia (e.g., Buss, 1994; Symons, 1995).

The evolutionary view of gender differences in preferences for mates remains speculative and may be an oversimplification. For one thing, people tend to seek mates who are similar to themselves in physical attractiveness rather than pursue the neighborhood equivalent of a Cameron Diaz or a Keanu Reeves. Note, too, that it is conceivable that cultural influences, rather than inherited dispositions, explain commonalities across cultures in gender differences in mate preferences. For example, in societies in which women are economically dependent on men, a man's appeal may depend to a large degree on his financial resources.

Stereotypes of Attractive People: Do Good Things Come in Pretty Packages?

By and large, we tend to apply the stereotype that what is beautiful is also good. Attractive children and adults tend to be judged and treated more positively than their unattractive peers (Langlois et al., 2000; Little, Burt, & Perret, 2006; Olson & Marshuetz, 2005). We also judge attractive people as more poised, sociable, popular, intelligent, mentally healthy, fulfilled, persuasive, and successful in their jobs and marriages. We expect attractive people to be persuasive and hold prestigious jobs. We even expect them to be good parents and have stable marriages. Given these stereotypes, it is not surprising that evidence links attractiveness with popularity, social skills, and sexual experience (Feingold, 1992).

Adults tend to rate physically attractive babies, even during the first year of life, as good, smart, likable, and unlikely to cause their parents problems (Langlois et al., 2000). Parents, teachers, and other children expect attractive children to do well in school and be popular, well behaved, and talented. Since our self-esteem reflects the admiration of others, it is not surprising that physically attractive people tend to have higher self-esteem.

Culture and Attractiveness: Who's Good-Looking?

Cultural differences certainly exist in attractiveness preferences. For example, among some tribal societies in Africa, plumpness takes the cake when it comes to the female ideal, whereas in contemporary Western cultures, "ultrathin is in" (though not a healthy ideal to which to aspire). Despite such cultural differences, though, researchers find a good deal of similarity across cultures (Langlois et al., 2000). For example, evolutionary psychologists report that such physical characteristics as symmetrical facial features and a clear complexion are universally preferred (Fink & Penton-Voak, 2002; Little et al., 2006).

People from different cultures also tend to rate physical beauty in similar ways. Consider a study in which European American college students and recently arrived Asian and Hispanic students were given photographs of Asian, Hispanic, black, and white women and then asked to rate the attractiveness of the women (Cunningham et al., 1995). The ratings showed a high degree of consistency across raters from these different ethnic groups. By and large, the features associated with feminine beauty included the following:

- High cheekbones and eyebrows
- Widely spaced eyes
- A small nose
- Thin cheeks
- A large smile
- Full lower lip
- Small chin
- Fuller hairstyle

Men and women also tended to judge the same faces as attractive. Perhaps not surprisingly, men and women generally prefer female faces that have more feminine features than those with more masculine features (Angier, 1998). But it may surprise you to learn that men and women generally find male faces that have more feminine features to be more attractive. Men and women prefer the more refined, delicate features of a Tom Cruise or Leonardo DiCaprio than the more rugged, masculinized features of, say, an Arnold Schwarzenegger (Angier, 1998).

11.1.2 The Matching Hypothesis: Who Is "Right" for You?

Have you ever refrained from asking out an extremely attractive person for fear of rejection? Do you feel more comfortable when you approach someone who is a bit less attractive? An answer of yes lends support to the **matching hypothesis**. According to the matching hypothesis, we are most likely to ask out people who are similar to ourselves in physical attractiveness rather than the local Justin Timberlake or Toni Braxton lookalike.

▮ **Matching hypothesis** The view that people generally seek to develop relationships with people who are similar to themselves in attractiveness and other attributes, such as attitudes.

Researchers find strong relationships between the attractiveness of dating partners and marital couples (Lee et al., 2008). In a recent study, investigators looked at dating patterns among members of a website (HotorNot.com) that focuses on having members rate the physical attractiveness of other members (Lee et al., 2008). More attractive members typically preferred dating more attractive partners. Married couples tend to be matched in physical attractiveness and even matched in weight. Matching extends beyond physical characteristics. For example, the extent to which one's partner's personality matches up with one's concept of the personality of an ideal mate turns out to be a strong predictor of a successful relationship (Zenter, 2005).

There are exceptions to the matching hypothesis. Now and then we find a beautiful woman married to a plain or ugly man (or vice versa). How do we explain it? When we find a mismatch in attractiveness, the less attractive partner usually compensates by having greater wealth or social position than the more attractive partner (Berscheid & Reis, 1998). An unseen factor may balance the differences in physical attractiveness between partners. For some mismatched couples, similarities in attitudes and personalities may balance out these physical differences.

The search for a match extends beyond physical attractiveness. Our marital and sex partners tend to be similar to us in race/ethnicity, age, level of education, and religion. Consider some findings of the National Health and Social Life Survey (Michael et al., 1994, pp. 45–47):

- Nearly 94% of single European American men have European American women as their sex partners; 2% are partnered with Latina American women, 2% with Asian American women, and less than 1% with African American women.

- About 82% of African American men have African American women as their sex partners; nearly 8% are partnered with European American women and almost 5% with Latina American women.

- About 83% of the women and men in the study chose partners within five years of their own age and of the same or a similar religion.

- Of nearly 2,000 women in the study, not one with a college degree had a partner who had not finished high school.

Why do most people have partners from the same background as their own? One reason is that marriages are made in the neighborhood, not in heaven. We tend to live among people who are similar to us in background, and we therefore come into contact with them more often than with people from other backgrounds. Another reason is that we are drawn to people whose attitudes are similar to ours. People from a similar background are more likely to have similar attitudes.

Caroline von Tuempling/Iconica/Getty Images, Inc.

Birds of a Feather?
Evidence shows that attitude similarity is an important determinant of romantic attraction. Similarities of preferences for the same-color bathing suit may be stretching a point, however.

11.1.3 Attraction and Similarity: Birds of a Feather Flock Together

This is the land of free speech. So do we respect the right of others to reveal their ignorance by disagreeing with us? Perhaps. But it has been observed since ancient times that we tend to like people who agree with us. Similarity in attitudes and tastes is a key contributor to initial attraction, friendships, love relationships, even choice of marital partners. People tend to select mates who are similar on many dimensions, including attitudes, religious views, values, and even body weight (e.g., Luo & Klohnen, 2005; Rushton & Bons, 2005). People are even more likely to select mates who have first or last names similar to their own (Jones et al., 2004). When it comes to liking or attraction, birds of a feather do indeed flock together (Angier, 2003; Buston & Emlen, 2003). Investigators also find that dating partners become more aligned in their attitudes over time (Davis & Rusbult, 2001).

Let us note a gender difference. It appears that women place greater emphasis than men do on attitude similarity as a determinant of attraction (Feingold, 1992). We should also not assume that all attitudes are necessarily equal. In an early study in this area, men at the University of Nevada were more influenced by similarity in sexual attitudes with partners on computer-assigned dates than by similarity in religious attitudes (Touhey, 1972). But women were more attracted to men whose religious views coincided with their own. The women may have been relatively less interested in a physical relationship and more concerned about creating a family with cohesive values. Physical attraction may motivate us to act as though differences in preferences, interests, tastes, and opinions don't exist—or at least don't matter. There are other ways of dealing with dissimilar attitudes and backgrounds. We can try to persuade others to adopt our views and attitudes, perhaps even to convert to our own religions. Or we can reevaluate our attitudes and explore the possibility of changing them. Or we can choose to end the relationship. But we can also choose to recognize that we needn't be carbon copies of each other to build a meaningful relationship. Though having some common ground is necessary to anchor a relationship, every relationship requires compromise, accommodation, and understanding to keep it afloat. We can also agree to disagree on some things, such as for tastes in music or perhaps political beliefs.

11.1.4 Proximity: Seeing You Is Liking You

You're more likely to develop friendships with people who live down the hall than those on the other side of town. When you grew up, you probably had more friends from the immediate neighborhood than those living farther away. Why? **Proximity**, or nearness, determines with whom we are likely to come into contact so that attraction can develop.

We might also expect that Sonya Deitrich was more likely to be friends with schoolmates Carmen Cruz and Nya Dillard than Rachel Wintersteen. The reason? Children are often assigned to seats in alphabetical order, so they're more likely to strike up a friendship with classmates sitting next to them whose names are also closer in the alphabet to their own.

How does proximity work its charms on attraction? One reason may be that proximity increases the chances of interacting with others. Greater opportunities for social interactions allow feelings of mutual attraction to grow. Another factor is mere exposure. Repeated contact with someone may kindle feelings of attraction. Put another way, the more I see you, the more I like you.

Yet another factor is similarity. People who live near each other may have more similar attitudes in common than people living farther away. But proximity does not always spill over into positive attraction. Repeated contact with someone you dislike might only intensify the negative feelings you have.

■ **Proximity** Nearness or propinquity.

Reciprocity: If You Like Me, You Must Have Excellent Judgment

Reciprocity is a powerful determinant of attraction (Nowak, Vallacher, & Miller, 2003). We tend to return feelings of admiration. When someone compliments us or does us a favor, we tend to respond in kind. We also tend to be more open, warm, and helpful when we are interacting with strangers who seem to like us (Curtis & Miller, 1986). Reciprocity also comes into play in determining tipping behavior in restaurants (Cialdini & Goldstein, 2004). In an experimental study, investigators found that waitresses received larger tips when they wrote helpful messages on the backs of customers' checks or gave customers a complimentary piece of chocolate when presenting their checks (Rind & Strohmetz, 1999; Strohmetz et al., 2002).

▎**Reciprocity** The tendency to return feelings and attitudes that are expressed about us.

11.1.5 Sexual Orientation: The Direction of Erotic Attraction

The topic of sexual orientation would seem at first blush to belong in a chapter on sexual behavior. But your authors broke with this convention to underscore an important point: Sexual orientation is a statement about sexual or erotic attraction, not sexual behavior per se. Sexual orientation is the direction of a person's erotic interests. People with a **heterosexual** orientation are sexually attracted to people of the other gender and interested in forming romantic relationships with them. People with a **homosexual** orientation are sexually attracted to people of their own gender and interested in forming romantic relationships with them. Homosexual males are also referred to as gay males and homosexual females as lesbians. People with a **bisexual** orientation are sexually attracted to, and interested in forming romantic relationships with, both women and men. People may consider themselves gay or heterosexual even before they become sexually active or even if they are not presently sexually active because of choice or lack of opportunity.

Just how many people identify themselves as gay? Surveys in the United States, Britain, France, and Denmark find that about 3% of men identify themselves as gay (Hamer et al., 1993; Janus & Janus, 1993; Laumann et al., 1994). About 2% of the U.S. women surveyed say that they have a lesbian sexual orientation (Janus & Janus, 1993; Laumann et al., 1994). U.S. Census data show that about 600,000 households are headed by same-sex partners ("Gay Couples," 2001).

▎**Heterosexual** Referring to people who are sexually aroused by, and interested in forming romantic relationships with, people of the other gender.

▎**Homosexual** Referring to people who are sexually aroused by, and interested in forming romantic relationships with, people of the same gender. (Derived from the Greek *homos*, meaning "same," not from the Latin *homo*, meaning "man.")

▎**Bisexual** A person who is sexually aroused by, and interested in forming romantic relationships with, people of either gender.

Sexual Orientation: Like the Colors of the Rainbow

The pioneering sex researcher Alfred Kinsey and his colleagues in the 1930s and 1940s added another wrinkle in our understanding of sexual orientation. They challenged the conventional wisdom that homosexuality and heterosexuality are mutually exclusive categories. Based on surveys conducted on thousands of people, they found a range of sexual interest and activity between the two ends of the dimension of homosexuality and heterosexuality. Many people reported that they were primarily but not exclusively homosexual or heterosexual. As Kinsey and his associates wrote, "The world is not to be divided into sheep and goats.... Only the human mind invents categories and tries to force facts into separated pigeonholes. The living world is a continuum in each and every one of its aspects" (1948, p. 639). Contemporary scholars concur that sexual orientation is more of a continuum with many gradations, similar in a way to the colors that comprise the spectrum of a rainbow (DeAngelis, 2001).

We should also point out that sexual behavior is not equivalent to sexual orientation. Sexual orientation is a statement of one's sexual interest in or attraction to members of one's own sex or the opposite sex. These attractions may or may not be expressed in actual behavior. We may be celibate but still identify ourselves as heterosexual, homosexual, or bisexual. Nor does behavior necessarily define sexual orientation. Men in prisons may have a heterosexual orientation but turn to each other as sexual outlets and then resume heterosexual activity once released from prison.

Frank Roth/Getty Images, Inc

A Spectrum of Sexual Orientations
Alfred Kinsey, the famed sex researcher, believed that sexual orientation is best represented in terms of a continuum or spectrum ranging from exclusive heterosexuality on one end to exclusive homosexuality on the other.

Research does not support the view that gay males and lesbians *choose* their sexual orientation any more than heterosexuals choose their orientation (American Psychological Association, 1998). Another common misconception: Since gay people are attracted to members of their own gender, some people assume that they would prefer to be members of the other gender. However, like heterosexuals but unlike transsexuals, gay people have a gender identity that is consistent with their anatomic gender. Gay males perceive themselves as males and lesbians perceive themselves as females.

Origins of Sexual Orientation

What are the causes of sexual orientation? The short answer is that we just don't know. Understandings of sexual orientation have been approached from both psychological and biological perspectives, but leading scholars recognize that we still have much to learn about the nature of sexual orientation (Gooren & Kruijver, 2002).

Freudian or psychodynamic theory attempted to explain sexual orientation on the basis of overidentification with the parent of the opposite sex, of boys identifying too strongly with their mothers and girls identifying too strongly with their fathers. In men, a reversal of identification stems from a "classic pattern" of child-rearing in which there is a "close binding" mother and a "detached hostile" father. Boys reared in such a home environment would come to identify with their mothers, not with their fathers. Gay males would thus be expected to develop effeminate behaviors. The reverse would be the case with lesbians, who would be expected to show tomboyish, masculine behaviors as a result of identifying more with their fathers than their mothers. Many critics of this traditional view point out that many gay males and lesbians do not show cross-gender behavior and many had excellent relationships with both parents. Also, the childhoods of many heterosexuals fit the "classic pattern."

More recent attempts to explain sexual orientation focus primarily on biological influences, including evidence of genetic contributions (Kohl, 2007; Sefcek et al., 2007). For example, studies show that identical (MZ or monozygotic) twins are more likely to share their sexual orientation in common than are fraternal (DZ or dizygotic) twins (Bailey, 2003; Hyde, 2005b). Recall that MZ twins share 100% of their genes in common as compared to 50% among fraternal twins (or other siblings). The greater similarity in sexual orientation among MZ twins is thus consistent with a genetic contribution. Although genetic factors may partly determine sexual orientation, they are not the only determinant. If genes did fully determine sexual orientation, we wouldn't find, as Bailey and Pillard (1991) reported, that nearly half of MZ twins have different sexual orientations. Moreover, evidence also suggests that genetics may play a stronger role in determining sexual orientation in men than in women (LeVay, 2003).

What about the effects of sex hormones on sexual orientation? Evidence shows that sexual orientation in humans is not linked to current (adult) levels of male or female sex hormones (LeVay, 2003). In other words, gay males and lesbians do not have lower levels of male or female sex hormones, respectively, than do their heterosexual counterparts. But investigators suspect that, like other species, exposure to sex hormones during prenatal development in humans may have an organizing effect on the developing brains (Lalumiére, Blanchard, & Zucker, 2000; LeVay, 2003). Sex hormones have **organizing effects** and **activating effects** on sexual behavior. We know that prenatal sex hormones can "masculinize" or "feminize" the brains of laboratory animals. That is, they can predispose lower animals toward masculine or feminine mating patterns—a directional or organizing effect (Crews, 1994). They also affect the sex drive and promote sexual response; these are activating effects. Investigators suspect that the brains of at least some gay males and lesbians may have been feminized or masculinized, respectively, prior to birth (Collaer & Hines, 1995; Ellis & Hellberg, 2005). However, we need to caution that such theories remain spec-

■ **Organizing effects** The directional effect of sex hormones—for example, along stereotypically masculine or feminine lines.

■ **Activating effects** The arousal-producing effects of sex hormones that increase the likelihood of sexual behavior.

ulative in the absence of direct evidence of the role of sex hormones in the development of sexual orientation.

In sum, the determinants of sexual orientation are obscure and complex. Sexual orientation may best be explained by a combination of factors, including genetic and hormonal influences interacting with environmental influences and life experiences. We also need to bear in mind that just as there are often many different roads that lead to the same destination, multiple pathways may be involved in explaining how different people develop their sexual orientations (Garnets, 2002).

Attitudes Toward Gay Males and Lesbians

In Western culture, few sexual practices have met with such widespread censure as sexual activities with members of one's own gender. Throughout much of history, male–male and female–female sexual behaviors were deemed sinful and criminal, an outrage against God and humanity. In the Judeo-Christian tradition, male–male sexual activity was regarded as a sin so vile that no one dared speak its name.

Most people in the United States believe that gay people should have equal access to employment opportunities (Eggers, 2000). But some people believe that gays should be barred from teaching and similar activities because they believe, erroneously, that gay people, given the chance, will seduce and recruit children into a gay lifestyle. These beliefs have been used to prevent gay couples from becoming adoptive or foster parents and to deny them custody or visitation rights to their own children following divorce. Some who would bar gay people from interactions with children fear that the children will be molested. Yet more than 90% of cases of child molestation involve heterosexual male assailants (Rathus et al., 2002). Recent research showed that a sample of children with lesbian parents were well adjusted and had positive relationships with their mothers (Golombok et al., 2003).

Many myths abound in the general public regarding sexual orientation. Table 11.2 debunks some of these common misconceptions.

Table 11.2 ▮ Myths vs. Facts about Sexual Orientation

Myth	Fact
A person's sexual orientation is a matter of choice.	Sexual orientation is not a matter of personal choice. One does not choose to be homosexual any more than one chooses to be heterosexual.
Children raised by gay or lesbian parents will turn out to be maladjusted or become gay themselves.	Children raised by gay or lesbian couples turn out to be as well adjusted as other children. Nor is there any evidence that children raised by gay parents are more likely than other children to become gay themselves.
You are either completely homosexual or completely heterosexual.	Since the time of Kinsey, investigators have classified sexual orientation on the basis of a continuum between exclusive homosexuality and exclusive heterosexuality.
Rates of homosexuality have increased sharply in recent years.	Though homosexuality is more openly discussed today, there is no evidence that underlying rates of homosexuality have changed in a significant way.
Gay males are responsible for most cases of sexual abuse of young boys.	Not true. The great majority of molesters of young boys and young girls are heterosexual men.
Gay males and lesbians really would prefer to be members of the opposite sex.	No, gay males and lesbians have a gender identity that is consistent with their anatomic gender.
Homosexuality is mostly about sex.	Not so. Homosexuality, like heterosexuality, is about patterns of sexual attraction, not how often—or even if—one engages in sexual relationships.

Source: Nevid, 2009. Reprinted with permission of Cengage Learning.

"Coming Out"

Because of the backdrop of social condemnation and discrimination, gay males and lesbians in our culture often struggle to come to terms with their sexual orientation (Meyer, 2003). The first challenge to adjustment experienced by gays and lesbians has to do with "coming out," also referred to as "coming out of the closet." Gay men and lesbians come out to themselves and to others. Many gay people have a difficult time coming out to themselves. Coming out to themselves involves recognizing, and accepting, their sexual orientation—in a hostile society. Because of problems in self-acceptance, some gays and lesbians have considered or attempted suicide.

Recognition of a gay sexual orientation as part of one's self-definition is the first step in a process of sexual identity formation. Some gay people come out to others by openly declaring their sexual orientation to the world. Others inform only one or a few select people, for example, friends but not family members. Many gay males and lesbians remain reluctant to declare their sexual orientation to anyone. Disclosure is fraught with the risk of loss of jobs, friendships, and social standing.

Gay men and lesbians often anticipate negative reactions from informing family members, including denial, anger, and rejection. Family members and loved ones may refuse to hear or be unwilling to accept reality, as Martha Barron Barrett notes in her book *Invisible Lives*, which chronicles the lives of a sample of lesbians in the United States:

> *Parents, children, neighbors, and friends of lesbians deny, or compartmentalize, or struggle with their knowledge in the same way the women themselves do. "My parents know I've lived with my partner for six years. She goes home with me. We sleep in the same bed there. The word lesbian has never been mentioned." "I told my mother and she said, 'Well, now that's over with. We don't need to mention it again.' She never has, and that was ten years ago. I don't know if she ever told my father." A husband may dismiss it as "just a phase," a boyfriend may interpret it as a sexual tease, a straight woman may believe "she's just saying that because she couldn't get a man."*
>
> *The strong message is, "Keep it quiet." Many lesbians do that by becoming invisible. … [They] leave their lesbian persona at home when they go to work on Monday morning. On Friday they do it again. (Barrett, 1990, p. 52)*

Some families are more accepting. They may in fact have had suspicions and prepared themselves for such news. Then, too, many families are initially rejecting but often eventually come to at least grudging acceptance that a family member is gay.

Adjustment of Gay Males and Lesbians

It is little wonder that many gay males and lesbians are distressed when they become aware of their sexual orientations, which often occurs during adolescence. Recent evidence indicates that gay males and lesbians are more likely than heterosexuals to experience feelings of anxiety and depression and that they are more prone to suicidal thinking and suicide attempts (Balsam et al., 2005; Skegg et al., 2003).

Psychologist J. Michael Bailey (1999) carefully reviewed the adjustment problems of gay males and lesbians. He proposed several alternative views of these problems, such as ascribing such problems to the influences of social oppression. "Surely," writes Bailey, "it must be difficult for young people to come to grips with their homosexuality in a world where homosexual people are often scorned, mocked, mourned, and feared." Declaring a gay male or lesbian sexual orientation to the world is difficult at best, and gay males and lesbians, especially as adolescents, are likely to have few friends and to encounter a great deal of disapproval and disgust. But Bailey allowed that atypical levels of prenatal sex hormones may affect later development or that differences in lifestyles may be involved, among other factors. On this latter point, he noted that gay males are more likely than heterosexual males to have eating disorders and also that "gay male culture emphasizes physical attractiveness and thinness, just as the heterosexual culture emphasizes female physical attractiveness

Adjustment and Modern Life

Ethnicity and Sexual Orientation: A Matter of Belonging

Lesbians and gay males frequently suffer the slings and arrows of an outraged society. Because of societal prejudices, it is difficult for many young people to come to terms with an emerging lesbian or gay male sexual orientation. You might assume that people who have been subjected to prejudice and discrimination—members of ethnic minority groups in the United States—would be more tolerant of a lesbian or gay male sexual orientation. However, members of ethnic minority groups in the United States tend to be less tolerant of homosexuals than European Americans are (Greene, 2005; Herek & Gonzalez-Rivera, 2006).

Our colleague Beverly Greene (2005) addresses the experiences of lesbians and gay men from ethnic minority groups. She notes that it is difficult to generalize about ethnic groups in the United States. For example, African Americans may find their cultural origins in the tribes of West Africa, but they have also been influenced by Christianity and the local subcultures of their North American towns and cities. Native Americans represent hundreds of tribal groups, languages, and cultures. By and large, however, a lesbian or gay male sexual orientation is rejected by ethnic minority groups in the United States. Lesbians and gay males are pressured to keep their sexual orientations a secret or to move to communities where they can live openly without sanction.

Within traditional Latino and Latina American culture, the family is the primary social unit. Men are expected to support and defend the family, and women are expected to be submissive, respectable, and deferential to men. Because women are expected to remain virgins until marriage, men sometimes engage in male–male sexual behavior without considering themselves gay (Barrett et al., 2005). Latino and Latina American culture frequently denies the sexuality of women. Thus, women who label themselves lesbians are doubly condemned because they are lesbians and because they are confronting others with their sexuality. Because lesbians are independent of men, most Latino and Latina American heterosexual people view Latina American lesbians as threats to the tradition of male dominance (Barrett et al., 2005).

Asian American cultures emphasize respect for elders, obedience to parents, and sharp distinctions in gender roles (Kumashiro, 2004). The topic of sex is generally taboo within the family. Asian Americans, like Latino and Latina Americans, tend to assume that sex is unimportant to women. Women are also considered less important than men. Open admission of a lesbian or gay male sexual orientation is seen as rejection of traditional cultural roles and a threat to the continuity of the family line (Collins, 2004). For all these reasons, it is not surprising that

Asian American college students report being more homophobic than their European American counterparts.

Because many African American men have had difficulty finding jobs, gender roles among African Americans have been more flexible than those found among European Americans and most other ethnic minority groups (Greene, 2000). Nevertheless, the African American community appears to strongly reject gay men and lesbians, pressuring them to remain secretive about their sexual orientations. Greene (2000) hypothesizes a number of factors that influence African Americans to be hostile toward lesbians and gay men. One is allegiance to Christianity and biblical scripture. Another is internalization of the dominant culture's stereotyping of African Americans as highly sexual beings. That is, many African Americans may feel a need to assert their sexual "normalcy."

Prior to European colonialization, sex may not have been discussed openly by Native Americans, but sex was generally seen as a natural part of life. Individuals who incorporated both traditional feminine and masculine styles were generally accepted and even admired. However, the influence of religious values of the mainstream culture led to greater rejection of lesbians and gay men within Native American communities, which in turn led to pressure on lesbian and gay male Native Americans to move off the reservation to the big cities (Adams & Phillips, 2006; Balsam et al., 2004). Native American lesbians and gay men, like Asian American lesbians and gay men, thus often feel doubly removed from their families.

If any generalization is possible, it may be that lesbians and gay men find more of a sense of belonging in the gay community than in their ethnic communities.

Source: Rathus, Nevid, & Fichner-Rathus, 2008. Reprinted with permission of Pearson Education.

and thinness." (The incidence of eating disorders among gay males could also be connected with atypical levels of prenatal hormones.)

We should reinforce the fact that Bailey insists that we must obtain more evidence before arriving at any judgments as to why gay males and lesbians are more prone to adjustment problems. Nevertheless, it is clear that gay males and lesbians do encounter stress from societal oppression and rejection and that their adjustment is connected with conflict over their sexual orientation (Simonsen, Blazine, & Watkins, 2000).

Researchers also find connections between lifestyle and adjustment among gay males and lesbians that appear to parallel the links between lifestyle and adjustment among heterosexual people. Generally speaking, gay and lesbian couples tend to be more similar to heterosexual couples than they are different (Kurdek, 2005). For example, gay and lesbian couples are likely to argue over the same issues as heterosexual couples—issues such as finances, affection, sex, and being overly critical. Overall, gay men and lesbians express as much satisfaction with their relationships as heterosexual couples (Kurdek, 2005; Means-Christensen, Snyder, & Negy, 2003). All in all, differences in adjustment may reflect the quality of the relationship, not a person's sexual orientation.

MODULE REVIEW

Review It

(1) The key factor determining attraction in romantic relationships is _____ _____.

(2) (Men or Women?) are more likely to look for vocational status, kindness, and fondness for children in a mate.

(3) Physically (attractive or unattractive?) individuals are more likely to be rated as maladjusted.

(4) According to the _____ hypothesis, we tend to ask out people who are similar to ourselves in attractiveness.

(5) _____ is the tendency to return feelings of admiration.

(6) _____ _____ refers to the direction of one's romantic or erotic interests.

(7) Sex hormones have _____ and activating effects.

(8) The process of _____ refers to recognizing and declaring one's sexual orientation.

(9) Gay males and lesbians are (more or less?) likely than heterosexuals to be anxious, depressed, or suicidal.

Think About It

How might the features found attractive by males and females provide humans with an evolutionary advantage? Explain.

MODULE 11.2

Positive
Psychology

Friendship: "Gotta Have Friends"

∎ What roles do friends play in our lives?
∎ What are the most important qualities in friends?

Friends play major roles in our lives from the time we are children through late adulthood. For primary school children, friendships are based largely on proximity, of who lives next door or who sits next to whom. "Friends" are classmates and those with whom kids do things and have fun. With middle-schoolers, similarity in interests enters the picture: Friendships begin to approach "perfect blendships." By puberty, people want someone with whom they can also share intimate feelings. In the teens, it becomes important that friends keep confidences. We want to be able to tell friends "everything" without worrying that they will spread stories. Girls find intimacy to be more important than boys do and typically form closer friendships (Berndt, 1982).

In high school and college, we tend to belong to **cliques** and **crowds**. A clique is a small number of close friends who share confidences. A crowd is a larger, loosely knit group of friends who share activities. The crowd may go to a football game together or to a party. But we tend to share our innermost feelings about people at the party within the clique. Friends also play an important role in late adulthood. The quality of friendliness is associated with psychological well-being among older people (Holmen, Ericsson, & Winblad, 2000; McAuley et al., 2000). People with confidants are generally less depressed and lonely. Having a confidant also heightens morale in the face of tragic events such as a significant illness or the death of a spouse.

What qualities define a good friend? A 1970s survey by *Psychology Today* magazine of some 40,000 readers highlighted some factors that are likely to be as important today as they were 40 years ago, or perhaps even 140 years ago. The ability to keep confidences and loyalty were the most sought-after qualities in a friend (Parlee, 1979). Overall, qualities deemed important in friends were these:

- Ability to keep confidences (endorsed by 89% of respondents)
- Loyalty (88%)
- Warmth and affection (82%)
- Supportiveness (75%)
- Honesty and frankness (73%)
- Humor (72%)
- Willingness to set aside time for me (62%)
- Independence (61%)
- Conversational skills (59%)
- Intelligence (58%)
- Social conscience (49%)

The results of this survey suggest that loyalty (keeping confidences is one aspect of loyalty) is the prime requisite for friendship. Also important are the supportive aspects of the relationship (including warmth, humor, and willingness to set aside time for the relationship). General positive traits also figure in—honesty, independence, intelligence, and so on.

When we consider how love—that many-splendored thing—exists in many forms, we may come to see that it is possible to be "in love" even if we are not true friends. Friendship and love, in other words, are not mutually defining. We shall see, however, that abiding love relationships tend to combine the two. First, however, we consider how the mass introduction of cell phones is changing the social landscape. Does it bring friends closer together, allowing them to remain in touch wherever they happen to be? Or might it lead them to retreat from face-to-face interactions?

▌ **Cliques** A small group of close friends who share confidences.

▌ **Crowds** A large number of loosely knit friends who share activities.

MODULE REVIEW

Review It

(10) (Boys or Girls?) are more likely to find intimacy to be important in friendship and to form closer friendships.

(11) Respondents to a *Psychology Today* poll reported that keeping confidences and_____ were the most sought-after qualities in a friend.

(12) _____ students are among the heaviest users of cell phones today.

Think About It

How would you distinguish between love and friendship? Explain.

Adjustment and Modern Life

Cell Phone Nation: Social Blessing or Curse?

In an episode from the classic 1990s TV show *Seinfeld,* two of the lead characters, Jerry Seinfeld and George Costanza, are traveling in separate cars to visit the Bubble Boy (don't ask). George, knowing the directions, suggests that Jerry follow him on the road. They set out on the road but soon lose sight of each other. Jerry gets lost and has no way of contacting George for help. While watching a rerun of the episode, my (J.N.) 14-year-old son asked, "Why doesn't Jerry just call George on the cell phone?" Why, indeed.

As recently as the 1990s, cell phones were considered a luxury. Today, many people regard them as a necessity. Fast forward to 2010. Mobile phones are virtually universal. The adoption of cell phones has occurred at a faster rate than that of any other technology in human history ("Social Serendipity," 2005).

College students are among the heaviest users of all. Cell phones have become as much a part of college life as textbooks and dormitory living. Here, a Denver student comments on just how dependent he has become on his cell phone: "Once, my cell didn't work. I couldn't get calls in or out, send or receive text messages or check voicemail.... I felt cut off from the rest of the world. What's worse was that I couldn't even order a pizza because I didn't know my dorm room phone number, so the delivery guy couldn't call me" ("The Ubiquitous Cell Phone," 2005).

Cell phones are no longer simply a convenient means of voice communication. Many people today, especially young people, are using cell phones not simply to chat with their friends but also to send text messages, play games, surf the web, listen to songs, and take pictures. In other words, cell phones are increasingly becoming integrated into our lifestyles. Many people would no sooner leave their homes without their cell phones than they would leave without getting dressed.

As cell phones become increasingly integrated into our daily lives, they offer new opportunities for social connections as well as new challenges to adjustment. Social scientists are beginning to study the effects of cell phones on our social behavior. Cell phones have the potential of increasing our social connections with others. You can share information with your friends by text messaging, keep in touch by calling them when you're on the go or away from home, or send them camera-phone snapshots of your experiences. New cell phone applications will even allow you to know when your friends are in your vicinity or to text message them en masse. In yet another application that may be commonplace by the time this book reaches your hands (woe to the writer trying to keep up with advances in technology!), cell phone users may be able to send anonymous text messages to people in their vicinity who share similar interests.

Ryan McVay/Stone/Getty Images, Inc.

Cell Phone Nation
Cell phones, once a luxury, have now become a staple of daily life. On many campuses, cell phones have become as much a part of college life as textbooks and dormitory living.

The recipient of these text alerts would need to respond "yes" to activate a personal communication. We can anticipate a brave new social world emerging in which people armed with their cell phone data banks scan their vicinities to find like-minded people to date or form friendships with.

On the other hand, cell phones have the potential to create social friction. Consider, for example, the rudeness associated with intrusive cell phone use in public places ("Can you ALL hear me now?"). Learning the ropes of cell phone etiquette is becoming as important a social-learning experience as learning good manners. Some municipalities have even instituted fines for inappropriate cell phone use in public places.

Our understanding of the effects of cell phone use on our social lives is still emerging. In the years ahead, we can anticipate that mobile communications will allow us to expand our social networks, such as by locating people with similar interests, as well as bringing us closer together to our friends and social contacts.

Yet we wonder about the potential challenges this technology poses in our daily lives: Will we feel a need to escape from the increasing numbers of messages, phone calls, and alerts? How might our sense of privacy be affected by carrying a device that keeps us constantly in touch on a 24/7 basis? Perhaps most significantly, will we retreat from face-to-face interactions with others as we come to increasingly rely on mobile communications?

Love: That Most Valued Emotion

■ What is love?

■ What are the components of love in Sternberg's theory?

■ How are these components related to different types of love?

Positive Psychology

What makes the world go round? **Love**, of course. But just what is love? Love is one of the most deeply stirring emotions, the ideal for which we will make great sacrifice, the emotion that launched a thousand ships in the Greek epic *The Iliad*. For thousands of years, poets have sought to capture love in words. A seventeenth-century poet wrote that his love was like "a red, red rose." In Sinclair Lewis's novel *Elmer Gantry*, love is "the morning and the evening star." Love is beautiful and elusive. It shines brilliantly and heavenly. Passionate love is also earthy and sexy, involving a solid ration of sexual desire.

Passionate or romantic love can also lead to a range of other emotions, from exhilaration that may come with new love to feelings of jealousy and fears of rejection. In fact, contemporary scholars believe that "falling in love" can send us on a rollercoaster of emotions that swing from one extreme to another, from exhilarating "ups" to crushing "downs" when the relationship ends (Fisher, 2000).

■ **Love** An intense, positive emotion that involves feelings of affection and desire to be with and to help another person.

11.3.1 Styles of Love

Psychologists find that love is a complex concept, involving many areas of experience—emotional, cognitive, and motivational (Sternberg, 1988). Psychologists also speak of different kinds of love and different *styles* of love. For example, Clyde and Susan Hendrick (1986) developed a love-attitude scale that suggests the existence of six styles of love among college students. Here are the styles and items, similar to those on the test, that identify them.

■ *Eros*, or romantic love. "My lover fits my ideal." "My lover and I were attracted to one another immediately." Eros is similar in meaning to the concept of passion. Eros was a character in Greek mythology (translated in Roman mythology into Cupido and now called Cupid) who would shoot unsuspecting people with his love arrows, causing them to fall madly in love with the person who was nearest to them at the time. Erotic love embraces sudden passionate desire: "love at first sight" and "falling head over heels in love." Younger college students are more likely to believe in love at first sight and that "love conquers all" than are older (and wiser?) college students (Knox et al., 1999).

Passion can be so gripping that one is convinced that life has been changed forever. This feeling of sudden transformation was captured by the Italian poet Dante Alighieri (1265–1321), who exclaimed upon first beholding his beloved Beatrice, *Incipit vita nuova*, which can be translated as "My life begins anew." Romantic love, as we have said, can also be earthy and sexy. In fact, sexual arousal and desire may be the strongest component of passionate or romantic love. Romantic love begins with a powerful physical attraction or feelings of passion and is associated with strong physiological arousal.

■ *Ludus*, or game-playing love. "I keep my lover up in the air about my commitment." "I get over love affairs pretty easily."

■ *Storge*, or friendship-love. "The best love grows out of an enduring friendship." Storge is loving attachment, deep friendship, or nonsexual affection. It is the emotion that binds friends and parents and children.

© Ron Chapple/Taxi/Getty Images

Ah, Love. Romance. Passion
How do psychologists define love? What styles or kinds of love are there?

▌ **Romantic love** A passionate form of love involving strong erotic attraction to another combined with desires for intimacy.

- *Pragma*, or pragmatic, logical love. "I consider a lover's potential in life before committing myself." "I consider whether my lover will be a good parent."
- *Mania*, or possessive, excited love. "I get so excited about my love that I cannot sleep." "When my lover ignores me, I get sick all over."
- *Agape*, or selfless love. "I would do anything I can to help my lover." "My lover's needs and wishes are more important than my own." Agape implies the wish to share one's bounty and is epitomized by anonymous donations of money. In relationships, it is characterized by selfless giving.

Most people who are "in love" combine a number of these styles. In an influential early study that examined these six styles of love, Hendrick and Hendrick (1986) found some interesting gender differences. Male college students are significantly more ludic (i.e., game-playing) than females. Female college students are significantly more storgic (friendly), pragmatic (long-term oriented), and manic[2] (possessive) than males. There were no gender differences in eros (passion) or agape (selflessness).

11.3.2 Romantic Love in Contemporary Western Culture

When people in Western culture speak of falling in love, they are referring to romantic love—not to the sort of loving attachment that binds parents to children. Nor are they referring to sexual arousal, which people may experience while they are reading an erotic story or looking at photographs in an erotic magazine. To experience **romantic love**, in contrast to attachment or sexual arousal, it may be that one must be exposed to a culture that idealizes the concept. In Western culture, romantic love blossoms with the fairytales of *Sleeping Beauty, Cinderella, Snow White*, and their "Prince Charmings." It matures with romantic novels, television tales and films, and the colorful narratives of friends and relatives.

We shouldn't think that the concept of romantic love is limited to Western cultures. A major cross-cultural study of 166 different cultures found evidence for the concept of romantic love in 147 of the 166 cultures studied, even in many preliterate societies (Jankowiak & Fischer, 1992). Even in the 19 other cultures in which the concept of romantic love was not revealed, the investigators suspected it probably existed but their methods were too limited to discover it. Romantic love may not make the world go round, but it does seem to go around the world.

The Love Triangle—That Is, the Triangular Model of Love

According to psychologist Robert Sternberg (1988), love consists of three primary components: intimacy, passion, and commitment.

1 *Intimacy* is the emotional component of love. It involves sharing intimate (deeply personal) information and developing feelings of mutual acceptance.
2 *Passion* is the motivational force behind love. It involves sexual attraction and the desire for sexual intimacy. Passion gives rise to fascination and preoccupation with the loved one. Passion is rapidly aroused but also quick to fade—especially among adolescents.
3 *Commitment* comprises the cognitive or decisional component of love. Initially, one decides that one is "in love." As time elapses, however, the initial decision becomes a lasting commitment to the other person and the relationship.

Different combinations of the components of love yield different kinds of love (see Figure 11.3 and Table 11.3). *Romantic love* involves passion and intimacy, but not necessarily commitment. Romantic love encourages lovers to champion the interests of the loved one even if it means sacrificing one's own interests. In fact, college

---

[2] Not to be confused with manic-depression (bipolar disorder), the problem discussed in Chapter 8.

Liking = Intimacy Alone
(true friendship without passion or long-term commitment)

Intimacy

**Romantic Love =
Intimacy + Passion**
(lovers physically and emotionally attracted to each other but without commitment, as in a summer romance)

**Companionate Love =
Intimacy + Commitment**
(long-term committed friendship such as a marriage in which the passion has faded)

**Consummate Love =
Intimacy + Passion + Commitment**
(a complete love consisting of all three components—an ideal difficult to attain)

Passion   Commitment

Infatuation = Passion Alone
(passionate, obsessive love at first sight without intimacy or commitment)

Fatuous Love = Passion + Commitment
(commitment based on passion but without time for intimacy to develop—shallow relationship such as a whirlwind courtship)

**Empty Love =
Commitment Alone**
(commitment to remain together without intimacy or passion)

Figure 11.3
The Triangular Model of Love
According to psychologist Robert Sternberg, love consists of three components, as shown by the vertices of this triangle. Various kinds of love consist of different combinations of these components. Romantic love, for example, consists of passion and intimacy. Consummate love—a state idealized in Western society—consists of all three.

∎ **Consummate love** In Sternberg's model, a form of love involving all three components of love: intimacy, commitment, and passion.

∎ **Empty love** In Sternberg's model, a form of love involving commitment but without passion or intimacy.

∎ **Fatuous love** A foolish type of love in which there is passion combined with commitment but without any true intimacy.

undergraduates see the desire to help or care for the loved one as central to the concept of romantic love (Steck et al., 1982).

During adolescence, strong sexual arousal along with an idealized image of the object of our desires leads us to label our feelings as love. We may learn to speak of "love" rather than "lust," because sexual desire in the absence of a committed relationship might be viewed as indecent or immoral. Being "in love" ennobles attraction and sexual arousal, not only to society but also to oneself. Unlike lust, love can be discussed even at the dinner table. If others think we are too young to experience "the real thing"—which presumably includes knowledge of and respect for the other person's personality traits—our feelings may be called "puppy love" or a "crush." Western society maintains much of the double standard toward sexuality. Thus, women are more often expected to justify sexual experiences as involving someone they love. Young men usually need not attribute sexual urges to love, so men are more apt to deem love a "mushy" concept. The great majority of people in the United States nonetheless view romantic love as a prerequisite for marriage.

Romantic lovers also idealize each other, magnifying positive features and overlooking flaws. Romantic love may burn brightly and then flicker out. If commitment develops, romantic love may evolve into **consummate love**, in which all three components flower. Consummate love is an ideal toward which many Westerners strive. **Empty love** is characterized by commitment alone. There is neither the warm emotional embrace of intimacy nor the flame of passion. In the case of empty love, one usually tolerates one's partner out of a sense of duty. Is there such a thing as love at first sight? Yes. Within Sternberg's model, love at first sight is a **fatuous love** (foolish love). People may be overwhelmed by passion and make a premature commitment before true intimacy develops. Fatuous love may propel whirlwind courtships and marriages that end when a partner wakes up one morning and realizes that the couple are poorly matched and the infatuation is over.

As time goes on, signs that distinguish infatuation from a lasting romantic love begin to emerge. The partners begin to view each other more realistically and determine whether or not the relationship should continue.

According to the Sternberg model, couples are matched if they possess corresponding levels of passion, intimacy, and commitment. A couple's compatibility can

Alamy Limited

Love or Infatuation?
How can you distinguish between love and infatuation? What are the different types of love in Sternberg's model? How do they differ?

Table 11.3 ▌ Types of Love According to Sternberg's Triangular Model	
Types of Love	**Description**
1. Nonlove	A relationship in which all three components of love are absent. Most of our personal relationships are of this type—casual interactions or acquaintances that do not involve any elements of love.
2. Liking	A loving experience with another person or a friendship in which intimacy is present but passion and commitment are lacking.
3. Infatuation	A kind of "love at first sight" in which one experiences passionate desires for another person in the absence of both intimacy and commitment.
4. Empty love	A kind of love characterized by commitment to maintain the relationship in the absence of either passion or intimacy. Stagnant relationships that no longer involve the emotional intimacy or physical attraction that once characterized them are of this type.
5. Romantic love	A loving experience characterized by the combination of passion and intimacy, but lacking commitment.
6. Companionate love	A kind of love that derives from the combination of intimacy and commitment. This kind of love often occurs in marriages in which passionate attraction between the partners has died down and has been replaced by a kind of committed friendship.
7. Fatuous love	The type of love associated with whirlwind romances and "quickie marriages" in which passion and commitment are present, but intimacy is not.
8. Consummate love	The full or complete measure of love involving the combination of passion, intimacy, and commitment. Many of us strive to attain this type of complete love in our romantic relationships. Maintaining it is often harder than achieving it.

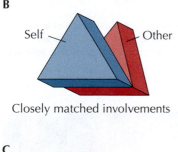

Perfectly matched involvements

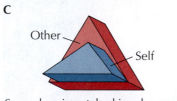

Closely matched involvements

Figure 11.4
Compatibility and Incompatibility, According to the Triangular Model of Love
Within Sternberg's model of love, compatibility can be conceptualized in terms of these "love triangles." In part A there is a perfect match; the triangles are congruent. In part B there is a good match; the levels of the components generally overlap. Part C reveals a mismatch, with large differences between the partners in terms of the components of love.

be represented in terms of the fit of the love triangles. Figure 11.4A shows a perfect match, in which the triangles are congruent. Figure 11.4B depicts a good match, one in which partners are similar in the three dimensions. Figure 11.4C shows a mismatch. There are large differences between the partners in all three components. Relationships suffer when partners are grossly mismatched. A relationship may fizzle, rather than sizzle, when one partner has a great deal more passion or when one wants a permanent commitment and the other's idea of commitment is to stay the night.

Romantic versus Companionate Love: Is Romantic Love Any Basis for a Marriage?

According to the American ideal, when people come of age, they will find their perfect match, fall in love, get married, and live happily ever after. In the next chapter we shall see that the high divorce rate sheds some doubt on this fantasy. But for the moment, let us confine ourselves to asking whether romantic love provides a sound basis for marriage.

There is cause for skepticism. Romantic love frequently assails us in a flash. Then it may dissipate as knowledge of the loved one grows. Some philosophers and social critics have argued that romantic love is but a "passing fancy." Marriage, therefore, must be a firm legal institution for the rearing of children and the transmission of wealth from one generation to another. So it is unwise to base marriage on romantic love. From this perspective, marriage is a sober instrument of social stability whereas love, after all, is *l'amour!* In many instances throughout Western history, it

Has Cupid Shot His Arrow into Your Heart? Sternberg's Triangular Love Scale

Self-Assessment

Which are the strongest components of your love relationship? Intimacy? Passion? Commitment? All three components? Two of them?

To complete the following rating scale, fill in the blank spaces with the name of one person you love or care about deeply. Then rate your agreement with each of the items by using a 9-point scale in which 1 = not at all, 5 = moderately, and 9 = extremely. Use points in between these values to indicate intermediate levels of agreement. Then consult the scoring key at the end of the chapter.

Intimacy Component

_____ 1. I am actively supportive of _____ 's well-being.
_____ 2. I have a warm relationship with _____ .
_____ 3. I am able to count on _____ in times of need.
_____ 4. _____ is able to count on me in times of need.
_____ 5. I am willing to share myself and my possessions with _____ .
_____ 6. I receive considerable emotional support from _____ .
_____ 7. I give considerable emotional support to _____ .
_____ 8. I communicate well with _____ .
_____ 9. I value _____ greatly in my life.
_____ 10. I feel close to _____ .
_____ 11. I have a comfortable relationship with _____ .
_____ 12. I feel that I really understand _____ .
_____ 13. I feel that _____ really understands me.
_____ 14. I feel that I can really trust _____ .
_____ 15. I share deeply personal information about myself with _____ .

Passion Component

_____ 1. Just seeing _____ excites me.
_____ 2. I find myself thinking about _____ frequently during the day.
_____ 3. My relationship with _____ is very romantic.
_____ 4. I find _____ to be very personally attractive.
_____ 5. I idealize _____ .
_____ 6. I cannot imagine another person making me as happy as _____ does.
_____ 7. I would rather be with _____ than anyone else.
_____ 8. There is nothing more important to me than my relationship with _____ .
_____ 9. I especially like physical contact with _____ .
_____ 10. There is something almost "magical" about my relationship with _____ .
_____ 11. I adore _____ .
_____ 12. I cannot imagine life without _____ .
_____ 13. My relationship with _____ is passionate.
_____ 14. When I see romantic movies and read romantic books, I think of _____ .
_____ 15. I fantasize about _____ .

Commitment Component

_____ 1. I know that I care about _____ .
_____ 2. I am committed to maintaining my relationship with _____ .
_____ 3. Because of my commitment to _____ , I would not let other people come between us.
_____ 4. I have confidence in the stability of my relationship with _____ .
_____ 5. I could not let anything get in the way of my commitment to _____ .
_____ 6. I expect my love for _____ to last for the rest of my life.
_____ 7. I will always feel a strong responsibility for _____ .
_____ 8. I view my commitment to _____ as a solid one.

_____ 9. I cannot imagine ending my relationship with _____ .

_____ 10. I am certain of my love for _____ .

_____ 11. I view my relationship with _____ as permanent.

_____ 12. I view my relationship with _____ as a good decision.

_____ 13. I feel a sense of responsibility toward _____ .

_____ 14. I plan to continue my relationship with _____ .

_____ 15. Even when _____ is hard to deal with, I remain committed to our relationship.

Source: Sternberg (1988). Reprinted by permission of Basic Books, Inc., New York.

For an interactive version of this self-assessment exercise, go to www.wileyplus.com

▮ **Companionate love** In Sternberg's model, a form of love involving intimacy and commitment but without a strong element of passion.

was assumed that husbands would take mistresses or visit prostitutes. In a few cases, wives have also been expected to take lovers, especially among the aristocratic upper classes. People are more likely to maintain their relationship once the romance begins to fade if they have developed **companionate love**. Companionate love requires trust, loyalty, sharing of feelings, mutual respect and appreciation, acceptance of imperfections, and willingness to sacrifice. Companionate love is based on genuine knowledge of the other person, not idealization.

If companionate love blooms, a relationship can survive the fading of extremes of passion. At this point, a couple can work together to meet each other's sexual as well as companionate needs. Skills can substitute for the excitement of novelty.

All in all, it sounds a bit like friendship.

In this chapter we have discussed interpersonal attraction—the force that initiates social contact. In the next chapter we follow the development of these social contacts into intimate relationships, particularly as they concern marriage and alternative styles of life.

MODULE REVIEW

Review It

(13) A friendship type of love is called _____.

(14) According to the triangular model of love, love can include combinations of_____, passion, and commitment.

(15) _____ love involves a combination of passion and intimacy.

(16) The type of love that brings together intimacy, passion, and commitment is called _____ love.

Think About It

"How do I love thee? Let me count the ways," wrote the nineteenth-century poet Elizabeth Barrett Browning (1806–1861). Based on conceptualizations of love in modern psychology, how would you interpret what Browning was saying?

Psychology in Daily Life

MODULE 11.4

Coping with Loneliness

In the classic song "Eleanor Rigby," the Beatles wondered where all the lonely people come from. Being lonely is not the same thing as being alone. Loneliness is a feeling state in which we sense ourselves as painfully isolated or cut off from other people. Being alone is a physical fact, and people with many close friends choose to be alone from time to time so that they can study, work, or just reflect on their feelings about being in the world (van Baarsen et al., 2001).

People who are lonely, as compared to people who are not, tend to show behavior patterns such as the following. They tend to spend more time by themselves; are more likely to eat dinner alone and spend weekends alone; are more self-critical; and are less likely to be dating (e.g., Wiseman, Mayseless, & Sharabany, 2006). Lonely people may report having as many friends as people who are not lonely, but upon closer examination, their friendships are relatively superficial. For example, they are not very likely to share confidences with their friends, and sometimes their so-called friends are surprised to learn that they were considered friends.

Loneliness tends to peak during adolescence, when most of us begin to replace close links to our parents with peer relationships. It is also a major problem of older adulthood, when children live elsewhere and, often, a spouse has died (van Baarsen et al., 2001). It is no surprise that loneliness is often associated with depression (Segrin et al., 2003). A study of 90 college students linked feelings of loneliness to low self-confidence, introversion, unhappiness, and emotional instability (Cheng & Furnham, 2002).

Loneliness is also linked to physical health problems, such as high blood pressure and poorer immune system functioning (Hawkley et al., 2003; Pressman et al., 2005). Lonely people, it seems, are actually more likely to get sick! People who are socially isolated also stand a greater risk of developing such serious diseases as cancer and heart disease (Hawkley & Cacioppo, 2003). Although causal connections are not clear, stress may be the pathway that connects loneliness and physical illness. Stress can impair our immune system and general health, and lonely people typically have greater difficulty coping with the effects of stress than others with more supportive social networks (Cacioppo, Hawkley, & Bernston, 2003).

11.4.1 Causes of Loneliness

Many factors contribute to loneliness, such as the loss of a spouse, development of a physical disability that impairs mobility, or loss of a social network because of relocation. Shyness, too, is a key contributor to loneliness. Because of shyness, people may avoid social contacts and lead isolated lives. Investigators also find a number of psychological characteristics associated with lonely people (e.g., Cramer, 2003; Prezza et al., 2001; Rokach & Bacanli, 2001; van Baarsen et al., 2001), including the following:

1. Lack of social skills. They may be insensitive to the feelings of others, or not know how to make friends, or not know how to cope with disagreements.
2. Lack of interest in other people.
3. Lack of empathy.
4. High self-criticism concerning social interactions and expectation of failure in dealing with other people.
5. Fear of rejection.
6. Failure to disclose information about themselves to potential friends.
7. Cynicism about human nature (e.g., perceiving people as only out for themselves).
8. Demanding too much too soon, as characterized by misperceptions of other people as cold and unfriendly in the early stages of developing a relationship.
9. Pessimistic attitudes in general.
10. An external locus of control—believing that their fate is beyond their control.
11. Lack of sense of community—as among college students who are new to campus life or among older people whose family, friends, and confidants have died or moved.

Ed Freeman/Image Bank/Getty Images, Inc.

Loneliness
Why are so many people lonely? Do they lack social skills? Have they been "burned" so badly that they fear getting involved? Do they fear rejection? All of the above apply, and more. Cognitive-behavioral psychologists have developed many methods for overcoming loneliness, such as those outlined in the text.

11.4.2 What To Do

Cognitive and behavioral treatment methods may help people overcome loneliness. Cognitive therapy for loneliness combats feelings of pessimism, cynicism about human nature ("Yes, many people are selfish and not worth knowing, but if we assume that everyone is like that, how can we develop fulfilling relationships?"), and fear of social failure.

Behavioral methods, such as assertiveness or social skills training, help lonely people develop ways of initiating conversations, talking on the telephone, giving and receiving compliments, and handling disagreements without being submissive or aggressive. You can refresh yourself on assertiveness training by reviewing Chapter 7. In the next chapter we'll have some suggestions for enhancing date-seeking skills. Also consider the following measures for making friends and combating loneliness:

1. *Make frequent social contacts.* Join committees for student-body activities. Engage in intramural sports. Join social-action groups or clubs such as the psychology club, ski club, or photography club. Get on the school newspaper staff.
2. *Combat shyness.* A leading authority on shyness, Bernardo Carducci of Indiana University, Southeast, offers some guidance on dealing with shyness in the *Adjustment and Modern Life* feature in Chapter 7.
3. *Be assertive.* Express opinions. Smile and say "Hi" to interesting-looking people. Sit down next to people at the cafeteria, not in a corner by yourself.
4. *Become a good listener.* Ask people how they're "doing" and what they think about classes or events of the day. Then *listen* to them. Be reasonably tolerant of divergent opinions; no two people are exactly alike. Maintain eye contact and a friendly face.

5. *Let people get to know you.* Try exchanging opinions and talking about your interests. Sure, you'll "turn off" some people—we all do—but how else can you learn whether you have something in common?

6. *Fight fair.* Now and then a friend will disappoint you and you'll want to tell him or her about it, but do so fairly. Begin by asking your friend if it's okay to be honest about something. Then say, "I feel upset because you..." Ask whether your friend realized that his or her behavior upset you. Work together to figure out a way to avoid repetition. End by thanking your friend for solving the problem with you.

7. *Tell yourself that you're worthy of friends.* None of us are perfect. Each of us has a unique pattern of traits and insights, and you'll connect with more people than you might expect. Give them a chance.

8. *Find an on-campus job.* Working with others can help you establish a social network that includes other students and possibly staff and faculty members.

9. *Make use of college counseling center services.* Thousands of students are lonely and don't know exactly what to do. Some know what to do but haven't quite got the courage. College counseling centers are familiar with the problem and are a valuable resource.

CHAPTER REVIEW

RECITE! RECITE! RECITE! RECITE! RECITE! RECITE! RECITE!

Study Tip: Reciting the answers to these study questions will help you become a more effective learner. First try answering the questions by yourself, either reciting them out loud or writing them in a notebook or on the computer. Then compare your answers with the sample answers provided below.

1. What factors contribute to attraction in our culture?
Physical appeal appears to be the key factor. In our culture, slenderness is considered attractive in both men and women, but especially so in women, whereas tallness is valued in men. Women tend to see themselves as heavier than the cultural ideal. Similarity in attitudes and sociocultural factors (ethnicity, education, and so on), proximity, and reciprocity in feelings of admiration also contribute to attraction.

2. What are some common stereotypes of attractive people?
There is an assumption that good things come in pretty packages. Physically attractive people are assumed to be more successful, sociable, popular, intelligent, and fulfilled, among other positive traits.

3. Do males and females find the same traits to be attractive in dating partners and mates?
Both males and females emphasize the importance of physical appeal and personal qualities. However, males tend to place somewhat more emphasis on physical attractiveness, and females tend to place relatively more emphasis than males do on traits like vocational status, earning potential, consideration, dependability, and fondness for children. Some behavioral and social scientists believe that evolutionary forces favored the survival of ancestral men and women with these mating preferences because they conferred reproductive advantages.

4. What is the matching hypothesis?
The matching hypothesis suggests that we are more likely to ask out and marry people who are similar to ourselves in attractiveness—largely because of fear of rejection.

5. What is sexual orientation?
Sexual orientation refers to the direction of erotic interests. People with a heterosexual orientation are sexually attracted to members of the opposite sex. People with a gay male or les-

bian sexual orientation are sexually attracted to people of their own gender. People with a bisexual orientation are attracted to both women and men.

6. How do researchers explain sexual orientation?
Evidence of a genetic contribution to sexual orientation is accumulating. Sex hormones are known to have both organizing and activating effects. Sex hormones may have an effect on the developing brain during prenatal development that affects later sexual orientation.

7. How do people in our society react to gay or bisexual people?
Gay males and lesbians have generally met with strong—sometimes violent—social disapproval. Most people in the United States today favor granting gay males and lesbians equal access to jobs, but many would bar them from activities—such as teaching—in which they fear (mistakenly) that their sexual orientation might affect the sexual orientations of children.

8. Given the general societal reaction to gay males and lesbians, what challenges to adjustment are they likely to encounter?
Gay males and lesbians frequently struggle with coming out, both to themselves and to others. They often have difficulty coming to terms with their sexual orientation—both recognizing and personally accepting their sexual orientations and then deciding whether they will declare their orientation to other people. Gay males and lesbians are more likely than heterosexuals to be anxious, depressed, or suicidal. Their adjustment problems may be connected with society's negative treatment of them.

9. What roles do friends play in our lives?
We share activities, interests, and confidences with friends.

10. What are the most important qualities in friends?
The key qualities we seek are ability to keep confidences, loyalty, social support, and general positive traits, such as frankness and intelligence.

11. What is love?

Love is a strong positive emotion characterized by feelings of attraction, attachment, and sexual arousal.

12. What are the components of love in Sternberg's theory?

His components of love are intimacy, passion, and commitment.

13. How are these components related to different types of love?

Romantic love is characterized by intimacy and passion; infatuation (fatuous love) by passion and commitment; companionate love by intimacy and commitment; and consummate love—which, to many, is the ideal form of love—by all three components.

YOUR PERSONAL JOURNAL

REFLECT   REFLECT   REFLECT   REFLECT   REFLECT   REFLECT   REFLECT

Study Tip: Reflecting on how the concepts in the chapter relate to your own experiences encourages deeper processing, which makes the material more personally meaningful and fosters more effective learning. Use additional pages if needed to complete your answers.

1. How important is physical appearance in determining whom you would like to date or with whom you would like to mate? Is there a difference between your dating and mating preferences? Explain.

_____

_____

_____

_____

2. Did reading about the origins of sexual orientation change your views in any way? How so?

_____

_____

_____

_____

_____

ANSWERS TO MODULE REVIEWS

Module 11.1

1. physical attractiveness
2. Women
3. unattractive
4. matching
5. Reciprocity
6. Sexual orientation
7. organizing
8. "coming out"
9. more

Module 11.2

10. Girls
11. loyalty
12. College

Module 11.3

13. storge
14. intimacy
15. Romantic
16. consummate

SCORING KEY FOR STERNBERG'S TRIANGULAR LOVE SCALE

First add your scores for the items on each of the three components—Intimacy, Passion, and Commitment—and divide each total by 15. This procedure will yield an average rating for each subscale. An average rating of 5 on a particular subscale indicates a moderate level of the component represented by the subscale. A higher rating indicates a greater level; a lower rating indicates a lower level. Examining your ratings on these components will give you an idea of the degree to which you perceive your love relationship to be characterized by these three components of love. For example, you might find that passion is stronger than commitment, a pattern that is common in the early stages of an intense romantic relationship. You might find it interesting to complete the questionnaire a few months or perhaps a year or so from now to see how your feelings about your relationship change over time. You might also ask your partner to complete the scale so that the two of you can compare your respective scores. Comparing your ratings for each component with those of your partner will give you an idea of the degree to which you and your partner see your relationship in a similar way.

Relationships and Communication: Getting from Here to There

OUTLINE

Did you know that...

- Moviegoers who saw a happy film with their partners later reported more positive feelings toward their partners than did those who watched a sad film? (p. 384)

- Many people seeking romantic partners go from "texting" to "webcam" dates before actually meeting the person? (p. 385)

- We are less likely to try to iron out the wrinkles in our relationships when new partners are available to us? (p. 392)

- Marriages are made in the neighborhood, not in heaven? (p. 395)

- People who remarry after divorce are less likely to make a go of it than people who marry for the first time? (p. 404)

- Disagreement is not destructive to a relationship? (p. 411)

Ed Bock/Corbis Images

Striking up a relationship requires some social skills. Those first few conversational steps can be big ones. In this chapter, we first explore stages in the development of **intimate relationships**. Then we discuss the institution of marriage, which remains the goal for most Americans. We examine the popular lifestyles of remaining single and cohabitation. Finally, we consider ways of enhancing intimate relationships, including improving communication skills.

Relationships, like people, can be thought of as undergoing stages of development. **Social-exchange theorists** view the stages of development as reflecting the unfolding of social exchanges, which involve the rewards and costs of maintaining the relationship as opposed to dissolving it. During each stage, positive factors lead partners toward maintaining and enhancing their relationship. Negative factors lead them to letting it deteriorate and end. In the first module in this chapter, we focus on how relationships change over time and how they can grow stronger and more enduring or weaken and deteriorate.

> **Intimate relationship** A relationship characterized by sharing of innermost feelings. The term *physical intimacy* implies a sexual relationship.

> **Social-exchange theory** A view of the stages of development as reflecting the unfolding of social exchanges, which involve the rewards and costs of maintaining the relationship.

MODULE 12.1

The ABC(DE)s of Relationships

- How do social scientists view stages in the development of relationships?
- What are Levinger's five stages of relationship development?
- What steps can people take to build a relationship?
- What factors contribute to the continuation or deterioration of a relationship?

383

Like individuals, relationships undergo different stages of development (Dindia & Timmerman, 2003). The sociologist George Levinger proposed a guiding conceptual model of relationship changes (Levinger, 1980). This model, called the **ABCDE model**, describes the life cycle of romantic relationships in terms of five stages of development: attraction, building, continuation, deterioration, and ending. During

> **ABCDE model** Levinger's theory of stages of development in a relationship: attraction, building, continuation, deterioration, and ending.

each stage, positive factors incline us to build or maintain the relationship; negative factors motivate us to dissolve the relationship. By learning more about these factors, we may be better prepared to strengthen our relationships rather than see them reach the ending stage. We use Levinger's model as a framework for exploring the factors that contribute to strengthening or weakening relationships.

12.1.1 A Is for Attraction

Initial attraction requires that people first become aware of one another. But how do relationships begin? How do we go from zero contact to initial attraction? Relationships may begin when we spot a new person across a crowded lunchroom, when we enter a class with new students, or when someone takes a job in a nearby office. We may also go from zero contact to initial attraction through computer matchups, blind dates, or even speed dating. Most often, however, we meet other people simply by accident. The greatest promoter of such accidents is propinquity, or nearness. We may live near the other person, have friends in common, attend the same school, or work in the same office or for the same company. Investigators find that most people report they met their spouses through mutual friends (35%) or by directly introducing themselves to others (32%) (Michael et al., 1994) (see Figure 12.1). However, times-are-a-changing.

As we see in the nearby *Adjustment and Modern Life* feature, many people today are meeting online. Not only are people meeting through online dating services, but young adults today are interacting through social networking sites such as MySpace and Facebook. A 2009 study at Georgetown University showed that the average student spent about 30 minutes a day using Facebook (Pempek, Yermolayeva, & Calvert, 2009). Students spent more time looking at other people's Facebook pages than posting information about themselves. Students primarily interacted on Facebook with friends and acquaintances with whom they had established relationships. Facebook and similar social networking sites serve as a medium not only for exchanging information with others but also for expressing one's own individual identity.

Many factors contribute to initial attraction, including physical attractiveness, similarity of attitudes, propinquity (nearness), and reciprocity. Other factors to consider include the **need for affiliation** (friendship and belonging) and the role of positive emotions. People with strong needs for belonging and friendship tend to seek out other people for relationships.

Positive emotions can also be catalysts for initial attraction. Levinger and his colleagues showed 128 male and female moviegoers either a happy or a sad film (Forgas, Levinger, & Moylan, 1994). Those exposed to the happy film reported more positive feelings about their partners and their relationships (so think twice before taking your date to a real downer). Negative factors include physical distance (lack of propinquity), negative emotions, and low need for affiliation.

It's important to make a positive first impression, especially because first impressions tend to become lasting impressions. Just how quickly are first impressions formed? Psychologists find that first impressions begin to be formed in less than a second, even before a person utters a word (Bar, Neta, & Linz, 2006; Willis & Todorov, 2006). When you are meeting someone on a first date, or being interviewed for a job, the person greeting you will begin sizing you up at first glimpse (Wargo, 2006). While initial impressions may change as the person gets to know you better, you never get a second chance to make a first impression. It's best to make that first impression count in your favor.

▌ **Need for affiliation** The need to have friends and belong to groups.

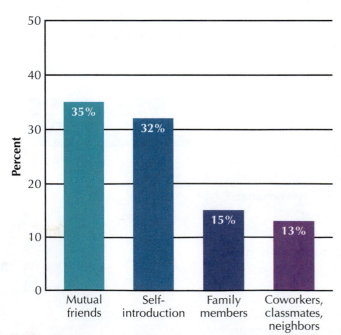

Figure 12.1

How Married People Met Their Spouses

Two out of three married people met their spouse either through mutual friends or self-introduction.

Adjustment and Modern Life

Twenty-First Century Dating: Matches Made in (Cyber) Heaven

Digital Vision/Getty Images, Inc.

Love to Tango
Looking for a partner in the dance of life
Age: Mid-twenties
Location: San Antonio, TX
Favorite activities: Dancing till dawn, outdoor sports, Mexican cooking
Dream vacation: Private beach on Maui (Right!)

Looking for a date? Or a mate? Millions of American adults seeking dates and mates have replaced bars and nightclubs as traditional meeting places with the computer as they search the web for Mr. or Ms. Right on the Net.

Online dating has shed its image of "Losers.com." We may need a whole new vocabulary for modem matchmaking. To answer the question "Are you seeing someone?" the proper form of a reply might become, "No, we're still just texting. But I'm hop-ing that soon we'll start having webcam dates." One observer of the Internet dating scene dubbed it "Google for people." Internet dating services have grown tremendously in recent years and now boast a million or more members. One large dating site, Match.com, boasts some 15 million members, slightly more men (55%) than women (45%) (Holstein, 2005; Wilkowe, 2005).

Each website has its own rules for playing the mating game. In some cases, users can browse the listings to find a suitable match. When they find someone who sparks their interest, they can become a registered member (for a fee, of course) and then chat with the person online. Some sites use interest patterns or psychological profiles to help users narrow their search to like-minded matches. Registered users typically post a profile of themselves, including a photograph, and select a user name or "date ID." The profile generally contains detailed information about themselves, such as their interests, physical features, religious and lifestyle background, age, and geographical location. Users are guaranteed anonymity (no real names, please) unless they decide to reveal their identity. They may search for prospective dates or mates on the basis of desired location, age, religious background, sexual orientation, even zip code.

The Stanfields met online, through Love at AOL, a service of AOL intended to help singles connect.

Bill Stanfield, 47, says he can't imagine marrying a woman after dating for only a few months. But he and his wife Jacqueline wed, "and I've never regretted it. There were no surprises."

Of course, they didn't really date. They met online. "We spent hundreds and hundreds of hours communicating. There were no distractions.... I knew my first wife for three years before we got married, but I didn't know her as well as I knew Jackie."

Before heading off to cyberspace to find that special some-one, consider the suggestions offered in Table 12.1 for safer cyberdating.

Table 12.1 ▮ Guidelines for Safer Cyberdating

- Never reveal your name, home address, or phone number to someone with whom you interact in cyberspace—whether it be through a chat room or through an Internet dating service.
- If you would like to meet someone in the real world, arrange to meet at a public place. Do not give the person your address or full name.
- Let someone else know where you will be and whom you will be meeting. Arrange to call that person during the meeting or have that person call you if you have a cell phone available.
- Recognize any red flags. Does the person's life story add up, or are there gaps or inconsistencies? Does the person change his or her life story from time to time?
- Be sensitive to your feelings. Does the person express an angry tone or put any pressure on you that makes you feel uncom-fortable? Take such signs as cues to end the contact then and there.
- Don't accept the person's word at face value. People with whom you interact on the Internet may not be who they say they are.
- When in doubt, leave him or her out. It's better to be safe than sorry. If you feel something is "off" about the person, move on by.
- Enjoy yourself, but be careful.

Ingram Publishing/SUPERSTOCK

You Never Get a Second Chance to Make a First Impression
First impressions begin to be formed in the mere glimpse of an eye. Make first impressions count in your favor.

12.1.2 *B* Is for Building

After initial attraction comes the stage of building. Positive factors in building a relationship include matching physical attractiveness (see discussion of the matching hypothesis in Chapter 11), attitudinal similarity, and mutual positive evaluations. Negative factors—factors that might encourage us to dissolve the relationship—include major differences in physical attractiveness, attitudinal dissimilarity, and mutual negative evaluations.

The "Opening Line": How Do You Get Things Started?

One type of small talk is the greeting, or opening line. Greetings are usually preceded by eye contact. Reciprocation of eye contact may mean that the other person is willing to be approached. Avoidance of eye contact may mean that he or she is not willing, but it can also be a sign of shyness. In any event, if you would like to venture from initial attraction to surface contact, try a smile and some eye contact. When the eye contact is reciprocated, choose an opening line.

Here is a list of greetings, or opening lines:

- Verbal "salutes," such as "Good morning."
- Personal inquiries, such as "How are you doing?" or "Hey, like, whassup?"
- Compliments, such as "You're very attractive."
- References to your mutual surroundings, such as "What do you think of that painting?" or "This is a nice apartment house, isn't it?"
- References to people or events outside the immediate setting, such as "How do you like this weather we've been having?"
- References to the other person's behavior, such as "I couldn't help noticing you were sitting alone" or "I see you out on this track every Sunday morning."
- References to your own behavior, or to yourself, such as "Hi, my name is John Smith." (Use your own name, if you like.)
- A simple "Hi" or "Hello" is very useful. A friendly glance followed by a cheerful "hello" ought to give you some idea as to whether your feelings of attraction are reciprocated. If the "hello" is returned with a friendly smile and inviting eye contact, follow it up with another greeting, such as a reference to your surroundings, the other person's behavior, or your name.

Exchanging "Name, Rank, and Serial Number"

▮ **Surface contact** According to Levinger, a phase of a relationship in which we seek common ground and test mutual attraction.

Once we have begun a relationship with an opening line, we experiment with **surface contact**: We seek common ground (e.g., attitudinal similarity, overlap of interests). Early exchanges are likely to include name, occupation, marital status, and hometown. This kind of interaction has been referred to as exchanging "name, rank, and serial number." Each person is seeking a profile of the other in the hope that common ground will provide the footing for pursuing a conversation.

An unspoken rule seems to be at work: "If I provide you with some information about myself, you will reciprocate by giving me an equal amount of information about yourself," or " 'I'll tell you my hometown if you tell me yours'" (Knapp, 1984, p. 170). If the person does not follow this rule, it may mean that he or she is not interested. But it could also be that he or she doesn't "know the rules" or that you are turning the other person off. Small talk may sound "phony," but premature self-disclosure of personal information may repel the other person.

Not-So-Small Talk: Auditioning for Love

▮ **Small talk** A superficial form of conversation that allows people to seek common ground to determine whether they wish to pursue a relationship. Small talk stresses breadth of topic coverage rather than in-depth discussion.

We test our feelings of attraction. Whether to pursue the relationship may be decided on the basis of **small talk**. At a cocktail party, people may flit about from person to person exchanging small talk, but now and then common ground is found and people begin to pair off.

Self-Disclosure: You Tell Me and I'll Tell You... Carefully

Opening up, or self-disclosure, is central to building intimate relationships. But when you meet someone for the first time, how much can you safely disclose? If you hold back completely, you may seem uninterested or you may appear to be hiding something. But if you tell a new acquaintance that your hemorrhoids have been acting up, you are being too intimate too soon.

Research warns us against disclosing certain types of information too rapidly (Punyanunt-Carter, 2006). Consider a classic study by psychologist Camille Wortman and colleagues (Wortman et al., 1976). In this study, **confederates** of the experimenters engaged in 10-minute conversations with subjects. Some confederates were "early disclosers." They shared intimate information early in the conversations. "Late disclosers" revealed the same information but toward the end of the conversation. Subjects rated early disclosers as less mature, less secure, less well adjusted, and more phony than late disclosers. Subjects wished to pursue relationships with late disclosers but not with early disclosers. In general, people who are considered well adjusted or mentally healthy disclose much about themselves but manage to keep a lid on information that could be self-damaging or prematurely revealing.

If the surface contact in the way of small talk and initial self-disclosure is mutually rewarding, the relationship may strengthen as feelings of liking for each other deepen (Abell et al., 2006). Self-disclosure may continue to build gradually as partners come to trust each other enough to share confidences and more intimate feelings.

Let us note an important gender difference. Women often complain that men are reluctant to disclose their feelings. As we noted in Chapter 10, women tend to be more expressive of their feelings than are men (LaFrance, Hecht, & Paluck, 2003). In part, men's reluctance to "open up" reflects adherence to the traditional "strong and silent" male stereotype. Yet gender differences in self-disclosure tend to be rather small. We should thus be careful not to rush to the conclusion that men are always more "tight-lipped."

▌ **Confederate** A person in league with the researcher who pretends to be a subject in an experiment.

12.1.3 C Is for Continuation

Once a relationship has been built, it enters the stage of continuation. Factors that contribute to the continuation of a relationship (i.e., positive factors) include looking for ways to enhance variety and maintain interest, trust, caring, commitment, showing evidence of continuing positive evaluation (e.g., Valentine's Day cards), absence of jealousy, perceived equity (e.g., a fair distribution of homemaking, childrearing, and breadwinning chores), and mutual overall satisfaction.

Trust

When there is trust in a relationship, partners feel secure that disclosing intimate feelings will not lead to ridicule, rejection, or other kinds of harm. Trust usually builds gradually, as partners learn whether it is safe to share confidences. Research shows that people come to trust their partners when they see that their partners have made sincere investments in the relationship, as by making sacrifices to be with one's partner (e.g., earning the disapproval of one's family, driving one's partner somewhere rather than studying, etc.) (Wieselquist et al., 1999). Commitment and trust in a relationship can be seen as developing according to a model of **mutual cyclical growth**. According to this view:

1 Feelings that one needs one's partner and the relationship promote a strong sense of commitment to and dependence on the relationship.

2 Commitment to the relationship encourages the individuals in the relationship to do things that are good for the relationship.

3 One's partner perceives the pro-relationship behaviors of the other partner.

▌ **Mutual cyclical growth** A process by which commitment and trust in a relationship develop. According to this view, needing one's partner encourages individuals to do things that are good for the relationship, which is perceived by the partner and encourages him or her to also develop commitment and trust.

4 Perception of these pro-relationship behaviors enhances the partner's trust in the other partner and in the relationship.

5 Feelings of trust increase the willingness of the partners to increase their feelings that they need each other and the relationship.

6 And so it continues, and grows.

Caring

Caring is an emotional bond that allows intimacy to develop. In caring relationships, partners seek to gratify each other's needs and interests. Caring also involves willingness to make sacrifices for the other person.

Mutuality: When the "We," Not the "I's," Have It

▌ **Mutuality** According to Levinger, a phase of a relationship in which two people think of themselves as "we."

As commitment to the relationship grows, a cognitive shift tends to occur in which the two "I's"—that is, two independent persons—come to perceive themselves as a "we"— that is, a couple (Deci et al., 2006; Neff & Harter, 2003). People are no longer just two "I's" who happen to occupy the same place at the same time. They have attained what Levinger terms **mutuality**. Mutuality favors continuation and further deepening of the relationship. Couples begin thinking in terms of "we"—planning for the future, in little ways (What will I do this weekend?) and big ways (What will I do about my education and my career?).

Commitment

Have you ever noticed that people may open up to strangers on airplanes or trains yet find it hard to talk openly with the people to whom they are closest? An intimate relationship involves more than the isolated act of baring one's soul to a stranger. Truly intimate relationships are marked by commitment or resolve to maintain the relationship through thick and thin. When we open up to strangers on a plane, we know we are unlikely to see them again.

Commitment carries an obligation that the couple will work to overcome problems in the relationship rather than run for the exit at the first sign of trouble. Relationships are more likely to endure when the partners demonstrate a mutual level of commitment. If one member of the couple is vowing undying love while the other has his or her foot out the door, the relationship hasn't much of a future. Factors in the continuation stage that can throw the relationship into a downward spiral include lack of commitment, boredom (e.g., falling into a rut), displaying evidence of negative evaluation (e.g., bickering, forgetting anniversaries and other important dates or pretending that they do not exist), perceiving unfairness in the relationship (such as one partner's always deciding how the couple will spend their free time), or feelings of jealousy.

Jealousy

O! beware, my lord, of jealousy;
It is the green-ey'd monster...

—WILLIAM SHAKESPEARE,
OTHELLO

Thus was Othello, the Moor of Venice, warned of jealousy in the Shakespearean play that bears his name. Even so, Othello could not control his feelings, and he ultimately killed his beloved wife, Desdemona. The English poet John Dryden labeled jealousy a "tyrant of the mind."

Sexual jealousy is aroused when we suspect that an intimate relationship is threatened by a rival. Lovers can become jealous when others show sexual interest in their partners or when their partners show an interest (even a casual or nonsexual interest) in another. Jealousy can lead to loss of feelings of affection, feelings of insecurity and

TRY THIS OUT   GET THAT DATE!

All right, now you're aware that your Mr. or Ms. Right exists. What do you do about it? How do you get him or her to go out with you? Psychologists have found that we may enhance social skills, such as date-seeking skills, through successive approximations. That is, we engage in a series of tasks of graded difficulty. We fine-tune our skills and gain confidence at each level. As suggested in the context of assertiveness training (see Chapter 7), we may try out some skills through "behavior rehearsal" with friends. Friends can role-play the person we would like to ask out and provide candid "feedback" about our effectiveness. Here is a graded series of tasks that can be practiced by readers who want to sharpen their date-seeking skills.

Easy Practice Level

Select a person of the of your preferred gender with whom you are friendly but one whom you have no desire to date. Practice making small talk about the weather or about new films that have come to town, television shows, concerts, museum exhibits, political events, and personal hobbies.

Select a person you might have some interest in dating. Smile when you pass this person at work, school, or elsewhere, and say "Hi." Engage in this activity with other people of both genders to increase your skills at greeting others.

Speak into your mirror, using behavior rehearsal and role playing. Pretend you are in the process of sitting next to the person you would like to date—say, at lunch or in the laundry room. Say "Hello" with a broad smile and introduce yourself. Work on the smile until it looks inviting and genuine. Make some comment about the food or the setting—the cafeteria, the office, whatever.

Use a family member or confidant to obtain feedback about the effectiveness of the smile, your tone of voice, posture, and choice of words.

Medium Practice Level

Sit down next to the person you want to date and engage him or her in small talk. If you are in a classroom, talk about a homework assignment, the seating arrangement, or the instructor (be kind!). If you are at work, talk about the building or some recent interesting event in the neighborhood. Ask your intended date how he or she feels about the situation. If you are at some group such as Parents Without Partners, tell the other person that you are there for the first time and ask for advice on how to relate to the group.

Engage in small talk about the weather and local events. Channel the conversation into an exchange of personal information. Give your "name, rank, and serial number"—who you are, your major field or your occupation, where you're from, why or how you came to the school or company. The other person is likely to reciprocate and provide equivalent information. Ask how he or she feels about the class, place of business, city, hometown, and so forth.

Practice asking the person out before your mirror, a family member, or a confidant. You may wish to ask the person out for "a cup of coffee" or to a film. It is somewhat less threatening to ask someone out to a gathering at which "some of us will be getting together." Or you may rehearse asking the person to accompany you to a cultural event, such as an exhibition at a museum or a concert—it's "sort of" a date but less intimidating.

Target Behavior Level

Ask the person out on a date. If the person says he or she has a previous engagement or can't make it, you may wish to say something like "That's too bad" or "I'm sorry you can't make it"—and add something like "Perhaps another time." You should be able to get a feeling for whether the person you asked out was just seeking an excuse or has a genuine interest in you and, as claimed, could not in fact accept the specific invitation.

Before asking the person out again, pay attention to his or her apparent comfort level when you return to small talk on a couple of occasions. If there is still a chance, the person should smile and return your eye contact. The other person may also offer you an invitation. In any event, if you are turned down twice, do not ask a third time. And don't catastrophize the refusal. Look up. Note that the roof hasn't fallen in. The birds are still chirping in the trees. You are still paying taxes. Then give someone else a chance to appreciate your fine qualities. Trust and caring also contributes to the development of mutuality.

© Dazzo/Masterfile

Hey, What's Your Sign?
Hopefully you can do better than that. Psychologists have devised a graduated series of steps to help build date-seeking skills.

rejection, anxiety and loss of self-esteem, feelings of mistrust of one's partner and potential rivals, and the ultimate failure of the relationship. Feelings of possessiveness, which are related to jealousy, can also place stress on a relationship. In extreme cases, jealousy can cause depression or give rise to spousal abuse, suicide, or, as with Othello, murder (Puente & Cohen, 2003; Sukru, Huner, & Yerlikaya, 2004; Tilley & Brackley, 2005). But milder forms of jealousy are not necessarily destructive to a relationship. They may even serve the positive function of revealing how much one cares for one's partner.

What causes jealousy? In some cases, people become mistrustful of their current partners because their former partners had cheated. Jealousy may also derive from low self-esteem or a lack of self-confidence. People with low self-esteem may experience sexual jealousy because they become overly dependent on their partners. They may also fear that they will not be able to find another partner if their present lover leaves.

Researchers find gender differences in jealousy. Males tend to feel more insecure and threatened by sexual infidelity, whereas females seem to be more upset by emotional infidelity (e.g., Murphy et al., 2006; Shackelford, Schmitt, & Buss, 2005; Wiederman & Kendall, 1999). That is, males are made more insecure and angry when their partners have sexual relations with someone else; females are made more insecure and angry when their partners become emotionally attached to someone else.

Adjustment in the New Millenium

They Say You Can't Hurry Love... But How About Speed Dating?

This is a short story about two cable news network reporters who tried speed dating in the line of duty. But of course they also thought that it wouldn't hurt if they found someone spectacular along the way.

Allie, 25, is a fresh field reporter from the Midwest who is looking for someone who is a professional, a bit older but not too much older, who loves animals, who likes traveling, who is well-groomed, who speaks well, and who meets her minimal physical standards. He doesn't have to be Daniel Craig, but he has to take care of himself, Allie says.

Michael is a 24-year-old news editor from Delaware who would like to find someone who knows a good bottle of wine, likes the theater, reads, and is good-looking.

Allie and Michael tried speed dating so they could do a story about it. The idea behind speed dating is that singles without a lot of time to spare can meet a whole bunch of people in a short amount of time. Using HurryDate, the Manhattan dating service, Allie and Michael talked to potential soul mates for only four minutes each.

They paid HurryDate a fee, signed up for an event, posted their profiles on the HurryDate website, and attended the event at a conveniently located bar where they were matched with other single people who were each assigned a number—no names.

Then the men played musical chairs, with a switch taking place every four minutes, except that no chairs were pulled out

of the bunch. A part of the bar was cordoned off and the men sat down across from the women, with just four minutes to chat them up, back and forth. Then a whistle blew—literally!—and the men moved over a seat, and the process continued, couple by couple. After each conversation, both parties jot down quick notes on a sheet provided by HurryDate next to their current partner's number so they can remember how they reacted to them later on.

Once the event is over and the participants have returned home, they can log on to the HurryDate website and search for the numbers of the people they met at the event. They can indicate whether they would like to hear from them by entering a "yes" or a "no." Then the yesses are matched and participants can send messages through HurryDate to their matches.

What happened with Allie and Michael? See below.

Allie

I did this for a story and I didn't expect much from it. To be honest, I got from it what I expected—very little. I thought it might be amusing, and sometimes it was, but it was also sort of hectic, and if I didn't distance myself from it a bit, I think I would have found it sort of emotionally churning, if you know what I mean. I didn't think for a minute there would be a chance of meeting Mr. Right, and I was right about that. Twenty faces in an hour and a half were sort of tough going if you take this sort of thing too seriously, I guess.

Almost all the guys told me what they did for a living, though I didn't ask. Maybe they thought that was strange, but when I saw them, I guess I really didn't feel like I had to know. Some

Some researchers seek explanations of the gender difference in evolutionary theory (Shackelford, Schmitt, & Buss, 2005). Perhaps males are more upset by sexual infidelity because it confuses the issue as to whose children a woman is bearing. Women may be more upset by emotional infidelity because it threatens to deprive them of the resources they need to rear their children. However, we should recognize that that women can be as upset by sexual infidelity as men can be.

Many lovers—including many college students—play jealousy games. They let their partners know that they are attracted to other people. They flirt openly or manufacture tales to make their partners pay more attention to them, to test the relationship, to inflict pain, or to take revenge for a partner's disloyalty.

Equity

Equity involves feelings that one is getting as much from the relationship as one is giving to it. We will make great sacrifices for people whom we love, but as a relationship continues over the years, the "accumulation of too much debt" makes the relationship lopsided and unwieldy. Even if the relationship is maintained, there are likely to be resentments that may be expressed openly or indirectly, as in loss of interest in sexual relations. Dating relationships and marriages are more stable when each partner feels that the relationship is equitable.

said they were into finance with some sort of emphasis as if that was supposed to mean millions. There were a couple of teachers, no college professors. No doctors. Oh, yes—"sales," generic. Some said they lived in Manhattan, again emphasizing Manhattan, like to say they could afford it.

They asked me what I did, as if I was supposed to contribute to the rent or the mortgage. They also wanted to know where I lived and what I liked to do in my spare time. I did ask them if they traveled or liked foreign films. I wound up with 15 guys saying "yes" on the website. Truth is, I'm going to find Mr. Right another way.

Caroline Cortizo/Alamy

Michael

Allie told me about her experience, and, frankly, I guess mine was a bit better than hers. She's sort of outgoing and guys sort of flock to her, if you know what I mean. I'm outgoing when I know people, but people don't flock to me the way they flock to Allie, so the idea of meeting twenty people in an hour and a half isn't a negative for me. In fact, six of them said "yes," meaning that they're willing to have more contact with me, and of that six, I find two attractive enough in one way or another. Now, you could say that's low odds, right? One in ten. I mean I met twenty women and something could happen with two of them. But that's not bad at all. If I were out with my friends at a bar on the weekend, I might wind up talking with one woman, and the chances of her having an interest in seeing me again might be, what, one in five?

I'll say this about the four minutes. It may sound like very little, but it's more than you think. I mean you say like what do you do and what do you like and stuff, and she asks you what do you do and what do you like, and a couple of more questions, and if the answers are pretty short, you can be done in pretty much two minutes. Well, let me put it this way: If you're both kind of shy and you're both not long-winded, you might run out of stuff to say fairly quickly. Well, that's one of my problems, looking at someone and wondering what to say next.

Anyhow, and don't ask me how, with one of the women who said yes, my favorite, somehow we wound up talking about Gilbert and Sullivan and all sorts of mutual cultural interests. I guess she's the one who did it. I'm really looking forward to seeing her again!

Source: Reprinted from Rathus, Nevid, & Fichner-Rathus, 2008. Reprinted with permission of Pearson Education.

12.1.4 *D* Is for Deterioration

Deterioration is the fourth stage in the development of relationships—certainly not a stage that is desirable or inevitable. Positive factors that can prevent deterioration from occurring include investing time and effort in the relationship, working at improving the relationship, and being patient—that is, giving the relationship time for improvement. Negative factors that can advance deterioration include failing to invest time and effort in the relationship, deciding to end the relationship, or simply allowing deterioration to continue unchecked. Deterioration begins when either or both partners perceive the relationship as less desirable or worthwhile than it had once been.

Active and Passive Responses to a Deteriorating Relationship

When partners perceive a relationship to be deteriorating, they may respond in active or passive ways. Active ways of responding include taking action that might improve the relationship (e.g., enhancing communication skills, negotiating differences, getting professional help) or deciding to end the relationship. Passive responses are essentially characterized by waiting or doing nothing—that is, by sitting back and waiting for the problems in the relationship to resolve themselves or to worsen to the point where the relationship ends.

As in coping with other sources of stress, we encourage readers to take an active approach to coping with deteriorating relationships. That is, don't just allow things to happen to you. Make a decision to work to improve things, and if improvement appears to be impossible, consider the possibility of dissolving the relationship. Later in the chapter we will see that it is irrational (and harmful to a relationship) to believe that ideal relationships need not be worked on. No two of us are matched perfectly. Unless one member of the pair is a doormat, conflicts are bound to emerge. When they do, it is helpful to work to resolve them rather than to let them continue indefinitely or to pretend that they do not exist.

12.1.5 *E* Is for Ending

The ending of a relationship is the fifth and final of Levinger's stages. As with deterioration, it is not inevitable that relationships end. Various factors can prevent a deteriorating relationship from ending. For example, people who continue to find some sources of satisfaction, who are committed to maintaining the relationship, or who believe they will eventually be able to overcome their problems are more likely to invest what they must to prevent the collapse.

According to social-exchange theory, relationships draw to a close when negative forces are in sway—when the partners find little satisfaction in the affiliation, when the barriers to leaving the relationship are low (i.e., the social, religious, and financial constraints are manageable), and especially when alternative partners are available.

Problems in communication and jealousy are among the most common reasons for ending a relationship. How do relationships end? About six out of seven students at a large southeastern university reported that they ended relationships by having frank discussions about them with their partners (Knox, Zusman, & Nieves, 1998). Honesty helped them maintain friendly feelings once the romantic relationship had ended.

The swan song of a relationship—moving on—is not always a bad thing. When people are definitely incompatible, and when genuine attempts to preserve the relationship have faltered, ending the relationship can offer each partner a chance for happiness with someone else. One reason we suggest taking an active approach to coping with deteriorating relationships is that they are more likely to be dissolved before marriage takes place—or when the partners are still young and have not yet established a family. As a consequence, fewer people are likely to get hurt, and each person is more likely to attract a new, more compatible partner.

Learning more about the factors that strengthen or weaken relationships may help us develop more satisfying and lasting relationships, whether those relationships occur in the context of marriage, cohabitation, or singlehood. This information can be applied to married as well as nonmarried couples. In the next several modules in this chapter, we discuss several of the major lifestyles in America today, including marriage, singlehood, cohabitation, and stepparenting.

MODULE REVIEW

Review It

(1) The rewards and costs of maintaining a relationship are called _____ exchanges.

(2) The ABCDE model of relationships refers to attraction, building, _____, deterioration, and ending.

(3) Intimacy can be built through self-_____.

(4) Most studies show that (men or women?) _____ are more disturbed by sexual infidelity, whereas (men or women?) _____ are more disturbed by emotional infidelity.

(5) The text suggests that readers take an active response to the _____ of a relationship.

Think About It

What is meant by mutuality? How does mutuality contribute to the continuation of a relationship?

MODULE 12.2

Marriage

∎ What is the role of marriage today?

∎ What factors contribute to marital satisfaction? Are married people happier than singles?

∎ What are the attitudes of Americans toward extramarital affairs?

∎ How does an affair affect a primary relationship?

∎ How widespread is domestic violence? What motivates it?

∎ How many marriages end in divorce? Why do people get divorced?

∎ What are the financial and emotional repercussions of divorce?

It is a truth universally acknowledged that a single man in possession of a good fortune must be in want of a wife.

—JANE AUSTEN

One should always be in love. That is the reason one should never marry.

—OSCAR WILDE

All tragedies are finished by death; all comedies are ended by a marriage.

—LORD BYRON

Marriage is a great institution, but I'm not ready for an institution, yet.

—MAE WEST

Views of marriage may differ, but the fact remains that marriage is our most common lifestyle. Even in today's more liberal times, people still see marriage as a permanent commitment. A poll by the *New York Times* asked the question, "If you got

Table 12.2 ∎ Percent Who Report They Are "Very Happy," According to Marital Status		
	Married	Single
Total	57%	36%
Men	53	35
Women	62	37

Source: Chambers (2000).

married today, would you expect to stay married for the rest of your life;" and 86% of respondents answered yes (Eggers, 2000), and only 11% said no. In some cultures, such as among Hindus in India, marriage is virtually universal, with more than 99% of the females eventually marrying. Even with the diversities of lifestyles in contemporary Western society, more than three of four families in the United States (76%) are headed by a married couple ("Married Households," 2003).

Throughout Western history, marriage has helped people adjust to personal and social needs. Marriage regulates and legitimizes sexual relations. Marriage creates a home life and provides an institution for the financial support and socialization of children. Marriage provides a means of determining the father of a woman's children. So marriage also permits the orderly transmission of wealth from one generation to another and from one family to another.

Notions such as romantic love, equality, and the concept that men, like women, should aspire to the ideal of faithfulness are recent additions to the structure of marriage. Today, with the high number of people who believe that sex is acceptable within the bounds of an affectionate relationship, the desire to engage in sexual intercourse is less likely to motivate marriage. But marriage still offers a sense of emotional and psychological security—a partner with whom to share feelings, experiences, and goals.

In general, people want to get married because they believe they will be happier. Opinion polls shows that, generally speaking, married people say they are happier than single folks (Gallup Organization, 2005) (see Table 12.2). But questions of cause and effect remain muddled because of the possibility that happier folks are more likely to get married and stay married (Stein, 2005; Wallis, 2005). Moreover, although some couples report a bounce in happiness shortly after marriage, findings based on a sample of more than 24,000 people showed that life satisfaction typically returned to the level of happiness couples had had before they walked down the aisle (Lucas et al., 2003). Personal happiness seems to be more a matter of one's personal disposition or general outlook on life than marital status.

∎ **Homogamy** The principle of like marrying like.

Made in Heaven?

Purestock

Are marriages made in heaven or in the neighborhood? What factors help account for our choice of mates?

12.2.1 Whom Do We Marry? Are Marriages Made in Heaven or in the Neighborhood?

Parents today may no longer arrange their children's marriages, but many of them still encourage their children to date the charming son or daughter of that solid churchgoing couple or respectable family down the street. We tend to marry people to whom we are attracted. They are usually similar to us in physical attractiveness and hold similar attitudes on major issues. They also seem likely to meet our material, sexual, and psychological needs.

Most marriages in the United States are based on **homogamy**, the concept of like marrying like. Americans typically marry people who are similar to themselves in race, socioeconomic status, and religion. However, the number of interracial or mixed marriages has been rising rapidly and now represents about 7% of all marriages (Carey, 2005; Kennedy, 2003).

More than 9 marriages in 10 are between people of the same religion. Marriages between individuals from similar backgrounds tend to be more stable, perhaps because they tend to share values and attitudes (Willetts, 2006). As we noted in Chapter 11, we also tend to be similar to our mates in attitudes, values, personality traits, and even body weight and similarities of names.

Let us also note a tendency for some marriages to show a *mating gradient* in which women marry men who are slightly older, taller, and higher in social status. Bridegrooms tend to be two to five years older than their wives, on the average, in European, North American, and South American countries (Buss, 1994). People who are getting remarried, or marrying for the first time at later ages, are less likely to marry partners so close in age.

By and large, we seem to be attracted to and to marry the boy or girl (almost) next door in a quite predictable manner. Marriages seem to be made in the neighborhood—not in heaven. But as we have seen in the *Adjustment and Modern Life* feature on pg. 385, some marriages are made online.

Many gay couples, like many heterosexual couples, are involved in long-term committed relationships ("Sexual Orientation & Marriage", 2004). Many gay couples also take marital vows, even if their marriages are not legally sanctioned by the state. The issue of gay marriages has emerged as one of the most divisive issues of our time. Do you believe the legal institution of marriage should be limited to a union between a man and a woman? Or do you believe that marriages between committed partners should be permitted regardless of sexual orientation or gender? Or might you believe that gay couples should be permitted to form civil unions that provide the legal benefits of marriage but are not sanctioned as marriages by the state? Where do you stand on the issue of gay marriage?

12.2.2 The Marriage Contract: A Way of Clarifying Your Expectations

We are not talking about "prenuptial agreements" that hit the front pages when wealthy couples obtain divorces. This is an informal marriage contract that helps couples clarify and communicate their expectations about their forthcoming unions. Such marriage contracts are not legally binding. They are intended to help prevent couples from entering nuptials with "blinders on."

Marriage contracts encourage couples to spell out their marital values and goals. If they desire a traditional marriage in which the husband acts as breadwinner while the wife cooks, cleans, and raises the kids, they can so specify. If they desire a marriage in which each partner has an equal right to personal fulfillment through careers, or through extramarital relationships, this, too, can be specified. By discussing who will do what before they get married, couples gain insight into potential sources of conflict and have an opportunity to resolve them—or to reevaluate the wisdom of maintaining their marital plans. Couples include items like the following in the marriage contract:

1. Whether the wife will take her husband's surname, or retain her maiden name, or whether both will use a hyphenated last name
2. How household tasks will be allocated and who will be responsible for everyday activities—such as cleaning, washing, cooking, minor home repairs, and so forth
3. Whether the couple will have children and, if so, how many and at what time in the marital life cycle
4. What type of contraception to use and who will take the responsibility for using it
5. How childcare responsibilities will be divided, as well as the techniques the couple will employ in rearing the children
6. Whether they will rent or buy a place to live, and whether residential decisions will accommodate the husband's or wife's career plans (will the husband, for example, be willing to move to another city so that the wife can take advantage of a better job offer?)
7. How the breadwinning functions will be divided, who will control the family finances, and how economic decisions will be made
8. How in-law relations will be handled, and whether vacations will be spent visiting relatives
9. What proportion of leisure activities will be done apart from the spouse and what leisure activities will be done together
10. How their sexual relations will be arranged and whether fidelity will be preserved
11. How they will go about changing parts of the marital contract as the marriage progresses

Sound like a tall order? It is. Some critics note that couples entering marriage at an early age are not in a position to foresee the consequences of their current ideas. Rigid adherence to contractual specifications may hamper rather than promote marital adjustment in such cases. Couples, they assert, must be free to change their minds on certain issues and to outgrow the declarations of youth.

That is true, but a marriage contract is a record of who was thinking what, and when—not a straitjacket. Such a contract can be used to explain why one partner now has certain expectations of the other. We need not demand absolute compliance. None of us need feel bound forever by ill-conceived or impractical declarations of youth. But it may be useful to have a record of early expectations, especially when they affect another person. We should also be aware of the tendency to assume that we can change our partner's behavior once we are married. Though we can ask or encourage people to change their behavior in ways that meet our expectations, they must make the decision to actually make the change.

Positive Psychology

12.2.3 Marital Satisfaction: Is Everybody Happy?

After ecstasy, the laundry.

—ANONYMOUS

How well do we adjust to marriage? What factors contribute to marital satisfaction? Such factors as feelings of intimacy in the relationship, demonstrated by, say, sharing innermost feelings as well as sharing values and power, sexual satisfaction, general life satisfaction, and communication ability are linked to greater marital satisfaction (e.g., Grote & Clark, 2001; Patrick et al., 2007; Perrone, Webb, & Jackson, 2007). A classic research study showed that styles of communication among couples planning marriage predict marital adjustment five and a half years after vows are taken (Markman, 1981). Later in the chapter, we describe ways of improving communication skills.

Snyder (1979) constructed a questionnaire concerning areas of marital distress (see Table 12.3) and found that four areas strongly predicted overall satisfaction: expression of affection and understanding; problem-solving communication, or ability to resolve disputes; sexual dissatisfaction; and disagreement about finances, or fighting over money management. Expression of affection and capacity to resolve problems were consistently more important than problems in childrearing, history of distress in the family of origin, and sex.

Table 12.3 ∎ Factors Contributing to Marital Dissatisfaction and Sample Questionnaire Items Used in their Measurement

1. *Global distress.* "My marriage has been disappointing in several ways."
2. *Affective communication.* "I'm not sure my spouse has ever really loved me."
3. *Problem-solving communication.* "My spouse and I seem to be able to go for days sometimes without settling our differences."
4. *Time together.* "My spouse and I don't have much in common to talk about."
5. *Disagreement about finances.* "My spouse buys too many things without consulting me first."
6. *Sexual dissatisfaction.* "My spouse sometimes shows too little enthusiasm for sex."
7. *Role orientation.* "A wife should not have to give up her job when it interferes with her husband's career."
8. *Family history of distress.* "I was very anxious as a young person to get away from my family."
9. *Dissatisfaction with children.* "My children rarely seem to care how I feel about things."
10. *Conflict over childrearing.* "My spouse doesn't assume his (her) fair share of taking care of the children."

Adjustment and Modern Life

Emotional Intelligence: The Emotional Pathway to Success

Theorists propose that the ability to recognize and manage emotions is a form of intelligent behavior, or EI (Salovey & Grewal, 2005; Mayer, Salovey, & Caruso, 2008). Emotional intelligence and IQ are largely independent of each other. You probably know people whom you consider "smart" but who seem to be clueless when it comes to recognizing or understanding their own emotions or those of others. Having superior intellectual abilities may help you to make scientific discoveries or prepare brilliant legal briefs, but emotional intelligence may be more important in helping you become a successful executive or a partner in a leading law firm.

Investigators are actively exploring links between EI and adjustment. They find a number of links, or statistical associations, between EI and positive outcomes, including emotional well-being and life satisfaction, happier marriages, higher GPAs in college, and the ability of physicians to relate to patients and communicate effectively with them (Gannon & Ranzijn, 2005; Gignac, 2006; Parker, Austin, et al., 2005; Parker, Duffy, et al., 2005; Salovey & Grewal, 2005). Also, the greater the ability of spouses to accurately perceive, express, and regulate emotions, the happier their marriages tend to be (Fitness, 2001).

But just what is emotional intelligence? Although it is difficult to define precisely, we can represent the construct in terms of five main features:

1. *Recognizing your emotions.* Your ability to identify your emotions—to recognize your true feelings—is a cardinal feature of emotional intelligence.

2. *Managing your emotions.* People with high levels of emotional intelligence effectively manage their emotions. They can soothe themselves during difficult times and bounce back quickly from disappointments or setbacks.

3. *Using your emotions effectively.* People with high levels of emotional intelligence use their emotions to motivate themselves in pursuing their goals. They bring their enthusiasm, zeal, and confidence to bear on whatever goals they pursue, which helps them achieve high levels of productivity. They can constrain their impulses and needs for immediate gratification to pursue long-term goals.

4. *Identifying emotions in others.* People with high levels of emotional intelligence are attuned not only to their own emotions but also to emotions in others. Their ability to be empathic—to accurately recognize emotions in others—helps them build strong relationships and succeed in professions requiring contact with people, such as teaching, sales, management, and the helping professions.

5. *Handling emotions in relationships.* Emotional intelligence is also measured by the ability to help others deal with troubling emotions and to handle emotion-laden conflicts in the context of intimate relationships.

Yellow Dog Productions/Taxi/Getty Images, Inc.

What's Your Emotional IQ?

Emotional intelligence may be an important contributor to a successful marriage as well as a successful career. People with high emotional intelligence are attuned not only to their own emotions but to the emotions of others.

Let's turn it around to you. Although we lack a validated self-report scale of emotional intelligence, the following questions should give you some insight into how you measure up on the construct. Your answers are not for public consumption, so answer them as honestly as you can in terms of your real self, not your imagined or ideal self.

1. Would you say (honestly now) that
   (a) you generally go through the day without paying attention to your emotions, OR
   (b) you are generally attuned to your feelings?

2. Would you say that
   (a) your emotions tend to get all lumped together, OR
   (b) you are able to clearly discriminate one emotion from another?

3. Would you say that
   (a) you seldom if ever experience negative emotions, such as anger or fear, OR
   (b) you are able to recognize these emotions when you experience them?

4. Would you say that
   (a) you deny feeling strong positive emotions, such as love or joy, OR
   (b) you recognize these feelings when they occur?

5. Would you say that
   (a) you are able to recognize emotions in others, OR
   (b) you have a hard time reading emotions in other people?
6. Would you say that
   (a) you try to understand what people are feeling, OR
   (b) you would rather not deal with that mushy stuff?
7. Would you say that
   (a) you tend to focus on what people say, not what they must be feeling, OR
   (b) you tend to focus on both what people say and what they must be feeling?
8. If someone starts crying or gets angry, do you
   (a) just want to leave the scene, OR
   (b) seek to calm or comfort the person?

9. If you get into an argument with your partner or a family member, do you
   (a) just try to stop the argument by becoming silent, OR
   (b) try to focus on the issues and resolve them?
10. If someone has a gripe with you, do you
    (a) immediately jump to defend yourself, OR
    (b) try to understand the situation from the other person's perspective?

Did you detect a pattern? These items are scaled such that (b) responses are keyed to be reflective of emotional intelligence. How did you do? Would you consider yourself to be emotionally intelligent or emotionally challenged? Do you think you can change how you deal with your own emotions and how you respond to emotions in others? How would you go about it?

12.2.4 Extramarital Affairs: On Truth and Consequences

Women seek soul mates; men seek playmates. Women believe that their affair is justified when it is for love; men, when it's not for love.

—JANIS ABRAHMS SPRING (1997)

There are times when it seems that nearly every married person is having an affair. Viewers of TV talk shows may get the impression that everyone cheats, but surveys paint a different picture: More than 90% of the married women and 75% of the married men in a landmark sex survey reported remaining loyal to their mates (Laumann et al., 1994). The overwhelming majority—86%—of respondents to a *New York Times* poll reported that they were "absolutely certain" that their partners were faithful to them (Eggers, 2000).

What can we conclude? Perhaps two things: One is that men are about twice as likely as women to admit to affairs. Yet only a minority of married people admit to affairs.

Those are the conclusions, but note that we said "admit to affairs." The fact is that the percentages of reported affairs cannot be verified. People may be reluctant to reveal that they have "cheated" on their spouses even when they are assured of anonymity. There is likely to be an overall tendency to underreport the incidence of extramarital sex.

Why do people have affairs? Some people have affairs for the sake of variety (Lamanna & Riedman, 2005; Reynolds, Barlow, & Pedersen, 2006). Others seek to break the routine of a confining marriage. Still others have affairs for reasons akin to the nonsexual reasons sometimes given by adolescents—for example, as a way of expressing hostility (in this case, toward a spouse, not a parent) or as a way of retaliating for injustice. People who have affairs often report that they are not happy with their marital relationships, but curiosity and the desire for personal growth are cited as more common reasons than marital dissatisfaction. Some middle-aged people have affairs to boost their self-esteem or to prove they are still attractive.

Do You Endorse a Traditional or a Liberal Marital Role?

Self-Assessment

What do you believe? Should the woman cook and clean, or should housework be shared? Should the man be the bread-winner, or should each couple define their own roles? Are you traditional or nontraditional in your views on marital roles for men and women?

Directions: The following items permit you to indicate the degree to which you endorse traditional roles for men and women in marriage. Answer each one by circling the letters (AS, AM, DM, or DS), according to the code given below. Then turn to the key at the end of the chapter to find out whether you tend to be traditional or nontraditional in your views. (Ignore the numbers beneath the codes for the time being.) You may also be interested in seeing whether the answers of your date or your spouse show some agreement with your own.

AS = agree strongly
AM = agree mildly
DM = disagree mildly
DS = disagree strongly

1. A wife should respond to her husband's sexual overtures even when she is not interested.

AS	AM	DM	DS
1	2	(3)	4

2. In general, the father should have greater authority than the mother in the bringing up of children.

AS	AM	DM	DS
1	2	3	(4)

3. Only when the wife works should the husband help with housework.

AS	AM	DM	DS
1	2	(3)	4

4. Husbands and wives should be equal partners in planning the family budget.

AS	AM	DM	DS
(1)	2	3	4

5. In marriage, the husband should make the major decisions.

AS	AM	DM	DS
1	2	(3)	4

6. If both husband and wife agree that sexual fidelity isn't important, there's no reason why both shouldn't have extramarital affairs if they want to.

AS	AM	DM	DS
1	2	3	(4)

7. If a child gets sick and his wife works, the husband should be just as willing as she to stay home from work and take care of that child.

AS	AM	DM	DS
(1)	2	3	4

8. In general, men should leave the housework to women.

AS	AM	DM	DS
1	2	3	(4)

9. Married women should keep their money and spend it as they please.

AS	AM	DM	DS
1	2	(3)	4

10. In the family, both of the spouses ought to have as much say on important matters.

AS	AM	DM	DS
(1)	2	3	4

Source: Karen Oppenheim Mason, with the assistance of Daniel R. Denison and Anita J. Schacht. *Sex-role attitude items and scales from U.S. sample surveys.* Rockville, MD: National Institute of Mental Health, 1975, pp. 16–19.

For an interactive version of this self-assessment exercise, go to www.wileyplus.com

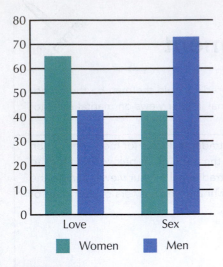

Figure 12.2
Why Do People Have Extramarital Affairs?
Women are more likely than men to justify affairs for reasons of love. Men are more likely than women to cite sexual excitement as the reason for the affair.
Sources: Glass & Wright, 1992; Townsend, 1995.

Sexual motives are frequently less pressing than the desire for emotional closeness. Some women say they are seeking someone to whom they can talk or with whom they can communicate (Lamanna & Riedmann, 2005). There is a notable gender difference here. According to Janis Abrahms Spring, author of *After the Affair* (a self-help book designed to help people save their marriages after an affair), men may be seeking sex in affairs ("playmates"). Women, however, are usually seeking "soul mates." Spring (1997) notes that "women believe that their affair is justified when it is for love; men, when it's not for love." As you can see in Figure 12.2, 77% of the women who have had affairs cite love as their justification, versus 43% of the men (Townsend, 1995).

Writing about how men and women differ, UCLA psychologist Letitia Anne Peplau notes that men are more likely than women to distinguish between sex and love, whereas women are more likely to see sex and love as closely linked together (Peplau, 2003). Consequently, women are more likely to regard love as a precondition for sexual intimacy. However, it is important to note that these are general group differences. Many men connect emotional and sexual intimacy, and many women seek sexual flings.

Despite a liberalization of sexual attitudes in recent years, most couples continue to value fidelity as a cornerstone of marriage (Silva, 2005; Smart, 2006). Three out of four Americans say that extramarital sex is "always wrong" (Berke, 1997). Another one in seven say that it is "almost always wrong." Only about 1% say that extramarital affairs are "not at all wrong." Most married couples embrace the value of monogamy as the cornerstone of their marital relationship.

Thus, even the majority of today's sophisticated young people see something wrong with an occasional fling. The sexual revolution never extended itself to affairs—at least among the majority of people who have primary relationships. The sexual revolution may have liberalized attitudes toward premarital sex, but the message here seems to be that once people make commitments, they are expected to keep them.

The discovery of infidelity can evoke strong emotional responses. The spouse (or cohabitant) may be filled with anger, jealousy, even shame. Feelings of inadequacy and doubts about one's attractiveness and desirability may surface. The betrayed individual may see infidelity as a serious breach of trust and intimacy. Primary relationships that are not terminated in the wake of the disclosure may survive only in damaged form.

The harm an affair does to a primary relationship may reflect the meaning of the affair to the individual and his or her partner. Deborah Lamberti, director of a counseling and psychotherapy center in New York City, points again to women's traditional intertwining of sex with relationships; she argues that "men don't view sex with another person as a reason to leave a primary relationship" (1997, pp. 131–132). Betrayed women may recognize this and be able to tell themselves that their partners are sleeping with someone else just for physical reasons. But women are more concerned about remaining monogamous. Therefore, if a woman is sleeping with another man, she may already have a foot out the door, so to speak. Whereas a woman's affair may be an unforgivable blow to a man's ego or pride, a woman may be more likely to see her partner's transgression as a threat to the structure of her life (Alterman, 1997).

If a person has an affair because the relationship is deeply troubled, the affair may be one more factor that speeds its dissolution. The effects on the relationship may depend on the nature of the affair. It may be easier to understand that one's partner has fallen prey to an isolated, unplanned encounter than to accept an extended affair. In some cases, the discovery of infidelity stimulates the couple to work to improve their relationship. If the extramarital activity continues, of course, it may undermine the couple's efforts to restore their relationship. Affairs frequently lead to divorce, a topic we will soon discuss.

12.2.5 Intimate Partner Violence

When it comes to the risk of physical assault, women are much more likely to be raped, injured, or killed by their current or former partners than by strangers or other assailants. Intimate partner violence, or IPV, has become a social epidemic in our society. Estimates are that as many as 1.5 million to 2 million women in the United States are physically assaulted or raped by their partners each year (Bell & Naugle, 2008; Murphy, 2003). Tragically, about 2,000 women in the United States are killed each year by their intimate partners.

Domestic violence knows no cultural boundaries. Worldwide, one of three women have been beaten or sexually or emotionally abused by their partners (Murphy, 2003).

It may surprise you to learn that women are just as likely as men to be violent in their intimate relationships. In about half of the couples in which domestic violence occurs, both partners are guilty of physical abuse. However, women are more likely than men to sustain physical injuries such as broken bones and other internal damage.

Male domestic violence often stems from factors that threaten their traditional dominance in relationships, such as unemployment and substance abuse. Women's violence often arises from the stress of coping with an abusive partner (Magdol et al., 1997).

Domestic violence is found at all levels in society, but it is reported more commonly among people of lower socioeconomic status. This difference may reflect the greater amount of stress experienced by people who are struggling financially. In many cases, a disparity in income between partners such that the woman earns more than the man, not poverty per se, may contribute to domestic violence.

Domestic violence often follows a triggering event such as criticism or rejection by one's partner or incidents that cause the man to feel trapped, insecure, or threatened. The use of alcohol or other drugs often plays a role with respect to inciting or triggering battering (Bell & Naugle, 2008; Foran & O'Leary, 2008). In addition, male batterers often have low self-esteem and a sense of personal inadequacy. They may become dependent on their partners for emotional support and feel threatened if they perceive their partners becoming more independent. Feminist theorists look upon domestic violence as a product of the power relationships that exist between men and women in our society. Men may be socialized into dominant roles in which they expect women to be subordinate to their wishes. Men learn that aggressive displays of masculine power are socially sanctioned and even glorified in some venues, such as athletics. These role expectations, together with a willingness to accept interpersonal violence as an appropriate means of resolving differences, create a context for domestic violence when the man perceives his partner to be threatening his sense of control or failing to meet his needs. Men who batter may also have less power in their relationships and may be attempting to make up for it by means of force.

Many social commentators and scholars argue that our society supports domestic violence by appearing to condone it. The man who beats his wife may be taken aside and "talked to" by a police officer, rather than arrested and prosecuted. Even if he is prosecuted and convicted, his punishment is likely to be less severe (sometimes just a "slap on the wrist") than if he had assaulted a stranger.

Michael Newman/PhotoEdit

Domestic Violence
Women stand a greater chance of being raped, injured, or killed by their current or former partners than by other assailants. Estimates suggest that about one in eight women are assaulted by their partners each year. About 2,000 women die each year as the result of domestic violence.

© David Young-Wolff/PhotoEdit

Children Are Listening
The effects of verbal or physical abuse in the marital relationship can affect the children as well as the spouses themselves. Children who are exposed to domestic violence may develop behavioral problems or emotional disorders, such as depression.

12.2.6 Divorce

My wife and I were considering a divorce, but after pricing lawyers we decided to buy a new car instead.

—COMEDIAN HENNY YOUNGMAN

Whenever I date a guy, I think, is this the man I want my children to spend their weekends with?

—COMEDIAN RITA RUDNER

In 1920, about one marriage in seven ended in divorce; by 1960, this figure had risen to one in four. Today, some 40% to 50% of first marriages in the United States end in divorce, and the percentage soars to about 65% for second marriages. Nearly 40% of European American children and about 75% of African American children in the United States who are born to married parents will spend at least part of their childhoods in single-parent families as a result of divorce (Marsiglio, 2004). Today, more than one-quarter (27%) of children below the age of 18 live in single-parent households. Divorced women outnumber divorced men, in part because men are more likely to remarry.

The relaxation of legal restrictions on divorce, especially the introduction of the so-called no-fault divorce, has made divorces easier to obtain. Until the mid-1960s, adultery was the only legal grounds for divorce in New York State. Other states were equally strict. But now no-fault divorce laws have been enacted in nearly every state, allowing a divorce to be granted without a finding of marital misconduct. The increased economic independence of women has also contributed to the rising divorce rate. More women today have the economic means of breaking away from a troubled marriage. Today, more people consider marriage an alterable condition than they did in prior generations.

People today hold higher expectations of marriage than did their parents or grandparents. They expect marriage to be personally fulfilling as well as meet the traditional expectation of marriage as an institution for rearing children. Many demand the right to be happy in marriage. The most common reasons given for a divorce today are problems in communication and a lack of understanding. Key predictors of divorce today include a husband's criticism, defensiveness, contempt, and stonewalling—not lack of support (Carrère et al., 2000).

Why do Americans believe that the divorce rate has risen so high? A Time/CNN poll asked a national sample, "Which is the main reason for the increase in the number of divorces?" Answers are shown in Table 12.4. Respondents were almost equally split in their answer to the question, "Do you believe it should be harder than it is for married couples to get a divorce?" Half (50%) said yes, and 46% said no.

Table 12.4 ▮ **Reasons Given for the Increased Number of Divorces in the United States, According to a *Time/CNN* Poll**

Reason	Percent of Respondents Citing Reason as the One Main Reason
Marriage is not taken seriously by the couples.	45%
Society has become more accepting of divorced people.	15%
It is easier to get divorced than it used to be.	10%
People who get divorced are selfish.	9%
The earning power of women and men has changed.	7%
All of the above	9%

The Cost of Divorce

When a household splits, the resources may not maintain the former standard of living for both partners (Donald et al., 2006; Lorenz et al., 2006). Women and children typically experience the most significant drop in standard of living after a divorce and are more likely to be living in poverty. The divorced woman who has not pursued a career may find herself competing for work with younger, more experienced people. The divorced man may not be able to manage alimony and child support and also establish a new home of his own.

Adjustment to divorce can be more difficult than adjustment to death of a spouse. When a spouse dies, legalities are minimal. But divorce may require legal conflict, reams of documents, and seemingly endless waiting periods. (The use of **divorce mediation**, in which the couple are guided through the decisions required by divorce in a cooperative spirit rather than as adversaries, may help reduce some of the stresses of the process.) When someone dies, the rest of the family remains intact. After a divorce, children and others may choose sides and assign blame. After a death, people receive "compassionate leave" from work and are expected to be less productive for a while. After a divorce, they are commonly criticized. Death is final, but divorced people may nourish "what-ifs?" and vacillate in their emotions.

People who are separated and divorced have the highest rates of adjustment problems and psychological disorders in the population (Carrère et al., 2000; Gottman et al., 1998). Divorced people are subject to greater stress and feel that they exert less control over their lives. Feelings of failure as a spouse and parent, loneliness, and uncertainty prompt feelings of depression.

The hardest aspect of divorce may be separating psychologically from one's "ex." Severing links to the past and becoming a whole, autonomous person once more—or in the case of women who had held traditional attitudes, for the first time—can be the greatest challenge but also the most constructive aspect of adjustment to divorce.

Generation EX: The Children of Divorce

Divorce takes a toll on children as well as parents (Amato, 2006; Barnes, 2005). Divorce can turn the child's world topsy-turvy. The simple things that had been taken for granted are no longer simple: Eating meals and going on trips with both parents, curling up with either parent to read a book or watch television, or kissing both parents at bedtime come to an end. Divorced parents must support two households, not one. Children of divorce thus most often suffer downward movement in socioeconomic status. If the downward movement is not severe, it may require minor adjustments. But many children who live in father-absent homes scrape by below the poverty level. In severe cases, the downward trend can mean moving from a house into a cramped apartment or from a more desirable to a less desirable neighborhood. Mother may suddenly be required to join or rejoin the workforce and place her children in day care. Such women typically suffer the stresses of task overload as well as the other problems of divorce.

One of the major conflicts between parents is differences in childrearing practices. Children of parents who get a divorce have frequently heard them arguing about how they should be reared, so young children may erroneously blame themselves. Younger children also tend to be fearful of the unknown. Adolescents have had more of an opportunity to learn that they can exert some control over what happens to them.

Ex-husbands, ex-wives, ex-families—one could say that about half the children in the United States belong to "generation ex." The great majority of the children of divorce live with their mothers. Visitation by their fathers may begin regularly in the months after the divorce but then drop off over time. Also, many divorced fathers fail to keep up their child-support payments, exacerbating the family's downward trend in socioeconomic status.

Research results are mixed concerning the effects of divorce. Studies show that the children of divorced people are more likely to have behavioral problems, engage in substance abuse, and earn lower grades in school (Amato, 2006; O'Connor et al.,

∎ **Divorce mediation** A process in which a couple getting a divorce are guided rationally and reasonably amicably through the decisions that must be made.

© Bob Daemmrich/The Image Works

The Costs of Divorce
Divorce usually creates serious adjustment problems for the couple and their children. The standard of living for all family members is usually lowered. Meals often become catch-as-catch-can as family life disintegrates. Divorce is connected with high rates of psychological disorders and suicide. Does this mean that battling couples should stay together? Not necessarily. Being in the midst of a parental war is no bed of roses for the children, and separation sometimes allows mismatched members of couples to grow. The choices are difficult, and the outcomes are almost always stressful in one way or another.

2000). Children's problems tend to increase during the first year after divorce, but they regain much of their equilibrium after two years. Boys tend to have greater problems adjusting to conflict or divorce, such as conduct problems at school and increased anxiety and dependence. After a couple of years go by, girls by and large cannot be distinguished in terms of general adjustment from girls from intact families.

We should recognize that children in troubled marriages may fare no better, and may even fare worse, than those in divorced families (Furstenberg & Kiernan, 2001; Troxel & Matthews, 2004). Yet we should be aware of potential "sleeper effects" in children affected by divorce. Children who were apparently adjusting to divorce may develop later problems, such as when they are about to enter their own intimate relationships (Wallerstein, Lewis, & Blakeslee, 2000). They may find, for example, that they do not trust their partners to make lasting commitments.

Researchers attribute children's problems not only to divorce itself but also to the emotional strain on the caretaking parent and the decline in the quality of parenting that may follow (Clarke-Stewart et al., 2000; Hetherington, 2006; Hetherington & Kelly, 2003). The organization of family life tends to deteriorate. The family is more likely to eat their meals "pickup style." Children are less likely to get to school on time or to bed at a regular hour. It is more difficult for single mothers to set limits on sons' behavior. In all likelihood, children will fare better in homes with capable and well-adjusted parents than in homes with constantly bickering parents.

Though divorce can be hard on the children, psychologists often advise that parents can protect their children and minimize the impact of divorce by taking steps such as the following (Nevid, 2007):

- Try, in spite of their differences, to agree on how to handle the children
- Help each other maintain important roles in the children's lives
- Do not criticize or disparage each other in front of the children

12.2.7 Adjustment in Stepparent Families

More than one in three children in the United States will spend part of childhood in a stepfamily (U.S. Bureau of the Census, 2005). So the effects of stepparenting are also a key issue in American family life today.

The adjustment of children in blended families depends in large part on the quality of the relationships with stepparents. Stepfathers can have positive effects on stepsons, and stepmothers on stepdaughters. In an influential early study of the effects of stepparenting on middle-schoolers, positive stepmother–stepchild relationships were associated with lower aggression in boys and girls and with higher self-esteem in girls (Clingempeel & Segal, 1986). Frequent visits with the nonresident natural mother appeared to impair stepmother–stepdaughter relations. Perhaps they encouraged resistance by stepdaughters to forming a relationship with the stepmother. On the other hand, stepmother–stepdaughter relationships generally improved over time.

Most divorced people, about 70% to 75%, eventually remarry, usually within five years. But are they more likely to "get it right" the second time around and stay married through "thick and thin"? Actually, later marriages are more likely than first marriages to end in divorce. One reason perhaps is that people who divorce are less likely than those who stay married to stick it out when they encounter significant relationship problems. Conflicts involving stepchildren can also contribute to marital strain in reconstituted families—

Digital Vision/Getty Images, Inc

Stepfamilies
More than one in three children in the United States spend part of their childhood in a stepfamily. What does psychological research teach about stepparent–stepchild relationships? What observations have you made about these relationships?

Adjustment and Modern Life

Dating Again

"Love is lovelier," goes the lyric from a popular song of the 1950s, "the second time around." Love may be lovelier, but for many newly single people reentering the dating scene after a divorce, death of a spouse, or marital separation, the prospects of dating again seem anything but "lovely." As one 39-year-old divorced man put it, "I felt like a failure going into a singles bar. It had been almost 20 years since I stepped into one of those places. I didn't feel comfortable dating back then. Now I feel like used goods." A 42-year-old widowed woman said, "I look around and all I can see is these younger women desperately seeking men. How am I going to compete with them? Do I look as desperate?"

In our society, in which nearly half of all marriages end in divorce, many people who felt that they had moved past the dating stage of life are finding themselves smack back in the middle of the singles scene. But dating at age 30 or 40 or 50 or above is unlike dating the first time around. For many long-married people, the idea of becoming sexually intimate with another person poses major hurdles. As one woman in her forties put it, "I was never that comfortable with my sexuality to begin with. I was raised with the idea of finding one partner for life. Now to take another man into my bed—the very thought gives me chills." People who are widowed may feel as if they are betraying their deceased spouse. Newly single parents may feel that having an intimate relationship with a new partner would send the "wrong message" to the kids. Said a 37-year-old divorced woman who established an intimate relationship with a man, "We do it in secret—during the day when the kids are in school. It makes me feel dirty, like I'm ashamed that there's a new man in my life. But I don't want the kids to think that they have a new daddy."

A 42-year-old divorced father expressed similar sentiments: "It's become so complicated. I know the kids still hold out hope that Janice [his ex-wife] and I will get back together. When I introduce them to a new woman I'm seeing, I can just see the disappointment in their faces. I can't expect them to be happy for me and it makes me feel guilty if I feel happy."

Although some divorced people prefer to remain single, the great majority remarry. On the downside, however, evidence shows that remarriages are even more likely than first marriages to end in divorce (Lown & Dolan, 1988). One reason may be that people who divorce in the first place have more accepting attitudes toward divorce than those who decide to stick with marriage through "thick and thin." If you are unattached again and contemplating reentering the dating scene, you may find it helpful to review the following tips, which are offered by a website specializing in providing resources and information to single-parent families:

1. *Give yourself time to heal before establishing a new relationship.* Jumping into a new relationship is sometimes tempting. However, rushing into another relationship is usually a way to avoid the pain of the breakup. Give yourself time to heal and rebuild your life.

2. *Establish good routines and structures in your family.*

3. *Children thrive on consistency.* Having predictable structures set up in the family will ease feelings of insecurity when a new person is introduced.

4. *Keep dating time and parenting time separate* (for noncustodial parents especially).

5. *Children need to know that their time is important.* Children will often resent the new person if they feel their special time is being intruded on.

6. *Avoid sleepovers with the new person when the children are present.*

7. *Introduce the new person only when you think the relationship has long-term potential.* New relationships might not work out, so wait awhile before you introduce the new person to your children. Introducing many people in the children's life creates confusion and insecurity.

8. *Don't have the children refer to the new person as a relative.*

9. *Telling the child to call the new person Mom, Dad, Uncle, etc., is too confusing, particularly if the relationship doesn't work out.* Have the children use the first name of the new person.

10. *Go slowly.* For instance, introduce the children to a new person first before including them in family activities. A new person who is worth having in your life will understand your need to ease them into your children's lives.

Source: Suggestions reprinted from Single Parent Central, www.single-parentcentral.com, which offers information and resources to single-parent families. ©2000 SingleParentCentral.com.

conflicts that often center around the financial strain of supporting children from two or more marriages or tendencies to favor one's biological children (Golish, 2003; Hofferth & Anderson, 2003).

Is it better for the children for parents to remain together despite their differences? Our answers cannot address moral issues, only psychological ones. Students will have to weigh moral questions about the advisability of divorce in terms of their own values. But let us note that marital conflict and constant bickering can lead to the same kinds of problems as divorce, causing psychological distress in both children and adolescents. Developmental psychologists E. Mavis Hetherington and John Kelly go even further in arguing that divorce can be a positive solution to destructive family functioning (Hetherington & Kelly, 2003).

MODULE REVIEW

Review It

(6) _____ is our most common lifestyle.

(7) (Married or Single?) people report that they are happier.

(8) The concept of like marrying like is termed _____.

(9) The text suggests the use of a _____ _____ to clarify and communicate one's expectations of marriage.

(10) Research suggests that most men who have extramarital affairs are seeking sex, whereas most women who do so are seeking _____ _____.

(11) The great majority of Americans (approve or disapprove?) of extramarital affairs.

(12) Today 40% to 50% of _____ marriages in the United States end in divorce.

(13) (Boys or Girls?) usually have greater problems in the first few years after a parental divorce.

(14) More than _____ in three children in the U.S. will spend some time growing up in a stepfamily.

(15) (Men or Women?) are more likely to be injured by domestic violence.

Think About It

Why do you think that marriage remains our most common lifestyle?

MODULE 12.3

Being Single

- What is the "singles scene" like today?
- What are some reasons couples cohabit?
- What is the relationship between cohabitation and later marital success?

More young people today are single than ever before. In fact, singlehood, not marriage, is the nation's most common lifestyle among people in their early to mid-twenties. There may be a saying that "marriages are made in heaven," but many people in the United States are saying that heaven can wait.

Remaining single has become more socially acceptable. There was a time when single women over the age of 30 were stereotyped as either "spinsters" or "loose" and single men as perennial bachelors. For many young people today, remaining single is not simply a way station while they wait for Mr. or Ms. Right to come along. Many view singlehood as a lifestyle choice that fits their personal and career needs. Social norms, too, are shifting, so people feel it is more acceptable to maintain a sexually intimate relationship without marriage or to raise a child without a spouse or partner. As more women enter careers, they are no longer financially dependent on men, and so a number of them choose to remain single. Table 12.5 presents a snapshot of single women today.

Table 12.5 ■ A Statistical Portrait of Single Women in the United States

1. Forty years ago, 83% of American women aged 25 to 55 were married, as compared with about 65% today.

2. When women were asked what they missed most due to being single, 75% answered "companionship" and only 4% said sex.

3. The birth rate has been falling among teenagers but climbing among single adult women. It is up 15% in the past 10 years among women in their thirties.

4. Three single women in five (61%), aged 18–49, say they would consider rearing a child on their own.

5. Single women have gained economic power. Single women bought about 20% of the homes for sale in 1999, double the percentage in 1985.

6. Only about one-third (34%) of single women said they would settle for a less-than-perfect mate if they had to, as compared with 41% of men.

Source: Poll results reported by Time Magazine/CNN.

Table 12.6 shows a steady increase in the percentage of never-married adults over the past 40 years. The proportions of 20- and early 30-somethings who have remained single have more than doubled since 1970 (Edwards, 2000). By the beginning of the new millennium, one woman in four and three men in ten in the United States 15 years of age and older had never been married. Half a century earlier, in 1950, one woman in five and about one man in three aged 15 or older had never been married.

In the United States, most people still get married, but today about 28% of people aged 15 and above have never married. Marriage may not be going out of fashion, but the traditional family unit (married couple with children under 18) is becoming less prevalent. The traditional family unit now comprises only about one quarter of American households, as compared to about four in ten in 1970.

Families today come in all varieties, from the traditional family unit to families consisting of stepparents and stepchildren, adoptive families with one or two parental figures, and gay partners with children. The number of single-mother family groups has doubled over the past 30 years, to more than a quarter of all family units (U.S. Bureau of the Census, 2005). Although some of these family units are the result of divorce, many women today started their families as single mothers.

Cohabitation is also increasing in the United States, having risen 10-fold from 1960, from less than half a million couples to about 5 or 6 million couples today (Kurdek, 2005; Whitehead & Popenoe, 2006). About one in nine of these households comprise

Lise Gagne/iStockphoto

The "Singles Scene"?
Actually, there is no single singles scene in the United States. Yes, some people are swinging singles who value sexual novelty and engage in a series of one-night stands. Other singles engage in sexual activity not at all, infrequently, or in serial monogamous relationships. Some people see being single as a preferred way of life. For others, singlehood is a way station on the path to an enduring, committed relationship.

Table 12.6 ■ Current Marital Status of People in the United States (15 Years and Older)

Year	Males		Females	
	Currently married	Never married	Currently married	Never married
2005	55.9%	31.0%	51.0%	25.5%
1990	60.7	29.9	56.9	22.8
1980	63.2	29.6	58.9	22.5
1970	66.8	28.1	61.9	22.1
1960	69.3	25.3	65.0	19.0
1950	67.5	26.4	65.8	20.0

Source: U.S. Census Bureau; 2005 data based on 2005 American Community Survey

Table 12.7 ❙ Changes in Median Age at First Marriage		
Year	Males	Females
2005	27.0	25.5
1990	26.1	23.9
1980	24.7	22.0
1970	23.2	20.8
1960	22.8	20.3
1950	22.8	20.3

Source: U.S. Census Bureau; 2005 data based on 2005 American Community Survey

same-sex partners (Simons & O'Connell, 2003). Cohabitation rates are about twice as high among African American couples as European American couples (Laumann, Mahay, & Youm, 2007).

Many factors contribute to the increased proportion of single people. One is that more people are postponing marriage to pursue educational and career goals. Many young people are deciding to live together (cohabit), at least for a while, rather than get married. People are also getting married at later ages. The typical man in the United States gets married at the age of 27 today, as compared with the age of 23 in 1950 (see Table 12.7). The typical woman gets married today at about the age of 25, as compared with the age of 20 in 1950. Many single people, of course, are not single by choice. Some remain single because they have not yet found Mr. or Ms. Right.

There is no single "singles scene." Being single is varied in intent and style of life. For some, it means singles bars and a string of one-night affairs. There are also singles apartment complexes, some of which permit nude sunbathing and swimming (children and married couples not allowed, thank you). Some "swinging singles" do not want to be "trapped" with a single partner. They opt for many partners for the sake of novel sexual stimulation, the personal growth that can be attained through meeting many people, and the maintenance of independence. Yet many singles have become disillusioned with frequent casual sexual involvements. The singles bar provokes anxieties about physical and sexual abuse, fear of sexually transmitted infections, and feelings of alienation as well as opportunities for sexual experience. Other single people limit sex to affectionate relationships only. Some singles achieve emotional security through a network of friends.

Many single people find that being single is not always as free as it seems. Some complain that employers and coworkers view them with skepticism and are reluctant to assign them responsibility. Their families may see them as selfish, as failures, or as sexually loose. Many single women complain that once they have entered their mid-twenties, men are less willing to accept a "No" at the end of a date. Men assume that they are no longer virgins and that their motives for saying no are to play games or snare them into marriage.

The goals and values that seem rock solid in the twenties may be shaken in the thirties. The singles scene, too, can pall. In their late twenties and thirties, many singles decide that they would prefer to get married and have children. For women, of course, the "biological clock" may seem to be running out during the thirties. Yet some people—of both genders—choose to remain single for a lifetime. Some who remain single live with their partners. It is that topic we discuss next.

12.3.1 Cohabitation: "Would You Be My POSSLQ"?

There's Nothing That I Wouldn't Do If You Would Be My POSSLQ is the name of a book by CBS newsperson Charles Osgood. POSSLQ? That's the unromantic abbreviation for "person of opposite sex sharing living quarters"—the official term used for cohabiters by the U.S. Census Bureau.

❙ **Cohabitation** An intimate relationship in which—pardon us—POSSLQ's (pronounced POSS-l-cues) live as though they are married, but without legal sanction.

Cohabitation may not yet be fully accepted in the social mainstream, but contemporary society has become more tolerant of it. Today we seldom hear of cohabitation as "living in sin" or "shacking up," as we once did. Instead, people are more likely to refer to cohabitation with value-free expressions such as "living together."

The greater public acceptance of cohabiting or nontraditional households may reflect society's adjustment to the increase in the number of cohabiting couples. Or perhaps the numbers of cohabiting couples have increased as a consequence of tolerance. The numbers of cohabiting households has risen from fewer than half a million in 1960 to about 5 million today (Whitehead & Popenoe, 2006). More than half of all marriages today are preceded by a period of cohabitation (Bramlett & Mosher, 2002).

Who Cohabits?

Although much attention is focused on college students living together, cohabitation cuts across all age groups and socioeconomic levels in our society. We are fast approaching a time when the majority of adults living in the United States will cohabit at some time.

Cohabitation also cuts across sexual orientations. Gay couples comprise about one in nine unmarried cohabitating couples (Simons & O'Connell, 2003). Investigators find that gay men and lesbians in cohabiting couples are about as happy with their relationships as are cohabiting heterosexual couples (Means-Christensen, Snyder, & Negy, 2003).

Children are common in cohabiting households. Nearly half of the divorced people who are cohabiting with new partners have children in the household (Smock, 2000). At least one out of three households with never-married cohabiting couples also have children living with them.

Why Do People Cohabit?

Cohabitation, like marriage, is an alternative to the loneliness that can accompany living alone. Cohabitation, like marriage, creates a home life. Romantic partners may have deep feelings for each other but not be ready to get married. Some couples prefer cohabitation because it provides a consistent relationship without the legal constraints of marriage (Marquis, 2003).

Many cohabiters feel less commitment toward their relationships than married people do. Ruth, an 84-year-old woman, has been living with her partner, age 85, for four years. "I'm a free spirit," she says. "I need my space. Sometimes we think of marriage, but then I think that I don't want to be tied down" (cited in Steinhauer, 1995, p. C7).

Ruth's comments are of interest because they counter stereotypes of women and older people. However, it is more often the man who is unwilling to make a marital commitment, as in the case of Mark. Mark, a 44-year-old computer consultant, lives with Nancy and their 7-year-old daughter, Janet. Mark says, "We feel we are not primarily a couple but rather primarily individuals who happen to be in a couple. It allows me to be a little more at arm's length. Men don't like committing, so maybe this is just some sort of excuse" (cited in Steinhauer, 1995, p. C7).

Economic factors come into play as well. Emotionally committed couples may decide to cohabit because of the economic advantages of sharing household expenses. Cohabiting individuals who receive public assistance (Social Security or welfare checks) risk losing support if they get married. Some older people live together rather than marry because of resistance from adult children. Some children fear that a parent will be victimized by a needy senior citizen. Others may not want their inheritances to come into question. Younger couples may cohabit secretly to maintain parental support that they might lose if they were to get married or to openly reveal their living arrangements.

Styles of Cohabitation

People come to cohabit in various ways, leading to different "styles" of cohabitation (Shehan & Kammeyer, 1997):

1 *Part-time/limited cohabitation.* In this style, people start dating, and one person starts spending more time at the other's residence. As the relationship deepens, she or he stays overnight more frequently. The visitor gradually brings in more clothes and other belongings. The couple thus drifts into cohabitation whether or not they arrive at a decision to do so. Since they did not make a formal arrangement, they may not have resolved issues such as whether to share expenses or date others. This style of cohabitation often ends because of an outside event, such as the end of the schoolyear. Part-time/limited cohabitation can also lead to premarital cohabitation, however.

2 *Premarital cohabitation.* In premarital cohabitation, people who expect to get married, or who may have made the decision to get married, live together beforehand. Premarital cohabitation sometimes takes the form of a trial marriage, in which the couple decides to test their relationship before making a more permanent commitment.

3 *Substitute marriage.* In this style, the couple decides to make a long-term commitment to live together without getting married. Some people enter into substitute marriages out of fear of a legal commitment. For example, a divorced person may be reluctant to enter another marriage. Some people may believe that a marriage certificate (a "piece of paper") is not necessary to certify their relationship. Many poor people and widows and widowers cohabit rather than get married because marriage would compromise their eligibility for welfare or Social Security payments.

Cohabitation and Later Marriage: Benefit or Risk?

More than half of marriages today in the United States are preceded by a period of living together (Smock, 2000). But does cohabitation help couples work out the kinks in their relationships and thus lower their risk of eventual divorce? The answer, it turns out, is no: Cohabiting couples who eventually get married are more likely to eventually get divorced than are those who do not cohabit prior to marriage (Cohan & Kleinbaum, 2002; Holman, 2000).

Why might cohabiting couples run a greater risk of divorce than couples who did not cohabit prior to marriage? Do not assume that cohabitation might somehow cause divorce. We must be cautious about drawing causal conclusions from correlational data. Note that none of the couples in these studies were randomly assigned to cohabitation or noncohabitation. Therefore, selection factors—the factors that lead some couples to cohabit and others not to cohabit—may explain the results. In general, cohabitors hold less traditional attitudes toward marriage and are less likely to say that religion is very important to them than are noncohabitors (Marquis, 2003). All in all, people who cohabit prior to marriage tend to be less committed to the values and interests traditionally associated with the institution of marriage. The cohabitors' attitudes, rather than cohabitation itself, may thus account for their higher rates of marital dissolution.

MODULE REVIEW

Review It

(16) The proportion of young adults in their twenties and early thirties who have remained single is (higher? lower?) today than it was in 1970.

(17) Career women can choose to remain single because they are (dependent on or independent of?) men.

(18) (More or Less?) than half of the marriages today are preceded by period of living together.

(19) Nearly _____ of the divorced people who are cohabiting with new partners have children in the household.

(20) Some couples prefer cohabitation to marriage because it provides a consistent relationship without the _____ constraints.

(21) Couples who cohabit before getting married appear to run a (lesser or greater?) risk of divorce than other couples if they eventually get married.

Think About It

How would you account for the popularity of cohabitation? What risks may be associated with cohabitation?

Psychology in Daily Life

MODULE 12.4

Making Relationships Work

Whether you are cohabiting or married, conflict is inevitable. Conflicts occur over money, communication, personal interests, sex, relatives and in-laws, friends, and children. If couples do not spell out their expectations of one another in advance, they are faced with the chore of deciding who does what. In traditional marriages, responsibilities are delegated according to gender-role stereotypes. The wife cooks, cleans, and diapers. The husband earns the bread and adjusts the carburetor. In nontraditional marriages, chores are usually shared or negotiated, especially when the wife also works. Not surprisingly, friction may develop when a nontraditional woman gets married to a traditional man.

The following list is a sampling of the risks that create conflict and endanger the stability of marriages (Booth & Edwards, 1985; Kornblum, 2000):

- Meeting "on the rebound"
- Living too close to, or too distant from, the families of origin
- Differences in race, religion, education, or social class
- Dependence on one or both families of origin for money, shelter, or emotional support
- Marriage before the couple know each other for six months or after an engagement of many years (couples who put off marriage for many years may have misgivings or conflicts that continue to harm the relationship)
- Marital instability in either family of origin
- Pregnancy prior to, or during the first year of, marriage
- Insensitivity to the partner's sexual needs
- Discomfort with the role of husband or wife
- Disputes over the division of labor

12.4.1 Resolving Conflicts

When conflicts arise in marriage, as they inevitably will, the following suggestions may be of help.

Challenge Irrational Expectations

People whose marriages are distressed are more likely than people with functional marriages to harbor a number of irrational beliefs (Rathus & Sanderson, 1999). Despite the fact that nearly all couples disagree now and then, they may believe that any disagreement is destructive. They assume that disagreement about in-laws, children, or sexual activities means that they do not love each other or that their marriage is on the rocks. They may believe that their partners should be able to read their minds (and know what they want), that their partners cannot change, that they must be perfect sex partners, and that men and women differ dramatically in personality and needs. It is rational, and healthy for a marriage , for partners to recognize that no two people can agree all the time, to express their wishes rather than depend on "mind-reading" (and a sullen face) to get the message across, to believe that we all can change (although change may come slowly), to tolerate some sexual blunders and frustrations, and to treat each other as equals.

In sum, disagreement in itself is not destructive to a marriage. Disagreement is found in every marriage. The issue is how well the partners manage disagreement. Belief that disagreement is destructive in itself is an irrational belief that can imperil marital adjustment. Gottman and Krokoff (1989) found that disagreement and the expression of anger could help marital satisfaction in the long run, as long as they were handled properly. Gottman and Krokoff followed marriages for three years and found that the following had long-term destructive effects:

- Being defensive, or making excuses instead of accepting responsibility for problems
- Making countercharges for every charge, without indicating that both partners' views may have some validity
- Telling partners only what they should stop doing, not what they should do more often
- Erroneously accusing partners of bad feelings, ideas, or motives that they don't really have—and then blaming them for these feelings, ideas, or motives
- Being stubborn; refusing to accept compromises or tolerate differences
- Making contemptuous remarks or hurling insults
- Whining

On the other hand, Gottman and Krokoff found that the following kinds of interactions led to increased marital satisfaction as time went on:

- At least partly acknowledging partners' points of view
- Carefully listening to accusations
- Understanding how partners feel, even in the heat of the argument
- Compromising
- Changing one's views

Belief that one's partner cannot change for the better is a type of stable attribution for marital problems. Stable attributions for problems make efforts to bring about change seem hopeless and are also linked to feelings of depression. Similarly, global attributions ("That's the way my partner is," as compared to the specific "That's what my partner's doing that's annoying me") exaggerate the magnitude of problems.

Here is a sampling of other irrational beliefs that increase marital distress:

- "My spouse doesn't love me if he/she doesn't support me at all times."
- "People who love one another don't raise their voices."
- "It's awful if a disagreement isn't resolved immediately."
- "If my spouse really cared about my anxiety/depression/ulcer/exam, he/she wouldn't be acting this way."
- "My spouse has that annoying habit just to bug me."
- "If she/he truly loved me, she/he would know what I want.

These irrational beliefs magnify differences and heighten rather than relieve marital stress. The last belief is extremely harmful. We may assume that people who really care for us will know what pleases or displeases us, even when we don't tell them. But other people cannot read our minds, and we should be open and direct about our feelings and preferences.

Negotiate Differences

In order to effectively negotiate differences about household responsibilities, leisure-time preferences, and so on, each spouse must be willing to share the power in the relationship (Rathus & Sanderson, 1999). If a marriage "gets off on the wrong foot," with one spouse dominating the other, the discrepancy in bargaining power may hamper all future negotiations. The disadvantaged spouse may not be heard, resentments may build, and the relationship may eventually dissolve. Research evidence shows that gay and lesbian couples tend to assign household tasks more fairly than do heterosexual couples (Kurdek, 2005). Whatever the couple's sexual orientation may be, however, a helpful strategy for averting discrepancies in bargaining power is to list day-to-day responsibilities. Then each spouse can scale them according to their desirability. Chris and Dana ranked the chores shown in Table 12.8 by using this code:

> 5 = most desirable
> 4 = desirable
> 3 = not sure, mixed feelings
> 2 = undesirable
> 1 = Are you kidding? Get lost!

Chris wound up washing the dishes and paying the bills. Dana did the cooking and toyed with the car. They agreed to alternate vacuuming and cleaning the bathroom—specifying a schedule for them so that they wouldn't procrastinate and eventually explode, "It's your turn!" Both had careers, so the breadwinning responsibility was divided evenly.

Make a Contract for Exchanging New Behaviors

In exchange contracting, you and your partner identify specific behaviors that you would like to see changed, and you offer to modify some of your own disturbing behavior patterns in exchange. A sample contract:

CHRIS: *I agree to talk to you at the dinner table rather than watch the news on TV if you in turn help me type my business reports one evening a week.*

DANA: *I agree never to insult your mother if you in return absolutely refuse to discuss our sexual behavior with her.*

Table 12.8 ▍ Chris and Dana's Rankings of Marital Chores		
Chore	**Chris's Ranking**	**Dana's Ranking**
Washing dishes	3	1
Cooking	1	4
Vacuuming	2	3
Cleaning the bathroom	1	3
Maintaining the automobile	3	5
Paying the bills	5	3

12.4.2 Increasing Pleasurable Marital Interactions

Satisfied couples tend to display higher rates of pleasurable behavior toward one another. One spouse also tends to reciprocate the pleasurable behavior shown by the other (Rathus & Sanderson, 1999). So consider trying out in your relationship the following behaviors that are associated with more satisfying relationships:

▪ Paying attention, listening
▪ Agreeing with your spouse (that is, when you do agree)
▪ Showing approval when pleased by your spouse
▪ Engaging in positive physical interactions such as touching and hugging
▪ Showing concern
▪ Showing humor; laughing and smiling
▪ Compromising on disagreements
▪ Complying with reasonable requests

Unfortunately, couples experiencing problems tend to underestimate the pleasurable behaviors shown by their spouses. It may be because poorly adjusted couples have come to expect the worst from one another and either ignore or do not "believe" efforts to change. If your partner has been trying to bring more pleasure into your life, it might help to show some appreciation. And if you have been trying to bring pleasure to your partner, and it has gone unnoticed, it might not hurt to say something like, "Hey! Look at me! I'm agreeing with you; I think you're pretty smart; and I'm smiling!" Now let us turn our attention to one of the best ways of resolving conflicts in relationships: improving communication skills.

12.4.3 Enhancing Communication Skills

How do you learn about your partner's needs? How do you let your partner know about your own needs? How do you criticize someone you love? How do you accept criticism and maintain your self-esteem? How do you say no? How do you get by impasses?

All these questions focus on the need for communication. Poor affective and problem-solving communication are two of the important factors that interfere with marital satisfaction. Moreover, people who are dissatisfied with their partners usually list difficulties in communication as one of the major rubs.

Some of us are better communicators than others, perhaps because we are more sensitive to others' needs or perhaps because we had the advantage of observing good communicators in our own homes. However, communication is a skill that can be learned. Learning takes time and work, but if you are willing, the following guidelines may be of help:

How to Get Started

One of the trickiest aspects of communicating is getting started.

1. *Talk about talking.* One possibility is to begin by talking about talking. That is, explain to your partner that it is hard to talk about your conflicts. Perhaps you can refer to some of the things that have happened in the past when you tried to resolve conflicts.

2. *Request permission to raise a topic.* You can also ask permission to bring up a topic. You can say something like, "Something's been on my mind. Is this a good time to bring it up?" Or try, "I need to get something off my chest, but I really don't know how to start. Will you help me?"

12.4.4 How to Listen

Listening to your partner is an essential part of communicating. Moreover, by being a good listener, you suggest ways that your partner can behave in listening to you. First, engage in "active listening." Don't stare off into space when your partner is talking or offer an occasional, begrudging "mmhmm" while you're watching TV. In active listening, you maintain eye contact with your partner. You change your facial expression in a demonstration of empathy for his or her feelings. You nod your head as appropriate and ask helpful questions such as, "Could you give me an example of what you mean?" or "How did you feel about that?"

1. *Use paraphrasing.* In paraphrasing, you recast what your partner is saying to show that you understand. For instance, if your partner says, "Last night it really bugged me when I wanted to talk about the movie but you were on the phone," you might say something like, "It seemed that I should have known that you wanted to talk about the movie" or "It seems that I'm talking more to other people than to you?"

2. *Reinforce your partner for communicating.* Even if you don't agree with what your partner said, you can genuinely say something like, "I'm glad you told me how you really feel about that" or "Look, even if I don't always agree with you, I care about you and I always want you to tell me what you're thinking."

3. *Use unconditional positive regard.* Keep in mind Carl Rogers's concept of unconditional positive regard, which is used by client-centered therapists. When you disagree with your partner, do so in a way that shows that you still value your partner as a person. In other words, say something like, "I love you very much, but it bugs me when you..." rather than "You're rotten for..."

12.4.5 How to Learn About Your Partner's Needs

Listening is essential to learning about your partner's needs, but sometimes you need to do more than just listen.

1. *Ask questions designed to encourage your partner to communicate.* Questions can either suggest a limited range of answers or be open-ended. The following "yes-or-no" questions require a specific response:

   ■ "Do you think I spend too much time on the phone with my sister?"

   ■ "Does it bother you that I wait until we're ready to go to bed before loading the dishwasher?"

   ■ "Do you think I don't value your opinions about cars?"
   Yes-or-no questions can provide a concrete piece of information. Open-ended questions, however, encourage exploration of broader issues. For example:

   ■ "What do you like best about the way we make love?" or "What bothers you about the way we make love?"

   ■ "What are your feelings about where we live?"

   ■ "How would you like to change things with us?"

   ■ "What do you think of me as a father/mother?"
   If your partner finds such questions too general, you can offer an example, or you can say something like, "Do you think we're living in an ideal situation? If you had your preferences, how would you change things?"

2. *Use self-disclosure.* Try self-disclosure, not only because you communicate your own ideas and feelings in this way but also because you invite reciprocation. For example, if you want to know whether your partner is concerned about your relationship with your parents, you can say something like, "You know, I have to admit that I get concerned when you call your folks from work. I get the feeling that there are things that you want to talk about with them but not have me know about..."

3. *Give your partner permission to say something that might be upsetting to you.* Tell your partner to level with you about a troublesome issue. Say that you realize that it might be clumsy to talk about it, but you promise to try to listen carefully without getting too upset. Consider limiting communication to, say, one difficult issue per conversation. When the entire emotional dam bursts, the chore of "mopping up" can be overwhelming.

How to Make Requests

1. *Take responsibility for what happens to you.* The first step in making requests is internal—that is, taking responsibility for the things that happen to you. If you want your partner to change behavior, you have to be willing to request the change. Then, if your partner refuses to change, you have to take responsibility for how you will cope with the impasse.

2. *Be specific.* It might be useless to say, "Be nicer to me," because your partner might not recognize the abrasive nature of his or her behavior and not know what you mean. It can be more useful to say something like, "Please don't cut me off in the middle of a sentence" or "Hey, you! Give me a smile!"

3. *Use "I" talk.* Also, make use of the word *I* where appropriate. "I would appreciate it if you would take out the garbage tonight" might get better results than "Do you think the garbage needs to be taken out?" Similarly, "I like you to kiss me more when we're making love" might be more effective than "Jamie told me about an article that said that kissing makes sex more enjoyable."

12.4.6 How to Deliver Criticism

You can't believe it! You've been waiting for an important business call, and it came. There's only one hitch: Your partner was home at the time—you were out—and your partner's not sure who called. If only your partner would be more responsible and write down messages!

You can't let it go this time. You're bound and determined to say something. But what?

Delivering criticism is tricky. Your goal should be to modify your partner's behavior without arousing extremes of anger or guilt. Consider these guidelines:

1. *Evaluate your motives.* First of all, be honest with yourself about your motives. Do you want to change behavior, or do you just want to punish your partner? If you want to punish your partner, you might as well be crude and insulting, but if you want to resolve conflicts, try a more diplomatic approach. We presume that your goal should be to modify your partner's behavior without reducing him or her to a quivering mass of fear or guilt.

2. *Pick a good time and place.* Express complaints privately— not in front of the neighbors, in-laws, or children. Your spouse has a right to be angry when you express intimate thoughts and feelings in public places. When you make private thoughts public, you cause resentment and cut off communication. If you're not sure that this is a good time and place, try asking permission. Say something like, "Something is on my mind. Is this a good time to bring it up?"

3. *Be specific.* As in making requests, be specific when making complaints. By being specific, you will communicate what behavior disturbs you. Don't insult your partner's personality. Say something like, "Please write down messages for me," not "You're totally irresponsible." Say, "Please throw your underwear in the hamper," not "You're a disgusting slob." It is easier (and less threatening) to change problem behavior than to try to overhaul personality traits.

4. *Express dissatisfaction in terms of your own feelings.* This is more effective than attacking the other person. Say, "You know, it upsets me when something that's important to me gets lost, or misplaced," not "You never think about anybody but yourself." Say, "You know, it upsets me that you don't seem to be paying attention to what I'm saying," not "You're always off in your own damn world. You never cared about anybody else and never will."

5. *Keep complaints to the present.* Say, "This was a very important phone call." It may not be helpful to say, "Last summer you didn't write that message from the computer company and as a result I didn't get the job." Forget who did what to whom last summer. It may also be counterproductive to say, "Every time I call my mother, there's a fight afterwards!" Bringing up the past muddles the current issue and heightens feelings of anger.

6. *Try to phrase the criticism positively.* Try to phrase criticism positively, and combine it with a specific request. Say something like, "You know, you're usually very considerate. When I need help, I always feel free to ask for it. Now I'm asking for help when I get a phone call. Will you please write down the message for me?" In another situation, say, "You really make my life much easier when you help me with the dishes. How about a hand tonight?" rather than "Would it really compromise your self-image as Mr. Macho if you gave me a hand with the dishes tonight?"

12.4.7 How to Receive Criticism

Honest criticism is hard to take, particularly from a relative, a friend, an acquaintance, or a stranger.

—Franklin P. Jones

Taking criticism on the job, at home—anywhere—isn't easy. It's helpful to recognize that you might not be perfect and to be prepared for occasional criticism. Your objectives in receiving criticism should be to learn about your partner's concerns, keep lines of communication open, and find, or negotiate, ways of changing the troublesome behavior. Yet you should not feel that you must take verbal abuse, and you should speak up if the criticism exceeds acceptable boundaries. For example, if your partner says, "You know, you're pretty damned obnoxious," you might say something like, "Say, how about telling me what I did that's troubling you and forgetting the character assassination?" In this way, you are also asking your partner to be specific.

1. *Ask clarifying questions.* Another way to help your partner be specific is to ask clarifying questions. If your partner criticizes you for spending so much time with your parents, you might ask something like, "Is it that I'm spending too much time with them, or do you feel they're having too much influence with me?"

2. *Paraphrase the criticism.* As with being a good listener in general, paraphrase the criticism to show that you understand it.

3. *Acknowledge the criticism.* Acknowledge the criticism even if you do not agree with it by saying something like, "I hear you" or "I can understand that you're upset that I've been investing so much time in the job lately."

4. *Acknowledge your mistake if you have made a mistake.* If you do not believe that you have, express your genuine feelings, using "I" statements and being as specific as possible.

5. Negotiate differences. Unless you feel that your partner is completely in the wrong, perhaps you can seek ways to negotiate your differences. Say something like, "Would it help if I...?"

12.4.8 How to Cope with Impasses

When we are learning to improve our communication skills, we may arrive at the erroneous idea that all of the world's problems, including our own, could be resolved if people would only make the effort of communicating with each other. Communication helps, but it is not the whole story. Sometimes people have deep, meaningful differences. Although they may have good communication skills, they now and then arrive at an impasse. When you and your partner do arrive at an impasse, the following suggestions may be of some use.

1. *Try to see the situation from your partner's perspective.* Maybe you can honestly say something like, "I don't agree with you, but I can see where you're coming from." In this way you validate your partner's feelings and, often, decrease the tension between you.

2. *Seek validating information.* Say something like, "I'm trying, but I honestly can't understand why you feel this way. Can you help me understand?"

3. *Take a break.* When we arrive at an impasse in solving a problem, allowing the problem to incubate frequently helps (Rathus, 2002). Allow each other's points of view to incubate, and perhaps a solution will dawn on one of you a bit later. You can also schedule a concrete time for a follow-up discussion so that the problem is not swept under the rug.

4. *Tolerate differentness.* Recognize that each of you is a unique individual and that you cannot agree on everything. Families function better when members tolerate each other's differentness. By and large, when we have a solid sense of ego identity (of who we are and what we stand for), we are more likely to be able to tolerate differentness in others.

5. *Agree to disagree.* Recognize that we can survive as individuals and as partners even when some conflicts remain unresolved. You can "agree to disagree" and maintain self-respect and respect for one another.

CHAPTER REVIEW

RECITE! RECITE! RECITE! RECITE! RECITE! RECITE! RECITE!

Study Tip: Reciting the answers to these study questions will help you become a more effective learner. First try answering the questions by yourself, either reciting them out loud or writing them in a notebook or on the computer. Then compare your answers with the sample answers provided below.

1. **How do social scientists view stages in the development of relationships?**
   According to social-exchange theory, stages of development involve social exchanges, which balance the rewards and costs of maintaining the relationship.

2. **What are Levinger's five stages of relationship development?**
   According to Levinger, relationships undergo a five-stage developmental sequence: attraction, building, continuation, deterioration, and ending. Relationships need not advance beyond any one of these stages.

3. **What steps can people take to build a relationship?**
   People can use opening lines, small talk, and self-disclosure to build relationships. Small talk is a broad exploration for common ground that permits us to decide whether we wish to advance the relationship beyond surface contact. Self-disclosure is the revelation of personal information. Self-disclosure invites reciprocity and can foster intimacy. However, premature self-disclosure suggests maladjustment and tends to repel people.

4. **What factors contribute to the continuation or deterioration of a relationship?**
   Factors that contribute to the continuation of a relationship include enhancing variety (to fight boredom), trust, caring, commitment, evidence of continuing positive evaluation (e.g., Valentine's Day cards), absence of jealousy, perceived equity (e.g., a fair distribution of homemaking, childrearing, and breadwinning chores), and mutual overall satisfaction.

5. **What is the role of marriage today?**
   Today's marriages still provide a home life and an institution for rearing children and transmitting wealth. However, they are usually based on attraction and feelings of love, and they provide for emotional and psychological intimacy and security.

6. **What factors contribute to marital satisfaction? Are married people happier than singles?**
   Factors that contribute to marital satisfaction include good affective communication, good problem-solving communication, sexual satisfaction, and agreement about finances and childrearing. A marriage contract may help clarify a couple's values and goals. For example, it can indicate whether the wife will take the husband's surname, who will be responsible for what chores, the type of contraception to be used, methods of childrearing, and how leisure activities will be decided on. By and large, married people seem to be happier with their lives than single people are.

7. **What are the attitudes of Americans toward extramarital affairs?**
   Extramarital sex is viewed negatively by the great majority of people in the United States. Although people have become more permissive about premarital sex, they generally remain opposed to extramarital sex.

8. **How does an affair affect a primary relationship?**
   The discovery of infidelity can evoke anger, jealousy, even shame. Affairs often, but not always, damage marriages.

9. **How widespread is domestic violence? What motivates it?**
   About one woman in eight is victimized by domestic violence each year. Women and men are equally likely to engage in domestic violence, but women are more likely to sustain serious injuries. Domestic violence is frequently connected with threats to men's dominance in relationships.

10. **How many marriages end in divorce? Why do people get divorced?**
    About half the marriages in the United States end in divorce. Reasons include relaxed restrictions on divorce, greater financial independence of women, and—ironically—continued positive expectations of marriage, particularly the belief that marriages should meet people's needs and be happy.

11. What are the financial and emotional repercussions of divorce?

Divorce typically lowers the standard of living for all parties involved. It is associated with emotional problems in the couple and in the children. Divorce is associated with an increased likelihood of suicide in men. Divorce can lead to family disorganization, making it more difficult to rear children.

12. What is the "singles scene" like today?

More people are remaining single today by choice, and many are delaying marriage to pursue educational and vocational goals. Some people remain single because they have not found the right marital partner. Others prefer sexual variety and wish to avoid making a commitment.

13. What are some reasons couples cohabit?

Cohabitation is living together without being married. For some, cohabitation is an alternative to marriage that confers many of the benefits of marriage without the depth of commitment. For others, cohabitation has, in effect, become a stage in courtship.

14. What is the relationship between cohabitation and later marital success?

Actually, people who cohabit before marriage are more likely to get divorced. However, we shouldn't assume that cohabitation prior to marriage is a cause of later divorce.

YOUR PERSONAL JOURNAL

REFLECT   REFLECT   REFLECT   REFLECT   REFLECT   REFLECT   REFLECT

Study Tip: Reflecting on how the concepts in the chapter relate to your own experiences encourages deeper processing, which makes the material more personally meaningful and fosters more effective learning. Use additional pages if needed to complete your answers.

1. How does the principle of homogamy come into play in the marriages of people you know?

_____

_____

_____

_____

_____

_____

2. Do you think cohabitation is helpful or harmful to an eventual marriage? Did reading about the research on cohabitation change your views in any way?

_____

_____

_____

_____

_____

_____

ANSWERS TO MODULE REVIEWS

Module 12.1

1. social
2. continuation
3. disclosure
4. men/women
5. deterioration

Module 12.2

6. Marriage
7. Married
8. homogamy
9. marriage contract
10. soul mates

11. disapprove
12. first
13. Boys
14. little
15. Women

Module 12.3

16. higher
17. independent of
18. More
19. half
20. legal
21. greater

SCORING KEY FOR QUESTIONNAIRE ON ENDORSEMENT OF TRADITIONAL OR LIBERAL MARITAL ROLES

Below each of the scoring codes (AS, AM, DM, and DS) there is a number. Underline the numbers beneath each of your answers. Then reverse the scoring for the following items: 4, 6, 7, 9, and 10 (a "1" becomes a "4," a "2" becomes a "3," a "3" becomes a "2," and a "4" becomes a "1"). Then add all the numbers to obtain your total score. The total score can vary from 10 to 40. A score of 10 to 20 shows moderate to high traditionalism concerning marital roles, whereas a score of 30 to 40 shows moderate to high liberalism. A score between 20 and 30 suggests that you are a middle-of-the-roader.

CHAPTER

13

Sexual Behavior

OUTLINE

Did you know that...

CHAPTER REVIEW   *RECITE! RECITE! RECITE!*

YOUR PERSONAL JOURNAL   *REFLECT REFLECT REFLECT*

- While people in the United States link romantic love with Valentine's Day, people in Japan eroticize another significant day—Christmas Eve? (p. 420)

- A word used to describe the female genital organs derives from Latin roots meaning "something to be ashamed of"? (p. 421)

- Only women have a sex organ that has sexual pleasure as its only function? (p. 421)

- The ancient Egyptians used crocodile dung as a contraceptive device? (p. 427)

- When people are sexually aroused, their earlobes swell? (p. 430)

- Obesity increases a person's risk not only of heart disease and diabetes but also of erectile dysfunction? (p. 442)

- The male sex hormone increases sexual drive and interest in both men and women suffering from a lack of desire? (p . 442)

- The virus that causes genital warts is also a major cause of cervical cancer, a potential killer? (p. 445)

Galina Barskaya/iStockphoto

Offshore from the misty coasts of Ireland lies the small island of Inis Beag. From the air, it is a green jewel, warm and inviting. At ground level, things are somewhat different.

For example, the residents of Inis Beag do not believe that women experience orgasm. The woman who chances to find pleasure in sex is considered deviant. Premarital sex is all but unknown. Women engage in sexual relations in order to conceive children and to appease their husbands' carnal cravings. They need not worry about being called on for frequent performances, however, since the men of Inis Beag believe, erroneously, that sex saps their strength. Sex on Inis Beag is carried out in the dark—literally and figuratively—and with the nightclothes on. The man lies on top in the so-called missionary position. In accord with local concepts of masculinity, he ejaculates as fast as he can. Then he rolls over and falls asleep.

If Inis Beag does not sound like your cup of tea, you may find the atmosphere of Mangaia more congenial. Mangaia is a Polynesian pearl of an island, lifting languidly from the blue waters of the Pacific. It is on the other side of the world from Inis Beag—in more ways than one.

From an early age, Mangaian children are encouraged to get in touch with their sexuality through masturbation. Mangaian adolescents are expected to engage in sexual intercourse. They may be found on secluded beaches or beneath the listing fronds of palms, diligently practicing techniques learned from village elders.

Mangaian women are expected to reach orgasm several times before their partners do. Young men want their partners to reach orgasm and compete to see who is more effective at bringing young women to multiple orgasms.

On the island of Inis Beag, a woman who has an orgasm is considered deviant, whereas on Mangaia multiple orgasms are the norm (Rathus, Nevid, & Fichner-Rathus,

2008). If we take a quick tour of the world of sexual diversity, we also find that the following are true:

- Nearly every society has an incest taboo, but some societies believe that a brother and sister who eat at the same table are engaging in a mildly sexual act and forbid it.

- What is considered sexually arousing varies enormously among different cultures. Women's breasts and armpits are considered sexual stimuli in some cultures but not in others.

- Kissing is nearly universal in the United States but is unpopular in Japan and is unknown in some cultures in Africa and South America. Upon seeing European visitors kissing, a member of an African tribe remarked, "Look at them—they eat each other's saliva and dirt."

- Sexual fidelity in marriage is highly valued in many cultures, but among the people of Alaska's Aleutian Islands, it is considered good manners for a man to offer his wife to a houseguest.

- The United States has its romantic Valentine's Day, but Japan has eroticized another day—Christmas Eve. (You read that right: Christmas Eve.) On Christmas Eve, single people seek a date that includes an overnight visit (Reid, 1990). During the weeks prior to Christmas, the media brim with reports on hotels for overnight stays, the correct attire, and breakfast ideas for the morning after. Where do Tokyo singles like to go before their overnighter? Tokyo Disneyland.

People the world over—including the residents of Inis Beag and Mangaia—have similar anatomic features. But people in different cultures, and even those within the same general cultures, may have vastly different attitudes toward sex. Personal values and cultural tradition influence sexual behavior and the pleasure people find—or do not find—in sex. Sex, like eating, is a natural function. But as we saw in our tour of the world, perhaps no other natural function has been influenced so strongly by religious and moral beliefs, traditions, values, folklore, and superstition.

In this chapter, we examine sexual anatomy and sexual response and see that women and men may be more alike in their sexual response than you thought. Although human sexuality provides meaningful relationships and a source of pleasure, it is also connected with many challenges to psychological adjustment. Among these is the social problem of combating rape and coping with its aftermath. We consider the causes of rape and rape prevention, and we find that widespread cultural attitudes contribute to the high incidence of rape. We also consider such adjustment challenges as sexual dysfunctions and their treatment. We also discuss contraception in an effort to help students make responsible sexual choices. Sexually transmitted diseases (STDs) (also called *sexually transmitted infections,* or STIs) such as HIV/AIDS[1] may yet pose the greatest challenge to adjustment in the realm of human sexuality. Preventing HIV/AIDS and other STDs is the topic of this chapter's *Adjustment and Modern Life* feature.

MODULE 13.1

The Biological Basis of Sex

▮ What are the woman's sexual organs?
▮ What are the man's sexual organs?
▮ How do sex hormones regulate the menstrual cycle?
▮ What effects do sex hormones have on sexual behavior?

[1] HIV stands for human immunodeficiency virus, the virus that causes AIDS. The STD is now generally referred to as HIV/AIDS to indicate that the condition begins with HIV infection but may not develop into a "full-blown" case of AIDS for a decade or more.

Although we may consider ourselves sophisticated about sex, it's surprising how little many of us know about the biology of sex. In this section we survey female and male sexual anatomy. Then we consider the sexual response cycle and the roles of sex hormones in sexual behavior.

13.1.1 Female Sexual Anatomy

The external female genital organs are called the **vulva**, from the Latin for "covering." The vulva is also known as the **pudendum**, from "something to be ashamed of"—a clear reflection of sexism in ancient Western culture. The vulva has several parts (see the bottom part of Figure 13.1): the mons veneris, clitoris, major and minor lips, and vaginal opening. Females urinate through the **urethral** opening. The **mons veneris** (Latin for "hill of love") is a fatty cushion that lies above the pubic bone and is covered with short, curly pubic hair. The mons and pubic hair cushion the woman's pelvis during sexual intercourse. The woman's most sensitive sex organ, the **clitoris** (from the Greek for "hill"), lies below the mons and above the urethral opening. The only known function of the clitoris is to receive and transmit pleasurable sensations. By contrast, the man has no one organ that serves the purpose of sexual pleasure exclusively. The penis does double and even triple duty as an organ for transmitting sperm, passing urine, and providing sexual stimulation. The clitoris is primarily responsible for the sensory input that triggers the orgasmic response in women (Mah & Binik, 2001). Even during intercourse, the clitoris is stimulated by the back-and-forth tugging action of the penis against the clitoral tissue.

During sexual arousal, the clitoris becomes engorged with blood and expands, much like the penis expands during erection. The clitoris has a shaft and a tip, or **glans**.

▍ **Vulva** The female external genital organs.

▍ **Pudendum** Another term for the vulva.

▍ **Urethral** Relating to the urethra, the tube that conducts urine from the body and, in males, the ejaculate.

▍ **Mons veneris** The mound of fatty tissue that covers the joint of the pubic bones and cushions the female during intercourse.

▍ **Clitoris** The female sex organ whose only known function is the reception and transmission of sensations of sexual pleasure.

▍ **Glans** Tip or head.

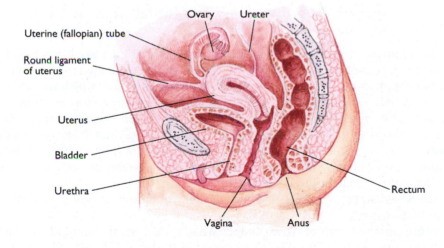

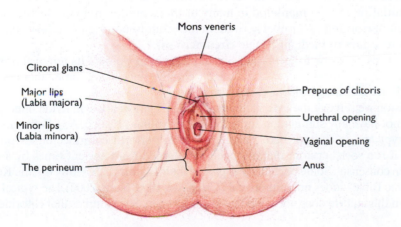

Figure 13.1
Female Sexual Anatomy
The above drawing is a cross section of the internal reproductive organs of the female. The drawing below is an external view of the vulva.

Major lips Large folds of skin that run along the sides of the vulva. (In Latin, *labia majora*.)

Minor lips Folds of skin that lie within the major lips and enclose the urethral and vaginal openings. (In Latin, *labia minora*.)

Vagina The tubular female sexual organ that receives the penis during intercourse and through which the baby passes during childbirth.

Cervix The lower part of the uterus that opens into the vagina.

Uterus The pear-shaped female reproductive organ in which the fertilized ovum implants and develops until childbirth.

Fallopian tubes The strawlike tubes through which the ovum passes between the ovaries and the uterus.

Ovaries Female reproductive organs that produce ova and the hormones estrogen and progesterone.

Ovum An egg cell (Plural: *ova*).

Clitoridectomy Removal of the clitoris.

Circumcision In men, the removal of the penile foreskin.

The glans is the more sensitive of the two and may become irritated by too early an approach during foreplay or by prolonged stimulation.

Two layers of fatty tissue, the outer or **major lips** and the inner or **minor lips**, line the entrance to the vagina. The outer lips are covered with hair and are less sensitive to touch than the smooth, pinkish inner lips.

We have learned about the woman's external sexual organs. The woman's internal sexual and reproductive organs consist of the vagina, cervix, fallopian tubes, and ovaries (see the top part of Figure 13.1). The **vagina** contains the penis during intercourse. At rest, the vagina is a flattened tube 3 to 5 inches in length. When aroused, it can lengthen by several inches and dilate (open) to a diameter of about 2 inches. A large penis is not required to "fill" the vagina in order for a woman to experience sexual pleasure. The vagina expands as needed. The pelvic muscles that surround the vagina may also be contracted during intercourse to heighten sensation. The outer third of the vagina is highly sensitive to touch.

When a woman is sexually aroused, the vaginal walls produce moisture that serves as lubrication during sexual intercourse. Sexual relations can be painful for unaroused, unlubricated women. Adequate arousal usually stems from a combination of sexual attraction, feelings of love, fantasies, and direct stimulation in the form of foreplay. Anxieties concerning sex or a partner may inhibit sexual arousal—for either gender.

High in the vagina is a small opening called the **cervix** (Latin for "neck") that connects the vagina to the **uterus**. Strawlike **fallopian tubes** lead from the uterus to the abdominal cavity. **Ovaries**, which produce ova and the hormones estrogen and progesterone, lie near the uterus and the fallopian tubes. When an **ovum** is released from an ovary, it normally finds its way into the nearby fallopian tube and makes its way to the uterus. Conception normally takes place in the tube, but the embryo becomes implanted and grows in the uterus. During labor the cervix dilates, and the baby passes through the cervix and distended vagina.

Cultural Bases of Clitoridectomy: The Ritual Destruction of Female Sexuality

Despite hundreds of years of tradition, Hajia Zuwera Kassindja would not let it happen to her 17-year-old daughter, Fauziya. Hajia's own sister had died from it. So Hajia gave her daughter her inheritance from her deceased husband, which amounted to only $3,500 but left Hajia a pauper. Fauziya used the money to buy a phony passport and flee from the African country of Togo to the United States (Dugger, 1996a). Upon arrival in the United States, Fauziya requested asylum from persecution. However, she was put into prison for more than a year. But then, in 1996, the Board of Immigration Appeals finally agreed that Fauziya was fleeing persecution, and she was allowed to remain in the United States.

From what had Hajia's sister died? From what was Fauziya escaping? Ritual genital mutilation.

Cultures in some parts of Africa and the Middle East ritually mutilate or remove the clitoris, not just the clitoral hood. Removal of the clitoris, or **clitoridectomy**, is a rite of initiation into womanhood in many of these predominantly Islamic cultures. It is often performed as a puberty ritual in late childhood or early adolescence (not within a few days of birth, like male **circumcision)**.

The clitoris gives rise to feelings of sexual pleasure in women. Its removal or mutilation represents an attempt to ensure the girl's chastity since it is assumed that uncircumcised girls are consumed with sexual desires. Cairo physician Said M. Thabit says, "With circumcision we remove the external parts, so when a girl wears tight nylon underclothes she will not have any stimulation" (cited in MacFarquhar, 1996, p. A3). Some groups in rural Egypt and in the northern Sudan, however, perform clitoridectomies primarily because it is a social custom that has been maintained from ancient times by a sort of unspoken consensus. Some perceive it as part of their Islamic faith. However, the Koran—the Islamic Bible—does not authorize it (Crossette, 1998; Nour, 2000). The typical young woman in this culture does not grasp that she is a victim. She assumes that clitoridectomy is part of being female. As one young woman told gynecologist Nawal M. Nour (2000), the clitoridectomy hurt but was a good thing because now she was a woman.

Clitoridectomies are performed under unsanitary conditions without benefit of anesthesia. Medical complications are common, including infections, bleeding, tissue scarring, painful menstruation, and obstructed labor. The procedure is psychologically traumatizing. An even more radical form of clitoridectomy, called *infibulation* or Pharaonic circumcision, is practiced widely in the Sudan. Pharaonic circumcision involves complete removal of the clitoris along with the labia minora and the inner layers of the labia majora. Only a tiny opening is left to allow passage of urine and menstrual discharge (Nour, 2000). The sewing together of the vulva is intended to ensure chastity until marriage. Medical complications are common, including menstrual and urinary problems, and even death. After marriage, the opening is enlarged to permit intercourse. Mutilation of the labia is now illegal in the Sudan, although the law continues to allow removal of the clitoris. Some African countries, including Egypt, have outlawed clitoridectomies, although such laws may not be enforced.

More than 100 million women in Africa and the Middle East have undergone removal of the clitoris and the labia minora. Clitoridectomies remain common or even universal in nearly 30 countries in Africa, in many countries in the Middle East, and in parts of Malaysia, Yemen, Oman, Indonesia, and the India–Pakistan subcontinent. Thousands of African immigrant girls living in European countries and the United States have also been mutilated (Nour, 2000).

Do not confuse male circumcision with the maiming inflicted on girls in the name of circumcision. Nour (2000) depicts the male equivalent of female genital mutilation as cutting off the penis. The Pulitzer Prize–winning African American novelist Alice Walker drew attention to the practice in her best-selling novel *Possessing the Secret of Joy*. She called for its abolition in her book and movie *Warrior Marks*.

In 1996, the United States outlawed ritual genital mutilation within its borders. The government also directed U.S. representatives to world financial institutions to deny aid to countries that have not established educational programs to bring an end to the practice. Yet calls from Westerners to ban the practice in parts of Africa and the Middle East have sparked controversy on grounds of "cultural condescension" — that people in one culture cannot dictate the cultural traditions of another. Yet for Alice Walker, "torture is not culture." As the debate continues, some 2 million African girls are ritually mutilated each year.

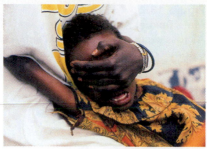
©AP/Wide World Photos

Clitoridectomy
Cultures in some parts of Africa and the Middle East ritually mutilate or remove the clitoris as a rite of initiation into womanhood. The removal or mutilation of the clitoris is an attempt to ensure the girl's chastity, since it is assumed that uncircumcised girls are consumed with sexual desires. Clitoridectomies are performed under unsanitary conditions without benefit of anesthesia, and serious medical complications are common.

13.1.2 Male Sexual Anatomy

The major male sex organs consist of the **penis** (from the Latin for "tail"); **testes** (or testicles); **scrotum**; and the series of ducts, canals, and glands that store and transport **sperm** and produce **semen**. Whereas the female vulva has been viewed historically as "something to be ashamed of," the male sex organs were prized in ancient Greece and Rome. Citizens wore phallic-shaped trinkets, and the Greeks held their testes when offering testimony, in the same way that we swear on a Bible. *Testimony* and *testicle* both derive from the Greek *testis*, meaning "witness." Given this tradition of masculine pride, it is not surprising that Sigmund Freud believed that girls were riddled with penis envy. Ingrained cultural attitudes cause many women to feel embarrassed about their genital organs.

The testes produce sperm and the male sex hormone **testosterone**. The scrotum allows the testes to hang away from the body (sperm require a lower-than-body temperature). Sperm travel through ducts up over the bladder and back down to the ejaculatory duct (see Figure 13.2), which empties into the urethra. In females, the urethral opening and the orifice for transporting the ejaculate are different; in males, they are one and the same. Although the male urethra transports urine as well as sperm, a valve shuts off the bladder during ejaculation. Thus, sperm and urine do not mix. Several glands, including the **prostate**, produce semen. Semen transports, activates, and nourishes sperm, enhancing their ability to swim and fertilize the ovum. The penis consists mainly of loose erectile

Penis The male organ that serves as a conduit for sperm during ejaculation and urine during urination.

Testes Male reproductive organs that produce sperm cells and male sex hormones. Also called *testicles*.

Scrotum A pouch of loose skin that houses the testes.

Sperm Male germ cell (From a Greek root, meaning "seed").

Semen The whitish fluid that carries sperm. Also called *the ejaculate*.

Testosterone A male sex hormone that promotes development of male sexual characteristics and has activating effects on sexual arousal.

Prostate A male reproductive organ that produces semen.

Figure 13.2
Male Sexual Anatomy
A cross section of the internal and external reproductive organs of the male.

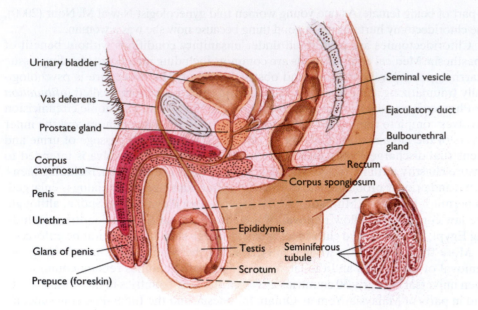

tissue. Like the clitoris, the penis has a shaft and tip, or glans, which is highly sensitive to sexual stimulation, especially on the underside. Within seconds following sexual stimulation, blood rushes reflexively into caverns within the penis, just as blood engorges the clitoris. Engorgement with blood—not bone—produces erection.

13.1.3 Sex Hormones and Sexual Behavior

Sex hormones have multiple roles. They promote the differentiation of male and female sex organs in the embryo. Under the influence of the male sex hormone testosterone, male fetuses develop male sexual organs. Lacking testosterone, the female fetus develops female sexual organs. In later development, sex hormones regulate the menstrual cycle in women and have more direct effects on sexual behavior.

Hormonal Regulation of the Menstrual Cycle

▮ **Estrogen** A generic term for several female sex hormones that foster growth of female sex characteristics and regulate the menstrual cycle.

▮ **Progesterone** A female sex hormone that promotes growth of the sex organs, helps maintain pregnancy, and is also involved in regulation of the menstrual cycle.

▮ **Menstruation** The monthly shedding of the inner lining of the uterus by women who are not pregnant.

▮ **Endometrium** The tissue forming the inner lining of the uterus.

▮ **Ovulation** The release of an ovum from an ovary.

The ovaries produce **estrogen** and **progesterone**. Estrogen spurs development of female reproductive capacity and secondary sex characteristics, such as accumulation of fat in the breasts and the hips. Progesterone also has multiple functions. It stimulates growth of the female reproductive organs and maintains pregnancy. Levels of estrogen and progesterone vary markedly and regulate the menstrual cycle. Following **menstruation**—the monthly sloughing off of the inner lining of the uterus—estrogen levels increase, leading to the ripening of an ovum (egg cell) and the growth of the **endometrium**, or inner lining of the uterus. **Ovulation** occurs—that is, the ovum is released by the ovary—halfway through the menstrual cycle, when estrogen reaches peak blood levels. Then, in response to secretion of progesterone, the inner lining of the uterus thickens, gaining the capacity to support an embryo if fertilization should occur. If the ovum is not fertilized, estrogen and progesterone levels drop suddenly, triggering menstruation once more.

Organizing and Activating Effects of Sex Hormones

Sexual behavior among many lower animals is almost completely governed by hormones (Crews, 1994). Sex hormones have two distinct kinds of behavioral effects: organizing and activating effects (Buchanan, Eccles, & Becker, 1992). They predispose lower animals toward performing masculine or feminine mating behaviors, a directional or *organizing effect*. Hormones also stimulate the sex drive and facilitate sexual response, which are *activating effects*.

In many species, if female fetuses are exposed to large doses of testosterone in the uterus (which occurs naturally when they share the uterus with many brothers or artificially as a result of hormone injections), their sex organs become masculine in structure (Crews, 1994). Prenatal testosterone also organizes the brains of females in the masculine direction, predisposing them toward masculine behaviors in adulthood. Testosterone in adulthood then apparently activates masculine behavior patterns. Testosterone is also important in the behavior of human males. Men who are castrated or given drugs that decrease the amount of testosterone in the bloodstream usually show gradual loss of sexual desire and of the capacities for erection and orgasm. Still, many castrated men remain sexually active for years, suggesting that for many people fantasies, memories, and other cognitive stimuli are as important as hormones in sexual motivation. Beyond minimal levels, there is no clear link between testosterone level and sexual arousal.

Female mice, rats, cats, and dogs are receptive to males only during **estrus**, when female sex hormones are plentiful. But women are sexually responsive during all phases of the menstrual cycle, even during menstruation and after **menopause**, when hormone levels are low.

Testosterone stokes sexual desire in both men and women (Davis et al., 2005; Shifren & Ferrari, 2004). Testosterone is produced in women's bodies by the ovaries and the adrenal glands, but in much smaller amounts as compared to men (Sweeney, 2005). (Men also produce small amounts of the hormone in their adrenal glands.) Women whose adrenal glands and ovaries have been removed (so that they no longer produce testosterone) may gradually lose sexual interest and the capacity for sexual response. Recent evidence shows that women 18 to 44 years of age who have very low levels of male sex hormones tend also to have lower levels of sexual desire and responsiveness (Davis et al., 2005). We have also learned that testosterone injections can increase sexual interest and desire in both men and women who present with low levels of the hormone (Davis et al., 2008; Brown & Haaser, 2005; Wang et al., 2004).

We need to understand, however, that whatever role sex hormones may play in human sexual behavior, our sexual behavior is not controlled by the biological dictates of hormones. Sex hormones promote the differentiation of our sex organs in a masculine or feminine direction. As adults, we also need minimal levels of sex hormones to maintain a healthy sexual appetite and arousal patterns. However, psychological factors greatly influence our sexual behavior. In human sexuality, biology is not destiny.

▮ **Estrus** The periodic sexual excitement of many female mammals, during which they can conceive and are receptive to the sexual advances of males.

▮ **Menopause** The cessation of menstruation.

MODULE REVIEW

Review It

(1) The external female genital organs are called the _____.

(2) The _____ produce ova and the hormones estrogen and progesterone.

(3) The testes in the male produce sperm and the male sex hormone _____.

(4) Sex hormones promote the _____ of male and female sex organs in the embryo.

(5) The hormone _____ spurs development of female reproductive capacity and secondary sex characteristics.

(6) The hormone _____ stimulates growth of the female reproductive organs and maintains pregnancy.

(7) If an ovum is not fertilized, levels of estrogen and progesterone (increase or decrease?) suddenly, triggering menstruation.

(8) Sex hormones have _____ and activating effects.

(9) Men who are given drugs that (increase or decrease?) _____ the amount of testosterone in the bloodstream usually show gradual loss of sexual desire and of the capacities for erection and orgasm.

Think About It

It has been said that in human sexuality, "Biology is not destiny." What does that mean to you?

MODULE 13.2

Sexual Behavior and Response

▌ Why do sexual practices and customs vary so widely around the world?

▌ What factors do we need to consider when selecting a method of contraception?

▌ What is the sexual response cycle?

We noted in the introduction to this chapter how our sexual behavior is influenced by our values and cultural backgrounds. The residents of Inis Beag and Mangaia, for instance, have the same hormones circulating throughout their bodies and the same biological capacity for sexual pleasure. However, they are polar opposites when it comes to their sexual patterns and customs because of differences in their cultural values and attitudes toward sexual expression.

Our bodies are exquisitely sensitive to sexual stimulation—and for good reason: Without the capacity to respond sexually, none of us would be around to tell our story. But the capacity of our bodies to respond sexually does not determine our sexual behavior. How we express ourselves sexually is a function not only of our capacity for reaping pleasure from sexual activity but also, more importantly, of our values, religious and cultural traditions, and personal choices.

13.2.1 Varieties of Sexual Expression

We needn't go to faraway places like Inis Beag and Mangaia to observe diversity of sexual experience. In our society we see a wide variety of sexual behaviors, ranging from self-stimulation (masturbation) to oral sex to vaginal and anal intercourse, to name several of the ways in which people express themselves sexually. We also see a wide variety of methods of contraception used to prevent unwanted pregnancy. According to a recent large-scale survey of sexual practices in the United States, 27% of adult men, though only 7.6% of women, report masturbating at least once monthly (Laumann et al., 1994). Since surveys are subject to certain response biases (people may not report intimate behavior accurately or honestly), we might assume that many other people actually do masturbate or engage in other sexual practices but fail to report that they do. Yet the evidence we have available does indicate that the bedroom has become a stage with more varied parts for the players. For example, survey evidence shows that oral sex has now become the norm, with more than 70% of people surveyed reporting some experience with oral sex (Laumann et al., 1994). Anal intercourse has also become more common but not as common as other forms of intimate sexual activity, with about one in four men (26%) and one in five women (20%) reporting that they have engaged in anal intercourse at some point in their lives. Variety of sexual expression is also found in differences among couples in reported frequency of sexual intercourse. Ten to twenty percent report engaging in intercourse "a few times per year," whereas more than 30% report a frequency of "2–3 times weekly" (see Figure 13.3). On average, married couples report having intercourse at a rate of slightly more than once a week (Deveny, 2003).

Values and Sexual Expression

Our values are important determinants of our sexual behavior. We North Americans live in pluralistic societies that embrace a wide range of cultural attitudes and values about sexuality. Some of us hold traditional or conservative values that may be grounded in certain religious traditions. Others hold more permissive or liberal values about sexual behavior. Young people are much more liberal today in their sexual attitudes and behaviors than they were a few generations ago. For example, acceptability

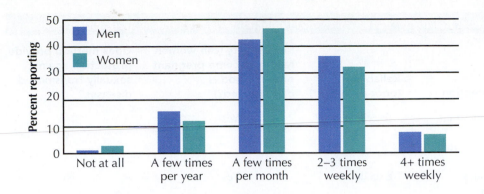

Figure 13.3
Reported Frequency of Sexual Intercourse in Marriage During the Past Year
Source: Adapted from Laumann et al. (1994).

of premarital intercourse increased from 12% in 1943 to 73% in 1999 among young women and from 40% to 79% among young men (Wells & Twenge, 2005).

Our sexual values may mirror those of our parents, religious leaders, and other important influences in our lives. But they may also reflect our efforts to arrive at a set of beliefs that reflect our own deeply held convictions, even if those beliefs deviate from the cultural traditions with which we were raised. In any event, our values come into play in determining how (and with whom) we express ourselves sexually. For example, our values determine whether we are willing to engage in premarital sex or in casual sex with a variety of partners.

Throughout this text we encourage you to explore your own values. Here, let us focus on clarifying values with respect to an extremely important issue in expressing your sexuality: protecting yourself or your partner from unwanted pregnancy. First, however, let us summarize the major methods of contraception.

Methods of Contraception

Familiarity breeds contempt—and children.

—MARK TWAIN

Contraception (prevention of pregnancy) has a fascinating history. For example, ancient Egyptians douched with wine and garlic after sex; they also soaked crocodile dung in sour milk and stuffed the mixture into the vagina. The dung blocked the passage of many—if not all—sperm and also soaked up sperm. A "social" mechanism may also have been at work. Perhaps the crocodile dung discouraged all but the most ardent suitors.

In any event, sexually active college students need to face the question of contraception, and today's methods of contraception are more reliable—if not more interesting—than those of the ancient Egyptians. Here we consider a number of methods of contraception. Table 13.1 summarizes the reliability, reversibility, and degree of protection against sexually transmitted diseases provided by various methods. Reliability is generally higher among people who use the methods carefully. For example, some women forget to take the pill regularly, and male condoms can tear or slip.

Table 13.2 shows the frequency of use of different methods of contraception among college students on the last occasion they engaged in vaginal intercourse. Note that the birth control pill is the method most widely reported by women, while condoms are reported by males to be the most widely used method, just barely surpassing "the pill."

Selecting a Method of Contraception

If you and your partner decide to use contraception, how can you determine which method is right for you? There is no one answer. What works for a friend may not work—or work as well—for you. We cannot tell you what to use, but we can suggest some issues that you may want to consider:

1 *Convenience.* Is the method convenient? For example, must it be purchased in advance? If so, is a prescription required? Does it work at a moment's notice, or, like the birth control pill, is time required to reach maximum effectiveness?

Dirk Anschutz/Photonica/Getty Images, Inc.

Intimacy Is More Than Skin Deep
Sexual activity can provide a way of sharing emotional, not just physical, intimacy.

■ **Contraception** Prevention of pregnancy.

Table 13.1 ▮ Methods of Contraception: Reliability, Reversibility, and Protection Against Sexually Transmitted Diseases

Method	Mode of Contraception	Reliability (poor-excellent[a])	Reversibility (can women readily become pregnant once method is discontinued?)	Does method provide protection against sexually transmitted diseases?
Birth control pills	Female sex hormones that inhibit ovulation or interfere with implantation of a fertilized egg	Excellent	Yes	No
Norplant	Female sex hormones delivered through match-stick-sized implants in upper arm	Excellent	Yes	No
Depo-Provera	Long-acting, synthetic form of the female sex hormone progesterone that inhibits ovulation	Excellent	Yes	No
Intrauterine device (IUD)	A device that is inserted and left in place in the uterus to prevent conception or implantation of a fertilized egg	Excellent	Yes (unless fertility is impaired by infection)	No
Diaphragm with spermicide	A barrier method that covers the cervix to prevent passage of sperm; spermicide kills sperm directly	Fair to good	Yes	Some protection
Cervical cap with spermicide	A rubber or plastic cap that is fitted over the cervix; works in similar ways as diaphragm	Fair to good	Yes	Some protection
Male condom	A barrier device worn on the penis that prevents passage of sperm	Fair to good[b]	Yes	No
Withdrawal (Coitus interruptus)	Withdrawal of the penis before ejaculation	Poor to fair	Yes	No
Rhythm methods	Methods of timing ovulation; used by couples to avoid intercourse during times of the month the woman may be most likely to conceive	Poor to fair	Yes	No
Vasectomy (male sterilization)	Surgical procedure in which the tube through which sperm is transported from the testes to the penis is severed, so that no sperm can be ejaculated	Excellent	Not usually	No
Tubal ligation (female sterilization)	Surgical procedure in which the fallopian tubes that carry egg cells (ova) from the ovary to the uterus are severed and tied back	Excellent	Not usually	No

[a]Excellent: Fewer than 5% of women who use method become pregnant within a year.
[b]About 10% of women whose partners wear a condom become pregnant within a year.

2 *Moral acceptability.* A method that is acceptable to one person may be unacceptable to another. The rhythm method may be acceptable to people from various faiths, but more intrusive or active methods of birth control may not. For example, some types of birth control pills prevent fertilization, whereas others allow fertilization to occur but then prevent implantation of the fertilized ovum in the uterus. The latter can be said to produce a form of early abortion, which would be of concern to people

Table 13.2	Reported Types of Contraception Students Used the Last Time They Engaged in Vaginal Intercourse					
	Total		**Female**		**Male**	
Contraceptive Method	*n*	%	*n*	%	*n*	%
Birth control pills	7,697	39.5	5,001	40.5	2,288	38.2
Condoms (male or female)	6,886	35.3	4,160	33.7	2,344	39.1
Withdrawal	2,888	14.8	1,874	15.2	828	13.8
Spermicide	698	3.6	402	3.3	247	4.1
Fertility awareness	520	2.7	344	2.8	148	2.5
Depo Provera	494	2.5	329	2.7	131	2.2
Diaphragm/cervical cap/sponge	64	0.3	37	0.3	22	0.4
Norplant	23	0.1	11	0.1	9	0.2
Other method	597	3.1	407	3.3	148	2.5
Nothing	708	3.6	425	3.4	239	4.0

Note: Refers to Question 28; "If you had vaginal intercourse, what method did you or your partner use to prevent pregnancy the last time? (select all that apply)." Because of missing data by sex, the response categories do not always equal the total.

Source: American College Health Association, 2005. Reprinted by permission of The American College Health Association.

who object to abortion on moral grounds. Yet the same people may have no moral objection to preventing fertilization.

3 *Cost.* Methods vary in cost. Some require medical visits in addition to the cost of the devices themselves.

4 *Sharing responsibility.* Most forms of contraception largely place the burden of responsibility on the woman. She must consult with her physician to obtain birth control pills or other prescription devices. She must take birth control pills reliably or check to see that her intrauterine device (IUD) remains in place. Of course, a man can share in the responsibility for the birth control pill by accompanying his partner on her medical visits and sharing the cost.

5 *Safety.* What are the method's side effects? What health risks are connected with its use?

6 *Reversibility.* Can the contraceptive effects of the birth control method be fully—and easily—reversed by discontinuing its use? How quickly? It is wise to consider sterilization to be irreversible, even though attempts at reversal are often successful.

7 *Protection against sexually transmitted diseases (STDs).* Does the method afford protection against STDs? For example, condoms do; oral contraceptives don't.

8 *Effectiveness.* What is the level of effectiveness of the particular method? Techniques vary in their effectiveness in actual use (if in doubt, ask your physician or health care provider). Some are almost perfectly effective; others are quite iffy.

All said, we can see that there is much variety in sexual expression, both around the world and around the neighborhood. Let us now turn to consider how our bodies respond to sexual stimulation by focusing on the stages of sexual response identified by famed sex researchers William Masters and Virginia Johnson. First, however, you may want to glimpse at a new challenge faced by many people in today's wired world—cybersex addiction.

13.2.2 The Sexual Response Cycle

Although we may be culturally attuned to focus on gender differences rather than similarities, Masters and Johnson (1966) found that the biological responses of males and females to sexual stimulation—that is, their sexual response cycles—are quite similar. Masters and Johnson used the term **sexual response cycle** to describe the changes that

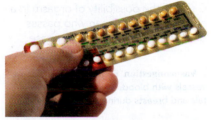
Clayton Hansen/iStockphoto

Marcin Bania/Stockphoto

Selecting a Method of Contraception
Many varieties of contraceptives are available today. Among the factors to consider in choosing a contraceptive method is the convenience, effectiveness, moral acceptability, reversibility, and cost. People may also wish to consider whether the method provides protection against STDs and whether it allows both partners to share the responsibility.

| **Sexual response cycle** Masters and Johnson's model of sexual response, which consists of four stages or phases.

Figure 13.4

Levels of Arousal During the Phases of the Sexual Response Cycle

Masters and Johnson divide the sexual response cycle into four phases: excitement, plateau, orgasm, and resolution. During the resolution phase, the level of sexual arousal returns to the prearoused state. For men there is a refractory period following orgasm. As shown by the broken line, however, men can become rearoused to orgasm once the refractory period is past and their levels of sexual arousal have returned to preplateau levels. Pattern A for women shows a response cycle with multiple orgasms. Pattern B shows the cycle of a woman who reaches the plateau phase but for whom arousal is "resolved" without reaching the orgasmic phase. Pattern C shows the possibility of orgasm in a highly aroused woman who passes quickly through the plateau phase.

▌ **Vasocongestion** Engorgement of blood vessels with blood, which swells the genitals and breasts during sexual arousal.

▌ **Myotonia** Muscle tension.

▌ **Excitement phase** The first phase of the sexual response cycle, which is characterized by erection in the male, vaginal lubrication in the female, myotonia (muscle tension), and increases in heart rate in both males and females.

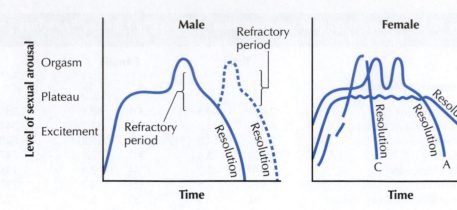

occur in the body as men and women become sexually aroused. They divided the sexual response cycle into four phases: excitement, plateau, orgasm, and resolution. Figure 13.4 suggests the levels of sexual arousal associated with each phase.

The sexual response cycle is characterized by **vasocongestion** and **myotonia**. Vasocongestion is the swelling of the genital tissues with blood. It causes erection of the penis and swelling of the area surrounding the vaginal opening. The testes, the nipples, and even the earlobes swell as blood vessels dilate in these areas (yes—the earlobes). Myotonia is muscle tension. It causes facial grimaces, spasms in the hands and feet, and then the spasms of orgasm.

13.2.3 Excitement Phase

Vasocongestion during the **excitement phase** can cause erection in young men as soon as 3 to 8 seconds after sexual stimulation begins. The scrotal skin also thickens, becoming less baggy. The testes increase in size and become elevated.

In the female, excitement is characterized by vaginal lubrication, which may start 10 to 30 seconds after sexual stimulation begins. Vasocongestion swells the clitoris and flattens and spreads the vaginal lips. The inner part of the vagina expands. The breasts enlarge, and blood vessels near the surface become more prominent.

In the excitement phase the skin may take on a rosy sex flush. This is more pronounced in women. The nipples may become erect in both men and women. Heart rate and blood pressure also increase.

Warning Signs of Cybersex Addiction

Self-Assessment

- Are you spending increasing amounts of time at sex-related sites on the Internet?
- Do you experience frequent urges to visit sex sites on the Internet?
- Have you clicked on sex sites in your place of employment or school, even though you knew you could get into trouble?
- Do you engage in sexual interchanges with people in chat rooms?
- Do you hide your Internet surfing from your spouse or children because you are ashamed of the sites you are visiting?
- Do you have difficulty stopping yourself from using the Internet for sexual gratification?
- Do you prefer seeking sexual experiences on the Internet to having sexual relations with your spouse or lover?
- Has your use of the Internet "spilled over" into your daily life, such as by using phone sex services or frequenting X-rated stores?
- Are you worried about your sexual behavior or inclinations? Should you be?

    If you answered "yes" to any of these questions, we suggest you speak about these concerns with a professional counselor. Like other forms of addictive behavior, cybersex addiction can lead to potentially damaging consequences.

Adjustment and Modern Life

"Cybersex Addiction"— A New Adjustment Problem

Online pornography has become a multi-billion dollar industry. Estimates are that at least a third of all Web visits involve sexually oriented sites, chat rooms, and news groups (Cooper et al., 2000, 2004). Although romps into cybersex may seem relatively harmless in many cases, psychologists say that the easy affordability, accessibility, and anonymity of surfing the Internet fuels a brand-new adjustment problem—cybersex addiction (Gerevich et al., 2005; Philaretou et al., 2005). The problem seems to be spreading rapidly and has the potential to bring turmoil into the lives of affected people.

A leading expert in cyberspace addiction, psychologist Al Cooper of the San Jose Marital and Sexuality Center in Santa Clara, California, and his colleagues (2000, 2004) report that many of the people who are spending dozens of hours a week seeking online sexual stimulation deny that they have a problem, just like other kinds of addicts frequently deny they have a problem. It is not uncommon for them to refuse help until their marriages or their jobs are in jeopardy. Yet they may spend hours a day masturbating to pornographic images, or they may have "mutual" online sex with someone they find in a chat room. Now and then, they progress to actual extramarital affairs with partners they meet online. In an interview with Jane Brody (2000a), sex therapist Dr. Mark Schwartz said that "sex on the Net is like heroin. It grabs [people] and takes over their lives. And it's very difficult to treat because the people affected don't want to give it up."

Cooper and his colleagues (2000) refer to the Internet as "the crack cocaine of sexual compulsivity." They conducted a survey online with 9,265 men and women who admitted surfing the Net for sex, and they found that at least 1% of the respondents appeared to be seriously hooked on online sex. The survey found that as many as a third of Internet users admitted to visiting a sexually oriented website. One male respondent in five and one female respondent in eight admitted to surfing for sex at work. Projecting this figure to Americans as a whole, we can estimate that there are at least a couple of hundred thousand cybersex addicts. We should also realize that the respondents were self-selected and that people tend to deny that they have lost control over some aspect of their behavior. Therefore, the figure of 1% is probably an underestimate. "This is a hidden public health hazard exploding, in part, because very few are recognizing it as such or taking it seriously," writes Cooper (Cooper et al., 2000).

Cooper compares cybersex compulsives with drug addicts. He notes that they "use the Internet as an important part of their sexual acting out, much like a drug addict who has a 'drug of choice,'" often with serious consequences for their occupational and social lives. People "whose sexuality may have been suppressed and limited all their lives [who] suddenly find an infinite supply of sexual opportunities" are especially vulnerable to becoming hooked on cybersex.

Cybersex, like many psychoactive drugs, has reinforcement value. Schwartz writes that "intense orgasms from the minimal investment of a few keystrokes are powerfully reinforcing. Cybersex affords easy, inexpensive access to a myriad of ritualized encounters with idealized partners" (cited in Cooper et al., 2000).

Sometimes the computer turns users on before the users turn the computer on. (Yes, we'll explain.) One contributor to the Cooper article noted that some cybersex addicts become conditioned such that that their computer elicits sexual arousal even before they turn it on. He suggested that these people become especially highly motivated to surf for sex whenever they approach a computer, even at work. Thus their jobs become jeopardized.

As with other addictions, people can develop tolerance to cybersex stimulation. Thus they need to take greater risks to recapture the initial high. Some surf for sex when their spouses or children are nearby. Others do so at work. And some compulsively seek to meet sex partners online and subsequently in the flesh. Surfing for sex on the job has become so common that many companies now monitor employees' online behavior. Repeated visits to sex sites have cost people their jobs. And some people land in prison for downloading child pornography. Possessing or distributing child pornography is a criminal act in the United States.

Children can be victimized by a parent's addiction to cybersex in other ways. They can stumble across the pornographic material that is downloaded or left on a monitor. They may walk in on a parent who is viewing online sexual material. As with other addictions, once people become dependent on cybersex, they often place themselves and others at risk and do things they wouldn't normally do.

Martyn Vickery/Alamy

Cybersex Addiction
Many people spend dozens of hours a week seeking online sexual stimulation. Although their surfing for sex may interfere with their work and home lives, they usually deny that they have an adjustment problem.

13.2.4 Plateau Phase

▮ **Plateau phase** The second phase of the sexual response cycle, which is characterized by increases in vasocongestion, muscle tension, heart rate, and blood pressure in preparation for orgasm.

The level of sexual arousal remains somewhat stable during the **plateau phase** of the cycle. Because of vasocongestion, men show some increase in the circumference of the head of the penis, which also takes on a purplish hue. The testes are elevated into position for ejaculation and may reach one and a half times their unaroused size.

In women, vasocongestion swells the outer part of the vagina, contracting the vaginal opening in preparation for grasping the penis. The inner part of the vagina expands further. The clitoris withdraws beneath the clitoral hood and shortens. Breathing becomes rapid, like panting. Heart rate may increase to 100 to 160 beats per minute. Blood pressure continues to rise.

13.2.5 Orgasmic Phase

▮ **Orgasmic phase** The third phase of the sexual response cycle, which is characterized by pelvic contractions and accompanied by intense pleasure.

The **orgasmic phase** in the male consists of two stages of muscular contractions. In the first stage, semen collects at the base of the penis. The internal sphincter of the urinary bladder prevents urine from mixing with semen. In the second stage, muscle contractions propel the ejaculate out of the body. Sensations of pleasure tend to be related to the strength of the contractions and the amount of seminal fluid present. The first three to four contractions are generally most intense and occur at 0.8-second intervals (five contractions every 4 seconds). Another two to four contractions occur at a somewhat slower pace. Rates and patterns can vary from one man to another. Orgasm in the female is characterized by 3 to 15 contractions of the pelvic muscles that surround the vaginal barrel. The first contractions occur at 0.8-second intervals. As in the male, they produce release of sexual tension. Weaker and slower contractions follow.

Erection, vaginal lubrication, and orgasm are all reflexes; that is, they occur automatically in response to adequate sexual stimulation. Of course, the decision to enter a sexual relationship is voluntary, as are the decisions to kiss and fondle each other, and so on. Blood pressure and heart rate reach a peak, with the heart beating up to 180 times per minute. Respiration may increase to 40 breaths per minute.

13.2.6 Resolution Phase

▮ **Resolution phase** The fourth phase of the sexual response cycle, during which the body gradually returns to its prearoused state.

After orgasm, the body returns to its unaroused state. This is called the **resolution phase**. After ejaculation, blood is released from engorged areas, causing the erection to disappear. The testes return to their normal size.

In women, orgasm also triggers the release of blood from engorged areas. The nipples return to their normal size. The clitoris and vaginal barrel gradually shrink to their unaroused sizes. Blood pressure, heart rate, and breathing also return to their levels before arousal. Both partners may feel relaxed and satisfied.

▮ **Refractory period** A period of time following a response (e.g., orgasm) during which an individual is not responsive to further sexual stimulation.

Unlike women, men enter a **refractory period** during which they cannot experience another orgasm or ejaculate. The refractory period of adolescent males may last only minutes, whereas that of men age 50 and above may last from several minutes to a day. Women do not undergo a refractory period and therefore can become quickly rearoused to the point of repeated (multiple) orgasm if they desire and receive continued sexual stimulation.

The changes in our bodies that occur during sexual stimulation are summarized in Table 13.3.

Table 13.3 ▮ Sexual Response Cycle: How Our Bodies Respond to Sexual Stimulation

In Males	In Females	In Both Genders
Excitement Phase		
Vasocongestion results in erection.	Vasocongestion swells vaginal tissue, clitoris, and the area surrounding the opening of the vagina.	Vasocongestion of genital tissues occurs.
The testes begin to elevate.	Vaginal lubrication appears.	Heart rate, muscle tension (*myotonia*), and blood pressure increase.
Skin on the scrotum tenses and thickens.	The inner two-thirds of the vagina expand and vaginal walls thicken and turn a deeper color.	Nipples may become erect.
Plateau Phase		
The tip of the penis turns a deep reddish-purple.	Inner two-thirds of vagina expand fully.	Vasocongestion increases.
Testes become completely elevated.	Outer third of vagina thickens.	Myotonia, heart rate, and blood pressure continue to increase.
Droplets of semen may be released from penile opening before ejaculation.	Clitoris retracts behind its hood. The uterus elevates and increases in size.	
Orgasmic Phase		
Sensations of impending ejaculation lasting 2 to 3 seconds precede the ejaculatory reflex.	Contractions of the pelvic muscles surrounding the vagina occur.	Orgasm releases sexual tension and produces intense feelings of pleasure.
Orgasmic contractions propel semen through the penis and out of the body.		Muscle spasms occur throughout the body; blood pressure, heart rate, and breathing rate reach a peak.
Resolution Phase		
Men become physiologically incapable of achieving another orgasm or ejaculation for a period of time called a refractory period.	Multiple orgasms may occur if the woman desires it and sexual stimulation continues.	Lacking continued sexual stimulation, myotonia and vasocongestion lessen and the body gradually returns to its prearoused state.

Adjustment and Modern Life

In Search of the Magic Fragrance: What Does the Nose Really Know?

For centuries, people have searched for aphrodisiacs, or love potions. Fragrance companies today are investing millions to discover chemicals that can arouse ardent passion. Some scientists suggest that such potions may already exist in the form of chemical secretions known as **pheromones**. Responses to pheromones are biologically wired into the organism and play an important role in other species in attracting mates, marking territory, establishing dominance hierarchies, and controlling aggression (Chamero et al., 2007; Nakagawa et al., 2005). But what role, if any, do pheromones play in determining human behavior? Let us consider the research evidence.

Pheromones are odorless chemicals that are detected through a "sixth sense"—the vomeronasal organ (VNO). People possess such an organ, located in the mucous lining of the nose (Liberles & Buck, 2006). During the embryonic period, the VNO acts as a pathway for sex hormones into the brain, aiding in the process by which the brain becomes sexually differentiated in a masculine or feminine direction. But prior to birth, the VNO in humans shrinks, and we lack evidence that it continues to work following birth. If it does continue to work, it might detect pheromones and communicate information about them to the hypothalamus, where certain pheromones might affect sexual response. People might also use pheromones in many other ways. Infants might use them to recognize their mothers, and adults might respond to them in seeking a mate.

We know that pheromones induce mating behavior in insects. So what about humans? (We thought you'd never ask.) Although more research needs to be done, we have some evidence that chemical substances found in the underarm secretions of young women can increase men's perceptions of women's sexual attractiveness (McCoy & Pitino, 2002). Other research with women volunteers shows that applying male perspiration (thankfully disguised by fragrance) to the women's lips induced feelings of relaxation and even sexual arousal in some of the participants (Pilcher, 2003; Preti et al., 2003; Wyart et al., 2007).

All told, we have yet to find compelling evidence that pheromones—or suspected pheromones—directly affect sexual behavior in humans in any meaningful way (Shepherd, 2006). Still, fragrance companies are forever searching for that magical chemical formula that will induce sexual desire. But as Richard Doty, a leading expert on olfaction and gestation, says of the search for pheromones in humans: "My view is that the whole thing is primarily driven by the perfume industry, and when looked at carefully sort of falls apart" (cited in Benson, 2002, p. 48). Although we should keep an open mind about the possible role of pheromones in human sexual behavior, we should also remember that human behavior is much more complex than the behavior of other animals and more dependent on social contexts.

Joey Nelson/iStockphoto

Love Potion Number 9?

What does the nose know? Might we humans be subject to the sexual attractants, or pheromones, that help regulate sexual behavior in many other species? What does the evidence suggest? What is your view?

❚ **Pheromones** Chemical substances secreted by many species that have various functions, including sexual attraction.

MODULE REVIEW

Review It

(10) The practice of oral sex has become the _____ among adult couples.

(11) Birth control pills have (excellent or fair?) reliability.

(12) Sterilization (is or is not?) considered to be a reversible birth control method.

(13) Masters and Johnson divide the sexual response cycle into four phases: excitement, _____, orgasm, and resolution.

(14) The excitement phase of the sexual response cycle is generally characterized by_____ and _____.

(15) Sexual excitement reaches a peak during the _____ _____ of the sexual response cycle.

(16) Only men experience a _____ _____ during the resolution phase.

Think About It

Would you characterize female and male sexual responses as being more alike or more different? Explain.

MODULE 13.3

Rape

- ❚ What motives underlie rape?
- ❚ What are some common myths about rape?
- ❚ How can we prevent rape?

❚ **Rape** Forced sexual intercourse.

Parents regularly encourage their daughters to be wary of strangers and strange places—places where they could fall prey to rapists. Certainly the threat of **rape** from strangers is real enough. Yet four out of five rapes are committed by people the victims know—dating partners, family members, spouses, or acquaintances (Laumann et al., 1994). Overall, as many as one in four women in the United States suffer a rape during their lifetimes (Brener et al., 1999; Koss & Kilpatrick, 2001).

Rape, especially date rape, is a pressing concern on college and high school campuses (Fisher et al., 2003). A recent nationwide survey of college students showed that 6.4% of college women and 2% of college men say that during the past year they have experienced either an attempted or completed rape (unwanted sexual penetration; see Table 13.4) (American College Health Association, 2005).

Consider one woman's account of date rape from the authors' files:

I first met him at a party. He was really good-looking and he had a great smile. I wanted to meet him but I wasn't sure how. I didn't want to appear too forward. Then he came over and introduced himself. We talked and found we had a lot in common. I really liked him. When he asked me over to his place for a drink, I thought it would be okay. He was such a good listener, and I wanted him to ask me out again.

When we got to his room, the only place to sit was on the bed. I didn't want him to get the wrong idea, but what else could I do? We talked for a while and then he made his move. I was so startled. He started by kissing. I really liked him so the kissing was nice. But then he pushed me down on the bed. I tried to get up and I told him to stop. He was so much bigger and stronger. I got scared and I started to cry. I froze and he raped me.

It took only a couple of minutes and it was terrible, he was so rough. When it was over he kept asking me what was wrong, like he didn't know. He had just forced himself on me and he thought that was okay. He drove me home and said he wanted to see me again. I'm so afraid to see him. I never thought it would happen to me.

Student surveys reveal that unwelcome touching and outright sexual assault are widespread problems in our society:

- A survey of female high school students in Massachusetts and Minnesota found that between 10% and 20% of these young women reported that they had been physically or sexually assaulted by a dating partner (Silverman et al., 2001; Stenson, 2001).
- A recent survey of college students showed that one in four reported experiences in which they were sexually touched, grabbed, or intentionally brushed upon (mashed) against their will (Schemo, 2006).
- A survey of college men from California and Ohio showed that more than one out of three admitted to coercing women into sexual activity by means of arguments, pressure, or force (Hall et al., 2000). About one man in seven had reportedly coerced a woman into sexual intercourse by means of arguments, pressure, or force.

Table 13.4 ▌ Types of Sexual Assault Students Reported Experiencing in the Past School Year

Sexual Assault Behavior	Total		Female		Male	
	n	%	*n*	%	*n*	%
Verbal threats for sex against your will	712	3.7	517	4.2	140	2.3
Sexual touching against your will	1,914	9.9	1,464	11.9	340	5.7
Attempted sexual penetration against your will	624	3.2	512	4.2	70	1.2
Sexual penetration against your will	339	1.8	269	2.2	49	0.8

Note: Refers to Question 7: "Within the last school year, have you experienced…?" Because of missing data by sex, the response categories do not always equal the total.

Source: American College Health Association, 2005. Reprinted by permission of the American College Health Association.

Make no mistake, coerced or forced sexual intercourse is rape. It doesn't matter what the woman was wearing or what sexual play she may have consented to beforehand; when she fails to consent to a sexual act, or says *no* or *stop*, it means *no*. Not *maybe*, not *perhaps*, but *no*.

13.3.1 Why Do Men Rape Women?

What motivates rape? Many social scientists believe that rape has more to do with motives of power, control, and revenge than sexual desire (Hall & Barongan, 1997). Rape is often a means by which a man seeks to control and dominate a woman, or to exact revenge because of a history of perceived mistreatment and humiliation by women. With some rapists, violence appears to enhance sexual arousal. They therefore seek to combine sex and aggression (Barbaree & Marshall, 1991).

Evolutionary psychologists suggest that among ancestral humans, males who were more sexually aggressive were more likely to transmit their genes to future generations (Fisher, 2000; Thornhill & Palmer, 2000). Thus, men may have a genetic tendency to be more sexually aggressive than women. However, evolutionary psychologists do not condone rape or sexual aggression. Human beings can choose whether or not to act aggressively.

Many social critics, however, contend that American culture also socializes young men—including perhaps the nice young man next door—into sexually aggressive roles by reinforcing them for aggressive and competitive behavior (Davis & Liddell, 2002; Holcomb et al., 2002). Young men learn from an early age that they are expected to dominate and overpower opponents on the playing fields. Unfortunately, these lessons may carry over into the bedroom when women resist their sexual overtures. Many young men view their dating partners as opponents whose resistance must be overcome by whatever means necessary, even if it requires the use of force. The addition of alcohol to the mix impairs judgment and ability to weigh the consequences of behavior, further raising the risk of sexual aggression (Testa, 2002).

We also need to consider the cognitive underpinnings to rape. Men may misread a woman's resistance as a form of coy game-playing on her part, thinking that "no" means "maybe" and "maybe" means "yes." They may misread other signals or delude themselves into believing that the woman truly "wanted it," as shown in these comments by the man who raped the woman whose story appeared earlier in the section:

> I first met her at a party. She looked really hot, wearing a sexy dress that showed off her great body. We started talking right away. I knew that she liked me by the way she kept smiling and touching my arm while she was speaking. She seemed pretty relaxed so I asked her back to my place for a drink.... When she said yes, I knew that I was going to be lucky!
>
> When we got to my place, we sat on the bed kissing. At first, everything was great. Then, when I started to lay her down on the bed, she started twisting and saying she didn't want to. Most women don't like to appear too easy, so I knew that she was just going through the motions. When she stopped struggling, I knew that she would have to throw in some tears before we did it.
>
> She was still very upset afterwards, and I just don't understand it! If she didn't want to have sex, why did she come back to the room with me? You could tell by the way she dressed and acted that she was no virgin, so why she had to put up such a big struggle I don't know.

Let us turn to another cognitive factor in rape—the belief in stereotypical myths about rape.

13.3.2 Myths About Rape

In the United States there are many myths about rape—myths that blame the victim (Bernat, Wilson, & Calhoun, 1999) (see Tables 13.5 and 13.6). One example is the belief that the woman is partly responsible for rape if she dresses provocatively. Other myths include the notions that "women say no when they mean yes" and "rapists are crazed by sexual desire" (Powell, 1996, p. 139). Still another myth is that deep down inside, women want to be raped. Such myths deny the impact of the assault and transfer blame onto the victim. Men who support traditional, rigidly defined gender roles are more likely to blame the victims of rape (Raichle & Lambert, 2000). The myths contribute to a social climate that is too often lenient toward rapists and unsympathetic toward victims. Moreover, the myths lead to hostility toward women, which, in turn, can lead to rape (Hall et al., 2000) (see Figure 13.5).

If you want to learn whether you harbor some of the more common myths about rape, complete the self-assessment on page 439.

Table 13.5 ▮ Would You Classify the Following as Rape or Not?

		Rape	Not Rape
A man has sex with a women who has passed out after drinking too much.	Female	88%	9%
	Male	77%	17%
A married man has sex with his wife even though she does not want him to.	Female	61%	30%
	Male	56%	38%
A man argues with a woman who does not want to have sex until she agrees to have sex.	Female	42%	53%
	Male	33%	59%
A man uses emotional pressure, but no physical force, to get a woman to have sex.	Female	39%	55%
	Male	33%	59%
		Yes	*No*
(Do you believe that some women like to be talked into having sex?)	Female	54%	33%
	Male	69%	20%

Table 13.6 ▮ Once Again, Would You Classify the Following as Rape or Not?

	Age	Rape	Not Rape
She is under the influence of drugs or alcohol.	18–34	31%	66%
	35–49	35%	58%
	50+	57%	36%
She initially says yes to having sex and then changes her mind.	18–34	34%	60%
	35–49	43%	53%
	50+	43%	46%
She dresses provocatively.	18–34	28%	70%
	35–49	31%	67%
	50+	53%	42%
She agrees to go to the man's room or home.	18–34	20%	76%
	35–49	29%	70%
	50+	53%	41%
		Yes	*No*
Have you ever been in a situation with a man in which you said no but ended up having sex anyway?	Asked of females	18%	80%

Figure 13.5

A Common Pathway to Sexual Aggression

A statistical technique called path analysis reveals the powerful cognitive aspects of sexual aggression. Belief in rape myths, such as the idea that women really want to be raped or that women who dress provocatively get what's coming to them, increases hostility toward women. Hostility toward women in turn may prompt sexual aggression.

Belief in rape myths (e.g., "Way deep down, women really want to be raped," "Women who dress provocatively get what's coming to them.") → Hostility toward women → Sex play or sexual intercourse by using arguments, pressure, threats, or force

13.3.3 Preventing Rape

Don't accept rides from strange men—and remember that all men are strange.
—ROBIN MORGAN

The aftermath of rape can include physical harm, anxiety, depression, sexual dysfunction, sexually transmitted disease, and/or pregnancy. From a sociocultural perspective, prevention of rape involves publicly examining and challenging the widely held cultural attitudes and ideals that contribute to rape. The traditions of male dominance and rewards for male aggressiveness take a daily toll on women. One thing we can do is encourage colleges and universities to require students to attend rape awareness lectures and seminars. These educational programs seek to promote more respectful attitudes toward women (O'Donohue, Yeater, & Fanetti, 2003). Among the objectives of these programs is to dispel myths about rape and for men to learn that "no" means "no." Although these programs can help change attitudes, we lack firm evidence that they reduce the incidence of sexual assault on campus (Breitenbecher, 2000). Nonetheless, they focus much-needed attention on the problem of rape on campus. On a societal level, we need to encourage our community and national leaders to pay more attention to the problem and to enact policies that send the clear and consistent message that sexual coercion of any form will not be tolerated.

On a personal level, there are things that women can do to protect themselves. *The New Our Bodies, Ourselves* (Boston Women's Health Book Collective, 1993) includes the following suggestions for preventing rape by strangers:

- Establish signals and arrangements with other women in an apartment building or neighborhood.
- List only first initials in the telephone directory or on the mailbox.
- Use deadbolt locks.
- Keep windows locked and obtain iron grids for first-floor windows.
- Keep entrances and doorways brightly lit.
- Have keys ready for the front door or the car.
- Do not walk alone in the dark.
- Never allow a strange man into your apartment or home without checking his credentials.
- Drive with the car windows up and the door locked.
- Check the rear seat of the car before entering.
- Avoid living in an unsafe building.
- Do not pick up hitchhikers (including women).
- Do not talk to strange men in the street.
- Shout "Fire!" not "Rape!" People crowd around fires but avoid scenes of violence.

Let us also offer some suggestions for preventing date rape (after Powell, 1996):

- *Communicate your sexual limits to your date.* Tell your partner how far you would like to go so that he will understand the limits. For example, if your partner starts fondling you in ways that make you uncomfortable, you might say, "I'd prefer if you didn't touch me there. I really like you, but I prefer not getting so intimate at this point in our relationship."

Bob Mahoney/Getty Images News and Sport Services

Rape Awareness Workshops

Many colleges offer rape awareness workshops which are intended to dispel myths about rape and promote more respectful attitudes toward women.

- *Meet new dates in public places, and avoid driving with a stranger or a group of people you've just met.* When meeting a new date, drive in your own car and meet your date at a public place. Don't drive with strangers or offer rides to strangers or groups of people. In some cases of date rape, the group disappears just prior to the assault.

- *State your refusal in definitive terms.* Be firm in refusing a sexual overture. Look your partner straight in the eye. The more definite you are, the less likely your partner will be to misinterpret your wishes.

- *Become aware of your fears.* Take notice of any fears of displeasing your partner that might stifle your assertiveness. If your partner is truly respectful of you, you need not fear an angry or demeaning response. But if your partner is not respectful, it is best to become aware of it early and end the relationship right away.

- *Pay attention to your "vibes."* Trust your gut-level feelings. Many victims of acquaintance rape said afterward that they had a strange feeling about the man but ignored it.

- *Be especially cautious if you are in a new environment, such as college or a foreign country.* You may be especially vulnerable to exploitation when you are becoming acquainted with a new environment, different people, and different customs.

- *If you have broken off a relationship with someone you don't really like or feel good about, don't let him into your place.* Many acquaintance rapes are committed by ex-lovers and ex-boyfriends.

- *Stay sober and see that your date does, too.* Alcohol can loosen inhibitions, cloud judgment, and make one more vulnerable to nonconsensual sex.

Cultural Myths That Create a Climate That Supports Rape

Self-Assessment

Read each of the following statements and indicate whether you believe it to be true or false by circling the T or the F. Then look below the statements to evaluate your beliefs.

T F   1. Women who dress provocatively in public places are just "asking for it."
T F   2. A woman who accompanies a man home from a club or a bar deserves whatever she gets.
T F   3. Women who claim they were raped are just looking for excuses for having engaged in sex.
T F   4. Any physically healthy woman could resist a man's advances if she really wanted to.
T F   5. If a woman allows a man to touch her in a sexual way, it means she wants to have intercourse.
T F   6. Most women who are raped probably did something to lead the man on.
T F   7. If a woman initiates touching or petting with a man, it's her own fault if things go too far.
T F   8. Women may not admit it, but they truly want to be overpowered by men.
T F   9. If a woman has too much to drink at a party, it's her fault if men take advantage of her.
T F 10. Rape is often a misunderstanding that gets out of hand.

Each of these items represents a rape myth. For example, a rapist who believes that women truly desire to be overpowered by men may think he was just giving the woman what she wanted. But how can anyone know what someone else truly wants unless that person reveals it? Such beliefs are often used as self-serving justifications to explain away unacceptable behavior. Let's be entirely clear about this: When it comes to sex, *no* means *no*. Not *maybe*. Not *sometimes*. *Not in a few minutes.*

Just *no*. Moreover, consenting to one sexual act (fondling, kissing, oral sex, etc.) does not imply consent for any other sexual act. Anyone has a right to say *no* at any time or to place limits on what they are willing to do. If you endorsed any of these items, apply your critical thinking skills to reexamine your beliefs.

Rape myths may also contribute to the greater leniency accorded sexual assailants than other types of assailants. If you believe that rape victims "get what they have coming to them," your sympathies may lie more with the assailant than with the victim.

Let's set the record straight: The responsibility for a sexual crime, as with any other crime, lies entirely with the assailant, not the victim.

Source: Adapted from Burt, 1980.

MODULE REVIEW

Review It

(17) Most rapes are committed by (strangers or acquaintances?).

(18) Many social scientists argue that rape mainly has to do with (sex or power?).

(19) Men who support traditional, rigidly defined gender roles are (more or less?) likely to blame the victims of rape.

Think About It

What role does cultural learning play in creating a social context for rape?

MODULE 13.4

Sexual Dysfunctions

■ What are sexual dysfunctions?

■ What are the major types of sexual dysfunctions?

■ What are the origins of sexual dysfunctions?

■ How are sexual dysfunctions treated?

■ **Sexual dysfunctions** Persistent, recurring problems in becoming sexually aroused or reaching orgasm.

Rolf Bruderer/Masterfile

Sexual Dysfunction or a Troubled Relationship?
Problems in a relationship can affect sexual desire and performance. Lack of sexual interest may then further strain the relationship.

Millions of Americans experience **sexual dysfunctions**, or persistent difficulties in sexual interest, arousal, or response. Estimates indicate that nearly half (43%) of American women and about a third of American men (31%) experience sexual dysfunctions at some points in their lives (Laumann, Paik, & Rosen, 1999; Rosen & Laumann, 2003).

Perhaps the best source of information on the frequency of sexual problems is the National Health and Social Life Survey (NHSLS) (Laumann et al., 1994) (see Table 13.7). The NHSLS group asked people for a yes-or-no answer to questions such as "During the last 12 months has there ever been a period of several months or more when you lacked interest in having sex?" Higher percentages of women reported problems in the areas of painful sex, lack of pleasure, inability to reach orgasm, and lack of interest in sex. Higher percentages of men reported reaching orgasm too early and being anxious about their performance. The NHSLS focused on persistent current problems that are characteristic of sexual dysfunctions. The occurrence of occasional problems is likely to be even higher.

Let us briefly review several of the major types of sexual dysfunctions that are classified by the American Psychiatric Association (2000): hypoactive sexual desire disorder, female sexual arousal disorder, male erectile disorder, orgasmic disorder, and premature ejaculation.

13.4.1 Types of Sexual Dysfunctions

In **hypoactive sexual desire disorder**, the person reports a lack of interest in sexual activity, low sexual drive, and, frequently, an absence of any sexual fantasies. The diagnosis reflects the belief that sexual interest, drive, and fantasies fall within the normal spectrum of human sexuality. Not surprisingly, the disorder is associated with lower levels of satisfaction with a relationship and lower levels of sexual activity (Leiblum et al., 2006). In the female, sexual arousal is characterized by vaginal lubri-

Table 13.7 ▪ Current Sexual Dysfunctions According to the NHSLS Study (Percent of Respondents Reporting the Problem Within the Past Year)

	Men	Women
Pain during sex	3.0	14.4
Sex not pleasurable	8.1	21.2
Unable to reach orgasm (orgasmic disorder)	8.3	24.1
Lack of interest in sex (hypoactive sexual desire)	11.8	33.4
Anxiety about performance[a]	17.0	11.5
Reaching climax too early (premature ejaculation in the male)	28.5	10.3
Unable to keep an erection (male erectile disorder, also called erectile dysfunction, or ED)[b]	10.4	—
Having trouble lubricating (female sexual arousal disorder)	—	18.8

Source: Adapted from Tables 10.8A and 10.8B, pages 370 and 371, in E. O. Laumann, J. H. Gagnon, R. T. Michael, and S. Michaels (1994), *The Social Organization of Sexuality: Sexual Practices in the United States.* Chicago: University of Chicago Press.

[a]Anxiety about performance is not itself a sexual dysfunction. However, it figures prominently in sexual dysfunction.

[b]Other studies shows that as many as half or more of men in middle and late adulthod have difficulty obtaining or maintaining an erection.

cation that prepares the vagina for penile penetration. Sexual arousal in the male is characterized by erection.

Almost all women now and then have difficulty becoming or remaining lubricated. Almost all men have occasional difficulty attaining an erection or maintaining an erection through intercourse. The diagnoses of **female sexual arousal disorder** and **male erectile disorder** are brought to bear when these problems are persistent or recurrent. In **orgasmic disorder**, the man or woman, though sexually excited, is persistently delayed in reaching orgasm or does not reach orgasm at all. Orgasmic disorder and low sexual drive are more common among women than men. Men more commonly have difficulty achieving orgasm too quickly, as in **premature ejaculation**, in which the man ejaculates following minimal sexual stimulation. In some cases, an individual can reach orgasm without difficulty while engaging in sexual relations with one partner, but not with another.

The NHSLS study found differences in the incidences of sexual problems associated with sexual dysfunctions between European Americans and African Americans (Laumann et al., 1994) (see Table 13.8). African American men reported a higher incidence of each sexual dysfunction surveyed than did European American men. African American women reported a higher incidence of most sexual dysfunctions, with the exceptions of painful sex and trouble lubricating.

Since not everyone experiences sexual dysfunctions, researchers have sought to determine why some do and others do not.

▪ **Hypoactive sexual desire disorder** A sexual dysfunction characterized by lack of interest in sexual activity.

▪ **Female sexual arousal disorder** A sexual dysfunction characterized by difficulty in becoming sexually aroused, as defined by vaginal lubrication, or sustaining arousal long enough to engage in satisfying sexual relations.

▪ **Male erectile disorder** A sexual dysfunction characterized by repeated difficulty becoming sexually aroused, as defined by failure to achieve or sustain erection.

▪ **Orgasmic disorder** A sexual dysfunction in which one has difficulty reaching orgasm, although one has become sufficiently sexually aroused.

▪ **Premature ejaculation** Rapid ejaculation that occurs with minimal sexual stimulation.

Table 13.8 ▪ Incidence of Current Sexual Problems Among European Americans and African American Respondents Reporting the Problem Within the Past Year

	European American Men (%)	African American Men (%)	European American Women (%)	African American Women (%)
Pain during sex	3.0	3.3	14.7	12.5
Sex not pleasurable	7.0	11.2	19.7	30.0
Unable to reach orgasm	7.4	9.9	23.2	29.2
Lack of interest in sex	14.7	20.0	30.9	44.5
Anxiety about performance	16.8	23.7	10.5	14.5
Reaching climax too early	27.7	33.8	7.5	20.4
Unable to keep an erection	9.9	14.5	—	—
Having trouble lubricating	—	—	20.7	13.0

13.4.2 Causes of Sexual Dysfunctions

The causes of sexual dysfunctions run the gamut from the biological to the psychological and cultural.

Biological Causes

Many cases of sexual dysfunctions reflect biological problems (Janssen, 2006; Taylor, Rudkin, & Hawton, 2005). Lack of sexual desire, for example, may result from deficient levels of the male sex hormone testosterone, the hormone that plays a key role in activating sexual drive in both men and women. Diabetes can damage blood vessels and nerves, including those that provide blood to the penis, leading to erectile dysfunction (difficulty attaining or maintaining erection). Erectile dysfunction may also involve other medical problems affecting the flow of blood to and through the penis or damage to nerves involved in erection.

We have also learned that obesity increases not only the risks of heart disease and diabetes, but also the risk of erectile dysfunction (Saigal et al., 2006). The underlying process explaining the connection is not clear, but the culprit might be high blood cholesterol levels, a frequent accompaniment of obesity. Cholesterol leads to formation of fatty deposits (plaque) in blood vessels that can impede the flow of blood to the penis just as it impedes the flow of blood to the heart. The good news is that health interventions that help obese men to lose weight and increase their activity levels also lead to better erectile functioning (Esposito et al., 2004).

Other physical causes, such as fatigue and use of alcohol and other drugs, also play roles in sexual problems. Fatigue can reduce sexual desire and inhibit orgasm. Depressants such as alcohol, narcotics, and tranquilizers can also impair sexual response. Lack of sexual drive or interest is often connected with mental health problems, especially depression. Health problems can affect orgasmic functioning in both men and women, including such problems as coronary heart disease; diabetes mellitus; multiple sclerosis; spinal-cord injuries; complications from certain surgical procedures (such as removal of the prostate in men), endocrinological (hormone) problems; and use of certain therapeutic drugs, such as drugs used to treat hypertension and mental health problems.

Adjusting to physical change associated with aging is yet another challenge. Whereas young people often wrestle with the question "Should I?" many older adults fret about the recurring question "Can I?" For example, the NHSLS study found that difficulty in obtaining or keeping an erection (erectile disorder) increases with age from about 6% in the 18- to 24-year-old age group to about 20% in the 55- to 59-year-old age group. A gradual decline in sexual desire, at least among men, may be explained in part by the reduction in testosterone levels that occurs in middle and later life. Injections of testosterone may help increase sexual interest or desire, but men are cautioned to consult with their health care providers in weighing the risks of hormone replacement therapy (Clay, 2009; Heiman, 2008). That said, most physically healthy people can continue to engage successfully in sexual relations well into their advanced years.

Female sexual arousal disorder, like male erectile disorder, may also have physical causes. We recommend a thorough evaluation by a medical specialist: a urologist in the case of a male, a gynecologist in the case of a female. Any neurological, vascular, or hormonal problem that interferes with the lubrication or swelling response of the vagina to sexual stimulation may contribute to female sexual arousal disorder. For example, diabetes mellitus may lead to diminished sexual excitement in women because of the degeneration of the nerves servicing the clitoris and the blood vessel (vascular) damage it causes. Reduced estrogen production—one of the effects of aging—can also result in vaginal dryness.

Pain during sexual activity, like any other kind of pain, is a sign that something is wrong—physically or psychologically. Pain during intercourse can be traced to physical causes, emotional causes, or both. The most common cause of sexual pain in women is inadequate lubrication. Sometimes the problem is solved as easily as providing additional foreplay or artificial lubrication. Vaginal infections or sexually transmitted diseases can also make sexual activity painful. Allergic reactions to spermicides, or the latex material in condoms, can cause pain or irritation during sex. Other physical causes are endometriosis, pelvic inflammatory disease (PID), or structural disorders of the reproductive organs, such as a retroverted uterus. Women who have borne children may even encounter painful sex from a slowly healing—or non-healing—episiotomy. Painful sex is not normal and does not have to be tolerated. Check with a gynecologist.

Psychological Causes

The underlying causes of sexual dysfunctions often involve psychological reasons, such as a history of sexual trauma, unresolved anger toward partners, lack of sexual competencies, and a form of anxiety called **performance anxiety**, or fear of not being able to perform sexually (Firestone, Firestone, & Catlett, 2006; Moore & Heiman, 2006). Problems in the relationship may not be so easily left at the bedroom door. Deep-seated feelings of anger and resentment may be difficult to turn off when the couple go to bed. In other cases, sexual trauma is implicated. Physically or psychologically painful sexual experiences, such as rape, can block future sexual response. Survivors of sexual abuse often find it difficult to respond sexually to their partners or may respond to sexual stimulation with deep feelings of revulsion or disgust rather than pleasure. Feelings of helplessness, anger, or guilt, or even flashbacks of the abuse, may surface when they begin sexual activity, dampening their ability to become aroused. Other psychosocial causes include anxiety or guilt about sex and ineffective stimulation by the partner.

Moreover, a sexual relationship is usually no better than other aspects of a relationship. General difficulties in communication also inhibit the expression of sexual desires.

Irrational beliefs, another psychological factor, can also contribute to sexual dysfunctions. If we believe that we need a lover's approval at all times, we may view a disappointing sexual episode as a catastrophe. If we demand that every sexual encounter be perfect, we set ourselves up for failure.

Sexual competencies, like other competencies, are based on knowledge and skill and derive largely from learning experiences. Although sex is a "natural function," we learn what makes us and others feel good through trial and error, by talking and reading about sex, and perhaps by watching erotic films. Many people do not acquire sexual competencies because of lack of knowledge and experimentation—even within marriage. The irrational belief that a man somehow knows what he is doing sexually—or ought to know—places great demands on couples. For one thing, it discourages many men from seeking (scientific) knowledge about sex or even asking their partners what they like. The belief also leads many women to be reluctant to guide their partners in sexually arousing them. They may think that if they are "forward," or express their sexual likes and dislikes, they will be viewed as sluttish. But it is irrational for people to expect that their lovers can read their minds. Physical or verbal guidance often leads the way to a more fulfilling sexual relationship.

People handicapped by performance anxiety may focus on past failures and expectations of another disaster rather than enjoying present erotic sensations and fantasies. Performance anxiety makes it difficult for a man to attain erection yet may also spur him to ejaculate prematurely. It can also prevent a woman from becoming adequately lubricated or reaching orgasm. Performance anxiety creates vicious cycles in which expectation of failure heightens anxiety. High anxiety levels then impair sexual performance, confirming the individual's—or couple's—fears. One young man with erectile dysfunction who developed a relationship with a young woman kept picturing her face and how disappointed she'd be if he failed to perform. "By the time we did go to bed," he reported, "I was paralyzed with anxiety" (cited in Nevid, Rathus, & Greene, 2006).

▮ **Performance anxiety** Fear concerning whether one will be able to perform adequately.

Sociocultural Causes

Cultural beliefs can also affect sexual response and sexual behavior. For example, the old-fashioned stereotype suggests that men find sex pleasurable but that sex is a duty for women. In this "liberated" day and age, it may seem hard to imagine that Americans are unaware of women's potential for experiencing sexual pleasure. But remember that this is a nation of nations; we have literally hundreds of subcultures. Women (and men) reared in various subcultures may learn quite different attitudes toward sexuality. Even if they "know" about sexual potential from the mass media and sex education programs, they may find it extremely different to relate to—or express—their knowledge. Women and men alike may be so handicapped by misinformation and sexual taboos that they are extremely anxious about sex. These anxieties may create a self-fulfilling prophecy, as we will see.

13.4.3 Sex Therapy

Sexual dysfunctions are often treated by means of sex therapy, which refers to a relatively brief and direct form of psychological treatment that generally incorporates cognitive and behavioral components. Sex therapy is largely indebted to the pioneering work of Masters and Johnson (1970), although other therapists have also developed important techniques to help couples improve their sexual functioning. Sex therapy techniques typically have the following goals in common:

1 *Reducing performance anxiety.* Therapists frequently prescribe that clients engage in activities such as massage or petting under "nondemand" circumstances for a while to reduce performance anxiety. Nondemand activity means that sexual arousal and intercourse are not expected at first. Lessened anxiety allows natural reflexes such as erection, lubrication, and orgasm to occur.

2 *Changing self-defeating attitudes and expectations.* Clients are shown how expectations of failure can raise anxiety levels and become self-fulfilling prophecies.

3 *Teaching sexual skills.* Clients may be taught how to provide each other with adequate sexual stimulation. In the case of premature ejaculation, they may also be shown how to delay ejaculation by means such as the *stop-and-go* method (repeatedly pausing as the man becomes highly aroused and then restarting, so that the man becomes better able to gauge the level of stimulation, or "point of no return," that triggers the ejaculation reflex).

4 *Enhancing sexual knowledge.* Some problems are connected with ignorance or misinformation about biological and sexual functioning.

5 *Improving sexual communication.* Partners are taught ways of showing each other what they like and do not like.

Today, a range of biological treatments are also available to help people with sexual dysfunctions. Testosterone therapy may help restore sexual interest or lack of desire in both men and women in some cases (Brown & Haaser, 2005; Davis et al., 2008; Wang et al., 2004). However, serious questions remain about the safety and side effects of these hormonal treatments.

Drugs such as Viagra and its chemical cousins can help produce erections in most men suffering from erectile disorder (Lehne, 2005; Naughton, 2004; Walker, 2004). These drugs relax the blood vessels in the penis, allowing the chambers of the penis to fill with blood, which leads to erection. Testing of these and other drugs in treating female sexual dysfunction is ongoing, although results have not been as consistent with women as they have been with men (Berman et al., 2003; O'Connor, 2004; Portner, 2008). All in all, most cases of sexual dysfunction can be treated successfully through either biological or psychological interventions (or a combination of treatments), which is a far better situation than that which existed several generations ago when no effective treatments were available.

Review It

(20) Survey evidence indicates that nearly _____ of American women and about a _____ of American men experience sexual dysfunctions at some point in their lives.

(21) Women with female sexual _____ disorder have difficulty lubricating.

(22) Men with persistent difficulty attaining or maintaining an erection have_____ _____ disorder.

(23) Males who ejaculate too quickly may be diagnosed with _____ _____.

(24) _____ _____ generally focuses on reducing performance anxiety, changing self-defeating attitudes, teaching sexual skills, enhancing sexual knowledge, and improving communication.

Think About It

Connect the different types of sexual dysfunctions with the various phases of the sexual response cycle.

Psychology in Daily Life

MODULE 13.5

Practicing Healthier Behaviors to Prevent the Spread of HIV/AIDS and Other Sexually Transmitted Diseases

Sexually transmitted diseases (STDs) are widespread in our society, especially among young people, with about 3 million cases among preteens and teens reported annually in the United States. Although media attention has focused largely on HIV/AIDS, other sexually transmitted diseases (also called *sexually transmitted infections,* or STIs) are far more widespread. For example, although nearly 1 million Americans may be infected with HIV, an estimated 45 million people, including more than one in five adolescents and adults, are infected with HSV-2, the virus causing genital herpes (NIAID, 2005b).

HPVs (*human papillomaviruses*), the viruses that cause genital warts, are found in at least one in five Americans over the age of 12 and produce more than 6 million new cases of HPV infection each year (Steinbrook, 2006). More than 1 million cases of *chlamydia*, a sexually transmitted bacterial infection, and more than 350,000 cases of gonorrhea, another bacterial STD, were reported in 2007, the most recent year for which statistics were available (CDC, 2009).

Most college students appear to be reasonably well informed about HIV transmission and AIDS, yet many are unaware that chlamydia can go undetected for years. Moreover, if it is not treated effectively, it can lead to pelvic inflammatory disease and infertility in women and reduced fertility in men. More than half of all new infections with chlamydia and gonorrhea, another potentially serious STD, go undiagnosed, underscoring the need for regular medical screening (CDC, 2009). Many students are also ignorant of HPV, which is a major cause of cervical cancer, a potential killer. None of this is meant to underscore the risk of AIDS, a deadly immune system disease caused by the *human immunodeficiency virus* (HIV).

Women bear a heavier burden of STDs than men (CDC, 2009). They are more likely to be affected by STDs such as chlamydia and gonorrhea and to develop infertility if an STD spreads through the reproductive system. In addition to their biological effects, STDs take an emotional toll and can strain relationships to the breaking point.

For the rest of this section we focus on AIDS, but there are many other STDs of which you should be aware (see Table 13.9). Readers who want more information are advised to talk to their health care provider or visit their college health center. Before proceeding, you can test your knowledge of HIV/AIDS by completing the self-assessment on page 448.

13.5.1 HIV/AIDS

HIV infection is a life-threatening viral disease in which a virus, the human immunodeficiency virus (HIV), invades the person's immune system, the body system that defends against disease-causing agents like bacteria and viruses. People with HIV infection may progress to full-blown AIDS (acquired immunodeficiency syndrome), a

Table 13.9 ▌ Causes, Methods of Transmission, Symptoms, Diagnosis, and Treatment of Sexually Transmitted Diseases (STDs)

STD and Cause	Methods of Transmission	Symptoms	Diagnosis	Treatment
Acquired Immunodeficiency Syndrome (AIDS): *Human immunodeficiency virus (HIV)*	HIV is transmitted by sexual intercourse, direct infusion of contaminated blood, or from mother to child during childbirth, or breastfeeding.	Infected people may not have any symptoms; they may develop mild flu-like symptoms that disappear for many years prior to the development of "full-blown" AIDS. Full-blown AIDS is symptomized by fever, weight loss, fatigue, diarrhea, and opportunistic infections such as Kaposi's sarcoma, pneumonia (PCP), and invasive cancer of the cervix.	Blood, saliva, and urine tests can detect HIV *antibodies* in the bloodstream. The Western blot blood test may be used to confirm positive results.	There is no safe, effective vaccine for HIV. Combinations of antiviral drugs offer the hope of managing HIV/AIDS as a chronic disease, but it remains prudent to treat AIDS as a lethal condition and to take appropriate steps to protect yourself and your sexual partners.
Bacterical Vaginosis: *Gardnerella vaginalis* bacterium and others	Can arise by overgrowth of organisms in vagina, allergic reactions, etc; transmitted by sexual contact.	In women, thin, foul-smelling vaginal discharge. Irritation of genitals and mild pain during urination. In men, inflammation of penile foreskin and glans, urethritis, and cystitis. May be asymptomatic in both genders.	Culture and examination of bacterium	Oral treatment with metronidazole (brand name: Flagyl)
Candidiasis moniliasis (thrush, "yeast infection"): *Candida albicans*—a yeast-like fungus	Can arise by overgrowth of fungus in vagina; transmitted by sexual contact, or by sharing a washcloth with an infected person.	In women, vulval itching; white, cheesy, foul-smelling discharge; soreness or swelling of vaginal and vulval tissues. In men, itching and buring on urination, or a reddening of the penis.	Diagnosis is usually made on basis of symptoms.	Vaginal suppositories, creams, or tablets containing miconazole, clotrimazole, or teraconazole; modification of use of other medicines and chemical agents; keeping infected area dry.
Chlamydia and Nongonococcal urethritis (NGU): *Chlamydia trachomatous* bacterium; NGU in men may also be caused by *Ureaplasma urealycticum* bacterium and other pathogens.	Transmitted by vaginal, oral, or anal sexual activity; to the eye by touching one's eyes after touching the genitals of an infected partner; or by passing through the birth canal of an infected mother.	In women, frequent and painful urination, lower abdominal pain and inflammation, and vaginal discharge (but most women are symptom-free). In men, symptoms are similar to but milder than those of gonorrhea—burning or painful urination, slight penile discharge (some men are also asymptomatic). Sore throat may indicate infection from oral/genital contact.	The Abbott Test-pack analyzes a cervical smear in women.	Antibiotics

Table 13.9 ▌ **Continued**

STD and Cause	Methods of Transmission	Symptoms	Diagnosis	Treatment
Genital herpes: *Herpes simplex virus-type 2 (HSV-2)*	Almost always by means of vaginal, oral, or anal sexual activity; most contagious during active outbreaks of the disease.	Painful, reddish bumps around the genitals, thigh, or buttocks; in women, may also be in the vagina or on the cervix. Bumps become blisters or sores that fill with pus and break, shedding viral particles. Other possible symptoms: burning urination, fever, aches and pains, swollen glands; in women, vaginal discharge.	Clinical inspection of sores; culture and examination of fluid drawn from the base of a genital sore.	The antiviral drug acyclovir may provide relief and prompt healing over, but is not a cure.
Genital warts (venereal warts): *Human papilloma virus (HPV)*	Transmission is by sexual and other forms of contact, as with infected towels or clothing. Women are especially vulnerable, particularly women who have multiple sex partners.	Appearance of painless warts, often resembling cauliflowers, on the penis, foreskin, scrotum, or internal urethra in men, and on the vulva, labia, wall of the vagina or cervix in women. May occur around the anus and in the rectum.	Clinical inspection. (Because HPV can cause cervical cancer, regular Pap tests are also advised.)	Methods of removal include cryotherapy (freezing), podophyllin, burning, and surgical removal (by a physician!).
Gonorrhea ("clap," "drip"): Gonococcus bacterium *(Neisseria gonorrhoeae)*	Transmitted by vaginal, oral, or anal sexual activity, or from mother to newborn during delivery.	In men, yellowish, thick penile discharge, burning urination. In women, increased vaginal discharge, burning urination, irregular menstrual bleeding (most women show no early symptoms)	Clinical inspection; culture of sample discharge.	Antibiotics

condition in which the body's immune system is so weakened that it cannot ward off opportunistic diseases—diseases that the body can normally fend off, but that flourish when the immune system is weakened.

HIV kills a type of white blood cell called a CD4 cell.[2] These immune system cells recognize viruses and "instruct" other white blood cells—called B lymphocytes—to make antibodies, which combat disease. Eventually, however, CD4 cells are depleted and the body is left vulnerable to opportunistic diseases.

AIDS is characterized by fatigue, fever, unexplained weight loss, swollen lymph nodes, diarrhea, and, in many cases, impairment of learning and memory. Among the opportunistic infections that may take hold are Kaposi's sarcoma, a cancer of the blood cells; PCP (*pneumocystis carinii pneumonia*), a kind of pneumonia; and, in women, invasive cancer of the cervix.

The Global Plague of HIV/AIDS

HIV infection and AIDS are a global plague. Health officials estimate that more than 40 million people worldwide and more than 1 million in the United States are infected with HIV (Hammer et al., 2006; Ostermann et al., 2007). About 55,000 new cases of HIV infection are reported annually in the United States (CDC, 2008). A majority of cases of HIV worldwide, and about one in three in the United States, occur through heterosexual sex.

AIDS has become one of history's worst epidemics, accounting for more than 430,000 deaths in the United States and more than 25 million deaths worldwide (National Women's Health Information Center, 2005; Stephenson, 2004). Sub-Saharan Africa has been hardest hit by the HIV/AIDS epidemic, with about two-thirds of cases of HIV/AIDS worldwide occurring in this part of the world.

[2] Also called T4 cells or helper cells.

The AIDS Awareness Inventory | *Self-Assessment*

Some readers are more knowledgeable than others about HIV and AIDS. To find out how much you know about them, place a T in the blank space for each item that you believe is true or mostly true. Place an F in the blank space for each item that you believe is false or mostly false. Then check your answers against those found at the end of the chapter.

Before you get started, let us issue a "warning." Some of the items in this self-assessment are "R" rated. If we were talking about a film, we would say that it contains some "sex" and "nudity." There is no violence, however. The purpose of the questionnaire, like the purpose of this book, is to help you prevent doing violence to yourself.

_____ 1. AIDS is synonymous with HIV. They are different names for the same thing.

_____ 2. AIDS is a form of cancer.

_____ 3. You can't get infected with HIV the first time you engage in sexual intercourse.

_____ 4. You can't be infected by HIV unless you engage in male–male sexual activity or share needles to inject ("shoot up") drugs.

_____ 5. You can be infected by HIV and not have any signs or symptoms of illness for many years.

_____ 6. You can't be infected with HIV by hugging someone, even if that person is infected with HIV.

_____ 7. You can't be infected with HIV by having regular sexual intercourse (intercourse with the penis in the vagina), even if your partner is infected with HIV.

_____ 8. You can't be infected with HIV through sexual activity if you're using contraception, even if your partner is infected with HIV.

_____ 9. You can't be infected with HIV by oral sex (that is, from kissing, licking, or sucking a penis or a vagina), even if your partner is infected with HIV.

_____ 10. Using condoms ("rubbers," "safes") guarantees protection against being infected with HIV, even if your partner is infected with HIV.

_____ 11. You can be infected with HIV by donating blood.

_____ 12. If you already have a sexually transmitted disease, like chlamydia or genital warts, you can't be infected with HIV.

_____ 13. You can't be infected with HIV if you and your sex partner are faithful to each other (don't have sex with anyone else).

_____ 14. Knowledge of how HIV is transmitted is sufficient to get people to abstain from risky behavior.

_____ 15. People are likely to be infected with HIV if they are bitten by insects such as mosquitoes that are carrying it.

Tragically, nearly an entire generation of African children are now without parents because of AIDS—some 11 million orphans by some estimates (National Women's Health Information Center, 2005).

Modes of Transmission

HIV is transmitted by infected blood, semen, vaginal and cervical secretions, and breast milk. We may contract the virus through vaginal, anal, or oral sex with an infected partner. The virus may also be transmitted from an infected mother to fetus during pregnancy or from the mother to child through childbirth or breastfeeding. Other means of infection include sharing a hypodermic needle with an infected person (as is common among people who inject illicit drugs) and transfusion with contaminated blood. There need be no concern about closed-mouth kissing. Note, too, that saliva does not transmit HIV. However, transmission through deep kissing is theoretically pos-

sible if blood in an infected person's mouth (e.g., from toothbrushing or gum disease) enters cuts (again, as from toothbrushing or gum disease) in the other person's mouth. There is no evidence that public toilets, insect bites, holding or hugging an infected person, or living or attending school with one, transmits HIV.

HIV is generally spread through intimate sexual contact or needle-sharing with an infected person. One psychological risk factor for HIV infection is that people tend to underestimate their risk of infection. Because AIDS has been characterized as mainly transmitted by anal intercourse (a practice that is fairly common among gay males) and the sharing of contaminated needles, many heterosexual Americans who do not use drugs dismiss the threat of AIDS. Yet male–female sexual intercourse can transmit the disease and already accounts for the majority of cases around the world. We should understand that while gay men and drug abusers and their partners have been hit hardest by the epidemic, HIV cuts across all bound-

Adjustment and Modern Life

Making Sex Safe(r) in the Age of AIDS

You've gone out with Chris a few times, and you're keenly attracted. Chris is attractive, bright, and witty; shares some of your attitudes; and, all in all, is a powerful turn-on. Now the evening is winding down. You've been cuddling, and you think you know where things are heading.

Something clicks in your mind! You realize that as wonderful as Chris is, you don't know every place Chris has "been." As healthy as Chris looks and acts, you don't know what's swimming around in Chris's bloodstream either.

What do you say now? How do you protect yourself without turning Chris off? Ah, the clumsiness! If you ask about STDs, it is sort of making a verbal commitment to have sexual relations, and perhaps you're not exactly sure that's what your partner intends. And even if it's clear that's where you're heading, will you seem too straightforward? Will you kill the romance? The spontaneity of the moment? Sure you might—life has its risks. But which is riskier: an awkward moment or being infected with a fatal illness? Let's put it another way: Are you really willing to die for sex? Given that few verbal responses are perfect, here are some things you can try:

1. Ask good-naturedly, "Do you have anything to tell me?" This question is open-ended, and if Chris is as bright as you think, Chris might very well take the hint and tell you what you need to know.

2. If Chris answers "I love you," be happy about it. You could respond with something like, "I'm crazy about you, too." A minute later, add "Do you have anything else to tell me?"

3. If Chris says "Like what?" you can beat around the bush one more time and say something like, "Well, I'm sure you weren't waiting for me all your life locked in a closet. I don't know everywhere you've been..."

4. If you're uncomfortable with that, or if you want to be more straightforward, you can say something like, "As far as I know, I'm perfectly healthy. Have there been any problems with you I should know about?" Saying that you are healthy invites reciprocity in self-disclosure.

5. Once Chris has expressed unawareness of being infected by any STDs, you might pursue it by mentioning your ideas about prevention. You can say something like, "I've brought something and I'd like to use it..." (referring to a condom).

6. Or you can say something like, "I know this is a bit clumsy" [you are assertively expressing a feeling and asking permission to pursue a clumsy topic; Chris is likely to respond with something like, "That's okay" or "Don't worry—what is it?"], but the world isn't as safe as it used to be, and I think we should talk about what we're going to do."

This is the point: Your partner hasn't been living in a remote cave. Your partner is also aware of the dangers of STDs, especially of AIDS, and ought to be working with you to make things safe and unpressured. If your partner is pressing for unsafe sex and is inconsiderate of your feelings and concerns, you need to reassess whether you really want to be with this person. We think you can do better.

---

aries of gender, sexual orientation, ethnicity, and socioeconomic status. No one is immune, and anyone can contract the virus from even a single sexual contact or needle-sharing with an infected person.

Treatment of HIV/AIDS

Although there is no safe, effective vaccine against HIV/AIDS, recent developments in drug therapy have raised hopes about controlling this deadly disease. A combination of antiviral drugs—the so-called drug cocktail—offers hope that AIDS will become a manageable chronic disease, not a terminal one. However, these hopes are tempered by the fact that many patients are not helped by them and that drug-resistant strains of the virus have begun to emerge. Moreover, treatment is expensive and requires a demanding regimen. Therefore, the most effective way of dealing with AIDS is prevention. At best, the antiviral drugs available today may help control the virus, but they do not produce a cure or eliminate the infectious organism from the body. For the latest information on AIDS, call the National AIDS Hotline at 1-800-342-AIDS. If you want to receive information in Spanish, call 1-800-344-SIDA. You can also go to the

website of the Centers for Disease Control and Prevention: www.cdc.gov. Once you're there, you can click on "Health Topics A–Z" and then on "AIDS."

13.5.2 What You Can Do to Prevent STDs in the Age of AIDS

You're not just sleeping with one person, you're sleeping with everyone they ever slept with.

—*Dr. Theresa Crenshaw, past president, American Association of Sex Educators, Counselors and Therapists*

As shown by the remarks of one young woman, it can be clumsy to try to protect oneself from STDs such as AIDS:

It's one thing to talk about "being responsible about STDs" and a much harder thing to do it at the very moment. It's just plain hard to say to someone I am feeling very erotic with, "Oh, yes, before we go any further, can we have a conversation about STD?" It's hard to imagine murmuring into someone's ear at a time of passion, "Would you mind slipping on this condom or using this cream just in case one of us has a STD?" Yet it seems awkward to bring it up beforehand, if it's not yet clear between us that we want to make love with one another. (Boston Women's Health Book Collective, 1993)

Because of the difficulties in discussing STDs with sex partners, some people admit that they "wing it." That is, they assume that a partner does not have an STD, or they hope for the best—even in the age of AIDS. Don't be one of them. The risks are too high. The only sure way to prevent the sexual transmission of HIV/AIDS, says Dr. Robert Janssen of the CDC's division of HIV/AIDS, is to either abstain from sexual activity or maintain a truly monogamous relationship with a partner who is also HIV-negative (Laino, 2002).

What can you do to prevent the transmission of HIV and other STD-causing organisms? A number of things:

1. *Don't ignore the threat of STDs.* Many people try to put AIDS and other STDs out of their minds. They just assume that their partners are uninfected, or they believe it would hurt the relationship to ask about STDs. The first aspect of prevention is psychological: Do not ignore STDs or assume that they will not affect you.

2. *Practice abstinence.* One way to curb the sexual transmission of HIV and other organisms that cause STDs is sexual abstinence. Of course, most people who remain abstinent do so while they are looking for Mr. or Ms. Right. Thus, they eventually face the risk of contracting STDs through sexual intercourse. Moreover, students want to know just what "abstinence" means. Does it mean avoiding sexual intercourse (yes) or any form of sexual activity with another person (not necessarily)? Kissing, hugging, and petting to orgasm (without coming into contact with semen or vaginal secretions) are generally considered safe in terms of HIV transmission. However, kissing can transmit oral herpes (as shown by the development of cold sores) and some types of bacterial STDs.

3. *Engage in a monogamous relationship with someone who is not infected.* Sexual activity within a monogamous relationship with an uninfected person is safe. The question here is how certain you can be that your partner is uninfected and monogamous.

4. *Practice safer sex.* Readers who do not abstain from sexual relationships or limit themselves to a monogamous relationship can do some things to make sex safer—if not perfectly safe—such as the following:

   ∎ *Be selective.* Engage in sexual activity only with people you know well. Consider whether they are likely to have engaged in the kinds of behaviors that transmit HIV or other STDs.

   ∎ *Inspect your partner's genitals.* People who have STDs often have a variety of symptoms. Examining your partner's genitals for blisters, discharges, chancres, rashes, warts, lice, and unpleasant odors during foreplay may reveal signs of such diseases.

   ∎ *Wash your own genitals before and after contact.* Washing beforehand helps protect your partner. Washing promptly afterward with soap and water helps remove germs.

   ∎ *Don't rely on spermicides for additional protection.*

   ∎ *Use condoms.* Latex condoms (but not condoms made from animal membrane) protect the woman from having HIV-infected semen enter the vagina and the man from contact with HIV-infected vaginal (or other) body fluids. Condoms also prevent transmission of bacterial STDs. Table 13.10 shows the frequency of condom use among U.S. college students based on a recent large-scale nationwide survey. Nearly half of college students reported using a condom during the last time they engaged in vaginal " intercourse; a lower percentage (23%) reported condom use during the last occasion of anal intercourse; and relatively few reported condom use during oral intercourse (American College Health Association, 2005).

5. *Don't use oral sex as a safe alternative.* Researchers report a significant number of new HIV infections linked to oral sex (Laino, 2002). But you can decrease your risk by using a condom during oral sex or any other type of sex, says leading AIDS expert Robert Janssen.

6. *If you fear that you have been exposed to HIV or another infectious organism, talk to your doctor about it.* Early treatment is usually more effective than later treatment. It may even prevent infection.

7. *When in doubt, stop.* If you are not sure that sex is safe, stop and think things over or seek expert advice.

Table 13.10 ∎ Reported Condom Use Among Sexually Active Students the Last Time They Had Sexual Intercourse

Types of Sexual Activity	Total		Female		Male	
	n	%	*n*	%	*n*	%
Oral intercourse	460	3.3	256	2.9	174	3.9
Vaginal intercourse	6,301	48.6	3,805	46.2	2,148	53.9
Anal intercourse	762	23.0	338	17.3	370	32.5

Note: Refers to Question 27: "If you are sexually active did you use a condom the last time you had: oral, vaginal, or anal intercourse?" (*Never, No, Yes, Don't Know/Don't Remember*). Students reporting "Never did this sexual activity" were excluded from the analysis. Because of missing data by sex, the response categories do not always equal the total.
Source: American College Health Association, 2005. Reprinted by permission of the American College Health Association.

If you think about it, the last item is rather good general advice. When in doubt, why not stop and think, regardless of whether the doubt is about your sex partner, your college major, or a financial investment?

Many health programs encourage sexually active people to engage in safer sexual techniques. What steps are you taking to protect yourself and your partners from HIV/AIDS and other sexually transmitted diseases?

CHAPTER REVIEW

RECITE! RECITE! RECITE! RECITE! RECITE! RECITE! RECITE!

Study Tip: Reciting the answers to these study questions will help you become a more effective learner. First try answering the questions by yourself, either reciting them out loud or writing them in a notebook or on the computer. Then compare your answers with the sample answers provided below.

1. **What are the woman's sexual organs?**
   The vulva, or external female sexual organs, includes the mons veneris, clitoris, major and minor lips, and vaginal opening. The woman's internal sexual organs consist of the vagina, cervix, fallopian tubes, and ovaries. The cervix is the opening that connects the upper vagina to the uterus. Fallopian tubes connect the uterus with the abdominal cavity. Ovaries lie in the abdomen and produce ova and the sex hormones estrogen and progesterone. When an ovum is released, it travels through a fallopian tube, where fertilization is most likely to occur.

2. **What are the man's sexual organs?**
   The major male sex organs include the penis; testes (or testicles); scrotum; and the series of ducts, canals, and glands that store and transport sperm and produce semen (the fluid that transports and nourishes sperm).

3. **How do sex hormones regulate the menstrual cycle?**
   Levels of estrogen and progesterone vary and regulate the menstrual cycle. Following menstruation, estrogen levels increase, causing an ovum to ripen and the uterine lining to thicken. An ovum is released (ovulation occurs) when estrogens reach peak blood levels. In response to secretion of progesterone, the inner lining of the uterus thickens, gaining the capacity to support an embryo. If the ovum is not fertilized, estrogen and progesterone levels drop suddenly, triggering menstruation.

4. **What effects do sex hormones have on sexual behavior?**
   As a directional or organizing effect, sex hormones predispose animals toward masculine or feminine mating patterns. The activating effects of sex hormones influence the sex drive and facilitate sexual response. The sex drive and sexual response of both males and females are facilitated by testosterone.

5. **Why do sexual practices and customs vary so widely around the world?**
   Sexual practices and customs vary largely because of differences in cultural attitudes and values concerning sex.

6. **What factors do we need to consider when selecting a method of contraception?**
   Considerations in the selection of a method of contraception include its convenience, its moral acceptability, its cost, the extent to which it enables partners to share the responsibility for contraception, its safety, its reversibility, whether it affords protection against sexually transmitted diseases (STDs), and its effectiveness.

7. **What is the sexual response cycle?**
   The sexual response cycle describes the body's response to sexual stimulation and consists of four phases: excitement, plateau, orgasm, and resolution. The sexual response cycle is characterized by vasocongestion and myotonia. Excitement is characterized by erection in the male and lubrication in the female. Orgasm is characterized by muscle contractions and release of sexual tension. Following orgasm, males enter a refractory period during which they are temporarily unresponsive to sexual stimulation.

8. **What motives underlie rape?**
   Rape apparently has more to do with power and aggressiveness than with sex per se. Social critics argue that men are socialized into sexual aggression by being generally reinforced for aggressiveness and competitiveness. Social and cognitive factors, such as viewing sex in adversarial terms and adopting rape myths that tend to blame the victim, also contribute to a social climate that encourages rape.

9. **What are some common myths about rape?**
   These include beliefs that women who dress provocatively deserve or are at least partially responsible for rape and that women who say "no" really mean "yes."

10. **How can we prevent rape?**
    From a cultural perspective, prevention of rape involves publicly examining and challenging the widely held cultural attitudes and ideals that contribute to rape. We can specifically encourage our colleges and universities to require students to attend lectures and seminars on rape. In terms of a woman's personal life, she can take cautionary measures to reduce the risk of rape, such as avoiding deserted areas, dating in groups, and being assertive in expressing her sexual limits. But let us not forget that the act of rape is a crime of violence and is always the fault of the rapist.

11. **What are sexual dysfunctions?**
    Sexual dysfunctions are persistent or recurrent problems in becoming sexually aroused or reaching orgasm.

12. What are the major types of sexual dysfunctions?
They include hypoactive sexual desire disorder (lack of interest in sex), female sexual arousal disorder and male erectile disorder, orgasmic disorder, and premature ejaculation.

13. What are the origins of sexual dysfunctions?
Sexual dysfunctions may be caused by physical health problems, negative attitudes toward sex, lack of sexual knowledge and skills, problems in the relationship, and performance anxiety.

14. How are sexual dysfunctions treated?
Sexual dysfunctions are treated by sex therapy, which focuses on reducing performance anxiety, changing self-defeating attitudes and expectations, teaching sexual skills, enhancing sexual knowledge, and improving sexual communication. There are also some biological treatments, such as drugs that enhance vasocongestion.

YOUR PERSONAL JOURNAL

REFLECT   REFLECT   REFLECT   REFLECT   REFLECT   REFLECT   REFLECT

Study Tip: Reflecting on how the concepts in the chapter relate to your own experiences encourages deeper processing, which makes the material more personally meaningful and fosters more effective learning. Use additional pages if needed to complete your answers.

1. The text contrasts a sexually restrictive society (Inis Baeg) with a sexually permissive society (Mangaia). In which society would you rather live? In which society would you rather rear your children? Explain.

_____

_____

_____

_____

_____

2. Did learning about rape myths lead you to rethink some of your own attitudes or beliefs? How so?

_____

_____

_____

_____

_____

ANSWERS TO MODULE REVIEWS

Module 13.1
1. vulva
2. ovaries
3. testosterone
4. differentiation
5. estrogen
6. progesterone
7. decrease
8. organizing
9. decrease

Module 13.2
10. norm
11. excellent
12. is not
13. plateau

14. vascongestion/myotonia
15. orgasmic phase
16. refractory period

Module 13.3
17. acquaintances
18. power
19. more

Module 13.4
20. half/third
21. arousal
22. male erectile
23. premature ejaculation
24. Sex therapy

ANSWERS TO THE AIDS AWARENESS INVENTORY

1. *False.* AIDS is the name of a disease syndrome. AIDS stands for *acquired immunodeficiency syndrome.* (A syndrome is a group of signs or symptoms of a disease.) HIV stands for *human immunodeficiency virus,* which is the microscopic disease organism that causes AIDS. When the immune system is weakened beyond a certain point, people are prey to illnesses that normally would not gain a foothold in the body. At this time, they are said to have AIDS.

2. *False.* The confusion about AIDS and cancer may stem from the fact that men with weakened immune systems are prone to developing a rare form of blood cancer, *Kaposi's sarcoma,* which leaves purplish spots all over the body.

3. *False.* Sure you can. There is also a myth that you cannot become pregnant the first time you engage in sexual intercourse, but you most certainly can.

4. *False.* Men who engage in sexual activity with other men and people who inject drugs have been at relatively higher risk for being infected by HIV, especially in the United States and Canada. However, *anyone* can be infected by HIV if the virus enters her or his bloodstream.

5. *True.* It generally takes years before people infected with HIV develop AIDS.

6. *True.* In order to be infected with HIV, the virus must get into your bloodstream. This will not happen through hugging someone, even if that person is infected. This is why people who care for HIV-infected children can lavish affection on them without fear of being infected themselves.

7. *False.* This mistaken belief may reflect the connection between sexual orientation and AIDS in many people's minds. Either the man or the woman can be infected with HIV through vaginal intercourse.

8. *False.* You most certainly can. Some forms of contraception such as the birth control pill and rhythm method afford no protection against infection by HIV. Latex condoms do offer some protection, but they are not perfect.

9. *False.* It appears that you can be infected by HIV through oral sex, even though this avenue of transmission is unlikely (digestive juices such as saliva and the normal acids that are found in the digestive tract kill HIV). Some people appear to have been infected in this manner, however.

10. *False.* Using latex condoms substantially reduces the risk of HIV infection but does not guarantee safety.

11. *False.* It is not true that you can be infected by HIV by donating blood. The needles are sterile (free of infection) and are used only once.

12. *False.* Some people believe, erroneously, that they cannot be placed in "double jeopardy" by sexually transmitted diseases. People who have another sexually transmitted disease are actually *more* likely, not less likely, to be infected by HIV. There are at least two reasons for this. One is that they may have sores in the genital region that provide convenient ports of entry for HIV into the bloodstream. The second is that the risky sexual behavior that led to one kind of infection can easily lead to others.

13. *False.* You cut your risks by limiting your sexual activity to a monogamous relationship, but you must consider two questions: First, what was your faithful partner doing before the two of you became a couple? Second, do you or your partner engage in *nonsexual* forms of behavior that could result in HIV infection, such as shooting up drugs?

14. *False.* Would that it were so! Knowledge of possible consequences alone is often not enough to encourage people to modify risky behavior.

15. *False.* You do not have to be concerned about the insects that mill about in next summer's heated air. There is no documented case of HIV having been transmitted in this manner.

CHAPTER 14

Adolescent and Adult Development: Going Through Changes

OUTLINE

Did you know that...

▍ Module 14.1: Adolescence

▍ Module 14.2: Young and Middle Adulthood

▍ Module 14.3: Late Adulthood

▍ Module 14.4: Psychology in Daily Life: Living Longer and Healthier Lives

CHAPTER REVIEW *RECITE! RECITE! RECITE!*

YOUR PERSONAL JOURNAL *REFLECT REFLECT REFLECT*

- The adolescent brain is still in the process of maturing, especially the part that puts the brakes on risky or impulsive behavior? (p. 460)

- Rates of sexual intercourse among teens have actually been dropping in recent years? (p. 462)

- Though men in later adulthood may father children, their sperm is more prone to genetic defects than sperm of younger men? (p. 467)

- Alzheimer's disease is not a result of normal aging? (p 483)

- Most people do not set off for the sunbelt when they reach their "golden years" but remain put in their home towns and cities? (p. 484)

- The rate of suicide is highest among older adults, not teenagers or young adults? (p. 485)

- The next best thing to a Fountain of Youth is your neighborhood gym? (p. 489)

Kevin Russ/iStockphoto

There is no cure for birth or death save to enjoy the interval.

—GEORGE SANTAYANA

Adjustment is a process, not a final state. We continually encounter challenges to adjustment as we develop, and development is a lifetime process. At what stage of development are you now? What adjustment issues do you face? Are you developing plans for a career and thinking about marriage and a family? Do you already have your career laid out? Does adjustment to you mean juggling classes and a job? Classes, a job, and a relationship? Some readers are juggling the demands of classes, jobs, relationships, and children—even grandchildren.

What's going to happen as you journey through the remaining years of life? Do you expect that everything will come up roses, right on course? Think again. We're all bound to encounter road bumps along the highway of life. What are the typical life experiences of 40-, 50-, and 60-year-olds in our culture? What types of adjustment issues do they encounter?

What do you think about middle age and late adulthood? Or are you so immersed in the seemingly endless possibilities of youth that you cannot imagine yourself ever aging, let alone reaching the "golden" years of 70 or 80? What do you think it feels like to be 80? The famed French entertainer Maurice Chevalier was asked the same question when he reached that milestone. He said, but let us paraphrase, "Fine, considering the alternative." Given the alternative, let us hope you do reach such a venerable age. What challenges might you expect as you turn the calendar on your sixth, seventh, eighth, or even ninth decade of life?

If you hold negative stereotypes of what it will be like to be a 50-year-old or a 60-year-old, let us also hope that this chapter will replace some of your prejudices with accurate information and positive expectations.

People are living longer than ever before and are freer than ever to choose how they will lead their lives. Changes are overleaping themselves at an accelerating pace. As we develop through our adult years, we may find that our homes and our work bear little resemblance to what they are today. Still, we have made enormous progress toward understanding the psychological and physical changes people undergo as they travel through young, middle, and late adulthood. In a sense, this chapter encourages you to get ready for the rest of your life. Let us begin this journey—no, your journey— by reviewing the challenges of adolescence and emerging adulthood. Then we will chronicle the human experience through young, middle, and late adulthood. We will see that each stage of development challenges us to adjust but also holds opportunities for personal growth and fulfillment.

MODULE 14.1

Adolescence

▪ What changes in physical development occur during adolescence?
▪ What changes in cognitive development occur during adolescence?
▪ What changes in social and personality development occur during adolescence?

▪ **Adolescence** The period of life bounded by puberty and early adulthood.

Do you still think of yourself as an adolescent? Or as coming out of **adolescence**? For older readers, adolescence may be a thing of the past; they may look upon memories of adolescence fondly, or they may think "Good riddance." This is not surprising since adolescence is something of a mixed bag.

Adolescence is a time of transition from childhood to adulthood. It begins at puberty and ends with early adulthood. In our society, adolescents often feel that they are "neither fish nor fowl," as the saying goes—neither children nor adults. Although adolescents may be physically as large as their parents and capable of reproducing, they are often treated quite differently than adults. They may not be eligible for a driver's license until they are 17 or 18. They cannot attend R-rated films unless they are accompanied by an adult. They are prevented from working long hours, and they may not marry until they reach the "age of consent."

14.1.1 Physical Changes of Adolescence

One of the most noticeable physical developments of adolescence is a growth spurt. The adolescent growth spurt lasts for two to three years and ends the stable patterns of growth in height and weight that characterize most of childhood. Within this short span of years, adolescents grow some 8 to 12 inches. Most boys wind up taller and heavier than most girls.

In boys, the weight of the muscle mass increases notably. The width of the shoulders and circumference of the chest also increase. Adolescents may eat enormous quantities of food to fuel their growth spurt. Adults fighting the "battle of the bulge" stare at them in wonder as they wolf down french fries and shakes at the fast-food counter and later go out for pizza.

The most dramatic changes during adolescence occur during the period of development called puberty.

Puberty

▪ **Puberty** The period of physical development during which sexual reproduction first becomes possible.

▪ **Secondary sex characteristics** Characteristics that distinguish the sexes, such as distribution of body hair and depth of voice, but that are not directly involved in reproduction.

Puberty is the period of development during which the body becomes sexually mature. It heralds the onset of adolescence. Puberty begins with the appearance of **secondary sex characteristics** such as body hair, deepening of the voice in males, and rounding of the breasts and hips in females (see Figure 14.1). It ends when bone growth stops, which usually occurs at about age 16 in girls and 17.5 in boys

(Schneider, 2004). By the end of puberty, young men and women have become capable of reproducing. The timing of puberty and the unfolding of the physical changes that occur during puberty are largely controlled by genetic factors (Beier & Dluhy, 2003; Mustanski et al., 2004).

In boys, pituitary hormones stimulate the testes to increase the output of testosterone, which in turn causes the penis and testes to grow and leads to the development of body hair. By their early teens, boys often experience erections and may begin to ejaculate. The ability to ejaculate usually precedes the presence of mature sperm by at least a year. Ejaculation thus is not evidence of reproductive capacity. In girls, a critical body weight in the neighborhood of 100 pounds is thought to trigger a cascade of hormonal secretions in the brain that cause the ovaries to secrete higher levels of the female sex hormone estrogen (Frisch, 1997). Estrogen stimulates the growth of breast tissue and fatty and supportive tissue in the hips and buttocks.

Thus, the pelvis widens, rounding the hips. Small amounts of male sex hormones called androgens, which include testosterone, along with estrogen, spur the growth of pubic and underarm hair. Estrogen and androgens promote the development of female sex organs. Estrogen production becomes cyclical during puberty and regulates the menstrual cycle. The beginning of menstruation, or **menarche**, usually occurs between the ages of 11 and 14. The average age of menstruation today is about 12.1 years for African American girls and about 12.6 years for European American girls (Anderson, Dallal, & Must, 2003). The average age of menarche has been declining for decades, likely as the result of improved nutrition and health care. Girls cannot become pregnant until they begin to ovulate, however, and this may occur as much as two years after menarche.

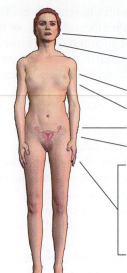

Pubertal Developments in Females:

Increased skin oils may produce acne.

The voice may deepen slightly (but not as much as in males).

Underarm hair appears.

The breasts grow and become more rounded.

Internal reproductive organs begin to grow.

Body fat rounds the hips.

Pubic hair becomes darker and coarser.

The ovaries increase production of estrogen.

Internal reproductive organs continue to develop.

Ovaries begin to release mature eggs capable of being fertilized.

Menarche occurs.

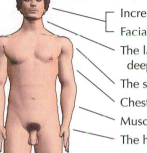

Pubertal Developments in Males:

Increased skin oils may produce acne.

Facial and underarm hair appears.

The larynx (voice box) enlarges, resulting in deepening of the voice.

The shoulders broaden.

Chest hair appears.

Muscle mass develops, and the boy grows taller.

The hips narrow.

Pubic hair appears, grows, coarsens, and curls.

The penis grows longer and widens.

The testes increase production of testosterone.

The testicles grow.

The skin of the scrotum reddens and coarsens.

Ejaculation occurs.

Figure 14.1
Changes of Puberty
Dramatic increases in the secretion of sex hormones usher in the physical changes of puberty.

▮ **Menarche** The beginning of menstruation.

14.1.2 Cognitive Development

I am a college student of extremely modest means. Some crazy psychologist interested in something called "formal operational thought" has just promised to pay me $20 if I can make a coherent logical argument for the proposition that the federal government should under no circumstances ever give or lend more to needy college students. Now what could people who believe that possibly say by way of supporting argument? Well, I suppose they could offer this line of reasoning....

— ADAPTED FROM FLAVELL, Miller, & Flavell (2002)

The adolescent thinker approaches problems very differently from the elementary school child. The child sticks to the facts, to concrete reality. Speculating about abstract possibilities and of what might be is very difficult. The adolescent, on the other hand, is able to deal with the abstract and the hypothetical. As shown in the above example, adolescents realize that one does not have to believe in the truth or justice of something in order to mount an argument in favor of it (Flavell et al., 2002). In this section, we explore some of the cognitive developments of adolescence by drawing on the contributions of two highly influential theorists, Jean Piaget and Lawrence Kohlberg. We begin with Piaget.

Piaget's Formal Operational Stage

According to the developmental psychologist Jean Piaget, the ability to engage in abstract thinking, or what he called *formal operations*, is what most clearly separates the cognitive abilities of children and adolescents. For many children in Western societies, the **formal operational stage** of cognitive development begins at about the start of adolescence—the age of 11 or 12. However, not all individuals enter this stage at this time, and some individuals never reach it.

■ **Formal operational stage** According to Piaget, the stage of cognitive development associated with abstract logical thought and deduction from principles.

Formal operational thought involves the ability to classify, hypothesize, and carry arguments to their logical conclusions. Central features are the ability to think about ideas as well as objects and to group and classify ideas—symbols, statements, entire theories. The flexibility and reversibility of operations, when applied to statements and theories, allow adolescents to follow arguments from their premises to their conclusions and back again. The formal operational thinker can apply deductive reasoning, such as in deducing the identity of the killer from a set of facts in a "who-done-it" mystery.

A 9-year-old may have no difficulty solving the following type of problem: "If Jim has more baseball cards than Jonas, and Jonas has more cards than Kamau, who has more cards—Kamau or Jim?" But 9-year-old Bhupin is likely to be stumped if the same problem is framed in hypothetical or logical terms, such as by asking, "If A is greater than B, and B is greater than C, is A greater than C?" In other words, the child who has not yet reached the stage of formal operations may be able to perform logical operations, but only when they are tied to concrete examples.

In a sense, it is during the stage of formal operations that adolescents tend to emerge as theoretical scientists—even though they may see themselves as having little or no interest in science. Like scientists, they become capable of dealing with hypothetical situations. They realize that situations can have different outcomes, and they think ahead, experimenting with different possibilities. They can also conduct personal experiments to determine whether their hypotheses are correct. These experiments are not conducted in the laboratory. Rather, adolescents may try out different tones of voice, and ways of carrying themselves and of treating others to see what works best for them. Yet the growing intellectual ability of the adolescent faces a challenge of adjustment: **egocentrism**.

■ **Egocentrism** Placing oneself at the center of one's psychological world; inability to view the world from the perspective of others.

Adolescent Egocentrism: "You Just Don't Understand!"

The thinking styles of preschoolers are characterized by a form of egocentrism in which they cannot take another's point of view. Adolescent thought is marked by the sort of egocentrism in which they can understand the thoughts of others but still have trouble separating things that are of concern to others and those that are of concern only to themselves (Elkind, 1985). Adolescent egocentrism gives rise to two important cognitive developments: the **imaginary audience** and the **personal fable**. The concept of the imaginary audience refers to the belief that other people are as concerned with our thoughts and behavior as we are. As a result, adolescents see themselves as the center of attention and assume that other people are about as preoccupied with their appearance and behavior as they are. Adolescents may feel they are on stage and all eyes are focused on them.

■ **Imaginary audience** The belief that other people are as concerned with our thoughts and behaviors as we are.

■ **Personal fable** The belief that our feelings and ideas are special and unique and that we are invulnerable.

The concept of the imaginary audience may fuel the intense adolescent desire for privacy. It helps explain why adolescents are so self-conscious about their appearance, why they worry about every facial blemish and spend long hours grooming. The personal fable is the belief that our feelings and ideas are special, even unique, and that we are somehow invulnerable to harm. The personal fable seems to underlie adolescent behavior patterns such as showing off and taking risks. Some adolescents adopt an "It can't happen to me" attitude; they assume they can smoke without risk of cancer or engage in sexual activity without risk of sexually transmitted diseases or pregnancy. "All youth—rich, poor, black, white—have this sense of invincibility, invulnerability," says Ronald King (2000) of the HIV Community Coalition of Washington, D.C., explaining why many teens who apparently know the risks still expose themselves to HIV. Teens are more likely than adults to underestimate the risks associated with such behaviors as drinking, smoking, and unsafe sex (Berger et al., 2005; Nowinski, 2007).

Another aspect of the personal fable is the idea that no one else has experienced or can understand one's "unique" feelings, such as needing independence or being in love. The personal fable may underlie the common teenage lament, "You just don't understand me!"

14.1.3 Social and Personality Development

Adolescence has long been recognized as a time of turbulence. In the nineteenth century, psychologist G. Stanley Hall, the founder of the American Psychological Association and its first president, described adolescence as a time of *sturm und drang*—storm and stress. Many adolescents experience storm and stress in dealing with such issues as family conflict, coping with physical and emotional changes, and carving out a personal identity for themselves. However, not all teens experience adolescence as a turbulent, pressure-ridden period. There are also important individual differences and cultural variations. Adolescents with strong traditional roots seem to experience less storm and stress than adolescents who are swayed by risk-taking peers or by media imagery that romanticizes people who live on the fringes of society. And one important factor in adolescent storm and stress for youths from minority cultural backgrounds is cultural disconnectedness. That is, many minority youths encounter stress in terms of whether they can adopt the attitudes and behavior patterns of the dominant culture—and over whether they ought to do so.

Many American teenagers do abuse drugs, get pregnant, contract sexually transmitted diseases (STDs), become involved in violence, fail in school, and even attempt suicide. Each year nearly 1 in 10 adolescent girls become pregnant. Nearly 10% of teenage boys and 20% of teenage girls attempt suicide. Motor vehicle crashes are the leading cause of death among adolescents in the United States, and many of these involve use of alcohol or distraction of the driver by passengers. Adolescents also stand a higher than average risk of death from homicide and suicide.

Some readers might be surprised by evidence showing that adolescents and their parents typically have love and respect for each other and tend to agree on most of the major issues in life (Arnett, 2004). Though disagreements with parents often occur, most adolescents surveyed in a recent poll reported that they got along "very well" or "extremely well" with their parents or guardians ("Teens Say," 2003).

The Quest for Independence: "I Gotta Be Me"

Adolescents strive to become more independent from their parents, which often leads to conflicts over issues such as homework, chores, money, appearance, curfews, and dating. Arguments are common when adolescents want to make their own choices about matters such as clothes and friends. The striving for independence is also characterized by withdrawal from family life, at least relative to prior involvement.

Some distancing from parents is a good thing. After all, adolescents do need to form relationships outside the family and to begin to spread their wings. But more independence does not mean that adolescents must become emotionally detached from their parents or fall completely under the influence of their peers.

Adolescents who feel close to their parents actually show greater self-reliance and independence than do those who are distant from their parents. Adolescents who retain close ties with their parents also tend to fare better in school and have fewer adjustment problems (Steinberg, 1996).

Image Source/Getty Images, Inc.

Everyone Will See It
Adolescents often assume that they are the center of everyone else's attention. They become overly self-conscious about their appearance, believing that every one notices even their slightest blemish.

Jacopo Pandolfi/Reportage/Getty Images, Inc.

Do You Take Unnecessary Risks?
Risky behavior is not limited to adolescents. More than half of Americans surveyed in a 2009 poll said they never use a helmet while riding a bicycle. Do you? Should you?

Adolescent Adjustment—Sometimes a Risky Business

Adolescents and parents are often in conflict because adolescents experiment with many things that can be harmful to their health, even their lives, such as reckless driving, unsafe sex, illicit drug use, and binge drinking (Curry & Youngblade, 2006). Yet—apparently because of the personal fable—adolescents often do not perceive such activities to be as risky as their parents often see them as being. Even adolescents who understand the risky consequences of their behavior may just decide that taking certain risks is just "worth it" (Reyna & Farley, 2006). One factor prompting risk-taking behavior is having friends who take risks.

Let's also note that the adolescent brain is still maturing, especially the part of the brain that puts the brakes on risky or impulsive behavior (Packard, 2007; Steinberg, 2007; Yurgelun-Todd & Killgore, 2006). It's not that adolescents can't think logically or rationally. But, as psychiatrist David Fassler, puts it, "... they (adolescents) are more likely to act impulsively, on instinct, without fully understanding or analyzing the consequences of their actions" (cited in "Teens' Brains," 2007).

Although adolescence is the period of life associated with greater risk-taking behavior, there are important individual differences in risk-taking among adolescents (and among older people). For example, being married, having children, and having strong traditional roots apparently tend to place the brakes on impulsive behavior (Arnett, 1999). Adolescents, of course, are less likely than adults to be married and have children (and we're not recommending that they curtail risky behavior by taking these routes).

Risk-taking is not limited to adolescents, of course. Many adults take unnecessary risks that pose threats to our safety or the safety of others. According to a 2009 Consumer Reports National Research Center poll, 58% of 1,000 Americans surveyed reported they never wear a helmet while riding a bicycle and 53% said they either occasionally or often talk on a cell phone while driving ("How Often Do Americans," 2009).

Individual differences in sensation-seeking come into play in determining risk-taking behaviors. Risk-takers tend to have a strong need for high levels of sensation. For example, Jacob is a couch potato, content to sit by the TV set all evening. Alexis doesn't feel right unless she's out on the tennis court or jogging. Matthew isn't content unless he has ridden his motorcycle over back trails at breakneck speeds, and Brianna feels exuberant when she's catching the big wave or free-fall diving from an airplane. Matthew and Brianna are high risk-takers. The nearby self-assessment exercise gives you an opportunity to evaluate your needs for sensation-seeking.

The Sensation-Seeking Scale

Self-Assessment

What about you? Are you content to read or watch television all day? Or must you catch the big wave or bounce the bike across the dunes of the Mojave Desert? Sensation-seeking scales measure the level of stimulation or arousal a person will seek.

Psychologist Marvin Zuckerman and his colleagues (1980) have identified four factors that are involved in sensation-seeking: (1) seeking thrill and adventure, (2) disinhibition (that is, tendency to express impulses), (3) seeking experience, and (4) susceptibility to boredom. People high in sensation-seeking are more likely to develop problems with alcohol and drug abuse (Dom, Hulstijn, & Sabbe, 2006). They are also likely to prefer activities like skydiving and hang gliding to less risky pastimes, such as rowing, bowling, and table tennis (Zarevski et al., 1998).

A shortened version of one of Zuckerman's scales follows. To gain insight into your own sensation-seeking tendencies, circle the choice, A or B, which best describes you. Then compare your answers to those in the scoring key at the end of the chapter.

1. a) I would like a job that requires a lot of traveling.
   b) I would prefer a job in one location.
2. a) I am invigorated by a brisk, cold day.
   b) I can't wait to get indoors on a cold day.
3. a) I get bored seeing the same old faces.
   b) I like the comfortable familiarity of everyday friends.

4. a) I would prefer living in an ideal society in which everyone is safe, secure, and happy.
   b) I would have preferred living in the unsettled days of our history.
5. a) I sometimes like to do things that are a little frightening.
   b) A sensible person avoids activities that are dangerous.
6. a) I would not like to be hypnotized.
   b) I would like to have the experience of being hypnotized.
7. a) The most important goal in life is to live it to the fullest and experience as much as possible.
   b) The most important goal in life is to find peace and happiness.
8. a) I would like to try parachute jumping.
   b) I would never want to try jumping out of a plane, with or without a parachute.
9. a) I enter cold water gradually, giving myself time to get used to it.
   b) I like to dive or jump right into the ocean or a cold pool.
10. a) When I go on a vacation, I prefer the change of camping out.
    b) When I go on a vacation, I prefer the comfort of a good room and bed.
11. a) I prefer people who are emotionally expressive, even if they are a bit unstable.
    b) I prefer people who are calm and even-tempered.
12. a) A good painting should shock or jolt the senses.
    b) A good painting should give one a feeling of peace and security.
13. a) People who ride motorcycles must have some kind of unconscious need to hurt themselves.
    b) I would like to drive or ride a motorcycle.

For an interactive version of this self-assessment exercise, go to www.wileyplus.com

Ego Identity versus Role Diffusion

We know that the brain continues to develop during adolescence, including strengthening of the neural connections involved in processes as varied as perception, thinking, and motor (movement) skills (Kuhn, 2006). One consequence of these changes is the increasing sense of personal identity involving questions of "who I am" and "what I am good at." The theorist Erik Erikson (1963) recognized that issues of ego identity take central stage during adolescence, a stage of psychosocial development he characterized as **ego identity versus role diffusion**. Erikson recognized that identity formation is a lifelong process. People face different challenges in their psychosocial development as they travel the road of life. In all, he charted eight stages of identity formation, each of which is characterized by a particular challenge or "crisis" in adjustment. Four of these stages, beginning with the stage of trust versus mistrust, occur during the years of childhood (see Chapter 2).

As Erikson saw it, the major challenge of adolescence is the creation of an adult identity or public role. He coined the term *identity crisis* to describe the period of personal turmoil or upheaval that adolescents may experience as they come to grapple with questions about their public role—their occupational choice and direction in life. This crisis may resolve successfully with the attainment of **ego identity**, or a deeply held commitment to a particular occupational or life goal. Other researchers have extended Erikson's model to examine identity formation in the context of developing other personal beliefs, such as sexual, political, and religious beliefs.

Erikson believed that an identity crisis is a healthy aspect of normal development. This period of personal struggle may result in the development of a stable sense of ego identity. A contemporary scholar, Jeffrey Arnett, prefers the term *exploration* to *crisis* so as to avoid the implication that the process of coming to terms with one's identity is necessarily fraught with anguish and struggle (Arnett, 2004). To Erikson (1963), ego identity is a firm sense of who one is and what one stands for. Adolescents who do not develop ego identity—who have not acquired a firm set of personal beliefs and sense of self—may experience a drifting form of identity that Erikson called **role diffusion**. They find themselves shifting their beliefs to suit the moment and placing themselves under the wing of strong-minded individuals who offer them a sense of identity and belongingness that they cannot find for themselves.

◼ **Ego identity versus role diffusion** Erikson's life crisis of adolescence, which is characterized by the challenge of developing a clear commitment to a set of personal beliefs and public role.

◼ **Ego identity** Erikson's term for a firm sense of who one is and what one stands for.

◼ **Role diffusion** Erikson's term for lack of clarity in one's life roles (due to failure to develop ego identity).

Taxi/Getty Images, Inc.

Teenage Motherhood
Most teenage pregnancies are unplanned. The medical, social, and economic costs of unplanned teenage pregnancies are enormous to teenage mothers and their children. Teenage mothers are more likely to have medical complications during pregnancy and to deliver babies that are premature and of low birthweight. Teenage mothers are also less likely to finish school and more likely to need assistance. Will the father help out? He probably cannot support himself, much less a family.

Adolescent Sexual Adjustment

Erikson stressed the importance during adolescence of coming to terms with one's public role, of what one wants to be in life. But to many adolescents, career aspirations take a backseat (literally) to a consuming interest in dating and sexuality. Some observers have even dubbed adolescents "hormones with feet." Adolescents wrestle with questions of how and when to express their awakening sexuality. To complicate matters, Western culture sends mixed messages about sex. Teenagers may be advised to wait until they have married or at least entered into meaningful relationships, but they are also bombarded by sexual messages in films, TV and radio commercials, and the like, as well as peer pressure and their own natural desires and curiosities. Whereas in traditional times young people "waited" to say their "I do's" before becoming sexually active, young people today hold more lenient attitudes toward premarital sex (Wells & Twenge, 2005). On the other hand, rates of sexual intercourse among teens have actually been dropping in recent years (Santelli et al., 2007). Among 15- to 17-year-old girls, about 30% have engaged in sexual intercourse, which is down from about 38% in the mid-1990s. More teens today are postponing or avoiding premarital sex, in part because of concerns about sexually transmitted diseases and unwanted pregnancies. Despite declines in sexual activity among teens, about 500,000 American teenagers give birth each year, a rate much higher than those in other Western, industrialized countries. Another troubling sign is an uptick in the teenage birth rate, which in 2006 rose for the first time since 1991 (Harris, 2007).

What's Your Identity Status?

Self-Assessment

This self-assessment exercise asks you to apply Erikson's model of psychosocial development to yourself. Many college-age students are in the process of creating their ego identities. But creation takes time, and the process need not be completed by graduation. You'll recall from Chapter 6 that psychologist James Marcia (1991) identified four identity statuses that describe where people stand with respect to their ego identities at any given time:

- *Identity achievement* describes people who have emerged from an identity crisis (a period of serious self-reflection) with a commitment to a relatively stable set of personal beliefs and to a course of action in pursuing a particular career. An example of a career commitment would be pursuing a course of study in engineering in preparation for becoming an engineer.
- *Foreclosure* describes people who have adopted a set of beliefs or a course of action, though with no period of serious self-exploration or self-examination. They did not go through an identity crisis to arrive at their beliefs and occupational choices. Most base their commitments on what others, especially their parents, instilled in them.
- *Moratorium* describes people who are presently in a state of identity crisis concerning their beliefs or career choices. People in moratorium are actively working through their personal beliefs or struggling to determine which career course to pursue.
- *Identity diffusion* describes people who are not yet committed to a set of personal beliefs or career choices and show no real interest in developing these commitments. Issues of ego identity have not yet taken center stage in their lives.

Now let's turn the discussion around to you. What identity status best describes your identity in the areas of occupational choice and personal (political and moral) beliefs? Bear in mind that you may have a different identity status in each area. What criteria did you apply? Has your ego identity status shifted over time? Might it change in the future? Why or why not?

Why is teenage pregnancy so common? Some teenage girls become pregnant as a way of eliciting a commitment from their partner or rebelling against their parents. But most become pregnant because they misunderstand reproduction and contraception or miscalculate the odds of conception. Even those who are well informed about contraception often do not use it consistently. Peers also play an important role in determining the sexual behavior of adolescents. When teenagers are asked why they do not wait to have sexual intercourse until they are older, the top reason cited is usually peer pressure (Dickson et al., 1998).

Adolescent girls by and large also obtain little advice at home or in school about how to resist sexual advances. Nor do most of them have ready access to effective contraception. Fewer than half of the adolescents who are sexually active report using contraceptives consistently (CDC, 2000b).

Unwed teenage mothers face many serious challenges and obstacles. They are more likely than their peers to live under the poverty line, to quit school prematurely, and to require public assistance (Arnett, 2004; CDC, 2000b). Few teenage mothers receive consistent financial or emotional help from the babies' fathers, who generally are unable to support themselves, let alone a family.

Many gay adolescents face the special challenge of coming to terms with their own developing sexuality in a culture that continues to harbor resentment and negative attitudes toward gays. For many gay males and lesbians, the process of "coming out" involves a struggle for self-acceptance in which they need to strip away layers of denial about their sexuality. Many young gay people may not come to fully accept their sexual orientation until young or middle adulthood. The process of achieving self-acceptance against this backdrop of societal intolerance of their sexuality can be so difficult that many gay adolescents seriously consider suicide or actually attempt to take their own lives (Bagley & D'Augelli, 2000).

MODULE REVIEW

Review It

(1) Puberty begins with the appearance of _____ _____ _____, such as the growth of bodily hair, deepening of the voice in males, and rounding of the breasts and hips in females.

(2) According to Piaget, the _____ _____ stage is characterized by hypothetical thinking and deductive logic.

(3) Adolescent egocentrism gives rise to the imaginary _____ and the personal _____.

(4) Psychologist G. Stanley Hall described adolescence as a time of *sturm und drang*, or _____.

(5) The leading cause of death among adolescents is _____ _____ accidents.

(6) Adolescents tend to see experimentation with cars, drugs, and sex as (more or less?) risky than their parents do.

(7) Parents and adolescents tend to (agree or disagree?) on social, political, religious, and economic issues.

(8) Erik Erikson considers the life crisis of adolescence to be _____ identity versus _____ diffusion.

Think About It

Apply your knowledge of cognitive development in adolescence to the understanding of adolescent risk-taking.

MODULE 14.2

Young and Middle Adulthood

▪ ▪

▪ What is adulthood?

▪ What is meant by "emerging adulthood"?

▪ What changes in physical development occur during young and middle adulthood?

▪ What changes in cognitive development occur during young and middle adulthood?

▪ What changes in social and personality development occur during young and middle adulthood?

▮ **Emerging adulthood** A hypothesized period of development found in wealthier societies that spans the ages of 18 to 25 and is characterized by prolonged role exploration.

When our mothers were our age, they were engaged.... They at least had some idea what they were going to do with their lives.... I, on the other hand, will have a dual degree in majors that are ambiguous at best and impractical at worst (English and political science), no ring on my finger and no idea who I am, much less what I want to do.... Under duress, I will admit that this is a pretty exciting time. Sometimes, when I look out across the wide expanse that is my future, I can see beyond the void. I realize that having nothing ahead to count on means I now have to count on myself; that having no direction means forging one of my own.

(Kristen, age 22, cited in Page, 1999, pp. 18, 20)

According to psychologist Jeffrey Arnett (2000a), Kristen is in a period of life that we can label **emerging adulthood**, a period of psychosocial development roughly spanning the ages of 18 through 25 that bridges adolescence and full adulthood. Previously, it was widely accepted that people undergo a transition from adolescence directly into young adulthood. However, Arnett recognizes that the process of achieving full adulthood tends to occur gradually over time. Arnett believes that this period of development, which he calls emerging adulthood, exists only in societies that permit young people extended periods of role exploration before assumption of full adult responsibilities. Relatively affluent societies, such as our own, are able to grant young people the luxury of more slowly developing their adult identities and individual life plans through a combination of parental help, government-funded student loans, and the like.

Young adults today are members of the Millennial generation that came of age during a time of emerging cultural trends such as iPods, "googling," and "facebooking." For many young adults today, the threshold of full-fledged adulthood has been moved up to age 30 (Grigoriadis, 2003). As you can see in Figure 14.2, the majority of today's adults do not perceive themselves to have achieved full adulthood until some point in their late twenties or early thirties. Many 20-somethings and even 30-somethings still live with their parents, a theme depicted in the recent movie *Failure to Launch*. Today, many young people are delaying the walk down the proverbial aisle. For today's youths who are emerging into adulthood, the markers for the transition to adulthood are more strongly linked to issues such as making independent decisions, accepting responsibility for oneself, and becoming financially independent. Getting married may no longer be a key marker of achieving adult status.

Young adulthood has been generally seen as the period of life during which people tend to establish themselves as independent members of society. Sure, this transition could be delayed, and some people are referred to as "perpetual adolescents" by family and friends—meaning, perhaps, that they have difficulty making lasting commitments, remain sort of egocentric, and have not achieved independence.

Survey results suggest that emerging adults in our society today tend to be generally optimistic and to believe that their lives will be as good as or better than those of their parents (Arnett, 2000b). Many still view personal relationships, especially

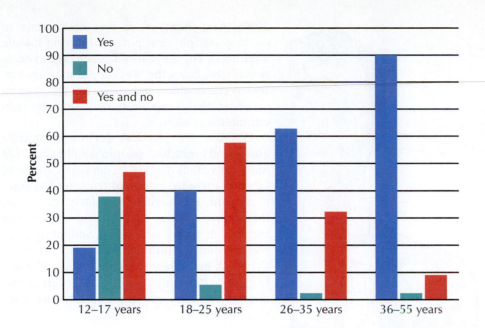

Figure 14.2
Becoming an Adult
Here we see the answers of people who were asked, "Do you feel you have reached adulthood?" For most young people today, it isn't until the late twenties or even the early thirties that they think of themselves as full-fledged adults.
Source: Arnett, 2004.

marriage, as the foundation of future happiness. However, most are deeply concerned about their economic prospects and about larger issues such as crime and destruction of the environment. Even so, most believe that they can succeed in their personal quest for fulfillment.

14.2.1 Physical Development in Adulthood

We continue to develop physically and psychologically throughout our lifespan. People today are living longer than ever before and are freer than ever to choose their own lifestyles and identities. Even 50- or 60-year-olds may still be struggling to "find themselves" or perhaps "reinvent" themselves. Adjustment thus becomes more creative.

In the following section, we consider the physical developments that take place during early adulthood, which roughly spans the period between the ages of 20 and 40, and middle adulthood, which roughly spans the ages of about 45 to 65. Figure 14.3 on the next page displays some of the physical changes that occur with aging.

Reaching Our Peak

Physical development peaks in the twenties and early thirties, then begins to decline slowly (Markham, 2006). Most people are at their height of sensory sharpness, strength, reaction time, and cardiovascular fitness. Women gymnasts find themselves going downhill in their early twenties because they accumulate body fat and lose suppleness and flexibility. Other athletes are more likely to experience a decline in their thirties. The great majority of professional athletes retire before they reach 40.

As we enter our middle years, we are likely to lose some of the strength, coordination, and stamina we had during our twenties and thirties. The decline is most obvious in the professional sports ranks, where peak performance is at a premium. The legendary hockey player Gordie Howe still played at age 50, and basketball great Michael Jordan took himself out of retirement two times and returned to play professional basketball into his forties. But eventually, all professional athletes hang up their skates or cleats for a final time or perhaps join the "senior circuit."

Although we may begin losing some of our physical abilities as we mature, the years between 40 and 60 are reasonably stable in terms of physical functioning, assuming we are fortunate enough to remain healthy. There is a gradual physical decline, but it is minor and likely to be of concern only if we insist on competing with young adults—or with idealized memories of ourselves (Morley & van den Berg,

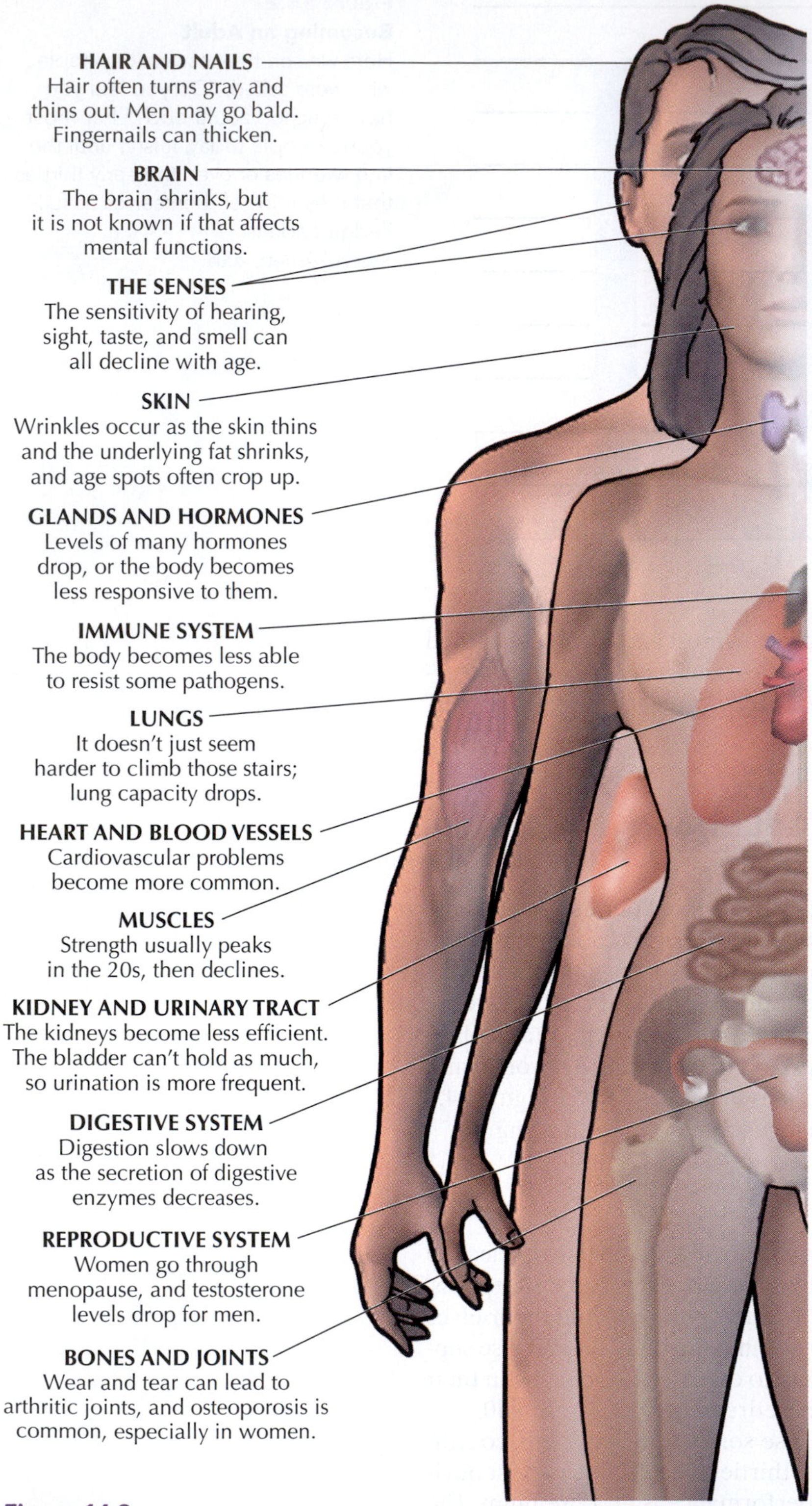

HAIR AND NAILS
Hair often turns gray and thins out. Men may go bald. Fingernails can thicken.

BRAIN
The brain shrinks, but it is not known if that affects mental functions.

THE SENSES
The sensitivity of hearing, sight, taste, and smell can all decline with age.

SKIN
Wrinkles occur as the skin thins and the underlying fat shrinks, and age spots often crop up.

GLANDS AND HORMONES
Levels of many hormones drop, or the body becomes less responsive to them.

IMMUNE SYSTEM
The body becomes less able to resist some pathogens.

LUNGS
It doesn't just seem harder to climb those stairs; lung capacity drops.

HEART AND BLOOD VESSELS
Cardiovascular problems become more common.

MUSCLES
Strength usually peaks in the 20s, then declines.

KIDNEY AND URINARY TRACT
The kidneys become less efficient. The bladder can't hold as much, so urination is more frequent.

DIGESTIVE SYSTEM
Digestion slows down as the secretion of digestive enzymes decreases.

REPRODUCTIVE SYSTEM
Women go through menopause, and testosterone levels drop for men.

BONES AND JOINTS
Wear and tear can lead to arthritic joints, and osteoporosis is common, especially in women.

Figure 14.3
Age-Related Changes
Many physical changes occur as we age. How we cope with these changes plays a large part in our adjustment in middle and later adulthood.

▌ **Menopause** The cessation of menstruation.

2000). And many of us first make time to develop our physical potential during middle adulthood. The 20-year-old couch potato occasionally becomes the 50-year-old marathoner. By any reasonable standard, we can maintain an excellent cardiorespiratory condition throughout middle adulthood.

Because the physical decline in middle adulthood is gradual, people who begin to eat more nutritious diets (e.g., decrease intake of fats and increase intake of fruits and vegetables) and to exercise regularly may find themselves looking and feeling better than they did in young adulthood. Sedentary people in young adulthood may gasp for air if they rush half a block to catch a bus, whereas fit people in middle adulthood—even in late adulthood—may run for miles before they feel fatigued.

Menopause

Menopause, or cessation of menstruation, usually occurs during the late forties or early fifties, although there are wide variations in the age at which it occurs. Menopause is the final stage of a broader female experience, the **climacteric**, which is caused by a falling off in the secretion of the hormones estrogen and progesterone (Morley & van den Berg, 2000). During menopause, ovulation draws to an end and women lose the ability to reproduce. There is also some loss of breast tissue and of elasticity in the skin. There can also be a loss of bone density that leads to **osteoporosis** (a bone disease characterized by loss of bone tissue that makes bones more brittle and susceptible to fractures) in late adulthood.

Many women experience unpleasant symptoms during menopause, such as hot flashes (uncomfortable sensations characterized by heat and perspiration) and loss of sleep. Loss of estrogen can be accompanied by feelings of anxiety and depression, but women appear to be more likely to experience serious depression prior to menopause, when they may feel overwhelmed by the combined demands of the workplace, childrearing, and homemaking ("Depression Research," 2000). Most women get through the mood changes that can accompany menopause without great difficulty. According to psychologist Karen Matthews, who followed a sample of hundreds of women through menopause, "The vast majority [of women] have no problem at all getting through the menopausal transition" (Matthews, 1994, p. 25).

Of course, many myths abound about menopause—myths that spread misinformation and can engender feelings of helplessness. Table 14.1 helps to debunk some of the more common of these myths.

Table 14.1 ∎ Some Myths vs. Facts About Menopause

Myth	Fact
A woman's body no longer produces estrogen after menopause.	Though estrogen production falls offs, some estrogen continues to be produced by the woman's adrenal glands, in fatty tissue, and in the brain.
Women normally become depressed or anxious during menopause as the result of hormonal changes.	Menopausal status is not related to either depression or anxiety. Of course, women who had psychological problems before menopause may continue to have difficulties following menopause. And women who equate menopause with loss of femininity may encounter more emotional distress than those who do not. But this is a statement about the meaning attributed to this period of life, not hormonal changes.
Menopause is a physical event, not a psychological event.	Although physical changes occur in the woman's body during menopause, the meaning she applies to these changes has a determining effect on her emotional response. If the woman considers menopause as the beginning of the end of her life, she may develop a sense of hopelessness that can lead to depression.
Women can expect to experience severe hot flashes during menopause.	Many women experience mild flashes or no flashes at all.
Women lose all desire for sexual activity after menopause.	Not so. Sexual interest and capability may continue throughout the woman's lifespan.
Following menopause, women can no longer bear children.	This was once true, but advances in reproductive technology make it possible for some postmenopausal women to bear children with donated eggs. Some women (including a 63-year-old woman in California) have carried to term babies that were conceived from donated ova that were fertilized in laboratory dishes and then implanted in their uteruses (Bohlen, 1995).

Source: Dennerstein et al, 2002; Jackson, Taylor, & Pyngolil, 1991; Jones, 1994; Matthews et al., 1990.

What About Men? Is There a Manopause?

Since men don't menstruate, they can't experience menopause. But people sometimes refer to the changes that men experience during midlife as a kind of male menopause, or "manopause." Another frequently used term is *andropause*, which refers to the dropoff in androgens, or male sex hormones, that normally occurs during this period of life. Testosterone production begins to decline at around age 40, at a rate of about 1% per year (Daw, 2002). The effects of testosterone reduction can include reduced muscle strength, diminished sex drive, and lack of energy. Still, the decline in both production of sex hormones and fertility is more gradual in men than in women (Tancredi et al., 2005). It therefore is not surprising to find a man in his seventies or older fathering a child. Yet research shows that sperm in older men is more prone to genetic defects than sperm of younger men (Sommerfeld, 2002). Defective sperm can lead to fertility problems, miscarriages, and even birth defects. Many men in their fifties and sixties also experience intermittent problems in achieving and maintaining erections, which may reflect circulatory problems and may or may not have to do with lower testosterone production.

Sexual performance is only one part of the story, however. As we age, we lose bone mass and an inch or more in height. Loss of bone mass puts men as well as women at risk of osteoporosis. They gain more body fat and lose muscle mass. The eardrums thicken, as do the lenses of the eyes, resulting in some loss of hearing and vision. There is also loss of endurance as the cardiovascular system and lungs become less capable of responding effectively to exertion.

Some of these changes can be slowed or even reversed. Exercise helps to maintain muscle tone and to keep the growth of fatty tissue in check. A diet rich in calcium and vitamin D can help ward off bone loss in men as well as in women. Hormone replacement may also help but is controversial. Although testosterone replacement appears to boost strength, energy, and the sex drive, it is connected with increased risks of prostate cancer and cardiovascular disease (Morley & van den Berg, 2000).

∎ **Climacteric** The multiyear process triggered by falloff in production of sex hormones in which menstrual periods become irregular and finally cease.

∎ **Osteoporosis** A condition characterized by porosity, and hence brittleness, of the bones; more common among women.

Ryan Mcvay/Getty Images, Inc.

Is There Such a Thing as a Manopause?

In a literal sense, no. Men have never menstruated, so they cannot experience menopause (the cessation of menstruation). However, people sometimes speak more loosely of "menopausal" changes in middle-aged men, possibly because of a falling off in production of testosterone. Proper diet and exercise helps both men and women ward off many of the effects of aging. Hormone replacement therapy is also sometimes used with individuals who are experiencing adjustment problems related to lower hormone levels. However, hormone replacement has its health risks.

▮ **Crystallized intelligence** A person's lifetime of intellectual attainments, as shown by vocabulary, accumulated facts about world affairs, and ability to solve problems within one's areas of expertise.

▮ **Fluid intelligence** Mental flexibility, as shown by the ability to process information rapidly, as in learning and solving problems in new areas of endeavor.

Even though sexual interest and performance decline, men can remain sexually active and father children at advanced ages. For both genders, attitudes toward the biological changes of aging—along with general happiness—may affect sexual behavior as much as biological changes do.

14.2.2 Cognitive Development

As is the case with physical development, people are also at the height of their cognitive powers during early adulthood. Some aspects of cognitive development show a general decline as we age. Memory functioning, for example, declines with age. We find it more difficult to remember newly acquired information and have trouble recalling the names of common objects or people we know (Hess, 2005; Jacoby & Rhode, 2006; Prull et al., 2006).

Memory lapses can be embarrassing, but they usually do not interfere with a person's ability to function effectively. Nor are declines in memory as large as many people assume. We should note that most memory tests measure ability to recall strings of meaningless information. But in daily life, our functioning depends more on applying our accumulated knowledge and experience. For example, who would do a better job of solving problems in chemistry—a 20-year-old college chemistry major or a 60-year-old full professor of chemistry?

People also obtain the highest intelligence test scores in young adulthood. Yet people typically retain their verbal skills and may even show improvement in certain skills as they age, such as vocabulary and general knowledge. It is their performance on tasks that require reasoning or problem-solving speed and visual-spatial skills, such as putting puzzles together, that tends to fall off as they age.

Consider the difference between **crystallized intelligence** and **fluid intelligence**. Crystallized intelligence, which represents a person's store of knowledge and ability to apply that knowledge in solving problems (what some might call "wisdom"), generally increases over the decades (Kim & Hasher, 2005; Leclerc & Hess, 2007). But fluid intelligence, that aspect of intelligence involved in the ability to process information rapidly, is more susceptible to the effects of aging (Salthouse, 2004; Stine-Morrow, 2007).

In terms of adjustment on the job, familiarity in solving the kinds of problems found at work (crystallized intelligence) may be more important than fluid intelligence. Experience on the job enhances people's specialized vocabularies and knowledge. People draw on fluid intelligence when the usual solutions fail, but experience can be more valuable than fluid intelligence.

14.2.3 Social and Personality Development

Let's begin with some good news. Research evidence suggests that people tend to grow psychologically healthier as they advance from adolescence through middle adulthood. They show higher levels of conscientiousness, emotional stability, and less negative and more positive emotions (Roberts et al., 2006; Sheldon, Houser-Marko, & Kasser, 2006). Other psychologists studied 236 participants in California who had been followed from early adolescence for about 50 years and found that they generally became more productive and had better interpersonal relationships as the years went on (Jones & Meredith, 2000). Certainly there are individual differences, but many individuals, even some with a turbulent adolescence, showed dramatically better psychological health at age 62 than they had half a century earlier.

Let's now recount some of the major themes that theorists identify with psychological development through young and middle adulthood.

Making Your Way in the World: The Challenges of Young Adulthood

Many theorists treat young adulthood as the period of life during which people tend to establish themselves as independent members of society. At some point during the twenties, many people become fueled by ambition. A leading commentator on developmental changes in adulthood, the journalist Gail Sheehy (1976), labeled the twenties the **trying twenties**—a period during which people strive to establish their pathways in life, such as by working to advance their careers. The experience of grounding oneself in an adult life role is often a trying one. Many young adults also adopt what theorist Daniel Levinson and his colleagues (1978) call "**the dream**"—the drive to "become" someone, to leave their mark on history—which serves as a tentative blueprint for their life. A limitation of Levinson's work was that it was based on a sample of men; we should add that holding a dream is not gender-specific.

Intimacy versus Isolation
Erik Erikson (1963) saw the establishment of intimate relationships as central to young adulthood and characterized the major identity challenge facing young adults as one pitting **intimacy versus isolation**. Young adults who have evolved a firm sense of identity during adolescence are ready to "fuse" their identities with those of other people through marriage and abiding friendships. People who do not reach out to develop intimate relationships risk retreating into isolation and loneliness.

Erikson warned that we might not be able to commit ourselves to others until we have achieved ego identity—that is, established stable life roles. To Erikson, achieving ego identity is the central task of adolescence. Lack of personal stability is connected with the high divorce rate for teenage marriages.

Personality Development and Gender
Many men in Western cultures consider separation and **individuation** to be key goals of personality development during young adulthood (Guisinger & Blatt, 1994). For many women, however, the establishment and maintenance of binding close relationships may be of primary importance (Gilligan, Lyons, & Hammer, 1990; Gilligan, Rogers, & Tolman, 1991). Women, as psychologist Carol Gilligan (1982) pointed out in her influential book, *In a Different Voice,* are likely to undergo a transition from being cared for by others to caring for others. In becoming adults, men are more likely to undergo a transition from being restricted by others to autonomy and perhaps control of other people.

But we shouldn't overgeneralize. Women, like men, seek increasing control over their own lives as they progress through their twenties. Although there may be some general differences in adult development of women and men, many women, especially college-educated women, also develop their identities in terms of individuation and autonomy.

The Age-30 Transition
Levinson labeled the ages of 28 to 33 the **age-30 transition**. For men and women, the late twenties and early thirties are commonly characterized by reassessment: "Where is my life going?" "Why am I doing this?" Sheehy (1976) labeled this period the **catch thirties** because of this tendency to catch up with the story of their lives and reassess where they are headed. During our thirties, we often find that the lifestyles we adopted during our twenties do not fit as comfortably as we had expected.

One response to the disillusionments of the thirties, according to Sheehy,

...is the tearing up of the life we have spent most of our twenties putting together. It may mean striking out on a secondary road toward a new vision or converting a dream of "running for president" into a more realistic goal. The single person feels a push to find a partner. The woman who was previously content at home with children chafes to venture into the world. The childless couple reconsiders children. And almost everybody who is married...feels a discontent. (Sheehy, 1976, p. 34)

Many psychologists find that the later thirties are characterized by settling down or planting roots. Many young adults feel a need to make a financial and emotional investment in their home. Their concerns become more focused on promotion or tenure, career advancement, and long-term mortgages.

iStockphoto

Establishing Intimate Relationships According to Erik Erikson, forming intimate relationships is a key task of young adulthood. He characterized the "life crisis" of young adulthood as one of intimacy versus isolation.

▪ **Trying twenties** Sheehy's term for the third decade of life, when people are frequently occupied with advancement in the career world.

▪ **The dream** In this usage, Levinson's term for the overriding drive of youth to become someone important, to leave one's mark on history.

▪ **Intimacy versus isolation** Erikson's life crisis of young adulthood, which is characterized by the task of developing abiding intimate relationships.

▪ **Individuation** The process by which one separates from others and gathers control over one's own behavior.

▪ **Age-30 transition** Levinson's term for the ages from 28 to 33, which are characterized by reassessment of the goals and values of the twenties.

▪ **Catch thirties** Sheehy's term for the fourth decade of life, when many people undergo major reassessments of their accomplishments and goals.

New credit: Digital Vision/Getty Images, Inc.

The "Catch Thirties"
For many people, the late twenties and early thirties are a time of self-examination, of catching up with how one's life is progressing and reassessing one's direction in life.

Developmental Tasks of Young Adulthood Developmental psychologist Robert Havighurst (1972) believed that each stage of development involves accomplishing certain "tasks." The developmental tasks he describes for young adulthood include the following:

1 Getting started in an occupation
2 Selecting and courting a mate
3 Learning to live contentedly with one's partner
4 Starting a family and becoming a parent
5 Assuming the responsibilities of managing a home
6 Assuming civic responsibilities
7 Finding a congenial social group

Erikson and Havighurst were actively theorizing more than 30 years ago, when it was widely assumed that young adults would want to get married and start families. Many young adults in the United States, perhaps most, still have these goals. But there is an increasing diversity of lifestyle choices today. Many people, for example, choose to delay marriage until their late twenties or thirties, whereas some opt to remain single as a permanent lifestyle. Others choose to live together without getting married.

14.2.4 Children: To Have or Not to Have

Once upon a time, marriage was equated with children. According to the "motherhood mandate," it was traditional for women to bear at least two children. Married women who could bear children usually did. Today the motherhood mandate, like other traditions, has come under reconsideration. More than ever, people see themselves as having the right to *choose* whether they will have children.

The decision to have or not to have children is a personal one—one of the most important decisions we make. The nearby self-assessment may be helpful in weighing this most personal and important life decision.

Should You Have a Child?	*Self-Assessment*

Whether to have a child is a heady decision. Children have a way of needing a generation (or a lifetime) of love and support. So we have no simplistic answers to this question, no standardized questionnaire that yields a score for a "Go." Instead, we review some of the considerations involved in choosing to have, or not to have, children. Researchers have found several for each choice. The lists may offer you some insight into your own motives. Sure, you can check the blank spaces of the pros and cons to see how many pros you come up with and how many cons. But we're not suggesting that each item in the list should be weighted equally or that the totals should be the determining factor. You be the judge. It's your life (and, perhaps, your children's lives) and your choice.

Reasons to Have Children

Following are a number of reasons for having children. Check those that seem to apply to you:

___ 1. *Personal experience.* Having children is a unique experience. To many people, no other experience compares with having the opportunity to love them, to experience their love, to help shape their lives, and to watch them develop.

___ 2. *Personal pleasure.* There is fun and pleasure in playing with children, taking them to the zoo and the circus, and viewing the world through their fresh, innocent eyes.

___ 3. *Personal extension.* Children carry on our genetic heritage, and some of our own wishes and dreams, beyond the confines of our own mortality. We name them after ourselves or our families and see them as extensions of ourselves. We identify with their successes.

_____ 4. *Relationship.* Parents have the opportunity to establish extremely close bonds with their children.

_____ 5. *Personal status.* In our culture, parents are afforded respect *just because* they are parents. Consider the commandment: "Honor thy father and thy mother."

_____ 6. *Personal competence.* Parenthood is a challenge. Competence in the social roles of mother and father is a potential source of gratification to people who cannot match this competence in their vocational or other social roles.

_____ 7. *Personal responsibility.* Parents have the opportunity to be responsible for the welfare and education of their children.

_____ 8. *Personal power.* The power that parents hold over their children is gratifying to some people.

_____ 9. *Moral worth.* Some people feel that having children provides the opportunity for a moral, selfless act in which they place the needs of others—their children—ahead of their own.

Reasons Not to Have Children

Following are reasons cited by many couples for deciding not to have children. Check those that apply:

_____ 1. *Strain on resources.* The world is overpopulated and it is wrong to place additional strain on limited resources.

_____ 2. *Increase in overpopulation.* More children will only geometrically increase the problem of overpopulation.

_____ 3. *Choice, not mandate.* Parenthood should be a choice, not a mandate.

_____ 4. *Time together.* Child-free couples can spend more time together and develop a more intimate relationship.

_____ 5. *Freedom.* Children can interfere with plans for leisure time, education, and vocational advancement. Child-free couples are more able to live spontaneously, to go where they please and do as they please.

_____ 6. *Other children.* People can enjoy helping children other than their own, such as by volunteering in Big Brother or Big Sister programs.

_____ 7. *Dual careers.* Members of child-free couples may both pursue meaningful careers without distraction.

_____ 8. *Financial security.* Children are a financial burden, especially considering the cost of a college education.

_____ 9. *Community welfare.* Child-free couples have a greater opportunity to become involved in civic concerns and community organizations.

_____ 10. *Difficulty.* Parenthood is demanding. It requires sacrifice of time, money, and energy, and not everyone makes a good parent.

_____ 11. *Irrevocable decision.* Once you have children, the decision cannot be changed.

_____ 12. *Failure.* Some people fear that they will not be good parents.

_____ 13. *Danger.* The world is a dangerous place, with the threats, for example, of crime and terrorism. It is better not to bring children into such a world.

14.2.5 Becoming an Authoritative Parent: Rearing Competent Children

This book has aimed to enhance readers' competence to cope with the challenges of their lives. Yet we can also help our children cope with the challenges they will face in their own lives. Research by psychologist Diana Baumrind suggests that we, as parents, may also be able to foster what Baumrind calls **instrumental competence** in our children. Instrumentally competent children manipulate their environments to achieve their goals. They are also energetic and friendly. Compared to other children, they show self-reliance and independence, maturity in the formation of goals, achievement motivation, cooperation, self-assertion, and exploratory behavior. The key to helping children develop instrumental competence begins with good parenting.

▮ **Instrumental competence** Ability to manipulate the environment to achieve desired effects.

Adjustment and Modern Life

Childbirth Advice Is Just Keystrokes Away

You're pregnant and it's midnight. You've just felt a couple of abdominal twinges and you're a little worried. You know your obstetrician is probably asleep, and since you still have a couple of weeks to go before the baby's due, you don't want to rush out to the emergency room. Right now, some good, solid medical information would be ever so reassuring.

If you've got an Internet connection, help could be just a few keystrokes away. These days, the web is teeming with birth-related sites. The Net-savvy mother-to-be can research labor issues, find a childbirth class, chat with other expectant women, and shop for everything from pregnancy vitamins to maternity fitness wear.

Of course, as with everything that appears on the web, there's a certain amount of drivel and misinformation. So MSNBC has rounded up some experts to help you find the best places to dock your surfboard.

For trustworthy medical advice, you should probably stick to sites that are affiliated with either an academic institution or an established professional organization, suggests Dr. David Toub, director of quality improvement at Keystone Mercy Health Plan and a member of the department of obstetrics and gynecology at the Pennsylvania Hospital in Philadelphia. One such site, Intelihealth, a joint venture between Johns Hopkins Medical Institutions and Aetna, offers its own experts and links to many reputable sources of information, says Dr. Pamela Yoder, medical director of women's health, obstetrics and gynecology, and maternal–fetal medicine at Provena Covenant Medical Center at the University of Illinois. Another option is to seek sites that have input from recognized experts, such as Obgyn.net. This site also contains chats and forums that focus on such subjects as pregnancy, birth, and breastfeeding.

When she was pregnant, Dr. Kelly Shanahan often drifted over to Obgyn.net's forums to talk with other mothers-to-be about such topics as swollen ankles. "Sometimes it's good to be able to vent to other people in the same situation," says Shanahan, a physician in private practice and chair of obstetrics and gynecology at the Barton Memorial Hospital in South Lake Tahoe, California.

And after the baby was born, Shanahan frequented the chat for new moms. "I may be an obstetrician, but I didn't know diddley about what to do with babies once they're out of the uterus," she says. "It was really helpful to get hints from other moms on how to cope with a newborn."

Another good site for conversation about pregnancy and baby-rearing is iVillage.com, Shanahan says. "This site also has an expert question and answer section," she adds. When it comes to bulletin boards, women should remember that anyone can post anything, experts say.

Some of the Best Websites

The American College of Obstetricians and Gynecologists
http://www.acog.org/

American College of Nurse-Midwives
http://www.midwife.org/

Intelihealth
http://www.intelihealth.com/

Obgyn.net
http://www.obgyn.net/

iVillage.com
http://www.parentsplace.com/pregnancy/

Childbirth.org
http://www.childbirth.org/

Fitness Wear for Pregnant Women
http://www.fitmaternity.com/index.html

Birth and labor section of Babycenter.com
http://www.babycenter.com/birthandlabor/

Types of Parenting Styles

How does competence develop? Diana Baumrind (1973, 1991a, b) studied the relationship between parenting styles and the development of competence. She focused on four aspects of parental behavior: strictness; demands for the child to achieve intellectual, emotional, and social maturity; communication ability; and warmth and involvement. The three most important parenting styles she found are the *authoritative, authoritarian*, and *permissive* styles.

1 *Authoritative parents.* The parents of the most competent children rate high in all four areas of behavior (see Table 14.2). They are strict (restrictive) and demand mature behavior. However, they temper their strictness and demands with willingness to reason with their children, and with love and support. They expect a lot, but they explain why and offer help. Baumrind labeled these parents **authoritative** parents to suggest that they are knowledgeable sources of guidance and support for their children but are also loving and respectful of their children.

▌**Authoritative** Descriptive of parents who demand mature behavior, reason with their children, and provide love and encouragement.

Table 14.2 ▮ Parenting Styles

Style of Parenting	Restrictiveness	Demands for Mature Behavior	Communication Ability	Warmth and Support
Authoritative	High (use of reasoning)	High	High	High
Authoritarian	High (use of force)	Moderate	Low	Low
Permissive	Low (easygoing)	Low	Low	High

2 *Authoritarian parents.* **Authoritarian** parents view obedience as a virtue to be pursued for its own sake. They have strict guidelines about what is right and wrong, and they demand that their children adhere to those guidelines. Both authoritative and authoritarian parents are strict. However, authoritative parents explain their demands and are supportive, whereas authoritarian parents rely on force and communicate poorly with their children. They do not respect their children's points of view, and they may be cold and rejecting. When their children ask them why they should behave in a certain way, authoritarian parents often answer, "Because I say so!"

3 *Permissive parents.* **Permissive** parents are generally easygoing with their children. As a result, the children do pretty much whatever they wish. Permissive parents are warm and supportive but poor at communicating.

Baumrind believes that authoritative parenting is the most successful parenting style. She points to evidence showing that children of authoritative parents generally achieve better outcomes in childhood and adolescence (Baumrind, 1991a, 1991b). For instance, they typically are more popular with their peers, have higher self-esteem, and are more self-reliant and competent than children of parents with other parenting styles (Parke & Buriel, 1997). Children of authoritarian parents are often withdrawn or aggressive, and they usually do not do as well in school as children of authoritative parents. Children of permissive parents seem to be the least mature. They are frequently impulsive, moody, and aggressive. In adolescence, lack of parental monitoring is often linked to delinquency and poor academic performance.

Parental strictness appears to pay off, provided that it is tempered by reason and warmth. The combination of flexibility and firmness in authoritative parents encourages children to become independent and assertive but in ways that show sensitivity and respect for the needs of others. Children whose parents treat them warmly with love and support, as authoritative parents do, tend to become socially and emotionally well adjusted and to internalize moral standards—that is, to develop a moral compass or conscience (Miller et al., 1993; Parke & Buriel, 1997).

We should recognize that parenting styles need to be examined through a cultural lens. Some cultures emphasize authoritarian styles more than others do. Even in our own society, an authoritarian parenting style may be adaptive in cases of poorer families coping with stresses they are likely to encounter, such as living in more dangerous, drug-ridden neighborhoods. Consequently, enforcing stricter obedience and setting stricter limits may be an adaptive strategy to protect their children from outside threats (Parke, 2004).

We should also note that while parenting styles influence children's development, children's behavior influences how their parents relate to them. We need to take a broader view of the parent–child relationship by recognizing that both children and parents influence each other (Kerr et al., 2003).

Becoming an Authoritative Parent

Parenting involves a complex set of behaviors that cannot be reduced to a few simple steps. But we can offer some guidance that may help parents promote competence in their child:

▪ *Be flexible, but not without limits.* Don't allow your children to "run wild" but exert control by using reasoning rather than force.

▮ **Authoritarian** Descriptive of parents who demand obedience for its own sake.

▮ **Permissive** Descriptive of parents who do not make demands of, or attempt to control, their children.

- *Set high but reasonable expectations.* Temper demands by knowledge of what your children *can* do at a given stage of development. If they struggle to perform a certain task, demonstrate how to perform the behavior and give them guidance and encouragement when they attempt the task themselves.

- *Explain to your children why you make certain demands.* Use reasoning, not force. At an early age, the explanation can be simple: "That hurts!" or "You're breaking things that are important to Mommy and Daddy!" The point is to help your child develop a sense of values that he or she can use to form judgments and self-regulate behavior.

- *Listen to your children's opinions.* Show them that you are concerned about how they feel and what they think, but also explain why it is important for them to follow rules.

- *Show warmth.* Frequently express love and caring—give lots of hugs and kisses. Praise them for accomplishing tasks; even small tasks such as playing independently for a few minutes at the age of 2 is an achievement.

Child Abuse: A Crisis in America

Dr. Linda Cahill is the medical director of the Child Protection Center at Montefiore Medical Center in the Bronx, New York. She reviewed the cases of six children who were scheduled to be seen one morning:

- A preschool girl whose mother feared that her interest in her genital organs was a sign that she had been molested.

- A disabled boy who reported that he had been sexually assaulted by a school aide. ["I can't believe people," Dr. Cahill said. "The idea that people who are supposed to watch children—disabled children—could do this" (cited in Fein, 1998).]

- A 6-year-old girl who was being neglected by her mother.

- A 9-year-old boy and his 6-year-old sister who were found to be involved in sexual playacting in their foster home (such playacting can be a sign of sexual abuse).

- A teenager who had been sexually molested by her stepfather.

- A boy with neurological problems who had been abandoned by his mother.

The numbers are staggering and have reached crisis proportions. Some 1 million children in the United States each year are identified as victims of abuse at the hands of their parents or caretakers (Eckenrode et al., 2000; Golden, 2000). More than half a million of these suffer serious injuries, and thousands die. Yet the numbers of children who suffer abuse are much greater, as the great majority of cases go unreported.

Factors Contributing to Child Abuse Child abuse does not develop in a vacuum but arises in families in which parents turn to increasingly coercive means of controlling their children's behavior. Many factors contribute to child abuse: stress, a history of child abuse in at least one of the parents' families of origin, parents with poor anger management skills, alcohol or substance abuse, acceptance of violence as a way of coping with stress, failure to become attached to the children, and rigid attitudes toward childrearing (Belsky, 1993). Unemployment and low socioeconomic status are among the more common stressors associated with child abuse, although abuse is found in all sectors of society.

Abused children are at increased risk of developing many different types of behavioral problems, including poor school performance, aggressiveness, low self-esteem, emotional problems such as depression and suicidal thinking and attempts, immature behaviors such as bed-wetting and thumb-sucking, and failure to venture out to explore the world (e.g., Shonk & Cicchetti, 2001; Wolfe et al., 2001). They are also more likely to have psychological problems in adulthood, such as anxiety, depression, bulimia, substance abuse, and low self-esteem (Evren, Kural, & Cakmak, 2006; Lipman, MacMillan, & Boyle, 2001).

Child abuse runs in families to some degree (Ertem, Leventhal, & Dobbs, 2000). That is, child abusers are more likely to have been abused than is true for the general population. Even so, the majority of children who are abused do not abuse their own children as adults.

Why does abuse run in some families? Several factors may be at work. For one, parents serve as role models. Exposure to their parent's use of harsh discipline may lead children to view this kind of abuse as normal, creating accepting attitudes toward using harsh discipline when they become parents themselves. In addition, being abused can create feelings of hostility that are then expressed against others, including one's own children.

Child Sexual Abuse—What to Do, Where to Turn

Sexual abuse is a form of child abuse in which children are subjected to fondling, exhibitionism, oral sex, or intercourse. An estimated 500,000 children in the United States are abused each year (Villarosa, 2002). Contrary to the stereotype of the sexual abuser as a stranger lurking in the shadows of the neighborhood playground, the perpetrator in most cases, perhaps in as many as 75% to 80% of cases, is someone who has a relationship with either the child or the child's family (Zielbauer, 2000). The typical abuser is a relative or step-relative of the child, a family friend, or a neighbor—people who may have held and then abused the child's trust. Ninety percent of molesters are men (Villarosa, 2002).

Although we cannot identify any one single syndrome that results from child sexual abuse, investigators find that sexually abused children are more likely to develop a wide range of physical and psychological health problems than are nonabused children (Saywitz et al., 2000). Child sexual abuse can also have lasting negative effects on children's relationships and psychological health in adulthood (Collishaw et al., 2008; Miller-Perrin et al., 2009; Sachs-Ericsson et al., 2005).

What can you do if you suspect that a child has been subject to sexual abuse? The American Psychological Association offers these guidelines:[1]

- Give the child a safe environment in which to talk to you or another trusted adult. Encourage the child to talk about what he or she has experienced, but be careful that you not suggest events to him or her that may not have happened. Guard against displaying emotions that would influence the child's telling of the information.
- Reassure the child that he or she did nothing wrong.
- Seek mental health assistance for the child.
- Arrange for a medical examination for the child. Select a medical provider who has experience in examining children and identifying sexual and physical trauma. It may be necessary to explain to the child the difference between a medical examination and the abuse incident.
- Be aware that many states have laws requiring that persons who know or have a reason to suspect that a child has been sexually abused must report that abuse to either local law enforcement officials or child protection officials. In all 50 states, medical personnel, mental health professionals, teachers, and law enforcement personnel are required by law to report suspected abuse.

The APA also lists the following resources that people can use to find help:

- American Professional Society on the Abuse of Children
  407 South Dearborn
  Suite 1300
  Chicago, IL 60605
  312-554-0166
  http://www.apsac.org/

[1]The Office of Public Communications, American Psychological Association, 750 First Street, NE, Washington, DC 20002-4242. 202-336-5700. http://www.apa.org/releases/sexabuse/.

- National Center for Missing and Exploited Children
  Charles B. Wang International Children's Building
  699 Prince Street
  Alexandria, VA 22314-3175
  24-hour hotline: 1-800-THE-LOST
  http://www.missingkids.com/

- Child Help USA
  15757 North 78th Street
  Scottsdale, AZ 85260
  800-4-A-CHILD
  http://www.childhelpusa.org/

- National Clearinghouse on Child Abuse and Neglect Information
  U.S. Department of Health and Human Services
  P.O. Box 1182
  Washington, DC 20013
  800-FYI-3366

14.2.6 Transitions to Mastery: Facing the Challenges of Midlife

▌ **Generativity versus stagnation** Erikson's term for the crisis of middle adulthood, characterized by the task of being productive and contributing to younger generations.

Theorist Erik Erikson (1963) described the life crisis of the middle years as one of **generativity versus stagnation**. Generativity is the process of contributing to children's development or the betterment of society in general, such as by investing one's efforts in raising one's own children or performing work that benefits others, such as transmitting values and mentoring younger workers. Evidence suggests that generativity tends to peak in midlife and may be the path toward greater personal fulfillment (Peterson & Duncan, 2007; Zucker, Ostrove, & Stewart, 2002). By contrast, stagnation involves letting time just pass by rather than making efforts to use time productively; it means maintaining the status quo rather than moving forward in one's life.

Midlife Transition

▌ **Midlife transition** Levinson's term for the ages from 40 to 45, which are characterized by a shift in psychological perspective from viewing ourselves in terms of years lived to viewing ourselves in terms of the years we have left.

Psychologist Daniel Levinson and colleagues (1978), who examined the life experiences of a group of 40 men, found that a **midlife transition** typically occurred at about age 40 to 45. This transition was characterized by a shift in psychological perspective. Previously, men had thought of their age in terms of the number of years that had elapsed since birth. Now they begin to think of their age in terms of the number of years they have left. Men in their thirties still think of themselves as older brothers to "kids" in their twenties. At about age 40 to 45, however, some marker event—illness, a change of job, the death of a friend or parent, or being beaten at tennis by their son—leads men to realize that they are a full generation older. Suddenly there seems to be more to look back on than forward to. It dawns on men that they will never be president or chairman of the board. They will never play shortstop for the Dodgers or point guard for the Heat. They mourn the passing of their own youth and begin to adjust to the specter of old age and the finality of death.

Research suggests that women may undergo a midlife transition a number of years earlier than men do (Stewart & Ostrove, 1998). Sheehy (1976) writes that women may enter midlife about five years earlier than men, at about age 35 instead of 40. Why? Much of it has to do with the winding down of the "biological clock"—that is, the abilities to conceive and bear children. Yet many women today are having children in their forties, and so we need to consider traditional time markers somewhat more flexibly.

The Midlife Crisis

According to Levinson, the midlife transition may trigger a crisis—the **midlife crisis**. The middle-level, middle-aged businessperson looking ahead to another 10 to 20 years of grinding out accounts in a Wall Street cubbyhole may encounter severe depression. The housewife with two teenagers, an empty house from 8:00 A.M. to 4:00 P.M., and a fortieth birthday on the way may feel that she is coming apart at the seams. Both feel a sense of entrapment and loss of purpose. Some people are propelled into extramarital affairs by the desire to prove to themselves that they are still attractive. That said, a midlife crisis may be more the exception than the rule. Evidence fails to bear out the widely held belief that a midlife crisis is a widespread occurrence (Lachman, 2004).

Toward Mastery

Sheehy (1995) is much more optimistic than Levinson. She terms the years from 45 to 65 the "age of mastery." Rather than viewing them as years of decline, her interviews suggest that many Americans find that these years present opportunities for new direction and fulfillment. Many people are at the height of their productive powers during this period. Sheehy believes that the key task for people aged 45 to 55 is to decide what they will do with their "second adulthoods"—the 30 to 40 healthy years that may be left for them once they reach 50. She believes that both men and women can experience great success and joy if they identify meaningful goals and pursue them wholeheartedly.

Middlescence

Yet people need to define themselves and their goals. Sheehy coined the term **middlescence** to describe a period of searching, a kind of midcourse correction through life in which people seek a new identity or find a new purpose or goal in life. Women frequently experience a renewed sense of self in their forties and fifties as they emerge from middlescence (Sheehy, 1995). Many women in their early forties are already emerging from some of the fears and uncertainties that are first confronting men. For example, women in their early forties are more likely than women in their early thirties to feel confident; to exert an influence on their community; to feel secure and committed; to feel productive, effective, and powerful; and to extend their interests beyond their family.

The Empty-Nest Syndrome

In earlier decades, psychologists placed great emphasis on a concept referred to as the **empty-nest syndrome**. This concept was applied most often to women. It was assumed that women experience a profound sense of loss when their youngest child goes off to college, gets married, or otherwise moves out of the home. The sense of loss is widely assumed to be greatest among women who had remained in the home. Research findings paint a more optimistic picture. Certainly, a sense of loss may be experienced when the children have left home, and the loss applies to both parents. Parents may find it difficult to let go of the children after so many years of mutual dependence. However, many mothers report increased marital satisfaction and personal changes such as greater mellowness, self-confidence, and stability once the children have left home (Stewart & Ostrove, 1998).

Many parents—fathers as well as mothers—report that the years after raising children can become a time for reconnecting with one another (Gorchoff, John, & Helson, 2008). Although "empty-nesters" may miss their children, their sense of loss tends to be offset by the greater freedom they enjoy and their ability to pursue their own interests. That said, many empty nests are refilling as adult children facing a tough job market and high housing costs are returning home or are deciding not to leave in the first place (Buss, 2005).

Steve Craft/Masterfile

Midlife Crisis?
Though many people believe that a midlife crisis is somehow unavoidable, evidence suggests that a period of serious personal crisis during the middle years is more of an exception than the rule.

■ **Midlife crisis** A crisis experienced by many people during the midlife transition when they realize that life may be more than halfway over and they reassess their achievements in terms of their dreams.

■ **Middlescence** Sheehy's term for a period of searching for identity that occurs during middle adulthood.

■ **Empty-nest syndrome** A sense of depression and loss of purpose experienced by some parents when the youngest child leaves home.

MODULE REVIEW

Review It

(9) The period that bridges adolescence and full adulthood is called _____ adulthood.

(10) This period of development exists in (wealthy or poor?) societies.

(11) Cessation of menstruation, termed _____, usually occurs during the late forties or early fifties.

(12) A dropoff in the hormone _____ can be accompanied by hot flashes and feelings of anxiety and depression.

(13) People tend to retain (verbal skills or performance on tasks that require speed and visual-spatial skills?) into advanced old age.

(14) _____ intelligence refers to one's lifetime of intellectual achievement, as shown by vocabulary and general knowledge.

(15) _____ intelligence entails mental flexibility, as shown by the ability to solve new kinds of problems.

(16) The term _____ _____ refers to the period of young adulthood in which people begin to establish themselves in their careers and assume more independent roles in society.

(17) Erikson characterized the major identity challenge of young adulthood in terms of _____ vs. isolation

(18) (High or Low?) socioeconomic status is a common stressor that leads to child abuse.

(19) Children who are abused are (more or less?) likely to be aggressive than other children.

(20) Most perpetrators of child sexual abuse (have had or have not had) a prior relationship with the child or the child's family.

(21) According to Levinson, the midlife transition may trigger a _____ _____ that is characterized by a sense of entrapment and loss of purpose.

(22) Sheehy characterized the period of midlife in terms of opportunities for new direction and fulfillment the "age of _____."

Think About It

Is there a difference between an extended adolescence and the concept of emerging adulthood?

MODULE 14.3

Late Adulthood

▪ What changes in physical development occur during late adulthood?

▪ What changes in cognitive development occur during adulthood?

▪ What is Alzheimer's disease?

▪ What are the gender and ethnic differences in life expectancy?

▪ What changes in cognitive development occur during late adulthood?

▪ What do we know of the psychology of death and dying?

Did you know that an age-quake is coming? With improved health care and knowledge of the importance of diet and exercise, more Americans are age 65 or older (see Figure 14.4). We are living in the midst of a continuing graying of America (Libow, 2005). Consider that in the year 1900, only one American in 30 was over 65. By the middle of the twenty-first century, more than one in five Americans will be 65 years of age or older (Clements,

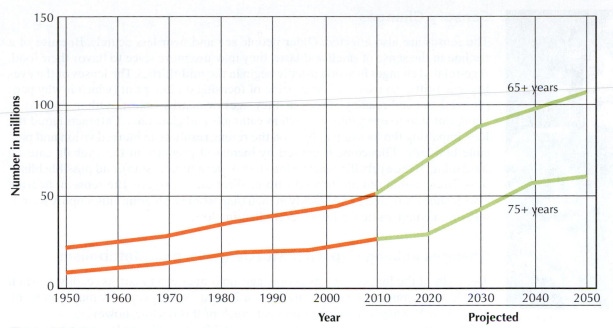

Figure 14.4

Population Growth Among Older Americans

The U.S. population is expected to continue to rise, along with the numbers of Americans 65 years of age and older.
Sources: Centers for Disease Control and Prevention, National Center fo *Health Statistics, Health, United States*, 2007, Figure 1. Data from the U.S. Census Bureau.

2003). Average life expectancy continues to rise, having reached a record 77.9 years in 2005 (Mueller, 2007). Today, the average 65-year-old man or woman in good health has a 50% chance of living to at least age 85 (for men) or 88 (for women) (see Table 14.3).

Let us recount some of the changes you can anticipate if you are fortunate enough to one day join the ranks of older adults.

14.3.1 Physical Development

We can expect a number of physical changes—some of them troublesome—as we progress through **late adulthood**. The skin becomes less elastic and so becomes more wrinkled. The hair grows gray as the production of *melanin*, the pigment responsible for hair color, declines. Hair loss also accelerates as people age, especially in men. Age-related changes in the nervous system increase **reaction time**—the amount of time it takes to respond to a stimulus (Der & Deary, 2006). Older drivers, for example, need more time to respond to traffic lights, other vehicles, and changing road conditions. Nor can older people catch rapidly moving baseballs or footballs. As we grow older, our immune system also functions less effectively, leaving us more vulnerable to diseases such as cancer. Organ systems deteriorate. Eventually, these changes result in death.

"Good news, honey—seventy is the new fifty."

Betsy Streeter

▪ **Late adulthood** The last stage of life, beginning at age 65.

▪ **Reaction time** The amount of time required to respond to a stimulus.

Table 14.3 ▪ Good Health, Long Life		
	50% Chance of Living to:	**25% Chance of Living to:**
65-year old male in good health	Age 85	Age 92
65-year old female in good health	Age 88	Age 94

Source: Adapted from Carnahan, 2005.

Michael Malfer/Retna

Old? Who, Me?
The continuing popularity of aging rock stars has blurred generational differences. Though aging involves a physical process, social conceptions of where the boundaries lie between youth and middle age and between middle age and old age have changed over time.

Sensory Changes

The senses are also affected. Older people see and hear less acutely. Because of a decline in the sense of smell and taste, they may use more spice to flavor their food. Age-related changes in vision usually begin in the mid-thirties. The lenses of the eyes become brittle, so they are less capable of focusing on fine print (which is why people tend to need reading glasses as they age) or nearby objects. Other changes of aging can lead to eye problems such as cataracts and glaucoma. Cataracts cloud the lens, impairing the focusing of light on the retina, resulting in blurred vision and possible blindness. Glaucoma is caused by increased pressure in the eyeball, causing hardening of the eyeball, tunnel vision (loss of peripheral vision), and possible blindness. These conditions are treated with medication or surgery. The sense of hearing also declines with age, more quickly in men than women. Hearing aids amplify sounds and often compensate for more severe hearing loss.

Changes in Lung Capacity, Muscle Mass, and Metabolism

The walls of the lungs stiffen as people age, no longer expanding as readily as when people were younger. Between the ages of 20 and 70, lung capacity may decline by 40% or so. Regular exercise can prevent much of this decline, however.

The very composition of the body changes. Muscle cells are lost with age, especially after the age of 45. Fat replaces muscle. There is a consequent reshaping of the body and loss of muscle strength. However, exercise can compensate for much of the loss by increasing the size of the muscle cells that remain.

The metabolic rate (the rate at which the body burns calories) declines as we age, largely because of the loss of muscle tissue and the corresponding increase in body fat. Muscle burns more calories—has a faster metabolic rate—than fat. People also require fewer calories to maintain their weight as they age, and extra calories are deposited as fat. Older people are thus likely to gain weight if they eat as much as they did when they were younger. Regular exercise helps older people maintain a healthful weight, just as it does with younger people. Not only does exercise burn calories; it also builds the muscle mass, and muscle burns calories more efficiently than fat. The cardiovascular system becomes less efficient with age. The heart pumps less blood and the blood vessels carry less blood, which has implications for sexual functioning, as we see later.

Changes in Bone Density

Bones consist mainly of calcium, and they begin to lose density in early middle age, frequently leading to osteoporosis. Osteoporosis literally translates as "porous bone," meaning that the bone becomes porous rather than maintaining its density. As a result, the risk of fractures increases. Osteoporosis poses a greater threat to women because men usually begin with a larger bone mass, providing some protection against the disease. Bone loss in women is associated with low levels of estrogen at menopause (Marwick, 2000). Bones break more readily, and some women develop curvature of the spine ("dowager's hump"). Osteoporosis can be handicapping, even life-threatening. Brittleness of the bones increases the risk of serious fractures, especially of the hip, and many older women never fully recover from them.

Changes in Sexual Functioning

Corbis/Alamy

Aging and Sexuality
People in good physical health can remain sexually active throughout their lives. The belief that older adults who retain sexual interest or activity are abnormal is a type of age-related prejudice.

As a joke, an 18-year-old college student gave her middle-aged parents a book called *Sex in Middle Age* that contained nothing but blank pages. The student laughed, but her parents smiled politely, knowing that the joke was on her. Despite lingering stereotypes that sex belongs to the young, most people in middle adulthood report having satisfying and rich sex lives (Duplassie & Daniluk, 2007; Vares et al., 2007). That said, there are important age-related changes that affect sexual functioning (see Table 14.4).

Table 14.4 ▌ Changes in Sexual Response Connected with Aging

Changes that Occur in Women	Changes that Occur in Men
Less interest in sex	Less interest in sex
Less blood flow to the genitals	Less blood flow to the genitals
Less vaginal lubrication	More time needed to attain erection and reach orgasm
Less elasticity in vaginal walls	More need for direct stimulation (touch) to attain erection
Smaller increases in breast size	Less firm erections
Less intense orgasms	Less ejaculate
	Less intense orgasms
	More time needed to become aroused (erect) again

The underlying point is that physically healthy people are capable of enjoying sexual experience for a lifetime if they make some adjustments, including adjustments to their expectations. Older men and women may both experience less interest in sex, which is apparently related to lowered levels of testosterone (yes, as noted earlier, women naturally produce some testosterone) in both genders.

For example, older men may need more time to attain erections, and the erections are less firm. Fantasy may no longer do it; extensive direct stimulation (stroking) may be needed. Many men, perhaps half, have at least intermittent problems in attaining erection in middle and late adulthood. They also usually require more time to reach orgasm. Couples can adjust to these changes by extending the length and variety of foreplay. Women will normally produce less vaginal lubrication as they age, but artificial lubrication may be sufficient to engage in intercourse. Orgasms become weaker as measured by the physical aspects of orgasm—that is, the strength and number of muscle contractions at the base of the penis. But physical measures do not translate exactly into pleasure. An older man may enjoy orgasms as much as he did when younger. A person's attitudes and expectations are crucial to the continued enjoyment of sexual activity.

In sum, late adulthood need not bring one's sex life to a halt. Expectations and the willingness of partners to adjust are crucial factors in sexual fulfillment.

What Are Your Attitudes Toward Aging?

Self-Assessment

What are your assumptions about late adulthood? Do you see older people as basically different from the young in their behavior patterns and their outlooks, or just as a few years more mature?

To evaluate the accuracy of your attitudes toward aging, mark each of the following items true (T) or false (F). Then turn to the answer key at the end of the chapter.

T F 1. By age 60 most couples have lost their capacity for satisfying sexual relations.
T F 2. The elderly cannot wait to retire.
T F 3. With advancing age, people become more externally oriented, less concerned with the self.
T F 4. As individuals age, they become less able to adapt satisfactorily to a changing environment.
T F 5. General satisfaction with life tends to decrease as people become older.
T F 6. As people age, they tend to become more homogeneous—that is, all old people tend to be alike in many ways.
T F 7. For the older person, having a stable intimate relationship is no longer highly important.
T F 8. The aged are more susceptible to a wider variety of psychological disorders than young and middle-aged adults.
T F 9. Most older people are depressed much of the time.
T F 10. Church attendance increases with age.
T F 11. The occupational performance of the older worker is typically less effective than that of the younger adult.
T F 12. Most older people are just not able to learn new skills.

For an interactive version of this self-assessment exercise, go to www.wileyplus.com

14.3.2 Cognitive Development

As people advance in years, they often experience problems with memory functioning. They may have difficulty recalling the names of people or solving math problems in their heads (DeDe et al., 2004; Henry et al., 2004; Peters et al., 2007). They also may have more difficulty solving problems requiring fluid intelligence, such as piecing together jigsaw puzzles. Yet performance on tasks that tap into crystallized intelligence tends to remain relatively intact as people age, including vocabulary skills and ability in applying acquired knowledge or information. Fortunately, most tasks we're likely to encounter in the workplace involve crystallized intelligence, such as those in which we need to apply our accumulated knowledge (Volz, 2000). Age-related changes in mental abilities may be reduced to some extent through training programs in memory and other cognitive skills and physical fitness training (Kramer & Willis, 2002).

Creativity, another cognitive skill, is not bound by age. At the age of 80, Merce Cunningham choreographed a dance that made use of computer-generated digital images. Hans Hofmann created some of his most vibrant paintings at 85, and Pablo Picasso was painting in his nineties. Grandma Moses did not begin painting until she was 78 years old, and she painted past the age of 100. Giuseppe Verdi wrote his joyous opera *Falstaff* at the age of 79. The architect Frank Lloyd Wright designed New York's innovative spiral-shaped Guggenheim Museum when he was 89 years old! Not too shabby.

Keeping the Mind Sharp: The Seattle Longitudinal Study

Psychologist Walter Schaie and his colleagues (Schaie, 1994) have been studying the cognitive development of adults for four decades and have discovered factors that contribute to preserved intellectual functioning across the lifespan:

1 *General health.* People in good health tend to retain higher levels of intellectual functioning into late adulthood. Therefore, paying attention to one's diet, exercising, and having regular medical checkups contribute to intellectual functioning as well as physical health.

2 *Socioeconomic status (SES).* People with high SES tend to maintain intellectual functioning more adequately than people with low SES. High SES is also connected with above-average income and levels of education, a history of stimulating occupational pursuits, maintenance of intact families, and better health.

3 *Stimulating activities.* Cultural events, travel, participation in professional organizations, and extensive reading contribute to intellectual functioning.

4 *Marriage to a spouse with a high level of intellectual functioning.* The spouse whose level of intellectual functioning is lower at the beginning of a marriage tends to increase in intellectual functioning as time goes by. Perhaps that partner is continually challenged by the other.

5 *Openness to new experience.* Being open to new challenges of life apparently helps keep us young—at any age.

Alzheimer's Disease: The Long Goodbye

▮ Alzheimer's disease An irreversible brain disease characterized by gradual deterioration in mental processes such as memory, language use, judgment, and problem solving.

Alzheimer's disease (AD) is an irreversible brain disease, resulting in the death of brain cells in many areas of the brain, that slowly but relentlessly robs people of their mental abilities (Gross, 2007). The final stages of the disease lead to loss of speech and ability to control body movement and eventually to death.

Alzheimer's disease afflicts more than 5 million Americans and has become the fourth leading cause of death among adults in the United States. It affects one in eight people age 65 or older and more than four in ten people over the age of 85 (Gross, 2007). As the U.S. population continues to age, the prevalence of Alzheimer's disease is expected to nearly quadruple, to about 16 million people ("Alzheimer's Cases," 2007). Although AD may affect younger people, it is rare in those under the age 65.

We discuss Alzheimer's disease in the section on cognitive development because it is characterized by deterioration in mental processes such as memory, language use, judgment, and problem solving and changes in personality. As the disease progresses, people may fail to recognize familiar faces or forget their names. At the most severe stage, people with Alzheimer's disease become essentially helpless. They become unable to communicate or walk and require help in toileting and feeding. More isolated memory losses (for example, forgetting where one put one's glasses) may be a normal feature of aging. Alzheimer's, in contrast, seriously impairs vocational and social functioning.

Alzheimer's is a disease, not a normal part of the aging process (Gatz, 2007). The toll it takes on its victims and on those who care for them, generally spouses who themselves are coping with the challenges of aging, is incalculable. Because of the slow but insidious nature of the disease, it has been likened to a "funeral without end."

The causes of Alzheimer's disease remain unknown, but recent evidence points to a genetic contribution (Bartzokis et al., 2006; Godbolt et al., 2006; Lesné et al. 2006). Scientists suspect a role for genes that regulate the production of a protein that is involved in the formation of the brain plaques and tangles associated with the disease.

Unfortunately, we lack an effective treatment for the disease. Presently available drugs achieve modest benefits at best. Scientists are working on the development of a vaccine that would stimulate the immune system to recognize and attack the plaque more vigorously. Such work remains experimental, however.

Aging, Gender, and Ethnicity: Different Patterns of Aging

Although Americans in general are living longer and living better, the good news is not spread around in equal measure. For example, women in our society typically live longer, but older men tend to live better ("Longer, Healthier, Better," 1997). European Americans live longer on the average than do Latino and Latina Americans, African Americans, and Native Americans (CDC, 2000e). Life expectancy for Latino and Latina Americans falls somewhere between the figures for African Americans and European Americans. The longevity of Asian Americans falls closer to that of European Americans than to that of African Americans. Native Americans have the lowest average longevity of the major racial/ethnic groups in the United States. Though gender and racial gaps in longevity remain, these gaps are narrowing.

Why the Gender Difference in Longevity?
Women in the United States outlive men by about five years on the average. Why? For one thing, heart disease, the nation's leading killer, typically develops later in women than in men. Men are also more likely to die because of accidents, cirrhosis of the liver, strokes, suicide, homicide, AIDS, and cancer. Many deaths from these causes are the result of unhealthy habits that are more typical of men, such as excessive drinking and reckless behavior. Many men are also reluctant to have regular physical exams or to talk to their doctors about their health problems.

Although women tend to outlive men, their prospects for a happy and healthy old age are dimmer. Men who beat the statistical odds by living beyond their seventies are far less likely than their female counterparts to live alone, suffer from disabling conditions, or be poor. Older women are more likely than men to live alone largely because they are more likely to be widowed. One reason that older women are more likely to be poor is that women who are now age 65 or older were less likely to have held high-paying jobs or have generous pension benefits.

What Roles Do Race and Social Class Play?
Socioeconomic differences play an important role in ethnic differences in life expectancy. Members of ethnic minority groups in our society are more likely to be poor, and poor people tend to eat less nutritious diets, encounter more stress, and have less access to quality health care. There is a seven-year difference in life expectancy between people in the highest income brackets and those in the lowest. Yet other factors, such as cultural differences in diet and lifestyle, the stress of coping with discrimination, and genetic differences, may partly account for ethnic group differences in life expectancy.

We also need to factor into the equation the unequal access that people of color have to medical services, including more aggressive and potentially life-saving medical treatments. Evidence shows that African Americans who suffer a heart attack receive less aggressive treatments than do their European American counterparts (Chen et al., 2001;

© Jeff Greenberg/PhotoEdit

Patterns of Aging
European Americans tend to outlive Latino and Latina Americans, African Americans, and Native Americans. When we hold ethnicity constant, women tend to outlive men by about five years. How do we explain these different patterns of aging?

Stolberg, 2001). America has a dual standard of health care, one that may reflect not only differential access to quality care but also discrimination by health care providers.

14.3.3 Personality and Social Development

▌ **Ego integrity versus despair** Erikson's term for the crisis of late adulthood, characterized by the task of maintaining one's sense of identity despite physical deterioration.

Erikson characterized late adulthood as the stage of **ego integrity versus despair**. The basic challenge is to maintain the belief that life is meaningful and worthwhile in the face of the inevitability of death. Ego integrity derives from wisdom, which we can define as expert knowledge about the meaning of life, balancing one's own needs and those of others, and pushing toward excellence in one's behavior and achievements. Erikson also believed that wisdom enabled people to accept their lifespan as occurring at a certain point in the sweep of history and as being limited in time.

According to Robert Peck (1968), who has extended Erikson's views, a number of shifts in our thinking and attitudes can help us adjust to the developmental challenges of late adulthood:

- Coming to value wisdom more than physical strength and power
- Coming to value friendship and social relationships more than sexual prowess[2]
- Retaining emotional flexibility so that we can adjust to changing family relationships and the ending of a career
- Retaining mental flexibility so that we can form new social relationships and undertake new leisure activities
- Keeping involved and active and concerned about others so that we do not become preoccupied with physical changes or the approach of death
- Shifting interest from the world of work to retirement activities

Havighurst also denotes a number of developmental tasks of late adulthood:

- Adjusting to physical changes
- Adjusting to retirement and to changes in financial status
- Establishing satisfying living arrangements
- Learning to live with one's spouse in retirement (e.g., coping with the spouse being home much of the time)
- Adjusting to the death of one's spouse
- Forming new relationships with aging peers
- Adopting flexible social roles

On Living Independently

There are some stereotypes concerning living arrangements for older people. One has them living with their grown children; another has them all living in institutions (Stock, 1995). Still another has them buying recreational vehicles and taking off for condominiums or retirement communities in the sunbelt.

First, let us put to rest the stereotype that older people are generally dependent on others. According to the U.S. Bureau of the Census (2000), the majority of heads of households who are 65 years of age or older own their own homes. Only a small minority (5%) of adults over the age of 65 are living in long-term care facilities, such as a nursing home (Hyer et al., 2005). However, upwards of 40% of older adults eventually spend at least some time in these facilities (Hyer et al., 2005). Evidence also shows that adults who are in good general health and who believe it is important to be independent are more likely to live on their own than are less healthy and independent peers (Ford et al., 2000). Despite the stereotype of taking off for the sunbelt, the majority of older people remain in their home towns and cities. Moving is stressful at any age. Most older people prefer to remain in familiar locales.

---

[2]However, most of us continue, or can continue, to enjoy sexual expression for a lifetime, and we should not fall prey to the stereotype of the elderly as asexual (Rathus, Nevid, & Fichner-Rathus, 2008).

Older people are often portrayed as living in poverty or at the mercy of their children and external forces, such as government support. Unfortunately, some of these stereotypes are based on reality. People who no longer work are usually dependent on savings and fixed incomes such as pensions and Social Security payments. The flip-side of the coin is that, nationwide, only about 13% of those aged 65 and above live below the poverty level (U.S. Bureau of the Census, 2000).

On Retirement

Although life changes can be stressful, retirement can be a positive step. Many retirees enjoy their leisure. Some continue in part-time labor, paid or voluntary. Most people who deteriorate rapidly after retirement were unhealthy prior to retirement (Crowley, 1985). Older people may delay retirement if they need to continue contributing to the support of their children. Atchley (1985) has theorized that many older people undergo a six-phase developmental sequence of retirement:

1 *The preretirement phase.* This phase involves fantasies about retirement—positive and negative. Company preretirement programs and retired friends can foster adjustment by providing accurate information about financial realities and postretirement lifestyles.

2 *The honeymoon phase.* This phase often involves the euphoria that accompanies newfound freedom. It is a busy period during which people do the things they had fantasized doing once they had the time—as financial resources permit.

3 *The disenchantment phase.* As one's schedule slows down and one discovers that fantasized activities are less stimulating than anticipated, disenchantment can set in.

4 *The reorientation phase.* Now a more realistic view of the possibilities of retirement develops. Now retirees frequently join volunteer groups and increase civic involvements.

5 *The stability phase.* The retirement role has been mastered. Routine and stability set in; there is more accurate self-awareness of one's needs and strengths and weaknesses.

6 *The termination phase.* Retirement can come to an end in different ways. One is death; another is the assumption of the sick role because of disability; still another is return to work.

As noted in Figure 14.5, many people return to some form of work after retiring. For them, the benefits of employment outweigh the lure of leisure. Some companies have instituted programs to lure retired workers back into part-time positions (Alexander, 2003). An increasing number of older workers are also opting not to retire or are returning to work, many in part-time positions.

On Psychological Well-Being

The most common emotional problem occurring in late adulthood is depression. As many as one in seven older adults may suffer from some level of depression (Beekman et al., 2002; Charney et al., 2003; Luijendijk et al., 2008;). Suicide is much higher among older adults, especially older white males, than in younger groups (Heisel & Duberstein, 2005; Zweig, 2005). Unfortunately, geriatric depression often goes untreated, in part because it is often overlooked by health care providers who focus more on the physical complaints of older adults than on their emotional states (Areán & Ayalon, 2005).

Despite the changes that accompany aging, most people in their seventies report being generally satisfied with their lives (Volz, 2000). Evidence from a recent large-scale study of adults indicates that life satisfaction tends to increase through adulthood, at least until about age 65 or 70, after which it declines (Mroczek & Spiro, 2005). However, more extraverted or outgoing people tend to maintain self-esteem through late adulthood, a tribute perhaps to the benefits of socializing with others. But even for those older adults who battle depression, substantial benefits can be achieved through use of available treatments, such as antidepressant medication and psychotherapy (Bruce et al., 2004; C.F. Reynolds et al., 2006; Scogin et al., 2005).

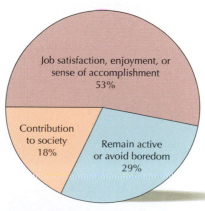

Figure 14.5
Why Retired People Return to Work
As reported in the *Wall Street Journal*, one-third of a surveyed group of retired senior executives returned to full-time work within 18 months of retirement. How do you think you will spend your retirement?

On Death and Dying

Death is the last great taboo. Psychiatrist Elisabeth Kübler-Ross comments on our denial of death in her landmark book *On Death and Dying:*

> We use euphemisms, we make the dead look as if they were asleep, we ship the children off to protect them from the anxiety and turmoil around the house if the [person] is fortunate enough to die at home, [and] we don't allow children to visit their dying parents in the hospitals. (Kübler-Ross, 1969, p. 8)

In this section we explore aspects of death and dying. First we consider the pioneering theoretical work of Kübler-Ross and the writings of more recent theorists. Then we examine issues concerning dying with dignity, the funeral, and bereavement.

Theoretical Perspectives From her work with terminally ill patients, Kübler-Ross found some common responses to news of impending death. She identified five stages of dying through which many patients pass. She suggests that older people who suspect the approach of death may undergo similar responses. The stages are the following:

1 *Denial.* In this stage people feel, "It can't be me. The diagnosis must be wrong." Denial can be flat and absolute. It can fluctuate so that one minute the patient accepts the medical verdict; the next, the patient starts chatting animatedly about distant plans.

2 *Anger.* Denial usually gives way to anger and resentment toward the young and healthy, and sometimes toward the medical establishment—"It's unfair. Why me?"

3 *Bargaining.* Next, people may bargain with God to postpone death, promising, for example, to do good deeds if they are given another six months, another year.

4 *Depression.* With depression come feelings of loss and hopelessness—grief at the specter of leaving loved ones and life itself.

5 *Final acceptance.* Ultimately, inner peace may come, quiet acceptance of the inevitable. This "peace" is not contentment; it is nearly devoid of feeling.

There are numerous critiques of the views of Kübler-Ross. For example, Joan Retsinas (1988) notes that its applicability is limited to those cases in which people receive a diagnosis of a terminal illness. Retsinas points out that most people die because of advanced years with no specific terminal diagnosis, and Kübler-Ross's approach may not be of much use in helping us understand their adjustment.

Edwin Shneidman (1984) offers another critique. He acknowledges the presence of feelings such as those described by Kübler-Ross in dying people. He does not see them linked in sequence, however. Shneidman suggests, instead, that people show a variety of emotional and cognitive responses. They can be fleeting or relatively stable, ebb and flow, and reflect pain and bewilderment. People's responses reflect their personalities and their philosophies of life.

Research supportive of Shneidman's views shows that reactions to nearing death turn out to be varied. Some people are reasonably accepting of the inevitable; others are despondent; still others are terrified. Some people have rapidly shifting emotions, ranging from rage to surrender, from envy of the young to yearning for the end (Shneidman, 1984).

Dying with Dignity Dying people, like other people, need self-confidence, security, and dignity. They may also need relief from pain, and a medical controversy is raging concerning giving them addictive painkilling drugs (e.g., narcotics) that are unavailable to the general public.

Even more controversial is **euthanasia**—also referred to as "mercy killing." Euthanasia is sometimes considered when there is no hope for a patient's recovery, when the patient is unconscious (as in a coma), or when the patient is in relentless pain and requests death (Emanuel, Fairclough, & Emanuel, 2000). There are two general forms of euthanasia. In positive or active euthanasia, the patient is given high doses of drugs, such as barbiturates or morphine, that induce death painlessly. Positive euthanasia has different legal standings in various states but is illegal in most states. One physi-

▌ **Euthanasia** Causing a painless death of someone suffering from an incurable and painful disease or condition.

cian—Jack Kevorkian, dubbed "Dr. Death" in the press—was found guilty of murder for helping terminally ill people commit suicide. Negative or passive euthanasia, by contrast, refers to not preventing death (Tadros & Salib, 2001). Negative euthanasia can involve denying comatose patients medicine, food, or life-support systems such as respirators. The legal status of negative euthanasia varies throughout the United States.

The dying often need to share their feelings. It may be helpful to encourage them to talk about what they are feeling. It can also be helpful just to be there—not to withdraw from them when they fear themselves withdrawing from what they hold dear. Pattison (1977) suggests a number of guidelines for helping dying people, such as the following:

- Providing social support
- Providing accurate information as to what might be experienced in terms of pain and loss of body functions and control
- Acknowledging the reality of the impending loss of family and other people
- Helping the person make final financial and legal arrangements
- Allowing the person to experience grief
- Assuming maintenance of necessary body functions in a way that allows the person to maintain dignity
- Pointing out that people should not blame themselves for loss of control over body functions

The Hospice Movement   The term **hospice** derives from the same root that gives rise to the words *hospital* and *hospitality*. It has come to refer to homelike environments in which terminally ill people can face death with physical and emotional supports that provide them with dignity (Lynn, 2001; McCarthy et al., 2003).

Family and friends work with specially trained staff to provide support. In contrast to hospital procedures, patients are given as much control over their lives as they can handle. As long as their physical conditions permit, patients are encouraged to make decisions as to their diets, activities, and medication. Relatives and friends may maintain contact with staff to work through their grief once the patient has died.

Bereavement   Those who are left behind, like those who learn of impending death, undergo a complex range of powerful emotions. The term **bereavement** refers to the state of the survivors. It implies feelings of sadness and loneliness as well as a process of mourning as survivors adjust to the loss of a loved one.

There are many aspects to bereavement: sorrow, emptiness and numbness, anger ("Why did he or she have to die?" "How could they let this happen?" "What do I do now?"), loneliness—even relief, as when the deceased person has suffered over a prolonged period and we feel that we have reached the limits of our abilities to help sustain him or her (McBride & Simms, 2001; Stroebe, 2001). Death also makes us mindful of our own mortality.

Investigators have also derived stages or phases of grief and mourning. First there is often numbness and shock, accompanied by the need to maintain as many routines as possible. Then there is preoccupation with and intense yearning for the loved one. Next, as the loss of the loved one sinks in more and more, there is depression, despair, and disorganization. Loss of appetite, insomnia, and forgetfulness are all normal reactions at this time. It may take two years or more for the mourner to accept the loss.

Usually, the most intense grief is encountered after the funeral, when the relatives and friends have gone home and the bereaved person is finally alone. Then he or she may have to finally come to grips with the reality of an empty house, of being truly alone. For this reason, it is helpful to space one's social support over a period of time, not do everything at once. Mourning takes time. Support is helpful throughout the process.

Bereaved people do usually come back from their losses. They may never forget the deceased person, but they become less preoccupied. They resume routines at work or in the home. They may never be as happy or satisfied with life, but most of the time they resume functioning. Sometimes they grow in compassion because of their loss. They gain a deeper appreciation of the value of life.

▮ **Hospice** As generally used, a residence, nursing home, or hospital facility providing supportive care to dying patients.

▮ **Bereavement** The saddened, lonely state of those who have experienced the death of a loved one.

MODULE REVIEW

Review It

(23) The time required to respond to stimuli—called _____ _____— increases as people age.

(24) Alzheimer's disease (is or is not?) a normal feature of the aging process.

(25) In the United States, (men or women?) tend to live longer.

(26) Erikson labeled late adulthood the stage of _____ _____ _____.

(27) Many retired people undergo a _____ phase during which they do things they had fantasized doing once they had the time.

(28) A (majority or minority?) of people in their seventies report being generally satisfied with their lives.

(29) Kübler-Ross identified five stages of dying: denial, anger, _____, depression, and final acceptance.

(30) Shneidman views the feelings described by Kübler-Ross as (linked or not linked?) in sequence.

(31) A _____ creates a homelike environment in which terminally ill people can face death with physical and emotional supports that provide them with dignity.

(32) The term _____ refers to feelings of sadness and loneliness as well as a process of mourning as survivors adjust to the loss of a loved one.

Think About It

What evidence would you use to argue against the proposition that people should face mandatory retirement because of age-related declines in mental abilities?

Psychology in Daily Life

Positive Psychology

MODULE 14.4

Living Longer and Healthier Lives

Americans are living longer than ever, and part of the reason is that many of them are taking charge of their own lives, influencing not only how long they live but how well they live. Regular medical evaluations, proper diet (for example, consuming less fat), and exercise can all help people live longer. Exercise helps older people maintain flexibility and cardiovascular condition. The exercise need not be of the type that pounds the body and produces rivers of sweat. Vigorous walking is an exercise that most healthy people of whatever age can integrate into their lifestyles.

Americans are eating more wisely and exercising at later ages, so many older people are robust. According to a national poll of nearly 1,600 adults by the *Los Angeles Times*, 75% of older people feel younger than their age—19 years on average (Stewart & Armet, 2000). People in their seventies and eighties felt as though they were in their sixties. People in their sixties reported feeling as though they were in their early fifties.

Let us also note that while social support is a key element to successful adjustment at any age, it may be better to give than to receive. Investigators find that among older adults, giving support to others is more closely linked to extended longevity than is receiving support (Brown et al., 2003).

14.4.1 Components of Successful Aging

Developmental psychologists do not use the term *successful aging* to put a positive spin on the inevitable. Rather, they mean that peo-

ple can take an active role in managing how they cope with aging. There are three general components of successful aging (Freund & Baltes, 1998; Volz, 2000).

1. *Reshaping one's life to concentrate on what one finds to be important and meaningful.* Laura Carstensen's (1997) research on people aged 70 and above reveals that successful agers form emotional goals that bring them satisfaction. For example, rather than cast about in multiple directions, they may focus on their family and friends. Successful agers may have less time left than younger people, but they tend to spend it more wisely (Garfinkel, 1995).

   Researchers use terms such as *selective optimization* and *compensation* to describe the manner in which successful agers lead their lives (Baltes, 1997). That is, successful agers no longer seek to compete in arenas best left to younger people—such as certain kinds of athletic or business activities. Rather, they optimize their time and skills by focusing on activities that allow them to maintain a sense of control over their own actions. Moreover, they learn to use available resources to compensate for losses. If their memory is not quite what it once was, they make greater use of notes or other reminders. If their senses are no longer as acute, they use devices such as hearing aids or allow themselves more time to take in information.

2. *Maintaining a positive outlook.* People who hold a more positive view of aging live longer on the average—about 7.5 years longer according to a recent study (Levy et al., 2002)—than do people with less positive self-perceptions of aging. The lead researcher in this

study, Becca Levy of Yale University, was quoted as saying, "The effect of more positive self-perceptions of aging on survival is greater than the physiological measures of low systolic blood pressure and cholesterol, each of which is associated with a longer lifespan of four years or less" ("Think Positive, Live Longer," 2002).

Older people may attribute occasional health problems such as aches and pains to specific and unstable factors like a cold or jogging too long. Others attribute aches and pains to global and stable factors such as aging itself. Not surprisingly, those who attribute these problems to specific, unstable factors are more optimistic about surmounting them. They thus have a more positive outlook or attitude. Of particular interest here is research conducted by William Rakowski (1995). Rakowski followed 1,400 people aged 70 or older with nonlethal health problems such as aches and pains. He found that those who blamed the problems on aging itself were significantly more likely to die in the near future than those who blamed the problems on specific, unstable factors.

3. *Seeking challenges.* Many people look forward to late adulthood as a time when they can rest from life's challenges. But sitting back and allowing the world to pass by is a prescription for vegetating, not for living life to its fullest. The old adage "use it or lose it" can apply to mental as well as physical functions (Salthouse, 2006). Keeping the mind active by engaging in mentally stimulating activities is linked to better mental and physical functioning and may even help lower lower the risks of Alzheimer's disease (Hopkin, 2004; Rabin, 2008). Holding a mentally stimulating job, engaging in interesting pastimes and leisure-time activities, and playing games or solving puzzles (such as playing chess or completing crossword puzzles) that challenge the mind are among the ways of keeping the mind active and alert.

14.4.2 Developing Healthy Exercise and Nutrition Habits

The Spanish explorer Ponce de León searched for the mythical "Fountain of Youth." Based on modern evidence, he might have been better off had he just stayed home and built a gym. Investigators find that regular exercise and a healthful diet have benefits at any age, but especially as we grow older (Adler & Raymond, 2001; Fukukawa et al., 2004; O'Neil, 2003).

How important is physical exercise? Well, evidence points to the many benefits of physical exercise, including the following (e.g., Blair & Church, 2004; Weinstein et al., 2004; Wessel et al., 2004):

- Slowing down the physical effects of aging, such as the loss of lean body mass, bone, and muscle strength
- Reducing the risk of certain cancers, such as cancer of the colon
- Reducing the risk of other major killers such as heart disease, stroke, and diabetes
- Reducing the risk of osteoporosis

Given the benefits of exercise, it should come as no surprise that people who exercise regularly tend to live longer (Gregg et al., 2003). But you might be surprised to learn that physical exercise has many positive effects on mental health. Exercise helps boost psychological well-being, preserve mental sharpness, including memory functioning, and may combat depression in later life (e.g., Gorman, 2006; Harris, Cronkite, & Moos, 2006; McAuley et al., 2005; Netz et a.l, 2005). Regular exercise is even linked to reduced risks of dementia in later life (Abbott et al., 2004).

There is much else we can do to live longer and live better, such as controlling stress, avoiding harmful substances such as tobacco and excessive alcohol consumption, having regular medical checkups, and keeping our weight down. All told, it makes sense to take stock of our healthy habits now. By developing healthy habits now and practicing them throughout our lives, we can improve our chances of living a longer and healthier life.

Successful Agers
The later years were once seen mainly as a prelude to dying. But today, not only are the numbers of older adults rising sharply, but many older adults are rising to the challenges of aging successfully. "Successful agers" seek new opportunities and challenges to give their life meaning in their later years.

CHAPTER REVIEW

RECITE! RECITE! RECITE! RECITE! RECITE! RECITE! RECITE!

Study Tip: Reciting the answers to these study questions will help you become a more effective learner. First try answering the questions by yourself, either reciting them out loud or writing them in a notebook or on the computer. Then compare your answers with the sample answers provided below.

1. **What changes in physical development occur during adolescence?** Adolescence is a period of life that begins at puberty and ends with assumption of adult responsibilities. Changes that lead to reproductive capacity and secondary sex characteristics are stimulated by increased levels of testosterone in the male and of estrogen and androgens in the female.

2. **What changes in cognitive development occur during adolescence?** Formal operational thinking appears in adolescence, but not everyone reaches this stage. Two consequences of adolescent egocentrism are the imaginary audience and the personal fable. The imaginary audience refers to adolescents' belief that they are the center of attention and that other people are as concerned with

their appearance and behavior as they are. The personal fable refers to adolescents' belief that one's feelings and ideas are special, even unique, and that one is invulnerable. Feelings of invulnerability can be connected with risky behavior.

3. What changes in social and personality development occur during adolescence?

Adolescents and parents are often in conflict because adolescents desire more independence and may experiment with things that can jeopardize their health. Despite bickering, most adolescents continue to love and respect their parents. According to Erikson, adolescents strive to forge an ego identity—a sense of who they are and what they stand for. The changes of puberty prepare the body for sexual activity and reproduction, but many adolescents lack the maturity to make responsible decisions regarding their sexual activities.

4. What is adulthood?

Historically speaking, marriage has been a marker of adulthood. In American society today, making independent decisions, accepting responsibility for oneself, and financial independence are the key markers.

5. What is meant by "emerging adulthood"?

Emerging adulthood is a hypothesized period that exists in wealthy societies. It roughly spans the ages of 18 to 25 and affords young people extended periods of role exploration.

6. What changes in physical development occur during young and middle adulthood?

People are usually at the height of their physical powers during young adulthood. Menopause, the cessation of menstruation, is associated with a great many myths, including the belief that hormonal changes naturally lead women to become depressed or anxious during this period of life. Men undergo a more gradual decline of reproductive functioning.

7. What changes in cognitive development occur during young and middle adulthood?

People are usually at the height of their cognitive powers during early adulthood, but people can be creative for a lifetime. Memory functioning declines with age, but the declines are not usually as large as people assume. People tend to retain verbal ability, as shown by vocabulary and general knowledge, into advanced old age. Crystallized intelligence—one's vocabulary and accumulated knowledge—generally remains intact. Fluid intelligence—the ability to process information rapidly—declines more rapidly, but workers' familiarity with solving specific kinds of problems is often more important than declines in fluid intelligence.

8. What changes in social and personality developments occur during young and middle adulthood?

Young adulthood is generally characterized by efforts to become established and advance in the business world as well as by the development of intimate ties. Many young adults reassess the directions of their lives during the "age-30 transition." Many theorists view middle adulthood as a time of crisis (the "midlife crisis") and further reassessment. Many adults try to come to terms with the discrepancies between their achievements and the dreams of youth during middle adulthood. Some middle-aged adults become depressed when their youngest child leaves home (the "empty-nest syndrome"), but many report increased satisfaction, stability, and self-confidence. Many people in middle adulthood experience "middlescence"—a phase during which they redefine themselves and their goals for the 30 to 40 healthy years they expect lie ahead.

9. What changes in physical development occur during late adulthood?

Older people show less sensory acuity, and their reaction time lengthens. Changes in the elasticity of the skin lead to wrinkling, and production of melanin declines, producing a graying of the hair. Our lung capacity, muscle mass, metabolic rate, and bone density decline. Our immune system weakens, and our cardiovascular system becomes less efficient. Though we also encounter age-related changes in sexual functioning, people who maintain their general health can adjust to these changes and continue to enjoy sexual experience throughout their lifetimes.

10. What changes in cognitive development occur during young and middle adulthood?

Cognitive changes beginning in middle adulthood continue, which mostly affect memory and tasks requiring fluid intelligence. Crystallized intelligence remains relatively intact, and people can continue to be creative throughout their lifetimes.

11. What is Alzheimer's disease?

Alzheimer's disease is a brain disease of unknown origin. It is not a consequence of normal aging. It is characterized by cognitive deterioration in memory, language, and problem solving.

12. What are the gender and ethnic differences in life expectancy?

Women outlive men by about five years, and European and Asian Americans tend to outlive other ethnic groups in the United States. By and large, the groups who live longer are more likely to have access to, and make use, of health care.

13. What changes in social and personality developments occur during late adulthood?

Erikson characterizes late adulthood as the stage of ego integrity versus despair. He saw the basic challenge as maintaining the belief that life is worthwhile in the face of physical deterioration. Despite common stereotypes, most older people live independently and are not living in poverty. Older adults rate their life satisfaction and health as generally good. Retirement can be a positive step, as long as it is voluntary. Having social support is a major contributor to emotional well-being among older people.

14. What do we know of the psychology of death and dying?

Kübler-Ross has identified five stages among people who are terminally ill: denial, anger, bargaining, depression, and final acceptance. However, other investigators find that psychological reactions to approaching death are more varied than Kübler-Ross suggests. Hospices support terminally ill patients and their families. Euthanasia is a controversial topic with varied legal status. Scholars have identified certain stages of bereavement that many people experience when they lose a loved one.

YOUR PERSONAL JOURNAL

REFLECT REFLECT REFLECT REFLECT REFLECT REFLECT REFLECT

Study Tip: Reflecting on how the concepts in the chapter relate to your own experiences encourages deeper processing, which makes the material more personally meaningful and fosters more effective learning. Use additional pages if needed to complete your answers.

1. Consider your own adolescence. Did it fit the stereotype of a period of "storm and stress" described in the text? Explain.

   _____

   _____

   _____

2. At what life stage do you see yourself? Adolescence? Emerging adulthood? Early or middle adulthood? Late adulthood? What is the basis of your self-perception?

   _____

   _____

   _____

ANSWERS TO MODULE REVIEWS

Module 14.1

1. secondary sex characteristics
2. formal operational
3. audience/fable
4. stress
5. motor vehicle
6. less
7. agree
8. ego/role

Module 14.2

9. emerging
10. wealthy
11. menopause
12. estrogen
13. verbal skills
14. Crystallized
15. Fluid
16. trying twenties
17. intimacy
18. Low
19. more
20. have had
21. midlife crisis
22. mastery

Module 14.3

23. reaction time
24. is not
25. women
26. ego integrity versus despair
27. honeymoon
28. majority
29. bargaining
30. not linked
31. hospice
32. bereavement

SCORING KEY TO SENSATION-SEEKING SCALE

Since this is a shortened version of a questionnaire, no norms are available. However, answers in agreement with the following key point in the direction of sensation seeking:

1. A	6. B	11. A
2. A	7. A	11. A
3. A	8. A	13. B
4. B	9. B	
5. A	10. A	

ANSWER KEY TO ATTITUDES TOWARD AGING

1. *False.* Most healthy couples continue to engage in satisfying sexual activities into their seventies and eighties.
2. *False.* This is too general a statement. Those who find their work satisfying are less desirous of retiring.
3. *False.* In late adulthood we tend to become more concerned with internal matters—our physical functioning and our emotions.
4. *False.* Adaptability remains reasonably stable throughout adulthood.
5. *False.* Age itself is not linked to noticeable declines in life satisfaction. Of course, we may respond negatively to disease and losses, such as death of a spouse.
6. *False.* Although we can predict some general trends for the elderly, we can also do so for the young. The elderly remain heterogeneous in personality and behavior patterns.
7. *False.* Elderly people with stable intimate relationships are more satisfied.
8. *False.* We are susceptible to a wide variety of psychological disorders at all ages.
9. *False.* Only a minority are depressed.
10. *False.* Actually church attendance declines, although there is no difference in verbally expressed religious beliefs.
11. *False.* Although reaction time may increase and general learning ability may undergo a slight decline, the elderly usually have little or no difficulty at familiar work tasks. In most jobs, experience and motivation are more important than age.
12. *False.* Learning may just take a bit longer.

- Million-dollar lottery winners often feel aimless and dissatisfied after quitting their jobs upon striking it rich? (p. 495)

- Women who wear perfume to interviews may be less likely to get the job, at least when they are interviewed by men? (p. 502)

- High tech still rules when it comes to the fastest-growing occupations? (p. 506)

- Job satisfaction may depend more on your general disposition than on the qualities of the job itself? (p. 509)

- An estimated 45 million workers call the office home? (p. 515)

- Despite the narrowing of the gender gap in earnings, women overall still earn only three-quarters the income of men? (p. 523)

- Experts estimate that as many as one in two women encounter sexual harassment on the job or in college? (p. 526)

Diane Deiderich/iStockphoto

f you are holding down a full-time job, chances are that you are spending more time with your coworkers and supervisors than you are with your family and friends. Work not only fills time but also provides opportunities to fill our lives in other ways. Work helps us pay our bills and make ends meet. But many of us also reap satisfaction and a sense of personal fulfillment from our work. Our sense of self may be closely identified with the work that we do. We may think of ourselves in relation to what we do. "I'm a teacher...a librarian...a _____" (you fill in the blanks). Note how we tend to say in social conversation, "I'm a _____" rather than "I work as a _____." Our work is a part of our social identity, the part that relates to the public roles we perform. It's no surprise that we identify ourselves with our work. Most of us spend many years training to do the work that we do. So much of ourselves is invested in developing a career or occupation that it's understandable that a part of our psychological identity is linked to what we do.

In this chapter we focus on the world of work, but we do so from a personal perspective. We reflect on our motives for working and the stages involved in career development. We will see how our knowledge of our personalities can enhance career decision making. We will also see how psychologists in the specialty field of industrial/organizational (I/O) psychology have contributed to our knowledge of factors that enhance job satisfaction. Then we shift the focus to examine a major social change in the workplace—the growing representation of women in the workforce. Finally, we turn the discussion around to you by inviting you to examine your own career interests and aspirations.

MODULE 15.1

Career Development

- Why do people work?
- What processes do people undergo as they decide on a career to pursue?
- What's a résumé? How do I write one?
- What goes into the cover letter?
- How do I "ace" the job interview?
- Okay, I've got the job. Now what do I do to get ahead?

Arnold Newman/Liason/Getty Images, Inc.

Work, a Meaningful Experience
The great artist Pablo Picasso expressed his personal needs, interests, and values through his work. Not only did he achieve recognition and wealth in his lifetime, he also found personal meaning and self-fulfillment. One might even go so far as to suggest that his work kept him young. The second author's spouse did her doctoral dissertation on the American artist Jack Tworkov, who wore blue jeans and a T-shirt into his eighties. "Every morning," he told her at the age of 80, "I go to the easel in a fever."

...if one advances confidently in the direction of his dreams, and endeavors to live the life which he has imagined, he will meet with a success unexpected in common hours.

—HENRY DAVID THOREAU, *WALDEN*

"Any child can grow up to be president."
"My child—the doctor."
"You can do anything if you set your mind to it."

The United States and Canada may be lands of opportunity, but opportunity comes with a cost: decision anxiety. What we "do" is an important aspect of our social standing. "What do you do?" is a more important question at social gatherings than "How do you do?" It is usually the first question raised in small talk. In a society free of traditional castes or hereditary aristocracies, occupational prestige becomes a major determinant of social status and respect.

Young people today face a bewildering array of career possibilities. The *Dictionary of Occupational Titles*, published by the U.S. Department of Labor, lists more than 20,000 occupations. Most of us do not select careers by leafing through the dictionary, of course. Most of us make our choices from a relatively narrow group of occupations, based on our experiences and our personalities (Herr, 2001).

Some people follow the paths of role models such as parents or respected members of the community. Others postpone career decisions so that when they have graduated from college they are no closer to settling on a career than when they began college.

Psychologists have identified a number of factors to help explain how adolescents and young adults choose a particular career (Hartman & Betz, 2007; Lent et al., 2007; Navarro, Flores, & Worthington, 2007). The factors include the following:

- *Competencies.* What am I good at? What am I capable of learning?
- *Comprehension.* Personal knowledge of careers and career opportunities
- *Expectancies.* Beliefs about what the person expects will happen in a given career. Expectancies also include expectations about the self, or *self-efficacy expectations*—that is, a person's beliefs about ability to handle the challenges and tasks in a given career

Some people carefully plan out their careers based on their self-appraisals of perceived abilities and personality traits (Skorikov, 2007). Others continue along a career path based on early work experiences that point them in certain directions (Creed, Patton, & Prideaux, 2007). But many of us basically "fall into" careers because of what is available at the time, family pressures, or the lure of high income or a certain lifestyle. Sometimes we take the first job that comes along after graduation. Sometimes we are lucky and things work out. Sometimes we are not and we hop from job to job. And it may be that the fifth job suits us better than the first. We need not rely on luck to find a career. By understanding the stages in career development, we may be better equipped to find an occupation that best fits us as individuals. Before discussing the stages in career development, we should first pose a more general question: *Why* work?

15.1.1 Motives for Working

Why do people work? The simple answer is the most obvious: to earn a living. Work provides us with the means to pay our bills. If we are lucky enough, we may have a little extra left over to buy things that we desire and, hopefully, even to squirrel some money away so that we will have it available for that proverbial rainy day. The paycheck, fringe benefits, security in old age—all these are external or **extrinsic motives** for working. But extrinsic motives alone do not explain why people work. Consider the world's richest man, Bill Gates, the founder and chairman of Microsoft, the leading software firm in the world whose flagship Windows operating system is installed in more than 90% of the world's computers. By recent estimates, Bill's net worth was valued at a whopping $40 billion ("The World's Billionaires," 2009). The sheer size of his fortune boggles the imagination, but does Bill just lounge around day after day in some secluded mansion? Hardly. He still trots off to the office, although he now divides his time between Microsoft and his humanitarian activities. What makes Bill run? What makes you run?

> **Extrinsic motives** Motives involving pursuit of external rewards, such as money or approval.

For Bill, there are always more mountains to climb, more challenges to test his mettle. He once explained to an interviewer that life for him is a continuous process of challenge and achievement. We work for extrinsic rewards, yes, but work also satisfies many internal or **intrinsic motives**, including the opportunity to engage in stimulating and satisfying activities and to climb yet another mountain. Interestingly, professional women, who must often balance the demands of jobs and families, are more likely to quit their jobs because of intrinsic factors such as boredom and lack of challenge than because of extrinsic factors such as lack of flexible work hours and availability of on-site day care (Deutsch, 1990).

> **Intrinsic motives** Involving pursuit of internal goals, such as self-satisfaction.

It may surprise you to learn that many million-dollar lottery winners who quit their jobs encounter feelings of aimlessness and dissatisfaction afterward (Kaplan, 1978). Moreover, the emotional boost that winning the lottery may produce tends to be short-lived; within a year of cashing their checks, lottery winners generally report happiness levels corresponding to their pre-winning levels (Corliss, 2003). This goes to show that not only does money not breed happiness but also that people seek more out of life than such extrinsic rewards as a paycheck and financial security. They also seek intrinsic rewards, such as opportunities to engage in activities that are personally fulfilling or challenging, to broaden their social contacts, and to fill their days with meaningful activity. A lottery jackpot would be nice, but it does not fill the day with purposeful activity. Other intrinsic reasons for working include the work ethic, self-identity, self-fulfillment, self-worth, social values of work, and social roles:

1 *The work ethic.* The work ethic holds that we are morally obligated to engage in productive labor, to avoid idleness. Adherents to the work ethic view life without work as unworthy or unethical, even for the wealthy.

2 *Self-identity.* We noted how occupational identity becomes intertwined with self-identity. We may think of ourselves as having careers or occupations, not simply as holding jobs.

3 *Self-fulfillment.* We often express our personal needs, interests, and values through our work. We may choose a profession that allows us to express these interests. The self-fulfilling values of the work of the astronaut, scientist, and athlete may seem obvious. But factory workers, plumbers, police officers, and firefighters can also find self-enrichment as well as cash rewards for their work.

4 *Self-worth.* Recognition and respect for a job well done contribute to self-esteem. For some, self-worth may ride on accumulating money. For a writer, self-worth may hinge on acceptance of a poem or an article by a magazine. When we fail at work, our self-esteem may plummet as sharply as our bank account.

5 *Social values of work.* The workplace extends our social contacts. It introduces us to friends, lovers, and challenging adversaries. At work, we may meet others who share our interests. We may form social networks that in our highly mobile society sometimes substitute for family.

6 *Social roles.* Work roles help define our functions in the community. Communities have their public identities: druggist, shoemaker, teacher, doctor.

15.1.2 Stages of Career Development

For most of us, career development is a process that can be described in terms of a number of stages. Not all these stages apply to each individual. But these stages are helpful in understanding how we come to decide on a career to pursue. Our discussion is informed by a major theory of career development developed by the psychologist Donald Super. However, we have made some modifications to reflect contemporary realities.

1 *Fantasy.* The first stage involves the child's unrealistic conception of self-potential and of the world of work. This stage of fantasy dominates from early childhood until about age 11. Young children focus on glamour professions, such as acting, medicine, sports, and law enforcement (Nauta & Kokaly, 2001; Wahl & Blackhurst, 2000). They show little regard for practical considerations, such as the fit between these occupations and their abilities or the likelihood of "getting anywhere" in them. For example, the second author's daughter, Allyn, at age 6, was thoroughly committed to becoming a "rock star." Her sister, Jordan, age 4 at the time, intended with equal intensity to become a ballerina. But they also intended to become teachers, authors, psychologists, art historians (like their mother), and physicians. The first author's son, Michael, was concerned at age 7 about picking the right college to improve his chances of being drafted by the NBA. His double-left-footed father was proud of his ambitions but wanted Michael to first learn to dribble.

2 *Tentative choice.* During the second stage, children narrow their choices and begin to show some realistic self-assessment and knowledge of occupations. From about age 11 through high school, children base their tentative choices on their interests, abilities, and limitations, as well as glamour.

3 *Realistic choice.* The following stage is characterized by realistic choice. Beyond age 17 or so, choices become narrowed and more realistic (Krieshok, 2001). Students weigh job requirements, rewards, even the futures of occupations. They appraise themselves more accurately. Ideally, they try to mesh their interests, abilities, and values with a job. They may also direct their educational plans to ensure they obtain the knowledge and skills they need to enter their intended occupation. Keep in mind, however, that many of us never make realistic choices and eventually "fall into" occupations we hadn't planned for.

4 *Maintenance.* During the maintenance stage, we begin "settling" into our career role, which often happens in the second half of our thirties. Although we may change positions within a company or within a career (such as moving from education to publishing), there is often a sense of our careers continuing to develop, a feeling of moving forward. The goal may not be perfectly clear, but we feel that we are moving upward in our career trajectory. But people can also get "trapped" into dead-end jobs during this stage. Their employers may come to view them as cogs in the wheel and attend to them only when and if something goes wrong. They may also face a midlife question that leads them to either hold on or let go: "Do I want to do this for the next 25 years?" (Savickas, 2002).

WoodyStock/Alamy

Making the Transition
College graduation is a crowning achievement, but it is just a start. For many newly minted college grads, negotiating the transition from college life to the workplace can be a daunting challenge. How prepared are you to make the leap?

5 *Career change.* Here is where present realities require that we diverge from the traditional view of career development. Because of corporate downsizing and mergers and acquisitions (M&A), many employees no longer feel the kind of loyalty to their employers that workers once did. Thus, they are more likely to job-hop when the opportunity arises. People are also living longer, healthier lives in rapidly changing times. They are staying in school longer and returning to school later for education, training, and retraining. We suspect that many students who are reading this text are returning students.

Fewer workers are putting in their time until the age of 65 in the hope of retiring. Rather, many are seeking fulfillment in the workplace and remain ambitious well into their middle years and often into late adulthood. Today it is the norm, rather than the exception, for people to switch jobs more than once. That said, vocational interests tend to be stable over the life course, especially after the college years (Low et al., 2005). Vocational interests are even more stable than personality traits over time. Though people often switch jobs, they generally maintain the same interests and look for jobs that reflect these interests.

Message to readers: Keep your eyes open and maintain a sense of flexibility. The opportunities you find in your thirties, forties, fifties, and even sixties and beyond may be things that are literally undreamt of today. When your first author began studying psychology, he used a calculator that filled the top of the desk.

Personal computers were unknown. Even the founder of IBM, John Watson, was known to have said in the 1940s that he couldn't imagine the need for more than about half a dozen computers throughout the world! Today, many large families own as many computers as Watson envisioned for the entire world.

If you are restless, it may be a sign of psychological health rather than instability. Take the time to explore your feelings and options. Have the courage to try new things.

6. *Retirement.* The final stage in Super's scheme is the retirement stage, during which the individual severs bonds with the workplace.

No, we won't leave you at the stage of retirement. We wouldn't be able to speak of career development in the first place if people weren't able to get started in their careers by landing that important first job.

15.1.3 Getting a Job

In the chapter's *Psychology in Daily Life* module, we return to the challenge of career development and offer some advice on finding a career that fits. For now, let's focus on getting a job.

Writing a Résumé

When you apply for a job, you usually send a résumé with a cover letter. A résumé is a summary of your background that is intended to convince a hiring manager that you are well qualified for the position and that interviewing you will be a worthwhile investment. But until you are called in for an interview, your résumé is you. In fact, it's the first impression you want others to form about you. So give it the same attention you would give grooming, wardrobe, and use of proper etiquette.

In a moment, we will get into the mechanics of the résumé. First, it helps to know who will be looking at it and deciding whether to toss it into the "circular file"—the wastepaper basket or the shredder. Résumés are usually first screened by a secretary or administrative assistant. That person may chuck it if it's sloppy, illegible, incomplete, and incompatible with the job requirements. Then it is usually seen by an employment or personnel manager. This individual may screen it out if it is incompatible with job requirements or does not show the required specifications. Employment managers also discard résumés that show inadequate experience or education, incompatible salary requirements, and lack of U.S. citizenship or lack of permanent resident status. They also eliminate résumés that are too long. A résumé is a summary of your qualifications. It's not a diary or a book. Keep your résumé to one page unless it is truly impossible to do so. One exception to this rule involves the learned or scholarly professions, where a *curriculum vitae* (CV) often takes the place of a résumé. A CV is a listing of professional accomplishments, including published works. The longer the CV, the more impressive the individual's scholarly record.

The hiring officer—this may be the person who would be supervising you in the job—may screen out your résumé if it shows that you lack the right qualifications. But you may also be eliminated if you're overqualified. Why? If you're too highly skilled or too well educated for the job, you probably won't be happy in it. If you're not happy, you won't give it your best. You may even quit early, and the company is unlikely to recoup the investment they made in hiring and training you.

What should your résumé look like? Should everything be boldfaced or capitalized? Should you use color and a variety of artistic fonts? How about colored paper? (How about crayons?) Automotive pioneer Henry Ford used to say that people could have his Model T (the early Ford) in any color, as long as it was black. Generally speaking, use black print on white paper. Make exceptions only for a reason that seems to be compelling—such as in applying for a position in graphic design. But remember that black print on white paper will never cause your résumé to be tossed into the wastepaper basket. Other approaches might. Use a common, readable font. If some line—for example, a heading like "Education"—seems in need of emphasis, you can boldface it or make it larger than the normal text, but do so sparingly. Try to look as if you're serious, as if you have substance, not superficial glitter.

In sum, be neat. Be serious. Show that you are right for the job. Don't use the same résumé for all positions. Instead, keep a general résumé on file. Then fine-tune it for the specific position.

And be honest. Use the job description to decide which of your qualifications to highlight—not as a basis for lying. Not only is lying morally wrong, it can lead to dire consequences for you in the long run. Many otherwise-successful individuals have been fired years after they began a job because it came to light that they had lied about their qualifications. Moreover, if you are truly not qualified for a job, you do your employer and yourself a service by accepting the fact and moving on.

Although the particular format and style of résumé may vary, most consist of the following sections or parts:

1 A heading
2 A statement of your job objective
3 A summary of your educational background
4 A summary of your work experience
5 A list of references

Let's look at each section in detail.

The Heading The heading contains your name, address, and telephone number. If you are living at home, center the heading as follows:

My Name
My Street Address
My City, State, and Zip Code
My Telephone Number
(landline and cell phone)

If you are living at school, you might want to provide both a temporary and a permanent address. Note that your cell phone number can follow you anywhere in the United States and that your e-mail address can follow you around the world. Today, in fact, applicants for some technical positions provide only their cell phone and e-mail addresses.

Job Objective   Tailor the job objective to the opening. Don't be too general or too blatantly specific. Is the advertised job for a computer sales trainee in Phoenix, Arizona? A job objective of "Marketing or Sales" might be too general. It might suggest that you do not know what specific job you are seeking. Also avoid saying things that will screen you out, like "Sales trainee with rapid advancement opportunities to management." You're being considered for the sales trainee position, not president of the company! A more reasonable objective would be "Sales, computer equipment," or "Sales of technical merchandise."

Educational Background   For each school attended, include the following:

1 The degree awarded (or expected)
2 Name of school (and address, if school is not well known)
3 Year graduated (or expected to graduate)
4 Major field or specialties
5 Grade point average (when 3.0 or better)
6 Honors and awards
7 Professional certificates (e.g., teaching, interior design)
8 Extracurricular activities

List schools attended in reverse order. That is, put the most recent school first. For example:

Education

BA	Northern Arizona University, Flagstaff, Arizona, 2009
Major	Psychology
GPA	3.7/4.0
Honors	Magna Cum Laude
Activities	President, Psi Chi, 2008–2009
AA	Glendale Community College, Glendale, Arizona, 2007
Major	Psychology
H.S. Diploma	Glendale High School, Glendale, Arizona, 2005

In the preceding hypothetical example, the solid GPA, the honors earned at Northern Arizona University, and the presidency of the Psi Chi campus organization are all listed. The less impressive performances in high school are not detailed. As suggested by a colleague, you are not required to say that you are short on your résumé. That is, don't draw attention to your shortcomings. Highlight your strengths. Job screeners expect you to present a favorable image of yourself. On the other hand, don't exaggerate or embellish your many fine features and accomplishments. Let the record speak for itself.

List your most important extracurricular activities. Be sure to indicate when and where you played a leadership role. Most students approaching graduation do not have extensive work experience. Having been editor of the yearbook, president of a club, or captain of a team is thus a notable achievement.

Work Experience   Don't list childhood jobs of babysitting and lawn mowing, unless you organized and ran babysitting or lawn-mowing businesses in your hometown. Pay particular attention to the jobs that are related to the position you are seeking. If you can show that you have been pursuing the same field for a number of years, you will look more organized and motivated. These are desirable job qualities. Of particular importance are internships and full-time positions. Also of interest are responsible summer and part-time positions. Don't pad your résumé with irrelevant, unimportant positions. Remember that you're applying for a job as a fresh graduate. You need not look like a mature professional on the move from one executive position to another.

For each position, include the following:

1 Title of position
2 Dates of employment
3 Whether job was full- or part-time; number of hours per week
4 Name of employer
5 Division of employer, or location of employment
6 Brief statement of job responsibilities, using action verbs (see sample below)
7 Brief statement of chief achievements

Don't list the names of your supervisors, unless you are willing to have all of them called by your prospective employer. List positions in reverse chronological order — most recent position first. Consider this hypothetical example:

Work Experience

1. January 2006–June 2008

Employer	San Diego State University
Position	Assistant to the Director, University Art Gallery
Responsibilities	Catalogued art works in permanent collection; arranged shipping of works for exhibitions; assisted in the hanging of exhibitions; arranged printing of exhibition catalogues and mailers
Major Achievements	Curated Christo exhibition; co-authored exhibition catalogue Conceptual Art.

2. 2008, 2009, 2010, etc.

Personal Information   Be careful about including any personal information, such as your age, marital status, number of children, citizenship, health, and so on. You do not need to disclose this information on a professional résumé. Though discrimination on the basis of ethnic and racial background or age is illegal, the law may not shield you from the prejudices in an employer's mind.

For example, although age discrimination is unlawful, some employers are prejudiced against people who begin their professional careers at later ages. Why tell them that you went back to school once your kids entered their teens? Also, consider omitting your high school education (why give away the graduation date?), another obvious sign that you may not be as youthful as the next applicant. Or you may omit your years of preprofessional work — unless, of course, you had notable achievements.

They'll see that you're older than 21 in the job interview. But then you have the opportunity to impress them with who you are, not with the dates printed on a piece of paper. You can show them how you bring mature judgment, strong motivation, and a clear sense of direction. But first, you've got to get to the interview.

References   References would be placed last on the résumé. It's probably best not to use them unless they are specifically requested. The prospective employer may check them out before inviting you to an interview. The slightest bit of negative information may knock you out of contention. Unless the employer specifically asks for references, it may be better to say "References will be furnished upon request" in your cover letter.

| Table 15.1 | Common Mistakes People Make on Their Résumés ... and How to Avoid Them |

Your résumé may not get you a job, but it can get you in the front door. Most hiring managers see hundreds of résumés for each job opening, so they literally only have a few seconds to scan each one—including yours. So make the most of those choice few seconds by avoiding common mistakes that lead to résumés being tossed in the old circular file:

1. *Typographical, grammatical, and spelling errors.* Use a spell-check and grammar-check program and ask someone else to review your résumé before submitting it.

2. *Use of exotic fonts, inappropriate formatting, and cutesy icons or decorative papers (e.g., little white clouds on blue paper).* Keep it simple and businesslike.

3. *Vague or poorly defined accomplishments.* Spell out clearly what you have accomplished: "Increased sales of _____ by 23%."

4. *Describing what the employer can do for you, such as wanting a job in which you could meet people and travel.* Rather, describe what you can do for the employer.

5. *Incomplete contact information.* Make sure to include your full contact information, including home phone and cell phone numbers, fax machine (if you have one), and both home and e-mail addresses.

6. *Excessive wordiness.* Keep it brief and simple.

7. *One-size-fits-all résumés.* Tailor the résumé to match the particular job you are seeking.

8. *Unrelated information.* Avoid giving information about your religion, political affiliation, pets, or even marital status or children. Stick to job-related experience and accomplishments.

Your résumé may not get you a job, but it can get you in the front door. Most hiring managers see hundreds of résumés for each job opening, so they literally only have a few seconds to scan each one—including yours. So make the most of those choice few seconds by avoiding common mistakes that lead to résumés being tossed in the old circular file (see Table 15.1).

The Cover Letter

The cover letter accompanies your résumé. Since you may be wondering, the cover letter should contain the following information:

1 Explanation of the purpose of the letter
2 Explanation of how you learned about the opening
3 Comparison of your qualifications and the job requirements
4 Statements of desired salary and geographic limitations (optional)
5 Request for an interview or other response to the letter
6 Statement that references will be sent on request
7 Thanks for the prospective employer's consideration

For additional suggestions about constructing cover letters, see Table 15.2.

Congratulations! Let's assume your résumé and cover letter were very good. In fact, they made such an impression that you've been invited to an interview. Now what?

Table 15.2 ∎ Samples of Cover Letters: The Good, the Bad, and the Blah	
Section of Letter	**About ...**
I enclose my résumé in application for the position of computer sales trainee, as described in the job notice sent to my college's placement office.	Refers to enclosed résumé (okay) States writer is applying for position (okay) Says how writer learned of position (okay)
My education and work experience appear to fit well indeed with your job requirements. My major field is business, with a specialty in marketing. I have four courses in computer science. I hold a part-time position in the college computer center, where I advise students how to use our computers and a variety of software programs. Moreover, I have held part-time and summer sales positions, as outlined in the résumé.	Good! The writer shows extensive experience (for a fresh college graduate) both in sales and in computers.
Salary is relatively unimportant to me. However, my wife is employed in town here, so I would not be able to relocate.	Mistakes! Visualize someone tossing your application into circular file (wastepaper basket). Salary is always important—to the employer if not to you. Say nothing about salary unless a statement of "salary requirement" is specifically required in the job listing. Also, don't go into marital status and possible relocation problems. You can deal with them after you get to the interview. Here you've knocked yourself out of contention by admitting that family commitments may prevent you from doing your job.
I look forward to the prospect of an interview. I can get off from work or miss a class or two if I have to.	Yes—no. Yes to desiring an interview; ditch the preoccupation with the mechanics of breaking free for the interview (nobody cares about such garbage details—yes, we're being tough on you so that you don't create a situation in which the person receiving your letter is tough on you). If getting to the interview creates so much stress that you must discuss it in your cover letter, how will you ever handle the stress of a real job in the real world?
Thanks a lot for your consideration.	Spell out "thank you"; "Thanks" is too informal. Delete "a lot"! *A lot*, meaning "much," is two words. But don't spell it properly; just delete it. It's also poor diction. Enter the real world!

How to Wow the Interviewer!

A job interview is both a social occasion and a test. First, remember that first impressions and neatness count, so dress well and look your best. Everything else being equal, people who look their best are more successful at getting the job. You may also wish to avoid using perfume or cologne. An early research study that put this advice to the test showed that women interviewers rated applicants who wore perfume or cologne more positively, whereas male interviewers rated fragranced applicants—male and female alike—more negatively (Baron, 1983). Male interviewers may be more rigid than their female counterparts and believe that people who adorn themselves with fragrances are not to be taken as serious workers.

Maintain direct eye contact with your interviewer, but look alert, cooperative, and friendly—don't stare. A hard stare is perceived as an aversive challenge. Flattery works, but only when it is specific to the abilities or accomplishments of the recipient. Psychologists find that people generally tend to like those who flatter them (Vonk, 2002). But idle flattery will likely appear to be self-serving and insincere. Perhaps the take-away message is to read up on the company and the interviewer, so that you can come across as knowledgeable, and be discerning in your use of flattery.

Anticipating the interviewer's questions will help prepare you for the interview. Once you have written down a list of likely questions, rehearse answers to them. Practice them aloud. You can recruit a friend to role play the interviewer.

A good student doesn't have to say something in every class. Similarly, a good job candidate does not monopolize the conversation during an interview. Be patient: Allow the interviewer to tell you about the job and the organization without feeling that you must jump in. Look interested. Nod now and then. Don't chomp at the bit.

When asked about your experiences and accomplishments, don't become Mr. or Ms. Bashful. Promote yourself by describing your strengths and accomplishments, but rein in your tendencies to overly embellish your many fine qualities. Evidence backs up the value of self-promotion, as investigators find that the use of self-promotion during job interviews is related to higher interviewer ratings of the interviewees (Aleksander et al., 2002).

Now let us consider the kinds of questions you will be asked in the interview. Some of the interviewer's questions will be specific to your field, and we cannot help you anticipate those. But we will discuss the ones that are likely to be found in most job interviews. Assume then that your résumé and cover letter have gotten your foot in the door. This exercise will help you prepare for that all-important job interview. In this exercise, we ask a question and then provide room for an answer. Next we offer our thoughts on the subject and try to alert you as to what your interviewer is looking for. We don't always supply a specific answer. The specific words will have to be consistent with the nature of your field, the organization to which you have applied, your geographical setting, and so on.

All right, the person ahead of you leaves and it's your turn for an interview! Here are the questions. Why not write down the answer that pops into your mind, and then check for our suggestions below?

1 *How are you today?*

_____

_____

Our recommendation: *Don't* get cute or fancy. Say something like, "Fine, thank you. How're you?"

2 *How did you learn about the opening?*

_____

_____

Don't say, "I indicated that in my application." (You're looking for a job, not for an argument.) Yes, you probably did explain how you learned about the job on your application or in the cover letter for your résumé, but your interviewer may not be familiar with the letter or may want to follow a standard procedure. So answer concisely and politely.

3 *What do you know about our organization?*

_____

_____

Be prepared. Do your homework by researching the organization before you set foot in the door. Your interviewer wants to learn whether you know something about his or her organization or applied everywhere with equal disinterest. Suggest how the organization fits your career goals.

4 *What are you looking for in this job?*

_____

_____

This is another opportunity to describe your concrete goals. Interviewers look for candidates who have a clear sense of direction or purpose. Mention things like the opportunity to work with noted professionals in your field, the organizational culture or climate, the organization's leadership in its field, and so on. Don't say, "It's close to home." Don't ask about the parking availability, bonuses, vacations, or the like—anything that smacks of a sense of entitlement, of what you expect the company to do for you. You can say that you know that salaries are good, but also refer to opportunities for personal growth and self-fulfillment.

Banana Stock/Alamy Limited

Get That Job!
Prepare for that job interview. Be well-groomed. Rehearse answers to likely questions. Also have some questions ready to ask the interviewer about the nature or location of the job. It's a good idea to research the company or organization so that the questions can sound sophisticated.

5 *What do you plan to be doing 10 years from now?*

_____

_____

Your interviewer wants to hear that you have a clear cognitive map of the corporate ladder and that your career goals are consistent with company needs. Preplan a coherent answer, but also show flexibility—perhaps that you're interested in exploring a couple of branches of the career ladder. You want your interviewer to think that you're not rigid and that you recognize that your experience within the organization may affect your future plans.

6 *Are you willing to relocate after a year or two if we need you in another office/plant?*

_____

_____

Your interviewer wants to hear that you are willing—that your ties to the company would be more important than your geographical ties. Don't say that your fiancé or spouse is flexible. It implies that he or she really is not, and you just don't want to get into this.

7 *What are your salary needs?*

_____

_____

Entry-level salaries are often fixed, especially in large organizations. But if this question is asked, don't fall into the trap of thinking you're more likely to get the job if you ask for less than what your background and qualifications call for. Mention a reasonably high, but not absurdly high figure. You can mention the figure—with an explanation—reemphasizing your experience and training. Good things don't come cheap, and organizations know this. And why should they think more of you than you think of yourself?

8 *What is the first thing you would do if you were to take the job?*

_____

_____

Your interviewer probably wants to know (a) if you're an active, take-charge type of person and (b) whether you do have an understanding of what is required. Don't say you'd be shocked or surprised. Say something like, "I'd get to know my supervisors and coworkers to learn the details of the organization's goals and expectations for the position." Or it might be appropriate to talk about "hitting the ground running," organizing your workspace, evaluating and ordering the equipment needed to get started, and so on—all depending on the nature of the job.

9 *Do you realize that this is a very difficult (or time-consuming) job?*

_____

_____

It is or it isn't, but the interviewer doesn't want to hear that you think the job's a snap. The interviewer wants to hear that you will dedicate yourself to your work and that you have boundless energy. One legitimate response is to ask your interviewer to amplify a bit on the remark so that you can fine-tune your eventual answer.

10 *What do you see as your weaknesses?*

_____

_____

This is arguably the toughest question you'll face. Come prepared with an answer—not a pat answer, but one that is specific to the particular job. Turn the question into an opportunity for emphasizing your strengths. You might say something like, "I feel I can benefit from the type of training this organization provides. I've been looking for the opportunity to expand my skills in this direction. I'm a quick study and I'm confident that I'll do a good job."

11 *Do you have any questions?*

_____

_____

Duh? Rather than show a blank expression on your face, prepare a few questions before the interview. Asking intelligent questions is a sign of your interest in the job and your ability to handle the job. In the unlikely event that the interviewer manages to cover them all during his or her presentation, you can say something like, "I was going to ask 'such and such' that you discussed during the interview. But perhaps you can expand on that a bit?"

12 *Finally, what do you say when the interview is over?*

_____

_____

Express appreciation, but don't go overboard with gushy enthusiasm. Say something like, "Thank you for the interview. It was a pleasure meeting you. I look forward to hearing from you."

Developmental Tasks in Taking a Job: How to Succeed in Business with Really Trying

Okay, you've got it! The job you've been dreaming about! Your academic work has paid off, and you did brilliantly at the interview. (Of course you did; we told you how.) Good salary, solid opportunities for advancement, and the promise of self-development in a field that you enjoy—all of these are yours. From here on in, it's smooth sailing, right? You've been reading this book long enough to predict our answer: not necessarily.

Okay, you've got the job. Now what do you do? If the job you have landed fits your education, experience, and personality, the chances are that you will indeed do well. But there are a number of developmental tasks that we undertake when we begin working.

- *Making the transition from school to the workplace.* You have already mastered the school world, and change can be threatening as well as exciting. You are also going from the "top" of the school world (graduation) to a relatively low position in the organizational hierarchy. Moreover, you are moving from a system in which there is measurable progress, including courses completed each term and movement up the educational ladder each year. In a job, one can go for years without a promotion.

- *Learning how to carry out the job tasks.* Job tasks include executing occupational skills and also meshing your own attitudes and values with those of the organization. Learning the organization's explicit (written) and implicit (unwritten) rules is a job in itself.

- *Accepting your subordinate status within the organization or profession.* Perhaps you were extremely popular on campus. Perhaps you were leader of an athletic team. Perhaps you were an honors student. Despite all these accomplishments and your sterling qualities, you are a newcomer on the job. Act accordingly. (You needn't grovel, of course, but accept the fact that you are new and sort of wet behind the ears.)

- *Learning how to get along with your coworkers and supervisor.* Sure, you have some social skills. But you are in a new setting with new people. They have new expectations of you. Expect a few bumps in the social road.

- *Showing that you can maintain the job, make improvements, and show progress.* Yes, this is not fourth grade, and you are not likely to be graded on your potential. You will have to show that you are worth what you are being paid.

- *Finding a sponsor or mentor to "show you the ropes."* If you find a helpful mentor, you are more likely to be satisfied with the job and to succeed at it (Murphy & Ensher, 2001).

- *Defining the boundaries between the job and other areas of life.* Where do work and concerns about work end? Where do your personal interests and social relationships begin? Try not to bring home your troubles on the job. (And try not to bring your troubles at home into the job!)

- *Evaluating your occupational choice in the light of supervisor appraisal and measurable outcomes of your work.* Is the job really for you? If you have given it a solid amount of time and evaluated it carefully, and it does not seem to fit you, investigate why and consider a change.

- *Learning to cope with daily hassles on the job, frustrations, and successes and failures.* Jobs have their stresses, and some stress management may be in order. Check out the suggestions in this chapter and in earlier chapters.

Adjustment and Modern Life

Careers: What's Hot, What's Not

What career are you planning for? Will you be writing software for video games and superefficient voice-recognition technology? Will you be teaching youngsters in primary schools? Will you be hashing out the ... hash in a restaurant? Will you start up your own business? Will you be Dr. _____ (fill in your name)? What career dreams do you entertain? And, importantly, in what fields are new jobs likely to be found?

Services, Services, Services

The government expects that service-producing industries will account for most of the new jobs. More than a million jobs will be lost among machine operators, fabricators, laborers, craftspeople, and repair people. Advances in technology, including new generations of robots, will continue to replace people on the assembly line. Jobs in agriculture, forestry, fishing, and related occupations are also expected to decline. Job openings in these fields will stem from replacement needs.

Within the burgeoning area of services, the lion's share of the new opportunities will be found in health, education, and business. Why health? Well, the population is aging, and older people require more health care. But many of these jobs will not require college graduates. To contain costs, hospitals are discharging patients sooner, which will increase the need for personal and home care aides as well as home health aides. But there will also be an increase in the use of innovative medical technology for diagnosis and treatment, and these jobs will require technical training at the very least. Nurses will also be in strong demand. Why education? Because there will be many young children, and because older people are retooling. Why business? The business of America, as they say, is business. And despite a recent downtrend in technology-related jobs, technology is not about to disappear from the scene. Not unless we all

iStockphoto

Tech Trek in the New Millennium
If it's got the adjective *digital* in front of it, chances are there's a job connected with it in today's world. But if high tech is not for you, careers in health care, education, and business are also in demand.

are willing to give up our cell phones, personal computers, PDAs, digital cameras, DVD players, and whatever newfangled device has hit the market by the time this book reaches your hands.

High-Tech Rules

What do you suppose are projected to be the fastest-growing occupations in the period spanning the years 2006 to 2016? Check out Table 15.3. Notice a pattern? Most of the fastest-growing occupations are in health care and computer-related fields. Health care also continues to shine in terms of employment growth, especially for people trained as medical, physician, social, and human service assistants. There will be very rapid growth in jobs for computer specialists—especially software engineers and systems analysts. The country is relying more heavily on computer software than ever before, and the demand for people who can develop and use software has vastly outstripped the supply. The shortage is expected to worsen because a million new programming jobs are expected to open up within the next decade. Systems analysts figure out how to piece it all together—that is, how to make computer hardware and software work for your business or organization. If you're going to need them, perhaps you want to join them.

There is especially good news for today's college students. Openings in occupations that require a bachelor's degree or more will grow at almost twice the rate projected for jobs that require less education and training. Moreover, these jobs will pay much better than average wages. As you can see in Table 15.3, jobs in the computer and health fields will be in especially high demand.

Want more specifics? Visit your college or university's placement office. (Tell them who sent you.)

Table 15.3 ∎ Where the Jobs Will Be: The 30 Fastest Growing Occupations in the United States

Here we see the occupations expected to show the largest growth in numbers of jobs by the year 2016. The fastest-growing job category, network systems and data communications, is expected to grow by 53.4% between 2006 and 2016.

Occupation	Employment Change 2006–16 Number	Percent	Most Significant Source of Postsecondary Education or Training[1]
Network systems and data communications	140	53.4	Bachelor's degree
Personal and home care aides	389	50.6	Short-term on-the-job training
Home health aides	384	48.7	Short-term on-the-job training
Computer software engineers, applications	226	44.6	Bachelor's degree
Veterinary technologists and technicians	29	41.0	Associate degree
Personal financial advisors	72	41.0	Bachelor's degree
Makeup artists, theatrical and performance	1	39.8	Postsecondary vocational award
Medical assistants	148	35.4	Moderate-term on-the-job training
Veterinarians	22	35.0	First professional degree
Substance abuse and behavioral disorder counselors	29	34.3	Bachelor's degree
Skin care specialists	13	34.3	Postsecondary vocational award
Financial analysts	75	33.8	Bachelor's degree
Social and human service assistants	114	33.6	Moderate-term on-the-job training
Gaming surveillance officers and gaming investigators	3	33.6	Moderate-term on-the-job training
Physical therapist assistants	20	32.4	Associate degree
Pharmacy technicians	91	32.0	Moderate-term on-the-job training
Forensic science technicians	4	30.7	Bachelor's degree
Dental hygienists	50	30.1	Associate degree
Mental health counselors	30	30.0	Master's degree
Mental health and substance abuse social workers	37	29.9	Master's degree
Marriage and family therapists	7	29.8	Master's degree
Dental assistants	82	29.2	Moderate-term on-the-job training
Computer systems analysts	146	29.0	Bachelor's degree
Database administrators	34	28.6	Bachelor's degree
Computer software engineers, systems software	99	28.2	Bachelor's degree
Gaming and sports book writers	5	28.0	Short-term on-the-job training
Environmental science and protection technicians, including health	10	28.0	Associate degree
Manicurists and pedicurists	22	27.6	Postsecondary vocational award
Physical therapists.	47	27.1	Master's degree
Physician assistants	18	27.0	Master's degree

[1] An occupation is placed into 1 of 11 categories that best describes the postsecondary education or training needed by most workers to become fully qualified in that occupation.

Source: *2008–09 Occupational Outlook Handbook*, U.S. Bureau of Labor Statistics, http://www.bls.gov/news.release/ooh.t01.htm

MODULE REVIEW

Review It

(1) Earning a paycheck is an (extrinsic or intrinsic?) motive for working.

(2) The work _____ holds that we are morally obligated to engage in productive labor.

(3) Recognition for a job well done contributes to self-_____.

(4) Some of us follow the career paths of role _____ such as parents or respected members of the community.

(5) The _____ stage of career development involves the child's unrealistic conception of self-potential and of the world of work.

(6) During the stage of _____ choice, children narrow their choices and begin to show some realistic self-assessment and knowledge of occupations.

(7) The stage of career _____ reflects the fact that today it is the norm, rather than the exception, for people to switch careers more than once.

(8) In applying for a job, your _____ is your summary of your background.

(9) In preparing for the job interview, remember that first _____ are very important.

(10) It (is or is not?) good to ask the interviewer questions.

(11) Your first task on the job is to learn how to carry out the _____ tasks.

Think About It

If you had to condense the advice for the developmental tasks in taking a new job to just two suggestions, what would they be?

MODULE 15.2

Adjustment in the Workplace

■ What factors are associated with job satisfaction?

■ What factors may enhance job satisfaction?

■ What are the sources of stress in the workplace?

■ How can I—or we—decrease stress in the workplace?

■ What is burnout? What causes it?

■ How can I prevent job burnout?

Although work provides an important opportunity for personal growth and a sense of fulfillment, it also imposes on us many demands that require adjustment. In this module we have a look at factors that contribute to job satisfaction, and then we examine the types of stresses we may face on the job.

15.2.1 Job Satisfaction

▮ **Job satisfaction** Degree to which workers have positive feelings toward their jobs.

It is one thing to land a job; it is another to be satisfied with it. **Job satisfaction** is the degree to which one has a positive feeling toward one's work or job. Two out of three employees reported being satisfied with their coworkers in a Gallup survey (Saad, 1999). More than half were satisfied with the physical safety of their workplaces, the flexibility of their work schedules, and the amount of vacation time. Figure 15.1 shows that workers were least satisfied with the stress they experienced on the job, the recognition they received, and their pay and benefits.

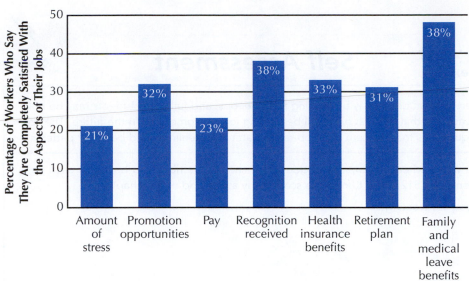

Figure 15.1
Areas in Which Workers Experience the Least Job Satisfaction
According to a Gallup survey, workers report that they are least likely to be completely satisfied with these aspects of their jobs.
Source: Saad, 1999.

Some workers—particularly assembly-line workers and those on the bottom rungs of the corporate ladder—report feelings of alienation and dissatisfaction. Some say their work is boring or dehumanizing. They complain that supervisors treat them with disrespect and fail to use them as resources for learning how to improve working conditions and productivity. In other words, their dissatisfaction is connected with feelings of having been "left out of the loop." They do not share in decision making, have no power, and feel that they have no control over their own jobs or what the organization does (Anderson & Betz, 2001; Judge & Bono, 2001). Control at work is not just important for job satisfaction; but also appears to be an important element in employees' health and well-being (Spector, 2003).

What Determines Job Satisfaction?

Job satisfaction depends on many factors, including good pay and fringe benefits, opportunities to perform personally fulfilling work and to form social relationships with coworkers, and availability of childcare services (Morgeson & Humphrey, 2006). Another important element in job satisfaction is a sense of control over the work itself. When workers have a sense of personal control over what they do, they are more likely to be satisfied with and remain in their jobs (Ashforth & Saks, 2000; Judge & Bono, 2001). Yet job satisfaction also depends on qualities the worker brings to the job (Bowling et al., 2005). It turns out that people who have a sunnier disposition in general also tend to be more satisfied with their jobs than people with a sourer general outlook (Judge & Ilies, 2002; Staw & Cohen-Charash, 2005).

Job satisfaction and life satisfaction may mutually influence each other, meaning that being happy with your life in general may influence your satisfaction with your job, while being happy with your job may spill over into your general satisfaction with your life. We've also learned that personality traits such as self-esteem, belief in being able to accomplish one's goals (self-efficacy), and emotional stability are also associated with greater job satisfaction (Judge, Heller, & Mount, 2002; Staw & Cohen-Charash, 2005). And consider this, too: Evidence points to a genetic influence in job satisfaction (Olson et al., 2001). Perhaps genetics affects job satisfaction by affecting our general ability to reap happiness from life experiences.

The cognitive factor of *attributional style* may also play a part (Hewlett, 2001). Many people prefer jobs that give them more control over their work. But investigators find that a subgroup of workers prefers having someone else take control (Schaubroeck, Jones, & Xie, 2001). These workers have a negative attributional style, which is a tendency to heap blame on themselves when things at work don't turn out well. They tend to prefer jobs in which others take control, which allows them to avert blaming themselves for negative outcomes.

© Alan Carey/The Image Works

What Factors Contribute to Job Satisfaction?
Most Americans are at least somewhat satisfied with their jobs, and nearly all see themselves as hard workers. What do they complain about? Many are unhappy with their pay, the amount of stress on the job, the feeling that they do not receive enough recognition, their inability to affect organizational policies and decision making, and their retirement and health benefits.

| How Do You Feel About Your Work?
The Job Satisfaction Index | Self-Assessment |

How satisfied are you with your work? Part-time students may be holding full-time jobs, and full-time students may be holding part-time jobs. In any event, you can assume that the rest of us will be holding jobs at some time in the future. The Job Satisfaction Index provides a number of questions that concern your job-related attitudes, feelings, and behavior patterns.

Directions: Consider your present job as you read each item, and decide which choice describes you best. For each item, mark your answer in the answer column on page 512. Then turn to the scoring key at the end of the chapter.

1. Do you watch the clock when you are working?
   a. Constantly
   b. At slack times
   c. Never

2. When Monday morning comes, do you
   a. Feel ready to go back to work?
   b. Think longingly of being able to lie in the hospital with a broken leg?
   c. Feel reluctant to start with, but fit into the work routine quite happily after an hour or so?

3. How do you feel at the end of a working day?
   a. Dead tired and fit for nothing
   b. Glad that you can start living
   c. Sometimes tired, but usually pretty satisfied

4. Do you worry about your work?
   a. Occasionally
   b. Never
   c. Often

5. Would you say that your job
   a. Underuses your ability?
   b. Overstrains your abilities?
   c. Makes you do things you never thought you could do before?

6. Which statement is true for you?
   a. I am rarely bored with my work.
   b. I am usually interested in my work, but there are patches of boredom.
   c. I am bored most of the time I am working.

7. How much of your work time is spent making personal telephone calls, or with other matters not connected with the job?
   a. Very little
   b. Some, especially at crisis times in my personal life
   c. Quite a lot

8. Do you daydream about having a different job?
   a. Very little
   b. Not a different job, but a better position in the same kind of job
   c. Yes

9. Would you say that you feel
   a. Pretty capable most of the time?
   b. Sometimes capable?
   c. Panicky and incapable most of the time?

10. Do you find that
    a. You like and respect your colleagues?
    b. You dislike your colleagues?
    c. You are indifferent to your colleagues?

11. Which statement is most true for you?
    a. I do not want to learn more about my work.
    b. I quite enjoyed learning my work when I first started.
    c. I like to go on learning as much as possible about my work.

12. Mark the qualities you think are your best points:
    __ a. Sympathy   __ b. Clear-thinking   __ c. Calmness
    __ d. Good memory   __ e. Concentration   __ f. Physical stamina
    __ g. Inventiveness   __ h. Expertise   __ i. Charm
    __ j. Humor

13. Now mark the qualities that are demanded by your job:
    __ a. Sympathy   __ b. Clear-thinking   __ c. Calmness
    __ d. Good memory   __ e. Concentration   __ f. Physical stamina
    __ g. Inventiveness   __ h. Expertise   __ i. Charm
    __ j. Humor

14. Which statement do you most agree with?
    a. A job is only a way to make enough money to keep yourself alive.
    b. A job is mainly a way of making money, but should be satisfying if possible.
    c. A job is a whole way of life.

15. Do you work overtime?
    a. Only when it is paid
    b. Never
    c. Often, even without pay

16. Have you been absent from work (other than for normal vacations or illness) in the last year?
    a. Not at all
    b. For a few days only
    c. Often, even without pay

17. Would you rate yourself as
    a. Very ambitious?
    b. Unambitious?
    c. Mildly ambitious?

18. Do you think that your colleagues
    a. Like you, enjoy your company, and get on well with you in general?
    b. Dislike you?
    c. Do not dislike you, but are not particularly friendly?

19. Do you talk about work
    a. Only with your colleagues?
    b. With friends and family?
    c. Not if you can avoid it?

20. Do you suffer from minor unexplained illnesses and vague pains?
    a. Seldom
    b. Not too often
    c. Frequently

21. How did you choose your present job?
    a. Your parents or teachers decided for you.
    b. It was all you could find.
    c. It seemed the right thing for you.

22. In a conflict between job and home, such as an illness of a member of the family, which would win?
    a. The family every time
    b. The job every time
    c. The family in a real emergency, but otherwise probably the job

23. Would you be happy to do the same job if it paid one-third less?
    a. Yes
    b. You would like to, but could not afford to
    c. No

24. If you were made redundant (unnecessary), which of these would you miss most?
    a. The money
    b. The work itself
    c. The company of your colleagues

25. Would you take a day off to have fun?
    a. Yes
    b. No
    c. Possibly, if there was nothing too urgent for you to do at work

26. Do you feel unappreciated at work?
    a. Occasionally
    b. Often
    c. Rarely

27. What do you most dislike about your job?
    a. That your time is not your own
    b. The boredom
    c. That you cannot always do things the way you want to

28. Do you keep your personal life separate from work? (Check with your partner on this one.)
    a. Pretty strictly
    b. Most of the time, but there is some overlap
    c. Not at all

29. Would you advise a child of yours to take up the same kind of work as you do?
    a. Yes, if he or she had the ability and temperament.
    b. No, you would warn him or her off.
    c. You would not press it, but you would not discourage him or her.

30. If you won or suddenly inherited a large sum of money, would you
    a. Stop work for the rest of your life?
    b. Take up some kind of work that you have always wanted to do?
    c. Decide to continue, in some way, the same work you do now?

Answer Column

1. a. _____ b. _____ c. _____
2. a. _____ b. _____ c. _____
3. a. _____ b. _____ c. _____
4. a. _____ b. _____ c. _____
5. a. _____ b. _____ c. _____
6. a. _____ b. _____ c. _____
7. a. _____ b. _____ c. _____
8. a. _____ b. _____ c. _____
9. a. _____ b. _____ c. _____
10. a. _____ b. _____ c. _____
11. a. _____ b. _____ c. _____
12. a. _____ b. _____ c. _____ d. _____ e. _____ f. _____ g. _____ h. _____ i. _____ j. _____
13. a. _____ b. _____ c. _____ d. _____ e. _____ f. _____ g. _____ h. _____ i. _____ j. _____
14. a. _____ b. _____ c. _____
15. a. _____ b. _____ c. _____
16. a. _____ b. _____ c. _____
17. a. _____ b. _____ c. _____
18. a. _____ b. _____ c. _____
19. a. _____ b. _____ c. _____

20. a. _____ b. _____ c. _____
21. a. _____ b. _____ c. _____
22. a. _____ b. _____ c. _____
23. a. _____ b. _____ c. _____
24. a. _____ b. _____ c. _____
25. a. _____ b. _____ c. _____
26. a. _____ b. _____ c. _____
27. a. _____ b. _____ c. _____
28. a. _____ b. _____ c. _____
29. a. _____ b. _____ c. _____
30. a. _____ b. _____ c. _____

Source: Copyright by Phoebus Publishing Co./BPC Publishing Ltd., 1975. Reprinted with permission.

For an interactive version of this self-assessment exercise, go to www.wileyplus.com

Enhancing Job Satisfaction: Improving the Quality of Work Life Is Also Good Business

Increasing the quality of work life turns out to be good business for everyone. First, increased job satisfaction is associated with lower employee turnover and absenteeism—two expensive measures of job dissatisfaction (Abbasi & Hollman, 2000; Traut, Larsen, & Feimer, 2000). Second, there is a link between enhanced productivity and the quality of work life. But how do we increase productivity and at the same time enhance job satisfaction? There are several methods.

Improved Recruitment and Placement   Worker motivation is enhanced right at the beginning by creating the right fit between the person and the job (Spector, 2003). When the company's needs mesh with the worker's, both profit. Unfortunately, people sometimes get hired for reasons that are irrelevant to their potential to perform well in the job. They may be hired because of their physical appearance or because of a personal or family connection. By and large, however, businesses seek employees that they believe are well suited to the jobs in which they are placed. Employees who are satisfied with their jobs are less likely to be absent or quit. I/O psychologists work with companies to establish employee screening programs that help facilitate good placement. They analyze the specific skills and personal attributes needed for particular jobs, and they construct tests and develop interview protocols to determine whether candidates possess the requisite skills and attributes.

Training and Instruction   Training and instruction help increase productivity and provide workers with the skills they need to perform their jobs well. They also reduce the stresses on workers by equipping them to solve the problems they will face. Capacity to solve challenging problems enhances worker feelings of self-worth.

Use of Constructive Criticism   Criticism is necessary if workers are to improve, but to be effective, criticism needs to be delivered constructively, not destructively (Johnson & Indvik, 2000). In Table 15.4 constructive criticisms ("the good") in appraisal of workers' performances are contrasted with destructive criticisms ("the bad and ugly"). Poor use of criticism is a great cause of conflict. It saps workers' motivation and self-efficacy expectancies, and it leads to lower job satisfaction. The most useful kind of criticism leads workers to feel that they are being helped to perform better.

Unbiased Appraisal of Workers' Performance   Not surprisingly, workers are more productive and effective when they receive guidance and reinforcers based on an accurate appraisal of their performance (Johnson & Indvik, 2000). In an ideal world, appraisal of workers' performances would be based solely on how well they

Table 15.4 ▌ Criticism, The Good, the Bad, and the Ugly	
Constructive Criticism (Good)	**Destructive Criticism (Bad and Ugly)**
Specific: The supervisor is specific about what the employee is doing wrong. For example, she or he says, "This is what you did that caused the problem, and this is why it caused the problem."	**Vague:** The supervisor makes a blanket condemnation, such as, "That was an awful thing to do" or "that was a lousy job." No specifics are given.
Supportive of the employee: The supervisor gives the employee the feeling that the criticism is meant to help him or her perform better on the job.	**Condemnatory of the employee:** The supervisor attributes the problem to an unchangeable cause such as the employee's personality.
Helpful in problem solving: The supervisor helps employees improve things or solve their problems on the job.	**Threatening:** The supervisor attacks the employee, as by saying, "If you do this again, you'll be docked" or "Next time, you're fired."
Timely: The supervisor offers the criticism as soon as possible after the problem occurs.	**Untimely:** The supervisor offers the criticism after a good deal of time passes, after the employee has "moved on" psychologically.
Optimistic: The supervisor appears to assume that the employee will be able to improve.	**Pessimistic:** The supervisor seems doubtful that the employee will be able to improve.

do their jobs. However, cognitive biases often affect workers' evaluations. For example, supervisors tend to focus on the worker rather than on the worker's performance. Supervisors may form general impressions of liking or disliking workers and base their evaluations on these impressions rather than on the work performed. The tendency to rate workers according to general impressions can be reduced by instructing raters to focus on how well the worker carries out specific tasks. Learning theorists have suggested that the criteria for appraisal be totally objective—based on publicly observable behaviors and outlined to workers and supervisors prior to performance. Ideally, workers are rated according to whether they engage in targeted behavior patterns. Workers are not penalized for intangibles such as "poor attitude." Another bias is the tendency to evaluate workers according to how much effort they put into their work. Though effort is important, hard work is not necessarily good work. (Do you think that students who work harder than you should be given higher grades on tests, even when you get better test scores? Should professional ballplayers be judged on their effort or their success? What do you think?)

Goal Setting   Setting clear work goals helps breed job satisfaction (Murphy & Ensher, 2001). Workers need to know precisely what is expected of them. In many cases, however, work goals are vague or poorly defined. Workers may be told that they should "work hard" or "be serious" about their jobs, but hard work and seriousness are ill defined. This lack of knowledge creates anxiety and contributes to poor performance. Setting concrete goals at high but attainable levels makes work challenging but keeps stress at acceptable levels.

Financial Compensation   Workers need to feel that their efforts are rewarded with salaries and bonuses that are commensurate with their performance. It can be demoralizing to productive workers when they receive no greater pay than nonproductive workers. Another demoralizing condition faced by many women is being paid less than men for the same work.

Work Redesign   Psychologists understand the importance of creating settings in which workers can feel pride and accomplishment. An assembly-line worker may repeat one task hundreds of times a day and never see the finished product. To make factory work more meaningful, workers at one Volvo assembly plant in Sweden have been organized into small groups that elect leaders and distribute tasks among themselves. In another work-redesign program, workers move along the assembly line with their truck chassis, which gives them the satisfaction of seeing their product take shape. The janitorial staff at a Texas Instruments worksite meets in small groups to set goals and distribute cleaning tasks among themselves. Texas Instruments reports a cleaner plant, lowered costs, and decreased turnover.

The **quality circle**, a management practice developed by Japanese companies, comprises a group of workers who meet regularly to discuss problems on the job and suggest solutions (Spector, 2003). Quality circles give workers a greater sense of control over their jobs and increase their commitment to the company. Workers who are committed to their organizations—as well as to their careers—are more satisfied with their jobs and less likely to switch jobs (Somers & Birnbaum, 2000). Control and commitment also enhance psychological hardiness. Moreover, workers are in the best position to understand problems that prevent them from performing optimally.

❙ **Quality circle** A regularly scheduled meeting in which a group of workers discusses problems and suggests solutions in order to enhance the quality of products.

Adjustment and Modern Life

Challenges of a Changing Workplace

There are many opportunities and many challenges for today's workers. Technology, already transforming in its effects on the workplace, will continue to influence the type of work we do and how we do it. Technological change helps people find better ways to do what they do (Lewis, 2002). New occupational categories will emerge as workers are needed to manage these technological advances. Technology also makes it possible to expand the workplace, to literally make the entire world an extension of the home office. New jobs will be designed, and then redesigned, all with dizzying speed. Even now, web-enabled cell phones allow workers to keep abreast of work-related e-mail, track customer orders, hold videoconference calls, and keep in touch with their customers and managers on a 24/7 basis—just about wherever they happen to be in the world.

Other changes are making the workplace a less secure environment than it was in past generations. Many workers in your parents' and grandparents' generations stayed with the same company, or in the same jobs, for much, if not all, of their occupational careers. Today, fewer companies are offering the same kind of long-term job security that workers formerly enjoyed. Workers will need to plan their careers in terms of moving from one position to another, perhaps every few years. They will also need to continually retool in order to keep their skills current.

Another transformation is the change in the traditional nine-to-five workday. Today, increasing numbers of companies are allowing more flexible work shifts and increased opportunities for *telecommuting*. Moreover, about 15% of American workers perform shift work, most commonly involving evening hours (U.S. Bureau of Labor Statistics, 2006) (see Figure 15.2). In addition, an estimated 45 million Americans call their office home. They are telecommuters—people whose only office is at home are now estimated to number about 45 million workers in the United States (*Telecommuting*, 2007). Many telecommuters feel they have greater control over their work environment than traditional office workers, so it's not surprising that telecommuting is linked to greater job satisfaction, better work performance, and lower turnover rates (Gajendran & Harrison, 2007).

Many companies provide satellite offices or telework centers where telecommuting workers can drop in to perform work they cannot complete at home. One emerging work model, referred to as **hoteling**, provides temporary office space in a central office for workers only as needed—much as they would check into a hotel when traveling.

©Daniel Bolsen/Getty Images, Inc

Pants Optional

Increasing numbers of workers are telecommuting. With e-mail, videoconferencing, and other technological advancements, many people can work from home, at least part of the time, whether they are fully dressed or not.

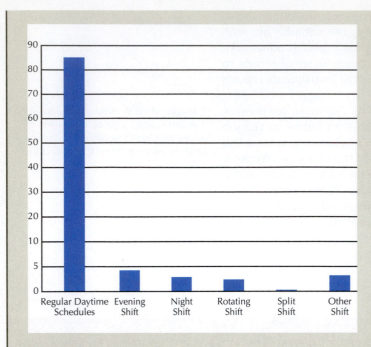

Figure 15.2
Shift Workers in America
About 15% of American workers today perform shift work, most commonly evening shifts.
Source: U.S. Bureau of Labor Statistics, 2006.

Industrial/organizational psychologists work with companies to help them adjust their corporate cultures to the changing workplace. For example, large companies today are typically multinational in their operations. Companies need to adapt to the demands of working with suppliers, manufacturers, and customers in many other cultures. Company representatives need to be sensitive to cultural differences and find ways of overcoming cultural barriers that may exist.

Another challenge to today's workers is the increased emphasis on entrepreneurship. By this we don't mean that workers will be expected to form their own companies, although many will. But we do mean that workers will need to assume an ever greater responsibility for their own career development. They will also need to keep apace of changing technology and job responsibilities and gear their occupational careers to take advantage of new opportunities. Industrial/organizational psychologists play important roles in helping companies select workers who can best adapt to the changing work environment. They also help workers adjust to these changes and help redesign the work environment to meet the demands of a changing workplace.

∎ **Hoteling** An emerging model in the workplace whereby workers are provided with temporary office space in the home office, which is available to them only when needed.

∎ **Flextime** A modification of one's work schedule from the standard 9:00 a.m. to 5:00 p.m.

Work Schedules Where is it written that work is performed best only between the hours of nine and five? Today, more and more companies are experimenting with **flextime**, or letting employees modify their own schedules to meet their personal needs (Grzywacz & Butler, 2005). In one approach to flextime, workers put in four 10-hour workdays, rather than five eight-hour days. One study found that flextime lowered absenteeism (Baltes et al., 1999). Flextime can help workers cope with parenthood, for example, and as a result boost their morale on the job (Seib & Muller, 1999). Job-sharing can have similar beneficial effects. At Honeywell, a "mothers' shift" allows women to coordinate their work schedules with school hours. Mothers may also have college students fill in for them during their children's summer vacations. Hasn't the time come to also consider the need for a "fathers' shift"? The message is beginning to resonate, as companies are now offering new dads the ability to take time off or adopt more flexible work schedules. One manager for a leading chip manufacturer was given a five-month leave after the birth of his son. One day, the proud father called his wife in her office, bubbling over with excitement in telling her that their son had rolled over for the first time (Stein, 2002).

Integration of New Workplace Technology Robots and other mechanical devices are increasingly replacing workers in some industries and are enabling others to enhance their productivity. Not very long ago, only computer specialists could operate a computer. Now it's standard issue for any new office worker. Fax machines and computerized payments are replacing the mail. Psychologists are involved in helping companies use technology in ways that make workers and the organizations in which they work more productive. They are also involved in helping workers retool so that workers keep abreast of the latest technological innovations.

Before moving on, let us offer one caveat. Although job satisfaction is linked to lower rates of absenteeism and employee turnover, the link between job satisfaction and productivity is only modestly strong at best (Judge et al., 2001). We shouldn't be surprised. Other factors may be stronger determinants of job performance and productivity than job satisfaction—factors such as fear of getting fired or losing future raises or bonuses if one's performance is just lacking.

15.2.2 Work and Stress

Many factors make jobs stressful, including heavy workloads, highly repetitive or boring work tasks, and conflicts with coworkers and supervisors (Spector, 2003). High levels of job-related stress are associated with increased physical symptoms. The left-hand part of Figure 15.3 shows how various features of the workplace can contribute to stress. Among the aspects of the physical environment that can produce stress are poor lighting, poor air quality, crowding, noise, and extremes of temperature. Individual stressors include work overload, boredom, conflict about one's work (e.g., producing products that may cause harm), excessive responsibility, and lack of forward movement in one's career or occupational standing. Group stressors include troublesome relationships with supervisors, subordinates, and peers. Organizational stressors include lack of opportunity to participate in decision making, ambiguous or conflicting company policies, too much or too little organizational structure, low pay, racism, and sexism (Gumbau, Soria, & Silla, 2000; Johnson & Indvik, 2000).

Stress at work also spills over into stress at home, and vice versa. Frustrations and resentments about the workplace can make us tired and short tempered. They can contribute to family arguments. In a vicious cycle, family conflict may then compound problems at work.

The Role of the Worker

The central part of Figure 15.3 shows the worker and the sources of stress that may be acting on him or her. For example, marital or inner conflict may compound conflicts encountered in the workplace. A person with a Type A personality may turn the easiest, most routine task into a race to beat the clock. Irrational needs for excessive approval may sap the benefits of rewards or appropriate recognition.

The right-hand side of Figure 15.3 suggests a number of subjective, behavioral, cognitive, physiological, and organizational outcomes from the interaction of these sources of stress.

On a subjective level, stressed workers can experience anxiety, depression, frustration, fatigue, boredom, loss of self-esteem, and burnout.

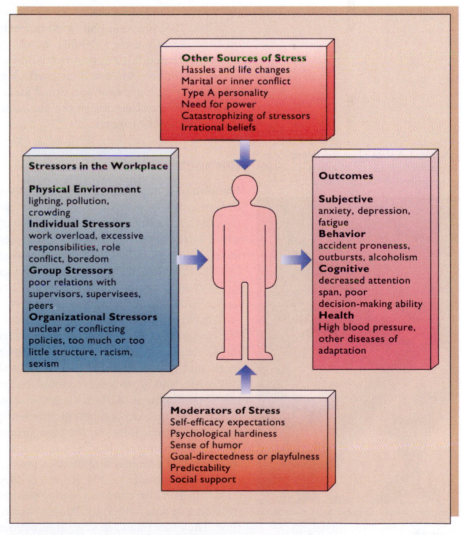

Figure 15.3
Effects of Stress in the Workplace
As shown in this model, various factors such as the physical environment and organizational stressors affect the worker. Workplace stressors can also interact with stress from home and personality factors to produce a range of negative outcomes.

How to Cope with Stress on the Job

Psychologists find that we can take many steps to decrease stress in the workplace. The organization or the individual can begin with an objective analysis of the workplace to determine whether physical conditions are hampering rather than enhancing the quality of life. Much job stress arises from a mismatch between job demands and the abilities and needs of the employee. To prevent mismatches, companies can use more careful screening measures (e.g., interviewing and psychological testing) to recruit employees whose personalities are compatible with job requirements and then provide the training and education needed to impart the specific skills that will enable workers to perform effectively. Job requirements should be as specific and clear as possible.

Workers need to feel they will find social support from their supervisors if they have complaints or suggestions. Companies can also help workers manage stress by offering counseling and supportive therapy, education about health, and gyms. Kimberly Clark, Xerox, Pepsi Cola, Weyerhauser, and Rockwell International, for example, have all made significant investments in gyms that include jogging tracks, exercise cycles, and other equipment. Johnson & Johnson's Live-for-Life program not only addresses stress management per se but also focuses on weight control, exercise, smoking reduction, nutrition, and alcohol abuse. Workers whose companies provide such programs are generally more fit, take fewer sick days, and report greater job satisfaction than workers at companies that provide medical screenings only.

Workers whose companies do not help them manage stress can tackle this task on their own by using methods such as relaxing, examining whether perfectionism or excessive needs for approval are heightening the tension they encounter at work, or attempting to enhance their psychological hardiness. Of course, they can always consult psychologists for additional ideas. If these measures are not sufficient, they may wish to carefully weigh the pluses and minuses and decide whether to change their jobs or shift careers.

▌ **Burnout** A state of mental and physical exhaustion brought on by overcommitment to work or other responsibilities.

Archivberlin Fotoagentur GmbH/Alamy Limited

Burnout

People who face excessive workload demands and overextend themselves may suffer burnout, a type of stress reaction associated with a state of emotional and physical exhaustion.

Burnout

Burnout is a state of mental and physical exhaustion brought on by excessive demands we face at work, or in caretaking roles, or in pursuing personal causes (Maslach & Leiter, 2008; Mommersteeg et al., 2006; Peeters et al., 2005). People who suffer burnout feel emotionally exhausted and lack motivation at work. They even have a sense of detachment or depersonalization ("This doesn't feel real"; "I can't believe I'm here"). Burnout is not just emotionally exhausting, it can also lead to stress-related health problems, such as headaches, stomach distress, sleep problems, and even hypertension and heart disease (Melamed et al., 2006).

Who is most likely to suffer burnout? Overly conscientious workers, frequently referred to as workaholics, can set the stage for burnout by extending themselves too far. College students, too, can suffer burnout, especially when they take on far more work, family, and school responsibilities than they can reasonably handle.

People who experience burnout become so consumed by their work that they neglect other areas of life, such as social relationships and leisure activities. Typically, burnout victims are competent, efficient people who become overwhelmed by the demands of their jobs and the recognition that they are unlikely to have the impact they had anticipated. Teachers, nurses, mental health workers, police officers, social workers, and criminal and divorce lawyers seem particularly prone to job burnout (Bakker & Schaufeli, 2000; Rupert & Morgan, 2005; Sternberg, 2000).

Burnout is also common among people who have high levels of role conflict, role overload, or role ambiguity. People in role conflict face competing demands for their time. They feel pulled in several directions at once. Their efforts to meet competing demands eventually lead to burnout. People with role overload find it hard to say "no." They take on more and more responsibilities until they burn out. People with role ambiguity are uncertain as to what other people expect of them. Thus, they work hard at trying to be all things to all people. It is not apathetic workers who are most likely to experience job burnout. Burnout tends to affect the most dedicated workers.

Behaviorally, stressed workers may become accident-prone, engage in excessive eating or smoking, turn to alcohol or other drugs, and show temperamental outbursts. Perhaps stress decreases workers' attention to potentially harmful details. Or perhaps some of the same conditions that are stressful are physically harmful.

The cognitive effects of excessive stress on the job include poor concentration and loss of ability to make sound decisions. Physiological effects include high blood pressure and the "diseases of adaptation." The organizational effects of excessive stress include absenteeism, alienation from coworkers, decreased productivity, high turnover rate, and loss of commitment and loyalty to the organization.

Burnout develops gradually. The warning signs may not appear for years, but here are some of the more common signs:

- Loss of energy and feelings of exhaustion, both physical and psychological
- Irritability and shortness of temper
- Stress-related problems, such as depression, headaches, backaches, or apathy
- Difficulty concentrating or feeling distanced from one's work
- Loss of motivation
- Lack of satisfaction or feelings of achievement at work
- Loss of concern about work in someone who was previously committed
- Feeling that one has nothing left to give

Preventing Burnout People may become burned out when they are overextended. Yet burnout is not inevitable. Here are some suggestions that may be helpful in preventing burnout:

1 *Establish your priorities.* Make a list of the things that are truly important to you. If your list starts and ends with work, rethink your values. Ask yourself some key questions: Am I making time for the relationships and activities that bring a sense of meaning, fulfillment, and satisfaction to life? Getting in touch with what's truly important to you may help you reorder your values and priorities.

2 *Set reasonable goals.* People at risk of burnout drive themselves to extremes. Set realistic long-term and short-term goals for yourself and don't push yourself beyond your limits.

3 *Take things one day at a time.* Work gradually toward your goals. Burning the candle at both ends is likely to leave you burned (out).

4 *Set limits.* People at risk of burnout often have difficulty saying "no." They are known as the ones who get things done. Yet the more responsibilities they assume, the greater their risk of burnout. Learn your limits and respect them. Share responsibilities with others. Delegate tasks. Cut back on your responsibilities before things pile up to the point where you have difficulty coping.

5 *Share your feelings.* Don't keep feelings bottled up, especially negative feelings like anger, frustration, and sadness. Share your feelings with people you trust. It is stressful to keep feelings under wraps.

6 *Build supportive relationships.* Developing and maintaining relationships helps buffer us against the effects of stress. People headed toward burnout may become so invested in their work that they let supportive relationships fall to the wayside.

7 *Do things you enjoy.* Balance work and recreation. Do something you enjoy every day. Breaks clear your mind and recharge your batteries. All work and no play makes Jack (or Jill) burn out.

8 *Take time for yourself.* Set aside time for yourself. Say "no" or "later." With all the demands that others place on your shoulders, you need some time for yourself. Make it part of your weekly schedule.

9 *Don't skip vacations.* People who are headed for burnout often find reasons to skip vacations. Big mistake: Vacations give you time off from the usual stresses.

10 *Be attuned to your health.* Be aware of stress-related symptoms. These include physical symptoms such as fatigue, headache or backache, and reduced resistance to colds and the flu. They include psychological symptoms such as anxiety, depression, irritability, or shortness of temper. Changes in health may represent the first signs of burnout. Take them as signals to examine the sources of stress in your life and do something about them. Consult health professionals about any symptoms that concern you. Get regular checkups to help identify developing health problems.

MODULE REVIEW

Review It

(12) The (majority or minority?) of American workers are at least somewhat satisfied with their jobs.

(13) Increased job satisfaction is linked to (higher or lower?) employed turnover and absenteism.

(14) Job satisfaction correlates (positively or negatively?) with the accuracy of appraisal of worker performance.

(15) The first method described in the text for increasing job satisfaction is improved _____ and placement.

(16) The most effective form of criticism is _____ criticism.

(17) A Japanese management practice involves the use of _____ circles in which workers meet regularly to discuss problems and suggest solutions relating to their jobs.

(18) Flextime (raises or lowers?) absenteeism.

(19) _____ stressors on the job include lack of opportunity to participate in decision making.

(20) The state of mental and physical exhaustion brought on by excessive demands is called _____

Think About It

What kinds of workplace stressors do workers create for themselves?

MODULE 15.3

Women in the Workplace

▪ Why do women work? What sources of stress in the workplace do women face?

▪ What is "men's work"? What is "women's work"?

▪ How much of a gender-related earnings gap is there? How do we explain it?

▪ How can we reduce the earnings gap for women?

▪ What is sexual harassment?

▪ What can people do if they are sexually harassed?

There was a time not long ago that women were denied a place in the boardroom, the factory assembly line, the firehouse, the naval vessel at sea, or the college classroom. Today, increasing numbers of women are taking their place in these and other worksites alongside men. Progress toward equality in the workplace has been made, but inequalities still exist. (For a timeline on notable dates in the history of women

Figure 15.4
Women in the Workplace:
A Timeline
Source: Adapted from *Working Mother magazine*, October 2002.

Women in the Workplace: A Timeline

1903	Maggie Lena Walker in Richmond, Virginia, becomes the first woman bank president.
1916	Jeannette Rankin of Montana becomes the first woman to serve as a representative in the U.S. Congress.
1920	The Nineteenth Amendment to the Constitution is ratified, granting women the right to vote.
1932	Amelia Earhart becomes the first woman, and second person, to fly solo across the Atlantic Ocean.
1943	Kaiser Shipbuilding establishes a childcare center for female workers building ships to support the U.S. war effort.
1948	Women are permitted to serve as full-time members of the military.
1960	Sirimavo Bandaranaike of Sri Lanka becomes the first woman in the world to serve as a prime minister.
1961	President Kennedy establishes a commission to study gender equality in education, the workplace, and the law.
1963	The United States enacts the Equal Pay Act, which makes it illegal for companies to pay women less simply on the basis of their gender.
1966	The National Organization for Women (NOW) is founded.
1966	The French designer Yves Saint Laurent introduces the women's pantsuit, which revolutionizes women's dress in the workplace.
1967	Muriel Siebert becomes the first woman to buy a seat on the New York Stock Exchange.
1972	The first women FBI agents are hired.
1972	Title IX is passed, banning sex discrimination in schools receiving federal funding.
1973	The U.S. Supreme Court holds that sex-segregated help-wanted ads in newspapers are unconstitutional.
1973	The first female pilot for a major airline is hired.
1973	Katherine Graham of the Washington Post Company becomes the first woman CEO of a Fortune 500 Company.
1974	Arlington County, Virginia, becomes the first municipality to hire a female career firefighter.
1976	Barbara Walters becomes the first female anchor of a network evening newscast.
1978	The Pregnancy Discrimination Act is passed, which, among other provisions, prohibits discrimination on the basis of pregnancy, childbirth, or related illness at work.
1981	Sandra Day O'Connor becomes the first woman to serve on the U.S. Supreme Court.
1983	Dr. Sally Ride becomes the first American woman in space as a member of the shuttle crew.
1984	Geraldine Ferraro becomes the first woman of a major political party to run for vice-president.
1986	The U.S. Supreme Court rules that sexual harassment can be used as a legal basis to support a claim for sex discrimination.
1993	The Family and Medical Leave Act is passed, allowing 12 weeks of unpaid leave to care for a newborn child after birth or adoptions.
1994	Psychologist Judith Rodin becomes the first woman to be appointed as president of an Ivy League school (University of Pennsylvania).
1996	Madeleine Albright becomes the first female U.S. secretary of state, making her the highest-ranking female government official in U.S. history.
2000+	To be continued …

Source: Adapted from *Working Mother* magazine, October 2002.

in the workplace, see Figure 15.4.) For example, women on the average still earn less than men. We also have evidence that many male managers tend to be biased toward giving male workers more favorable evaluations (Bowen, Swim, & Jacobs, 2000). A similar bias is not found for women managers (Bowen et al., 2000). Such bias as there is, then, tends to victimize women more than men. (Big surprise?) As we see next, women also tend to face a greater role overload than do men.

So why do women work? As you can see in the following section, the answer is that women work for the same reasons as men do: to earn money, structure their time, meet people, and find challenge and self-fulfillment. Nevertheless, it is sometimes heard that women are less committed than men to their jobs. Employers who deny women equal access to training and promotions sometimes justify discrimination by citing higher quit rates for women. However, evidence shows that women and men in the same job categories show comparable quit rates (Deutsch, 1990). The fact of the matter is that women are overrepresented in lower-echelon and dead-end jobs. It turns out that workers of both genders in such jobs have higher quit rates than workers in higher-paying, challenging positions. The job role, not the gender of the worker, is the major predictor of job commitment.

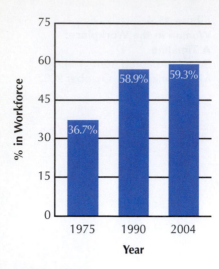

Figure 15.5
Working Mothers
Notice the sharp rise in workforce participation among married women with husbands present and young children under the age of 6.

15.3.1 Why Do Women Work?

Women, like men, work to support their families. Even asking the question "Why do women work?" is condescending. Why not ask, "Why do men work?" Women work for the same reasons men work—to earn a living, to support their families, to pursue personal interests that make their lives more fulfilling. Today, nearly three out of four married mothers of children under age 18 are employed outside the home (U.S. Bureau of the Census, 2007) (see Figure 15.5). Yet many women today are expected not only to bring home the bacon but to fry it up in the pan. That is, they still carry out the great majority of the household chores—including cooking, cleaning, and shopping (see Figure 15.6). Nine of 10 working mothers still bear the primary responsibility for the children, the cooking, and the cleaning. Between work, commuting, childcare, and housework, American working women are putting in nearly 15 hours a day! (Klein et al., 1998).

Are these mothers overburdened? Perhaps. A Harris poll survey found that working mothers are pressed for time. They are worried about not having enough time with their families and about balancing the demands of work and a home life. Nevertheless, when they were asked whether they would like to surrender some of their responsibilities, 53% of working women said no. Even more ironic, full-time working mothers reported that they felt more likely to feel valued for their contributions at home than full-time homemakers were.

Despite their new earning power, working mothers are still primarily concerned about their children. When they were asked what made them feel successful at home, about one man and woman in four mentioned good relationships and spending time together. The next-largest group of women (22%) reported good, well-adjusted, healthy children. But 20% of men mentioned money, or being able to afford things. Only 8% of the men mentioned well-adjusted kids. Just 5% of the women mentioned money. When we speak about role overload, we should keep in mind that we are talking about the situation of the typical American woman who has children who have not yet left the home. Let us momentarily climb atop our soapbox to note that the

Figure 15.6
When Mommy's Got a Job, Who Does the Cleaning, Cooking, and Shopping? You Guessed It
Most American women put in a second shift when they get home from the workplace. Most childcare and homemaking chores are left to women; the only exception is making repairs.

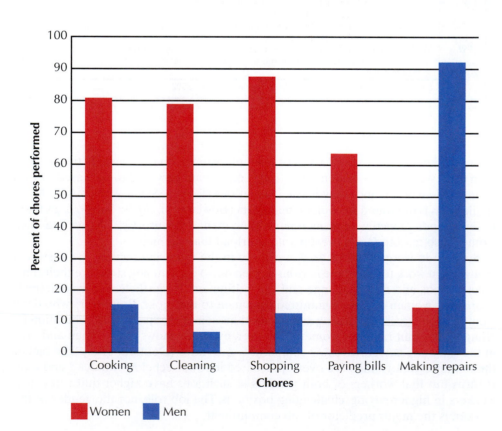

United States is somewhat unusual in that it still lacks coherent policies for helping dual-wage-earning families. Most industrialized nations provide families with allowances for children and paid leave when babies are born. Only a minority of companies in the United States do so.

Perhaps more companies in the United States should do so. Helping families manage pregnancies and the infancy of their children helps breed loyalty to the company (Lyness et al., 1999). Otherwise, working women are sort of held hostage by the company and switch jobs when the opportunity arises.

So working women usually work two shifts, one in the workplace and one at home. For example, about 90% of working women—including married and single mothers—continue to bear the major responsibility for childcare (Senecal, Vallerand, & Guay, 2001). When it comes to Mom or Dad staying home when Junior is running a fever, guess who most often gets the nod? Women miss work twice as often as men do when the kids are sick (Wasserman, 1993).

15.3.2 Women in the Workplace

Despite some recent breaking down of traditional gender segregation, many occupations largely remain "men's work" or "women's work." Those jobs we consider men's work or women's work usually involve a history of tradition—and just as often, of flat-out prejudice.

Because of a combination of tradition, prejudice, and individual preference, women still account for the great majority of secretaries and schoolteachers but only a small percentage of police officers and mechanics. On the other hand, the percentage of women in medical and law schools has recently risen to levels equal to those of men entering these professions (Glater, 2001).In psychology, women now constitute nearly three-quarters of new doctorate recipients, as compared to fewer than half some 25 years earlier (Gill, 2006). But the gap in some other professional fields has not narrowed as much, particularly in fields such as math, science, and engineering.

The Earnings Gap

Overall, women earn only three-quarters of the income of men (Stein, 2002). Men also tend to outearn women even when they are of the same educational level (U.S. Bureau of the Census, 2006) (see Figure 15.7).Yet women are gaining ground on the wage front (Uchitelle, 2004). Although a gap remains, women's earnings are moving toward parity with men's earnings.

The gender gap in earnings has implications not only for women but also for their families. Good earnings are connected with a lower likelihood of divorce, greater likelihood of marital satisfaction, and even greater well-being in the children. It might be—in part—that the same competencies that lead to high income also lead to better marriages and better-adjusted children. At the same time, research of this sort would seem to put to rest the notion that women with high earnings strain the family because of spouses' jealousy.

Why is there this gap in earnings? Although outright discrimination may account for some of the gap, much of it results from the fact that many women still work in traditionally low-paying occupations such as waitress, housekeeper, clerk, sales, and light factory work. Even in the same

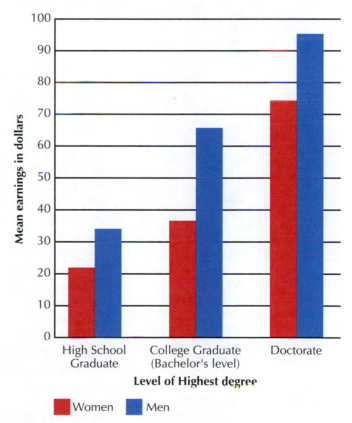

Figure 15.7
The Gender Gap in Wages
Despite a narrowing of the wage gap in recent years, on the average men still outearn women of the same educational level.
Source: U.S. Census Bureau, *Statistical Abstract of the United States,* 126th ed., 2006.

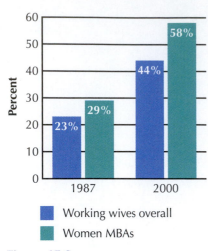

Figure 15.8

Who's Bringing Home More of the Bacon? Percentages of Wives Who Outearn Their Husbands

Though a gender disparity in earnings continues to exist, the gap has been narrowing in recent years. *Source:* Adapted from Conlin, 2003.

Digital Vision/SuperStock

Women in the Workplace

Women are making significant gains in fields once considered part of the male preserve. The numbers of new female doctors and lawyers are nearly equal to those of males, and, over time, women will be found in a higher percentage of top jobs in these fields and others. There remains a gender-related earnings gap, but this gap has also been declining. On the other hand, many women still face discrimination, and many others select traditional, low-paying, "nurturing" and "helping" jobs, such as in schoolteaching and secretarial work.

job area, such as sales, men are often given higher-paying, more responsible positions. Men in sales are more likely to vend high-ticket items such as military equipment, automobiles, computers, and appliances.

Even though nearly as many women as men now graduate from medical schools, men tend to gravitate toward higher-paying specialties, such as surgery. Female physicians are more likely to enter lower-paying medical specialties with traditional "nurturing" aspects, such as pediatrics and psychiatry (Stone & McKee, 2000). Men are also more likely than women to be in positions of power on medical school faculties—partly because they have been there longer.

Male college professors earn more than their women counterparts for several reasons. Since women are relative newcomers to academia, they are more likely to be found in lower-paying entry positions, such as assistant professorships. The gap narrows considerably as women move up the professorial ranks. Another reason for the academic pay gap is that women are more likely than men to choose lower-paying academic fields, such as education and English. Men are more likely to be found on faculties in business, engineering, and the hard sciences, where the pay is higher.

Progress in narrowing the earnings gap has been made and is continuing still. In fact, nearly one in three working wives now outearn their husbands, up from about one in five in 1980 (Conlin, 2003) (see Figure 15.8). Women MBAs are doing even better, with nearly 60% outearning their husbands, as compared to about 45% in 1987. And women now constitute nearly half of the ranks of high-paying managerial or executive positions (Tyre & McGinn, 2003). Still, more progress needs to be made to equalize the playing field for women workers overall, as we see next. Sexist attitudes in the workplace also linger. For example, a seasoned male manager may be accorded a respected social role as a "gray-beard" and venerated for his wisdom. But a seasoned female manager may not be valued as highly or accorded a similarly respected social role.

Reducing the Earnings Gap   The Equal Pay Act of 1963 requires equal pay for equal work. The Civil Rights Act of 1964 prohibits discrimination in hiring, firing, or promotion on the basis of race, ethnic origin, or gender. Measures such as the following can improve the quality of work life and reduce the earnings gap for women:

- *Encourage more realistic career planning.* The average woman today spends about 28 years in the workforce but plans for a much shorter tenure. Young women should assume that they will be working for several decades so that they will avail themselves of opportunities for education and training.

- *Provide employers with accurate information about women in the workforce.* If more employers recognized that women spend so many years in the workforce, and that commitment to a job reflects the type of work rather than the gender of the worker, they might be more motivated to open the doors to women.

- *Heighten awareness of the importance of the woman's career in dual-career marriages.* Husbands may also hold stereotypes that damage their wives' chances for career advancement and fulfillment. A couple should not blindly assume that the man's career always comes first. The man can share childrearing and housekeeping chores so that each may reap the benefits of employment.

- *Maintain employment continuity and stability.* Promotions and entry into training programs are usually earned by showing a stable commitment to a career and, often, one's employer. Many couples permit both partners to achieve these benefits by postponing childbearing or sharing childrearing tasks.

- *Increase job flexibility and provide childcare facilities.* Employers can also assist women workers through flextime, providing on-site childcare facilities, and granting extended maternity and paternity leaves.

- *Recruit qualified women into training programs and jobs.* Educational institutions, unions, and employers can actively recruit qualified women for positions that have traditionally been held by men.

15.3.3 Sexual Harassment

Sexual harassment is one of the common and troubling adjustment problems that women—and sometimes men—face in the workplace (Cortina & Wasti, 2005). But just what is sexual harassment? Where can we draw the line between an "innocent" flirtation and sexual harassment?

Let us draw the line by adopting a widely accepted definition of sexual harassment as behavior that consists of deliberate or repeated unsolicited verbal comments, gestures, or physical contacts of a sexual nature that are not wanted by the recipient. Examples of sexual harassment can range from unwelcome sexual jokes, overtures, suggestive comments, and sexual innuendos to outright sexual assault, and it includes behaviors such as the following (Powell 1996):

- Verbal harassment or abuse
- Subtle pressure for sexual activity
- Remarks about a person's clothing, body, or sexual activities
- Leering at or ogling a person's body
- Unwelcome touching, patting, or pinching
- Brushing against a person's body
- Demands for sexual favors accompanied by implied or overt threats concerning one's job or student status
- Physical assault

Both men and women can engage in sexual harassment or be subject to it. Nevertheless, women are much more likely than men to suffer harassment, and women of color are more likely to suffer harassment than are white women (Berdahl & Moore, 2006). Charges of sexual harassment are often ignored or trivialized by coworkers and employers. The victim may hear, "Why make a big deal out of it? It's not like you were attacked in the street." Evidence shows, however, that persons subjected to sexual harassment are harmed (Buchanan & Fitzgerald, 2008; Harned, 2000). The majority of people subjected to sexual harassment report significant adjustment problems that range from anxiety, irritability, and lower self-esteem to anger and disturbed eating behavior. Harassment on the job is also linked among women workers to a greater likelihood of switching jobs, even to less preferable jobs (Sims, Drasgow, & Fitzgerald, 2005). College women have dropped courses, switched majors, or changed graduate programs or even colleges because they were unable to stop professors from sexually harassing them.

One reason that sexual harassment is so stressful is that, as with so many other forms of sexual exploitation or coercion, the blame tends to fall on the victim. Sexual harassers often claim that charges of harassment are exaggerated. They say that the victim "overreacted" to normal male–female interactions or "took me too seriously." In our society, women are expected to be "nice"—to be passive, not to "make a scene." The woman who assertively protects her rights may be seen as "strange" or a "troublemaker." Women are "damned if they assert themselves and victimized if they don't" (Powell, 1991, p. 114).

Motives for Sexual Harassment

Experts agree that sexual harassment has more to do with aggressiveness and the abuse of power than with sexual desire (Lim & Cortina, 2005; O'Leary-Kelly, Paetzold, & Griffin, 2000). In sexual harassment, sexual advances

Image State/Alamy Limited

Sexual Harassment?
Men and women often have different views of behaviors that constitute sexual harassment. Men also tend to see sexual harassment as less serious a problem than do women and to underestimate its occurrence. Sexual harassment can take many forms, including unwelcome touching, verbal abuse, and pressure for sexual activity.

become expressions of power that are used as a tactic to control or frighten someone, usually a woman. The harasser is usually in a dominant position and abuses that position by exploiting the victim's vulnerability. Sexual harassment may be used as a tactic of social control. It may be a means of keeping women "in their place." This is especially so in work settings that are traditional male preserves, such as the firehouse, the construction site, or the military academy. Sexual harassment expresses resentment and hostility toward women who venture beyond the boundaries of the traditional feminine role (Fitzgerald, 1993).

How Widespread Is the Problem?

How common is sexual harassment in the workplace? Men tend to see sexual harassment as a less serious problem than women do and also tend to underestimate its incidence (Corr & Jackson, 2001). We lack precise figures on the frequency of sexual harassment, in large part because it often goes unreported. Most women who are sexually harassed do not file complaints, largely because they believe it would be futile or because of fear of reprisals (Cortina & Wasti, 2005). When women perceive leaders of the organizations in which they work as making sincere efforts to stop harassment, they typically feel freer to report harassment than do those who view leaders as more tolerant of harassment (Offermann & Malamut, 2002).

Experts estimate that as many as one in two women encounter some form of sexual harassment on the job or in college (Fitzgerald, 1993). In all likelihood, sexual harassment is the most common form of sexual victimization. Sexual harassment against women is more common in workplaces in which women have traditionally been underrepresented, such as the construction site or the shipyard. Yet, despite the prevalence of sexual harassment, incidents generally are not reported.

Resisting Sexual Harassment

What would you do if you were sexually harassed by an employer? How would you handle it? Would you try to ignore it and hope that it would stop? What actions might you take? We offer some suggestions that may be helpful (adapted from Powell, 1996, and Rathus, Nevid, & Fichner-Rathus, 2008). Recognize, however, that responsibility for sexual harassment always lies with the perpetrator and the organization that permits sexual harassment to take place, not with the person subjected to the harassment.

1 *Convey a professional attitude.* Harassment may be stopped cold by responding to the harasser with a businesslike, professional attitude.

2 *Discourage harassing behavior and encourage appropriate behavior.*
Harassment may also be stopped cold by shaping the harasser's behavior. Your reactions to the harasser may encourage businesslike behavior and discourage flirtatious or suggestive behavior. If a harassing supervisor suggests that you come back once the office is closed to review your project so that the two of you will be undisturbed, set limits assertively. Tell him that you'd feel more comfortable discussing work during office hours. Remain task-oriented. Stick to business. The harasser should quickly get the message that you wish to maintain a strictly professional relationship. If the harasser persists, do not blame yourself. You are responsible only for your own actions. When the harasser persists, a more direct response may be appropriate: "Mr. Jones, I'd like to keep our relationship on a purely professional basis, okay?"

3 *Avoid being alone with the harasser.* If you are being harassed by your supervisor but need some advice about your work, approach him at a time when other workers are milling about, not when the workplace is deserted. Or arrange for a coworker to come in with you or wait outside the office while you consult your supervisor.

4 *Keep a record.* Keep a record of all incidents of harassment as documentation in the event you decide to lodge an official complaint. The record should include the following: (1) where the incident took place; (2) the date and time; (3) what happened, including the exact words that were used, if you can recall them; (4) how you felt; and (5) the names of witnesses. Some people who have been subjected to sexual harassment have carried a hidden tape recorder during contacts with the harasser. Such recordings may not be admissible in a court of law, but they are persuasive in organizational grievance procedures. A hidden tape recorder may be illegal in your state, however. It is advisable to check the law.

5 *Talk with the harasser.* It may be uncomfortable to address the issue directly with a harasser, but doing so puts the offender on notice that you are aware of the harassment and want it to stop. It may be helpful to frame your approach in terms of a description of the specific offending actions (e.g., "When we were alone in the office, you repeatedly attempted to touch me or brush up against me"), your feelings about the offending behavior ("It made me feel like my privacy was being violated; I'm very upset about this and haven't been sleeping well"), and what you would like the offender to do ("So I'd like you to agree never to attempt to touch me again, okay?"). Having a talk with the harasser may stop the harassment. If the harasser denies the accusations, it may be necessary to take further action.

6 *Write a letter to the harasser.* Set down on paper a record of the offending behavior, and put the harasser on notice that the harassment must stop. Your letter might (1) describe what happened ("Several times you have made sexist comments about my body"), (2) describe how you feel ("It made me feel like a sexual object when you talked to me that way"), and (3) describe what you would like the harasser to do ("I want you to stop making sexist comments to me").

7 *Seek support.* Support from people you trust can help you through the often-trying process of resisting sexual harassment. Talking with others allows you to express your feelings and receive emotional support, encouragement, and advice. In addition, it may strengthen your case if you have the opportunity to identify and talk with other people who have been harassed by the offender.

8 *File a complaint.* Companies and organizations are required by law to explain policies concerning sexual harassment and to respond reasonably to complaints of sexual harassment (Stokes, Stewart-Belle, & Barnes, 2000). In large organizations, a designated official (sometimes an ombudsman, affirmative action officer, or sexual harassment adviser) is usually charged to handle such complaints. Set up an appointment with this official to discuss your experiences. Ask about the grievance procedures in the organization and your right to confidentiality. Have available a record of the dates of the incidents, what happened, how you felt about it, and so on. The two major government agencies that handle charges of sexual harassment are the Equal Employment Opportunity Commission (look under the government section of your phonebook for the telephone number of the nearest office) and your state's Human Rights Commission (listed in your phonebook under state or municipal government). These agencies may offer advice on how you can protect your legal rights and proceed with a formal complaint.

9 *Seek legal remedies.* Sexual harassment is illegal and actionable. If you are considering legal action, consult an attorney familiar with this area of law. You may be entitled to back pay (if you were fired for reasons arising from the sexual harassment), job reinstatement, and punitive damages.

Let us not leave this chapter on a negative note. The *Psychology in Daily Life* module concludes with advice on how to find a career that may best fit you as an individual.

Review It

(21) Research suggests that many male raters of job performance tend to be biased toward giving (male or female?) workers more favorable evaluations.

(22) The typical American working woman whose children are in the home experiences _____ overload.

(23) The reasons that women work are mainly (the same as or different from?) the reasons that men work.

(24) Women account for the (majority or minority?) of secretaries and schoolteachers.

(25) The gender-related earnings gap is (increasing or decreasing?).

(26) The average woman today spends (more than or less than?) 25 years in the workforce but expects to spend (more or less?) time there.

(27) _____ _____ consists of deliberate or repeated unsolicited verbal comments, gestures, or physical contacts of a sexual nature that are not wanted by the recipient.

(28) One reason that sexual harassment is so stressful is that the _____ tends to fall on the victim.

Think About It

Agree or disagree with the following statement and explain your point of view: Some work should be men's work and some should be women's work.

Psychology in Daily Life   MODULE 15.4

Finding a Career That Fits

Finding a job we will enjoy and stick with requires that we take into account not only how the job fits our personality but also how it fits our aptitudes, interests, and personal traits. Let's put it another way: It may matter little that we are bringing home the bacon if we hate getting up in the morning to face our jobs. If we do not fit our jobs, we find them more stressful and are unlikely to try to do our best. Finding the right fit requires that we first take stock of ourselves, which may begin with the nearby self-assessment feature.

Many occupations call for combinations of personality traits (Darcy & Tracey, 2007; Nauta, 2007). A copywriter in an advertising agency might be both artistic and enterprising. Clinical and counseling psychologists tend to be investigative, artistic, and socially oriented. Military people and beauticians tend to be realistic and conventional. (But military leaders who plan major operations and form governments are also enterprising, and individuals who create new hairstyles and fashions are also artistic.)

Let us consider ways in which psychology can help us make sound career choices. Two key approaches involve the balance sheet and the use of psychological tests.

15.4.1 How to Use the Balance Sheet and Psychological Tests to Make Career Decisions

Balance sheets can be helpful in making personal decisions, such as career decisions. The balance sheet can help you weigh the pluses and minuses of each decision, pinpoint potential sources of frustration, and plan how to get more information or to surmount obstacles.

There is nothing new in the concept of weighing pluses and minuses, but Janis and Mann (1977) find that use of a balance sheet can help us make sure that we have considered the information available to us. The balance sheet also helps highlight gaps in information. The balance sheet has been shown to help high school students select a college and to help adults decide whether or not to go on diets and attend exercise classes. Balance sheet users show fewer regrets about the road not taken and are more likely to stick to their decisions.

To use the balance sheet, jot down the following information for each choice:

1. Projected tangible gains and losses for oneself
2. Projected tangible gains and losses for others
3. Projected self-approval or self-disapproval
4. Projected approval or disapproval of others

Emily, a first-year liberal arts major, wondered whether she should strive to become a physician. There were no physicians in her family with whom to explore the idea. A psychologist in her college counseling center advised her to fill out the balance sheet shown in Table 15.5 to help weigh the pluses and minuses of medicine.

Emily's balance sheet helped her see that she needed dozens of pieces of information to decide. For example, how would she react to intense, prolonged studying? What were her chances of being accepted by a medical school? How did the day-to-day nitty-gritty of medical work fit her personality?

Table 15.5 ▌ Emily's Balance Sheet for the Alternative of Pursuing Premedical Studies

Emily's balance sheet of the alternatives showed that although she knew that other people admired physicians, she had not considered how she would feel about herself as a physician. It encouraged her to seek further information about her psychological needs.

Areas of Consideration	Positive Expectations	Negative Expectations
Tangible gains and losses for Emily	1. Solid income	1. Long hours studying 2. Worry about acceptance by medical school 3. High financial debt upon graduation
Tangible gains and losses for others	1. Solid income for the benefit of the family	1. Little time for family life
Self-approval or disapproval	1. Pride in being a physician	
Social approval or disapproval	1. Other people admire doctors	1. Some women (still!) frown on women doctors

The need for information is not limited to those contemplating a career in medicine. The types of questions that we must consider about any career are shown in Table 15.6.

To gather more information, Emily's counselor used a number of psychological tests. Most career counselors test to some degree. They combine test results with interview information and knowledge of their clients' personal histories to attain a rounded picture of their clients' interests, abilities, and personalities.

One of the tests Emily took was the Wechsler Adult Intelligence Scale (WAIS). The WAIS and the Stanford-Binet Intelligence Scales are the most widely used intelligence tests. Emily's WAIS score was in the 130s, which means that her general level of intellectual functioning was on a par with that of people who performed well in medicine. Her verbal, mathematical, and spatial-relations skills showed no deficiencies. Thus, any academic problems were likely to reflect lack of motivation or of specific prerequisites, not lack of ability. But her counselor also told Emily that "the best predictor of future behavior is past behavior." Since premedical programs are dominated by chemistry, Emily's solid performance in high school chemistry was promising.

Table 15.6 ▌ Types of Information Needed to Make Satisfying Career Decisions

1. **Intellectual and Educational Appropriateness: Is your intended career compatible with your own intellectual and educational abilities and background?** Have you taken any "preprofessional" courses that lead to the career? Have you done well in them? What level of intellectual functioning is shown by people already in the career? Is your own level of intellectual functioning comparable? What kinds of special talents and intellectual skills are required for this career? Are there any psychological or educational tests that can identify where you stand in your possession of these talents or in the development of these skills? If you do not have these skills, can they be developed? How are they developed? Is there any way of predicting how well you can do at developing them? Would you find this field intellectually demanding and challenging? Would you find the field intellectually sterile and boring?

   Information Resources: College or university counseling or testing center, college placement center, private psychologist or career counselor, people working in the field, professors in or allied to the field.

2. **Intrinsic Factors: Is your intended career compatible with your personality?** Does the job require elements of the realistic personality type? Of the investigative, artistic, social, enterprising. or conventional types? What is your personality type, according to Holland's theory (see nearby Self-Assessment)? Is there a good "person–job environment fit"? Is the work repetitious, or is it varied? Do you have a marked need for change (perpetual novel stimulation), or do you have a greater need for order and consistency? Would you be working primarily with machinery, with papers, or with other people? Do you prefer manipulating objects, doing paperwork, or interacting with other people? Is the work indoors or outdoors? Are you an "indoors" or an "outdoors person"? Do you have strong needs for autonomy and dominance, or do you prefer to defer to others? Does the field allow you to make your own decisions, permit you to direct others, or require that you closely take direction from others? Do you have strong aesthetic needs? Is the work artistic? Are you Type A or Type B, or somewhere in between? Is this field strongly competitive or more relaxed?

   Information Resources: Successful people in the field (Do you feel similar to people in the field? Do you have common interests? Do you like them and enjoy their company?), written job descriptions, psychological tests of personality and interests.

3. **Extrinsic Factors: What is the balance between the investment you would have to make in the career and the probable payoff?** How much time, work, and money would you have to invest in your educational and professional development in order to enter this career? Do you have the financial resources? If not, can you get them? (Do the sacrifices you would have to make to get them—such as long-term debt—seem worthwhile?) Do you have the endurance? The patience? What will the market for your skills be like when you are ready to enter the career? In 20 years? Will the financial rewards adequately compensate you for your investment?

   Information Resources: College financial aid office, college placement office, college counseling center, family, people in the field.

The balance sheet suggested that Emily had only superficially asked herself about how she would enjoy being a physician. She had recognized that physicians are generally admired and assumed that she would have feelings of pride. But would the work of a physician be consistent with her personality type? Would her psychological needs be met? The counselor provided helpful personality information through an interest inventory and a widely used personality scale, the Edwards Personal Preference Schedule (EPPS). Interest inventories are widely used in college counseling and testing centers.

Most items require that test-takers indicate whether they like, are indifferent to, or dislike various occupations (e.g., actor/actress, architect), school subjects (algebra, art), activities (adjusting a carburetor, making a speech), amusements (golf, chess, jazz or rock concerts), and types of people (babies, nonconformists). The preferences of test-takers are compared with those of people in various occupations. Areas of general interest (e.g., sales, science, teaching, agriculture) and specific interest (e.g., mathematician, guidance counselor, beautician) are derived from these comparisons. Test-takers may also gather information about their personality type.

The EPPS pairs a number of statements expressive of psychological needs, and test-takers indicate which of each pair of statements is more descriptive of them. In this way it can be determined, for example, whether test-takers have a stronger need for dominance than for deference (taking direction from others) or a strong need for order or to be helped by others. All in all, the relative strength of 15 psychological needs is examined.

The interest inventory suggested that Emily would enjoy investigative work, science—including medical science—and mathematics. However, she was not particularly socially oriented. Well-adjusted physicians usually show a combination of investigative and social types. The EPPS showed relatively strong needs for achievement, order, dominance, and endurance. All these factors meshed well with premedical studies—the long hours, the willingness to delay gratification, and the desire to learn about things—to make them fit together and work properly. The EPPS report dovetailed with the interest inventory's report to the effect that Emily was not particularly socially oriented: The EPPS suggested that Emily had a low need for **nurturance**, for caring for others and promoting their well-being.

Thus, we can see that people with the ability to enter prestigious vocations such as college professor, psychologist, physician, or lawyer might not be happy with them. We may be miserable in occupations that are inconsistent with our personalities.

With this information in hand, Emily recognized that she really did not sense a strong desire to help others through medicine. Her medical interests were mainly academic. But after some reflection, she chose to pursue premedical studies and to expand her college work in chemistry and other sciences to lay the groundwork for alternative careers in medically related sciences. The courses promised to be of interest even if she did not develop a strong desire to help others or was not accepted by medical school. Contingency plans like these are useful for all of us. If we can consider alternatives, even as we head down the path toward a concrete goal, we are better equipped to deal with unanticipated roadblocks.

15.4.2 Finding Your Dream Job

Learning more about your interests and personality traits may help you identify the kind of work for which you are best suited. But once you land a job, you need to continually evaluate whether the job meets your personal needs. You need to be asking yourself questions like: Do I find it fulfilling? Does it allow me to pursue my dreams?

Industrial/organizational psychologist Nashá London-Vargas (2001) offers a set of self-directed questions that you may find helpful in sizing up whether your present job, or a job you may hold in the future, meets your personal—not just your financial— needs.

- Is the job associated with your interests or passions in life?
- Will the job help you pursue your dreams?
- Are you passionate about your work?
- Did you seek out the job, or did you just happen to fall into it?
- Does your work make you feel like you've accomplished a job well done? Or do you leave work feeling unfulfilled or depressed?

London-Vargas points out that connecting our work with our interests, passions, personal fulfillment, and needs for challenge helps imbue our lives with meaning and adds value not only to our own lives but to those of others who benefit from the work we do.

▮ **Nurturance** A psychological trait or need characterized by caring for people (or other living organisms) and/or rearing them.

| **What's Your Career Type? Attend the Job Fair and Find Out!** | ***Self-Assessment*** |

There are a number of different approaches to predicting whether we are likely to adjust to various job environments or occupations. By and large, they involve matching our traits to the job. Psychologist John Holland (1997) has developed a theory of matching six types of personality to occupations. To obtain insight into your own personality type—or types—let's attend a job fair.

Imagine a job fair held in a college gymnasium. What happened is this. When the fair got under way, students and prospective employers began to chat. As time elapsed, they found mutual interests and collected into parts of the gym according to those interests.

All right, now you enter the room. Groups have already formed, but you decide not to stay by yourself. You catch snatches of conversation in an effort to decide which group to join.

Now consider the types of people in the six groups by reading the descriptions in Figure 15.9:
Which group would you most like to join? Write the letter that signifies the group (R, I, A, S, E, or C) here: _____

What is your second choice? After you had met and chatted with the folks in the first group, with whom else might you like to chat? Write the letter here:_____

Now, which group looks most boring to you? With which group do you have nothing in common? Which group would you most like to avoid? Write the letter signifying the group that should have stayed at home here: _____

Where, then, did you fit in at the fair? What might it mean for your career adjustment? Predicting our adjustment involves matching our traits to the job. The job fair helps people decide where they do and do not "fit in."

Holland (1997) has predicted how well people will enjoy a certain kind of work by matching six personality types—realistic, investigative, artistic, social, enterprising, and conventional—to the job. Each of the groups in Figure 15.9 represents a type of personality (Brown, 2002; Holland, 1997; Spokane, Luchetta, & Richwine, 2002):

1. *Realistic.* Realistic people tend to be concrete in their thinking, mechanically oriented, and interested in jobs that involve motor activity. Examples include farming; unskilled labor, such as attending gas stations; and skilled trades, such as construction and electrical work.

2. *Investigative.* Investigative people tend to be abstract in their thinking, creative, and introverted. They are frequently well adjusted in research and college and university teaching.

3. *Artistic.* Artistic individuals tend to be creative, emotional, interested in subjective feelings, and intuitive. They tend to gravitate toward the visual and performing arts.

4. *Social.* Socially oriented people tend to be extraverted and socially concerned. They frequently show high verbal ability and strong needs for affiliating with others. Jobs such as social work, counseling, and teaching children often fit them well.

5. *Enterprising.* Enterprising individuals tend to be adventurous and impulsive, domineering, and extraverted. They gravitate toward leadership and planning roles in industry, government, and social organizations. The successful real estate developer or tycoon is usually enterprising.

6. *Conventional.* Conventional people tend to enjoy routines. They show high self-control, needs for order, and the desire for social approval; they are not particularly imaginative. Jobs that suit them include banking, accounting, and clerical work.

Figure 15.9
Personality Types and Careers
Picture yourself at a job fair like the one pictured here. At such fairs, students and prospective employers begin to chat. As time elapses, they find mutual interests and collect into groups accordingly. Consider the types of people in the six groups by reading the descriptions for each. In which group do you feel you would be best suited? What does your choice suggest about your personality type?

C
These people have clerical or numerical skills. They like to work with data, to carry out other people's directions, or to carry things out in detail.

E
These people like to work with people. They like to lead and influence others for economic or organizational gains.

R
These people have mechanical or athletic abilities. They like to work with machines and tools, to be outdoors, or to work with animals or plants.

I
These people like to learn new things. They enjoy investigating and solving problems and advancing knowledge.

S
This group enjoys working with people. They like to help others, including the sick. They enjoy informing and enlightening people.

A
This group is highly imaginative and creative. They enjoy working in unstructured situations. They are artistic and innovative.

CHAPTER REVIEW

RECITE! RECITE! RECITE! RECITE! RECITE! RECITE! RECITE!

Study Tip: Reciting the answers to these study questions will help you become a more effective learner. First try answering the questions by yourself, either reciting them out loud or writing them in a notebook or on the computer. Then compare your answers with the sample answers provided below.

1. Why do people work?

Workers are motivated both by extrinsic rewards (money, status, security) and intrinsic rewards (the work ethic, self-identity, self-fulfillment, self-worth, and the social values of work).

2. What processes do people undergo as they decide on a career to pursue?

Stage theorists identify various stages of career development, including the fantasy, tentative, realistic choice, maintenance, career change, and retirement stages.

3. What's a résumé? How do I write one?

Your résumé is a summary of your background and qualifications. Your résumé is you—until the interview. It should summarize your background in education and work experience, most recent experiences first. General rule to break (sometimes): Any color ink is fine as long as it's black. Include e-mail address and cell phone number. Don't lie! You may lie your way into a job for which you're not qualified—then what do you do?

4. What goes into the cover letter?

The cover letter can explain how you learned about the opening, briefly show how you are qualified, state salary and geographical needs, request an interview, offer to send references upon request, and thank the prospective employer for her or his consideration.

5. How do I "ace" the job interview?

Make a good first impression by being well-groomed, well-dressed, and as well-spoken as you can be. Maintain eye contact, but look engaged, not challenging. Answer questions briefly and have some questions of your own to ask. Emphasize how your qualifications fit this job. Never be sarcastic or impatient. Ask for a reasonably high salary. Don't volunteer weaknesses.

6. Okay, I've got the job. Now what do I do to get ahead?

Your adjustment may begin with recognizing that you're going from the "top" of your educational experience to a relatively low rung in the world outside. Learn how to do your specific job tasks and take responsibility for them. Show that you can get along with coworkers and supervisors. Seek a mentor to "show you the ropes."

7. What factors are associated with job satisfaction?

Actually, the great majority of workers in the United States report being completely or somewhat satisfied with their jobs. Older workers and workers with higher incomes are more likely to say they are satisfied. Workers do not like being left out of decision-making processes and profit from constructive rather than destructive criticism. Many workers complain of stress, low pay, lack of recognition, and unsatisfactory job benefits in areas like health insurance and retirement.

8. What factors may enhance job satisfaction?

Measures that contribute to job satisfaction include careful recruitment and selection of workers, training and instruction, unbiased appraisal and feedback, goal setting, linking financial compensation to productivity, allowing workers to make appropriate decisions, and flexible schedules such as flextime and job-sharing.

9. What are the sources of stress in the workplace?

There are physical, individual, group, and organizational stressors. For example, the workplace can be polluted. The worker's personality may not fit the job. Coworkers may be criticizers or "back-stabbers." Organizations may have strict hierarchies that do not permit input from lower-level workers.

10. How can I—or we—decrease stress in the workplace?

For one thing, the organization can study the workplace environment to reduce stressors such as pollution and abrasive supervisor–employee relationships. Many organizations provide health or fitness facilities and activities. Workers also need to evaluate whether their jobs truly fit their personalities and skills.

11. What is burnout? What causes it?

Burnout is characterized by emotional exhaustion, feelings of depersonalization, and reduced achievement. The typical "setup" for burnout is frustration on the job when encountered by highly conscientious workers.

12. How can I prevent job burnout?

Workers can prevent burnout by measures such as creating clear priorities, setting reasonable goals and limits, sharing their feelings (with people they can trust!), building supportive relationships, and setting aside time to pursue personally rewarding activities outside the workplace.

13. Why do women work? What sources of stress in the workplace do women face?

Mainly, work means for a woman what it means for a man—financial independence, self-esteem, social interaction, self-identity. However, women often encounter greater stress in the workplace, such as the pressures of balancing childbearing and career needs, role overload, sexism and sexual harassment, and dealing with the gender-related earnings gap.

14. What is "men's work"? What is "women's work"?

The very question is sexist because it assumes that there are such things as "men's work" and "women's work." Areas that have been traditional male preserves—especially medicine and law—are now seeing equal or nearly equal numbers of women entering them. However, because these areas were shut off to women, older men usually remain in positions of power. Other areas are still dominated by men—for example, the military, science and engineering, truck driving, and the construction industry.

15. How much of a gender-related earnings gap is there? How do we explain it?

The earnings gap narrowed at the end of the twentieth century such that women earned about 75% of the income of men. There is no simple explanation for the remaining earnings gap. Reasons include discrimination, women's "choices" (based on a lifetime of exposure to gender-role stereotypes) to enter traditionally lower-paying fields, and the fact that the fields formerly restricted to women tend to remain dominated by older men.

16. How can we reduce the earnings gap for women?

Women profit from realistic career planning, employment continuity, childcare facilities, and training programs. (Lack of discrimination wouldn't hurt, either.)

17. What is sexual harassment?

One commonly accepted definition of sexual harassment consists of deliberate or repeated unsolicited verbal comments, gestures, or physical contacts of a sexual nature that are unwelcome.

18. What can people do if they are sexually harassed?

People who are sexually harassed can adopt a cool (not necessarily nasty) "professional" attitude in relating to harassers, directly inform the harasser to stop, avoid being alone with the harasser, keep a record of incidents, complain to the organization, and seek legal remedies. Harassment usually will not go away "by itself."

YOUR PERSONAL JOURNAL

REFLECT REFLECT REFLECT REFLECT REFLECT REFLECT REFLECT

Study Tip: Reflecting on how the concepts in the chapter relate to your own experiences encourages deeper processing, which makes the material more personally meaningful and fosters more effective learning. Use additional pages if needed to complete your answers.

1. What intrinsic and extrinsic factors underlie your motivation to be in college and join the workforce?

2. The text discusses different stages of career development. In what stage of career development are you? Explain.

ANSWERS TO MODULE REVIEWS

Module 15.1

1. extrinsic
2. ethic
3. esteem
4. models
5. fantasy
6. tentative
7. change
8. résumé
9. impressions
10. is
11. job

Module 15.2

12. majority
13. lower
14. positively
15. recruitment
16. constructive
17. quality
18. lowers
19. Organizational
20. burnout

Module 15.3

21. male
22. role
23. the same as
24. majority
25. decreasing
26. more than/less
27. Sexual harassment
28. blame

SCORING KEY FOR JOB SATISFACTION INDEX

To find your score, compare your answers to those shown in the scoring key. Allot yourself the number of points indicated by each answer. Add your points and write your total here: _____

SCORING KEY

1. a. 1 b. 3 c. 5   2. a. 5 b. 1 c. 3   3. a. 3 b. 1 c. 5
4. a. 5 b. 3 c. 1   5. a. 1 b. 3 c. 5   6. a. 5 b. 3 c. 1
7. a. 5 b. 3 c. 1   8. a. 5 b. 3 c. 1   9. a. 5 b. 3 c. 1
10. a. 5 b. 3 c. 1   11. a. 1 b. 3 c. 5

12 and 13: Give yourself 5 points each time the qualities you marked are a match:

a.____   b.____   c.____   d.____
e.____   f.____   g.____   h.____
i.____   j.____

14. a. 1 b. 3 c. 5   15. a. 3 b. 1 c. 5   16. a. 5 b. 3 c. 1
17. a. 5 b. 1 c. 3   18. a. 5 b. 1 c. 3   19. a. 3 b. 5 c. 1
20. a. 5 b. 3 c. 1   21. a. 3 b. 1 c. 5   22. a. 1 b. 5 c. 3
23. a. 5 b. 3 c. 1   24. a. 1 b. 5 c. 3   25. a. 1 b. 5 c. 3
26. a. 3 b. 1 c. 5   27. a. 3 b. 1 c. 5   28. a. 1 b. 3 c. 5
29. a. 5 b. 1 c. 3   30. a. 1 b. 3 c. 5

INTERPRETATION

How did you score? Low scores range between 28 and 80, average scores fall between 81 and 150, and high scores are 151 and above.

LOW SCORERS (28–80): Your score suggests that you are dissatisfied with your current job, but it does not suggest *why*.

Examine your situation and ask yourself whether your dissatisfaction is related to factors such as a mismatch of your personal characteristics and the behaviors required by the job or personal conflicts with a supervisor. If you suspect a mismatch between your traits and the job requirements, vocational testing and counseling may be of help. If interpersonal problems or other factors are preventing you from finding satisfaction with your work, you may be interested in pursuing methods of conflict resolution discussed in Chapter 12 or other solutions. Why not share your concerns with a counselor, a trusted coworker, or a family member?

AVERAGE SCORERS (81–150): Your level of job satisfaction is about average. Perhaps you would like better pay, a bit less job-related stress, and some more appreciation, but by and large your job seems to provide you with some social and/or personal benefits in addition to the paycheck.

HIGH SCORERS (151 and above): Your job seems to be a source of great satisfaction to you. You apparently enjoy the daily ins and outs of your work, get along with most of your colleagues, and feel that what you are doing is right for you. If something is lacking in your life, it probably is not to be found in the job. On the other hand, is it possible that your commitment to your work is interfering with your development of a fully satisfying family and leisure life?

References

AAUW (1992). See American Association of University Women.

Abbasi, S. M., & Hollman, K. W. (2000). Turnover: The real bottom line. *Public Personnel Management, 29,* 333–342.

Abbott, R. D., White, L. R., Ross, G. W., Masaki, K. H., Curb, J. D., & Petrovitch, H. (2004). Walking and dementia in physically capable elderly men. *Journal of the American Medical Association, 292,* 1447–1453.

Abell, J., Locke, A., Condor, S., Gibson, S., & Stevenson, C. (2006). Trying similarity, doing difference: The role of interviewer self-disclosure in interview talk with young people. *Qualitative Research, 6,* 221–244.

Abramson, L. T., Seligman, M. E. P., & Teasdale, J. D. (1978). Learned helplessness in humans: Critique and reformulation. *Journal of Abnormal Psychology, 87,* 49–74.

Aboa-Éboulé, C., Brisson, C., Maunsell, E., Mâsse, B., Bourbonnais, R., Vézina, M., et al. (2007). Job strain and risk of acute recurrent coronary heart disease events. *Journal of the American Medical Association, 298,* 1652–1660.

Aboud, F. E. (2003). The formation of in-group favoritism and out-group prejudice in young children: Are they distinct attitudes? *Developmental Psychology, 39,* 48–60.

Abramowitz, J. S., Olatunji, B. O., & Deacon, B. J. (2008). Health anxiety, hypochondriasis, and the anxiety disorders. *Behavior Therapy, 38,* 86–94.

Adams, H., & Phillips, L. (2006). Experiences of two-spirit lesbian and gay Native Americans: An argument for standpoint theory in identity research. *Identity, 6,* 273–291.

Adelson, A. (1990, November 19). Study attacks women's roles in TV. *New York Times,* p. C18.

Ader, R., Felten, D. L., & Cohen, N. (Eds.). (2001). *Psychoneuroimmunology* (3rd ed.). San Diego: Academic Press.

Adler, J., & Raymond, J. (2001, Fall/Winter). Fight back, with sweat. *Newsweek* [Special Issue], pp. 35–41.

Aleksander, P. J. E., West, B. J., Ryan, A. M., &. DeShon, R. P. (2002). The use of impression management tactics in structured interviews: A function of question type? *Journal of Applied Psychology, 87*(6), 1200–1208.

Alexander, K. (2003, March 18). Retired, but still on the job. *New York Times,* pp. G1, G8.

Alexander, M. (2007, October). Deadly distraction. *Reader's Digest,* 92–105.

Allport, G. W. (1954). *The nature of prejudice.* Reading, MA: Addison-Wesley.

Alterman, E. (1997, November). Sex in the '90s. *Elle,* pp. 128–134.

Alzheimer's cases may quadruple by 2050. (2007, June 11). *Associated Press News Release.* Retrieved June 26, 2007, from *http://news.aol.com/top-news/articles/a/alzheimers-cases-may-quadruple-by-2050/n20070610021509990003*

Amato, P. R. (2006). Marital discord, divorce, and children's well-being: Results from a 20-year longitudinal study of two generations. In A. Clarke-Stewart & J. Dunn (Eds.), *Families count: Effects on child and adolescent development. The Jacobs Foundation series on adolescence* (pp. 179–202). Cambridge, UK: Cambridge University Press.

American Association of University Women (AAUW) (1992). *How schools shortchange women: The A.A.U.W. report.* Washington, DC: A.A.U.W. Educational Foundation.

American Cancer Society. (2005a). *Signs and symptoms of cancer, what are symptoms and signs? Detailed guide: Cancer (general information).* American Cancer Society: Author.

American Cancer Society. (2005b). *Can prostate cancer be prevented?* Retrieved November 12, 2005, from *http://www.cancer.org/docroot/cri/content/cri_2_4_2x_can_prostate_cancer_be_prevented_36.asp*

American College Health Association. (2005). National College Health Assessment (ACHA-NCHA), Spring 2003 Reference Group Report. *Journal of American College Health, 53,* 199–210.

American Heart Association. (2005). *High-protein diets.* Retrieved June 18, 2005, from *http://216.185.112.5/presenter.jhtml?identifier=11234*

American Lung Association. (2007). *Fact sheets.* Retrieved July 5, 2007, from *http://www.lungusa.org/*

American Psychiatric Association. (2000). *Diagnostic and statistical manual of mental disorders.* Washington, DC: Author.

American Psychological Association. (1998, March 16). *Sexual harassment: Myths and realities.* Retrieved March 19, 1998, from www.apa.org

American Psychological Association. (2006, March 4). *Americans engage in unhealthy behaviors to manage stress.* Retrieved March 15, 2006, from *http://apahelpcenter.mediaroom.com/index.php?s=press_releases &item=23*

American Psychological Association (APA) (2007a, October 25). *Stress a major health problem in the U.S., warns APA.* Retrieved October 26, 2007 from *http://www.apa.org/releases/stressproblem.html*

American Psychological Association. (2007b, October 24). *Stress in America Survey.* Retrieved December 14, 2008, from *http://74.125.45.104/search?q=cache:UAeL3kDHQdoJ:apahelpcenter. mediaroom.com/file.php/138/Stress%2Bin%2BAmerica%2BRE-PORT%2BFINAL.doc+Stress+in+America+Survey&hl=en&ct=clnk&c d=1&gl=us*

Americans engage in unhealthy behaviors to manage stress. (2006, March 4). *APA Press Release.* Retrieved March 15, 2006, from *http://apahelpcenter.mediaroom.com/index.php?s=press_releases&item=23*

Andersen, B. L., Yang, H.-C., Farrar, W. B., Golden-Kreutz, D. M., Emery, C. F., Thornton, L. M., et al. (2008). Psychologic intervention improves survival for breast cancer patients: A randomized clinical trial. *Cancer, 113,* 3450–3458.

Anderson, C. A., & DeNeve, K. M. (1992). Temperature, aggression, and the negative affect escape model. *Psychological Bulletin, 111,* 347–351.

Anderson, E. M., & Lambert, M. J. (2001). A survival analysis of clinically significant change in outpatient psychotherapy. *Journal of Clinical Psychology, 57,* 875–888.

Anderson, J. W., Liu, C., & Kryscio, R. J. (2008). Blood pressure response to transcendental meditation: A meta-analysis. *American Journal of Hypertension.* Retrieved June 14, 2008, from *http://www.nature.com/ajh/journal/v21/n3/abs/ajh200765a.html*

Anderson, S. E., Dallal, G. E., & Must, A. (2003). Relative weight and race influence average age at menarche: Results from two nationally representative surveys of US girls studied 25 years apart. *Pediatrics, 111,* 844–850.

Anderson, S. L., & Betz, N. E. (2001). Sources of social self-efficacy expectations: Their measurement and relation to career development. *Journal of Vocational Behavior, 58*(1), 98–117.

Andersson, G., Carlbring, P., Holmström, A., Sparthan, E., Furmark, T., et al. (2006). Internet-based self-help with therapist feedback and in vivo group exposure for social phobia: A randomized controlled trial. *Journal of Consulting and Clinical Psychology, 74,* 677–686.

Angier, N. (1998, September 1). Nothing becomes a man more than a woman's face. *New York Times,* p. F3.

Angier, N. (2003, February 25). Not just genes: Moving beyond nature vs. nurture. *New York Times,* pp. F1, F10.

Antill, J. K. (1983). Sex role complementarity versus similarity in married couples. *Journal of Personality and Social Psychology, 45,* 145–155.

Anton, R. F. (2008). Naltrexone for the management of alcohol dependence. *New England Journal of Medicine, 359,* 715–721.

APA Presidential Task Force on Evidence-Based Practice. (2006). Evidence-based practice in psychology. *American Psychologist, 61,* 271–285.

Arbona, C. (2000). Practice and research in career counseling and development. *Career Development Quarterly, 49,* 98–134.

Archer, J. (2004). Sex differences in aggression in real-world settings: A meta-analytic review. *Review of General Psychology, 8,* 291–322.

Areán, P. A., & Ayalon, L. (2005). Assessment and treatment of depressed older adults in primary care. *Clinical Psychology: Science and Practice, 12,* 321–335

Armeli, S., Carney. M. A., Tennen, H., Affleck, G., & O'Neil T.P. (2000). Stress and alcohol use: A daily process examination of the stressor/vulnerability model. *Journal of Personality and Social Psychology, 78,* 979–994.

Armfield, J. M. (2006). Cognitive vulnerability: A model of the etiology of fear. *Clinical Psychology Review, 26,* 746–768.

Arnett, J. J. (1999). Adolescent storm and stress, reconsidered. *American Psychologist, 54,* 317–326.

Arnett, J. J. (2000a). Emerging adulthood. *American Psychologist, 55,* 469–480.

Arnett, J. J. (2000b). High hopes in a grim world: Emerging adults' view of their futures and Generation X. *Youth & Society, 31,* 267–286.

Arnett, J. J. (2004). *Adolescence and emerging adulthood: A cultural approach* (2nd ed.). Upper Saddle River, NJ: Pearson/Prentice Hall.

Arthritis Foundation. (2000, April 6). Pain in America: Highlights from a Gallup survey. Retrieved October 30, 2006 from *http://www.arthritis.org/answers/sop_factsheet.asp.*

Asch, S. E. (1956). Studies of independence and conformity: I. A minority of one against a unanimous majority. *Psychological Monographs, 70,* 70.

Ashforth, B. E., & Saks, A. M. (2000). Personal control in organizations: A longitudinal investigation with newcomers. *Human Relations, 53,* 311–339.

Assad, K. K., Donnellan, M. B., & Conger, R. D. (2007). Optimism: An enduring resource for romantic relationships. *Journal of Personality and Social Psychology, 93,* 285–297.

Atchley, R. C. (1985). *Social forces and aging: An introduction to social gerontology.* Belmont, CA: Wadsworth.

Awad, G. H., & Ladhani, S. (2007). Review of counseling and psychotherapy with Arabs and Muslims: A culturally sensitive approach. *Cultural Diversity and Ethnic Minority Psychology, 13,* 374–375.

Babyak, M., Blumenthal, J. A., Herman, S., Khatri, P., Doraiswamy, M., Moore, K., et al. (2000). Exercise treatment for major depression: Maintenance of therapeutic benefit at 10 months. *Psychosomatic Medicine, 62,* 633–638.

Bach, P. B., Schrag, D., Brawley, O. W., Galaznik, A., Yakren, S., & Begg, C. B. (2003). Survival of blacks and whites after a cancer diagnosis. *Journal of the American Medical Association, 287,* 2106-–2113.

Bäckström T., et al. (2003). The role of hormones and hormonal treatments in premenstrual syndrome. *CNS Drugs, 17*(5), 325–342.

Bagley, C., & D'Augelli, A. R. (2000). Suicidal behaviour in gay, lesbian, and bisexual youth. *British Medical Journal, 320,* 1617–1618.

Bailey, D. S. (2003). The "Sylvia Plath" effect. *Monitor on Psychology, 34,* 42–43

Bailey, J. M. (1999). Homosexuality and mental illness. *Archives of General Psychiatry, 56*(10), 883–884.

Bailey, J. M., Dunne, M. P., & Martin, N. G. (2000). Genetic and environmental influences on sexual orientation and its correlates in an Australian twin sample. *Journal of Personality and Social Psychology, 78*(3), 524 536.

Bailey, J. M., & Pillard, R. C. (1991). A genetic study of male sexual orientation. *Archives of General Psychiatry, 48,* 1089–1096.

Baillargeon, R. H., Zoccolillo, M., Keenan, K., Côté, S., Pérusse, D., Wu, H.-Z., et al. (2007). Gender differences in physical aggression: A prospective population-based survey of children before and after 2 years of age. *Developmental Psychology, 43,* 13–26.

Baker, C. W., Whisman, M. A., & Brownell, K. D. (2000). Studying intergenerational transmission of eating attitudes and behaviors: Methodological and conceptual questions. *Health Psychology, 19*(4), 376–381.

Baker, F., Ainsworth, S. R., Dye, J. T., Crammer, C., Thun, M. J., Hoffman, D., et al. (2000). Health risks associated with cigar smoking. *Journal of the American Medical Association, 284,* 735–740.

Bakker, A. B., & Schaufeli, W. B. (2000). Burnout contagion processes among teachers. *Journal of Applied Social Psychology, 30,* 2289–2308.

Baldwin, S. A., Wampold, B. E., & Imel, Z. E. (2007). Untangling the alliance-outcome correlation: Exploring the relative importance of therapist and patient variability in the alliance. *Journal of Consulting and Clinical Psychology, 75,* 842–852.

Ballie, R (2002, January). Kay Redfield Jamison receives $500,000 "genius award." *Monitor on Psychology.* Retrieved March, 15, 2003, from *http://www.apa.org/monitor/jan02/redfield.html*

Balsam, K. F., Beauchaine, T. P., Mickey, R. M., & Rothblum, E. D. (2005). Mental health of lesbian, gay, bisexual, and heterosexual siblings: Effects of gender, sexual orientation, and family. *Journal of Abnormal Psychology, 114,* 471–476.

Balsam, K. F., Huang, B. U., Fieland, K. C., Simonikarina, J. M., & Walters, K. (2004). Culture, trauma, and wellness: A comparison of heterosexual and lesbian, gay, bisexual, and two-spirit Native Americans. *Cultural Diversity & Ethnic Minority Psychology, 10,* 287–301.

Baltes, B. B., Briggs, T. E., Huff, J. W., Wright, J. A., & Neuman, G. A. (1999). Flexible and compressed workweek schedules: A meta-analysis of their effects on work-related criteria. *Journal of Applied Psychology, 84*(4), 496–513.

Baltes, P. B. (1997). On the incomplete architecture of human ontogeny: Selection, optimization, and compensation as foundation of developmental theory. *American Psychologist, 52,* 366–380.

Bandelow, B., Wedekind, D., Sandvoss, V., Broocks, A., Hajak, G., Pauls, J., et al. (2000). Salivary cortisol in panic attacks. *American Journal of Psychiatry, 157,* 454–456.

Bandura, A. (1986). *Social foundations of thought and action: A social-cognitive theory.* Englewood Cliffs, NJ: Prentice-Hall.

Bandura, A. (1999). Social cognitive theory: An agentic perspective. *Asian Journal of Social Psychology, 2*(1), 21–41.

Bandura, A. (2004). Swimming against the mainstream: The early years from chilly tributary to transformative mainstream. *Behaviour Research and Therapy, 42,* 613–630.

Bandura, A., Blanchard, E. B., & Ritter, B. (1969). The relative efficacy of desensitization and modeling approaches for inducing behavioral, affective, and cognitive changes. *Journal of Personality and Social Psychology, 13,* 173–199.

Bandura, A., & Bussey, K. (2004). On broadening the cognitive, motivational, and sociostructural scope of theorizing about gender development and functioning: Comment on Martin, Ruble, and Szkrybalo (2002). *Psychological Bulletin, 130,* 691–701.

Bandura, A., & Locke, E. A. (2003). Negative self-efficacy and goal effects revisited. *Journal of Applied Psychology, 88,* 87–89.

Bandura, A., Pastorelli, C., Barbaranelli, C., & Caprara, G. V. (1999). Self-efficacy pathways to childhood depression. *Journal of Personality & Social Psychology, 76,* 258–269.

Bank, B. J., & Hansford, S. L. (2000). Gender and friendship: Why are men's best same-sex friendships less intimate and supportive? *Personal Relationships, 7,* 63–78.

Banks, S. M., et al. (1995). The effects of message framing on mammography utilization. *Health Psychology, 14,* 178–184.

Bar, M., Neta, M., & Linz, H. (2006). Very first impressions. *Emotion, 6,* 269–278.

Barbaree, H. E., & Marshall, W. L. (1991). The role of male sexual arousal in rape: Six models. *Journal of Consulting and Clinical Psychology, 59,* 621–631.

Barch, D. M., & Csernansky, J. G. (2007). Abnormal parietal cortex activation during working memory in schizophrenia: Verbal phonological coding disturbances versus domain-general executive dysfunction. *American Journal of Psychiatry, 164,* 1090–1098.

Barnes, G. G. (2005). Divorcing children: Children's experience of their parent's divorce. *Child & Adolescent Mental Health, 10*(1), 47.

Barnes, V. A., Treiber, F. A., & Johnson, M. H. (2004). Impact of transcendental meditation on ambulatory blood pressure in African-American adolescents. *American Journal of Hypertension, 17,* 366–369.

Baron, R. A. (1983). *Behavior in organizations.* Boston: Allyn & Bacon.

Baron, R. A., & Byrne, D. (2000). *Social psychology: Understanding human interaction* (9th ed.). Boston: Allyn & Bacon.

Barrett, M. B. (1990). *Invisible lives: The truth about millions of women-loving women.* New York: Harper & Row.

Barrett, M. B. (1990). *Invisible lives: The truth about millions of women-loving women.* New York: Harper & Row (Perennial Library).

Barrett, S. E., Chin, J. L., Comas-Diaz, L., Espin, O., Greene, B., & McGoldrick, M. (2005). Multicultural feminist therapy: Theory in context. *Women & Therapy, 28*(3–4), 27–61.

Barry, D. T., & Grilo, C. M. (2002). Cultural, psychological, and demographic correlates of willingness to use psychological services among East Asian immigrants. *Journal of Nervous and Mental Disease, 190,* 32–39.

Barsky, A. J., Ahern, D. K., Bailey, E. D., Saintfort, R., Liu, E. B., & Peekna, H. M. (2003). Hypochondriacal patients' appraisal of health and physical risks. *American Journal of Psychiatry, 158,* 783–787.

Barsky, A. J., & Ahern, D. K. (2004). Cognitive behavior therapy for hypochondriasis: A randomized controlled trial. *Journal of the American Medical Association, 291,* 1464–1470.

Bartzokis, G., Lu, P. H., Geschwind, D. H., Edwards, N., Mintz, J., &. Cummings, J. L. (2006). Apolipoprotein e genotype and age-related myelin breakdown in healthy individuals: Implications for cognitive decline and dementia. *Archives of General Psychiatry, 63,* 63–72.

Basch, M. F. (1980). *Doing psychotherapy.* New York: Basic Books.

Batson, C. D., & Powell, A. A. (2003). Altruism and prosocial behavior. In T. Millon & M. J. Lerner (Eds.), *Handbook of psychology: Personality and social psychology.* (Vol. 5, pp. 463–484). New York: Wiley.

Baucom, D. H., & Aiken, P. A. (1984). Sex role identity, marital satisfaction, and response to behavioral marital therapy. *Journal of Consulting and Clinical Psychology, 52,* 438–444.

Baucom, D. H., & Danker-Brown, P. (1983). Peer ratings of males and females possessing different sex-role identities. *Journal of Personality Assessment, 47,* 494–506.

Baum, A. E., Akula, N., Cabanero, M., Cardona, I., Corona, W., Klemens, B., et al. (2007). A genome-wide association study implicates diacylglycerol kinase eta (DGKH) and several other genes in the etiology of bipolar disorder. *Molecular Psychiatry.* Retrieved June 22, 2007, from *http://www.ncbi.nlm.nih.gov/sites/entrez?cmd=Retrieve&db=PubMed& list_uids=17486107&dopt=Abstract*

Baumrind, D. (1973). The development of instrumental competence through socialization. In A. D. Pick (Ed.), *Minnesota Symposia on Child Development* (Vol. 7). Minneapolis: University of Minnesota Press.

Baumrind, D. (1991a). The influence of parenting style on adolescent competence and substance abuse. *Journal of Early Adolescence, 11,* 56–95.

Baumrind, D. (1991b). Parenting styles and adolescent development. In J. Brooks-Gunn, R. Lerner, & A. C. Petersen (Eds.), *Encyclopedia of Adolescence* (Vol. 2). New York: Garland.

Beck, A. T. (2005). The current state of cognitive therapy: A 40-year retrospective. *Archives of General Psychiatry, 62,* 953–959.

Beck, A. T., & Weishaar, M. E. (2008). Cognitive therapy. In R. J. Corsini & D. Wedding (Eds.), *Current psychotherapies* (8th ed., pp. 263–294). Belmont, CA: Thomson Higher Education.

Beck, A. T., Rush, A. J., Shaw, B. F., & Emery, G. (1979). *Cognitive therapy of depression.* New York: Guilford Press.

Beekman, A. T. F., Geerlings, S. W., Deeg, D. J. H., Smit, J. H., Schoevers, R. S., de Beurs, E., et al. (2002). The natural history of late-life depression: A 6-year prospective study in the community. *Archives of General Psychiatry, 59,* 605–611.

Beevers, C. G., Wells, T. T., & Miller, I. W. (2007). Predicting response to depression treatment: The role of negative cognition. *Journal of Consulting and Clinical Psychology, 75,* 422–431.

Beier, D. R., & Dluhy, R. G. (2003). Bench and bedside — the g protein-coupled receptor GPR54 and puberty. *New England Journal of Medicine, 349,* 1589–1592.

Beilock, S. L., Carr, T. H., MacMahon, C., & Starkes, J. L. (2002). When paying attention becomes counterproductive: impact of divided versus skill-focused attention on novice and experienced performance of sensorimotor skills. *Journal of Experimental Psychology-Applied, 8,* 6–16.

Beitman, B. D., Goldfried, M. R., & Norcross, J. C. (1989). The movement toward integrating the psychotherapies: An overview. *American Journal of Psychiatry, 146,* 138–147.

Bell, K. M., & Naugle, A. E. (2008). Intimate partner violence theoretical considerations: Moving towards a contextual framework. *Clinical Psychology Review, 28,* 1096–1107.

Bell, P. A. (2005). Reanalysis and perspective in the heat-aggression debate. *Journal of Personality and Social Psychology, 89,* 71–73.

Belluck, P. (2003, February 9). Methadone, once the way out, suddenly grows as a killer drug. *New York Times,* pp. A1, A30.

Belmaker, R. H., & Agam, G. (2008). Major depressive disorder. *New England Journal of Medicine, 35,* 55–68.

Belsky, J. (1993). Etiology of child maltreatment. *Psychological Bulletin, 114,* 413–434.

Bem, S. L. (1993). *The lenses of gender.* New Haven, CT: Yale University Press.

Benight, C. C., & Bandura, A. (2004). Social cognitive theory of posttraumatic recovery: The role of perceived self-efficacy. *Behaviour Research and Therapy, 10,,* 1129–1148.

Benincasa, R. (2008, November 13). Fewer than 1 in 5 U.S. adults now smoke. *NPR.org.* Retrieved November 16, 2008, from *http://www.npr.org/templates/story/story.php?storyId=96950224*

Benjamin, J., Ebstein, R., & Belmaker, R. (Eds.). (2002). *Molecular genetics and the human personality.* Washington, DC: American Psychiatric Publishing.

Benson, E. (2002, October). Pheromones, in context. *Monitor on Psychology, 33,* p. 46.

Benotsch, E. G., Kalichman, S., & Weinhardt, L. S. (2004). HIV–AIDS patients' evaluation of health information on the Internet: The digital divide and vulnerability to fraudulent claims. *Journal of Consulting and Clinical Psychology, 72,* 1004–1011.

Berdahl, J. L., & Moore, C. (2006). Workplace harassment: Double jeopardy for minority women. *Journal of Applied Psychology, 91,* 426–436.

Berenbaum, S. A., & Bailey, J. M. (2003). Effects on gender identity of prenatal androgens and genital appearance: Evidence from girls with congenital adrenal hyperplasia. *Journal of Clinical Endocrinology and Metabolism, 88,* 1102–1106.

Berenson, A. (2007, September 3). Schizophrenia medicine shows promise in trial. *New York Times,* p. A9.

Berger, L. E., Jodl, K. M., Allen, J. P., McElhaney, K. B., & Kuperminc, G. P. (2005). When adolescents disagree with others about their symptoms: Differences in attachment organization as an explanation of discrepancies between adolescent, parent, and peer reports of behavior problems. *Development and Psychopathology, 17,* 509–528.

Berke, R. L. (1997, June 15). Suddenly, the new politics of morality. *New York Times,* p. E3.

Berle, D., Starcevic, V., Hannan, A., Milicevica, D., Lamplugh, C., & Fenech, P. (2008). Cognitive factors in panic disorder, agoraphobic avoidance and agoraphobia. *Behaviour Research and Therapy, 46,* 282–291.

Berman, J. R., Berman, L. A., Toler, S. M., Gill, J., Haughie, S., & Sildenafil Study Group. (2003). Safety and efficacy of sildenafil citrate for the treatment of female sexual arousal disorder: A double-blind, placebo controlled study. *Journal of Urology, 170,* 2333–2338.

Bernal, M., Haro, J. M., Bernert, S., Brugha, T., de Graaf, R., Bruffaerts, R., et al. (2007). Risk factors for suicidality in Europe: Results from the ESEMED study. *Journal of Affective Disorders, 101,* 27–34.

Bernardin, H. J., Cooke, D. K., & Villanova, P. (2000). Conscientiousness and agreeableness as predictors of rating leniency. *Journal of Applied Psychology, 85,* 232–236.

Bernat, J. A., Wilson, A. E., & Calhoun, K. S. (1999). Sexual coercion history, calloused sexual beliefs and judgments of sexual coercion in a date rape analogue. *Violence and Victims, 14(2),* 147–160.

Berndt, T. J. (1982). The features and effects of friendships in early adolescence. *Child Development, 53,* 1447–1460.

Berne, E, (1976). *Games people play.* New York: Ballantine Books.

Berscheid, E., & Reis, H. T. (1998). Attraction and close relationships. In D. T. Gilbert, S. T., Fiske, et al. (Eds.), The *handbook of social psychology, Vol. 2* (4th ed.). (pp. 193–281). New York: McGraw-Hill.

Berzins, J. I., Welling, M. A., & Wetter, R. E. (1977). The PRF ANDRO Scale: User's manual. Unpublished manuscript: University of Kentucky.

Bettencourt, B. A., Dorr, N., Charlton, K., & Hume, D. L. (2001). Status differences and in-group bias: A meta-analytic examination of the effects of status stability, status legitimacy, and group permeability. *Psychological Bulletin, 127,* 520–542.

Beyer, S., Rynes, K., Perrault, J., Hay, K., & Haller, S. (2003). Gender differences in computer science students. *Proceedings of the Thirty-Fourth SIGCSE Technical Symposium on Computer Science Education* (pp. 49–53). New York. ACM.

Billings, D. W., Folkman, S., Acree, M., & Moskowitz, J. T. (2000). Coping and physical health during caregiving: The roles of positive and negative affect. *Journal of Personality and Social Psychology, 79*(1), 131–142.

Birch, C. D., Stewart, S. H., & Brown, C. G. (2007). Exploring differential patterns of situational risk for binge eating and heavy drinking. *Addictive Behaviors, 32*, 433–448.

Birnbaum, M. H., Martin, H., & Thomann, K. (1996). Visual function in multiple personality disorder. *Journal of the American Optometric Association, 67*, 327–334.

Bjerklie, D. (2005, January 17). Can sunny thoughts halt cancer? *Time*, p. A14.

Bjorklund, D. F., & Kipp, K. (1996). Parental investment theory and gender differences in the evolution of inhibition mechanisms. *Psychological Bulletin, 120*, 163–188.

Blair, S. N., & Church, T. S. (2004). The fitness, obesity, and health equation: Is physical activity the common denominator? *Journal of the American Medical Association, 292*, 1232–1234.

Blanchard, E. B., & Hickling, E. J. (2004). *After the crash: Psychological assessment and treatment of survivors of motor vehicle accidents*. (2nd ed.). Washington, DC: American Psychological Association.

Blass, T. (2004). *The man who shocked the world*. New York: Basic Books.

Blatt, S. J., Quinlan, D. M., Pilkonis, P. A., & Shea, M. T. (1995). Impact of perfectionism and need for approval on the brief treatment of depression: The National Institutes of Mental Health Treatment of Depression Collaborative Research Program revisited. *Journal of Consulting and Clinical Psychology, 63*, 125–132.

Blumenthal, J. A., Sherwood, A., Babyak, M. A., Watkins, L. L., Waugh, R., Georgiades, A., et al. (2005). Effects of exercise and stress management training on markers of cardiovascular risk in patients with ischemic heart disease: A randomized controlled trial. *Journal of the American Medical Association, 293*, 1626–1634.

Bogg, T., & Roberts, B. W. (2004). Conscientiousness and health-related behaviors: A meta-analysis of the leading behavioral contributors to mortality. *Psychological Bulletin, 130*, 887–919.

Booth, A., & Edwards, J. N. (1985). Age at marriage and marital instability. *Journal of Marriage and the Family, 47*, 67–75.

Borges, G., Angst, J., Nock, M. K., Rusciof, Y. M., & Kessler, R. C. (2008). Risk factors for the incidence and persistence of suicide-related outcomes: A 10-year follow-up study using the National Comorbidity Surveys. *Journal of Affective Disorders, 105*, 25–33.

Borjesson, M., & Dahlof, B. (2005). Physical activity has a key role in hypertension therapy. *Lakartidningen, 102*, 123–124, 126, 128–129.

Boskind-White, M., & White, W. C. (1983). *Bulimarexia: The binge/purge cycle*. New York: Norton.

Boston Women's Health Book Collective. (1993). *The new our bodies, ourselves*. New York: Simon and Schuster.

Bouchard, T. J., Jr. (2004). Genetic influence on human psychological traits. *Current Directions in Psychological Science, 13*, 148–151.

Boyatzis, R. E. (1974). The effect of alcohol consumption on the aggressive behavior of men. *Quarterly Journal of Studies on Alcohol, 35*, 929–972.

Bowen, C.-C., Swim, J. K., & Jacobs, R. R. (2000). Evaluating gender biases on actual job performance of real people: A meta-analysis. *Journal of Applied Social Psychology, 30*, 2194–2215.

Bowling, N. A., Beehr, T. A., Wagner, S. H., & Libkuman, T. M. (2005). Adaptation-level theory, opponent process theory, and dispositions: An integrated approach to the stability of job satisfaction. *Journal of Applied Psychology, 90*, 1044–1053.

Boyd-Franklin, N. (1995, August). *A multisystems model for treatment interventions with inner-city African American families*. Master lecture delivered at the annual meeting of the American Psychological Association, New York.

Boykin, A. W., & Ellison, C. M. (1995). The multiple ecologies of black youth socialization: An Afrographic analysis. In R. L. Taylor (Ed.), *African American youth: Their social and economic status in the United States*. (pp. 93–128) Westport, CT: Praeger.

Boyle, S. H., Jackson, W. G., &. Suarez, E. C. (2007). Hostility, anger, and depression predict increases in C3 over a 10-year period. *Brain, Behavior, and Immunity, 21*, 816–823.

Boynton, R. S. (2004, January 11). In the Jung archives. *New York Times Book Review*, p. 8.

Bradley, R., Greene, J., Russ, E., Dutra, L., & Westen, D. (2005). A multidimensional meta-analysis of psychotherapy for PTSD. *American Journal of Psychiatry, 162*, 214–227.

Bradshaw, J. (2008, July/August). Consulting authority expanding for RxP psychologist. *National Psychologist*, p. 7.

Braff, D., Schork, N. J., &. Gottesman, I. I. (2007). Endophenotyping schizophrenia. *American Journal of Psychiatry, 164*, 705–707.

Bramlett, M. D., & Mosher, W. D. (2002). *Cohabitation, marriage, divorce, and remarriage*. National Center for Health Statistics, Vital Health Statistics, 23(22). *http://www.cdc.gov/nchs/data/series/sr_23/sr23_022.pdf*.

Braun, B. G. (1988). *Treatment of multiple personality disorder*. Washington, DC: American Psychiatric Press.

Brehm, S. S. (2008). Looking ahead: The future of psychology and APA. *American Psychologist, 63*, 337–344.

Breitenbecher, K., H. (2000). Sexual assault on college campuses: Is an ounce of prevention enough? *Applied and Preventive Psychology, 9*, 23–52.

Brener, N. D., McMahon, P. M., Warren, C. W., & Douglas, K. A. (1999). Forced sexual intercourse and associated health-risk behaviors among female college students in the United States. *Journal of Consulting and Clinical Psychology, 67*, 252–259.

Brewer, M. B., & Brown, R. J. (1998). Intergroup relations. In D. T. Gilbert, S. T. Fiske, & G. Lindzey (Eds.), *The handbook of social psychology* (4th ed., Vol. 2, pp. 554–594). Boston: McGraw-Hill.

Brewer, R. D., & Swahn, M. H. (2005). Binge drinking and violence. *Journal of the American Medical Association, 294*, 616–618.

Bridge, J. A., Iyengar, S., Salary, C. B., Barbe, R. P., Birmaher, B., Pincus, H. A., et al. (2007). Clinical response and risk for reported suicidal ideation and suicide attempts in pediatric antidepressant treatment: A meta-analysis of randomized controlled trials. *Journal of the American Medical Association, 297*, 1683–1696.

Brinkhaus, B., Witt, C. M., Jena, S., Linde, K., Streng, A., Wagenpfeil, S., et al. (2006). Acupuncture in patients with chronic low back pain: A randomized controlled trial. *Archives of Internal Medicine, 166*, 450–457.

Brody, J. E. (1996b, September 4). Osteoporosis can threaten men as well as women. *New York Times*, p. C9.

Brody, J. E. (2000, May 16). Cybersex gives birth to a psychological disorder. *New York Times*, pp. F7, F12.

Brown, D. (2002). Introduction to theories of career development and choice: Origins, evolution, and current efforts. In D. Brown & Associates (Eds.), *Career choice and development* (4th ed.) (pp. 3–23). San Francisco: Jossey-Bass.

Brown, G. R., & Haaser, R. C. (2005). Sexual disorders. In Levenson, J. L. (Ed.). *The American psychiatric publishing textbook of psychosomatic medicine* (pp. 359–386). Washington, DC: American Psychiatric Publishing, Inc.

Brown, M. J. (2006). Hypertension and ethnic group. *British Medical Journal, 332*, 833–836.

Brown, S. L., Nesse, R. M., Vinokur, A. D., & Smith, D. M. (2003). Providing social support may be more beneficial than receiving it: Results from a prospective study of mortality. *Psychological Science, 14*, 320–327.

Bruce, M. L., Ten Have, T. R., Reynolds, C. F., III, Katz, I. I., Schulberg, H. C., Mulsant, B. H., Brown, G. K., et al. (2004). Reducing suicidal ideation and depressive symptoms in depressed older primary care patients: A randomized controlled trial. *Journal of the American Medical Association, 291*, 1081–1091.

Bryant, A., & Check, E. (2000, Fall/Winter). How parents raise boys & girls. A sense of self. *Newsweek* [Special Issue], 64–65.

Buchanan, C. M., Eccles, J. S., & Becker, J. B. (1992). Are adolescents the victims of raging hormones? Evidence for activational effects of hormones on moods and behavior at adolescence. *Psychological Bulletin, 111*, 62–107.

Buchanan, N. T., & Fitzgerald, L. F. (2008). Effects of racial and sexual harassment on work and the psychological well-being of African American women. *Journal of Occupational Health Psychology, 13*, 137–151.

Budney, A. J., Vandrey, R. G., Hughes, J. R., Moore, B. A., & Bahrenburg, B. (2007). Oral delta-9tetrahydrocannabinol suppresses cannabis withdrawal symptoms. *Drug and Alcohol Dependence, 86*, 22–29.

Bulik, C. M., Sullivan, P. F., Tozzi, F., Furberg, H., Lichtenstein, P., & Pedersen, N. L. (2006). *Archives of General Psychiatry, 63,* 305–312.

Burger, J. M. (2009). Replicating Milgram: Would people still obey today? *American Psychologist, 64,* 1–11.

Burns, D. D. (1980). *Feeling good: The new mood therapy.* New York: Morris.

Burt, M. R. (1980). Cultural myths and supports for rape. *Journal of Personality and Social Psychology, 38,* 217–230.

Burton, C. M., & King, L. A. (2004). The health benefits of writing about intensely positive experiences. *Journal of Research in Personality, 38,* 150–163.

Burton, N., & Lane, R. C. (2001). The relational treatment of dissociative identity disorder. *Clinical Psychology Review, 21,* 301–320.

Buscemi, N., Vandermeer, B., Hooton, N., Pandya, R., Tjosvold, L., et al. (2006). Efficacy and safety of exogenous melatonin for secondary sleep disorders and sleep disorders accompanying sleep restriction: Meta-analysis. *British Medical Journal, 332,* 385–393.

Bushman, B. J., & Anderson, C. A. (2001). Media violence and the American public: Scientific facts versus media misinformation. *American Psychologist, 56,* 477–489.

Bushman, B. J., Wang, M. C., & Anderson, C. A. (2005). Is the curve relating temperature to aggression linear or curvilinear? Assaults and temperature in Minneapolis reexamined. *Journal of Personality and Social Psychology, 89,* 62–66.

Buss, D. (2005, January 23). Sure, come back to the nest. Here are the rules. *New York Times,* Section 3, p. 8.

Buss, D. M. (1994). *The evolution of desire: Strategies of human mating.* New York: Basic Books.

Buss, D. M. (2000). The evolution of happiness. *American Psychologist, 55,* 15–23.

Buston, P. M., & Emlen, S. T. (2003). Cognitive processes underlying human mate choice: The relationship between self-perception and mate preference in Western society. *Proceedings of the National Academy of Sciences, 100,* 8805–8810.

Butler, A. C., Chapman, J. E., Forman, E. M., & Beck, A. T. (2006). The empirical status of cognitive-behavioral therapy: A review of meta-analyses. *Clinical Psychology Review, 26,* 17–33.

Cacioppo, J. T., Hawkley, L. C., & Bernston, G. G. (2003). The anatomy of loneliness. *Current Directions in Psychological Science, 12*(3), 71–74.

Cale, E. M., & Lilienfeld, S. O. (2002). Sex differences in psychopathy and antisocial personality disorder. A review and integration. *Clinical Psychology Review, 22,* 1179–1207.

Camara, W. J., Nathan, J. S., & Puente, A. E. (2000). Psychological test usage: Implications in professional psychology. *Professional Psychology: Research and Practice, 31,* 141–154.

Campbell, W. K., Sedikides, C., Reeder, G. D., & Elliott, A. J. (2000). Among friends? An examination of friendship and the self-serving bias. *British Journal of Social Psychology, 39*(2), 229–239.

Canli, T., Desmond, J. E., Zhao, Z., & Gabrieli, J. D. E. (2002). Sex differences in the neural basis of emotional memories. *Proceedings of the National Academy of Sciences, 99*(16), 10789–10794.

Cannon, W. B. (1920). *Bodily changes in pain, hunger, fear, and rage.* New York: Appleton.

Carducci, B. J. (1999). *The pocket guide to making successful small talk: How to talk to anyone anytime anywhere about anything.* New Albany, IN: Pocket Guide Publishing.

Carducci, B. J. (2000a). *Shyness: A bold new approach.* New York: HarperCollins.

Carducci, B. J. (2000b, February). Shyness: The new solution. *Psychology Today, 33,* 38–40, 42–45, 78.

Carey, B. (2005, December 18). In-laws in the age of the outsider. *New York Times,* Section 4, pp. 1, 3.

Carlbring, P., Bohman, S., Brunt, S., Buhrman, M., Westling, B. E., Ekselius, L., et al. (2006). Remote treatment of panic disorder: A randomized trial of Internet-based cognitive behavior therapy supplemented with telephone calls. *American Journal of Psychiatry, 163,* 2119–2125.

Carmichael, M. (2003, May 5). The fat factor. *Newsweek,* p. 69.

Carnahan, I. (2005, June 6). Do-it-yourself retirement. *Forbes,* p. 93.

Carpenter, W. T., Jr., & Buchanan, R. W. (1994). Schizophrenia. *New England Journal of Medicine, 330,* 681–690.

Carrère, S., Buehlman, K. T., Gottman, J. M., Coan, J. A., & Ruckstuhl, L. (2000). Predicting marital stability and divorce in newlywed couples. *Journal of Family Psychology, 14*(1), 42–58.

Carroll, K. M., & Onken, L. S. (2005). Behavioral therapies for drug abuse. *American Journal of Psychiatry, 162,* 1452–1460.

Carstensen, L. (1997, August 17). *The evolution of social goals across the life span.* Paper presented at the American Psychological Association, Chicago.

Carver, C. S., Smith, R. G., Antoni, M., Petronis, V. M., Weiss, S., & Derhagopian, R. P. (2005). Optimistic personality and psychosocial well-being during treatment predict psychosocial well-being among long-term survivors of breast cancer. *Health Psychology, 24,* 508–516.

Caspi, A., Roberts, B. W., & Shiner, R. L. (2005). Personality development: Stability and change. *Annual Review of Psychology, 56,* 453–484.

Cellar, D. F., Nelson, Z. C., & Yorke, C. M. (2000). The five-factor model and driving behavior: Personality and involvement in vehicular accidents. *Psychological Reports, 86*(2) 454–456.

Centers for Disease Control and Prevention (CDC). (2000b, June 9). Youth risk behavior surveillance—United States, 1999. *Morbidity and Mortality Weekly Report, 49*(SS05), 1–96.

Centers for Disease Control and Prevention (CDC). (2000c). Suicide in the United States. Retrieved November 30, 2000. from *http://www.cdc.gov/ncipc/factsheets/suifacts.htm*

Centers for Disease Control and Prevention (CDC). (2000e). *National Vital Statistics Reports, 48*(3).

Centers for Disease Control and Prevention (CDC). (2001, March 9.) Physical activity trends in the United States, 1990–1998. *Morbidity and Mortality Weekly Report 50,* 166–169.

Centers for Disease Control (CDC). (2009, January 13). *Annual CDC report finds high burden of sexually transmitted diseases, especially among women and racial minorities.* Retrieved January 13, 2009, from *http://www.cdc.gov/nchhstp/Newsroom/PressRelease011309.html*

Cepeda-Benito, A., Reynoso, J. T., & Erath, S. (2004). Meta-analysis of the efficacy of nicotine replacement. *Journal of Consulting and Clinical Psychology, 72,* 712–722.

Ceron-Litvoc, D., Soares, B. G., Geddes, J., Litvoc, J., & de Lima, M. S. (2009). Comparison of carbamazepine and lithium in treatment of bipolar disorder: A systematic review of randomized controlled trials. *Human Psychopharmacology: Clinical and Experimental, 24,* 19–28.

Chambers, C. (2000, October 143). *Americans are overwhelmingly happy and optimistic about the future of the U.S.* Princeton, NJ: Gallup News Service.

Chambless, D. L., et al. (1998, Winter). Update on empirically validated therapies, II. *Clinical Psychologist, 51,* 3–16.

Chambless, D. L., & Hollon, S. D. (1998). Defining empirically supported therapies. *Journal of Consulting and Clinical Psychology, 66,* 7–18.

Chambless, D. L., & Ollindick, T. H. (2001). Empirically supported psychological interventions: Controversies and evidence. *Annual Review of Psychology, 52,* 685–716.

Chamero, P., Marton, T. F., Logan, D. W., Flanagan, K., Cruz, J. R., Saghatelian, A., et al. (2007). Identification of protein pheromones that promote aggressive behavior. *Nature, 450,* 899–902.

Chamorro-Premuzic, T., & Furnham, A. (2003). Personality predicts academic performance: Evidence from two longitudinal university samples. *Journal of Research in Personality, 37,* 319–338.

Chang, E. C., & Asakawa, K. (2003). Cultural variations on optimistic and pessimistic bias for self versus a sibling: Is there evidence for self-enhancement in the West and for self-criticism in the East when the referent group is specified? *Journal of Personality and Social Psychology, 84,* 569–581.

Charney, D. S., Nemeroff, C. B., Lewis, L., Laden, S. K., Gorman, J. M., & Laska, E. M. (2003). National depressive and manic-depressive association consensus statement on the use of placebo in clinical trials of mood disorders. *Archives of General Psychiatry, 59,* 262–270.

Charney, D. S., Reynolds, C. F., III, Lewis, L., Lebowitz, B. D., Sunderland, T., Alexopoulos, G. S., et al. (2003). Depression and bipolar support alliance consensus statement on the unmet needs in diagnosis and treatment of mood disorders in late life [Review]. *Archives of General Psychiatry, 60,* 664–672.

Chen, J., Rathore, S. S., Radford, M. J., Wang, Y., & Krumholz, H. M. (2001). Racial differences in the use of cardiac catheterization after acute myocardial infarction. *New England Journal of Medicine, 344,* 1443–1449.

Cheng, H., & Furnham, A. (2002). Personality, peer relations, and self-confidence as predictors of happiness and loneliness. *Journal of Adolescence, 25,* 327–339.

Choi, I., Dalal, R., Kim-Prieto, C., & Park, H. (2003). Culture and judgment of causal relevance. *Journal of Personality and Social Psychology, 84,* 46–59.

Choy, Y., Fyer, A. J., & Lipsitz, J. D. (2007). Treatment of specific phobia in adults. *Clinical Psychology Review, 27,* 266–286.

Christakis, N. A., & Fowler, J. H. (2007). The spread of obesity in a large social network over 32 years. *New England Journal of Medicine, 357,* 370–379.

Christensen, A., Atkins, D. C., Berns, S., Wheeler, J., Baucom, D. H., & Simpson, L. E. (2004). Traditional versus integrative behavioral couple therapy for significantly and chronically distressed married couples. *Journal of Consulting and Clinical Psychology, 72,* 176–191.

Cialdini, R. B., & Goldstein, N. J. (2004). Social influence: Compliance and conformity. *Annual Review of Psychology, 55,* 591–621.

Cialdini, R. B., & Trost, M. R. (1998). Social influence: Social norms, conformity, and compliance. In D. T. Gilbert, S. T. Fiske, & G. Lindzey (Eds.), *The handbook of social psychology* (4th ed., Vol. 2, pp. 151–192). Boston: McGraw-Hill.

Cialdini, R. B., et al. (1999). Compliance with a request in two cultures: The differential influence of social proof and commitment/consistency on collectivists and individualists. *Personality & Social Psychology Bulletin, 25,* 1242–1253.

Cigars increase lung cancer risk fivefold study. (2000, February 15). *Reuters News Agency.* Retrieved February 23, 2006, from *http://www.cancer.org/docroot/NWS/content/NWS_1_1x_Cigars_Increase_Lung_Cancer_Risk_Five_Fold.asp*

Clancy, S. M., & Dollinger, S. J. (1993). Identity, self, and personality: I. Identity status and the five-factor model of personality. *Journal of Research on Adolescence, 3,* 227–245.

Clarke-Stewart, K. A., Vandell, D. L., McCartney, K., Owen, M. T., & Booth, C. (2000). Effects of parental separation and divorce on very young children. *Journal of Family Psychology, 14,* 304–326.

Clay, R. A. (2000). Staying in control. *Monitor on Psychology, 31*(1), 32–34.

Clay, R. A. (2009, April). The debate over low libidos. *Monitor on Psychology, 40,* pp. 32–35.

Clements, J. (2003, March 5). Working late: Your friends won't retire at age 65, but here's how you can. *Wall Street Journal,* p. D1.

Clingempeel, W. G., & Segal, S. (1986). Stepparent-stepchild relationships and the psychological adjustment of children in stepmother and stepfather families. *Child Development, 57,* 474–484.

Cocaine impairs brain's "pleasure circuits." (2003, January 1). *CNN.com.* Retrieved January 2, 2003, from *http://www.cnn.com/2003/HEALTH/01/01/cocaine.brain.ap/index.html*

Cochran, S. V., & Rabinowitz, F. E. (2003). Gender-sensitive recommendations for assessment and treatment of depression in men. *Professional Psychology: Research and Practice, 34,* 132–140.

Cockell, S. J., Hewitt, P. L., Seal, B., Sherry, S., Goldner, E. M., Flett, G. L., et al. (2002). Trait and self-presentational dimensions of perfectionism among women with anorexia nervosa. *Cognitive Therapy and Research, 26,* 745–758.

Coderre, T. J., Mogil, J. S., & Bushnell, M. C. (2003). The biological psychology of pain. In M. Gallagher & R. J. Nelson (Eds.), *Handbook of psychology: Vol. 3. Biological psychology* (pp. 237–268). New York: Wiley.

Cohan, C. L., & Kleinbaum, S. (2002). Toward a greater understanding of the cohabitation effect: Premarital cohabitation and marital communication. *Journal of Marriage and the Family, 64,* 180–192.

Cohen, J. (2001, July/August)). Time spent playing with peers influences gender-typed behaviors in young children. *Monitor on Psychology,* p. 17

Cohen, L. A. (1987, November). Diet and cancer. *Scientific American,* pp. 42–48, 533–534.

Cohen, S., Doyle, W. J., Skoner, D. P., Rabin, B. S., Gwaltney, J. M., Jr., et al. (1997). Social ties and susceptibility to the common cold. *Journal of the American Medical Association, 277,* 1940–1944.

Cohen, S., Janicki-Deverts, D., & Miller, G. E. (2007). Psychological stress and disease. *Journal of the American Medical Association, 298,* 1685–1687.

Cohen, S., & Williamson, G. M. (1991). Stress and infectious disease in humans. *Psychological Bulletin, 109,* 5–24.

Cohn, E. G. (1990). Weather and violent crime. *Environment and Behavior, 22,* 280–294.

Cohn, E. G., & Rotton, J. (2000). Weather, seasonal trends, and property crimes in Minneapolis, 1987–1988. A moderator-variable time-series analysis of routine activities. *Journal of Environmental Psychology, 20*(3), 257–272.

Coleman, L. (1990). Cited in D. Goleman (1990, August 2). The quiet comeback of electroshock therapy. *New York Times,* p. B5.

Coleman, M., & Ganong, L. H. (1985). Love and sex role stereotypes: Do macho men and feminine women make better lovers? *Journal of Personality and Social Psychology, 49,* 170–176.

Collaer, M. L., & Hill, E. M. (2006). Large sex difference in adolescents on a timed line judgment task: Attentional contributors and task relationship to mathematics. *Perception, 35,* 561–572.

Collaer, M. L., & Hines, M. (1995). Human behavioral sex differences: A role for gonadal hormones during early development? *Psychological Bulletin, 118,* 55–107.

Collins, J. F. (2000). Biracial Japanese American identity: An evolving process. *Cultural Diversity & Ethnic Minority Psychology, 6,* 115–133.

Collins, L. (2004). We are not gay. In K. K. Kumashiro (Ed.), *Restoried selves: Autobiographies of queer Asian/Pacific American activists* (pp. 13–17). New York: Harrington Park Press/Haworth Press.

Collishaw, S., Pickles, A., Messer, J., Rutter, M, Shearer, C., & Maughan, B. (2008). Resilience to adult psychopathology following childhood maltreatment: Evidence from a community sample. *Child Abuse & Neglect, 31,* 211–229.

Coltraine, S., & Messineo, M. (2000). The perpetuation of subtle prejudice: Race and gender imagery in 1990s television advertising. *Sex Roles, 42,* 363–389.

Comas-Diaz, L. (2006). The present and future of clinical psychology in private practice. *Clinical Psychology: Science and Practice, 13,* 273–277.

Conkle, A., & West, C. (2008, June/July). *APS Observer, 21,* 18–23.

Conlin, M. (2003, January 27). Look who's bringing home more bacon. *Business Week,* p. 85.

Contrada, R. J., & Guyll, M. (2001). On who gets sick and why: The role of personality and stress. In A. Baum, T. A. Revenson, & J. E. Singer (Eds), *Handbook of health psychology* (pp. 59–84). Mahwah, NJ: Erlbaum.

Conway, K. P., Compton, W., Stinson, F. S., & Grant, B. F. (2006). Lifetime comorbidity of DSM-IV mood and anxiety disorders and specific drug use disorders: Results from the National Epidemiologic Survey on Alcohol and Related Conditions. *Journal of Clinical Psychiatry, 67,* 247–257.

Cooper, A., Delmonico, D. L., & Burg, R. (2000). Cybersex users, abusers, and compulsives: New findings and implications. *Sexual Addiction & Compulsivity, 7,* 5–29.

Cooper, A., Delmonico, D. L., Griffin-Shelley, E., & Mathy, R. M. (2004). Online sexual activity: An examination of potentially problematic behaviors. *Sexual Addiction & Compulsivity, 11,* 129–143.

Cooper, A., Scherer, C. R., Boies, S. C., & Gordon, B. L. (1999). Sexuality on the Internet: From sexual exploration to pathological expression. *Professional Psychology: Research & Practice, 30*(2), 154–164.

Coopersmith, S. (1967). *The antecedents of self esteem.* San Francisco: Freeman.

Corliss, R. (2003, January 20). Is there a formula for joy? *Time,* pp. 44–46.

Cororve, M. B., & Gleaves, D. H. (2001). Body dysmorphic disorder: A review of conceptualizations, assessment, and treatment strategies. *Clinical Psychology Review, 21,* 949–970.

Corr, P. J., & Jackson, C. J. (2001). Dimensions of perceived sexual harassment: Effects of gender, and status/liking of protagonist. *Personality & Individual Differences, 30*(3), 525–539.

Cortina, L. M., & Wasti, S. A. (2005). Profiles in coping: responses to sexual harassment across persons, organizations, and cultures. *Journal of Applied Psychology, 90,* 182–192.

Coryell, W., Pine, D., Fyer, A., & Klein, D. (2006). Anxiety responses to CO_2 inhalation in subjects at high-risk for panic disorder. *Journal of Affective Disorders, 92,* 63–70.

Costa, P. T., & McCrae, R. R. (2006). Changes in personality and their origins: Comment on Roberts, Walton, and Viechtbauer (2006). *Psychological Bulletin, 132,* 26–28.

Costa, P., Jr., Terracciano, A., & McCrae, R. R. (2002). Gender differences in personality traits across cultures: Robust and surprising findings. *Journal of Personality and Social Psychology, 81,* 322–331.

Courtenay, W. H. (2000). Engendering health: A social constructionist examination of men's health beliefs and behaviors. *Psychology of Men & Masculinity, 1*(1), 4–15.

Couzin, J. (2006, April 13). Gene variant may boost obesity risk. *ScienceNOW Daily News.* Retrieved May 26, 2006, from *http://sciencenow.sciencemag.org/cgi/content/full/2006/413/1.*

Couzin, J. (2007, November 8). Deciphering an obesity gene. *ScienceNOW Daily News.* Retrieved November 10, 2007, from *http://sciencenow.sciencemag.org/cgi/content/full/2007/1108/1.*

Cramer, D. (2003). Facilitativeness, conflict, demand for approval, self-esteem, and satisfaction with romantic relationships. *Journal of Psychology, 137,* 85–98.

Cramer, P. (2000). Defense mechanisms in psychology today: Further processes for adaptation. *American Psychologist, 55,* 637–646.

Creed, F., & Barsky, A. (2004). A systematic review of the epidemiology of somatisation disorder and hypochondriasis. *Journal of Psychosomatic Research, 56,* 391–408.

Creed, P. A., Patton, W., & Prideaux, L-A. (2007). Predicting change over time in career planning and career exploration for high school students. *Journal of Adolescence, 30,* 377–392.

Crews, D. (1994). Animal sexuality. *Scientific American, 270*(1), 108–114.

Crockett, L. J., Iturbide, M. I., Torres Stone, R. A., McGinley, M., Raffaelli, M., et al. (2007). Acculturative stress, social support, and coping: Relations to psychological adjustment among Mexican American college students. *Cultural Diversity and Ethnic Minority Psychology, 13,* 347–355.

Crockett, M. J., Clark, L., Robbins, T. W., Tabibnia, G., & Lieberman, M. D. (2008). Serotonin modulates behavioural reactions to unfairness. *Science.* Retrieved June 7, 2008, from *http://www.sciencedaily.com≠/releases/2008/06/080605150908.htm*

Crossette, B. (1998, March 23). Mutilation seen as risk for the girls of immigrants. *New York Times,* p. A3.

Crowley, J. (1985). Cited in D. Zuckerman (1985). Retirement: R & R or risky? *Psychology Today, 19*(2), 80.

Cunningham, M. R., Roberts, A. R., Barbee, A. P., Druen, P. B., et al. (1995). "Their ideas of beauty are, on the whole, the same as ours": Consistency and variability in the cross-cultural perception of female physical attractiveness. *Journal of Personality and Social Psychology, 68,* 261–279.

Curry, L. A., & Youngblade, L. M. (2006). Negative affect, risk perception, and adolescent risk behavior. *Journal of Applied Developmental Psychology, 27,* 468–485.

Curtis, R. C., & Miller, K. (1986). Believing another likes or dislikes you: Behavior making the beliefs come true. *Journal of Personality and Social Psychology, 51,* 284–290.

Cynkar, A. (2007, June). The changing gender composition of psychology. *Monitor on Psychology,* pp. 46–47.

Dabbs, J. M., Jr., Chang, E.-L., Strong, R. A., & Milun, R. (1998). Spatial ability, navigation strategy, and geographic knowledge among men and women. *Evolution & Human Behavior, 19*(2), 89–98.

Damasio, R. (2000). A neural basis for sociopathy. *Archives of General Psychiatry, 57,* 128–129.

Danielsen, L. M., Lorem, A. E., & Kroger, J. (2000). The impact of social context on the identity-formation process of Norwegian late adolescents. *Youth & Society, 31,* 332–362.

Darcy, M. U. A., & Tracey, T. J. G. (2007). Circumplex structure of Holland's RIASEC interests across gender and time. *Journal of Counseling Psychology, 54,* 17–31.

Darley, J. M. (1993). Research on morality. *Psychological Science, 4,* 353–357.

Darley, J. M., & Latané, B. (1968). Bystander intervention in emergencies: Diffusion of responsibility. *Journal of Personality and Social Psychology, 8,* 377–383.

Davidson, J. R. T., Foa, E. B., Huppert, J. D., Keefe, F. J., Franklin, M. E., Compton, J. S., et al. (2004). Fluoxetine, comprehensive cognitive behavioral therapy, and placebo in generalized social phobia. *Archives of General Psychiatry, 61,* 1005–1013.

Davis, A. M., Grattan, D. R., & McCarthy, M. M. (2000). Decreasing GAD neonatally attenuates steroid-induced sexual differentiation of the rat brain. *Behavioral Neuroscience, 114,* 923–933.

Davis, J. L., & Rusbult, C. E. (2001). Attitude alignment in close relationships. *Journal of Personality and Social Psychology, 81,* 65–84.

Davis, J. M., Chen, N., & Glick, I. D. (2003). A meta-analysis of the efficacy of second-generation antipsychotics. *Archives of General Psychiatry, 60,* 553–564.

Davis, S. R., Davison, S. L., Donath, S., & Bell, R. J. (2005). Circulating androgen levels and self-reported sexual function in women. *Journal of the American Medical Association, 294,* 91–96.

Davis, S. R., Moreau, M., M.D., Kroll, R., Bouchard, C., Panay, N., et al. (2008). Testosterone for low libido in postmenopausal women not taking estrogen. *New England Journal of Medicine, 359,* 2005–2017.

Davis, T. L., & Liddell, D. L. (2002). Getting inside the house: The effectiveness of a rape prevention program for college fraternity men. *Journal of College Student Development, 43,* 35–50.

Davison, G. C. (2000). Stepped care: Doing more with less? *Journal of Consulting and Clinical Psychology, 68,* 580–585.

Daw, J. (2002, October). Hormone therapy for men? *Monitor on Psychology,* p. 53.

DeAngelis, T. (2001). Our erotic personalities are as unique as our fingerprints. *Monitor on Psychology, 32,* p. 25.

Deci, E. L., La Guardia, J. G., Moller, A. C., Scheiner, M. J., & Ryan, R. M. (2006). On the benefits of giving as well as receiving autonomy support: Mutuality in close friendships. *Personality and Social Psychology Bulletin, 32,* 313–327.

DeDe, G., Caplan, D., Kemtes, K., & Waters, G. (2004). The relationship between age, verbal working memory, and language comprehension. *Psychology and Aging, 19,* 601–616.

Deegear, J., & Lawson, D. M. (2003). The utility of empirically supported treatments. *Professional Psychology: Research and Practice, 34,* 271–277.

De La Cancela, V., & Guzman, L. P. (1991). Latino mental health service needs: Implications for training psychologists. In H. F. Myers et al. (Eds.), *Ethnic minority perspectives on clinical training and services in psychology* (pp. 59–64). Washington, DC: American Psychological Association.

Delahanty, D. L., & Baum, A. (2001). Stress and breast cancer. In A. Baum, T. A. Revenson, & J. E. Singer (Eds), *Handbook of health psychology* (pp. 747–756). Mahwah, NJ: Erlbaum.

DelVecchio, T., & O'Leary, K. D. (2004). Effectiveness of anger treatments for specific anger problems: A meta-analytic review. *Clinical Psychology Review, 24,* 15–34.

de Moor, C., Sterner, J., Hall, M., Warneke, C., Gilani, Z, Amato, R., et al. (2003). A pilot study of the effects of expressive writing on psychological and behavioral adjustment in patients enrolled in a phase II trial of vaccine therapy for metastatic renal cell carcinoma. *Health Psychology, 21,* 615–619.

Denizel-Lewis, B. (2005, January 9). Ban of brothers. *New York Times Magazine,* pp. 32–39, 52, 73, 74.

Dennerstein, L., Randolph, J., Taffe, J., Dudley, E., & Burger, H. (2002). Hormones, mood, sexuality, and the menopausal transition *Fertility and Sterility, 77,* 42–48.

Depression research at the National Institutes of Mental Health. (2000). NIH Publication No. 00–4501. Retrieved January 15, 2001, from *http://www.nimh.nih.gov/publicat/depresfact.cfm*

Der, G., & Deary, I. J. (2006). Age and sex differences in reaction time in adulthood: Results from the United Kingdom Health and Lifestyle Survey. *Psychology and Aging, 21,* 62–73.

DeRubeis, R. J., Hollon, S. D., Amsterdam, J. D., Shelton, R. C., Young, P. R., Salomon, R.M., et al. (2005). Cognitive therapy vs medications in the treatment of moderate to severe depression. *Archives of General Psychiatry, 62,* 409–416.

DeRubeis, R. J., Tang, T. Z., & Beck, A. T. (2001). Cognitive therapy. In K. S. Dobson (Ed.), *Handbook of cognitive-behavioral therapies* (2nd ed., pp. 349–392). New York: Guilford Press.

Deutsch, C. H. (1990, April 29). Why women walk out on jobs. *New York Times*, p. F27.

Deveny, K. (2003, June 30). We're not in the mood. *Newsweek*, pp. 41–46.

Diamond, A. (2009). The interplay of biology and the environment broadly defined. *Developmental Psychology, 45*, 1–8.

Dickerson, F. B., Tenhula, W. N., & Green-Paden, L. D. (2005). The token economy for schizophrenia: review of the literature and recommendations for future research. *Schizophrenia Research, 75*, 405–416.

Dickson, N., Paul, C., Herbison, P., & Silva, P. (1998). First sexual intercourse: Age, coercion, and later regrets reported by a birth cohort. *British Medical Journal, 316*, 29–33.

Dietz, W. H. (2004). Overweight in childhood and adolescence. *New England Journal of Medicine, 350*, 855–857.

Di Fabio, A., & Busoni, L. (2007). Fluid intelligence, personality traits and scholastic success: Empirical evidence in a sample of Italian high school students. *Personality and Individual Differences, 43*, 2095-2104.

DiGiuseppe, R., & Tafrate, R. C. (2003). Anger treatment for adults: A meta-analytic review. *Clinical Psychology: Science and Practice, 10*, 70–84.

DiGiuseppe, R., & Tafrate, R. C. (2007). *Understanding anger disorders*. New York: Oxford University Press.

Dindia, K., & Timmerman, L. (2003). Accomplishing romantic relationships. In J. O. Greene & B. R. Burleson (Eds.), *Handbook of communication and social interaction skills* (pp. 685–721). Mahwah, NJ: Erlbaum.

Di Paula, A., & Campbell, J. D. (2002). Self-esteem and persistence in the face of failure. *Journal of Personality and Social Psychology, 83*, 711–724.

Dittmann, M. (2003, March). Anger across the gender divide. *Monitor on Psychology, 34*, 52–53.

Dittmann, M. (2004, July/August). Standing tall pays off, study finds. *Monitor on Psychology, 35*, 14.

Dittmar, H., Halliwell, E., & Ive, S. (2006). Does Barbie make girls want to be thin? The effect of experimental exposure to images of dolls on the body image of 5- to 8-year-old girls. *Developmental Psychology, 42*, 283–292.

Ditzen, B., Schmidt, S., Strauss, B., Nater, U. M., Ehlert, U., & Heinrichs, M. (2008). Adult attachment and social support interact to reduce psychological but not cortisol responses to stress. *Journal of Psychosomatic Research, 64*, 479–486.

Dixon, J., Durrheim, K., & Tredoux, C. (2007). Intergroup contact and attitudes toward the principle and practice of racial equality. *Psychological Science, 18*, 867–872.

Dodge, K. A., Laird, R., Lochman, J. E., & Zelli, A. (2002). Multidimensional latent-construct analysis of children's social information processing patterns. *Psychological Assessment, 14*, 60–73.

Dohrenwend, B. P. (2006). Inventorying stressful life events as risk factors for psychopathology: Toward resolution of the problem of intracategory variability. *Psychological Bulletin, 132*, 477–495.

Dolbier, C. L., Cocke, R. R., Leiferman, J. A., Steinhardt, M. A., Schapiro, S. J., Nehete, P. N., et al. (2001). Differences in functional immune responses of high vs. low hardy healthy individuals. *Journal of Behavioral Medicine, 24*, 219–229.

Dom, G., Hulstijn, W., & Sabbe, B. (2006). Differences in impulsivity and sensation seeking between early- and late-onset alcoholics. *Addictive Behaviors, 31*, 298–308.

Domino, M. E., Burns, B. J., Silva, S. G., Kratochvil, C. J., Vitiello, B., Reinecke, M. A., et al. (2008). Cost-effectiveness of treatments for adolescent depression: Results from TADS. *American Journal of Psychiatry, 165*, 588–596.

Donald, M., Dower, J., Correa-Velez, I., & Jones, M. (2006). Risk and protective factors for medically serious suicide attempts: A comparison of hospital-based with population-based samples of young adults. *Australian and New Zealand Journal of Psychiatry, 40*, 87–96.

Donohue, K. F., Curtin, J. J., Patrick, C. J., & Lang, A. R. (2007). Intoxication level and emotional response. *Emotion, 7*, 103–112.

Dorahy, M. J. (2001). Dissociative identity disorder and memory dysfunction: The current state of experimental research and its future directions. *Clinical Psychology Review, 21*, 771–795.

Dougall, A. L., & Baum, A. (2001). Stress, health, and illness. In A. Baum, T. A. Revenson, & J. E. Singer (Eds), *Handbook of health psychology* (pp. 339–348). Mahwah, NJ: Erlbaum.

Dovidio, J. F., Gaertner, S. L., Esses, V. M., & Brewer, M. B. (2003). Social conflict, harmony, and integration. In T. Millon & M. J. Lerner (Eds.), *Handbook of psychology: Vol. 5. Personality and social psychology* (pp. 485–506). New York: Wiley.

Drapers, P. (1975). !Kung women: Contrasts in sexual egalitarianism in foraging and sedentary contexts. In R. R. Reiter (Ed.), *Toward an anthropology of women* (pp. 77–109). New York: Monthly Review Press.

Drescher, J., & Merlino, J. P. (2007). (Eds.). *American psychiatry and homosexuality: An oral history.* New York: Haworth.

Drieling, T., van Calker, D., & Hecht, H. (2006). Stress, personality and depressive symptoms in a 6.5 year follow-up of subjects at familial risk for affective disorders and controls. *Journal of Affective Disorders, 91*, 195–203.

Dryden, W., & Ellis, A. (2001). Rational emotive behavior therapy. In K. S. Dobson (Ed.), *Handbook of cognitive-behavioral therapies* (2nd ed., pp. 295–348). New York: Guilford.

DuBois, D. L., & Flay, B. R. (2004). The healthy pursuit of self-esteem: Comment on and alternative to the Crocker and Park (2004) formulation. *Psychological Bulletin, 130*, 415–420.

Dubovsky, S. (2008, May 12). Neurosurgery for depression: Pinpointing the way to success. *Journal Watch Psychiatry*. Retrieved June 26, 2008, from *http://psychiatry.jwatch.org/cgi/content/full/2008/512/2*

Duenweld, M. (2003, June 18). More Americans seeking help for depression. *New York Times*, pp. A1, A22.

Dugas, M. L., Ladouceur, R., Léger, E., Freeston, M. H., Langlis, F., Provencher, M. D., et al. (2003). Group cognitive-behavioral therapy for generalized anxiety disorder: Treatment outcome and long-term follow-up. *Journal of Consulting and Clinical Psychology, 71*, 821–825.

Dugger, C. W. (1996, September 11). A refugee's body is intact but her family is torn. *New York Times*, pp. A1, B6.

Duplassie, D., & Daniluk, J. C. (2007). Sexuality: Young and middle adulthood. In M. S. Tepper & A. F. Owens (Eds.), *Sexual health: Vol 1. Psychological foundations* (pp. 263–289). Westport, CT: Praeger/Greenwood.

Durham, P. L. (2004). CGRP-receptor antagonists—a fresh approach to migraine therapy? *New England Journal of Medicine, 350*, 1073–1075.

Dwairy, M. (2002). Foundations of psychosocial dynamic personality theory of collective people. *Clinical Psychology Review, 22*, 343–360.

Dyer, K. R., et al. (2001). The relationship between mood state and plasma methadone concentration in maintenance patients. *Journal of Clinical Psychopharmacology, 21*, 78–84.

Eagle, M. (2000). Repression, part I of II. *Psychoanalytic Review, 87*, 1–38.

Easterbrook, G. (2005, January 17). The real truth about money. *Time*, pp. A32–A34.

Ebmeier, K. P., Donaghey, C., & Steele, J. D. (2006). Recent developments and current controversies in depression. *Lancet, 367*, 153–167.

Eckenrode, J., et al. (2000). Preventing child abuse and neglect with a program of nursing home visitation. *Journal of the American Medical Association, 284*, 1385–1391.

Eckhardt, C., Norlander, B., & Deffenbacher, J. (2004). The assessment of anger and hostility: A critical review. *Aggression and Violent Behavior, 9*, 17–43.

Eddleston, K. A., Veiga, J. F., & Powell, G. N. (2006). Explaining sex differences in managerial career satisfier preferences: The role of gender self-schema. *Journal of Applied Psychology, 91*, 437–445.

Edenberg, H. J., Strother, W. N., McClintick, J. N., Tian, H., Stephens, M., Jerome, R. E., et al. (2005). Gene expression in the hippocampus of inbred alcohol-preferring and -nonpreferring rats. *Genes, Brain & Behavior, 4*, 20–30.

Edinger, J. D., et al. (2001). Cognitive behavioral therapy for treatment of chronic primary insomnia. *Journal of the American Medical Association, 285*(14), 1856–1864.

Edmundson, M. (1999, August 22). Psychoanalysis, American style. Retrieved August 30, 2000, from www.nytimes.com.

Edwards, T. M. (2000, August 28). Single by choice. *Time, 156*(9). Retrieved June 23, 2004, from www.wtamu.edu/~rbrammer/edpd5529/articles/singlewomen.htm

Egerton, A., Allison, C., Brett, R. R., & Pratt, J. A. (2006). Cannabinoids and prefrontal cortical function: Insights from preclinical studies. *Neuroscience & Biobehavioral Reviews, 30*, 680–695.

Egger, J. I. M., De Mey, H. R. A., Derksen, J. J. L., & van der Staak, C. P. F. (2003). Cross-cultural replication of the five-factor model and comparison of the NEO-PI-R and MMPI-2 PSY-5 scales in a Dutch psychiatric sample. *Psychological Assessment, 15*, 81–88.

Eggers, D. (2000, May 7). Intimacies. *New York Times Magazine,* pp. 76–77.

Ehlers, A., Clark, D. M., Hackmann, A., McManus, F., Fennell, M., Herbert, C., & Mayou, R. (2003). A randomized controlled trial of cognitive therapy, a self-help booklet, and repeated assessments as early interventions for posttraumatic stress disorder. *Archives of General Psychiatry, 60,* 1024–1032.

Ehrlinger, J., & Dunning, D. (2003). How chronic self-views influence (and potentially mislead) estimates of performance. *Journal of Personality and Social Psychology, 84*, 5–17.

Eisner, R. (2005, January). Study suggests cognitive deficits in MDMA-only drug abusers. *NIDA Notes, 19*(5). Retrieved February 9, 2005, from *http://www.-nida.nih.gov/NIDA_notes/NNvol19N5/Study.html*

Elkind, D. (1985). Egocentrism redux. *Developmental Review, 5*, 218–226.

Ellemers, N., Spears, R., & Doosje, B. (2002). Self and social identity. *Annual Review of Psychology, 53,* 161–186.

Ellington, J. E., Marsh, L. A., & Critelli, J. E. (1980). Personality characteristics of women with masculine names. *Journal of Social Psychology, 111,* 211–218.

Ellis, A. (2001, January). "Intellectual" and "emotional" insight revisited. *NYS Psychologist, 13,* 2–6.

Ellis, A. (2008). Rational emotive behavior therapy. In R. J. Corsini & D. Wedding (Eds.), *Current psychotherapies* (8th ed., pp. 187–222). Belmont, CA: Thomson Higher Education.

Ellis, A., & Dryden, W. (1996). *The practice of rational emotive behavior therapy.* New York: Springer.

Ellis, B. J., Jackson, J. J., & Boyce, W. T. (2006). The stress response systems: Universality and adaptive individual differences. *Developmental Review, 26,* 175–212.

Ellis, L., & Bonin, S. L. (2003). Genetics and occupation-related preferences. Evidence from adoptive and non-adoptive families. *Personality and Individual Differences, 35,* 929–937.

Ellis, L., & Hellberg, J. (2005). Fetal exposure to prescription drugs and adult sexual orientation. *Personality and Individual Differences, 38,* 225–236.

Ellsworth, P. C., Carlsmith, J. M., & Henson, A. (1972). The stare as a stimulus to flight in human subjects. *Journal of Personality and Social Psychology, 21,* 302–311.

Elms, A. C. (2009). Obedience lite. *American Psychologist, 64,* 32–36.

El Nasser, H. (2004, March 18). Census projects growing diversity. *USA Today,* p. A1.

Elvins, R., & Green, J. (2008). The conceptualization and measurement of therapeutic alliance: An empirical review. *Clinical Psychology Review, 28,* 1167–1187.

Emanuel, E. J., Fairclough, D. L., & Emanuel, L. L. (2000). Attitudes and desires related to euthanasia and physician-assisted suicide among terminally ill patients and their caregivers. *Journal of the American Medical Association, 284,* 2460–2468.

Engels, R. C. M. E., Scholte, R. H. J., van Lieshout, C. F. M., de Kemp, R., & Ovebeek, G. (2006). Peer group reputation and smoking and alcohol consumption in early adolescence. *Addictive Behaviors, 31,* 440–449.

Epstein, A. M., & Ayanian, J. Z. (2001). Racial disparities in medical care. *New England Journal of Medicine, 345,* 839.

Erikson, E. H. (1963). *Childhood and society.* New York: Norton.

Ertem, I. O., Leventhal, J. M., & Dobbs, S. (2000). Intergenerational continuity of child physical abuse: How good is the evidence? *Lancet, 356,* 814–819.

Escobar, J. I., Hoyos-Nervi, C., & Gara, M. (2000). Immigration and mental health: Mexican-Americans in the United States. *Harvard Review of Psychiatry, 8,* 64–72.

Escobar, J. I., & Vega, W. A. (2000). Commentary: Mental health and immigration's AAAs: Where are we and where do we go from here? *Journal of Nervous and Mental Disease, 188,* 736–740.

Esposito, K., Giugliano, F., Di Palo, C., Giugliano, G., Marfella, R., D'Andrea, F., et al. (2004). Effect of lifestyle changes on erectile dysfunction in obese men: A randomized controlled trial. *Journal of the American Medical Association, 291,* 2978–2984.

Essock, S. M., Frisman, L. K., Covell, N. H., & Hargreaves, W. A. (2000). Cost-effectiveness of clozapine compared with conventional antipsychotic medication for patients in state hospitals. *Archives of General Psychiatry, 57,* 987–994.

Ettinger, U., Picchioni, M., Landau, S., Matsumoto, K., van Haren, N. E., Marshall, N., et al. (2007). Magnetic resonance imaging of the thalamus and adhesio interthalamica in twins with schizophrenia. *Archives of General Psychiatry, 64,* 401–409.

Evans, S. W., Pelham, W. E., Smith, B. H., et al. (2001). Dose-response effects of methylphenidate on ecologically valid measures of academic performance and classroom behavior in adolescents with ADHD. *Experimental and Clinical Psychopharmacology, 9,* 163–175.

Evren, C., Kural, S., & Cakmak, D. (2006). Clinical correlates of childhood abuse and neglect in substance dependents. *Addictive Behaviors, 31,* 475–485.

Eysenbach, G., Powell, J., Kuss, O., & Sa, E-R. (2003). Empirical studies assessing the quality of health information for consumers on the World Wide Web: A systematic review. *Journal of the American Medical Association, 287,* 2691–2700.

Eysenck, H. J., & Eysenck, M. W. (1985). *Personality and individual differences.* New York: Plenum.

Fairfield, H. (2009, February 28). Why Is Her Paycheck Smaller? The New York Times. Retrieved May 4, 2009, from *http://www.nytimes.com/2009/03/01/business/01metrics.html*

Fallon, A. E., & Rozin, P. (1985). Sex differences in perceptions of desirable body shape. *Journal of Abnormal Psychology, 94,* 102–105.

Fals-Stewart, W. (2003). The occurrence of partner physical aggression on days of alcohol consumption: A longitudinal diary study. *Journal of Consulting and Clinical Psychology, 71,* 41–52.

Fan, Y., Tang, Y., Lu, Q., Feng, S., Yu, Q., Sui, D. et al. (2009). Dynamic changes in salivary cortisol and secretory immunoglobulin A response to acute stress. *Stress and Health, 25,* 189–194.

Farber, B. A., Brink, D. C., & Raskin, P. M. (1996). *The psychotherapy of Carl Rogers: Cases and commentary* (pp. 74–75). New York: The Guilford Press.

Feder, J., Levant, R. F., & Dean, J. (2007). Boys and violence: A gender-informed analysis. *Professional Psychology: Research and Practice, 38,* 385–391.

Fein, E. (1998, January 5). A doctor puts herself in the world of abused children. *New York Times,* p. C3.

Feingold, A. (1992). Good-looking people are not what we think. *Psychological Bulletin, 111,* 304–341.

Feingold, A. (1994). Gender differences in personality: A meta-analysis. *Psychological Bulletin, 116,* 429–456.

Feldman, L. B., & Rivas-Vazquez, R. A. (2003). Assessment and treatment of social anxiety disorder. *Professional Psychology: Research and Practice, 34,* 396–405.

Feng, J., Spence, I., & Pratt, J. (2007). Playing an action video game reduces gender differences in spatial cognition. *Psychological Science, 18,* 850–855.

Ferdinand, K. C. (2006). Coronary artery disease in minority racial and ethnic groups in the United States. *The American Journal of Cardiology, 97,* 12–19.

Ferraz, L., Vállez, M., Navarro, B., Gelabert, E., Martín-Santos, R., & Subirà, S. (2009). Dimensional assessment of personality and impulsiveness in borderline personality disorder. *Personality and Individual Differences, 46,* 140–146.

Fewer youths using marijuana; alcohol abuse steady. (2004, September 9). *CNN.com*. Retrieved September 10, 2004, from *http://www.cnn.com/2004/HEALTH/09/09/drug.use.ap/index.html*.

Fibel, B., & Hale, W. D. (1978). The generalized expectancy for success scale—A new measure. *Journal of Consulting and Clinical Psychology, 46*, 924–931.

Fink, B., & Penton-Voak, I. (2002). Evolutionary psychology of facial attractiveness. *Current Directions in Psychological Science, 11*, 154–158.

Fink, M., & Taylor, M. A. (2007). Electroconvulsive therapy: Evidence and challenges. *Journal of the American Medical Association, 298*, 330–332.

Firestone, R. W., Firestone, L. A., & Catlett, J. (2006). *Sex and love in intimate relationships*. Washington, DC: American Psychological Association.

Fisher, B. S., Daigle, L. E., Cullen, F. T., & Turner, M. G. (2003). Reporting sexual victimization to the police and others: Results from a national-level study of college women. *Criminal Justice & Behavior, 30*, 6–38.

Fisher, H. E. (2000). Brains do it: Lust, attraction and attachment. *Cerebrum, 2*, 23–42.

Fitness, J. (2001). Emotional intelligence and intimate relationships. In J. Ciarrochi & J. P. Forgas, et al. (Eds.), *Emotional intelligence in everyday life: A scientific inquiry* (pp. 98–112). Philadelphia, PA: Psychology Press.

Fitzgerald, L. F. (1993). Sexual harassment: Violence against women in the workplace. *American Psychologist, 48*, 1070–1076.

Flavell, J. H., Miller, P. H., & Miller, S. A. (2002). *Cognitive development* (4th ed.). Upper Saddle River, NJ: Prentice Hall.

Fleeson, W. (2004). Moving personality beyond the person-situation debate: The challenge and the opportunity of within-person variability. *Current Directions in Psychological Science, 13*, 83–87.

Flegal, K. M., Graubard, B. I., Williamson, D. F., & Gail, M. H. (2007). Cause-specific excess deaths associated with underweight, overweight, and obesity. *Journal of the American Medical Association, 298*, 2028–2037.

Flegal, K. M., Graubard, B. I., Williamson, D. F., & Gail, M. H. (2007). Excess deaths associated with underweight, overweight, and obesity. *Journal of the American Medical Association, 293*, 1861–1867.

Fogel, J. (2003). Use of the Internet for health information and communication [Letter to the editor]. *Journal of the American Medical Association, 290*, 2256.

Folkman, S., & Moskowitz, T. (2000a). Positive affect and the other side of coping. *American Psychologist, 55*, 647–654.

Folkman, S., & Moskowitz, J. T. (2000b). The context matters. *Personality & Social Psychology Bulletin, 26*, 150–151.

Fontaine, K. R., Redden, D. T., Wang, C., Westfall, A. O., & Allison, D. B. (2003). Years of life lost due to obesity. *Journal of the American Medical Association, 289*, 187–193.

Foran, H. M., & O'Leary, K. D. (2008). Alcohol and intimate partner violence: A meta-analytic review. *Clinical Psychology Review, 28*, 1222–1234.

Forbush, K., Heatherton, T. F., & Keel, P. K. (2007). Relationships between perfectionism and specific disordered eating behaviors. *International Journal of Eating Disorders, 40*, 37–41.

Ford, A. B., Haug, M. R., Stange, K. C., Gaines, A. D., Noelker, L. S., & Jones, P. K. (2000). Sustained personal autonomy: A measure of successful aging. *Journal of Aging & Health, 12*, 470–489.

Forestell, C. A., Humphrey, T. M., & Stewart, S. H. (2004). Is beauty in the eye of the beholder? Effects of weight and shape on attractiveness ratings of female line drawings by restrained and nonrestrained eaters. *Eating Behaviors, 5*, 89–101.

Forgas, J. P., Levinger, G., & Moylan, S. J. (1994). Feeling good and feeling close: Affective influences on the perception of intimate relationships. *Personal Relationships, 1*, 165–184.

Fountoulakis, K. N., Grunze, H., Panagiotidis, P., & Kaprinis, G. (2008). Treatment of bipolar depression: An update. *Journal of Affective Disorders, 109*, 21–343.

Fowler, J. H., & Christakis, N. A. (2008). Dynamic spread of happiness in a large social network: Longitudinal analysis over 20 years in the Framingham Heart Study. *British Medical Journal, 337*, 2338.

Frattaroli, J. (2006). Experimental disclosure and its moderators: A meta-analysis. *Psychological Bulletin, 132*, 823–865.

Freeman, H. P., & Payne, R. (2000). Racial injustice in health care. *New England Journal of Medicine, 342*, 1045–1047.

French, S. E., Seidman, E., Allen, L., & Aber, J. L. (2006). The development of ethnic identity during adolescence. *Developmental Psychology, 42*, 1–10.

Fresco, A. (2005, October 31). Texting teenagers are proving 'more literate than ever before'. *The Times*. Retrieved November 24, 2005, from *http://www.timesonline.co.uk/article/0,,2–1850922,00.html*

Freud, S. (1933). New introductory lectures. In *Standard edition of the complete psychological works of Sigmund Freud* (Vol. 22). London: Hogarth Press, 1964.

Freud, S. (1964). New introductory lectures. In *Standard edition of the complete psychological works of Sigmund Freud* (Vol. 22). London: Hogarth. (Original work published 1933.)

Freund, A. M., & Baltes, P. B. (1998). Selection, optimization, and compensation as strategies of life management: Correlations with subjective indicators of successful aging. *Psychology & Aging, 13*(4), 531–543.

Friedman, L. J. (1999). *Identity's architect: A biography of Erik H. Erikson*. New York: Scribner.

Friedman, M., & Rosenhan, R. H. (1974). *Type A behavior and your heart*. New York: Knopf.

Friedman, M., & Ulmer, D. (1984). *Treating Type A behavior and your heart*. New York: Fawcett Crest.

Friedman, R. A. (2006). The changing face of teenage drug abuse—the trend toward prescription drugs. *New England Journal of Medicine, 354*, 1448–1450.

Friedman, R. A., &. Leon, A. C. (2007). Expanding the black box—depression, antidepressants, and the risk of suicide. *New England Journal of Medicine, 356*, 2343–2346.

Frisch, R. (1997). Cited in N. Angier (1997). Chemical tied to fat control could help trigger puberty. *New York Times*, pp. C1, C3.

Fujita, F., & Diener, E. (2005). Life satisfaction set point: Stability and change. *Journal of Personality and Social Psychology, 88*, 158–164.

Fukukawa, Y., Nakashima, C., Tsuboi, S., Kozakai, R., Doyo, W., Niino, N., et al. (2004). Age differences in the effect of physical activity on depressive symptoms. *Psychology and Aging, 19*, 346–351.

Fuligni, A. J., Witkow, M., & Garcia, C. (2005). Ethnic identity and the academic adjustment of adolescents from Mexican, Chinese, and European backgrounds. *Developmental Psychology, 41*, 799–811.

Furnham, A., Petrides, K. V., & Constantinides, A. (2005). The effects of body mass index and waist-to-hip ratio on ratings of female attractiveness, fecundity, and health. *Personality and Individual Differences, 38*, 1823–1834.

Furstenberg, F. F., & Kiernan, K. E. (2001). Delayed parental divorce: How much do children benefit? *Journal of Marriage & the Family, 63*, 446–457

Futrelle, D. (2006, August). Can money buy happiness? *Money*, pp. 127–131.

Gabbard, G. O. (2005). Mind, brain, and personality disorders. *American Journal of Psychiatry, 162*, 648–655.

Gaines, S. O., Jr., Marelich, W. D., Bledsoe, K. L., Steers, W. N., et al. (1997). Links between race/ethnicity and cultural values as mediated by racial/ethnic identity and moderated by gender. *Journal of Personality and Social Psychology, 72*, 1460–1476.

Gajendran, R. S., & Harrison, D. A. (2007). The good, the bad, and the unknown about telecommuting: Meta-analysis of psychological mediators and individual consequences. *Journal of Applied Psychology, 92*, 1524–1546.

Gallagher, R. (1996). Cited in B. Murray (1996). College youth haunted by increased pressures. *APA Monitor, 26*(4), 47.

Gallup Organization. (2005). *Americans' personal satisfaction*. Retrieved April 20, 2005, from *http://www.gallup.com/poll/content/default.aspx?ci14506*

Gannon, N., & Ranzijn, R. (2005). Does emotional intelligence predict unique variance in life satisfaction beyond IQ and personality? *Personality and Individual Differences, 38*, 1353–1364.

Garb, H. N., Wood, J. M., Lilienfeld, S. O., & Nezworski, M .T. (2002). Effective use of projective techniques in clinical practice: Let the data help with selection and interpretation. *Professional Psychology: Research and Practice, 33,* 454–463.

Garb, H. N., Wood, J. M., Lilienfeld, S. O., & Nezworski, M. T. (2005). Roots of the Rorschach controversy. *Clinical Psychology Review, 25,* 97–118.

Garcia, S. M., Weaver, K., Moskowitz, G. B., & Darley, J. M. (2002). Crowded minds: The implicit bystander effect. *Journal of Personality and Social Psychology, 83,* 843–853.

Garfinkel, R. (1995). Cited in P. Margoshes (1995). For many, old age is the prime of life. *APA Monitor, 26*(5), 36–37.

Garlow, S. J., Purselle, D., & Heninger, M. (2005). Ethnic differences in patterns of suicide across the life cycle. *American Journal of Psychiatry, 162,* 319–323.

Garnets, L. D. (2002). Sexual orientations in perspective. *Cultural Diversity and Ethnic Minority Psychology, 8,* 115–129.

Gartlehner, G., Gaynes, B. N., Hansen, R. A., Thieda, P., DeVeaugh-Geiss, A., Krebs, E. E., et al. (2008). Comparative benefits and harms of second-generation antidepressants: Background paper for the American College of Physicians. *Annals of Internal Medicine, 149,* 734–750.

Garwood, S. G., Cox, L., Kaplan, V., Wasserman, N., et al. (1980). Beauty is only "name deep": The effect of first name in ratings of physical attraction. *Journal of Applied Social Psychology, 10,* 431–435.

Gatchel, R. J. (2001). Biofeedback and self-regulation of physiological activity: A major adjunctive treatment modality in health psychology. In A. Baum, T. A. Revenson, & J. E. Singer (Eds), *Handbook of health psychology* (pp. 95–104). Mahwah, NJ: Erlbaum.

Gatz, M. (2007). Genetics, dementia, and the elderly. *Current Directions in Psychological Science, 16,* 123–127.

Gaulin, S. J. C., & McBurney, D. H. (2001). *Psychology: An evolutionary approach.* Upper Saddle River, NJ: Prentice Hall.

Gay couples found to head more homes. (2001, August 22). *New York Times,* p. A16.

Geddes, J. R., Burgess, S., Hawton, K., Jamison, K., & Goodwin, G. M. (2004). Long-term lithium therapy for bipolar disorder: Systematic review and meta-analysis of randomized controlled trials. *American Journal of Psychiatry, 161,* 217–222.

Geier, A. B., Rozin, P., & Doros, G. (2006). Unit bias: A new heuristic that helps explain the effect of portion size on food intake. *Psychological Science, 17,* 521–525.

Geipert, N. (2007, January). Don't be mad: More research links hostility to coronary risk. *Monitor on Psychology, 38,* pp. 50–51.

Gelernter, J., Panhuysen, C., Weiss, R., Brady, K., Polinga, J., Krauthammer, M., Farrer, L., et al. (2007). Genomewide linkage scan for nicotine dependence: Identification of a chromosome 5 risk locus. *Biological Psychiatry, 61,* 119–126.

Gelman, D., with P. Kandell. (1993, January 18). Isn't it romantic? *Newsweek,* pp. 60–61.

Gerevich, J., Treuer, T., Danics, Z., & Herr, J. (2005). Diagnostic and psychodynamic aspects of sexual addiction appearing as a non-paraphiliac form of compulsive sexual behaviour. *Journal of Substance Use, 10,* 253–259.

Getting high. (2008, January 30). *Journal Watch Pediatrics and Adolescent Medicine.* Retrieved April 24, 2008, from *http://monitoringthefuture.org/data/07data.html#2007data-drugs)*

Giancola, P. R., & Corman, M. D. (2007). Alcohol and aggression: A test of the attention-allocation model. *Psychological Science, 18,* 649–655.

Gignac, G. E. (2006). Self-reported emotional intelligence and life satisfaction: Testing incremental predictive validity hypotheses via structural equation modeling (SEM) in a small sample. *Personality and Individual Differences, 40,* 1569–1577.

Gilbert, S. (1997, June 25). Social ties reduce risk of a cold. *New York Times,* p. C11.

Gilbert, S. (2004, March 16). New clues to women veiled in black. *New York Times,* pp. F1, F7.

Gilbert, S. C. (2003). Eating disorders in women of color. *Clinical Psychology: Science and Practice, 10,* 444–455.

Gill, R. E. (2006, January/February). *The National Psychologist, 15,* 1–2.

Gilligan, C. (1982). *In a different voice: Psychological theory and women's development.* Cambridge, MA: Harvard University Press.

Gilligan, C., Lyons, P., & Hanmer, T. J. (Eds.). (1990). *Making connections.* Cambridge, MA: Harvard University Press.

Gilligan, C., Rogers, A. G., & Tolman, D. L. (Eds.). (1991). *Women, girls, and psychotherapy.* New York: Haworth.

Gillis, J. S., & Avis, W. E. (1980). The male-taller norm in mate selection. *Personality and Social Psychology Bulletin, 6,* 396–401.

Giltay, E. J., Kamphuis, M. H., Kalmijn, S., Zitman, F. G., & Kromhout, D. (2006). Dispositional optimism and the risk of cardiovascular death: The Zutphen Elderly Study. *Archives of Internal Medicine, 166,* 431–436.

Glass, S. P., & Wright, T. L. (1992). Justifications of extramarital relationships: The association between attitudes, behaviors, and gender. *Journal of Sex Research, 29,* 361–387.

Glater, J. D. (2001, March 16). Women are close to being majority of law students. *New York Times,* pp. A1, A16.

Godbolt, A. K., Waldman, A. D., MacManus, D. G., Schott, J. M., Frost, C., Cipolotti, L., et al. (2006). MRS shows abnormalities before symptoms in familial Alzheimer disease. *Neurology, 66,* 718–722

Goldberg, I. J., Mosca, L., Piano, M. R., & Fisher, E. A. (2001). AHA science advisory: Wine and your heart. *Circulation, 103,* 472–475.

Golden, O. (2000). The federal response to child abuse and neglect. *American Psychologist, 55,* 1050–1053.

Goldstat, R., Briganti, E., Tran, J., Wolfe, R., & Davis, S. R. (2003). Transdermal testosterone therapy improves well-being, mood, and sexual function in premenopausal women. *Menopause, 10,* 390–398.

Goldstein, R. B., Grant, B. F., Huang, B., Smith, S. M., Stinson, F. S., Dawson, D. A., et al. (2006). Lack of remorse in antisocial personality disorder: Sociodemographic correlates, symptomatic presentation, and comorbidity with Axis I and Axis II disorders in the National Epidemiologic Survey on Alcohol and Related Conditions. *Comprehensive Psychiatry, 47,* 289–297.

Goldston, K., & Baillie, A. J. (2007). Depression and coronary heart disease: A review of the epidemiological evidence, explanatory mechanisms and management. *Clinical Psychology Review, 28,* 288–306.

Golish, T. D. (2003). Stepfamily communication strengths: Understanding the ties that bind. *Human Communication Research, 29,* 41–80.

Golombok, S., Perry, B., Burston, A., Murray, C., Mooney-Somers, J., Stevens, M., et al. (2003). Children with lesbian parents: A community study. *Developmental Psychology, 39,* 20–33.

Good, C., Aronson, J., & Harder, J. A. (2008). Problems in the pipeline: Stereotype threat and women's achievement in high-level math courses. *Journal of Applied Developmental Psychology, 29,* 17–28.

Goode, E. (2000, June 25). Thinner: The male battle with anorexia. *New York Times Magazine,* p. 8.

Goode, E. (2001, February 20). What's in an inkblot? Some say, not much. *New York Times,* pp. F1, F4.

Gooren, L. J. G., & Kruijver, P. M. (2002). Androgens and male behavior. *Molecular and Cellular Endocrinology, 198,* 31–40.

Gorchoff, S. M., John, O. P., & Helson, R. (2008). Contextualizing change in marital satisfaction during middle age: An 18-year longitudinal study. *Psychological Science, 19,* 1194–1200.

Gorman, C. (2006, January 16). Can you prevent Alzheimer's disease? *Time,* pp. 110–113.

Gorman, C. (2007, January 29). 6 lessons for handling stress. *Newsweek,* pp. 80–85.

Gottman, J. M., Coan, J., Carrère, S., & Swanson, C. (1998). Predicting marital happiness and stability from newlywed interactions. *Journal of Marriage and the Family, 60,* 5–22.

Gottman, J. M., & Krokoff, L. J. (1989). Marital interaction and satisfaction: A longitudinal view. *Journal of Consulting and Clinical Psychology, 57,* 47–52.

Grabe, S., Ward, L. M., & Hyde, J. S. (2008). The role of the media in body image concerns among women: A meta-analysis of experimental and correlational studies. *Psychological Bulletin, 134,* 460–476.

Graham, J. R. (2000). *MMPI-2: Assessing personality and psychopathology* (3rd ed.). New York: Oxford University Press.

Grant, B. F., Harford, T. C., Muthen, B. O., Yi, H. Y., Hasin, D. S., & Stinson, F. S. (2006a). DSM-IV alcohol dependence and abuse: Further evidence of validity in the general population. *Drug and Alcohol Dependence, 86,* 154–166.

Grant, B. F., Hasin, D. S., Blanco, C., Stinson, F. S., Chou, S. P., Goldstein, R. B., et al. (2006a). The epidemiology of social anxiety disorder in the

United States: Results from the National Epidemiologic Survey on Alcohol and Related Conditions. *Journal of Clinical Psychiatry, 66,* 1351–1361.

Grant, B. F., Hasin, D. S., Stinson, F. S., Dawson, D. A., Goldstein, R. B., Smith, S., et al. (2006b). The epidemiology of DSM-IV panic disorder and agoraphobia in the United States: Results from the National Epidemiologic Survey on Alcohol and Related Conditions. *Journal of Clinical Psychiatry, 67,* 363–374.

Gray, M. J., & Acierno, R. (2002). Posttraumatic stress disorder. In M. Hersen (Ed.), *Clinical behavior therapy: Adults and children* (pp. 106–124). New York: Wiley.

Gray-Little, B., & Hafdahl, A. R. (2000). Factors influencing racial comparisons of self-esteem: A quantitative review. *Psychological Bulletin, 126,* 26–54.

Green, D. P., Glaser, J., & Rich, A. (1998). From lynching to gay bashing: The elusive connection between economic condition and hate crime. *Journal of Personality and Social Psychology, 75,* 82–92.

Greenbaum, P., & Rosenfeld, H. M. (1978). Patterns of avoidance in response to interpersonal staring and proximity: Effects of bystanders on drivers at a traffic intersection. *Journal of Personality and Social Psychology, 36,* 575–587.

Greenberg, L. S., & Malcolm, W. (2002). Resolving unfinished business: Relating process to outcome. *Journal of Consulting and Clinical Psychology, 70,* 406–416.

Greenberg, S. T., & Schoen, E. G. (2008). Males and eating disorders: Gender-based therapy for eating disorder recovery. *Professional Psychology: Research and Practice, 39,* 464–471.

Greene, B. (2000). African American lesbian and bisexual women. *Journal of Social Issues, 56,* 239–249.

Greene, B. (2005). Psychology, diversity and social justice: Beyond heterosexism and across the cultural divide. *Counseling Psychology Quarterly, 18,* 295–306.

Greene, B. A. (1993). African American women. In L. Comas-Diaz & B. Greene (Eds.), *Women of color and mental health.* New York: Guilford.

Greene, M. L., Way, Niobe, N., & Pahl, K. (2006). Trajectories of perceived adult and peer discrimination among Black, Latino, and Asian American adolescents: Patterns and psychological correlates. *Developmental Psychology, 42,* 218–238.

Greenwood, A. (2006, April 25). Natural killer cells power immune system response to cancer. *NCI Cancer Bulletin, 3,* 17. Retrieved April 28, 2006, from *http://www.cancer.gov/ncicancerbulletin/NCI_Cancer_Bulletin_042506/page4*

Gregg, E. W., Cauley, J. A., Stone, K., Thompson, T. J., Bauer, D. C., Cummings, S. R., et al. (2003). Relationship of changes in physical activity and mortality among older women. *Journal of the American Medical Association, 289,* 2379–2386.

Grigoriadis, V. (2003, July 20). Smiling through the 30th, a birthday once apocalyptic. *New York Times,* Section 9, pp. 1, 8.

Grimsley, K. D. (2000, June 9). Panel asks why women still earn less. *Washington Post,* p. E3.

Gross, J. (2007, March 21). Prevalence of Alzheimer's rises 10% in 5 years. *New York Times,* p. A14.

Grossman, P. (2008). On measuring mindfulness in psychosomatic and psychological research. *Journal of Psychosomatic Research, 64,* 405–408.

Grote, N. K., & Clark, M. S. (2001). Perceiving unfairness in the family: Cause or consequence of marital distress? *Journal of Personality & Social Psychology, 80,* 281–293.

Grzywacz, J. G., & Butler, A. B. (2005). The impact of job characteristics on work-to-family facilitation: Testing a theory and distinguishing a construct. *Journal of Occupational Health Psychology, 10,* 97–109.

Guisinger, S., & Blatt, S. J. (1994). Individuality and relatedness: Evolution of a fundamental dialectic. *American Psychologist, 49,* 104–111.

Gumbau, R. G., Soria, M. S., & Silla, J. M. P. (2000). Efectos moduladores de la autoeficacia en el estres laboral. *Apuntes de Psicologia, 18,* 57–75.

Gunderson, J. G. (2007). Disturbed relationships as a phenotype for borderline personality disorder. *American Journal of Psychiatry, 164,* 1637–1640.

Gur, R. E., Nimgaonkar, V. L., Almasy, L., Calkins, M. E., Ragland, J. D., Pogue-Geile, M. F., et al. (2007). Neurocognitive endophenotypes in a multiplex multigenerational family study of schizophrenia. *American Journal of Psychiatry, 164,* 813–819.

Guralnik, O., Schmeidler, J., & Simeon, D. (2000). Feeling unreal: Cognitive processes in depersonalization. *American Journal of Psychiatry, 157,* 103–109.

Gurling, H. M. D., Critchley, H., Datta, S. R., McQuillin, A., Blaveri, E., Thirumalai, S., et al. (2006). Association and brain morphology studies and the chromosome 8p22 Pericentriolar Material 1 (PCM1) gene in susceptibility to schizophrenia. *Archives of General Psychiatry, 63,* 844–854.

Gyatso, T. (2003, April 26). The monk in the lab. *New York Times,* p. A29.

Haaga, D. A. F. (2000). Introduction to the special section on stepped care models in psychotherapy. *Journal of Consulting and Clinical Psychology, 68,* 547–548.

Haake, M., Müller, H.-H., Schade-Brittinger, C., Basler, H. D., Schäfer, H., Maie, C., et al. (2007). German Acupuncture Trials (GERAC) for chronic low back pain: Randomized, multicenter, blinded, parallel-group trial with 3 groups. *Archives of Internal Medicine, 167,* 1892–1898.

Haas, D. C., Chaplin, W. F., Shimbo, D., Pickering, T. G., Burg, M., & Davidson, K. W. (2005). Hostility is an independent predictor of recurrent coronary heart disease events in men but not women: Results from a population based study. *Heart, 91,* 1609–1610.

Haeffel, G. J., Getchell, M., Koposov, R. A., Yrigollen, C. M., DeYoung, C. G., af Klinteberg, B., et al. (2008). Association between polymorphisms in the dopamine transporter gene and depression: Evidence for a gene-environment interaction in a sample of juvenile detainees. *Psychological Science, 19,* 62–69.

Hafdahl, A. R., & Gray-Little, B. (2002). Explicating methods in reviews of race and self-esteem: Reply to Twenge and Crocker (2002). *Psychological Bulletin, 128,* 409–416.

Hajjar, I., & Kotchen, T. A. (2003). Trends in prevalence, awareness, treatment, and control of hypertension in the United States, 1988–2000. *Journal of the American Medical Association, 290,* 199–206.

Haley, W. E., et al. (1996). Appraisal, coping, and social support as mediators of well-being in black and white caregivers of patients with Alzheimer's disease. *Journal of Consulting and Clinical Psychology, 64,* 121–129.

Hall, G. C. N., & Barongan, C. (1997). Prevention of sexual aggression. *American Psychologist, 52,* 5–14.

Hall, G. C. N., Sue, S., Narang, D. S., & Lilly, R. S. (2000). Culture-specific models of men's sexual aggression: Intra- and interpersonal determinants. *Cultural Diversity & Ethnic Minority Psychology, 6,* 252–267.

Halmi, K. A., Sunday, S. R., Strober, M., Kaplan, A., Woodside, D. B., Fichter, M., et al. (2000). Perfectionism in anorexia nervosa: Variation by clinical subtype, obsessionality, and pathological eating behavior. *American Journal of Psychiatry, 157,* 1799–1805.

Halpern, D. F. (2004). A cognitive-process taxonomy for sex differences in cognitive abilities. *Current Directions in Psychological Science, 13,* 135–139.

Halpern, D. F., Benbow, C. P., Geary, D. C., Gur, R. C., Shibley Hyde, J., & Gernsbacher, M. A. (2007). The science of sex differences in science and mathematics. *Psychological Science in the Public Interest, 8,* 1–51.

Halpern, D. F., & LaMay, M. L. (2000). The smarter sex: A critical review of sex differences in intelligence. *Educational Psychology Review, 12,* 229–246.

Ham, L. S., & Hope, D. A. (2003). College students and problematic drinking: A review of the literature. *Clinical Psychology Review, 23,* 719–759.

Hamel, M., Shafer, T. W., & Erdberg, P. (2003). A study of nonpatient preadolescent Rorschach protocols. *Journal of Personality Assessment, 75,* 280–294.

Hamer, D., et al. (1993). Cited in W. A. Henry (1993, July 26). Born gay? *Time,* pp. 36–39.

Hamilton, S. P. (2008). Schizophrenia candidate genes: Are we really coming up blank? *American Journal of Psychiatry, 165,* 420–423.

Hammer, S. M., Saag, M. S., Schechter, M., Montaner, J. S. G., Schooley, R. T., et al. (2006). Treatment for adult HIV infection: 2006 recommendations of the International AIDS Society–USA Panel. *Journal of the American Medical Association, 295,* 190–198.

Hampton, T. (2006). Alcoholism genes. *Journal of the American Medical Association, 295,* 190–198.

Hampton, T. (2008). Sleep deprivation. *Journal of the American Medical Association, 299,* 513.

Hansen, N. D., Randazzo, K. V., Schwartz, A., Marshall, M., Kalis, D., Frazier, E., et al. (2006). Do we practice what we preach? An exploratory survey of multicultural psychotherapy competencies. *Professional Psychology: Research and Practice, 37,* 66–74.

Hardin, E. E., & Leong, F. T. L. (2005). Optimism and pessimism as mediators of the relations between self-discrepancies and distress among Asian and European Americans. *Journal of Counseling Psychology, 52,* 25–35.

Hariri, A. R., Mattay, V. S., Tessitore, A., Kolachana, B., Fera, F., Goldman, D., & Egan, M. F. (2002). Serotonin transporter genetic variation and the response of the human amydgala. *Science, 297,* 400–403.

Harmon, A. (2003, July 6). Online dating sheds its stigma as losers.com. *New York Times.* Retrieved November 24, 2006, from *http://query.nytimes.com/gst/ abstract.html*

Harned, M. (2000). Harassed bodies: An examination of the relationships among women's experiences of sexual harassment, body image and eating disturbances. *Psychology of Women Quarterly, 24,* 336–348.

Harris, A. H. S., Cronkite, R., & Moos, R. (2006). Physical activity, exercise coping, and depression in a 10-year cohort study of depressed patients. *Journal of Affective Disorders, 93,* 79–85.

Harris, G. (2004, October 16). F.D.A. toughens warning on antidepressant drugs. *New York Times,* p. A9.

Harris, G. (2007, December 6). Teenage birth rate rises for first time since '91. *New York Times,* p. A26.

Harro, J., Merenäkk, L., Nordquist, N., Konstabel, K., Comascoe, E., & Oreland, L. (2009). Personality and the serotonin transporter gene: Associations in a longitudinal population-based study. *Biological Psychology, 81,* 9–13.

Hartman, R. O., & Betz, N. E. (2007). The five-factor model and career self-efficacy: General and domain-specific relationships. *Journal of Career Assessment, 15,* 145–161.

Hartmann, P., Reuter, M., & Nyborg, H. (2006). The relationship between date of birth and individual differences in personality and general intelligence: A large-scale study. *Personality and Individual Differences, 40,* 1349–1362.

Hassinger, H. J., Semenchuk, E. M., & O'Brien, W. H. (1999). Appraisal and coping responses to pain and stress in migraine headache sufferers. *Journal of Behavioral Medicine, 22*(4), 327–340.

Havighurst, R. J. (1972). *Developmental tasks and education* (3rd ed.). New York: McKay.

Hawkley, L. C., Burleson, M. H., Berntson, G. G., & Cacioppo, J. T. (2003). Loneliness in everyday life: Cardiovascular activity, psychosocial context, and health behaviors. *Journal of Personality & Social Psychology, 85,* 105–120.

Hawkley, L. C., & Cacioppo, J. T. (2003). Loneliness and pathways to disease. *Brain, Behavior & Immunity, 17*(Suppl. 11), S98–S105.

Hedley, A. A., Ogden, C. L., Johnson, C. L., Carroll, M. D., Curtin, L. R., & Flegal, K. M. (2004). Prevalence of overweight and obesity among US children, adolescents, and adults, 1999–2002. *Journal of the American Medical Association, 291,* 2847–2850.

Heiman, J. R. (2008). Treating low sexual desire—new findings for testosterone in women. *New England Journal of Medicine, 359,* 2047–2049.

Heisel, M. J., & Duberstein, P. R. (2005). Suicide prevention in older adults. *Clinical Psychology: Science and Practice, 12,* 242–259.

Helderman, R. S. (2003, May 20). Click by click, teens polish writing; instant messaging teaches more than TTYL and ROFL. *Washington Post,* p. B1.

Helgeson, V. S. (2005). Recent advances in psychosocial oncology. *Journal of Consulting and Clinical Psychology, 73,* 268–271.

Hendrick, C. D., Wells, K. S., & Faletti, M. V. (1982). Social and emotional effects of geographical relocation on elderly retirees. *Journal of Personality and Social Psychology, 42,* 951–962.

Hendrick, C., & Hendrick, S. (1986). A theory and method of love. *Journal of Personality and Social Psychology, 50,* 392–402.

Henry, J. D., MacLeod, M. S., Phillips, L., H., & Crawford, J. R. (2004). A meta-analytic review of prospective memory and aging. *Psychology and Aging, 19,* 27–39.

Herdt, G. H. (1981). *Guardians of the flutes: Idioms of masculinity.* New York: McGraw-Hill.

Herek, G. M., & Gonzalez-Rivera, M. (2006). Attitudes toward homosexuality among U.S. residents of Mexican descent. *Journal of Sex Research, 43,* 122–135.

Herr, E. L. (2001). Career development and its practice: A historical perspective. *Career Development Quarterly, 49*(3), 196–211.

Herzog, T. R., & Chernick, K. K. (2000). Tranquility and danger in urban and natural settings. *Journal of Environmental Psychology, 20,* 29–39.

Hess, T. M. (2005). Memory and aging in context. *Psychological Bulletin, 131,* 383–406.

Het, S., & Wolf, O. T. (2007). Mood changes in response to psychosocial stress in healthy young women: Effects of pretreatment with cortisol. *Behavioral Neuroscience, 121,* 11–20.

Hetherington, E. M. (2006). The influence of conflict, marital problem solving and parenting on children's adjustment in nondivorced, divorced and remarried families. In A. Clarke-Stewart & J. Dunn (Eds.), *Families count: Effects on child and adolescent development* (pp. 203–237). New York: Cambridge University Press.

Hetherington, E. M., & Kelly, J. (2003). For better or for worse: Divorce reconsidered. *American Journal of Psychiatry, 160,* 601–602.

Hewlett, K. (2001, July/August). Can low self-esteem and self-blame on the job make you sick? *Monitor on Psychology, 32,* 58–60.

Hewstone, M., & Hamberger, J. (2000). Perceived variability and stereotype change. *Journal of Experimental Social Psychology, 36,* 103–124.

Hill, J. O., Wyatt, H. R., Reed, G.W., & Peters, J. C. (2003). Obesity and the environment: Where do we go from here? [Editorial]. *Science, 299,* 853–855.

Hingson, R. W., et al. (2000). Age of drinking onset and unintentional injury involvement after drinking. *Journal of the American Medical Association, 284,* 1527–1533.

Hobza, C. L., Walker, K. E., Yakushko, O., & Peugh, J. L. (2007). What about men? Social comparison and the effects of media images on body and self-esteem. *Psychology of Men & and Masculinity, 8,* 161–172.

Hofferth, D. G., & Anderson, K. G. (2003). Are all dads equal? Biology versus marriage as a basis for paternal investment. *Journal of Marriage and the Family, 65,* 213–232.

Hoffman, S. G. (2000). Treatment of social phobia: Potential mediators and moderators. *Clinical Psychology: Science and Practice, 7*(1), 3–16.

Hofmann, S. G. (2008). Cognitive processes during fear acquisition and extinction in animals and humans: Implications for exposure therapy of anxiety disorders. *Clinical Psychology Review, 28,* 200–211.

Holcomb, D. R., Savage, M. P., Seehafer, R., & Waalkes, D. M. (2002). A mixed-gender date rape prevention intervention targeting freshman college athletes. *College Student Journal, 36,* 165–179.

Holland, J. L. (1997). *Making vocational choices: A theory of vocational personalities and work environments* (3rd ed.). Odessa, FL: Psychological Assessment Resources.

Holloway, J. D. (2000, December). Snapshot from the therapy room. *Monitor on Psychology, 34,* 31.

Holman, B. (2000, August 2). Experts doubt value of living together before marriage. *Star Tribune Company.* Retrieved August 23, 2000, from *http://www.psycport.com/news/2000/08/02/eng-startribune_variety/eng-*

Holmans, P., Weissman, M., Zubenko, G. S., Scheftner, W. A., Crowe, R. R., DePaulo, J. R., Jr., et al. (2007). Genetics of recurrent early-onset major depression (genred): Final genome scan report. *American Journal of Psychiatry, 164,* 248–258.

Holmen, K., Ericsson, K., & Winblad, B. (2000). Social and emotional loneliness among non-demented and demented elderly people. *Archives of Gerontology & Geriatrics, 31*(3), 177–192.

Holroyd, K. A. (2002). Assessment and psychological management of recurrent headache disorders. *Journal of Consulting and Clinical Psychology, 70,* 656–677.

Holstein, W. J. (2005, November 6). For some searches, Google won't do. *New York Times,* p. B9.

Hoover, R. N. (2000). Cancer—Nature, nurture, or both? *New England Journal of Medicine, 343,* 135–136.

Hopkin, M. (2004, August 10). Alzheimer's linked to lowbrow jobs. *Nature.com.* Retrieved August 11, 2004, from *http://www.nature. com/news/2004/040809/full/040809–3.html*

Horwitz, B. N., Luong, G., & Charles, S. T. (2008). Neuroticism and extraversion share genetic and environmental effects with negative and positive mood spillover in a nationally representative sample. *Personality and Individual Differences, 45,* 636–642.

Hossain, P., Kawar, B., & El Nahas, M. (2007). Obesity and diabetes in the developing world—a growing challenge. *New England Journal of Medicine, 356,* 213–215.

Houry, D. (2004). Suicidal patients in the emergency department: Who is at greatest risk? *Annals of Emergency Medicine, 43,* 731–732.

Hovey, J. D. (2000). Acculturative stress, depression, and suicidal ideation in Mexican immigrants. *Cultural Diversity and Ethnic Minority Psychology, 6,* 134–151.

How often do Americans take risks? (2009, February). *Consumer Reports,* pp. 8–9.

Howard, B. V., Manson, J. E., Stefanick, M. L., Beresford, S. A., Frank, G., Jones, B., et al. (2006). Low-fat dietary pattern and weight change over 7 years: The Women's Health Initiative Dietary Modification Trial. *Journal of the American Medical Association, 295,* 39–49.

Hu, P., Stylos-Allan, M., & Walker, M. (2006). Sleep facilitates consolidation of emotional declarative memory. *Psychological Science, 17,* 891–898.

Huang, L. H. (1994). An integrative approach to clinical assessment and intervention with Asian-American adolescents. *Journal of Clinical Child Psychology, 23,* 21–31.

Hudson, J. I., Hiripi, E., Pope, H. G., Jr., & Kessler, R. C. (2006). Prevalence and correlates of eating disorders in the National Comorbidity Survey Replication. *Biological Psychiatry, 61,* 348–358.

Huesmann, L. R., Moise-Titus, J., Podolski, C.-L., & Eron, L. D. (2003). Longitudinal relations between children's exposure to TV violence and their aggressive and violent behavior in young adulthood: 1977–1992. *Developmental Psychology, 39,* 201–221.

Hunsley, J., & Bailey, J. M. (2001). Whither the Rorschach? An analysis of the evidence. *Psychological Assessment, 13,* 472–485.

Huntjens, R. J. C., Peters, M. L., Postma, A., Woertman, L., Effting, M., & van der Hart, O. (2005). Transfer of newly acquired stimulus valence between identities in dissociative identity disorder (DID). *Behaviour Research and Therapy, 43,* 243–255.

Huttunen, J., Heinimaa, M., Svirskis, T., Nyman, M., Kajander, J., Forsback, S., et al. (2008). Striatal dopamine synthesis in first-degree relatives of patients with schizophrenia. *Biological Psychiatry, 63,* 114–117.

Hwang, W.-C. (2006). The psychotherapy adaptation and modification framework: Application to Asian Americans. *American Psychologist, 61,* 702–715.

Hyde, J. S. (2005a). The gender similarities hypothesis. *American Psychologist, 60,* 581–592.

Hyde, J. S. (2005b). The genetics of sexual orientation. In J. S. Hyde (Ed.), *Biological substrates of human sexuality* (pp. 9–20). Washington, DC: American Psychological Association.

Hyde, J. S, Mezulis, A. H., & Abramson, L. Y. (2008). The ABCs of depression: Integrating affective, biological, and cognitive models to explain the emergence of the gender difference in depression. *Psychological Review, 115,* 291–313.

Hyer, L., Carpenter, B., Bishmann, D., & Wu, H.-S. (2005). Depression in long-term care. *Clinical Psychology: Science and Practice, 12,* 280–299.

Hyman, D. J., & Pavlik, V. N. (2001). Characteristics of patients with uncontrolled hypertension in the United States. *New England Journal of Medicine, 345,* 479–486.

Ilgen, M., McKellar, J., & Tiet, Q. (2005). Abstinence self-efficacy and abstinence 1 year after substance use disorder treatment. *Journal of Consulting and Clinical Psychology, 73,* 1175–1180.

Iribarren, C., Sidney, S., Bild, D. E., Liu, K., Markovitz, J. H., Roseman, J. M., & Matthews, K. (2000). Association of hostility with coronary artery calcification in young adults: The CARDIA study. *Journal of the American Medical Association, 283,* 2546–2551.

̶ks, J. Z., & Devine, P. G. (2000). Attitude importance, forewarning of ̶̶sage content, and resistance to persuasion. *Basic & Applied Social ̶ogy, 22.* 19–29.

Jacoby, L. L., & Rhode, M. G. (2006). False remembering in the aged. *Current Directions in Psychological Science, 15,* 49–53.

Jamison, K. R. (1995). *An unquiet mind.* New York: Knopf.

Jamison, K. R. (1997). Manic-depressive illness and creativity. *Scientific American mysteries of the mind* [Special Issue], 7 (1), 44–49.

Jamison, K. R. (2000). Cited in K. Krehbiel (2000). Diagnosis and treatment of bipolar disorder. *Monitor on Psychology, 31*(9), 22.

Janis, I. L., & Mann, L. (1977). *Decision-making.* New York: Free Press.

Jankowiak, W. R., & Fischer, E. F. (1992). A cross-cultural perspective on romantic love. *Ethnology, 31,* 149–155.

Janssen, E. (Ed.). (2006). *The psychophysiology of sex.* Bloomington: Indiana University Press.

Janus, S. S., & Janus, C. L. (1993). *The Janus report on sexual behavior.* New York: Wiley.

Jefferson, D. J. (2005, August 8). America's most dangerous drug. *Newsweek,* p. 41–48.

Jeffery, R. W., Epstein, L. H., Wilson, G. T., Drewnowski, A., Stunkard, A. J, & Wing, R. R. (2000). Long-term maintenance of weight loss: Current status. *Health Psychology, 19*(Suppl. 1), 5–16.

Jeffery, R. W., Hennrikus, D. J., Lando, H. A., Murray, D. M., & Liu, J. W. (2000). Reconciling conflicting findings regarding postcessation weight concerns and success in smoking cessation. *Health Psychology, 19,* 242–246.

Jemmott, J. B., et al. (1983). Academic stress, power motivation, and decrease in secretion rate of salivary secretory immunoglobin A. *Lancet, 1,* 1400–1402.

Jiang, H., & Chess, L. (2006). Regulation of immune responses by T cells. *New England Journal of Medicine, 354,* 1166–1176.

Joe, S., Baser, E., Breeden, G., Neighbors, H. W., & Jackson, J. S. (2006). Prevalence of and risk factors for lifetime suicide attempts among blacks in the United States. *Journal of the American Medical Association, 296,* 2112–2123.

Johnson, P. R., & Indvik, J. (2000). Rebels, criticizers, backstabbers, and busybodies: Anger and aggression at work. *Public Personnel Management, 29,* 165–174.

Johnson, R. E., Chutuape, M. A., Strain, E. C., Walsh, S. L., Stitzer, M. L., & Bigelow, G. E. (2000). A comparison of levomethadyl acetate, buprenorphine, and methadone for opioid dependence. *New England Journal of Medicine, 343,* 1290–1297.

Johnson, W., & Bouchard, T. J., Jr. (2007). Sex differences in mental abilities: *g* masks the dimensions on which they lie. *Intelligence, 35,* 23–39.

Johnson, W., McGue, M., Krueger, R. J., & Bouchard, T. J., Jr. (2004). Marriage and personality: A genetic analysis. *Journal of Personality and Social Psychology, 86,* 285–294.

Joiner, T. E., Jr., Brown, J. S, & Wingate, L. R. (2005). The psychology and neurobiology of suicidal behavior. *Annual Review of Psychology, 56,* 287–314.

Jokinen, J., Mårtensson, B., Nordström, A.-L., & Nordström, P. (2008). CSF 5-HIAA and DST non-suppression-independent biomarkers in suicide attempters. *Journal of Affective Disorders, 105,* 241–245.

Jones, C. J., & Meredith, W. (2000). Developmental paths of psychological health from early adolescence to later adulthood. *Psychology and Aging, 15,* 351–360.

Jones, D. W., Chambless, L. E., Folsom, A. R., Heiss, G., Hutchinson, R. G., Sharrett, A. R., et al. (2002). Risk factors for coronary heart disease in African Americans: The atherosclerosis risk in communities study, 1987–1997. *Archives of Internal Medicine, 162,* 2565–2571.

Jones, J. (1994). Embodied meaning: Menopause and the change of life. [Special Issue: Women's health and social work: Feminist perspectives]. *Social Work in Health Care, 19*(3–4), 43–65.

Jones, J. L., & Leary, M. R. (1994). Effects of appearance-based admonitions against sun exposure on tanning intentions in young adults. *Health Psychology, 13,* 86–90.

Jones, J. T., Pelham, B. W., Carvallo, M., & Mirenberg, M. C. (2004). How do I love thee? Let me count the Js: Implicit egotism and interpersonal attraction. *Journal of Personality and Social Psychology, 87,* 665–683.

Jonkman, S. (2006). Sensitization facilitates habit formation: Implications for addiction. *Journal of Neuroscience, 26,* 7319–7320.

Judge, T. A., & Cable, D. M. (2004). Income: Preliminary test of a theoretical model. *Journal of Applied Psychology, 89*, 428–441.

Judge, T. A., & Bono, J. E. (2001). Relationship of core self-evaluation traits—self-esteem, generalized self-efficacy, locus of control, and emotional stability—with job satisfaction and job performance: A meta-analysis. *Journal of Applied Psychology, 86*, 80–92.

Judge, T. A., Heller, D., & Mount, M. K. (2002). Five-factor model of personality and job satisfaction: A meta-analysis. *Journal of Applied Psychology, 87*, 530–541.

Judge, T. A., & Ilies, R. (2002). Relationship of personality to performance motivation: A meta-analytic review. *Journal of Applied Psychology, 87*, 797–807.

Judge, T. A., Thoresen, C. J., Bono, J. E., & Patton, G. K. (2001). The job satisfaction–job performance relationship: A qualitative and quantitative review. *Psychological Bulletin, 127*, 376–407.

Just, N., & Alloy, L. B. (1997). The response styles theory of depression: Tests and an extension of the theory. *Journal of Abnormal Psychology, 106*, 221–229.

Kahnemann, D., Krueger, A. B., Schkade, D., Schwarz, N., & Stone, A. A. (2006). Would you be happier if you were richer? A focusing illusion. *Science, 312*, 1908–1910.

Kaiser, C. R., Vick, S. B., & Major, B. (2006). Prejudice expectations moderate preconscious attention to cues that are threatening to social identity. *Psychological Science, 17*, 332–338.

Kallgren, C. A., Reno, R. R., & Cialdini, R. B. (2000). A focus theory of normative conduct: When norms do and do not affect behavior. *Personality & Social Psychology Bulletin, 26*, 1002–1012.

Kamphaus, R. W., Petoskey, M. D., & Rowe, E. W. (2000). Current trends in psychological testing of children. *Professional Psychology: Research and Practice, 31*, 155–164.

Kant, A. K., Schatzkin, A., Graubard, B. I., & Schairer, C. (2000). A prospective study of diet quality and mortality in women. *Journal of the American Medical Association, 283*, 2109–2115.

Kantrowitz, B., & Springen, K. (2003, September 22). Why sleep matters. *Newsweek*, pp. 75–77.

Kaplan, H. R. (1978). *Lottery winners.* New York: Harper & Row.

Kashima, Y. (2000). Maintaining cultural stereotypes in the serial reproduction of narratives. *Personality & Social Psychology Bulletin, 26*, 594–604.

Katon, W. J. (2006). Panic disorder. *New England Journal of Medicine, 354*, 2360–2367.

Katon, W., Russo, J., Sherbourne, C., Russo, J., Sherbourne, C., Stein, M. B., et al. (2006). Incremental cost-effectiveness of a collaborative care intervention for panic disorder. *Psychological Medicine, 36*, 353–363.

Kay, A. B. (2006). Natural killer T cells and asthma [Editorial]. *New England Journal of Medicine, 354*, 1186–1188.

Kaya, N., & Erkip, F. (1999). Invasion of personal space under the condition of short-term crowding: A case study on an automatic teller machine. *Journal of Environmental Psychology, 19*(2), 183–189.

Keating, C. F., Randall, D., Kendrick, T., & Gutshall, K. (2003). Do baby-faced adults receive more help? The (cross-cultural) case of the lost resume. *Journal of Nonverbal Behavior, 27*, 89–109.

Keefe, F. J., Abernethy, A. P., & Campbell, L. C. (2005). Psychological approaches to understanding and treating disease-related pain. *Annual Review of Psychology, 56*, 601–630.

Keller, S. N., & Brown, J. D. (2002). Media interventions to promote responsible sexual behavior. *The Journal of Sex Research, 39*, 1–6.

Keller, S., Maddock, J. E., Laforge, R. G., Velicer, W. F., & Basler, H-D. (2007). Binge drinking and health behavior in medical students. *Addictive Behaviors, 32*, 505–515.

Kellerman, J., Lewis, J., & Laird, J. D. (1989). Looking and loving: The effects of mutual gaze on feelings of romantic love. *Journal of Research in Personality, 23*, 145–161.

Kemeny, M. E. (2003). The psychobiology of stress. *Current Directions in Psychological Science, 12*, 124–129.

Kendler, K. S., et al. (2000). Illicit psychoactive substance use, heavy use, abuse, and dependence in a US population-based sample of male twins. *Archives of General Psychiatry, 57*, 261–269.

Kennedy, R. (2003). *Interracial intimacies: Sex, marriage, identity, and adoption.* New York: Knopf.

Kenrick, D. T., Li, N. P., & Butner, J. (2003). Dynamical evolutionary psychology: Individual decision rules and emergent social norms. *Psychological Review, 110*, 3–28.

Kenrick, D. T., & MacFarlane, S. W. (1986). Ambient temperature and horn honking: A field study of the heat/aggression relationship. *Environment and Behavior, 18*, 179–191.

Kern, M. L., & Friedman, H. S. (2008). Do conscientious individuals live longer? A quantitative review. *Health Psychology, 27*, 505–512.

Kerr, M., Stattin, H., Biesecker, G., & Ferrer-Wreder, L. (2003). Relationships with parents and peers in adolescence. In R. M. Lerner, M. A. Easterbrooks, & J. Mistry (Eds.), *Handbook of psychology: Developmental psychology* (Vol. 6, pp. 395–422). New York: Wiley.

Kessler, R. C., Berglund, P., Demler, O., Jin, R., Koretz, D., Merikangas, K. R., et al. (2003). The epidemiology of major depressive disorder: Results from the National Comorbidity Survey Replication (NCS-R). *Journal of the American Medical Association, 289*, 3095–3105.

Kessler, R. C., Berglund, P. A., Demler, O., Jin, R., & Walters, E. E. (2005). Lifetime prevalence and age-of-onset distributions of DSM-IV disorders in the National Comorbidity Survey Replication (NCS-R). *Archives of General Psychiatry, 62*, 593–602.

Kessler, R. C., Chiu, W. T., Demler, O., & Walters, E. E. (2005). Prevalence, severity, and comorbidity of 12-month DSM-IV disorders in the National Comorbidity Survey Replication. *Archives of General Psychiatry, 62*, 617–627.

Kiecolt-Glaser, J. K., Preacher, K. J., MacCallum, R. C., Atkinson, C., Malarkey, W. B., & Glaser, R. (2003). Chronic stress and age-related increases in the proinflammatory cytokine IL-6. *Proceedings of the National Academy of Sciences, 100*, 9090–9095.

Kiecolt-Glaser, J. K., Speicher, C. E., Holliday, J. E., & Glaser, R. (1984). Stress and the transformation of lymphocytes in Epstein-Barr virus. *Journal of Behavioral Medicine, 7*, 1–12.

Kiefer, A. K., & Sekaquaptewa, D. (2007). Implicit stereotypes, gender identification, and math-related outcomes: A prospective study of female college students. *Psychological Science, 18*, 13–18.

Kiehl, K. A. (2006). A cognitive neuroscience perspective on psychopathy: Evidence for paralimbic system dysfunction. *Psychiatry Research, 142*, 107–128.

Kim, S., & Hasher, L. (2005). The attraction effect in decision making: Superior performance by older adults. *The Quarterly Journal of Experimental Psychology: Human Experimental Psychology, 58A*(1), 120–133.

Kimura, D. (2002, May 13). Sex differences in the brain. *Scientific American.* Retrieved June 23, 2002, from *http://www.sciam.com/article.cfm?articleID=00018E9D-879D-1D06-8E498 09EC588EEDF*

King, K. R. (2005). Why is discrimination stressful? The mediating role of cognitive appraisal. *Cultural Diversity & Ethnic Minority Psychology, 11*, 202–212.

King, R. (2000). Cited in L. Frazier (2000, July 16). The new face of HIV is young, black. *Washington Post*, p. C1.

Kinsey, A. C., Pomeroy, W. B., & Martin, C. E. (1948). *Sexual behavior in the human male.* Philadelphia: W. B. Saunders.

Kirsch, I., Moore, T. J., Scoboria, A., & Nicholls, S. S. (2002a, July). The emperor's new drugs: An analysis of antidepressant medication data submitted to the U.S. Food and Drug Administration. *Prevention & Treatment, 5.* Retrieved July 16, 2003, from *http://journals.apa.org/preveniton/volume5/pre0050023a.html*

Kirsch, I., Scoboria, A., & Moore, T. J. (2002b). Antidepressants and placebos: Secrets, revelations, and unanswered questions. *Prevention and Treatment, 5.* Retrieved August 8, 2005, from *http://www.journals.apa.org/prevention/volume5/pre0050033r.html*

Kitayama, S., Duffy, S., Kawamura, T., & Larsen, J. T. (2003). Perceiving an object and its context in different cultures: A cultural look at new look. *Psychological Science, 14*, 201–206.

Klein, M. H., Hyde, J. S., Essex, M. J., & Clark, R. (1998). Maternity leave, role quality, work involvement, and mental health one year after delivery. *Psychology of Women Quarterly, 22*(2), 239–266.

Kleinke, C. L. (1977). Compliance to requests made by gazing and touching experimenters in field settings. *Journal of Experimental Social Psychology, 13,* 218–223.

Kleinke, C. L., & Staneski, R. A. (1980). First impressions of female bust size. *Journal of Social Psychology, 110,* 123–134.

Klump, K. L., & Culbert, K. M. (2007). Molecular genetic studies of eating disorders: Current status and future directions. *Current Directions in Psychological Science, 16,* 37–41.

Knapp, M. L. (1984). *Interpersonal communication and human relationships.* Needham Heights, MA: Allyn & Bacon.

Knox, D., Zusman, M. E., & Nieves, W. (1998). Breaking away: How college students end love relationships. *College Student Journal, 32,* 482–484.

Knox, D., Zusman, & Zusman, M. E. (1999). Love relationships among college students. *College Student Journal, 33,* 149–151.

Kobasa, S. C. O., Maddi, S. R., Puccetti, M. C., & Zola, M. A. (1994). Effectiveness of hardiness, exercise, and social support as resources against illness. In A. Steptoe & J. Wardle (Eds.), *Psychosocial processes and health* (pp. 247–260). Cambridge, UK: Cambridge University Press.

Koenen, K. C., Fu, Q. J., Ertel, K., Lyons, M. J., Eisen, S. A., et al. (2008). Common genetic liability to major depression and posttraumatic stress disorder in men. *Journal of Affective Disorders, 105,* 109–115.

Kohl, J. V. (2007). Pospartum psychoses: Closer to schizophrenia or the affective spectrum? *Current Opinion in Psychiatry, 17,* 87–90.

Kohlberg, L. (1981). *The philosophy of moral development: Moral stages and the idea of justice.* San Francisco: Harper & Row.

Kolata, G. (2000, June 25). Men in denial: The doctor's tale. *New York Times.* Retrieved February 22, 2002, from *http://www. nytimes.com/2000/06/25/health/men-in-denial-the-doctors-tale.html*

Kornblum, W. (2000). *Sociology in a changing world* (5th ed.). Fort Worth: Harcourt College Publishers.

Koss, M. P., & Kilpatrick, D. G. (2001). Rape and sexual assault. In Gerrity, E., et al. (Eds.). *The mental health consequences of torture.* (pp. 177–193). Dordrecht, Netherlands: Kluwer Academic Publishers.

Kosson, D. S., Lorenz, A. R., & Newman, J. P. (2006). Effects of comorbid psychopathy on criminal offending and emotion processing in male offenders with antisocial personality disorder. *Journal of Abnormal Psychology, 115,* 798–780.

Kramer, A. F., & Willis, S. L. (2002). Enhancing the cognitive vitality of older adults. *Current Directions in Psychological Science, 11,* 173–177.

Krantz, D. S., Contrada, R. J., Hill, D. R., & Friedler, E. (1988). Environmental stress and biobehavioral antecedents of coronary heart disease. *Journal of Consulting and Clinical Psychology, 56,* 333–341.

Krantz, M. J., & Mehler, P. S. (2004). Treating opioid dependence: Growing implications for primary care. *Archives of Internal Medicine, 164,* 277–288.

Kranzler, H. R. (2000). Medications for alcohol dependence: New vistas [Editorial]. *Journal of the American Medical Association, 284.*

Krendl, A. C., Richeson, J. A., Kelley, W. M., & Heatherton, T. F. (2008). The negative consequences of threat: A functional magnetic resonance imaging investigation of the neural mechanisms underlying women's underperformance in math. *Psychological Science, 19,* 168–175.

Krieshok, T. S. (2001). How the decision-making literature might inform career center practice. *Journal of Career Development, 27*(3), 207–216.

Kroger, J. (2000). Ego identity status research in the new millennium. *International Journal of Behavioral Development, 24,* 145–148.

Krueger, R. F., & Markon, K. E. (2006). Understanding psychopathology: Melding behavior genetics, personality, and quantitative psychology to develop an empirically based model. *Current Directions in Psychological Science, 15,* 113–117.

Krug, E. G., et al. (1998). Suicide after natural disasters. *New England Journal of Medicine, 338,* 373–378.

Kubiszyn, T. W., Meyer, G. J., Finn, S. E., Eyde, L. D., Kay, G. G., Moreland, K. L., et al. (2000). Empirical support for psychological assessment in clinical health care settings. *Professional Psychology: Research and Practice, 31,* 119–130.

E. (1969). *On death and dying.* New York: Macmillan.

Kuhn, C. M., & Wilson, W. A. (2001, Spring). Our dangerous love affair with ecstasy. *Cerebrum,* pp. 22–33.

Kuhn, D. (2006). Do cognitive changes accompany developments in the adolescent brain? *Perspectives on Psychological Science, 1,* 59–67.

Kumashiro, K. K. (Ed.). (2004). *Restoried selves: Autobiographies of queer Asian/Pacific American activists.* New York: Haworth Press.

Kumsta, R., Entringer, S., Hellhammer, D. H., & Wüst, S. (2007). Cortisol and ACTH responses to psychosocial stress are modulated by corticosteroid binding globulin levels. *Psychoneuroendocrinology, 32,* 1153–1157.

Kunda, Z., & Spencer, S. J. (2003). When do stereotypes come to mind and when do they color judgment? A goal-based theoretical framework for stereotype activation and application. *Psychological Bulletin, 129,* 522–544.

Kupfersmid, J. (1995). Does the Oedipus complex exist? *Psychotherapy, 32,* 535–547.

Kurdek, L. A. (2005). What do we know about gay and lesbian couples? *Current Directions in Psychological Science, 14*(5), 251.

Kurzban, R., & Weeden, J. (2005). HurryDate: Mate preferences in action. *Evolution and Human Behavior, 26,* 227–244.

Lachman, M. E. (2004). Development in midlife. *Annual Review of Psychology, 55,* 305–331.

LaFramboise, T. (1994). Cited in T. DeAngelis (1994). History, culture affect treatment for Indians. *APA Monitor, 27*(10), 36.

LaFrance, M., Hecht, M. A., & Paluck, E. L. (2003). The contingent smile: A meta-analysis of sex differences in smiling. *Psychological Bulletin, 129,* 305–334.

Lahti, J., Räikkönen, K., Ekelund, J., Peltonen, L, Raitakari, O. T., & Keltikangas-Järvinen, L. (2006). Socio-demographic characteristics moderate the association between DRD4 and novelty seeking. *Personality and Individual Differences, 40,* 533–543.

Laino, C. (2000, July 18). Cybersex addiction widespread. *MSNBC.* Retrieved July 23, 2000, from *http://www.msnbc.com/news/596355.asp*

Laino, C. (2002, April 25) Gender gap in longevity narrowing. *MSNBC.* Retrieved May 5, 2002, from *http://www.msnbc.com/news/743069.asp*

Lalumière, M. L., Blanchard, R., & Zucker, K. J. (2000). Sexual orientation and handedness in men and women: A meta-analysis. *Psychological Bulletin, 126,* 575–592.

Lamanna, M. A., & Riedmann, A. (2005). *Marriages and families* (8th ed). Belmont, CA: Wadsworth.

Lamberg, L. (2003). Advances in eating disorders offer food for thought. *Journal of the American Medical Association, 290,* 1437–1442.

Lamberg, L. (2006). Rx for obesity: Eat less, exercise more, and—maybe—get more sleep. *Journal of the American Medical Association, 295,* 2341–2344.

Lamberg, L. (2008). Despite effectiveness, behavioral therapy for chronic insomnia still underused. *Journal of the American Medical Association, 300,* 2474–2475.

Lamberti, D. (1997). Cited in Alterman, E. (1997, November). Sex in the '90s. *Elle.*

Lamers, C. T. J., Bechara, A., Rizzo, M., & Ramaekers, J. G. (2006). Cognitive function and mood in MDMA/THC users, THC users and non-drug using controls. *Journal of Psychopharmacology, 20,* 302–311.

Lancaster, T., Stead, L., Silagy, C., & Sowden, A. (2000). Regular review: Effectiveness of interventions to help people stop smoking: Findings from the Cochrane Library. *British Medical Journal, 321,* 355–358.

Lang, A. R., Goeckner, D. J., Adesso, V. J., & Marlatt, G. A. (1975). Effects of alcohol on aggression in male social drinkers. *Journal of Abnormal Psychology, 84,* 508–518.

Langens, T. A., & Schüler, J. (2007). Effects of written emotional expression: The role of positive expectancies. *Health Psychology, 26,* 174–182.

Langlois, J. H., Kalakanis, L., Rubenstein, A. J., Larson, A., Hallam, M., & Smoot, M. (2000). Maxims or myths of beauty? A meta-analytic and theoretical review. *Psychological Bulletin, 126,* 390–423.

Laroche, L. (2003). *Managing cross-cultural differences in international projects.* Retrieved May 8, 2003, from *http://www.itapintl.com/mngdifintproj.htm*

Latane, B., & Darley, J. M. (1970). *The unresponsive bystander: Why doesn't he help?* New York: Appleton-Century-Crofts.

Latta, F., & Van Cauter, E. (2003). Sleep and biological clocks. In M. Gallagher & R. J. Nelson (Eds.), *Handbook of psychology: Vol. 3. Biological psychology* (pp. 355–378). New York: Wiley.

Lauerman, C. (2000, November 7). Psychological counseling is now just a computer click away. *Chicago Tribune.* Retrieved October 15, 2001, from *http://www.psycport.com/news/2000/11/07/knigt/3822–0076-MED-ETHERAPY.TB.html*

Laumann, E. O., Gagnon, J. H., Michael, R. T., & Michaels, S. (1994). *The social organization of sexuality.* Chicago: University of Chicago Press.

Laumann, E. O., Mahay, J., & Youm, Y. (2007). Sex, intimacy, and family life in the United States. In M. Kimmel (Ed), *The sexual self: The construction of sexual scripts* (pp. 165–190). Nashville, TN: Vanderbilt University Press.

Laumann, E. O., Paik, A., & Rosen, R. C. (1999). Sexual dysfunction in the United States: Prevalence and predictors. *Journal of the American Medical Association, 281,* 537–544.

Lawrence, J., Mayers, D. L., Hullsiek, K. H., Collins, G., Abrams, D. I., Reisler, R. B., et al. (2003). Structured treatment interruption in patients with multidrug-resistant human immunodeficiency virus. *New England Journal of Medicine, 349,* 837–846.

Lazarus, R. S., DeLongis, A., Folkman, S., & Gruen, R. (1985). Stress and adaptational outcomes: The problem of confounded measures. *American Psychologist, 40,* 770–779.

Lazarus, R. S., & Folkman, S. (1984). *Stress, appraisal, and coping.* New York: Springer.

Leaper, C. (2000). Gender, affiliation, assertion, and the interactive context of parent–child play. *Developmental Psychology, 36,* 381–393.

Leaper, C., & Ayres, M. M. (2007). A meta-analytic review of gender variations in adults' language use: Talkativeness, affiliative speech, and assertive speech. *Personality and Social Psychology Review, 11,* 328–363.

Lear, J. (2000, February 27). Freud's second thoughts. *New York Times Book Review,* p. 39.

Leber, P. (2000). Placebo controls: No news is good news. *Archives of General Psychiatry, 57,* 319–320.

Leckman, J. F., & Kim, Y. S. (2006). A primary candidate gene for obsessive-compulsive disorder. *Archives of General Psychiatry, 63,* 717–720.

Leclerc, C. M., & Hess, T. M. (2007). Age differences in the bases for social judgments: Tests of a social expertise perspective. *Experimental Aging Research, 33,* 95–120.

Lee, I.-M. (2007). Dose-response relation between physical activity and fitness: Even a little is good; more is better. *Journal of the American Medical Association, 297,* 2137–2139.

Lee, J. (2002, September 19). I think, therefore IM. *New York Times,* p. G1.

Lee, L., Loewenstein, G., Ariely, D., Hong, J., Young, J. (2008). If I'm not hot, are you hot or not? Physical-attractiveness evaluations and dating preferences as a function of one's own attractiveness. *Psychological Science, 19,* 669–677.

Lefley, H. P. (1990). Culture and chronic mental illness. *Hospital and Community Psychiatry, 41,* 277–286.

Lehne, G. K. (2005). Sexual dysfunction. *Journal of Nervous and Mental Disease, 193,* 429–430.

Leiblum, S. R., Koochaki, P. E., Rodenberg, C. A., Barton, I. P., & Rosen, R. C. (2006). Hypoactive sexual desire disorder in postmenopausal women: US results from the women's International Study of Health and Sexuality (WISHeS). *Menopause, 13,* 46–56.

Lent, R. W., Singley, D., Shou, H. B., Schmidt, J. A., & Schmidt, L. C. (2007). Relation of social-cognitive factors to academic satisfaction in engineering students. *Journal of Career Assessment, 15,* 87–97.

Leon, A. C. (2000). Placebo protects subjects from nonresponse: A paradox of power. *Archives of General Psychiatry, 57,* 329–330.

Leonardo, E. D., & Hen, R. (2006). Genetics of affective and anxiety disorders. *Annual Review of Psychology, 57,* 117–137.

Lesné, S., Koh, M. T., Kotilinek, L., Kayed, R., Glabe, C. G., Yang, A., et al. (2006). A specific amyloid-bold beta protein assembly in the brain impairs memory. *Nature, 440,* 352–357.

Lespérance F., Frasure-Smith, N., Koszycki, D., Laliberté, M.-A., van Zyl, L. T., Baker, B., et al. (2007). Effects of citalopram and interpersonal psychotherapy on depression in patients with coronary artery disease: The Canadian Cardiac Randomized Evaluation of Antidepressant and Psychotherapy Efficacy (CREATE) trial. *Journal of the American Medical Association, 297,* 367–379.

LeVay, S. (2003). *The biology of sexual orientation.* Retrieved December 19, 2003, from *http://members.aol.com/slevay/page22.html*

Levine, E. S., & Schmelkin, L. P. (2006). The move to prescribe: A change in paradigm? *Professional Psychology: Research and Practice, 37,* 205–209.

Levine, R. V., & Norenzayan, A. (1999). The pace of life in 31 countries. *Journal of Cross-Cultural Psychology, 30,* 178–205.

Levine, S. C., Vasilyeva, M., Lourenco, S. F., Newcombe, N. S., & Huttenlocher, J. (2005). Socioeconomic status modifies the sex difference in spatial skill. *Psychological Science, 16,* 841–845.

Levinson, D. J., Darrow, C. N., Klein, E. B., Levinson, M. H., & McKee, B. (1978). *The seasons of a man's life.* New York: Knopf.

Levy, B. R., Slade, M. D., Kunkel, S. R., & Kasl, S. V. (2002). Longevity increased by positive self-perceptions of aging. *Journal of Personality and Social Psychology, 83,* 261–270.

Lewinsohn, P. M., Rohde, P., Seeley, J. R., Klein, D. N., & Gotlib, I. H. (2000). Natural course of adolescent major depressive disorder in a community sample: Predictors of recurrence in young adults. *American Journal of Psychiatry, 157,* 1584–1591.

Lewis, M. (2002, October 27). In defense of the boom. *New York Times Magazine,* pp. 44–49, 60, 71–72, 84, 94.

Leyton, M., et al. (2000). Acute tyrosine depletion and alcohol ingestion in healthy women. *Alcoholism: Clinical & Experimental Research, 24,* 459–464.

Li, G., Baker, S. P., Smialek, J. E., & Soderstrom, C. A. (2001). Use of alcohol as a risk factor for bicycling injury. *Journal of the American Medical Association, 284,* 893–896.

Li, N. P., & Kenrick, D. T. (2006). Sex similarities and differences in preferences for short-term mates: what, whether, and why. *Journal of Personality and Social Psychology, 90,* 468–489.

Liberles, S., D., & Buck, L. B. (2006). A second class of chemosensory receptors in the olfactory epithelium. *Nature, 442,* 645–650.

Libow, L. S. (2005). Geriatrics in the United States—baby boomers' boon? *New England Journal of Medicine, 352,* 750–752.

Lieber, C. S. (1990, January 14). Cited in Barroom biology: How alcohol goes to a woman's head, *New York Times,* p. E24.

Lieberman, J. A., Stroup, T. S., McEvoy, J. P., Swartz, M. S., Rosenheck, R. A., Perkins, D. O., et al. (2005). Effectiveness of antipsychotic drugs in patients with chronic schizophrenia. *New England Journal of Medicine, 353,* 1209–1223.

Lilienfeld, S. O., Fowler, K. A., & Lohr, J. M. (2003). And the band played on: Science, pseudoscience, and the Rorschach Inkblot method. *The Clinical Psychologist, 56*(1), 6–7.

Lilienfeld, S. O., Kirsch, I., Sarbin, T. R., Lynn, S. J., Chaves, J. F., Ganaway, G. K., et al. (1999). Dissociative identity disorder and the sociocognitive model: Recalling the lessons of the past. *Psychological Bulletin, 125,* 507–523.

Lim, S., & Cortina, L. M. (2005). Interpersonal mistreatment in the workplace: The interface and impact of general incivility and sexual harassment. *Journal of Applied Psychology, 90,* 483–496.

Linde, K., Streng, A., Jurgens, S., Hoppe, A., Brinkhaus, B., Witt, C., Wagenpfeil S, et al. (2005). Acupuncture for patients with migraine: A randomized controlled trial. *Journal of the American Medical Association, 293,* 2118–2125.

Lindenmayer, J. P., & Khan, A. (2004). Pharmacological treatment strategies for schizophrenia. *Expert Review of Neurotherapeutics, 4,* 705–723.

Lipman, E. L., MacMillan, H. L., & Boyle, M. H. (2001). Childhood abuse and psychiatric disorders among single and married mothers. *American Journal of Psychiatry, 158,* 73–77.

Lisanby, S. H., Maddox, J. H., Prudic, J., Devanand, D. P., & Sackeim, H. A. (2000). The effects of electroconvulsive therapy on memory of autobiographical and public events. *Archives of General Psychiatry, 57,* 581–590.

Little, A. C., Burt, D. M., & Perrett, D. I. (2006). What is good is beautiful: Face preference reflects desired personality. *Personality and Individual Differences, 41,* 1107–1118.

Little, S. J., Holte, S., Routy, J. P., Daar, E. S., Markowitz, M., Collier, A. C., et al. (2002). Antiretroviral-drug resistance among patients recently infected with HIV. *New England Journal of Medicine, 347,* 385–394.

Livingston, R. W., & Drwecki, B. B. (2007). Why are some individuals not racially biased? Susceptibility to affective conditioning predicts non-prejudice toward blacks. *Psychological Science, 18,* 816–823.

Lo, C. S. L., Ho, S. M. Y., & Hollon, S. D. (2008). The effects of rumination and negative cognitive styles on depression: A mediation analysis. *Behaviour Research and Therapy, 46,* 487–495.

Lobb, R., Suarez, E. G., Fay, M. E., Gutheil, C. M., Hunt, M. K., Fletcher, R. H., & Emmons, K. M. (2004). Implementation of a cancer prevention program for working class, multiethnic populations. *Preventive Medicine, 38,* 766–776.

Lobel, M., DeVincent, C.J., Kaminer, A., & Meyer, B.A. (2000). The impact of prenatal maternal stress and optimistic disposition on birth outcomes in medically high-risk women. *Health Psychology, 19,* 544–553.

Lohman, J. J. H. M. (2001). Treatment strategies for migraine headache. *Journal of the American Medical Association, 285,* 1014.

London-Vargas, N. (2001, July). Organizing a life's work: Finding your dream job. *TIP: The Industrial-Organizational Psychologist, Vol. 39*(1). Retrieved August 13, 2001, from *http://www.siop.org/TIP/backissues/TipJul01/Jul01TOC.htm.*

Longer, healthier, better. (1997, March 9). *New York Times Magazine,* pp. 44–45.

López-León, S., Janssens, A. C., González-Zuloeta Ladd, A. M., Del-Favero, J., Claes, S. J., Oostra, B. A., et al.. (2008). Meta-analysis of genetic studies on major depressive disorder. *Molecular Psychiatry, 13,* 7772.

Lorenz, F. O., Wickrama, K. A. S., Conger, R. D., & Elder, G. H., Jr. (2006). The short-term and decade-long effects of divorce on women's midlife health. *Journal of Health and Social Behavior, 47,* 111–125.

Los Angeles Unified School District. (2000). *Youth suicide prevention information.* Los Angeles: Author.

Low, C. A., Stanton, A. L., & Danoff-Burg, S. (2006). Expressive disclosure and benefit finding among breast cancer patients: Mechanisms for positive health effects. *Health Psychology, 25,* 181–189.

Low, K. S. D., Yoon, M., Mijung; R., Roberts, B. W., & Rounds, J. (2005). The stability of vocational interests from early adolescence to middle adulthood: a quantitative review of longitudinal studies. *Psychological Bulletin, 131,* 713–737.

Lown, J. M., & Dolan, E. M. (1988). Financial challenges in remarriage. *Lifestyles, 9,* 73–88.

Lucas, R. E. (2007). Adaptation and the set-point model of subjective well-being: Does happiness change after major life events? *Current Directions in Psychological Science, 16,* 75–79.

Lucas, R. E., Clark, A. E., Georgellis, Y., & Diener, E. (2003). Reexamining adaptation and the set point model of happiness: Reactions to changes in marital status. *Journal of Personality and Social Psychology, 84,* 527–539.

Ludwick-Rosenthal, R., & Neufeld, R. W. J. (1993). Preparation for undergoing an invasive medical procedure. *Journal of Consulting and Clinical Psychology, 61,* 156–164.

Ludwig, D. S., & Kabat-Zinn, J. (2008). Mindfulness in medicine. *Journal of the American Medical Association, 300,* 1350–1352.

Luijendijk, H. J., van den Berg, J. F., Marieke, J. H. J., Dekker, M. D., van Tuijl, H. R., Otte, W., et al. (2008). Incidence and recurrence of late-life depression. *Archives of General Psychiatry, 65,* 1394–1401.

Luo, S., & Klohnen, E. C. (2005). Assortative mating and marital quality in newlyweds: A couple-centered approach. *Journal of Personality and Social Psychology, 88,* 304–326.

Luoma, J. B., Martin, C. E., & Pearson, J. L. (2002). Contact with mental health and primary care providers before suicide: A review of the evidence. *American Journal of Psychiatry, 159,* 909–916.

Lurie, N. (2005). Health disparities—less talk, more action. *New England Journal of Medicine, 353,* 727–729.

Lurie, N., et al. (1993). Preventive care for women: Does the sex of the physician matter? *New England Journal of Medicine, 329,* 478–482.

Lykken, D., & Csikszentmihalyi, M. (2001). Happiness—stuck with what you've got? *American Psychologist, 14,* 470–472.

Lynch, H. T., Coronel, S. M., Okimoto, R., Hampel, H., Sweet, K., Lynch, J. F., et al. (2004). A founder mutation of the MSH2 gene and hereditary nonpolyposis colorectal cancer in the United States. *Journal of the American Medical Association, 291,* 718–724.

Lyness, K. S., Thompson, C. A., Francesco, A. M., & Judiesch, M. K. (1999). Work and pregnancy: Individual and organizational factors influencing organizational commitment, time of maternity leave and return to work. *Sex Roles, 41,* 485–508.

Lynn, J. (2001). Serving patients who may die soon and their families: The role of hospice and other services. *Journal of the American Medical Association, 285,* 925–932.

Lynskey, M. T., Grant, J. D., Li, L., Nelson, E. C., Bucholz, K. K., Madden, P. A., Statham, D., et al. (2007). Stimulant use and symptoms of abuse/dependence: Epidemiology and associations with cannabis use—a twin study. *Drug and Alcohol Dependence, 86,* 147–153.

Lyssenko, V., Jonsson, A., Almgren, P., Pulizzi, N., Isomaa, B., Tuomi, R., et al. (2008). Clinical risk factors, DNA variants, and the development of type 2 diabetes. *New England Journal of Medicine, 359,* 2220–2232.

MacFarquhar, N. (1996, August 8). Mutilation of Egyptian girls: Despite ban, it goes on. *New York Times,* p. A3.

Maccoby, E. E., & Jacklin, C. N. (1974). *The psychology of sex differences.* Stanford, CA: Stanford University Press.

Machleit, K. A., Eroglu, S. A., & Mantel, S. P. (2000). Perceived retail crowding and shopping satisfaction: What modifies this relationship? *Journal of Consumer Psychology, 9,* 29–42.

Maestripieri, D., & Roney, J. R. (2006). Evolutionary developmental psychology: Contributions from comparative research with nonhuman primates. *Developmental Review, 26,* 120–137.

Magdol, L., Moffitt, T. E., Caspi, A., et al. (1997). Gender differences in partner violence in a birth cohort of 21-year-olds: Bridging the gap between clinical and epidemiological approaches. *Journal of Consulting and Clinical Psychology, 65,* 68–78.

Mah, K., & Binik, Y. M. (2001). The nature of human orgasm: A critical review of major trends. *Clinical Psychology Review, 21,* 823–856.

Mahmut, M., Homewood, J., & Stevenson, R. (2007). The characteristics of non-criminals with high psychopathy traits: Are they similar to criminal psychopaths? *Journal of Research in Personality, 42,* 679–692.

Major, G. C., Doucet, E., Trayhurn, P., Astrup, A., & Tremblay, A. (2007). Clinical significance of adaptive thermogenesis. *International Journal of Obesity, 31,* 204–212.

Maldonado, J. R., Butler, L. D., & Spiegel, D. (1998). Treatments for dissociative disorders. In P. E. Nathan & J. M. Gorman (Eds.), *A guide to treatments that work* (pp. 423–446). New York: Oxford University Press.

Malgady, R. G., Rogler, L. H., & Costantino, G. (1990). Culturally sensitive psychotherapy for Puerto Rican children and adolescents: A program of treatment outcome research. *Journal of Consulting and Clinical Psychology, 58,* 704–712.

Malouff, J., Rooke, S., & Schutte, N. (2008). The heritability of human behavior: Results of aggregating meta-analyses. *Current Psychology, 27,* 153–161.

Mann, T., Tomiyama, A.J., Westling, E., Lew, A., Samuels, B., & Chatman, J. (2007). Medicare's search for effective obesity treatments: Diets are not the answer. *American Psychologist, 62,* 220–233.

Manning, R., Levine, M., & Collins, A. (2007). The Kitty Genovese murder and the social psychology of helping: The parable of the 38 witnesses. *American Psychologist, 62,* 555–562.

Mansell, W., & Pedley, R. (2008). The ascent into mania: A review of psychological processes associated with the development of manic symptoms. *Clinical Psychology Review, 28,* 494–520.

Manson, J. E., & Bassuk, S. S. (2003). Obesity in the United States: A fresh look at its high toll. *Journal of the American Medical Association, 289,* 229–230.

Manson, J. E., Greenland, P., LaCroix, A. Z., Stefanick, M. L., Mouton, C. P., et al. (2002). Walking compared with vigorous exercise for the prevention of cardiovascular events in women. *New England Journal of Medicine, 347,* 716–725.

Manson, J. E., Skerrett, P. J., Greenland, P., & VanItallie, T. B. (2004). The escalating pandemics of obesity and sedentary lifestyle: A call to action for clinicians. *Archives of Internal Medicine, 164,* 249–258.

Marcia, J. E. (1991). Identity and self-development. In R. M. Lerner, A. C. Petersen, & J. Brooks-Gunn (Eds.), *Encyclopedia of adolescence* (Vol. 1). New York: Garland.

Marin, T. J., Martin, T. M., Blackwell, E., Stetler, C., & Miller, G. E. (2007). Differentiating the impact of episodic and chronic stressors on hypothalamic-pituitary-adrenocortical axis regulation in young women. *Health Psychology, 26*, 447–455.

Markel, H. (2003, September 3). Lack of sleep takes it toll on student psyches. *New York Times*, p. F6.

Markham, B. (2006). Older women and security. In J. Worell & C. D. Goodheart (Eds.), *Handbook of girls' and women's psychological health: Gender and well-being across the lifespan* (pp. 388–396). New York: Oxford University Press.

Markman, H. J. (1981). Prediction of marital distress: A five-year follow-up. *Journal of Consulting and Clinical Psychology, 49*, 760–762.

Marks, I., & Dar, R. (2000). Fear reduction by psychotherapies: Recent findings, future directions. *British Journal of Psychiatry, 176*, 507–511.

Markus, H., & Kitayama, S. (1991). Culture and the self. *Psychological Review, 98*(2), 224–253.

Marquis, C. (2003, March 16). Living in sin. *New York Times*, p. WK2.

Married households rise again among blacks, census finds. (2003, April 26). *New York Times*, p. A13.

Marsiglio, W. (2004). When stepfathers claim stepchildren: A conceptual analysis. *Journal of Marriage & Family, 66*, 22–39.

Martella, D., & Maass, A. (2000). Unemployment and life satisfaction: The moderating role of time structure and collectivism. *Journal of Applied Social Psychology, 30*, 1095–1108.

Martin, A. (2007, March 25). Will diners still swallow this? *New York Times*, Section 3, pp. 1, 9, 10.

Martin, C. L., & Fabes, R. A. (2001). The stability and consequences of young children's same-sex peer interactions. *Developmental Psychology, 37*, 431–446.

Martin, C. L., & Halverson, C. F. (1983). The effects of sex-typing schemas on young children's memory. *Child Development, 54*, 563–574.

Marwick, C. (2000). Consensus panel considers osteoporosis. *Journal of the American Medical Association, 283*(16). Retrieved May 14, 2009, from *http://womenshealth.about.com/library/weekly//aa040300a.html*

Marx, J. (2007). Evidence linking DISC1 gene to mental illness builds. *Science, 318*, 1062–1063.

Maslach, C., & Leiter, M. P. (2008). Early predictors of job burnout and engagement. *Journal of Applied Psychology, 93*, 498–512.

Masters, W. H., & Johnson, V. E. (1966). *Human sexual response.* Boston: Little, Brown.

Masters, W. H., & Johnson, V. E. (1970). *Human sexual inadequacy.* Boston: Little, Brown.

Matlin, M. W. (1999). *The psychology of women* (4th ed.). Fort Worth, TX: Harcourt College.

Matthews, K. (1994). Cited in Azar, B. (1994). Women are barraged by media on "the change." *APA Monitor, 25*(5), 24–25.

Maxwell, L. E., & Evans, G. W. (2000). The effects of noise on pre-school children's pre-reading skills. *Journal of Environmental Psychology, 20*, 91–97.

Mayer, J. D., Salovey, P., & Caruso, D. R. (2008). Emotional intelligence: New ability or eclectic traits. *American Psychologist, 63*, 503.

Mays, V. M., Cochran, S. D., & Barnes, N. W. (2007). Race, race-based discrimination, and health outcomes among African Americans. *Annual Review of Psychology, 58*, 201–225.

Mazure, C. M., & Keita, G. P. (Eds.).(2006). *Understanding depression in women: Applying empirical research to practice and policy.* Washington, DC: American Psychological Association.

McAuley, E., Blissmer, B., Marquez, D. X., Jerome, G. J., Kramer, A. G., & Katula, J. (2000). Social relations, physical activity and well-being in older adults. *Preventive Medicine, 31*, 608–617.

McAuley, E., Elavsky, S., Jerome, G. J., Konopack, J. F., & Marquez, D. X. (2005). Physical activity-related well-being in older adults: Social cognitive influences. *Psychology and Aging, 20*, 295–302.

McBride, J., & Simms, S. (2001). Death in the family: Adapting a family systems framework to the grief process. *American Journal of Family Therapy, 29*(1), 59–73.

McCarthy, E. P., Burns, R. B., Ngo-Metzger, Q., Davis, R. B., & Phillips, R. S. (2003). Hospice use among Medicare managed care and fee-for-service patients dying with cancer. *Journal of the American Medical Association, 289*, 2238–2245.

McCoy, N. L., & Pitino, L. (2002). Pheromonal influences on sociosexual behavior in young women. *Physiology and Behavior, 75*, 367–375.

McCrae, R. R., Costa, P. T., Jr., Martin, T. A., Oryol, V. E., Rukavishnikov, A. A., Senin, I. G., et al. (2004). Consensual validation of personality traits across cultures. *Journal of Research in Personality, 38*, 179–201.

McCrae, R. R., Costa, P. T., Jr., Ostendorf, F., Angleitner, A., Hrebickova, M., Avia, M., et al. (2000). Nature over nurture: Temperament, personality, and life span development. *Journal of Personality and Social Psychology, 78*, 173–186.

McCrae, R. R., & Terracciano, A. (2005). Personality profiles of cultures: Aggregate personality traits. *Journal of Personality and Social Psychology, 89*, 407–425.

McCurry, S. M., Logsdon, R. G., Teri, L., & Vitiello, M. V. (2007). Evidence-based psychological treatments for insomnia in older adults. *Psychology and Aging, 22*, 18–27.

McDermott, J. F. (2001). Emily Dickinson revisited: A study of periodicity in her work *American Journal of Psychiatry, 158*, 686–690.

McDermut, W., Miller, I. W., & Brown, R. A. (2001). The efficacy of group psychotherapy for depression: A meta-analysis and review of the empirical research. *Clinical Psychology: Science and Practice, 8*, 98–116.

McEvoy, P. M. (2008). Effectiveness of cognitive behavioural group therapy for social phobia in a community clinic: A benchmarking study. *Behaviour Research and Therapy, 45*, 3030–3040.

McGowan, S., Lawrence, A. D., Sales, T., Quested, D., & Grasby, P. (2004). Presynaptic dopaminergic dysfunction in schizophrenia: A positron emission tomographic [18f]fluorodopa study. *Archives of General Psychiatry, 61*, 134–142.

McKellar, J., Stewart, E., & Humphreys, K. (2003). Alcoholics Anonymous involvement and positive alcohol-related outcomes: Cause, consequence, or just a correlate? A prospective 2-year study of 2,319 alcohol-dependent men. *Journal of Consulting and Clinical Psychology, 71*, 302–308.

McKnight Investigators. (2003). Risk factors for the onset of eating disorders in adolescent girls: Results of the McKnight Longitudinal Risk Factor Study. *American Journal of Psychiatry, 160*, 248–254.

McMahon, M. J., et al. (1996). Comparison of a trial of labor with an elective second cesarean section. *New England Journal of Medicine, 335*, 689–695.

McNeil, D. G., Jr. (2005, August 24). Obesity rate is nearly 25 percent, group says. *New York Times*, p. A13.

Mead, M. (1935). *Sex and temperament in three primitive societies.* New York: Dell.

Means-Christensen, A. J., Snyder, D. K., & Negy, C. (2003). Assessing nontraditional couples: Validity of the Marital Satisfaction Inventory-Revised with gay, lesbian, and cohabiting heterosexual couples. *Journal of Marital and Family Therapy, 29*, 69–83.

Mehl, M. R., Vazire, S., Ramírez-Esparza, N., Slatcher, R. B., & Pennebaker, J. W. (2007). Are women really more talkative than men? *Science, 317*, 82.

Melamed, S., Shirom, A., Toker, S., Berliner, S., & Shapira, I. (2006). Burnout and risk of cardiovascular disease: Evidence, possible causal paths, and promising research directions. *Psychological Bulletin, 132*, 327–353.

Melzack, R. (1999, August). From the gate to the neuromatrix. *Pain* (Suppl. 6), S121–S126.

Mendelsohn, M. E., & Karas, R. H. (2005). Molecular and cellular basis of cardiovascular gender differences. *Science, 308*, 583–587.

Menza, M. (2006). STAR*D: The results begin to roll in. *American Journal of Psychiatry, 163*, 1123.

Menzies, L., Achard, S., Chamberlain, S. R., Fineberg, N., Chen, C.-H., del Campo, N., et al. (2007) . Neurocognitive endophenotypes of obsessive-compulsive disorder. *Brain, 130*, 3223–3236.

Meyer, G. J. (2000). Incremental validity of the Rorschach Prognostic Rating Scale over the MMPI Ego Strength Scale and IQ. *Journal of Personality Assessment, 74*, 365–370.

Meyer, G. J., Finn, S. E., Eyde, L. D., Kay, G. G., Moreland, K. L., Dies, R. R., et al. (2001). Psychological testing and psychological assessment: A review of evidence and issues. *American Psychologist, 56,* 128–165.

Meyer, I. H. (2003). Prejudice, social stress, and mental health in lesbian, gay, and bisexual populations: Conceptual issues and research evidence. *Psychological Bulletin, 129,* 674–697.

Meyers, L (2007, February). A struggle for hope. *Monitor on Psychology, 38,* 30–31.

Meyer, T. (2001, August 6). The Thief of Time. *The New York Times.* Retrieved February 23, 2009, from *http://www.umich.edu/~bcalab/articles/NPRArticle2001.pdf*

Mezulis, A. H., Abramson, L. Y., Hyde, J. S., & Hankin, B. L. (2004). Is there a universal positivity bias in attributions? A meta-analytic review of individual, developmental, and cultural differences in the self-serving attributional bias. *Psychological Bulletin, 130,* 711–747.

Michael, R. T., Gagnon, J. H., Laumann, E. O., & Kolata, G. (1994). *Sex in America: A definitive survey.* Boston: Little, Brown.

Milgram, S. (1963). Behavioral study of obedience. *Journal of Abnormal and Social Psychology, 67,* 371–378.

Milgram, S. (1974). *Obedience to authority.* New York: Harper & Row.

Miller, A. G. (2009). Reflections on "Replicating Milgram" (Burger, 2009). *American Psychologist, 64,* 20–27.

Miller, G. E., Chen, E., & Zhou, E. S. (2007). If it goes up, must it come down? Chronic stress and the hypothalamic-pituitary-adrenocortical axis in humans. *Psychological Bulletin, 133,* 25–45.

Miller, M., Azrael, D., & Hemenway, D. (2004). The epidemiology of case fatality rates for suicide in the northeast. *Annals of Emergency Medicine, 43,* 723–730.

Miller, N. B., Cowan, P. A., Cowan, C. P., Hetherington, E. M., & Clingempeel, W. G. (1993). Externalizing in preschoolers and early adolescents. *Developmental Psychology, 29,* 3–18.

Miller, N. E., & Dollard, J. (1941). *Social learning and imitation.* New Haven, CT: Yale University Press.

Miller-Perrin, C. L., Perrin, R. D., & Kocur, K. L. (2009). Parental physical and psychological aggression: Psychological symptoms in young adults. *Child Abuse & Neglect, 33,* 1–11.

Minerd, J., & Jasmer, R. (2006, April). Forty winks or more to make a healthier America. *MedPage Today.* Retrieved April 7, 2006, from *http://www.medpagetoday.com/PrimaryCare/SleepDisorders/tb/3009*

Mischel, W. (2004). Toward an integrative science of the person. *Annual Review of Psychology, 55,* 1–22.

Mischel, W., & Shoda, Y. (1995). A cognitive-affective system theory of personality. *Psychological Review, 102,* 246–268.

Mitka, M. (2003). Economist takes aim at "big fat" US lifestyle. *Journal of the American Medical Association, 289,* 33–34.

Modelska, K., & Cumming, S. (2003). Female sexual dysfunction in postmenopausal women: Systematic review of placebo-controlled trials. *American Journal of Obstetrics and Gynecology, 188,* 286–293.

Moffitt, T. E., Caspi, A., & Rutter, M. (2006). Measured gene-environment interactions in psychopathology concepts, research strategies, and implications for research, intervention, and public understanding of genetics. *Perspectives on Psychological Science, 1,* 5–27.

Mokdad, A. H., Ford, E. S., Bowman, B. A., Dietz, W. H., Vinicor, F., Bales, V. S., et al. (2003). Prevalence of obesity, diabetes, and obesity-related health risk factors, 2001. *Journal of the American Medical Association, 289,* 76–79.

Mokdad, A. H., Marks, J. S., & Stroup, D. F. (2004). Modifiable behavioral factors as causes of death—reply. *Journal of the American Medical Association, 291,* 2942–2943.

Mommersteeg, P. M. C., Keijsers, G. P. J., Heijnen, C. J., Verbraak, M. J. P M., & van Doornen, L. J. P. (2006). Cortisol deviations in people with burnout before and after psychotherapy: A pilot study. *Health Psychology, 25,* 243–248.

Monroe, S. M., Slavich, G. M., Torres, L. D., & Gotlib, I. H. (2007). Major life events and major chronic difficulties are differentially associated with history of major depressive episodes. *Journal of Abnormal Psychology, 116,* 116–124.

Montpetit, M. A., & Bergeman, C. S. (2007). Dimensions of control: Mediational analyses of the stress–health relationship. *Personality and Individual Differences, 43,* 2237–2248.

Moore, D. R., & Heiman, J. R. (2006). Women's sexuality in context: Relationship factors and female sexual functioning. In I. Goldstein, C. Meston, S. Davis, & A. Traish (Eds.), *Female sexual dysfunction.* New York: Parthenon.

Moos, R. H., & Moos, B. S. (2004). Long-term influence of duration and frequency of participation in Alcoholics Anonymous on individuals with alcohol use disorders. *Journal of Consulting and Clinical Psychology, 72,* 81–90.

Morawska, A., & Oei, T. P. S. (2005). Binge drinking in university students: A test of the cognitive model. *Addictive Behaviors, 30,* 203–218.

Morgan, R. D., Patrick, A. R., & Magaletta, P. R. (2008). Does the use of telemental health alter the treatment experience? Inmates' perceptions of telemental health versus face-to-face treatment modalities. *Journal of Consulting and Clinical Psychology, 76,* 158–162.

Morgenstern, J., Bux, D., Labouvie, E., Blanchard, K. A., & Morgan, T. I. (2002). Examining mechanisms of action in 12-step treatment: The role of 12-step cognitions. *Journal of Studies on Alcohol, 63,* 665–672.

Morgeson, F. P., & Humphrey, S. E. (2006). The Work Design Questionnaire (WDQ): Developing and validating a comprehensive measure for assessing job design and the nature of work. *Journal of Applied Psychology, 91,* 1321–1339.

Morley, J. E., & van den Berg, L., (Eds.). (2000). *Endocrinology of aging.* Totowa, NJ: Humana Press.

Morphy, H., Dunn, K. M., Lewis, M., Boardman, H. F., & Croft, P. R. (2007). Epidemiology of insomnia: A longitudinal study in a UK population. *Sleep, 30,* 274–280.

Morris, W. N., Miller, R. S., & Spangenberg, S. (1977). The effects of dissenter position and task difficulty on conformity and response conflict. *Journal of Personality, 45,* 251–256.

Mortola, J. F. (1998). Premenstrual syndrome: Pathophysiologic considerations. *New England Journal of Medicine, 338,* 256–257.

Motl, R. W., Dishman, R. K., Saunders, R. P., Dowda, M., Felton, G., Ward, D. S., et al. (2002). Examining social-cognitive determinants of intention and physical activity among black and white adolescent girls using structural equation modeling. *Health Psychology, 21,* 459–467.

Mroczek, D. K., & Spiro, A. (2005). Change in life satisfaction during adulthood: Findings from the Veterans Affairs Normative Aging Study. *Journal of Personality and Social Psychology, 88,* 189–202.

Mueller, S. (2007, September 14). *U.S. life expectancy now is 77.9 years, falling behind 41 other countries.* Retrieved September 16, 2007, from *http://foodconsumer.org/7777/8888/Non-food_Things_27/091409102007_U_S_life_expectancy_now_is_78_9_years_falling_behind_41_other_countries.shtml*

Mukamal, K. J, Conigrave, K. M., Mittleman, M. A., Camargo, C. A., Jr., Stampfer, M. J., Willett, W. C., et al. (2003). Roles of drinking pattern and type of alcohol consumed in coronary heart disease in men. *New England Journal of Medicine, 348,* 109–118.

Multitasking: You can't pay full attention to both sights and sounds. NewsWise /John Hopkins University. Retrieved October 23, 2005, from *http://newswise.com/articles/view/512657*

Mulvihill, K. (2000, March 14). Many miss out on migraine remedies. *New York Times.* Retrieved May 15, 2009, from *http://www.nytimes.com/2000/03/14/health/many-mis-out-on-migraine-remedies.html*

Munro, G. D., & Munro, J. E. (2000). Using daily horoscopes to demonstrate expectancy confirmation. *Teaching of Psychology, 27,* 114–116.

Murphy, E. M. (2003). Being born female is dangerous for your health. *American Psychologist, 58,* 205–210.

Murphy, S. E., & Ensher, E. A. (2001). The role of mentoring support and self-management strategies on reported career outcomes. *Journal of Career Development, 27,* 229–246.

Murphy, S. M., Vallacher, R. R., Shackelford, T. K., Bjorklund, D. F., & Unger, J. L. (2006). Relationship experience as a predictor of romantic jealousy. *Personality and Individual Differences, 40,* 761–769.

Murstein, B. I., & Mathes, S. (1996). Projection on projective techniques pathology: The problem that is not being addressed. *Journal of Personality Assessment, 66,* 337–349.

Murtagh, D. R. R., & Greenwood, K. M. (1995). Identifying effective psychological treatments for insomnia: A meta-analysis. *Journal of Consulting and Clinical Psychology, 63,* 79–89.

Muslim women bridging culture gap. (1993, November 8). *The New York Times,* p. B9.

Mustanski, B. S., Viken, R. J., Kaprio, J., Pulkkinen, L., & Rose, R. J. (2004). Genetic and environmental influences on pubertal development: Longitudinal data from Finnish twins at ages 11 and 14. *Developmental Psychology, 40,* 1188–1198.

Muzzatti, B., & Agnoli, F. (2007). Gender and mathematics: Attitudes and stereotype threat susceptibility in Italian children. *Developmental Psychology, 4,* 747–759.

Myrick, H., Anton, R. F., Li, X., Henderson, S., Randall, P, K., & Voronin, K. (2008). Effect of naltrexone and ondansetron on alcohol cue–induced activation of the ventral striatum in alcohol-dependent people. *Archives of General Psychiatry, 65,* 466–475.

Nakagawa, T., Sakurai, T., Nishioka, T., & Touhara, K. (2005). Insect sex-pheromone signals mediated by specific combinations of olfactory receptors. *Science, 307,* 1638–1642.

Nasser, H. (2000, June 9). Mom's career sacrifice: Study: Women yield ambitions when children come to two-career couples. *CNN.* Retrieved May 15, 2009, from *http://www.bio.net/bionet/mm/womenbio/2000-June/008607.html*

National Cancer Institute (2000a). Cited in Jetter, A. (2000, February 22). Breast cancer in blacks spurs hunt for answers. *New York Times,* p. D5.

National Institute of Allergy and Infectious Diseases (NIAID), National Institutes of Health. (2005b, November). *Genital herpes.* Retrieved April 16, 2006, from *http://www.niaid.nih.gov/factsheets/stdherp.htm.*

National Sleep Foundation (2000). *2000 Omnibus Sleep in America Poll.* Retrieved January 14, 2001, from *http://www.sleepfoundation.org/publications/2000poll.html#3.*

National Sleep Foundation. (2005). *Sleep in America.* Retrieved March 30, 2005, from *http://www.sleepfoundation.org/hottopics/index.php?secid=16*

National Women's Health Information Center, U.S. Department of Health and Human Services. (2005, April). *AIDS worldwide.* Retrieved July 1, 2005, from *http://www.4woman.gov/HIV/world.cfm*

Naughton, K. (2004, February 2). "The soft sell." *Newsweek,* pp. 46–47.

Nauta, M. M. (2007). Career interests, self-efficacy, and personality as antecedents of career exploration. *Journal of Career Assessment, 15,* 162–180.

Nauta, M. M., & Kokaly, M. L. (2001). Assessing role model influences on students' academic and vocational decisions. *Journal of Career Assessment, 9,* 81–99.

Navarro, R. L., Flores, L. Y., & Worthington, R. L. (2007). Mexican American middle school students' goal intentions in mathematics and science: A test of social cognitive career theory. *Journal of Counseling Psychology, 54,* 320–335.

Neff, K. D., & Harter, S. (2003). Relationship styles of self-focused autonomy, other-focused connectedness, and mutuality across multiple relationship contexts. *Journal of Social & Personal Relationships, 20,* 81–99.

Neighbors, C., Lee, C. M., Lewis, M. A., Fossos, N., & Walter, T. (2009). Internet-based personalized feedback to reduce 21st-birthday drinking: A randomized controlled trial of an event-specific prevention intervention. *Journal of Consulting and Clinical Psychology, 77,* 51–63.

Nelson, T. D. (2002). *The psychology of prejudice.* Boston, MA: Allyn and Bacon.

Nestoriuc, Y., Rief, W., & Martin, A. (2008). Meta-analysis of biofeedback for tension-type headache: Efficacy, specificity, and treatment moderators. *Journal of Consulting and Clinical Psychology, 76,* 379–396.

Nettle, D. (2001). *Strong imagination: Madness, creativity, and human nature.* New York: Oxford University Press.

Netz, Y., Wu, M.-J., Becker, B. J., & Tenenbaum, G. (2005). Physical activity and psychological well-being in advanced age: A meta-analysis of intervention studies. *Psychology and Aging, 20,* 272–284.

Nevid, J. S. (1984). Sex differences in factors of romantic attraction. *Sex Roles, 11,* 401–411.

Nevid, J. S. (2006). *Essentials of psychology: Concepts and applications.* Boston: Houghton Mifflin Company.

Nevid, J. S. (2007). *Psychology: Concepts and applications.* (2nd ed.). Boston: Houghton Mifflin Company.

Nevid, J. S. (2009). *Psychology: Concepts and applications.* (3rd ed.). Belmont, CA: Cengage.

Nevid, J. S., & Rathus, S. A. (2007). *Your health.* Mason, OH: Thomson Custom Solutions.

Nevid, J. S., Rathus, S. A., & Greene, B. (2003). *Abnormal psychology in a changing world* (5th ed.). Upper Saddle River, NJ: Prentice-Hall, Inc.

Nevid, J. S., Rathus, S. A., & Greene, B. (2006). *Abnormal psychology in a changing world* (6th ed.). Upper Saddle River, NJ: Prentice-Hall.

Nevid, J. S., Rathus, S. A., & Greene, B. A. (2008). *Abnormal psychology in a changing world* (7th ed.). Upper Saddle River, NJ: Pearson Education.

Nevid, J. S. Rathus, S. A., & Greene, B. (2006). *Abnormal psychology in a changing world* (6th ed.). Upper Saddle River, NJ: Prentice-Hall.

Nezlek, J. B., & Plesko, R. M. (2001). Day-to-day relationships among self-concept clarity, self-esteem, daily events, and mood. *Personality & Social Psychology Bulletin, 27,* 201–211.

NIDA Notes (2004, December). 2003 surveys reveals increase in prescription drug abuse, sharp drop in abuse of hallucinogens. *NIDA Notes, 19*(4), p. 14.

Nides, M. A., et al. (1995). Predictors of initial smoking cessation and relapse through the first 2 years of the lung health study. *Journal of Consulting and Clinical Psychology, 63,* 60–69.

NIH Consensus Development Panel on Osteoporosis Prevention, Diagnosis, and Therapy. (2001). Osteoporosis prevention, diagnosis, and therapy. *Journal of the American Medical Association, 285,* 785–795.

Nisbett, R. E. (2003). *The geography of thought: How Asians and Westerners think differently . . . and why.* New York: The Free Press.

Nolen-Hoeksema, S., Stice, E., Wade, E., & Bohon, C. (2007). Reciprocal relations between rumination and bulimic, substance abuse, and depressive symptoms in female adolescents. *Journal of Abnormal Psychology, 116,* 198–207.

Nolen-Hoeksema, S. (2006). The etiology of gender differences in depression. In C. M. Mazure & G. Puryear (Eds.), *Understanding depression in women: Applying empirical research to practice and policy.* Washington, DC: American Psychological Association.

Nonnemaker, J. M., & Homsi, G. (2007). Measurement of properties of the Fagerstrom Test for nicotine dependence adapted for use in an adolescent sample. *Addictive Behaviors, 32,* 181–186.

Norcross, J. C. (2002). (Ed.). *Psychotherapy relationships that work: Therapist contributions and responsiveness to patients.* London: Oxford University Press.

Norcross, J. C., Karpiak, C. P., & Santoro, S. O. (2005). Clinical psychologists across the years: The division of clinical psychology from 1960 to 2003. *Journal of Clinical Psychology, 61,* 1467–1483.

Norlander, T., Erixon, A., & Archer, T. (2000). Psychological androgyny and creativity: Dynamics of gender-role and personality trait. *Social Behavior & Personality, 28,* 423–435.

Norris, F N., Murphy, A.D., Baker, C. K., Perilla, J. L., Rodriguez, F. G, & Rodriguez, J.D. (2003). Epidemiology of trauma and posttraumatic stress disorder in Mexico. *Journal of Abnormal Psychology, 112,* 646–656.

Nosek, B. A., Banaji, M. R., & Greenwald, A. G. (2003). Math = male, me = female, therefore math ≠ me. *Journal of Personality and Social Psychology, 83,* 44–59.

Nour, N. M. (2000). Female circumcision and genital mutilation: A practical and sensitive approach. *Contemporary Ob/Gyn, 45,* 50–55.

Nowak, A., Vallacher, R. R., & Miller, M. E. (2003). Social influence and group dynamics. In T. Millon & M. J. Lerner (Eds.), *Handbook of psychology: Vol. 5. Personality and social psychology* (pp. 383–418). New York: Wiley.

Nowicki, S., & Strickland, B. R. (1973). A locus of control scale for children. *Journal of Consulting and Clinical Psychology, 40,* 148–154.

Nowinski, J. (2007). *The identity trap: Saving our teens from themselves.* New York: AMACOM.

Nuland, S. (2003, May 19). "Where doesn't it hurt?" *Newsweek,* p. 62.

Oberauer, K., & Kliegl, R. (2004). Simultaneous cognitive operations in working memory after dual-task practice. *Journal of Experimental Psychology–Human Perception and Performance, 30,* 689–707.

O'Brien, C. P. (2008). Prospects for a genomic approach to the treatment of alcoholism. *Archives of General Psychiatry, 65,* 132–133.

O'Connor, A. (2004, March 16). In sex, brain studies show, "la difference" still holds. *New York Times,* p. F5.

O'Connor, A. (2005, March). Instant messaging: Friend or foe of student writing? *NewHorizons.* Retrieved August 25, 2005, from *http://www.newhorizons.org/strategies/literacy/oconnor.htm.*

O'Connor, T. G., Caspi, A., DeFries, J. C., & Plomin, R. (2000). Are associations between parental divorce and children's adjustment genetically mediated? An adoption study. *Developmental Psychology, 36,* 429–437.

O'Donohue, W., Yeater, E. A., & Fanetti, M. (2003). Rape prevention with college males: The roles of rape myth acceptance, victim empathy, and outcome expectancies. *Journal of Interpersonal Violence, 18,* 513–531.

Ogden, C. L., Carroll, M. D., Curtin, L. R., McDowell, M. A., Tabak, C. J., & Flegal, K. M. (2006). Prevalence of overweight and obesity in the United States, 1999–2004. *Journal of the American Medical Association, 295,* 190–198.

Offermann, L. R.., & Malamut, A. B. (2002). When leaders harass: The impact of target perceptions of organizational leadership and climate on harassment reporting and outcomes. *Journal of Applied Psychology, 87,* 885–893.

O'Leary-Kelly, A. M., Paetzold, R. L., & Griffin, R. W. (2000). Sexual harassment as aggressive behavior: An actor-based perspective. *Academy of Management Review, 25,* 372–388.

Olfson, M., Gameroff, M. J., Marcus, S. C., Greenberg T., & Shaffer, D. (2005). Emergency treatment of young people following deliberate self-harm. *Archives of General Psychiatry, 62,* 1122–1128.

Olson, J. M., Vernon, P. A., Harris, J. A., & Jang, K. L. (2001). The heritability of attitudes: a study of twins. *Journal of Personality and Social Psychology, 80,* 845–860.

O'Neil, J. (2003, February 4). Jog your memory? At the gym? *New York Times,* p. F6.

Olshansky, S. J., Passaro, D. J., Hershow, R. C., Layden, J., Carnes, B. A., Brody, J., et al. (2005). A potential decline in life expectancy in the United States in the 21st century. *New England Journal of Medicine, 352,* 1138–1145.

Olson, I. R., & Marshuetz, C. (2005). Facial attractiveness is appraised in a glance. *Emotion, 5,* 498–502.

Olson, M. B., Krantz, D. S., Kelsey, S. F., Pepine, C. J., Sopko, G., Handberg, E., et al. (2006). Hostility scores are associated with increased risk of cardiovascular events in women undergoing coronary angiography: A report from the NHLBI-sponsored WISE study. *Psychosomatic Medicine, 67,* 546–552.

Onishi, N. (2004, January 8). Never lost, but found daily: Japanese honesty. *New York Times,* pp. A1, A4.

Oquendo, M. A., Hastings, R. S., Huang, Y., Simpson, N., Ogden, R. T., Hu, X.-Z., Goldman, D., et al. (2007). Brain serotonin transporter binding in depressed patients with bipolar disorder using positron emission tomography. *Archives of General Psychiatry, 64,* 201–208.

Orbach, G., Lindsay, S., & Grey, S. (2007). A randomised placebo-controlled trial of a self-help Internet-based intervention for test anxiety. *Behaviour Research and Therapy, 45,* 483–496.

Ortega, A. N., Rosenheck, R., Alegria, M., & Desai, R. A. (2000). Acculturation and the lifetime risk of psychiatric and substance use disorders among Hispanics. *Journal of Nervous and Mental Disease, 188,* 728–735.

Ostermann, J., Kumar, V., Pence, B. W., & Whetten, K. (2007). Trends in HIV testing and differences between planned and actual testing in the United States, 2000–2005. *Archives of Internal Medicine, 167,* 2128–2135.

Otto, M. W., Teachman, B. A., Cohen, L. S., Soares, C. N., Vitonis, A. F., Allison, F., et al. (2007). Dysfunctional attitudes and episodes of major depression: Predictive validity and temporal stability in never-depressed, depressed, and recovered women. *Journal of Abnormal Psychology, 116*(3), 475–483.

Ouellette, S. C., & DiPlacido, J. (2001). Personality's role in the protection and enhancements of health: Where the research has been, where it is stuck, how it might move. In A. Baum, T. A. Revenson, & J. E. Singer (Eds.), *Handbook of health psychology* (pp. 175–194). Mahwah, NJ: Erlbaum.

Ouimette, P. C., Finney, J. W., & Moos, R. H. (1997). Twelve-step and cognitive-behavioral treatment for substance abuse. *Journal of Consulting and Clinical Psychology, 65,* 230–240.

Overmier, J. B., & Seligman, M. E. P. (1967). Effects of inescapable shock upon subsequent escape and avoidance learning. *Journal of Comparative and Physiological Psychology, 63,* 23–33.

Oyserman, D., Coon, H. M., & Kemmelmeier, M. (2002). Rethinking individualism and collectivism: evaluation of theoretical assumptions and meta-analyses. *Psychological Bulletin, 128,* 3–72.

Oyserman, D., Gant, L., & Ager, J. (1995). A socially contextualized model of African American identity: Possible selves and school persistence. *Journal of Personality and Social Psychology, 69,* 1216–1232.

Oyserman, D., Kemmelmeier, M., & Coon, H. M., (2002). Cultural psychology, a new look: Reply to Bond (2002), Fiske (2002), Kitayama (2002), and Miller (2002). *Psychological Bulletin, 128,* 110–117.

Ozer, E. J., & Weiss, D. S. (2004). Who develops posttraumatic stress disorder? *Current Directions in Psychological Science, 13,* 169–172.

Packard, E. (2007, April). That teenage feeling. *Monitor on Psychology, 38*(4), 20–22.

Packer, D. J. (2008). Identifying systematic disobedience in Milgram's obedience experiments: A meta-analytic review. *Perspectives on Psychological Science, 3,* 301–304.

Page, K. (1999, May 16). The graduate. *Washington Post Magazine, 152,* pp.18, 20.

Park, A., Sher, K. J., & Krull, J. L. (2006). Individual differences in the "Greek effect" on risky drinking: The role of self-consciousness. *Psychology of Addictive Behaviors, 20,* 85–90.

Park, J., & Banaji, M. R. (2000). Mood and heuristics: The influence of happy and sad states on sensitivity and bias in stereotyping. *Journal of Personality and Social Psychology, 78,* 1005–1023.

Parke, R. D. (2004). Development in the family. *Annual Review of Psychology, 55,* 365–399.

Parke, R. D., & Buriel, R. (1997). Socialization in the family: Ethnic and ecological perspectives. In W. Damon & N. Eisenberg, *Handbook of child psychology*(5th ed.,): *Vol. 3. Social, emotional, and personality development* (pp. 463–552). New York: Wiley.

Parker, J. D. A., Austin, E. J., Hogan, M. J., Wood, L. M., & Bond, B. J. (2005). Alexithymia and academic success: Examining the transition from high school to university. *Personality and Individual Differences, 38,* 1257–1267.

Parker, J. D. A., Creque, R. E., Sr., Barnhart, D. L., Harris, J., I., Majeski, S. A., et al. (2004). Academic achievement in high school: Does emotional intelligence matter? *Personality and Individual Differences, 37,* 1321–1330.

Parkes, L. P., Bochner, S., & Schneider, S. K. (2001). Person-organisation fit across cultures: An empirical investigation of individualism and collectivism. *Applied Psychology: An International Review, 50*(1), 81–108.

Parlee, M. B. (1979). The friendship bond: *Psychology Today's* survey report on friendship in America. *Psychology Today, 13*(4), 43–54, 113.

Parloff, R. (2003, February 3). Is fat the next tobacco? *Fortune,* pp. 51–54.

Pate, J. L. (2000). Psyhcological organizations in the United States. *American Psychologist, 55,* 1139–1143.

Patrick, S., Sells, J. N., Giordano, F. G., & Tollerud, T. R. (2007). Intimacy, differentiation, and personality variables as predictors of marital satisfaction. *The Family Journal, 15,* 359–367.

Pattison, E. M. (1977). *The experience of dying.* Englewood Cliffs, NJ: Prentice Hall.

Paul, E. L., & Brier, S. (2001). Friendsickness in the transition to college: Precollege predictors and college adjustment correlates. *Journal of Counseling & Development, 79*(1), 77–89.

Paul, P. (2005, January 17). The power to uplift. *Time,* pp. A46-A48.

Paunonen, S. V. (2003). Big five factors of personality and replicated predictions of behavior. *Journal of Personality and Social Psychology, 84,* 411–424.

Pavlov, I. (1927). *Conditioned reflexes.* London: Oxford University Press.

Pawlowski, B., & Koziel, S. (2002). The impact of traits offered in personal advertisements on response rates. *Evolution & Human Behavior, 23*(2), 139–149.

Pearson, J. L., & Brown, G. K. (2000). Suicide prevention in late life: Direction for science and practice. *Clinical Psychology Review, 20,* 685–705.

Peck, R. C. (1968). Psychological developments in the second half of life. In B. L. Neugarten (Ed.), *Middle age and aging.* Chicago: University of Chicago Press.

Pedersen, S. S., Lemos, P. A., van Vooren, P. R., Liu, T. K., et al. (2004). Type D Personality predicts death or myocardial infarction after bare metal stent or sirolimus-eluting stent implantation: a rapamycin-eluting stent evaluated at Rotterdam Cardiology Hospital (RESEARCH) registry substudy. *Journal of the American College of Cardiology, 44,* 997–1001.

Peeters, M. C., Bakker, A. B., Schaufeli, W. B., & Wilmar, B. (2005). Balancing work and home: How job and home demands are related to burnout. *International Journal of Stress Management, 12,* 43–61.

Pempek, T. A., Yermolayeva, Y. A., & Calvert. S. L. (2009). College students' social networking experiences on Facebook. *Journal of Applied Developmental Psychology, 43,* 438–443.

Pengilly, J. W., & Dowd, E. T. (2000). Hardiness and social support as moderators of stress. *Journal of Clinical Psychology, 56,* 813–820.

Pennebaker, J. W. (2004). Theories, therapies, and taxpayers: On the complexities of the expressive writing paradigm. *Clinical Psychology: Science and Practice, 11,* 138–142.

Penner, L. A., Dovidio, J. F., Piliavin, J. A., & Schroeder, D. A. (2005). Prosocial behavior: Multilevel perspectives. *Annual Review of Psychology, 56,* 365–392.

Peplau, L. A. (2003). Human sexuality: How do men and women differ? *Current Directions in Psychological Science, 12,* 37–40.

Perälä, J., Suvisaari, J., Saarni, S. I., Kuoppasalmi, K., Isometsä, E., Pirkola, S., Partonen, T., et al. (2007). Lifetime prevalence of psychotic and bipolar I disorders in a general population. *Archives of General Psychiatry, 64,* 19–28.

Pereira, M. A., O'Reilly, E., Augustsson, K., Fraser, G. E., Goldbourt, U., Heitmann, et al. (2004). Dietary fiber and risk of coronary heart disease: A pooled analysis of cohort studies. *Archives of Internal Medicine, 164,* 370–376.

Perlis, M. L., Jungquist, C., Smith, M. T., & Posner, D. (2008). *Cognitive behavioral treatment of insomnia: A session by session guide.* New York: Springer.

Perls, F. S. (1971). *Gestalt therapy verbatim.* New York: Bantam Books.

Perrett, D. L. (1994, March 21). Nature. In J. E. Brody, Notions of beauty transcend culture, new study suggests. *The New York Times,* p. A14.

Perrone, K. M., Webb, L. K., & Jackson, Z. V. (2007). Relationships between parental attachment, work and family roles, and life satisfaction. *The Career Development Quarterly, 55,* 237–248.

Perry, D. G., & Bussey, K. (1979). The social learning theory of sex differences: Imitation is alive and well. *Journal of Personality and Social Psychology, 37,* 1699–1712.

Perry, W. (2003). Let's call the whole thing off: A response to Dawes (2001). *Psychological Assessment, 15,* 582–585.

Persons, J. B., Davidson, J., & Tompkins, M. A. (2001). *Essential components of cognitive-behavior therapy for depression.* Washington, DC: American Psychological Association.

Peters, E., Hess, T. M., Västfjäll, D., & Auman, C. (2007). Adult age differences in dual information processes: Implications for the role of affective and deliberative processes in older adults' decision making. *Perspectives on Psychological Science, 2,* 1–23.

Peterson, B. E., & Duncan, L. E. (2007). Midlife women's generativity and authoritarianism: Marriage, motherhood, and 10 years of aging. *Psychology and Aging, 22,* 411–419.

Pettigrew, T. F., & Tropp, L. R. A. (2006). A meta-analytic test of intergroup contact theory. *Journal of Personality and Social Psychology, 90,* 751–783.

Petty, R. E., & Brinol, P. A. (2006). A metacognitive approach to "implicit" and "explicit" evaluations: Comment on Gawronski and Bodenhausen (2006). *Psychological Bulletin, 132,* 740–744.

Petty, R. E., Wheeler, S. C., & Tormala, Z. L. (2003). Persuasion and attitude change. In T. Millon & M. J. Lerner (Eds.), *Handbook of psychology: Vol. 5. Personality and social psychology* (pp. 353–382). New York: Wiley.

Philaretou, A. G., Mahfouz, A. Y., & Allen, K. R. (2005). Use of Internet pornography and men's well-being. *International Journal of Men's Health, 4,* 149–169.

Phinney, J., & Alipuria, L. (1990). Ethnic identity in older adolescents from four ethnic groups. *Journal of Adolescence, 13,* 171–183.

Phinney, J. S. (2000). Identity formation across cultures: The interaction of personal, societal, and historical change. *Human Development, 43,* 27–31.

Phinney, J. S., & Devich-Navarro, M. (1997). Variations in bicultural identification among African American and Mexican American adolescents. *Journal of Research on Adolescence, 7*(1), 3–32.

Phinney, J. S., Cantu, C. L., & Kurtz, D. A. (1997). Ethnic and American identity as predictors of self-esteem among African American, Latino, and white adolescents. *Journal of Youth & Adolescence, 26*(2), 165–185.

Pilcher, H. R. (2003, May 28). Men's underarms may hold clue to new fertility drug. *Nature Science Update.* Retrieved June 10, 2003, from *http://www.nature.com/nsu/030527/030527–2.html.*

Pilkonis, P. (1996). Cited in Goleman, D. J. (1996, May 1). Higher suicide risk for perfectionists. *The New York Times,* p. C12.

Pincus, A. L., Lukowitsky, M. R., Wright, A. G. C., & Eichler, W. C. (2009). The interpersonal nexus of persons, situations, and psychopathology. *Journal of Research in Personality, 43,* 264–265.

Piñol; V., et al. (2005). Accuracy of Revised Bethesda Guidelines, microsatellite instability, and immunohistochemistry for the identification of patients with hereditary nonpolyposis colorectal cancer. *Journal of the American Medical Association, 293,* 986–1994;

Plaisier, I., de Bruijn, J. G. M., Smit, J. H., de Graafd, R., ten Have, M., Beekman, A. T. F., van Dyck, R., et al. (2008). Work and family roles and the association with depressive and anxiety disorders: Differences between men and women. *Journal of Affective Disorders, 105,* 63–72.

Plomin, R., & Crabbe, J. (2000). DNA. *Psychological Bulletin, 126,* 806–828.

Plomin, R., & McGuffin, P. (2003). Psychopathology in the postgenomic era. *Annual Review of Psychology, 54,* 205–228.

Polinko, N. K., & Popovich, P. M (2001). Evil thoughts but angelic actions: Responses to overweight job applicants. *Journal of Applied Social Psychology, 31,* 905–924.

Pollack, A. (2004, January 13). Sleep experts debate root of insomnia: Body, mind or a little of each. *New York Times,* p. F8.

Pope, H. G., Kouri, E. M., & Hudson, J. I. (2000). Effects of supraphysiologic doses of testosterone on mood and aggression in normal men: A randomized controlled trial. *Archives of General Psychiatry, 57,* 133–140.

Poppy, J. (1995, October). Easy does it. *Health,* p. 42.

Powell, E. (1991). *Talking back to sexual pressure.* Minneapolis: CompCare Publishers.

Powell, E. (1996). *Sex on your terms.* Boston: Allyn & Bacon.

Powell, L. H., Calvin, J. E., 3rd, & Calvin, J. E., Jr. (2007). Effective obesity treatments. *American Psychologist, 62,* 234–246.

Powers, R. (2000, May 7). American dreaming. The New York Times Magazine, pp. 66–67.

Pratt, L. A., & Brody, D. J. (2008, September). Depression in the United States household population, 2005–2006. *NCHS Data Brief, Number 7.* Retrieved October 14, 2008, from *http://www.cdc.gov/nchs/data/databriefs/db07.htm*

Pressman, S. D., & Cohen, S. (2005). Does positive affect influence health? *Psychological Bulletin, 131,* 925–971.

Pressman, S. D., Cohen, S., Miller, G. E., Barkin, A., Rabin, B. S., & Treanor J. J. (2005). Loneliness, social network size, and immune response to influenza vaccination in college freshmen. *Health Psychology, 24,* 297–306.

Preti, G., Wysocki, C. J., Barnhart, K. T., Sondheimer, S. J., & Leyden, J. J. (2003). Male axillary extracts contain pheromones that affect pulsatile secretion of luteinizing hormone and mood in women recipients. *Biology of Reproduction, 68,* 2107–2103.

Preston, S. H. (2003). Deadweight?—the influence of obesity on longevity. *New England Journal of Medicine, 352,* 1135–1137.

Preti, G., Wysocki, C. J., Barnhart, K. T., Sondheimer, S. J., & Leyden, J. J. (2003). Male axillary extracts contain pheromones that affect pulsatile secretion of luteinizing hormone and mood in women recipients. *Biology of Reproduction, 68,* 2107–2103.

Prezza, M., Amici, M., Roberti, T., & Tedeschi, G. (2001). The effects of culture on the causes of loneliness. *Journal of Community Psychology, 29,* 29–52.

Price, T. S., & Jaffee, S. R. (2008). Effects of the family environment: Gene-environment interaction and passive gene-environment correlation. *Developmental Psychology, 44,* 305–315.

Pronin, E., Gilovich, T., & Ross, L. (2004). Objectivity in the eye of the beholder: Divergent perceptions of bias in self versus others. *Psychological Review, 111,* 781–799.

Prudic, J., Olfson, M., Marcus, S. C., Fuller, R. B., & Sackeim, H. A. (2004). Effectiveness of electroconvulsive therapy in community settings. *Biological Psychiatry, 55,* 301–312.

Prull, M. W., Dawes, L. L., Crandell, M., McLeish, A., Rosenberg, H. F., & Light, L. L. (2006). Recollection and familiarity in recognition memory: Adult age differences and neuropsychological test correlates. *Psychology and Aging, 21,* 107–118.

Puente, S., & Cohen, D. (2003). Jealousy and the meaning (or nonmeaning) of violence. *Personality & Social Psychology Bulletin, 29,* 449–460.

Punyanunt-Carter, N. M. (2006). An analysis of college students' self-disclosure behaviors on the Internet. *College Student Journal, 40,* 329–331.

Qaseem, A., Snow, V., Denberg, T. D., Forciea, M. A., Owens, D. K., et al. (2008). Using second-generation antidepressants to treat depressive disorders: A clinical practice guideline from the American College of Physicians. *Annals of Internal Medicine, 149,* 725–733.

Quaiser-Pohl, C., Geiser, C., & Lehmann, W. (2006). The relationship between computer-game preference, gender, and mental-rotation ability. *Personality and Individual Differences, 40,* 609–619.

R ur txt msgs? (2003). *CNN.* Retrieved November 10, 2005, from *http://www.cnn.com/2003/TECH/ptech/02/13/text.messaging.ap/*

Rabasca, L. (2000a). Listening instead of preaching. *Monitor on Psychology, 31*(3), pp. 50-51.

Rabasca, L. (2000b). Pre-empting racism. *Monitor on Psychology, 31*(11), 60.

Rabin, R. C. (2008, May 13). For a sharp brain, stimulation. *New York Times,* p. H4.

Radel, M., Vallejo, R. L., Iwata, N., Aragon, R., Long, J. C., Virkkunen, M., et al. (2005). Haplotype based localization of an alcohol dependence gene to the 5q34 ? Aminobutyric acid type A gene cluster. *Archives of General Psychiatry, 62,* 47–55.

Raichle, K., & Lambert, A. J. (2000). The role of political ideology in mediating judgments of blame in rape victims and their assailants: A test of the just world, personal responsibility, and legitimization hypotheses. *Personality & Social Psychology Bulletin, 26,* 853–863.

Rakoff, D. (2000, January 2). Candid classroom: Questions for James B. Maas. *The New York Times Magazine,* p. 6.

Rakowski, W. (1995). Cited in Margoshes, P. (1995). For many, old age is the prime of life. *APA Monitor, 26*(5), 36–37.

Rasch, B., Büchel, C., Gais, S., & Born, J. (2007). Odor cues during slow-wave sleep prompt declarative memory consolidation. *Science, 315,* 1426–1429.

Raskin, N. J., Rogers, C. R., & Witty, M. C. (2008). Person-centered therapy. In R. J. Corsini & D. Wedding (Eds.) (8th ed.), *Current psychotherapies* (pp. 141–186). Belmont, CA: Thomson Higher Education.

Rathus, J. H., & Sanderson, J. H. (1999). *Marital distress: Cognitive behavioral interventions for couples.* Northvale, NJ: Jason Aronson.

Rathus, S. A. (1973). A 30-item schedule for assessing assertive behavior. *Behavior Therapy, 4,* 398–406.

Rathus, S. A., Nevid, J. S., & Fichner-Rathus, L. (2005). *Human sexuality in a world of diversity,* 6th ed. Boston: Allyn & Bacon.

Rathus, S. A., Nevid, J. S., & Fichner-Rathus, L. (2008). *Human sexuality in a world of diversity.* (7th ed.). Boston: Allyn & Bacon.

Rathus, S. A. (2002). *Psychology in the new millennium* (8th ed.). Fort Worth: Harcourt College Publishers.

Rathus, S. A., & Fichner-Rathus, L. (1994). *The right start.* New York: Addison Wesley Longman.

Rathus, S. A., Nevid, J. S., & Fichner-Rathus, L. (2002). *Human sexuality in a world of diversity* (5th ed.). Boston: Allyn & Bacon.

Rathus, S. A., Nevid, J. S., & Fichner-Rathus, L. (2008). *Human sexuality in a world of diversity* (7th ed.). Boston: Allyn & Bacon.

Rawe, J., & Kingsbury, K. (2006, May 22). When colleges go on suicide watch. *Time,* pp. 62- 63.

Reas, D. L., & Grilo, C. M. (2007). Timing and sequence of the onset of overweight, dieting, and binge eating in overweight patients with binge eating disorder. *International Journal of Eating Disorders, 40,* 165–170.

Redd, W. H., & Jacobsen, P.B.(2001). Behavioral intervention in comprehensive cancer care. In A. S. Baum, T. A. Ravenson, & J. E. Singer (Eds.), *Handbook of Health Psychology* (pp. 757–776). Mahwah, NJ: Lawrence Erlbaum Associates.

Redgrave, G. W., Coughlin, J. W., Heinberg, L. J., & Guarda, A. S. (2007). First-degree relative history of alcoholism in eating disorder inpatients: Relationship to eating and substance use psychopathology. *Eating Behaviors, 8,* 15–22.

Reeves, G. K., Pirie, K., Beral, V., Green, J., & Spencer, E. (2007). Cancer incidence and mortality in relation to body mass index in the Million Women Study: Cohort study. *British Medical Journal, 335,* 1134–1138.

Rehm, L. P. (2008). How far have we come in teletherapy? Comment on "telephone-administered psychotherapy." *Clinical Psychology: Science and Practice, 15,* 259–261.

Reichenberg, A., & Harvey, P. D. (2007). Neuropsychological impairments in schizophrenia: Integration of performance-based and brain imaging findings. *Psychological Bulletin, 133,* 833–858.

Reid, T. R. (1990, December 24). Snug in their beds for Christmas Eve: In Japan, December 24th has become the hottest night of the year. *Washington Post,* pp. B1–B3

Reifler, B. V. (2006). Play it again, Sam—depression is recurring. *New England Journal of Medicine, 354,* 1189–1190.

Reis, H. T., Wilson, I. M., Monestere, C., Bernstein, S., et al. (1990). What is smiling is beautiful and good. *European Journal of Social Psychology, 20,* 259–267.

Resnick, H. S., Kilpatrick, D. G., Dansky, B. S., Saunders, B. E., & Best, C. L. (1993). Prevalence of civilian trauma and posttraumatic stress disorder in a representative national sample of women. *Journal of Consulting and Clinical Psychology,* 61, 984–991.

Retsinas, J. (1988). A theoretical reassessment of the applicability of Kübler-Ross's stages of dying. *Death Studies, 12,* 207–216.

Revenson, T. A., & Baum, A. (2001). Introduction. In *Handbook of health psychology* (pp. xv–xx). Mahwah, NJ: Erlbaum.

Reyna, V. F., & Farley, F. (2006). Risk and rationality in adolescent decision making: Implications for theory, practice, and public policy. *Psychological Science in the Public Interest, 7,* 2–44.

Reynolds, C. A., Barlow, T., & Pedersen, N. L. (2006). Alcohol, tobacco and caffeine use: Spouse similarity processes. *Behavior Genetics, 36,* 201–215.

Reynolds, C. F., Dew, M. A., Pollock, B. J., Mulsant, B. H., Frank, E., Miller, M. D., Houck, P. R., Mazumdar, S., et al. (2006). Maintenance treatment of major depression in old age. *New England Journal of Medicine, 354,* 1130–1138.

Ricciardelli, L. A., & McCabe, M. P. (2001). Children's body image concerns and eating disturbance: A review of the literature. *Clinical Psychology Review, 21,* 325–344.

Ricciardelli, L. A., McCabe, M. P., Williams, R. J., & Thompson, J. K. (2007). The role of ethnicity and culture in body image and disordered eating among males. *Clinical Psychology Review, 27,* 582–606.

Ridgell, S. D., & Lounsbury, J. W. (2004). Predicting academic success: General intelligence, "Big Five" personality traits, and work drive. *College Student Journal, 38,* 607–614.

Rieckmann, T. R., Wadsworth, M. E., & Deyhle, D. (2004). Cultural identity, explanatory style, and depression in Navajo adolescents. *Cultural Diversity and Ethnic Minority Psychology, 10,* 365–382.

Rief, W., & Sharpe, M. (2004). Somatoform disorders—new approaches to classification, conceptualization, and treatment. *Journal of Psychosomatic Research, 56,* 387–390.

Riepe, M. (2000). Cited in Ritter, M. (2000, March 21). Brains differ in navigation skills. *Associated Press.*

Rimm, E. B. & Stampfer, M. J. (2005). Diet, lifestyle, and longevity—the next step. *Journal of the American Medical Association, 292,* 1490–492.

Rind, B., & Strohmetz, D. (1999). Effect on restaurant tipping of a helpful message written on the back of customers' checks. *Journal of Applied Social Psychology, 29,* 139–144.

Ripley, A. (2005, March 7). Who says a woman can't be Einstein? *Time,* pp. 51–60.

Riso, L. P., duToit, P. L., Blandino, J. A., Penna, S., Dacey, S., Duin, J. S., et al. (2003). Cognitive aspects of chronic depression. *Journal of Abnormal Psychology, 112,* 72–80.

Ritter, M. (2000, March 21). Brains differ in navigation skills. *Associated Press.*

Robbins, J. (2000, September 26). Some see hope in biofeedback for attention disorder. *New York Times,* p. F7.

Roberts, A., Cash, T. F., Feingold, A., & Johnson, B. T. (2006). Are black-white differences in females' body dissatisfaction decreasing? A meta-analytic review. *Journal of Consulting and Clinical Psychology, 74,* 1121–1131.

Roberts, B. W., Walton, K. E., & Viechtbauer, W. (2006). Patterns of mean-level change in personality traits across the life course: A meta-analysis of longitudinal studies.

Roberts, R. E. (2008). Persistence and change in symptoms of insomnia among adolescents. *Sleep, 31,* 177.

Roberts, S. (2005, March 27). Ms. Rose, by any other name, might still be a florist. *New York Times,* Section 4, p. 12.

Robins, R. W., & Trzesniewski, K .H. (2005). Self-esteem development across the lifespan. *Current Directions in Psychological Science, 14* 158–162.

Robins, R. W., Trzesniewski, K. H., Tracy, J. L., Gosling, S. D., & Potter, J. (2002). Global self-esteem across the life span. *Psychology and Aging,17,* 423–434.

Robinson, F. P. (1970). *Effective study* (4th ed.). New York: Harper & Row.

Robles, T. F., Glaser, R., & Kiecolot-Glaser, J. K. (2005). Out of balance: A new look at chronic stress, depression, and immunity. *Current Directions in Psychological Science, 14,* 111–115.

Rodriguez, N., Myers, H. F., Mira, C. B., Flores, T., & Garcia-Hernandez, L. (2002). Development of the Multidimensional Acculturative Stress Inventory for adults of Mexican origin. *Psychological Assessment, 14,* 451–461.

Roese, N. J., & Olson, J. M. (2007). Better, stronger, faster: Self-serving judgment, affect regulation, and the optimal vigilance hypothesis. *Perspectives on Psychological Science, 2,* 124–141.

Rokach, A., & Bacanli, H. (2001). Perceived causes of loneliness: A cross-cultural comparison. *Social Behavior & Personality, 29,* 169–182.

Rosen, R. C., & Laumann, E. O. (2003). The prevalence of sexual problems in women: How valid are comparisons across studies? Commentary on Bancroft, Loftus, and Long's (2003) "Distress about sex: A national survey of women in heterosexual relationships." *Archives of Sexual Behavior, 32,* 209–211.

Rotter, J. B. (1990). Internal versus external control of reinforcement. *American Psychologist, 45,* 489–493.

Roy-Byrne, P. (2009, January 12). With a little help from my friends: the happiness effect. *Journal Watch Psychiatry.* Retrieved January 12, 2009, from *http://psychiatry.jwatch.org/cgi/content/full/2009/112/1*

Rozin, P., Bauer, R., & Catanese, D. (2003). Food and life, pleasure and worry, among American college students: Gender differences and regional similarities. *Journal of Personality and Social Psychology, 85,* 132–141.

Rubin, R. (2003, April 3). Newly approved HPV test must be used wisely, experts say. *USA Today,* p. 10D.

Rubinstein, J. S., Meyer, D. E., & Evans, J. E. (2001). Executive control of cognitive processes in task switching. *Journal of Experimental Psychology: Human Perception and Performance, 27,* 763–797.

Rubinstein, S., & Caballero, B. (2000). Is Miss America an undernourished role model? *Journal of the American Medical Association, 283,* 1569.

Rupert, P. A., & Morgan, D. J. (2005). Work setting and burnout among professional psychologists. *Professional Psychology: Research and Practice, 36,* 544–550.

Rush, A. J., Khatami, M., & Beck, A. T. (1975). Cognitive and behavior therapy in chronic depression. *Behavior Therapy, 6,* 398–404.

Rushton, J. P., & Bons, T. A. (2005). Mate choice and friendship in twins: Evidence for genetic similarity. *Psychological Science, 16,* 555–559.

Rüstemli, A. (1986). Male and female personal space needs and escape reactions under intrusion: A Turkish sample. *International Journal of Psychology.*

Rutledge, P. C., Park, A., & Sher, K. J. (2008). 21st birthday drinking: Extremely extreme. *Journal of Consulting and Clinical Psychology, 76,* 517–523.

Rutter, M. (2008). Biological implications of gene–environment interaction. *Journal of Abnormal Child Psychology, 36,* 969–975.

Rutter, M., Caspi, A., Fergusson, D., Horwood, L. J., Goodman, R., Maughan, B., et al. (2004). Sex differences in developmental reading disability: New findings from 4 epidemiological studies. *Journal of the American Medical Association, 291,* 2007–2012.

Ryder, A. G., Alden, L. E., & Paulhus, D. L.(2000). Is acculturation unidimensional or bidimensional? A head-to-head comparison in the prediction of personality, self-identity, and adjustment. *Journal of Personality and Social Psychology, 79,* 49–65.

Saad, L. (1999, September 3). American workers generally satisfied, but indicate their jobs leave much to be desired. *Gallup News Service.*

Sachs-Ericsson, N., Blazer, D., Plant, E. A., & Arnow, B. (2005). Childhood sexual and physical abuse and the 1-year prevalence of medical problems in the National Comorbidity Survey. *Health Psychology, 24,* 32–40.

Saigal, C. S. (2004). Obesity and erectile dysfunction: Common problems, common solution? *Journal of the American Medical Association, 291,* 3011–3012.

Saigal, C. S., Wessells, H., Pace, J., Schonlau, M., & Wilt, T. J. (2006). Predictors and prevalence of erectile dysfunction in a racially diverse population. *Archives of Internal Medicine, 166,* 207–212.

Salgado de Snyder, V. N., Cervantes, R. C., & Padilla, A. M. (1990). Gender and ethnic differences in psychosocial stress and generalized distress among Hispanics. *Sex Roles, 22,* 441–453.

Salovey, P., & Grewal, D. (2005). The science of emotional intelligence. *Current Directions in Psychological Science, 14,* 281–285.

Salthouse, T. A. (2004). What and when of cognitive aging. *Current Directions in Psychological Science, 13,* 140–144.

Salthouse, T. A. (2006). Mental exercise and mental aging: Evaluating the validity of the "use it or lose it" hypothesis. *Perspectives on Psychological Science, 1,* 68–87.

Samet, J. M., Dominici, F., Curriero, F. C., Coursac, I., & Zeger, S. L. (2000). Fine particulate air pollution and mortality in 20 U.S. cities, 1987–1994. *New England Journal of Medicine, 343,* 1742–1749.

Sanders, L. (2007, December 16). Gut problem. *New York Times Magazine,* pp. 42–44.

Sanna, L. J., & Meier, S. (2000). Looking for clouds in a silver lining: Self-esteem, mental simulations, and temporal confidence changes. *Journal of Research in Personality, 34*(2), 236–251.

Santelli, J. S., Lindberg, L. D., Finer, L. B., & Singh, S. (2007). Explaining recent declines in adolescent pregnancy in the United States: The contribution of abstinence and improved contraceptive use. *American Journal of Public Health, 97,* 150–156.

Sar, V., Akyuz, G., Kundakci, T., Kiziltan, E., & Dogan, O. (2004). Childhood trauma, dissociation, and psychiatric comorbidity in patients with conversion disorder. *American Journal of Psychiatry, 161,* 2271–2276.

Saucier, D. A., Miller, C. T., & Doucet, N. (2005). Differences in helping whites and blacks: A meta-analysis. *Personality and Social Psychology Review, 9,* 2–16.

Savickas, M. L. (2002). Career construction: A developmental theory of vocational behavior. In D. Brown & Associates (Eds.), *Career choice and development.* (4th ed., pp. 149–205). San Francisco: Jossey-Bass.

Saywitz, K. J., Mannarino, A P., Berliner, L, & Cohen, J. A. (2000). Treatment for sexually abused children and adolescents. *American Psychologist, 55,* 1040–1049.

Schaie, K. W. (1994). The course of adult intellectual development. *American Psychologist, 49,* 304–313.

Schaubroeck, J., Jones, J. R., & Xie, J. L. (2001). Individual differences in utilizing control to cope with job demands: Effects on susceptibility to infectious disease. *Journal of Applied Psychology, 86,* 265–278.

Scheier, M. F., & Carver, C. S. (1985). Optimism, coping, and health: Assessment and implications of generalized outcome expectancies. *Health Psychology, 4,* 219–247.

Scheier, M. F., Matthews, K. A., Owens, J. F., Schulz, R., Bridges, M. W., Magovern, G. J. et al. (1999). Optimism and rehospitalization after coronary artery bypass graft surgery. *Archives of Internal Medicine, 159,* 829–935.

Schemo, D. J. (2006, January 25). One-quarter of college students cite unwanted sexual contact *New York Times,* p. B7.

Schiedel, D. G., & Marcia, J. E. (1985). Ego identity, intimacy, sex-role orientation, and gender. *Developmental Psychology, 21,* 149–160.

Schmader, T., Johns, M., & Forbes, C. (2008). An integrated process model of stereotype threat effects on performance. *Psychological Review, 115,* 336–356.

Schmidt, U., Lee, S., Beecham, J., Perkins, S., Treasure, J., Yi, I., Winn, S., et al. (2007). A randomized controlled trial of family therapy and cognitive behavior therapy guided self-care for adolescents with bulimia nervosa and related disorders. *American Journal of Psychiatry, 164,* 591–598.

Schneider, L. S. (2004). Estrogen and dementia: Insights from the Women's Health Initiative Memory Study. *Journal of the American Medical Association, 291,* 3005–3007.

Schneiderman, N. (2004). Psychosocial, behavioral, and biological aspects of chronic diseases. *Current Directions in Psychological Science, 13,* 247–251.

Schneier, F. R. (2006). Social anxiety disorder. *New England Journal of Medicine, 355,* 1029–1036.

Schroeder, S. A. (2007). We can do better — improving the health of the American people. *New England Journal of Medicine, 357,* 1221–1228.

Schultz, L. T., & Heimberg, R. G. (2008). Attentional focus in social anxiety disorder: Potential for interactive processes. *Clinical Psychology Review, 28,* 1206–1221.

Schwartz, C. E., Wright, C. I., Shin, L. M., Kagan, J., & Rauch, S. L. (2003). Inhibited and uninhibited infants "grown up:" Adult amygdalar response to novelty. *Science, 300,* 1952–1953.

Schwartz, R. M., & Gottman, J. M. (1976). Toward a task analysis of assertive behavior. *Journal of Consulting and Clinical Psychology, 44,* 910–920.

Schwartz, S. J., Mullis, R. L., Waterman, A. S., & Dunham, R. M. (2000). Ego identity status, identity style, and personal expressiveness: An empirical investigation of three convergent constructs. *Journal of Adolescent Research, 15,* 504–521.

Schwartz, S. J., Zamboanga, B. L., & Jarvis, L. H. (2007). Ethnic identity and acculturation in Hispanic early adolescents: Mediated relationships to academic grades, prosocial behaviors, and externalizing symptoms. *Cultural Diversity and Ethnic Minority Psychology, 13,* 364–373.

Scott, J. (1994, May 9). Multiple personality cases perplex legal system. *New York Times,* pp. A1, B10, B11.

Sedikides, C., Gaertner, L, & Toguchi, Y. (2003). Pancultural self-enhancement. *Journal of Personality and Social Psychology, 84,* 60–79.

Sefcek, J. A., Brumbach, B. H., Vasquez, G., & Miller, G. F. (2007). The evolutionary psychology of human mater choice: How ecology, genes, fertility, and fashion influence mating strategies. *Journal of Psychology & Human Sexuality, 18,* 125–182

Segrin, C., Powell, H. L., Givertz, M., & Brackin, A. (2003). Symptoms of depression, relational quality, and loneliness in dating relationships. *Personal Relationships, 10,* 25–36.

Seib, B., & Muller, J. (1999). The effect of different work schedules on role strain of Australian working mothers: A pilot study. *Journal of Applied Health Behaviour, 1*(2), 9–15.

Seligman, M. E. P. (2003, August). *Positive psychology: Applications to work, love, and sports.* Paper presented at the meeting of the American Psychological Association, Toronto, CA.

Seligman, M. E. P., & Maier, S. F. (1967). Failure to escape traumatic shock. *Journal of Experimental Psychology, 74,* 1–9.

Seligman, M. E. P., Steen, T. A., Park, N., & Peterson, C. (2005). Positive psychology progress: Empirical validation of interventions. *American Psychologist, 60,* 410–421.

Selye, H. (1976). *The stress of life* (rev. ed.). New York: McGraw-Hill.

Senecal, C., Vallerand, R. J., & Guay, F. (2001). Antecedents and outcomes of work-family conflict: Toward a motivational model. *Personality & Social Psychology Bulletin, 27*(2), 176–186.

Serrano-Blanco, A., Gabarron, E., Garcia-Bayo, I., Soler-Vila, M., Caramés, E., Peñarrubia-Maria, M.T., et al. (2006). Effectiveness and cost-effectiveness of antidepressant treatment in primary health care: A six-month randomised study comparing fluoxetine to imipramine. *Journal of Affective Disorders, 91,* 153–163.

Sexual Orientation & Marriage. (2004, July). American Psychological Association Policy Statement. Retrieved March 24, 2006, from *http://www.apa.org/pi/lgbc/policy/marriage.html*

Shackelford, T. K., Schmitt. D. P., & Buss, D. M. (2005). Universal dimensions of human mate preferences. *Personality and Individual Differences, 39,* 447–458.

Shadish, W. R., & Baldwin, S. A. (2005). Effects of behavioral marital therapy: A meta-analysis of randomized controlled trials. *Journal of Consulting and Clinical Psychology, 73,* 6–14.

Shadish, W. R., Matt, G. E., Navarro, A. M., & Phillips, G. (2000). The effects of psychological therapies under clinically representative conditions: A meta-analysis. *Psychological Bulletin, 126,* 512–529.

Shafran, R., & Mansell, W. (2001). Perfectionism and psychopathology: A review of research and treatment. *Clinical Psychology Review, 21,* 879–906.

Sharp, T. A. (2006). New molecule to brighten the mood. *Science, 311,* 45–46

Shea, C. (2007, December 9). The height tax. *New York Times Magazine,* p. 74.

Sheard, M., & Golby, J. (2007). Hardiness and undergraduate academic study: The moderating role of commitment. *Personality and Individual Differences, 43,* 579–588.

Sheehy, G. (1976). *Passages: Predictable crises of adult life.* New York: Dutton.

Sheehy, G. (1995). *New passages: Mapping your life across time.* New York: Random House.

Shehan, C., & Kammeyer, K. (1997). *Marriages and families: Reflections of a gendered society.* Boston: Allyn & Bacon.

Sheldon, K. M. (2004). The benefits of a "sidelong" approach to self-esteem need satisfaction: Comment on Crocker and Park (2004). *Psychological Bulletin, 130,* 421–424.

Sheldon, K. M., Houser-Marko, L., & Kasser, T. (2006). Does autonomy increase with age? Comparing the goal motivations of college students and their parents. *Journal of Research in Personality, 40,* 168–178.

Shellenbarger, S. (2003b, March 20). Female rats are better multitaskers; with humans, the debate rages on. *Wall Street Journal,* p. D1.

Shellenbarger, S. (2003, February 27). Multitasking makes you stupid: Studies show pitfalls of doing too much at once. *The Wall Street Journal,* p. D1.

Shepherd, G. M. (2006). Behaviour: Smells, brains and hormones. *Nature, 439,* 149–151.

Shields, D. C., Asaad, W., Eskandar, E. N., Jain, F. A., Cosgrove, G. R., Flaherty, A. W., et al. (2008). Prospective assessment of stereotactic ablative surgery for intractable major depression. *Biological Psychiatry, 64,* 449.

Shiffman, S., Balabanis, M. H., Paty, J. A., Engberg, J., Gwaltney, C. J., Liu, K. S., et al. (2000). Dynamic effects of self-efficacy on smoking lapse and relapse. *Health Psychology, 19,* 315–323.

Shifren, J., & Ferrari, N. A. (2004, May 10). A better sex life. *Newsweek,* pp. 86–87.

Shneidman, E. S. (Ed.). (1984). *Death: Current perspectives* (3rd ed.). Palo Alto, CA: Mayfield.

Shneidman, E. S. (1999). The Psychological Pain Assessment Scale. *Suicide & Life-Threatening Behavior, 29*(4), 287–294.

Shnek, Z. M., Irvine, J., Stewart, D., & Abbey, S. (2001). Psychological factors and depressive symptoms in ischemic heart disease. *Health Psychology,* 141–145.

Shonk, S. M., & Cicchetti, D. (2001). Maltreatment, competency deficits, and risk for academic and behavioral maladjustment. *Developmental Psychology, 37,* 3–17.

Sibille, E., & Lewis, D. A. (2006). SERT-ainly involved in depression, but when? *American Journal of Psychiatry, 163,* 8–11.

Siegle, G. J. (2008). Brain mechanisms of borderline personality disorder at the intersection of cognition, emotion, and the clinic [Editorial]. *American Journal of Psychiatry, 164,* 1776–1779.

Siegler, I., Bosworth, H. B., & Poon, L. W. (2003). Disease, health, and aging. In R. M. Lerner, M. A. Easterbrooks, & J. Mistry (Eds.), *Handbook of psychology: Developmental psychology* (Vol. 6., pp. 423–442). New York: Wiley.

Silberstein, S. D., Massiou, H., Le Jeunne, C., Johnson-Pratt, L., McCarroll, K. A., & Lines, C. R. (2000). Rizatriptan in the treatment of menstrual migraine. *Obstetrics and Gynecology, 96,* 237–242.

Silva, P. (2005). The state of affairs. *Sexual and Relationship Therapy, 20,* 261–262.

Silventoinen, K., Pietiläinen, K. H., Tynelius, P., Serensen, T. I. A., & Kaprio, J., & Rasmussen, F. (2007). Genetic and environmental factors in relative weight from birth to age 18: The Swedish young male twins study. *International Journal of Obesity, 31,* 615–621.

Silverman, J. G., Raj, A., Mucci, L. A., & Hathaway, J. E. (2001). Dating violence against adolescent girls and associated substance use, unhealthy weight control, sexual risk behavior, pregnancy, and suicidality. *Journal of the American Medical Association, 286,* 572–579.

Simons, T., & O'Connell, M. (2003). Married-couple and unmarried-partner households: 2000. Washington, D.C.: U.S. Census Bureau. Retrieved October 25, 2004, from *http://www.census.gov/prod/2003pubs/censr-5.pdf*

Simonsen, G., Blazina, C., & Watkins, C. E., Jr. (2000). Gender role conflict and psychological well-being among gay men. *Journal of Counseling Psychology, 47,* 85–89.

Simpson, H. B., Foa, E. B., Liebowitz, M. R., Ledley, D. R., Huppert, J. D., & Cahill, S. (2008). A randomized, controlled trial of cognitive-behavioral therapy for augmenting pharmacotherapy in obsessive-compulsive disorder. *American Journal of Psychiatry, 165,* 621–630.

Sims, C. S., Drasgow, F., & Fitzgerald, L. F. (2005). The effects of sexual harassment on turnover in the military: time-dependent modeling. *Journal of Applied Psychology, 90,* 1141–1152.

Singer, T., Verhaeghen, P., Ghisletta, P., Lindenberger, U., & Baltes, P. B. (2003). The fate of cognition in very old age: Six-year longitudinal findings in the Berlin Aging Study (BASE). *Psychology and Aging, 18,* 318–331.

Singh, D. (1994a). Body fat distribution and perception of desirable female body shape by young Black men and women. *International Journal of Eating Disorders, 16,* 289–294.

Singh, D. (1994b). Is thin really beautiful and good? Relationship between waist-to-hip ratio (WHR) and female attractiveness. *Personality and Individual Differences, 16,* 123–132.

Sink, M. (2004, November 9). Drinking deaths draw attention to old campus problem. *New York Times,* p. A16.

Skegg, K., Nada-Raja, S., Dickson, N., Paul, C., & Williams, S. (2003). Sexual orientation and self-harm in men and women. *American Journal of Psychiatry, 160,* 541–546.

Skinner, B. F. (1938). *The behavior of organisms: An experimental analysis.* New York: Appleton.

Skorikov, V. (2007). Continuity in adolescent career preparation and its effects on adjustment. *Journal of Vocational Behavior, 70,* 8–24.

Sleek, S. (1997). Resolution raises concerns about conversion therapy. *APA Monitor, 27*(10), 15.

Slijper, F. M., Drop, S. L. S., Molenaar, J. C., & de Muinck Keizer Schrama, S. M. P. F. (1998). Long-term psychological evaluation of intersex children. *Archives of Sexual Behavior, 27,* 125–144.

Sloan, D. M., & Marx, B. P. (2004). A closer examination of the structured written disclosure procedure. *Journal of Consulting and Clinical Psychology, 72,* 165–175.

Smart, C. (2006). The state of affairs: Explorations in infidelity and commitment. *Sexualities, 9,* 259–262.

Smith, M. L., Glass, G. V., & Miller, T. I. (1980). *The benefits of psychotherapy.* Baltimore, MD: Johns Hopkins University Press.

Smith, M. T., & Perlis, M. L. (2006). Who is a candidate for cognitive-behavioral therapy for insomnia? *Health Psychology, 25,* 15–19.

Smith, T. W. (2006). Personality as risk and resilience in physical health. *Current Directions in Psychological Science, 15,* 227–231.

Smock, P. J. (2000). *Annual Review of Sociology.* Cited in Nagourney, E. (2000, February 15). Study finds families bypassing marriage. *New York Times,* p. F8.

Smoller, J. W., Paulus, M. P., Fagerness, J. A., Purcell, S., Yamaki, L. H., Hirshfeld-Becker, D., et al. (2008). Influence of RGS2 on anxiety-related temperament, personality, and brain function. *Archives of General Psychiatry, 65,* 298–308.

Smyth, K. A., Fritsch, T., Cook, T. B., McClendon, M. J., Santillan, C. E., & Friedland R. P. (2004). Worker functions and traits associated with occupations and the development of AD. *Neurology, 63,* 498–503.

Snibbe, A. C. (2004, November). Taking the "vs." out of nature vs. nurture. *Monitor on Psychology, 35* (10), pp. 22–25.

Snyder, C. R., & Lopez, S. J. (2007). *Positive psychology: The science and practical explorations of human strength.* Thousand Oaks, CA: Sage.

Snyder, D. (1979). Multidimensional assessment of marital satisfaction. *Journal of Marriage and the Family, 41,* 813–823.

Social serendipity. (2005) *MIT Media Lab.* Retrieved June 23, 2005, from *http://reality.media.mit.edu/serendipity.php*

Solowij, N., Stephens, R. S., Roffman, R. A., et al. (2002). Cognitive functioning of long-term heavy cannabis users seeking treatment. *Journal of the American Medical Association, 287,* 1123–1131.

Somers, M., & Birnbaum, D. (2000). Exploring the relationship between commitment profiles and work attitudes, employee withdrawal, and job performance. *Public Personnel Management, 29*(3), 353–365.

Sommerfeld, J. (2002, August 13). Coveting a clone. *MSNBC.* Retrieved May 13, 2005, from *http://www.msnbc.com/news/768363.asp?pne=msn*

Song, S. (2006, January 16). Sleeping your way to the top. *Time,* p. 83.

Spanos, N. P. (1994). Multiple identity enactments and multiple personality disorder: A sociocognitive perspective. *Psychological Bulletin, 116,* 143–165.

Spataro, J., Mullen, P. E., Burgess, P. M., Wells, D. L., & Moss, S. A. (2004). Impact of child sexual abuse on mental health: Prospective study in males and females. *British Journal of Psychiatry, 184,* 416–421.

Spector, P. E. (2003). *Industrial and organizational psychology: Research and practice.* (3rd ed.). New York: Wiley.

Spelke, E. S. (2005). Sex differences in intrinsic aptitude for mathematics and science? A critical review. *American Psychologist, 60,* 950–958.

Spokane, A. R., Luchetta, E. J., & Richwine, M. H. (2002). Holland's theory of personalities in work environments. In D. Brown & Associates (Eds.), *Career choice and development.* (4th ed., pp. 373–426). San Francisco: Jossey-Bass.

Sprecher, S., Sullivan, Q., & Hatfield, E. (1994). Mate selection preferences. *Journal of Personality and Social Psychology, 66*(6), 1074–1080.

Spring, J. A. (1997). Cited in Alterman, E. (1997, November). Sex in the '90s. *Elle.*

Stambor, Z. (2006, April). Extraversion, agreeableness linked to happiness in orangutans. *Monitor on Psychology, 37*(4), 10.

Stampfer, M. J., Hu, F. B., Manson, J. E., Rimm, E. B., & Willett, W. C. (2000). Primary prevention of coronary heart disease in women through diet and lifestyle. *New England Journal of Medicine, 343,* 16–22.

Staples, S. I. (1996). Human responses to environmental noise. *American Psychologist, 51,* 143–150.

Statistics Canada (2003). 2001 Census: Analysis series. *Canada's ethnocultural portrait.* Retrieved March 26, 2005, from *http://www12.statcan.ca/english/census01/products/analytic/companion/etoimm/contents.cfm*

Staub, E. (2000). Genocide and mass killing: Origins, prevention, healing and reconciliation. *Political Psychology, 21,* 367–382.

Staw, B. M., & Cohen-Charash, Y. (2005). The dispositional approach to job satisfaction: More than a mirage, but not yet an oasis. *Journal of Organizational Behavior, 26,* 59–78.

Steck, L., Levitan, D., McLane, D., & Kelley, H. H. (1982). Care, need, and conceptions of love. *Journal of Personality and Social Psychology, 43,* 481–491.

Steele, J. D., Christmas, D., Eljamel, M. S., & Matthews, K. (2008). Anterior cingulotomy for major depression: Clinical outcome and relationship to lesion characteristics. *Biological Psychiatry, 63,* 670.

Steele, J. R., & Ambady, N. (2006). "Math is hard!" The effect of gender priming on women's attitudes. *Journal of Experimental Social Psychology, 42,* 428–436.

Stein, J. (2005, January 17). Is there a hitch? *Time,* pp. A37–A40.

Stein, M. B., & Stein, D. J. (2008). Social anxiety disorder. *Lancet, 371,* 1115–1125.

Stein, S. (2002, October). Make room for daddy. *Working Mother,* pp. 44–49.

Steinberg, L. (1996). *Beyond the classroom*. New York: Simon & Schuster.

Steinberg, L. (2007). Risk taking in adolescence: New perspectives from brain and behavioral science. *Current Directions in Psychological Science, 16,* 55–59.

Steinbrook, R., (2004). The AIDS epidemic in 2004. *New England Journal of Medicine, 351,* 115–117.

Steinbrook, R. (2006). The potential of human papillomavirus vaccines. *New England Journal of Medicine, 354,* 1109–1112

Steinhauer, J. & Holson, J. M. (2008). Cellular alert: As texts fly, danger lurks. *New York Times,* pp. A1, A17.

Steinhauer, J. (1995, July 6). No marriage, no apologies. *New York Times,* pp. C1, C7.

Stenson, J. (2001, August 26). Burden of mental illness in America falls on minorities. *MSNBC.* Retrieved August 28, 2001, from *http://www.msnbc.com/news/619545.asp*

Stenson, J. (2003, May 14). How much exercise is enough? *MSNBC.* Retrieved May 15, 2003, from *http://www.msnbc.com/news/910636.asp*

Stephenson, J. (2004). Global AIDS epidemic worsens. *Journal of the American Medical Association, 291,* 31–32.

Sternberg, E. M. (2000). *The balance within: The science connecting health and emotions.* New York: Freeman.

Sternberg, R. J. (1988). *The triangle of love: Intimacy, passion, commitment.* New York: Basic Books.

Stevens, S. E., Hynan, M. T., & Allen, M. (2000). A meta-analysis of common factor and specific treatment effects across the outcome domains of the phase model of psychotherapy. *Clinical Psychology: Science and Practice, 7,* 273–290.

Stewart, A. J., & McDermott, C. (2004). Gender in psychology. *Annual Review of Psychology, 55,* 519–544.

Stewart, A. J., & Ostrove, J. M. (1998). Women's personality in middle age: Gender, history, and midcourse corrections. *American Psychologist, 53*(11), 1185–1194.

Stewart, J. Y., & Armet, E. (2000, April 3). Aging in America: Retirees reinvent the concept. *Los Angeles Times.* Retrieved May 14, 2009, from *http://articles.latimes.com/apr/03/news/mn-15453*

Stice, E., Hayward, C., Cameron, R. P., Killen, J. D., & Taylor, C. B. (2000). Body-image and eating disturbances predict onset of depression among female adolescents: A longitudinal study. *Journal of Abnormal Psychology, 109,* 438–444.

Stier, D. S., & Hall, J. A. (1984). Gender differences in touch: An empirical and theoretical review. *Journal of Personality and Social Psychology, 47,* 440–459.

Stine-Morrow, E. A. L. (2007). The Dumbledore hypothesis of cognitive aging. *Current Directions in Psychological Science, 16,* 295–299.

Stock, R. (1995, June 1). Wrongheaded views persist about the old. *New York Times,* p. C8.

Stokes, P. P., Stewart-Belle, S., & Barnes, J. M. (2000). The Supreme Court holds class on sexual harassment: How to avoid a failing grade. *Employee Responsibilities & Rights Journal, 12,* 79–91.

Stolberg, S. G. (2001, May 10). Blacks found on short end of heart attack procedure. *New York Times,* p. A20.

Stone, L., & McKee, N. P. (2000). Gendered futures: Student visions of career and family on a college campus. *Anthropology & Education Quarterly, 31,* 67–89.

Stoney, C. M. (2003). Gender and cardiovascular disease: A psychobiological and integrative approach. *Current Directions in Psychological Science, 12,* 129–133.

Stout, D. (2000, September 1). Use of illegal drugs is down among young, survey finds. *New York Times,* p. A18.

Strasser, A. A., Kaufmann, V., Jepson, C., Perkins, K. A., Pickworth, W. B., & Wileyto, E. P. (2005). Effects of different nicotine replacement therapies on postcessation psychological responses. *Addictive Behaviors, 30,* 9–17.

Stricker, G., & Gold, J. R. (1999). The Rorschach: Toward a nomothetically based, idiographically applicable configurational model. *Psychological Assessment, 11,* 240–250.

Striegel-Moore, R. H., Dohm, F. A., Kraemer, H. C., Taylor, C. B., Daniels, S. D., Crawford, P. B., et al. (2003). Eating disorders in white and black women. *American Journal of Psychiatry, 160,* 1326–1331.

Striegel-Moore, R. H., & Bulik, C. M. (2007). Factors for eating disorders. *American Psychologist, 62,* 181–198.

Stroebe, M. (2001). Gender differences in adjustment to bereavement: An empirical and theoretical review. *Review of General Psychology, 5,* 62–83.

Strohmetz, D. B., Rind, B., Fisher, R., & Lynn, M. (2002). Sweetening the till: The use of candy to increase restaurant tipping. *Journal of Applied Social Psychology, 32,* 300–309.

Strong, S. M., Williamson, D. A., Netemeyer, R. G., & Geer, J. H. (2000). Eating disorder symptoms and concerns about body differ as a function of gender and sexual orientation. *Journal of Social & Clinical Psychology, 19,* 240–255.

Stuart, R. B. (2004). Twelve practical suggestions for achieving multicultural competence. *Professional Psychology: Research and Practice, 35,* 3–9.

Studies focus on acculturation and Hispanic Youth. (2007, February). *NIDA Notes, 21*(2), p. 3

Substance Abuse and Mental Health Services Administration (SAMHSA). (2005). *Overview of findings from the 2002 National Survey on Drug Use and Health* (Office of Applied Studies, NHSDA Series H-21 DHHS Publication No. MA 03–3774). Rockville, MD. Retrieved February 9, 2005, from *http://www.nida.nih.gov/NIDA_notes/NNvol19N5/Study.html*

Sue, S. (1991). In Goodchilds, J. D. (1991). (Ed.). *Psychological perspectives on human diversity in America.* Washington, DC: American Psychological Association.

Sue, S. (2003). In defense of cultural competency in psychotherapy and treatment. *American Psychologist, 58,* 964–970.

Suedfeld, P. (2000). Reverberations of the Holocaust fifty years later: Psychology's contributions to understanding persecution and genocide. *Canadian Psychology, 41,* 1–9.

Suinn, R. M. (1982). Intervention with Type A behaviors. *Journal of Consulting and Clinical Psychology, 50,* 933–949.

Suinn, R. A. (1995). Anxiety management training. In K. Craig (Ed.), *Anxiety and depression in children and adults* (pp. 159–179). New York: Sage.

Suinn, R. M. (2001). The terrible twos—anger and anxiety: Hazardous to your health. *American Psychologist, 56,* 27–36.

Sukru, U., Huner, A., & Yerlikaya, E. E. (2004). Violence by proxy in Othello syndrome. *Primary Care Psychiatry, 9,* 121–123.

Suler, J. R. (2002). Identity management in cyberspace. *Journal of Applied Psychoanalytic Studies, 4,* 455–460.

Sullivan, A. (2000, April 2). The He hormone. *New York Times Magazine,* pp. 46–51ff.

Surgeon General warns of other cancers, pneumonia, cataracts and more. *The Associated Press Online.* Retrieved June 2, 2004, from *http://www.msnbc.msn.com/id/5077308*

Swami, V., & Furnham, A. (2008). *The psychology of physical attraction.* London: Routledge

Sweeney, C. (2005, June 5). Not tonight. *New York Times,* Section 15, pp. 1, 7.

Sweeny, K., Carroll, P. J., & Shepperd, J. A. (2006). Thinking about the future: Is optimism always best? *Current Directions in Psychological Science, 15,* 302–306.

Symons, D. (1995). Cited in Goleman, D. (1995, June 14). Sex fantasy research said to neglect women. *New York Times,* p. C14.

Szeszko, P. R., Ardekani, B. A., Ashtari, M., Malhotra, A. K., Robinson, D. G., Bilder, R. M., & Lim, K. O. (2005). White matter abnormalities in obsessive-compulsive disorder: A diffusion tensor imaging study. *Archives of General Psychiatry, 62,* 782–790.

Szeszko, P. R., MacMillan, S., McMeniman, M., Chen, S., Baribault, K., Lim, K. O., et al. (2004). Brain structural abnormalities in psychotropic drug-naive pediatric patients with obsessive-compulsive disorder. *American Journal of Psychiatry, 161,* 1049–1056.

Szeszko, P. R., Ardekani, B. A., Ashtari, M., Malhotra, A. K., Robinson, D. G., Bilder, R. M., & Lim, K. O. (2005). White matter abnormalities in obsessive-compulsive disorder: A diffusion tensor imaging study. *Archives of General Psychiatry, 62,* 782–790.

Szinovacz, M. E., DeViney, S., & Davey, A. (2001). Influences of family obligations and relationships on retirement: Variations by gender, race, and marital status. *Journals of Gerontology: Series B: Psychological Sciences & Social Sciences, 56B*(1), S20–S27.

Tadros, G., & Salib, E. (2001). Carer's views on passive euthanasia. *International Journal of Geriatric Psychiatry, 16*(2), 230–231.

Tancredi, A., Reginster, J-Y, Luyckx, F., & Legros, J-J. (2005). No major month to month variation in free testosterone levels in aging males. Minor impact on the biological diagnosis of "andropause." *Psychoneuroendocrinology, 30,* 638–646.

Tandon, R., Keshavan, M. S., & Nasralla, H. A. (2008). Schizophrenia, "just the facts," what we know in 2008. 2. Epidemiology and etiology. *Schizophrenia Research, 102,* 1–3.

Tang, T. Z., DeRubeis, R. J., Hollon, S. D., Amsterdam, J., & Shelton, R. (2007). Sudden gains in cognitive therapy of depression and depression relapse/recurrence. *Journal of Consulting and Clinical Psychology, 75,* 404–408.

Taylor, M. J. (2000). The influence of self-efficacy on alcohol use among American Indians. *Cultural Diversity and Ethnic Minority Psychology, 6,* 152–167.

Taylor, M. J., Rudkin, L., & Hawton, K. (2005). Strategies for managing antidepressant-induced sexual dysfunction: Systematic review of randomised controlled trials. *Journal of Affective Disorders, 88,* 241–254.

Taylor, S. E. (2000). Cited in Goode, E. (2000, May 19). Response to stress found that's particularly female. *New York Times,* p. A20.

Taylor, S. E., Klein, L. C., Lewis, B. P., Gurung, R. A. R., Gruenewald, T. L., & Updegraff, J. A. (2000). Biobehavioral responses to stress in females: Tend-and-befriend, not fight-or-flight. *Psychological Review, 107,* 411–429.

Taylor, S. E., Lerner, J. S., Sherman, D. K., Sage, R. M., & McDowell, N. K. (2003). Portrait of the self-enhancer: Well adjusted and well liked or maladjusted and friendless? *Journal of Personality and Social Psychology, 84,* 165–176.

Taylor, W. E., Welch, W. T., Kim, H. S., & Sherman, D. K. (2007) Cultural differences in the impact of social support on psychological and biological stress responses. *Psychological Science, 18,* 831–837.

Teens' brains hold key to their impulsiveness. (2007, December 3). Associated Press. Retrieved December 10, 2007, from *http://www.msnbc.msn.com/id/21997683/*

Teens say they get along with parents. (2003, August 5). *Associated Press, MSNBC.com.*. Retrieved August 8, 2003, from *http://www.msnbc.com/news/948480.asp*

Telecommuting has mostly positive consequences for employees and employers, say researchers. (2007, November 19). American Psychological Association press release. Retrieved December 24, 2007, from *http://www.apa.org/releases/telecommuting.html*

Tenenbaum, H. R., & Leaper, C. (2003). Parent–child conversations about science: The socialization of gender inequities? *Developmental Psychology, 39,* 34–47.

Tennen, H. & Affleck, G. (2000). The perception of personal control: Sufficiently important to warrant careful scrutiny. *Personality & Social Psychology Bulletin, 26,* 152–156.

Terry, D. (2000, July 16). Getting under my skin. *New York Times.* Retrieved May 14, 2009, from *http://partners.nytimes.com/library/national/race/071600terry-mag.html*

The ubiquitous cell phone. (2005, Summer). *The University of Denver Magazine.* Retrieved October 8, 2005, from *http://www.du.edu/dumagazine/studentLife.html*

The world's billionaires (2009, March 11). *Forbes.com.* Retrieved May 12, 2009, from *http://www.forbes.com/2009/03/11/worlds-richest-people-billionaires-2009-billionaires_land.html*

Thiederman, S. (2002). *Body language, Part II, Where do I stand?* Retrieved May 8, 2003, from *http://equalopportunity.monster.com/articles/body2/*

Think positive, live longer (2002, July 28). *MSNBC.* Retrieved July 30, 2002, from *http://www.msnbc.com/news/786749.asp*

Thompson, C. P., Anderson, L. P., & Bakeman, R. A. (2000). Effects of racial socialization and racial identity on acculturative stress in African American college students. *Cultural Diversity and Ethnic Minority Psychology, 6,* 196–210.

Thompson, J. K., & Tantleff, S. (1992). Female and male ratings of upper torso: Actual, ideal, and stereotypical conceptions. *Journal of Social Behavior and Personality, 7,* 345–354.

Thompson, P. M., Hayashi, K. M., Simon, S. L., Geaga, J. A., Hong, M. S., Sui, Y., et al. (2004). Structural abnormalities in the brains of human subjects who use methamphetamine. *Journal of Neuroscience, 30,* 6028–6036.

Thomsen, D. K., Mehlsen, M. Y., Christensen, S., & Zachariae, R. (2003). Rumination—relationship with negative mood and sleep quality. *Personality and Individual Differences, 34,* 1293–1301.

Thorne, S. L., Malarcher, A., Maurice, E., & Caraballo, R. (2009).Cigarette smoking among adults—United States, 2007. *Journal of the American Medical Association, 301,* 373–375.

Thornhill, R., & Palmer, C. (2000). *A natural history of rape: Biological bases of sexual coercion.* Cambridge, MA: MIT Press.

Tierney, J. M. (2008, March 11). A boy named Sue and a theory of names. *New York Times,* p. F1.

Tiggemann, M., Martins, Y., & Kirkbride, A. (2007). Oh to be lean and muscular: Body image ideals in gay and heterosexual men. *Psychology of Men & Masculinity, 8,* 15–24.

Tilley, D. S., & Brackley, M. (2005). Men who batter intimate partners: A grounded theory study of the development of male violence in intimate partner relationships. *Issues in Mental Health Nursing, 26,* 281–297.

Tomlinson, K. L., Tate, S. R., Anderson, K. G., McCarthy, D. M., & Brown, S. A. (2006). An examination of self-medication and rebound effects: Psychiatric symptomatology before and after alcohol or drug relapse. *Addictive Behaviors, 31,* 461–474.

Toomey, R., Lyons, M. J., Eisen, S. A., Xian, H., Chantarujikapong, S., Seidman, L. J., et al. (2003). A twin study of the neuropsychological consequences of stimulant abuse. *Archives of General Psychiatry, 60,* 303–310.

Touhey, J. C. (1972). Comparison of two dimensions of attitude similarity on heterosexual attraction. *Journal of Personality and Social Psychology, 23,* 8–10.

Townsend, J. M. (1995). Sex without emotional involvement: An evolutionary interpretation of sex differences. *Archives of Sexual Behavior, 24,* 173–206.

Traut, C. A., Larsen, R., & Feimer, S. H. (2000). Hanging on or fading out? Job satisfaction and the long-term worker. *Public Personnel Management, 29,* 343–351.

Tregellas, J. (2009). Connecting brain structure and function in schizophrenia. *American Journal of Psychiatry, 166,* 134–136.

Triandis, H. C. (1995). *Individualism and collectivism.* Boulder, CO: Westview Press.

Triandis, H. C., & Suh, E. M. (2002). Cultural influences on personality. *Annual Review of Psychology, 53,* 133–160.

Trobst, K. K., Collins, R. L., & Embree, J. M. (1994). The role of emotion in social support provision. *Journal of Social and Personal Relationships, 11,* 45–62

Troxel, W. M., & Matthews, K. A. (2004). What are the costs of marital conflict and dissolution to children's physical health? *Clinical Child & Family Psychology Review, 7*(1), 29–57.

Trull, T., J., Solhan, M. B., Tragesser, S. L., Jahng, S., Wood, P. K., Piasecki, T. M., et al. (2008). Affective instability: Measuring a core feature of borderline personality disorder with ecological momentary assessment. *Journal of Abnormal Psychology, 117,* 647–661.

Trunzo, J. J., & Pinto, B. M. (2003). Social support as a mediator of optimism and distress in breast cancer survivors. *Journal of Consulting and Clinical Psychology, 71,* 805–811.

Trzesniewski, K. H., Donnellan, M. B., Moffitt, T. E., Robins, R. W., Poulton, R., & Caspi, A. (2006). Low self-esteem during adolescence predicts poor health, criminal behavior, and limited economic prospects during adulthood. *Developmental Psychology. 42,* 381–390.

Trzesniewski, K. H., Donnellan, M. B., & Robins, R. W. (2003). Stability of self-esteem across the life span. *Journal of Personality and Social Psychology, 84,* 205–220.

Tsai, J. L., Mortensen, H., Wong, Y., & Hess, D. (2002). What does "being American" mean? A comparison of Asian American and European

American young adults. *Cultural Diversity and Ethnic Minority Psychology, 8,* 257–273.

Tuiten, A., Van Honk, J., Koppeschaar, H., Bernaards, C., Thijssen, J., & Verbaten, R. (2000). Time course of effects of testosterone administration on sexual arousal in women. *Archives of General Psychiatry, 57,* 149–153.

Turner, R. J., Lloyd, D. A., & Taylor, J. (2006). Stress burden, drug dependence, and the Hispanic nativity paradox. *Drug and Alcohol Dependence, 83,* 79–89.

Turner, R. N., Hewstone, M., & Voci, A. (2007). Reducing explicit and implicit outgroup prejudice via direct and extended contact: The mediating role of self-disclosure and intergroup anxiety. *Journal of Personality and Social Psychology, 93,* 369–388.

Twenge, J. M. (2009). Change over time in obedience: The jury's still out, but it might be decreasing. *American Psychologist, 64,* 28–31.

Twenge, J. M., & Crocker, J. (2002). Race and self-esteem: Meta-analyses comparing whites, blacks, Hispanics, Asians, and American Indians and comment on Gray-Little and Hafdahl (2000). *Psychological Bulletin, 128,* 371–408.

Tyre, P. (2004, October 4). Combination therapy. *Newsweek.* Retrieved July 2, 2005, from msnbc.msn.com/id/6100257/site/newsweek/

Tyre, P., & McGinn, D. (2003, May 12). She works, he doesn't. *Newsweek,* pp. 45–52.

U.S. Bureau of Labor Statistics. (2006). *Workers on flexible and shift schedules, News.* USDL 05–1198. Retrieved April 16, 2006, from www.bls.gov/bls/newrels.htm#OEUS

U.S. Bureau of the Census (USBC). (2000). *Statistical abstract of the United States,* 120th ed. Washington, DC: U.S. Government Printing Office.

U.S. Bureau of the Census. (2005). *Statistical abstract of the United States* (125th ed.). Washington, DC: U.S. Government Printing Office.

U.S. Bureau of the Census (USBC). (2006). Current Population Report, P2-550. *Statistical Abstract of the United States, 2006.* Retrieved April 16, 2006, from www.census/gov/population/www/socdemo/educ-attn.html

U.S. Bureau of the Census. (2007). *Statistical abstract of the United States* (127th ed.). Washington, DC: U.S. Government Printing Office.

U.S. Department of Health and Human Services, Substance Abuse and Mental Health Services Administration, Center for Mental Health Services, National Institutes of Health, National Institutes of Mental Health. (2001). *Mental health: Culture, race, and ethnicity: A supplement to Mental Health: A Report of the Surgeon General—executive summary.* Rockville, MD: Author.

U.S. minority population tops 100 million. (2007, May 15). *MSNBC.* Retrieved May 15, 2007, from *http://www.msnbc.msn.com/id/ 18715129/*

Uchitelle, L. (2004, December 31). Women are gaining ground on the wage front. *New York Times,* pp. C1, C2.

Uhl, G. R., & Grow, R. W. (2004). The burden of complex genetics in brain disorders. *Archives of General Psychiatry, 61,* 223–229.

Uhlmann, E., & Swanson, J. (2004). Exposure to violent video games increases automatic aggressiveness. *Journal of Adolescence, 27,* 41–52.

Umaña-Taylor, A. J. (2004). Ethnic identity and self-esteem: Examining the role of social context. *Journal of Adolescence, 27,* 139–146.

Underwood, A. (2004, October 11). We've got rhythm . *Newsweek.* Retrieved October 14, 2004, from *http://www.msnbc.msn.com/ id/6161341/site/newsweek/*

Underwood, A., & Adler, J. (2004, August 23). What you don't know about fat. *Newsweek,* pp. 40–47.

Unger, J. B., Cruz, T. B., Rohrbach, L. A., Ribisl, K. M., Baezconde-Garbanati, L., Chen, X., et al. (2000). English language use as a risk factor for smoking initiation among Hispanic and Asian American adolescents: Evidence for mediation by tobacco-related beliefs and social norms. *Health Psychology, 19,* 403–410.

Unger, T., Calderon, G., Bradley, L., Sena-Esteves, M., & Rios, M. (2007). Selective deletion of BDNF in the ventromedial and dorsomedial hypothalamus of adult mice results in hyperphagic behavior and obesity. *Journal of Neuroscience, 27,* 14265–14274.

Vaillant, G. E. (1994). Ego mechanisms of defense and personality psychopathology. *Journal of Abnormal Psychology, 103,* 44–50.

Valian, V. (1998). *Why so slow? The advancement of women.* Cambridge, MA: MIT Press.

Vallea, M. F., Huebner, E. S., & Suldo, S. M. (2006). An analysis of hope as a psychological strength. *Journal of School Psychology, 44,* 393–406.

van Baarsen, B., Snijders, T. A. B., Smit, J. H., & van Duijn, M. A. J.(2001). Lonely but not alone: Emotional isolation and social isolation as two distinct dimensions of loneliness in older people. *Educational & Psychological Measurement, 61,* 119–135.

Vancouver, J. B., Thompson, C. M., Tischner, E. C., & Putka, D. J. (2002). Two studies examining the negative effect of self-efficacy on performance. *Journal of Applied Psychology, 87,* 506–516.

Vares, T., Potts, A., Gavey, N., & Grace, V. M. (2007). Reconceptualizing cultural narratives of mature women's sexuality in the Viagra era. *Journal of Aging Studies, 21,* 153–164.

Vasquez, M. J. T. (2007). Cultural difference and the therapeutic alliance: An evidence-based analysis. *American Psychologist, 62,* 878–885.

Verkuyten, M., & De Wolf, A. (2007). The development of in-group favoritism: Between social reality and group identity. *Developmental Psychology, 43,* 901–911.

Vermeer, H. J., Boekaerts, M., & Seegers, G. (2000). Motivational and gender differences: Sixth-grade students' mathematical problem-solving behavior. *Journal of Educational Psychology, 92*(2), 308–315.

Vickers, A. J., Rees, R. W., Zollman, C. E., McCarney, R., Smith, C. M., Ellis, N., et al. (2004). Acupuncture for chronic headache in primary care: Large, pragmatic, randomised trial. *British Medical Journal, 328,* 744–747.

Villarosa, L. (2002, December 3). To prevent sexual abuse, abusers step forward. *The New York Times,* p. F5.

Vincent, N., Lewycky, S., & Finnegan, H. (2008). Barriers to engagement in sleep restriction and stimulus control in chronic insomnia. *Journal of Consulting and Clinical Psychology, 76,* 820–828.

Volkow, N. D. (2007). Genes and smoking. *NIDA Notes, 21*(3), 2.

Volkow, N. D., Chang, L., Wang, G. J., Fowler, J. S., Leonido-Yee, M., Franceschi, D., et al. (2001). Association of dopamine transporter reduction with psychomotor impairment in methamphetamine abusers. *American Journal of Psychiatry, 158,* 377–382.

Volz, J. (2000). Successful aging: The second 50. *Monitor on Psychology, 30*(1), 24–28.

Vonk, R. (2002). Self-Serving Interpretations of Flattery: Why Ingratiation Works. *Journal of Personality and Social Psychology, 82,* 515–526.

Wadden, T. A., Berkowitz, R. I., Womble, L. G., Sarwer, D. B., Phelan, S., Cato, R. K., Hesson, L. A., et al. (2005). Randomized trial of lifestyle modification and pharmacotherapy for obesity. *New England Journal of Medicine, 353,* 2111–2120.

Wagner-Moore, L. E. (2004). Gestalt therapy: Past, present, theory, and research. *Psychotherapy: Theory, Research, Practice, Training, 41,* 180–189.

Wahl, K. H., & Blackhurst, A. (2000). Factors affecting the occupational and educational aspirations of children and adolescents. *Professional School Counseling, 3,* 367–374.

Walker, E., Kestler, L., Bollini, A., & Hochman, K. M. (2004). Schizophrenia: Etiology and course. *Annual Review of Psychology, 55,* 401–430.

Walker, E., & Tessner, K. (2008). Schizophrenia. *Perspectives on Psychological Science, 3,* 30–37.

Walker, R. (2004, February 8). Cialis. *New York Times Magazine,* p. 26.

Wallerstein, J., Lewis, J., & Blakeslee, S. (2000*). The unexpected legacy of divorce: A 25-year landmark study.* New York: Hyperion.

Wallis, C. (2005). The new science of happiness. *Time,* pp. A3–A9.

Wallis, C., & Steptoe, S. (2006, January 16). Help! I've lost my focus. *Time,* pp. 73–78.

Walsh, B. T., Fairburn, C. G., Mickley, D., Sysko, R., & Parides, M. K. (2004). Treatment of bulimia nervosa in a primary care setting. *American Journal of Psychiatry, 161,* 556–561.

Walsh, B. T., Kaplan, A. S., Attia, E., Olmsted, M., Parides, M., Carter, J. C., et al. (2006). Fluoxetine after weight restoration in anorexia nervosa: A randomized controlled trial. *Journal of the American Medical Association, 295,* 2605–2612.

Walsh, T., Casadei, S., Coats, K. H., Swisher, E., Stray, S. M., & Higgins, J. (2006). Spectrum of mutations in BRCA1, BRCA2, CHEK2, and TP53 in families at high risk of breast cancer. *Journal of the American Medical Association, 295*, 1379–1388.

Walters, S. T., Wright, J. A., & Shegog, R. (2006). A review of computer and Internet-based interventions for smoking behavior. *Addictive Behaviors, 31*, 264–277.

Wampold, B. E. (2007). Bruce E. Wampold: Award for distinguished professional contributions to applied research. *American Psychologist, 62*, 855–873.

Wang, C., Cunningham, G., Dobs, A., Iranmanesh, A., Matsumoto, A. M., Snyder, P. J., et al. (2004). Long-term testosterone gel (AndroGel) treatment maintains beneficial effects on sexual function and mood, lean and fat mass, and bone mineral density in hypogonadal men. *Journal of Clinical Endocrinology and Metabolism, 89*, 2085–2098.

Wang, P. S., Lane, M., Olfson, M., Pincus, H. A., Wells, K. B., & Kessler, R. C. (2005). Twelve-month use of mental health services in the United States: Results from the National Comorbidity Survey Replication. *Archives of General Psychiatry, 62*, 629–640.

Ward, C. A. (2000). Models and measurements of psychological androgyny: A cross-cultural extension of theory and research. *Sex Roles, 43*, 529–552.

Wargo, E. (2006, July). How many seconds to a first impression? *APS Observer, 19*(7), 11.

Wargo, E. (2007, November). Understanding the have-nots. *APS Observer, 20*(11). Retrieved November 20, 2008, from *http://www.psychologicalscience.org/observer/getArticle.cfm?id=2265.*

Warneken, F., & Tomasello, M. (2006). Altruistic helping in human infants and young chimpanzees. *Science, 311*, 1301–1303.

Warner, J. (2004, September 27). Suburbs may be hazardous to your health. *WebMD Medical News.* Retrieved September 28, 2004, from *http://content.health.msn.com/content/article/94/102926.htm*

Wartik, N. (2000, June 25). Depression comes out of hiding. *New York Times*, pp. MH1, MH4.

Wasserman, J. (1993, September 3). It's still women's work. *New York Daily News*, p. 7.

Waterman, C. K., & Nevid, J. S. (1977). Sex differences in the resolution of the identity crisis. *Journal of Youth and Adolescence, 6*, 337–342.

Watson, D., Suls, J., & Haig, J. (2002). Global self-esteem in relation to structural models of personality and affectivity. *Journal of Personality and Social Psychology, 83*, 185–197.

Watson, J. B. (1924). *Behaviorism.* New York: Norton.

Watson, J. B., & Rayner, R. (1920). Conditioned emotional reactions. *Journal of Experimental Psychology, 3*, 1–14.

Webster, G. D. (2009). The person-situation interaction is increasingly outpacing the person-situation debate in the scientific literature: A 30-year analysis of publication trends, 1978–2007. *Journal of Research in Personality, 43*, 278–279.

Weiner, M. J., & Wright, F.E. (1973). Effects of undergoing arbitrary discrimination upon subsequent attitudes toward a minority group. *Journal of Applied Social Psychology, 3*, 94–102.

Weiner, R. D. (2000). Retrograde amnesia with electroconvulsive therapy. *Archives of General Psychiatry, 57*, 591–592.

Weinstein, A. R., Sesso, H. D., Lee, I. M., Cook, N. R., Manson, J. E., Buring, J. E., & Gaziano, J. M. (2004). Relationship of physical activity vs body mass index with type 2 diabetes in women. *Journal of the American Medical Association, 292*, 1188–1194.

Weisler, R. H., Calabrese, J. R., Bowden, C. L., Ascher, J. A., DeVeaugh-Geisse, J., & Evoniuk, K. (2008). Discovery and development of lamotrigine for bipolar disorder: A story of serendipity, clinical observations, risk taking, and persistence. *Journal of Affective Disorders, 108*, 1–9.

Weisz, J. R, Pilkonis, P. A., Woody, S. R., & Follette, W. C. (2000). Stressing the (other) three Rs in the search for empirically supported treatments: Review procedures, research quality, relevance to practice and the public interest. *Clinical Psychology: Science and Practice, 7*, 243–258.

Weisz, J. R., Jensen-Doss, A., & Hawley, K., M. (2006). Evidence-based youth psychotherapies versus usual clinical care: A meta-analysis of direct comparisons. *American Psychologist, 61*, 671–689.

Weisz, J. R., Sweeney, L., Proffitt, V., & Carr, T. (1993). Control-related beliefs and self-reported depressive symptoms in late childhood. *Journal of Abnormal Psychology, 102*, 411–418.

Wells, B. E., & Twenge, J. M. (2005). Changes in young people's sexual behavior and attitudes, 1943–1999: A cross-temporal meta-analysis. *Review of General Psychology, 9*, 249–261.

Wessel, T. R., Arant, C. B., Olson, M. B., Johnson, B. D., Reis, S. E., Sharaf, B. L., et al. (2004). Relationship of physical fitness vs body mass index with coronary artery disease and cardiovascular events in women. *Journal of the American Medical Association, 292*, 1179–1187.

Westen, D. (2002). Implications of developments in cognitive neuroscience for psychoanalytic psychotherapy. *Harvard Review of Psychiatry, 10*, 369–373.

Westen, D., & Gabbard, G. O. (2002). Developments in cognitive neuroscience: 1. Conflict, compromise, and connectionism. *Journal of the American Psychoanalytic Association, 50*, 53–98.

Weuve, J., Kang, J. H., Manson, J. E., Breteler, M. M. B., Ware, J. H., & Grodstein, F. (2004). Physical activity, including walking, and cognitive function in older women. *Journal of the American Medical Association, 292*, 1454–1461.

White, J. K., Hendrick, S. S., & Hendrick, C. (2004). Big five personality variables and relationship constructs. *Personality and Individual Differences, 37*, 1519–1530.

White, K. S., Brown, T. W., Somers, T. J., & Barlow, D. H. (2006). Avoidance behavior in panic disorder: The moderating influence of perceived control. *Behaviour Research and Therapy, 44*, 147–157.

Whitehead, B. D., & Popenoe, D. (2006). *The state of our unions: The social health of marriage in America.* Retrieved December 22, 2008, from *http://marriage.rutgers.edu/Publications/SOOU/TEXTSOOU2006.htm*

Wideroff, L., et al. (2005) Hereditary breast/ovarian and colorectal cancer genetics knowledge in a national sample of U.S. physicians. *Journal of Medical Genetics. 42*, 749–755.

Widiger, T. A. (2005). Five factor model of personality disorder: Integrating science and practice. *Journal of Research in Personality, 39*, 67–83.

Wieselquist, J., Rusbult, C. E., Foster, C. A., & Agnew, C. R. (1999). Commitment, pro-relationship behavior, and trust in close relationships. *Journal of Personality & Social Psychology, 77*(5), 942–966.

Wilkowe, E. S. (2005, September 11). Looking for love on the web: Internet expands the dating pool for young, old. *DailyRecord.* Retrieved November 13, 2005, from *http://www.dailyrecord.com/apps/pbcs.dll/article?AID=/20050911/LIFE/509110310/1004/ARCHIVES*

Willett, W. C. (2005). Diet and cancer: An evolving picture. *Journal of the American Medical Association, 293*, 233–234.

Willetts, M. C. (2006). Union quality comparisons between long-term heterosexual cohabitation and legal marriages. *Journal of Family Issues, 27*, 110–127.

Williams, D. E., & D'Alessandro, J. D. (1994) A comparison of three measures of androgyny and their relationship to psychological adjustment. *Journal of Social Behavior and Personality, 9*(3) 469 480.

Williams, J. E., & Best, D. L. (1994). Cross-cultural views of women and men. In W. J. Lonner & R. Malpass (Eds.), *Psychology and culture.* Boston: Allyn & Bacon.

Williams, J. E., Paton, C. C., Siegler, I. C., Eigenbrodt, M. L., Nieto, F. J., & Tyroler, H. A. (2000). Anger proneness predicts coronary heart disease risk: Prospective analysis from the Atherosclerosis Risk in Communities (ARIC) study. *Circulation, 101*, 2034–2039.

Williams, L. (1992, February 6). Woman's image in a mirror: Who defines what she sees? *New York Times*, pp. A1, B7.

Williams, S. M., Addy, J. H., Phillips, J. A., 3rd, Dai, M., Kpodonu, J., Afful, J., et al. (2000). Combinations of variations in multiple genes are associated with hypertension. *Hypertension, 36*, 2–6.

Willis, J., & Todorov, A. (2006). First impressions: Making up your mind after a 100-ms exposure to a face. *Psychological Science, 17*, 592–598.

Wills, T. A., & Filer Fegan, M. (2001). Social networks and social support. In A. Baum, T. A. Revenson, & J. E. Singer (Eds.), *Handbook of health psychology* (pp. 209–234). Mahwah, NJ: Erlbaum.

Wilson, G. T., Grilo, C. M., & Vitousek, K. M. (2007). Psychological treatment of eating disorders. *American Psychologist, 62*, 199–216.

Wilson, J. M. B., Tripp, D. A., & Boland, F. J. (2005). The relative contributions of waist-to-hip ratio and body mass to judgments of attractiveness. *Sexualities, Evolution & Gender, 7,* 245–267.

Winerip, M. (1998, January 4). Binge nights. *New York Times,* Section 4A, pp. 28–31, 42.

Winerman, L. (2004, July/August). Sleep deprivation threatens public health, says research award winner. *Monitor on Psychology, 35,* 61.

Winzelberg, A. J., et al. (2000). Effectiveness of an Internet-based program for reducing risk factors for eating disorders. *Journal of Consulting and Clinical Psychology, 68,* 346–350.

Wiseman, H., Mayseless, O., & Sharabany, R. (2006). Why are they lonely? Perceived quality of early relationships with parents, attachment, personality predispositions and loneliness in first-year university students. *Personality and Individual Differences, 40,* 237–248.

Wolfe, D. A., et al. (2001). Child maltreatment: Risk of adjustment problems and dating violence in adolescence. *Journal of American Academy of Child & Adolescent Psychiatry, 40,* 282–289.

Wonderlich, S. A., Joiner, T. E., Jr., Keel, P. K., Williamson, D. A., & Crosby, R. D. (2007). Eating disorder diagnoses: Empirical approaches to classification. *American Psychologist, 62,* 167–180.

Wong, E. C., Kim, B. S. K., Zane, N. W. S., Kim, I. J., & Huang, J. S. (2003). Examining culturally based variables associated with ethnicity: Influences on credibility perceptions of empirically supported interventions. *Cultural Diversity and Ethnic Minority Psychology, 9,* 88–96.

Wood, M. D., Vinson, D. C., & Sher, K. J. (2001). Alcohol use and misuse. In A. Baum, T. A. Revenson, & J. E. Singer (Eds.), *Handbook of health psychology* (pp. 280–320). Mahwah, NJ: Erlbaum.

Wood, W., & Quinn, J. M. (2003). Forewarned and forearmed? Two meta-analytic syntheses of forewarnings of influence appeals. *Psychological Bulletin, 129,* 119–138.

Woods, S. C., Schwartz, M. W., Baskin, D. G., & Seeley, R. J. (2000). Food intake and the regulation of body weight. *Annual Review of Psychology, 51,* 255–277.

Wortman, C. B., Adesman, P., Herman, E., & Greenberg, P. (1976). Self-disclosure: An attributional perspective. *Journal of Personality and Social Psychology, 33,* 184–191.

Wright, J. T., Jr., Dunn, K., Cutler, J. A., Davis, B. R., Cushman, W. C, et al. (2005). Outcomes in hypertensive Black and nonblack patients treated with chlorthalidone, amlodipine, and lisinopril. *Journal of the American Medical Association, 293,* 1595–1608.

Wright, K. P., Jr., Hull, J. T., Hughes, R. J., Ronda, J. M., & Czeisler, C. A. (2006). Sleep and wakefulness out of phase with internal biological time impairs learning in humans. *Journal of Cognitive Neuroscience, 18,* 508–521.

Wu, K. D., & Clark, L. A. (2003). Relations between personality traits and self-reports of daily behavior. *Journal of Research in Personality, 37,* 231–256.

Wyart, C., Webster, W. W., Chen, J. H., Wilson, S. R., McClary, A., Khan, M., & Sobel, N. (2007). Male sweat as a possible chemosignal. *The Journal of Neuroscience, 27,* 1261–1265.

Yager, J. (2006, October 16). Which patients with major depression will relapse despite maintenance fluoxetine? *Journal Watch Psychiatry.* Retrieved October 16, 2006, from *http://psychiatry.jwatch.org/cgi/content/full/2006/1016/4*

Yang, Q., She, H., Gearing, M., Colla, E., Lee, M., Shacka, J. J., & Mao, Z. (2009). Regulation of neuronal survival factor MEF2D by chaperone-mediated autophagy. *Science, 323,* 124–127.

Yates, W. R. (2000). Testosterone in psychiatry: Risks and benefits. *Archives of General Psychiatry, 57,* 155–156.

Yeo, R. A., Gangestad, S. W., & Thoma, R. J. (2007). Developmental instability and individual variation in brain development: Implications for the origin of neurodevelopmental disorders. *Current Directions in Psychological Science, 16,* 245–249.

Yoder, A. E. (2000). Barriers to ego identity status formation: A contextual qualification of Marcia's identity status paradigm. *Journal of Adolescence, 23,* 95–106.

Yonkers, K. A., O'Brien, P. M. S., & Eriksson, E. (2008). Premenstrual syndrome. *Lancet, 371,* 1200–1210.

Yücel, M., Solowij, N., Respondek, C., Whittle, S., Fornito, A., Pantelis, C., et al. (2008). Regional brain abnormalities associated with long-term heavy cannabis use. *Archives of General Psychiatry, 65,* 694–701.

Yurgelun-Todd, D. A., & Killgore, W. D. S. (2006). Fear-related activity in the prefrontal cortex increases with age during adolescence: A preliminary fMRI study. *Neuroscience Letters, 406,* 194–199.

Zajonc, R. B. (1968). Attitudinal effects of mere exposure. *Journal of Personality and Social Psychology, 9,* 1–27.

Zane, N., & Sue, S. (1991). Culturally responsive mental health services for Asian Americans: Treatment and training issues. In H. F. Myers et al. (Eds.), *Ethnic minority perspectives on clinical training and services in psychology* (pp. 49–58). Washington, DC: American Psychological Association.

Zarevski, P., Marusic, I., Zolotic, S., Bunjevac, T., & Vukosav, Z. (1998). Contribution of Arnett's inventory of sensation seeking and Zuckerman's sensation seeking scale to the differentiation of athletes engaged in high and low risk sports. *Personality & Individual Differences, 25,* 763–768.

Zautra, A. J., Davis, M. C., Reich, J. W., Nicassario, P., Tennen, H., Finan, P., et al. (2008). Comparison of cognitive behavioral and mindfulness meditation interventions on adaptation to rheumatoid arthritis for patients with and without history of recurrent depression. *Journal of Consulting and Clinical Psychology, 76,* 408–421.

Zea, M. C., Mason, M., & Murguita, A. (2000). Psychotherapy with members of Latino/Latina religions and spiritual traditions. In P. S. Richards & A. E. Bergin (Eds.), *Handbook of psychotherapy and religious diversity* (pp. 397–419). Washington, DC: American Psychological Association.

Zenter, M. R. (2005). Ideal mate personality concepts and compatibility in close relationships: A longitudinal analysis. *Journal of Personality and Social Psychology, 89,* 242–256.

Zernike, K. (2005, March 12). A 21st-birthday drinking game can be a deadly rite of passage. *New York Times,* pp. A1, A13.

Zhang, Z.-J., Tan, Q.-R., Tong, Y., Lic, W., Kang, W.-H., Zhen, X.-C., & Post, R. M. (2008). The effectiveness of carbamazepine in unipolar depression: A double-blind, randomized, placebo-controlled study. *Journal of Affective Disorders, 109,* 91–97.

Zielbauer, P. (2000, May 22). Sex offender listings on web set off debate. *New York Times.*

Zucker, A. N., Ostrove, J. M., & Stewart, A. J. (2002). College-educated women's personality development in adulthood: Perceptions and age differences. *Psychology and Aging, 2,* 236–244.

Zuckerman, M. (1980). Sensation seeking. In H. London & J. Exner (Eds.), *Dimensions of personality.* New York: Wiley.

Zuckerman, M. (2006). Biosocial bases of sensation seeking. In T. Canli (Ed.), *Biology of personality and individual differences* (pp. 37–59). New York: Guilford.

Zweig, R. A. (2005). Suicide prevention in older adults: An interdisciplinary challenge. *Clinical Psychology: Science and Practice, 12,* 260–263.

Name Index

Subject Index